The firstwriter.com
Writers' Handbook
2026

The firstwriter.com
Writers' Handbook
2026

EDITOR
J. PAUL DYSON

Published in 2025 by JP&A Dyson
27 Old Gloucester Street, London WC1N 3AX, United Kingdom
Copyright JP&A Dyson

https://www.jpandadyson.com
https://www.firstwriter.com

ISBN 978-1-909935-57-0

All rights reserved. No part of this publication may be reproduced or transmitted in any form or by any means, or stored in any retrieval system without prior written permission. firstwriter.com, the firstwriter.com logo, and the firstwriter.com oval are trademarks of JP&A Dyson trading as firstwriter.com. Whilst every effort is made to ensure that all information contained within this publication is accurate, no liability can be accepted for any mistakes or omissions, or for losses incurred as a result of actions taken in relation to information provided. Unless otherwise stated, firstwriter.com is not associated with and does not endorse, recommend, or guarantee any of the organisations or persons listed within this publication. Inclusion does not constitute recommendation.

**Registered with the IP Rights Office
Copyright Registration Service
Ref: 3536156568**

Foreword

The firstwriter.com Writers' Handbook returns for its 2026 edition with over 1,400 listings of literary agents, literary agencies, publishers, and magazines that have been updated in firstwriter.com's online databases between 2023 and 2025. This includes revised and updated listings from the previous edition and over 200 new entries.

Previous editions of this handbook have been bought by writers across the United States, Canada, and Europe; and ranked in the United Kingdom as the number one bestselling writing and publishing directory on Amazon. The 2026 edition continues this international outlook, giving writers all over the English-speaking world access to the global publishing markets.

Finding the information you need is made quick and easy with multiple tables, a detailed index, and unique paragraph numbers to help you get to the listings you're looking for.

The variety of tables helps you navigate the listings in different ways, and includes a Table of Authors, which lists over 5,000 authors and tells you who represents them, or who publishes them, or both.

The number of genres in the index has expanded to over 950. So, for example, while there was only one option for "Romance" in previous editions, you can now narrow this down to Historical Romance, Fantasy Romance, Supernatural / Paranormal Romance, Contemporary Romance, Diverse Romance, Erotic Romance, Feminist Romance, Christian Romance, or even Amish Romance.

The handbook also provides free online access to the entire current firstwriter.com databases, including over 2,100 magazines, over 2,400 literary agents and agencies, over 2,700 book publishers that don't charge fees, and constantly updated listings of current writing competitions, with typically more than 50 added each month.

For details on how to claim your free access, please see the end of this book.

Included in the subscription

A subscription to the full website can be taken out for free with the code included at the end of this book, and comes packed with all the following features:

Advanced search features

- Save searches and save time – set up to 15 search parameters specific to your work, save them, and then access the search results with a single click whenever you log in. You can even save multiple different searches if you have different types of work you are looking to place.
- Add personal notes to listings, visible only to you and fully searchable – helping you to organise your actions.
- Set reminders on listings to notify you when to submit your work, when to follow up, when to expect a reply, or any other custom action.
- Track which listings you've viewed and when, to help you organise your search – any listings which have changed since you last viewed them will be highlighted for your attention.

Daily email updates

As a subscriber you will be able to take advantage of our email alert service, meaning you can specify your particular interests and we'll send you automatic email updates when we change or add a listing that matches them. So if you're interested in agents dealing in romantic fiction in the United States you can have us send you emails with the latest updates about them – keeping you up to date without even having to log in.

User feedback

Our agent, publisher, and magazine databases all include a user feedback feature that allows our subscribers to leave feedback on each listing – giving you not only the chance to have your say about the markets you contact, but giving a unique authors' perspective on the listings.

Save on copyright protection fees

If you're sending your work away to publishers, competitions, or literary agents, it's vital that you first protect your copyright. As a subscriber to firstwriter.com you can do this through our site and save 10% on the copyright registration fees normally payable for protecting your work internationally through the Intellectual Property Rights Office (https://www.CopyrightRegistrationService.com).

Monthly newsletter

When you subscribe to firstwriter.com you also receive our monthly email newsletter – described by one publishing company as "the best in the business" – including articles, news, and interviews for writers. And the best part is that you can continue to receive the newsletter even after you stop your paid subscription – at no cost!

For details on how to claim your free access please see the back of this book.

Contents

Foreword v
Contents vii
Glossary of Terms ix

Guidance

The Writer's Roadmap 1
Why Choose Traditional Publishing 3
Formatting Your Manuscript 5
Protecting Your Copyright 7
Should You Self-Publish 11
The Self Publishing Process 13

Tables

Table of US Literary Agencies 15
Table of UK Literary Agencies 17
Table of US Literary Agents 19
Table of UK Literary Agents 23
Table of Canadian Literary Agents 27
Table of US Magazines 29
Table of UK Magazines 31
Table of Canadian Magazines 33
Table of US Book Publishers 35
Table of UK Book Publishers 37
Table of Canadian Book Publishers 39
Table of Authors 41

Listings

Literary Agents and Agencies 75
Magazines 187
Book Publishers 235

Claim your free access to www.firstwriter.com: See p.367

Index

Index 293

Free Access

Get Free Access to the firstwriter.com Website 367

Glossary of Terms

This section explains common terms used in this handbook, and in the publishing industry more generally.

Academic
Listings in this book will be marked as targeting the academic market only if they publish material of an academic nature; e.g. academic theses, scientific papers, etc. The term is not used to indicate publications that publish general material aimed at people who happen to be in academia, or who are described as academic by virtue of being educated.

Adult
In publishing, "adult" simply refers to books that are aimed at adults, as opposed to books that are aimed at children, or young adults, etc. It is not a euphemism for pornographic or erotic content. Nor does it necessarily refer to content which is unsuitable for children; it is just not targeted at them. In this book, most ordinary mainstream publishers will be described as "adult", unless their books are specifically targeted at other groups (such as children, professionals, etc.).

Advance
Advances are up-front payments made by traditional publishers to authors, which are offset against future royalties.

Agented
An *agented* submission is one which is submitted by a literary agent. If a publisher accepts only *agented* submissions then you will need a literary agent to submit the work on your behalf.

Author bio
A brief description of you and your life – normally in relation to your writing activity, but if intended for publication (particularly in magazines) may be broader in scope. May be similar to *Curriculum Vitae* (CV) or résumé, depending on context.

Bio
See *Author bio*.

Curriculum Vitae
A brief description of you, your qualifications, and accomplishments – normally in this context in relation to writing (any previous publications, or awards, etc.), but in the case of nonfiction proposals may also include relevant experience that qualifies you to write on the subject. Commonly abbreviated to "CV". May also be referred to as a résumé. May be similar to *Author bio*, depending on context.

CV
See *Curriculum Vitae*.

International Reply Coupon
When submitting material overseas you may be required to enclose *International Reply Coupons*, which will enable the recipient to send a response and/or return your material at your cost. Not applicable/available in all countries, so check with your local Post Office for more information.

IRC
See *International Reply Coupon*.

Manuscript
Your complete piece of work – be it a novel, short story, or article, etc. – will be referred to as your manuscript. Commonly abbreviated to "ms" (singular) or "mss" (plural).

MS
See *Manuscript*.

MSS
See *Manuscript*.

Professional
Listings in this book will be marked as targeting the professional market if they publish material serving a particular profession: e.g. legal journals, medical journals, etc. The term is not used to indicate publications that publish general material aimed at a notional "professional class".

Proposal
A proposal is normally requested for nonfiction projects (where the book may not yet have been completed, or even begun). Proposals can consist of a number of components, such as an outline, table of contents, CV, marketing information, etc. but the exact requirements will vary from one publisher to another.

Query
Many agents and publishers will prefer to receive a query in the first instance, rather than your full *manuscript*. A query will typically consist of a cover letter accompanied by a *synopsis* and/or sample chapter(s). Specific requirements will vary, however, so always check on a case by case basis.

Recommendation
If an agent is only accepting approaches by recommendation this means that they will only consider your work if it comes with a recommendation from an established professional in the industry, or an existing client.

RoW
Rest of world.

SAE
See *Stamped Addressed Envelope*. Can also be referred to as SASE.

SASE
Self-Addressed Stamped Envelope. Variation of SAE. See *Stamped Addressed Envelope*.

Simultaneous submission
A simultaneous submission is one which is sent to more than one market at the same time. Normally you will be sending your work to numerous different magazines, agents, and publishers at the same time, but some demand the right to consider it exclusively – i.e. they don't accept simultaneous submissions.

Stamped Addressed Envelope
Commonly abbreviated to "SAE". Can also be referred to as Self-Addressed Stamped Envelope, or SASE. When supplying an SAE, ensure that the envelope and postage is adequate for a reply or the return of your material, as required. If you are submitting overseas, remember that postage from your own country will not be accepted, and you may need to provide an *International Reply Coupon*.

Synopsis
A short outline of your story. This should cover all the main characters and events, including the ending. It is not the kind of "teaser" found on a book's back cover. The length of synopsis required can vary, but is generally between one and three pages.

TOC
Table of Contents. These are often requested as part of nonfiction proposals.

Unagented
An unagented submission is one which is not submitted through a literary agent. If a publisher accepts unagented submissions then you can approach them directly.

Unsolicited mss
A manuscript which has not been requested. Many agents and publishers will not accept unsolicited mss, but this does not necessarily mean they are closed to approaches – many will prefer to receive a short *query* in the first instance. If they like the idea, they will request the full work, which will then be a solicited manuscript.

The Writer's Roadmap

With most objectives in life, people recognise that there is a path to follow. Whether it is career progression, developing a relationship, or chasing your dreams, we normally understand that there are foundations to lay and baby steps to take before we'll be ready for the main event.

But for some reason, with writing (perhaps because so much of the journey of a writer happens in private, behind closed doors), people often overlook the process involved. They often have a plan of action which runs something like this:

1. Write novel.
2. Get novel published.

This is a bit like having a plan for success in tennis which runs:

1. Buy tennis racket.
2. Win Wimbledon.

It misses out all the practice that is going to be required; the competing in the minor competitions and the learning of the craft that will be needed in order to succeed in the major events; the time that will need to be spent gaining reputation and experience.

In this roadmap we'll be laying out what we think is the best path to follow to try and give yourself the best shot of success in the world of writing. You don't necessarily have to jump through all the hoops, and there will always be people who, like Pop Idol or reality TV contestants, get a lucky break that propels them to stardom without laying any of the foundations laid out below, but the aim here is to limit your reliance on luck and maximise your ability to shape your destiny yourself.

1: Write short material

Writers will very often start off by writing a novel. We would advise strongly against this. It's like leaving school one day and applying for a job as a CEO of an international corporation the next. Novels are the big league. They are expensive to produce, market, and distribute. They require significant investment and pose a significant financial risk to publishers. They are not a good place for new writers to try and cut their teeth. If you've already written your novel that's great – it's great experience and you'll have learned a lot – but we'd recommend shelving it for now (you can always come back to it later) and getting stuck into writing some short form material, such as poetry and short fiction.

This is what novelist George R. R. Martin, author of *A Game of Thrones*, has to say on the subject:

> "I would also suggest that any aspiring writer begin with short stories. These days, I meet far too many young writers who try to start off with a novel right off, or a trilogy, or even a nine-book series. That's like starting in at rock climbing by tackling Mt Everest. Short stories help you learn your craft."

You will find that writing short material will improve your writing no end. Writing short fiction allows you to play with lots of different stories and characters very quickly. Because you will probably only spend a few days on any given story you will quickly gain a lot of experience with plotting stories and will learn a lot about what works, what doesn't work, and what you personally are good at. When you write a novel, by contrast, you may spend years on a single story and one set of characters, making this learning process much slower.

Your writing will also be improved by the need to stick to a word limit. Writers who start their career by writing a novel often produce huge epics, the word counts of which they wear as a badge of honour, as if they demonstrate their commitment to and enthusiasm for writing. What they actually demonstrate is a naivety about the realities of getting published. The odds are already stacked against new writers getting a novel published, because of the cost and financial risk of publishing a novel. The bigger the novel, the more it will cost to print, warehouse, and distribute. Publishers will not look at a large word count and be impressed – they will be terrified. The longer the novel, the less chance it has of getting published.

A lengthy first novel also suggests that the writer has yet to learn one of the most critical skills a writer must possess to succeed: brevity. By writing short stories that fit the limits imposed by competitions and magazines you will learn this critical skill. You will learn to remove unnecessary words and passages, and you will find that your writing becomes leaner, more engaging, and more exciting as a result. Lengthy first novels are often rambling and sometimes boring – but once you've been forced to learn how to "trim the fat" by writing short stories, the good habits you've got into will transfer across when you start writing long form works, allowing you to write novels that are pacier and better to read. They will stand a better chance of publication not just because they are shorter and cheaper to produce, but they are also likely to be better written.

2: Get a professional critique

It's a good idea to get some professional feedback on your work at some point, and it's probably better to do this sooner, rather than later. There's no point spending a long time doing something that doesn't quite work if a little advice early on could have got you on the right track sooner. It's also a lot cheaper to get a short story critiqued than a whole novel, and if you can learn the necessary lessons now it will both minimise the cost and maximise the benefit of the advice.

Should you protect the copyright of short works before showing them to anyone?

This is a matter of personal preference. We'd suggest that it certainly isn't as important to register short works as full novels, as your short works are unlikely to be of much financial value to you. Having said that, films do sometimes get made which are based on short stories, in which case you'd want to have all your rights in order. If you do choose to register your short works this can be done for a relatively small amount online at https://www.copyrightregistrationservice.com/register.

3: Submit to competitions and magazines, and build a list of writing credits

Once you have got some short works that you are happy with you can start submitting them to competitions and small magazines. You can search for competitions at https://www.firstwriter.com/competitions and magazines at https://www.firstwriter.com/magazines. Prize money may not be huge, and you probably won't be paid for having your work appear in the kind of small literary magazines you will probably be approaching at first, but the objective here is to build up a list of writing credits to give you more credibility when approaching agents and publishers. You'll be much more likely to grab their attention if you can reel off a list of places where you have already been published, or prizes you have won.

4: Finish your novel and protect your copyright

Okay – so you've built up a list of writing credits, and you've decided it's time to either write a novel, or go back to the one you had already started (in which case you'll probably find yourself cutting out large chunks and making it a lot shorter!). Once you've got your novel to the point where you're happy to start submitting it for publication you should get it registered for copyright. Unlike the registration of short works, which we think is a matter of personal preference, we'd definitely recommend registering a novel, and doing so before you show it to anybody. That *includes* family and friends. Don't worry that you might want to change it – as long as you don't rewrite it to the point where it's not recognisable it will still be protected – the important thing is to get it registered without delay. You can protect it online at https://www.copyrightregistrationservice.com/register.

If you've already shown it to other people then just register it as soon as you can. Proving a claim to copyright is all about proving you had a copy of the work before anyone else, so time is of the essence.

5: Editing

These days, agents and publishers increasingly seem to expect manuscripts to have been professionally edited before being submitted to them – and no, getting your husband / wife / friend / relative to do it doesn't count. Ideally, you should have the whole manuscript professionally edited, but this can be expensive. Since most agents and publishers aren't going to want to see the whole manuscript in the first instance you can probably get away with just having the first three chapters edited. It may also be worth having your query letter and synopsis edited at the same time.

6: Submit to literary agents

There will be many publishers out there who will accept your submission directly, and on the face of it that might seem like a good idea, since you won't have to pay an agent 15% of your earnings.

However, all the biggest publishers are generally closed to direct submissions from authors, meaning that if you want the chance of getting a top publisher you're going to need a literary agent. You'll also probably find that their 15% fee is more than offset by the higher earnings you'll be likely to achieve.

To search for literary agents go to https://www.firstwriter.com/Agents. Start by being as specific in your search as possible. So if you've written a historical romance select "Fiction", "Romance", and "Historical". Once you've approached all the agents that specifically mention all three elements broaden your search to just "Fiction" and "Romance". As long as the new results don't specifically say they don't handle historical romance, these are still valid markets to approach. Finally, search for just "Fiction", as there are many agents who are willing to consider all kinds of fiction but don't specifically mention romance or historical.

Don't limit your approaches to just agents in your own country. With more and more agents accepting electronic queries it's now as easy to approach agents in other countries as in your own, and if you're ignoring either London or New York (the two main centres of English language publishing) you're cutting your chances of success in two.

7: Submit directly to publishers

Once you're certain that you've exhausted all potential agents for your work, you can start looking for publishers to submit your work directly to. You can search for publishers at https://www.firstwriter.com/publishers. Apply the same filtering as when you were searching for agents: start specific and gradually broaden, until you've exhausted all possibilities.

8: Self-publishing

In the past, once you got to the point where you'd submitted to all the publishers and agents who might be interested in your book, it would be time to pack away the manuscript in the attic, chalk it up to experience, and start writing another. However, these days writers have the option to take their book directly to market by publishing it themselves.

Before you decide to switch to self-publishing you must be sure that you've exhausted all traditional publishing possibilities – because once you've self-published your book you're unlikely to be able to submit it to agents and publishers. It will probably take a few years of exploring the world of traditional publishing to reach this point, but if you do then you've nothing to lose by giving self-publishing a shot. See our guide to self-publishing for details on how to proceed.

Why Choose Traditional Publishing

When **firstwriter.com** first started, back in 2001, there were only two games in town when it came to getting your book published: traditional publishing, and vanity publishing – and which you should pick was a no-brainer. Vanity publishing was little more than a scam that would leave you with an empty bank account and a house full of unsold books. If you were serious about being a writer, you had to follow the traditional publishing path.

Since then, there has been a self-publishing revolution, with new technologies and new printing methods giving writers a genuine opportunity to get their books into the market by themselves. So, is there still a reason for writers to choose traditional publishing?

The benefits of traditional publishing

Despite the allure and apparent ease of self-publishing, the traditional path still offers you the best chance of making a success of being a writer. There are rare cases where self-published writers make staggering fortunes and become internationally renowned on the back of their self-published books, but these cases are few and far between, and a tiny drop in the rapidly expanding ocean of self-published works. The vast majority of successful books – and the vast majority of successful writers – have their homes firmly in the established publishing houses. Even those self-published authors who find success usually end up moving to a traditional publisher in the end.

This is because the traditional publishers have the systems, the market presence, and the financial clout to *make* a book a bestseller. While successful self-published authors often owe their success in no small part to a decent dose of luck (a social media comment that goes viral; the right mention on the right media outlet at the right time), traditional publishers are in the business of engineering that success. They might not always succeed, but they have the marketing budgets and the distribution channels in place to give themselves, and the book they are promoting, the best possible chance.

And it's not just the marketing and the distribution. Getting signed with a traditional publisher brings a whole team of people with a wealth of expertise that will all work towards the success of the book. It will provide you with an editor who may have experience of working on previous bestsellers, who will not only help you get rid of mistakes in your work but may also help you refine it into a better book. They will help make sure that the quality of your content is good enough to make it in the marketplace.

The publishers will source a professional cover designer who will make your book look the part on the shelves and on the pages of the bookselling websites. They will have accountants who will handle the technicalities of tax regimes both home and abroad. They will have overseas contacts for establishing foreign publishing rights; translations; etc. They may even have contacts in the film industry, should there be a prospect of a movie adaptation. They will have experts working on every aspect of your book, right down to the printing and the warehousing and the shipping of the physical products. They will have people to manage the ebook conversion and the electronic distribution. As an author, you don't need to worry about any of this.

This means you get more time to simply be a writer. You may have to go on book tours, but even these will be organised for you by PR experts, who will also be handling all the press releases, etc.

And then there's the advances. Advances are up-front payments made by traditional publishers to authors, which are off-set against future royalties. So, an author might receive a $5,000 advance before their book is published. When the royalties start coming in, the publisher keeps the first $5,000 to off-set the advance. The good news for the author is that if the book flops and doesn't make $5,000 in royalties they still get to keep the full advance. In an uncertain profession, the security of an advance can be invaluable for an author – and of course it's not something available to self-published authors.

The drawbacks of traditional publishing

The main downside of traditional publishing is just that it's so hard to get into. If you choose to self-publish then – provided you have enough perseverance, the right help and advice, and perhaps a little bit of money – you are guaranteed to succeed and see your book in print and for sale. With traditional publishing, the cold hard fact is that most people who try will not succeed.

And for many of those people who fail it may not even be their fault. That aspect of traditional publishing which can bring so many benefits as compared to self-publishing – that of being part of a team – can also be part of its biggest drawback. It means that you have to get other people to buy into your book. It means that you have to rely on other people being competent enough to spot a bestseller. Many failed to spot the potential of the Harry Potter books. How many potential bestsellers never make it into print just because none of the professionals at the publishers' gates manage to recognise their potential?

So if you choose traditional publishing your destiny is not in your own hands – and for some writers the lack of exclusive control can also be a problem. Sometimes writers get defensive when editors try to tinker with their work, or annoyed when cover artists don't realise their vision the way they expect. But this is hardly a fair criticism of traditional publishing, as most writers (particularly when they are starting out) will benefit from advice from experienced professionals in the field, and will often only be shooting themselves in the foot if they insist on ignoring it.

The final main drawback with traditional publishing is that less of the sale price of each copy makes it to the writer. A typical royalty contract will give the writer 15%. With a self-published book, the author can expect to receive much more. So, all other things being equal, the self-published route can be more profitable – but, of course, all things are not equal. If self-publishing means lower sales (as is likely), then you will probably make less money overall. Remember, it's better to have 15% of something than 50% of nothing.

Conclusion

In conclusion, our advice to writers would be to aim for traditional publishing first. It might be a long shot, but if it works then you stand a much better chance of being successful. If you don't manage to get signed by an agent or a publisher then you still have the option of self-publishing, but make sure you don't get tempted to resort to self-publishing too soon – most agents and publishers won't consider self-published works, so this is a one-way street. Once you've self-published your work, you probably won't be able to change your mind and go back to the traditional publishers with your book unless it becomes a huge hit without them. It's therefore important that you exhaust all your traditional publishing options before

*Claim your free access to **www.firstwriter.com**: See p.367*

making the leap to self-publishing. Be prepared for this to take perhaps a few years (lots of agents and publishers can take six months just to respond), and make sure you've submitted to everyone you can on *both* sides of the Atlantic (publishing is a global game these days, and you need to concentrate on the two main centres of English-language publishing (New York and London) equally) before you make the decision to self-publish instead.

Formatting Your Manuscript

Before submitting a manuscript to an agent, magazine, or publisher, it's important that you get the formatting right. There are industry norms covering everything from the size of your margins to the font you choose – get them wrong and you'll be marking yourself out as an amateur. Get them right, and agents and editors will be far more likely to take you seriously.

Fonts

Don't be tempted to "make your book stand out" by using fancy fonts. It *will* stand out, but not for any reason you'd want. Your entire manuscript should be in a monospaced font like Courier (not a proportional font, like Times Roman) at 12 points. (A monospaced font is one where each character takes up the same amount of space; a proportional font is where the letter "i" takes up less space than the letter "m".)

This goes for your text, your headings, your title, your name – everything. Your objective is to produce a manuscript that looks like it has been produced on a simple typewriter.

Italics / bold

Your job as the author is to indicate words that require emphasis, not to pick particular styles of font. This will be determined by the house style of the publisher in question. You indicate emphasis by underlining text; the publisher will decide whether they will use bold or italic to achieve this emphasis – you shouldn't use either in your text.

Margins

You should have a one inch (2.5 centimetre) margin around your entire page: top, bottom, left, and right.

Spacing

In terms of line spacing, your entire manuscript should be double spaced. Your word processor should provide an option for this, so you don't have to insert blank lines manually.

While line spacing should be double, spaces after punctuation should be single. If you're in the habit of putting two spaces after full stops this is the time to get out of that habit, and remove them from your manuscript. You're just creating extra work for the editor who will have to strip them all out.

Do not put blank lines between paragraphs. Start every paragraph (even those at the start of chapters) with an indent equivalent to five spaces. If you want a scene break then create a line with the "#" character centred in the middle. You don't need blank lines above or below this line.

Word count

You will need to provide an estimated word count on the front page of your manuscript. Tempting as it will be to simply use the word processor's word counting function to tell you exactly how many words there are in your manuscript, this is not what you should do. Instead, you should work out the maximum number of characters on a line, divide this number by six, and then multiply by the total number of lines in your manuscript.

Once you have got your estimated word count you need to round it to an approximate value. How you round will depend on the overall length of your manuscript:

- up to 1,500 words: round to the nearest 100;
- 1,500–10,000 words: round to the nearest 500;
- 10,000–25,000 words: round to the nearest 1,000;
- Over 25,000 words: round to the nearest 5,000.

The reason an agent or editor will need to know your word count is so that they can estimate how many pages it will make. Since actual pages include varying amounts of white space due to breaks in paragraphs, sections of speech, etc. the formula above will actually provide a better idea of how many pages will be required than an exact word count would.

And – perhaps more importantly – providing an exact word count will highlight you immediately as an amateur.

Layout of the front page

On the first page of the manuscript, place your name, address, and any other relevant contact details (such as phone number, email address, etc.) in the top left-hand corner. In the top right-hand corner write your approximate word count.

If you have registered your work for copyright protection, place the reference number two single lines (one double line) beneath your contact details. Since your manuscript will only be seen by agents or editors, not the public, this should be done as discreetly as possible, and you should refrain from using any official seal you may have been granted permissions to use. (For information on registering for copyright protection see "Protecting Your Copyright", below.)

Place your title halfway down the front page. Your title should be centred and would normally be in capital letters. You can make it bold or underlined if you want, but it should be the same size as the rest of the text.

From your title, go down two single lines (or one double line) and insert your byline. This should be centred and start with the word "By", followed by the name you are writing under. This can be your name or a pen name, but should be the name you want the work published under. However, make sure that the name in the top left-hand corner is your real, legal name.

From your byline, go down four single lines (or two double lines) and begin your manuscript.

Layout of the text

Print on only one side of the paper, even if your printer can print on both sides.

In the top right-hand corner of all pages except the first should be your running head. This should be comprised of the surname used in your byline; a keyword from your title, and the page number, e.g. "Myname / Mynovel Page 5".

Text should be left-aligned, *not* justified. This means that you should have a ragged right-hand edge to the text, with lines ending at different points. Make sure you don't have any sort of hyphenation function switched on in your word processor: if a word is too long to fit on a line it should be taken over to the next.

Start each new chapter a third of the way down the page with the centred chapter number / title, underlined. Drop down four single lines (two double lines) to the main text.

At the end of the manuscript you do not need to indicate the ending in any way: you don't need to write "The End", or "Ends", etc. The only exception to this is if your manuscript happens to end at the bottom of a page, in which case you can handwrite the word "End" at the bottom of the last page, after you have printed it out.

Protecting Your Copyright

Protecting your copyright is by no means a requirement before submitting your work, but you may feel that it is a prudent step that you would like to take before allowing strangers to see your material.

These days, you can register your work for copyright protection quickly and easily online. The Intellectual Property Rights Office operates a website called the "Copyright Registration Service" which allows you to do this:

- *https://www.CopyrightRegistrationService.com*

This website can be used for material created in any nation signed up to the Berne Convention. This includes the United States, United Kingdom, Canada, Australia, Ireland, New Zealand, and most other countries. There are around 180 countries in the world, and over 160 of them are part of the Berne Convention.

Provided you created your work in one of the Berne Convention nations, your work should be protected by copyright in all other Berne Convention nations. You can therefore protect your copyright around most of the world with a single registration, and because the process is entirely online you can have your work protected in a matter of minutes, without having to print and post a copy of your manuscript.

What is copyright?

Copyright is a form of intellectual property (often referred to as "IP"). Other forms of intellectual property include trade marks, designs, and patents. These categories refer to different kinds of ideas which may not exist in a physical form that can be owned as property in the traditional sense, but may nonetheless have value to the people who created them. These forms of intellectual property can be owned in the same way that physical property is owned, but – as with physical property – they can be subject to dispute and proper documentation is required to prove ownership.

The different types of intellectual property divide into these categories as follows:

- **Copyright:** copyright protects creative output such as books, poems, pictures, drawings, music, films, etc. Any work which can be recorded in some way can be protected by copyright, as long as it is original and of sufficient length. Copyright does not cover short phrases or names.
- **Trade marks:** trade marks cover words and/or images which distinguish the goods or services of one trader from another. Unlike copyright, trade marks can cover names and short phrases.
- **Designs:** designs cover the overall visual appearance of a product, such as its shape, etc.
- **Patents:** patents protect the technical or functional aspects of designs or inventions.

The specifics of the legal protection surrounding these various forms of intellectual property will vary from nation to nation, but there are also generally international conventions to which a lot if not most of the nations of the world subscribe. The information provided below outlines the common situation in many countries but you should be aware that this may not reflect the exact situation in every territory.

The two types of intellectual property most relevant to writers are copyright and trade marks. If a writer has written a novel, a short story, a poem, a script, or any other piece of writing then the contents themselves can be protected by copyright. The title, however, cannot be protected by copyright as it is a name. An author may therefore feel that they wish to consider protecting the title of their work by registering it as a trade mark, if they feel that it is particularly important and/or more valuable in itself than the cost of registering a trade mark.

If a writer wants to register the copyright for their work, or register the title of their work as a trade mark, there are generally registration fees to be paid. Despite the fact that copyright covers long works that could be hundreds of thousands of words long, while trade marks cover single words and short phrases, the cost for registering a trade mark is likely to be many times higher than that for registering a work for copyright protection. This is because trade marks must be unique and are checked against existing trade marks for potential conflicts. While works to be registered for copyright must also not infringe existing works, it is not practical to check the huge volume of new works to be registered for copyright against the even larger volume of all previously copyrighted works. Copyright registration therefore tends to simply archive the work in question as proof of the date at which the person registering the work was in possession of it.

In the case of both copyright and trade marks the law generally provides some protection even without any kind of registration, but registration provides the owner of the intellectual property with greater and more enforceable protection. In the case of copyright, the creator of a work usually automatically owns the copyright as soon as the work is recorded in some way (i.e. by writing it down or recording it electronically, etc.), however these rights can be difficult to prove if disputed, and therefore many countries (such as the United States) also offer an internal country-specific means of registering works. Some countries, like the United Kingdom, do not offer any such means of registration, however an international registration is available through the Intellectual Property Rights Office's Copyright Registration Service, and can be used regardless of any country-specific provisions. This can help protect copyright in all of the nations which are signatories of the Berne Convention.

In the case of trade marks, the symbol "™" can be applied to any mark which is being used as a trade mark, however greater protection is provided if this mark is registered, in which case the symbol "®" can be applied to the mark. It is often illegal to apply the "®" symbol to a trade mark which has not been registered. There are also options for international registrations of trade marks, which are administered by the World Intellectual Property Organization, however applications cannot be made to the WIPO directly – applications must be made through the relevant office of the applicant's country.

Copyright law and its history

The modern concept of copyright can be traced back to 1710 and the "Statute of Anne", which applied to England, Scotland, and Wales. Prior to this Act, governments had granted monopoly rights to publishers to produce works, but the 1710 Act was the first time that a right of ownership was acknowledged for the actual creator of a work.

From the outset, the attempt to protect the creator's rights was beset with problems due to the local nature of the laws, which applied in Britain only. This meant that lots of copyrighted works were reproduced without the

*Claim your free access to **www.firstwriter.com**: See p.367*

permission of the author in Ireland, America, and in European countries. This not only hindered the ability of the London publishers to sell their legitimate copies of their books in these territories, but the unauthorised reproductions would also find their way into Britain, harming the home market as well.

A natural progression for copyright law was therefore its internationalisation, beginning in 1846 with a reciprocal agreement between Britain and Prussia, and culminating in a series of international treaties, the principal of which is the Berne Convention, which applies to over 160 countries.

Traditionally in the United Kingdom and the United States there has been a requirement to register a work with an official body in order to be able to claim copyright over it (Stationers Hall and the US Library of Congress respectively), however this has been changed by the Berne Convention, which requires signatory countries to grant copyright as an automatic right: i.e. the creator of a work immediately owns its copyright by virtue of creating it and recording it in some physical way (for instance by writing it down or making a recording of it, etc.). The United Kingdom and the United States have both been slow to fully adopt this approach. Though the United Kingdom signed the Berne Convention in 1887, it took 100 years for it to be fully implemented by the Copyright Designs and Patents Act 1988. The United States did not even sign the convention until 1989.

In the United States the US Library of Congress continues to provide archiving services for the purposes of copyright protection, but these are now optional. US citizens no longer need to register their work in order to be able to claim copyright over it. It is necessary, however, to be able to prove when the person who created it did so, and this is essentially the purpose of the registration today. In the United Kingdom, Stationers Hall has ceased to exist, and there is no longer any state-run means of registering the copyright to unpublished works, leaving the only available options as independent and/or international solutions such as the copyright registration service provided by the IP Rights Office.

Registering your work for copyright protection

Registering your work for copyright protection can help you protect your rights in relation to your work. Generally (particularly if you live in a Berne Convention country, as most people do) registration will not be compulsory in order to have rights over your work. Any time you create a unique original work you will in theory own the copyright over it, however you will need to be able to prove when you created it, which is the purpose of registering your work for copyright protection. There are other ways in which you might attempt to prove this, but registration provides better evidence than most other forms.

There are a range of different options for protecting your copyright that vary depending on where you live and the kind of coverage you want. Some countries, like the United States, provide internal means of registering the copyright of unpublished works, however the scope of these will tend to be restricted to the country in question. Other countries, like the United Kingdom, do not offer any specific government-sponsored system for registering the copyright of unpublished works. An international option is provided by the Intellectual Property Rights Office, which is not affiliated to any particular government or country. As long as you live in a Berne Convention country you should be able to benefit from using their Copyright Registration Service. You can register your work with the Intellectual Property Rights Office regardless of whether or not there are any specific arrangements in your home country (you may even choose to register with both to offer your work greater protection). Registration with the Intellectual Property Rights Office should provide you with protection throughout the area covered by the Berne Convention, which is most of the world.

Registering your work for copyright protection through the Intellectual Property Rights Office is an online process that can be completed in a few minutes, provided you have your file in an accepted format and your file isn't too large (if your file is too large and cannot be reduced you may have to split it and take out two or more registrations covering it). There is a registration fee to pay ($45 / £25 / €40 at the time of writing) per file for registration, however if you are a subscriber to **firstwriter.com** you can benefit from a 10% discount when you start the registration process on our site.

When registering your work, you will need to give some consideration to what your work actually consists of. This is a straightforward question if your work is a novel, or a screenplay, but if it is a collection of poetry or short stories then the issue is more difficult. Should you register your collection as one file, or register each poem separately, which would be more expensive? Usually, you can answer this question by asking yourself what you propose to do with your collection. Do you intend to submit it to publishers as a collection only? Or do you intend to send the constituent parts separately to individual magazines? If the former is the case, then register the collection as a single work under the title of the collection. If the latter is the case then this could be unwise, as your copyright registration certificate will give the name of the collection only – which will not match the names of the individual poems or stories. If you can afford to, you should therefore register them separately. If you have so many poems and / or stories to register that you cannot afford to register them all separately, then registering them as a collection will be better than nothing.

Proper use of the copyright symbol

The first thing to note is that for copyright there is only one form of the symbol (©), unlike trade marks, where there is a symbol for registered trade marks (®) and a symbol for unregistered trade marks (™).

To qualify for use of the registered trade mark symbol (®) you must register your trade mark with the appropriate authority in your country, whereas the trade mark symbol (™) can be applied to any symbol you are using as a trade mark. Use of the copyright symbol is more similar to use of the trade mark symbol, as work does not need to be registered in order to use it.

You can place the copyright symbol on any original piece of work you have created. The normal format would be to include alongside the copyright symbol the year of first publication and the name of the copyright holder, however there are no particular legal requirements regarding this. While it has historically been a requirement in some jurisdictions to include a copyright notice on a work in order to be able to claim copyright over it, the Berne Convention does not allow such restrictions, and so any country signed up to the convention no longer has this requirement. However, in some jurisdictions failure to include such a notice can affect the damages you may be able to claim if anyone infringes your copyright.

A similar situation exists in relation to the phrase "All Rights Reserved". This phrase was a requirement in order to claim international copyright protection in countries signed up to the 1910 Buenos Aires Convention. However, since all countries signed up to the Buenos Aires Convention are now also signed up to the Berne Convention (which grants automatic copyright) this phrase has become superfluous. The phrase continues to be used frequently but is unlikely to have any legal consequences.

The Berne Convention

The Berne Convention covers 162 of the approximately 190 countries in the world, including most major nations. Countries which are signed up to the convention are compelled to offer the same protection to works created in other signatory nations as they would to works created in their own. Nations not signed up to the Berne Convention may have their own arrangements regarding copyright protection.

You can check if your country is signed up to the Berne Convention at the following website:

- *https://www.CopyrightRegistrationService.com*

The status of your country should be shown automatically on the right side of the screen. If not, you can select your country manually from the drop-down menu near the top right of the page.

Should You Self-Publish

Over recent years there has been an explosion in self-published books, as it has become easier and easier to publish your book yourself. This poses writers with a new quandary: continue to pursue publication through the traditional means, or jump into the world of self-publishing? As the rejections from traditional publishers pile up it can be tempting to reach for the control and certainty of self-publishing. Should you give into the temptation, or stick to your guns?

Isn't it just vanity publishing?

Modern self-publishing is quite different from the vanity publishing of times gone by. A vanity publisher would often pose or at least seek to appear to be a traditional publisher, inviting submissions and issuing congratulatory letters of acceptance to everyone who submitted – only slowly revealing the large fees the author would have to pay to cover the cost of printing the books.

Once the books were printed, the vanity publisher would deliver them to the author then cut and run. The author would be left with a big hole in their pocket and a mountain of boxes of books that they would be unlikely to ever sell a fraction of.

Modern self-publishing, on the other hand, is provided not by shady dealers but by some of the biggest companies involved in the publishing industry, including Penguin and Amazon. It doesn't have the large fees that vanity publishing did (depending on the path you choose and your own knowledge and technical ability it can cost almost nothing to get your book published); it *does* offer a viable means of selling your books (they can appear on the biggest bookselling websites around the world); and it *doesn't* leave you with a house full of unwanted books, because modern technology means that a copy of your book only gets printed when it's actually ordered.

That isn't to say that there aren't still shady characters out there trying to take advantage of authors' vanity by charging them enormous fees for publishing a book that stands very little chance of success, but it does mean that self-publishing – done right – can be a viable and cost effective way of an author taking their book to market.

The benefits of self-publishing

The main benefit of self-publishing, of course, is that the author gets control of whether their book is published or not. There is no need to spend years submitting to countless agents and publishers, building up countless heartbreaking rejection letters, and possibly accepting in the end that your dreams of publication will never come true – you can make them come true.

And this need not be pure vanity on the author's part. Almost every successful book – even such massive hits as *Harry Potter* – usually build up a string of rejections before someone finally accepts them. The professionals that authors rely on when going through the traditional publishing process – the literary agents and the editors – are often, it seems, just not that good at spotting what the public are going to buy. How many potential bestsellers might languish forever in the slush pile, just because agents and editors fail to spot them? What if your book is one of them? The traditional publishing process forces you to rely on the good judgment of others, but the self-publishing process enables you to sidestep that barrier and take your book directly to the public, so that readers can decide for themselves.

Self-publishing also allows you to keep control in other areas. You won't have an editor trying to change your text, and you'll have complete control over what kind of cover your book receives.

Finally, with no publisher or team of editors and accountants taking their slice, you'll probably get to keep a lot more of the retail price of every book you sell. So if you can sell the same amount of books as if you were traditionally published, you'll stand to make a lot more money.

The drawbacks of self-publishing

While self-publishing can guarantee that your book will be available for sale, it cannot guarantee that it will actually sell. Your self-published book will probably have a much lower chance of achieving significant sales than if it had been published traditionally, because it will lack the support that a mainstream publisher could bring. You will have no marketing support, no established position in the marketplace, and no PR – unless you do it yourself. You will have to arrange your own book tours; you will have to do your own sales pitches; you will have to set your own pricing structure; and you will have to manage your own accounts and tax affairs. If you're selling through Amazon or Smashwords or Apple (and if you're not, then why did you bother self-publishing in the first place?) you're going to need to fill in the relevant forms with the IRS (the US tax office) – whether you're a US citizen or not. If you're not a US citizen then you'll have to register with the IRS and complete the necessary tax forms, and potentially other forms for claiming treaty benefits so that you don't get taxed twice (in the US and your home country). And then of course you'll also have to register for tax purposes in your home nation and complete your own tax return there (though you would also have to do this as a traditionally published author).

It can all get very complicated, very confusing, and very lonely. Instead of being able to just be a writer you can find yourself writing less and less and becoming more and more embroiled in the business of publishing a book.

And while it's great to have control over your text and your cover, you'd be ill advised to ignore the value that professionals such as editors and cover designers can bring. It's tempting to think that you don't need an editor – that you've checked the book and had a friend or family member check it too, so it's probably fine – but a professional editor brings a totally different mindset to the process and will check things that won't have even occurred to you and your reader. Without a professional editor, you will almost certainly end up publishing a book which is full of embarrassing mistakes, and trust me – there is no feeling quite as deflating as opening up the first copy of your freshly printed book to see an obvious error jump out – or, even worse, to have it pointed out in an Amazon review, for all to see.

The cover is also incredibly important. Whether for sale on the shelf or on a website, the cover is normally the first point of contact your potential reader has with your book, and will cause them to form immediate opinions about it. A good cover can help a book sell well, but a bad one can kill its chances – and all too often self-published books have amateurish covers that will have readers flicking past them without a second glance.

Finally, the financial benefits of self-publishing can often be illusory. For starters, getting a higher proportion of the retail price is pretty irrelevant if you don't sell any copies. Fifty per cent of nothing is still nothing. Far better to have 15% of something. And then there's the advances. Advances are up-front payments made by traditional publishers to authors, which are off-set against future royalties. So, an author might receive a $5,000 advance before their book is published. When the royalties start coming in, the publisher keeps the first $5,000 to off-set the advance. The good news for the author is that if the book flops and doesn't make $5,000 in royalties they still get to keep the full advance. In an uncertain profession, the security of an advance can be invaluable for an author – and of course it's not something available to self-published authors.

Conclusion

Self-publishing can seem like a tempting shortcut to publication, but in reality it has its own challenges and difficulties. For the moment at least, traditional publishing still offers you the best shot of not only financial success, but also quality of life as a writer. With other people to handle all the other elements of publishing, you get to concentrate on doing what you love.

So we think that writers should always aim for traditional publishing first. It might be a long shot, but if it works then you stand a much better chance of being successful. If you don't manage to get signed by an agent or a publisher then you still have the option of self-publishing, but make sure you don't get tempted to resort to self-publishing too soon – most agents and publishers won't consider self-published works, so this is a one-way street. Once you've self-published your work, you probably won't be able to change your mind and go back to the traditional publishers with your book unless it becomes a huge hit without them. It's therefore important that you exhaust all your traditional publishing options before making the leap to self-publishing. Be prepared for this to take perhaps a few years (lots of agents and publishers can take six months just to respond), and make sure you've submitted to everyone you can on *both* sides of the Atlantic (publishing is a global game these days, and you need to concentrate on the two main centres of English-language publishing (New York and London) equally) before you make the decision to self-publish instead.

However, once you have exhausted all options for traditional publishing, modern self-publishing does offer a genuine alternative path to success, and there are a growing number of self-published authors who have managed to sell millions of copies of their books. If you don't think traditional publishing is going to be an option, we definitely think you should give self-publishing a shot.

For directions on your path through the traditional publishing process see our Writers' Roadmap, above.

If you're sure you've already exhausted all your options for traditional publishing then see below for our quick guide to the self-publishing process.

The Self Publishing Process

Thinking about self-publishing your book? Make sure you go through all these steps first – and in the right order! Do them the wrong way round and you could find yourself wasting time and/or money.

1. Be sure you want to self-publish

You need to be 100% sure that you want to self-publish, because after you've done it there is no going back. Publishers and literary agents will not normally consider books that have been self-published, so if you wanted to get your book to print the old fashioned way you should stop now and rethink. Make absolutely sure that you've exhausted every possible opportunity for traditional publishing before you head down the self-publishing path.

For more information, see "Why choose traditional publishing?" and "Should you self-publish?", above.

2. Protect your copyright

Authors often wonder about what stage in the process they should protect their copyright – often thinking that it's best to leave it till the end so that there are no more changes to make to the book after it is registered.

However, this isn't the case. The key thing is to protect your work before you let other people see it – or, if you've already let other people see it, as soon as possible thereafter.

Don't worry about making small changes to your work after registering it – as long as the work is still recognisable as the same piece of work it will still be protected. Obviously, if you completely change everything you've written then you're going to need another registration, as it will effectively be a different book, but if you've just edited it and made minor alterations this won't affect your protection.

You can register you copyright online at https://www.copyrightregistrationservice.com.

3. Get your work edited

Editing is a vital step often overlooked by authors who self-publish. The result can often be an amateurish book littered with embarrassing mistakes. Any professionally published book will go through an editing process, and it's important that the same applies to your self-published book. It's also important to complete the editing process before beginning the layout, or you could find yourself having to start the layout again from scratch.

4. Choose your self-publishing path

Before you can go any further you are going to need to choose a size for your book, and in order to do that you are going to need to choose a self-publishing path.

There are various different ways of getting self-published, but in general these range from the expensive hands off approach, where you pay a company to do the hard work for you, to the cheap DIY approach, where you do as much as you can yourself.

At the top end, the hands off approach can cost you thousands. At the bottom end, the DIY approach allows you to publish your book for almost nothing.

5. Finalise your layout / typesetting

Before you can finalise your layout (often referred to in the industry as "typesetting") you need to be sure that you've finalised your content – which means having your full work professionally edited and all the necessary changes made. If you decide to make changes after this point it will be difficult and potentially costly, and will require you to go through many of the following steps all over again.

You also need to have selected your path to publication, so that you know what page sizes are available to you, and what page margins you are going to need to apply. If you create a layout that doesn't meet printing requirements (for instance, includes text too close to the edge of the page) then you will have to start the typesetting process all over again.

6. Organise your ISBN

Your book needs to have an ISBN. If you are using a self-publishing service then they may provide you with one of their own, but it is likely to come with restrictions, and the international record for your book will show your self-publishing service as the publisher.

You can acquire your own ISBNs directly from the ISBN issuer, but they do not sell them individually, so you will end up spending quite a lot of money buying more ISBNs than you need. You will, however, have control of the ISBN, and you will be shown as the publisher.

Alternatively, you can purchase a single ISBN at a lower price from an ISBN retailer. This should give you control over the ISBN, however the record for the book will show the ISBN retailer as the publisher, which you may not consider to be ideal.

Whatever you choose, you need to arrange your ISBN no later than this point, because it needs to appear in the preliminary pages (prelims) of your book.

7. Compile your prelims

Your prelims may include a variety of pages, but should always include a title page, a half title page, and an imprint/copyright page. You might then also include other elements, such as a foreword, table of contents, etc. You can only compile your table of contents at this stage, because you need to know your ISBN (this will be included on the copyright/imprint page) and the page numbers for your table of contents. You therefore need to make sure that you are happy with the typesetting and have no further changes to make before compiling your prelims.

8. Create your final press proof

Depending on the self-publishing path you have chosen, you may be able to use a Word file as your final document. However, you need to be careful. In order to print your book it will have to be converted into a press-ready PDF at some point. If a self-publishing service is doing this for you then you will probably find that they own the PDF file that is created, meaning you don't have control over your own press files. Some services will impose hefty charges (hundreds or even more than a thousand dollars) to release these press files.

It might also be the case that you won't get to see the final PDF, and therefore won't get chance to check it for any errors introduced by the conversion process. If it's an automated system, it may also be difficult to control the output you get from it.

We'd suggest that it's best to produce your own PDF files if possible. To do this you will need a copy of Adobe Acrobat Professional, and you will need to be familiar with the correct settings for creating print ready PDFs. Be careful to embed all fonts and make sure that all images are at 300 DPI.

9. Create your cover

Only once your press proof is finalised can you complete your cover design. That's because your cover includes not only the front cover and the back cover, but also (critically) the spine – and the width of the spine will vary according to the number of pages in your final press proof. In order to complete your cover design you therefore need to know your page size, your page count (including all prelims), and your ISBN, as this will appear on the back cover. You also need to get a barcode for your ISBN.

10. Produce your book

Once your cover and press proof are ready you can go through whichever self-publishing path you have chosen to create your book. With some pathways the production of a print proof can be an optional extra that is only available at an extra cost – but we'd recommend standing that cost and getting a print version of your book to check. You never know exactly how it's going to come out until you have a physical copy in your hand.

If you're happy with the proof you can clear your book for release. You don't need to do anything to get it on online retailers like Amazon – they will automatically pick up the ISBN and add your book to their websites themselves.

11. Create an ebook version

In the modern day, having an ebook version of your book is imperative. Ebooks account for a significant proportion of all book sales and are a particularly effective vehicle for unknown and self-published authors.

There are various different file formats used by the different platforms, but .epub is emerging as a standard, and having your book in .epub format should enable you to access all the platforms with a single file.

12. Distribute your ebook

Unlike with print books, you will need to act yourself to get your ebooks into sales channels. At a minimum, you need to ensure that you get your ebook available for sale through Amazon, Apple, and Google Play.

Table of US Literary Agencies

3 Seas Literary Agency L001
Ambassador Speakers Bureau & Literary
    Agency..L013
Barone Literary Agency L036
Baror International, Inc. L037
Bent Agency, The..L052
Betancourt Literary..L057
Betsy Amster Literary Enterprises..................L059
Book Group, The..L068
Bradford Literary Agency L073
Brattle Agency LLC, The L077
Bright Agency (US), The..................................L079
CAA (Creative Artists Agency, LLC) L090
Carol Mann Agency L098
Carolyn Jenks Agency.....................................L100
Compass Talent...L124
Dana Newman Literary, LLC L138
Darhansoff & Verrill Literary Agents...............L142
Diana Finch Literary Agency L154
Don Congdon Associates, Inc.........................L159
Donald Maass Literary Agency L160
Doug Grad Literary Agency L161
Dunham Literary, Inc. L163
Dunow, Carlson & Lerner Agency L166
Ekus Group, The L176
    also L299
Elaine Markson Literary Agency L178
Evan Marshall Agency, The............................L183
Flannery Literary L204
Folio Jr...L207
Folio Literary Management, LLC L207
Friedrich Agency LLC, The.............................L220
Ghosh Literary L231
Glass Literary Management LLC...................L236
Global Lion Intellectual Property
    Management, Inc. L239
Gurman Agency, LLC L257
High Line Literary Collective L279
Inscriptions Literary Agency...........................L289
Inspired Ink Literary L290
Irene Goodman Literary Agency (IGLA).........L291
Javelin..L298
Jean V. Naggar Literary Agency, The.............L299
Joelle Delbourgo Associates, Inc. L301
Joy Harris Literary Agency, Inc.......................L308
Karen Gantz Literary Management L319
Kathryn Green Literary Agency, LLC L322
Kimberley Cameron & Associates L337
KT Literary..L345
Langtons International L354
Leigh Feldman Literary L359
Looking Glass Literary & Media
    Management..L370
Lotus Lane Literary L371
MacGregor & Luedeke....................................L380
Mad Woman Literary Agency L384
Massie McQuilkin & Altman L394
McCormick Literary...L400
Metamorphosis Literary Agency L406
Movable Type Management...........................L420
Nelson Literary Agency, LLC L435
Olswanger Literary LLC L449
Paradigm Talent and Literary Agency L454
Paul S. Levine Literary Agency......................L459
Perry Literary L466
Regina Ryan Books...L489
Root Literary L503
Rosenberg Group, The...................................L505
Rubin Pfeffer Content, LLC L509
Rudy Agency, The...L510
Selectric Artists L525
Sheree Bykofsky Associates, Inc...................L532
Sternig & Byrne Literary Agency....................L550
Stringer Literary Agency LLC, The.................L553
Stuart Krichevsky Literary Agency, Inc. L556
Susan Schulman Literary Agency...................L557
Susanna Lea Associates.................................L558
Victoria Sanders & Associates LLC L584
Wallace Literary Agency, The........................L016
Zack Company, Inc, The L615

Table of UK Literary Agencies

A.M. Heath & Company Limited, Author's Agents L002
Aevitas Creative Management (ACM) UK L006
Agency (London) Ltd, The L008
Alice Williams Literary L012
Andlyn L014
Andrew Nurnberg Associates, Ltd L016
Anne Clark Literary Agency L020
Annette Green Authors' Agency L021
Antony Harwood Limited L022
Apple Tree Literary Ltd L023
AVAnti Productions & Management L029
Bath Literary Agency L042
Bent Agency (UK), The L051
   also L052
BKS Agency, The L063
Blair Partnership, The L064
Blake Friedmann Literary Agency Ltd L065
Bookseeker Agency L069
Bright Agency (UK), The L078
Brotherstone Creative Management L081
CAA (London) L091
   also L090
Canterbury Literary Agency L096
Caroline Davidson Literary Agency L099
Children's Books North Agency L112
Creative Roots Studio L131
Curtis Brown L135
Darley Anderson Agency, The L143
Darley Anderson Children's L144
David Godwin Associates L145
David Higham Associates Ltd L146
DHH Literary Agency Ltd L152
Diamond Kahn and Woods (DKW) Literary Agency Ltd L153
DunnFogg L165

Eddison Pearson Ltd L170
Elaine Steel L179
Eunice McMullen Children's Literary Agent Ltd L182
Feldstein Agency, The L191
Felicity Bryan Associates L192
for Authors, A L209
FRA (Futerman, Rose, & Associates) L214
Fraser Ross Associates L216
Frog Literary Agency L221
Gemma Cooper Literary L228
Graham Maw Christie Literary Agency L246
Greene & Heaton Ltd L251
Greenstone Literary L252
Hanbury Agency, The L261
Hannah Sheppard Literary Agency L262
Hardman & Swainson L265
Janklow & Nesbit UK Ltd L297
JFL Agency L300
Johnson & Alcock L302
Jonathan Clowes Ltd L304
Judith Murdoch Literary Agency L309
Judy Daish Associates Ltd L310
Julie Crisp Literary Agency L311
Kane Literary Agency L316
Kate Barker Literary, TV, & Film Agency L320
Kate Nash Literary Agency L321
Keane Kataria Literary Agency L325
Ki Agency Ltd L331
Knight Features L340
Kruger Cowne L344
Laxfield Literary Associates L356
Lewinsohn Literary L363
Lindsay Literary Agency L366
Liverpool Literary Agency, The L369
Lutyens and Rubinstein L375

Madeleine Milburn Literary, TV & Film Agency L385
Marsh Agency, The L390
Mic Cheetham Literary Agency L407
Mulcahy Sweeney Literary Agency L423
Narrow Road Company, The L432
Northbank Talent Management L442
Originate Literary Agency L451
Perez Literary & Entertainment L463
PEW Literary L468
Plot Agency, The L478
Portobello Literary L479
Rachel Mills Literary L485
Rebecca Carter Literary L487
Redhammer L488
Robertson Murray Literary Agency L496
Rochelle Stevens & Co L498
Rocking Chair Books L499
Rogers, Coleridge & White Ltd L501
Rupert Crew Ltd L511
Sayle Literary Agency, The L521
Seventh Agency L527
Shaw Agency, The L529
Shesto Literary L533
Skylark Literary L540
Sophie Hicks Agency L545
StoryWise L552
Theseus Agency, The L573
Valerie Hoskins Associates L582
Viney Agency, The L585
Wade & Co Literary Agency L588
Watson, Little Ltd L590
Whispering Buffalo Literary Agency L599
YMU Books L613
Zeno Agency L617

Table of US Literary Agents

Abellera, Lisa	L337
Abou, Stephanie	L394
Acheampong, Kwaku	L003
also	L100
Aldridge, Kaylyn	L010
also	L406
Alekseii, Keir	L011
Altman, Elias	L394
Amling, Eric	L142
Amster, Betsy	L059
Andrade, Hannah	L015
also	L073
Ange, Anna	L019
Arms, Victoria Wells	L025
Bajek, Lauren	L031
Baker-Baughman, Bernadette	L584
Balow, Dan	L033
Barbara, Stephen	L034
Barer, Julie	L068
Barone, Denise	L036
Baror, Danny	L037
Baror-Shapiro, Heather	L037
Barr, Anjanette	L038
also	L163
Bassoff, Ethan	L394
Bauman, Erica	L043
Baumer, Jan	L044
also	L207
Beek, Emily Van	L207
Bender, Faye	L068
Bent, Jenny	L053
also	L052
Berdinsky, Kendall	L054
Bernardi, Amanda	L056
also	L279
Betancourt, Rose	L058
also	L057
Bewley, Elizabeth	L061
Bloom, Brettne	L068
Borstel, Stefanie Sanchez Von	L070
Bowlin, Sarah	L071
Bradford, Laura	L074
also	L073
Brailsford, Karen	L075
Brewer, Amy	L406
Brooks, Savannah	L080
also	L345
Brouckaert, Justin	L083
Brown, Megan	L084
Bukowski, Danielle	L086
Burby, Danielle	L087
also	L384
Burl, Emelie	L557
Bykofsky, Sheree	L532
Byrne, Jack	L550
Cabello, Analia	L092
Cameron, Kimberley	L093
also	L337
Campos, Vanessa	L095
Cappello, Victoria	L097
also	L052
Carlson, Jennifer	L166
Carr, Heather	L220
Carr, Jamie	L101
also	L068
Carson, Lucy	L220
Chambliss, Jamie	L207
Chanchani, Sonali	L108
also	L207
Chiotti, Danielle	L113
Christensen, Erica	L115
also	L406
Chromy, Adam	L420
Cichello, Kayla	L117
Cloughley, Amy	L337
Combemale, Chris	L122
Comparato, Andrea	L123
also	L289
Concepcion, Cristina	L159
Congdon, Michael	L159
Cooper, Maggie	L129
Crandall, Becca	L130
also	L100
Cross, Claudia	L207
Curry, Michael	L160
Cusick, John	L136
also	L207
Dail, Laura	L137
Danaczko, Melissa	L139
also	L556
Danko, Margaret	L140
also	L279
Darga, Jon Michael	L141
Darhansoff, Liz	L142
Datz, Arielle	L166
Dawson, Liza	L148
Decker, Stacia	L166
Delbourgo, Joelle	L301
Derviskadic, Dado	L151
also	L207
Deyoe, Cori	L001
Dickerson, Donya	L155
Dolin, Lily	L157
Dominguez, Adriana	L158
Doraswamy, Priya	L371
Draper, Claire	L162
Dunham, Jennie	L163
Dunow, Henry	L166
Dystel, Jane	L167
Eason, Lynette	L169
Edelstein, Anne	L171
Einstein, Susanna	L173
also	L166
Eisenbraun, Nicole	L174
Eisenmann, Caroline	L175
Ekstrom, Rachel	L207
Ekus, Lisa	L176
Ekus, Sally	L177
also	L176
also	L299
Ericka T. Phillips	L181
Esersky, Gareth	L098
Fabien, Samantha	L186
also	L503
Fazzari, Hillary	L188
also	L073
Feldman, Leigh	L189
also	L359
Feldmann, Kait Lee	L190
also	L345
Ferguson, T.S.	L195
Fernando, Kimberly	L198
also	L449
Figueroa, Melanie	L199
also	L503
Finch, Diana	L201
also	L154
Flannery, Jennifer	L204
Flynn, Amy Thrall	L205
Fox, Aram	L212
also	L394
Frankel, Valerie	L215
Friedman, Claire	L217
Friedman, Jessica	L218
Friedman, Rebecca	L219
Friedrich, Molly	L220
Fuentes, Sarah	L222
Galvin, Lori	L226
Gantz, Karen	L319
Geiger, Ellen	L227
Gerecke, Jeff	L178
Getzler, Josh	L229
Ghahremani, Lilly	L230
Ghosh, Anna	L232
also	L231
Gilbert, Tara	L233
also	L345
Gisondi, Katie	L235
Glass, Alex	L236
Goderich, Miriam	L240
Goetz, Adria	L241
also	L345
Goff, Ellen	L242
Goldstein, Veronica	L244
Goloboy, Jennifer	L160
Goodman, Irene	L291
Grad, Doug	L161
Graham, Stacey	L247
also	L001
Graham, Susan	L248
also	L166
Grajkowski, Kara	L249
also	L001
Grajkowski, Michelle	L001
Granger, David	L250
Green, Kathryn	L322
Grossman, Loren R.	L459
Gruber, Pam	L253
also	L279
Guinsler, Robert	L255
Gunic, Masha	L256
Gurman, Susan	L257
Haggerty, Taylor	L258
also	L503
Hakim, Serene	L259
Haley, Jolene	L260
also	L160
Hannigan, Carrie	L263
Hansen, Stephanie	L264
also	L406
Harper, Logan	L267
Harris, Erin	L268
also	L207
Harris, Joy	L308
Hawk, Susan	L269
Hensley, Chelsea	L274
also	L384
Hernandez, Saritza	L275
Hernando, Paloma	L276
Heymont, Lane	L277

Name	Page	Name	Page	Name	Page
Hildebrand, Cole	L280	McClure, Cameron	L160	Richesin, Nicki	L166
also	L299	McCormick, David	L400	Richter, Rick	L493
Hogrebe, Christina	L283	McDonald, Caitlin	L160	Roberts, Soumeya Bendimerad	L495
Hosier, Erin	L166	McNicol, Andy	L402	Robinson, Quressa	L497
Hwang, Annie	L288	McQuilkin, Rob	L394	also	L207
Jackson, Amanda Hepp	L295	Mendia, Isabel	L403	Rofe, Jennifer	L500
Jackson, Eleanor	L166	Milusich, Grace	L412	Romano, Annie	L502
Jackson, Jennifer	L160	also	L370	also	L449
Jenks, Carolyn	L100	Moore, Mary C.	L415	Root, Holly	L504
Johnson, Jared	L303	Moorhead, Max	L416	also	L503
also	L449	also	L394	Rosenberg, Barbara Collins	L506
Jones, Barbara	L305	Mortimer, Michele	L418	also	L505
also	L556	also	L142	Ross, Whitney	L507
Julien, Ria	L312	Murgolo, Karen	L427	also	L279
Kantor, Camille	L317	Murphy, Dana	L068	Rossitto, Stefanie	L508
also	L337	Muscato, Nate	L429	Rushall, Kathleen	L512
Kardon, Julia	L318	Mustelier, James	L052	Rutman, Jim	L514
Karinch, Maryann	L510	Napolitano, Maria	L431	Ryan, Regina	L489
Kean, Taylor Martindale	L324	also	L345	Salazar, Des	L515
Kellerman, Carly	L328	Nasson, Melissa	L509	also	L406
Kenny, Julia	L329	Necarsulmer, Edward	L166	Sanchez, Kaitlyn	L516
also	L166	Nelson, Kristin	L436	also	L073
Kerr, Kat	L160	also	L435	Sanders, Rayhane	L517
Kim, Jennifer	L333	Nelson, Patricia	L437	also	L394
Kim, Sally M.	L335	also	L370	Sanders, Victoria	L584
Kleinman, Jeff	L207	Newman, Dana	L138	Sant, Kelly Van	L518
Knigge, Sheyla	L339	Nguyen, Kiana	L160	also	L345
also	L279	Nichols, Mariah	L438	Schelling, Christopher	L525
Kotchman, Katie	L159	Niumata, Erin	L439	Schroder, Heather	L124
Kracht, Elizabeth	L341	also	L207	Schulman, Susan	L557
also	L337	Niv, Daniel	L440	Schwartz, Hannah	L556
Krichevsky, Stuart	L342	also	L449	Seidman, Yishai	L166
also	L556	Nolan, Laura	L441	Shreve, Jeff	L133
Krienke, Mary	L343	Nyen, Renee	L443	Silberman, Jeff	L207
Kye-Casella, Maura	L159	also	L345	Silbersack, John	L052
Lakosil, Natalie	L347	O'Brien, Lee	L444	Siobhan, Aiden	L539
also	L370	also	L370	Sluytman, Antoinette Van	L541
Langton, Linda	L354	O'Neill, Molly	L446	also	L370
Latshaw, Katherine	L355	also	L503	Soler, Shania N.	L543
also	L207	Oefelein, Colleen	L448	also	L406
Lerner, Betsy	L166	also	L380	Soloway, Jennifer March	L544
Levine, Paul S.	L459	Olson, Neil	L394	Sorg, Arley	L546
Levitt, Sarah	L361	Olswanger, Anna	L450	also	L345
Levy, Yael	L362	also	L449	Stephens, Jenny	L549
also	L449	Orloff, Edward	L400	Stevenson, Julie	L394
Lewis, Alison	L364	Ostby, Kristin	L452	Stone, Geoffrey	L510
Lightner, Kayla	L365	Pages, Saribel	L453	Stringer, Marlene	L554
Liss, Laurie	L368	Pareja, Sandra	L394	also	L553
Lovell, Jake	L372	Parker, Elana Roth	L455	Strothman, Wendy	L555
Luedeke, Amanda	L373	Patterson, David	L457	Sutherland, Kari	L559
also	L380	also	L556	also	L345
Maass, Donald	L377	Patterson, Emma	L458	Sweren, Becky	L564
also	L160	Perel, Kim	L462	Symonds, Laurel	L565
Mack, Kate	L381	also	L279	also	L345
MacKenzie, Joanna	L382	Perry, Joseph	L466	Takikawa, Marin	L566
also	L435	Pestritto, Carrie	L467	also	L220
MacLeod, Lauren	L383	Pfeffer, Rubin	L469	Tannenbaum, Amy	L568
Maffei, Dorian	L337	also	L509	Tasman, Alice	L569
Malin, Hester	L319	Phelan, Beth	L470	also	L299
Maltese, Alyssa	L387	Philips, Ariana	L471	Terlip, Paige	L570
also	L503	also	L299	Testerman, Kate	L571
Mann, Carol	L098	Phillips, Aemilia	L472	also	L345
Marini, Victoria	L388	also	L556	Thayer, Henry	L572
also	L279	Pine, Gideon	L475	Tibbets, Anne	L576
Marr, Jill	L389	Plant, Zoe	L476	also	L160
Marshall, Evan	L183	also	L052	Tran, Jennifer Chen	L578
Marshall, Jen	L391	Pomerance, Ruth	L207	also	L236
Marsiglia, Caroline	L392	Posner, Marcy	L480	Troha, Steve	L207
Massie, Maria	L394	also	L207	Udden, Jennifer	L580
Matte, Rebecca	L395	Potter, Madison	L481	Uh, Cindy	L090
also	L073	also	L449	Usselman, Laura	L581
Mattson, Jennifer	L396	Queen, Pilar	L400	also	L556
Maurer, Shari	L397	Ramer, Susan	L486	Vance, Lisa Erbach	L583
also	L553	also	L159	Watson, Mackenzie Brady	L556
McBride, Juliana	L399	Reed, Adam	L308	Watterson, Jessica	L591
McCarthy, Bridget	L400	Reid, Janet	L490	Weed, Elisabeth	L068

Weiman, Paula L592	Whatnall, Michaela L598	Zachary, Lane L394
Weimann, Frank L207	White, Melissa L207	Zack, Andrew L615
Weiss, Alexandra L593	Wickers, Chandler L600	Zacker, Marietta B L616
Weitzner, Tess L594	*also* L556	Zuckerbrot, Renee L618
Weltz, Jennifer L596	Wilson, Desiree L606	*also* L394
also L299	*also* L370	Zuraw-Friedland, Ayla L619
Westin, Erin Casey L597	Wyckoff, Joanne L098	

Table of UK Literary Agents

Adams, Seren	L004	
Alcock, Michael	L009	
also	L302	
Anderson, Darley	L143	
Andrew, Nelle	L485	
Andrew-Lynch, Davinia	L017	
also	L135	
Andrews, Gina	L018	
also	L008	
Armstrong, Susan	L026	
Arnold, Frances	L498	
Atyeo, Charlotte	L028	
Azis, Ollie	L030	
Bagnell, Becky	L366	
Bal, Emma	L032	
also	L385	
Barker, Kate	L320	
Barnard, Arthur	L035	
also	L008	
Barr, Nicola	L039	
also	L051	
Barrett, Emily	L040	
also	L064	
Bartholomew, Jason	L041	
also	L063	
Baxter, Veronique	L045	
also	L146	
Beaumont, Diana	L046	
also	L152	
Begum, Salma	L047	
Bell, Eva	L048	
Belton, Maddy	L049	
also	L385	
Bennett, Laura	L050	
also	L369	
Benson, Ian	L008	
Berlyne, John	L055	
also	L617	
Biltoo, Nicola	L008	
Blakey, Simon	L008	
Blunt, Felicity	L135	
Bolger, Maeve	L066	
also	L008	
Bolton, Camilla	L067	
also	L143	
Boulton, Hannah	L008	
Brace, Samantha	L072	
Brannan, Maria	L076	
Brotherstone, Charlie	L082	
also	L006	
also	L081	
Buckley, Louise	L085	
also	L262	
Burke, Kate	L088	
also	L065	
Burns, Camille	L089	
also	L153	
Calder, Rachel	L521	
Campbell, Charlie	L094	
Caravéo, Amber J.	L540	
Carroll, Megan	L102	
also	L590	
Carter, Rebecca	L103	
also	L487	
Cartey, Claire	L104	
Caskie, Robert	L105	
Cavaciuti, Maddalena	L106	
also	L146	
Chang, Nicola	L109	
also	L146	
Charnace, Edwina de	L110	
also	L423	
Cheetham, Mic	L407	
Cho, Catherine	L114	
also	L348	
Christie, Jennifer	L116	
also	L246	
Churchill, Julia	L002	
Clark, Anne	L020	
Clarke, Caro	L118	
also	L479	
Clarke, Catherine	L119	
also	L192	
Cochran, Alexander	L120	
Coleridge, Gill	L501	
Colwill, Charlotte	L121	
Conrad, Claire Paterson	L125	
also	L297	
Conville, Clare	L126	
Coombes, Clare	L127	
also	L369	
Cooper, Gemma	L128	
also	L228	
Copeland, Sam	L501	
Cox, Peter	L488	
Crossland, Annette	L209	
Crowley, Sheila	L132	
also	L135	
Curran, Sabhbh	L134	
also	L135	
Daish, Judy	L310	
Davidson, Caroline	L099	
Davies, Olivia	L147	
also	L338	
Davis, Meg	L331	
DeBlock, Liza	L149	
Delamere, Hilary	L008	
Demblon, Gabrielle	L150	
also	L590	
Dillsworth, Elise	L156	
also	L146	
Dixon, Isobel	L065	
Doherty, Broo	L152	
Dolby, Trevor	L006	
Dunn, Ben	L164	
also	L165	
Durbridge, Stephen	L008	
Edenborough, Sam	L172	
Edwards, Max	L006	
also	L023	
Edwards, Stephen	L501	
Ellis-Martin, Sian	L180	
also	L065	
Elliston, Tracey	L310	
Evans, Ann	L304	
Evans, Bethan	L008	
Evans, David	L184	
also	L146	
also	L146	
also	L245	
Evans, Kate	L185	
Fairweather, Natasha	L501	
Faulks, Holly	L187	
also	L251	
Feldstein, Paul	L191	
Feldstein, Susan	L191	
Fellows, Abi	L193	
also	L152	
Ferguson, Hannah	L194	
also	L265	
Fergusson, Julie	L196	
Finan, Ciara	L200	
also	L135	
Finch, Alison	L300	
Finch, Rebeka	L202	
also	L143	
Finegan, Stevie	L203	
also	L617	
Fogg, Jack	L206	
also	L165	
Fontaine, Melissa	L208	
Forrester, Jemima	L210	
also	L146	
Foster, Clara	L211	
also	L006	
Francis, Will	L297	
Fraser, Lindsey	L216	
Gahan, Isobel	L225	
Garrett, Georgia	L501	
Geller, Jonny	L135	
Gillam, Bianca	L234	
also	L617	
Glencross, Stephanie	L237	
also	L146	
Glenister, Emily	L238	
also	L152	
Glover, Georgia	L146	
Godman, Susannah	L375	
Godwin, David	L145	
Goldblatt, Rachel	L243	
also	L135	
Goodall, Bill	L209	
Gordon, Andrew	L245	
also	L146	
Grunewald, Hattie	L254	
also	L064	
Haines, Katie	L008	
Hamilton, Bill	L002	
Hammam, Samar	L499	
Hanbury, Margaret	L261	
Hardman, Caroline	L265	
Hare, Jessica	L266	
also	L008	
Harwood, Antony	L022	
Hawn, Molly Ker	L270	
also	L051	
Hayden, Viola	L271	
also	L135	
Headley, David H.	L272	
also	L152	
Heathfield, Laura	L273	
also	L252	
Heaton, Carol	L251	
Heller, Jenny	L496	
Hewson, Andrew	L302	
Hewson, Jenny	L501	
Hickman, Emily	L278	
also	L008	

Hicks, Sophie	L545
Hobbs, Victoria	L002
Hodges, Jodie	L282
Holloway, Sally	L284
also	L192
Holroyde, Penny	L285
Hordern, Kate	L286
Hornsley, Sarah	L287
also	L430
Hoskins, Valerie	L582
Illingworth, Harry	L152
Ireson, Amy	L432
Ireson, Dan	L432
Ireson, James	L432
Ireson, Richard	L432
Irvine, Lucy	L292
Irving, Dotti	L293
Israel, Clare	L294
also	L146
Jamieson, Molly	L296
also	L282
Jones, Cara	L501
Jones, Philip Gwyn	L307
Jones, Rebecca	L501
Kahn, Ella Diamond	L314
also	L153
Kaliszewska, Joanna	L315
also	L063
Kataria, Kiran	L325
Kavanagh, Jade	L323
also	L143
Kavanagh, Simon	L407
Keane, Sara	L325
Keeffe, Sara O'	L326
also	L016
Keen, Mariam	L599
Kelleher, Sophie	L327
also	L008
Kendrick, Tristan	L501
Keren, Eli	L330
Killingley, Jessica	L332
also	L063
Kinnersley, Jonathan	L008
Kirby, Robert	L338
Kreitman, Julia	L008
Kremer, Lizzy	L146
Laluyaux, Laurence	L501
Lambert, Sophie	L348
Lane, Helen	L349
also	L331
Langham, Sara	L351
also	L146
Langlee, Lina	L352
Langton, Becca	L353
also	L143
Lazar, Veronica	L029
Leach, Saskia	L357
also	L321
Leeke, Jessica	L358
also	L385
Leon, Nina	L360
also	L463
Lineberry, Isabel	L367
also	L463
Little, Mandy	L590
Lloyd, Jonathan	L135
Lloyd, Rozzy	L432
Lord, Dominic	L300
Lund, Nicky	L374
also	L146
Lutyens, Alice	L135
Lyon, Rebecca	L376
MacDonald, Emily	L378
Macdougall, Laura	L379
Maidment, Olivia	L386
also	L385
Marland, Matthew	L501
Martin, Olivia	L393
Maw, Jane Graham	L398
also	L246
McKinley, Christabel	L401
also	L146
McLay, Gill	L042
McMullen, Eunice	L182
Mendlesohn, Adam	L432
Merullo, Annabel	L405
Michel, Caroline	L408
Middleton, Leah	L409
Milburn, Madeleine	L411
also	L385
Mills, Rachel	L485
Molloy, Jess	L414
also	L135
Montgomery, Caroline	L511
Morrell, Imogen	L417
also	L251
Moult, Joanna	L540
Moylett, Lisa	L421
Mozley, Jack	L422
also	L463
Mulcahy, Ivan	L424
also	L423
Mumby, Helen	L425
Mundy, Toby	L426
also	L006
Munson, Oli	L002
Murdoch, Judith	L309
Murray, Hilary	L496
Murray, Judith	L428
also	L251
Mushens, Juliet	L430
Nash, Justin	L321
Nash, Kate	L321
Neely, Rachel	L434
Nelson, Zoe	L501
Nicklin, Susie	L390
Nundy, Sarah	L016
Nurnberg, Andrew	L016
O'Grady, Niamh	L445
O'Shea, Amy	L447
also	L246
Pass, Marina de	L456
Pearson, Clare	L170
Peddle, Kay	L460
Pelham, Imogen	L461
Perez, Kristina	L464
also	L463
Perotto-Wills, Martha	L465
also	L051
Petty, Rachel	L064
Pickering, Juliet	L473
also	L065
Pierce, Rosie	L474
also	L135
Plitt, Carrie	L477
also	L192
Power, Anna	L482
also	L302
Power, Deirdre	L483
also	L146
Preston, Amanda	L484
Rees, Florence	L002
Reilly, Milly	L491
Riccardi, Francesca	L492
also	L321
Ripley-Duggan, Louise	L494
also	L573
Ritchie, Rebecca	L002
Robertson, Charlotte	L496
Robinson, Peter	L501
Roderick, Nemonie Craven	L304
Rose, Guy	L214
Ross, Kathryn	L216
Rutherford, Laetitia	L513
also	L590
Sang, Angelique Tran Van	L192
Savvides, Marilia	L520
also	L478
Scarfe, Rory	L064
Schmidt, Leah	L008
Schofield, Hannah	L522
Schwizer, Fabienne	L523
also	L331
Seager, Chloe	L524
also	L385
Seymour, Charlotte	L528
also	L302
Shaw, Kate	L529
Sheldon, Caroline	L530
also	L501
Sheppard, Hannah	L531
also	L262
Shestopal, Camilla	L534
also	L533
Silk, Julia	L535
Silver, Lydia	L143
Simons, Tanera	L536
also	L252
Simpson, Cara Lee	L537
Singh, Amandeep	L538
also	L246
Smith, Emily	L008
Smith, Georgie	L542
also	L146
Spackman, James	L547
also	L063
Standen, Yasmin	L316
Steed, Hayley	L548
also	L297
Stevens, Rochelle	L498
Straus, Peter	L501
Summerhayes, Cathryn	L135
Sutherland-Hawes, Alice	L560
Swainson, Joanna	L561
also	L265
Sweeney, Sallyanne	L562
also	L423
Sweet, Emily	L563
also	L006
Talbot, Emily	L567
also	L282
Thompson, Paul	L069
Thorneycroft, Euan	L574
also	L002
Thwaites, Steph	L575
also	L135
Tillett, Tanya	L008
Topping, Antony	L577
also	L251
Turner, Matthew	L501
Veecock, Sarah	L432
Viney, Charlie	L586
also	L006
also	L585
Vogt-Vincent, Orli	L587
also	L146
Wade, Robin	L588
Waldie, Zoe	L501
Wallace, Clare	L143
also	L144
Walsh, Caroline	L589
also	L146
Walsh, Patrick	L468
Watson, Rebecca	L582
White, Pat	L501
Wild, Gary	L300
Williams, Alice	L601
also	L012

Williams, Katie L602	Wilson, Ed L607	Woods, Bryony L610
also L008	*also* L302	*also* L153
Williams, Laura L603	Winchester, Donald L590	Woollard, Jessica L611
also L251	Wise, Gordon L135	*also* L146
Williams, Sarah L545	Wood, Caroline L608	Yeoh, Rachel L612
Williamson, Jo L604	*also* L192	*also* L385
also L022	Wood, Ed L609	Young, Claudia L614
Wills, James L590	*also* L064	*also* L251
Wilson, Claire L501		

Table of Canadian Literary Agents

Armada, Kurestin L024
   also L503
Arthurson, Wayne L027
Bhasin, Tamanna L062
Cavanagh, Claire L107
Chevais, Jennifer L111

Foxx, Kat L213
Hiyate, Sam L281
Kim, Julia L334
Kimber, Natalie L336
Kong, Kelvin L313
Mihell, Natasha L410

Motala, Tasneem L419
Slopen, Beverley L060
Trudel, Jes L579
Wells, Karmen L595
Willms, Kathryn L605

Table of US Magazines

30 North	M001
32 Poems	M002
aaduna	M003
About Place Journal	M004
Account, The	M006
African American Golfer's Digest	M008
African American Review	M009
African Voices	M010
Agni	M011
Agricultural History	M012
Alabama Heritage	M013
Alaska Quarterly Review	M014
Albemarle	M015
Alfred Hitchcock Mystery Magazine	M016
American Short Fiction	M018
Ann Arbor Observer	M022
Arboreal	M023
Arts & Letters	M027
Asimov's Science Fiction	M029
Atlanta Magazine	M030
Atlanta Review	M031
Atlantic Northeast	M032
AZ Foothills Magazine	M036
Babybug	M037
Bacopa Literary Review	M038
Baffler, The	M039
Barren Magazine	M041
Bear Deluxe Magazine, The	M044
Belmont Story Review	M047
Beloit Fiction Journal	M048
Berks County Living	M049
Better Homes and Gardens	M051
Better Than Starbucks	M052
Big Fiction	M055
Black Moon Magazine	M056
Black Warrior Review	M058
Blue Earth Review	M059
Blue Mesa Review	M060
Bluegrass Unlimited	M061
Boston Review	M062
Bowhunter	M063
Boyfriend Village	M064
also	M058
Cafe Irreal, The	M071
Caribbean Writer, The	M073
Carolina Woman	M074
CharlottesvilleFamily	M076
Chautauqua Literary Journal	M077
Cheshire	M078
also	M094
Cobblestone	M079
Coil, The	P010
Cola	M081
Commonweal	M082
Concho River Review	M083
Conjunctions	M084
Conjunctions Online	M085
also	M084
Cowboys & Indians	M091
Crazyhorse / Swamp Pink	M093
Cream City Review	M094
Creative Nonfiction	M095
Cricket	M096
Cruising World	M097
CutBank	M099
Deep Overstock Magazine	M103
El Portal	M110
Emerge Literary Journal	M111
Entrepreneur	M112
Fabula Argentea	M115
Fate	M117
Faultline	M118
Feminist Studies	M119
Fiction	M120
First For Women	M122
First Line, The	M123
Five Points	M124
Folio	M126
Fourth River, The	M131
Fugue	M133
Funeral Business Solutions	M134
Gargoyle Online	M137
Georgia Review, The	M139
Ginosko Literary Journal	M140
Glacier, The	M141
Go World Travel Magazine	M142
Graywolf Lab	M145
also	P152
Gulf Coast: A Journal of Literature and Fine Arts	M147
Half Mystic Journal	M149
also	P157
Hanging Loose	M150
Harpur Palate	M151
Heavy Traffic	M153
Helix, The	M154
Horse & Rider	M159
Hotel Amerika	M160
Hunger Mountain	M161
I-70 Review	M162
Idaho Review	M163
Identity Theory	M164
Image	M166
Indiana Review	M167
Kenyon Review, The	M179
Leisure Group Travel	M183
Literary Mama	M187
Lost Lake Folk Opera Magazine	M193
also	P336
Louisiana Literature	M194
MacGuffin, The	M195
Manoa	M199
marie claire	M200
Marlin	M201
Massachusetts Review, The	M202
Meetinghouse	M203
Michigan Quarterly Review	M204
Micromance Magazine	M205
Mid-American Review	M206
Midsummer Dream House	M207
Midway Journal	M208
Missouri Review, The	M209
Modern Haiku	M211
Moonday Mag	M213
MQR Mixtape	M214
also	M204
Mystery Magazine	M216
Nashville Review	M217
New England Review	M220
Obsidian: Literature in the African Diaspora	M227
Pacifica Literary Review	M231
Paris Review, The	M233
Pleiades	M238
Ploughshares	M239
Poetry	M241
Preservation Magazine	M248
Qu Literary Magazine	M253
Radar Poetry	M256
Reactor	M258
River Hills Traveler	M263
River Styx	M264
Ruralite	M266
Saddlebag Dispatches	M267
Savannah Magazine	M269
Scifaikuest	M270
Second Factory	M274
also	P399
Seventeen	M275
Shenandoah	M277
Sierra	M281
Sinister Wisdom	M282
SmokeLong Quarterly	M283
SOMA	M285
South Carolina Review	M289
Southern Humanities Review	M290
Southern Review, The	M291
Southern Theatre	M292
Southwest Review	M293
Spa Magazine	M295
Spitball	M297
Story Unlikely	M300
Strange Horizons	M301
Strategic Finance	M302
Studio One	M304
Sunspot Literary Journal	M305
Tahoma Literary Review	M308
Thin Air Magazine	M314
Third Coast	M315
Threepenny Review, The	M317
Tributaries	M320
also	M131
Tusculum Review, The	M321
UCity Review	M322
Unfit Magazine	M326
Vagabond City	M327
Vestal Review	M329
Virginia Quarterly Review, The	M330
Virginia Wine & Country Life	M331
Virginia Wine & Country Weddings	M332
Waccamaw	M335
West Branch	M339
WestWard Quarterly	M340
Wine Enthusiast	M343
Yale Review, The	M344
Yankee Magazine	M345
Yellow Mama Webzine	M346
Zoetrope: All-Story	M352
Zone 3	M353

Table of UK Magazines

Abridged M005
Acumen M007
Allegro Poetry Magazine M017
Amethyst Review M019
And Other Poems M020
Architectural Review, The M025
Art Quarterly M026
Atrium M033
Auroras & Blossoms PoArtMo Anthology M035
Bandit Fiction M040
BBC History Magazine M042
Beano, The M043
Bee, The M045
Bella M046
Best of British M050
BFS Horizons M053
BFS Journal M054
Black Static M057
Britain Magazine M066
BSFA Review, The M067
Business & Accountancy Daily M068
Business Traveller M069
Butcher's Dog M070
Chapman M075
Cocoa Girl M080
Conversation (UK), The M087
Crystal Magazine M098
Dark Horse, The M101
Dawntreader, The M102
Descent M104
Dream Catcher M106
Dumfries and Galloway Life M108
Facts & Fiction M116
Flash: The International Short-Short Story
  Magazine M125
Fortean Times: The Journal of Strange
  Phenomena M127
Forty20 .... M128
  also P331
Foundation: The International Review of
  Science Fiction M129
Fourteen Poems M130
Frogmore Papers, The M132
Future Fire, The M135
Garden Answers M136
Geographical Journal, The M138
Granta M144
Great Outdoors (TGO), The M146
Gutter Magazine M148

Healthy M152
Hello! M155
Hertfordshire Life M156
History Today M157
Homes & Antiques M158
Idler, The M165
Ink Sweat and Tears M168
Insurance Post M169
International Piano M170
Interzone M171
Irish Pages M173
Journal, The M176
Kent Life M178
Kids Alive! M180
Lake, The M181
Leisure Painter M184
Lighthouse M185
Linguist, The M186
London Grip M188
London Grip New Poetry M189
  also M188
London Magazine, The M190
London Review of Books M191
Long Poem Magazine M192
Magma M196
Manchester Review, The M198
Modern Poetry in Translation M212
My Weekly M215
Neon M219
New Internationalist M221
New Statesman M222
New Welsh Reader M223
Norfolk & Suffolk Bride M224
North, The M225
Northern Gravy M226
OK! Magazine M228
Oxford Poetry M229
Oxford Review of Books M230
Panorama M232
Passionfruit Review, The M234
PC Pro M235
People's Friend Pocket Novels M236
  also M237
People's Friend, The M237
PN Review M240
Poetry Birmingham Literary Journal M242
Poetry London M244
Poetry Wales M245
Political Quarterly, The M246

Power Cut Lite M247
Present Tense P104
Pride M249
Prole M250
Pulsar Poetry Magazine M251
Pushing Out the Boat M252
Racecar Engineering M255
Rail Express M257
Red Magazine M259
Rialto, The M261
Riposte M262
Rugby World M265
Sailing Today M268
Scots Magazine, The M271
Scottish Field M272
Scribble M273
Shearsman M276
Ships Monthly Magazine M278
Shooter Literary Magazine M279
Shoreline of Infinity M280
Snowflake Magazine M284
Somerset Life M286
South M288
Speciality Food M296
Square Mile Magazine M298
Structo Magazine M303
Supplement, The M306
Swimming Pool News M307
Take a Break's Take a Puzzle M310
Tears in the Fence M311
That's Life! M313
This England M316
Times Literary Supplement (TLS), The M318
Ulster Business M323
Uncut M324
Under the Radar M325
  also P257
Viz M333
Vogue M334
Wallpaper M337
Wasafiri M338
Wet Grain M341
Yorkshire Dalesman, The M347
Yorkshire Life M348
Yorkshire Women's Life Magazine M349
Yours M350
Yours Fiction – Women's Special Series M351

Table of Canadian Magazines

Angela Poetry Magazine M021
Arc M024
Asian Social Science M028
Brick M065
Canadian Dimension M072
Contemporary Verse 2......................................M086
Cottage Life..M090
Dalhousie Review, The....................................M100
Diver...M105
Ekphrastic Review, The M109
Event M113
Every Day Fiction M114
Fiddlehead, The M121
Grain Literary Magazine M143
Malahat Review, The M197
Modern Applied Science M210
Neo-opsis Science Fiction Magazine M218
Temz Review, The M312
Vallum M328
Windsor Review...M342

Table of US Book Publishers

4 Color Books P103	Cleis Press P091	Jewish Lights Publishing P394
ABC-CLIO P002	Coaches Choice P093	Judson Press P201
also P053	College Press Publishing P094	Kane Press P202
ABC-CLIO / Greenwood P002	Crossway P100	also P023
Able Muse Press P003	Crown P101	Kar-Ben Publishing P213
Afterglow Books P006	also P103	Kensington Publishing Corp. P204
Albert Whitman & Company P007	Crown Publishing Group, The P103	KidHaven Press P139
Algonquin Books P008	Currency P103	Kore Press P207
Alternating Current Press P010	Dancing Girl Press P105	Leapfrog Press P212
American Mystery Classics P012	Darby Creek P213	Lerner Publishing Group P213
also P282	DAW Books P023	Libraries Unlimited P002
Andrews McMeel Publishing P015	Del Rey P108	Liguori Publications P216
Anhinga Press P016	Denis Kitchen Publishing Company Co., LLC P109	Little Bigfoot P218
Applause P145		also P325
April Gloaming P018	Diversion Books P111	Little, Brown and Company P156
Arcadia Publishing P020	DK Publishing P112	Llewellyn Worldwide Ltd P219
Arte Publico Press P021	Down East Books P145	Loft Press, Inc. P220
Arthur A. Levine Books P329	Dreamspinner Press P115	LSU Press P223
Asabi Publishing P022	DSP Publications P116	Lucent Books P139
Astra House P023	also P115	Lyons Press P145
Astra Publishing House P023	Eerdmans Books for Young Readers P120	Lyrical Press P225
Astra Young Readers P023	Enslow Publishers, Inc. P123	also P204
Astragal Press P145	Epicenter Press Inc P124	Margaret K. McElderry Books P228
AUWA Books P026	Evan-Moor Educational Publishers P125	MB Media P230
Backbeat Books P027	FalconGuides P145	Mcbooks Press P145
also P145	Farrar, Straus & Giroux P129	MCD Books P231
Baen Books P029	Feminist Press, The P130	Medical Physics Publishing P234
Bald and Bonkers Network LLC P030	Focal Press P378	Milkweed Editions P239
Banter Press P033	Forge P388	MineditionUS P023
Basalt Books P034	Free Spirit Publishing P136	Minnesota Historical Society Press P241
Basic Books P035	FrontLine P137	Minotaur Books P242
also P036	Future Horizons P138	Missouri Historical Society Press P243
Basic Books Group P036	Gale P139	MIT Press, The P244
also P156	Glass Poetry Press P144	Monacelli Press, The P245
Basic Health Publications, Inc. P037	Globe Pequot Press, The P145	also P287
also P394	Gold SF P146	Moody Publishers P247
Basic Liberty P038	Goodman Beck Publishing P147	Morgan Kaufmann Publishers P121
also P036	Grand Central Publishing P156	Muddy Boots P145
Basic Venture P039	Graywolf Press P152	Mysterious Press, The P252
also P036	Greenhaven Publishing P139	also P282
BatCat Press P040	Hachette Book Group P156	NAHB BuilderBooks P253
Baylor University Press P041	Half Mystic Press P157	NBM Publishing P254
becker&mayer! books P307	Hancock House Publishers P159	New Harbinger Publications P255
Bentley Publishers P044	Hardie Grant (North America) P163	Nightfire P388
Berrett-Koehler Publishers P046	also P162	No Starch Press, Inc. P258
Bess Press P047	Harmony Ink Press P115	Oh MG Press P260
Black Dog & Leventhal P050	Harvard Common Press P307	also P230
also P437	Harvard University Press P165	Ohio University Press P261
Blue Poppy Enterprises P055	Hawthorne Books P167	Ooligan Press P265
Blue Star Press P056	Hell's Hundred P170	Orchard Books P329
BOA Editions, Ltd. P057	also P348	Pacific Press Publishing Association P273
Books For All Times P060	Henry Holt & Co. P172	PB and Yay! Books P277
Bramble P061	Hippo Park P023	Pelican Publishing Company P020
also P388	Host Publications P177	Penzler Publishers P282
Calkins Creek P023	Idyll Arbor P181	Perseus Books P156
Candlemark & Gleam P069	Ig Publishing P182	Perugia Press P284
Captivate Press P072	IgKids P183	Peter Pauper Press P286
Carina Press P073	also P182	Phoenix Moirai P288
Cedar Fort P076	Imagine Publishing P186	Picador P290
Celadon Books P077	also P081	Pinata Books P021
Charisma House P079	Indiana University Press P187	Pineapple Press P293
Charles River Press P080	Information Today, Inc. P188	also P145
Charlesbridge Publishing P081	International Publishers P191	Poisoned Pen Press P297
Charlesbridge Teen P081	International Society for Technology in Education (ISTE) P192	also P350
Chelsea House Publishers P082		Praeger P002
Cherry Lake Publishing Group P083	Jain Publishing Company, Inc. P195	Press 53 .... P301
Clarkson Potter P103	Jamii Publishing P196	Procrastinating Writers United P303

Claim your free access to www.firstwriter.com: See p.367

Prometheus P145	Sourcebooks Landmark P356	Turtle Press P395
PublicAffairs... P304	also P350	Two Fine Crows Books................................. P396
also P036	Sourcebooks Wonderland P357	TwoDot P145
Purdue University Press P305	also P350	Tyndale House Publishers, Inc. P397
Pureplay Press.. P306	Sourcebooks Young Readers P358	Ugly Duckling Presse..................................... P399
Quirk Books.. P308	also P350	Unbridled Books... P401
Rand McNally.. P310	Spout Press.. P360	Union Park Press.. P145
Running Press.. P320	Spruce Books P325	University of Akron Press, The.................... P403
also P437	St Martin's Press P362	University of California Press P406
Sasquatch Books P325	St. Martin's Essentials P363	University of Georgia Press P407
Scarlet.. P327	St. Martin's Griffin.. P364	University of Iowa Press P408
also P282	St. Martin's Publishing Group P365	University of Maine Press.............................. P409
Schiffer Military History P328	Stackpole Books P145	University of Michigan Press, The................ P410
Scholastic.. P329	Stanford University Press P367	University of Missouri Press P411
Seal Press.. P332	Steward House Publishers P369	University of North Texas Press................... P412
also P036	Stipes Publishing P371	University of Tennessee Press...................... P413
Seaworthy Publications................................. P333	Storey Publishing P437	University of Texas Press.............................. P414
Sentient Publications..................................... P334	Sunbelt Publications, Inc. P373	University of Virginia Press.......................... P415
Shipwreckt Books Publishing Company P336	Sweetgum Press... P375	University Press of Colorado P416
Siloam.. P338	Tailwinds Press... P376	Unseen Press.. P417
Sinister Stoat Press.. P341	Ten Speed Press P380	Utah State University Press.......................... P416
Skip Jack Press... P145	also P103	Voyageur Press.. P307
Soho Crime P347	Texas A&M University Press P381	W.W. Norton & Company, Inc. P423
also P348	Thames & Hudson Inc................................... P382	Walter Foster Publishing............................... P307
Soho Press P348	also P383	Washington Writers' Publishing House P425
Soho Teen P349	Tilbury House Publishers P385	Watson-Guptill Publications P103
also P348	also P083	Whitford Press P428
Sourcebooks.. P350	Toad Hall Editions... P387	Wisdom Publications P431
Sourcebooks Casablanca P351	Toon Books P023	Wolfpack Publishing...................................... P432
also P350	Tor... P388	WordSong.. P023
Sourcebooks eXplore P352	Tor Publishing Group P388	Workman Publishing...................................... P437
also P350	Tor Teen P389	also P156
Sourcebooks Fire P353	also P388	YesYes Books.. P439
also P350	Tor.com Publishing P388	Zebra... P204
Sourcebooks Horror P354	Torrey House Press, LLC P390	Zibby Books P440
also P350	Turner Publishing... P394	

Access more listings online at www.firstwriter.com

Table of UK Book Publishers

404 Ink	P001	
Adventure Books by Vertebrate Publishing	P004	
Afsana Press	P005	
Amber Books Ltd	P011	
And Other Stories	P013	
Andersen Press Ltd	P014	
Arachne Press	P019	
Ashgate Publishing Limited	P378	
Aurora Metro Press	P024	
Autumn Publishing Ltd	P025	
also	P184	
Bad Betty	P028	
BCS (British Computer Society)	P042	
Bearded Badger Publishing Co.	P043	
Berghahn Books Ltd	P045	
BFI Publishing	P053	
Bird Eye Books	P048	
also	P150	
Black & White Publishing Ltd	P049	
Blackstaff Press	P051	
also	P095	
Bloodhound Books	P052	
Bloomsbury Academic	P053	
Blue Diode Publishing	P054	
Bonnier Books (UK)	P059	
Breedon Books	P062	
Brewin Books	P062	
Brewin Books Ltd	P062	
Bright Press	P307	
British Academy, The	P063	
British Museum Press, The	P064	
Broken Sleep Books	P066	
Cadno	P067	
also	P150	
Cambridge University Press	P068	
Candy Jar Books	P070	
Canterbury Press	P071	
Cassava Republic Press UK	P074	
CB Editions	P075	
CGI (Chartered Governance Institute) Publishing	P078	
Chambers	P200	
Chicken House Publishing	P329	
Child's Play (International) Ltd	P084	
Choc Lit	P085	
also	P199	
Cicada Books	P087	
Cinnamon Press	P088	
Claret Press	P089	
Classical Comics	P090	
Colourpoint Educational	P095	
Comma Press	P096	
Compassiviste Publishing	P097	
Countryside Books	P099	
Creative Essentials	P264	
Crime & Mystery Club	P264	
Dahlia Books	P104	
Daunt Books Publishing	P106	
Dedalus Ltd	P107	
Dodo Ink	P113	
Doubleday (UK)	P114	
also	P393	
Duncan Petersen Publishing Limited	P117	
East of Centre	P119	
also	P043	
Elsevier Ltd	P121	
Enitharmon Editions	P122	
Everything With Words	P126	
Facet Publishing	P127	
Fairlight Books	P128	
Fighting High	P132	
Fircone Books Ltd	P221	
Firefly	P133	
Frances Lincoln Children's Books	P307	
Free Association Books Ltd	P135	
Frontline Books	P281	
Gemini Books	P140	
Goss & Crested China Club	P149	
Graffeg	P150	
Graffeg Childrens	P151	
also	P150	
Guinness World Records	P154	
Guppy Books	P155	
Hammersmith Books	P158	
Handspring Publishing	P160	
also	P197	
Happy Yak	P161	
also	P307	
Hashtag Press	P166	
Hay House Publishers	P168	
Hearing Eye	P169	
Henley Hall Press	P171	
High Stakes Publishing	P173	
also	P264	
History into Print	P062	
History Press, The	P174	
Hodder & Stoughton Ltd	P175	
Hodder Faith	P175	
HopeRoad	P176	
Howgate Publishing	P178	
Hunt End Books	P062	
Icon Books Ltd	P180	
Igloo Books Limited	P184	
Inkandescent	P190	
InterVarsity Press (IVP)	P193	
Jessica Kingsley Publishers	P197	
also	P200	
JMD Media / DB Publishing	P198	
Joffe Books	P199	
John Murray Press	P200	
Jordan Publishing	P214	
Kamera Books	P264	
Kates Hill Press, The	P203	
Kitchen Press	P205	
Kogan Page Ltd	P206	
Korero Press	P208	
Kube Publishing	P209	
Lantana Publishing	P210	
Leamington Books	P211	
LexisNexis	P214	
Lightning Books	P215	
Logaston Press	P221	
Loudhailer Books	P222	
Lund Humphries Limited	P224	
Macmillan Children's Books	P226	
Manilla Press	P227	
also	P059	
Marion Boyars Publishers	P229	
McNidder & Grace	P232	
Medina Publishing	P235	
Merlin Unwin Books	P237	
Methuen Publishing Ltd	P238	
Mills & Boon	P240	
Monoray	P246	
Murdoch Books UK Ltd	P249	
Muswell Press	P250	
Myrmidon Books Ltd	P251	
New Walk Editions	P256	
Nicholas Brealey Publishing	P175	
Nine Arches Press	P257	
Old Pond Publishing	P262	
Old Street Publishing Ltd	P263	
Oldcastle Books	P264	
Oldcastle Books Group	P264	
Orenda Books	P267	
Orphans Publishing	P268	
Out-Spoken Press	P270	
Oxbow Books	P271	
Oxford University Press	P272	
Parthian Books	P275	
Pavilion Poetry	P276	
Peepal Tree Press	P278	
Pelagic	P279	
Pen & Ink Designs Publishing	P280	
Pen & Sword Books Ltd	P281	
Perspectives Books	P283	
Peter Lang	P285	
Phaidon Press	P287	
Phillimore	P174	
Piatkus Books	P289	
Piccadilly Press	P291	
Pimpernel Press	P292	
also	P140	
Plexus Publishing Limited	P294	
Pluto Press	P295	
Pocket Mountains	P296	
Polygon	P298	
Popular Chess	P299	
Practical Pre-School Books	P300	
Prestel Publishing Ltd	P302	
Psychology Press	P378	
Pulp! The Classics	P264	
Quarto Group, Inc., The	P307	
Radio Society of Great Britain	P309	
Ransom Publishing Ltd	P312	
Remember When	P281	
Renard Press Ltd	P313	
Richards Publishing	P062	
Routledge	P378	
Ruby Fiction	P319	
also	P085	
Salt Publishing	P322	
Sandstone Press	P323	
also	P004	
Saqi Books	P324	
Scala Arts & Heritage Publishers	P326	
Scholastic UK	P330	
also	P329	
Scratching Shed Publishing	P331	
Seren Books	P335	
Sigma Press	P337	
Singing Dragon	P340	
also	P197	
SmashBear Publishing	P342	
Smokestack Books	P343	
Snowbooks	P344	
Society for Promoting Christian Knowledge (SPCK)	P345	
Society of Genealogists	P346	
Sourcebooks Jabberwocky	P355	
also	P350	

Table of UK Book Publishers

Publisher	Page
Sparsile Books	P359
SRL Publishing	P361
Stainer & Bell Ltd	P366
Stanley Gibbons	P368
Stewed Rhubarb Press	P370
Sweet & Maxwell	P374
Tall-Lighthouse	P377
Taylor & Francis Group	P378
Telegram Books	P324
Templar Books	P059
Thames and Hudson Ltd	P383
Thinkwell Books, UK	P384
Tippermuir Books	P386
Torva	P391
also	P393
Tra[verse]	P392
also	P043
Transworld Publishers	P393
UCL Press	P398
Unbound Press	P400
Unicorn	P402
Valley Press	P418
Vane Women Press	P419
Velocity Press	P420
Verve Poetry Press	P421
W.W. Norton & Company Ltd	P422
Walker Books	P424
Wee Book Company, The	P427
Wharncliffe Books	P281
Wide-Eyed Editions	P429
also	P307
Windhorse Publications Ltd	P430
Words & Pictures	P433
also	P307
Wordsworth Editions	P435
Yale University Press (London)	P438

*Access more listings online at **www.firstwriter.com***

Table of Canadian Book Publishers

Anvil Press Publishers P017	Guernica Editions P153	Roseway P317
Broadview Press P065	Icehouse P179	*also* P131
Coach House Books P092	*also* P148	Simply Read Books P339
Dundurn P118	J. Gordon Shillingford Publishing P194	University of Alberta Press P404
Fernwood Publishing P131	Orca Book Publishers P266	University of Calgary Press P405
Goose Lane Editions P148	Rocky Mountain Books P315	

Table of Authors

Aaddam, Safia El L526
Abbas, Abigail L147
Abbott, Diane L065
also L473
Abbott, Rachel L146
Abdaal, Ali L185
Abdelnoor, Amy L348
Abdoo, Matt L141
Abdul-Jabbar, Kareem L207
Abdur-Rashid, Tasneem L152
also L193
Abe, Sally L149
Abeysekara, Shalini L296
Abrahams, Jodie L064
Abramović, Marina L064
Abrams, Brooke L382
also L435
Abrams, Dan L207
Abrams, Rebecca L513
also L590
Acker, Tanya L301
Ackerley, J. R. L146
Ackroyd, Claire L287
Acosta, Carlos L192
also L608
Acton, Johnny L192
also L284
Adair, Gilbert L065
Adams, Char L083
Adams, Gaar L348
Adams, Guy L094
Adams, Luci L102
also L590
Adams, Nathaniel L166
Adams, Nicola L064
Adams, Nicole L135
also L474
Adams, Poppy L428
Adams, Richard L045
also L146
Adams, Tim L006
also L426
Adams, Tom L102
also L590
Adams, Victoria M. L016
also L326
Adamson, Jean L102
also L590
Adcock, Siobhan L166
Addis, Ferdie L379
Addison, Katherine L550
Adebisi, Maria Motunrayo L143
Adee, Sally L192
also L477
Adelman, Juliana L251
also L417
Adesina, Precious L187
also L251
Adkins, Mary L153
Adlam, Emily L484
Admans, Jaimie L484
Adshead, Gwen L348
Aedin, M. Jules P115
Afrika, Tatamkhulu L065
Agbaimoni, Luke L082
Agbaje, Foluso L152
also L238
Agbaje-Williams, Ore L109
also L146
Agg, Henry L135
also L200
also L474
Agnew, Katie L146
Aguirre, Lauren L083
Ahlqvist, Emma L129
Ahluwalia, Jassa L064
also L254
Ahmadi, Arvin L052
also L053
Ahmed, Emad L522
Ahmed, Imran L064
Ahmed, K Anis L094
Ahmed, Saladin L160
Ahmed, Samira L119
also L192
Ahmed, Sara L109
also L146
Ahmed, Tufayel L537
Aile, Rhianne P115
Ailes, Kat L146
also L210
Ainsworth, Eve L603
Akala, ... L344
Akbar, Sam L614
Akers, Mary L065
Akilah, Shani L065
also L180
Akin, Sara L205
Akpan, Paula L152
also L193
Al-Hassan, Alwia L064
Al-Sabawi, Dina L560
Alabed, Bana L064
Alagiah, George L261
Alais, Saskia L065
also L473
Alameda, Courtney L136
Albano, Laurie L036
Albert, Elisa L071
Albert, Maria P115
Albuquerque, Telênia L043
Alcántara, Jacqueline L158
Alden, Darrell L588
Alder, Mark L428
Alderman, Naomi L045
also L146
Aldern, Clayton Page L251
also L577
Alderson, Sarah L484
Alderton, Dolly L126
Aldred, James L006
also L426
Aldred, Tanya L094
Alegre, Susie L082
Alexander, Becky L094
Alexander, Claire L430
Alexander, Grace L026
Alexander, Jane L098
Alexander, Malcolm L379
Alexander, Rose L102
also L590
Alexander, Tracy L146
Alford, Allison M. L427
Algharíz, Ahmed L205
Ali, Kasim L065
also L473
Ali, Moeen L094
Ali, Nimco L064
Ali, Rahaman L082
Ali-Afzal, Aliya L430
Alker, Elizabeth L146
also L207
also L245
Alkon, Amy L059
Allaf, Rime L207
Allan, Jo L216
Allbeury, Ted L065
Allen, Anthea L082
Allen, Denise L586
Allen, Diane L309
Allen, Dwight L059
Allen, Matt L064
Allen, Nikki L065
also L088
Allen, P. David L301
Allen, Preston L166
Allen, Rachael L146
Allen, Wendy L513
also L590
Allen, Will L059
Allen-Paisant, Jason L146
Allison, John L331
Allman, Esme L004
Allman, Gregg L207
Allnutt, Luke L430
Allport, Alan L146
also L207
also L245
also L555
Allueva, Oscar L281
Almond, David L119
also L192
Alonge, Amen L251
also L577
Alonso, Kassten P167
Alpsten, Ellen L408
Alsadir, Nuar L146
Altman, Mara L166
Altmann, Danny L064
also L254
Alton, Steve L588
Alvarez, Jennifer Lynn L301
Alvior, Jose L016
also L326
Amaka, Rosanna L109
Amati, Federica L613
Ambridge, Ben L192
also L284
Ambrose, David L586
Amidon, Stephen L166
Amuah, Marie-Claire L430
Ana Aranda L158
Anastasia, George L207
Anastasiu, Heather L301
Anatole, Alexina L491
Anaxagorou, Anthony L251
also L614
Anders, Adriana L136
Anderson, Brett L082
Anderson, Celia J L379
Anderson, Cynthia L166

42 Table of Authors

Anderson, G. V. L120
Anderson, Geraint L146
Anderson, Ho Che L281
Anderson, Jill L214
Anderson, Michelle Collins L553
Anderson, Michelle Wilde L555
Anderson, Pamela L429
Anderson, R. J. L146
also L589
Anderson, Rebecca L016
also L326
Anderson, Ros L065
also L180
Anderson, Sorrel L216
Anderson-Wheeler, Claire L026
Andrade, Tonio L555
Andress, David L586
Andrew, Kelly L146
also L589
Andrew, Kerry L146
also L611
Andrew, Sally L065
Andrews, Abi L146
Andrews, Casey Jay L135
also L414
Andrés López L158
Angelico, Karen L348
Anie, Sussie L430
Ann, Rebecca L560
Annukka, Sui L135
also L414
Anselmo, Lisa L301
Anshaw, Carol L146
Ante, Romalyn L065
Anthony, Carl Sferrazza L429
Antiglio, Dominique L484
Antrobus, Raymond L109
Appachana, Anjana L393
Appiah, Krystle Zara L430
Applestone, Jessica L166
Applestone, Josh & Jessica L166
Apps, Peter L251
also L577
Appy, Christian G. L555
Aquila, Richard L166
Araujo, Jess J. L059
Arbuthnot, Leaf L379
Arbuthnott, Gill L216
Arcanjo, JJ L064
Archbold, Tim L216
Archer, Amy L292
Archer, Deborah N. L555
Archer, Juliet P085
Archer, Micha L469
Archer, Rosie L102
also L590
Arditti, Michael L146
Ardizzone, Edward L146
Are, Carolina L152
also L193
Areguy, Fitsum L334
Arikha, Alba L405
Arikha, Noga L207
Ariyo, Lopè L082
Arlen, Michael L146
Armstrong, Addison L139
also L556
Armstrong, Graeme L065
also L473
Armstrong, Karen L119
also L192
Armstrong, Lindsey L252
Armstrong, Thomas L301
Arnold, Elana K. L469
Arnold, Luke L120
Arnott, Paul L586
Aron, Elaine N. L059
Arrowsmith, Simon L316
Arsenault, Ray L555
Arthur, Karen L152
also L193
Arvin, Eric P115
Aryan, Stephen L430
Asare, Tobi L535
Asbridge, Thomas L146
also L207
also L245
Asgarian, Roxanna L556
Ash, Lamorna L146
also L611
Ash, Lucy L119
also L192
Ashcroft, Frances L192
also L477
Ashe, Lucy L251
also L577
Asher, Jane L064
Ashley, Trisha L309
also P032
Ashling, Mickie B. P115
Ashton, James L006
also L426
Ashton, Paul L065
Ashworth, Jenn L045
also L146
Atack, Timothy X L135
also L243
Atapattu, Tanya L046
Atherton, Carol L028
Atkin, Polly L118
also L479
Atkins, Dani L065
also L088
Atkins, Jennifer L146
Atkins, Lucy L428
Atkinson, Kate P114
Atkinson, Ros L614
Atogun, Odafe L006
also L426
Attah, Ayesha Harruna L526
Attlee, Helena L577
Attlee, James L119
also L192
Attwell, Ciara L287
Au, Sara L301
Aubrey, Daniel L153
Augar, Philip L006
also L426
Ault, Sandi L059
Austin, Sophie L265
Austro, Ben L489
Avery, Mark L192
also L284
Avillez, Joana L381
Awwad, Aysha L567
Axat, Federico L526
Aye, MiMi L065
also L473
Ayscough, Aaron L441
Azerrad, Michael L441
Azoulay, Karen L381
Azzam, Abdul Rahman L065
Azzopardi, Trezza L065
also L473
Babakar, Mevan L251
also L577
Babalola, Bolu L065
also L473
Bacchus-Garrick, Nadine L185
Bacon, Beth L166
Baden, Michael L207
Badr, Ahmed L472
also L556
Baer, Kate L382
also L435
Baggini, Julian L146
Baggot, Mandy L252
Bailey, Connie P115
Bailey, Louis L479
Bailey, Samantha M. L052
also L053
Bailey, Susanna L567
Bainbridge, John L493
Bainbridge, Rebecca L613
Bakar, Faima L102
also L590
Baker, Harriet L146
Baker, Kevin L166
Baker, Livvy Jane L331
Baker, Modern L192
also L608
Bakunina, Jana L135
also L243
Balbirer, Nancy L166
Baldree, Travis L203
also L617
Bale, Anthony L045
also L146
Balen, Katya L119
also L192
Balfe, Abigail L567
Balfour, Alice L216
Balfour, Sandy L065
Ball, Jesse L564
Ballantine, Carol L187
also L251
Ballantine, Poe P167
Ballantyne, Lisa L348
Balls, Katy L146
also L207
also L245
Bamford, Emma L067
also L143
Bang, Michelle L187
also L251
Banissy, Michael L405
Banks, Gina L382
also L435
Bannan, Sarah L545
Bannon, Tia L004
Banta, Isabel L068
also L101
Barber, Antonia L146
also L589
Barcenilla, Lerah Mae L292
Barclay, Humphrey L300
Barclay, Jennifer L265
Bardell, Hannah L379
Bareham, Lindsey L146
also L207
also L245
Bareilles, Sara L441
Barker, Larry L214
Barker, Raffaella L251
also L428
Barker, Xanthi L491
Barley, Nigel L146
Barnard, Joanna L430
Barnard, Robert L146
Barnes, Hannah L006
also L426
Barnes, J. S. L120
Barnett, Daniel L595
Barnett, David M L251
also L603

Access more listings online at **www.firstwriter.com**

Barnett, Fiona	L331
Barnett, Laura	L428
Barnett, Rob	L493
Barnfield, Jessica	L135
also	L243
Barnhardt, Wilton	L166
Barnsley, Rhiannon	L434
Barokka, Khairani	L152
also	L193
Barr, Damian	L126
Barr, James	L119
also	L192
Barr, Lois	L059
Barr-Green, Craig	L135
also	L225
Barrett, Duncan	L379
Barrett, Kerry	L484
Barrett, Natasha S.	L391
Barri, Zahra	L047
Barrie, David	L119
also	L192
Barrington, C F	L379
Barron, Kay	L192
also	L608
Barroux,	L216
Barrow, Alex	L567
Barrow, Cathy	L427
Barrow-Belisle, Michele	L036
Barrowcliffe, Mark	L428
Barrows, Annie	L148
Barry, Rebecca Rego	L301
Barry, Shannon Lee	L234
also	L617
Barter, Catherine	L251
also	L603
Bartkowski, Frances	L301
Bartlett, Ciaran	L553
Bartlett, Graham	L152
also	L272
Bartlett, Jamie	L408
Bartlett, Neil	L126
Bartlett, Steven	L344
Barton, John	L119
also	L192
Bartsch, Shadi	L555
Barve, Nivedita	L004
Basilières, Michel	L281
Baskaran, Lucia	L526
Baskerville, Katie	L152
also	L193
Basra, Gurki	L107
Basu, Laura	L479
Batchelor, John	L119
also	L192
Bateman, Jackie	L265
Bateman, Sonya	L160
Bates, Stephen	L586
Batmanghelidjh, Camila	L408
Battenfield, Jackie	L166
Battersby, Matilda	L287
Battle, Nick	L214
Battle-Felton, Yvonne	L146
also	L156
Bauer, Belinda	L045
also	L146
Bauer, Charlotte	L251
also	L428
Bauer, Douglas	L166
Baughan, Emily	L192
also	L477
Bauman, Whitney	L613
Baumgartner, Alice	L555
Baur, Becky	L567
Bausch, Richard	L166
Bautista-Carolina, Suhaly	L068
also	L101
Baxter, Holly	L046
Baxter, Neil	L135
also	L243
Bay, Samara	L429
Bayley, Chloe	L135
also	L200
Bayley, Stephen	L082
Bays, Jill	L390
Bazalgette, Felix	L146
Beale, Susan	L192
also	L608
Beardsall, Jonny	L192
also	L284
Beashel, Amy	L064
also	L254
Beasley, Heidi Lauth	L185
Beatley, Meaghan	L526
Beaton, Roderick	L192
also	L477
Beauman, Francesca	L126
Beaumont, Dan	L379
Beaumont, Matt	L126
Bechtel, Greg	L027
Becker, Robin	L490
Bedell, Elaine	L408
Bee, Ishbelle	L153
Bee, J Y	L316
Beech, Ella	L146
also	L589
Beech, Louise	L152
also	L238
Beecheno, Pippa	L379
Beers, Laura	L146
also	L207
also	L245
Beetner, Eric	L027
Beezmohun, Sharmilla	L047
Begbie, Hannah	L045
also	L146
Begin, Mary Jane	L493
Behr, Rafael	L064
Beilock, Sian	L555
Beirne, Liam	L300
Beirne, Olivia	L287
Bekins, Alix	P115
Belim, Victoria	L094
Bell, A. D.	L152
also	L272
Bell, Alex	L265
Bell, Alice	L135
also	L203
also	L474
also	L617
Bell, Anna	L265
Bell, Annie	L146
Bell, Darcey	L428
Bell, Emma J.	L064
also	L254
Bell, Gary	L064
Bell, Johanna	L065
also	L088
Bell, Juliet	L535
Bellamacina, Greta	L126
Bellamy, Tomas	L065
also	L473
Beller, Elizabeth	L429
Bellezza, Audrey	L301
Belte, Nicola	L153
Belton, Catherine	L192
also	L477
Benavides, Lucía	L526
Bendavid, Marc	L071
Bender, Aimee	L146
also	L166
Benedict, Alexandra K	L046
Benedict, Alexandra K.	L046
also	L152
Benedictus, Leo	L348
Benjamin, Ruha	L361
Benn, Tom	L065
Benner, Erica	L119
also	L192
Bennett, Anne	L309
Bennett, Cathy	L036
Bennett, James	L331
Bennett, Joshua	L429
Bennett, Maggie	L309
Bennett, Margot	L146
Bennett, Nicki	P115
Bennett, SJ	L094
Bennett, Victoria	L118
also	L479
Benoist, Jessica	L043
Benoist, Melissa	L043
Benson, Harry	L405
Benson, Jendella	L065
also	L473
Benson, Patrick	L126
Bent, Arianna	L331
Bentley, Dorothy	L579
Benyon, Kaddy	L135
also	L474
Beorn, Waitman	L301
Beresford, Jason	L216
Beresiner, Sophie	L185
Berg, Meliz	L065
also	L473
Berger, Joe	L146
also	L589
Bergman, Ronen	L064
Bergstrom, Abigail	L185
Berk, Sheryl	L493
Berney, Jennifer	L166
Bernières, Louis De	L192
also	L608
Bernstein, Ariel	L059
Bernstein, Sarah	L146
Berridge, Elizabeth	L146
Berry, Anne	L309
Berry, Christine	L022
Berry, Mary	L192
also	L608
Berson, Josh	L047
Bertera-Berwick, Meg	L118
also	L479
Bertrand, Lynne	L205
Bertschinger, Claire	L119
also	L192
Berwin, Margot	L281
Bestwick, Simon	L331
Betke-Brunswick, Will	L129
Betley, Christian Piers	L214
Betts, Paul	L119
also	L192
Bhadreshwar, Nina	L192
also	L608
Bhaskar, Michael	L348
Bhathena, Tanaz	L166
Bhatia, Rahul	L006
also	L426
Bhatt, Chetan	L265
Bhattacharya, Santanu	L146
also	L611
Bhojwani, Kaamna	L334
Bibra, Suleena	L406
Bickers, Tessa	L146
also	L210
Bickerton, Chris	L006
also	L426
Biden, Hunter	L441

Biehler, L. L087
also L435
Bigg, Marieke L330
Biggs, Kathy L016
also L326
Bigland, Charlotte L252
Biglow, Sarah L036
Bindel, Julie L064
Binge, Nicholas L120
Bingham, Frances L304
Birch, Carol L407
Birch, Ian L065
also L473
Birch, James L126
Bird, A.L. L484
Bird, Brandon L166
Bird, Michael L119
also L192
Birkhead, Tim L192
also L477
Birkhold, Matthew H. L083
Birrell, Rebecca L146
Bishop, Gary John L052
also L053
Bishop, Patrick L405
Bishop, Sienna P115
Bishop, Sylvia L153
Bissonnette, Zac L141
Black, Fiona L118
also L479
Black, George L166
Black, Lea L166
Black, Leona Nichole L535
Black, Louise Soraya L102
also L590
Black, Robin L166
Black, Sue P114
Blackburn, Victor Lloret L526
Blackhurst, Chris L586
Blackhurst, Jenny L513
Blackmore, Neil L045
also L146
Blackmore, Rachel L065
also L473
Blacksell, Lily L251
also L614
Blackwell, Scarlett P115
Blaise, S. P115
Blaize, Immodesty L126
Blake, Laura L251
also L603
Blake, Matt L293
Blakeman, Rob P062
Blakeway, Jill L441
Blanch, Lesley L408
Blaxill, Gina L143
Bleeker, Emily L553
Blight, David W. L555
Bliss, Laura L361
Block, Cierra L203
also L617
Blom, Jen K L553
Bloodworth, James L146
also L207
also L245
Bloom, Emily L556
also L581
Bloom, Valerie L170
Bloor, Thomas L216
Blow, Charles L429
Blue, Maame L526
Blue-Williams, Steven P115
Bluestein, Greg L083
Blum, Andrew L192
also L284
Blunden, Edmund L146
Blunt, James L405
Blunt, Katherine L556
also L581
Bobelian, Michael L166
Bock, Kenneth L441
Boden, Margaret L146
Boehme, Jillian L087
also L435
Boehmer, Elleke L119
also L192
Boff, Jonathan L146
also L207
also L245
Boggio, Julia L016
also L326
Bohan, Suzanne L301
Bohn, Katie L252
Boissoneault, Lorraine L166
Bojanowski, Marc L361
Bolchover, David L064
Boleyn, Darcie L484
Bolingbroke-Kent, Antonia L461
Bonanno, Joe L207
Bonasia, Lynn Kiele L301
Bond, Caroline L428
Bond, Charlotte L120
Bond, Tara L143
Bongers, Charles L281
Bonnaffons, Amy L166
Bonnett, Alastair L022
Bono, Katie L579
Bonsu, Osei L082
Booker, Simon L405
Booles, Gill L118
also L479
Booth, Owen L535
Booth, Tom L493
Bootle, Emily L187
also L251
Borba, Michele L301
Borgh, Kate van der L135
also L474
Borisade, A.J. L331
Bornstein, Robert L301
Borum, Jeremy L586
Boss, Shira L166
Bossiere, Zoë L129
Bostock-Smith, Adam L300
Bostwick, Marie L148
Bosworth, Patricia L429
Botchway, Stella L119
also L192
Bothwick, Justine L072
Boudreau, Hélène L383
Bounds, Jon L265
also L561
Bourdillon, Roxy L379
Bourgeois, Francis L613
Bourggraff, Morgana L120
Bourgon, Lyndsie L556
Bourke, Jordan L614
Bourne-Taylor, Hannah L348
Bowdler, Michelle L166
Bowen, Innes L006
also L426
Bowen, Sesali L166
Bowers, Nadia L166
Bowie, Nikolas L555
Bowie, Sarah L143
Bowker, John L119
also L192
Bowlby, Will L082
Bowles, Peter L408
Bowman, Dan L040
also L064
Boy, Clerkenwell L082
Boyce, Kim L059
Boyce, Lee L545
Boycott, Rosie L408
Boyd, Elizabeth Reid L301
Boyd, Pattie L408
Boyle, Kenny L065
Boym, Svetlana L166
Boyne, John P114
Boytchev, Oggy L265
also L561
Bozeman, Darby L522
Bracewell, Michael L022
Bradbury, Megan L348
Bradbury-Haehl, Nora L301
Braddon, Paul L265
also L561
Bradford, Chris L586
Bradford, Maria L146
also L156
Bradley, Anna L553
Bradley, Christina L484
Bradley, Mark L143
Bradley, Mark Philip L555
Bradley, Vicki L067
also L143
Bradshaw, Terry L207
Brady, Ali L382
also L435
Brady, Fern L135
also L414
Brady, Susan MacKenty L155
Brager, Sol L472
also L556
Bragg, G.B. L166
Bragg, Melvyn L408
Bragg, Sara L252
Brahin, Lisa L605
Brahmachari, Sita L064
Braithwaite, E. R. L146
Bramley, Cathy L265
Brammer, Mikki L146
also L210
Bramwell-Lawes, Stephanie L613
Brandom, Helen L366
Brandon, Ruth L006
also L426
Brandt, Charles L207
Brandt, K.L. L331
Brar, Amman L109
Braude, Mark L564
Braun, Gabriella L461
Bravo, Lauren L146
also L210
Bray, Carys L045
also L146
Braybrooke, Neville L146
Brazier, Lucy L251
also L577
Brazil, Kevin L146
Breen, Benjamin L166
Brellend, Kay L102
also L590
Brencher, Hannah L556
Brennan, Marie L203
also L617
Brenner, Helene L059
Breslin, Theresa L146
also L589
Brett, Luce L535
Bridges, Chris L522
Bridgestock, R.C. L152
also L272
Bridget, ... L251
Bridgewater, Marcus L006
also L426
Bridle, James L577

Brier, Bob	L148
Brigden, Susan	L119
also	L192
Briggs, Andy	L065
also	L088
Brill, Francesca	L192
also	L608
Briner, Karen	L059
Briscoe, Constance	L143
Brizec, Isabelle	L316
Broach, Elise	L166
Broadbent, Jim	L379
Broadstock, Daniel	L064
Brockett, Catheryn J.	L059
Brockmeier, Kevin	L166
Brody, Frances	L309
Brook, Rhidian	L192
also	L608
Brooke, Amanda	L522
Brooke, Anne	P115
Brooke-Hitching, Edward	L094
Brooke-Smith, James	L192
also	L284
Brooke-Taylor, Tim	L300
Brooker, Will	L082
Brookes, Adam	L119
also	L192
Brookes, Catherine	L484
Brooks, Elizabeth	L265
also	L361
also	L561
Broom, Isabelle	L265
Broome, Iain	L348
Broomfield, Mark	L265
also	L561
Brotherson, Corey	L613
Brotherton, Marcus	L493
Brottman, Mikita	L166
Broudie, Ian	L082
Brovig, Dea	L348
Brower, Elena	L391
Brown, Anne Greenwood	L301
Brown, Archie	L192
also	L284
Brown, Bethany	P115
Brown, Colwill	L045
also	L146
Brown, Dan	P032
Brown, Danielle	L143
Brown, David W.	L166
Brown, Derren	P032
Brown, Don	L380
Brown, Glen James	L045
also	L146
Brown, Ian	L300
Brown, Jackson P.	L296
Brown, Kathy	L153
Brown, Larisa	L192
also	L284
Brown, Martin	L146
also	L589
Brown, Michelle Poirier	L027
Brown, Nora Anne	L065
also	L473
Brown, Stacia	L166
Brown, Steve	L064
Brown, Symeon	L109
Brown, Tom	L152
also	L272
Browne, David	L166
Browne, Gay	L301
Browne, Hester	L146
Browne, Janet	L146
Browne, Nm	L407
Brownfield, HF	L560
Brownlie, Rebecca	L203
also	L617
Brownlow, Mike	L146
also	L589
Brownrigg, Jess	L153
Brubach, Holly	L429
Bruder, Jessica	L146
Brueckmann, Alex	L281
Brume, Rukky	L146
also	L210
Brumm, Michael	L205
Brun, Theodore	L016
also	L326
Bryan, Jonathan	L408
Bryan, Lynne	L251
also	L428
Bryan, Mike	L586
Bryant, Anabelle	L553
Bryant, Arthur	L146
Brynard, Karin	L065
Bryson, Bill	P114
Bublitz, Jacqueline	L537
Buccola, Allison	L166
Buchan, Elizabeth	L428
Buchan, Ursula	L192
also	L477
Buchanan, Daisy	L046
also	L152
Buchanan, Kyle	L493
Buchanan, Tracy	L265
Buck, Libby	L493
Buck, Louisa	L126
Buck, Tobias	L006
also	L426
Bucknall, Ella	L146
Bucksbaum, Sydney	L141
Budde, Mariann Edgar	L441
Bueno, Julia	L192
also	L477
Bull, Andy	L094
Bull, Jessica	L430
Bullen, Chiara	L040
also	L064
Bullock, Maggie	L391
Bullock-Prado, Gesine	L441
Bunn, Davis	L380
Bunting, Erin	L065
also	L473
Bunzl, Peter	L022
Buoro, Stephen	L109
Burfoot, Ella	L216
Burger, Ariel	L301
Burgess, Anthony	L146
Burgess, Zoe	L187
also	L251
Burgis, Tom	L348
Burke, Kevin	L429
Burke, Stephen	L192
also	L608
Burke, Wren	L251
also	L428
Burn, Joanne	L153
Burnell, Mark	L146
Burnet, Graeme Macrae	L065
Burnett, R. S.	L146
also	L210
Burnford, Sheila	L146
Burnham, Amanda	L111
Burns, Jimmy	L405
Burns, Karen	L059
Burns, Nicole	L331
Burstein, Nicole	L153
Burston, Paul	L152
also	L272
Burt, Caroline	L146
also	L207
also	L245
Burtka, David	L441
Burton, Jessie	L430
Burton, Matthew	L119
also	L192
Burton, Sarah	L330
Burton-Morgan, P.	L379
Bush, Stephen	L006
also	L426
Bushby, Karl	L192
also	L284
Busk, Michael	L281
Bussey-Chamberlain, Prudence	L251
also	L417
Bustamante, Andrew	L493
Bustamante, Mónica	L059
also	L166
Butchart, Pamela	L366
Butcher, Jim	L160
Butcher, Sally	L045
also	L146
Butler, Dave	L281
Butler, Dawn	P391
Butler, Letty	L120
Butler, Sarah Jane	L535
Butler-Adams, William	L545
Butler-Bowdon, Tom	L192
also	L284
Butterfield, Charlotte	L522
Butterfield, Lanisha	L143
Butterwick, Caroline	L152
also	L193
Butterworth, Nick	L045
also	L146
Byrne, Emma	L192
also	L477
Byrne, Jason	L251
also	L577
Byrne, Lucy Sweeney	L147
Byrne, Michael	L064
Cabot, Meg	L265
Cadigan, Pat	L407
Cagan, Kayla	L136
Cagney, Liam	L147
Cahill, James	L065
Cain, Hamilton	L166
Cain, Kelly	L406
Caine, Michael	L408
Calder, Emma	L408
Calder, Jill	L216
Callaghan, Helen	L428
Callaghan, Jo	L026
Callahan, Eliza Barry	L146
Calleja, Jen	L004
Callow, Simon	L261
Calon, Sophie	L307
Calvi, Nuala	L379
Calvin, Michael	L064
Calvo, Paco	L146
also	L611
Cambanis, Thanassis	L555
Cameron, Bill	L490
Cameron, Cecil	L046
also	L152
Cameron, Josephine	L136
Cameron, Lucy	L064
also	L254
Cameron, Stella	L148
Cammaratta, Natalie	L406
Campbell, Alan	L407
Campbell, Hayley	L379
Campbell, James	L046

Campbell, Jen	L094	
Campbell, John	L307	
Campbell, Karen	L065	
also	L473	
Campbell, Steuart	L588	
Campbell, Susan	L301	
Campbell, Tom	L251	
also	L577	
Campbell-Johnston, Rachel	L126	
Campbell-Smith, Judy	L553	
Canellos, Peter	L555	
Canepa-Anson, Abi	L537	
Cannon, Joanna	L026	
Cantor, Melanie	L135	
also	L474	
Caporn, Sam	L522	
Cardwell, Diane	L083	
Carey, Anna	L136	
Carey, Edward	L065	
Carey, Linda	L331	
Carey, Louise	L331	
Carey, Mike	L331	
Cargill-Martin, Honor	L143	
Carlin, Laura	L379	
Carlin, Aine	L614	
Carlisle, Tom	L064	
Carlson, Craig	L301	
Carnegie, Jo	L484	
Carney, Mark	L408	
Carney, Scott	L441	
Carol, James	L067	
also	L143	
Carpenter, Elisabeth	L265	
Carr, Joe P.	L059	
Carr, John Dickson	L146	
Carr, Robyn	L148	
Carrasco, Katrina	L166	
Carraway, Tayler	L381	
Carrey, Jim	L429	
Carson, Paul	L143	
Carter, Andrea	L152	
also	L272	
Carter, Bill	L166	
Carter, Chris	L143	
Carter, Erika	L166	
Carter, Laura	L252	
Carter, Paul	L301	
Carter, Steven	L059	
Carthew, Natasha	L065	
also	L473	
Cartmel, Andrew	L203	
also	L617	
Cartner-Morley, Jess	L146	
Carver, Will	L152	
also	L272	
Casale, Alexia	L463	
also	L464	
Casares, Whitney	L427	
Casely-Hayford, Augustus	L408	
Casey, Anne-Marie	L146	
Cassidy, Amanda	L046	
also	L152	
Castillo-Speed, Lillian	L059	
Castle, Barbara	L146	
Castle, Jill	L301	
Castro, Orsola De	L185	
Castro, Pablo Valcárcel	L311	
Catchpool, Michael	L170	
Cathcart, Brian	L405	
Cathrall, Sylvie	L410	
Cathro, Grant	L300	
Causley, Charles	L146	
Cave, Holly	L026	
Cave, Kathryn	L146	
also	L589	
Cave, Lucie	L484	
Cavenagh, Clare	L251	
also	L428	
Cavendish, Lucy	L192	
also	L608	
Caveney, Graham	L192	
also	L284	
Caves, SB	L251	
also	L603	
Cayton-Holland, Adam	L166	
Cecil, Lila	L281	
Central, Climate	L166	
Cenziper, Debbie	L301	
Cerrotti, Rachael	L301	
Cervantes, Angela	L158	
Cervantes, Fernando	L192	
also	L477	
Chadwick, Angela	L537	
Chadwick, Elizabeth	L065	
Chaffin, Joshua	L006	
also	L426	
Chaiton, Sam	L605	
Chakkalakal, Tess	L555	
Chakrabortty, Aditya	L146	
also	L207	
also	L245	
Chalice, Lucy	L331	
Challis, Sarah	L192	
also	L608	
Chalmers, Ashley	L135	
also	L200	
Chalmers, John	L296	
Chamarette, Jenny	L479	
Chamberlain, Laura	L102	
also	L590	
Chamberlain, Mary	L430	
Chan, Eliza	L120	
Chan, Vanessa	L109	
also	L146	
Chance, Rebecca	L484	
Chancellor, Bryn	L166	
Chandler, Adam	L361	
Chandler, Natalie	L149	
Chandler-Wilde, Helen	L545	
Chang, Fran	L065	
also	L473	
Chapel, Janey	P115	
Chapman, Jason	L146	
also	L589	
Chapman, Peter	L192	
also	L284	
Chapman, Simon	L216	
Chapman, Sital Gorasia	L366	
Chapple, Matt	L614	
Charbonneau, Joelle	L166	
Charles, Georgina	L135	
also	L414	
Charles, Shavone	L472	
also	L556	
Charlesworth, Monique	L405	
Charlier, Marj	L301	
Charlton, Paul	L300	
Charlton, Richard	L405	
Charlton-Dailey, Rachel	L118	
also	L479	
Charney, Noah	L166	
Charter, David	L586	
Charters, Charlie	L586	
Chase, Eve	L146	
Chase, James Hadley	L146	
Chase, Paula	L166	
Chater, Nick	L119	
also	L192	
Chaupoly, Ratha	L441	
Chawdhary, Sunita	L292	
Chawla, Seerut K.	L146	
also	L210	
Chayka, Kyle	L175	
Chayka, Meghan	L605	
Che, Hannah	L082	
Cheek, Mavis	L408	
Cheetham, Tracey	L214	
Chen, Angela	L556	
also	L581	
Chen, Chengde	L214	
Chen, Tiffany	L082	
Chen, Wendy	L071	
Cheng, Ken	L135	
also	L414	
Cheng, Linda	L136	
also	L207	
Chenoweth, Emily	L166	
Chern, Lina	L382	
also	L435	
Chernoff, Marc and Angel	L493	
Chernoff, Scott	L141	
Cheshire, Simon	L265	
Chess, K	L166	
Chester, Fliss	L563	
Chien, Windy	L391	
Chigudu, Simukai	L192	
also	L477	
Child, Heather	L311	
Child, Lee	L143	
also	P032	
Childress, Mark	L166	
Childs, Tera Lynn	L052	
also	L053	
Chin, Rita Zoey	L129	
Chin-Quee, Tony	L141	
Chin-Tanner, Wendy	L068	
also	L101	
Chinn, Adrienne	L265	
also	L561	
Chinn, Carl	P062	
Chislett, Helen	L408	
Chiu, Christina	L166	
Chiusolo, Samantha	L190	
also	L345	
Cho, Catherine	L114	
also	L348	
Choate, Judith	L427	
Chong, Camille	L292	
Choo, Yangsze	L052	
also	L053	
Chotzinoff, Robin	L059	
Chowdhury, Ajay	L513	
Chown, Marcus	L192	
also	L477	
Christensen, Julia F.	L185	
Christian, Timothy	L281	
Christiansen, Morten H.	L119	
also	L192	
Christianson, John	L301	
Christie-Miller, Amelia	L563	
Christopher, Adam	L166	
Chu, Deborah	L613	
Chu, Vikki	L190	
also	L345	
Chubb, Mimi	L166	
Chun, Ye	L175	
Chung, Bonnie	L094	
Chung, Julien	L205	
Church, Daniel	L331	
Churchill, Amanda	L071	
Ciccarelli, Kristen	L087	
also	L435	
Ciccone, Carla	L556	
also	L581	
CityLab, Bloomberg	L361	
Claesson, Jonas	L304	
Clair, Kassia St	L461	

Claire, Sophie	L102
also	L590
Clammer, Paul	L586
Clancy, Christi	L207
also	L480
Clancy, Christina	L207
also	L480
Clare, Tim	L348
Clark, Alex	L065
also	L180
Clark, Emma Chichester	L146
also	L589
Clark, Lloyd	L586
Clark, Nicky	L064
Clark, Tara L.	L301
Clark, Tiana	L068
also	L101
Clark-Flory, Tracy	L068
also	L101
Clark-Junkins, Margot	L301
Clarke, Angela	L046
also	L152
Clarke, Arthur C.	L146
Clarke, Cassandra Rose	L166
Clarke, Chris	L082
Clarke, Clare	L082
Clarke, Georgina	L379
Clarke, Kevin	L214
Clarke, Lucy	L428
Clarke, Maxine Beneba	L026
Clarke, Norie	L065
also	L473
Clarke, Roger	L126
Clarke, Rosie	L309
Clayton, Mathew	L046
Clements, Abby	L265
Cliff, Aimee	L491
Cliff, Nigel	L166
Cliffe-Minns, Louise	L316
Clifford, David	L172
Clifford, Frank	L059
Clifton, Rita	L408
Clinning, Shauna	L463
also	L464
Clive, Lady Mary	L146
Cloepfil, Georgia	L556
also	L581
Cobb, Yvonne	L046
also	L152
Cochrane, Lauren	L082
Cockell, Charles	L251
also	L577
Cody, Liza	L119
also	L192
Cody, Sara	L594
Coe, Jonathan	L192
also	L608
Coe, Reuben	L293
Coe, Sebastian	L408
Coelho, Mário	L203
also	L617
Coetzee, J. M.	L146
Coffelt, Nancy	L166
Coffey, Laura	L135
also	L414
Coffin, Jaed	L166
Coggan, Helena	L331
Cohen, Cole	L166
Cohen, Deb	L265
Cohen, Miriam	L166
Cohen, Rob	L059
Cohen, Sir Ronald	L064
Cohen, Tal	L111
Cohu, Will	L192
also	L608
Colail, J. M.	P115
Colbert, Jaimee Wriston	L166
Cole, Chloe	L068
also	L101
Cole, Daniel	L026
Cole, Jessi	L087
also	L435
Cole, Julia	L065
also	L473
Cole, Martina	L143
Coleman, Ashley M.	L406
Coleman, Rowan	L064
also	L254
Coleman, Sarah J.	L102
also	L590
Colgan, Annette	L072
Colins, Katy	L430
Collard, Paul Fraser	L152
also	L272
Collett, Ryan	L064
also	L254
Collier, Deryn	L027
Collins, Christina	L366
Collins, David	L094
Collins, Fiona	L046
also	L152
Collins, Kathleen	L146
Collins, Sophie	L146
Collison, Martha	L614
Colville, Zoë	L094
Colwell, Chip	L555
Colyer, Howard	L152
Colón, Angel Luis	L141
Comite, Florence	L215
Conaboy, Chelsea	L139
also	L556
Conis, Elena	L555
Connelly, Charlie	L146
Connelly, Jaymz	P115
Connolly, Hannah	L135
also	L200
Connor, Alan	L146
also	L207
also	L245
Connor, Erin	L522
Conroy, Natalia	L408
Conroy, Paul	L405
Constable, John	L147
Constantine, Liv	L052
also	L053
Constantine, Susannah	L211
Conte, Marie Le	L461
Conti-Brown, Peter	L555
Conway, James	L152
also	L272
Conybeare, Catherine	L555
Cook, Emma	L428
Cook, Gloria	L067
also	L143
Cook, Jesselyn	L083
Cook, Melinda Chiu	L553
Cook, Peter	L146
Cook, Sheena	L064
also	L609
Cook, Sue	L065
also	L473
Cooke, Jack	L614
Cooke, Pan	L493
Cooke, Trish	L146
also	L589
Coolidge, Jennifer	L348
Coombs, Howard	L309
Cooper, Artemis	L119
also	L192
Cooper, Caren	L556
Cooper, Carol	L072
Cooper, Emily S.	L146
Cooper, Emma	L484
Cooper, Jilly	P032
Cooper, Mark	L586
Cooper, Natalie	L252
Cooper, Natasha	L146
Cooper, Roxie	L287
Cooper, Yvette	L348
Copeland, Rashawn	L380
Copp, Lucy Tandon	L143
Coppers, Toni	L135
also	L474
Copperthwaite, Barbara	L152
also	L238
Corbin, Pam	L251
also	L577
Corbishley, Nicky	L563
Corby, Gary	L490
Corcoran, Caroline	L046
also	L152
Corey, Deborah Joy	L166
Corlett, Anne	L251
also	L603
Cornelius, Olivia Jordan	L185
Cornell, Paul	L166
Cornwell, Bernard	L146
also	L207
Corrigan, Caroline	L071
Costello, Isabel	L046
also	L152
Costello, Jamie	L045
also	L146
Costello, Tara	L102
also	L590
Costeloe, Diney	L309
Cotterell, T.A.	L192
also	L608
Coulter-Cruttenden, Dawn	L064
Courcy, Anne de	L065
Courogen, Carrie	L166
Courter, Gay	L301
Cousens, Sophie	L143
Cousins, Bryony	L102
also	L590
Cove-Smith, Chris	L146
Cowan, Ashley	L107
Cowan, Nancy	L301
Cowan-Hall, Paige	L135
also	L200
Coward, Joseph	L187
Cowell, Cressida	L045
also	L146
Cowell, Emma	L065
also	L088
Cowen, Rob	L146
also	L611
Cowie, Jayne	L153
Cowing, Emma	L613
Cowley, Jason	L146
also	L207
also	L245
also	M222
Cownie, Jen	L153
Cox, Carl	L545
Cox, Helen	L265
also	L561
Crabtree, James	L006
also	L426
Craddock, Jeremy	L265
also	L561
Craig, Amanda	L022
also	L493
Craig, Holly	L143
also	L323
Craig, Jeremy	L166
Craig, Robin	L251
also	L417

Crampton, Caroline	L348
Crane, Marisa	L129
Craven, M.W.	L152
also	L272
Crawford, Katherine Scott	L301
Crawford, Robyn	L381
Crawford, Ryan	L560
Crawford, Susan	L083
Crenshaw, Kimberlé	L429
Crewe, Candida	L022
Crewe, Lesley	L214
Crisell, Hattie	L461
Crispell, Susan	L052
also	L053
Critchley, Simon	L304
Croce, Melissa	L141
Crocker, Bridget	L383
Croft, Adam	L405
Crone, Mackenzie	L331
Cronin, Marianne	L026
Crooks, Jacqueline	L109
Crosby, Polly	L430
Crosby, Sarah	L545
Cross, A J.	L067
also	L143
Cross, Charles R.	L441
Cross, Robin	L586
Crosskey, N.J.	L563
Crossley, Becki Jayne	L560
Crouch, Gabby Hutchinson	L300
Crowe, Duncan	L094
Crowe, Sara	L065
also	L265
also	L473
also	L561
Crowley, Katherine	L166
Crowley, Sinead	L016
also	L326
Crowley, Vivianne	L513
Croxford, Rianna	L207
Crumpton, Nick	L045
also	L146
Cruz-Borja, Vida	L203
also	L617
Cryer, Bob	L405
Cullen, Dave	L166
Cullins, Ashley	L141
Cumberbatch, Judy	L216
Cummins, Fiona	L348
Cundy, David	L059
Cunliffe, John	L146
Cunnell, Howard	L348
Cunningham, Emily	L526
Cunningham, Joshua	L265
Cunningham, Matt	L135
also	L474
Cunningham, Sue H	L064
Curran, Avery	L251
also	L417
Curran, John	L152
also	L272
Curran, Kim	L064
Curry, Tim	L141
Curtis, Cheyenne	L166
Curtis, James	L146
Curtis, Lauren Aimee	L004
Curtis, Norma	L309
Cutler, Georgina	L287
Cyca, Michelle	L556
also	L581
Cyd, Leela	L059
Czerski, Helen	P391
D'Amato, Jamie	L136
Dabel, David	L594
Dabydeen, David	L022
Dahl, Roald	L146
Dahlia, Fia	L107
Daiches, David	L146
Daitz, Ben	L441
Dale, Aaron	L152
also	L193
Dale, Katie	L292
Daly, Jim	L366
Daly, Tess	P032
Dangarembga, Tsitsi	L109
also	L146
Danger, Laura	L382
also	L435
Dangor, Achmat	L065
Daniel Fishel	L158
Daniels, Benjamin	L192
also	L608
Daniels, Sandra	L379
Daniels, Sarah	L135
also	L474
Dannatt, Richard	L586
Dapin, Mark	L166
Dar, Azma	L152
also	L193
Darcy, Dame	L166
Dare, Bill	L300
Dargie, Michael	L281
Dark, Alice Elliott	L166
Darlington, Miriam	L126
Darnton, Tracy	L022
Dart, Michael	L166
Darwent, Heather	L152
also	L238
Darwin, Emma	L265
also	L561
Das, Rijula	L526
Das, Subhadra	L109
Daseler, Graham	L006
also	L426
Dash, Mona	L118
also	L479
Davey, Ed	L588
David, Donna	L366
David, Iona	L185
David, Stuart	L265
also	L561
Davies, Kate	L428
Davies, Katie	L126
Davies, Nicola	L045
also	L146
Davies, Russell	L251
also	L577
Davies, Sara	P032
Davies, Sharron	L265
Davies, Tom	L064
also	L254
Davis, Anna	L251
also	L577
Davis, Daniel M.	L265
also	L361
Davis, Danielle	L205
Davis, Elizabeth	L166
Davis, James	L366
Davis, Kevan	L614
Davis, Lisa Marie	P115
Davis, Lydia	L428
Davis, Margaret Leslie	L059
Davison, Caroline	L265
also	L561
Dawn, Kimberly G.	L331
Dawnay, Gabby	L567
Dawson, Delilah S.	L166
Dawson, Ella	L068
also	L101
Dawson, J.R.	L203
also	L617
Dawson, Mark	L405
Dawson, Rachel	L251
also	L417
Dawson, Tim	L300
Day, Alex	L102
also	L590
Day, Anna	L603
Day, Becca	L152
also	L238
Day, Felicity	L153
Day, Martin	L300
Day, Rosie	L613
Day, Sarah	L430
Day, Susie	L146
also	L589
Daykin, Chloe	L119
also	L192
Daykin, Lizzie	L210
Daykin, Sarah	L210
Deacon, Caroline	L216
Deakin, Leona	L251
also	L603
Dean, Abigail	L430
Dean, Jason	L067
also	L143
Dean, Will	L065
also	L088
DeAngelo, Darcie	L555
Dear, Ian	L390
Dearman, Lara	L348
Deb, Mimi	L434
deBlanc-Knowles, Jaime	L166
DeBlieu, Jan	L059
Dederer, Claire	L348
Deen, Sophie	L567
Deepak, Sharanya	L251
also	L417
Deeren, R.S.	L083
Delahaye, Michael	L152
Delaney, Tish	L146
Delany, Ella	L139
Delderfield, R. F.	L556
Delderfield, R. F.	L146
Dempsey-Multack, Michelle	L301
Denizet-Lewis, Benoit	L083
Dennis, Essie	L064
Dennis, Roy	L022
Dent, Lizzy	L064
also	L254
Denton, Kady MacDonald	L146
also	L589
Denton, Rebecca	L064
also	L254
DePoy, Phillip	L490
Depp, Daniel	L331
DePree, Hopwood	L391
Derbyshire, Jonathan	L006
also	L426
Derome, Marie	L251
also	L577
Derrible, Sybil	L301
Despres, Mk Smith	L205
Detwiler-George, Jacqueline	L250
Devan, K.	L152
also	L193
Deverell, William	L083
Devine, Rachel	L434
DeVita, James	L016
also	L326
deVos, Kelly	L463
also	L464
Dewar, Elaine	L281
Dey, Iain	L094
Dhairyawan, Rageshri	L187
also	L251
Dhaliwal, Sharan	L152
also	L193

Dhand, A. A. L152
  also L272
Dhand, Roxane L064
  also L254
Dhillon, Preeti L152
  also L193
Diamond, David J. L059
Diamond, Lucy L146
Diamond, Martha O. L059
Diamond, Rebekah L083
Diaz, Juano L348
Dick, Gethan L307
Dick, Morgan L146
  also L210
Dickenson, Lisa L265
Dickie, Gloria L555
Dickie, John L119
  also L192
Dickinson, Margaret L143
Dickinson, Miranda L265
DiDonato, Tiffanie L215
Diffee, Matt L493
Difford, Chris L126
Digance, Richard L214
Dillamore, Lucy L146
  also L589
Dillon, Alena L166
Dillon, Lucy L146
Dillsworth, LM L430
Dimbleby, Jonathan L045
  also L146
Dinan, Nicola P114
Dine, Michael L006
  also L426
Ditum, Sarah L265
  also L361
Divin, Sue L251
  also L603
Dix, ...L379
Dixon, Heather L166
Dixon, Jack L588
Dixon, Phyllis L553
Do, Tuyen L065
  also L473
Dobbie, Peter L214
Dobkin, Adin L564
Dobson, W. Y. L292
Docton, Becky L152
  also L272
Dodd, Chris L094
Dodd, Emily L216
Dodsworth, Laura L064
Doherty, Berlie L045
  also L146
Dohrn, Zayd Ayers L441
Dolan, Naoise L146
Dolby, Freya L016
  also L326
Dolby, Hannah L046
  also L152
Dominczyk, Dagmara L441
Domingo, Sareeta L146
Domoney, David L146
  also L207
  also L245
Don, Lari L216
Donahue, Helen L556
Donahue, Peter P167
Donaldson, Carol L265
  also L561
Done, Stephen L072
Donkin, Susie L484
Donkor, Michael L065
  also L473
Donlea, Charlie L553
Donnelly, Joe L479

Donnelly, Liza L381
Donoghue, Emma L099
Donoghue, John "Chick" L207
Donohue, Rachel L016
  also L326
Donovan, Kim L522
Donwood, Stanley L146
  also L611
Dooey-Miles, Samantha L118
  also L479
Doran, Gregory L407
Doran, Phil L059
Dore, Madeleine L441
Dorey-Stein, Beck L564
Dorion, Christiane L216
Dorricott, Francesca L046
  also L152
Dorsey, Candas Jane L027
Doshi, Avni L526
Dotson, Drew L111
Doty, Max L076
Douaihy, Margot L379
Dougherty, Karla L301
Doughty, Anne L309
Doughty, Louise L022
Douglas, Alton P062
Douglas, Ashley L479
Douglas, Claire L430
Douglas, John L207
Douglas, Keighley L366
Douglass, Chloe L567
Douglass, Olivia L004
Doust, Kelly L146
Dowling, Clare L143
Dowling, Finuala L065
Dowling, Mike L405
Downes, Lawrence L166
Downes, Melvyn L613
Downey, Allyson L166
Downham, Jenny L119
  also L192
Downing, David L586
Downs-Barton, Karen L146
  also L156
Dowswell, Paul L586
Doyle, Hannah L484
Doyle, Hayley L067
  also L143
Doyle, Lisa L052
  also L053
Dozal, Gabriel L472
  also L556
Drake, Alicia L146
Drake, Monica P167
Drake, Patrick L251
  also L577
Drayton, Joanne L331
Dreilinger, Danielle L391
Dreisinger, Baz L361
Drew, Brian P062
Drew, Kimberly L068
  also L101
Dreyfus, Nancy L301
Dring, Helen L251
  also L603
Driscoll, Rachel Louise L287
Drucker, Ali L083
Druckman, Charlotte L441
Drummond, Elizabeth L522
Dryburgh, Nicole L216
Duane, Diane L331
duBois, Jennifer L166
DuBois, Laurent L555
Duchene, Remmy P115
Duckworth, Charlotte L265
Duckworth, Chloe L522

Dudley, Renee L564
Duenwald, Sarah L361
Duffy, Bobby L207
Duffy, Lisa L087
  also L435
Duffy, Maureen L304
Duggan, Audrey P062
Duggan, Helena L064
Duguid, Sarah L146
Duke, Kim L251
  also L614
Dumaine, Brian L083
Dumond, Susie L068
  also L101
Dunaway, Suzanne L059
Dunbar, Helene L383
Dunbar, Michaela L545
Duncan, Mike L166
Duncan, Oonagh L281
Dunham, Lacey L068
  also L101
Dunk, Anja L563
Dunlop, Hayley L251
  also L603
Dunlop, Rory L126
Dunn, Jane L613
Dunn, John L006
  also L426
Dunn, Katherine L348
Dunn, Lily L251
Dunn, Roxy L537
Dunn, Suzannah L251
  also L577
Dunne, Jacob L082
Dunne, Patrick L143
Dunne, Peter L126
Dunning, Mari Ellis L251
  also L603
Duns, Jeremy L251
  also L577
Duong, Stephanie L334
Duplessis, Trevor L027
Durant-Rogers, Annabel L292
Durantez, Miriam Gonzalez L405
Durrant, Sabine L428
Durst, Sarah Beth L153
Dusen, Kodie Van L410
Dye, Kerry Douglas L052
  also L053
Dyer, Nick L059
Dyer, Serena L192
  also L477
Dylan, Kate L434
Dyson, DK L166
Dyson, Ed L300
Dyson, Katherine L484
Dzukogi, Saddiq L047
D'Aguiar, Fred L045
  also L146
D'Angour, Armand L006
  also L426
Eagland, Jane L216
Eagle, Judith L292
Eakin, Hugh L429
East, Philippa L287
Eastham, Kate L309
Easthope, Lucy L491
Easton, Rosa Kwon L301
Eastwood, Owen L064
Eaton, Ellie L166
Eaves, Ed L567
Eaves, Will L192
  also L477
Ebert, Lilly L046
Ebuehi, Benjamina L491
Echols, Damien L166

Eddo-Lodge, Reni	L192	
also	L477	
Eden, Caroline	L146	
also	L611	
Eden, Polly	L300	
Eden, Scott	L250	
Eden, Simon David	L265	
also	L561	
Edge, Joanne	L331	
Edge, Suzie	L152	
also	L238	
Edger, Stephen	L152	
also	L238	
Edgers, Geoff	L493	
Eding, Stephanie	L406	
Edmonds, David	L045	
also	L146	
Edric, Robert	L022	
Edwards, Alan	L135	
also	L200	
Edwards, Eve	L146	
also	L589	
Edwards, Nick	L192	
also	L608	
Edwards, Rachel	L152	
also	L272	
Edwards, Scott V.	L555	
Edwards, Yvvette	L047	
Eerkens, Mieke	L361	
Eglinton, Mark	L082	
Egner, Jeremy	L493	
Ehrenhaft, Daniel	L166	
Eijk, Maggy Van	L251	
also	L603	
Eilberg-Schwartz, Penina	L564	
El-Arifi, Saara	L430	
El-Arifi, Sally	L149	
El-Baghdadi, Iyad	L006	
also	L426	
Elder, Charity	L301	
Eldon, Sindri	L613	
Eldred, Ava	L292	
Elkins, J. Theron	L059	
Elledge, Jonn	L251	
also	L577	
Ellen, Tom	L143	
Ellenson, Ruth Andrew	L059	
Ellingwood, Ken	L083	
Elliott, Bobby	L214	
Elliott, Laura	L479	
Elliott, Lexie	L207	
also	L480	
Elliott, Rebecca	L513	
Elliott, Simon	L586	
Ellis, David	M035	
Ellis, Giselle	P115	
Ellis, Rhian	L166	
Ellis, Samantha	L428	
Ellory, Anna	L152	
also	L193	
Ellsworth, Loretta	L059	
Elnoury, Tamer	L207	
Eloise, Marianne	L102	
also	L590	
Elster, Katherine Crowley & Kathy	L166	
Elster, Kathy	L166	
Elven, Lucie	L004	
Ely, Neil	L393	
Emberley, Michael	L493	
Emerson, Tracey	L082	
Emery, Léa Rose	L185	
Emily, Rachel	L366	
Emmerichs, Sharon	L463	
also	L464	
Emmerson, Miranda	L265	
Emmett, Jonathan	L146	
also	L589	
Empson, Clare	L064	
also	L254	
Emswiler, James P.	L059	
Emswiler, Mary Ann	L059	
Eng, Tan Twan	L146	
also	L611	
English, Richard	L146	
also	L207	
also	L245	
Engstrom, Doug	L087	
also	L435	
Ennes, Hiron	L120	
Epel, Naomi	L059	
Epstein, Alex	L059	
Epstein, Jenny	L287	
Erades, Guillermo	L526	
Erdal, Melek	L491	
Erichsen, Helen	L379	
Errett, Benjamin	L281	
Erskine, Barbara	L065	
Erskine, Fiona	L430	
Eschmann, Reese	L087	
also	L435	
Esden, Trish	L553	
Esfandiari-Denney, Eve	L146	
Esiri, Allie	L126	
Esler, Gavin	L146	
also	L207	
also	L245	
Espluga, Eudald	L526	
Essex, Charlotte	L064	
also	L609	
Estate, Anthony Price	L379	
Estate, Donald J. Sobol	L166	
Estate, Jim Carroll	L166	
Estate, John Steptoe	L166	
Estate, Joseph Mitchell	L166	
Estate, Katharine Briggs	L379	
Estate, Scott O'Dell	L166	
Estate, William Lee Miller	L166	
Esterhammer, Karin	L059	
Etherington, Jan	L300	
Ettlinger, Marion	L166	
Eure, Joshua	L016	
also	L326	
Evangelou, Gabriela	L251	
also	L614	
Evangelou, Lucia	L251	
also	L614	
Evans, Alex	L379	
Evans, Claire	L361	
Evans, Clio	L203	
also	L617	
Evans, James	L082	
Evans, Kate	L185	
Evans, Marina	L463	
also	L464	
Evans, Maz	L045	
also	L146	
Evans, Rowan	L146	
Evans, Stephanie	L490	
Evelyn, Alex	L143	
Evergreen, Katie	L252	
Ewan, C. M.	L067	
also	L143	
Ewing, Barbara	L407	
Ewing, Hope	L556	
Excell, Becky	L563	
Eyre, Kirsty	L535	
Eyre-Morgan, Lloyd	L393	
Facelli, Victoria	L556	
also	L581	
Facer, Jo	L065	
also	L473	
Fagan, Sinéad	L300	
Fairbairn, Emily	L613	
Fairhead, James	L192	
also	L284	
Fairless, Chelsea	L556	
Faith, Adelaide	L004	
Faith, Paloma	L613	
Falafel, Olaf	L251	
also	L577	
Falase-Koya, Alex	L560	
Falaye, Deborah	L052	
also	L053	
Falk, Seb	L146	
also	L207	
also	L245	
Fallanca, Vittoria	L251	
also	L417	
Fallon, D'Arcy	P167	
Fallon, Felice	L065	
Fallon, Rebecca	L135	
also	L474	
Famurewa, Jimi	L461	
Farias, Miguel	L265	
Farjeon, Eleanor	L146	
Farjeon, J. Jefferson	L146	
Farmelo, Graham	L006	
also	L426	
Farmer, Addy	L143	
Farmer, Penelope	L126	
Farnsworth, Lauren	L251	
also	L603	
Farooqi, Saad T.	L281	
Farquhar, Michael	L052	
also	L053	
Farrant, Natasha	L119	
also	L192	
Farrarons, Emma	L064	
Farrell, Chris	L301	
Farrell, Marchelle	L535	
Farrelly, Seán	L064	
Farren, Tracey	L065	
Farrer, Maria	L430	
Farrier, David	L192	
also	L477	
Fashola, Abimbola	L560	
Fast, Brooke	L143	
also	L202	
Faulke, Kathryn	L065	
Faulks, Ben	L146	
also	L589	
Faurot, Jeannette	L059	
Favereau, Marie	L166	
Fawcett, Edmund	L119	
also	L192	
Fearnley, James	L192	
also	L608	
Fearnley-Whittingstall, Hugh	L251	
also	L577	
Fearnley-Whittingstall, Jane	L251	
also	L577	
Fears, Mina	L052	
also	L053	
Fedewa, Marilyn	L301	
Fee, Meg	L153	
Feeney, Zoe	L251	
also	L603	
Feldman, Matthew	L331	
Feldman, Ruth	L361	
Feldman, Stephanie	L166	
Felicelli, Anita	L139	
also	L556	
Feng, Linda Rui	L175	
Fennell, David	L152	
also	L272	
Ferguson, Katherine	L153	
Ferguson, Kitty	L331	

*Access more listings online at **firstwriter.com***

Fergusson, Adam	L094
Fernandes, Sujatha	L526
Fernandez, Carla	L129
Fernie, Ewan	L304
Fernie, Gabrielle	L251
also	L603
Ferrars, Elizabeth	L146
Ferreira, Becky	L361
Ferrera, America	L381
Ferrier, Rebecca	L120
Ferris, Paul	L214
Ferry, Georgina	L192
also	L284
Fetuga, Rakaya	L004
Feuer, Michael	L301
Fewery, Jamie	L094
Fibert, Timna	L513
also	L590
Field, Anji Loman	L300
Field, Jean	P062
Field, Ophelia	L146
Field, Patricia	L381
Fields, Helen	L265
Fields-Meyer, Tom	L059
Filby, Eliza	L006
also	L426
Filer, Nathan	L348
Finch, Louise	L366
Finch, Paul	L065
also	L088
Fine, Anne	L146
Fine, Cordelia	L146
also	L207
also	L245
Finger, Aria	L441
Finkel, Eugene	L265
Finkelstein, Danny	L006
also	L426
Finkemeyer, Pip	L146
also	L210
Finnerty, Deirdre	L152
also	L193
Finney, Kathryn	L556
Finnigan, Louise	L251
also	L603
Fiore, Rosie	L265
Firdaus, A P	L535
Fischer, Becca	L281
Fischer, Bronwyn	L281
Fischer, Neal E.	L083
Fishell, Katy	L381
Fisher, Clare	L535
Fisher, Helen	L428
Fisher, Kerry	L143
Fisher, Richard	L185
Fishman, Boris	L166
Fisk, Nicholas	L146
Fisk, Pauline	L146
Fitz, Caitlin	L555
Fitz-Simon, Christopher	L251
also	L577
Fitzgerald, Ronan	L004
Fitzgibbon, Theodora	L146
Fitzhigham, Tim	L586
Fitzmaurice, Ruth	L545
Fitzpatrick, Noel	L613
FitzSimons, Amanda	L391
Flahive, Grace	L026
Flannery-Schroeder, Ellen	L301
Flavin, Teresa	L216
Fleet, Rebecca	L192
also	L608
Fleming, Anna	L022
Fleming, Leah	L309
Flemington, Sara	L281
Fletcher, Carrie Hope	L265
Fletcher, Catherine	L119
also	L192
Fletcher, Corina	L146
also	L589
Fletcher, Giovanna	L265
Fletcher, Susan	L205
Fletcher, Tom	L082
Flicker, Felix	L251
also	L577
Flint, Sarah	L309
Flitter, Emily	L166
Flood, Ciara	L216
Flood, CJ	L119
also	L192
Flood, Nancy Bo	L205
Flood, Patrick	L405
Florence, Kelly	L595
Flyn, Cal	L348
Flynn, Caroline	L406
Flynn, Megan	L331
Fogerty, John	L441
Fogtdal, Peter	P167
Folds, Ben	L441
Foley, Hannah	L216
Fonteyn, Margot	L146
Footz, Nona	L493
Force, Amy de la	L287
Ford, Catt	P115
Ford, Fiona	L065
also	L088
Ford, Ford Madox	L146
Ford, Harper	L379
Ford, Jack	L143
Ford, JR	L129
Ford, JR and Vanessa	L493
Ford, Kate	L545
Ford, Lauren	L102
also	L590
Ford, Martyn	L143
Ford, Matthew	L307
Ford, Nicola	L265
also	L561
Ford, Phil	L300
Ford, Richard T	L555
Ford, Vanessa	L129
Forman, Dov	L046
also	L152
Forman, Lily Ebert	L046
also	L152
Foroohar, Darya	L281
Forrest, Susanna	L428
Forster, Julia	L348
Fort, Adrian	L405
Fortgang, Laura Berman	L301
Fortin, Sue	L064
also	L254
Fortune, Brooke	L016
also	L326
Forward, Susan	L301
Fossen, Delores	L052
also	L053
Foster, Charles	L146
also	L611
Foster, Fred	L146
also	L210
Foster, Kennedy	L490
Foster, Nick	L251
also	L577
Fowler, Karen Joy	L146
Fowler, Yara Rodrigues	L461
Fowles, Sam	L348
Fox, Alix	L065
also	L473
Fox, Catherine	L146
Fox, Debbie	L281
Fox, Essie	L152
also	L272
Fox, James	L348
Fox, Jeffrey	L532
Fox, Kit	L556
Foxwood, Rowan	L292
Frainier, Lizzie	L613
Fram, John	L139
also	L556
Frances, Claire	L434
Franco, Marisa	L083
Frank, Anita	L152
also	L272
Frank, Matthew	L146
also	L207
also	L245
Franklin, Jonathan	L405
Franklin, Mariel	L109
also	L146
Franklin, Sarah	L065
also	L473
Frankopan, Peter	L119
also	L192
Franks, Dominic	L149
Fransman, Karrie	L348
Fraser, Caro	L309
Fraser, Emma	L309
Fraser, Eve	L379
Fraser, Henry	L064
Fraser, Jennifer Petersen	L036
Fraser, Jill	P062
Fraser, Liz	L535
Fraser, Rebecca	L094
Fraser-Cavassoni, Natasha	L082
Frears, Ella	L614
Frederick, Brendan	L166
Freedman, Harry	L265
also	L561
Freedman, Lawrence	L119
also	L192
Freeman, Gwen	P062
Freeman, Joanne B.	L555
Freeman, Mark	L064
also	L254
Freeman, Philip	L301
Freeman, Roxy	L065
also	L473
Freeman, Sara	L348
Freemantle, Brian	L304
Freestone, P. M.	L146
also	L589
Freitas, Irena	L158
French, John	L214
French, Tana	L143
French, Vivian	L216
Freston, Tom de	L146
Freud, Esther	L126
Frey, Pia	L166
Fricas, Katie	L556
Fridland, Valerie	L564
Fridman, Leora	L594
Fried, Seth	L166
Friedman, Joe	L216
Friedman, Rabbi Moshe	L040
also	L064
Friend, Holly	L187
also	L251
Friend, William	L064
Frigo, Christina	L594
Frisby, Dominic	L192
also	L284
Frizzell, Nell	P032
Front, Rebecca	L094
Frost, Claire	L252
Fry, Hannah	P391

52 Table of Authors

Fry, Stephen L045
also L146
Frye, Joe L410
Frye, Lacey-Anne P115
Fuller, Adam Hossein L111
Fullerton, Jean L065
also L088
Fulton, Patricia L281
Furniss, Clare L119
also L192
Furniss, Jo L064
also L254
Fury, John L064
Fury, Paris L064
Fury, Tyson L064
Gabbay, Tom L094
Gacioppo, Amaryllis L004
Gailey, Georgia L234
also L617
Galbraith, James K. L555
Galen, Shana L382
also L435
Galer, Dustin L605
Galfard, Christophe L251
also L577
Galgut, Damon L192
also L608
Gallagher, Patrick L300
Gallant, Mavis L146
Gallardo, Adriana L472
also L556
Galligan, John L382
also L435
Gallon, Harry L461
Galloway, Janice L065
also L473
Galloway, Steven L166
Galway, Caitlin L334
Gamble, Ed P032
Gamble, Ione L185
Game, Shannah L427
Gamp, Gary L064
also L254
Ganjei, Babak L135
also L414
Gannon, Emma P391
Gannon, Ted L300
Gapper, John L006
also L426
Garber, Stephanie L052
also L053
Garcia, Rhonda J. L595
Garcia, Rogelio L383
Gardam, Jane L146
also L589
Gardner, Hazel L064
Gardner, Michael and Ava L493
Gardner, Sally L119
also L192
Garelick, Rhonda L429
Garland, Emma L187
Garland, Sarah L146
also L589
Garner, Ian L094
Garner, Paula L136
Garnett, Eve L146
Garrard, Nicola L152
also L193
Garrett, A.D. L135
also L474
Garrison, Reve P115
Garroni, Lauren L556
Garthwaite, Annie L461
Gartner, John L166
Gaspard, Terry L301
Gastaldi, Federico L205
Gate, Darren L216
Gates, Susan L146
also L589
Gathorne-Hardy, Jonathan L146
Gatrell, Peter L192
also L477
Gattis, Ryan L146
Gatwood, Olivia L556
Gaudet, John L301
Gautier, Amina L166
Gavin, Gareth L251
also L417
Gavin, Jamila L045
also L146
Gay, Ross L148
Gaylord, Joshua L166
Gayton, Sam L366
Gbadamosi, Gabriel L348
Gearhart, Sarah L083
Gearing, Tessa L292
Geary, Karl L348
Geary, Valerie L166
Gebbia, Karen L205
Gee, Poppy L166
Geer, Yvette L036
Geissinger, J. T. L052
also L053
Gelfuso, Hayley L251
also L603
Gendron, Alice L064
also L254
George, Jessica L146
also L210
George, Susan L214
George-Warren, Holly L441
Geras, Adèle L146
also L589
Gerber, Michael L166
Gerner, Marina L064
also L254
Geronimus, Arline T. L429
Gerritsen, Tess P032
Getten, Kereen L560
Gettleman, Jeffrey L083
Ghelani, Divya L152
also L193
Ghosh, Mina Ikemoto L143
Gibbons, Moyette L522
Gibbs, Tessa L102
also L590
Gibson, Jasper L126
Gibson, Marion L361
Gibson, Michael L006
also L426
Gibson, Miles L304
Gibson, Rebecca L135
also L414
Gibson, Sarah L022
Gibson, Susannah L146
also L207
also L245
Gibson, Tamika L560
Giddens, Rhiannon L441
Gidney, Craig Laurance L203
also L617
Giesecke, Annette L361
Gifford, Lisa L300
Gilani, Nadia L152
also L193
Gilbert, Bob L022
Gilbert, Kenny L383
Gilbert-Collins, Susan L301
Gildea, Robert L119
also L192
Giles, Harry Josephine L118
also L479
Gill, Elizabeth L309
Gill, Flora L082
Gill, Josie L491
Gill, Nikita L109
Gill, Roy L216
Gill, Rupinder L281
Gillespie, Keith L214
Gillespie, Tyler L383
Gillett, Ed L082
Gillies, Andrea L428
Gilligan, Ruth L348
Gillingham, Erica L152
also L193
Gilliss, Meghan L071
Gilman, David L065
Gilmore, Olesya Salnikova L251
also L603
Gilmour, Jesse L281
Giltrow, Helen L251
Gimblett, Francis L251
also L614
Gimson, Andrew L146
also L207
also L245
Gingold, Alfred L166
Giorno, John L429
Giron, Maria L004
Gittell, Noah L083
Gittins, Rob L300
Giudici, Amelia L192
Giugni, Lilia L586
Gladstone, Xanthe L563
Gladwin, Faith L434
Glanfield, Jenny L065
also L180
Glasfurd, Guinevere L045
also L146
Glass, Emma L109
Glass, Seressia L052
also L053
Glasser, Ralph L146
Glazebrook, Olivia L461
Gleeson, Claire L535
Gleiberman, Owen L166
Glen, Joanna L026
Glenn, Ebony L190
also L345
Glenny, Misha L126
Glickman, Adina L560
Glogovac, Michelle L301
Glover, Jane L261
Glover, Jonathan L119
also L192
Glover, Julian L006
also L426
Goacher, Lucy L522
Godfrey, Joline L059
Godfrey-Isaacs, Laura L379
Gold, Mara L251
also L417
Gold, Robert L430
Goldbach, Eliese Colette L361
Goldberg, Danny L441
Goldberg, Ron L383
Goldblatt, Amanda L175
Goldblatt, David L192
also L284
Golding, Julia L146
also L589
Goldman, Dan L493
Goldreich, Anna L004
Goldsmith, Paul L207
Goldsmith, William L292
Goldstein, Brandt L166
Golio, Gary L166

Access more listings online at **www.firstwriter.com**

Golombok, Susan	L192
also	L477
Golus, Carrie	L579
Gomez, Erica	L560
Gonsalves, Florence	L087
also	L435
Gonzales, Gina	L560
Gonzalez, Clarissa Trinidad	L334
Gonzalez, Nicky	L071
Goodall, Lewis	L614
Goodan, Chelsey	L427
Goodavage, Clifton Hoodl Maria	L098
Goodhart, David	L006
also	L426
Goodman, Elyssa	L139
also	L556
Goodman, Jonah	L207
Goodman, Lee	L490
Goodman, Matthew	L166
Goodman, Tanya Ward	L059
Goodwin, Matthew	L082
Goodwin, Sarah	L251
also	L603
Goran, Michael I.	L059
Gordon, Kat	L192
also	L608
Gordon, Lyndall	L065
Gordon, Marianne	L331
Gorman, Michele	L265
Gosden, Chris	L119
also	L192
Gosling, Paula	L428
Gosling, Sharon	L153
Gosling, Victoria	L428
Gottlieb, Eli	L166
Goudeau, Jessica	L556
Goudge, Elizabeth	L146
Gough, Julian	L094
Gould-Bourn, James	L265
also	L561
Goulet, Nancy	L579
Govani, Shinan	L281
Gover, Janet	L535
Gowan, Lee	L281
Gower, Jon	L307
Gracie, Rickson	L207
Graetz, Michael	L555
Graff, Andrew J.	L129
Graham, Bre	L185
Graham, Caroline	L146
Graham, Elyse	L361
Graham, Joe	L432
Graham, Sarah	L535
Graham, Wade	L083
also	L361
Gramazio, Holly	L045
also	L146
Granados, Marlowe	L146
Grandin, Temple	L166
Grange, Pippa	L064
Granger, Ann	L065
Grant, Ann E.	L301
Grant, Carrie	L082
Grant, Colin	L348
Grant, David	L082
Grant, Kester	L146
also	L589
Grant, Oliver	L251
also	L603
Grant, Stephen Starring	L250
Graudin, Ryan	L146
also	L589
Graver, Elizabeth	L166
Gray, Casey	L166
Gray, John	L207
Gray, Kate	L430
Graydon, Samuel	L006
also	L426
Grayson, Jonathon	L301
Graystone, C.C.	L410
Graziosi, Barbara	L119
also	L192
Greanais, Margaret	L493
Greathouse, J.T.	L203
also	L617
Greaves, Abbie	L379
Greeley, Molly	L251
also	L603
Green, Caroline	L135
also	L474
Green, Carys	L149
Green, Catherine	L064
Green, Dominic	L146
Green, Ian	L407
Green, Lauren	L068
Green, Linda	L101
Green, Linda	L146
Green, Peter	L146
Greenan, Tracy	L107
Greenberg, Hindi	L059
Greene, Andy	L493
Greene, Brenda	L301
Greene, Graham	L146
also	L207
Greene, Kimberly	L588
Greene, Vanessa	L265
Greenfeld, Karl Taro	L429
Greenhalgh, Huho	L330
Greenhouse, Linda	L555
Greening, Fee	L147
Greenland, Seth	L166
Greenwald, Charlie	L205
Greenwald, Tommy	L205
Greenwood, Kirsty	L265
Gregersen, Elaine	L535
Gregoire, Sheila	L380
Gregor, James	L175
Gregory, Alexis	L152
also	L193
Gregory, Norma	L292
Greifeld, Bob	L429
Grey, Andrew	P115
Grey, Stella	L428
Gribbin, John	L146
also	L207
also	L245
Griffin, Anne	L026
also	L085
Griffin, Nicholas	L564
Griffin, Sarah Maria	L153
Griffin, Stephen	L214
Griffith, Gabriella	L065
also	L473
Griffiths, Jay	L146
also	L611
Griffiths, Kareen	L064
Griffiths, Nick	L588
Grigorescu, Alexandra	L281
Grigson, Geoffrey	L146
Grigson, Jane	L146
Groskop, Viv	P391
Gross, Gwendolen	L166
Gross, Neil	L391
Grosshans, Beth A.	L301
Grover, Elliott	L152
also	L272
Groves, Richard	L432
Grunenwald, Jill	L382
also	L435
Grynbaum, Michael	L429
Gubicza, Jen	L190
also	L345
Gude, Erik	L493
Gudowska, Malwina	L185
Guess, Jessica	L595
Guile, Alison	L567
Guillain, Adam	L588
Guillory, Sarah	L560
Guinness, Jack	L430
Gullen, Hayley	L535
Gunaratne, Guy	L348
Gunn, Alastair	L265
Gunn, Kirsty	L126
Guo, Nadia	L281
Gupta, Kamal	L281
Guralnick, Peter	L493
Gurney, Karen	L535
Guron, Ravena	L560
Gutierrez, Katie	L026
Gutierrez, Rudy	L166
Gutiérrez-Glik, Andrea	L441
Gutteridge, Toby	L064
Gwinn, Saskia	L028
Gwynne, John	L311
Hackett, Lily	L187
Hackman, Rose	L556
Hackworthy, Kate	L484
Haddad, Rana	L304
Haefele, John	L550
Hafdahl, Meg	L595
Hafiza, Radiya	L560
Hahn, Taylor	L068
also	L101
Haig, Francesca	L430
Haig, Matt	L126
Hakakian, Roya	L064
Hakes, Jasmin 'Iolani	L071
Hakim, Yalda	L064
Hale, Kathleen	L166
Hale, Lisa	L166
Hale, Steven	L383
Hales, Gabrielle	L082
Haley, Guy	L296
Hall, Araminta	L146
Hall, Bronwyn	L331
Hall, Catherine	L192
also	L608
Hall, Clare Leslie	L064
also	L254
Hall, Jake	L187
also	L251
Hall, Joanna	L428
Hall, Julie L.	L301
Hall, Lori Inglis	L026
Hall, Simon	L192
also	L284
Hall, Wes	L281
Hallberg, David	L429
Halliburton, Rachel	L006
also	L426
Halliday, G.R.	L067
also	L143
Halliday, Thomas	L119
also	L192
Halligan, Liam	L006
also	L426
Halliwell, Ed	L390
Halls, Ben	L537
Halls, Stacey	L430
Hamel-Akré, Jessica	L185
Hamid, Omar Shahid	L094
Hamilton, A.B.	L006
also	L211
Hamilton, Bridget Helen	L292
Hamilton, Henrietta	L072
Hamilton, James	L192
also	L477
Hamilton, Karen	L348

Hamilton, Lou	L126
Hamilton, Sophie	L143
also	L202
Hamilton-Bannis, Karissa	L613
Hamilton-McKenzie, Isaac	L064
Hamlyn, Lili	L004
Hammer, Alison	L382
also	L435
Hammond, Ryan	L143
Hampton, Leah	L166
Hamya, Jo	L146
Hancock, Penny	L146
also	L210
Handrick, Michael	L152
also	L193
Handy, Charles	L006
also	L426
Hankinson, Andrew	L006
also	L426
Hanley, James	L146
Hannah, James	L026
Hannibal, Mary Ellen	L166
Hannig, Anita	L556
Hannity, Mary	L146
Hansen, Kim-Julie	L082
Haque, Sarah	L185
Haran, Maeve	L428
Harcourt, Isabella	L522
Harcourt, Lou Morgan / Maggie	L430
Harding, Angela	L040
also	L064
Harding, Debora	L126
Harding, Emily	L301
Harding, Kate	L301
Hardman, Isabel	L146
also	L207
also	L245
Hardy, Alyssa	L166
Hardy, Chips	L064
Hardy, Edward	L216
Hardy, Elle	L064
Hardy, Reina	L361
Hare, Bernard	L261
Harffy, Matthew	L588
Harford, Tim	L192
also	L284
Hargreaves, Mary	L143
also	L202
Harlan, Charlie	L064
Harley, Belinda	L428
Harman, Alice	L143
Harman, Sophie	L146
also	L207
also	L245
Harmer, Joyce Efia	L143
Harper, Candida	L146
also	L589
Harper, Elodie	L430
Harper, K.C.	L331
Harper, Mireille	L152
also	L193
Harper, Peter	L614
Harris, Ali	L146
Harris, Anstey	L287
Harris, Ben	L300
Harris, Charlotte	L331
Harris, James	L567
Harris, Mish	L379
Harris, Neil Patrick	L441
Harris, Oliver	L045
also	L146
Harris, Sarah	L316
Harris, Will	L109
Harris, Windy Lynn	L166
Harrison, M John	L407
Harrison, Michael	L586
Harrison, Phil	L251
also	L428
Harry, Anneka	L379
Hart, Alice	L614
Hart, B. H. Liddell	L146
Hart, Ericka	L391
Hart, Gracie	L309
Hart, Natalie	L153
Hartema, Laura	L301
Hartley, Gabrielle	L083
also	L391
Hartley, Jack	L393
Hartley, Sarah	L065
also	L473
Harvey, Alyxandra	L553
Hasbun, Sabrin	L379
Hashimoto, Reiko	L082
Haslam, David	L065
also	L473
Hasler, Susan	L148
Haslett, Emma Forsyth	L065
also	L473
Hassan, Ramsey	L064
Hassett, Brenna Ryan	L153
Hastings, Elaine	L252
Hatch, Evie	L251
also	L417
Hatfield, Ruth	L366
Hattrick, Alice	L146
Hatzistefanis, Maria	L064
Hauck, Rachel	L380
Hauser, Ethan	L166
Havelin, Karen	L526
Hawdon, Lindsay	L026
Hawke, Sam	L311
Hawkins, Ed	L028
Hawkins, Paula	L146
also	P032
Hawley, Ellen	L059
Haworth, Julie	L379
Hay, Suzanne	L036
Hayder, Mo	L045
also	L146
Haydock, Sophie	L430
Hayes, Erica	L553
Hayes, Larry	L366
Hayes, Nick	L146
also	L611
Hayes, Patrick	P062
Haynes, Dana	L490
Hays, Kate	L064
Hayward, Cathy	L072
Hayward, Julie	L187
also	L251
Hazeley, Jason	L379
Hazell, Lottie	L146
also	P114
Hazzard, Oli	L146
He, Joan	L136
Healey, Cherry	L613
Healy, Claire Marie	L146
Heap, Joe	L379
Heap, Sue	L170
Heard, Gerald	L146
Hearn, Sam	L567
Hearne, Kevin	L166
Heath, Sue	L484
Heath-Stubbs, John	L146
Heather, Peter	L119
also	L192
Heatherington, Emma	L287
Heaton, Natalie	L484
Hecker, Tim	L192
also	L477
Heckler, Kimberly	L301
Hedges, Kristi	L301
Hedrick, Lucy	L553
Heerden, Etienne van	L065
Hehir, Sarah	L613
Heidicker, Christian McKay	L136
Heisenfelt, Ann	L215
Helen, Elizabeth	L203
also	L617
Hellenga, Robert	L166
Heller, Miranda Cowley	L026
Heller, Ted	L215
Hellisen, CL	L118
also	L479
Heminsley, Alexandra	L348
Hemnani, Ritu	L205
Henderson, Alexis	L052
also	L053
Henderson, Caspar	L022
Henderson, Christine Rose	L579
Henderson, Emma	L045
also	L146
Henderson, Jordan	L064
Henderson, Julietta	L026
Hendricks, Steve	L166
Hendrie, James	L300
Hendrix, Grady	L203
also	L617
Hendrix, Michael	L493
Hendry, Ali	L152
also	L193
Hendry, Diana	L216
Hendry, Sharon	L082
Hendy, Paul	L214
Henley, Amelia	L064
also	L254
Henley, Marian	L059
Hennigan, Jane	L149
Henry, Joe	L166
Hepburn, Cat	L251
also	L603
Hepburn, Jessica	L082
Hepinstall, Becky	L166
Hepworth, David	L586
also	P032
Herbert, James	L146
Heritage, Stuart	L251
also	L577
Herlich, Taryn	L410
Herrick, Holly	L301
Herrick, Richard	P080
Herriot, James	L146
Herron, Mick	L146
Herron, Rita	L052
also	L053
Herst, Charney	L059
Herz, Rachel	L383
Hesketh, Scott	L094
Hesse, Josiah	L441
Hewitt, Deborah	L146
also	L210
Hewlett, Rosie	L146
also	L210
Heyam, Kit	L187
also	L251
Hibberd, James	L493
Hibbert, Christopher	L146
Hickam, Homer	L207
Hicks, Dan	L082
Hicks, Josh	L064
Higginbotham, Adam	L348
Higgins, Carter	L205
Higgins, Chris	L216
Higgins, David	L094
Higham, Tom	L265
also	L561

Hill, Justin	L586
Hill, Kat	L251
also	L417
Hill, Louis	L119
also	L192
Hill, Maisie	L535
Hill, Matt Rowland	L348
Hill, Nathan	L045
also	L146
Hill, Will	L094
Hillman, Jonathan	L006
also	L426
Hilsum, Lindsey	L192
also	L477
Hilton, Lisa	L152
also	L272
Hincenbergs, Sue	L434
Hine, Lewis	L545
Hirschman, Leigh Ann	L059
Hirshman, Linda	L429
Hirst, Chris	L146
also	L207
also	L245
Hirst, Lindsay	L292
Hise, Brian Van	L072
Hitch, Julian	L251
also	L577
Hitchman, Beatrice	L251
also	L379
Hitzmann, Sue	L532
Ho, Karen	L472
also	L556
Ho-Yen, Polly	L143
Hoban, Russell	L146
also	L207
also	L245
Hobhouse, Penelope	L119
also	L192
Hobsbawm, Eric	L146
also	L207
also	L245
Hodes, Martha	L555
Hodge, Gavanndra	L146
Hodges, Kate	L065
also	L473
Hodges, Michael	L126
Hodgkin, Emily Jane	L166
Hodgkinson, Leigh	L146
also	L589
Hodgkinson, Thomas W.	L094
Hodgman, George	L166
Hodgson, Antonia	L126
Hodgson, Jesse	L146
also	L589
Hoffman, Paul	L045
also	L146
Hoffman, Roy	L301
Hogan, Edward	L045
also	L146
Hogan, Faith	L309
Hogan, Michael	L065
also	L473
Hogerton, Sam	L107
Hogg, Nicholas	L094
Hoggarth, Janet	L586
Hogge, Fred	L082
Hoghton, Anna	L146
also	L589
Hohenegger, Beatrice	L166
Holborn, Stark	L331
Holden, Amanda	L068
also	L101
Holding, Michael	L028
Holland, James	P032
Holland, Jesse J.	L203
also	L617
Holland, Merlin	L126
Hollander, Julia	L251
also	L428
Hollinger, David	L555
Hollingshead, Iain	L094
Hollingsworth, Mark	L586
Holloway-Smith, Wayne	L251
also	L614
Holman, Rebecca	L153
Holme, Lucy	L147
Holmes, Andrew	L251
also	L577
Holmes, David	L064
Holmes, Kelly	L344
Holmes, Marianne	L072
Holmes, Natasha	L102
also	L590
Holness, Nevin	L135
also	L225
Holwell, Hannah-Marie	L296
Honeywell, Antonia	L379
Hong, Euny	L146
Hong, Liu	L146
also	L611
Hood, Christopher M.	L166
Hood, Evelyn	L072
Hooper, Meredith	L146
also	L589
Hooper, Rebecca	L251
also	L603
Hoopes, Alex	L068
also	L101
Hope, Anna	L192
also	L608
Hope, Maggie	L309
Hopkins, Megan	L064
Hopkinson, Simon	L045
also	L146
Hopper, Jill	L022
Hopwood, Sharon	L366
Horn, Ariel	L059
Horn, Trevor	L146
also	L245
Hornak, Francesca	L304
Hornby, Emma	L309
Hornby, Gill	L192
also	L608
Horne, Eileen	L348
Hornsley, Sarah	L287
also	L430
Horowitz, Sarah	L141
Horrocks, Allison	L383
Horwitz, Jesse	L083
Hosier, Erin	L166
Hosken, Andrew	L094
Hoskins, Hayley	L102
also	L590
Hoskins, Tansy	L146
also	L207
also	L245
Hosy-Pickett, Leigh	L064
Hough, Richard	L146
Houghton, Eleanor	L149
Houghton, Emily	L287
Hounsom, Lucy	L045
also	L146
Hourston, Alex	L251
also	L577
House, Richard	L192
also	L608
Housham, Jane	L379
Housley, Sarah	L251
also	L417
Hovitz, Helaina	L301
Howard, A. G.	L052
also	L053
Howard, Alex	L309
Howard, Ayanna	L361
Howard, Catherine Ryan	L016
also	L326
Howard, David	L251
Howard, Jules	L379
Howard, Minna	L309
Howard, Sally	L461
Howard, Scott Alexander	L251
also	L603
Howell, C.R.	L537
Howell, Daniel	L135
also	L414
Howells, April	L252
Howells, Debbie	L430
Howes, Emily	L026
Howes, Theresa	L430
Howie, Vicki	L316
Howkins, John	L586
Hoy, Chris	L040
also	L064
Hoyer, Katja	L006
also	L426
Hoyland, Graham	L586
Hsieh-yung, Pai	L147
Hu, Tung-Hui	L361
Huang, Yunte	L555
Huband, Sally	L022
Huber, Sam	L429
Huchu, Tendai	L390
Huddleston, Tom	L153
Hudson, Kerry	L065
also	L473
Hudson, Lexy	L292
Hudson, Lincoln	L432
Huerta, Lizz	L472
also	L556
Huf, Tammye	L252
Huggins, James Byron	L380
Hughes, Alrene	L309
Hughes, Benjamin	L567
Hughes, Egan	L067
also	L143
Hughes, Gwyneth	L179
Hughes, Langston	L146
Hughes, Pascal	L040
also	L064
Hughes, Richard	L146
Hugo, Ilze	L166
Hui, Angela	L109
Huizing, Alyssa	L605
Hulland, Louise	L046
Humble, Catherine	L004
Hummer, Maria	L251
also	L603
Humphrey, Nicholas	L006
also	L426
Hung, Daisy J.	L251
also	L417
Hunt, Alice	L119
also	L192
Hunt, Kenya	L185
Hunter, Becky	L287
Hunter, Lisa	L059
Hunter-Gault, Charlayne	L429
Huntley, Alex	L281
Hurley, Michael	L307
Hurlock, Kathryn	L119
also	L192
Husain, Masud	L146
also	L611
Hussain, Anika	L560
Hussain, Iqbal	L292
Huston, Allegra	L192
also	L608
Hutchinson, Lindsey	L309

Table of Authors

Hutchinson, Michael L028
Hutchinson, Barry L216
Hutson, Shaun L331
Hutton, Alice L379
Hutton, Robert L192
  also L284
Hyatt, Oli L064
Hyde, Deborah L072
Hyland, Tara L143
Hyslop, Leah L065
  also L473
Høeg, Mette Leonard L307
Iacopelli, Jennifer L560
Idehen, Joshua L047
Iglesias, Gabino L139
  also L556
Ilott, Terry L214
Imdad, Ali L430
Ince, Robin L586
Ingalls, Bea L064
Innes, Catriona L046
  also L152
Innes, Kirstin L082
Inverne, James L064
Iqbal, Anam L522
Irankunda, Pacifique L555
Ireland, Amelia L152
  also L238
Ireland, Perrin L361
Irving, Ellie L028
Irwin, J D (Julie) L216
Isaacs, Robert L052
  also L053
Iselin, Josie L166
Issa, Hanan L152
  also L193
Ivey, Felicitas P115
Izadi, Shahroo L545
J, Sailor L136
Jabr, Ferris L251
  also L577
Jack, Belinda L119
  also L192
Jack, Valerie L152
Jackie, ... L059
Jackman, Wayne L300
Jackson, Alex L563
Jackson, Andrew L586
Jackson, Barry L493
Jackson, E A L379
Jackson, Erik Forrest L301
Jackson, Jeffrey H. L493
Jackson, Jeremy L166
Jackson, Julian L146
  also L207
  also L245
Jackson, Lawrence L564
Jackson, Olivia L331
Jackson, Steve L380
Jackson, Tiffany D. L052
  also L053
Jackson, Tom L563
Jacob, Catherine L143
Jacobs, John Hornor L166
Jacobs, Melissa L059
Jacobson, Gavin L006
  also L426
Jacques, Juliet L187
Jade, Holly L484
Jaeger, Meredith L052
  also L053
Jaffe, Janet L059
Jaffe, Sarah L556
  also L581
Jager, Liz De L430
Jahanshahi-Edlin, Gabby L491

Jahn, Ryan David L152
  also L272
Jahshan, Elias L102
  also L590
Jai, Sophie L152
  also L193
Jakeman, Jo L461
James, Alice L407
James, Blair L004
James, Brenda L588
James, Cate L216
James, Charlee L406
James, Charlie Hamilton L006
James, Cormac L065
James, Heidi L535
James, Liza St. L004
James, Lynsey L287
James, Peter L065
James, Rachel McCarthy L556
  also L581
James-Mackey, Tess L560
Janakievska, Irina L563
Jardine, Lis L292
Jarman, Julia L146
  also L589
Jarrett, Gene L555
Jarrett-Macauley, Delia L047
Jasmine, Lucretia Tye L381
Jasmon, Sarah L192
  also L477
Jayaraman, Saru L361
Jayatissa, Amanda L139
  also L556
Jaye, Lola L309
Jeans, Crystal L026
Jebara, Mohamad L564
Jebelli, Joseph L192
  also L477
Jecks, Michael L265
  also L561
Jedrowski, Tomasz L065
Jefferies, Dinah L265
Jeffries, Sheila L309
Jeffries, Stuart L307
Jellicoe, Alexandra L065
  also L473
Jeng, Sarah Zachrich L382
  also L435
Jenkins, Sophie L309
Jenkins, Tiffany L006
  also L426
Jenner, Genevieve L563
Jennings, Charles L251
Jennings, Elizabeth L146
Jensen, Helga L152
  also L272
Jensen, Louise L064
  also L254
Jensen, Nancy McSharry L361
Jensen, Oskar Cox L265
  also L561
Jesmond, Jane L484
Jewell, Hannah L586
Joan, ... L251
Jobin, Matthew L166
Joffe, Daron L166
Johansen, Signe L545
John Parra L158
John, D.B. L251
  also L577
John, Lauren St. L119
  also L192
Johncock, Benjamin L065
  also L473
Johns, Chris L281
Johnson, Betsey L381

Johnson, Daisy May L153
Johnson, Daniel Brock L555
Johnson, Harriet L046
  also L152
Johnson, Katerina L185
Johnson, Milly L146
Johnson, R. Dean L556
Johnson, Rebecca May L146
Johnson, Sophie Lucido L556
Johnson-Schlee, Sam L251
  also L417
Johnston, C.R. L107
Johnstone, Leigh L072
Johnstone, Lindsay L118
  also L479
Johnstone, Stuart L265
  also L561
Jolly, Joanna L006
  also L426
Jonasson, Ragnar L152
  also L272
Jones, Amy L046
  also L152
Jones, Arden L296
Jones, Becca L087
  also L435
Jones, Carol L309
Jones, Colin L119
  also L192
Jones, Diana Wynne L045
  also L146
Jones, Faith L564
Jones, Gaynor L251
  also L603
Jones, Ginger L535
Jones, Hannah Karena L522
Jones, Harold L146
Jones, Helen L251
  also L428
Jones, Ioan Marc L330
Jones, Jacqueline L251
  also L428
Jones, Lizzie Huxley L152
  also L193
Jones, Lucy L146
  also L611
Jones, Mary L166
Jones, Michael L586
Jones, Noah Z. L166
Jones, Owen L146
  also L207
  also L245
Jones, Peter L366
Jones, Rob Lloyd L126
Jones, Ruth P032
Jones, Sandie L143
Jones, Shane L071
Jones, Simon L094
Jones, Vanessa L296
Jooste, Pamela L309
Jordan, Amie L143
Jordan, Amy L016
  also L326
Jordan, Don L586
Jordan, Elise L429
Jordan-Baker, Craig L379
Jory, Chloe L087
  also L435
Joseph, Anjali L428
Joseph, Anthony L146
  also L156
Joseph, Jay L366
Joseph, R.J. L410
Joy, David L166
Joyce, Rachel L126
  also P114

Jr., Frank Wheeler, ... L166
Jr., Henry Louis Gates L429
Jubber, Nick L192
also L477
Judd, Alan L146
also L207
Jukes, Helen L146
also L611
Jukes, Matthew L147
Juliet Menéndez L158
June, Valerie L166
Jung, Grace L301
Juric, Sam L281
Jónasson, Jón Atli L152
Júlíusdóttir, Katrín L152
also L272
Kabler, Jackie L588
Kadri, Sadakat L126
Kahn-Harris, Keith L251
also L577
Kaiserman, Alex L119
also L192
Kalia, Ammar L004
Kallmayer, Line L004
Kam, Jennifer Wolf L463
also L464
Kamal, Isabella L553
Kambalu, Samson L513
Kaminski, Theresa L301
Kamler, Celina L553
Kane, Ashlyn P115
Kane, Karen L166
Kaner, Hannah L430
Kapil, Bhanu L109
Kaplan, Bonnie J. L441
Kaplan, Hester L166
Kar-Purkayastha, Ishani L265
Kara, Lesley L484
Kardas-Nelson, Mara L555
Karim, Noaah L334
Karim-Cooper, Farah L082
Karlie, Logan L135
also L200
Kashner, Sam L381
Kasket, Elaine L265
Kastens, Alegra L493
Kate, Jessica L380
Katz, Ani L166
Katz, Emily L059
Katz, Rachelle L301
Kaufman, Andrew L281
Kaufman, Charlotte L472
also L556
Kaufman, Kenn L555
Kaufman, Sashi L383
Kaufman, Sophie Monks L545
Kaufmann, Miranda L586
Kaur, Hardeep L064
Kavan, Anna L146
Kavanagh, Anthony L152
also L238
Kavanagh, Emma L067
also L143
Kavasch, E. Barrie L059
Kawa, Abraham L126
Kaye, M. M. L146
Keane, Jessie L146
also L210
Keane, Molly L146
Kearney, Fionnuala L287
Kearsley, Kelly L068
also L101
Kearsley, Susanna L135
also L474
Keating, Fiona L251
also L417
Keay, Anna L146
also L207
also L245
Keay, John L146
also L207
also L245
Keen, Andrew L006
also L426
Keen, Greg L135
also L414
Keenan, David L126
Keenan, Jillian L564
Keer, Jenni L085
also L522
Keiser, Jake L564
Keller, Jon L166
Keller, Joy L059
Kelley, Ann L216
Kelley, Nancy L152
also L193
Kelly, David L040
also L064
Kelly, Greta L111
Kelly, Helena L192
also L284
Kelly, Jacqueline L207
also L480
Kelly, Jason L532
Kelly, Joseph L301
Kelly, Louise L216
Kelly, Nicola L348
Kelly, Rachel L098
Kelly, Ruth L064
also L254
Kelly, Stephen L301
Kelly, Thomas Forrest L555
Kelman, Stephen L045
also L126
also L146
Kemp, Laura L146
Kempton, Beth L265
Kenani, Stanley L192
also L608
Kendrick, Erika J. L207
also L480
Kendrick, Mollie L064
also L254
Kennedy, Brynne S. L301
Kennedy, James L136
also L207
Kennedy, John L065
also L088
Kennedy, Jonathan L146
also L611
also P391
Kennedy, Katie L040
also L064
Kennedy, Nancy L301
Kennedy, Paul L146
also L207
also L245
Kennedy, Sean P115
Kennedy-Moore, Eileen L059
Kenward, Louise L479
Kenyon, Rachel Tawil L059
Kernick, Simon L484
Kerr, Emily L484
Kershaw, Claire L252
Kershaw, Robert L586
Kershaw, Scott L064
Kertzer, David L555
Kessler, Brad L166
Kessler, Diana L152
Kessler, Liz L119
also L192
Key, Amy L192
Keyes, Sidney L146
Keys, Barbara L146
also L207
also L245
also L555
Khalili, Nasser David L064
Khambete-Sharma, Vedashree L251
also L428
Khan, Amana Fontanella L348
Khan, Ausma Zehanat L087
also L435
Khan, Hiba Noor L102
also L590
Khan, Imran L261
also L613
Khan, Katie L430
Khan, Sara L214
Khan, Sulmaan Wasif L146
also L207
also L245
Khan, Sunnah L526
Khatib, Sulaiman L564
Khoo, Rachel L146
Khoury, Philip L563
Khurana, Vijay L307
Kidd, Jess L026
Kiefer, Christian L166
Kiernan, Olivia L026
Kildaire, V.B. P115
Kilkerr, Justine L026
Killham, Nina L135
also L200
Kim, Angela Jia L441
Kim, Erin Rose L463
also L464
Kim, Michelle L281
Kim, Sang L334
Kimble, Megan L556
Kimm, Gabrielle L251
Kimmerer, Robin Wall L361
Kimmerle, Erin L493
Kimutai, Kiprop L537
Kinavey, Hilary L301
Kincade, Sierra L382
also L435
Kincaid, Shay P115
Kinchen, Rosie L348
King, Claire L045
also L146
King, Clive L146
also L589
King, Danny James L135
also L414
King, Ella L484
King, Esme L251
also L428
King, Lizzie L614
King, Tracy P114
King, Vanessa L614
Kingori, Patricia L307
Kingsley, Sean L301
Kingston, Holly L265
Kinn, Julie L065
also L088
Kinnings, Max L251
also L577
Kino, Shilo L537
Kinsella, Ana L004
Kinsella, Sophie P032
Kirby, Annie L026
Kirk, David L251
also L577
Kirkbride, Jasmin L120
Kirshenbaum, Binnie L146
Kispert, Peter L175
Kissick, Lucy L311

Kisska, Kristin ... L553
Kissling, Chris ... L588
Kitamura, Katie ... L126
Kitchen, Bert ... L146
also ... L589
Kitchin, C. H. B. ... L146
Kite, Gerad ... L126
Kitson, Euan ... L135
also ... L474
Kjærgaard, Rikke Schmidt ... L251
also ... L577
Klaussmann, Liza ... L192
also ... L608
Kleine, Andrea ... L166
Klidonas, Caroline ... L064
Kliman, Stuart ... L155
Kline, Harriet ... L126
Kling, Rebecca ... L129
also ... L493
Knight, Caedis ... L484
Knight, Rebecca Dinerstein ... L251
also ... L428
Knopman, Jaime ... L427
Knox, Joseph ... L251
also ... L577
Knox-Mawer, June ... L146
Koch, Richard ... L192
also ... L284
Kochanski, Halik ... L146
also ... L207
also ... L245
Kochhar, Atul ... L082
Koekkoek, Taylor ... L166
Koh, Karen ... L382
also ... L435
Kohda, Claire ... L026
Kohler, Camri ... L331
Kolaya, Chrissy ... L166
Kole, William J. ... L493
Komolafe, Peter ... L064
also ... L254
Konditor, ... L065
also ... L473
Koonar, Sohan ... L281
Kooper, Zoya ... L064
Korman, Amanda ... L166
Korn, Gabrielle ... L166
Korpon, Nik ... L166
Koska, Anna ... L563
Koslowski, Chris ... L083
Kova, Elise ... L052
also ... L053
Kraatz, Jeramey ... L136
Kramer, J. Kasper ... L166
Kramer, Kathryn ... L594
Krantz, Laura ... L441
Krastev, Ivan ... L006
also ... L426
Kressley, Carson ... L441
Kriegsman, Ali ... L564
Krimpas, Titania ... L366
Kriss, Sam ... L390
Kristoff, Jay ... L146
also ... L589
Kronman, Anthony ... L555
Krug, Cassidy ... L472
also ... L556
Kudei, Sonya ... L251
Kuhlmann, Arkadi ... L281
Kuo, Fifi ... L146
also ... L589
Kuritzkes, Justin ... L166
Kurtz, Catherine ... L152
also ... L193
Kuyken, Willem ... L301
Kuznetsova, Maria ... L166
Kwak, Gene ... L071
Kwakye, Chelsea ... L192
also ... L477
Kwon, Mya ... L072
Kynge, James ... L192
also ... L284
Kyriacou, Eleni ... L152
also ... L193
LaBarge, Emily ... L146
LaBarge, Melanie ... L071
Labbe, Marguerite ... P115
Lacera, Jorge ... L136
Lacera, Megan ... L136
Lacey, Stephen ... L146
Lachlan, M.D. ... L428
Lagos, Leah ... L441
Lagrève, Manon ... L251
also ... L577
Lahti, Christine ... L441
Lake, Joanne ... L064
Lam, L.R. ... L430
Lamanna, Gina ... L287
Lamb, Nicola ... L563
Lambert, Charles ... L065
Lamm, August ... L187
also ... L251
Lammy, David ... L146
also ... L207
also ... L245
Lamond, Caroline ... L152
also ... L238
Lampard, Frank ... L064
Lancaster, Mike ... L366
Lancaster, Simon ... L192
also ... L284
Land, Ali ... L430
Landau, Camille ... L059
Landau, Deb Miller ... L493
Landdeck, Katherine Sharp ... L391
Landman, Tanya ... L216
Lane, Jennifer ... L028
Lane, Johanna ... L166
Lane, Mitch ... L563
Lane, Neil ... L493
Lang, Nico ... L493
Langan, Michael ... L379
Langan, Sarah ... L166
Lange, Richard ... L166
Langley, Philippa ... L586
Langmead, Oliver K. ... L120
Langrish, Katherine ... L119
also ... L192
Languirand, Mary ... L301
Lankina, Tomila ... L192
also ... L284
Lanzen, Meredith ... L331
Lapena, Shari ... P032
Lapidus, Jennifer ... L441
Lapine, Missy Chase ... L301
Larocca, Amy ... L429
Larsen, Casey ... L207
Larsen, Melissa ... L068
also ... L101
Larsen, Reif ... L428
Larson, Carlton F. W. ... L555
Larwood, Kieran ... L064
Laski, Marghanita ... L146
Laskow, Sarah ... L166
Lassoued, Alex ... L064
also ... L254
Laszlo, Mary de ... L309
Latham, Martin ... L348
Lattimore, Ashton ... L068
also ... L101
Laurie, Hugh ... L045
also ... L146
Lavelle, Amy ... L484
also ... L522
Lavender, Eleanor ... L146
also ... L589
Lavery, Grace ... L192
also ... L477
Law, Catherine ... L309
Law, Phyllida ... L192
also ... L608
Lawler, Liz ... L064
also ... L254
Lawrence, Ann ... L146
Lawrence, Caroline ... L170
Lawrence, Derek ... L493
Lawrence, Lee ... L064
Lawrence, Natalie ... L146
also ... L611
Lawrence, Sandra ... L153
Lawrie, Lucy ... L265
also ... L561
Laws, Chloe ... L135
also ... L200
Laws, Peter ... L265
also ... L561
Lawson, Davey ... L594
Lawson, Mike ... L076
Lawson, Persia ... L126
Lawton, Graham ... L006
also ... L426
Lawton, Sarah ... L135
also ... L474
Lay, Carol ... L059
Lazenby, John ... L586
LDN, Iggy ... L187
Leach, David ... L281
Leach, Tim ... L192
also ... L608
Leadbeater, Charles ... L006
also ... L426
Leadbeater, Cory ... L071
Leah, Bryony ... L153
Leake, Elisabeth ... L146
also ... L207
also ... L245
Leaver, Kate ... L146
also ... L210
LeCraw, Holly ... L166
Lee, Hali ... L129
Lee, Jenny ... L614
Lee, Jeremy ... L146
Lee, Julia ... L148
Lee, Kyo ... L334
Lee, Mirinae ... L166
Lee, Patrick ... L490
Lee, Sam ... L082
Lee, Shu Han ... L563
Lee, Tommy ... L166
Lee, Tony ... L300
Lee-Kennedy, Brydie ... L461
Leech, Frances ... L006
also ... L426
Leeds, Thomas ... L152
also ... L193
Leendertz, Lia ... L344
Lees, Georgina ... L484
Lefler, Anna ... L059
Legend, The Urban ... L064
Leger, Arizona ... L064
Leggo, Michael ... L152
Lehnen, Christine ... L265
Leider, Jerry ... L214
Leiggi, Miranda ... L560
Leiper, Kate ... L216
Leitch, Maurice ... L586
Leith, William ... L251
also ... L577

Leivaditaki, Marianna	L082
Lelic, Simon	L192
also	L608
Lemmey, Huw	L109
Lenier, Sue	L214
Lennon, Joan	L216
Lennon, Patrick	L143
Lennox, Judith	L261
Lennox, Lee	L064
Lent, James	L567
Leonard, Mark	L006
also	L426
Leonard, S.V.	L152
also	L238
Lepard, Dan	L251
also	L577
Lepucki, Edan	L166
Lerner, Claire	L301
Leslie, Barbra	L281
Leslie, Ian	L006
also	L426
Lesniak, Caroline	L553
Lesser, Elizabeth	L166
Lessore, Nathanael	L143
Lester, CN	L379
Lester, Jem	L251
also	L603
Letemendia, Claire	L281
Lethbridge, Lucy	L119
also	L192
Lette, Kathy	L152
Letwin, Oliver	L006
also	L426
Levene, Alysa	L192
also	L284
Levin, Daniel	L564
Levine, Irene S.	L301
Levitt, Alexandra	L301
Levitt, Theresa	L175
Levy, Ashley Nelson	L071
Levy, Paul	L094
Levy-Chehebar, Esther	L068
also	L101
Lewis, Ben	L307
Lewis, Beth	L152
also	L272
Lewis, Damien	L146
also	L207
also	L245
Lewis, Dan	L472
also	L556
Lewis, Daniel	L555
Lewis, David	L553
Lewis, Gwyneth	L022
Lewis, Ian	L072
Lewis, Jacqui	L083
Lewis, Jemima	L348
Lewis, Jenny	L107
Lewis, Jerry Lee	L166
Lewis, Lisa L.	L301
Lewis, Richard Leslie	L300
Lewis, Robert	L251
also	L577
Lewis, Robin	L166
Lewis, Ted	L146
Lewis-Oakes, Rebecca	L567
Lewis-Stempel, John	P114
Ley, Rebecca	L348
Leyes, Emilie	L215
Leyser, Matilda	L251
also	L603
Li, Maggie	L567
Li, Wenying	L479
Liang, Holan	L513
Libaire, Jardine	L428
Libby, Gillian	L382
also	L435
Lida, David	L166
Liebelson, Dana	L068
also	L101
Liftig, Anya	L166
Light, Alan	L441
Light, Daniel	L146
also	L207
also	L245
Lightfoot, Freda	L484
Lihou, Rose	L064
Lillie, Vanessa	L068
also	L101
Lim, Audrea	L556
Lim, Roselle	L052
also	L053
Lima, Ananda	L071
Lin, Jeremy Atherton	L379
Lin, Patty	L141
Linden, Rachel	L380
Lindop, Grevel	L586
Lindsay, Chantelle	L152
also	L193
Lindsay, Jack	L146
Lindsay, Keith R.	L214
Lindstrom, Eric	L251
Linfoot, Jane	L484
Lingard, Joan	L146
also	L216
Linic, Claire and Alan	L383
Linton, Marisa	L292
Lipinski, Emily	L281
Lippett, Ben	L563
Lippman, Thomas	L490
Lipscomb, Suzannah	L192
also	L477
Lipson, Molly	L004
Liptrot, Amy	L022
Lister, Kat	L065
also	L473
Lister, S E	L153
Lister, Simon	L082
Lister-Kaye, John	L119
also	L192
Listfield, Emily	L215
Listi, Brad	L166
Litman, Caroline	L251
also	L577
Littke, Lael	L550
Little, Hannah	L120
Little, Mary Ann	L301
Little, Tess	L192
also	L477
Littler, Richard	L065
also	L473
Littlewood, Clayton	L065
also	L473
Litvinoff, Emanuel	L146
Litvinova, Natalia	L526
Lively, Penelope	L146
Livingston, A. A.	L111
Livingston, Dan	L111
Llewellyn, David	L304
Lloyd, Chris	L153
Lloyd, John	L006
also	L426
Lloyd, Saci	L045
also	L146
Lo, Anita	L441
Lo, Catherine	L556
Lo, Malinda	L265
Lobato, Bruna Dantas	L071
Lobenstine, Margaret	L059
Lodge, Gytha	L135
also	L474
Lodge, Jo	L146
also	L589
Logan, T M	L067
also	L143
Logan, William Bryant	L166
Loh, Jonathan	L119
also	L192
Loiseau, Benoît	L004
Lombard, Jenny	L166
London, Clare	P115
London, Julia	L052
also	L053
Long, Kieran	L251
also	L577
Longmuir, Fiona	L535
Lopez, Loretta	L594
Lord, Annie	L479
Lord, Craig	L265
Lorincz, Holly	L380
Losada, Isabel	L006
also	L426
Lott, Tim	L146
also	L589
Louie, Nicole	L522
Louis, Lia	L430
Lovatt, Elizabeth	L152
also	L193
Love, Ryan	L331
Lovell, Julia	L146
also	L611
Lovelock, James	L179
Lovett, Jo	L287
Lovric, Michelle	L028
Lowe, Brigid	L307
Lowe, Katie	L430
Lowe, Rebecca	L192
also	L477
Lowe, Stephen	L214
Lowenthal, Mark	L059
Lowkis, Carmella	L434
Lowndes, Leil	L166
Lowther, Emma	L434
Loxton, Alice	L265
Loyn, David	L586
Loynd, Michael	L556
Lozada, Evelyn	L380
Lucas, Anneke	L281
Lucas, Fiona	L484
Lucas, Geralyn	L301
Lucas, Rachael	L484
Luckhurst, Phoebe	L379
Lucia Franco	L158
Lukate, Johanna	L330
Lumani, Violet	L141
Lumley, Joanna	L045
also	L146
Lumsden, Katie	L085
Lumsden, Richard	L146
also	L210
Lunde, Julie	L472
also	L556
Lunden, Jennifer	L556
Lunn, Natasha	L192
also	L477
Lupo, Kesia	L045
also	L146
Lury, Max	L146
Lusk, Sean	L152
also	L272
Luttichau, Chris	L588
Lutz, John	L064
also	L254
luxx, lisa	L152
also	L193
Lycett, Andrew	L006
also	L426

Lyman, Monty	L586
also	P391
Lyman, Robert	L586
Lynch, Karen	L406
Lynch, P J	L126
Lynes, S. E.	L045
also	L146
Lynskey, Dorian	L251
also	L577
Lyon, Joshua	L166
Lyons, Annie	L379
Lyons, David B.	L265
also	L561
Lyons, Zoe	L152
also	L272
Lyttelton, Celia	L126
Lytton, Charlotte	L064
also	L254
López, Lucas Sogas	L393
Ma, Lulee	L064
Macallum, Simon	L432
MacArthur, Robin	L166
MacBird, Bonnie	L094
Macciochi, Jenna	L185
Macculloch, Diarmaid	L119
also	L192
MacDonald, Cathy	L064
also	L254
MacDonald, Chris	L430
MacDonald, Dee	L484
MacDonald, Fraser	L022
Macdonald, Malcolm Ross	L146
Macdonald, Marianne	L146
MacDougall, Kate	L379
Mace, Guy	L553
Macfarlane, Robert	L146
also	L611
MacGillivray, Kirsten	L304
MacGowan, Siobhan	L016
also	L326
Macgregor, Virginia	L153
Machias, Jules	L136
Machin, Anna	L192
also	L284
Machray, Elle	L434
Macias, Maryann Jacob	L087
also	L435
MacInnes, Eric	L214
Mackay, Janis	L216
Mackenzie, Caroline	L026
Mackenzie, Polly	L006
also	L426
Mackenzie, Rebecca	L428
Mackie, Mary	L102
also	L590
Mackintosh, Anneliese	L065
also	L473
Mackintosh, Sophie	L146
Mackler, Lauren	L301
MacLachlan, Patricia	L469
Maclean, Charles	L094
MacLean, David Stuart	L166
MacLean, Natalie	L281
Maclean, Will	L120
MacLeod, Ken	L407
Macleod, Tatty	L135
also	L414
MacNeice, Louis	L146
Macneil, Kevin	L265
also	L561
MacRae, L. A.	L251
Macwhirter, L J	L216
Madden, Anne	L166
Madden, Gary	L006
also	L426
Maddocks, Fiona	L192
also	L477
Madeleine, Laura	L331
Madison, Juliet	L301
Madson, Devin	L311
Maestas, Carrie	L072
Magan, Manchan	L146
also	L611
Magazine, Rookie	L381
Mager, Kim	L493
Maggar, Carina	L187
also	L251
Maglaque, Erin	L146
Magrane, Paddy	L251
also	L603
Maguire, Aileen	L004
Maguire, Gráinne	L135
also	L414
Maguire, Laurie	L119
also	L192
Mahmood, Imran	L067
also	L143
Mahmoud, Doma	L361
Mahnke, Aaron	L493
Mahoney, Dennis	L166
Mahoney, Mary	L383
Mahood, Katy	L348
Maines, Nicole	L383
Maisonet, Illyanna	L427
Majka, Sara	L361
Major, Cesca	L143
Makepeace, Mark	L006
also	L426
Makis, Eve	L046
Malakin, Dan	L064
also	L254
Malchik, Antonia	L361
Malhotra, Aseem	L064
Malik, Kenan	L006
also	L426
Malik, Shiv	L348
Malik, Tania	L166
Malloy, Lauretta	L427
Malone, Ailbhe	L065
also	L473
Malone, Nana	L391
Malossi, Dan	L111
Manawer, Hussain	L064
Mance, Henry	L192
also	L477
Mancini, Ruth	L251
also	L428
Mandelbaum, Paul	L059
Manes, Eileen	L579
Mangan, Lucy	L065
also	L473
Manicka, Rani	L143
Mann, Michael	L135
also	L166
also	L225
Mannah, Foday	L146
also	L156
Manning, Ivy	L059
Manning, Joseph	L555
Manning, Olivia	L146
Mannix, Kathryn	L146
also	L207
also	L245
Manuel, Rob	L251
also	L577
Manuelpillai, Arji	L047
Manzoor, Sarfraz	L146
also	L207
also	L245
Mapp, Rue	L129
Maqhubela, Lindiwe	L102
also	L590
Mara, Andrea	L046
also	L152
also	P032
Mararike, Shingi	L094
Marber, Ian	L484
Marcelo Verdad	L158
March, Kerstin	L301
Marchant, Clare	L153
Marchetti, Donna	L143
also	L202
Marcus, Ben	L428
Marcus, Greil	L045
also	L146
Marcus, Halimah	L071
Maria Hinojosa	L158
Marin, Hugo Huerta	L141
Maris, Kathryn	L146
Mark, Jan	L146
also	L589
Mark, Sabrina Orah	L071
Markopolos, Harry	L207
Marks, Ann	L141
Marks, Jeff	L490
Marlow, Jane	L300
Marlow, Natalie	L152
also	L193
Marmery, Nikki	L153
Marney, Ellie	L146
also	L589
Marnham, Patrick	L045
also	L146
Marple, Mieke	L281
Marquand, David	L146
Marquardt, Tanya	L166
Marquart, Debra	L166
Marr, Elle	L052
also	L053
Marr, Sarah K	L192
also	L608
Marriott, Zoe	L316
Marrone, Amanda	L493
Marrouat, Cendrine	M035
Marrs, Sandra	L296
Marsden, Paul	L214
Marsden, Sam	L613
Marsh, Beezy	L379
Marsh, David J.	L301
Marsh, Katie	L094
also	L265
Marshall, Alex	L166
Marshall, Laura	L135
also	L474
Martelli, Joan	L215
Marten, Helen	L146
Martin, Barry	L052
also	L053
Martin, Chuck	L301
Martin, Emer	L147
Martin, Gina	P032
Martin, Jessica	L129
Martin, Kristen	L068
also	L101
Martin, Melissa	L059
Martin, S.I.	L586
Martinez, Claudia Guadalupe	L158
Martynoga, Ben	L192
also	L477
Martínez, Lucía Alba	L526
Marufu, Aneesa	L292
Marut, Lama	L301
Marvin, Cate	L166
Marwood, Alex	L513
Marx, Paul	L214

Marz, Megan	L004	McCarthy, Helen	L146	McKenzie, Elizabeth	L146
Masciola, Carol	L301	also	L207	McKinley, Barry	L094
Mascull, Rebecca	L379	also	L245	McKowen, Laura	L068
Mashigo, Mohale	L120	McCaughrean, Geraldine	L045	also	L101
Masing, Anna Sulan	L187	also	L146	Mclaughlin, Cressida	L265
also	L251	McCaulay, Diana	L513	Mclaughlin, Rosanna	L146
Maslo, Lina	L205	also	L590	McLaughlin, Tom	L146
Mason, Amanda	L535	McCauley, Claire	L252	also	L589
Mason, Mark	L586	McCausland, Elly	L082	McLeod, Ella	L135
Mason, Ruthy	L064	McCay, Layla	L152	also	L225
also	L254	McClorey, Kelly	L193	Mcloughlin, Kate	L119
Mason, Simon	L045	McClure, Jesse	L071	also	L192
also	L146	McCluskey, Laura	L545	McMahon, Tony	L214
Masters, Alexandra	L379	McConnell, Freddy	L135	McManus, Sarah	L331
Masters, Ben	L146	McCorkle, Jill	L474	McMullan, Thomas	L146
also	L611	McCormick, Neil	L379	McMullen, John	P080
Masters, Nicola	L016	McCracken, Elizabeth	L166	Mcnamara, Ali	L265
also	L326	also	L146	McNamara, Luna	L064
Masters, S R	L265	McCrea, Ronan	L166	also	L254
also	L561	McCrum, Robert	L265	McNaughton, Kate	L379
Matharu, Taran	L430	McCulloch, Amy	L126	McNeil, Jean	L045
Matheson, Hugh	L094	McCullough, Kelly	L430	also	L146
Maton, Tracy	L265	McDaniel, W. Caleb	L550	McNeil, Joanne	L071
Matson, Suzanne	L166	McDermid, Val	L555	McNeur, Catherine	L555
Matthews, Beryl	L065	McDermott, Andy	L146	McNuff, Anna	L203
also	L088	McDonald, Chris	L588	also	L617
Matthews, L V	L067	also	L152	McNulty, Phil	L545
also	L143	McDonald, Ed	L272	McOmber, Adam	L166
Matthews, Owen	L006	McDonald, Margaret	L120	Mcphee, Susy	L265
also	L426	McDonald-Gibson, Charlotte	L064	McPherson, Ben	L428
Matthews, Sadie	L146	McDonnell, Patrick	L348	Mcpherson, Kira	L537
Matthewson, Janina	L614	Mcdougall, James	L166	McPhillips, Fiona	L434
Matthiesen, Toby	L119	also	L119	McQueer, Chris	L461
also	L192	McDowell, Colin	L192	McSwiggan, Calum	L153
Matyjaszek, Kasia	L216	McDowell, Marta	L484	McTague, Tom	L006
Maugham, Jolyon	L251	also	L052	also	L426
also	L577	McFadden, Bernice	L053	Mda, Zakes	L065
Maur, Melissa Auf der	L429	also	L139	Mead, Peter	L006
Maure, Melanie	L016	McGarrity, Michael	L556	Meadows, Jodi	L383
also	L326	also	L207	Meals, Roy	L301
Maurer, Kevin	L207	McGee, James	L480	Medaglia, Mike	L499
Mavison, Dar	P115	also	L251	Medel, Elena	L526
Mavity, Roger	L082	McGilchrist, Iain	L577	Medhurst, Jennifer	L344
Maw, Laura	L004	McGill, C.E.	L146	Medinger, Gez	L064
Mawdsley, Evan	L146	McGilloway, Brian	L026	also	L254
Maxwell, Abi	L166	also	L152	Mednick, Sara C.	L441
May, Francesca	L046	McGinnis, Mindy	L272	Medrano, Emma	L152
also	L152	McGinty, Sean	L136	also	L238
May, Kiirsten	L281	McGivering, Jill	L166	Medved, Lisa	L484
May, Peter	L045	McGlasson, Claire	L309	Medved, Maureen	L281
also	L146	also	L251	Meehan, Andrew	L545
Maya Wei-Haas	L158	McGlynn, Clare	L603	Meekings, S. K.	L463
also	L564	McGoran, Jon	L265	also	L464
Mayeda, Andrew	L605	McGough, Roger	L166	Mehmood, Jamal	L004
Mayer, Shannon	L203	McGowan, Anthony	L567	Mehr, Bob	L166
also	L617	McGowan, Claire	L094	Mehri, Momtaza	L109
Mayhew, Emily	L461	also	L046	Melisse, Shane	L047
Mays, Hannah	L135	Mcgrath, Chris	L152	Melkonian, Sir Vartan	L214
also	L243	also	L119	Meller, Gill	L251
Mazarura, Rufaro Faith	L146	McGrath, Robyn	L192	also	L577
also	L210	McGrath, Mary	L205	Meller, Rachel	L152
Mazzola, Anna	L045	McGrath, Will	L166	Mellon, Mary	L281
also	L146	McGuffey, Charmaine	L215	Meltzer, Marisa	L391
McAllister, Gillian	L143	McGuire, Ian	L428	Mendelsohn, Joshua	L083
McAndrew, Tony	L214	McHugh, Laura	L428	Menon, Anand	L006
Mcauley, Paul	L407	McInerney, Kerry	L251	also	L426
McAuley, Roisin	L586	also	L417	Mensah, Elvin James	L430
McBride, Hazel	L135	McInnes, Mike	L588	Menzies, Jean	L152
also	L200	McIvor, Michelle	L605	also	L238
McBride, Matthew	L166	McKay, Rebecca Taylor	L251	Mercado, Richard	L560
McBride, Regina	L226	also	L603	Mercer, Alison	L309
McBride, Shane	L141	Mckechnie, Sam	L126	Merciel, Liane	L553
McCarron, Marina	L522	McKellar, Danica	L441	Mercurio, Peter	L556
McCarthy, Andrew	L429			also	L581

Meredith, Martin	L119
also	L192
Merrell, Susan Scarf	L166
Merrill, Emily	L147
Merritt, Chris	L152
also	L272
Mertens, Maggie	L361
Meslow, Scott	L493
Mesrati, Mohamed	L304
Messinger, Jonathan	L382
also	L435
Metcalfe, Anna	L109
also	L146
Metcalfe, Daniel	L006
also	L426
Meyer, Deon	L065
Meyers, Jeff	P167
Meyler, Deborah	L166
Mhaoileoin, Niamh Ní	L537
Michael, Darcy	L493
Middlemiss, LaRonda Gardner	L406
Middleton, Lia	L065
also	L088
Miers, Thomasina	L251
also	L577
Mihell, Natasha	L281
Mikhail, Alain	L555
Milan, Joe	L083
Milchman, Jenny	L166
Miles, David	L330
Miles, Rosalind	L586
Miliband, Ed	L146
also	L207
also	L245
Millar, Louise	L146
Miller, Barnabas	L166
Miller, Beth	L309
Miller, Catherine	L064
also	L254
Miller, Chris	L006
also	L426
Miller, Daphne	L166
Miller, Harland	L126
Miller, Kei	L146
Miller, Paul	L166
Miller, Richard J.	L166
Miller, Siobhan	L265
Miller, Tamara L.	L226
Millman, Janie	L152
also	L272
Mills, Liberty	L135
also	L200
Mills, Major Scotty	L064
Mills, SSG Travis	L493
Millward, Myfanwy	L146
also	L589
Milman, Oliver	L192
also	L284
Milne, Gemma	L251
also	L603
Milner, Kate	L146
also	L589
Milusich, Janice	L406
Min, Juli	L026
Mina, Denise	L166
Mincemeyer, Damascus	L111
Minchilli, Domenico	L059
Minchilli, Elizabeth Helman	L059
Minetor, Randi	L489
Minor, Wendell	L205
Minshall, Tim	L379
Minson, Shona	L491
Minton, Jenny	L391
Mir, Moin	L094
Mir, Saima	L152
also	L193
Miralles, Nina-Sophia	L065
also	L473
Miron, Rebekah	L135
also	L243
Mirza, Munira	L006
also	L426
Misick, Michael	L214
Misra, Jaishree	L309
Mitchell, Emma	L065
also	L473
Mitchell, Gladys	L146
Mitchell, Julian	L147
Mitchell, Kara	L493
Mitchell, Katie	L129
Mitchell, Malcolm	L493
Mitchell, Marie	L491
Mitchell, Sarah	L045
also	L146
Mitton, Tony	L146
also	L589
Miéville, China	L407
Moaveni, Azadeh	L391
Modafferi, Christine	L296
Moffatt, Hannah	L143
Mogel, Wendy	L059
Moggach, Lottie	L251
also	L577
Mohammadi, Kamin	L428
Mohamud, Ayaan	L143
Moldavsky, Goldy	L052
also	L053
Molho, Tony	L555
Molin, Meghan Scott	L382
also	L435
Molinaro, Joanne	L082
Molloy, Serena	L016
also	L326
Moncrieff, Ada	L379
Monday, T. T.	L166
Mone, Gregory	L166
Monette, Sarah	L550
Monroe, Jack	L344
Monroe, Jo	L430
Monroe, Katrina	L382
also	L435
Montalban, Vanessa	L087
also	L435
Montell, Amanda	L166
Monterey, Emmett de	L348
Montgomery, Heather L.	L205
Montrose, Sharon	L059
Moolla, Zeena	L152
also	L193
Mooney, Lauren	L045
also	L146
Mooney, Sinéad	L004
Moor, Becka	L567
Moor, Zewlan	L205
Moorcroft, Sue	L065
also	L473
Moore, Elizabeth S.	L152
also	L272
Moore, Jen	L535
Moore, Marianne	L461
Moore, Moira	L550
Moore, Richard	L036
Moore, Sally	L281
Moore, Sam	L141
Moore, Victoria	L146
Moore, Yashka	L207
Moorer, Allison	L441
Moorhead, Kr	L265
Moorhouse, Tom	L119
also	L192
Mooro, Alya	L461
Morain, Daniel	L075
Morales, Bonnie Frumkin	L059
Morales, Gerardo Ivan	L158
Morales, Zoraida Rivera	L205
Moran, Katy	L119
also	L192
Mordue, Mark	P167
Morelli, Laura	L052
also	L053
Moreno, Heidi	L158
Morgan, Abi	L068
also	L101
Morgan, Alistair	L192
also	L608
Morgan, Ann	L361
Morgan, Christine	L344
Morgan, Elian J.	L192
Morgan, Huey	L064
Morgan, Pete	L146
Morgan, Phoebe	L067
also	L143
Morgan-Witts, Max	L214
Moriarty, Bryan	L251
also	L603
Morita, Jennifer	L226
Morland, Paul	L006
also	L426
Morpurgo, Michael	L045
also	L146
Morr, Gemma	L251
also	L428
Morris, Amelia	L071
Morris, Elizabeth	L526
Morris, Emily	L251
also	L428
Morris, Jackie	L146
also	L611
Morris, Joel H.	L052
also	L053
Morris, Jonathan	L300
Morris, Mandy	L441
Morris, Priscilla	L348
Morris, Sir Derek	L214
Morrison, Jonathan	L172
Morrison, Kate	L428
Morrison, Rebecca	L136
Morrisroe, Rachel	L143
Morrow, Bradford	L166
Mort, Sophie	L185
Morten, Anais	P115
Mortimer, Grace	L065
also	L473
Morton, Brian	L166
Morton, Kate	L146
Mosimann, Anton	L094
Moskowitz, Eric	L555
Mosler, Layne	L166
Mosley, Beth	L379
Mosqueda, Andrea	L383
Moss, Adam	L429
Moss, Emma-Lee	L109
also	L146
Moss, Sarah	L166
Mossman, Kate	L586
Mottershead, Heather	L522
Motum, Markus	L064
Mountain, David	L563
Moussa, Tarek El	L141
Mowll, Joshua	L126
Moynes, Riley E.	L605
Mucha, Laura	L146
also	L461
also	L589
Muchamore, Robert	L170
Muchemi-Ndiritu, Irene	L526
Mufleh, Luma	L083

Muir, Evie	L152	
also	L193	
Mukendi, Tanya	L563	
Mukerji, Ritu	L166	
Muldoon, Eilidh	L216	
Mulgan, Geoff	L006	
also	L426	
Mulholland, Aefa	L118	
also	L479	
Mulholland, Hélène	L251	
also	L603	
Mulligan, Owain	L094	
Munda, Rosaria	L087	
also	L435	
Munder, Chrissy	P115	
Munhóz, Carolina	L410	
Murgatroyd, Erin	L102	
also	L590	
Murguia, Bethanie	L205	
Muroki, Mercy	L064	
Murphy, Bernadette	L427	
Murphy, Julie	L136	
Murphy, Kimberly Shannon	L166	
Murphy, Margaret	L135	
also	L474	
Murphy, Martina	L265	
Murphy, Mary	L170	
Murphy, Meagan B	L441	
Murphy, Megan	L143	
also	L202	
Murphy, Peter	L214	
Murray, Andrew	L316	
Murray, Annie	L143	
Murray, Struan	L135	
also	L225	
Murray, Victoria Christopher	L148	
Murrin, Alan	L192	
also	L608	
Musgrove, Myra	L166	
Musolino, Julien	L265	
Musson, Hester	L430	
Mutch, Barbara	L309	
Mutyora, Jade	L152	
also	L193	
Myers, Benjamin	L146	
also	L611	
Myers, Rebecca	L094	
Myint, Arnold	L141	
Mykura, Kim	L463	
also	L464	
Myrie, Clive	L006	
also	L426	
Nadel, Barbara	L513	
also	L590	
Nadel, Jennifer	L192	
also	L608	
Nadelson, Scott	P167	
Nagaki, Nicole	L522	
Naghdi, Yasmine	L560	
Nagle, Emily	L316	
Nair, Anita	L390	
Nakate, Vanessa	L192	
also	L477	
Nance, Sarafina	L139	
also	L556	
Nancollas, Tom	L192	
also	L477	
Narayan, Natasha	L119	
also	L192	
Nasimi, Shabnam	L064	
Nathan, Debbie	L166	
Nathan, Einat	L441	
Nathan, L.M.	L135	
also	L200	
Nathans, Benjamin	L555	
Naudus, Natalie	L052	
also	L053	
Naughtie, James	L119	
also	L192	
Nava, Eva Wong	L143	
Nava, Yolanda	L059	
Navai, Ramita	L348	
Nawaz, Maajid	L064	
Nawaz, Sabina	L441	
Nawotka, Ed	L166	
Nayeri, Farah	L472	
also	L556	
Naylor, Helen	L265	
Nazemian, Abdi	L136	
Neal, Jennifer	L491	
Neale, Kitty	L309	
Nehring, Cristina	L301	
Neima, Luke	L004	
Nelson, Alissa Jones	L613	
Nelson, Caleb Azumah	L004	
Nelson, Fraser	L146	
also	L207	
also	L245	
Nelson, Selene	L344	
Nemerever, Micah	L175	
Neri, Greg	L166	
Network, Real Sports Entertainment	L493	
Neuwith, Robert	L166	
Newberry, Sheila	L309	
Newbery, Linda	L119	
also	L192	
Newhouse, Alana	L166	
Newlands, Tom	L348	
Newman, Catherine	P114	
Newman, Cathy	L251	
also	L577	
Newman, Grace	L102	
also	L590	
Newman, Judith	L215	
Newman, Nathan	L082	
Newman, Peter	L430	
Newman, Richard	L588	
Newsome, Amy	L563	
Newson, Louise	L348	
Newstead, Briana J.	L102	
also	L590	
Newton, Hollie	L348	
Ng, Jasmine	L410	
Nguyen, Kevin	L071	
Niala, JC	L118	
also	L479	
Nice, Nicola	L301	
Nicholson, Christopher	L065	
Nicholson, Joy	L059	
Nicholson, Judge Chris	L214	
Nicholson, Lindsay	L064	
Nicholson, Norman	L146	
Nicolau, Maria	L526	
Nicolson, Juliet	L126	
Niedzviecki, Hal	L281	
Niekerk, Marlene van	L065	
Nies, Judith	L059	
Nimmo, Jenny	L146	
also	L589	
Ninan, TN	L119	
also	L192	
Nison, Rebecca	L281	
Nissenson, Carol	L579	
Nissley, Jennifer	L087	
also	L435	
Nixon, Pippa	L251	
also	L428	
Niño, Oliver	L441	
Noakes, Grace	L522	
Noakes, Laura	L143	
Noble, LeeAnet	L427	
Noelle, Marisa	L316	
Nolan, Hayley	L026	
Noni, Lynette	L087	
also	L435	
Noonan, Danny	L072	
Nooney, Laine	L361	
Norberg, Johan	L146	
also	L207	
also	L245	
Nord, Camilla	L192	
also	L477	
Norfolk, Lawrence	L065	
Norman, Charity	L045	
also	L146	
Norman, Stephen	L588	
Norminton, Gregory	L065	
Norms, Leena	L064	
also	L254	
Norrie, Kirsten	L304	
Norris, Barney	L603	
Norris, Mary	L429	
Norris, Susie	L059	
North, L. C.	L484	
Northedge, Charlotte	L348	
Norton, Chris and Emily	L493	
Norton, Madeleine	L135	
also	L474	
Norton, Preston	L052	
also	L053	
Norton, Sheila	L102	
also	L590	
Norwood, Robin	L331	
Nott, David	L146	
also	L207	
also	L245	
Noxon, Christopher	L059	
Noyce, Eleanor	L479	
Nunez, Sigrid	L045	
also	L146	
Nutt, Amy Ellis	L555	
Nuttall, Jenni	L361	
Nwanoku, Chi-chi	L408	
Nwoka, Okezie	L472	
also	L556	
Nyquist, Katy	L203	
also	L617	
Nzelu, Okechukwu	L537	
O'Callaghan, Jennifer	L301	
O'Connor, Joseph	L065	
O'Connor, Scott	L166	
O'Dair, Marcus	L348	
O'Dell, Emily J.	L301	
O'Donnell, Lisa	L026	
O'Donoghue, Lauren	L135	
also	L474	
O'Flanagan, Sheila	L065	
O'Grady, Colleen	L301	
O'Keeffe, Bernard	L379	
O'Leary, Beth	L252	
O'Neill, Louise	L430	
O'Regan, Marie	L331	
O'Reilly, Callie Rae	L107	
O'Reilly, Kaite	L065	
O'Reilly, Noel	L152	
also	L272	
O'Riordan, Valerie	L152	
O'Sullivan, Sadhbh	L187	
also	L251	
O'Sullivan, Tara	L135	
also	L414	
Oates, Nathan	L348	
Obergefell, Jim	L301	
Obidike, Jennifer	L185	
Oborne, Peter	L146	
also	L207	
also	L245	

Ochota, Mary-Ann L251
also L577
Ochs, Sara L065
also L088
Odell, Jenny L175
also L192
also L477
Offill, Jenny L428
Ogene, Timothy L004
Ogunbiyi, Ore L192
also L477
Ogundiran, Tobi L120
Oh, Temi L428
Ohajura, Michael L586
Ohanesian, Aline L166
Ohartghaile, Ciara L251
also L614
Oldfield, Elizabeth L348
Olding, Catriona L064
Olivarez, José L472
also L556
Oliver, Abi L143
Oliver, Aimee L296
Oliver, Diane L146
also L156
Oliver, Joshua L135
also L200
Olorunnipa, Toluse L075
Olsen, Erik L152
also L193
Olshaker, Mark L207
Olson, Liesl L555
Olson, Toby P167
Omand, David L006
also L426
Omond, Tam L513
Omotoso, Yewande L146
also L156
Oness, Elizabeth L166
Onoh, Nuzo L331
Onuzo, Chibundu L026
Ooi, Yen L152
also L193
Opie, Frederick Douglass L383
Oppenheimer, Mark L429
Orchard, Emma L046
also L152
Orchard, Erica Mary L216
Ord, Charlotte L535
Ordorica, Andrés N. L118
also L479
Orion, Ell L281
Ormerod, Jan L146
Orr, David L166
Orr, Elaine Neil L301
Orsted, Brad L281
Orton, Katharine L153
Orwin, Rebecca L153
Orzel, Chad L166
Osborn, Cate L493
Osborn, Christopher L251
also L577
Osei, Adjoa L119
also L192
Oshman, Michal L064
Oskis, Andrea L135
also L200
Osman, Richard L430
Ostlere, Emily L348
Ostrander, Madeline L556
also L581
Ostrovsky, Arkady L006
also L426
Oswald, James L430
Otheguy, Emma L158
Otis, Mary L071
Ovenden, Richard L119
also L192
Overton, Iain L251
also L577
Owen, Antonia L214
Owen, David L153
Owen, Joanne L119
also L192
Owen, Nick P062
Owen, Nikki L064
also L254
Owen, Orla L026
Owen, Polly L567
Owen, Tom L214
Owens, Laurie L146
Owens, Susan L146
also L207
also L245
Owens, Zahra P115
Owolade, Tomiwa L006
also L426
Oyebanji, Adam L203
also L617
Oza, Janika L071
Ozbek, Sara-Ella L187
O'Brien, Beth L366
O'Brien, Fiona L102
also L590
O'Brien, Kate L146
O'Brien, Vanessa L391
O'Connell, John L251
also L577
O'Connor, Sean L428
O'Dell, Tawni L148
O'Donnell, Cardy L300
O'Donnell, Leeanne L065
also L180
O'donnell, Svenja L192
also L608
O'Donoghue, Caroline L153
O'Donoghue, Deborah L146
also L210
O'gorman, Colm L192
also L608
O'Hara, Mary L214
O'Keeffe, Ciarán L214
O'Neill, Eric M. L564
O'Neill, Penelope L064
O'Neill, Poppy L613
O'Reilly, Jane L153
O'Reilly, Josephine L153
O'Reilly, Miriam L214
Pacat, C. S. L146
also L589
Packer, Ann L071
Packer, Nigel L265
Padamsee, Nicolas L187
also L251
Padua, Sydney L126
Padwa, Lynette L059
Pagan, Matthew A. L334
Page, Elliot P114
Page, Janice L215
Page, Jonathan L537
Page, Louise L135
also L225
Page, Robin L556
also L581
Page, Sally L252
Page, Sarah-Jane L153
Paine, Tom L166
Paley, Dan L205
Pallant, Stuart L064
Palmer, Alan L390
Palmer, Andrew L071
Palmer, Lindsey J. L301
Palmer, Soraya L556
also L581
Palà, Gemma Ruiz L526
Panagos, Angelique L484
Panay, Panos L493
Panciroli, Elsa L192
also L477
Panek, Richard L166
also L250
Paniz, Neela L059
Pantony, Ali L287
Paphides, Pete L251
also L577
Paphitis, Zoe L214
Papillon, Buki L430
Paradis, Michel L166
Parazynski, Scott L380
Parente, Stephanie L522
Parham, Taylor Riley L203
also L617
Paris, B.A. L067
also L143
Paris, Helen L428
Park, Haejin L190
also L345
Park, James L141
Parker, Andrew L586
Parker, Anna L251
also L417
Parker, Anna Chapman L004
Parker, D. G. P115
Parker, Della L309
Parker, Derek L146
Parker, Geoffrey L251
Parker, Julia L146
Parker, Nina L065
also L473
Parker, Sam L461
Parks, Alan L065
Parks, Shoshi L083
Parlato, Terri L553
Parmar, Sandeep L146
Parr, Helen L146
also L207
also L245
Parsons, Vic L491
Parten, Bennett L555
Partington, Richard L146
also L207
also L245
Pascali-Bonaro, Debra L166
Pascoe, Sara L348
Pass, Emma L153
Pass, Nina De L251
also L603
Pastan, Rachel L166
Patel, Jyoti L187
also L251
Patel, Neel L187
also L251
Paterson, Judy L216
Patis, Vikki L152
also L238
Patrick, Den L311
Patrick, Phaedra L143
Patrikarakos, David L064
Pattison, Justine L064
Pattison, Nell L430
Paula, Ju De L072
Pavliscak, Pamela L083
Payleitner, Jay L380
Payne, Robert L146
Payne, Rogba L064
Payne, Val L614
Payton, Theresa L301
Peacock, Justin L166

Peak, James	L094
Peall, Philippa	L152
also	L193
Pearce, AJ	L146
Pearce, Daisy	L064
also	L609
Pearce, Fred	L146
also	L611
Pearce, Michelle	L301
Pearce, Philippa	L146
Pearl, Mariane	L526
Pearlberg, Jamie	L166
Pearlstein, Howard	L579
Pears, Iain	L192
also	L608
Pearson, Adam	L046
also	L152
Pearson, Harry	L146
also	L207
also	L245
Pearson, Nancy	L605
Peate, Claire	L135
also	L200
Peaty, Adam	L064
Pechey, Ben	L102
also	L590
Pedder, Cato	L045
also	L146
Peel, Kit	L126
Peel, Megan	L126
Peeples, Scott	L301
Peet, Mal	L094
Peisner, David	L441
Pejic, Igor	L155
Pelham, Nicolas	L006
also	L426
Pell, Tanya	L207
also	L480
Pendleton, Madeline	L493
Penman, Sharon	L407
Penn, Thomas	L119
also	L192
Pennington, John	L072
Pennock, Matthew	L281
Penny, Eleanor	L146
Pepper, Penny	L152
also	L193
Percy, Ely	L120
Pereira, Lindsay	L107
Perera, Anna	L586
Perera, Kishani	L059
Peridot, Kate	L366
Perrin, Fiona	L046
Perrin, Nigel	L588
Perrine, Liz	L553
Perrottet, Tony	L166
Perry, Anne	L331
Perry, Matteson	L564
Perry, Rebecca	L004
Perry, Rob	L064
also	L254
Persichetti, James	L087
also	L435
Peters, Cash	L059
Peters, Shawn	L493
Peterson, Alice	L046
also	L152
Peterson, Amy	L556
Peterson, Gilles	L146
also	L207
also	L245
Peterson, Holly	L429
Pettegree, Andrew	L119
also	L192
Petty, Kate Reed	L146
Peyton, Katie	L281
Phibbs, John	L099
Philby, Charlotte	L045
also	L146
Phillips, Emily	L461
Phillips, Gin	P167
Phillips, Jess	L379
Phillips, Jonathan	L119
also	L192
Phillips, Leigh	L006
also	L426
Phillips, Marie	L251
also	L577
Phillips, Max	L166
Phillips, Riaz	L109
Phillips, Tom	L251
also	L577
Phillips, Trevor	L064
Philpott, William	L586
Phipps, Rachel	L046
also	L152
Phoon, Katy	L522
Piazza, Jo	L026
Pichon, Liz	L146
also	L589
Piddington, Catherine	L484
Pielichaty, Helena	L216
Pienaar, Erin	L153
Piepenburg, Erik	L141
Pierce, Karen	L605
Pierce, Molly	L553
Pierce, Wendell	L441
Piercey, Joshua	L072
Pierre, DBC	L126
Pierson, Melissa Holbrook	L166
Pilcher, Eleanor	L522
Pilgrim, Alake	L135
Pilling, David	L192
also	L284
Pimsleur, Julia	L301
Pinborough, Sarah	L045
also	L146
Pinchbeck, Dan	L120
Pinchin, Karen	L556
Pincus, Steven	L555
Pine, Courtney	L146
also	L156
Pinede, Nadine	L205
Pinfield, Matt	L441
Piper, Brittany	L427
Pirmohamed, Alycia	L479
Pishiris, Christina	L146
also	L210
Pistone, Joe	L207
Pitcher, Annabel	L119
also	L192
Pitt, Leah	L135
also	L474
Pizzolatto, Nic	L166
Plackett, Jon	L348
Platt, Jo	L067
also	L143
Plessis, Lauren du	L152
also	L193
Pliego, Ande	L522
Ploszajski, Anna	L379
Plunkett, Tammy	L111
Pocock, Joanna	L004
Poet, George The	L082
Poffenroth, Mary	L006
also	L426
Pointer, Anna	L484
Pokwatka, Aimee	L166
Polichetti, Daria	L166
Pollen, Samuel	L560
Pollock, Allyson	L390
Polo, Claudia	L526
Polonsky, Rachel	L119
also	L192
Polt, Richard	L166
Pompeo, Joe	L391
Ponseca, Nicole	L441
Popkey, Miranda	L428
Poplett, Georgia	L251
also	L417
Portero, Alana S.	L526
Posner, Gerald	L429
Possanza, Amelia	L361
Poster, Jem	L330
Postman, Andrew	L215
Potter, Nick	L192
also	L608
Potter, Rupert	L072
Pouncey, Maggie	L166
Powell, Anthony	L146
Powell, Des	L146
also	L207
also	L245
Powell, Huw	L126
Powell, Margaret	L146
Powell, Melissa	L296
Powell, Rosalind	L065
also	L473
Powers, Jessica	L166
Powers, Lindsay	L083
Powers, Michael	P115
Powling, Chris	L146
also	L589
Poynor, Elizabeth	L441
Pratchett, Terry	P114
Pratt, Laura	L605
Pratt, Wendy	L118
also	L479
Prempeh, Charlene	L348
Prentice, Andrew	L119
also	L192
Prepon, Laura	L207
Pressman, Gene	L391
Presto, Greg	L493
Preston, Caroline	L166
Preston, Elizabeth	L361
Price, Alfred	L390
Price, David Mark	L586
Price, Katie	L261
Price, Laura	L348
Price, Lauren	L265
also	L561
Pride, Christine	L026
Prideaux, Sue	L119
also	L192
Priest, Cherie	L166
Pringle, Paul	L391
Prins, Mark	L166
Prior, Hazel	L143
Pritchard, Joanna	L135
also	L474
Prizant, Barry	L059
Prochaska, Elizabeth	L348
Procter, Alice	L614
Prum, Eric	L441
Prusa, Carolyn	L129
Ptacin, Mira	L139
also	L556
Pufahl, Shannon	L146
Pugh, Tom	L586
Puhak, Shelley	L556
Pullen, Nicholas	L410
Pulley, D. M.	L166
Pullin, Jim	L300
Punwani, Seema	L107
Purbrick, Martin	L464
also	L617

Purcell, Laura	L430	
Purdie, Kathryn	L146	
also	L589	
Purdy, Rebekah	L036	
Purington, Carol	L166	
Purington, Susan Todd & Carol	L166	
Purkayastha, Ian	L381	
Purkiss, Diane	L119	
also	L192	
Purkiss, Sue	L216	
Purser, Ann	L146	
Purvis, Xenobe	L187	
also	L251	
Pyo, Rejina	L614	
Quach, Michelle	L052	
also	L053	
Quaid, Amanda	L135	
also	L243	
Quaintrell, Philip C	L265	
also	L561	
Quantick, David	L304	
Quantock, Grace	L152	
also	L193	
Quatro, Jamie	L348	
Quigley, Joan	L166	
Quinn, Anthony J.	L152	
also	L272	
Quinn, Bonnie	L076	
Quinn, Josephine	L119	
also	L192	
Quinn, Karina Lickorish	L004	
Quintana, Jenny	L152	
also	L272	
Qureshi, Jasmine	L152	
also	L193	
Qureshi, Sadiah	L146	
also	L207	
also	L245	
R, Rebecca	L560	
Radcliffe, Jenny	L006	
Radecki, Barbara	L281	
Rader, Mark	L166	
Rader, Peter	L429	
Radeva, Sabina	L045	
also	L146	
Radford, Sian	L203	
also	L617	
Radio, National Public	L441	
Radloff, Jessica	L493	
Radojevic, Monika	L152	
also	L193	
Radzinsky, Edvard	L094	
Raeside, Julia	L028	
Raheem, Zara	L526	
Rahim, Shoaib	L334	
Rajan, Amol	L146	
also	L207	
also	L245	
Ralat, José R.	L472	
also	L556	
Ramadorai, Tarun	L307	
Ramani, Madhvi	L146	
also	L589	
Ramaswamy, Chitra	L348	
Ramirez, Reyes	L472	
also	L556	
Ramirez, Steve	L265	
also	L361	
Ramoutar, Shivi	L251	
also	L577	
Ramsay, Adam	L118	
also	L479	
Ramsay, Francesca	L187	
also	L251	
Ramsden, James	L614	
Ramsden, Rosie	L614	
Randall, Emily	L292
Rankin, Joan	L146
Ransom, Jon	L152
also	L193
Ransom, Sue	L094
Raphael, Amy	L094
Rapley, John	L207
Rappaport, Captain Elliot	L192
also	L284
Rath, Emily	L203
also	L617
Rattle, Kayleigh	L613
Ravella, Shilpa	L192
also	L284
Rawlence, Ben	L348
Rawsthorn, Alice	L006
also	L426
Rawsthorne, Paula	L126
Ray, Cate	L072
Ray, Jonathan	L428
Ray, Reagan Lee	L238
Ray, Reagan Lee	L152
also	L238
Raygorodetsky, Gleb	L301
Rayner, Abigail	L043
Rayner, Catherine	L146
also	L589
Rayner, Jacqui	L146
also	L589
Razak, Melody	L192
also	L608
Razzouk, Assaad	L006
also	L426
Rea, Julie	L065
also	L473
Read, Herbert	L146
Read, Lorna	L588
Reading, Anna	L513
also	L590
Readman, Angela	L461
Realf, Maria	L428
Rebain, Erik	L383
Redd, Dani	L153
Reddy, Jini	L152
also	L193
Redgold, Eliza	L301
Redmond, Markus	L111
Reed, Richard	L251
also	L577
Reeder, Elizabeth	L379
Reeder, Lydia	L556
Reekles, Beth	L143
Rees, Owen	L119
also	L192
Reese, Ashanté	L361
Reeve, Alex	L192
also	L477
Reeves, Ben	L251
also	L603
Reeves, Gemma	L004
Reeves, James	L146
Reeves, Jordan	L136
Reeves, Megan	L064
Reeves, Richard	L006
also	L426
Regan, Katy	L146
Rege, Devika	L526
Regel, Hannah	L146
Reginato, James	L429
Reich, Susanna	L166
Reichard, Raquel	L472
also	L556
Reichert, Michael	L301
Reid, Aimee	L205
Reid, Andrew	L430
Reid, Carmen	L046
Reid, Ebony	L348
Reifler, Nelly	L166
Reihana, Victoria	L556
Reilly, Martina	L265
Reilly, Winifred	L059
Reimer, Heidi	L166
Reiss, Benjamin	L555
Reiter, Chris	L207
Relth, Michael	L493
Remington, Laurel	L149
Renan, Daphna	L555
Rendell, Matt	L513
Renke, Samantha	L046
Renner, James	L166
also	L301
Rensburg, Laure Van	L430
Rensten, John	L499
Renwick, Chris	L146
also	L245
Resnik, Judith	L555
Rettig, Liz	L214
Revell, Tim	L006
also	L426
Reyes, Ana	L187
also	L251
Reyes, Paul	L166
Reyes, Ruben	L472
also	L556
Reynolds, Brittlestar aka Stewart	L027
Reynolds, David	L192
also	L284
Reynolds, Sheri	L207
also	L480
Rhian Parry	L102
also	L590
Rhodeen, Pen	L564
Rhodes, David	L143
Rhodes-Courter, Ashley	L301
Rhush, Becky	L152
also	L238
Rhyno, Greg	L281
Rhys, Gruff	L304
Riaz, Farrah	L203
also	L617
Ricciardi, David	L493
Rice, Lynette	L141
Rice, Sam	L251
also	L577
Richard, Alison F.	L555
Richard, Will	L102
also	L590
Richards, Andrea	L059
Richards, Dan	L192
also	L477
Richards, David	L586
Richards, Steve	L146
also	L207
also	L245
Richardson, Lisa	L143
Richardson, Susan	L028
Riches, Anthony	L016
also	L326
also	L588
Richey, Warren	L490
Richmond, Gillian	L484
Richter, Jennifer Ann	L205
Rickards, Lynne	L216
Ricketts, Peter	L006
also	L426
Rickman, Eloise	L192
also	L477
Rid, Thomas	L119
also	L192
Ridgard, Sarah	L045
also	L146
Ridley, Lee	L046

Rien, Paige	L301
Riesman, Robert	L166
Rifaat, Laila	L292
Rijswijk, Honni Van	L166
Riley, Alex	L192
also	L477
Riley, Catherine	L348
Riley, CE	L348
Riley, Charlotte Lydia	L192
also	L477
Riley, Christina	L118
also	L479
Riley, Gillian	L390
Rimer, Alexandra	L301
Rimington, Celesta	L087
also	L435
Rinaldi, Nicholas	L166
Rio, M. L.	L045
also	L146
also	L166
Rippee, Christopher	L111
Risen, Alexandra	L281
Ritz, The	L082
Rivers, Carol	L309
Rix, Jamie	L216
Rix, Megan	L170
Rixon, Charlotte	L265
also	L361
Rizzuto, Rachel	L579
Robb, Jackie	L300
Robbie, Lou	L287
Roberton, Fiona	L146
also	L589
Roberts, Adam	L331
Roberts, Bethan	L045
also	L146
Roberts, Caroline	L265
Roberts, Gareth	L265
Roberts, Genevieve	L379
Roberts, Jillian	L301
Roberts, Nadim	L556
also	L581
Roberts, Patrick	L265
also	L561
Roberts, Richard Owain	L513
also	L590
also	P275
Roberts, Sophy	L348
Roberts, Tom	L207
Robertson, Al	L026
Robertson, Annie	L065
also	L473
Robertson, Emma	L046
also	L152
Robertson, Ian	L192
also	L284
Robertson, Ritchie	L119
also	L192
Robertson, Tatsha	L301
Robinson, Alan	L102
also	L590
Robinson, Ava	L068
also	L101
Robinson, Callum	L348
Robinson, Ellie	L143
Robinson, Jane	L045
also	L146
Robinson, Keith	L567
Robinson, Lucy	L146
Robinson, Nicole	L152
also	L238
Robinson, Roger	L047
Robinson, Tony	L251
also	L577
Robinson-Textor, Marisa	L166
Robson, David	L192
also	L477
Robson, Laura Brooke	L087
also	L435
Rocero, Geena	L141
Roche, Juno	L152
also	L193
Rockman, Seth	L555
Rockwell, Marsheila (Marcy)	L027
Roden, Claudia	L146
Rodriguez, Marianeli	L553
Rodriguez, Prisca Dorcas Mojica	L472
also	L556
Roe, Duncan	L064
Roelen, Keetie	L135
also	L200
Roffey, Monique	L065
Roffman, Karin	L429
Rogan, Eugene	L119
also	L192
Rogers, Annie	L166
Rogers, Paula	L187
also	L251
Rogers, Rebecca	L535
Rogerson, Phoenicia	L331
Rogoff, Seth	L215
Rogoyska, Jane	L146
also	L207
also	L245
Rojstaczer, Stuart	L166
Rollock, Nicola	L192
also	L477
Rolls-Bentley, Gemma	L379
Romano, Angela	P115
Romano, Tricia	L166
Romeo, Lisa	L301
Romero-Montalvo, Leon	L152
Romm, James	L429
Ronald, Terry	L064
Ronson, Mark	L429
Ronson, Stephen	L064
also	L254
Ronstadt, Linda	L166
Rooney, Graeme	L300
Rooney, Rachel	L146
also	L589
Root, Neil	L006
Roper, Jane	L166
Rosa, Brunello	L146
also	L207
also	L245
Rose, Alex	L166
Rose, Clare	L491
Rose, Jacqui	L143
Rose-Innes, Henrietta	L065
Rosen, Michael J	L205
Rosenberg, Allegra	L129
Rosenthall, Olivia	L004
Rosie, Diana	L046
Rosoff, Meg	L119
also	L192
Ross, Kenneth G.	L214
Ross, Leone	L109
also	L146
Ross, Marissa A.	L166
Rossi, Alan	L004
Rotert, Rebecca	L166
Roth, Eileen	L059
Rothstein, Marilyn Simon	L301
Rourke-Mooney, Beck	L383
Rouss, Shannan	L166
Roux, Abigail	P115
Rowan, Anthea	L293
Rowan, Iain	L152
Rowan, Isabella	P115
Rowell, Maud	L118
also	L479
Rowland, Katherine	L166
Rowling, J.K.	L064
Rowson, Jonathan	L006
also	L426
Roy, Jacqueline	L491
Roy, Lena	L166
Roz, Emily	L563
Rubel, David	L166
Rubenhold, Hallie	P114
Rubin, Miri	L119
also	L192
Rublack, Ulinka	L119
also	L192
Ruck, Adam	L192
also	L608
Rucklidge, Julia J.	L441
Rude, Curt	L036
Ruderman, Anne	L555
Rudge, Penny	L192
also	L608
Rudra, Suchi	L594
Ruffles, Lydia	L126
Rufus, Anneli	L441
Rumble, Taylor-Dior	L004
Rumfitt, Alison	L120
Rush, Lyndsay	L382
also	L435
Russakoff, Dale	L301
Russell, Bill	L207
Russell, Gary	L300
Russell, Jamie	L153
Russell, Karen	L428
Russell, Rupert	L146
also	L245
Russell, Thaddeus	L429
Russell-Brown, Katheryn	L158
Russell-Pavier, Nick	L265
also	L561
Russell-Walling, Edward	L192
also	L608
Rustin, Susanna	L265
Rutgers, Leonard	L172
Rutherford, Geo	L493
Rutherford, Robert	L152
also	L272
Rutt, Stephen	L022
Rutter, Thomas	L004
Ruzickova, Zuzana	L251
also	L603
Rwizi, C. T.	L311
Ryan, Elliot	L065
also	L473
Ryan, Frances	L046
also	L152
Ryan, Joan	L166
Ryan, Mike	P080
Ryan, Morgan	L052
also	L053
Ryan, Frances	L046
Ryle, Matthew	L563
Ryrie, Alec	L119
also	L192
Ryrie, Charlie	L614
Sachdeva, Anjali	L361
Sachsse, Emma	L111
Sacks, Alexandra	L429
Sackur, Stephen	L251
also	L577
Sadowski, Michael	L301
Sadr, Ehsaneh	L087
also	L435
Safi, Aminah Mae	L383
Sagar, Andy	L567

Sahota, Kohinoor	L102	Scanlan, Kathryn	L146	Sebastian, Tim	L614
also	L590	Scanlon, Suzanne	L265	Sebold, Alice	L146
Saint, Jennifer	L430	also	L361	Secker, Allison	L046
Saintclare, Celine	L064	Scarlett, Fiona	L085	also	L152
also	L254	also	L348	Seddon, Delphine	L064
Salam, Anbara	L064	Schaitkin, Alexis	L166	Seddon, Holly	L348
also	L254	Schapira, Kate	L391	Sedgwick, Mark	L006
Salge, Erinn	L382	Schechter, Florence	L379	also	L426
also	L435	Scheer, Kodi	L166	Sediment, Paul Keers:	L251
Salinari, Karla	L301	Scheff, Sue	L301	Seeber, Claire	L330
Salter, Cassidy Ellis	L203	Schelter, Kate	L381	Seesequasis, Coltrane	L027
also	L617	Schemel, Patty	L166	Segall, Laurie	L564
Salu, Michael	L004	Schesventer, Faith Williams	L143	Seiffert, Rachel	L045
Samadder, Rhik	L348	also	L353	also	L146
Samanani, Farhan	L192	Scheynius, Lina	L004	Selinger, Hannah	L493
also	L477	Schiavone, Tony	P080	Selman, Victoria	L152
Samaraweera, Darryl	L016	Schickel, Erika	L441	also	L272
also	L326	Schickler, David	L166	Semple, David	L300
Samawi, Mohammed Al	L564	Schiffer, Zoë	L556	Senior, Antonia	L146
Samet, Elizabeth	L429	also	L581	also	L207
Sampson, Steve	P115	Schiller, Rebecca	L535	also	L245
Sams, Saba	L109	Schiot, Molly	L166	Sentelik, Ian	P115
also	L146	Schmidt, Heidi Jon	L166	Serafinowicz, James	L300
Samson, Polly	L126	Schmitt, Sally	L166	Sergeant, David	L016
Samuel, Julia	L064	Schmitz, Anthony	L059	also	L326
Samuels, Robert	L075	Schmitz, Elisa A.	L301	Setchfield, Nick	L311
Sancton, Julian	L083	Schneider, Indyana	L251	Setoodeh, Ramin	L381
Sandenbergh, Roberta	L301	also	L428	Sevilla, Cate	L586
Sanders, Ella Frances	L187	Schneider, M.D. Edward	L059	Seville, Jane	P115
Sanders, Rob	L205	Schneiderhan, Caitlin	L136	Sewell, Zakia	L192
Sanderson, Jane	L146	also	L207	also	L477
also	L207	Schock, Gina	L207	Sexton, Tara	L102
also	L245	Scholfield, Yah Yah	L203	also	L590
Sandor, Steven	L027	also	L617	Seymour, Ingrid	L052
Sandoval, Richard	L166	Schonfeld, David	L472	also	L053
Sands, Lynsay	L052	also	L556	Seymour, Jeff	L087
also	L053	Schories, Pat	L166	also	L435
Sansom, C. J.	L251	Schorr, Melissa	L301	Seymour, John	L146
also	L577	Schroeder, Kate	L493	Seymour, Miranda	L146
Sansom, Clive	L146	Schulman, Michael	L429	Seymour, Richard	L390
Sansom, William	L251	Schulte, Anitra Rowe	L406	Shabi, Rachel	L146
Santos, Lucy Jane	L379	Schultz, Claire	L006	also	L207
Santos, Madrid	L158	also	L211	also	L245
Santos, Marisa de los	L166	Schultz, Ellen E.	L301	Shackelford, Elizabeth	L429
Santos, Vanessa	L004	Schultz, William Todd	L166	Shadbolt, Nigel	L006
Santos, Yaffa S.	L526	Schuneman, Kyle	L059	also	L426
Sanz, Marta	L526	Schwartz, A. Brad	L556	Shah, Mira V.	L067
Sapiro, Mike	L427	also	L581	also	L143
Sappington, Adam	L059	Schwartz, Adara	L135	Shah, Oliver	L006
Sargeant, Rachel	L252	also	L243	also	L426
Saro-Wiwa, Noo	L146	Schwartz, Lynne Sharon	P167	Shaha, Alom	L119
also	L156	Schwartzel, Erich	L429	also	L192
Sarsfield, Margie	L129	Schwarz, Viviane	L614	Shakur, Maurice "Mopreme"	L141
Sasson, Jean	L148	Scott, Alev	L251	Shalmiyev, Sophia	L068
Sassoon, Donald	L006	also	L577	also	L101
also	L426	Scott, Anika	L513	Shames, Terry	L490
Sassoon, Joseph	L119	Scott, Eddie	L251	Shanker, Samara	L406
also	L192	also	L417	Shannon, George	L059
Satterly, Tom	L380	Scott, Helen	L152	Shanté, Angela	L406
Saunders, Dan	L064	also	L193	Shapiro, Elizabeth	L153
Saunders, Karen	L216	Scott, Izabella	L146	Share, Amber	L083
Sautoy, Marcus du	L251	Scott, Marina	L139	also	L381
also	L577	also	L556	Sharkey, Lauren	L064
Savage, Jon	L192	Scott, Nikola	L265	also	L254
also	L284	Scott, Paul	L146	Sharma, Babita	L064
Savage, Marjorie Barton	L059	Scott, Su	L563	Sharma, Nina	L129
Savage, Vanessa	L430	Scott-Brown, Sophie	L004	Sharma, Priya	L120
Savanh, Victoria	L068	Scull, Luke	L120	Sharot, Tali	L348
also	L101	Seabright, Paul	L119	Sharp, Cathy	L309
Savaş, Ayşegül	L071	also	L192	Sharratt, Nick	L045
Savill, David	L348	Seal, Clare	L535	also	L146
Savin, Jennifer	L046	Seal, Rebecca	L251	Sharrer, Jos	L588
also	L152	also	L577	Shavick, Andrea	L588
Sayers, Dorothy L.	L146	Seale, Yasmine	L126	Shavit, Shabtai	L564
Scales, Helen	L028	Sebastian, Laura	L136	Shaw, Ali	L026

Shaw, Christine	L390
Shaw, Dale	L614
Shaw, L C	L052
also	L053
Shaw, Liam	L119
also	L192
Shaw, Martin	L146
also	L611
Shaw, Rebecca	L067
also	L143
Shea, Kieran	L166
Shearing, Neil	L307
Sheibani, Jion	L567
Shelby, Jeff	L166
Sheldrake, Merlin	L146
also	L611
Shenk, Joshua Wolf	L166
Shephard, Sarah	L028
Shepherd, Megan	L146
also	L589
Shepherd-Robinson, Laura	L251
also	L577
Sheppard, Kathleen	L361
Sher, Antony	L407
Sherbill, Sara	L301
Sheridan, Nick	L143
Sherlock, Alison	L309
Sherratt, Mel	L152
also	L272
Shertok, Heidi	L522
Sherwood, Kim	L026
Shetterly, Margot Lee	L556
Shev, Wyatt	L036
Shi, Qian	L567
Shields, Lauren	L361
Shih, David	L556
also	L581
Shimotakahara, Leslie	L281
Shingler, Tina	L293
Shoneyin, Lola	L146
also	L611
Shore, Gareth	L331
Short, Philip	L045
also	L146
Shortall, Eithne	L016
also	L326
Shorter, Louise	L064
Shoulder, Jack	L129
Shrubsole, Guy	L022
Shuker, Carl	L461
Shuldiner, Joseph	L441
Shumaker, Heather	L301
Shute, Jenefer	L166
Shuttle, Penelope	L146
Siadatan, Tim	L563
Sidibe, Gabourey	L564
Sidley, Kate	L381
Signer, Rachel	L441
Sikes, Kaitlin M	L205
Silas, Shelley	L379
Silber, Alexandra	L301
Silva, Hannah	L513
also	L590
Silva, Ingrid	L166
Silvani, Celia	L522
Silver, Elizabeth L	L071
Silver, Josh	L366
Silver, Marisa	L166
Silvey, Catriona	L153
Simants, Kate	L045
also	L146
Simmonds, Natali	L484
Simmons, Cécile	L028
Simmons, Gail	L348
Simmons, Kristen	L382
also	L435
Simone, Sierra	L136
Simons, Tom	L484
Simpson, Catherine	L265
also	L561
Simpson, John	L344
also	P115
Simpson, Travis	L553
Sims, Cat	L613
Sinclair, Jenna Hilary	P115
Sinclair, Pete	L300
Singleton, Calah	L203
also	L617
Sinotok, Karen	L146
also	L210
Sirdeshpande, Rashmi	L143
Sissay, Lemn	L126
Sitoy, Lakimbini	L499
Sittenfeld, Curtis	P114
Sivasundaram, Sujit	L146
also	L207
also	L245
Skinner, Dan	P115
Skinner, Richard	L126
Skoda, Amélie	L152
also	L193
Skuy, David	L281
Skye, Ione	L166
Skye, Sasha	P115
Slade, Emma	L265
Slahi, Mohamedou	L166
Slapper, Emily	L434
Slater, Alexander	L064
Slater, Kim	L067
also	L143
Slater, KL	L067
also	L143
Slater, Sean	L067
also	L143
Slater, Sofia	L126
Slim, Pamela	L301
Sliwa, Joanna	L301
Small, Mark	L129
Smalls, Chris	L391
Smith, Alexander McCall	L146
also	L589
Smith, Bruce	L406
Smith, Dan	L153
Smith, Danny	L265
also	L561
Smith, David	L158
Smith, Emma	L119
also	L192
Smith, Freddie	L215
Smith, Jon	L064
Smith, Julia Ridley	L129
Smith, Karen Ingala	L265
Smith, Kate Galloway	L252
Smith, Leslie C.	L155
Smith, Lisa	L109
also	L146
Smith, Luanne G.	L553
Smith, Luke	L207
Smith, Mark B.	L146
also	L207
also	L245
Smith, Mark David	L111
Smith, Max Sydney	L461
Smith, Nicholas Boys	L344
Smith, Nikki	L348
Smith, Patti	L166
Smith, Paul	L300
Smith, Robin Callender	L214
Smith, Rt. Hon Iain Duncan	L214
Smith, Sherry	L166
Smith, Talmon Joseph	L071
Smith, Tiffany Watt	L192
also	L477
Smith, Victoria	L265
Smoke, Ben	L491
Smokler, Kevin	L166
Smolyansky, Julie	L441
Smythe, James	L251
also	L603
Snider, Laura	L406
Snow, Anna	L036
Snow, Philippa	L461
Snyder, Christopher A.	L301
So, Cynthia	L560
Sobiech, Laura	L301
Sokol, Josh	L361
Sole, Linda	L309
Soli, Tatjana	L166
Solomon, Jemma	L613
Solomons, Natasha	L026
Somers, Carry	L535
Somers, Jeff	L490
Somerville, Christopher	P114
Something, Airy	L613
Sommer, Tim	L493
Sommerville, Anniki	L085
Sopel, Jon	L064
Sorrel, O.R.	L296
Sosna-Spear, Quinn	L136
Soundar, Chitra	L560
South, Alex	L348
South, Mary	L146
Southby-Tailyour, Ewen	L588
Southgate, Laura	L004
Southon, Emma	L586
Southwell, Gareth	L265
Sowa, Pat	L143
Sowden, Stephanie	L135
also	L474
Sowemimo, Annabel	L491
Spall, Shane	L513
Spanbauer, Tom	P167
Spangler, Brie	L556
Spark, Muriel	L146
Sparks, Lily	L166
Spector, Shira	L166
Spector, Tim	L348
Spencer, Ashley	L141
Spencer, Dan	L537
Spencer, Elisabeth	L265
Spencer, Mimi	L251
also	L577
Spencer, Sonja	P115
Spencer, Tom	L064
Sperling, Jason	L141
Spielman, Lori Nelson	L052
also	L053
Spiers, Johanna	L484
Spiller, Nancy	L059
Spiller, Tatton	L028
Spoelman, Colin	L429
Spohr, Kristina	L207
Spooner, Meagan	L146
also	L589
Spraggs, Gillian	L331
Spring, Howard	L146
Spring, Marianna	L006
Spring, Olivia	L004
Springer, Lisa	L087
also	L435
Springer, Nancy	L251
also	L603
Springsteen, Jennifer	L382
also	L435
Spurling, Hilary	L146
also	L207

Stacey, Alex	L563
Stadlen, Lexi	L119
also	L192
Staff, P. A.	L064
Stafford, Rebecca	L207
also	L480
Stamm, Julie M.	L301
Stanley, Jessica	L146
Stanley, Kelli	L166
Starcher, Allison Mia	L059
Starling, Boris	L430
Starling, Hollie	L265
also	L561
Staub, Leslie	L205
Stauffer, Rainesford	L068
also	L101
Stavinoha, Peter L.	L301
Steadman, Catherine	L067
also	L143
Stears, Marc	L119
also	L192
Stedman, M L	L026
Steele, Emma	L252
Steele, Francesca	L379
Steele, Fraser	L300
Steele, Jaxx	P115
Steer, Dugald	L216
Steer, Emily	L379
Stefanovich-Thomson, Alexis	L334
Stegert, Ali	L292
Stein, Gertrude	L146
Stein, Judith E.	L564
Stein, Leigh	L166
Steinacker-Clark, Alexandra	L211
Steiner, Ben	L179
Steiner, Guenther	P032
Steinman, Louise	L059
Steinmetz, Greg	L429
Stephens, Isaiah	L493
Stephens, Savannah	L331
Steptoe, Javaka	L166
Sterling, Michelle	L348
Sterling, Michelle Min	L348
Sterling, Siena	L586
Stern, Bill	L059
Stern, Lindsay	L166
Sterner-Radley, Emma	L331
Stevens, Andrew	L085
Stevens, Georgina	L567
Stevens, Mark	L126
Stevenson, Mark	L586
Stewart, Andrea	L430
Stewart, Dave	L344
Stewart, Heather Grace	L406
Stewart, J I M	L379
Stewart, Jude	L166
Stewart, Maryon	L301
Stewart, Polly	L251
also	L428
Stewart, Sam	L292
Stewart, Sarah	L479
Stieger, Allison	L281
Stimson, Lora	L065
also	L473
Stinchcombe, Paul	L214
Stirling, Joss	L146
also	L589
Stirling, Richard	L152
Stockwin, Julian	L065
Stohn, Stephen	L281
Stoker, Sean	L004
Stokes, Stacy	L382
also	L435
Stokes-Chapman, Susan	L430
Stolworthy, Jacob	L135
also	L243
Stone, Jennifer	L064
also	L254
Stoppard, Miriam	L192
also	L477
Storey, Erik	L143
Storey, Rosie	L146
also	L210
Storm, Jaelyn	P115
Storti, Kara	L469
Stott, Dean	L064
Stott, Peter	L146
also	L245
Stovell, Sarah	L064
also	L254
Stowe, Hannah	L146
also	L611
Strachan, Hew	L146
also	L207
Straight, Susan	L166
Strathie, Chae	L216
Strauss, Elissa	L068
also	L101
Strawson, John	L146
Streeting, Wes	L379
Strelow, Michael	P167
Strong, Count Arthur	L251
also	L577
Strong, Jarom	L331
Strong, Jeremy	L146
Strong, Lynn Steger	L071
Strong, Roy	L119
also	L192
Stroud, Clover	P114
Stroud, Jonathan	L045
also	L146
Stuart, Andrea	L094
Stuart, Jesse	L331
Stuart, Kimberly	L380
Stuart, Nancy Rubin	L301
Stuart-Smith, Sue	L192
also	L608
Stubblefield, Robert	L490
Studer, Kate Pawson	L553
Stults, Shannon	L406
Sturge, Georgina	L185
Sturgeon, Nicola	L146
also	L207
also	L245
Sturtevant, Dana	L301
Subko, C.J.	L076
Sudbury, Rowena	P115
Suggars, Philip	L172
Sukumar, Hema	L046
also	L152
Suleyman, Mustafa	L348
Sullivan, Deirdre	L143
Sullivan, Joy	L382
also	L435
Sullivan-Craver, Sharon	L036
Summers, Julie	L119
also	L192
Summers, Katy	L152
also	L238
Sumrow, Melanie	L493
Sung, Crystal	L522
Surrey, Ellen	L205
also	L469
Sussman, Fiona	L265
Sutcliff, Rosemary	L146
Sutherland, Fae	P115
Sutherland, Jacqueline	L251
also	L428
Sutherland, John	L251
also	L603
Sutherland, Krystal	L119
also	L192
Sutter, James L.	L146
also	L589
Sutton, Colin	L588
Sutton, Henry	L192
also	L608
Swaby, Rachel	L556
Swain, Heidi	L484
Swan, Annalyn	L126
Swan, Karen	L484
Swarup, Shubhangi	L526
Sweeney, Cynthia D'Aprix	L166
Sweeney, Emma Claire	L045
also	L146
Swift, Katherine	L192
also	L608
Swift, Vivian	L166
Swiss, Deborah J.	L301
Sword-Williams, Stefanie	L185
Sydnor, Charisma	L441
Sylva, Tasha	L146
also	L210
Symes, Sally	L146
also	L589
Sypeck, Jeff	L301
Szewczyk, Jesse	L141
Sánchez, María	L526
Sánchez-Andrade, Cristina	L526
Sóuter, Ericka	L301
Tachna, Ariel	P115
Tagliareni, Sonia	L430
Tagouri, Noor	L068
also	L101
Tait, Amelia	L185
Tait, Vanessa	L146
also	L589
Takaoka, Shannon	L166
Tallis, Raymond	L006
also	L426
Tamani, Liara	L166
Tangka, Eulalie	L135
also	L200
Tangorra, Zahra	L068
also	L101
Tania de Regil	L158
Tanner, Sophie	L484
Tanzer, Ben	L382
also	L435
Tanzer, Eliska	L265
also	L561
Tarlo, Emma	L563
Tarlow, Ellen	L205
also	L469
Tassier, Troy	L463
also	L464
Tate, Dizz	L146
Tate, June	L309
Tawse, Daniel	L366
Tay, Tania	L522
Taylor, A. J. P.	L146
Taylor, Andrew	L251
also	L577
Taylor, Annie	L152
also	L238
Taylor, Ayowa	L588
Taylor, Benjamin	L555
Taylor, E. J.	L153
Taylor, Ian	L207
Taylor, Jessica	L064
Taylor, Joelle	L379
Taylor, Jordyn	L087
also	L435
Taylor, Katie	L563
Taylor, Katrina	L166
Taylor, Lili	L429
Taylor, Lulu	L146
Taylor, Nick	L166

Taylor-Pitt, Paul	L152	
also	L193	
Tchaikovsky, Adrian	L407	
Teague, David	L166	
Telfer, Tori	L166	
Tempest, Daisy	L135	
also	L200	
Tempest, Kae	L109	
also	L146	
Temple, John	L301	
Temple, Rob	L430	
Templeton, Rebecca	L152	
also	L238	
Tennyson, Tre	L281	
Terrana, Diane	L281	
Tey, Josephine	L146	
Thai, Kim	L472	
also	L556	
Thammavongsa, Souvankham	L071	
Thample, Rachel de	L614	
Thanenthiran-Dharuman, Sureka	L146	
also	L210	
Thanhauser, Sofi	L556	
also	L581	
Thao, Dustin	L052	
also	L053	
Thayer, A.P.	L331	
Thebo, Mimi	L143	
Theise, Terry	L059	
Theodoridou, Natalia	L026	
Thernstrom, Melanie	L166	
Thom, Alessandra	L004	
Thomas Hertog	P391	
Thomas, Cathy	L192	
also	L477	
Thomas, David	L380	
Thomas, Dylan	L146	
also	L207	
also	L245	
Thomas, Frances	L146	
also	L589	
Thomas, Jo	L152	
also	L272	
Thomas, June	L129	
Thomas, Michelle	L348	
Thomas, Orla	L135	
also	L474	
Thomas, Scarlett	L045	
also	L146	
Thomas, Stacey	L149	
Thompson, Felicity Fair	L214	
Thompson, Jean	L166	
Thompson, Jo	L094	
Thompson, Kate	L065	
also	L088	
Thompson, Lara	L026	
Thompson, Shirley	P062	
Thompson, Tade	L120	
Thomson, Amanda	L379	
Thomson, Pat	L146	
also	L589	
Thomson-Spires, Nafissa	L348	
Thorne, Rebecca	L152	
also	L238	
Thurley, Simon	L146	
also	L207	
also	L245	
Tidy, Bill	L214	
Tidy, Joe	L265	
Tierney, Sarah	L265	
also	L561	
Tiffany, Kaitlyn	L556	
also	L581	
Tiffin, John	L588	
Tilburg, Christopher Van	L301	
Tilney, Georgie	L251	
also	L614	
Timms, Barry	L567	
Timoney, Lisa	L251	
also	L603	
Tinari, Leah	L493	
Tinglof, Christina Baglivi	L059	
Tinline, Phil	L146	
also	L207	
also	L245	
Tinniswood, Adrian	L192	
also	L284	
Tipler, Eric	L427	
Tipping, Liz	L430	
Tirado, Vincent	L463	
also	L464	
Tishby, Noa	L564	
Tivnan, Tom	L094	
Tizzard, Gemma	L535	
Tobin, Max	L393	
Todd, G X	L067	
also	L143	
Todd, Richard	L166	
Todd, Susan	L166	
Tomasi, Claire	L560	
Tomba, Neil	L493	
Tomba, Sheree	L493	
Tomlinson, David	L166	
Tomlinson, Theresa	L146	
also	L589	
Tomás, Teresa Jacinta	L434	
Tonge, Samantha	L143	
Tonkin, Peter	L146	
Toon, Nigel	L146	
also	L611	
Torday, Piers	L126	
Torjussen, Mary	L065	
also	L088	
Toumine, Ana	L410	
Towns, Krista	L605	
Townsend, Tracy	L203	
also	L617	
Townshend, Pete	L064	
Tracey, Kevin	L427	
Trail, Gayla	L441	
Tran, Ly Ky	L361	
Tran, Phuc	L361	
Treave, Hannah	L065	
also	L088	
Tregenza, Sharon	L366	
Treggiden, Katie	L545	
Trenhaile, John	L065	
also	L088	
Trenow, Liz	L265	
Trigell, Jonathan	L484	
Trinidad, Miguel	L441	
Trivelli, Joe	L563	
Trogen, Kari	L064	
Trott, Nikki	L535	
Trueblood, Amy	L463	
also	L464	
Trueblood, Amy True / Amy	L464	
also	L617	
Truss, Lynne	L146	
Tsong, Jing Jing	L469	
Tuama, Pádraig Ó	L126	
Tucker, Chelsea	L301	
Tucker, Jacqueline	L567	
Tucker, Nancy	L064	
also	L254	
Tudor, Kael	L567	
Tuke, Amanda	L152	
Tundun, Ola	L152	
also	L238	
Tunstall, KT	L613	
Turkot, Joseph	L052	
also	L053	
Turman, Lawrence	L166	
Turnbull, Ann	L146	
also	L589	
Turner, A. K.	L045	
also	L146	
Turner, Brian	L499	
Turner, Chris	L281	
Turner, David	L522	
Turner, Jane	L348	
Turner, Jon Lys	L126	
Turner, Katy	L379	
Turner, Rosie	L152	
also	L193	
Turner, Sarah	L265	
also	L361	
Turns, Anna	L484	
Twitchell, James	L166	
Tyce, Harriet	L045	
also	L146	
Tyler, L.C.	L152	
also	L272	
Tyler, Simon	L146	
also	L207	
also	L245	
Tyson, Neil deGrasse	L166	
Uddin, Zakia	L004	
Ujifusa, Steven	L564	
Underwood, Jack	L146	
Unger, Craig	L429	
Unsworth, Emma Jane	L126	
Unwin, Lucy	L567	
Uose, Hanna Thomas	L109	
also	L146	
Upano, Alicia	L026	
Upchurch, Gail	L292	
Updale, Eleanor	L119	
also	L192	
Upson, Nicola	L045	
also	L146	
Urban, Madeleine	P115	
Urwin, Jack	L065	
also	L473	
Urwin, Rosamund	L146	
also	L207	
also	L245	
Urzaiz, Begoña Gómez	L526	
Usher, M.D.	L301	
Usmani, Sumayya	L563	
Utley, Robert	L166	
Uzor, Kenechi	L004	
Vachon, Dana	L429	
Vadaketh, Sudhir Thomas	L006	
also	L426	
Valby, Karen	L166	
Valdez, Damian	L307	
Valentine, Jenny	L045	
also	L146	
Valentine, Rachel	L366	
Valerie, Julie	L301	
Vallance, Sarah	L361	
VanBrakle, Khadija L.	L464	
VanBrakle, Khadijah	L463	
also	L464	
Vanderbilt, Tom	L192	
also	L284	
VanderLugt, Dana	L205	
Vannicola, Joanne	L281	
VanSickle, Vikki	L382	
also	L435	
Vara, Geeta	L513	
Varaidzo,	L109	
also	L146	
Vardalos, Nia	L441	

Vardiashvili, Leo	L016
also	L326
Varga, Anne-Marie	L065
also	L088
Variyar, Rajasree	L430
Varnes, Allison	L493
Varoufakis, Yanis	L146
also	L207
also	L245
also	L555
Varouxakis, Georgios	L006
also	L426
Varricchio, Alex	L281
Varshney, Vani	L410
Vasagar, Jeevan	L006
also	L426
Vatomsky, Sonya	L251
also	L428
Vaughan, Carson	L556
Vaughan, Laura	L026
Vaughan, Sarah	L146
Vaughn, Lauren Roedy	L111
Vaz, Katherine	L166
Veen, Johanna van	L463
also	L464
Velasquez, Eric	L469
Velde, Simon Van Der	L016
also	L326
Vellekoop, Maurice	L281
Velton, Sonia	L430
Venis, Linda	L059
Ventura, MPH Emily	L059
Vera, Marisel	L059
Verde, Eva	L152
also	L193
Verdick, Elizabeth	L059
Veselka, Vanessa	L071
Veste, Luca	L065
also	L088
Vialleron, Margaux	L251
also	L417
Vian, Maddy	L567
Vick, Christopher	L119
also	L192
Victoire, Stephanie	L146
also	L156
Videen, Hana	L094
Vieira, Toby	L304
Viera, Rebecca Lynn	L301
Viertel, Jack	L564
Vieten, Cassandra	L427
Vigurs, Kate	L094
Vilden, Lynx	L441
Vince, Ian	L251
also	L577
Vincent, John	L251
also	L577
Vincent, Sarah St.	L166
Vincent, Yvonne	L331
Vine, Lucy	L046
also	L152
Vines, Stephen	L463
also	L464
Vinti, Lucia	L567
Virdi, R.R.	L203
also	L617
Vitiello, Cory	L281
Vladic, Sara	L493
Vladislavic, Ivan	L065
Vlock, Deb	L490
Voake, Steve	L126
Vogel, Sarah	L556
Vogl, James	L006
also	L426
Volanthen, John	L064
Volpatt, Michael	L301
Vondriska, Meg	L083
Voors, Barbara	L304
Vorhaus, John	L059
Voskuil, Hannah	L059
Vyner, Harriet	L126
Waal, Edmund De	L192
also	L608
Wabuke, Hope	L071
Waddell, James	L006
also	L426
Waddell, Martin	L146
also	L589
Wade, Christine	L166
Wade, Claire	L484
Wade, Lizzie	L361
Wadham, Lucy	L146
Wagner, Adam	L251
also	L577
Wagner, Benjamin	L215
Wagner, Kate	L175
Wainwright, Martha	L441
Wait, Rebecca	L265
Waite, Elizabeth	L143
Waite, Evan	L083
Wakeling, Kate	L216
Waldon, Laura	L166
Walker, Alice	L045
also	L146
Walker, Andy	L281
Walker, Casey	L166
Walker, Darren	L429
Walker, Harriet	L379
Walker, Jennie	L251
also	L577
Walker, Kandace Siobhan	L152
also	L193
Walker, Kay	L281
Walker, Martin	L192
also	L608
Walker, Owen	L006
also	L426
Walker, Sarai	L251
Walker, Sophie	L064
also	L254
Walker, Tash	L348
Walker-Edwards, Ryan	L393
Wallace, Rosie	L216
Walle, Mark Van de	L166
Waller, Sharon Biggs	L136
Wallfisch, Maya Lasker	L064
Wallis, Max	L126
Wallman, James	L046
Wallman, Sue	L366
Walmsley-Johnson, Helen	L065
also	L473
Walsh, Bridget	L065
Walsh, Bryan	L083
Walsh, Catherine	L522
Walsh, Claire	L545
Walsh, Jill Paton	L045
also	L146
Walsh, Joanna	L146
Walsh, Melanie	L146
also	L589
Walsh, Rosie	L146
Walsh, Stephen	L146
Walter, B P	L265
also	L561
Walters, Louise	L265
Walters, Minette	L146
also	L210
Walters, Vanessa	L146
also	L210
Walters, Victoria	L265
Walton, Jo	L550
Walton, Mollie	L379
Walton, Samantha	L192
also	L477
Wang, Dan	L006
also	L426
Wangtechawat, Pim	L149
Wansbrough, Barbara	L307
Wappler, Margaret	L166
Ward, Amanda Eyre	L126
Ward, Becky	L331
Ward, Catherine	L292
Ward, Miranda	L146
Ward, Rachel	L287
Ward, Sophie	L379
Wardell, M.A.	L203
also	L617
Wark, Kirsty	L192
also	L608
Warner, Tamsin	L153
Warren, Alyssa	L251
also	L603
Warren, Dakota	L613
Warren, Rossalyn	L185
Warren, Özlem	L491
Warrick, Eva	L004
Warwick, Hugh	L022
Washington, Brigid	L427
Washington, Janelle	L158
Wason, Wendy	L094
Wasserstein, Bernard	L146
also	L245
Wassmer, MJ	L203
also	L617
Wastvedt, Patricia	L428
Waterhouse, Keith	L146
Waters, Sarah	L428
Watkin, Sean	L064
also	L254
Watkins, Ali Marie	L083
Watkins, Roz	L046
also	L152
Watkins, Tionne	L441
Watson, Amy	L141
Watson, Christie	L348
Watson, Jesse Joshua	L469
Watson, Richard Jesse	L469
Watson, S J	L126
Watson, Stephanie Venn	L427
Watson, Sue	L265
Watson, Tom	L064
Watt, Holly	L146
also	L207
also	L245
Watters, Aisling	L146
also	L156
Watts, Anne	L065
Watts, Jonathan	L348
Watts, Rob	L251
also	L577
Wayne, Jemma	L065
also	L473
Wearing, Judy	L265
Weatherby, Alison	L292
Weatherford, Carole Boston	L469
Weatherford, Jeffery Boston	L469
Weatherley, Anna-Lou	L143
Weaver, Christian	L109
also	L146
Weaver, Pam	L102
also	L590
Weaver, Tim	L067
also	L143
Webb, Andrew	L251
also	L577
Webb, Catherine	L331
Webb, Clive	L192
also	L284

Webb, Justin	L006	
also	L426	
Webb, Ralf	L004	
Webb, Veronica	L427	
Webb-Carter, Oliver	L207	
Webber, Imogen Lloyd	L281	
Webster, Hayley	L535	
Webster, Lucy	L135	
also	L414	
Webster, Molly	L493	
Webster, Rachel J.	L207	
also	L480	
Webster-Hein, Michelle	L175	
Weduwen, Arthur Der	L119	
also	L192	
Wee, Lisa	L190	
also	L345	
Weeks, Josh	L135	
also	L243	
Weetman, Frances	L006	
also	L426	
Wegman, Jesse	L429	
Weil, Jonathan	L119	
also	L192	
Weinberg, Elizabeth	L166	
Weingarten, Lynn	L052	
also	L053	
Weinman, Jaime	L605	
Weinman, Sarah	L472	
also	L556	
Weir, Keziah	L391	
Weise, Jillian	L166	
Weiss, Jan Merete	L166	
Weissman, Michaele	L166	
Weitzman, Elizabeth	L166	
Welch, Caroline	L301	
Wellham, Melissa	L251	
also	L428	
Welliver, Melissa	L292	
Wells, Diana	L059	
Wells, Ione	L187	
also	L251	
Wells, Jenny	L379	
Wells, Kate	L484	
Welman, Kimberley	L556	
Wels, Susan	L301	
Welsh, Kaite	L379	
Wendig, Chuck	L166	
Wesley, Mary	L045	
also	L146	
West, Genevieve	L429	
West, Kate	L004	
West, Kathleen	L382	
also	L435	
West, Kevin	L381	
Westhead, Jessica	L281	
Wetherell, Sam	L146	
also	L207	
also	L245	
Wetzel, Paige	L493	
Weymouth, Adam	L348	
Weze, Clare	L152	
also	L193	
Whatley, Claire	L135	
also	L414	
Wheatcroft, Geoffrey	L006	
also	L426	
Wheeler, Frank	L166	
Whelan, David	L461	
Whipple, Dorothy	L146	
Whipple, Tom	L545	
Whitaker, Helen	L287	
White, Alison	L265	
White, Bryony	L379	
White, Elizabeth	L301	
White, Elizabeth "Barry"	L301	
White, Jim	L545	
White, Kali	L166	
White, Kristin M.	L301	
White, Mark	L214	
White, Sam	L330	
White, Shane	L555	
White, Sophie	L252	
White, Steve	L064	
also	L254	
White, T. H.	L146	
White, Tiare	L059	
Whitehart, Jacqueline	L366	
Whitehead, Harry	L065	
Whitehead, Kylie	L461	
Whitelock, Anna	L119	
also	L192	
Whitfield, Clare	L152	
also	L272	
Whitfield, Russell	L588	
Whitlam, Dan	L135	
also	L200	
also	L474	
Whitmarsh, Tim	L119	
also	L192	
Whitnell, Dee	L379	
Whitney, Rebecca	L026	
Whittaker, K.J.	L119	
also	L192	
Whittle, Kerry	L072	
Whyman, Kathleen	L152	
also	L238	
Whynott, Doug	L489	
Wicker, Alden	L381	
Wickins, Anna	L251	
also	L603	
Wiedemann, Elettra	L441	
Wiegle, Matt	L166	
Wiggins, Bethany	L553	
Wiggins, Marianne	L166	
Wigglesworth, Gary	L203	
also	L617	
Wigham, Jasmine	L203	
also	L617	
Wight, Jen	L028	
Wightwick, Charlotte	L434	
Wijeratne, Yudhanjaya	L203	
also	L617	
Wikholm, Catherine	L265	
Wilcox, Christina	L472	
also	L556	
Wilde, Lori	L052	
also	L053	
Wilder, Robyn	L251	
also	L577	
Wilder, Thornton	L146	
Wilding, Rose	L185	
Wilentz, Amy	L166	
Wiles, Ellen	L379	
Wiles, Will	L251	
also	L577	
Wiley, G.S.	P115	
Wiley, Richard	P167	
Wilford, Hugh	L192	
also	L284	
Wilhide, Elizabeth	L146	
Wiliam, Sioned	L094	
Wilkes, Will	L207	
Wilkin, Sam	L192	
also	L284	
Wilkinson, Annie	L309	
Wilkinson, Corban	L166	
Willard, Barbara	L146	
Willcox, Toyah	L214	
Willetts, Imogen	L192	
also	L284	
Williams, Charles	L146	
Williams, Cristin	L463	
also	L464	
Williams, David Michael	L550	
Williams, Elizabeth Lewis	L479	
Williams, Gray	L430	
Williams, Hattie	L430	
Williams, James	L006	
also	L426	
Williams, Jen	L430	
Williams, Jeremy	L102	
also	L513	
also	L590	
Williams, John L	L251	
also	L577	
Williams, Josh	L441	
Williams, Kat	L135	
also	L225	
Williams, Laura Jane	L153	
Williams, Rusty	L141	
Williams, Sophie	L491	
Williams, Zoe	L348	
Williamson, Lisa	L119	
also	L192	
Williamson, Sophie	L553	
Willner, Nina	L556	
Wilson, Alexandra	L265	
Wilson, Antoine	L348	
Wilson, Barrie	L301	
Wilson, Ben	L126	
Wilson, Casey	L429	
Wilson, Catelyn	L203	
also	L617	
Wilson, Claire	L152	
also	L272	
Wilson, Elspeth	L118	
also	L479	
Wilson, Eric	L391	
Wilson, Jacqueline	L146	
also	L589	
Wilson, Jason	L251	
also	L577	
Wilson, Joe	L366	
Wilson, Jon	L146	
also	L207	
also	L245	
Wilson, Miranda	L586	
Wilson, S.M.	L287	
Wilson, Samantha	L265	
also	L561	
Wilson-Lee, Edward	L065	
Wilton, Robert	L126	
Wincer, Penny	L535	
Windo, Nick Clark	L430	
Winn, Alice	L348	
Winning, Josh	L463	
also	L464	
Winstone, Keely	L006	
also	L426	
Winter, Kate	L484	
Winter, L. C.	L152	
also	L238	
Winter, Molly Roden	L281	
Winter, Tom	L430	
Winters, Ben H.	L301	
Winters, Ed	L064	
also	L254	
Winton, Tim	L045	
also	L146	
Wirkus, Tim	L166	
Wise, Greg	L192	
also	L608	
Wise, Susannah	L379	
Witt, Chris	L059	
Witynski, Karen	L059	
Wixey, Matt	L120	
Wodicka, Tod	L348	

Woghiren, Annabelle L064
Wojtowycz, David L146
   also L589
Wolf, Cristina L065
   also L180
Wolf, Hope L146
   also L207
   also L245
Wolf, Steve D. L059
Wolfe, Sean Fay L493
Wolff, Isabel L126
Wolff, Mishna L166
Wolitzer, Hilma L166
Wollock, David L059
Wolmar, Christian L006
   also L426
Womack, Jonathan P080
Womack, Marian L120
Womack, Rowena P080
Won, Annie L469
Won, Brian L469
Wong, Andrew L065
   also L473
Wong, Dalton L484
Wong, Regina L614
Wood, Alisson L166
Wood, Alistair L586
Wood, Aubrey L166
Wood, Benjamin L428
Wood, Bill L192
Wood, Brian L064
Wood, Charlotte L045
   also L146
Wood, Mary L309
Wood, Michael L119
   also L192
Wood, Olivia L026
Wood, Patricia L207
   also L480
Woodham, Simon L214
Woodhead, Matt L135
   also L225
Woodhouse, Joe L563
Woodhouse, Mike L094
Wooding, Lucy L119
   also L192
Woods, Billy L166
Woods, Carolyn L146
   also L245
Woods, Eva L046
Woods, Kell L311
Woods, Tom L064
Woodward, Kelly L064
Woof, Emily L135
   also L243
Wooldridge, Michael L192
   also L477
Woolf, Rebecca L166
Woolhouse, Alex L102
   also L590
WoonHeng, Chia L082
Worsley, Kate L045
   also L146
Worsley, Lucy L119
   also L192
Woster, Sara L166
Wozencraft, Kim L166
Wright, Ben L082
Wright, Claire L085
Wright, David L251
   also L614
Wright, John C. L550
Wright, Ronald L166
Wright, Tappy L214
Wroblewski, David L166
Wroe, Jo Browning L026
Wroe, Simon L026
Wu, Duncan L586
Wuebben, Jon L301
Wullschläger, Jackie L251
Wyatt, Stuart L588
Wyatt-Smith, Laura L535
Wyndham, John L146
Wyness, Gill L251
   also L603
Wythe, James L192
   also L608
Wärnberg, Jessica L119
   also L192
Xie, Jenny L071
Xinran L045
   also L146
Yamada, Taichi L146
   also L611
Yang, Jeff L166
Yang, Kelly L135
   also L225
Yang, Susie L251
   also L428
Yano, Naomi L281
Yates, Jon L006
   also L426
Yates, Karen L111
Yates, Kieran L192
   also L477
Yeboah, Stephanie L064
   also L254
Yeung, Adelle L560
Yeung, Bernice L556
Yi, Charlyne L139
   also L556
Yin, Mandy L109
   also L146
Yip, Vern L441
Yoo, David L166
Yoon, Helen L205
   also L469
Yoshida, Keio L379
Yoshino, Kenji L166
Young, Alora L383
Young, David L152
   also L272
Young, Dawn L059
Young, Emma L006
   also L426
Young, Erin L251
   also L577
Young, Eris L120
Young, Lola L064
   also L254
Young, Lucy L192
   also L608
Young, Robyn L251
   also L577
Younger, Bella L251
   also L603
Youngson, Anne L428
Yousefzada, Osman L126
Yu, Cindy L207
Yunis, Alia L166
Zackman, Gabra L301
Zadeh, Joe L251
   also L417
Zahawi, Nadhim L064
Zamani, Payam L564
Zambreno, Kate L146
Zandri, Vincent L380
Zappia, Corina L491
Zarei, Fatemeh L410
Zarrow, Rachel L068
   also L101
Zaza, Agatha L072
Zeleski, Allen L214
Zeller, Tom L556
Zenk, Molly L036
Zeschky, Clare L553
Zetterberg, Ally L252
Zha, Zed L605
Zhang, Angel Di L141
Zhang, Lijia L564
Zheutlin, Peter L301
Zichermann, Gabe L301
Ziegesar, Peter von L361
Ziegler, Alan L166
Ziegler, Sheryl Gonzalez L391
Ziepe, Laura L265
Ziminski, Andrew L251
   also L577
Zin, Sara L556
Zmith, Adam L348
Zolidis, Don L136
Zook, Kristal L441
Zuk, Marlene L383
Zuritsky, Elisa L215
Zweibel, Alan L441
Ægisdottir, Eva Björg L152
   also L272
Şode, Yomi L047

Literary Agents and Agencies

For the most up-to-date listings of these and hundreds of other literary agents and agencies, visit https://www.firstwriter.com/Agents

To claim your free access to the site, please see the back of this book.

L001 3 Seas Literary Agency
Literary Agency
PO Box 444, Sun Prairie, WI 53590
United States
Tel: +1 (608) 332-3430

https://www.threeseasagency.com
https://www.facebook.com/3-Seas-Literary-Agency-75205869856/
https://twitter.com/threeseaslit?lang=en

ADULT > **Fiction** > *Novels*
Fantasy; Romance; Science Fiction; Thrillers; Women's Fiction

CHILDREN'S > **Fiction** > *Middle Grade*

YOUNG ADULT > **Fiction** > *Novels*

How to send: Query Tracker
How not to send: Email

Accepts queries through online submission system only. See website for full guidelines.

Literary Agents: Cori Deyoe; Stacey Graham (**L247**); Kara Grajkowski (**L249**); Michelle Grajkowski

L002 A.M. Heath & Company Limited, Author's Agents
Literary Agency
6 Warwick Court, Holborn, London, WC1R 5DJ
United Kingdom
Tel: +44 (0) 20 7242 2811

submissions@amheath.com

https://amheath.com
https://twitter.com/AMHeathLtd
https://www.instagram.com/a.m.heath

Professional Body: The Association of Authors' Agents (AAA)

Fiction > *Novels*

Nonfiction > *Nonfiction Books*

Send: Query; Synopsis; Writing sample
How to send: Online submission system
How not to send: Post; Email

Handles general commercial and literary fiction and nonfiction. Submit work with cover letter, synopsis, and writing sample up to 10,000 words, via online submission system only. No paper submissions or submissions by email. Aims to respond within six weeks.

Agency Assistant: Jessica Lee

Agency Assistant / Associate Agent: Florence Rees

Literary Agents: Julia Churchill; Bill Hamilton; Victoria Hobbs; Oli Munson; Rebecca Ritchie; Euan Thorneycroft (**L574**)

L003 Kwaku Acheampong
Literary Agent
United States

carolyn@carolynjenksagency.com

https://www.carolynjenksagency.com/agent/Kwaku-Acheampong

Literary Agency: Carolyn Jenks Agency (**L100**)

ADULT
Fiction > *Novels*
Nonfiction > *Nonfiction Books*

NEW ADULT
Fiction > *Novels*
Nonfiction > *Nonfiction Books*

Send: Query; Writing sample
How to send: In the body of an email

Looking for fiction and nonfiction across most genres, though he has a special passion for new adult.

L004 Seren Adams
Literary Agent
United Kingdom

SAdams@unitedagents.co.uk

https://www.unitedagents.co.uk/sadamsunitedagentscouk
https://twitter.com/serenadams

Literary Agency: United Agents

Fiction > *Novels*
High Concept; Literary

Nonfiction > *Nonfiction Books*
Crime; Narrative Nonfiction; Nature

Send: Query; Synopsis; Pitch; Market info
How to send: Email

I am looking for literary novels, novellas and stories set anywhere in the world. Increasingly I am drawn to fiction with a distinctive and off-kilter voice which holds my attention, often wryly funny and/or full of feeling, usually inflected with strangeness, intensity or longing of some kind. While I tend not to read historical fiction or genre fiction, I enjoy books which are primarily literary but draw upon other genres; I would love to find an unforgettable high-concept literary novel which could become an instant classic. I also love realist novels which explore moral, philosophical or political questions, complex relationships, and/or troubling memories. I will always be interested in novels about intimacy, desire, love and loss. I am excited by big ideas books with a radical edge, and keen to see proposals that are doing something new within an established non-fiction genre, such as nature writing. I also love literary true crime. I enjoy anything with a compelling story and investigative elements based on meticulous and sensitive research.

Author Estates: The Estate of Dornford Yates; The Estate of Maurice Baring OBE

Authors: Esme Allman; Tia Bannon; Nivedita Barve; Jen Calleja; Lauren Aimee Curtis; Olivia Douglass; Lucie Elven; Adelaide Faith; Rakaya Fetuga; Ronan Fitzgerald; Amaryllis Gacioppo; Maria Giron; Anna Goldreich; Lili Hamlyn; Catherine Humble; Blair James; Liza St. James; Ammar Kalia; Line Kallmayer; Ana Kinsella; Molly Lipson; Benoît Loiseau; Aileen Maguire; Megan Marz; Laura Maw; Jamal Mehmood; Sinéad Mooney; Luke Neima; Caleb Azumah Nelson; Timothy Ogene; Anna Chapman Parker; Rebecca Perry; Joanna Pocock; Karina Lickorish Quinn; Gemma Reeves; Olivia Rosenthall; Alan Rossi; Taylor-Dior Rumble; Thomas Rutter; Michael Salu; Vanessa Santos; Lina Scheynius; Sophie Scott-Brown; Laura Southgate; Olivia Spring; Sean Stoker; Alessandra Thom; Zakia Uddin; Kenechi Uzor; Eva Warrick; Ralf Webb; Kate West

L005 Alex Adsett
Literary Agent; Consultant
Australia

https://alexadsett.com.au/literary-agency/
https://querymanager.com/query/AlexAdsettQueries
https://twitter.com/alexadsett

Literary Agency: Alex Adsett Literary

ADULT
  Fiction > *Novels*
    Commercial; Crime; Fantasy; Historical Romance; Literary; Mystery; Romantasy; Romantic Comedy; Romantic Mystery; Science Fiction

  Nonfiction > *Nonfiction Books*: Narrative Nonfiction

YOUNG ADULT > **Fiction** > *Novels*

Does not want:

  Fiction > *Novels*: Urban Fantasy

Send: Query; Author bio; Synopsis
How to send: Query Tracker; By referral

Costs: Offers services that writers have to pay for. Provides commercial and strategic advice to authors and independent publishers, particularly regarding publishing contracts.

An Australian literary agent and publishing consultant, who has been working in the publishing and bookselling industry for almost twenty-five years. She is always seeking amazing manuscripts, with a focus on fiction and narrative non-fiction, especially SFF, crime and romance, for all ages from picture books to adults.

L006 Aevitas Creative Management (ACM) UK
Literary Agency
43 Great Ormond Street, London, WC1N 3HZ
United Kingdom

ukenquiries@aevitascreative.com

https://aevitascreative.com/home/acm-uk/
https://twitter.com/AevitasCreative
https://www.facebook.com/AevitasCreative/

Literary Agency: Aevitas
Professional Body: The Association of Authors' Agents (AAA)

UK branch of a US agency, founded in 2019, representing writers and brands throughout the world.

Authors: Tim Adams; James Aldred; James Ashton; Odafe Atogun; Philip Augar; Hannah Barnes; Rahul Bhatia; Chris Bickerton; Innes Bowen; Ruth Brandon; Marcus Bridgewater; Tobias Buck; Stephen Bush; Joshua Chaffin; James Crabtree; Graham Daseler; Jonathan Derbyshire; Michael Dine; John Dunn; Armand D'Angour; Iyad El-Baghdadi; Graham Farmelo; Eliza Filby; Danny Finkelstein; John Gapper; Michael Gibson; Julian Glover; David Goodhart; Samuel Graydon; Rachel Halliburton; Liam Halligan; A.B. Hamilton; Charles Handy; Andrew Hankinson; Jonathan Hillman; Katja Hoyer; Nicholas Humphrey; Gavin Jacobson; Charlie Hamilton James; Tiffany Jenkins; Joanna Jolly; Andrew Keen; Ivan Krastev; Graham Lawton; Charles Leadbeater; Frances Leech; Mark Leonard; Ian Leslie; Oliver Letwin; John Lloyd; Isabel Losada; Andrew Lycett; Polly Mackenzie; Gary Madden; Mark Makepeace; Kenan Malik; Owen Matthews; Tom McTague; Peter Mead; Anand Menon; Daniel Metcalfe; Chris Miller; Munira Mirza; Paul Morland; Geoff Mulgan; Clive Myrie; David Omand; Arkady Ostrovsky; Tomiwa Owolade; Nicolas Pelham; Leigh Phillips; Mary Poffenroth; Jenny Radcliffe; Alice Rawsthorn; Assaad Razzouk; Richard Reeves; Tim Revell; Peter Ricketts; Neil Root; Jonathan Rowson; Donald Sassoon; Claire Schultz; Mark Sedgwick; Nigel Shadbolt; Oliver Shah; Marianna Spring; Raymond Tallis; Sudhir Thomas Vadaketh; Georgios Varoufakis; Jeevan Vasagar; James Vogl; James Waddell; Owen Walker; Dan Wang; Justin Webb; Frances Weetman; Geoffrey Wheatcroft; James Williams; Keely Winstone; Christian Wolmar; Jon Yates; Emma Young

Company Director / Senior Agent: Charlie Viney (**L586**)

Literary Agents: Trevor Dolby; Max Edwards; Clara Foster (**L211**); Maria Cardona Serra (**L526**); Emily Sweet (**L563**)

Senior Agents / Vice Presidents: Charlie Brotherstone (**L082**); Toby Mundy (**L426**)

L007 Thais Afonso
Associate Agent
Rio de Janeiro
Brazil

https://www.azantianlitagency.com
https://www.azantianlitagency.com/about-us/thais-afonso

Literary Agency: Azantian Literary Agency

ADULT > **Fiction** > *Novels*
  Commercial; Contemporary Romance; Cyberpunk; Fantasy; Folklore, Myths, and Legends; Gothic; Horror; LGBTQIA; Mystery; Romantic Comedy; Science Fiction; Speculative; Suspense; Thrillers; Women's Fiction

YOUNG ADULT > **Fiction** > *Novels*
  Fantasy; Horror; Mystery; Romantasy; Science Fiction; Speculative; Supernatural / Paranormal Thrillers; Thrillers

Does not want:

  Fiction > *Novels*: Grimdark

Closed to approaches.

Intends to represent marginalized authors, and she's especially seeking to uplift BIPOC born and raised in the Global South. An Afro-Brazilian lesbian, she currently lives and works out of Rio de Janeiro, Brazil.

L008 The Agency (London) Ltd
Literary Agency
24 Pottery Lane, Holland Park, London, W11 4LZ
United Kingdom
Tel: +44 (0) 20 7727 1346

info@theagency.co.uk
submissions@theagency.co.uk
childrensbooksubmissions@theagency.co.uk

https://theagency.co.uk

Professional Body: The Association of Authors' Agents (AAA)

ADULT > **Scripts**
  Film Scripts; TV Scripts; Theatre Scripts
CHILDREN'S > **Fiction**
  Middle Grade; Novels; Picture Books
TEEN > **Fiction** > *Novels*

YOUNG ADULT > **Fiction** > *Novels*

Send: Query; Synopsis; Writing sample
How to send: Email

Represents writers and authors for film, television, radio and the theatre. Also represents directors, producers, composers, and film and television rights in books, as well as authors of children's books from picture books to teen fiction. More likely to consider material from script writers if it has been recommended by a producer, development executive or course tutor. If this is the case send CV, covering letter and details of your referee by email. Do not email more than one agent at a time. For directors, send CV, showreel and cover letter by email. For children's authors, send query by email with synopsis and first three chapters (middle grade, teen, or Young Adult) or complete ms (picture books). All submissions should be sent directly to the relevant agent. Film, TV and theatre writers and composers should also CC the submissions email address.

Associate Agents: Arthur Barnard (**L035**); Sophie Kelleher (**L327**)

Literary Agents: Gina Andrews (**L018**); Ian Benson; Nicola Biltoo; Simon Blakey; Maeve Bolger (**L066**); Hannah Boulton; Hilary Delamere; Stephen Durbridge; Bethan Evans; Katie Haines; Jessica Hare (**L266**); Emily Hickman (**L278**); Jonathan Kinnersley; Julia Kreitman; Leah Schmidt; Emily Smith; Tanya Tillett; Katie Williams (**L602**)

L009 Michael Alcock
Literary Agent
United Kingdom

michael@johnsonandalcock.co.uk

http://www.johnsonandalcock.co.uk/michael-alcock

Literary Agency: Johnson & Alcock (**L302**)

Nonfiction > *Nonfiction Books*
Arts; Biography; Current Affairs; Food; Health; History; Popular Science

Send: Query; Writing sample; Synopsis

Client list covers non-fiction mainly in the fields of history and biography, current affairs, food, health, the arts and popular science.

L010 Kaylyn Aldridge
Assistant Agent
United States

https://www.metamorphosisliteraryagency.com
https://querytracker.net/query/3684/

Literary Agency: Metamorphosis Literary Agency (**L406**)

ADULT > **Fiction** > *Novels*
Coming of Age; Contemporary Romance; LGBTQIA; Romance; Romantic Comedy; Supernatural / Paranormal Romance

YOUNG ADULT > **Fiction** > *Novels*

How to send: Query Tracker

Loves to research underground internet subcultures. She believes that diverse perspectives are key to understanding cultures, communities, and nuances of the human experience. Accepts submissions in December, June, and July.

L011 Keir Alekseii
Associate Agent
United States

http://www.azantianlitagency.com/pages/team-ka.html
https://querymanager.com/query/keiralekseii
https://querymanager.com/query/keiralekseii/BIPOC

Literary Agency: Azantian Literary Agency

ADULT > **Fiction** > *Novels*
Fantasy; Horror; Science Fiction

YOUNG ADULT > **Fiction** > *Novels*
Contemporary; Fantasy; Horror; Science Fiction

How to send: Query Tracker

An educator and anti-GBV activist born and raised in Trinidad and Tobago, a twin island country in the West Indies. She is a writer, gamer, lover of folklore, and former research scientist. As a neurodivergent, queer woman of color, she is invested in discovering engaging work with similar representation, and is passionate about creating space for voices not often recognized. She is especially interested in stories from BIPOC who are born and raised in the Global South.

She is seeking YA & Adult SFFH and YA contemporary novels. She is ONLY open to receiving queries from writers who identify as belonging to a marginalized or underrepresented community.

L012 Alice Williams Literary
Literary Agency
United Kingdom
Tel: +44 (0) 20 7385 2118

submissions@alicewilliamsliterary.co.uk

https://www.alicewilliamsliterary.co.uk
http://instagram.com/agentalicewilliams

Professional Body: The Association of Authors' Agents (AAA)

CHILDREN'S
Fiction
Middle Grade; Novels; Picture Books
Nonfiction > *Nonfiction Books*

YOUNG ADULT
Fiction > *Novels*
Nonfiction > *Nonfiction Books*

How to send: Email

A specialist literary agency proudly representing writers and illustrators of picture books, young fiction, middle-grade, YA and non-fiction.

Literary Agent: Alice Williams (**L601**)

L013 Ambassador Speakers Bureau & Literary Agency
Literary Agency
United States
Tel: +1 (615) 370-4700

info@ambassadorspeakers.com

https://www.ambassadorspeakers.com

Fiction > *Novels*: Christianity

Nonfiction > *Nonfiction Books*: Christianity

Send: Query
How to send: Email

Represents select authors and writers who are published by religious and general market publishers in the US and Europe. Send query by email with short description.

L014 Andlyn
Literary Agency
United Kingdom

davinia@andlynliterary.co.uk

https://www.andlynliterary.co.uk

Professional Body: The Association of Authors' Agents (AAA)

CHILDREN'S > **Fiction**
Chapter Books; Early Readers; Middle Grade; Picture Books
TEEN > **Fiction** > *Novels*

YOUNG ADULT > **Fiction** > *Novels*

Specialises in children's/teen fiction and content. Handles picture books, middle-grade, young adult, and cross-over.

L015 Hannah Andrade
Literary Agent
United States

https://bradfordlit.com/hannah-andrade-agent/
https://twitter.com/hhandrade93
https://querymanager.com/hannahandrade

Literary Agency: Bradford Literary Agency (**L073**)

ADULT
Fiction > *Novels*: Mystery

Nonfiction > *Nonfiction Books*
Commercial; Crime; Investigative Journalism; Narrative Nonfiction

CHILDREN'S > **Fiction**
Graphic Novels: General
Middle Grade: General, and in particular: Dark Humour; Folklore, Myths, and Legends; Ghost Stories; Historical Fiction

YOUNG ADULT > **Fiction**
Graphic Novels: General
Novels: General, and in particular: Dark Fantasy; Folklore, Myths, and Legends; Historical Fiction; Mystery

Closed to approaches.

Likes to think of herself as an editorial-focused agent and is particularly eager to acquire BIPOC/underrepresented voices. She is prioritizing stories of joy where identity isn't the focus and is especially excited about stories rooted in history, mythology, and legends, particularly those that are lesser-known or underrepresented in traditional publishing.

Very interested in stories that explore the intricacies of multicultural identities. She loves stories of immigration (not relegated to America) and of first/second generation Americans who struggle balancing the values of their country with the culture and heritage of their parents (as in the tv shows Ramy or Gentefied). As a Mexican-American, she would particularly love to see the stories that she grew up with showcased in new and creative ways.

L016 Andrew Nurnberg Associates, Ltd
Literary Agency
43 Great Russell Street, London, WC1B 3PD
United Kingdom
Tel: +44 (0) 20 3327 0400

info@nurnberg.co.uk
submissions@nurnberg.co.uk

http://www.andrewnurnberg.com
https://twitter.com/nurnberg_agency
https://www.instagram.com/andrewnurnbergassociates/?hl=en

Professional Body: The Association of Authors' Agents (AAA)

ADULT
Fiction > *Novels*
Nonfiction > *Nonfiction Books*

CHILDREN'S > Fiction > *Novels*

Does not want:

> ADULT > Scripts
> *Film Scripts*; *Radio Scripts*; *TV Scripts*; *Theatre Scripts*
> CHILDREN'S > Fiction > *Picture Books*

Send: Query; Synopsis; Writing sample
How to send: Email

Handles adult fiction and nonfiction, and children's fiction. No poetry, children's picture books, or scripts for film, TV, radio or theatre. Send query by email with one-page synopsis and first three chapters or 50 pages as attachments.

Affiliated Agent: Sara O' Keeffe (**L326**)

Authors: Victoria M. Adams; Jose Alvior; Rebecca Anderson; Kathy Biggs; Julia Boggio; Theodore Brun; Sinead Crowley; James DeVita; Freya Dolby; Rachel Donohue; Joshua Eure; Brooke Fortune; Catherine Ryan Howard; Amy Jordan; Siobhan MacGowan; Nicola Masters; Melanie Maure; Serena Molloy; Anthony Riches; Darryl Samaraweera; David Sergeant; Eithne Shortall; Leo Vardiashvili; Simon Van Der Velde

Literary Agency: The Wallace Literary Agency

Literary Agents: Sarah Nundy; Andrew Nurnberg

L017 Davinia Andrew-Lynch
Literary Agent
United Kingdom

Literary Agency: Curtis Brown (**L135**)

L018 Gina Andrews
Literary Agent
United Kingdom

https://theagency.co.uk/the-agents/gina-andrews/

Literary Agency: The Agency (London) Ltd (**L008**)

Scripts
Film Scripts; *TV Scripts*

Representing clients across TV and film, she enjoys giving feedback on drafts and acting as a sounding board for new ideas. She's also acted as a consultant for script development for production companies. She is always grateful for the opportunity to discover and champion new talent.

L019 Anna Ange
Literary Agent
United States

QueryAnna@lizadawson.com

https://www.lizadawsonassociates.com
https://www.lizadawsonassociates.com/anna-ange

Literary Agency: Liza Dawson Associates

ADULT
Fiction
Graphic Novels: Fantasy; Gothic; Historical Fantasy; Horror; Noir; Romance
Novels: Historical Fantasy; Historical Fiction; Horror; LGBTQIA; Literary; Satire; Speculative
Nonfiction
Graphic Nonfiction: History; Memoir
Nonfiction Books: Narrative Essays; Narrative Nonfiction

CHILDREN'S > Fiction
Graphic Novels: Horror
Middle Grade: Horror

Send: Query; Writing sample; Synopsis
How to send: Email

Looking for adult literary/genre crossover. Literary forward novels that play with horror, speculative, or "weird" elements. Interesting prose, mind boggling premises. Satire also welcome. Fiction that is not technically horror, but evokes a sense of horror, nonetheless. True genre horror. No holds barred. Queer historical fiction and historical fantasy, especially set before the year 1900. Narrative non-fiction or essays that center on niche and surprising topics. Adult Graphic novels (fiction): Small-scale, intimate but existential stories set against fantastical backgrounds, historical fantasy, horror/gothic/noir with romantic subplots. Unique and inventive art styles. Adult Graphic novels (non-fiction): history and memoir. Autumnal, spooky/horror-adjacent, middle grade prose or graphic novels that take on complicated, relevant issues.

L020 Anne Clark Literary Agency
Literary Agency
United Kingdom

submissions@anneclarkliteraryagency.co.uk

https://www.anneclarkliteraryagency.co.uk

Professional Body: The Association of Authors' Agents (AAA)

CHILDREN'S
Fiction > *Middle Grade*
Nonfiction > *Nonfiction Books*

YOUNG ADULT
Fiction > *Novels*
Nonfiction > *Nonfiction Books*

Closed to approaches.

Handles fiction for children and young adults. Send query by email only with the following pasted into the body of the email (not as an attachment): for fiction, include brief synopsis and first 3,000 words; for nonfiction, send short proposal and the text of three sample pages. No submissions by post. See website for full guidelines.

Literary Agent: Anne Clark

L021 Annette Green Authors' Agency
Literary Agency
5 Henwoods Mount, Pembury, Kent, TN2 4BH
United Kingdom

annette@annettegreenagency.co.uk

https://www.annettegreenagency.co.uk
https://www.instagram.com/agacwc/
https://www.linkedin.com/in/annette-green-authors-agency-39040018b/
https://twitter.com/agacwc
https://www.facebook.com/Annette-Green-Authors-Agency-363774892041/

ADULT
Fiction > *Novels*
General, and in particular: Comedy / Humour; Current Affairs; Horror; Literary; Thrillers

Nonfiction > *Nonfiction Books*
Biography; Current Affairs; Films; History; Memoir; Music; Politics; Popular Culture; Science; Sport; TV

CHILDREN'S > Fiction > *Middle Grade*

TEEN > Fiction > *Novels*

Send: Query; Synopsis; Writing sample
How to send: Word file email attachment
How not to send: PDF file email attachment

Costs: Offers services that writers have to pay for.

Send query by email with a brief synopsis (fiction) or overview (nonfiction), and the opening few chapters (up to about 10,000 words). No poetry, scripts, science fiction, or fantasy. Send Word documents rather than PDFs.

L022 Antony Harwood Limited
Literary Agency
103 Walton Street, Oxford, OX2 6EB
United Kingdom
Tel: +44 (0) 1865 559615

mail@antonyharwood.com

http://www.antonyharwood.com

Fiction > *Novels*

Nonfiction > *Nonfiction Books*

Send: Query; Synopsis; Writing sample; Self-addressed stamped envelope (SASE)
How to send: Email; Post

Handles fiction and nonfiction in every genre and category, except for screenwriting and poetry. Send brief outline and first 50 pages by email, or by post with SASE.

Authors: Christine Berry; Alastair Bonnett; Michael Bracewell; Peter Bunzl; Amanda Craig; Candida Crewe; David Dabydeen; Tracy Darnton; Roy Dennis; Louise Doughty; Robert Edric; Anna Fleming; Sarah Gibson; Bob Gilbert; Caspar Henderson; Jill Hopper; Sally Huband; Gwyneth Lewis; Amy Liptrot; Fraser MacDonald; Stephen Rutt; Guy Shrubsole; Hugh Warwick

Literary Agents: Antony Harwood; Jo Williamson (**L604**)

L023 Apple Tree Literary Ltd
Literary Agency
United Kingdom

submissions@appletreeliterary.com

https://appletreeliterary.com
https://x.com/AppleTreeLit

Professional Body: The Association of Authors' Agents (AAA)

ADULT
  Fiction > *Novels*
    General, and in particular: Literary; Speculative

  Nonfiction > *Nonfiction Books*

YOUNG ADULT > **Fiction** > *Novels*

Send: Query; Synopsis; Writing sample; Proposal
How to send: Email

In fiction, we are particularly interested in literary and speculative fiction of all types – particularly where the two overlap. We are, however, interested in all adult and YA fiction – you never know, we may just fall in love with it. Please note we do not represent children's fiction below Young Adult. List of non-fiction authors across academics, journalists, memoirists, experts and high-profile names. We are particularly keen to hear from those telling untold or unknown stories, and experts writing about fascinating new ways of understanding our world.

Literary Agent: Max Edwards

L024 Kurestin Armada
Literary Agent
Canada

https://www.rootliterary.com/agents
https://querymanager.com/query/kurestinarmada
https://www.publishersmarketplace.com/members/kurestinarmada/

Literary Agency: Root Literary (**L503**)

ADULT > **Fiction** > *Novels*
  Fantasy; High / Epic Fantasy; Historical Romance; Horror; Romance; Romantasy; Science Fiction; Space Opera; Speculative; Spy Thrilllers; Upmarket; Westerns

CHILDREN'S > **Fiction**
  Chapter Books: General

  Graphic Novels: General
  Middle Grade: Adventure; Comedy / Humour; Contemporary; Fantasy; Historical Fiction; Literary; Mystery; Science Fiction; Upmarket
  Picture Books: Comedy / Humour

How to send: Query Tracker

I love working with creators to form a roadmap for the rest of their career. Talking to people with projects that are ambitious, strange, personal, and just outrageously fun is the spark that keeps me going. I'm here to be their advocate and make sure they can keep writing for years and years to come.

L025 Victoria Wells Arms
Literary Agent
United States

victoria@hgliterary.com

https://www.hgliterary.com/victoria
https://twitter.com/VWArms
https://querymanager.com/query/VictoriaWellsArms

Literary Agency: HG Literary
Professional Bodies: Association of American Literary Agents (AALA); Society of Children's Book Writers and Illustrators (SCBWI)

ADULT
  Fiction > *Novels*

  Nonfiction > *Nonfiction Books*: Food

CHILDREN'S > **Fiction**
  Middle Grade; *Picture Books*
YOUNG ADULT > **Fiction** > *Novels*

Closed to approaches.

Represents authors of children's books of all ages, select adult authors, food authors, and many talented picture book illustrators.

L026 Susan Armstrong
Literary Agent
United Kingdom
Tel: +44 (0) 20 7393 4200

susan.submissions@cwagency.co.uk
susan.armstrong@cwagency.co.uk

https://cwagency.co.uk/agent/susan-armstrong
https://twitter.com/SusanW1F

Literary Agency: C&W (Conville & Walsh)

Fiction > *Novels*
  Book Club Fiction; Contemporary; Crime; Family Saga; Fantasy; Gothic; Historical Fiction; Horror; Literary; Magical Realism; Science Fiction; Speculative; Suspense; Thrillers; Upmarket Commercial Fiction; Women's Fiction

How to send: Word file email attachment

I love to see literary fiction, book group/upmarket commercial women's fiction, contemporary stories, family dramas, historical, crime, thrillers and suspense. I'm also keen to see high-quality magical realism and speculative fiction i.e. books with an edge of SFF, horror, gothic or 'otherness'. I enjoy novels that blend genres, are unusual in setting or circumstance, have unexpected twists, have a little darkness, pull at the heart-strings, and/or contain some sort of moral dilemma. Books that make me laugh are always welcome!

So that's the writing, but what about the writer? There are no prerequisites except that I'm always looking for authors who want a long-term career and in return I will do everything to help shape, edit and sell their books along with offering support and guidance.

I'm not currently taking on new YA/children's books or espionage thrillers.

I am open to submissions from anyone anywhere in the world but I particularly love to hear from British, Irish, Greek and ANZ writers.

Authors: Grace Alexander; Claire Anderson-Wheeler; Jo Callaghan; Joanna Cannon; Holly Cave; Maxine Beneba Clarke; Daniel Cole; Marianne Cronin; Grace Flahive; Joanna Glen; Anne Griffin; Katie Gutierrez; Lori Inglis Hall; James Hannah; Lindsay Hawdon; Miranda Cowley Heller; Julietta Henderson; Emily Howes; Crystal Jeans; Jess Kidd; Olivia Kiernan; Justine Kilkerr; Annie Kirby; Claire Kohda; Caroline Mackenzie; C.E. McGill; Juli Min; Hayley Nolan; Lisa O'Donnell; Chibundu Onuzo; Orla Owen; Jo Piazza; Christine Pride; Al Robertson; Ali Shaw; Kim Sherwood; Natasha Solomons; M L Stedman; Natalia Theodoridou; Lara Thompson; Alicia Upano; Laura Vaughan; Rebecca Whitney; Olivia Wood; Jo Browning Wroe; Simon Wroe

L027 Wayne Arthurson
Literary Agent
Canada

https://www.therightsfactory.com/Agents/Wayne-Arthurson

Literary Agency: The Rights Factory

ADULT
  Fiction > *Novels*
    Crime; Fantasy; Literary; Science Fiction

  Nonfiction > *Nonfiction Books*
    Memoir; Narrative Nonfiction

YOUNG ADULT
  Fiction > *Novels*
    Crime; Fantasy; Literary; Science Fiction

  Nonfiction > *Nonfiction Books*
    Memoir; Narrative Nonfiction

Currently building his list of talent, looking specifically for YA or adult literary, crime and SFF and narrative nonfiction and memoir. He's actively seeking works by Indigenous writers.

Authors: Greg Bechtel; Eric Beetner; Michelle Poirier Brown; Deryn Collier; Candas Jane Dorsey; Trevor Duplessis; Brittlestar aka Stewart Reynolds; Marsheila (Marcy) Rockwell; Steven Sandor; Coltrane Seesequasis

L028 Charlotte Atyeo
Literary Agent
United Kingdom

charlotte@greyhoundliterary.co.uk

https://greyhoundliterary.co.uk/agent/charlotte-atyeo/
https://twitter.com/EverSoBookish

Literary Agency: Greyhound Literary

ADULT
Fiction > *Novels*: Literary

Nonfiction > *Nonfiction Books*
General, and in particular: Equality; Feminism; Gender Issues; Music; Nature; Sport

CHILDREN'S
Fiction > *Picture Books*

Nonfiction
Middle Grade; *Nonfiction Books*
YOUNG ADULT > Fiction > *Novels*

Does not want:

Nonfiction > *Nonfiction Books*
Religion; Self Help

Send: Query; Synopsis; Writing sample; Outline
How to send: Email
How not to send: Post

Represents non-fiction authors as well as a select number of children's and fiction authors. She is primarily looking for original and brilliantly written general non-fiction, sport, music, nature writing, and feminism, gender and equality issues. She is not taking on poetry or books about religion, self-help or memoirs that deal with abuse and/or trauma. When it comes to children's books, she is open to submissions of picture books (particularly non-rhyming texts) and non-fiction (ideally from authors with expert knowledge of their subject). She is especially excited to hear from author/illustrators and from under-represented voices. She is not looking for MG or YA fiction at the moment. She is currently closed to fiction submissions.

Authors: Carol Atherton; Saskia Gwinn; Ed Hawkins; Michael Holding; Michael Hutchinson; Ellie Irving; Jennifer Lane; Michelle Lovric; Julia Raeside; Susan Richardson; Helen Scales; Sarah Shephard; Cécile Simmons; Tatton Spiller; Jen Wight

L029 AVAnti Productions & Management
Literary Agency
124 City Road, The City, London, EC1V 2NX
United Kingdom
Tel: +44 (0) 7999 193311

avantiproductions@live.co.uk

https://www.avantiproductions.co.uk

Scripts > *Film Scripts*

Send: Full text
How to send: Email
How not to send: Post

Costs: Author covers sundry admin costs.

Talent and literary representation. Open to screenplay submissions for short films and feature films, but no theatre scripts.

Literary Agent: Veronica Lazar

L030 Ollie Azis
Literary Agent
United Kingdom

Literary Agency: Independent Talent Group Ltd

L031 Lauren Bajek
Junior Agent
United States

querylauren@lizadawson.com

https://www.lizadawsonassociates.com/lauren-bajek

Literary Agency: Liza Dawson Associates

Fiction > *Novels*
Fantasy; Horror; Literary; Science Fiction; Speculative; Upmarket

Nonfiction > *Nonfiction Books*
Crafts; Nature; Science

Send: Query; Writing sample
How to send: In the body of an email

Currently building a select list of fiction and nonfiction, with an emphasis in SFFH, upmarket speculative fiction, craft/DIY nonfiction, and science/nature nonfiction. Across the board, she is drawn to literary prose, queer and anticolonial perspectives, unusual or hybrid forms, and an ambitious sense of imagination. She is always interested in animal cognition, translation, and sentient houses.

L032 Emma Bal
Literary Agent
United Kingdom

https://madeleinemilburn.co.uk/looking-for/emma-bal-what-im-looking-for/

Literary Agency: Madeleine Milburn Literary, TV & Film Agency (**L385**)

Nonfiction > *Nonfiction Books*
Arts; Cookery; Food; Investigative Journalism; Memoir; Narrative Nonfiction; Nature; Science; Travel

Looking for non-fiction across the arts, humanities and sciences; narrative non-fiction; investigative journalism: cookery and food writing; travel and nature writing; memoir; illustrated projects.

L033 Dan Balow
Literary Agent
United States

vseem@stevelaube.com

https://stevelaube.com/what-i-am-looking-for/

Literary Agency: The Steve Laube Agency

Nonfiction > *Nonfiction Books*: Christianity

Send: Query; Proposal; Writing sample
How to send: Email attachment
How not to send: Post; In the body of an email

Represents nonfiction works mainly to Christian-themed publishers. No fiction.

L034 Stephen Barbara
Literary Agent
United States

submissions@inkwellmanagement.com

https://www.inkwellmanagement.com
https://www.inkwellmanagement.com/staff/stephen-barbara
https://twitter.com/Stephen_Barbara

Literary Agency: InkWell Management

ADULT
Fiction > *Novels*
Nonfiction > *Nonfiction Books*

YOUNG ADULT > Fiction > *Novels*

Send: Query; Writing sample
How to send: Email

Selective in taking on new clients but remains excited to discover great new writers and would be thrilled to find a novel that hits big on an emotional level or, if nonfiction, changes the way he thinks about the world.

L035 Arthur Barnard
Associate Agent
United Kingdom

abarnard@theagency.co.uk

https://theagency.co.uk/the-agents/arthur-barnard/

Literary Agency: The Agency (London) Ltd (**L008**)

Scripts
Film Scripts; *TV Scripts*; *Theatre Scripts*

Send: Query; Writing sample
How to send: Email

Started working at the agency in 2019, after graduating with a degree in English from The University of Cambridge. In 2020 he began work as an assistant, expanding his knowledge across television, film and theatre. He currently holds the position of associate agent and is starting to build his own list of clients.

L036 Barone Literary Agency

Literary Agency
United States

DSBLawyer@outlook.com

https://www.baroneliterary.com

ADULT > **Fiction** > *Novels*
  Erotic Romance; Historical Fiction; Horror; Romance; Women's Fiction

NEW ADULT > **Fiction** > *Novels*

YOUNG ADULT > **Fiction** > *Novels*

Does not want:

> **NEW ADULT** > **Fiction** > *Novels*
>   Science Fiction; Supernatural / Paranormal
>
> **YOUNG ADULT** > **Fiction** > *Novels*
>   Science Fiction; Supernatural / Paranormal

Closed to approaches.

Closed to submissions as at July 2023. Check website for current status.

Send query online form on website. Include synopsis and first three chapters. No plays, screenplays, picture books, middle grade, science fiction, paranormal, or nonfiction.

Authors: Laurie Albano; Michele Barrow-Belisle; Cathy Bennett; Sarah Biglow; Jennifer Petersen Fraser; Yvette Geer; Suzanne Hay; Richard Moore; Rebekah Purdy; Curt Rude; Wyatt Shev; Anna Snow; Sharon Sullivan-Craver; Molly Zenk

Literary Agent: Denise Barone

L037 Baror International, Inc.

Literary Agency
P.O. Box 868, Armonk, NY 10504-0868
United States

https://barorint.com

ADULT
  Fiction > *Novels*
    Commercial; Fantasy; Historical Fiction; Literary; Science Fiction; Suspense; Thrillers

  Nonfiction > *Nonfiction Books*

CHILDREN'S > **Fiction** > *Middle Grade*

YOUNG ADULT > **Fiction** > *Novels*

Closed to approaches.

Specialises in the international and domestic representation of literary works in both fiction and non-fiction ranging in genre including commercial fiction, literary, historical, suspense, thrillers, narrative, science fiction, fantasy, young adult, middle grade and more.

Literary Agents: Danny Baror; Heather Baror-Shapiro

L038 Anjanette Barr

Literary Agent
United States

query@dunhamlit.com

https://www.dunhamlit.com/anjanette-barr.html
https://aalitagents.org/author/anjanettebarr/
https://www.facebook.com/BookBarrista
https://twitter.com/bookbarrista
https://www.instagram.com/bookbarrista/
https://www.linkedin.com/in/anjanette-barr-34193765/
https://youtube.com/AnjanetteBarrtheBookBarr

Literary Agency: Dunham Literary, Inc. (**L163**)
Professional Bodies: Association of American Literary Agents (AALA); Society of Children's Book Writers and Illustrators (SCBWI)

ADULT
  Fiction > *Novels*
    General, and in particular: Gothic; Magical Realism

  Nonfiction > *Nonfiction Books*
    Arts; Biography; Culture; Folklore, Myths, and Legends; History; Memoir; Nature; Popular Science; Poverty; Religion

CHILDREN'S > **Fiction** > *Picture Books*

Send: Query; Writing sample
How to send: In the body of an email
How not to send: Google Docs shared document; Email attachment

She loves genre and popular fiction with substance, and literary and non-fiction titles infused with living ideas that leave readers with a new desire to immerse themselves in the subject matter. In non-fiction she is looking for well-researched biography written in beautiful literary prose, popular science and other disciplines titles that make lay-people enchanted and invested in topics previously over their heads, and memoir with the ability to connect diverse readers. She's also interested in books that shed light on poverty and justice in a new way. She prefers picture books that are winsome and pleasant to read aloud. Particular interests are the exploration of culture, history, faith, myth, fine arts, and nature. She has a soft spot for gothic novels and magical realism. As a mother of four, she's is especially fond of books that can be read aloud and shared with the whole family.

L039 Nicola Barr

Literary Agent
United Kingdom

https://www.thebentagency.com
https://www.thebentagency.com/nicola-barr
https://twitter.com/NicolaBarr123

Literary Agency: The Bent Agency (UK) (**L051**)

ADULT
  Fiction > *Novels*
    Commercial Women's Fiction; Commercial; Crime; Literary; Social Issues; Upmarket Commercial Fiction

  Nonfiction > *Nonfiction Books*
    Comedy / Humour; Europe; Feminism; Houses and Homes; Sport

YOUNG ADULT > **Fiction** > *Novels*: Contemporary

Closed to approaches.

I have over the years represented many bestselling commercial fiction authors, Richard & Judy bestsellers, and award-winning crime fiction and commercial women's fiction. I am still very much on the lookout for upmarket commercial well-written fiction in these areas, particularly if they speak to a social issue, shine a light on a true-life injustice, have an atypical hero or heroine. I adore literary fiction, whether experimental or traditional, and will certainly not turn away a novel for seeming lack of... anything happening.

But, whether you are writing commercial fiction or literary fiction, I am endlessly fascinated by dysfunctional or unusual families, oddballs, women struggling and women achieving, the disenfranchised, outsiders. I embrace fiction that explores the darker side of life, but do respond well to points of view that don't take the world too seriously.

In YA, I'm most passionate about grounded contemporary.

I'm a committed Londoner, but was born and raised in Northern Ireland, then studied at the University of Glasgow. I am actively looking to build on the brilliant Irish, Northern Irish and Scottish writers I already have. I do have a natural tendency to be drawn to working-class voices and regional stories. I also love nothing more than getting stuck in editorially on a story if I see brilliance there.

Like many in these odd times, I find myself increasingly drawn to non-fiction that allows for a collective vent. In the past year or so I have represented books on housing, Europe, feminism, millennials, sexual harassment. I love illustrators, cartoonists. I love sport and comedy and I might even show an interest in your food blog. As long as it doesn't mention cupcakes.

L040 Emily Barrett
Literary Agent
United Kingdom

emilysubmissions@theblairpartnership.com

https://www.theblairpartnership.com
https://www.theblairpartnership.com/literary-agents/emily-barrett/
https://twitter.com/emilyebarrett

Literary Agency: The Blair Partnership (**L064**)

Nonfiction
Nonfiction Books: Animals; Career Development; Climate Science; Comedy / Humour; Cookery; Crime; Health; History; Nature; Parenting; Personal Development; Politics; Popular Science; Wellbeing
Puzzles: General

How to send: Email

I'd love to see engaging history (both broad brushstrokes and specific stories from the past that read as compellingly as fiction); eye-opening but sympathetic true crime; supportive parenting guides backed up by a digital community; accessible pop science; stories with animals at their heart; useful cookery that does something new; and puzzle and humour books. I'm also keen to see books that are seeking to bring readers joy, could improve their health, wellbeing, career or lives in general, and will help readers understand the world today (e.g. books on politics, climate, nature etc).

Authors: Dan Bowman; Chiara Bullen; Rabbi Moshe Friedman; Angela Harding; Chris Hoy; Pascal Hughes; David Kelly; Katie Kennedy

L041 Jason Bartholomew
Literary Agent
United Kingdom

https://www.thebksagency.com/submissions

Literary Agency: The BKS Agency (**L063**)

Fiction > *Novels*
  Crime; Thrillers

Nonfiction > *Nonfiction Books*
  Biography; Current Affairs; History; Memoir; Narrative Nonfiction; Politics

Closed to approaches.

Originally from America. Spent ten years working in New York publishing, primarily for Hachette Book Group USA. He moved to Hachette UK in 2008 where he was the Rights Director across Hodder & Stoughton, Headline Publishing Group, Quercus Books, and John Murray Press.

L042 Bath Literary Agency
Literary Agency
5 Gloucester Road, Bath, BA1 7BH
United Kingdom

john.mclay@btinternet.com

https://www.bathliteraryagency.com
https://twitter.com/BathLitAgency
http://instagram.com/bathlitagency

Professional Body: The Association of Authors' Agents (AAA)

CHILDREN'S
  Fiction
    Middle Grade; *Picture Books*
  Poetry > *Picture Books*

YOUNG ADULT
  Fiction > *Novels*
  Nonfiction > *Nonfiction Books*

Send: Query; Synopsis; Writing sample; Full text; Self-addressed stamped envelope (SASE)
How to send: Email; Post

Handles fiction and nonfiction for children, from picture books to Young Adult. Send query by email or by post with SAE for reply and return of materials if required, along with the first three chapters (fiction) or the full manuscript (picture books). See website for full details.

Literary Agent: Gill McLay

L043 Erica Bauman
Literary Agent
United States

https://aevitascreative.com/agents/
https://querymanager.com/query/EricaBauman

Literary Agency: Aevitas

ADULT > **Fiction**
  Graphic Novels: General
  Novels: Commercial; Folklore, Myths, and Legends; Magic; Romantic Comedy; Speculative

CHILDREN'S > **Fiction** > *Graphic Novels*

YOUNG ADULT > **Fiction** > *Graphic Novels*

How to send: Query Tracker

Open to submissions the first week of every month. Most interested in commercial novels that feature an exciting premise and lyrical, atmospheric writing; imaginative, genre-blending tales; speculative worlds filled with haunting, quietly wondrous magic; fresh retellings of mythology, ballet, opera, and classic literature; sharply funny rom-coms; graphic novels for all ages; fearless storytellers that tackle big ideas and contemporary issues; and working with and supporting marginalized authors and stories that represent the wide range of humanity.

Authors: Telênia Albuquerque; Jessica Benoist; Melissa Benoist; Abigail Rayner

L044 Jan Baumer
Literary Agent
United States

jan@foliolit.com

https://www.foliolit.com/agent/jan-baumer

Literary Agency: Folio Literary Management, LLC (**L207**)

Nonfiction > *Nonfiction Books*
  Business; Comedy / Humour; Cookery; Health; Memoir; Narrative Nonfiction; Parenting; Prescriptive Nonfiction; Religion; Self Help; Spirituality; Wellbeing

Closed to approaches.

Interests as an agent are largely nonfiction, specifically spirituality, religion, self-help, health and wellness, parenting, memoir, and business with a spirituality or self-help angle. Response only if interested. If no response in 60 days, assume rejection.

L045 Veronique Baxter
Literary Agent; Company Director
United Kingdom

veroniquemanuscripts@davidhigham.co.uk
childrenssubmissions@davidhigham.co.uk

https://www.davidhigham.co.uk/agents-dh/veronique-baxter/

Literary Agency: David Higham Associates Ltd (**L146**)

ADULT
  Fiction > *Novels*
    Book Club Fiction; Comedy / Humour; Crime; Domestic; Family Saga; High Concept; Historical Fiction; Horror; Literary; Speculative; Thrillers

  Nonfiction > *Nonfiction Books*
    Crime; Current Affairs; Feminism; Food; History; Memoir; Psychology; Travel

CHILDREN'S > **Fiction** > *Middle Grade*
  Comedy / Humour; High Concept; Mystery

Send: Query; Synopsis; Writing sample
How to send: Email

In fiction, looking for: Literary fiction of all kinds including historical, horror and speculative; multi-generational novels; High concept book club fiction; Devil-in-the-detail domestic dramas; Crime and thrillers – particularly those set in unusual places or that take the genre conventions and do something a bit different with them; fictionalised true crime (gravitating towards the darker end of the spectrum); Caustic, funny novels.

In nonfiction, looking for true crime, history, current affairs, travel, food, psychology, feminism and memoir.

In children's, looking for high concept stories told with humour and heart, and mysteries and whodunnits at the older end.

Agency Assistant: Sara Langham

Authors: Richard Adams; Naomi Alderman; Jenn Ashworth; Anthony Bale; Belinda Bauer; Hannah Begbie; Neil Blackmore; Carys Bray; Colwill Brown; Glen James Brown; Sally Butcher; Nick Butterworth; Jamie Costello; Cressida Cowell; Nick Crumpton; Nicola

Davies; Jonathan Dimbleby; Berlie Doherty; Fred D'Aguiar; David Edmonds; Maz Evans; Stephen Fry; Jamila Gavin; Guinevere Glasfurd; Holly Gramazio; Oliver Harris; Mo Hayder; Emma Henderson; Nathan Hill; Paul Hoffman; Edward Hogan; Simon Hopkinson; Lucy Hounsom; Diana Wynne Jones; Stephen Kelman; Claire King; Hugh Laurie; Saci Lloyd; Joanna Lumley; Kesia Lupo; S. E. Lynes; Greil Marcus; Patrick Marnham; Simon Mason; Peter May; Anna Mazzola; Geraldine McCaughrean; Jean McNeil; Sarah Mitchell; Lauren Mooney; Michael Morpurgo; Charity Norman; Sigrid Nunez; Cato Pedder; Charlotte Philby; Sarah Pinborough; Sabina Radeva; Sarah Ridgard; M. L. Rio; Bethan Roberts; Jane Robinson; Rachel Seiffert; Nick Sharratt; Philip Short; Kate Simants; Jonathan Stroud; Emma Claire Sweeney; Scarlett Thomas; A. K. Turner; Harriet Tyce; Nicola Upson; Jenny Valentine; Alice Walker; Jill Paton Walsh; Mary Wesley; Tim Winton; Charlotte Wood; Kate Worsley; Xinran

L046 Diana Beaumont
Literary Agent
United Kingdom

db.submission@dhhliteraryagency.com

https://www.dhhliteraryagency.com
https://www.dhhliteraryagency.com/diana-beaumont

Literary Agency: DHH Literary Agency Ltd (**L152**)

Fiction > *Novels*
  Book Club Fiction; Commercial; Contemporary; Family Saga; Gothic; High Concept Crime; High Concept Thrillers; Historical Fiction; Romance; Romantic Comedy; Upmarket Commercial Fiction

Nonfiction > *Nonfiction Books*
  Comedy / Humour; Cookery; Lifestyle; Memoir; Social Justice

Closed to approaches.

Send your cover letter, first three chapters and a one-page synopsis, and ensure your chapters and synopsis are saved as Word Documents and sent as attachments.

Authors: Tanya Atapattu; Holly Baxter; Alexandra K Benedict; Alexandra K. Benedict; Daisy Buchanan; Cecil Cameron; James Campbell; Amanda Cassidy; Angela Clarke; Mathew Clayton; Yvonne Cobb; Fiona Collins; Caroline Corcoran; Isabel Costello; Hannah Dolby; Francesca Dorricott; Lilly Ebert; Dov Forman; Lily Ebert Forman; Louise Hulland; Catriona Innes; Harriet Johnson; Amy Jones; Eve Makis; Andrea Mara; Francesca May; Claire McGowan; Emma Orchard; Adam Pearson; Fiona Perrin; Alice Peterson; Rachel Phipps; Carmen Reid; Samantha Renke; Lee Ridley; Emma Robertson; Diana Rosie; Frances Ryan; Frances Ryan; Jennifer Savin; Allison Secker; Hema Sukumar; Lucy Vine; James Wallman; Roz Watkins; Eva Woods

L047 Salma Begum
Literary Agent
United Kingdom

salma@greyhoundliterary.co.uk

https://greyhoundliterary.co.uk
https://greyhoundliterary.co.uk/agents/salma-begum

Literary Agency: Greyhound Literary

Fiction > *Novels*
  General, and in particular: High Concept; Horror; Literary; Romance; Time Travel; Urban

Nonfiction > *Nonfiction Books*
  General, and in particular: Journalism; Memoir; Music; Social Media

Poetry > *Poetry Collections*

Send: Query; Synopsis; Writing sample
How to send: Email

Seeking confident, immersive, ambitious, narrative-driven writing. She works under the tenet that quality need not be to the sacrifice of commercial success. Her submission wishlist includes a sweeping love story set against a gritty urban backdrop; ingenious tales of time travel; and a masterfully crafted multi-generational epic. In non-fiction, she is looking for subject experts, journalists and memoirists who appreciate long-form literature and can breathe life into an idea, an event, a memory. Her non-fiction wishlist includes interrogations of social media use and its sometimes-devastating consequences as explored in the Netflix docudrama The Social Dilemma; captivating music writing such as Grime Kids by DJ Target and On Michael Jackson by Margo Jefferson; and ground-shifting journalism like Empire of Pain by Patrick Radden Keefe. She has published the work of a number of prize-winning poets. As an agent, her preference is for the colloquial, rhythmic, or playful, written with the ambition of forming a cohesive collection. She is keen to work with spoken word poets who are looking to bring their work to the page.

Authors: Zahra Barri; Sharmilla Beezmohun; Josh Berson; Saddiq Dzukogi; Yvvette Edwards; Joshua Idehen; Delia Jarrett-Macauley; Arji Manuelpillai; Shane Melisse; Roger Robinson; Yomi Ṣode

L048 Eva Bell
Literary Agent
United Kingdom

https://saylescreen.com/about-us/

Literary Agency: Sayle Screen Ltd

Scripts
  Film Scripts; TV Scripts; Theatre Scripts

How to send: By referral

Predominantly represents writers and writer/directors working across film, tv and theatre. Also represents script editors/script execs as well as dramatic rights in fiction and non-fiction books. Taste is varied across genres and tone, but the linking factor is always characterful storytellers that have a unique point of view or perspective on the worlds they are inviting their audience into.

L049 Maddy Belton
Literary Agent
United Kingdom

https://www.madeleinemilburn.co.uk/agents/maddy-belton/
https://twitter.com/MadsPhyllis

Literary Agency: Madeleine Milburn Literary, TV & Film Agency (**L385**)

ADULT > **Fiction** > *Novels*
  Contemporary Fantasy; Cozy Fantasy; Dark; Fairy Tales; Fantasy; Folklore, Myths, and Legends; High / Epic Fantasy; Historical Fiction; LGBTQIA; Romance; Science Fiction; Thrillers

CHILDREN'S
  Fiction > *Middle Grade*
    Comedy / Humour; Fantasy; Magic

  Nonfiction > *Nonfiction Books*

YOUNG ADULT > **Fiction** > *Novels*
  Contemporary Fantasy; Cozy Fantasy; Fantasy; High / Epic Fantasy; LGBTQIA; Romance

Send: Outline; Author bio; Market info; Marketing plan; Writing sample
How to send: Email

SFF across all genres for all ages, including: grim dark, thriller, historical, romance, cosy fantasy, sci-fi, epic, YA fantasy, dark academia, contemporary fantasy, fantasy middle-grade, mythology, fairy tale and queer fantasy. Inspiring children's non-fiction.

L050 Laura Bennett
Associate Agent; Editor
United Kingdom

https://www.liverpool-literary.agency/about

Literary Agency: The Liverpool Literary Agency (**L369**)

ADULT > **Fiction** > *Novels*
  Dystopian Fiction; Fantasy; Post-Apocalyptic; Science Fiction; Steampunk; Urban Fantasy

YOUNG ADULT > **Fiction** > *Novels*
  Dystopian Fiction; Fantasy; Post-Apocalyptic; Science Fiction; Steampunk; Urban Fantasy

Closed to approaches.

L051 The Bent Agency (UK)
Literary Agency
Greyhound House, 23/24 George Street, Richmond, TW9 1HY
United Kingdom

info@thebentagency.com

https://www.thebentagency.com
https://www.instagram.com/thebentagency/

Professional Body: The Association of Authors' Agents (AAA)
Literary Agency: The Bent Agency (**L052**)

ADULT
  Fiction
    Graphic Novels; *Novels*
  Nonfiction > *Nonfiction Books*

CHILDREN'S > **Fiction**
  Chapter Books; *Graphic Novels*; *Middle Grade*

YOUNG ADULT
  Fiction
    Graphic Novels; *Novels*
  Nonfiction > *Nonfiction Books*

Send: Query
How to send: Email; Query Tracker

UK office of established US agency. See website for individual agent interests and contact details and approach appropriate agent. Do not send submissions to general agency email address. See website for full submission guidelines.

Associate Agent: Martha Perotto-Wills (**L465**)

Literary Agent: Nicola Barr (**L039**)

Literary Agent / Managing Director: Molly Ker Hawn (**L270**)

L052 The Bent Agency
Literary Agency
PO Box 55772, Birmingham, AL 35205
United States

info@thebentagency.com

https://www.thebentagency.com
https://www.instagram.com/thebentagency/

ADULT
  Fiction
    Graphic Novels; *Novels*
  Nonfiction > *Nonfiction Books*

CHILDREN'S > **Fiction**
  Chapter Books; *Graphic Novels*; *Middle Grade*

YOUNG ADULT
  Fiction
    Graphic Novels; *Novels*
  Nonfiction > *Nonfiction Books*

Send: Query
How to send: Email; Query Tracker

Accepts email or Query Manager queries only. See website for agent bios and specific interests and email addresses, then query one agent only. See website for full submission guidelines.

Authors: Arvin Ahmadi; Samantha M. Bailey; Gary John Bishop; Tera Lynn Childs; Yangsze Choo; Liv Constantine; Susan Crispell; Lisa Doyle; Kerry Douglas Dye; Deborah Falaye; Michael Farquhar; Mina Fears; Delores Fossen; Stephanie Garber; J. T. Geissinger; Seressia Glass; Alexis Henderson; Rita Herron; A. G. Howard; Robert Isaacs; Tiffany D. Jackson; Meredith Jaeger; Elise Kova; Roselle Lim; Julia London; Elle Marr; Barry Martin; Marta McDowell; Goldy Moldavsky; Laura Morelli; Joel H. Morris; Natalie Naudus; Preston Norton; Michelle Quach; Morgan Ryan; Lynsay Sands; Ingrid Seymour; L C. Shaw; Lori Nelson Spielman; Dustin Thao; Joseph Turkot; Lynn Weingarten; Lori Wilde

Literary Agency: The Bent Agency (UK) (**L051**)

Literary Agent / President: Jenny Bent (**L053**)

Literary Agent / Vice President: Victoria Cappello (*L097*)

Literary Agents: James Mustelier; Zoe Plant (**L476**); John Silbersack

L053 Jenny Bent
Literary Agent; President
United States

queries@thebentagency.com

https://www.thebentagency.com/jenny-bent

Literary Agency: The Bent Agency (**L052**)

ADULT
  Fiction > *Novels*
    Commercial; Domestic Suspense; Grounded Fantasy; High Concept; Horror; Literary; Romance; Romantic Comedy; Speculative; Upmarket Women's Fiction

  Nonfiction > *Nonfiction Books*
    Lifestyle; Self Help

YOUNG ADULT > **Fiction** > *Novels*
  General, and in particular: Contemporary; Fantasy; Magic; Romantic Comedy; Suspense

Does not want:

> **Fiction** > *Novels*
>   Cozy Mysteries; High / Epic Fantasy; Science Fiction

Send: Query; Writing sample
How to send: Email
How not to send: Post

I'm currently looking for literary and commercial fiction and young adult fiction as well as select non-fiction in the areas of self-help and lifestyle. My client list is diverse and I welcome submissions from BIPOC authors.

In adult fiction, I'm looking for high concept, upmarket women's fiction; grounded fantasy; speculative fiction and horror (I particularly love a good ghost story, along the lines of writing by Simone St. James and Jennifer McMahon); and domestic suspense, but the bar is very high in suspense right now so it has to be an extremely creative concept. I also rep some romance and rom-com, but no other genre fiction: I'm not a good choice for high fantasy, cozy mystery, or sci-fi.

In young adult fiction, I'm pretty open to genre – I love fantasy, rom-coms, suspense, contemporary, almost anything except for sci-fi. I do notice that my YA taste does tend to skew towards older readers, more in a crossover direction.

In general, I tend to prefer plot-driven books to character-driven ones and pacing is very important to me. I also love novels – for adults or young adults – that have an element of magic or fantasy to them or that take me into a world that is new to me, whether real or imaginary. And while I love books to be dark and weird in terms of content, I find that I am more drawn to traditional, rather than experimental, methods of structure and storytelling.

In nonfiction, I am looking for authors with a unique approach and a very large existing platform. I'm not generally the right choice for memoir or narrative non-fiction, but I'm always open to hearing a pitch just in case.

All of the books that I represent speak to the heart in some way: they are linked by genuine emotion, inspiration, and great writing and storytelling. I love books that make me laugh, make me cry, or ideally do both.

Authors: Arvin Ahmadi; Samantha M. Bailey; Gary John Bishop; Tera Lynn Childs; Yangsze Choo; Liv Constantine; Susan Crispell; Lisa Doyle; Kerry Douglas Dye; Deborah Falaye; Michael Farquhar; Mina Fears; Delores Fossen; Stephanie Garber; J. T. Geissinger; Seressia Glass; Alexis Henderson; Rita Herron; A. G. Howard; Robert Isaacs; Tiffany D. Jackson; Meredith Jaeger; Elise Kova; Roselle Lim; Julia London; Elle Marr; Barry Martin; Marta McDowell; Goldy Moldavsky; Laura Morelli; Joel H. Morris; Natalie Naudus; Preston Norton; Michelle Quach; Morgan Ryan; Lynsay Sands; Ingrid Seymour; L C. Shaw; Lori Nelson Spielman; Dustin Thao; Joseph Turkot; Lynn Weingarten; Lori Wilde

L054 Kendall Berdinsky
Literary Agent
United States

kberdinsky@dystel.com

https://www.dystel.com
https://www.dystel.com/kendall-berdinsky
https://querymanager.com/query/kendallb
https://twitter.com/klberdinsky

Literary Agency: Dystel, Goderich & Bourret LLC

Fiction > *Novels*
  Book Club Fiction; Psychological Thrillers; Upmarket Romance

Nonfiction > *Nonfiction Books*: Narrative Nonfiction

How to send: Query Tracker

Interested in seeing upmarket romance, book club fiction, psychological thrillers, and narrative nonfiction. Overall, she is looking for work from underrepresented communities with new stories to tell.

L055 John Berlyne
Literary Agent
United Kingdom

http://zenoagency.com/about-us/

Literary Agency: Zeno Agency (**L617**)

ADULT > Fiction > *Novels*
  Crime; Fantasy; Historical Fiction; Horror; Science Fiction; Space Opera; Thrillers; Urban Fantasy

YOUNG ADULT > Fiction > *Novels*

Closed to approaches.

L056 Amanda Bernardi
Literary Agent
United States

https://www.highlineliterary.com
https://www.highlineliterary.com/agent-amanda
https://querymanager.com/query/3002
https://www.instagram.com/amandabernardibooks

Literary Agency: High Line Literary Collective (**L279**)

Nonfiction > *Nonfiction Books*
  Arts; Cookery; Design; Environment; Health; Houses and Homes; Investigative Journalism; Nature; Parenting; Popular Culture; Popular History; Popular Science; Social Justice; Sociology; Sport; Wellbeing

How to send: Query Tracker

Actively building her client list and works exclusively with non-fiction. She is interested in platform- or expertise-driven cookbooks, home & design, art, investigative journalism, social justice, pop science, wellness, social science, sports, health, pop history, parenting, nature, environmentalism, pop culture and anything that advances our community dialogue towards a better tomorrow. She is looking for projects that are thoughtful, actionable, and engaging for a general audience.

L057 Betancourt Literary
Literary Agency
United States

query@betancourtliterary.com

https://www.betancourtliterary.com

Fiction > *Novels*
  Literary; Mystery; Psychological Thrillers; Romance; Women's Fiction

Nonfiction > *Nonfiction Books*: Narrative Nonfiction

Send: Query; Synopsis; Writing sample
How to send: In the body of an email
How not to send: Email attachment

We believe powerful storytelling deserves powerful support. Our agency is dedicated to representing bold voices and unforgettable narratives in mystery, psychological thrillers, romance, women's fiction, literary fiction, and select non-fiction.

The agency was founded by a USA Today bestselling mystery author and experienced publishing professional. She holds a bachelor's degree in Communications and is currently earning her J.D., bringing both creativity and legal insight to the business of books. Her many years of writing experience allows her to advocate strategically and compassionately for the authors she represents.

She created this agency with a single mission: to empower authors. Whether you're seeking your first publishing deal or are ready to elevate your career, we offer the transparency, guidance, and enthusiasm every writer deserves.

We don't just shop books—we build careers.

Literary Agent: Rose Betancourt (*L058*)

L058 Rose Betancourt
Literary Agent
United States

Literary Agency: Betancourt Literary (**L057**)

L059 Betsy Amster Literary Enterprises
Literary Agency
607 Foothill Blvd #1061, La Canada Flintridge, CA 91012
United States

b.amster.assistant@gmail.com

http://amsterlit.com

Fiction > *Novels*
  Literary; Mystery; Thrillers; Upmarket Commercial Fiction; Upmarket Women's Fiction

Nonfiction
  Gift Books: General
  Nonfiction Books: Biography; Career Development; Cookery; Gardening; Health; History; Lifestyle; Medicine; Narrative Nonfiction; Nutrition; Parenting; Popular Culture; Psychology; Self Help; Social Issues; Travel; Women's Issues

How to send: Email
How not to send: Post

A full-service literary agency based in Los Angeles, California. No romances, screenplays, poetry, westerns, fantasy, horror, science fiction, techno thrillers, spy capers, apocalyptic scenarios, political or religious arguments, or self-published books. See website for full guidelines.

Authors: Amy Alkon; Dwight Allen; Will Allen; Jess J. Araujo; Elaine N. Aron; Sandi Ault; Lois Barr; Ariel Bernstein; Kim Boyce; Helene Brenner; Karen Briner; Catheryn J. Brockett; Karen Burns; Mónica Bustamante; Joe P. Carr; Steven Carter; Lillian Castillo-Speed; Robin Chotzinoff; Frank Clifford; Rob Cohen; David Cundy; Leela Cyd; Margaret Leslie Davis; Jan DeBlieu; David J. Diamond; Martha O. Diamond; Phil Doran; Suzanne Dunaway; Nick Dyer; J. Theron Elkins; Ruth Andrew Ellenson; Loretta Ellsworth; James P. Emswiler; Mary Ann Emswiler; Naomi Epel; Alex Epstein; Karin Esterhammer; Jeannette Faurot; Tom Fields-Meyer; Joline Godfrey; Tanya Ward Goodman; Michael I. Goran; Hindi Greenberg; Ellen Hawley; Marian Henley; Charney Herst; Leigh Ann Hirschman; Ariel Horn; Lisa Hunter; Jackie; Melissa Jacobs; Janet Jaffe; Emily Katz; E. Barrie Kavasch; Joy Keller; Eileen Kennedy-Moore; Rachel Tawil Kenyon; Camille Landau; Carol Lay; Anna Lefler; Margaret Lobenstine; Mark Lowenthal; Paul Mandelbaum; Ivy Manning; Melissa Martin; Domenico Minchilli; Elizabeth Helman Minchilli; Wendy Mogel; Sharon Montrose; Bonnie Frumkin Morales; Yolanda Nava; Joy Nicholson; Judith Nies; Susie Norris; Christopher Noxon; Lynette Padwa; Neela Paniz; Kishani Perera; Cash Peters; Barry Prizant; Winifred Reilly; Andrea Richards; Eileen Roth; Adam Sappington; Marjorie Barton Savage; Anthony Schmitz; M.D. Edward Schneider; Kyle Schuneman; George Shannon; Nancy Spiller; Allison Mia Starcher; Louise Steinman; Bill Stern; Terry Theise; Christina Baglivi Tinglof; Linda Venis; MPH Emily Ventura; Marisel Vera; Elizabeth Verdick; John Vorhaus; Hannah Voskuil; Diana Wells; Tiare White; Chris Witt; Karen Witynski; Steve D. Wolf; David Wollock; Dawn Young

Literary Agent: Betsy Amster

L060 Beverley Slopen Literary Agency
Literary Agency
131 Bloor St. W., Suite 711, Toronto, M5S 1S3
Canada
Tel: +1 (416) 964-9598

beverley@slopenagency.ca

https://slopenagency.com

Fiction > *Novels*
  Commercial; Literary
Nonfiction > *Nonfiction Books*
Closed to approaches.

One of Canada's leading literary agents. Based in Toronto, her list includes serious non-fiction and literary and commercial fiction.

Literary Agent: Beverley Slopen

L061 Elizabeth Bewley
Literary Agent
United States

ebewley@sll.com

https://www.sll.com/our-team

Literary Agency: Sterling Lord Literistic, Inc.

ADULT > **Fiction** > *Novels*
  Historical Fiction; Romance; Upmarket Women's Fiction
CHILDREN'S > **Fiction** > *Middle Grade*
YOUNG ADULT > **Fiction** > *Novels*

Send: Query; Synopsis; Writing sample
How to send: Online submission system; Email

She represents books for kids, with a focus on middle-grade and young adult fiction, as well as books for adults, with an eye towards upmarket women's fiction. She loves books that explore romantic relationships, stories that have a very specific point of view, and characters that make a lasting impression. Loves realistic fiction (our world is a fascinating place!), and she is currently on the hunt for historical fiction.

L062 Tamanna Bhasin
Assistant Agent
Canada

https://www.therightsfactory.com
https://www.therightsfactory.com/Agents/tamanna-bhasin
https://querymanager.com/query/tbhasin

Literary Agency: The Rights Factory

ADULT > **Fiction** > *Novels*
  Fantasy; Historical Fiction; Romance
YOUNG ADULT > **Fiction** > *Novels*
  Fantasy; Historical Fiction

Closed to approaches.

Her dedication to diverse narratives shines through as a literary agent—where she now combines her love for reading with her expertise in spotting compelling manuscripts across genres.

L063 The BKS Agency
Literary Agency
Penway Place, 2A Charing Cross Road,
London, WC2H 0FH
United Kingdom

https://www.thebksagency.com
https://www.facebook.com/thebksagency
https://twitter.com/ThebksAgency

Professional Body: The Association of Authors' Agents (AAA)

A literary management agency based in London. Founded in 2018 by three friends, each of whom has spent over two decades working across the biggest publishing houses in London and New York.

Literary Agents: Jason Bartholomew (**L041**); Joanna Kaliszewska (**L315**); Jessica Killingley (**L332**); James Spackman (**L547**)

L064 The Blair Partnership
Literary Agency
PO Box, 7828, London, W1A 4GE
United Kingdom
Tel: +44 (0) 20 3857 7555

info@theblairpartnership.com

https://www.theblairpartnership.com

Professional Body: The Association of Authors' Agents (AAA)

ADULT
  Fiction > *Novels*
    Book Club Fiction; Commercial; Crime; Detective Fiction; Dystopian Fiction; High Concept; Historical Fiction; Literary; Speculative; Thrillers; Upmarket Women's Fiction
  Nonfiction > *Nonfiction Books*
    Crime; Lifestyle; Personal Development
CHILDREN'S
  Fiction
    Middle Grade: Adventure
    Novels: General, and in particular: Commercial
  Nonfiction > *Nonfiction Books*
TEEN > **Fiction** > *Novels*
YOUNG ADULT > **Fiction** > *Novels*

Send: Query; Synopsis; Proposal; Writing sample
How to send: Word file email attachment; PDF file email attachment

We welcome all submissions and consider everything that is sent to the agency, though we are not currently accepting submissions for screenplays, short stories or poetry.

We welcome approaches from both debut writers and established authors. We're very happy to receive submissions from overseas, as long as they're written in English.

Authors: Jodie Abrahams; Marina Abramović; Nicola Adams; Jassa Ahluwalia; Imran Ahmed; Alwia Al-Hassan; Bana Alabed; Nimco Ali; Matt Allen; Danny Altmann; JJ Arcanjo; Jane Asher; Amy Beashel; Rafael Behr; Emma J. Bell; Gary Bell; Ronen Bergman; Julie Bindel; David Bolchover; Dan Bowman; Sita Brahmachari; Daniel Broadstock; Steve Brown; Chiara Bullen; Michael Byrne; Michael Calvin; Lucy Cameron; Tom Carlisle; Nicky Clark; Sir Ronald Cohen; Rowan Coleman; Ryan Collett; Sheena Cook; Dawn Coulter-Cruttenden; Sue H Cunningham; Kim Curran; Tom Davies; Essie Dennis; Lizzy Dent; Rebecca Denton; Roxane Dhand; Laura Dodsworth; Helena Duggan; Owen Eastwood; Clare Empson; Charlotte Essex; Emma Farrarons; Seán Farrelly; Sue Fortin; Henry Fraser; Mark Freeman; Rabbi Moshe Friedman; William Friend; Jo Furniss; John Fury; Paris Fury; Tyson Fury; Gary Gamp; Hazel Gardner; Alice Gendron; Marina Gerner; Pippa Grange; Catherine Green; Kareen Griffiths; Toby Gutteridge; Roya Hakakian; Yalda Hakim; Clare Leslie Hall; Isaac Hamilton-McKenzie; Angela Harding; Chips Hardy; Elle Hardy; Charlie Harlan; Ramsey Hassan; Maria Hatzistefanis; Kate Hays; Jordan Henderson; Amelia Henley; Josh Hicks; David Holmes; Megan Hopkins; Leigh Hosy-Pickett; Chris Hoy; Pascal Hughes; Oli Hyatt; Bea Ingalls; James Inverne; Louise Jensen; Hardeep Kaur; David Kelly; Ruth Kelly; Mollie Kendrick; Katie Kennedy; Scott Kershaw; Nasser David Khalili; Caroline Klidonas; Peter Komolafe; Zoya Kooper; Joanne Lake; Frank Lampard; Kieran Larwood; Alex Lassoued; Liz Lawler; Lee Lawrence; The Urban Legend; Arizona Leger; Lee Lennox; Rose Lihou; John Lutz; Charlotte Lytton; Lulee Ma; Cathy MacDonald; Dan Malakin; Aseem Malhotra; Hussain Manawer; Ruthy Mason; Margaret McDonald; Luna McNamara; Gez Medinger; Catherine Miller; Major Scotty Mills; Huey Morgan; Markus Motum; Mercy Muroki; Shabnam Nasimi; Maajid Nawaz; Lindsay Nicholson; Leena Norms; Catriona Olding; Michal Oshman; Nikki Owen; Penelope O'Neill; Stuart Pallant; David Patrikarakos; Justine Pattison; Rogba Payne; Daisy Pearce; Adam Peaty; Rob Perry; Trevor Phillips; Megan Reeves; Duncan Roe; Terry Ronald; Stephen Ronson; J.K. Rowling; Celine Saintclare; Anbara Salam; Julia Samuel; Dan Saunders; Delphine Seddon; Lauren Sharkey; Babita Sharma; Louise Shorter; Alexander Slater; Jon Smith; Jon Sopel; Tom Spencer; P. A. Staff; Jennifer Stone; Dean Stott; Sarah Stovell; Jessica Taylor; Pete Townshend; Kari Trogen; Nancy Tucker; John Volanthen; Sophie Walker; Maya Lasker Wallfisch; Sean Watkin; Tom Watson; Steve White; Ed Winters; Annabelle Woghiren; Brian Wood; Tom Woods; Kelly Woodward; Stephanie Yeboah; Lola Young; Nadhim Zahawi

Company Director / Literary Agent: Rory Scarfe

Literary Agents: Emily Barrett (**L040**); Hattie Grunewald (**L254**); Rachel Petty; Ed Wood (**L609**)

L065 Blake Friedmann Literary Agency Ltd
Literary Agency
15 Highbury Place, London, N5 1QP
United Kingdom
Tel: +44 (0) 20 7387 0842

info@blakefriedmann.co.uk

http://www.blakefriedmann.co.uk
https://twitter.com/BlakeFriedmann
https://www.instagram.com/blakefriedmannliteraryagency/

Professional Body: The Association of Authors' Agents (AAA)

Fiction > *Novels*

Nonfiction > *Nonfiction Books*

Send: Query; Synopsis; Writing sample
How to send: Word file email attachment

Always on the lookout for exciting new work and welcomes submissions from both published and debut authors, across many genres, and from any background. No submissions originated, written or edited by Artificial Intelligence (AI) technology.

Associate Agent: Sian Ellis-Martin (**L180**)

Authors: Diane Abbott; Gilbert Adair; Tatamkhulu Afrika; Mary Akers; Shani Akilah; Saskia Alais; Kasim Ali; Ted Allbeury; Nikki Allen; Ros Anderson; Sally Andrew; Romalyn Ante; Graeme Armstrong; Paul Ashton; Dani Atkins; MiMi Aye; Abdul Rahman Azzam; Trezza Azzopardi; Bolu Babalola; Sandy Balfour; Johanna Bell; Tomas Bellamy; Tom Benn; Jendella Benson; Meliz Berg; Ian Birch; Rachel Blackmore; Kenny Boyle; Andy Briggs; Nora Anne Brown; Karin Brynard; Erin Bunting; Graeme Macrae Burnet; James Cahill; Karen Campbell; Edward Carey; Natasha Carthew; Elizabeth Chadwick; Fran Chang; Alex Clark; Norie Clarke; Julia Cole; Sue Cook; Anne de Courcy; Emma Cowell; Sara Crowe; Achmat Dangor; Will Dean; Tuyen Do; Michael Donkor; Finuala Dowling; Barbara Erskine; Jo Facer; Felice Fallon; Tracey Farren; Kathryn Faulke; Paul Finch; Fiona Ford; Alix Fox; Sarah Franklin; Roxy Freeman; Jean Fullerton; Janice Galloway; David Gilman; Jenny Glanfield; Lyndall Gordon; Ann Granger; Gabriella Griffith; Sarah Hartley; David Haslam; Emma Forsyth Haslett; Etienne van Heerden; Kate Hodges; Michael Hogan; Kerry Hudson; Leah Hyslop; Cormac James; Peter James; Tomasz Jedrowski; Alexandra Jellicoe; Benjamin Johncock; John Kennedy; Julie Kinn; Konditor; Charles Lambert; Kat Lister; Richard Littler; Clayton Littlewood; Anneliese Mackintosh; Ailbhe Malone; Lucy Mangan; Beryl Matthews; Zakes Mda; Deon Meyer; Lia Middleton; Nina-Sophia Miralles; Emma Mitchell; Sue Moorcroft; Grace Mortimer; Christopher Nicholson; Marlene van Niekerk; Lawrence Norfolk; Gregory Norminton; Joseph O'Connor; Sheila O'Flanagan; Kaite O'Reilly; Sara Ochs; Leeanne O'Donnell; Nina Parker; Alan Parks; Rosalind Powell; Julie Rea; Annie Robertson; Monique Roffey; Henrietta Rose-Innes; Elliot Ryan; Lora Stimson; Julian Stockwin; Kate Thompson; Mary Torjussen; Hannah Treave; John Trenhaile; Jack Urwin; Anne-Marie Varga; Luca Veste; Ivan Vladislavic; Helen Walmsley-Johnson; Bridget Walsh; Anne Watts; Jemma Wayne; Harry Whitehead; Edward Wilson-Lee; Cristina Wolf; Andrew Wong

Literary Agent: Juliet Pickering (**L473**)

Literary Agent / Managing Director: Isobel Dixon

Senior Agent: Kate Burke (**L088**)

L066 Maeve Bolger
Literary Agent
United Kingdom

mbolger@theagency.co.uk

https://theagency.co.uk
https://theagency.co.uk/the-agents/maeve-bolger/

Literary Agency: The Agency (London) Ltd (**L008**)

Scripts
  Film Scripts; Radio Scripts; TV Scripts; Theatre Scripts

Send: Writing sample
How to send: Email

Trained at RADA and worked as a Stage Manager before becoming an agent in 2016. She represents Sound Designers, Composers, Musical Directors, Set and Costume Designers, Lighting Designers and Directors in Theatre, alongside a list of Writers across all disciplines.

L067 Camilla Bolton
Literary Agent; Managing Director
United Kingdom

camilla@darleyanderson.com

https://www.darleyanderson.com/our-team
https://twitter.com/CamillaJBolton

Literary Agency: The Darley Anderson Agency (**L143**)

Fiction > *Novels*
  Book Club Fiction; Crime; Mystery; Suspense; Thrillers; Women's Fiction

How to send: Email attachment

Looking for accessible and commercial crime, thrillers, mysteries, suspense and women's fiction.

Authors: Emma Bamford; Vicki Bradley; James Carol; Gloria Cook; A J Cross; Jason Dean; Hayley Doyle; C. M. Ewan; G.R. Halliday; Egan Hughes; Emma Kavanagh; T M Logan; Imran Mahmood; L V Matthews; Phoebe Morgan; B.A. Paris; Jo Platt; Mira V. Shah; Rebecca Shaw; KL Slater; Kim Slater; Sean Slater; Catherine Steadman; G X Todd; Tim Weaver

L068 The Book Group
Literary Agency
United States
Tel: +1 (212) 803-3360

submissions@thebookgroup.com
info@thebookgroup.com

http://www.thebookgroup.com
https://www.facebook.com/thebookgrp
https://twitter.com/thebookgrp
https://www.instagram.com/thebookgrp/

Fiction > *Novels*

Nonfiction > *Nonfiction Books*

Send: Query; Writing sample
How to send: In the body of an email
How not to send: Email attachment; Post; Phone

Represents a broad range of fiction and nonfiction. No poetry or screenplays. Send query by email only with ten sample pages and the first and last name of the agent you are querying in the subject line (see website for individual agent interests). No attachments. Include all material in the body of the email. See website for full guidelines. Response only if interested.

Authors: Isabel Banta; Suhaly Bautista-Carolina; Wendy Chin-Tanner; Tiana Clark; Tracy Clark-Flory; Chloe Cole; Ella Dawson; Kimberly Drew; Susie Dumond; Lacey Dunham; Lauren Green; Taylor Hahn; Amanda Holden; Alex Hoopes; Kelly Kearsley; Melissa Larsen; Ashton Lattimore; Esther Levy-Chehebar; Dana Liebelson; Vanessa Lillie; Kristen Martin; Laura McKowen; Abi Morgan; Ava Robinson; Victoria Savanh; Sophia Shalmiyev; Rainesford Stauffer; Elissa Strauss; Noor Tagouri; Zahra Tangorra; Rachel Zarrow

Literary Agents: Julie Barer; Faye Bender; Brettne Bloom; Jamie Carr (**L101**); Dana Murphy; Elisabeth Weed

L069 Bookseeker Agency
Literary Agency
United Kingdom

bookseller@blueyonder.co.uk

https://bookseekeragency.com
https://twitter.com/BookseekerAgent

Fiction > *Novels*

Poetry > *Any Poetic Form*

Send: Query; Synopsis; Writing sample
How to send: Email

Handles fiction and (under some circumstances) poetry. No nonfiction. Send query by email outlining what you have written and your current projects, along with synopsis and sample chapter (novels).

Literary Agent: Paul Thompson

L070 Stefanie Sanchez Von Borstel
Literary Agent
United States

https://www.fullcircleliterary.com/our-agents/stefanie-von-borstel/

Literary Agency: Full Circle Literary, LLC
Professional Bodies: Society of Children's Book Writers and Illustrators (SCBWI); Association of American Literary Agents (AALA)

ADULT > **Nonfiction** > *Nonfiction Books*
Activism; Inspirational

CHILDREN'S
Fiction > *Middle Grade*
Contemporary; Historical Fiction

Poetry > *Novels in Verse*
Contemporary; History

How to send: By referral

Represents children's books from toddler to tween and select adult nonfiction. In adult nonfiction, her focus is on activism and inspiration.

L071 Sarah Bowlin
Senior Agent
Los Angeles
United States

https://aevitascreative.com/agents/
https://querymanager.com/query/S_Bowlin_queries

Literary Agency: Aevitas

Fiction > *Novels*
General, and in particular: Literary

Nonfiction > *Nonfiction Books*
General, and in particular: Comedy / Humour; Dance; Food History; History; Narrative Nonfiction; Popular Culture; Wine

Send: Query; Market info; Author bio; Writing sample
How to send: Online submission system

Focused on bold, diverse voices in fiction and nonfiction. She's especially interested in stories of strong or difficult women and unexpected narratives of place, of identity, and of the shifting ways we see ourselves and each other. She's also interested in food history, wine, and dance.

Authors: Elisa Albert; Marc Bendavid; Wendy Chen; Amanda Churchill; Caroline Corrigan; Meghan Gilliss; Nicky Gonzalez; Jasmin 'Iolani Hakes; Shane Jones; Gene Kwak; Melanie LaBarge; Cory Leadbeater; Ashley Nelson Levy; Ananda Lima; Bruna Dantas Lobato; Halimah Marcus; Sabrina Orah Mark; Kelly McClorey; Joanne McNeil; Amelia Morris; Kevin Nguyen; Mary Otis; Janika Oza; Ann Packer; Andrew Palmer; Ayşegül Savaş; Elizabeth L. Silver; Talmon Joseph Smith; Lynn Steger Strong; Souvankham Thammavongsa; Vanessa Veselka; Hope Wabuke; Jenny Xie

L072 Samantha Brace
Literary Agent
United Kingdom

sbrace@pfd.co.uk

https://petersfraserdunlop.com/agent/samantha-brace/

Literary Agency: Peters Fraser + Dunlop

Fiction > *Novels*
Book Club Fiction; Coming of Age; Crime; Family; Historical Fiction; Literary; Mystery; Psychological Suspense; Thrillers

Send: Query; Synopsis; Writing sample; Author bio
How to send: Email
How not to send: Post

I'm looking for anything a bit dark and twisty. I'm desperate for psych-suspense and thrillers with a sinister twist. I also love a mysterious family drama – weave together a moody historical setting with a few dark family secrets and I'm hooked. I also like historical fiction, coming of age stories, and literary fiction, but I always prefer a mystery at the heart. No children's, YA, fantasy, or sci-fi.

Authors: Justine Bothwick; Annette Colgan; Carol Cooper; Stephen Done; Henrietta Hamilton; Cathy Hayward; Brian Van Hise; Marianne Holmes; Evelyn Hood; Deborah Hyde; Leigh Johnstone; Mya Kwon; Ian Lewis; Carrie Maestas; Danny Noonan; Ju De Paula; John Pennington; Joshua Piercey; Rupert Potter; Cate Ray; Kerry Whittle; Agatha Zaza

L073 Bradford Literary Agency
Literary Agency
5694 Mission Center Road # 347, San Diego, CA 92108
United States
Tel: +1 (619) 521-1201

bradfordassistant@bradfordlit.com

https://bradfordlit.com

ADULT
Fiction
Graphic Novels: General
Novels: Contemporary Romance; Erotic Romance; Fantasy; Historical Romance; Literary; Mystery; Romance; Romantasy; Romantic Comedy; Romantic Suspense; Science Fiction; Supernatural / Paranormal Romance; Thrillers; Upmarket Commercial Fiction; Women's Fiction

Nonfiction > *Nonfiction Books*
Biography; Business; Comedy / Humour; Cookery; Food; History; Memoir; Parenting; Popular Culture; Relationships; Self Help; Social Issues

CHILDREN'S > **Fiction**
Graphic Novels; *Novels*; *Picture Books*
YOUNG ADULT > **Fiction** > *Novels*

How to send: Query Tracker

Represents a wide range of fiction and nonfiction. Select a particular agent at the agency to submit to, and submit to only one agent at a time.

Literary Agents: Hannah Andrade (**L015**); Laura Bradford (**L074**); Hillary Fazzari (**L188**); Rebecca Matte (**L395**); Kaitlyn Sanchez (**L516**)

L074 Laura Bradford
Literary Agent
United States

https://bradfordlit.com/about/laura-bradford/
https://querymanager.com/query/laurabradford
http://www.twitter.com/bradfordlit

Literary Agency: Bradford Literary Agency (**L073**)
Professional Bodies: Association of American Literary Agents (AALA); Romance Writers of America (RWA); Society of Children's Book Writers and Illustrators (SCBWI)

ADULT
Fiction
Graphic Novels: General
Novels: Contemporary Romance; Erotic Romance; Historical Fiction; Historical Romance; Mystery; Romance; Romantic Suspense; Speculative; Thrillers; Women's Fiction
Nonfiction > *Nonfiction Books*

CHILDREN'S > **Fiction** > *Middle Grade*

YOUNG ADULT > **Fiction** > *Novels*

How to send: Query Tracker

Interested in romance (historical, romantic suspense, category, contemporary, erotic), speculative fiction, women's fiction, mystery, thrillers, young adult, upper middle grade, illustration as well as some select non-fiction.

L075 Karen Brailsford
Consulting Agent
United States

https://aevitascreative.com/agents
https://querymanager.com/query/KarenBrailsford

Literary Agency: Aevitas

Nonfiction > *Nonfiction Books*
Arts; Biography; Entertainment; Health; Memoir; Spirituality; Wellbeing

Closed to approaches.

Based in Los Angeles and is especially interested in arts and entertainment, memoir, biography, health and wellness, spirituality and works of non-fiction that inspire and shine a light on contemporary conditions.

Authors: Daniel Morain; Toluse Olorunnipa; Robert Samuels

L076 Maria Brannan
Literary Agent
United Kingdom

maria@greyhoundliterary.co.uk

https://greyhoundliterary.co.uk
https://greyhoundliterary.co.uk/agents/maria-brannan

Literary Agency: Greyhound Literary

ADULT
  Fiction > *Novels*
    General, and in particular: Book Club Fiction; Commercial; Fantasy; Gothic; High Concept; Horror; Romance; Romantic Comedy; Soft Science Fiction; Speculative; Thrillers; Upmarket

  Nonfiction > *Nonfiction Books*
    History; Memoir; Nature; Science

NEW ADULT > **Fiction** > *Novels*
    General, and in particular: Book Club Fiction; Commercial; Fantasy; High Concept; Horror; Romance; Romantic Comedy; Soft Science Fiction; Speculative; Thrillers; Upmarket

YOUNG ADULT > **Fiction** > *Novels*
    General, and in particular: Book Club Fiction; Commercial; Fantasy; High Concept; Horror; Romance; Romantic Comedy; Soft Science Fiction; Speculative; Thrillers; Upmarket

Send: Query; Synopsis; Outline; Writing sample
How to send: Email

Has very wide ranging tastes in fiction and is interested in writing for adult, new adult/crossover and YA readers. She loves character-driven novels with a commercial bent that spark imagination or discussion and is always looking for stories that explore under-represented and diverse experiences with authenticity and sensitivity. She has a passion for genre fiction – especially all kinds of fantasy, whether that be epic, cosy, dark or romantic– that has memorable characters and vivid world-building; horror with a unique concept or perspective that can send a chill down your spine; and softer, genre-crossing science fiction that explores the experience of being human. She is also keen on voice-led and emotive reading group and upmarket fiction; love stories and rom-coms that make you fall for both the leads; unnerving, twisty crime writing; thrillers with a great hook that will leave you floored and anything with a high concept, speculative or gothic edge. On the nonfiction side, she is drawn to anything that draws the reader into the immediacy and tangibility of an author's personal experiences; history and biography that explores overlooked or underrepresented people and events; and nature and science writing that evokes fascination and wonder in the reader, books that intrigue and act as a door into underexplored or unfamiliar worlds.

Authors: Max Doty; Mike Lawson; Bonnie Quinn; C.J. Subko

L077 The Brattle Agency LLC
Literary Agency
PO Box 380537, Cambridge, MA 02238
United States

submissions@thebrattleagency.com

https://thebrattleagency.com

Fiction
  Graphic Novels: General
  Novels: Literary

Nonfiction > *Nonfiction Books*
  American History; Art History; Culture; European History; Music; Politics; Sport

Closed to approaches.

Accepts submissions only during one-month reading periods. See website for details.

L078 The Bright Agency (UK)
Literary Agency
103-105 St John's Hill, London, SW11 1SY
United Kingdom
Tel: +44 (0) 20 7326 9140

mail@thebrightagency.com
literarysubmissions@thebrightagency.com

https://thebrightagency.com
https://thebrightagency.com/uk/submissions/new

Media Company: The Bright Group International Limited
Professional Body: The Association of Authors' Agents (AAA)

CHILDREN'S
  Fiction
    Chapter Books; *Graphic Novels*; *Middle Grade*; *Picture Books*
  Nonfiction > *Nonfiction Books*

Send: Query; Synopsis; Writing sample
How to send: Email

We love seeing new work, and we'd love to see yours. Talent is exciting, and when you help it grow, it's incredible. We're proud of our ability to discover and establish new artists and authors. We're also proud that we still represent people who were with us when we first opened, and who've truly bloomed over the years. Could you be next?

L079 The Bright Agency (US)
Literary Agency
157 – A First Street, C/O – Bright Group US Inc #339, Jersey City, NJ 07302
United States
Tel: +1 (646) 525 9040

mail@thebrightagency.com
literarysubmissions@thebrightagency.com

https://thebrightagency.com
https://thebrightagency.com/us/submissions/new

Media Company: The Bright Group International Limited

CHILDREN'S
  Fiction
    Chapter Books; *Graphic Novels*; *Middle Grade*; *Picture Books*
  Nonfiction > *Nonfiction Books*

Send: Query; Synopsis; Writing sample
How to send: Email

We love seeing new work, and we'd love to see yours. Talent is exciting, and when you help it grow, it's incredible. We're proud of our ability to discover and establish new artists and authors. We're also proud that we still represent people who were with us when we first opened, and who've truly bloomed over the years. Could you be next?

L080 Savannah Brooks
Literary Agent
United States

https://www.sblitagent.com
https://ktliterary.com/about/
https://twitter.com/SBLitAgent
https://querymanager.com/query/1346

Literary Agency: KT Literary (**L345**)

ADULT > **Fiction** > *Short Fiction Collections*
  Contemporary; Horror; Mystery; Romantic Comedy; Speculative; Suspense; Thrillers

CHILDREN'S > **Fiction**
  Chapter Books; *Middle Grade*; *Picture Books*

YOUNG ADULT
  Fiction > *Novels*
  Nonfiction > *Nonfiction Books*

Closed to approaches.

Represents all of kid lit and adult contemporary and spec fiction, romcoms, thrillers/mystery/suspense, and horror. She's especially interested in stories that teach her something new, add to a larger sociopolitical conversation, and highlight underrepresented identities and cultures.

L081 Brotherstone Creative Management
Literary Agency
Mortimer House, 37-41 Mortimer Street,

London, W1T 3JH
United Kingdom

submissions@bcm-agency.com
info@bcm-agency.com

http://bcm-agency.com

Fiction > *Novels*
  Commercial; Literary

Nonfiction > *Nonfiction Books*

Send: Query; Writing sample; Synopsis
How to send: Email

Always on the search for talented new writers. Send query by email. For fiction, include the first three chapters or 50 pages and 2-page synopsis. For nonfiction, include detailed outline and sample chapter. No children's and young adult fiction, sci-fi and fantasy novels or unsolicited short story and poetry collections, or scripts.

Senior Agent / Vice President: Charlie Brotherstone (**L082**)

L082 Charlie Brotherstone

Senior Agent; Vice President
United Kingdom

https://charliebrotherstone.com
https://www.aevitascreative.com/agent/charlie-brotherstone
https://bcm-agency.com/about/

Literary Agencies: Aevitas Creative Management (ACM) UK (**L006**); Brotherstone Creative Management (**L081**)

Fiction > *Novels*
  Commercial; Literary

Nonfiction > *Nonfiction Books*

Represents an eclectic list of authors, from academics, journalists, musicians, online creators and food writers, through to novelists of commercial and literary fiction and including numerous New York Times and Sunday Times bestsellers.

Authors: Luke Agbaimoni; Susie Alegre; Rahaman Ali; Anthea Allen; Brett Anderson; Lopè Ariyo; Stephen Bayley; Osei Bonsu; Will Bowlby; Clerkenwell Boy; Will Brooker; Ian Broudie; Hannah Che; Tiffany Chen; Chris Clarke; Clare Clarke; Lauren Cochrane; Jacob Dunne; Mark Eglinton; Tracey Emerson; James Evans; Tom Fletcher; Natasha Fraser-Cavassoni; Flora Gill; Ed Gillett; Matthew Goodwin; Carrie Grant; David Grant; Gabrielle Hales; Kim-Julie Hansen; Reiko Hashimoto; Sharon Hendry; Jessica Hepburn; Dan Hicks; Fred Hogge; Kirstin Innes; Farah Karim-Cooper; Atul Kochhar; Sam Lee; Marianna Leivaditaki; Simon Lister; Roger Mavity; Elly McCausland; Joanne Molinaro; Nathan Newman; George The Poet; The Ritz; Chia WoonHeng; Ben Wright

L083 Justin Brouckaert

Literary Agent
New York
United States

https://aevitascreative.com/agents/
https://querymanager.com/query/justinbrouckaert

Literary Agency: Aevitas

Nonfiction > *Nonfiction Books*
  Current Affairs; History; Internet Culture; Narrative Nonfiction; Politics; Science; Sport

Send: Author bio; Outline; Market info; Writing sample
How to send: Query Tracker

Actively seeking narrative nonfiction in the areas of history, current affairs, sports, internet culture, politics, and science.

Authors: Char Adams; Lauren Aguirre; Matthew H. Birkhold; Greg Bluestein; Diane Cardwell; Jesselyn Cook; Susan Crawford; R.S. Deeren; Benoit Denizet-Lewis; William Deverell; Rebekah Diamond; Ali Drucker; Brian Dumaine; Ken Ellingwood; Neal E. Fischer; Marisa Franco; Sarah Gearhart; Jeffrey Gettleman; Noah Gittell; Wade Graham; Gabrielle Hartley; Jesse Horwitz; Chris Koslowski; Jacqui Lewis; Joshua Mendelsohn; Joe Milan; Luma Mufleh; Shoshi Parks; Pamela Pavliscak; Lindsay Powers; Julian Sancton; Amber Share; Meg Vondriska; Evan Waite; Bryan Walsh; Ali Marie Watkins

L084 Megan Brown

Literary Agent
United States

jsanders@stevelaube.com

https://stevelaube.com/what-im-looking-for-megan-brown/

Literary Agency: The Steve Laube Agency

Nonfiction
  Nonfiction Books: Bible Studies; Christian Living; Christianity; Evangelism; Family; Military; Spirituality
  Reference: Christianity

Closed to approaches.

I am interested in nonfiction books. Specifically, I am most excited about pursuing projects in Bible study, reference, theology, Christian living and devotionals, spiritual formation, the integration of work and faith, marriage and family, church life, ministry, leadership, evangelism, and missions.

L085 Louise Buckley

Literary Agent
United Kingdom

http://zenoagency.com
https://hs-la.com/louise-buckley/
https://twitter.com/LouiseMBuckley
https://www.instagram.com/louise_buckley_literary_agent

Literary Agency: Hannah Sheppard Literary Agency (**L262**)

Fiction > *Novels*
  Book Club Fiction; Commercial; Contemporary; Cozy Fantasy; Cozy Mysteries; Crime; Dark Academia; Disabilities; Gothic; Historical Fiction; Horror; Literary; Magic; Supernatural / Paranormal; Thrillers; Upmarket; Witches

Nonfiction > *Nonfiction Books*
  Motherhood; Neuroscience; Science

Closed to approaches.

I like literary and book-club novels that focus on the underdog, the repressed, the suppressed, especially novels that represent working-class people or children going through difficult circumstances. I am known for representing Irish literary and book-club fiction and I would very much welcome submissions from Irish authors writing upmarket fiction featuring characters that I can't help but root for. I would LOVE to see some cosy fantasy. Think witches, magical bookshops, talking cats. I am a big crime and thriller fan and welcome submissions in this area. At the moment I am especially enjoying reading cosy or humorous crime. I would love to see some dark academia. More generally, I would also love to see novels with a disabled protagonist or someone (like me) who is living with an invisible disability. In non-fiction, I would love to see any submissions that focus on motherhood, especially through the lens of a scientific or neurological perspective.

Authors: Anne Griffin; Jenni Keer; Katie Lumsden; Fíona Scarlett; Anniki Sommerville; Andrew Stevens; Claire Wright

L086 Danielle Bukowski

Literary Agent
United States

https://www.sll.com/our-team

Literary Agency: Sterling Lord Literistic, Inc.

Fiction > *Novels*

Nonfiction > *Nonfiction Books*

Send: Query; Synopsis; Writing sample
How to send: Online submission system

Represents fiction for adults, from smart bookclub to literary, and select nonfiction, Particularly looking for narratives from writers traditionally excluded from the publishing industry. For fiction, she likes books that balance plot with voice, have a strong sense of place, a unique hook, and are stylistically bold; for nonfiction, she's looking for work grounded in the author's personal interest, rigorously reported and researched, and will expand the reader's view of the world.

L087 Danielle Burby

Literary Agent
United States

https://www.madwomanliterary.com/danielleburby
https://querymanager.com/query/1352
http://www.publishersmarketplace.com/members/dburby/
https://twitter.com/DanielleBurby
https://www.facebook.com/danielle.burby

Literary Agency: Mad Woman Literary Agency (**L384**)

ADULT > Fiction
  Graphic Novels: General
  Novels: Adventure; Fairy Tales; Fantasy; Feminism; Folklore, Myths, and Legends; LGBTQIA; Social Justice; Women's Fiction
CHILDREN'S > Fiction
  Graphic Novels; *Middle Grade*; *Picture Books*
YOUNG ADULT > Fiction
  Graphic Novels; *Novels*

Closed to approaches.

I am particularly drawn to: complex female characters, seaside novels, girls with swords, magical realism, LGBTQ+ love, sister stories, toxic friendships, feminist fairytales, social justice themes, folklore, creepy forests, complicated family dynamics, quirky adventures, protagonists who change systems and break rules, heartwarming love stories, whimsy.

Authors: L. Biehler; Jillian Boehme; Kristen Ciccarelli; Jessi Cole; Lisa Duffy; Doug Engstrom; Reese Eschmann; Florence Gonsalves; Becca Jones; Chloe Jory; Ausma Zehanat Khan; Maryann Jacob Macias; Vanessa Montalban; Rosaria Munda; Jennifer Nissley; Lynette Noni; James Persichetti; Celesta Rimington; Laura Brooke Robson; Ehsaneh Sadr; Jeff Seymour; Lisa Springer; Jordyn Taylor

L088 Kate Burke

Senior Agent
United Kingdom

kate@blakefriedmann.co.uk

http://blakefriedmann.co.uk/kate-burke
https://twitter.com/kbbooks

Literary Agency: Blake Friedmann Literary Agency Ltd (**L065**)

Fiction > *Novels*
  Book Club Women's Fiction; Contemporary; Crime; Dark; Family; Gothic; High Concept Thrillers; Historical Fiction; Mystery; Thrillers; Women's Fiction

Does not want:

> **Fiction > *Novels***
> Political Thrillers; Spy Thrillers

Send: Query; Synopsis; Writing sample
How to send: Word file email attachment

My list is made up of everything I like to read – gripping fiction featuring characters you can't get enough of and whom you don't want to part with at the end of a novel. I love dark stories but also uplifting love stories, too, and I'm keen to find more stories set in unusual or far-flung places. I love to learn more about a place and its inhabitants as I think fiction is all about escapism!

In terms of what I'm looking for: on the crime side, I love dark thrillers that keep me turning the page long into the night and that surprise me with plot twists and interesting narrative structures; crime series featuring new and fresh lead investigators; high-concept thrillers (contemporary or historical) that have a 'what if?' plot structure and say something about our society now or then.

On the historical fiction side, I love stories which combine a great sense of place and time (ideally, post-1800, please) with a mystery. I'm also a huge fan of anything set in a spooky old house so Gothic, atmospheric historical thrillers are also top of my wishlist!

Contemporary-wise, I love novels which have a discussable issue at their heart – and could work well for a heated book club discussion – as well as sweeping family stories about mothers, sisters and daughters (set anywhere in the world).

In case it's helpful to know what I don't represent: non-fiction, children's and young adult books, science fiction, fantasy, spy, conspiracy or political thrillers.

Authors: Nikki Allen; Dani Atkins; Johanna Bell; Andy Briggs; Emma Cowell; Will Dean; Paul Finch; Fiona Ford; Jean Fullerton; John Kennedy; Julie Kinn; Beryl Matthews; Lia Middleton; Sara Ochs; Kate Thompson; Mary Torjussen; Hannah Treave; John Trenhaile; Anne-Marie Varga; Luca Veste

L089 Camille Burns

Literary Agent
United Kingdom

https://dkwlitagency.co.uk
https://dkwlitagency.co.uk/agents/camille/
https://querymanager.com/query/Camille

Literary Agency: Diamond Kahn and Woods (DKW) Literary Agency Ltd (**L153**)

ADULT
  Fiction > *Novels*
  Nonfiction > *Nonfiction Books*
CHILDREN'S
  Fiction > *Middle Grade*
  Nonfiction > *Nonfiction Books*
YOUNG ADULT
  Fiction > *Novels*
  Nonfiction > *Nonfiction Books*

How to send: Query Tracker

I'm looking to grow my list with a particular focus on middle grade, young adult and adult/crossover fiction, as well as non-fiction for all ages.

L090 CAA (Creative Artists Agency, LLC)

Literary Agency
2000 Avenue of the Stars, Los Angeles, CA 90067, 405 Lexington Avenue, 22nd Floor, New York, NY 10174
United States
Tel: +1 (424) 288-2000
Fax: +1 (424) 288-2900

https://www.caa.com

Literary Agency: CAA (London) (**L091**)

Literary Agent: Cindy Uh

L091 CAA (London)

Literary Agency
United Kingdom

https://www.caa.com
https://www.caa.com/entertainmenttalent/publishing

Literary Agency: CAA (Creative Artists Agency, LLC) (**L090**)
Professional Body: The Association of Authors' Agents (AAA)

ADULT
  Fiction > *Novels*
  Nonfiction > *Nonfiction Books*

CHILDREN'S > Fiction > *Picture Books*

Represents award-winning and bestselling storytellers across a wide range of disciplines. Our authors include media personalities, musicians, actors, political figures, trendsetters, and more. We take an active role in every step of the book process, from developing the concept to amplifying author platforms and launching industry-leading book tours.

L092 Analia Cabello

Associate Agent
United States

analia@andreabrownlit.com

https://www.analiacabello.com
https://www.andreabrownlit.com/Team/analia-cabello
https://querytracker.net/query/3738
https://aalitagents.org/author/analiacabello/

Literary Agency: Andrea Brown Literary Agency, Inc.
Professional Body: Association of American Literary Agents (AALA)

CHILDREN'S > Fiction
  Middle Grade: Contemporary; Magic; Magical Realism; Supernatural / Paranormal
  Picture Books: Family; Food; Gardening

YOUNG ADULT > Fiction > *Novels*
Contemporary; Magic; Magical Realism; Supernatural / Paranormal

Looking to represent picture book illustrators, authors, and author-illustrators; middle grade fiction; and young adult fiction. In all categories, she is a fan of characters who feel in-between in any sense (identity, friend groups, transitional period of life, etc.); stories of self-discovery and character growth; explorations of sibling relationships and intergenerational families; and stories from creators whose voices have been traditionally underrepresented in the industry. She values cultural specificity and stories borne from personal experience.

L093 Kimberley Cameron
Literary Agent
United States

https://kimberleycameron.com
https://kimberleycameron.com/team/
https://querymanager.com/query/kimberleycameron
https://aalitagents.org/author/bookfemme/

Literary Agency: Kimberley Cameron & Associates (**L337**)
Professional Bodies: Association of American Literary Agents (AALA); The Authors Guild

Fiction > *Novels*

Nonfiction > *Nonfiction Books*

Does not want:

Fiction > *Novels*: Romance

Closed to approaches.

Has been a successful agent for 30 years and is enjoying mentoring and fostering the careers of her agents. While working largely by referral, she's always looking for exceptional writing in any field, particularly writing that touches the heart and makes us feel something. She's found success with many different genres and especially loves the thrill of securing representation for debut authors. She represents both fiction and nonfiction manuscripts, with the exception of romance, children's books, and screenplays.

L094 Charlie Campbell
Literary Agent
United Kingdom

charlie@greyhoundliterary.co.uk
https://greyhoundliterary.co.uk/agent/charlie-campbell/
https://twitter.com/ScapegoatCC

Literary Agency: Greyhound Literary

Fiction > *Novels*
Commercial; Crime; Literary; Thrillers

Nonfiction > *Nonfiction Books*
Commercial; Economics; Literary; Sport; Travel

Send: Query; Synopsis; Writing sample
How to send: Email

Represents a wide range of fiction and non-fiction, both literary and commercial. He is looking for original work and to build long-lasting and significant careers for his clients.

Authors: Guy Adams; K Anis Ahmed; Tanya Aldred; Becky Alexander; Moeen Ali; Victoria Belim; SJ Bennett; Edward Brooke-Hitching; Andy Bull; Jen Campbell; Bonnie Chung; David Collins; Zoë Colville; Duncan Crowe; Iain Dey; Chris Dodd; Adam Fergusson; Jamie Fewery; Rebecca Fraser; Rebecca Front; Tom Gabbay; Ian Garner; Julian Gough; Omar Shahid Hamid; Scott Hesketh; David Higgins; Will Hill; Thomas W. Hodgkinson; Nicholas Hogg; Iain Hollingshead; Andrew Hosken; Simon Jones; Paul Levy; Bonnie MacBird; Charles Maclean; Shingi Mararike; Katie Marsh; Hugh Matheson; Neil McCormick; Anthony McGowan; Barry McKinley; Moin Mir; Anton Mosimann; Owain Mulligan; Rebecca Myers; James Peak; Mal Peet; Edvard Radzinsky; Sue Ransom; Amy Raphael; Andrea Stuart; Jo Thompson; Tom Tivnan; Hana Videen; Kate Vigurs; Wendy Wason; Sioned Wiliam; Mike Woodhouse

L095 Vanessa Campos
Literary Agent
United States

Vanessa@d4eo.com
https://www.d4eoliteraryagency.com/p/vanessa-campos.html
https://querymanager.com/query/Vanessa_Reads
https://twitter.com/VanessaShares

Literary Agency: D4EO Literary Agency

Nonfiction > *Nonfiction Books*
Business; Entrepreneurship; Self Help

Send: Outline; Table of contents; Writing sample; Marketing plan
How to send: Query Tracker

Looking to help bring more diverse voices to the business, entrepreneurship, and self-help publishing space.

L096 Canterbury Literary Agency
Literary Agency
43 Nunnery Fields, Canterbury, Kent, CT1 3JT
United Kingdom
Tel: +44 (0) 7947 827860

francesca@canterburyliteraryagency.com
http://www.canterburyliteraryagency.com

Fiction > *Novels*

Nonfiction > *Nonfiction Books*
Autobiography; Biography; Women's Interests

"We are based in the UK, and actively welcome submissions from writers based in the United States and Canada. We sell to publishers in the UK an in the United States and Canada, and we sell translation rights worldwide.

Founded in 2011, we pride ourselves on being a literary agency devoted to the needs of writers. We welcome all kinds of submissions, including fiction, non-fiction, memoirs, collections of short stories and collections of poems. Our aim is to respond to all submissions in no more than two weeks. We will do all we can to give you the best chance of a literary career.

We believe in transparency and friendliness and we realise that, as a writer trying to get your literary career started, you may often feel the literary world is not very friendly to you; we will be friendly and positive and will do all we can to help you.

Also, we will get back to you. At a time when you are more likely to get an email reply from Charles Dickens than from most literary agencies, we aim to get back to you within two weeks. We reply to ALL emails we receive.

We are very well connected with publishers, we understand what needs to happen with a book to take it from a draft stage to being accepted by a publisher and we spare no effort for our writer clients."

Writers should be aware that there seems to a be a strong connection between this agency and The Conrad Press, a fee-charging publishing service. Listings for both were submitted within 17 minutes of each other at around 1am of the same morning, and their logos are almost identical. The postal address provided for this agency is the same address as was originally provided for The Conrad Press (which has subsequently been changed).

The agency website states that Francesca Garratt carries out editing work for The Conrad Press, and the other agent, Helen Komatsu, is listed as an editor at Conrad Press on her LinkedIn profile.

Oddly, her profile makes no mention of being a literary agent (at this agency or otherwise), despite apparently having been involved with the agency since 2011 and her LinkedIn profile containing changes as recent as 2018, when she became an editor at Conrad Press. The agency website describes her as "a highly experienced writer and literary agent", who "has been involved with the publishing industry for more than twenty years", however her LinkedIn profile lists only PR and marketing roles prior to becoming an editor with Conrad Press in 2018. The majority of that time (over 22 years) was spent in a marketing role working for a PR firm operated by the same person who now runs Conrad Press.

A post-pandemic interview with Helen Komatsu where she discusses her past and present career also fails to make any mention of work as a literary agent (https://www.careershifters.org/success-stories/from-business-owner-to-portfolio-career).

The agency website states that she is a published author, "having written books for the Financial Times organisation, Pearson and Reuters and other well-respected publishing houses", however searches on Amazon return no results for her name. She may, of course, have published under a different name.

Given the close connection between this agency and The Conrad Press, writers should be aware of the possibility that this agency may simply be a front for The Conrad Press, intended to generate customers for their publishing services.

Writers should also note that the agency states that "Our authors prefer us to keep their names confidential". This is highly irregular and raises red flags. Agencies routinely publish lists of their clients and authors appreciate publicity. If the agency has been in operation since 2011 you would expect them to have a number of clients, and the idea that every single one of those clients would want to have their association with this agency kept secret for some reason is both hard to believe, and, if true, suspicious in itself.

In light of these concerns, we would advise against approaching this agency.

Update: *On April 2, 2023, we were contacted by James Essinger, the person who runs Conrad Press, who asked us to include the following clarification: "Helen Komatsu co-authored several books with me some years ago when her name was Helen Wylie. Here is one: https://www.amazon.com/Seven-Deadly-Skills-Competing/dp/1861523742/ref=sr_1_1?crid=3Q3ZPTPTYQ5&keywords=Essinger+Wylie&qid=1680394116&sprefix=essinger+wylie%2Caps%2C173&sr=8-1"*

L097 Victoria Cappello

Literary Agent; Vice President
United States

Literary Agency: The Bent Agency (**L052**)

Closed to approaches.

L098 Carol Mann Agency

Literary Agency
New York, NY
United States
Tel: +1 (212) 206-5635

submissions@carolmannagency.com

https://www.carolmannagency.com

Send: Query; Author bio; Writing sample
How to send: In the body of an email
How not to send: Email attachment; Post; Phone

Send query by email only, including synopsis, brief bio, and first 25 pages, all pasted into the body of your email. No attachments. No submissions by post, or phone calls. Allow 3-4 weeks for response.

Authors: Jane Alexander; Clifton Hoodl Maria Goodavage; Rachel Kelly

Literary Agents: Gareth Esersky; Carol Mann; Joanne Wyckoff

L099 Caroline Davidson Literary Agency

Literary Agency
5 Queen Anne's Gardens, London, W4 1TU
United Kingdom
Tel: +44 (0) 20 8995 5768

enquiries@cdla.co.uk

https://www.cdla.co.uk

Professional Body: The Association of Authors' Agents (AAA)

Fiction > *Novels*

Nonfiction > *Nonfiction Books*

Does not want:

> **Nonfiction** > *Nonfiction Books*
> Autobiography; Crime; Education; Memoir; Personal Experiences; Self Help; Supernatural / Paranormal; Warfare

Send: Query; Author bio; Pitch; Synopsis; Writing sample; Self-addressed stamped envelope (SASE)
How to send: Post
How not to send: Email

Send query by post only. See website for full guidelines.

Authors: Emma Donoghue; John Phibbs

Literary Agent: Caroline Davidson

L100 Carolyn Jenks Agency

Literary Agency
30 Cambridge Park Drive, #5115, Cambridge, MA 02140
United States

https://www.carolynjenksagency.com
https://www.facebook.com/carolynjenksagency
https://twitter.com/TheJenksAgency

Company Director / Literary Agent: Carolyn Jenks

Literary Agents: Kwaku Acheampong (**L003**); Becca Crandall (**L130**)

L101 Jamie Carr

Literary Agent
United States

http://www.thebookgroup.com/jamie-carr

Literary Agency: The Book Group (**L068**)

Fiction > *Novels*
Comedy / Humour; Friends; Motherhood; Relationships; Suspense

Nonfiction > *Nonfiction Books*
Culture; Finance; Food; Journalism; Judaism; Millennial; Narrative Nonfiction

Send: Query; Writing sample
How to send: In the body of an email

Represents novelists, journalists, and experts in culture, food, sobriety, finance, millennial and Jewish issues, and more. In fiction, she's drawn to stories about navigating mid-thirties and forties marriage/divorce, motherhood, and complicated friendship. She likes a book with big biting humour or big twisty suspense to also have heart. She's especially a sucker for a multi-POV story and an atmospheric setting. On the whole, she is drawn to writing that is voice-driven, highly transporting, from unique perspectives and marginalized voices, and that seeks to disrupt or reframe what appears to be known. While born and raised in New York City, she prefers stories set in other areas of the country.

Authors: Isabel Banta; Suhaly Bautista-Carolina; Wendy Chin-Tanner; Tiana Clark; Tracy Clark-Flory; Chloe Cole; Ella Dawson; Kimberly Drew; Susie Dumond; Lacey Dunham; Lauren Green; Taylor Hahn; Amanda Holden; Alex Hoopes; Kelly Kearsley; Melissa Larsen; Ashton Lattimore; Esther Levy-Chehebar; Dana Liebelson; Vanessa Lillie; Kristen Martin; Laura McKowen; Abi Morgan; Ava Robinson; Victoria Savanh; Sophia Shalmiyev; Rainesford Stauffer; Elissa Strauss; Noor Tagouri; Zahra Tangorra; Rachel Zarrow

L102 Megan Carroll

Literary Agent
United Kingdom

https://www.watsonlittle.com/agent/megan-carroll/
https://twitter.com/MeganACarroll

Literary Agency: Watson, Little Ltd (**L590**)

ADULT > **Fiction** > *Novels*
Book Club Fiction; Coming of Age; Commercial; Contemporary; Dark Humour; Family; High Concept; Romance; Romantasy; Upmarket Romance; Upmarket

CHILDREN'S
Fiction > *Middle Grade*
Adventure; Comedy / Humour; Contemporary; Fantasy

Nonfiction > *Nonfiction Books*

YOUNG ADULT > Fiction > *Novels*
Book Club Fiction; Comedy / Humour; Commercial; Contemporary; High / Epic Fantasy; Horror; Romance; Romantasy; Thrillers; Upmarket Romance

Send: Query; Synopsis; Writing sample
How to send: Word file email attachment
How not to send: PDF file email attachment

Keen to see all kinds of love stories from the very commercial through to upmarket/reading group for adults and YA readers, both contemporary and in the 'romantasy' space. She'd especially love to see those familiar romance tropes – enemies to lovers, friends to lovers, love triangles, forbidden love etc. – with underrepresented characters at the centre. Also actively looking for upmarket fiction and would love to see high concept love stories, layered family drama, coming of age narratives, contemporary stories about life today and darkly comic novels that explore a specific time, place or experience. In YA, she is keen to see contemporary stories with humour, and romance at the heart – fun and emotional novels that appeal to the interests and issues of the teenage readers. She'd also love to see thrillers and horror stories for this age group too, as well as epic fantasy as long as there is a thread of romance throughout. On the younger end, she is looking for funny, contemporary middle grade and is keen to find original adventure stories in both fantasy and realistic settings.

Authors: Luci Adams; Tom Adams; Jean Adamson; Rose Alexander; Rosie Archer; Faima Bakar; Louise Soraya Black; Kay Brellend; Laura Chamberlain; Sophie Claire; Sarah J. Coleman; Tara Costello; Bryony Cousins; Alex Day; Marianne Eloise; Lauren Ford; Tessa Gibbs; Natasha Holmes; Hayley Hoskins; Elias Jahshan; Hiba Noor Khan; Mary Mackie; Lindiwe Maqhubela; Erin Murgatroyd; Grace Newman; Briana J. Newstead; Sheila Norton; Fiona O'Brien; Ben Pechey; Rhian Parry; Will Richard; Alan Robinson; Kohinoor Sahota; Tara Sexton; Pam Weaver; Jeremy Williams; Alex Woolhouse

L103 Rebecca Carter
Literary Agent
United Kingdom

https://rebeccacarterliteraryagent.wordpress.com/
https://twitter.com/RebeccasBooks

Literary Agency: Rebecca Carter Literary (**L487**)

ADULT
Fiction > *Novels*
Crime; Experimental

Nonfiction > *Nonfiction Books*
Biography; Creative Nonfiction; Cultural Commentary; Design; Environment; History; Memoir; Politics; Social Commentary; Technology; Travel

CHILDREN'S
Fiction > *Novels*
Nonfiction > *Nonfiction Books*

L104 Claire Cartey
Literary Agent
United Kingdom

claire@holroydecartey.com

https://www.holroydecartey.com/about.html
https://www.holroydecartey.com/submissions.html

Literary Agency: Holroyde Cartey

CHILDREN'S
Fiction
Novels; Picture Books
Nonfiction > *Nonfiction Books*

Send: Synopsis; Full text
How to send: Email attachment

I have worked in children's publishing for over twenty years as Art Director at Hodder Children's Books and in design for Random House. I am looking for author and illustrator proposals for picture books, young fiction and non-fiction. In illustration I'm also looking for creative brand building potential in markets outside of publishing.

L105 Robert Caskie
Literary Agent
United Kingdom

robert@robertcaskie.com
submissions@robertcaskie.com

https://www.robertcaskie.com
https://twitter.com/rcaskie1

Literary Agency: Robert Caskie Ltd

Fiction > *Novels*
Book Club Fiction; Commercial; Literary

Nonfiction > *Nonfiction Books*
Memoir; Narrative Nonfiction; Nature; Politics; Social Issues

Send: Query; Writing sample; Proposal
How to send: Email

Interested in fiction and nonfiction writing that stimulates debate, comments on the world around us, and invokes an emotional response. Currently closed to fiction submissions, but still welcomes nonfiction submissions.

L106 Maddalena Cavaciuti
Literary Agent
United Kingdom

Literary Agency: David Higham Associates Ltd (**L146**)

L107 Claire Cavanagh
Assistant Agent
Canada

https://www.therightsfactory.com
https://www.therightsfactory.com/Agents/claire-cavanagh
https://querymanager.com/query/2784

Literary Agency: The Rights Factory

Fiction > *Novels*
High Concept; Romantic Comedy

Nonfiction > *Nonfiction Books*
Arts; Biography; Celebrity; Cultural Criticism; Culture; Fashion; History; Memoir; Popular Culture; Society

Closed to approaches.

Currently seeking non-fiction on a range of topics and select fiction. For non-fiction she is particularly interested in pop culture/celebrity, gift books, memoir/hybrid memoir, biography, history, art, fashion, cultural criticism, and society/culture. She gravitates towards insightful projects on a less explored topic particularly when done with humour and is always keen to dive into niche topics and sub-cultures, including pop culture obsessions and analyses or insights into real or imagined communities. For fiction, she is currently only accepting rom coms. She loves high concept rom coms with an emphasis on the com and is always hoping to read something unique or less explored in this genre.

Authors: Gurki Basra; Ashley Cowan; Fia Dahlia; Tracy Greenan; Sam Hogerton; C.R. Johnston; Jenny Lewis; Callie Rae O'Reilly; Lindsay Pereira; Seema Punwani

L108 Sonali Chanchani
Literary Agent
United States

sonali@foliolit.com

https://www.foliolit.com/agents-1/sonali-chanchani

Literary Agency: Folio Literary Management, LLC (**L207**)
Professional Body: Association of American Literary Agents (AALA)

Fiction > *Novels*
Book Club Fiction; Coming of Age; Family; Friends; Literary Mystery; Literary; Speculative; Thrillers; Women's Fiction

Nonfiction > *Nonfiction Books*
Culture; Ethnic Groups; Gender; Investigative Journalism; Narrative Nonfiction; Politics; Social Class; Social Justice; Society

Send: Query; Writing sample
How to send: In the body of an email

In fiction, she is looking for literary fiction and book club fiction with a strong, distinctive voice. She's particularly interested in smart, funny coming of age novels; braided narratives of friendship or family; literary mysteries; and atmospheric stories with a speculative or fabulist twist. She loves novels that subvert dominant cultural narratives and engage with themes of identity, belonging, community, inheritance, and diaspora. In nonfiction, she is looking for narratives and collections that illuminate some aspect of our society or culture with an eye towards social justice. She is especially drawn to investigative journalism and deeply researched narratives that advance our current conversations about race, class, gender, and politics.

L109 Nicola Chang
Literary Agent
United Kingdom

nicolachang@davidhigham.co.uk
nicolasubmissions@davidhigham.co.uk

https://www.davidhigham.co.uk/agents-dh/nicola-chang/

Literary Agency: David Higham Associates Ltd (**L146**)

Fiction
 Novels: General, and in particular: Friends; Historical Fiction; Literary Thrillers; Literary; Romance; Saga
 Short Fiction Collections: General

Nonfiction > *Nonfiction Books*
 Cookery; Food

Poetry > *Any Poetic Form*

Send: Query; Writing sample
How to send: Email

On the lookout for precise, perspicacious books that examine and play with selfhood and the nature of identity; novel approaches to love stories; fiction set in decades gone by; stories that unspool over generations; literary thrillers; fiction about friends; writing with a global, transnational sensibility; places and characters not often represented in literature; stories concerning community and society; select short story collections; cookbooks—beautiful, timeless texts and recipes that are returned to again and again; food writing—what we do and don't think about when we are in the kitchen, around the dining table, on the sofa and eating out.

Authors: Ore Agbaje-Williams; Sara Ahmed; Rosanna Amaka; Raymond Antrobus; Amman Brar; Symeon Brown; Stephen Buoro; Vanessa Chan; Jacqueline Crooks; Tsitsi Dangarembga; Subhadra Das; Melissa Franklin; Nikita Gill; Emma Glass; Will Harris; Angela Hui; Bhanu Kapil; Huw Lemmey; Momtaza Mehri; Anna Metcalfe; Emma-Lee Moss; Riaz Phillips; Leone Ross; Saba Sams; Lisa Smith; Kae Tempest; Hanna Thomas Uose; Varaidzo; Christian Weaver; Mandy Yin

L110 Edwina de Charnace
Literary Agent
United Kingdom

https://mmbcreative.com/agents/edwina-de-charnace/

Literary Agency: Mulcahy Sweeney Literary Agency (**L423**)

Fiction in Translation > *Novels*

Fiction > *Novels*
 Dark Humour; East Asia; Family Saga; Horror; Psychological Thrillers; Romantasy

Nonfiction in Translation > *Nonfiction Books*

Nonfiction > *Nonfiction Books*
 Art History; East Asia; Investigative Journalism; Literature; Personal Development; Self Help

Send: Query; Author bio; Synopsis; Writing sample
How to send: Email

Her Korean heritage and upbringing in Asia explain her soft spot for writing from or about East Asia in both original English and in translation. At the top of her present wishlist are family sagas, stories spanning multiple generations, horror amplified (rather than lightened) by dark humour, fantasy with romance (rather than romance with fantasy), socially-inflected psychological thrillers, expert-led non-fiction in self-help/personal development, investigative journalism on topics related to the beauty industry (like plastic surgery) and writing by academics on art history and non-canonical literature.

L111 Jennifer Chevais
Associate Agent
Canada

https://www.therightsfactory.com/Agents/Jennifer-Chevais/
https://querymanager.com/query/JChevais
https://twitter.com/jchevais

Literary Agency: The Rights Factory

ADULT
 Fiction > *Novels*
  Fantasy; Horror; Science Fiction; Thrillers
 Nonfiction > *Nonfiction Books*

CHILDREN'S > **Fiction** > *Novels*

How to send: Query Tracker

A generalist with a strong interest in commercial horror, speculative fiction, as well as children's fiction and "just the right fit" nonfiction project. As a generalist she is primarily drawn to character-driven stories peopled by characters so strong they'll either break your heart or pull it right out of your body.

Authors: Amanda Burnham; Tal Cohen; Drew Dotson; Adam Hossein Fuller; Greta Kelly; A. A. Livingston; Dan Livingston; Dan Malossi; Damascus Mincemeyer; Tammy Plunkett; Markus Redmond; Christopher Rippee; Emma Sachsse; Mark David Smith; Lauren Roedy Vaughn; Karen Yates

L112 Children's Books North Agency
Literary Agency
United Kingdom

submissions@childrensbooksnorthagency.co.uk

https://www.childrensbooksnorthagency.co.uk
https://bsky.app/profile/cbnagency.bsky.social
https://www.instagram.com/childrensbooksnorthagency_
https://x.com/CBNAgency
https://www.linkedin.com/company/children-s-books-north-agency

Professional Body: The Association of Authors' Agents (AAA)

CHILDREN'S
 Fiction
  Chapter Books; *Graphic Novels*; *Middle Grade*; *Picture Books*
 Nonfiction > *Illustrated Books*

Send: Query; Synopsis; Full text; Author bio
How to send: Email

Represents authors, illustrators and author-illustrators, and specialises in picture books, pre-school, illustrated non-fiction, young fiction and graphic novels. Accepts submissions from debut and established authors and illustrators who are based in the north of England (Northwest, Northeast and Yorkshire) and Scotland.

L113 Danielle Chiotti
Literary Agent
United States

danielle.submission@gmail.com

https://www.upstartcrowliterary.com/agents/danielle-chiotti

Literary Agency: Upstart Crow Literary

ADULT
 Fiction > *Novels*
  Literary; Upmarket Commercial Fiction
 Nonfiction > *Nonfiction Books*
  Comedy / Humour; Cookery; Current Affairs; Food; Lifestyle; Memoir; Narrative Nonfiction; Relationships; Wine

CHILDREN'S > **Fiction** > *Middle Grade*

YOUNG ADULT > **Fiction** > *Novels*

How to send: Email

For adult fiction, she is seeking upmarket commercial fiction and literary fiction. She prefers books that explore deep emotional relationships in an interesting or unusual way.

For middle grade and YA: She is actively seeking fresh young adult and middle grade fiction across all genres. She is drawn toward gorgeous writing and strong, flawed characters. Her dream project for young readers is one that challenges and inspires, with a compelling voice that will make her stay up all night reading.

For nonfiction: she is looking for compelling, voice-driven projects that shed a humorous or thought-provoking light on a previously unknown topic in the areas of narrative nonfiction/memoir, lifestyle, relationships, humor, current events, food, wine, and cooking.

L114 Catherine Cho
Literary Agent; Author
United Kingdom

https://www.paperliterary.com/submissions-catherine/
https://twitter.com/catkcho

Literary Agencies: Paper Literary; C&W (Conville & Walsh)
Literary Agent: Sophie Lambert (**L348**)

ADULT
  Fiction > *Novels*
    Book Club Fiction; Family; Folklore, Myths, and Legends; High Concept; Historical Fiction; Literary; Magical Realism; Multicultural; Relationships; Speculative; Suspense
  Nonfiction > *Nonfiction Books*: Narrative Nonfiction

YOUNG ADULT > **Fiction** > *Novels*: Fantasy

Send: Query; Synopsis; Writing sample

Originally from Kentucky. After a background in law and public affairs, she began her publishing career in New York at Folio Literary Management before moving to London.

L115 Erica Christensen
Senior Agent
United States

https://www.metamorphosisliteraryagency.com/about
https://querymanager.com/query/ericachristensen
https://twitter.com/literaryerica

Literary Agency: Metamorphosis Literary Agency (**L406**)

ADULT > **Fiction** > *Novels*
  Romance; Thrillers

YOUNG ADULT > **Fiction** > *Novels*
  Contemporary; Romance

Does not want:

> **ADULT** > **Fiction** > *Novels*
>   Historical Romance; Supernatural / Paranormal Romance
> **YOUNG ADULT** > **Fiction** > *Novels*
>   Historical Romance; Supernatural / Paranormal Romance

Closed to approaches.

Only open to SUBSIDIARY RIGHTS queries for established Romance and Thriller authors (Self-Published/Indie and Traditional) who retain the subsidiary rights (audio, foreign, gaming, film/tv) for their book(s). The book(s) must have a minimum of 50 reviews. Please include your Amazon author page and Goodreads page in the Bio section.

L116 Jennifer Christie
Literary Agent
United Kingdom
Tel: +44 (0) 7971 268342

jen@grahammawchristie.com

https://www.grahammawchristie.com
https://www.grahammawchristie.com/about

Literary Agency: Graham Maw Christie Literary Agency (**L246**)

Nonfiction > *Nonfiction Books*
  General, and in particular: Business; Comedy / Humour; Economics; History; Memoir; Personal Development; Personal Experiences; Philosophy; Popular Science; Psychology; Science; Social Issues

Send: Outline; Author bio; Market info; Writing sample
How to send: Email

Interests are wide ranging, from popular science, philosophy and humour to business and memoir.

L117 Kayla Cichello
Literary Agent
United States

kayla.submission@gmail.com

https://www.upstartcrowliterary.com/agents/kayla-cichelloa
https://twitter.com/SeriousKayla

Literary Agency: Upstart Crow Literary

ADULT > **Fiction** > *Novels*
  Contemporary Romance; Upmarket

CHILDREN'S > **Fiction**
  Middle Grade: General
  Picture Books: Comedy / Humour

YOUNG ADULT > **Fiction** > *Novels*
  Commercial; Dark Humour; Literary; Magical Realism; Mystery; Romance; Romantic Comedy; Suspense

Closed to approaches.

Open to picture books through YA and illustrators, and select adult manuscripts in the upmarket and contemporary romance categories. She is searching for those voices that make her laugh and keep the page turning.

L118 Caro Clarke
Literary Agent
United Kingdom

submissions@portobelloliterary.co.uk
https://www.portobelloliterary.co.uk

Literary Agency: Portobello Literary (**L479**)

Fiction > *Novels*
  Crime; Fantasy; Literary; Speculative

Nonfiction
  Essays: General
  Nonfiction Books: Cookery; Culture; Food; Intersectional Feminism; LGBTQIA; Memoir; Narrative Nonfiction; Nature; Popular Science; Travel

Send: Synopsis; Author bio; Writing sample
How to send: Email
How not to send: Post

I am actively building a list of authors writing fiction and non-fiction. I have very broad taste in fiction and I'm attracted to excellent writing, clever plots, unusual settings and complex characters. I love all types of stories from niche literary novels, to speculative fiction and fantasy, gripping crime and novels with wide appeal. I am partial to fiction that transports you, steals your heart and makes you think. On the non-fiction side, I'm looking for narrative non-fiction, memoir, popular science, big ideas, travel, culture, essays, queer culture and intersectional feminism. I'm also interested in food writing and cookbooks. I have a particular soft spot for nature writing of any type. What I look for in non-fiction are fascinating topics, a unique perspective or one that disrupts the status quo and an engaging voice. Most of all, I'm looking for writers who are passionate about the topic of their book.

Authors: Polly Atkin; Victoria Bennett; Meg Bertera-Berwick; Fiona Black; Gill Booles; Rachel Charlton-Dailey; Mona Dash; Samantha Dooey-Miles; Harry Josephine Giles; CL Hellisen; Lindsay Johnstone; Aefa Mulholland; JC Niala; Andrés N. Ordorica; Wendy Pratt; Adam Ramsay; Christina Riley; Maud Rowell; Elspeth Wilson

L119 Catherine Clarke
Literary Agent; Managing Director
United Kingdom

https://felicitybryan.com/fba-agent/catherine-clarke/

Literary Agency: Felicity Bryan Associates (**L192**)

ADULT > **Nonfiction** > *Nonfiction Books*
  Biography; History; Memoir; Nature; Philosophy

CHILDREN'S > **Fiction** > *Novels*

I have been building a list of adult non-fiction and children's fiction writers since 2001. In non-fiction, I particularly love history and philosophy and biography, especially from authors who have the academic credentials or expertise but also have the ambition and vision and writerly skill to make us see their subjects in a new light, or to overturn received wisdom. I also love outstanding nature writing with a dash of compelling memoir.

Authors: Samira Ahmed; David Almond; Karen Armstrong; Lucy Ash; James Attlee; Katya Balen; James Barr; David Barrie; John Barton; John Batchelor; Erica Benner; Claire Bertschinger; Paul Betts; Michael Bird; Elleke Boehmer; Stella Botchway; John Bowker; Susan Brigden; Adam Brookes; Matthew Burton; Nick Chater; Morten H. Christiansen; Liza Cody; Artemis Cooper; Chloe Daykin; John Dickie; Jenny Downham; Natasha Farrant; Edmund Fawcett; Catherine Fletcher; CJ Flood; Peter Frankopan; Lawrence Freedman; Clare Furniss; Sally Gardner; Robert Gildea; Jonathan Glover; Chris Gosden; Barbara Graziosi; Thomas Halliday; Peter Heather; Louis Hill; Penelope Hobhouse; Alice Hunt; Kathryn Hurlock; Belinda Jack; Lauren St John; Colin Jones; Alex Kaiserman; Liz Kessler; Katherine Langrish; Lucy Lethbridge; John Lister-Kaye; Jonathan Loh; Diarmaid Macculloch; Laurie Maguire; Toby Matthiesen; James Mcdougall; Chris Mcgrath; Kate Mcloughlin; Martin Meredith; Tom Moorhouse; Katy Moran; Natasha Narayan; James Naughtie; Linda Newbery; TN Ninan; Adjoa Osei; Richard Ovenden; Joanne Owen; Thomas Penn; Andrew Pettegree; Jonathan Phillips; Annabel Pitcher; Rachel Polonsky; Andrew Prentice; Sue Prideaux; Diane Purkiss; Josephine Quinn; Owen Rees; Thomas Rid; Ritchie Robertson; Eugene Rogan; Meg Rosoff; Miri Rubin; Ulinka Rublack; Alec Ryrie; Joseph Sassoon; Paul Seabright; Alom Shaha; Liam Shaw; Emma Smith; Lexi Stadlen; Marc Stears; Roy Strong; Julie Summers; Krystal Sutherland; Eleanor Updale; Christopher Vick; Arthur Der Weduwen; Jonathan Weil; Anna Whitelock; Tim Whitmarsh; K.J. Whittaker; Lisa Williamson; Michael Wood; Lucy Wooding; Lucy Worsley; Jessica Wärnberg

L120 Alexander Cochran
Literary Agent
United Kingdom

alexander@greyhoundliterary.co.uk

https://greyhoundliterary.co.uk/agents/alexander-cochran
https://instagram.com/agentalexcochran

Literary Agency: Greyhound Literary

Fiction > *Novels*
 Crime; Dark Thrillers; Fantasy; Literary; Science Fiction; Speculative; Thrillers

Nonfiction > *Nonfiction Books*

Send: Query; Synopsis; Writing sample
How to send: Email

Actively building his list and is always on the lookout for new writers of speculative fiction, literary fiction, crime and thriller and serious non-fiction. His tastes range widely, and in fiction he's particularly interested in dark thrillers and crime novels, sci-fi and fantasy that push boundaries or cross genres, but are rooted in the believable, playful literary fiction, and novels that don't shy away from the darker aspects of humanity. On the non-fiction side, he tends towards the serious and is looking for books with big ideas that subvert our assumptions, serious histories, and narrative non-fiction with a focus on contemporary events and issues.

Authors: G. V. Anderson; Luke Arnold; J. S. Barnes; Nicholas Binge; Charlotte Bond; Morgana Bourggraff; Letty Butler; Eliza Chan; Hiron Ennes; Rebecca Ferrier; Jasmin Kirkbride; Oliver K. Langmead; Hannah Little; Will Maclean; Mohale Mashigo; Ed McDonald; Tobi Ogundiran; Ely Percy; Dan Pinchbeck; Alison Rumfitt; Luke Scull; Priya Sharma; Tade Thompson; Matt Wixey; Marian Womack; Eris Young

L121 Charlotte Colwill
Literary Agent
United Kingdom

submissions@colwillandpeddle.com
https://www.colwillandpeddle.com/about

Literary Agency: Colwill & Peddle

ADULT > **Fiction** > *Novels*
 General, and in particular: Comedy / Humour; Crime; Horror; Literary Horror; Literary; Romance

CHILDREN'S
Fiction > *Novels*

Nonfiction
 Middle Grade: Real Life Stories
 Nonfiction Books: General

YOUNG ADULT
Fiction > *Novels*
 Contemporary; Fantasy; High Concept

Nonfiction > *Nonfiction Books*: Real Life Stories

Send: Query; Synopsis; Writing sample; Author bio; Market info; Outline

Looking for adult fiction and children's fiction and non-fiction.

Always looking for fiction with a unique voice and compelling story, with something new to say. Loves unusual perspectives, dark twists and sharp writing. Particularly on the lookout for smart romance with an edge, really fresh and page-turning crime fiction, horror and literary horror with a contemporary resonance and literary fiction that is funny and moving, with a brand-new hook.

In children's books she is open to both fiction and non-fiction for all ages, from chapter books to Young Adult. At the moment she is really looking for a funny and engaging author/illustrator with a fresh new series for young readers (5+), middle grade fiction with a new hook, brilliant world-building and characters we haven't seen before, and in YA she's looking for homegrown fantasy fiction, high concept contemporary stories and books about unusual relationships. In children's non-fiction she'd love to see books that tackle curriculum subjects in a brand new and super engaging way, and real-life stories for middle grade and YA readers.

No picture books or submissions from the USA.

L122 Chris Combemale
Associate Agent
United States

https://www.sll.com
https://www.sll.com/christopher-combemale

Literary Agency: Sterling Lord Literistic, Inc.

Fiction > *Novels*
 Literary; Upmarket

Nonfiction > *Nonfiction Books*
 Cultural Criticism; Narrative Nonfiction

Send: Query; Synopsis; Proposal; Writing sample
How to send: Online submission system

Looking for a broad range of literary fiction and voice driven upmarket fiction with an unexpected hook. He is on the hunt for a literary campus novel. In non-fiction he is interested in narrative nonfiction, cultural criticism/essay, and expert-driven projects.

L123 Andrea Comparato
Literary Agent
United States

andrea@inscriptionsliterary.com

https://inscriptionsliterary.com/agents/
https://aalitagents.org/author/acomparato/
https://www.publishersmarketplace.com/members/inscriplit/
https://querymanager.com/query/InscriptionsLit_Query

Literary Agency: Inscriptions Literary Agency (**L289**)
Professional Body: Association of American Literary Agents (AALA)

ADULT
 Fiction > *Novels*
  Mystery; Suspense

 Nonfiction > *Nonfiction Books*: Memoir

CHILDREN'S
Fiction
 Middle Grade; *Picture Books*
Scripts > *Film Scripts*

How to send: Query Tracker

All manuscript submissions should be sent through Query Manager.

L124 Compass Talent
Literary Agency
New York, NY
United States
Tel: +1 (646) 822-4691

https://www.compasstalent.com
https://x.com/CompassTalentNY

ADULT
  Fiction > *Novels*

  Nonfiction > *Nonfiction Books*
    General, and in particular: Food; Journalism; Memoir; Science; Technology

YOUNG ADULT > Fiction > *Novels*

Literary agency in NYC, specializing in non-fiction, fiction, YA, food writing, memoir, journalism, and science and technology. No phone calls about submissions.

Literary Agent: Heather Schroder

L125 Claire Paterson Conrad
Literary Agent; Company Director
United Kingdom

http://www.janklowandnesbit.co.uk/node/671

Literary Agency: Janklow & Nesbit UK Ltd (**L297**)

Fiction > *Novels*
  Commercial; Experimental; Feminism; Literary

Nonfiction > *Nonfiction Books*
  Biology; Creative Nonfiction; Environment; Nature; Popular Science

Send: Query; Synopsis; Writing sample; Outline
How to send: Email
How not to send: Post

In fiction, I work across upmarket commercial to literary fiction and mistrust pigeon-holing books into genres. I'm actively looking to take on distinctive fiction which is voice or character driven; a strong hook or unusual perspective is always a bonus. I'm currently keen to find an all-consuming multi-generational novel or gripping love stories, particularly if it's warm-hearted and wise. I'd also like to find more novels that make you laugh out loud, and fiction that subverts the norm, even in subtle ways. I love beautifully written literary fiction that has a strong sense of place, feminist fiction with a revisionary twist and experimental novels that play with structure or form, especially when this is used to illuminate the complexities of human experience. I'd particularly like to hear from novelists who have started writing later in life.

In non-fiction, currently, I'm looking for writers who show us new ways of looking at things or help us understand the world better, or books that start conversations and change minds. I'm also passionate about finding and amplifying voices from under-represented backgrounds. I'm looking for memoir and narrative non-fiction by writers, journalists or historians who can retell fascinating stories or little-known periods of history. I'm searching for good food writing and books about the food system, or books that highlight our need to protect and care for our precious planet, especially nature writing. I'm looking for books that are a call to arms for other issues of our day, ones that challenge orthodoxies in ways that aren't necessarily prescriptive. I'd love to find more good popular science writing, written by great communicators. Lastly, I'm a huge fan of non-fiction that melds genres.

L126 Clare Conville
Literary Agent
United Kingdom
Tel: +44 (0) 20 7393 4203

convilleoffice@cwagency.co.uk

https://cwagency.co.uk/agent/clare-conville

Literary Agency: C&W (Conville & Walsh)

Fiction > *Novels*
  Comedy / Humour; Family; Literary

Nonfiction > *Nonfiction Books*
  General, and in particular: Memoir

How to send: Email

Currently looking for an engrossing literary novel; a funny, compelling novel about family dynamics; expert-led nonfiction; and memoir that makes you rethink your place in the world.

Authors: Dolly Alderton; Damian Barr; Neil Bartlett; Francesca Beauman; Matt Beaumont; Greta Bellamacina; Patrick Benson; James Birch; Immodesty Blaize; Louisa Buck; Rachel Campbell-Johnston; Roger Clarke; Miriam Darlington; Katie Davies; Chris Difford; Rory Dunlop; Peter Dunne; Allie Esiri; Penelope Farmer; Esther Freud; Jasper Gibson; Misha Glenny; Kirsty Gunn; Matt Haig; Lou Hamilton; Debora Harding; Michael Hodges; Antonia Hodgson; Merlin Holland; Rob Lloyd Jones; Rachel Joyce; Sadakat Kadri; Abraham Kawa; David Keenan; Stephen Kelman; Katie Kitamura; Gerad Kite; Harriet Kline; Persia Lawson; P J Lynch; Celia Lyttelton; Robert McCrum; Sam Mckechnie; Harland Miller; Joshua Mowll; Juliet Nicolson; Sydney Padua; Kit Peel; Megan Peel; DBC Pierre; Huw Powell; Paula Rawsthorne; Lydia Ruffles; Polly Samson; Yasmine Seale; Lemn Sissay; Richard Skinner; Sofia Slater; Mark Stevens; Annalyn Swan; Piers Torday; Pádraig Ó Tuama; Jon Lys Turner; Emma Jane Unsworth; Steve Voake; Harriet Vyner; Max Wallis; Amanda Eyre Ward; S J Watson; Ben Wilson; Robert Wilton; Isabel Wolff; Osman Yousefzada

L127 Clare Coombes
Literary Agent
United Kingdom

https://www.liverpool-literary.agency/about

Literary Agency: The Liverpool Literary Agency (**L369**)

Fiction > *Novels*
  General, and in particular: Crime; Historical Fiction; Psychological Thrillers; Women's Fiction

Would love to see historical fiction, crime fiction, psychological thrillers and women's fiction, but as a new agent, she is open to all great writing with a strong hook in any area (excluding non-fiction, children's and YA).

L128 Gemma Cooper
Literary Agent
United Kingdom

https://www.gemmacooperliterary.com
https://www.gemmacooperliterary.com/about-us

Literary Agency: Gemma Cooper Literary (**L228**)

ADULT > Fiction > *Novels:* Cozy Crime

CHILDREN'S > Fiction
  Chapter Books: General, and in particular: High Concept
  Graphic Novels: General
  Middle Grade: General, and in particular: Adventure; Comedy / Humour; Fantasy; Historical Fiction; Mystery

YOUNG ADULT > Fiction
  Graphic Novels: General
  Novels: Contemporary; Family; Friends; High Concept; Historical Fiction; Mystery; Romantic Comedy; Speculative; Thrillers

I adore middle-grade fiction and have the widest taste in this readership: anything from mystery to fantasy, historical to funny, adventure stories to serious topics, verse, illustrated, animal perspectives and everything in between. Really, any middle-grade novel with a strong voice and/or a big hook will get my attention. Bonus points if it's also funny.

In young adult fiction, I want contemporary novels – I'd love a rom-com with a hook, or something high-concept with strong friendships or sibling relationships, or a mystery or thriller. I will consider historical novels if they have action or a good murder. I'm not the agent for YA fantasy but will consider light speculative fiction with a twist.

I enjoy high-concept funny chapter books with series potential aimed at ages 7+. I'm also looking for graphic novels across all ages of children's and YA. I am not currently taking on picture books clients and will not reply to these submissions.

Right now, I'm only open to the following adult genres: cosy crime, smart contemporary crime with humour, crime with a fantasy twist, and crime with a sci-fi spin like murder on a spaceship.

L129 Maggie Cooper
Literary Agent
Boston, MA
United States

https://aevitascreative.com/agents/
https://querymanager.com/query/cooper

Literary Agency: Aevitas

Fiction > *Novels*
  Cozy Fantasy; Fabulism; Feminist Romance; Historical Fiction; LGBTQIA; Literary; Magical Realism

Nonfiction > *Nonfiction Books*
  Climate Science; Creative Nonfiction; Culture; Food; Gender; Social Justice; Sustainable Living

Closed to approaches.

I'm seeking imaginative, genre-bending literary fiction; beautifully told queer stories; and smart, feminist vacation reads. I love retellings of classic stories, epistolary novels, and well-earned happy endings. I don't typically work on "hard" science fiction and fantasy, although I'm drawn to stories that blend the realist and speculative in the traditions of magical realism, fabulism, or otherwise—and right now, I'm very open to seeing cozy or quirky fantasy, especially if it overlaps with my other interests. I'm particularly attracted to structural innovation, language that makes the reader pause over its peculiar specificity, and books that make our world a weirder, kinder, and/or more joyful place.

In nonfiction, I'm looking for graphic projects with a literary sensibility, self-aware creative nonfiction, and projects with a quirky, joyful, or humorous bent. Across genres, I'm always interested in food, literary culture, gender, sustainability and climate crisis, social justice, schools and education, and projects that engage our current cultural moment, whether directly or slantwise.

Authors: Emma Ahlqvist; Will Betke-Brunswick; Zoë Bossiere; Rita Zoey Chin; Marisa Crane; Carla Fernandez; JR Ford; Vanessa Ford; Andrew J. Graff; Rebecca Kling; Hali Lee; Rue Mapp; Jessica Martin; Katie Mitchell; Carolyn Prusa; Allegra Rosenberg; Margie Sarsfield; Nina Sharma; Jack Shoulder; Mark Small; Julia Ridley Smith; June Thomas

L130 Becca Crandall
Literary Agent
United States

carolyn@carolynjenksagency.com

https://www.carolynjenksagency.com/agent/BECCA-CRANDALL

Literary Agency: Carolyn Jenks Agency (**L100**)

ADULT
  Fiction
    Graphic Novels; *Novels*
  Nonfiction > *Nonfiction Books*

CHILDREN'S > **Fiction**
  Middle Grade; *Picture Books*
YOUNG ADULT > **Fiction** > *Novels*

Closed to approaches.

L131 Creative Roots Studio
Literary Agency
United Kingdom

https://www.creativerootsstudio.com
https://x.com/Creative_Roots_
https://www.instagram.com/creative.roots.studio
https://www.linkedin.com/company/creativerootsstudio/

Professional Body: The Association of Authors' Agents (AAA)

CHILDREN'S > **Fiction** > *Picture Books*

Send: Query; Author bio
How to send: Online contact form
How not to send: Post

Costs: Offers services that writers have to pay for. Offers coaching sessions starting at £100 for one-hour sessions.

We're building sustainable, long-term careers for children's book creatives. We developed the three pillars of our business specifically for authors, illustrators and publishing professionals, to maximise creativity, industry knowledge and the opportunity for success. We only accept submissions from traditionally published authors and illustrators. However, we do open our submissions to self-published and non-published creatives from time to time. Please check our social media for these dates and/or subscribe to our newsletter. For published creatives, please enquire using our contact form, telling us a bit about you and your publishing career, including a list of your published books and the publishers you've worked with. Unfortunately, we do not accept physical submissions via post or courier.

L132 Sheila Crowley
Literary Agent
United Kingdom

crowleyofficesubmissions@curtisbrown.co.uk

https://curtisbrown.co.uk
https://curtisbrown.co.uk/agent/sheila-crowley

Literary Agency: Curtis Brown (**L135**)

Fiction > *Novels*
  Book Club Fiction; Commercial; Family; Mystery; Romance; Saga; Suspense; Thrillers

Nonfiction > *Nonfiction Books*

Send: Query; Author bio; Writing sample; Proposal
How to send: Email

I represent a wide range of authors from award-winning novelists to million-copy-selling non-fiction writers. Authors are at the centre of everything I do as an agent – one of the best things about the job is working closely with writers across all stages of the publishing process. I am looking for the best new talent in bookclub and commercial fiction, be that an epic romance, family drama, transporting saga or a page-turning thriller. As well as helping debut authors launch a publishing career, I'm also interested in taking on published writers who may want to reinvigorate their career or change direction.

L133 Curious Minds
Literary Agency
Scheideweg 34C, Hamburg, 20253
Germany

info@curiousmindsagency.com

https://curiousmindsagency.com
https://x.com/curiouslitag

Professional Body: The Association of Authors' Agents (AAA)

ACADEMIC > **Nonfiction** > *Nonfiction Books*
  General, and in particular: Health; History; Mathematics; Medicine; Nature; Philosophy; Science; Technology

ADULT > **Nonfiction** > *Nonfiction Books*
  General, and in particular: Health; History; Mathematics; Medicine; Nature; Philosophy; Science; Technology

Send: Query; Proposal; Pitch; Market info; Author bio; Table of contents; Writing sample
Don't send: Full text
How to send: Email

We represent authors writing about the sciences, as well as mathematics, natural history, philosophy, health and medicine, technology, history and many other areas of nonfiction.

Literary Agents: Jeff Shreve; Tisse Takagi; Peter Tallack

L134 Sabhbh Curran
Literary Agent
United Kingdom

sabhbh.curran@curtisbrown.co.uk

http://submissions.curtisbrown.co.uk/agents/

Literary Agency: Curtis Brown (**L135**)

Fiction > *Novels*
Book Club Fiction; Dark; Historical Fiction; Literary; Psychological Suspense

Nonfiction > *Nonfiction Books*
Art History; Arts; Current Affairs; Fashion; Food; History; Mind, Body, Spirit; Narrative Nonfiction; Popular Culture; Popular Science; Psychology; Travel

Send: Query; Synopsis; Writing sample; Proposal
How to send: Email

I am on the hunt for literary, book club fiction and psychological suspense fiction. What I look for is well-crafted and stylish prose, complex characterisations and probably at least a hint of darkness: obsessive friendships and relationships; loneliness; trauma; dysfunctional families; the strangeness of urban life. I'm also drawn to beautifully written, researched and evoked historical fiction.

In non-fiction, I'm particularly keen to hear from chefs, mixologists and food writers but I am also interested in narrative non-fiction, history, travel writing, current affairs, popular science, psychology, MBS, fashion and popular culture. I would like to hear from non-fiction writers (especially journalists and activists) who speak to a younger audience. I have a real soft spot for anything related to art or art history, whatever the genre.

L135 Curtis Brown

Literary Agency
Cunard House, 15 Regent Street, London, SW1Y 4LR
United Kingdom
Tel: +44 (0) 20 7393 4400

info@curtisbrown.co.uk

https://www.curtisbrown.co.uk
http://submissions.curtisbrown.co.uk/

Professional Body: The Association of Authors' Agents (AAA)
Literary Agency: United Talent Agency (UTA)

ADULT
Fiction > *Novels*
General, and in particular: Commercial Women's Fiction; Crime; Erotic; Historical Fiction; Horror; Literary; Memoir; Romance; Thrillers

Nonfiction > *Nonfiction Books*

Scripts
Film Scripts; *TV Scripts*; *Theatre Scripts*

CHILDREN'S > Fiction
Early Readers: General
Middle Grade: General, and in particular: Fantasy; Science Fiction
Picture Books: General

YOUNG ADULT > Fiction > *Novels*
General, and in particular: Fantasy; Science Fiction

Send: Query; Synopsis; Writing sample

Costs: Offers services that writers have to pay for. Offers writing courses.

Renowned and long-established London agency. Handles general fiction and nonfiction, and scripts. Also represents directors, designers, and presenters. Also offers services such as writing courses for which authors are charged.

Associate Agent: Rachel Goldblatt (**L243**)

Authors: Nicole Adams; Henry Agg; Casey Jay Andrews; Sui Annukka; Timothy X Atack; Jana Bakunina; Jessica Barnfield; Craig Barr-Green; Neil Baxter; Chloe Bayley; Alice Bell; Kaddy Benyon; Kate van der Borgh; Fern Brady; Melanie Cantor; Ashley Chalmers; Georgina Charles; Ken Cheng; Laura Coffey; Hannah Connolly; Toni Coppers; Paige Cowan-Hall; Matt Cunningham; Sarah Daniels; Alan Edwards; Rebecca Fallon; Babak Ganjei; A.D. Garrett; Rebecca Gibson; Caroline Green; Nevin Holness; Daniel Howell; Logan Karlie; Susanna Kearsley; Greg Keen; Nina Killham; Danny James King; Euan Kitson; Chloe Laws; Sarah Lawton; Gytha Lodge; Tatty Macleod; Gráinne Maguire; Michael Mann; Laura Marshall; Hannah Mays; Hazel McBride; Laura McCluskey; Ella McLeod; Liberty Mills; Rebekah Miron; Margaret Murphy; Struan Murray; L.M. Nathan; Madeleine Norton; Lauren O'Donoghue; Tara O'Sullivan; Joshua Oliver; Andrea Oskis; Louise Page; Claire Peate; Alake Pilgrim; Leah Pitt; Joanna Pritchard; Amanda Quaid; Keetie Roelen; Adara Schwartz; Stephanie Sowden; Jacob Stolworthy; Eulalie Tangka; Daisy Tempest; Orla Thomas; Lucy Webster; Josh Weeks; Claire Whatley; Dan Whitlam; Kat Williams; Matt Woodhead; Emily Woof; Kelly Yang

Literary Agent / President: Jonathan Lloyd

Literary Agents: Davinia Andrew-Lynch (**L017**); Felicity Blunt; Sheila Crowley (**L132**); Sabhbh Curran (**L134**); Ciara Finan (**L200**); Jonny Geller; Viola Hayden (**L271**); Alice Lutyens; Jess Molloy (**L414**); Rosie Pierce (**L474**); Cathryn Summerhayes; Steph Thwaites (**L575**); Gordon Wise

L136 John Cusick

Literary Agent; Vice President
United States

https://www.foliojr.com/john-cusick
https://www.publishersmarketplace.com/members/JohnC/
https://twitter.com/johnmcusick

Literary Agencies: Folio Literary Management, LLC (**L207**); Folio Jr.

ADULT > Fiction > *Novels*
Fantasy; Horror; Romance; Romantic Comedy; Science Fiction; Suspense; Thrillers

CHILDREN'S > Fiction > *Middle Grade*
Comedy / Humour; Contemporary; Fantasy; Science Fiction; Speculative

YOUNG ADULT > Fiction > *Novels*
Comedy / Humour; Contemporary; Fantasy; Science Fiction; Speculative

Send: Query; Writing sample
How to send: Email

I'm seeking unique voices in middle-grade, young adult, and young adult/adult-crossover fiction. I want stories that move readers, moments that make me look up and say "Wow, yes. I've felt that."

I want compelling page-turners that create life-long readers, stories that will inspire fandoms, characters readers will cosplay as, obsess over, and never forget. I want #ownvoices stories of all styles and genres, and am particularly interested in sci-fi, fantasy, and genre fiction from under-represented voices. I love the strange, iconoclastic, and unusual. Send me the books kids will sneak / steal / borrow in secret. Those intimate, dangerous, life-saving stories.

I love proactive protagonists, kids and teens chasing a dream or a hero who swings in with a song in her heart and a knife in her teeth. I am not seeking picture book authors or illustrators, or non-fiction, at this time.

Authors: Courtney Alameda; Adriana Anders; Kayla Cagan; Josephine Cameron; Anna Carey; Linda Cheng; Jamie D'Amato; Paula Garner; Joan He; Christian McKay Heidicker; Sailor J; James Kennedy; Jeramey Kraatz; Jorge Lacera; Megan Lacera; Jules Machias; Mindy McGinnis; Rebecca Morrison; Julie Murphy; Abdi Nazemian; Jordan Reeves; Caitlin Schneiderhan; Laura Sebastian; Sierra Simone; Quinn Sosna-Spear; Sharon Biggs Waller; Don Zolidis

L137 Laura Dail

Literary Agent; President
United States

http://www.ldlainc.com/about
http://twitter.com/lcdail
http://aaronline.org/Sys/PublicProfile/2176649/417813

Literary Agency: Laura Dail Literary Agency
Professional Body: Association of American Literary Agents (AALA)

Closed to approaches.

L138 Dana Newman Literary, LLC

Literary Agency
1900 Avenue of the Stars, 19th Floor, Los Angeles, CA 90067
United States

dananewmanliterary@gmail.com

https://www.dananewman.com
https://twitter.com/DanaNewman

https://www.linkedin.com/in/dananewman/
https://www.instagram.com/danamnewman/

Fiction > *Novels*
Literary; Suspense; Thrillers; Upmarket

Nonfiction > *Nonfiction Books*
Biography; Business; Current Affairs; Fitness; Health; History; Literary; Memoir; Mind, Body, Spirit; Narrative Nonfiction; Parenting; Popular Culture; Psychology; Social Issues; Sport; Technology; Wellbeing; Women's Interests

Send: Query; Outline; Author bio
How to send: Email

We are interested in practical nonfiction (business, health and wellness, mind/body/spirit, psychology, parenting, technology) by authors with smart, unique perspectives and established platforms who are committed to actively marketing and promoting their books.

We love compelling, inspiring narrative nonfiction in the areas of memoir, biography, history, pop culture, current affairs/women's interest, social trends, and sports/fitness. A favorite genre is literary nonfiction: true stories, well told, that read like a novel you can't put down.

On the fiction side we consider a select amount of literary fiction, upmarket fiction, and suspense/thriller. We look for character-driven stories written in a distinctive voice that are emotionally truthful.

Submissions are accepted via email only.

Literary Agent: Dana Newman

L139 Melissa Danaczko
Literary Agent
United States

mdquery@skagency.com

http://skagency.com
http://skagency.com/agents/melissa-danaczko/

Literary Agency: Stuart Krichevsky Literary Agency, Inc. (**L556**)

Fiction > *Novels*
Book Club Fiction; Commercial; Contemporary; Family; Friends; Historical Fiction; International; Literary; Magic; Psychological Thrillers; Sub-Culture

Nonfiction > *Nonfiction Books*
History; Memoir; Science

Focuses on literary and commercial fiction and gravitates towards plot-driven novels with a fresh perspective, energetic writing and deep sense of place. Favorite categories include historical fiction, psychological thrillers, and contemporary book club fiction. She has a soft spot for novels with international settings, unreliable narrators, elements of magic, dysfunctional families, intense friendships, and unique subcultures. She is also representing select history, science, memoir and idea-driven non-fiction. In all categories, it's a big plus if a book can introduce her to a new world, make her think differently about one she already knows or tap into the cultural climate.

Authors: Addison Armstrong; Chelsea Conaboy; Ella Delany; Anita Felicelli; John Fram; Elyssa Goodman; Gabino Iglesias; Amanda Jayatissa; Bernice McFadden; Sarafina Nance; Mira Ptacin; Marina Scott; Charlyne Yi

L140 Margaret Danko
Literary Agent
United States

https://www.highlineliterary.com/agent-margaret
https://querymanager.com/query/margaretdanko

Literary Agency: High Line Literary Collective (**L279**)

ADULT
Fiction > *Novels*
Contemporary Women's Fiction; Family; Mental Health; Psychological Suspense; Romance; Speculative Romance; Women's Issues

Nonfiction > *Nonfiction Books*
Comedy / Humour; Cookery; Crime; Environment; Lifestyle; Mental Health; New Age; Politics; Popular Science; Spirituality

YOUNG ADULT
Fiction > *Novels*
Commercial; Contemporary; Fantasy

Nonfiction > *Nonfiction Books*
Crime; Culture; Environment; History; Lifestyle; Narrative Essays; Personal Finance; Politics; Self Help; Social Commentary; Spirituality; Wellbeing; Witchcraft; Women

How to send: By referral

A multi-faceted agent, highly skilled at representing both fiction and nonfiction titles. Her clients include environmental scientists, high-ranking government officials, CEOs, groundbreaking journalists, spiritual leaders, culture makers, and award-winning novelists. She is passionate about projects that encourage readers to view themselves and the world around them in a new light.

L141 Jon Michael Darga
Senior Agent
New York
United States

https://aevitascreative.com/agents/
https://querymanager.com/query/jonmichaeldarga

Literary Agency: Aevitas

Fiction > *Novels:* Commercial

Nonfiction > *Nonfiction Books*
Biography; Cookery; History; Photography; Popular Culture

Send: Author bio; Outline; Pitch; Market info; Writing sample
How to send: Online submission system

Represents both nonfiction and fiction. He is most interested in voice-driven pop culture writing and histories that re-cast the narrative by emphasizing unexpected or unheard voices.

Authors: Matt Abdoo; Zac Bissonnette; Sydney Bucksbaum; Scott Chernoff; Tony Chin-Quee; Angel Luis Colón; Melissa Croce; Ashley Cullins; Tim Curry; Sarah Horowitz; Patty Lin; Violet Lumani; Hugo Huerta Marin; Ann Marks; Shane McBride; Sam Moore; Tarek El Moussa; Arnold Myint; James Park; Erik Piepenburg; Lynette Rice; Geena Rocero; Maurice "Mopreme" Shakur; Ashley Spencer; Jason Sperling; Jesse Szewczyk; Amy Watson; Rusty Williams; Angel Di Zhang

L142 Darhansoff & Verrill Literary Agents
Literary Agency
275 Fair Street, Suite 17D, Kingston NY, 12401
United States
Tel: +1 (845) 514-2070

submissions@dvagency.com
info@dvagency.com

https://www.dvagency.com

ADULT
Fiction > *Novels*
Nonfiction > *Nonfiction Books*

YOUNG ADULT > **Fiction** > *Novels*

Send: Query; Writing sample
How to send: In the body of an email
How not to send: Post

Response only if interested. If no response within eight weeks, assume rejection.

Foreign Rights Director / Literary Agent: Eric Amling

Literary Agents: Liz Darhansoff; Michele Mortimer (**L418**)

L143 The Darley Anderson Agency
Literary Agency
Estelle House, 11 Eustace Road, London, SW6 1JB
United Kingdom
Tel: +44 (0) 20 7385 6652

https://darleyanderson.com
https://twitter.com/DA_Agency
https://www.instagram.com/darleyanderson_agency/

Professional Body: The Association of Authors' Agents (AAA)

Fiction > *Novels*
 Commercial; Crime; Historical Fiction; Romance; Romantasy; Romantic Comedy; Thrillers

Send: Query; Synopsis; Writing sample
How to send: Online submission system; Post

We specialise in commercial, page-turning, conversation-starting fiction. We're talking heart stopping thrillers, 'have you read this yet?!' books, laugh out loud rom-coms, steamy romances, addictive crime, sweeping love stories, breathtaking romantasy and glamorous regency dramas, to name but a few.

Associate Agent: Rebeka Finch (**L202**)

Authors: Maria Motunrayo Adebisi; Emma Bamford; Gina Blaxill; Tara Bond; Sarah Bowie; Mark Bradley; Vicki Bradley; Constance Briscoe; Danielle Brown; Lanisha Butterfield; Honor Cargill-Martin; James Carol; Paul Carson; Chris Carter; Lee Child; Martina Cole; Gloria Cook; Lucy Tandon Copp; Sophie Cousens; Holly Craig; A J Cross; Jason Dean; Margaret Dickinson; Clare Dowling; Hayley Doyle; Patrick Dunne; Tom Ellen; Alex Evelyn; C. M. Ewan; Addy Farmer; Brooke Fast; Kerry Fisher; Jack Ford; Martyn Ford; Tana French; Mina Ikemoto Ghosh; G.R. Halliday; Sophie Hamilton; Ryan Hammond; Mary Hargreaves; Alice Harman; Joyce Efia Harmer; Polly Ho-Yen; Egan Hughes; Tara Hyland; Catherine Jacob; Sandie Jones; Amie Jordan; Emma Kavanagh; Patrick Lennon; Nathanael Lessore; T M Logan; Imran Mahmood; Cesca Major; Rani Manicka; Donna Marchetti; L V Matthews; Gillian McAllister; Hannah Moffatt; Ayaan Mohamud; Phoebe Morgan; Rachel Morrisroe; Megan Murphy; Annie Murray; Eva Wong Nava; Laura Noakes; Abi Oliver; B.A. Paris; Phaedra Patrick; Jo Platt; Hazel Prior; Beth Reekles; David Rhodes; Lisa Richardson; Ellie Robinson; Jacqui Rose; Faith Williams Schesventer; Mira V. Shah; Rebecca Shaw; Nick Sheridan; Rashmi Sirdeshpande; KL Slater; Kim Slater; Sean Slater; Pat Sowa; Catherine Steadman; Erik Storey; Deirdre Sullivan; Mimi Thebo; G X Todd; Samantha Tonge; Elizabeth Waite; Anna-Lou Weatherley; Tim Weaver

Literary Agent / Managing Director: Camilla Bolton (**L067**)

Literary Agents: Darley Anderson; Jade Kavanagh (**L323**); Becca Langton (**L353**); Lydia Silver; Clare Wallace

L144 Darley Anderson Children's

Literary Agency
United Kingdom
Tel: +44 (0) 20 3940 9012

childrens@darleyanderson.com

http://www.darleyandersonchildrens.com
http://twitter.com/DA_Childrens

Professional Body: The Association of Authors' Agents (AAA)

CHILDREN'S
Fiction
 Chapter Books; *Middle Grade*; *Picture Books*
Nonfiction > *Nonfiction Books*

YOUNG ADULT > **Fiction** > *Novels*

Send: Query; Synopsis; Writing sample; Author bio; Pitch
How to send: Word file email attachment; PDF file email attachment
How not to send: Post

Always on the look out for exciting, inspiring and original novels for both Young Adult and Middle-Grade readers, chapter books, picture books, and nonfiction.

Literary Agent: Clare Wallace

L145 David Godwin Associates

Literary Agency
2nd Floor, 40 Rosebery Avenue, Clerkenwell, London, EC1R 4RX
United Kingdom
Tel: +44 (0) 20 7240 9992

submissions@davidgodwinassociates.co.uk

http://www.davidgodwinassociates.com

Professional Body: The Association of Authors' Agents (AAA)

Fiction > *Novels*

Nonfiction > *Nonfiction Books*

Send: Query; Synopsis; Writing sample
How to send: Email

Handles a range of nonfiction and fiction. Send query by email with synopsis and first 30 pages. No poetry. No picture books, except for existing clients.

Literary Agent: David Godwin

L146 David Higham Associates Ltd

Literary Agency
6th Floor, Waverley House, 7-12 Noel Street, London, W1F 8GQ
United Kingdom
Tel: +44 (0) 20 7434 5900

reception@davidhigham.co.uk
submissions@davidhigham.co.uk
childrenssubmissions@davidhigham.co.uk

https://davidhigham.co.uk
https://twitter.com/DHAbooks
https://www.linkedin.com/company/david-higham-associates-limited
https://www.instagram.com/davidhighambooks/?hl=en

Professional Body: The Association of Authors' Agents (AAA)

We are always on the lookout for exciting new voices. From pioneering non-fiction, to meticulously-plotted thrillers, life-changing love stories, and bold literary debuts, we are committed to storytelling in all forms. We are keen to hear from writers from under-represented backgrounds.

Agency Assistant: Sara Langham

Associate Agent: David Evans

Author / Editor-in-Chief: Jason Cowley

Authors: Rachel Abbott; J. R. Ackerley; Richard Adams; Ore Agbaje-Williams; Katie Agnew; Sara Ahmed; Kat Ailes; Naomi Alderman; Tracy Alexander; Elizabeth Alker; Rachael Allen; Jason Allen-Paisant; Alan Allport; Nuar Alsadir; Geraint Anderson; R. J. Anderson; Kelly Andrew; Kerry Andrew; Abi Andrews; Carol Anshaw; Michael Arditti; Edward Ardizzone; Michael Arlen; Thomas Asbridge; Lamorna Ash; Jenn Ashworth; Jennifer Atkins; Julian Baggini; Harriet Baker; Anthony Bale; Katy Balls; Antonia Barber; Lindsey Bareham; Nigel Barley; Robert Barnard; Yvonne Battle-Felton; Belinda Bauer; Felix Bazalgette; Ella Beech; Laura Beers; Hannah Begbie; Annie Bell; Aimee Bender; Margot Bennett; Joe Berger; Sarah Bernstein; Elizabeth Berridge; Santanu Bhattacharya; Tessa Bickers; Rebecca Birrell; Neil Blackmore; James Bloodworth; Edmund Blunden; Margaret Boden; Jonathan Boff; Maria Bradford; E. R. Braithwaite; Mikki Brammer; Lauren Bravo; Carys Bray; Neville Braybrooke; Kevin Brazil; Theresa Breslin; Colwill Brown; Glen James Brown; Martin Brown; Hester Browne; Janet Browne; Mike Brownlow; Jessica Bruder; Rukky Brume; Arthur Bryant; Ella Bucknall; Anthony Burgess; Mark Burnell; R. S. Burnett; Sheila Burnford; Caroline Burt; Sally Butcher; Nick Butterworth; Eliza Barry Callahan; Paco Calvo; John Dickson Carr; Jess Cartner-Morley; Anne-Marie Casey; Barbara Castle; Charles Causley; Kathryn Cave; Aditya Chakrabortty; Vanessa Chan; Jason Chapman; Eve Chase; James Hadley Chase; Seerut K. Chawla; Emma Chichester Clark; Arthur C. Clarke; Lady Mary Clive; J. M. Coetzee; Kathleen Collins; Sophie Collins; Charlie Connelly; Alan Connor; Peter Cook; Trish Cooke; Emily S. Cooper; Natasha Cooper; Bernard Cornwell; Jamie Costello; Chris Cove-Smith; Cressida Cowell; Rob Cowen; Nick Crumpton; John Cunliffe; James Curtis; Roald Dahl; David Daiches; Tsitsi Dangarembga; Nicola Davies; Susie Day; Tish Delaney; R. F. Delderfield; Kady MacDonald Denton; Lucy Diamond; Morgan Dick; Lucy Dillamore; Lucy Dillon; Jonathan Dimbleby; Berlie Doherty; Naoise Dolan; Sareeta Domingo; David Domoney; Stanley Donwood; Kelly Doust; Karen Downs-Barton; Alicia Drake;

Sarah Duguid; Fred D'Aguiar; Caroline Eden; David Edmonds; Eve Edwards; Jonathan Emmett; Tan Twan Eng; Richard English; Eve Esfandiari-Denney; Gavin Esler; Maz Evans; Rowan Evans; Seb Falk; Eleanor Farjeon; J. Jefferson Farjeon; Ben Faulks; Elizabeth Ferrars; Ophelia Field; Anne Fine; Cordelia Fine; Pip Finkemeyer; Nicholas Fisk; Pauline Fisk; Theodora Fitzgibbon; Corina Fletcher; Margot Fonteyn; Ford Madox Ford; Charles Foster; Fred Foster; Karen Joy Fowler; Catherine Fox; Matthew Frank; Melissa Franklin; P. M. Freestone; Tom de Freston; Stephen Fry; Mavis Gallant; Jane Gardam; Sarah Garland; Eve Garnett; Susan Gates; Jonathan Gathorne-Hardy; Ryan Gattis; Jamila Gavin; Jessica George; Adèle Geras; Susannah Gibson; Andrew Gimson; Guinevere Glasfurd; Ralph Glasser; Julia Golding; Elizabeth Goudge; Caroline Graham; Holly Gramazio; Marlowe Granados; Kester Grant; Ryan Graudin; Dominic Green; Linda Green; Peter Green; Graham Greene; John Gribbin; Jay Griffiths; Geoffrey Grigson; Jane Grigson; Araminta Hall; Jo Hamya; Penny Hancock; James Hanley; Mary Hannity; Isabel Hardman; Sophie Harman; Candida Harper; Ali Harris; Oliver Harris; B. H. Liddell Hart; Alice Hattrick; Paula Hawkins; Mo Hayder; Nick Hayes; Lottie Hazell; Oli Hazzard; Claire Marie Healy; Gerald Heard; John Heath-Stubbs; Emma Henderson; James Herbert; James Herriot; Mick Herron; Deborah Hewitt; Rosie Hewlett; Christopher Hibbert; Nathan Hill; Chris Hirst; Russell Hoban; Eric Hobsbawm; Gavandra Hodge; Leigh Hodgkinson; Jesse Hodgson; Paul Hoffman; Edward Hogan; Anna Hoghton; Euny Hong; Liu Hong; Meredith Hooper; Simon Hopkinson; Trevor Horn; Tansy Hoskins; Richard Hough; Lucy Hounsom; Langston Hughes; Richard Hughes; Masud Husain; Julian Jackson; Julia Jarman; Elizabeth Jennings; Milly Johnson; Rebecca May Johnson; Diana Wynne Jones; Harold Jones; Lucy Jones; Owen Jones; Anthony Joseph; Alan Judd; Helen Jukes; Anna Kavan; M. M. Kaye; Jessie Keane; Molly Keane; Anna Keay; John Keay; Stephen Kelman; Laura Kemp; Jonathan Kennedy; Paul Kennedy; Sidney Keyes; Barbara Keys; Sulmaan Wasif Khan; Rachel Khoo; Claire King; Clive King; Binnie Kirshenbaum; Bert Kitchen; C. H. B. Kitchin; June Knox-Mawer; Halik Kochanski; Jay Kristoff; Fifi Kuo; Emily LaBarge; Stephen Lacey; David Lammy; Marghanita Laski; Hugh Laurie; Eleanor Lavender; Ann Lawrence; Natalie Lawrence; Elisabeth Leake; Kate Leaver; Jeremy Lee; Damien Lewis; Ted Lewis; Daniel Light; Jack Lindsay; Joan Lingard; Emanuel Litvinoff; Penelope Lively; Saci Lloyd; Jo Lodge; Tim Lott; Julia Lovell; Joanna Lumley; Richard Lumsden; Kesia Lupo; Max Lury; S. E. Lynes; Louis MacNeice; Malcolm Ross Macdonald; Marianne Macdonald; Robert Macfarlane;

Sophie Mackintosh; Manchan Magan; Erin Maglaque; Foday Mannah; Olivia Manning; Kathryn Mannix; Sarfraz Manzoor; Greil Marcus; Kathryn Maris; Jan Mark; Ellie Marney; Patrick Marnham; David Marquand; Helen Marten; Simon Mason; Ben Masters; Sadie Matthews; Evan Mawdsley; Peter May; Rufaro Faith Mazarura; Anna Mazzola; Helen McCarthy; Geraldine McCaughrean; Elizabeth McCracken; Val McDermid; Iain McGilchrist; Elizabeth McKenzie; Tom McLaughlin; Thomas McMullan; Jean McNeil; Rosanna Mclaughlin; Anna Metcalfe; Ed Miliband; Louise Millar; Kei Miller; Myfanwy Millward; Kate Milner; Gladys Mitchell; Sarah Mitchell; Tony Mitton; Lauren Mooney; Victoria Moore; Pete Morgan; Michael Morpurgo; Jackie Morris; Kate Morton; Emma-Lee Moss; Laura Mucha; Benjamin Myers; Fraser Nelson; Norman Nicholson; Jenny Nimmo; Johan Norberg; Charity Norman; David Nott; Sigrid Nunez; Peter Oborne; Diane Oliver; Yewande Omotoso; Jan Ormerod; Laurie Owens; Susan Owens; Kate O'Brien; Deborah O'Donoghue; C. S. Pacat; Derek Parker; Julia Parker; Sandeep Parmar; Helen Parr; Richard Partington; Robert Payne; AJ Pearce; Fred Pearce; Philippa Pearce; Harry Pearson; Cato Pedder; Eleanor Penny; Gilles Peterson; Kate Reed Petty; Charlotte Philby; Liz Pichon; Sarah Pinborough; Courtney Pine; Christina Pishiris; Anthony Powell; Des Powell; Margaret Powell; Chris Powling; Shannon Pufahl; Kathryn Purdie; Ann Purser; Sadiah Qureshi; Sabina Radeva; Amol Rajan; Madhvi Ramani; Joan Rankin; Catherine Rayner; Jacqui Rayner; Herbert Read; James Reeves; Katy Regan; Hannah Regel; Chris Renwick; Steve Richards; Sarah Ridgard; M. L. Rio; Fiona Roberton; Bethan Roberts; Jane Robinson; Lucy Robinson; Claudia Roden; Jane Rogoyska; Rachel Rooney; Brunello Rosa; Leone Ross; Rupert Russell; Saba Sams; Jane Sanderson; Clive Sansom; Noo Saro-Wiwa; Dorothy L. Sayers; Kathryn Scanlan; Izabella Scott; Paul Scott; Alice Sebold; Rachel Seiffert; Antonia Senior; John Seymour; Miranda Seymour; Rachel Shabi; Nick Sharratt; Martin Shaw; Merlin Sheldrake; Megan Shepherd; Lola Shoneyin; Philip Short; Penelope Shuttle; Kate Simants; Karen Sinotok; Sujit Sivasundaram; Alexander McCall Smith; Lisa Smith; Mark B. Smith; Mary South; Muriel Spark; Meagan Spooner; Howard Spring; Hilary Spurling; Jessica Stanley; Gertrude Stein; Joss Stirling; Rosie Storey; Peter Stott; Hannah Stowe; Hew Strachan; John Strawson; Jeremy Strong; Jonathan Stroud; Nicola Sturgeon; Rosemary Sutcliff; James L. Sutter; Emma Claire Sweeney; Tasha Sylva; Sally Symes; Vanessa Tait; Dizz Tate; A. J. P. Taylor; Lulu Taylor; Kae Tempest; Josephine Tey; Sureka Thanenthiran-Dharuman; Dylan Thomas; Frances Thomas; Scarlett Thomas; Pat Thomson; Simon Thurley; Phil Tinline;

Theresa Tomlinson; Peter Tonkin; Nigel Toon; Lynne Truss; Ann Turnbull; A. K. Turner; Harriet Tyce; Simon Tyler; Jack Underwood; Hanna Thomas Uose; Nicola Upson; Rosamund Urwin; Jenny Valentine; Varaidzo; Yanis Varoufakis; Sarah Vaughan; Stephanie Victoire; Martin Waddell; Lucy Wadham; Alice Walker; Jill Paton Walsh; Joanna Walsh; Melanie Walsh; Rosie Walsh; Stephen Walsh; Minette Walters; Vanessa Walters; Miranda Ward; Bernard Wasserstein; Keith Waterhouse; Holly Watt; Aisling Watters; Christian Weaver; Mary Wesley; Sam Wetherell; Dorothy Whipple; T. H. White; Thornton Wilder; Elizabeth Wilhide; Barbara Willard; Charles Williams; Jacqueline Wilson; Jon Wilson; Tim Winton; David Wojtowycz; Hope Wolf; Charlotte Wood; Carolyn Woods; Kate Worsley; John Wyndham; Xinran; Taichi Yamada; Mandy Yin; Kate Zambreno

Company Director / Literary Agent: Veronique Baxter (**L045**)

Literary Agents: Maddalena Cavaciuti (*L106*); Nicola Chang (**L109**); Elise Dillsworth (**L156**); David Evans (*L184*); Jemima Forrester (**L210**); Stephanie Glencross (*L237*); Georgia Glover; Andrew Gordon (**L245**); Clare Israel (*L294*); Lizzy Kremer; Sara Langham (*L351*); Nicky Lund (*L374*); Christabel McKinley (*L401*); Deirdre Power (*L483*); Georgie Smith (*L542*); Orli Vogt-Vincent (*L587*); Caroline Walsh (**L589**); Jessica Woollard (**L611**)

L147 Olivia Davies

Assistant Agent
United Kingdom

odavies@unitedagents.co.uk

https://www.unitedagents.co.uk
https://www.unitedagents.co.uk/odaviesunitedagentscouk
https://x.com/oliviamdavies1

Literary Agency: United Agents
Literary Agent / Company Director: Robert Kirby (**L338**)

Fiction > *Novels*

Nonfiction
  Gift Books: General
  Illustrated Books: General
  Nonfiction Books: Arts; Food; History; Literary Criticism; Popular Culture; Religion; Travel; Warfare

Send: Query; Synopsis; Writing sample; Proposal
How to send: Email

Looking for bold voices and stories that evoke feeling. She reads and represents a broad range of fiction and remains fundamentally curious as to how writers can open life to new perspectives. In non-fiction, she enjoys being guided by a warm, expert voice through topics such as history, religion, war, art, literary criticism, travel, pop culture, and food. More specifically, she's often drawn to personal narratives which upend monolithic constructions of cultural or national identity. For novels, send email with a synopsis and 10,000 words. For nonfiction, if you are an expert in your field, it's fine to contact her at an earlier stage of development.

Authors: Abigail Abbas; Lucy Sweeney Byrne; Liam Cagney; John Constable; Fee Greening; Lucy Holme; Pai Hsieh-yung; Matthew Jukes; Emer Martin; Emily Merrill; Julian Mitchell

L148 Liza Dawson
Senior Agent; President
United States

queryliza@lizadawsonassociates.com

https://www.lizadawsonassociates.com/liza-dawson

Literary Agency: Liza Dawson Associates
Professional Bodies: The Authors Guild; Mystery Writers of America (MWA)

Fiction > *Novels*
 Book Club Fiction; Contemporary; Historical Fiction; Literary; Mystery; Social Class; Spy Thrilllers; Thrillers

Nonfiction > *Nonfiction Books*
 Comedy / Humour; Culture; Environment; Ethnic Groups; Finance; Memoir; Narrative History; Politics; US Southern States; Women's Issues

Closed to approaches.

She specializes in: Smart, plot-driven bestselling fiction. Memorable, confidently-written, literary fiction. Page-turning thrillers that teach you about spycraft, foreign intrigue or an unusual career. Mysteries – featuring brainy detectives. Literary fiction for book clubs. Breakout historical novels. In nonfiction, she is drawn to cross-cultural and women's issues written by experts. She is looking for narrative history, memoirs about women and men who have escaped from closed, repressive societies and books by journalists and poets who are trying to make sense of exotic locations, race, the environment, Wall Street, Washington, and the South. Humor and tenderness are a plus, and she has a weakness for cartoonists and quirky humor.

Authors: Annie Barrows; Marie Bostwick; Bob Brier; Stella Cameron; Robyn Carr; Ross Gay; Susan Hasler; Julia Lee; Victoria Christopher Murray; Tawni O'Dell; Jean Sasson

L149 Liza DeBlock
Literary Agent
United Kingdom

submissions@mushens-entertainment.com

https://www.mushens-entertainment.com/liza-deblock

https://x.com/lizadeblock
https://www.instagram.com/lizathelitagent/

Literary Agency: Mushens Entertainment

Fiction > *Novels*
 Grounded Fantasy; High Concept; Historical Fiction; Literary; Romantasy; Speculative; Thrillers; Upmarket; Urban Fantasy; Vampires; Werewolves; Witches

Nonfiction > *Nonfiction Books*
 Cookery; Popular Science; Social History

Closed to approaches.

Looking for both fiction and non fiction.

For fiction, she is interested in adult only – do not send her children's, middle grade, or YA. She is looking for historical fiction that is well researched, immerses readers in the era, and looks at overlooked characters from the past, or perhaps gives a new spin on someone we think we know. On the literary and upmarket side, she is looking for novels infused with emotions that capture the human experience and make readers think. If your literary novel is something set at A24 productions might turn into a movie, this is her taste. When it comes to fantasy, she loves urban and grounded fantasy (no sci-fi please!), and is always happy to look at anything with a vampire, werewolf, witches, warlocks, fairies, and perhaps a sinister selkie or two. She is also very much looking for romantasy and is the best person at the agency to submit that too. For thrillers, send her anything set in an exotic location, high-concept, or things with a speculative twist. She loves when characters are put in situations she would never want to be in, and then they have to get out of it.

On the non fiction side, she is looking for books that teach her something new or reframe a topic from an alternative point of view. This can include cookery, pop science, and social history.

Please do not send her: novellas or unfinished manuscripts, sci-fi, horror, erotica, graphic novels, children's books, middle grade, or poetry.

Authors: Sally Abe; Natalie Chandler; Sally El-Arifi; Dominic Franks; Carys Green; Jane Hennigan; Eleanor Houghton; Laurel Remington; Stacey Thomas; Pim Wangtechawat

L150 Gabrielle Demblon
Literary Agent; Foreign Rights Manager
United Kingdom

submissions@watsonlittle.com

https://www.watsonlittle.com
https://www.watsonlittle.com/agent/gabrielle-demblon/

Literary Agency: Watson, Little Ltd (**L590**)

Fiction > *Novels*
 Crime; High Concept; Horror; LGBTQIA; Literary; Psychological Suspense Thrillers; Speculative; Thrillers; Upmarket

Nonfiction > *Nonfiction Books*
 Career Development; Crime; Nutrition; Parenting; Personal Finance; Politics; Popular Science; Psychology; Relationships

Does not want:

> Fiction > *Novels*: Police Procedural

Send: Query; Synopsis; Writing sample
How to send: Email
How not to send: Post

I'm looking for literary and upmarket fiction, particularly with queer themes or from unusual / underrepresented perspectives, as well as select thrillers and nonfiction. I'm open to debut authors at all life stages. I'm looking for literary speculative/high concept fiction from queer/female/transnational perspectives. In crime, I'm looking for a fun, pulpy thriller with a high concept twist or standout setting. In nonfiction, I'm drawn to popular science, politics, and true crime. I'm also looking to work with experts and influencers specialising in personal style, nutrition, psychology, relationships, personal finance, career guidance, parenting and alternative family formation.

L151 Dado Derviskadic
Literary Agent
United States
Tel: +1 (212) 400-1494

dado@foliolitmanagement.com

http://foliolit.com/dado-derviskadic

Literary Agency: Folio Literary Management, LLC (**L207**)

Nonfiction > *Nonfiction Books*
 Art History; Biography; Cookery; Cultural History; Fashion; Films; Food; Health; Motivational Self-Help; Nutrition; Philosophy; Popular Culture; Popular Science; Psychology; Religion; Spirituality; Sub-Culture

Send: Query; Writing sample; Proposal
How to send: In the body of an email

I am primarily interested in: cultural history; biography; art history; film; religion and spirituality; psychology; philosophy; pop science and motivational self-help; health and nutrition; pop culture and subcultures; fashion; and food narrative and cookbooks.

L152 DHH Literary Agency Ltd
Literary Agency
23-27 Cecil Court, London, WC2N 4EZ
United Kingdom
Tel: +44 (0) 20 3990 2452

enquiries@dhhliteraryagency.com

https://www.dhhliteraryagency.com

Professional Body: The Association of Authors' Agents (AAA)

ADULT
  Fiction > *Novels*
  Nonfiction > *Nonfiction Books*

CHILDREN'S > Fiction > *Novels*

YOUNG ADULT > Fiction > *Novels*

Send: Query; Synopsis; Writing sample
How to send: Email
How not to send: Post

Accepts submissions by email only. No postal submissions. See website for specific agent interests and email addresses and approach one agent only. Do not send submissions to generic "enquiries" email address.

Authors: Tasneem Abdur-Rashid; Foluso Agbaje; Paula Akpan; Carolina Are; Karen Arthur; Khairani Barokka; Graham Bartlett; Katie Baskerville; Louise Beech; A. D. Bell; Alexandra K. Benedict; R.C. Bridgestock; Tom Brown; Daisy Buchanan; Paul Burston; Caroline Butterwick; Cecil Cameron; Andrea Carter; Will Carver; Amanda Cassidy; Angela Clarke; Yvonne Cobb; Paul Fraser Collard; Fiona Collins; Howard Colyer; James Conway; Barbara Copperthwaite; Caroline Corcoran; Isabel Costello; M.W. Craven; John Curran; Aaron Dale; Azma Dar; Heather Darwent; Becca Day; Michael Delahaye; K Devan; Sharan Dhaliwal; A. A. Dhand; Preeti Dhillon; Becky Docton; Hannah Dolby; Francesca Dorricott; Suzie Edge; Stephen Edger; Rachel Edwards; Anna Ellory; David Fennell; Deirdre Finnerty; Dov Forman; Lily Ebert Forman; Essie Fox; Anita Frank; Nicola Garrard; Divya Ghelani; Nadia Gilani; Erica Gillingham; Alexis Gregory; Elliott Grover; Michael Handrick; Mireille Harper; Ali Hendry; Lisa Hilton; Catriona Innes; Amelia Ireland; Hanan Issa; Valerie Jack; Ryan David Jahn; Sophie Jai; Helga Jensen; Harriet Johnson; Ragnar Jonasson; Amy Jones; Lizzie Huxley Jones; Jón Atli Jónasson; Katrín Júlíusdóttir; Anthony Kavanagh; Nancy Kelley; Diana Kessler; Catherine Kurtz; Eleni Kyriacou; Caroline Lamond; Thomas Leeds; Michael Leggo; S.V. Leonard; Kathy Lette; Beth Lewis; Chantelle Lindsay; Elizabeth Lovatt; Sean Lusk; Zoe Lyons; Andrea Mara; Natalie Marlow; Francesca May; Layla McCay; Chris McDonald; Brian McGilloway; Claire McGowan; Emma Medrano; Rachel Meller; Jean Menzies; Chris Merritt; Janie Millman; Saima Mir; Zeena Moolla; Elizabeth S. Moore; Evie Muir; Jade Mutyora; Noel O'Reilly; Valerie O'Riordan; Erik Olsen; Yen Ooi; Emma Orchard; Vikki Patis; Philippa Peall; Adam Pearson; Penny Pepper; Alice Peterson; Rachel Phipps; Lauren du Plessis; Grace Quantock; Anthony J. Quinn; Jenny Quintana; Jasmine Qureshi; Monika Radojevic; Jon Ransom; Reagan Lee Ray; Jini Reddy; Becky Rhush; Emma Robertson; Nicole Robinson; Juno Roche; Leon Romero-Montalvo; Iain Rowan; Robert Rutherford; Frances Ryan; Jennifer Savin; Helen Scott; Allison Secker; Victoria Selman; Mel Sherratt; Amélie Skoda; Richard Stirling; Hema Sukumar; Katy Summers; Annie Taylor; Paul Taylor-Pitt; Rebecca Templeton; Jo Thomas; Rebecca Thorne; Amanda Tuke; Ola Tundun; Rosie Turner; L.C. Tyler; Eva Verde; Lucy Vine; Kandace Siobhan Walker; Roz Watkins; Clare Weze; Clare Whitfield; Kathleen Whyman; Claire Wilson; L. C. Winter; David Young; lisa luxx; Eva Björg Ægisdottir

Company Director / Literary Agent: Emily Glenister (**L238**)

Literary Agent / Managing Director: David H. Headley (**L272**)

Literary Agents: Diana Beaumont (**L046**); Broo Doherty; Abi Fellows (**L193**); Harry Illingworth

L153 Diamond Kahn and Woods (DKW) Literary Agency Ltd

Literary Agency
Salisbury House, 29 Finsbury Circus, London, EC2M 5QQ
United Kingdom
Tel: +44 (0) 20 3514 6544

info@dkwlitagency.co.uk

http://dkwlitagency.co.uk

Professional Body: The Association of Authors' Agents (AAA)

Fiction > *Novels*

Nonfiction > *Nonfiction Books*

We are always excited to read submissions from potential new clients. We welcome and actively encourage submissions from authors of all backgrounds, including those currently under-represented in publishing.

Whilst we do consider submissions from international authors, given that we are based in the United Kingdom, we feel that US-based authors will generally be better served by a US-based agent.

See individual agent listings for details on their interests and how to submit to each.

Authors: Mary Adkins; Daniel Aubrey; Ishbelle Bee; Nicola Belte; Sylvia Bishop; Kathy Brown; Jess Brownrigg; Joanne Burn; Nicole Burstein; Jayne Cowie; Jen Cownie; Felicity Day; Sarah Beth Durst; Meg Fee; Katherine Ferguson; Sharon Gosling; Sarah Maria Griffin; Natalie Hart; Brenna Ryan Hassett; Rebecca Holman; Tom Huddleston; Daisy May Johnson; Sandra Lawrence; Bryony Leah; S E Lister; Chris Lloyd; Virginia Macgregor; Clare Marchant; Nikki Marmery; Calum McSwiggan; Katharine Orton; Rebecca Orwin; David Owen; Caroline O'Donoghue; Jane O'Reilly; Josephine O'Reilly; Sarah-Jane Page; Emma Pass; Erin Pienaar; Dani Redd; Jamie Russell; Elizabeth Shapiro; Catriona Silvey; Dan Smith; E. J. Taylor; Tamsin Warner; Laura Jane Williams

Literary Agents: Camille Burns (**L089**); Ella Diamond Kahn (**L314**); Bryony Woods (**L610**)

L154 Diana Finch Literary Agency

Literary Agency
116 West 23rd Street, Suite 500, New York, NY 10011
United States
Tel: +1 (917) 544-4470

http://dianafinchliteraryagency.blogspot.com
https://dianafinchliteraryagency.submittable.com/submit
https://www.facebook.com/DianaFinchLitAg/

Nonfiction > *Nonfiction Books*
  Adventure; Business; Environment; History; Lifestyle; Mathematics; Memoir; Narrative Nonfiction; Politics; Science

How to send: Submittable

The agency is closed to all fiction submissions, and taking only nonfiction queries, including memoir, until further notice.

Literary Agent: Diana Finch (**L201**)

L155 Donya Dickerson

Literary Agent
United States

https://www.aevitascreative.com
https://www.aevitascreative.com/agent/donya-dickerson
https://querymanager.com/query/3213

Literary Agency: Aevitas

Nonfiction > *Nonfiction Books*
  Business; History; Parenting; Personal Development; Popular Culture; Science; Self Help; Technology

How to send: Query Tracker

Focuses primarily on nonfiction in the categories of business, personal development, self-help, pop culture, science, technology, history, and parenting. She is looking for breakthrough thinking, experts with a fresh voice, and new approaches to solving the problems people face daily. She is especially drawn to books that help others be their best self and succeed in both their professional and personal lives. She is based in New York.

Authors: Susan MacKenty Brady; Stuart Kliman; Igor Pejic; Leslie C. Smith

L156 Elise Dillsworth

Literary Agent
United Kingdom

elise@elisedillsworthagency.com

https://www.davidhigham.co.uk/agents-dh/elise-dillsworth/

Literary Agencies: Elise Dillsworth Agency (EDA); David Higham Associates Ltd (**L146**)

Fiction > *Novels*
  General, and in particular: International; Literary

Nonfiction > *Nonfiction Books*
  General, and in particular: Autobiography; International; Literary; Memoir

Represents literary and general fiction and non-fiction – especially autobiography and memoir, with a keen aim to reflect writing that is international.

Authors: Yvonne Battle-Felton; Maria Bradford; Karen Downs-Barton; Anthony Joseph; Foday Mannah; Diane Oliver; Yewande Omotoso; Courtney Pine; Noo Saro-Wiwa; Stephanie Victoire; Aisling Watters

L157 Lily Dolin
Associate Agent
United States

https://www.sll.com
https://www.sll.com/lily-dolin

Literary Agency: Sterling Lord Literistic, Inc.

ADULT
  Fiction > *Novels*
    Commercial; Dark Humour; Family Saga; Literary; Speculative
  Nonfiction > *Nonfiction Books*
    Crime; Feminism; Food; History; Memoir; Narrative Essays; Narrative Nonfiction; Popular Culture

YOUNG ADULT > **Fiction** > *Novels*

She represents authors in both fiction and nonfiction, including YA, with books ranging from commercial to literary and everything in between. She is actively looking for novels with strong hooks, propulsive plots, dark and offbeat humor, and nuanced female perspectives. She especially loves sweeping family dramas, strange and unusual women in strange and unusual circumstances, and smart speculative bents. In nonfiction, she is looking for narrative nonfiction, memoirs, or essay collections that are funny, outrageous, shocking, emotional, or all of the above. She particularly loves food stories, true crime, pop culture, and untold history with a feminist angle.

L158 Adriana Dominguez
Senior Agent; Partner
United States

https://aevitascreative.com/agents/
https://querymanager.com/query/2243

Literary Agency: Aevitas

ADULT > **Nonfiction** > *Nonfiction Books*: Narrative Nonfiction

CHILDREN'S
  Fiction
    Middle Grade; Picture Books
  Nonfiction > *Nonfiction Books*

How to send: Query Tracker

Interested in illustrators with fresh, unmistakable styles, platform-driven narrative nonfiction from children to adult, and select children's fiction from picture books to middle grade.

Authors: Jacqueline Alcántara; Ana Aranda; Andrés López; Angela Cervantes; Daniel Fishel; Irena Freitas; John Parra; Juliet Menéndez; Lucía Franco; Marcelo Verdad; Maria Hinojosa; Claudia Guadalupe Martinez; Maya Wei-Haas; Gerardo Ivan Morales; Heidi Moreno; Emma Otheguy; Katheryn Russell-Brown; Madrid Santos; David Smith; Tania de Regil; Janelle Washington

L159 Don Congdon Associates, Inc.
Literary Agency
88 Pine Street, Suite 730, New York, NY 10005
United States
Tel: +1 (212) 645-1229

dca@doncongdon.com
https://doncongdon.com

Professional Body: Association of American Literary Agents (AALA)

Fiction > *Novels*

Nonfiction > *Nonfiction Books*

Send: Query; Synopsis; Writing sample; Market info; Author bio
How to send: Email; Query Tracker

Send query by email (no attachments) or by Query Manager, per agent preference. Include one-page synopsis including genre, word count and comparative titles; relevant background info; and first chapter, all within the body of the email if submitting by email. Include the word "Query" in the subject line. See website for full guidelines. No unsolicited MSS.

Foreign Rights Manager / Literary Agent: Cristina Concepcion

Literary Agents: Michael Congdon; Katie Kotchman; Maura Kye-Casella; Susan Ramer (**L486**)

L160 Donald Maass Literary Agency
Literary Agency
121 West 27th Street, Suite 1201, New York, NY 10001
United States
Tel: +1 (212) 727-8383

info@maassagency.com
https://maassagency.com

Professional Body: Association of American Literary Agents (AALA)

ADULT
  Fiction > *Novels*
  Nonfiction > *Nonfiction Books*

YOUNG ADULT > **Fiction** > *Novels*

Send: Query; Synopsis; Writing sample
How to send: Email
How not to send: Post; Phone; Social Media

Welcomes all genres, in particular science fiction, fantasy, mystery, suspense, horror, romance, historical, literary and mainstream novels. Send query to a specific agent, by email, with "query" in the subject line. No queries by post, phone, or social media. See website for individual agent interests and email addresses.

Authors: Saladin Ahmed; Sonya Bateman; Jim Butcher

Literary Agents: Michael Curry; Jennifer Goloboy; Jolene Haley (**L260**); Jennifer Jackson; Kat Kerr; Donald Maass (*L377*); Cameron McClure; Caitlin McDonald; Kiana Nguyen; Anne Tibbets (**L576**)

Vice President: Katie Shea Boutillier

L161 Doug Grad Literary Agency
Literary Agency
156 Prospect Park West, #3L, Brooklyn, NY 11215
United States
Tel: +1 (718) 788-6067

doug.grad@dgliterary.com
http://www.dgliterary.com
https://www.facebook.com/DGLit

Fiction
  Graphic Novels: General
  Novels: Comedy / Humour; Crime; Historical Fiction; Mystery; Romance; Science Fiction; Thrillers; Westerns; Women's Fiction
Nonfiction
  Illustrated Books: Comedy / Humour; Photography
  Nonfiction Books: Adventure; Biography; Business; Cars; Comedy / Humour; Cookery; Crime; Dogs; Films; Gardening; Health; History; How To; Journalism; Language; Memoir; Military; Music; Politics; Religion; Self Help; Sport; Theatre; Travel

Send: Query
Don't send: Writing sample
How to send: Email
How not to send: Post; Phone

Send query letter by email. Do not include sample material until requested.

Literary Agent: Doug Grad

L162 Claire Draper
Literary Agent
United States

https://querymanager.com/query/draper_claire

Literary Agency: Azantian Literary Agency

ADULT
Fiction > *Novels*
Feminism; LGBTQIA; Romance

Nonfiction > *Nonfiction Books*
General, and in particular: Arts; Cookery; Crafts; Feminism; Home Improvement; LGBTQIA; Media; Memoir; Parenting; Plants

CHILDREN'S > Fiction
Graphic Novels; Middle Grade
YOUNG ADULT > Fiction
Graphic Novels; Novels

How not to send: Query Tracker

Prefers to work with queer and BIPOC creators. Likes lighthearted, emotional, hopeful, adventurous reads. Largely genre-agnostic, but prefers books with a fast pace, high stakes, and strong emotional development for the main character(s). Does not want to see books from authors writing identity-based books not of their own identity.

L163 Dunham Literary, Inc.
Literary Agency
United States

query@dunhamlit.com
https://www.dunhamlit.com

ADULT
Fiction > *Novels*

Nonfiction > *Nonfiction Books*: Narrative Nonfiction

CHILDREN'S > Fiction
Novels; Picture Books

Closed to approaches.

Handles quality fiction and nonfiction for adults and children. Send query by email only. See website for full guidelines. No approaches by post, phone or fax. No email attachments or links to Google docs.

Literary Agents: Anjanette Barr (**L038**); Jennie Dunham

L164 Ben Dunn
Literary Agent
United Kingdom

https://dunnfogg.co.uk
https://dunnfogg.co.uk/about-us/

Literary Agency: DunnFogg (**L165**)

Fiction > *Novels*
Book Club Fiction; Speculative; Thrillers; Women's Fiction

Nonfiction > *Nonfiction Books*
High Concept; Memoir; Narrative Nonfiction; Nature; Popular Science

How to send: Online submission system

I am happy to consider submissions in the following areas:

Fiction: off-beat thriller, reading group, speculative, issue-led women's fiction.

Non-fiction: Memoir, narrative-led non-fiction, nature writing, media tie-in (TV, Radio, Social Media, Podcast), pop-science, and big ideas.

For fiction, I enjoy off-beat characters, unusual plots and writing that extends the margins of what is traditionally expected within a genre. I am drawn to unique voices, and often novels written with humour, not 'funny' novels per se, but writing that stands out as different and unexpected.

For non-fiction, I made my start in publishing just as it was embracing popular culture. This led me into a career of following and anticipating trends, and I have continued that course into my time as an agent.

L165 DunnFogg
Literary Agency
PO Box 78047, London, N4 9LP
United Kingdom

https://dunnfogg.co.uk

Professional Body: The Association of Authors' Agents (AAA)

Fiction > *Novels*

Nonfiction > *Nonfiction Books*

Send: Query; Author bio; Synopsis; Writing sample
How to send: Online submission system

A high-profile independent literary agency that specialises in quality and commercial non-fiction and fiction. Set up in 2021, the agency represents numerous award-winning, bestselling and renowned writers and artists.

Literary Agents: Ben Dunn (**L164**); Jack Fogg (**L206**)

L166 Dunow, Carlson & Lerner Agency
Literary Agency
27 West 20th Street, Suite 1103, New York, NY 10011
United States
Tel: +1 (212) 645-7606

mail@dclagency.com

https://www.dclagency.com

Professional Body: Association of American Literary Agents (AALA)

ADULT
Fiction > *Novels*
Commercial; Literary

Nonfiction > *Nonfiction Books*

CHILDREN'S > Fiction
Chapter Books; Early Readers; Middle Grade

Send: Query; Writing sample; Self-addressed stamped envelope (SASE)
How to send: In the body of an email; Post
How not to send: Email attachment

Represents literary and commercial fiction, a wide range of nonfiction, and children's literature for all ages. Prefers queries by email, but will also accept queries by post with SASE. No attachments. Does not respond to all email queries.

Author Estates: The Estate of Donald J. Sobol; The Estate of Jim Carroll; The Estate of John Steptoe; The Estate of Joseph Mitchell; The Estate of William Lee Miller

Authors: Nathaniel Adams; Siobhan Adcock; Preston Allen; Mara Altman; Stephen Amidon; Cynthia Anderson; Jessica Applestone; Josh & Jessica Applestone; Richard Aquila; Beth Bacon; Kevin Baker; Nancy Balbirer; Wilton Barnhardt; Jackie Battenfield; Douglas Bauer; Richard Bausch; Aimee Bender; Jennifer Berney; Tanaz Bhathena; Brandon Bird; George Black; Lea Black; Robin Black; Michael Bobelian; Lorraine Boissoneault; Amy Bonnaffons; Shira Boss; Michelle Bowdler; Sesali Bowen; Nadia Bowers; Svetlana Boym; G.B. Bragg; Benjamin Breen; Elise Broach; Kevin Brockmeier; Mikita Brottman; David W. Brown; Stacia Brown; David Browne; Allison Buccola; Mónica Bustamante; Hamilton Cain; Katrina Carrasco; Bill Carter; Erika Carter; Adam Cayton-Holland; Climate Central; Bryn Chancellor; Joelle Charbonneau; Noah Charney; Paula Chase; Emily Chenoweth; K Chess; Mark Childress; Christina Chiu; Adam Christopher; Mimi Chubb; Cassandra Rose Clarke; Nigel Cliff; Nancy Coffelt; Jaed Coffin; Cole Cohen; Miriam Cohen; Jaimee Wriston Colbert; Deborah Joy Corey; Paul Cornell; Carrie Courogen; Jeremy Craig; Katherine Crowley; Dave Cullen; Cheyenne Curtis; Mark Dapin; Dame Darcy; Alice Elliott Dark; Michael Dart; Elizabeth Davis; Delilah S. Dawson; Alena Dillon; Heather Dixon; Lawrence Downes; Allyson Downey; Mike Duncan; DK Dyson; Ellie Eaton; Damien Echols; Daniel Ehrenhaft; Rhian Ellis; Katherine Crowley & Kathy Elster; Kathy Elster; Donald J. Sobol Estate; Jim Carroll Estate; John Steptoe Estate; Joseph Mitchell Estate; Scott O'Dell Estate; William Lee Miller Estate; Marion Ettlinger; Marie Favereau; Stephanie Feldman; Boris Fishman; Emily Flitter; Brendan Frederick; Pia Frey; Seth Fried; Steven Galloway; John Gartner; Amina Gautier; Joshua Gaylord; Valerie Geary; Poppy Gee; Michael Gerber; Alfred Gingold; Owen Gleiberman; Brandt Goldstein; Gary Golio; Matthew Goodman; Eli Gottlieb; Temple Grandin; Elizabeth Graver; Casey

Gray; Seth Greenland; Gwendolen Gross; Rudy Gutierrez; Kathleen Hale; Lisa Hale; Leah Hampton; Mary Ellen Hannibal; Alyssa Hardy; Windy Lynn Harris; Ethan Hauser; Kevin Hearne; Robert Hellenga; Steve Hendricks; Joe Henry; Becky Hepinstall; Emily Jane Hodgkin; George Hodgman; Beatrice Hohenegger; Christopher M. Hood; Erin Hosier; Ilze Hugo; Josie Iselin; Jeremy Jackson; John Hornor Jacobs; Matthew Jobin; Daron Joffe; Mary Jones; Noah Z. Jones; David Joy; Frank Wheeler, Jr.; Valerie June; Karen Kane; Hester Kaplan; Ani Katz; Jon Keller; Brad Kessler; Christian Kiefer; Andrea Kleine; Taylor Koekkoek; Chrissy Kolaya; Amanda Korman; Gabrielle Korn; Nik Korpon; J. Kasper Kramer; Justin Kuritzkes; Maria Kuznetsova; Johanna Lane; Sarah Langan; Richard Lange; Sarah Laskow; Holly LeCraw; Mirinae Lee; Tommy Lee; Edan Lepucki; Elizabeth Lesser; Jerry Lee Lewis; Robin Lewis; David Lida; Anya Liftig; Brad Listi; William Bryant Logan; Jenny Lombard; Leil Lowndes; Joshua Lyon; Robin MacArthur; David Stuart MacLean; Anne Madden; Dennis Mahoney; Tania Malik; Michael Mann; Tanya Marquardt; Debra Marquart; Alex Marshall; Cate Marvin; Suzanne Matson; Abi Maxwell; Matthew McBride; Jill McCorkle; Elizabeth McCracken; Patrick McDonnell; Sean McGinty; Jon McGoran; Will McGrath; Adam McOmber; Bob Mehr; Susan Scarf Merrell; Deborah Meyler; Jenny Milchman; Barnabas Miller; Daphne Miller; Paul Miller; Richard J. Miller; Denise Mina; T. T. Monday; Gregory Mone; Amanda Montell; Bradford Morrow; Brian Morton; Layne Mosler; Sarah Moss; Ritu Mukerji; Kimberly Shannon Murphy; Myra Musgrove; Debbie Nathan; Ed Nawotka; Greg Neri; Robert Neuwith; Alana Newhouse; Scott O'Connor; Aline Ohanesian; Elizabeth Oness; David Orr; Chad Orzel; Tom Paine; Richard Panek; Michel Paradis; Debra Pascali-Bonaro; Rachel Pastan; Justin Peacock; Jamie Pearlberg; Tony Perrottet; Annie Rogers, Ph.D.; Chad Orzel, Ph.D.; Max Phillips; Melissa Holbrook Pierson; Nic Pizzolatto; Aimee Pokwatka; Daria Polichetti; Richard Polt; Maggie Pouncey; Jessica Powers; Caroline Preston; Cherie Priest; Mark Prins; D. M. Pulley; Carol Purington; Susan Todd & Carol Purington; Joan Quigley; Mark Rader; Susanna Reich; Nelly Reifler; Heidi Reimer; James Renner; Paul Reyes; Robert Riesman; Honni Van Rijswijk; Nicholas Rinaldi; M. L. Rio; Marisa Robinson-Textor; Annie Rogers; Stuart Rojstaczer; Tricia Romano; Linda Ronstadt; Jane Roper; Alex Rose; Marissa A. Ross; Rebecca Rotert; Shannan Rouss; Katherine Rowland; Lena Roy; David Rubel; Joan Ryan; Richard Sandoval; Marisa de los Santos; Alexis Schaitkin; Kodi Scheer; Patty Schemel; David Schickler; Molly Schiot; Heidi Jon Schmidt; Sally Schmitt; Pat Schories; William Todd Schultz; Kieran Shea; Jeff Shelby; Joshua Wolf Shenk; Jenefer Shute; Ingrid Silva; Marisa Silver; Ione Skye; Mohamedou Slahi; Patti Smith; Sherry Smith; Kevin Smokler; Tatjana Soli; Lily Sparks; Shira Spector; Kelli Stanley; Leigh Stein; Javaka Steptoe; Lindsay Stern; Jude Stewart; Susan Straight; Cynthia D'Aprix Sweeney; Vivian Swift; Shannon Takaoka; Liara Tamani; Katrina Taylor; Nick Taylor; David Teague; Tori Telfer; Melanie Thernstrom; Jean Thompson; Richard Todd; Susan Todd; David Tomlinson; Lawrence Turman; James Twitchell; Neil deGrasse Tyson; Robert Utley; Karen Valby; Katherine Vaz; Sarah St. Vincent; Christine Wade; Laura Waldon; Casey Walker; Mark Van de Walle; Margaret Wappler; Elizabeth Weinberg; Jillian Weise; Jan Merete Weiss; Michaele Weissman; Elizabeth Weitzman; Chuck Wendig; Frank Wheeler; Kali White; Matt Wiegle; Marianne Wiggins; Amy Wilentz; Corban Wilkinson; Tim Wirkus; Mishna Wolff; Hilma Wolitzer; Alisson Wood; Aubrey Wood; Billy Woods; Rebecca Woolf; Sara Woster; Kim Wozencraft; Ronald Wright; David Wroblewski; Jeff Yang; David Yoo; Kenji Yoshino; Alia Yunis; Alan Ziegler; Jaime deBlanc-Knowles; Jennifer duBois

Literary Agents: Jennifer Carlson; Arielle Datz; Stacia Decker; Henry Dunow; Susanna Einstein (**L173**); Susan Graham (**L248**); Erin Hosier; Eleanor Jackson; Julia Kenny (**L329**); Betsy Lerner; Edward Necarsulmer; Nicki Richesin; Yishai Seidman

L167 Jane Dystel
President; Literary Agent
United States

https://www.dystel.com
https://x.com/jdystel

Literary Agency: Dystel, Goderich & Bourret LLC

Fiction > *Novels*
Commercial Women's Fiction; Commercial; Literary

Nonfiction > *Nonfiction Books*
Biography; Current Affairs; History; Legal; Medicine; Memoir; Politics; Science

Send: Query
How to send: In the body of an email
How not to send: Email attachment; Links to material online; Google Docs shared document; Dropbox

I love to read commercial and literary fiction, memoir, biography and history. I am very interested in current events, politics, legal subjects and women's commercial fiction of all kinds. I find science fascinating and am passionate about science and medical narratives.

L168 Molly Eagles
Literary Agent

Literary Agency: Independent Talent Group Ltd

L169 Lynette Eason
Literary Agent
United States

ehumphries@stevelaube.com

https://stevelaube.com/what-i-am-looking-for-lynette-eason/

Literary Agency: The Steve Laube Agency

ADULT
Fiction > *Novels*
Christianity; Contemporary Women's Fiction; Historical Fiction; Mystery; Romantic Suspense; Speculative; Thrillers

Nonfiction > *Nonfiction Books*: Christianity

YOUNG ADULT
Fiction > *Novels*: Christianity

Nonfiction > *Nonfiction Books*: Christianity

Send: Query; Writing sample
How to send: Email
How not to send: Post

I am looking for Christian authors wishing to write and sell to the Christian market. This means that I'm searching for clients who adhere to the teachings of Christ and Scripture. I'm looking to represent authors of all types of Christian fiction. I'm also interested in YA nonfiction and may be interested in some adult nonfiction, depending on the topic. I am not looking for children's books.

L170 Eddison Pearson Ltd
Literary Agency
West Hill House, 6 Swain's Lane, London, N6 6QS
United Kingdom
Tel: +44 (0) 20 7700 7763

enquiries@eddisonpearson.com

https://www.eddisonpearson.com
https://linktr.ee/ClarePearson
https://eddisonpearson.blog
https://www.linkedin.com/in/clare-pearson-epla
https://twitter.com/ClarePearson_EP

Professional Body: The Association of Authors' Agents (AAA)

CHILDREN'S
Fiction
Novels: Contemporary; Historical Fiction
Picture Books: General

Poetry > *Any Poetic Form*

YOUNG ADULT > **Fiction** > *Novels*

Send: Query; Writing sample
How to send: Email
How not to send: Social Media; Post

A London-based literary agency providing a personal service to a small stable of talented authors, mainly of books for children and young adults. Send query by email only for auto-response containing up-to-date submission guidelines and email address for submissions. No submissions or enquiries by post.

Authors: Valerie Bloom; Michael Catchpool; Sue Heap; Caroline Lawrence; Robert Muchamore; Mary Murphy; Megan Rix

Literary Agent: Clare Pearson

L171 Anne Edelstein
Literary Agent
United States

https://www.pandeliterary.com
https://www.pandeliterary.com/our-team-pandeliterary

Literary Agency: Ayesha Pande Literary

Fiction > *Novels*

Nonfiction > *Nonfiction Books*
  Culture; Memoir; Narrative History; Philosophy; Religion; Science; Spirituality

Closed to approaches.

Over the decades, her work with authors is led by passion for their subjects and their writing. This encompasses a range of narrative history, culture, philosophy, religion, spirituality, science, memoir and fiction

L172 Sam Edenborough
Literary Agent; Foreign Rights Director
United Kingdom

sam@greyhoundliterary.co.uk

https://greyhoundliterary.co.uk/agent/sam-edenborough/
https://twitter.com/SamEdenborough

Literary Agency: Greyhound Literary

Fiction > *Novels*
  Cyberpunk; Fantasy; Folklore, Myths, and Legends; Hard Science Fiction; Horror; Speculative; Upmarket

Nonfiction > *Nonfiction Books*
  Classical Music; Culture; History; Jazz; Music; Science

Send: Synopsis; Outline; Writing sample
How to send: Email

A life-long reader of speculative fiction. He loves hard SF and cyberpunk that explores the biggest questions about what it means to be human; fantasy with wit, brilliantly deep world-building and characters with an edge. He is interested in upmarket, folkloric or horror-tinged fiction. He is also looking for fiction and non-fiction which engages with landscape or the sea in a profound and original way; books about jazz and classical music and musicians; work by historians and novelists who challenge us to rethink comfortable assumptions about an era or a culture; and writing by scientists who are able to communicate complex ideas to a wide readership with verve.

Authors: David Clifford; Jonathan Morrison; Leonard Rutgers; Philip Suggars

L173 Susanna Einstein
Literary Agent
United States

https://www.dclagency.com
https://aalitagents.org/author/susannaeinsteinliterary-com/

Literary Agency: Dunow, Carlson & Lerner Agency (**L166**)
Professional Body: Association of American Literary Agents (AALA)

ADULT
  Fiction > *Novels*
    Crime; Upmarket Commercial Fiction

  Nonfiction > *Nonfiction Books*
    Biography; Business; Cookery; History; Memoir

CHILDREN'S > **Fiction** > *Middle Grade*

YOUNG ADULT > **Fiction** > *Novels*

Works primarily on upmarket commercial and crime fiction for adults, selectively on YA and MG projects, and idiosyncratically on non-fiction that has included biography, business, cookbooks, history and memoir.

L174 Nicole Eisenbraun
Literary Agent
United States

nme@gingerclarkliterary.com

https://gingerclarkliterary.com/About
https://gingerclarkliterary.com/Submissions
http://aaronline.org/Sys/PublicProfile/51483163/417813

Literary Agency: Ginger Clark Literary
Professional Body: Association of American Literary Agents (AALA)

CHILDREN'S > **Fiction** > *Middle Grade*
  General, and in particular: Fairy Tales

YOUNG ADULT > **Fiction** > *Novels*
  General, and in particular: Fairy Tales

Send: Query; Writing sample
How to send: Email

Looking for middle grade and young adult in all genres. She is particularly interested in great fairytale retellings with colorful twists and stories that tackle difficult subjects in unexpected ways.

L175 Caroline Eisenmann
Senior Agent; Vice President
United States

ce@goldinlit.com

https://goldinlit.com/agents/

Literary Agency: Frances Goldin Literary Agency, Inc.
Professional Body: Association of American Literary Agents (AALA)

Fiction > *Novels*
  Literary; Social Issues; Upmarket

Nonfiction
  Essays: General
  Nonfiction Books: Biography; Cultural Criticism; History; Literary Memoir; Sub-Culture

How to send: Email

Particularly drawn to novels that engage with social issues, stories about obsession, and work that centers around intimacy and its discontents. Her nonfiction interests include deeply reported narratives (especially those that take the reader into the heart of a subculture), literary memoir, cultural criticism, essay collections, and history and biography with a surprising point of view.

Authors: Kyle Chayka; Ye Chun; Linda Rui Feng; Amanda Goldblatt; James Gregor; Peter Kispert; Theresa Levitt; Micah Nemerever; Jenny Odell; Kate Wagner; Michelle Webster-Hein

L176 The Ekus Group
Literary Agency
216 East 75th Street, Suite 1E, New York, NY 10021
United States

https://ekusgroup.com

Literary Agency: The Jean V. Naggar Literary Agency (**L299**)

Nonfiction > *Nonfiction Books*: Cookery

How to send: Online submission system

Handles cookery books only. Submit proposal through submission system on website.

Literary Agent: Lisa Ekus
Senior Agent: Sally Ekus (**L177**)

L177 Sally Ekus
Senior Agent
United States

sally@ekusgroup.com

https://ekusgroup.com
https://ekusgroup.com/people/sally-ekus/
https://www.jvnla.com/our-team.php
https://aalitagents.org/author/sallylisaekus-com/
https://www.linkedin.com/in/sally-ekus-b8116554/
https://www.instagram.com/sallyekus/

Literary Agencies: The Ekus Group (**L176**); The Jean V. Naggar Literary Agency (**L299**)
Professional Body: Association of American Literary Agents (AALA)

Nonfiction > *Nonfiction Books*
  Cookery; Health; Lifestyle; Wellbeing

Send: Query; Proposal; Author bio; Market info; Marketing plan; Table of contents
How to send: Email

Represents a wide range of culinary, health, wellness, and lifestyle talent, from first-time cookbook authors to seasoned chefs, RDs, professional food writers, bloggers, online creators, and journalists.

L178 Elaine Markson Literary Agency
Literary Agency
116 West 23rd Street, 5th flr, New York, NY 10011
United States

gagencyquery@gmail.com

https://www.marksonagency.com

Fiction > *Novels*

Nonfiction > *Nonfiction Books*

Literary Agent: Jeff Gerecke

L179 Elaine Steel
Literary Agency
49 Greek Street, London, W1D 4EG
United Kingdom
Tel: +44 (0) 1273 739022

es@elainesteel.com

https://www.elainesteel.com

Professional Body: The Association of Authors' Agents (AAA)

Fiction > *Novels*

Nonfiction > *Nonfiction Books*

Scripts
  Film Scripts; Radio Scripts; TV Scripts; Theatre Scripts

Send: Query; Author bio; Outline
Don't send: Full text
How to send: Email

Represents writers and directors in film, television, stage and radio as well as book writers. Send query by email with CV and outline, along with details of experience. No unsolicited mss.

Authors: Gwyneth Hughes; James Lovelock; Ben Steiner

L180 Sian Ellis-Martin
Associate Agent
United Kingdom

sian@blakefriedmann.co.uk

http://blakefriedmann.co.uk/sianellis-martin
https://twitter.com/sianellismartin

Literary Agency: Blake Friedmann Literary Agency Ltd (**L065**)

Fiction > *Novels*
  Coming of Age; Commercial; Contemporary; Crime; Ethnic Groups; Family Saga; Family; Friends; Historical Fiction; LGBTQIA; Literary; Love; Relationships; Romance; Romantic Comedy; Sex; Sexuality; Social Class; Thrillers

Nonfiction > *Nonfiction Books*
  Cookery; Food; History; Love; Narrative Nonfiction; Politics; Popular Culture; Relationships

Does not want:

  Fiction > *Novels*: Police Procedural

Send: Query; Synopsis; Writing sample
How to send: Email attachment

I'm building a list of fiction and non-fiction across genres. I'm keen to hear from authors who feel their voice is underrepresented in publishing and it's important to me to work with authors and books from a wide variety of backgrounds.

Authors: Shani Akilah; Ros Anderson; Alex Clark; Jenny Glanfield; Leeanne O'Donnell; Cristina Wolf

L181 Ericka T. Phillips
Literary Agent
United States

https://www.stephanietadeagency.com/aboutus

Literary Agency: Stephanie Tade Literary Agency

Nonfiction > *Nonfiction Books*
  Buddhism; Health; Mind, Body, Spirit; Spirituality

Interested in non-fiction authors working in the Buddhist and mindfulness arena with a focus on health and spiritual well-being. She has a passion for developing projects and building platforms that help amplify the voices of women of color and black women writers in particular. She is experienced in platform development, marketing, and publicity and helps authors translate their message into brand strategy.

L182 Eunice McMullen Children's Literary Agent Ltd
Literary Agency
Low Ibbotsholme Cottage, Off Bridge Lane, Troutbeck Bridge, Windermere, Cumbria, LA23 1HU
United Kingdom
Tel: +44 (0) 1539 448551

eunice@eunicemcmullen.co.uk

https://www.eunicemcmullen.co.uk

CHILDREN'S > Fiction
  Middle Grade; *Novels*; *Picture Books*
TEEN > Fiction > *Novels*

Closed to approaches.

Most of my clients have been with me a considerable time so my list tends not to change. The agency is no longer accepting new submissions.

Literary Agent: Eunice McMullen

L183 The Evan Marshall Agency
Literary Agency
1 Pacio Court, Roseland, NJ 07068-1121
United States
Tel: +1 (973) 287-6216

evan@evanmarshallagency.com

https://www.evanmarshallagency.com

Professional Body: Association of American Literary Agents (AALA)
Types: Fiction; Nonfiction
Markets: Adult; Young Adult

Closed to approaches.

Represents all genres of adult and young-adult full-length fiction. New clients by referral only.

Literary Agent: Evan Marshall

L184 David Evans
Literary Agent
United Kingdom

Literary Agency: David Higham Associates Ltd (**L146**)

L185 Kate Evans
Literary Agent
United Kingdom
Tel: +44 (0) 20 7344 1047

kevans@pfd.co.uk

https://petersfraserdunlop.com/agent/kate-evans/
https://twitter.com/kateeevans

Literary Agency: Peters Fraser + Dunlop

Fiction > *Novels*
  General, and in particular: Family Saga; Literary Suspense; Romance

Nonfiction > *Nonfiction Books*
  Cookery; Economics; Food; History; Literary; Memoir; Narrative Nonfiction; Nature; Personal Development; Philosophy; Politics; Popular Culture; Popular Science; Science; Social Issues

Does not want:

  Fiction > *Novels*
    Hard Science Fiction; High / Epic Fantasy

Send: Query; Synopsis; Writing sample; Proposal; Author bio

How to send: Email
How not to send: Post

I am actively looking for exciting new voices across both fiction and non-fiction.

I'm interested in non-fiction that says something about the way we live- from beautiful narrative non-fiction with a strong voice to passionate manifestos from experts in their fields. Whether it's popular science, big ideas, nature writing, memoir, fresh approaches to history or insightful takes on pop culture, I am drawn to writing that makes social, political, and economic issues accessible and engaging.

I read very widely in fiction but the common thread that runs through most novels I love is a sharply observed take on relationships and strong characters I'll think about long after I've left them on the page. I want a book I can gleefully, greedily consume- that kind of crying in public, ignoring your friends level compulsiveness… but I also want it to be beautifully put together.

I would love to see more literary suspense, a funny-sad family drama and I am forever on the lookout for a great love story.

I am largely genre-agnostic and if you're using genre (crime, horror, speculative) in an interesting way underpinned by exceptional writing I'd love to see it. Having said this, I'm probably not the best agent for hard SFF or YA.

Authors: Ali Abdaal; Nadine Bacchus-Garrick; Heidi Lauth Beasley; Sophie Beresiner; Abigail Bergstrom; Orsola De Castro; Julia F. Christensen; Olivia Jordan Cornelius; Iona David; Léa Rose Emery; Kate Evans; Richard Fisher; Ione Gamble; Bre Graham; Malwina Gudowska; Jessica Hamel-Akré; Sarah Haque; Kenya Hunt; Katerina Johnson; Jenna Macciochi; Sophie Mort; Jennifer Obidike; Georgina Sturge; Stefanie Sword-Williams; Amelia Tait; Rossalyn Warren; Rose Wilding

L186 Samantha Fabien
Literary Agent
United States

https://www.rootliterary.com/agents
https://www.publishersmarketplace.com/members/samfabien/
https://twitter.com/samanthashnh
https://aalitagents.org/author/samanthashnh/
https://querymanager.com/query/samanthafabien

Literary Agency: Root Literary (**L503**)
Professional Body: Association of American Literary Agents (AALA)

ADULT > **Fiction** > *Novels*
Book Club Fiction; Commercial; Contemporary Romance; Fantasy; High Concept; Horror; Mystery; Romantic Comedy; Speculative; Suspense; Thrillers; Upmarket; Women's Fiction

CHILDREN'S > **Fiction** > *Middle Grade*
YOUNG ADULT > **Fiction** > *Novels*

Send: Query; Synopsis; Writing sample
How to send: Query Tracker

I live for the rollercoaster of emotions that characters and stories can take me on. Whether I'm swooning or gasping, I want to feel strongly enough about a project that I desperately need to share it with the world.

L187 Holly Faulks
Literary Agent
United Kingdom

https://greeneheaton.co.uk/agents/holly-faulks/
https://x.com/hollycfaulks

Literary Agency: Greene & Heaton Ltd (**L251**)

Fiction > *Novels*
General, and in particular: Commercial; Cozy Fantasy; Crime; Dark Academia; High Concept; Literary; Romance; Romantasy; Social Commentary; Social Media; Thrillers

Nonfiction > *Nonfiction Books*
General, and in particular: Health; Language; Lifestyle; Personal Finance; Politics; Society; Wellbeing

Send: Synopsis; Writing sample
How to send: Email

In fiction I read widely across genre and am happy to be surprised by the next thing I fall for. I've had a lot of fun with romance recently and am always keen to be swept up in a gorgeous love story. This might be anything from a classic of the genre, to something high-concept or even something that totally subverts expectations. I've been getting excited about romance that seeps into fantasy – my favourites in this area tend to be either cosy or lean into dark academia but as I say, I'm open to being surprised! I like my fiction to maintain a real warmth, whether that's in commercial fiction or more literary writing. I love sharp and witty prose, but that sense of warmth is (almost always!) crucial. My all-time favourites are Katheirne Heiny and Maria Semple. I'd particularly love to find some new authors writing accessible literary fiction with a high-concept hook – if you think that could be you, please do submit to me! I'm always looking for new voices in crime and thriller. I love writers like Rumaan Alam and Sabine Durrant who weave social commentary into the genre but ultimately, I'm just looking for anything that makes me want to keep turning the pages! I'd really like to find a smart and original take on the world of influencers and social media so please do send me anything in that vein too.

Most of the non-fiction I work on is socially and politically engaged and I'm always looking for more writers in this area exploring new subjects. As in fiction, I'm drawn to books that explore the way we live, particularly in the modern world. At the moment I'm also keen to take on more writers interested in helping us live our lives better – perhaps that's soft business or finance, health and wellness or practical guides for everyday living. I'm always keen to hear from people who have something new to add to our current understandings and conversations on the way we live. I studied languages at university so I'm always keen to find books about the spoken word, and more particularly about the way it relates to the way we experience the world. In non-fiction I often take on books in areas I didn't even know I was looking so if you've got a fabulous idea, whatever the area, do get in touch!

And one final, more specific plea – I think we're overdue a book on teeth and gums, particularly as they pertain to our overall health. If you're a dentist ready to write a book – please get in touch!

Authors: Precious Adesina; Carol Ballantine; Michelle Bang; Emily Bootle; Zoe Burgess; Joseph Coward; Rageshri Dhairyawan; Holly Friend; Emma Garland; Lily Hackett; Jake Hall; Julie Hayward; Kit Heyam; Juliet Jacques; Iggy LDN; August Lamm; Carina Maggar; Anna Sulan Masing; Sadhbh O'Sullivan; Sara-Ella Ozbek; Nicolas Padamsee; Jyoti Patel; Neel Patel; Xenobe Purvis; Francesca Ramsay; Ana Reyes; Paula Rogers; Ella Frances Sanders; Ione Wells

L188 Hillary Fazzari
Literary Agent
United States

https://bradfordlit.com
https://bradfordlit.com/hillary-fazzari-agent/
https://querymanager.com/query/3240
https://aalitagents.org/author/hillaryfazzari/
https://twitter.com/HillaryFazzari

Literary Agency: Bradford Literary Agency (**L073**)
Professional Body: Association of American Literary Agents (AALA)

ADULT
Fiction > *Novels*
Book Club Fiction; Commercial Fantasy; Culture; Dark Romance; Family; Gothic; High Concept; Historical Fiction; Horrorromance; Literary; Romance; Romantasy; Romantic Comedy; Science Fiction Romance; Speculative Historical Fiction; Upmarket Fantasy; Upmarket; Women's Fiction

Nonfiction > *Nonfiction Books*
Archaeology; History; Literature; Popular Culture

CHILDREN'S > **Fiction** > *Middle Grade*

NEW ADULT > Fiction > *Novels*
  General, and in particular: Commercial
YOUNG ADULT > Fiction > *Novels*
Closed to approaches.

On the lookout for: Highly accessible, super high concept kids' books in all age bands; Very commercial books for New Adult and Adult Gen-Z and Millennial audiences that feature sticky hooks and feel like they're doing something fun, new, and BIGGER with their genre; Select Adult upmarket/literary work that is also super high concept and feels fresh and hyper relevant; and Adult Nonfiction in areas of History, Archaeology, Pop Culture, and Literature.

In terms of material, she acquires Middle Grade, YA, and New Adult fiction (including "gap area" stories) in all genres, and in the Adult sphere, she acquires more selectively and is open to unsolicited queries in: Rom-coms and rom-com adjacent material (especially when projects feel like they're evolving the genre ahead!); Horrormance and Dark Romance (big concept, not too gruesome, and I like consent); Romantasy and other mashups of SFF/romance (especially work that plays with concepts/foundations of fandoms and/or pop culture but doesn't specifically mimic an already extent fandom such as ACOTAR); Commercial or upmarket fantasy, speculative historical, and/or gothic work with a strong appeal to book club, romance, or women's fiction audiences; High concept, upmarket work that explores family/culture/history à la THE JOY LUCK CLUB; and Nonfiction that focuses on History, Archaeology, Pop Culture, and Literature.

L189 Leigh Feldman
Literary Agent
United States

Literary Agency: Leigh Feldman Literary (**L359**)

L190 Kait Lee Feldmann
Literary Agent
United States

kait@ktliterary.com
querykait@ktliterary.com

https://www.kaitfeldmann.com
https://www.kaitfeldmann.com/mswl
https://ktliterary.com/agents

Literary Agency: KT Literary (**L345**)

CHILDREN'S > Fiction
  Graphic Novels; Picture Books

Send: Query; Full text
How to send: Email attachment; Links to material online

Costs: Offers services that writers have to pay for.

I represent illustrators and illustrator-authors who are primarily interested in working on picture books and graphic novels. We'd be a good match if you enjoy wholesome chaos. Let's make books for the kids who get in trouble for their imagination, the next generation of mad scientists, supervillains, and witches at the end of the street.

Authors: Samantha Chiusolo; Vikki Chu; Ebony Glenn; Jen Gubicza; Haejin Park; Lisa Wee

L191 The Feldstein Agency
Literary Agency; Editorial Service; Consultancy
52 Ashley Drive, Bangor, Northern Ireland, BT20 5RD
United Kingdom
Tel: +44 (0) 2891 312485

submissions@thefeldsteinagency.co.uk

https://www.thefeldsteinagency.co.uk
https://twitter.com/feldsteinagency

Fiction > *Novels*

Nonfiction > *Nonfiction Books*

Does not want:

> Fiction > *Novels*
>   Fantasy; Historical Fiction; Romance; Science Fiction

Send: Query; Synopsis; Proposal; Author bio
How to send: Word file email attachment; PDF file email attachment

Costs: Offers services that writers have to pay for. Offers editing, ghostwriting, and consultancy services.

Handles adult fiction and nonfiction only. No children's, young adult, romance, science fiction, fantasy, poetry, scripts, short stories, or already-published works (including self-published). For fiction, please email a cover letter, a 1-2 page synopsis of your novel, and a brief biography. For non-fiction, please email a cover letter, a detailed proposal, and a brief biography. No reading fees or evaluation fees. The only instance in which an author would be charged a fee is for ghost-writing.

Consultant / Literary Agent: Paul Feldstein

Editor / Literary Agent: Susan Feldstein

L192 Felicity Bryan Associates
Literary Agency
2a North Parade Avenue, Banbury Road, Oxford, OX2 6LX
United Kingdom
Tel: +44 (0) 1865 513816

submissions@felicitybryan.com

https://felicitybryan.com

Professional Body: The Association of Authors' Agents (AAA)

Fiction > *Novels*

Nonfiction > *Nonfiction Books*

Does not want:

> Fiction > *Novels*
>   Fantasy; Romantasy; Science Fiction

Send: Query; Synopsis; Proposal; Writing sample
How to send: Online submission system
How not to send: Post

As an agency we are always searching for talented new writers. Whether you write beautifully crafted literary fiction, immersive middle-grade novels, or fascinating and informative non-fiction, we would love the opportunity to consider your work. We look for ambitious, confident writing that feels fresh and distinctive, and we welcome voices from all backgrounds. There is no expectation for writers to have existing connections to the publishing industry or a formal creative writing qualification. We take the time to carefully read and review every submission we receive.

Associate Agent: Sally Holloway (**L284**)

Authors: Carlos Acosta; Johnny Acton; Sally Adee; Samira Ahmed; David Almond; Ben Ambridge; Karen Armstrong; Lucy Ash; Frances Ashcroft; James Attlee; Mark Avery; Modern Baker; Katya Balen; James Barr; David Barrie; Kay Barron; John Barton; John Batchelor; Emily Baughan; Susan Beale; Jonny Beardsall; Roderick Beaton; Catherine Belton; Erica Benner; Louis De Bernières; Mary Berry; Claire Bertschinger; Paul Betts; Nina Bhadreshwar; Michael Bird; Tim Birkhead; Andrew Blum; Elleke Boehmer; Stella Botchway; John Bowker; Susan Brigden; Francesca Brill; Rhidian Brook; James Brooke-Smith; Adam Brookes; Archie Brown; Larisa Brown; Ursula Buchan; Julia Bueno; Stephen Burke; Matthew Burton; Karl Bushby; Tom Butler-Bowdon; Emma Byrne; Lucy Cavendish; Graham Caveney; Fernando Cervantes; Sarah Challis; Peter Chapman; Nick Chater; Simukai Chigudu; Marcus Chown; Morten H. Christiansen; Liza Cody; Jonathan Coe; Will Cohu; Artemis Cooper; T.A. Cotterell; Benjamin Daniels; Chloe Daykin; John Dickie; Jenny Downham; Serena Dyer; Will Eaves; Reni Eddo-Lodge; Nick Edwards; James Fairhead; Natasha Farrant; David Farrier; Edmund Fawcett; James Fearnley; Georgina Ferry; Rebecca Fleet; Catherine Fletcher; CJ Flood; Peter Frankopan; Lawrence Freedman; Dominic Frisby; Clare Furniss; Damon Galgut; Sally Gardner; Peter Gatrell; Robert Gildea; Amelia Giudici; Jonathan Glover; David Goldblatt; Susan Golombok; Kat Gordon; Chris Gosden; Barbara Graziosi; Catherine Hall; Simon Hall; Thomas Halliday; James Hamilton; Tim Harford; Peter Heather; Tim Hecker; Louis Hill; Lindsey Hilsum; Penelope Hobhouse; Anna Hope; Gill Hornby;

Richard House; Alice Hunt; Kathryn Hurlock; Allegra Huston; Robert Hutton; Belinda Jack; Sarah Jasmon; Joseph Jebelli; Lauren St John; Colin Jones; Nick Jubber; Alex Kaiserman; Helena Kelly; Stanley Kenani; Liz Kessler; Amy Key; Liza Klaussmann; Richard Koch; Chelsea Kwakye; James Kynge; Simon Lancaster; Katherine Langrish; Tomila Lankina; Grace Lavery; Phyllida Law; Tim Leach; Simon Lelic; Lucy Lethbridge; Alysa Levene; Suzannah Lipscomb; John Lister-Kaye; Tess Little; Jonathan Loh; Rebecca Lowe; Natasha Lunn; Diarmaid Macculloch; Anna Machin; Fiona Maddocks; Laurie Maguire; Henry Mance; Sarah K Marr; Ben Martynoga; Toby Matthiesen; James Mcdougall; Chris Mcgrath; Kate Mcloughlin; Martin Meredith; Oliver Milman; Tom Moorhouse; Katy Moran; Alistair Morgan; Elian J Morgan; Alan Murrin; Jennifer Nadel; Vanessa Nakate; Tom Nancollas; Natasha Narayan; James Naughtie; Linda Newbery; TN Ninan; Camilla Nord; Jenny Odell; Ore Ogunbiyi; Adjoa Osei; Richard Ovenden; Joanne Owen; Svenja O'donnell; Colm O'gorman; Elsa Panciroli; Iain Pears; Thomas Penn; Andrew Pettegree; Jonathan Phillips; David Pilling; Annabel Pitcher; Rachel Polonsky; Nick Potter; Andrew Prentice; Sue Prideaux; Diane Purkiss; Josephine Quinn; Captain Elliot Rappaport; Shilpa Ravella; Melody Razak; Owen Rees; Alex Reeve; David Reynolds; Dan Richards; Eloise Rickman; Thomas Rid; Alex Riley; Charlotte Lydia Riley; Ian Robertson; Ritchie Robertson; David Robson; Eugene Rogan; Nicola Rollock; Meg Rosoff; Miri Rubin; Ulinka Rublack; Adam Ruck; Penny Rudge; Edward Russell-Walling; Alec Ryrie; Farhan Samanani; Joseph Sassoon; Jon Savage; Paul Seabright; Zakia Sewell; Alom Shaha; Liam Shaw; Emma Smith; Tiffany Watt Smith; Lexi Stadlen; Marc Stears; Miriam Stoppard; Roy Strong; Sue Stuart-Smith; Julie Summers; Krystal Sutherland; Henry Sutton; Katherine Swift; Cathy Thomas; Adrian Tinniswood; Eleanor Updale; Tom Vanderbilt; Christopher Vick; Edmund De Waal; Martin Walker; Samantha Walton; Kirsty Wark; Clive Webb; Arthur Der Weduwen; Jonathan Weil; Anna Whitelock; Tim Whitmarsh; K.J. Whittaker; Hugh Wilford; Sam Wilkin; Imogen Willetts; Lisa Williamson; Greg Wise; Bill Wood; Michael Wood; Lucy Wooding; Michael Wooldridge; Lucy Worsley; James Wythe; Jessica Wärnberg; Kieran Yates; Lucy Young

Company Directors / Literary Agents: Carrie Plitt (**L477**); Caroline Wood (**L608**)

Literary Agent: Angelique Tran Van Sang

Literary Agent / Managing Director: Catherine Clarke (**L119**)

L193 Abi Fellows
Literary Agent
United Kingdom

af.submission@dhhliteraryagency.com
https://www.dhhliteraryagency.com
https://www.dhhliteraryagency.com/abi-fellows

Literary Agency: DHH Literary Agency Ltd (**L152**)

ADULT
Fiction > *Novels*
General, and in particular: Dark; Historical Fiction; Literary; Romantic Comedy

Nonfiction > *Nonfiction Books*
General, and in particular: Commercial; Culture; History; Literary Memoir; Self Help

CHILDREN'S > **Fiction** > *Middle Grade*
YOUNG ADULT > **Fiction** > *Novels*

Does not want:

> **Fiction** > *Novels*
> Cookery; Fantasy; Horror; Science Fiction

Send: Query; Synopsis; Proposal; Writing sample; Outline; Market info
How to send: Email

For fiction, please send your cover letter, one-page synopsis and first three chapters. For non-fiction, please send a proposal (including overview of book's main idea, information about you the author / why you are the person to write the book, an outline of full book with chapter breakdowns / descriptions and sources, a sample chapter and, if these are available to you, media links, advance praise, comparable titles).

Authors: Tasneem Abdur-Rashid; Paula Akpan; Carolina Are; Karen Arthur; Khairani Barokka; Katie Baskerville; Caroline Butterwick; Aaron Dale; Azma Dar; K Devan; Sharan Dhaliwal; Preeti Dhillon; Anna Ellory; Deirdre Finnerty; Nicola Garrard; Divya Ghelani; Nadia Gilani; Erica Gillingham; Alexis Gregory; Michael Handrick; Mireille Harper; Ali Hendry; Hanan Issa; Sophie Jai; Lizzie Huxley Jones; Nancy Kelley; Catherine Kurtz; Eleni Kyriacou; Thomas Leeds; Chantelle Lindsay; Elizabeth Lovatt; Natalie Marlow; Layla McCay; Saima Mir; Zeena Moolla; Evie Muir; Jade Mutyora; Erik Olsen; Yen Ooi; Philippa Peall; Penny Pepper; Lauren du Plessis; Grace Quantock; Jasmine Qureshi; Monika Radojevic; Jon Ransom; Jini Reddy; Juno Roche; Helen Scott; Amélie Skoda; Paul Taylor-Pitt; Rosie Turner; Eva Verde; Kandace Siobhan Walker; Clare Weze; lisa luxx

L194 Hannah Ferguson
Literary Agent
United Kingdom

hannah@hardmanswainson.com
submissions@hardmanswainson.com
https://www.hardmanswainson.com/agent/hannah-ferguson/
https://twitter.com/AgentFergie

Literary Agency: Hardman & Swainson (**L265**)

Fiction > *Novels*
General, and in particular: Book Club Fiction; Commercial; Crime; Literary; Thrillers; Women's Fiction

Nonfiction > *Nonfiction Books*: Narrative Nonfiction

Send: Query; Synopsis; Full text
How to send: Email

Represents women's fiction, from the more literary to the very commercial. Likes book club reads that really capture a reader's attention or heart. Always on the lookout for great crime and thrillers and interesting non-fiction.

L195 T.S. Ferguson
Literary Agent
United States

http://www.azantianlitagency.com/pages/team-tf.html
https://querymanager.com/query/TSFerguson

Literary Agency: Azantian Literary Agency

CHILDREN'S > **Fiction**
Graphic Novels: General
Middle Grade: General, and in particular: Adventure; Commercial; Dark; Fairy Tales; Fantasy; Folklore, Myths, and Legends; High / Epic Fantasy; High Concept; Horror; LGBTQIA
YOUNG ADULT > **Fiction**
Graphic Novels: General
Novels: General, and in particular: Adventure; Dark; Fairy Tales; Fantasy; Folklore, Myths, and Legends; High / Epic Fantasy; High Concept; Horror; LGBTQIA

Does not want:

> **CHILDREN'S** > **Fiction** > *Middle Grade*
> Hard Science Fiction; Religion; Sport
> **YOUNG ADULT** > **Fiction** > *Novels*
> Hard Science Fiction; Religion; Sport

Closed to approaches.

Looking for young adult and middle grade fiction across all genres that combines high-concept, hooky stories with writing and voice that feel standout. An addicting, page-turning quality is always a plus! He has a special place in his heart for dark and edgy stories (including but not limited to horror), fairy tales, mythology, action-adventure, LGBTQ stories, graphic novels, and stories by and about under-represented voices. He is not the best fit for sports-centric stories, high sci-fi, or non-fiction.

L196 Julie Fergusson
Literary Agent
United Kingdom

http://thenorthlitagency.com/our-friends-in-the-north/
https://twitter.com/julie_fergusson

Literary Agency: The North Literary Agency

Fiction > *Novels*
  Book Club Fiction; Domestic Suspense; Literary; Psychological Thrillers; Romantic Comedy; Speculative

Closed to approaches.

Looking for fiction across a range of genres, particularly psychological thrillers, domestic suspense, near-future speculative, romcoms, reading group and literary fiction. No submissions from authors who live in North America.

L197 Rochelle Fernandez
Literary Agent
Australia

rochelle@alexadsett.com.au

https://alexadsett.com.au/literary-agency/
https://querymanager.com/query/3065

Literary Agency: Alex Adsett Literary

ADULT
  Fiction > *Novels*
    Commercial; Crime; Fantasy; Mystery; Romantic Comedy; Science Fiction

  Nonfiction > *Nonfiction Books*: Memoir

CHILDREN'S > **Fiction**
  Middle Grade; *Picture Books*

How to send: Query Tracker

Seeking well written manuscripts of any genre with a compelling premise and three dimensional, interesting characters. Based in Sydney, she is passionate about hearing and seeing diverse stories that represent the wonderful multicultural multifaceted society that comprises Australia.

L198 Kimberly Fernando
Literary Agent
United States

https://www.kfernandobooks.com
https://www.olswanger.com
https://querytracker.net/query/2640
https://querytracker.net/query/2640/NonfictionProjects
https://aalitagents.org/author/kimfern/
https://x.com/books4kimberly

Literary Agency: Olswanger Literary LLC (**L449**)
Professional Body: Association of American Literary Agents (AALA)

Nonfiction > *Nonfiction Books*
  Cookery; Crime; Fitness; Food; Gardening; Health; Lifestyle; Memoir; Relationships; Self Help; Spirituality

How to send: Query Tracker

Represents clients in the adult fiction space. She is passionate about representing all voices and backgrounds and she's especially interested in elevating underrepresented voices.

L199 Melanie Figueroa
Literary Agent
United States

https://www.melaniefigueroa.com
https://www.rootliterary.com/agents
https://querymanager.com/query/melaniefigueroa
https://twitter.com/wellmelsbells/
https://www.linkedin.com/in/melaniefigueroa
https://www.instagram.com/wellmelsbells/

Literary Agency: Root Literary (**L503**)
Professional Body: Association of American Literary Agents (AALA)

ADULT > **Fiction** > *Novels*
  Commercial; Contemporary; Family Saga; Fantasy; Historical Fiction; Horror; Literary; Magical Realism; Mystery; Speculative; Suspense; Thrillers; Upmarket; Women's Fiction

CHILDREN'S > **Fiction** > *Middle Grade*
  Contemporary; Fantasy; Historical Fiction; Literary; Mystery; Science Fiction

YOUNG ADULT > **Fiction** > *Novels*
  Contemporary; Fantasy; Historical Fiction; Literary; Mystery; Romance; Science Fiction

How to send: Query Tracker

I want to work with the kind of stories that both create and sustain life-long readers—books that make me sigh with contentment, learn something new, or take delight in the unexpected. Those stories stay with you, and they're a gift I want to help give readers by lifting up the voices of talented and hard-working creatives.

L200 Ciara Finan
Literary Agent
United Kingdom
Tel: + 44 (0) 207 393 4357

ciara.finan@curtisbrown.co.uk

https://curtisbrown.co.uk
https://curtisbrown.co.uk/agent/ciara-finan

Literary Agency: Curtis Brown (**L135**)

Fiction > *Novels*
  Book Club Fiction; Cozy Fantasy; Crime; Fantasy; Historical Fiction; Politics; Psychological Thrillers; Romance; Romantasy; Romantic Comedy; Thrillers

Nonfiction > *Nonfiction Books*
  Beauty; Commercial; Economics; Feminism; Health; History; Politics; Relationships

Send: Query; Synopsis; Writing sample; Proposal
How to send: Email

I am looking for fantasy, romantasy, dark academia, rom-coms and romance, book club fiction, psychological thrillers, historical fiction and commercial non-fiction. I'm particularly interested in finding and championing stories by writers from underrepresented backgrounds and communities.

Authors: Henry Agg; Chloe Bayley; Ashley Chalmers; Hannah Connolly; Paige Cowan-Hall; Alan Edwards; Logan Karlie; Nina Killham; Chloe Laws; Hazel McBride; Liberty Mills; L.M. Nathan; Joshua Oliver; Andrea Oskis; Claire Peate; Keetie Roelen; Eulalie Tangka; Daisy Tempest; Dan Whitlam

L201 Diana Finch
Literary Agent
United States

dianafinchagent@gmail.com

http://dianafinchliteraryagency.blogspot.com/
https://dianafinchliteraryagency.submittable.com/submit
https://aalitagents.org/author/dianagent/
https://twitter.com/DianaFinch

Literary Agency: Diana Finch Literary Agency (**L154**)
Professional Body: Association of American Literary Agents (AALA)

How to send: Submittable

L202 Rebeka Finch
Associate Agent
United Kingdom

rebeka@darleyanderson.com

https://darleyanderson.com
https://darleyanderson.com/team/rebeka-finch/
https://twitter.com/Beka_finch
https://www.instagram.com/rebeka.finch/

Literary Agency: The Darley Anderson Agency (**L143**)

ADULT > **Fiction** > *Novels*
  Commercial; Contemporary; Folklore, Myths, and Legends; Romance; Romantasy; Romantic Comedy; Women's Fiction

NEW ADULT > **Fiction** > *Novels*
  Commercial; Contemporary; Folklore, Myths, and Legends; Romance; Romantasy; Romantic Comedy; Women's Fiction

How to send: Online submission system

As an agent and reader, I am always on the lookout for commercial romance and romantasy fiction. Whatever the story, I want books with romance at the very heart of the narrative.

Authors: Brooke Fast; Sophie Hamilton; Mary Hargreaves; Donna Marchetti; Megan Murphy

L203 Stevie Finegan
Literary Agent
United Kingdom

https://zenoagency.com
https://zenoagency.com/agents/stevie-finegan/
https://querytracker.net/query/StevieFinegan
https://twitter.com/StevieFinegan

Literary Agency: Zeno Agency (**L617**)

ADULT
Fiction
Graphic Novels: Feminism; LGBTQIA
Novels: High / Epic Fantasy; Soft Science Fiction
Nonfiction > *Nonfiction Books*
Feminism; Mental Health; Politics; Social Issues

CHILDREN'S > **Fiction**
Early Readers; *Middle Grade*; *Picture Books*

Closed to approaches.

Authors: Travis Baldree; Alice Bell; Cierra Block; Marie Brennan; Rebecca Brownlie; Andrew Cartmel; Mário Coelho; Vida Cruz-Borja; J.R. Dawson; Clio Evans; Craig Laurance Gidney; J.T. Greathouse; Elizabeth Helen; Grady Hendrix; Jesse J. Holland; Shannon Mayer; Anna McNuff; Katy Nyquist; Adam Oyebanji; Taylor Riley Parham; Sian Radford; Emily Rath; Farrah Riaz; Cassidy Ellis Salter; Yah Yah Scholfield; Calah Singleton; Tracy Townsend; R.R. Virdi; M.A. Wardell; MJ Wassmer; Gary Wigglesworth; Jasmine Wigham; Yudhanjaya Wijeratne; Catelyn Wilson

L204 Flannery Literary
Literary Agency
United States

jennifer@flanneryliterary.com

https://flanneryliterary.com

CHILDREN'S
Fiction > *Middle Grade*
Nonfiction > *Nonfiction Books*

YOUNG ADULT > **Fiction** > *Novels*

Closed to approaches.

Send query by email, with the word "Query" in the subject line. Include first 5-10 pages of your novel or full picture book text. Deals exclusively in children's and young adults' fiction and nonfiction, including picture books. See website for full guidelines.

Literary Agent: Jennifer Flannery

L205 Amy Thrall Flynn
Senior Agent
United States

https://www.aevitascreative.com
https://www.aevitascreative.com/agent/amy-thrall-flynn
https://querymanager.com/query/flynn

Literary Agency: Aevitas

CHILDREN'S > **Fiction**
Chapter Books; *Early Readers*; *Middle Grade*; *Picture Books*
YOUNG ADULT > **Fiction** > *Novels*

Closed to approaches.

Represents writers and illustrators of fiction and nonfiction for children, from picture books to young adult novels.

Authors: Sara Akin; Ahmed Alghariz; Lynne Bertrand; Michael Brumm; Julien Chung; Danielle Davis; Mk Smith Despres; Susan Fletcher; Nancy Bo Flood; Federico Gastaldi; Karen Gebbia; Charlie Greenwald; Tommy Greenwald; Ritu Hemnani; Carter Higgins; Lina Maslo; Robyn McGrath; Wendell Minor; Heather L. Montgomery; Zewlan Moor; Zoraida Rivera Morales; Bethanie Murguia; Dan Paley; Nadine Pinede; Aimee Reid; Jennifer Ann Richter; Michael J. Rosen; Rob Sanders; Kaitlin M Sikes; Leslie Staub; Ellen Surrey; Ellen Tarlow; Dana VanderLugt; Helen Yoon

L206 Jack Fogg
Literary Agent
United Kingdom

https://dunnfogg.co.uk
https://dunnfogg.co.uk/about-us/

Literary Agency: DunnFogg (**L165**)

Fiction > *Novels*
Literary; Psychology; Speculative; Suspense

Nonfiction > *Nonfiction Books*
Business; Crafts; Design; Food; Investigative Journalism; Memoir; Narrative Nonfiction; Nature; Psychology; Sociology; Sport

How to send: Online submission system

In fiction, I'm drawn to books which combine compelling storytelling, engaging characters and strong plotting, whether they be considered commercial or literary. I particularly love novels of ambition and scope, which are full of big-hearted characters and aren't afraid to entertain. In non-fiction, my tastes are broad, and I read widely in the areas of memoir, current affairs, politics, biography, sport, history, psychology, pop science, food and nature writing. I'm especially drawn to great narrative non-fiction which has a deep focus and then expands outwards to explain a whole culture or subculture.

L207 Folio Literary Management, LLC
Literary Agency
630 9th Avenue, Suite 1009, New York, NY 10036
United States
Tel: +1 (212) 400-1494
Fax: +1 (212) 967-0977

http://www.foliolit.com
https://www.facebook.com/folio.literary
https://twitter.com/FolioLiterary

Fiction > *Novels*
Commercial; Literary; Upmarket

Nonfiction > *Nonfiction Books*
Memoir; Narrative Nonfiction

Read agent bios on website and decide which agent to approach. Do not submit to multiple agents simultaneously. Each agent has different submission requirements: consult website for details. No unsolicited MSS or multiple submissions.

Affiliated Agents: Ruth Pomerance; Jeff Silberman

Author / Editor-in-Chief: Jason Cowley

Authors: Kareem Abdul-Jabbar; Dan Abrams; Elizabeth Alker; Rime Allaf; Gregg Allman; Alan Allport; George Anastasia; Noga Arikha; Thomas Asbridge; Michael Baden; Katy Balls; Lindsey Bareham; Laura Beers; James Bloodworth; Jonathan Boff; Joe Bonanno; Terry Bradshaw; Charles Brandt; Caroline Burt; Aditya Chakrabortty; Linda Cheng; Christi Clancy; Christina Clancy; Alan Connor; Bernard Cornwell; Rianna Croxford; David Domoney; John "Chick" Donohue; John Douglas; Bobby Duffy; Lexie Elliott; Tamer Elnoury; Richard English; Gavin Esler; Seb Falk; Cordelia Fine; Matthew Frank; Susannah Gibson; Andrew Gimson; Paul Goldsmith; Jonah Goodman; Rickson Gracie; John Gray; Graham Greene; John Gribbin; Isabel Hardman; Sophie Harman; Homer Hickam; Chris Hirst; Russell Hoban; Eric Hobsbawm; Tansy Hoskins; Julian Jackson; Owen Jones; Alan Judd; Anna Keay; John Keay; Jacqueline Kelly; Erika J. Kendrick; James Kennedy; Paul Kennedy; Barbara Keys; Sulmaan Wasif Khan; Halik Kochanski; David Lammy; Casey Larsen; Elisabeth Leake; Damien Lewis; Daniel Light; Kathryn Mannix; Sarfraz Manzoor; Harry Markopolos; Kevin Maurer; Helen McCarthy; Michael McGarrity; Ed Miliband; Yashka Moore; Fraser Nelson; Johan Norberg; David Nott; Peter Oborne; Mark Olshaker; Susan Owens; Helen Parr; Richard Partington; Harry Pearson; Tanya Pell; Gilles Peterson; Joe Pistone; Des Powell; Laura Prepon; Sadiah Qureshi; Amol Rajan; John Rapley; Chris Reiter; Sheri Reynolds; Steve Richards; Tom Roberts; Jane Rogoyska; Brunello Rosa; Bill Russell; Jane Sanderson; Caitlin Schneiderhan; Gina Schock; Antonia Senior; Rachel Shabi; Sujit Sivasundaram;

Luke Smith; Mark B. Smith; Kristina Spohr; Hilary Spurling; Rebecca Stafford; Hew Strachan; Nicola Sturgeon; Ian Taylor; Dylan Thomas; Simon Thurley; Phil Tinline; Simon Tyler; Rosamund Urwin; Yanis Varoufakis; Holly Watt; Oliver Webb-Carter; Rachel J. Webster; Sam Wetherell; Will Wilkes; Jon Wilson; Hope Wolf; Patricia Wood; Cindy Yu

Literary Agency: Folio Jr.

Literary Agents: Jan Baumer (**L044**); Jamie Chambliss; Sonali Chanchani (**L108**); Dado Derviskadic (**L151**); Rachel Ekstrom; Quressa Robinson (**L497**); Melissa White

Literary Agents / Partners: Emily Van Beek; Claudia Cross; Jeff Kleinman; Steve Troha; Frank Weimann

Literary Agents / Senior Vice Presidents: Erin Niumata (**L439**); Marcy Posner (**L480**)

Literary Agents / Vice Presidents: John Cusick (**L136**); Erin Harris (**L268**); Katherine Latshaw (**L355**)

L208 Melissa Fontaine
Associate Agent
United Kingdom

https://thesohoagency.co.uk
https://thesohoagency.co.uk/agent/melissa-fontaine/

Literary Agency: The Soho Agency

Scripts > *TV Scripts*

Works across the list of television and brand talent. She began her career in theatre, before moving into the world of agenting. She is a self-confessed TV addict and can be found watching everything from reality shows to feature length documentaries.

L209 A for Authors
Literary Agency
73 Hurlingham Road, Bexleyheath, Kent, DA7 5PE
United Kingdom
Tel: +44 (0) 1322 463479

enquiries@aforauthors.co.uk

http://aforauthors.co.uk

Fiction > *Novels*
Commercial; Crime; Historical Fiction; Literary; Thrillers

How to send: Word file email attachment; PDF file email attachment

Query by email only. Include synopsis and first three chapters (or up to 50 pages) and short author bio. All attachments must be Word format documents. No submissions by post or by downloadable link.

Literary Agents: Annette Crossland; Bill Goodall

L210 Jemima Forrester
Literary Agent
United Kingdom

jemimaforrester@davidhigham.co.uk

https://www.davidhigham.co.uk/agents-dh/jemima-forrester/

Literary Agency: David Higham Associates Ltd (**L146**)

Fiction > *Novels*
Book Club Fiction; Commercial; Crime; Fantasy; High Concept; Historical Fiction; Literary; Magic; Psychological Suspense; Speculative; Thrillers; Upmarket; Women's Fiction

Nonfiction > *Nonfiction Books*
Comedy / Humour; Feminism; Lifestyle; Popular Culture

Send: Query; Synopsis; Writing sample
How to send: Email

Actively growing her list of commercial and upmarket fiction and has wide-ranging tastes within this space. She is looking for: book club and accessible literary fiction; crime and thrillers; upmarket historical fiction; psychological suspense; women's fiction; speculative/high-concept novels; novels with a lightly magical or fantastical edge. She loves distinctive narrative voices, well-paced plots with a great hook, and complex female characters. She's often drawn to humour, quirky or unusual narrators, moral dilemmas and stories about sisters. In non-fiction, she is looking for innovative lifestyle and popular-culture projects, unique personal stories and humour.

Authors: Kat Ailes; Tessa Bickers; Mikki Brammer; Lauren Bravo; Rukky Brume; R. S. Burnett; Seerut K. Chawla; Lizzie Daykin; Sarah Daykin; Morgan Dick; Pip Finkemeyer; Fred Foster; Jessica George; Penny Hancock; Deborah Hewitt; Rosie Hewlett; Jessie Keane; Kate Leaver; Richard Lumsden; Rufaro Faith Mazarura; Deborah O'Donoghue; Christina Pishiris; Karen Sinotok; Rosie Storey; Tasha Sylva; Sureka Thanenthiran-Dharuman; Minette Walters; Vanessa Walters

L211 Clara Foster
Literary Agent
United Kingdom

https://www.aevitascreative.com/agent/clara-foster
https://querymanager.com/query/2979

Literary Agency: Aevitas Creative Management (ACM) UK (**L006**)

ADULT
Fiction > *Novels*
Fantasy; Folklore, Myths, and Legends; Historical Fiction; Literary; Speculative; Upmarket

Nonfiction > *Nonfiction Books*
Culture; Politics; Science; Women

YOUNG ADULT > **Fiction** > *Novels*
High Concept; Romance

Closed to approaches.

Represents adult fiction, YA, and select non-fiction, and is particularly looking to partner with writers who are looking to build a career from their words, wherever that might take them. Her fiction tastes tend towards the accessible literary and upmarket, often with a strong female focus, as well as genre titles in the fantasy, speculative, and historical arenas. Anything written with beautiful prose, a high-stakes plot, and/or a folkloric, legendary, or mythical grounding is likely to be a good bet. In non-fiction, she finds herself drawn to expert-led narratives which sit at the juncture of either women, politics, and culture, or women, politics, and science. In the YA/Crossover space, she wants to see clever world-building, emotional (and flawed) characters, and preferably a romantic sub-plot—or main plot. Here however she would like to find writing from authors who push the boundaries even further: new twists on old tropes, high concepts (an idea you can pitch in a sentence), and perspectives we rarely get to see.

Authors: Susannah Constantine; A.B. Hamilton; Claire Schultz; Alexandra Steinacker-Clark

L212 Aram Fox
Literary Agent
United States

https://www.mmqalit.com
https://www.mmqalit.com/about/

Literary Agency: Massie McQuilkin & Altman (**L394**)

Fiction > *Novels*
Commercial; Literary

Nonfiction > *Nonfiction Books*
Culture; History; Memoir; Narrative Nonfiction; Nature; Politics; Science

Send: Query; Writing sample; Proposal; Synopsis; Author bio
How to send: In the body of an email

Represents adult fiction and nonfiction. Looking for novelists – literary and commercial – who put immersive storytelling front and center. Regardless of genre, what gets his attention is a writer who brings authentic emotional consequences to their fiction. In nonfiction, he's a ferocious advocate for deeply reported narrative nonfiction and singular memoir, including eye-opening writing about culture, politics, science, history and natural history.

L213 Kat Foxx
Assistant Agent
Canada

https://www.therightsfactory.com
https://www.therightsfactory.com/Agents/kat-foxx
https://querymanager.com/query/KatFoxx

Literary Agency: The Rights Factory

ADULT
  Fiction > *Novels*
    Book Club Fiction; Commercial; Gothic; Historical Fantasy; Historical Fiction; Magical Realism; Mystery; Nostalgia; Romance; Romantic Comedy; Supernatural / Paranormal Horror; Suspense; Thrillers

  Nonfiction > *Nonfiction Books*
    Childbirth; Classics / Ancient World; Crime; Food; Memoir; Motherhood; Parenting; Pregnancy; Travel; Wine; Witchcraft; Witches

YOUNG ADULT > Fiction > *Novels*
  Gothic; Historical Fantasy; Historical Fiction; Magical Realism; Mystery; Romance; Romantic Comedy; Supernatural / Paranormal Horror; Suspense; Thrillers

Closed to approaches.

Building her list of exceptionally talented authors in commercial and book club fiction as well as some select nonfiction topics. In fiction, she's looking for Adult and YA thriller/mystery/suspense, gothic and supernatural horror, historical fiction (preferably pre-20th century), historical fantasy/magical realism (less magicians / wizards / kings / queens and more witches, ghosts, time travel, past lives, etc.), and romcom and romance (light spice). She also enjoys anything nostalgic and anything to do with past lives and soul connections, haunted houses, ancestry, and midwifery/natural childbirth. She *loves* creepy, scary stories that make her eyes water and give her goosebumps! Across ages and genres, stories that normalize blended, single-parent, adoptive, racially and/or culturally diverse, and same-sex relationships and families are high on her list. For nonfiction, she is seeking compelling memoirs that read like fiction, motherhood/natural pregnancy and childbirth/midwifery/planned unassisted births, single parenthood (especially if paired with overcoming an abusive relationship with the other parent), past life/reincarnation, the "brotherhood" mentality of law enforcement, narcissistic abuse recovery, true crime, wine/food/travel, a history of witches and witchcraft, and ancient locations/civilizations.

L214 FRA (Futerman, Rose, & Associates)
Literary Agency
91 St Leonards Road, London, SW14 7BL
United Kingdom
Tel: +44 (0) 20 8255 7755

guy@futermanrose.co.uk

http://www.futermanrose.co.uk

Professional Body: The Association of Authors' Agents (AAA)

Nonfiction > *Nonfiction Books*
  General, and in particular: Entertainment; Media; Music; Politics; Sports Celebrity

Send: Query
Don't send: Full text
How to send: Email

We have a strong reputation for non-fiction, especially books about show business, the music profession and politics, and in recent years we've had particular success with sports biographies and memoirs. We have successfully placed film and TV rights to many of our authors' works with major studios and producers, in some cases even ahead of the book rights.

Authors: Jill Anderson; Larry Barker; Nick Battle; Christian Piers Betley; Tracey Cheetham; Chengde Chen; Kevin Clarke; Lesley Crewe; Richard Digance; Peter Dobbie; Bobby Elliott; Paul Ferris; John French; Susan George; Keith Gillespie; Stephen Griffin; Paul Hendy; Terry Ilott; Sara Khan; Jerry Leider; Sue Lenier; Keith R. Lindsay; Stephen Lowe; Eric MacInnes; Paul Marsden; Paul Marx; Tony McAndrew; Tony McMahon; Sir Vartan Melkonian; Michael Misick; Max Morgan-Witts; Sir Derek Morris; Peter Murphy; Judge Chris Nicholson; Antonia Owen; Tom Owen; Mary O'Hara; Ciarán O'Keeffe; Miriam O'Reilly; Zoe Paphitis; Liz Rettig; Kenneth G. Ross; Robin Callender Smith; Rt. Hon Iain Duncan Smith; Paul Stinchcombe; Felicity Fair Thompson; Bill Tidy; Mark White; Toyah Willcox; Simon Woodham; Tappy Wright; Allen Zeleski

Literary Agent: Guy Rose

L215 Valerie Frankel
Literary Agent
Brooklyn, NY
United States

https://www.aevitascreative.com/agent/valerie-frankel

Literary Agency: Aevitas

ADULT
  Fiction > *Novels*
    Mystery; Romance; Thrillers

  Nonfiction > *Nonfiction Books*
    Business; Health; Lifestyle; Memoir; Wellbeing

YOUNG ADULT > Fiction > *Novels*

Closed to approaches.

Literary agent based in Brooklyn, New York. Has 35 years of editorial experience, and has collaborated with celebrities, public figures, and experts on more than thirty books, including two #1 New York Times bestsellers. She's interested in non-fiction (memoir, health and wellness, business, lifestyle) and fiction (thriller, mystery, romance, YA).

Authors: Florence Comite; Tiffanie DiDonato; Ann Heisenfelt; Ted Heller; Emilie Leyes; Emily Listfield; Joan Martelli; Charmaine McGuffey; Judith Newman; Janice Page; Andrew Postman; Seth Rogoff; Freddie Smith; Benjamin Wagner; Elisa Zuritsky

L216 Fraser Ross Associates
Literary Agency
42 Hadfast Road, Cousland, Midlothian, EH22 2NZ
United Kingdom

fraserrossassociates@gmail.com

http://www.fraserross.co.uk

ADULT
  Fiction > *Novels*
  Nonfiction > *Nonfiction Books*

CHILDREN'S > Fiction > *Picture Books*

Send: Query; Synopsis; Proposal; Writing sample; Full text
How to send: Email; Post

Send query by email or by post, including CV, the first three chapters and synopsis for fiction, or a one page proposal and the opening chapter and a further two chapter outlines for nonfiction. For picture books, send complete MS, without illustrations. No poetry, playscripts, screenplays, or individual short stories.

Authors: Jo Allan; Sorrel Anderson; Gill Arbuthnott; Tim Archbold; Alice Balfour; Barroux; Jason Beresford; Thomas Bloor; Ella Burfoot; Jill Calder; Simon Chapman; Judy Cumberbatch; Caroline Deacon; Emily Dodd; Lari Don; Christiane Dorion; Nicole Dryburgh; Jane Eagland; Teresa Flavin; Ciara Flood; Hannah Foley; Vivian French; Joe Friedman; Darren Gate; Roy Gill; Edward Hardy; Diana Hendry; Chris Higgins; Barry Hutchison; J D (Julie) Irwin; Cate James; Ann Kelley; Louise Kelly; Tanya Landman; Kate Leiper; Joan Lennon; Joan Lingard; Janis Mackay; L J Macwhirter; Kasia Matyjaszek; Eilidh Muldoon; Erica Mary Orchard; Judy Paterson; Helena Pielichaty; Sue Purkiss; Lynne Rickards; Jamie Rix; Karen Saunders; Dugald Steer; Chae Strathie; Kate Wakeling; Rosie Wallace

Literary Agents: Lindsey Fraser; Kathryn Ross

L217 Claire Friedman
Literary Agent
United States

http://www.inkwellmanagement.com/staff/claire-friedman

Literary Agency: InkWell Management

ADULT
  Fiction > *Novels*
    Book Club Fiction; Commercial; Romance; Speculative; Suspense; Thrillers; Upmarket
  Nonfiction > *Nonfiction Books*: Narrative Nonfiction

CHILDREN'S > **Fiction** > *Novels*

YOUNG ADULT > **Fiction** > *Novels*
  Book Club Fiction; Commercial; Romance; Speculative; Suspense; Thrillers; Upmarket

Send: Query; Writing sample
How to send: In the body of an email

Actively seeking upmarket and commercial fiction in the adult and YA categories, with a special focus on book club fiction, thrillers and suspense, romance, and anything with a speculative edge.

L218 Jessica Friedman
Literary Agent
United States

https://www.sll.com/our-team

Literary Agency: Sterling Lord Literistic, Inc.

Fiction in Translation > *Novels*

Fiction
  Graphic Novels: General
  Novels: Literary; Upmarket
Nonfiction > *Nonfiction Books*: Narrative Nonfiction

Represents literary and upmarket fiction and narrative nonfiction, as well as literature in translation and select graphic novels. She is interested in distinctive voices and writing that challenges the expected–stylistically, formally, or otherwise. She is particularly drawn to voice-driven prose, thoughtful criticism, genre-bending writing, and underrepresented narratives.

L219 Rebecca Friedman
Literary Agent
United States

queries@rfliterary.com

https://rfliterary.com/about/
https://twitter.com/rebeccalitagent

Literary Agency: Rebecca Friedman Literary Agency

ADULT
  Fiction > *Novels*
    Commercial; Contemporary Romance; Literary; Suspense; Women's Fiction
  Nonfiction > *Nonfiction Books*
    Journalism; Memoir

YOUNG ADULT > **Fiction** > *Novels*

Send: Query; Writing sample
How to send: Email

Interested in commercial and literary fiction with a focus on literary novels of suspense, women's fiction, contemporary romance, and young adult, as well as journalistic non-fiction and memoir. Most of all, she is looking for great stories told in strong voices.

L220 The Friedrich Agency LLC
Literary Agency
United States

https://www.friedrichagency.com

Fiction > *Novels*

Nonfiction > *Nonfiction Books*

Send: Query; Writing sample
How to send: Email

See website for agent bios and individual contact details, then submit to one by email only. See website for full guidelines.

Associate Agent: Marin Takikawa (**L566**)

Literary Agents: Heather Carr; Lucy Carson; Molly Friedrich

L221 Frog Literary Agency
Literary Agency
United Kingdom
Tel: +44 (0) 7221 660990

hello@frogliterary.agency
submissions@frogliterary.agency

https://www.frogliterary.agency
https://twitter.com/frogliterary
http://www.instagram.com/frogliterary

Nonfiction > *Nonfiction Books*

Closed to approaches.

LGBTQIA+ writers only. No submissions from heterosexuals. Writing need not have a queer focus, so heterosexual content may be accepted if it is written by someone who says they are gay. However, the same content would be rejected if the person who wrote it says they are straight.

L222 Sarah Fuentes
Literary Agent
United States

https://www.unitedtalent.com
https://www.unitedtalent.com/bio/sarah-fuentes

Literary Agency: United Talent Agency (UTA)

Fiction > *Novels*
  Comedy / Humour; Dark; Literary; Speculative; Upmarket

Nonfiction > *Nonfiction Books*
  Cultural Criticism; History; Investigative Journalism; Literary Memoir; Popular Science; Social History

Send: Query; Full text; Proposal
How to send: Online submission system

Across genres she is looking for sharp and distinct contemporary voices, compelling prose, and singular points of view. In fiction she's interested in novels that dig into the complicated inner workings of relationships and bring readers deep in the messy minds of their characters, and particularly those that wrestle with class, sexuality, race, and power in all its forms. She also loves a twist of humor, a dark bent, or a speculative or uncanny edge. In nonfiction, she's drawn to idea-driven narratives that help explain how we see and construct the world around us or that bring some hidden architecture into view. Her interests span literary memoir, popular science, investigative journalism, history (social, intellectual, and overlooked histories in particular), and cultural criticism and essays.

L223 Lisa Fuller
Literary Agent
Australia

https://alexadsett.com.au
https://alexadsett.com.au/literary-agency/

Literary Agency: Alex Adsett Literary

ADULT > **Fiction** > *Novels*: Speculative

CHILDREN'S > **Fiction** > *Novels*

YOUNG ADULT > **Fiction** > *Novels*

Interested in Own Voices works, YA, children's literature and all things speculative fiction.

L224 Eugenie Furniss
Literary Agent

eugeniefurniss@42mp.com

https://www.42mp.com/agents
https://twitter.com/Furniss

Literary Agency: 42 Management and Production

Fiction > *Novels*
  Comedy / Humour; Crime; Historical Fiction

Nonfiction > *Nonfiction Books*
  Biography; Finance; Memoir; Politics; Popular History

Closed to approaches.

Drawn to crime in all its guises and historical fiction. On the nonfiction front seeks biography and popular history, and politics.

L225 Isobel Gahan
Associate Agent
United Kingdom
Tel: +44 (0) 207 393 4411

isobel.gahan@curtisbrown.co.uk

https://curtisbrown.co.uk
https://curtisbrown.co.uk/agent/isobel-gahan

CHILDREN'S
Fiction
Graphic Novels: Coming of Age; Fantasy; Historical Fantasy; Science Fiction; Space Opera
Middle Grade: Fantasy; Historical Fantasy; Science Fiction; Space Opera
Nonfiction > *Nonfiction Books*

YOUNG ADULT
Fiction
Graphic Novels: Coming of Age; Fantasy; Historical Fantasy; Science Fiction; Space Opera
Novels: Fantasy; Historical Fantasy; Science Fiction; Space Opera
Nonfiction > *Nonfiction Books*

Closed to approaches.

I'm currently building my own list, looking for YA and middle grade fantasy, sci-fi, graphic novels and non-fiction. I read widely, but I have a particular love for fantasy and especially plots with ambitious world-building and immersive mythologies. I also enjoy coming-of-age stories that explore growing up, particularly in graphic novel form. I read widely in adult fantasy and sci-fi and I love historical fantasy and ambitious space-operas that explore the universe.

Authors: Craig Barr-Green; Nevin Holness; Michael Mann; Ella McLeod; Struan Murray; Louise Page; Alake Pilgrim; Kat Williams; Matt Woodhead; Kelly Yang

L226 Lori Galvin
Senior Agent
Boston
United States

https://aevitascreative.com/agents/
https://querymanager.com/query/QueryLoriGalvin

Literary Agency: Aevitas

Fiction > *Novels*
Domestic Suspense; Mystery; Psychological Thrillers

Nonfiction > *Nonfiction Books*
Cookery; Food; Memoir

Send: Author bio; Query; Synopsis; Writing sample; Pitch; Market info
How to send: Query Tracker

Represents both adult fiction (especially domestic suspense, psychological thrillers and mysteries) and nonfiction (memoir, food writing, and cookbooks).

Authors: Regina McBride; Tamara L. Miller; Jennifer Morita

L227 Ellen Geiger
Literary Agent
United States

https://goldinlit.com/agents/

Literary Agency: Frances Goldin Literary Agency, Inc.

Fiction > *Novels*
Culture; Historical Fiction; Literary Thrillers; Multicultural

Nonfiction > *Nonfiction Books*
Biography; History; Investigative Journalism; Multicultural; Politics; Psychology; Religion; Social Issues; Women's Issues

Closed to approaches.

Represents a broad range of fiction and non-fiction. She has a lifelong interest in multicultural and social issues embracing change. History, biography, progressive politics, psychology, women's issues, religion and serious investigative journalism are special interests.

In fiction, she loves a good literary thriller, and novels in general that provoke and challenge the status quo, as well as historical and multicultural works. She is drawn to big themes which make a larger point about the culture and times we live in, such as Barbara Kingsolver's Poisonwood Bible. She is not the right agent for New Age, romance, how-to or right-wing politics.

L228 Gemma Cooper Literary
Literary Agency
United Kingdom

info@gemmacooperliterary.com

https://www.gemmacooperliterary.com
https://www.instagram.com/gemmacooperliterary

Professional Body: The Association of Authors' Agents (AAA)

Literary Agent: Gemma Cooper (**L128**)

L229 Josh Getzler
Literary Agent; Partner
United States

josh@hgliterary.com

https://www.hgliterary.com/josh
https://twitter.com/jgetzler
http://www.publishersmarketplace.com/members/jgetzler/
http://aaronline.org/Sys/PublicProfile/2902758/417813
http://queryme.online/Getzler

Literary Agency: HG Literary
Professional Body: Association of American Literary Agents (AALA)

ADULT
Fiction > *Novels*
Crime; Historical Fiction; Mystery; Thrillers; Upmarket; Women's Fiction

Nonfiction > *Nonfiction Books*
Business; History; Politics

CHILDREN'S > **Fiction** > *Middle Grade*
Comedy / Humour; Contemporary

Closed to approaches.

L230 Lilly Ghahremani
Literary Agent
United States

https://www.fullcircleliterary.com/our-agents/lilly-ghahremani/
https://querymanager.com/query/LillyFCL
https://twitter.com/Wonderlilly

Literary Agency: Full Circle Literary, LLC

ADULT > **Nonfiction**
Gift Books: High Concept; Photography
Illustrated Books: General

CHILDREN'S
Fiction
Middle Grade: Comedy / Humour; Culture; Middle East
Picture Books: Comedy / Humour; Culture; Middle East
Nonfiction > *Nonfiction Books*

YOUNG ADULT > **Fiction** > *Novels*: Middle East

Closed to approaches.

Seeks to partner up with creatives who have done their homework on the industry, their place in it, and have a concept that stays with her. Wants: Children's books that infuse traditional cultural wisdoms in a modern, relatable way; Children's nonfiction books by experts; Funny but smart picture books that surprise; Books for kids of any age that center disabled characters without necessarily being about disability; High-concept gift books with illustration/photography included; Picture book, middle grade, and YA with Middle Eastern characters, settings, or themes; and Joyous middle grade.

L231 Ghosh Literary
Literary Agency
United States

submissions@ghoshliterary.com

https://www.ghoshliterary.com

Fiction > *Novels*

Nonfiction > *Nonfiction Books*

Send: Query; Author bio; Market info
How to send: Email

An independent literary agency offering worldwide literary representation for print and digital media and all allied rights, including motion picture, theatrical and multimedia rights.

Literary Agent: Anna Ghosh (**L232**)

L232 Anna Ghosh
Literary Agent
United States

submissions@ghoshliterary.com
annaghosh@ghoshliterary.com

https://www.ghoshliterary.com

Literary Agency: Ghosh Literary (**L231**)

Fiction > *Novels*

Nonfiction > *Nonfiction Books*

Send: Query; Author bio; Market info
How to send: Email

Particularly interested in literary narratives and books that illuminate some aspect of human endeavour or the natural world. Does not typically represent genre fiction but is drawn to compelling storytelling in most guises.

L233 Tara Gilbert
Literary Agent
United States

https://taragilbert.com
https://querymanager.com/query/TaraGilbert
https://ktliterary.com/about/
https://www.publishersmarketplace.com/members/tsgilbert/
https://twitter.com/Literary_Tara
https://www.pinterest.com/tarashilohgilbert/
https://www.instagram.com/literary.tara/
https://www.facebook.com/taragilbertlitagent

Literary Agency: KT Literary (**L345**)

ADULT > **Fiction** > *Novels*
  Historical Fantasy; Horror; Low Fantasy; Mystery; Romance; Speculative; Suspense; Thrillers; Upmarket

CHILDREN'S > **Fiction** > *Graphic Novels*

YOUNG ADULT > **Fiction** > *Novels*
  Comedy / Humour; Contemporary; Fantasy; Horror; Romance; Romantic Comedy

Closed to approaches.

Passion is working with LGBTQ+, BIPOC, Neurodiverse, body diverse, and underrepresented authors and illustrators, focusing on fiction and graphic novels for MG, YA, and adults.

L234 Bianca Gillam
Literary Agent
United Kingdom

gillam@zenoagency.com

https://zenoagency.com
https://zenoagency.com/agents/bianca-gillam/

Literary Agency: Zeno Agency (**L617**)

Fiction > *Novels*
  Romantasy; Romantic Comedy; Thrillers; Women's Fiction

Nonfiction > *Nonfiction Books*: Narrative Nonfiction

Closed to approaches.

When open, I am looking for: Romantasy, Rom-coms with an edge, women's fiction with a strong hook and deep emotional narrative (think Taylor Jenkins-Reid), atmospheric thrillers with a strong sense of place (think In My Dreams I Hold a Knife by Ashley Winstead). My primary focus is fiction, but I am open to a select number of narrative non-fiction projects, with a focus on stories that have particular relevance for young women (think I'm Glad My Mom Died by Jeannette McCurdy), or are so gripping they read like fiction (think Educated by Tara Westover).

Authors: Shannon Lee Barry; Georgia Gailey

L235 Katie Gisondi
Literary Agent
United States

http://www.ldlainc.com/about
https://querymanager.com/query/2696
https://www.manuscriptwishlist.com/mswl-post/katie-gisondi/
https://twitter.com/GisondiKatie

Literary Agency: Laura Dail Literary Agency

ADULT > **Fiction**
  Graphic Novels: Fantasy; High Concept; Romance
  Novels: Cozy Mysteries; Fantasy; High Concept; Mystery; Romance; Romantasy; Romantic Comedy

CHILDREN'S > **Fiction**
  Graphic Novels: Fantasy; High Concept; Romance
  Middle Grade: Adventure; Fantasy; High Concept

YOUNG ADULT > **Fiction**
  Graphic Novels: Fantasy; High Concept; Romance
  Novels: Adventure; Fantasy

How to send: Query Tracker
How not to send: Email; Social Media; Phone; Post

In all genres I prioritize diversity and marginalized voices. Specifically, I would love to see more Indigenous, Native American, and First Nations, as well as Latinx, disabled, chronically ill, and trans/nonbinary/queer stories and voices. In general, I am looking for commercial fiction and non-fiction with a clear, distinct voice and a unique hook.

L236 Glass Literary Management LLC
Literary Agency
138 West 25th Street, 10th Floor, New York, NY 10001
United States
Tel: +1 (646) 237-4881

info@glassliterary.com

https://glassliterary.com
https://www.facebook.com/glassliterary
https://www.publishersmarketplace.com/members/GlassLiterary/

ADULT
  Fiction > *Novels*
  Nonfiction > *Nonfiction Books*

CHILDREN'S
  Fiction > *Novels*
  Nonfiction > *Nonfiction Books*

Send: Query
How to send: Online contact form

Represents fiction and nonfiction for adults and children. Send query through online contact form. Prefers queries that describe your book concisely; are well-written and typo-free; show an understanding of the marketplace and where your book would fit into it; and, for nonfiction, show why you are the best person to be writing the book you're proposing. Response not guaranteed unless interested.

Literary Agents: Alex Glass; Jennifer Chen Tran (**L578**)

L237 Stephanie Glencross
Literary Agent
United Kingdom

Literary Agency: David Higham Associates Ltd (**L146**)

L238 Emily Glenister
Literary Agent; Company Director
United Kingdom

eg.submission@dhhliteraryagency.com

http://www.dhhliteraryagency.com/emily-glenister.html
http://www.twitter.com/emily_glenister

Literary Agency: DHH Literary Agency Ltd (**L152**)

Fiction
  Novels: Book Club Fiction; Commercial; Contemporary; Crime; Ghost Stories; Gothic; Historical Fiction; Horror; Magical Realism; Psychological Thrillers; Romance; Romantic Comedy; Upmarket Commercial Fiction; Urban Fantasy
  Short Fiction Collections: Ghost Stories; Horror
Nonfiction > *Nonfiction Books*
  Autobiography; Biography; Crime; History; Medicine; Memoir; Popular Culture; Royalty; Women

Does not want:

  Fiction > *Novels*: Police Procedural

Closed to approaches.

Looking for female-led commercial fiction; upmarket commercial fiction; diverse and unique voices; crime and psychological thrillers; witty, contemporary and observant romcoms; epic love stories; smart and quick-witted historical fiction; gothic fiction (historical OR contemporary); female focus and dual timeline narrative; book club fiction; magical realism and urban fantasy; fun retellings (not Greek mythology, please); horror novel / ghost story; short story collections with a ghost / horror theme. In nonfiction: historical (monarchy, medicine or women); pop culture; biographies, autobiographies and memoirs; true crime.

Authors: Foluso Agbaje; Louise Beech; Barbara Copperthwaite; Heather Darwent; Becca Day; Suzie Edge; Stephen Edger; Amelia Ireland; Anthony Kavanagh; Caroline Lamond; S.V. Leonard; Emma Medrano; Jean Menzies; Vikki Patis; Reagan Lee Ray; Reagan Lee Ray; Becky Rhush; Nicole Robinson; Katy Summers; Annie Taylor; Rebecca Templeton; Rebecca Thorne; Ola Tundun; Kathleen Whyman; L. C. Winter

L239 Global Lion Intellectual Property Management, Inc.
Literary Agency
PO BOX 669238, Pompano Beach, FL 33066
United States
Tel: +1 (754) 222-6948

queriesgloballionmgt@gmail.com

https://globallionmanagement.com
https://www.facebook.com/GlobalLionMgt/
https://twitter.com/globallionmgt
https://www.instagram.com/globallionmgt/

Fiction > *Novels*
  Commercial; Fantasy; Science Fiction

Nonfiction > *Nonfiction Books*
  Arts; Business; Commercial; Education; Film Industry; Self Help; TV; Technology

Send: Query; Synopsis; Writing sample; Author bio
How to send: Online submission system

Currently looking for commercial fiction, fantasy, science fiction, and intriguing studies of interesting subjects, art, and "making of" books on the film and television industry. Will not turn down anything with sharp prose, modern takes on classic concepts, a great mystery to solve or intriguing characters.

L240 Miriam Goderich
Literary Agent
United States

miriam@dystel.com

https://www.dystel.com
https://www.dystel.com/miriam-goderich
https://x.com/miriamgoderich

Literary Agency: Dystel, Goderich & Bourret LLC

Fiction > *Novels*: Commercial

Nonfiction > *Nonfiction Books*
  Biography; Inspirational Memoir; Narrative Nonfiction; Self Help

Send: Query; Writing sample
How to send: In the body of an email

Looking for the next brilliant novel, fun beach read, gripping nonfiction narrative, inspirational memoir or biography, or instructional self-help title. Wants to see more commercial fiction.

L241 Adria Goetz
Literary Agent
United States

https://ktliterary.com/submissions/
https://querymanager.com/query/adriastreasuretrove
https://adriagoetz.wpcomstaging.com/manuscript-wishlist/

Literary Agency: KT Literary (**L345**)

ADULT > **Fiction** > *Novels*
  Cozy Fantasy; Romantic Comedy; Thrillers; Upmarket

CHILDREN'S > **Fiction**
  Graphic Novels; *Middle Grade*; *Picture Books*

Closed to approaches.

Seeking picture books (especially by author-illustrators), middle grade fiction, graphic novels, and adult fiction—particularly rom coms, thrillers, upmarket fiction, and cozy fantasy.

L242 Ellen Goff
Associate Agent
United States

ellen@hgliterary.com

https://www.hgliterary.com/ellen

Literary Agency: HG Literary

ADULT
Fiction > *Novels*
  Fantasy; Romance; Romantasy

Nonfiction > *Nonfiction Books*
  General, and in particular: Food; Gender; Intersectional Feminism

CHILDREN'S > **Fiction**
  Middle Grade; *Picture Books*
YOUNG ADULT
Fiction
  Graphic Novels: General
  Novels: General, and in particular: Ghost Stories; Gothic; Romance
Nonfiction > *Nonfiction Books*
  General, and in particular: Food

List consists of authors writing for all age groups, from picture books to middle grade to young adult to adult, in both fiction and nonfiction. She also represents illustrators, for kidlit and adult projects, as well as graphic novelists. She is always hungry for stories celebrating girl power and intersectional feminism, but also narratives that don't shy away from asking questions about gender and exploring gender roles. She has a soft spot for southern stories that remind her of her home state of Kentucky, and is a perpetual sucker for a darn good love story. For picture books, she is only taking on new clients who are author-illustrators, and gravitates toward projects that highlight the sparse and simple. She is interested in all genres and formats of MG and YA, especially anything spooky, graphic novels, novels-in-verse, and projects that allow her to travel vicariously through place and time. In adult, she represents fantasy and romance and their intersection. She might be convinced on a nonfiction project if it involves food.

L243 Rachel Goldblatt
Associate Agent
United Kingdom
Tel: +44 (0) 20 7393 4418

rachel.goldblatt@curtisbrown.co.uk

https://curtisbrown.co.uk

Literary Agency: Curtis Brown (**L135**)
Literary Agent / President: Jonathan Lloyd

Fiction > *Novels*
  Dark; Domestic; Family; Historical Fiction; Relationships; Speculative; Women

Nonfiction > *Nonfiction Books*
  Arts; Biography; History; Literary Criticism; Memoir; Narrative Nonfiction; Nature; Sociology

Send: Query; Writing sample; Proposal
How to send: Email

In terms of fiction, I'm particularly drawn to character and voice driven narratives that make me feel deeply and think hard about the world around us. If the writing is compelling, agile, atmospheric and intelligent I can fall for any kind of story, but I especially enjoy those that have a strong sense of time and place, are clear and bold in their intent and style and that interrogate what it means to be human. I love books that explore complicated or outsider characters, complex family dynamics, the domestic space, modern life, relationships in all forms, identity and the female experience. I always love reading clever novels with a dark edge. I want to read absorbing narrative non-fiction that challenges and broadens our perspective and offers a fresh take on or new approach to big subjects. I am especially drawn to literary biography and criticism as well as books about nature, art, history and contemporary social issues, and I'm always interested in extraordinary stories about real people or events. I also enjoy reading creative, formally inventive memoir and life writing.

Authors: Timothy X Atack; Jana Bakunina; Jessica Barnfield; Neil Baxter; Hannah Mays; Rebekah Miron; Amanda Quaid; Adara Schwartz; Jacob Stolworthy; Josh Weeks; Emily Woof

L244 Veronica Goldstein
Literary Agent
United States

https://www.unitedtalent.com
https://www.unitedtalent.com/bio/veronica-goldstein

Literary Agency: United Talent Agency (UTA)

Fiction > *Novels*
  Autofiction; Contemporary; Culture; Experimental; Literary; Politics; Society; Speculative

Nonfiction > *Nonfiction Books*
  Culture; Investigative Journalism; Memoir; Nature; Politics; Popular Culture; Science; Sociology; Technology

Send: Query; Full text; Proposal
How to send: Online submission system

In fiction, she looks for literary novels with an original, contemporary voice that balance the complexities of culture and politics with storytelling that explores the inner worlds of its characters in a way that challenges expectations and deepens the emotional stakes of the story. Autofiction, grounded speculative fiction, and experimental forms are always of interest. She's also looking for compelling critical takes on cultural and sociological trends and overlooked or misunderstood histories; investigative and issue-focused narrative nonfiction; and memoir that makes the personal political and vice versa. Pop culture, science, technology, politics, and writing about the natural world are always of interest.

L245 Andrew Gordon
Literary Agent
United Kingdom

andrewgordon@davidhigham.co.uk

https://www.davidhigham.co.uk/agents-dh/andrew-gordon/

Literary Agency: David Higham Associates Ltd (**L146**)

Fiction > *Novels*
  Commercial; High Concept Crime; Literary; Thrillers

Nonfiction > *Nonfiction Books*
  Adventure; Biography; Business; Current Affairs; Economics; Films; History; Memoir; Music; Narrative Nonfiction; Politics; Popular Culture; Popular Science; Psychology; Sport

List is primarily non-fiction. On the lookout for Non-fiction: – history (whether narrative, popular or serious) – current affairs, politics and economics – biography and memoir – narrative and literary non-fiction including books that blur genre boundaries – sport and tales of adventure – popular culture, film and music – popular science and psychology – 'smart thinking' or ideas books – business books with a strong narrative (rather than 'how to'); and Fiction: – novels that grab the attention, whether literary or commercial – strong stories evocative of a period or place – big, brassy 'airport' thrillers and high-concept crime.

Associate Agent: David Evans

Author / Editor-in-Chief: Jason Cowley

Authors: Elizabeth Alker; Alan Allport; Thomas Asbridge; Katy Balls; Lindsey Bareham; Laura Beers; James Bloodworth; Jonathan Boff; Caroline Burt; Aditya Chakrabortty; Alan Connor; David Domoney; Richard English; Gavin Esler; Seb Falk; Cordelia Fine; Matthew Frank; Susannah Gibson; Andrew Gimson; John Gribbin; Isabel Hardman; Sophie Harman; Chris Hirst; Russell Hoban; Eric Hobsbawm; Trevor Horn; Tansy Hoskins; Julian Jackson; Owen Jones; Anna Keay; John Keay; Paul Kennedy; Barbara Keys; Sulmaan Wasif Khan; Halik Kochanski; David Lammy; Elisabeth Leake; Damien Lewis; Daniel Light; Kathryn Mannix; Sarfraz Manzoor; Helen McCarthy; Ed Miliband; Fraser Nelson; Johan Norberg; David Nott; Peter Oborne; Susan Owens; Helen Parr; Richard Partington; Harry Pearson; Gilles Peterson; Des Powell; Sadiah Qureshi; Amol Rajan; Chris Renwick; Steve Richards; Jane Rogoyska; Brunello Rosa; Rupert Russell; Jane Sanderson; Antonia Senior; Rachel Shabi; Sujit Sivasundaram; Mark B. Smith; Peter Stott; Nicola Sturgeon; Dylan Thomas; Simon Thurley; Phil Tinline; Simon Tyler; Rosamund Urwin; Yanis Varoufakis; Bernard Wasserstein; Holly Watt; Sam Wetherell; Jon Wilson; Hope Wolf; Carolyn Woods

L246 Graham Maw Christie Literary Agency
Literary Agency
37 Highbury Place, London, N5 1QP
United Kingdom
Tel: +44 (0) 7971 268342

nonfiction@grahammawchristie.com
fiction@grahammawchristie.com

https://www.grahammawchristie.com
https://twitter.com/litagencygmc
https://www.instagram.com/litagencygmc/

Professional Body: The Association of Authors' Agents (AAA)

Fiction > *Novels*

Nonfiction > *Nonfiction Books*

Send: Query; Outline; Author bio; Market info; Marketing plan; Writing sample
How to send: Email

When we launched in 2005, we set out to focus on non-fiction and wanted to build a collaborative, creative, market-driven agency. Twenty years on, a few of our clients also write fiction. We still believe that authors can change the world through books, and that a successful career as a writer starts with an excellent book proposal. Authors need someone in their corner – not only to find the right publisher but to navigate and prepare for each stage of the publishing process, from pitch to publication, from the lonely days of honing the manuscript to building a writing career from the first book onwards.

Associate Agent: Amandeep Singh (**L538**)

Junior Agent: Amy O'Shea (**L447**)

Literary Agents: Jennifer Christie (**L116**); Jane Graham Maw (**L398**)

L247 Stacey Graham
Literary Agent
United States

stacey@threeseaslit.com

https://www.threeseasagency.com/agents/stacey-graham
http://querymanager.com/Stacey3Seas

Literary Agency: 3 Seas Literary Agency (**L001**)

ADULT
  Fiction
    Graphic Novels: General
    Novels: Comedy / Humour; Commercial; Mystery; Popular Culture; Romantic Comedy
  Nonfiction > *Nonfiction Books*
    Antiques; Commercial; Cookery; Crafts; How To; Lifestyle; Pets

YOUNG ADULT > **Fiction** > *Graphic Novels*

How to send: Query Tracker

Currently looking to expand her list with adult romance (referral only); quirky, fascinating nonfiction with strong commercial appear and a great platform; graphic novels for adult / young adult; mystery; commercial fiction; humour; and pop culture.

L248 Susan Graham
Literary Agent
United States

https://www.dclagency.com
https://aalitagents.org/author/sgraham/

Literary Agency: Dunow, Carlson & Lerner Agency (**L166**)
Professional Body: Association of American Literary Agents (AALA)

ADULT
  Fiction > *Novels:* Speculative
  Nonfiction > *Nonfiction Books*

CHILDREN'S > **Fiction** > *Novels*

YOUNG ADULT > **Fiction** > *Novels*

Represents illustrators across format and age categories, children's and young adult prose, genre and speculative fiction, and select non-fiction.

L249 Kara Grajkowski
Literary Agent
United States

threeseasagency.kara@gmail.com

https://www.threeseasagency.com/agents/kara-grajkowski
https://querymanager.com/query/2761

Literary Agency: 3 Seas Literary Agency (**L001**)

CHILDREN'S > *Fiction* > *Novels*: Contemporary

YOUNG ADULT > *Fiction* > *Novels*: Contemporary

Closed to approaches.

Looking for contemporary middle grade fiction; contemporary young adult fiction; and own voices.

L250 David Granger
Literary Agent
New York
United States

https://aevitascreative.com/agents/

Literary Agency: Aevitas

Nonfiction > *Nonfiction Books*
Celebrity; Culture; Food; Journalism; Politics

Closed to approaches.

Represents primarily non-fiction and is obsessed with topics across an extremely wide spectrum – politics; food culture; actual innovation in design, tech and science; fame. What binds these things is a yen for intensely original ideas and writing that pushes boundaries.

Authors: Jacqueline Detwiler-George; Scott Eden; Stephen Starring Grant; Richard Panek

L251 Greene & Heaton Ltd
Literary Agency
T18, West Wing, Somerset House, Strand,
London, WC2R 1LA
United Kingdom

submissions@greeneheaton.co.uk
info@greeneheaton.co.uk

http://www.greeneheaton.co.uk
https://twitter.com/greeneandheaton

Professional Body: The Association of Authors' Agents (AAA)

Fiction > *Novels*

Nonfiction > *Nonfiction Books*

Does not want:

> **CHILDREN'S** > *Fiction* > *Picture Books*

Send: Query; Synopsis; Writing sample
Don't send: Full text

How to send: Email
How not to send: Post

Send query by email only, including synopsis and three chapters or approximately 50 pages. No submissions by post. No response unless interested. Handles all types of fiction and nonfiction, but no scripts or children's picture books.

Author Estates: The Estate of Julia Darling; The Estate of Sarah Gainham

Authors: Juliana Adelman; Precious Adesina; Clayton Page Aldern; Amen Alonge; Anthony Anaxagorou; Peter Apps; Lucy Ashe; Mevan Babakar; Carol Ballantine; Michelle Bang; Raffaella Barker; David M Barnett; Catherine Barter; Charlotte Bauer; Lily Blacksell; Laura Blake; Emily Bootle; Lucy Brazier; Bridget; Lynne Bryan; Zoe Burgess; Wren Burke; Prudence Bussey-Chamberlain; Jason Byrne; Tom Campbell; Clare Cavenagh; SB Caves; Charles Cockell; Pam Corbin; Anne Corlett; Robin Craig; Avery Curran; Russell Davies; Anna Davis; Rachel Dawson; Leona Deakin; Sharanya Deepak; Marie Derome; Rageshri Dhairyawan; Sue Divin; Patrick Drake; Helen Dring; Kim Duke; Hayley Dunlop; Lily Dunn; Suzannah Dunn; Mari Ellis Dunning; Jeremy Duns; Maggy Van Eijk; Jonn Elledge; Gabriela Evangelou; Lucia Evangelou; Olaf Falafel; Vittoria Fallanca; Lauren Farnsworth; Hugh Fearnley-Whittingstall; Jane Fearnley-Whittingstall; Zoe Feeney; Gabrielle Fernie; Louise Finnigan; Christopher Fitz-Simon; Felix Flicker; Nick Foster; Holly Friend; Christophe Galfard; Gareth Gavin; Hayley Gelfuso; Olesya Salnikova Gilmore; Helen Giltrow; Francis Gimblett; Mara Gold; Sarah Goodwin; Oliver Grant; Molly Greeley; Jake Hall; Phil Harrison; Evie Hatch; Julie Hayward; Cat Hepburn; Stuart Heritage; Kit Heyam; Kat Hill; Julian Hitch; Beatrice Hitchman; Julia Hollander; Wayne Holloway-Smith; Andrew Holmes; Rebecca Hooper; Alex Hourston; Sarah Housley; David Howard; Scott Alexander Howard; Maria Hummer; Daisy J. Hung; Ferris Jabr; Charles Jennings; Joan; D.B. John; Sam Johnson-Schlee; Gaynor Jones; Helen Jones; Jacqueline Jones; Keith Kahn-Harris; Fiona Keating; Vedashree Khambete-Sharma; Gabrielle Kimm; Esme King; Max Kinnings; David Kirk; Rikke Schmidt Kjærgaard; Rebecca Dinerstein Knight; Joseph Knox; Sonya Kudei; Manon Lagrève; August Lamm; William Leith; Dan Lepard; Jem Lester; Robert Lewis; Matilda Leyser; Eric Lindstrom; Caroline Litman; Kieran Long; Dorian Lynskey; L. A. MacRae; Carina Maggar; Paddy Magrane; Ruth Mancini; Rob Manuel; Anna Sulan Masing; Jolyon Maugham; James McGee; Claire McGlasson; Kerry McInerney; Rebecca Taylor McKay; Gill Meller; Thomasina Miers; Gemma Milne; Lottie Moggach; Bryan Moriarty; Gemma Morr; Emily Morris; Hélène Mulholland; Cathy Newman; Pippa Nixon; Sadhbh O'Sullivan; Mary-Ann Ochota; Ciara Ohartghaile; Christopher Osborn; Iain Overton; John O'Connell; Nicolas Padamsee; Pete Paphides; Anna Parker; Geoffrey Parker; Nina De Pass; Jyoti Patel; Neel Patel; Marie Phillips; Tom Phillips; Georgia Poplett; Xenobe Purvis; Shivi Ramoutar; Francesca Ramsay; Richard Reed; Ben Reeves; Ana Reyes; Sam Rice; Tony Robinson; Paula Rogers; Zuzana Ruzickova; Stephen Sackur; C. J. Sansom; William Sansom; Marcus du Sautoy; Indyana Schneider; Alev Scott; Eddie Scott; Rebecca Seal; Paul Keers: Sediment; Laura Shepherd-Robinson; James Smythe; Mimi Spencer; Nancy Springer; Polly Stewart; Count Arthur Strong; Jacqueline Sutherland; John Sutherland; Andrew Taylor; Georgie Tilney; Lisa Timoney; Sonya Vatomsky; Margaux Vialleron; Ian Vince; John Vincent; Adam Wagner; Jennie Walker; Sarai Walker; Alyssa Warren; Rob Watts; Andrew Webb; Melissa Wellham; Ione Wells; Anna Wickins; Robyn Wilder; Will Wiles; John L Williams; Jason Wilson; David Wright; Jackie Wullschläger; Gill Wyness; Susie Yang; Erin Young; Robyn Young; Bella Younger; Joe Zadeh; Andrew Ziminski

Literary Agents: Holly Faulks (**L187**); Carol Heaton; Imogen Morrell (**L417**); Judith Murray (**L428**); Antony Topping (**L577**); Laura Williams (**L603**); Claudia Young (**L614**)

L252 Greenstone Literary
Literary Agency
United Kingdom

Hello@GreenstoneLiterary.com

https://www.greenstoneliterary.com
https://x.com/GreenstoneLit
https://www.instagram.com/greenstoneliterary/
https://www.tiktok.com/@greenstoneliterary

Professional Body: The Association of Authors' Agents (AAA)

Fiction > *Novels*: Commercial

Send: Query; Synopsis; Writing sample
How to send: Online submission system

Represents bestselling, established authors as well as debut writers. We are passionate about great stories and getting them out into the world. Specialising in commercial fiction, our authors' work has reached millions of readers, listeners and viewers.

Authors: Lindsey Armstrong; Mandy Baggot; Charlotte Bigland; Katie Bohn; Sara Bragg; Laura Carter; Natalie Cooper; Katie Evergreen; Claire Frost; Elaine Hastings; April Howells; Tammye Huf; Claire Kershaw; Claire McCauley; Beth O'Leary; Sally Page; Rachel Sargeant; Kate Galloway Smith; Emma Steele; Sophie White; Ally Zetterberg

Company Directors / Literary Agents: Laura Heathfield (**L273**); Tanera Simons (**L536**)

L253 Pam Gruber
Literary Agent
United States

https://www.highlineliterary.com/agent-pam
https://querymanager.com/query/Pam_Gruber
https://www.instagram.com/pjgruber/
https://twitter.com/Pamlet606

Literary Agency: High Line Literary Collective (**L279**)

ADULT
  Fiction > *Novels*
    Coming of Age; Commercial; Folklore, Myths, and Legends; Grounded Fantasy; Literary; Speculative

  Nonfiction > *Nonfiction Books*: Narrative Nonfiction

CHILDREN'S > **Fiction**
  Graphic Novels: General
  Middle Grade: Coming of Age; Commercial; Folklore, Myths, and Legends; Grounded Fantasy; Literary; Speculative

YOUNG ADULT > **Fiction**
  Graphic Novels: General
  Novels: Coming of Age; Commercial; Folklore, Myths, and Legends; Grounded Fantasy; Literary; Speculative

Closed to approaches.

Actively looking for adult, young adult, and middle grade fiction with literary voices and commercial hooks. In all categories, she is particularly interested in finding grounded fantasy that feels like folklore, stories exploring an under-represented mythology, twisty speculative fiction, fantastical realism, and coming-of-age stories (any age). She is also open to graphic novels (chapter book, middle grade, and YA only), preferably with art attached. In nonfiction, she is drawn to a more narrative style, with an honest, relatable voice that has something to say about life or can fascinate her with new information about the world.

L254 Hattie Grunewald
Literary Agent
United Kingdom

hattiesubmissions@theblairpartnership.com
https://www.theblairpartnership.com/literary-agents/hattie-grunewald/
https://twitter.com/hatteatime

Literary Agency: The Blair Partnership (**L064**)

Fiction > *Novels*
  Book Club Fiction; Commercial Women's Fiction; Commercial; Cozy Mysteries; Crime; Detective Fiction; Family; High Concept Romance; Historical Fiction; Mystery; Romance; Romantic Comedy; Thrillers; Upmarket

Nonfiction > *Nonfiction Books*
  Lifestyle; Mental Health; Personal Development

Send: Pitch; Market info; Synopsis; Writing sample
How to send: Email

Represents commercial and upmarket fiction, including book club fiction, crime and thriller, historical and contemporary fiction, and some non-fiction in the areas of lifestyle and personal development.

Authors: Jassa Ahluwalia; Danny Altmann; Amy Beashel; Emma J. Bell; Lucy Cameron; Rowan Coleman; Ryan Collett; Tom Davies; Lizzy Dent; Rebecca Denton; Roxane Dhand; Clare Empson; Sue Fortin; Mark Freeman; Jo Furniss; Gary Gamp; Alice Gendron; Marina Gerner; Clare Leslie Hall; Amelia Henley; Louise Jensen; Ruth Kelly; Mollie Kendrick; Peter Komolafe; Alex Lassoued; Liz Lawler; John Lutz; Charlotte Lytton; Cathy MacDonald; Dan Malakin; Ruthy Mason; Luna McNamara; Gez Medinger; Catherine Miller; Leena Norms; Nikki Owen; Rob Perry; Stephen Ronson; Celine Saintclare; Anbara Salam; Lauren Sharkey; Jennifer Stone; Sarah Stovell; Nancy Tucker; Sophie Walker; Sean Watkin; Steve White; Ed Winters; Stephanie Yeboah; Lola Young

L255 Robert Guinsler
Senior Agent
United States

https://www.sll.com/our-team

Literary Agency: Sterling Lord Literistic, Inc.

Nonfiction > *Nonfiction Books*

Send: Query; Synopsis; Writing sample
How to send: Online submission system

His general curiosity in all things has allowed him the opportunity to represent a wide variety of prize-winning and New York Times bestselling nonfiction authors and projects. Most every avenue of the nonfiction spectrum can be found on his list. As well, he has been a champion of LGBTQ+ voices his entire career.

L256 Masha Gunic
Associate Agent
United States

http://www.azantianlitagency.com/pages/team-mg.html
https://querymanager.com/query/MashaGunic

Literary Agency: Azantian Literary Agency

CHILDREN'S > **Fiction** > *Middle Grade*
  Adventure; Comedy / Humour; Contemporary; Fantasy; Historical Fiction; Horror

YOUNG ADULT > **Fiction** > *Novels*
  Commercial; Contemporary; Fantasy; High Concept; Historical Fiction; Literary; Magical Realism; Mystery; Science Fiction; Space Opera; Thrillers

Closed to approaches.

Represents middle grade and young adult novels.

L257 Gurman Agency, LLC
Literary Agency
United States

https://gurmanagency.com

Professional Body: Writers Guild of America (WGA)

Scripts > *Theatre Scripts*

How to send: By referral

Represents playwrights, directors, choreographers, composers and lyricists. New clients by referral only, so prospective clients should seek a referral rather than querying. No queries accepted.

Literary Agent: Susan Gurman

L258 Taylor Haggerty
Literary Agent
United States

submissions@rootliterary.com
taylor@rootliterary.com

https://www.rootliterary.com/agents
https://www.publishersmarketplace.com/members/taylorhaggerty/
https://twitter.com/tayhaggerty

Literary Agency: Root Literary (**L503**)

ADULT > **Fiction** > *Novels*
  Book Club Fiction; Commercial; Romance

TEEN > **Fiction** > *Novels*
  Book Club Fiction; Commercial; Romance

Send: Query; Writing sample
How to send: In the body of an email

I represent commercial fiction for teens and adults – particularly in the romance and book club spaces. I gravitate toward smart, funny, voice-driven projects and welcome all the longing, pining, heart-breaking and heart-mending emotional rollercoasters you want to send my way. I have a tendency to fall for books that blur the lines between genres and am a big novelty seeker as a reader, so always love to be surprised by the fresh and unexpected!

L259 Serene Hakim
Literary Agent
United States

https://www.pandeliterary.com/about-pandeliterary
https://twitter.com/serenemaria
http://aaronline.org/Sys/PublicProfile/52119398/417813

Literary Agency: Ayesha Pande Literary
Professional Body: Association of American Literary Agents (AALA)

ADULT > Fiction > *Novels*
Culture; International; Literary

CHILDREN'S > Fiction > *Middle Grade*: Fantasy

YOUNG ADULT > Fiction > *Novels*
Contemporary; Culture; International

Closed to approaches.

Represents authors in a variety of genres, from MG fantasy to adult literary fiction to contemporary YA. Particularly interested in both YA and adult fiction that has international themes, highlights a variety of cultures, and focuses on underrepresented and/or marginalized voices. At the moment, she is mostly focusing on YA/MG and taking on adult writers more selectively. Specifically, she's looking for writing that explores different meanings of identity, home, and family, and in general would love to find more Middle Eastern writers.

L260 Jolene Haley
Literary Agent
United States

https://www.jolenehaley.com
http://maassagency.com/jolene-haley/
https://querymanager.com/query/QueryJolene
https://twitter.com/JoleneHaley
https://www.instagram.com/jolenehaleybooks/

Literary Agency: Donald Maass Literary Agency (**L160**)

ADULT
Fiction > *Novels*
Cozy Mysteries; Crime; Ghost Stories; Mystery; Romantic Comedy; Romantic Suspense

Nonfiction > *Nonfiction Books*
Crime; Magic; Mind, Body, Spirit; Spirituality; Witchcraft

CHILDREN'S > Fiction > *Middle Grade*
Adventure; Comedy / Humour; Contemporary; Family; Horror; Magic; Magical Realism; Mystery

YOUNG ADULT > Fiction > *Novels*
Adventure; Coming of Age; Contemporary; Folklore, Myths, and Legends; Ghost Stories; Horror; Magical Realism; Mystery; Romance; Tarot; Thrillers; Witches

Closed to approaches.

Has been in the publishing industry since 2012 on both the publisher and agency sides in editorial, marketing, publicity, contracts, and agent positions.

L261 The Hanbury Agency
Literary Agency
Suite 103, 88 Lower Marsh, London, SE1 7AB
United Kingdom

enquiries@hanburyagency.com
http://www.hanburyagency.com
https://www.facebook.com/HanburyAgency/
https://twitter.com/hanburyagency
https://www.instagram.com/the_hanbury_agency/

Fiction > *Novels*

Nonfiction > *Nonfiction Books*
Current Affairs; History; Popular Culture

Closed to approaches.

Closed to submissions as at August 2019. Check website for current status.

No film scripts, plays, poetry, books for children, self-help. Not accepting fantasy, science fiction, or misery memoirs. Send query by post with brief synopsis, first 30 pages (roughly), and your email address and phone number. No submissions by email. Do not include SAE, as no material is returned. Response not guaranteed, so assume rejection if no reply after 8 weeks.

Authors: George Alagiah; Simon Callow; Jane Glover; Bernard Hare; Imran Khan; Judith Lennox; Katie Price

Literary Agent: Margaret Hanbury

L262 Hannah Sheppard Literary Agency
Literary Agency
United Kingdom

https://hs-la.com
https://twitter.com/hannah_litagent
https://instagram.com/hannah_litagent
https://www.facebook.com/hannahsheppard.editor

Professional Body: The Association of Authors' Agents (AAA)

ADULT
Fiction > *Novels*
Crime Thrillers; Family; Friends; High Concept; Horror; Romantasy; Speculative Romance; Speculative; Thrillers

Nonfiction > *Nonfiction Books*
Feminism; Narrative Nonfiction

CHILDREN'S > Fiction
Graphic Novels: General
Middle Grade: Comedy / Humour; Ghost Stories; Horror; Romance; Romantasy

YOUNG ADULT > Fiction > *Graphic Novels*

Send: Query; Synopsis; Writing sample
How to send: Online submission system

I represent both adult and children's fiction (as well as a small amount of non-fiction) and, more than anything, I want to be entertained by a great story while caring deeply about your characters. In general, I love bold, distinctive voices, intriguing stories with a strong hook and flawed characters with something to learn. I want characters who are truly diverse – let's be inclusive, body positive and joyful in our representation. I also like big, mind-bending ideas and combinations of genres that feel fresh and create something new...

Literary Agents: Louise Buckley (**L085**); Hannah Sheppard (*L531*)

L263 Carrie Hannigan
Literary Agent; Partner
United States

carrie@hgliterary.com

https://www.hgliterary.com/carrie
http://queryme.online/Hannigan

Literary Agency: HG Literary
Professional Body: Association of American Literary Agents (AALA)

ADULT > Nonfiction > *Nonfiction Books*

CHILDREN'S
Fiction
Graphic Novels: General
Novels: Comedy / Humour; Contemporary; Fantasy
Nonfiction > *Nonfiction Books*

Closed to approaches.

L264 Stephanie Hansen
Senior Agent
United States

https://www.metamorphosisliteraryagency.com/about
https://querymanager.com/query/Query_Metamorphosis

Literary Agency: Metamorphosis Literary Agency (**L406**)
Professional Body: Association of American Literary Agents (AALA)

ADULT
Fiction > *Novels*: Thrillers

Nonfiction > *Nonfiction Books*

YOUNG ADULT > Fiction > *Novels*
Contemporary; Thrillers

How to send: Query Tracker

Represents authors with their debut novels and New York Times-bestsellers and has brokered deals with small presses, mid-size publishers, major publishing houses, foreign publishers, audio producers, gaming app companies, reading app companies, and film producers. Looks for Thrillers (YA & Adult); YA contemporary with unexpected antagonists; Prose that flows as smoothly as poetry; Unforgettable plot twists; Well-rounded characters; and Non-fiction with heart.

L265 Hardman & Swainson
Literary Agency
S106, New Wing, Somerset House, Strand, London, WC2R 1LA
United Kingdom
Tel: +44 (0) 20 3701 7449

submissions@hardmanswainson.com

https://www.hardmanswainson.com
https://twitter.com/HardmanSwainson

Professional Body: The Association of Authors' Agents (AAA)

Send: Query; Proposal; Writing sample; Full text
How to send: Email

Agency launched June 2012 by former colleagues at an established agency. Represents a range of fiction and nonfiction. See website for full submission guidelines.

Authors: Sophie Austin; Jennifer Barclay; Jackie Bateman; Alex Bell; Anna Bell; Chetan Bhatt; Jon Bounds; Oggy Boytchev; Paul Braddon; Cathy Bramley; Elizabeth Brooks; Isabelle Broom; Mark Broomfield; Tracy Buchanan; Meg Cabot; Elisabeth Carpenter; Simon Cheshire; Adrienne Chinn; Abby Clements; Deb Cohen; Helen Cox; Jeremy Craddock; Sara Crowe; Joshua Cunningham; Emma Darwin; Stuart David; Sharron Davies; Daniel M. Davis; Caroline Davison; Lisa Dickenson; Miranda Dickinson; Sarah Ditum; Carol Donaldson; Charlotte Duckworth; Simon David Eden; Miranda Emmerson; Miguel Farias; Helen Fields; Eugene Finkel; Rosie Fiore; Carrie Hope Fletcher; Giovanna Fletcher; Nicola Ford; Harry Freedman; Michele Gorman; James Gould-Bourn; Vanessa Greene; Kirsty Greenwood; Alastair Gunn; Tom Higham; Michael Jecks; Dinah Jefferies; Oskar Cox Jensen; Stuart Johnstone; Ishani Kar-Purkayastha; Elaine Kasket; Beth Kempton; Holly Kingston; Lucy Lawrie; Peter Laws; Christine Lehnen; Malinda Lo; Craig Lord; Alice Loxton; David B. Lyons; Kevin Macneil; Katie Marsh; S R Masters; Tracy Maton; Ronan McCrea; Clare McGlynn; Cressida Mclaughlin; Ali Mcnamara; Susy Mcphee; Siobhan Miller; Kr Moorhead; Martina Murphy; Julien Musolino; Helen Naylor; Nigel Packer; Lauren Price; Philip C Quaintrell; Steve Ramirez; Martina Reilly; Charlotte Rixon; Caroline Roberts; Gareth Roberts; Patrick Roberts; Nick Russell-Pavier; Susanna Rustin; Suzanne Scanlon; Nikola Scott; Catherine Simpson; Emma Slade; Danny Smith; Karen Ingala Smith; Victoria Smith; Gareth Southwell; Elisabeth Spencer; Hollie Starling; Fiona Sussman; Eliska Tanzer; Joe Tidy; Sarah Tierney; Liz Trenow; Sarah Turner; Rebecca Wait; B P Walter; Louise Walters; Victoria Walters; Sue Watson; Judy Wearing; Alison White; Catherine Wikholm; Alexandra Wilson; Samantha Wilson; Laura Ziepe

Literary Agents: Hannah Ferguson (**L194**); Caroline Hardman; Joanna Swainson (**L561**)

L266 Jessica Hare

Literary Agent
United Kingdom

jhare@theagency.co.uk
https://theagency.co.uk/the-agents/jessica-hare/
https://twitter.com/jcehare
https://instagram.com/jcehare

Literary Agency: The Agency (London) Ltd (**L008**)

CHILDREN'S
  Fiction
    Board Books; *Chapter Books*; *Early Readers*; *Middle Grade*; *Picture Books*
  Nonfiction > *Nonfiction Books*

Runs the Children's Books department. Represents established and emerging children's books authors and illustrators across every age range and genre.

L267 Logan Harper

Literary Agent
United States

https://www.janerotrosen.com/agents

Literary Agency: Jane Rotrosen Agency

Fiction > *Novels*
  Book Club Fiction; Contemporary Romance; Crime; Domestic Suspense; Horror; Literary; Mystery; Psychological Thrillers; Romantic Comedy; Upmarket

Send: Query
How to send: Online contact form

Seeking a wide range of character-driven fiction and is particularly drawn to book club fiction, contemporary romance and romantic comedies, psychological thrillers, domestic suspense, horror, mystery/crime, upmarket and literary fiction.

L268 Erin Harris

Literary Agent; Vice President
United States

eharris@foliolitmanagement.com
https://www.publishersmarketplace.com/members/eharris/
https://twitter.com/ErinHarrisFolio

Literary Agency: Folio Literary Management, LLC (**L207**)
Professional Body: Association of American Literary Agents (AALA)

ADULT
  Fiction > *Novels*
    Alternative History; Book Club Fiction; Contemporary; Fabulism; Fairy Tales; Family Saga; Folklore, Myths, and Legends; High Concept; Historical Fiction; Horror; Literary Mystery; Literary; Science Fiction; Suspense
  Nonfiction > *Nonfiction Books*
    High Concept; Memoir; Narrative Nonfiction
  Poetry > *Poetry Collections*

YOUNG ADULT > **Fiction** > *Novels*
  Contemporary; High Concept; Magic; Speculative; Suspense

Send: Query; Writing sample
How to send: In the body of an email

Passionate about books that interrogate our collective and personal histories with heart and intelligence; characters that make us feel and stories that make us think, even as they keep us feverishly turning pages; and book club and literary fiction that is high concept, whether it be contemporary, historical, or genre-bending (i.e. an accessible, elevated dash of fabulism, sci-fi, horror, suspense, alt. history, etc.)

L269 Susan Hawk

Literary Agent
United States

susanhawk.submission@gmail.com

http://www.upstartcrowliterary.com/agent/susan-hawk/
https://twitter.com/@susanhawk

Literary Agency: Upstart Crow Literary

CHILDREN'S
  Fiction
    Chapter Books; *Middle Grade*; *Picture Books*
  Nonfiction > *Nonfiction Books*

TEEN > **Fiction** > *Novels*

YOUNG ADULT > **Fiction** > *Novels*

How to send: Email

Represents work for children and teens only: picture books, chapter books, middle grade, and young adult, along with some non-fiction for young readers. She doesn't represent adult projects. Open to queries the first week of each month.

L270 Molly Ker Hawn

Literary Agent; Managing Director
United Kingdom

hawnqueries@thebentagency.com

http://www.thebentagency.com/molly-ker-hawn
http://www.twitter.com/mollykh
https://www.publishersmarketplace.com/members/mkhawn

Literary Agency: The Bent Agency (UK) (**L051**)

ADULT > **Fiction** > *Novels*
  Fantasy; Science Fiction; Speculative

CHILDREN'S
  Fiction
    Graphic Novels; *Middle Grade*
  Nonfiction > *Nonfiction Books*

YOUNG ADULT > **Fiction**
  Graphic Novels; *Novels*

Closed to approaches.

I'm looking for exceptional middle-grade and young adult fiction with global commercial appeal, as well as graphic novels for children and young adults with illustrations in place and fantasy, science fiction and speculative fiction for adults.

For children's and YA, I'm open to any genre and almost any topic. Contemporary, historical, fantasy, science fiction, romance, horror…I've loved and sold books that fit all those descriptions. For adult fantasy, science fiction and speculative fiction, I'm looking for fast-paced stories that would appeal to a broad audience, set either in new worlds or one that could be our own, with vividly drawn characters.

No matter the genre or age category, the writing needs to be polished and assured; the story needs to be captivating. I like to be astonished! I'm especially drawn to stories with a strong sense of place, told by authors who fundamentally understand the world they're writing about, whether it's real or imaginary.

L271 Viola Hayden
Literary Agent
United Kingdom
Tel: +44 (0)20 7393 4391

viola.hayden@curtisbrown.co.uk

https://curtisbrown.co.uk
https://curtisbrown.co.uk/agent/viola-hayden

Literary Agency: Curtis Brown (**L135**)

Fiction > *Novels*
Book Club Fiction; Commercial; Crime; Historical Fiction; Suspense

Nonfiction > *Nonfiction Books*
General, and in particular: Memoir; Narrative Nonfiction

Send: Query; Synopsis; Writing sample
How to send: Email
How not to send: Online submission system

I am looking for commercial and reading group fiction, but also narrative non-fiction and some memoir.

L272 David H. Headley
Literary Agent; Managing Director
United Kingdom

submission@dhhliteraryagency.com

http://www.dhhliteraryagency.com/david-h-headley.html
https://twitter.com/davidhheadley

Literary Agency: DHH Literary Agency Ltd (**L152**)

Fiction > *Novels*
General, and in particular: High Concept

Does not want:

Fiction > *Novels*
Fantasy; Science Fiction

Closed to approaches.

Looking for: character-driven debuts; sweeping stories with big universal themes; high concepts; thought-provoking stories; uplifting fiction; original narrative voices; and emotional journeys.

Authors: Graham Bartlett; A. D. Bell; R.C. Bridgestock; Tom Brown; Paul Burston; Andrea Carter; Will Carver; Paul Fraser Collard; James Conway; M.W. Craven; John Curran; A. A. Dhand; Becky Docton; Rachel Edwards; David Fennell; Essie Fox; Anita Frank; Elliott Grover; Lisa Hilton; Ryan David Jahn; Helga Jensen; Ragnar Jonasson; Katrin Júlíusdóttir; Beth Lewis; Sean Lusk; Zoe Lyons; Chris McDonald; Brian McGilloway; Chris Merritt; Janie Millman; Elizabeth S. Moore; Noel O'Reilly; Anthony J. Quinn; Jenny Quintana; Robert Rutherford; Victoria Selman; Mel Sherratt; Jo Thomas; L.C. Tyler; Clare Whitfield; Claire Wilson; David Young; Eva Björg Ægisdottir

L273 Laura Heathfield
Literary Agent; Company Director
United Kingdom

laura@greenstoneliterary.com

https://www.greenstoneliterary.com
https://www.greenstoneliterary.com/agents/amet-elit-sed
https://www.instagram.com/laura.heathfield/

Literary Agency: Greenstone Literary (**L252**)

Fiction > *Novels*
Book Club Fiction; Commercial; Crime; Historical Fiction; Romance; Suspense; Thrillers

Nonfiction > *Nonfiction Books*

Send: Query; Synopsis; Writing sample
How to send: Online submission system

I am looking for commercial crime, thriller, suspense, book club, historical and romance fiction as well as select non-fiction. Above everything I want to be entertained. I'm looking for a book you can't wait to talk to someone about, in the same way as a new film or the latest release on Netflix. A book that engrosses me from the first page to the last, desperate for someone I know to read so we can discuss as soon as possible. In non-fiction, I'm looking for an untold story or perspective or an unexplored area where you have expertise or real-life experience. As a reader of non-fiction, I want to be engaged in a relatable, accessible way. I am not looking for poetry, novellas, short story collections, screenplays, children's or middle-grade books.

L274 Chelsea Hensley
Literary Agent
United States

https://www.chelseahensley.com
https://www.madwomanliterary.com/chelseahensley
https://www.chelseahensley.com/mswl
https://querymanager.com/query/Chelseahensley

Literary Agency: Mad Woman Literary Agency (**L384**)

ADULT
Fiction > *Novels*
Fantasy; Horror; Mystery; Romance; Science Fiction; Suspense; Thrillers

Nonfiction > *Nonfiction Books*
Astrology; Media; Popular Culture; Tarot; Women's Football / Soccer; Women's Sports

CHILDREN'S
Fiction
Middle Grade: Horror; Mystery
Picture Books: Adventure; Animals; Comedy / Humour; Contemporary; Lyrical
Nonfiction > *Picture Books*: Biography

YOUNG ADULT > **Fiction** > *Novels*
Fantasy; Horror; Mystery; Science Fiction; Suspense; Thrillers

How to send: Query Tracker

In all areas I'm looking for lyrical prose, voice that comes off the page, intricate plots, complex emotional arcs, and immersive worlds. I'd love to see some ambitious works that play with form and narration as well as works that blend genre, aren't afraid to get a little weird, and surprise me. The bolder the better. I'm also eager to find authors who write across multiple genres and age categories, so if you have ambitions to write beyond the project you're currently querying, take a look at other areas of my wishlist and see if we may be a good fit for future works of yours, too.

L275 Saritza Hernandez
Literary Agent
United States

saritza@andreabrownlit.com

https://www.andreabrownlit.com
https://www.andreabrownlit.com/Team/saritza-hern%C3%A1ndez
https://querymanager.com/query/Saritza
https://bsky.app/profile/litagentsaritza.bsky.social
https://instagram.com/saritzah/
https://www.facebook.com/LitAgentSaritza

Literary Agency: Andrea Brown Literary Agency, Inc.

ADULT
Fiction > *Novels*
Romance; Science Fiction

Nonfiction > *Nonfiction Books*
  Food and Drink; Narrative Nonfiction; Popular Culture; Science

CHILDREN'S > *Fiction* > *Middle Grade*

YOUNG ADULT > *Fiction* > *Novels*

Does not want:

> Nonfiction > *Nonfiction Books*: Cookery

How to send: Query Tracker

Specializes in romance and young adult fiction by and for diverse audiences but also represents writers and illustrators for picture books, middle grade, young adult, and adult (fiction and nonfiction).

L276 Paloma Hernando
Associate Agent
United States

https://www.pandeliterary.com
https://www.pandeliterary.com/our-team-pandeliterary
https://x.com/AgentPaloma

Literary Agency: Ayesha Pande Literary

ADULT
  Fiction
    Graphic Novels: High / Epic Fantasy; LGBTQIA; Magic; Romance; Science Fiction
    Novels: High / Epic Fantasy; LGBTQIA; Magic; Romance; Science Fiction
  Nonfiction > *Nonfiction Books*
    General, and in particular: History; Media

CHILDREN'S
  Fiction > *Middle Grade*: Comedy / Humour
  Nonfiction > *Nonfiction Books*
    General, and in particular: History; Media

YOUNG ADULT > *Fiction*
  Graphic Novels: High / Epic Fantasy; LGBTQIA; Magic; Romance; Science Fiction
  Novels: High / Epic Fantasy; LGBTQIA; Magic; Romance; Science Fiction

How to send: Online submission system

Has built a list focusing on graphic novels and illustrated books. Coming from a background of independent comics and the DIY scene, she has always been attracted to well-told stories with a passionate drive behind them. She is also accepting prose works and is seeking any book that tells genre stories in new ways. The only thing she likes more than trope-y fun is the chance to break it down into something new. She also represents illustrators for literary projects and is always on the lookout for strong visual styles. As a daughter of Argentinian immigrants, she views publishing globally and would love to work with any bilingual or international projects.

L277 Lane Heymont
President; Literary Agent
United States

https://www.thetobiasagency.com/lane-heymont
https://querymanager.com/query/1291
http://aaronline.org/Sys/PublicProfile/27203936/417813

Literary Agency: The Tobias Literary Agency
Professional Body: Association of American Literary Agents (AALA)

ADULT
  Fiction > *Novels*
    Commercial; Horror
  Nonfiction > *Nonfiction Books*
    Celebrity; Culture; History; Popular Culture; Science

YOUNG ADULT > *Fiction* > *Novels*: Horror

Send: Author bio; Query; Market info; Writing sample
How to send: Query Tracker

Represents a broad range of commercial fiction and serious nonfiction. In fiction, he is especially interested in projects broadly defined as horror. This includes select young adult horror. He is always looking for projects by underrepresented voices both in horror, fiction in general, and nonfiction. In nonfiction, he focuses on the sciences, cultural studies, history, pop-culture, and celebrity projects.

L278 Emily Hickman
Literary Agent
United Kingdom
Tel: +44 (0) 20 7908 0977

ehickman@theagency.co.uk

https://theagency.co.uk/the-agents/emily-hickman/

Literary Agency: The Agency (London) Ltd (**L008**)

Scripts
  Film Scripts; TV Scripts; Theatre Scripts

Represents a diverse list of writers and writer/directors across stage and screen, alongside the dramatic rights for a variety of fiction and non-fiction authors.

L279 High Line Literary Collective
Literary Agency
United States

https://www.highlineliterary.com

Standing at the cross-section between art and commerce, our agents facilitate thriving, vibrant careers for writers, artists and creators. From the moment we begin working with a client, we establish full-spectrum representation dedicated to each creator's unique needs. From audience engagement, to career orientation, to strategic long-term management, our holistic guidance charts your most successful publishing journey.

Literary Agents: Amanda Bernardi (**L056**); Margaret Danko (**L140**); Pam Gruber (**L253**); Sheyla Knigge (**L339**); Victoria Marini (**L388**); Kim Perel (**L462**); Whitney Ross (**L507**)

L280 Cole Hildebrand
Literary Agent
United States

https://www.cole-hildebrand.com
https://www.jvnla.com/submitch
https://querytracker.net/query/colehildebrandqueries

Literary Agency: The Jean V. Naggar Literary Agency (**L299**)

Fiction > *Novels*
  Contemporary; Experimental; LGBTQIA; Literary; Upmarket

Nonfiction > *Nonfiction Books*
  Arts; Culture; Environment; History; Investigative Journalism; LGBTQIA; Memoir; Mental Health; Narrative Nonfiction; Politics; Popular Culture

How to send: Query Tracker

Represents adult literary and upmarket fiction, and narrative non-fiction, with particular focus on queer themes and stories.

In non-fiction, he is drawn to narrative and/or investigative work that blends personal, cultural, political, and historical threads – books that engage with radical thought, queer history, art, pop culture, environmental studies, and mental health. He is also interested in outward-focused memoirs and well-researched accounts of understudied historical periods or movements.

In fiction, he is looking for contemporary upmarket, literary, and experimental work, and is open to novels that blur genre elements in surprising or unconventional ways. He is drawn to stories driven by character and voice that play with form and narrative structure, written with stylistically distinctive prose.

L281 Sam Hiyate
Literary Agent; President; Chief Executive Officer
Canada

shiyate@therightsfactory.com

https://www.therightsfactory.com/Agents/Sam-Hiyate
https://www.therightsfactory.com/submit-sam

Literary Agency: The Rights Factory

Fiction > *Novels*
  Crime; Literary; Mystery; Thrillers; Upmarket Commercial Fiction

Nonfiction > *Nonfiction Books*
Business; Food; Health; Lifestyle; Memoir; Personal Development

Send: Query; Author bio; Writing sample
How to send: Email

Handles various categories, including memoir, literary and commercial fiction, narrative non-fiction and graphic novels. He's looking for works of all categories with distinct and compelling voices. He loved to discover and help new writers prepare their works for the market, and to help them build a career with their talent.

Authors: Oscar Allueva; Ho Che Anderson; Michel Basilières; Margot Berwin; Charles Bongers; Alex Brueckmann; Michael Busk; Dave Butler; Lila Cecil; Timothy Christian; Michael Dargie; Elaine Dewar; Oonagh Duncan; Benjamin Errett; Saad T. Farooqi; Becca Fischer; Bronwyn Fischer; Sara Flemington; Darya Foroohar; Debbie Fox; Patricia Fulton; Rupinder Gill; Jesse Gilmour; Shinan Govani; Lee Gowan; Alexandra Grigorescu; Nadia Guo; Kamal Gupta; Wes Hall; Alex Huntley; Chris Johns; Sam Juric; Andrew Kaufman; Michelle Kim; Sohan Koonar; Arkadi Kuhlmann; David Leach; Barbra Leslie; Claire Letemendia; Emily Lipinski; Anneke Lucas; Natalie MacLean; Mieke Marple; Kiirsten May; Maureen Medved; Mary Mellon; Natasha Mihell; Sally Moore; Hal Niedzviecki; Rebecca Nison; Ell Orion; Brad Orsted; Matthew Pennock; Katie Peyton; Barbara Radecki; Greg Rhyno; Alexandra Risen; Leslie Shimotakahara; David Skuy; Allison Stieger; Stephen Stohn; Tre Tennyson; Diane Terrana; Chris Turner; Joanne Vannicola; Alex Varricchio; Maurice Vellekoop; Cory Vitiello; Andy Walker; Kay Walker; Imogen Lloyd Webber; Jessica Westhead; Molly Roden Winter; Naomi Yano

L282 Jodie Hodges
Literary Agent
United Kingdom
Tel: +44 (0) 20 3214 0891

jhodges@unitedagents.co.uk

https://www.unitedagents.co.uk/jhodgesunitedagentscouk
http://twitter.com/jodiehodges31

Literary Agency: United Agents

CHILDREN'S > **Fiction**
Comics: General
Graphic Novels: General
Middle Grade: Adventure; Comedy / Humour; Domestic; Fantasy; Historical Fiction
Picture Books: General

Send: Query; Synopsis; Writing sample; Full text
How to send: Email attachment
How not to send: Post

I'll always be keen to see classic storytelling for 8-12s be it an adventure, a fantasy, historical, domestic, a comedy. Anything and everything to appeal to the both the voracious child reader I was and those children for whom books aren't an everyday part of life. Additionally, I'm always searching for children's book illustrators or writer/illustrators who know their own style and are attuned to the children's book market. I also represent creators of comics and graphic novels for children and very happy to see more.

Associate Agent: Molly Jamieson (**L296**)

Literary Agent: Emily Talbot (**L567**)

L283 Christina Hogrebe
Literary Agent
United States

https://www.janerotrosen.com/
https://www.janerotrosen.com/contact-christina-hogrebe

Literary Agency: Jane Rotrosen Agency

Fiction > *Novels*
Fantasy; Romance; Thrillers

How not to send: Online submission system

Drawn to the kind of fun, escapist stories that also spark lively debate in her book club, especially in the areas of fantasy, thriller, and romance, and would love to champion an author underrepresented in those categories.

L284 Sally Holloway
Associate Agent
United Kingdom

https://felicitybryan.com/fba-agent/sally-holloway/

Literary Agency: Felicity Bryan Associates (**L192**)

Nonfiction > *Nonfiction Books*
Biography; Business; Contemporary; Economics; High Concept; History; Investigative Journalism; Literature; Narrative Nonfiction; Popular Culture; Popular Psychology; Popular Science

Send: Query; Proposal; Writing sample; Synopsis
How to send: Online submission system

I am always on the look-out for authors who can write with authority, wit and originality in the fields of 'Big Ideas', popular psychology, contemporary issues, economics and business (though not 'how to' books). I also like writers who can explain complex ideas entertainingly or who are able to transport me into a different world, in areas as diverse as popular science, history, biography, literature, popular culture. I would love to find more writers of narrative non-fiction who have important stories to tell, especially investigative journalists.

Authors: Johnny Acton; Ben Ambridge; Mark Avery; Jonny Beardsall; Andrew Blum; James Brooke-Smith; Archie Brown; Larisa Brown; Karl Bushby; Tom Butler-Bowdon; Graham Caveney; Peter Chapman; James Fairhead; Georgina Ferry; Dominic Frisby; David Goldblatt; Simon Hall; Tim Harford; Robert Hutton; Helena Kelly; Richard Koch; James Kynge; Simon Lancaster; Tomila Lankina; Alysa Levene; Anna Machin; Oliver Milman; David Pilling; Captain Elliot Rappaport; Shilpa Ravella; David Reynolds; Ian Robertson; Jon Savage; Adrian Tinniswood; Tom Vanderbilt; Clive Webb; Hugh Wilford; Sam Wilkin; Imogen Willetts

L285 Penny Holroyde
Literary Agent
United Kingdom

penny@holroydecartey.com

https://www.holroydecartey.com/about.html
https://www.holroydecartey.com/submissions.html

Literary Agency: Holroyde Cartey

CHILDREN'S
Fiction
Board Books; Chapter Books; Early Readers; Middle Grade; Picture Books
Nonfiction > *Nonfiction Books*

Send: Synopsis; Full text
How to send: Email attachment

I've worked in publishing for nearly thirty years at publishers Walker Books in the UK and Candlewick Press in the US and then as an agent with Caroline Sheldon. I have a particular love for the picture book but am looking for authors and illustrators working across fiction and non-fiction for all ages.

L286 Kate Hordern
Literary Agent
United Kingdom

kate@khla.co.uk

https://twitter.com/katehordern

Literary Agency: Kate Hordern Literary Agency

ADULT
Fiction > *Novels*
General, and in particular: Book Club Fiction; Commercial; Crime; Historical Fiction; Psychological Suspense; Speculative; Upmarket Women's Fiction

Nonfiction > *Nonfiction Books*
History; Memoir

CHILDREN'S > **Fiction** > *Middle Grade*

I'm looking for fiction across the range, from bookclub through to psychological suspense, crime, speculative, historical, commercial and upmarket women's fiction, with a unique hook, whether that is a very special voice or a high-concept plot or compelling characters or a combination of these. In non-fiction I'm looking for history, where the author has the appropriate platform, and memoir. My middle-grade kids fiction list is currently closed to new submissions.

L287 Sarah Hornsley
Literary Agent; Author
United Kingdom

shornsley@pfd.co.uk

https://petersfraserdunlop.com/agent/sarah-hornsley/
https://twitter.com/SarahHornsley

Literary Agencies: Peters Fraser + Dunlop; Mushens Entertainment
Literary Agent: Juliet Mushens (**L430**)

Fiction > *Novels*
  Book Club Fiction; Commercial; Historical Fiction; Romance; Speculative; Suspense; Thrillers; Women's Fiction

Nonfiction > *Nonfiction Books*

Send: Query; Synopsis; Writing sample; Proposal; Author bio
How to send: Email
How not to send: Post

I'm looking for adult commercial and book club fiction across all genres. I'm always on the look-out for a strong hook – a setting or scenario which captures my imagination straight away. Generally, I am drawn to strong, emotive writing matched with a gripping fast-paced plot. I am very hands-on editorially and am looking to only take on a few select really special writers this year. I'd love to find a really high-concept twisty thriller or suspense novel. Something that subverts my expectations and keeps me on the edge of my seat. I also never tire of exploring dark sibling relationships and as a mother myself I love a complex mother/daughter relationship. In general and women's fiction, I'm really keen to find something with heart and brilliant emotive storytelling. I absolutely adore historical fiction. I'm also a huge fan of romantic fiction and have had a number of authors shortlisted for the RNA Awards. I enjoy anything from genre-bending rom-coms and laugh-out-loud escapist spicy romance with fresh hooks to emotive epic love stories.

Authors: Claire Ackroyd; Ciara Attwell; Matilda Battersby; Olivia Beirne; Roxie Cooper; Georgina Cutler; Rachel Louise Driscoll; Philippa East; Jenny Epstein; Amy de la Force; Anstey Harris; Emma Heatherington; Emily Houghton; Becky Hunter; Lynsey James; Fionnuala Kearney; Gina Lamanna; Jo Lovett; Ali Pantony; Lou Robbie; Rachel Ward; Helen Whitaker; S.M. Wilson

L288 Annie Hwang
Literary Agent
United States

https://twitter.com/AnnieAHwang
https://www.publishersmarketplace.com/members/hwangan/

Literary Agency: Ayesha Pande Literary

Fiction > *Novels*: Literary

Nonfiction > *Nonfiction Books*: Narrative Nonfiction

Poetry > *Poetry Collections*

Send: Pitch; Author bio; Synopsis; Writing sample
How to send: Online submission system

Primarily represents voice-driven literary fiction that plays with genre, though she also takes on nonfiction and poetry on occasion. In particular, she is drawn to what she likes to think of as "literary fiction with teeth"—ambitious novels that are daring in their approach that also grapple with the complexities of the world with nuance and finesse.

L289 Inscriptions Literary Agency
Literary Agency
United States
Tel: +1 (636) 633-7846

https://inscriptionsliterary.com
https://querymanager.com/query/InscriptionsLit_Query

ADULT
  Fiction > *Novels*
    General, and in particular: Christian Romance; Contemporary Romance; Hardboiled Crime; Mystery; Science Fiction; Suspense

  Nonfiction > *Nonfiction Books*
    Christianity; Crime; Memoir

  Scripts > *Film Scripts*

CHILDREN'S > **Fiction**
  Middle Grade; Picture Books

Does not want:

> **CHILDREN'S** > **Fiction** > *Middle Grade*
>   Dark Magic; Gender Issues; Science Fiction; Voodoo; Witchcraft

Send: Query; Synopsis; Writing sample; Full text; Pitch
How to send: Query Tracker; Email

A boutique literary agency which offers representation services to authors who are both published and pre-published. Our mission is to form strong partnerships with our clients and build long-term relationships that extend from writing the first draft through the entire length of the author's career.

What is a boutique literary agency? A small, but mighty agency that has less than 12 agents. We specialize in quality, not quantity. We limit the amount of clients we take on, in order to give each client our full attention.

We are not looking for books containing: political agenda, controversies, AI content, alternative religion books, books labeled "Christian" that do not follow the standards of the Bible, Sci-Fi-Christian, illustrated children's books.

We are not looking for: Erotic, board books, baby or toddler books, lyrical books, SEL books, or topics in children's books that contradict basic Christian standards. We believe Christian values should always be portrayed in Children's fiction.

Submit literary submissions via QueryManager. Submit pitches for screenplay representation by email.

Literary Agent: Andrea Comparato (**L123**)

L290 Inspired Ink Literary
Literary Agency
2520 Glaicer Drive, Pine Mountain Club, CA 93225
United States
Tel: +1 (661) 645-2065

g.seeholzer@gmail.com

https://gisaseeholzer.com
https://www.facebook.com/profile.php?id=100091319542373
https://www.instagram.com/gisaseeholzer

Fiction > *Novels*
  General, and in particular: Historical Fiction

Nonfiction > *Nonfiction Books*: Creative Nonfiction

Send: Query; Synopsis; Writing sample; Proposal; Outline
How to send: PDF file email attachment; In the body of an email

We are passionate about discovering exceptional voices and powerful storytelling. We welcome submissions in Historical Fiction, Fiction, and Creative Non-Fiction, with a particular interest in works that captivate, provoke thought, and spark meaningful conversations. Our agency is dedicated to representing authors whose stories resonate with readers, transport them to new worlds, and leave a lasting impression. If you believe your work embodies these qualities, we would love to hear from you.

L291 Irene Goodman Literary Agency (IGLA)
Literary Agency
United States

irene.queries@irenegoodman.com

https://www.irenegoodman.com
https://twitter.com/IGLAbooks
http://instagram.com/iglabooks
https://www.facebook.com/IreneGoodmanAgency

ADULT
  Fiction > *Novels*
    Historical Fiction; Mystery; Romance; Thrillers
  Nonfiction > *Nonfiction Books*
    Business; Cookery; France; Health; History; Judaism; Lifestyle; Politics; Popular Culture
YOUNG ADULT > Fiction > *Novels*

Send: Query; Writing sample; Synopsis; Outline; Proposal; Market info
How to send: Email

Interests include business, health, politics and history, cookbooks, pop culture, Jewish interest, Francophilia, lifestyle, upmarket fiction, historical fiction, and mysteries. All non-fiction proposals should include an overview, descriptions of each chapter, comp titles, and a healthy platform. Fiction should include the first ten pages, a complete synopsis, and a total word count. If you are published by a commercial publisher, please tell me who published you and give me an idea of the sales history.

Literary Agent: Irene Goodman

L292 Lucy Irvine
Literary Agent
United Kingdom
Tel: +44 (0) 20 7344 1087

lirvine@pfd.co.uk

https://petersfraserdunlop.com/agent/lucy-irvine/

Literary Agency: Peters Fraser + Dunlop

ADULT > Fiction > *Novels*
  Cozy Fantasy; Fantasy; High / Epic Fantasy; Horror; Romantasy; Science Fiction; Space Opera; Speculative Horror; Steampunk; Urban Fantasy; Werewolves
CHILDREN'S > Fiction
  Chapter Books: General
  Early Readers: General
  Middle Grade: General, and in particular: Adventure; Commercial; Contemporary; Fantasy; Folklore, Myths, and Legends
  Picture Books: General, and in particular: Comedy / Humour
YOUNG ADULT > Fiction > *Novels*
  Fantasy; Historical Romance; Mystery; Romance

Does not want:

Fiction > *Novels:* Grimdark

Send: Query; Synopsis; Writing sample; Proposal; Author bio
How to send: Email

My taste is generally very broad; I represent anything that falls under the children's umbrella, with a focus on middle-grade, YA, and science-fiction/fantasy/horror in the adult market. I'm currently not looking for picture books.

My taste in middle-grade books veers towards the commercial; I'm drawn to quick-paced, adventurous narratives with series potential. I love stories set in worlds that pull you in and stay with you long after you've finished reading, and am particularly keen to see original world-building and hooky, plot driven narratives. I'm always looking for fantasy in this space, but would also love contemporary, realistic settings – whether these are silly and humorous or emotional and issue-led. I would love to find something in the vein of Louie Stowell's LOKI series or Elle McNicoll's KEEDIE. I'm also very drawn to re-imagined folktales, myths, and legends, especially from voices traditionally underrepresented within publishing. Some middle-grade books I grew up on and adored include THE ROMAN MYSTERIES, THE CHRONICLES OF ANCIENT DARKNESS, and the PERCY JACKSON series.

On the YA side, I love all kinds of genre fiction, from fantasy to historical to romance to murder mystery. I'm keen to build the romance side of my list, and here I'm really looking for compelling character writing that makes me invested in the romance arc whatever the setting. I love twists and subversions on beloved tropes, and to really believe in the conflict (if you're writing enemies-to-lovers, make them ENEMIES). Fantasy wise, I'm keen to see original world-building, and love anything that genre blends or offers a fresh take on traditional themes. I recently read and loved Moira Buffini's SONGLIGHT and S.F. Williamson's A LANGUAGE OF DRAGONS, and would love to find something similarly ambitious.

In terms of crossover and adult science-fiction/fantasy, I accept submissions in anything that falls under the general SFF umbrella, from urban to epic fantasy, from space opera to steampunk, but am not the right person for anything too grimdark. I would love to find something with the ambition and wit of GIDEON THE NINTH, or the scope and narrative-weaving of THE PRIORY OF THE ORANGE TREE. I'm also really keen to find more cozy fantasy, and I really want a werewolf story after reading and loving Ali Hazelwood's BRIDE! I'll happily read romantasy submissions, but here am looking for fresh approaches to the genre. I'm dipping my toes into speculative horror and am keen to read more submissions in this space.

I am always looking for diverse writers and protagonists across race, sexuality, gender, class, and disability.

Across the board, I'd love to find stories with characters that I can see a fandom forming around.

Authors: Amy Archer; Lerah Mae Barcenilla; Sunita Chawdhary; Camille Chong; Katie Dale; W. Y. Dobson; Annabel Durant-Rogers; Judith Eagle; Ava Eldred; Rowan Foxwood; Tessa Gearing; William Goldsmith; Norma Gregory; Bridget Helen Hamilton; Lindsay Hirst; Lexy Hudson; Iqbal Hussain; Lis Jardine; Marisa Linton; Aneesa Marufu; Emily Randall; Laila Rifaat; Ali Stegert; Sam Stewart; Gail Upchurch; Catherine Ward; Alison Weatherby; Melissa Welliver

L293 Dotti Irving
Literary Agent
United Kingdom

dotti@greyhoundliterary.co.uk

https://greyhoundliterary.co.uk/agents/dotti-irving

Literary Agency: Greyhound Literary

Nonfiction > *Nonfiction Books:* Narrative Nonfiction

Send: Query; Synopsis; Writing sample
How to send: Email

Primarily interested in narrative non-fiction, in books that tell a story that rings true and speaks to a wider world.

Authors: Matt Blake; Reuben Coe; Anthea Rowan; Tina Shingler

L294 Clare Israel
Literary Agent
United Kingdom

Literary Agency: David Higham Associates Ltd (**L146**)

L295 Amanda Hepp Jackson
Associate Agent
United States

https://www.stephanietadeagency.com/aboutus

Literary Agency: Stephanie Tade Literary Agency

L296 Molly Jamieson
Associate Agent
United Kingdom
Tel: +44 (0) 20 3214 0973

mjamieson@unitedagents.co.uk

https://www.unitedagents.co.uk/mjamiesonunitedagentscouk

Literary Agency: United Agents
Literary Agent: Jodie Hodges (**L282**)

ADULT > **Fiction** > *Novels*
  Commercial; Fantasy; Folk Horror; Gothic; Horror; Romance; Science Fiction

CHILDREN'S > **Fiction** > *Novels*
  Fantasy; Science Fiction

Send: Query; Synopsis; Writing sample
How to send: Email

Has a particular interest in scifi and fantasy across both adult and children's books. She loves anything with high stakes, characters you would follow anywhere, big stories, expansive worldbuilding, breathless romance, and threads of adventure running throughout. She would be keen to see gothic horror and folk horror, stories that mess with your mind, rather than showcasing gratuitous violence.

Author Estates: The Estate of Algernon Blackwood; The Estate of R Austin Freeman; The Estate of Rafael Sabatini; The Estate of Sir Alan (A P) Herbert

Authors: Shalini Abeysekara; Jackson P. Brown; John Chalmers; Guy Haley; Hannah-Marie Holwell; Arden Jones; Vanessa Jones; Sandra Marrs; Christine Modafferi; Aimee Oliver; Melissa Powell; O.R. Sorrel

L297 Janklow & Nesbit UK Ltd
Literary Agency
Holborn Town Hall, 193-197 High Holborn, London, WC1V 7BD
United Kingdom
Tel: +44 (0) 20 3411 6550

submissions@janklow.co.uk

http://www.janklowandnesbit.co.uk
https://twitter.com/JanklowUK

Professional Body: The Association of Authors' Agents (AAA)

ADULT
  Fiction > *Novels*
    General, and in particular: Commercial; Literary
  Nonfiction > *Nonfiction Books*

CHILDREN'S > **Fiction** > *Novels*

YOUNG ADULT > **Fiction** > *Novels*

Send: Query; Synopsis; Writing sample
How to send: Email

Send query by email, including informative covering letter providing background about yourself and your writing; first three chapters / approx. 50 pages; a brief synopsis for fiction, or a full outline for nonfiction. For poetry, submit a short pitch and small sample of 3-5 poems.

Company Director / Literary Agent: Claire Paterson Conrad (**L125**)

Literary Agents: Will Francis; Hayley Steed (**L548**)

L298 Javelin
Literary Agency
203 South Union Street, Alexandria, VA 22314
United States
Tel: +1 (703) 490-8845

hello@javelindc.com

http://javelindc.com

Nonfiction > *Nonfiction Books*
  History; Journalism; Politics; Science

Send: Pitch
How to send: Online contact form

Represents presidential contenders, diplomats, journalists, historians, scientists – and others with a unique and compelling story to share.

L299 The Jean V. Naggar Literary Agency
Literary Agency
216 East 75th Street, Suite 1E, New York, NY 10021
United States

https://www.jvnla.com
https://www.instagram.com/jvnlainc/
http://x.com/JVNLA
https://www.facebook.com/JVNLA

ADULT
  Fiction > *Novels*
  Nonfiction > *Nonfiction Books*

CHILDREN'S > **Fiction** > *Middle Grade*

YOUNG ADULT > **Fiction** > *Novels*

Send: Query; Outline; Author bio
How to send: Online submission system
How not to send: Post

View agent details and submit to only one agent. Your query should include a brief description of your work and a short author bio. No submissions by post. Response only if interested.

Literary Agency: The Ekus Group (**L176**)

Literary Agent / President: Jennifer Weltz (**L596**)

Literary Agents: Cole Hildebrand (**L280**); Ariana Philips (**L471**); Alice Tasman (**L569**)

Senior Agent: Sally Ekus (**L177**)

L300 JFL Agency
Literary Agency
60 St Martin's Lane, London, WC2N 4JS
United Kingdom
Tel: +44 (0) 20 3137 8182

representation@jflagency.com
agents@jflagency.com

http://www.jflagency.com

Scripts
  Film Scripts; *Radio Scripts*; *TV Scripts*; *Theatre Scripts*

Send: Query
How to send: Email

Handles scripts only (for television, film, theatre and radio). Considers approaches from established writers with broadcast experience, but only accepts submissions from new writers during specific periods – consult website for details.

Authors: Humphrey Barclay; Liam Beirne; Adam Bostock-Smith; Tim Brooke-Taylor; Ian Brown; Grant Cathro; Paul Charlton; Gabby Hutchinson Crouch; Bill Dare; Tim Dawson; Martin Day; Ed Dyson; Polly Eden; Jan Etherington; Sinéad Fagan; Anji Loman Field; Phil Ford; Patrick Gallagher; Ted Gannon; Lisa Gifford; Rob Gittins; Ben Harris; James Hendrie; Wayne Jackman; Tony Lee; Richard Leslie Lewis; Jane Marlow; Jonathan Morris; Cardy O'Donnell; Jim Pullin; Jackie Robb; Graeme Rooney; Gary Russell; David Semple; James Serafinowicz; Pete Sinclair; Paul Smith; Fraser Steele

Literary Agents: Alison Finch; Dominic Lord; Gary Wild

L301 Joelle Delbourgo Associates, Inc.
Literary Agency
101 Park St., Montclair, Montclair, NJ 07042
United States
Tel: +1 (973) 773-0836

submissions@delbourgo.com

https://www.delbourgo.com

ADULT
  Fiction > *Novels*
    Commercial; Fantasy; Literary; Mystery; Science Fiction; Thrillers; Women's Fiction

  Nonfiction
    Nonfiction Books: Biography; Cookery; Current Affairs; Food; Health; History; Memoir; Mind, Body, Spirit; Narrative Nonfiction; Parenting; Popular Culture; Psychology; Science
    Reference: Popular

CHILDREN'S
  Fiction
    Middle Grade; *Picture Books*
  Nonfiction > *Middle Grade*

YOUNG ADULT > **Fiction** > *Novels*

Closed to approaches.

Costs: Author covers sundry admin costs.

A boutique literary agency based in the greater New York City area. We represent a wide range of authors writing for the adult trade market, from creative nonfiction to expert-driven nonfiction, commercial fiction to literary fiction, as well as middle grade fiction and nonfiction.

Authors: Tanya Acker; P. David Allen; Jennifer Lynn Alvarez; Heather Anastasiu; Lisa Anselmo; Thomas Armstrong; Sara Au; Rebecca Rego Barry; Frances Bartkowski; Audrey Bellezza; Waitman Beorn; Suzanne Bohan; Lynn Kiele Bonasia; Michele Borba; Robert Bornstein; Elizabeth Reid Boyd; Nora Bradbury-Haehl; Anne Greenwood Brown; Gay Browne; Ariel Burger; Susan Campbell; Craig Carlson; Paul Carter; Jill Castle; Debbie Cenziper; Rachael Cerrotti; Marj Charlier; John Christianson; Tara L. Clark; Margot Clark-Junkins; Gay Courter; Nancy Cowan; Katherine Scott Crawford; Michelle Dempsey-Multack; Sybil Derrible; Karla Dougherty; Nancy Dreyfus; Rosa Kwon Easton; Charity Elder; Chris Farrell; Marilyn Fedewa; Michael Feuer; Ellen Flannery-Schroeder; Laura Berman Fortgang; Susan Forward; Philip Freeman; Terry Gaspard; John Gaudet; Susan Gilbert-Collins; Michelle Glogovac; Ann E. Grant; Jonathon Grayson; Brenda Greene; Beth A. Grosshans; Julie L. Hall; Emily Harding; Kate Harding; Laura Hartema; Kimberly Heckler; Kristi Hedges; Holly Herrick; Roy Hoffman; Helaina Hovitz; Erik Forrest Jackson; Grace Jung; Theresa Kaminski; Rachelle Katz; Joseph Kelly; Stephen Kelly; Brynne S. Kennedy; Nancy Kennedy; Hilary Kinavey; Sean Kingsley; Willem Kuyken; Mary Languirand; Missy Chase Lapine; Claire Lerner; Irene S. Levine; Alexandra Levitt; Lisa L. Lewis; Mary Ann Little; Geralyn Lucas; Lauren Mackler; Juliet Madison; Kerstin March; David J. Marsh; Chuck Martin; Lama Marut; Carol Masciola; Roy Meals; Cristina Nehring; Nicola Nice; Jennifer O'Callaghan; Emily J. O'Dell; Colleen O'Grady; Jim Obergefell; Elaine Neil Orr; Lindsey J. Palmer; Theresa Payton; Michelle Pearce; Scott Peeples; Julia Pimsleur; Gleb Raygorodetsky; Eliza Redgold; Michael Reichert; James Renner; Ashley Rhodes-Courter; Paige Rien; Alexandra Rimer; Jillian Roberts; Tatsha Robertson; Lisa Romeo; Marilyn Simon Rothstein; Dale Russakoff; Michael Sadowski; Karla Salinari; Roberta Sandenbergh; Sue Scheff; Elisa A. Schmitz; Melissa Schorr; Ellen E. Schultz; Sara Sherbill; Heather Shumaker; Alexandra Silber; Pamela Slim; Joanna Sliwa; Christopher A. Snyder; Laura Sobiech; Julie M. Stamm; Peter L. Stavinoha; Maryon Stewart; Nancy Rubin Stuart; Dana Sturtevant; Deborah J. Swiss; Jeff Sypeck; Ericka Sóuter; John Temple; Christopher Van Tilburg; Chelsea Tucker; M.D. Usher; Julie Valerie; Rebecca Lynn Viera; Michael Volpatt; Caroline Welch; Susan Wels; Elizabeth White; Elizabeth "Barry" White; Kristin M. White; Barrie Wilson; Ben H. Winters; Jon Wuebben; Gabra Zackman; Peter Zheutlin; Gabe Zichermann

Literary Agent: Joelle Delbourgo

L302 Johnson & Alcock

Literary Agency
West Wing, Somerset House, Strand, London, WC2R 1LA
United Kingdom
Tel: +44 (0) 20 7251 0125

http://www.johnsonandalcock.co.uk

Professional Body: The Association of Authors' Agents (AAA)

Send: Query; Synopsis; Writing sample
How to send: Email attachment
How not to send: Post

Send query by email to specific agent. Response only if interested. Include synopsis and first three chapters (approximately 50 pages).

Company Directors / Literary Agents: Andrew Hewson; Ed Wilson (**L607**)

Literary Agent / Managing Director: Anna Power (**L482**)

Literary Agents: Michael Alcock (**L009**); Charlotte Seymour (**L528**)

L303 Jared Johnson

Associate Agent
United States

jared@olswangerliterary.com

https://www.jaredhjohnson.com
https://www.olswanger.com
https://querytracker.net/query/jaredjohnson
https://x.com/_jaredhjohnson
https://bsky.app/profile/litjared.bsky.social

Literary Agency: Olswanger Literary LLC (**L449**)

Fiction > *Novels*
  Comedy / Humour; Culture; Family; Fantasy; Horror; Magic; Science Fiction; Speculative

Nonfiction > *Nonfiction Books*
  Culture; History; Language; Society

Does not want:

  Fiction > *Novels*: Romantasy

How to send: Query Tracker

I'm a recovering academic. After several years of academic research in the humanities and teaching writing and history, I realized academia wasn't for me, but I always loved sharing good stories with others. I wanted a job that would still let me do that, so I pursued a career in publishing. I represent a range of nonfiction and fiction genres.

L304 Jonathan Clowes Ltd

Literary Agency
United Kingdom
Tel: +44 (0) 20 7722 7674

admin@jonathanclowes.co.uk

https://www.jonathanclowes.co.uk

Professional Body: The Association of Authors' Agents (AAA)

Fiction > *Novels*

Nonfiction > *Nonfiction Books*

Send: Query; Synopsis; Writing sample
How to send: Email
How not to send: Post

Send query with synopsis and three chapters (or equivalent sample) by email.

Authors: Frances Bingham; Jonas Claesson; Simon Critchley; Maureen Duffy; Ewan Fernie; Brian Freemantle; Miles Gibson; Rana Haddad; Francesca Hornak; David Llewellyn; Kirsten MacGillivray; Mohamed Mesrati; Kirsten Norrie; David Quantick; Gruff Rhys; Toby Vieira; Barbara Voors

Literary Agents: Ann Evans; Nemonie Craven Roderick

L305 Barbara Jones

Literary Agent
United States

bjquery@skagency.com

http://skagency.com/submission-guidelines/

Literary Agency: Stuart Krichevsky Literary Agency, Inc. (**L556**)

Closed to approaches.

L306 Jessica Jones

Literary Agent

Literary Agency: Independent Talent Group Ltd

L307 Philip Gwyn Jones

Literary Agent
United Kingdom

https://greyhoundliterary.co.uk/agents/philip-gwyn-jones
https://twitter.com/PGJPublishing

Literary Agency: Greyhound Literary

Fiction > *Novels*

Thirty-three years of experience as an editor and publisher, just over half of them in corporate publishing and just under half in independent publishing.

Authors: Sophie Calon; John Campbell; Gethan Dick; Matthew Ford; Jon Gower; Michael Hurley; Mette Leonard Høeg; Stuart Jeffries; Vijay Khurana; Patricia Kingori; Ben Lewis; Brigid Lowe; Tarun Ramadorai; Neil Shearing; Damian Valdez; Barbara Wansbrough

L308 Joy Harris Literary Agency, Inc.
Literary Agency
1501 Broadway, Suite 2605, New York, NY 10036
United States
Tel: +1 (212) 924-6269

contact@joyharrisliterary.com

https://www.joyharrisliterary.com

Professional Body: Association of American Literary Agents (AALA)

Types: Fiction; Nonfiction; Translations
Formats: Short Fiction
Subjects: Autobiography; Comedy / Humour; Commercial; Culture; Experimental; History; Literary; Media; Mystery; Satire; Spirituality; Suspense; Women's Interests
Markets: Adult; Young Adult

Closed to approaches.

Costs: Author covers sundry admin costs.

Send query by email, including sample chapter or outline. No poetry, screenplays, genre fiction, self-help, or unsolicited mss. See website for full guidelines.

Literary Agents: Joy Harris; Adam Reed

L309 Judith Murdoch Literary Agency
Literary Agency
19 Chalcot Square, London, NW1 8YA
United Kingdom
Tel: +44 (0) 20 7722 4197

jmlitag@btinternet.com

http://www.judithmurdoch.co.uk

Fiction > *Novels*
   Commercial; Crime; Literary

Send: Query; Synopsis; Writing sample
How to send: Post
How not to send: Email

Send query by post with SAE or email address for response, brief synopsis, and first three chapters. No science fiction, fantasy, children's stories, or email submissions.

Author Estates: The Estate of Catherine King; The Estate of Meg Hutchinson

Authors: Diane Allen; Trisha Ashley; Anne Bennett; Maggie Bennett; Anne Berry; Frances Brody; Rosie Clarke; Howard Coombs; Diney Costeloe; Norma Curtis; Anne Doughty; Kate Eastham; Leah Fleming; Sarah Flint; Caro Fraser; Emma Fraser; Elizabeth Gill; Gracie Hart; Faith Hogan; Maggie Hope; Emma Hornby; Alex Howard; Minna Howard; Alrene Hughes; Lindsey Hutchinson; Lola Jaye; Sheila Jeffries; Sophie Jenkins; Carol Jones; Pamela Jooste; Mary de Laszlo; Catherine Law; Jill McGivering; Alison Mercer; Beth Miller; Jaishree Misra; Barbara Mutch; Kitty Neale; Sheila Newberry; Della Parker; Carol Rivers; Cathy Sharp; Alison Sherlock; Linda Sole; June Tate; Annie Wilkinson; Mary Wood

Literary Agent: Judith Murdoch

L310 Judy Daish Associates Ltd
Literary Agency
2 St Charles Place, London, W10 6EG
United Kingdom
Tel: +44 (0) 20 8964 8811
Fax: +44 (0) 20 8964 8966

judy@judydaish.com

http://www.judydaish.com

Literary Agency: United Agents

Scripts
   Film Scripts; *Radio Scripts*; *TV Scripts*; *Theatre Scripts*

Represents writers, directors, designers and choreographers for theatre, film, television, radio and opera. No books or unsolicited mss.

Literary Agents: Judy Daish; Tracey Elliston

L311 Julie Crisp Literary Agency
Literary Agency; Editorial Service
United Kingdom

julieacrisp@gmail.com

http://www.juliecrisp.co.uk
https://querymanager.com/query/2079

Professional Body: The Association of Authors' Agents (AAA)

Fiction > *Novels*
   Fantasy; Magical Realism; Science Fiction; Speculative Horror

Closed to approaches.

Costs: Offers services that writers have to pay for.

Open to queries and actively looking for full length, adult, fantasy, science fiction, magical realism and speculative fiction.

Authors: Pablo Valcárcel Castro; Heather Child; John Gwynne; Sam Hawke; Lucy Kissick; Devin Madson; Den Patrick; C. T. Rwizi; Nick Setchfield; Kell Woods

L312 Ria Julien
Literary Agent
United States

rj@goldinlit.com

https://www.goldinlit.com/ria-julien
https://www.goldinlit.com/ria-julien

Literary Agency: Frances Goldin Literary Agency, Inc.

Fiction in Translation > *Novels*

Fiction > *Novels*: African Diaspora

Nonfiction > *Nonfiction Books*
   Culture; Economics; Environment; Gender; History; Legal; Social Justice; Women

An agent and attorney who has worked in publishing since 1999. Her interests include literature in translation, diaspora fiction, and nonfiction works of conscience on a wide range of topics including law, history, economics, women and gender, environmental and cultural studies. She represents authors whose works offer a critique of power and social injustice.

L313 K2 Literary
Literary Agency
Canada

https://k2literary.com
https://www.facebook.com/k2literary/
https://twitter.com/k2literary
https://instagram.com/k2literary

ADULT > **Fiction** > *Novels*

CHILDREN'S > **Fiction** > *Novels*

How to send: By referral

Currently accepts submissions by referral only. Unsolicited submissions, queries, submission emails, or phone calls will not be answered.

Literary Agent: Kelvin Kong

L314 Ella Diamond Kahn
Literary Agent
United Kingdom

https://dkwlitagency.co.uk/
https://dkwlitagency.co.uk/agents/ella/
https://twitter.com/elladkahn

Literary Agency: Diamond Kahn and Woods (DKW) Literary Agency Ltd (**L153**)

ADULT
   Fiction > *Novels*
      Commercial; Contemporary; Crime; Historical Fiction; Speculative; Thrillers; Upmarket; Women's Fiction

   Nonfiction > *Nonfiction Books*
      Archaeology; Biography; Contemporary Culture; Cultural History; Culture; Memoir; Narrative Nonfiction; Social History; Society

CHILDREN'S > **Fiction** > *Middle Grade*

YOUNG ADULT > **Fiction** > *Novels*

Closed to approaches.

I'm particularly looking for commercial and upmarket fiction with a compelling story and a confident, distinctive writing voice, whether it's historical, contemporary, uplifting women's fiction, crime/thriller, or speculative fiction. I am also looking for children's fiction for the 9-12 and YA age groups in any genre. Please note I am not looking for any adult fantasy for the time being. I am also interested in distinctive memoir, and in narrative nonfiction, focusing on social and cultural topics (both contemporary and historical), historical biography and archaeology.

L315 Joanna Kaliszewska
Literary Agent
United Kingdom

https://www.thebksagency.com/about
https://www.thebksagency.com/submissions

Literary Agency: The BKS Agency (**L063**)

Fiction > *Novels*
  Book Club Fiction; Crime; Thrillers; Upmarket Commercial Fiction

Nonfiction > *Nonfiction Books*
  Health; Wellbeing

Send: Query; Outline; Author bio
How to send: Online submission system

I am looking for crime, thriller, reading group and upmarket commercial fiction. On the non-fiction side, I am looking for expert-lead books on health and wellness. Please note that I DO NOT represent experimental literary fiction, speculative, science fiction, fantasy, YA or children's.

L316 Kane Literary Agency
Literary Agency
United Kingdom

submissions@kaneliteraryagency.com
getintouch@kaneliteraryagency.com

https://www.kaneliteraryagency.com
https://www.facebook.com/kaneliteraryagency/
https://www.twitter.com/YasminKane3
https://www.instagram.com/YasminKane3/

Professional Body: The Association of Authors' Agents (AAA)

Fiction > *Novels*
  Crime; Domestic Thriller; Noir; Police Procedural; Psychological Thrillers; Thrillers

Send: Query; Synopsis; Writing sample; Pitch; Market info
How to send: Email

Currently only looking for: crime fiction, thrillers, police procedurals, psychological thrillers, and domestic thrillers. Bring on the noir!

Authors: Simon Arrowsmith; J Y Bee; Isabelle Brizec; Louise Cliffe-Minns; Sarah Harris; Vicki Howie; Zoe Marriott; Andrew Murray; Emily Nagle; Marisa Noelle

Literary Agent: Yasmin Standen

L317 Camille Kantor
Literary Agent
United States

https://www.camillekantor.com
https://www.kimberleycameron.com/team/
https://querymanager.com/query/camillekantor/
https://www.instagram.com/lady_reads_alot/
https://twitter.com/CamilleKantor/
https://www.manuscriptwishlist.com/mswl-post/camille-kantor/

Literary Agency: Kimberley Cameron & Associates (**L337**)

Fiction > *Novels*
  High Concept; Literary; Nature

Nonfiction > *Nonfiction Books*
  Nature; Popular Science

Closed to approaches.

Looking for titles, whether fiction or non-fiction, that will inspire the public to engage with nature while imparting fascinating knowledge about our planet and its inhabitants. She is particularly interested in popular science non-fiction work. Her fiction tastes include books that immerse the reader in descriptive but clear imagery and that have themes of nature-human interactions. She especially loves interesting, well-developed characters and high concept literary fiction that approaches philosophical topics about our relationship with our planet.

L318 Julia Kardon
Literary Agent; Vice President
United States

julia@hgliterary.com

https://www.hgliterary.com/julia
https://twitter.com/jlkardon
https://querymanager.com/query/JuliaKardon

Literary Agency: HG Literary

Fiction > *Novels*
  Literary; Upmarket

Nonfiction > *Nonfiction Books*
  History; Journalism; Memoir; Narrative Nonfiction

How to send: Query Tracker

She is interested primarily in literary and upmarket fiction and memoir, and especially stories grappling with racial, religious, sexual or national identity, narrative nonfiction, journalism, and history. She does not represent thrillers, any children's literature or books about spirituality or Christianity.

L319 Karen Gantz Literary Management
Literary Agency
United States

kgzahler@aol.com

https://karengantzliterarymanagement.com
https://www.facebook.com/Karengantzliterarymanagement/
https://twitter.com/karengantz
https://www.instagram.com/karen_gantz/

Fiction > *Novels*

Nonfiction > *Nonfiction Books*
  Cookery; Current Affairs; History; Lifestyle; Memoir; Narrative Nonfiction; Politics; Psychology; Religion

Send: Query; Synopsis
How to send: Email

Considers all genres but specialises in nonfiction. Send query and summary by email only. While all submissions will be read, due to the high volume of submissions not all queries will be answered.

Assistant Agent: Hester Malin

Literary Agent: Karen Gantz

L320 Kate Barker Literary, TV, & Film Agency
Literary Agency
London,
United Kingdom
Tel: +44 (0) 20 7688 1638

kate@katebarker.net

https://www.katebarker.net

Professional Body: The Association of Authors' Agents (AAA)

Fiction > *Novels*
  Book Club Fiction; Commercial; Contemporary; High Concept; Historical Fiction; Literary

Nonfiction > *Nonfiction Books*
  History; Lifestyle; Memoir; Nature; Popular Psychology; Science; Wellbeing

Send: Query; Writing sample
How to send: Online submission system

I'm looking for commercial, literary and reading group novels: my taste in fiction is broad. I like strong stories, interesting settings (contemporary or historical) and high concept novels. I especially love books that make me cry. Please note that I do not represent science fiction, fantasy or books for children. Work in those genres will not be read. Non-fiction: I'm looking for smart thinking, history, memoir, popular psychology and science, nature writing, lifestyle and wellbeing. Big ideas and subjects that get people talking. I particularly enjoy helping experts translate their work for a general audience.

Literary Agent: Kate Barker

L321 Kate Nash Literary Agency
Literary Agency
United Kingdom

https://katenashlit.co.uk
https://www.facebook.com/KateNashLiteraryAgency/
https://twitter.com/katenashagent
https://www.youtube.com/channel/UCAugaYbUoZXD7wldntZ8DwQ

Professional Body: The Association of Authors' Agents (AAA)

ADULT
  Fiction > *Novels*

  Nonfiction > *Nonfiction Books*: Commercial

CHILDREN'S > **Fiction** > *Middle Grade*

YOUNG ADULT > **Fiction** > *Novels*

Send: Query; Synopsis; Writing sample; Pitch; Author bio
How to send: Online submission system

Open to approaches from both new and established authors. Represents general and genre fiction and popular nonfiction. No poetry, drama, or genre SFF. Send query via online submission form with synopsis and first chapter (fiction) or up to three chapters (nonfiction) pasted into the body of the email (no attachments).

Junior Agent: Saskia Leach (**L357**)

Literary Agent / Managing Director: Justin Nash

Literary Agents: Kate Nash; Francesca Riccardi (**L492**)

L322 Kathryn Green Literary Agency, LLC
Literary Agency
157 Columbus Avenue, Suite 510, New York, NY 10023
United States
Tel: +1 (212) 245-4225

query@kgreenagency.com
kathy@kgreenagency.com

https://www.kathryngreenliteraryagency.com
https://twitter.com/kathygreenlit

ADULT
  Fiction > *Novels*
    General, and in particular: Cozy Mysteries; Historical Fiction

  Nonfiction > *Nonfiction Books*
    General, and in particular: Comedy / Humour; History; Memoir; Parenting; Popular Culture

CHILDREN'S > **Fiction** > *Middle Grade*

YOUNG ADULT > **Fiction** > *Novels*

Does not want:

> **ADULT** > **Fiction** > *Novels*
>   Fantasy; Science Fiction
>
> **CHILDREN'S** > **Fiction**
>   *Middle Grade*: Fantasy; Science Fiction
>   *Picture Books*: General
>
> **YOUNG ADULT** > **Fiction** > *Novels*
>   Fantasy; Science Fiction

Closed to approaches.

Send query by email. Do not send samples unless requested. No science fiction, fantasy, children's picture books, screenplays, or poetry.

Literary Agent: Kathryn Green

L323 Jade Kavanagh
Literary Agent
United Kingdom

jade@darleyanderson.com

https://darleyanderson.com
https://darleyanderson.com/team/jade-kavanagh/
https://twitter.com/jadekav_
https://www.instagram.com/jade_kavanagh_agent/

Literary Agency: The Darley Anderson Agency (**L143**)

Fiction > *Novels*
  Book Club Fiction; Dark; Horror; Psychological Suspense; Speculative; Suspense; Thrillers

How to send: Online submission system

My primary genres and areas of interest include, thriller, glam suspense, psychological suspense, horror, book club and speculative fiction with a darker edge.

Author: Holly Craig

L324 Taylor Martindale Kean
Literary Agent
United States

https://www.fullcircleliterary.com/our-agents/taylor-martindale-kean/
https://querymanager.com/query/TaylorFCL

Literary Agency: Full Circle Literary, LLC

CHILDREN'S > **Fiction** > *Middle Grade*
  General, and in particular: Contemporary; Fantasy; Historical Fiction; Literary; Magical Realism

YOUNG ADULT > **Fiction** > *Novels*
  General, and in particular: Fantasy; Magical Realism

Closed to approaches.

She is looking for young adult fiction and literary middle grade fiction, across all genres. She is interested in finding unique and unforgettable voices in contemporary, fantasy, historical and magical realism novels. She is looking for books that demand to be read. More than anything, she is looking for diverse, character-driven stories that bring their worlds vividly to life, and voices that are honest, original and interesting.

L325 Keane Kataria Literary Agency
Literary Agency
United Kingdom

info@keanekataria.co.uk
https://www.keanekataria.co.uk/submissions/

Fiction > *Novels*
  Book Club Fiction; Commercial Women's Fiction; Contemporary; Cozy Mysteries; Historical Fiction; Romance; Saga

Closed to approaches.

Currently accepting submissions in the crime, domestic noir and commercial women's fiction genres. No thrillers, science fiction, fantasy or children's books. Send query by email only with synopsis and first three chapters. Attachments in PDF format only.

Literary Agents: Kiran Kataria; Sara Keane

L326 Sara O' Keeffe
Affiliated Agent
United Kingdom

https://www.saraokeeffe.co.uk
https://andrewnurnberg.com/team-member/sara-okeeffe/
https://querymanager.com/query/SaraOK_QueryForm
https://www.instagram.com/sarabookcrazy/
https://twitter.com/okeeffe05

Literary Agency: Andrew Nurnberg Associates, Ltd (**L016**)

Fiction > *Novels*
  Book Club Fiction; Literary; Thrillers

How to send: Query Tracker

Specialises in fiction, representing accessible literary fiction, reading group fiction and upmarket genre fiction (especially thrillers).

Authors: Victoria M. Adams; Jose Alvior; Rebecca Anderson; Kathy Biggs; Julia Boggio; Theodore Brun; Sinead Crowley; James DeVita; Freya Dolby; Rachel Donohue; Joshua Eure; Brooke Fortune; Catherine Ryan Howard; Amy Jordan; Siobhan MacGowan; Nicola Masters; Melanie Maure; Serena Molloy; Anthony Riches; Darryl Samaraweera; David Sergeant; Eithne Shortall; Leo Vardiashvili; Simon Van Der Velde

L327 Sophie Kelleher
Associate Agent
United Kingdom
Tel: +44 (0) 20 7727 1346

skelleher@theagency.co.uk

https://theagency.co.uk/the-agents/sophie-kelleher/

Literary Agency: The Agency (London) Ltd (**L008**)
Literary Agent: Tanya Tillett

Scripts
  Film Scripts; *TV Scripts*; *Theatre Scripts*

Joined the agency in January 2020, originally working as an assistant. In 2022, she covered an agent's maternity leave, expanding her knowledge as an agent across film, television and theatre. She now works as an associate agent with her own list of writers. Prior to her career in film and TV, she worked in publishing.

L328 Carly Kellerman
Literary Agent
United States

https://aliveliterary.com

Literary Agency: Alive Literary Agency

Nonfiction > *Nonfiction Books*

How to send: By referral

Has spent more than fifteen years helping writers find their voice and hone their message. With a professional background that spans editorial development and sales, she has a proven knack for finding the sweet spot between profoundly meaningful and commercially viable content. Her unique blend of business acumen and love for storytelling makes her an excellent advocate and guide for authors navigating the publishing world.

L329 Julia Kenny
Literary Agent
United States

https://www.dclagency.com

Literary Agency: Dunow, Carlson & Lerner Agency (**L166**)

Fiction > *Novels*
Dark; Literary; Suspense

Primarily works on fiction and has a soft spot for dark, literary suspense. She is on the lookout for writing that immediately draws her in, bold voices, "unlikeable" narrators, and stories that linger.

L330 Eli Keren
Associate Agent
United Kingdom
Tel: +44 (0) 20 3214 0775

ekeren@unitedagents.co.uk

https://www.unitedagents.co.uk/ekerenunitedagentscouk
https://twitter.com/EliArieh

Literary Agency: United Agents

Fiction > *Novels*
Commercial; Crime; Domestic Suspense; Historical Fiction; LGBTQIA; Literary; Magical Realism; Mystery; Speculative; Thrillers; Upmarket

Nonfiction > *Nonfiction Books*
General, and in particular: Cultural History; LGBTQIA; Popular Science

Closed to approaches.

In non-fiction, I am particularly interested in expert-led smart and engaging popular science. My own background is in chemistry, but I'm fairly omnivorous and happy to look at any non-fiction that grips me, be that science, cultural history or something unexpected. I enjoy books by writers completely obsessed with a niche subject who are skilled enough communicators to make the rest of the world fall in love with their passion too, whatever that passion might be. I am interested in any book that will change the world for the better. I'm probably not the right agent for books on religion or spirituality.

In fiction, I mostly work with commercial and upmarket fiction, not so much with the very literary. In commercial fiction, I'm interested in crime/thriller and domestic suspense with a strong hook and addictive storytelling. I love mysteries and whodunnits, and am also open to uplifting general fiction. I'm happy to look at historical fiction with a contemporary outlook. Towards the more literary side, I'm looking for books with plot and pace that set out to achieve something, change the way I see the world, challenge me and subvert my expectations. I don't typically work with science-fiction or fantasy, but am open to some grounded speculative fiction and magical realism. I don't work with holocaust novels.

I do not represent authors for children's and YA literature.

Authors: Marieke Bigg; Sarah Burton; Huho Greenhalgh; Ioan Marc Jones; Johanna Lukate; David Miles; Jem Poster; Claire Seeber; Sam White

L331 Ki Agency Ltd
Literary Agency
Primrose Hill Business Centre, 110 Gloucester Avenue, London, NW1 8HX
United Kingdom
Tel: +44 (0) 20 3214 8287

https://ki-agency.co.uk

Professional Bodies: The Association of Authors' Agents (AAA); Personal Managers' Association (PMA); Writers' Guild of Great Britain (WGGB)

Fiction > *Novels*

Nonfiction > *Nonfiction Books*
Leadership; Personal Coaching; Personal Development

Scripts
Film Scripts; TV Scripts; Theatre Scripts

Send: Synopsis; Writing sample
How to send: Email attachment

Represents novelists and scriptwriters in all media. No children's or poetry, or submissions from writers in the US or Canada. Send synopsis and first three chapters / first 50 pages by email.

Authors: John Allison; Livvy Jane Baker; Fiona Barnett; James Bennett; Arianna Bent; Simon Bestwick; A.J. Borisade; K.L. Brandt; Nicole Burns; Linda Carey; Louise Carey; Mike Carey; Lucy Chalice; Daniel Church; Helena Coggan; Mackenzie Crone; Kimberly G. Dawn; Daniel Depp; Joanne Drayton; Diane Duane; Joanne Edge; Matthew Feldman; Kitty Ferguson; Megan Flynn; Marianne Gordon; Bronwyn Hall; K.C. Harper; Charlotte Harris; Stark Holborn; Shaun Hutson; Olivia Jackson; Camri Kohler; Meredith Lanzen; Ryan Love; Laura Madeleine; Sarah McManus; Robin Norwood; Marie O'Regan; Nuzo Onoh; Anne Perry; Adam Roberts; Phoenicia Rogerson; Gareth Shore; Gillian Spraggs; Savannah Stephens; Emma Sterner-Radley; Jarom Strong; Jesse Stuart; A.P. Thayer; Yvonne Vincent; Becky Ward; Catherine Webb

Literary Agents: Meg Davis; Helen Lane (**L349**); Fabienne Schwizer (**L523**)

L332 Jessica Killingley
Literary Agent
United Kingdom

https://www.thebksagency.com/about
https://www.thebksagency.com/submissions

Literary Agency: The BKS Agency (**L063**)

Fiction > *Novels*
Dark Humour; Fantasy; High Concept; Literary; Science Fiction; Speculative

Nonfiction > *Nonfiction Books*
Business; Personal Development

Closed to approaches.

I am looking for personal development, business and smart thinking from authors with strong platforms and engaged audiences. I am also currently open for original, high-concept, speculative/literary adult fiction. Within genre fiction, my taste tends to lean more towards SF than epic fantasy (I'm more spaceships than dragons) and I love anything with very dark humour.

L333 Jennifer Kim
Literary Agent
United States

https://www.dijkstraagency.com
https://www.dijkstraagency.com/agent-page.php?agent_id=Kim
https://querymanager.com/query/JenniferKim

Literary Agency: Sandra Dijkstra Literary Agency

Fiction in Translation > *Novels*

Fiction > *Novels*
Culture; Family Saga; Fantasy; Ghost Stories; Gothic; Horror; Literary; Science Fiction; Speculative

Nonfiction > *Nonfiction Books*
History; Journalism; Music; Politics; Popular Culture

Does not want:

> **Fiction** > *Novels*
> Hard Science Fiction; High / Epic Fantasy

How to send: Query Tracker

Most interested in literary fiction, speculative fiction, and translated fiction for the adult market, unusual history, journalism, politics, and pop-culture and music history. She is particularly drawn to eccentric and unusual stories and values a distinct narrative voice and a strong sense of place. She loves literary fiction with genre elements (horror, sci-fi, or fantasy), but isn't a great fit for high fantasy or straightforward science fiction. She's a fit for anything described as gothic, alternative, or weird, ghost stories that explore culture and trauma, family sagas (both blood and chosen), and anything that dismantles oppressive systems. As a third culture kid, she's interested in stories that reflect that experience.

Open to submissions during the first week of every month.

L334 Julia Kim
Assistant Agent
Canada

https://www.therightsfactory.com
https://www.therightsfactory.com/Agents/julia-kim
https://querymanager.com/query/3602

Literary Agency: The Rights Factory

Fiction > *Novels*
Crime; Historical Fiction; Horror; Literary; Mystery

Nonfiction > *Nonfiction Books*
Arts; Biography; Culture; Current Affairs; Films; Food; History; Lifestyle; Memoir; Politics; Popular Culture; TV; Women's Issues

How to send: Query Tracker

Looking for literary fiction and select genre fiction (mystery, crime, horror, historical). She is also seeking a range of nonfiction topics including history, politics, current affairs, women's issues, biography and memoir, food and lifestyle, art and culture, film and TV, pop culture.

Authors: Fitsum Areguy; Kaamna Bhojwani; Stephanie Duong; Caitlin Galway; Clarissa Trinidad Gonzalez; Noaah Karim; Sang Kim; Kyo Lee; Matthew A. Pagan; Shoaib Rahim; Alexis Stefanovich-Thomson

L335 Sally M. Kim
Associate Agent
United States

sally@andreabrownlit.com
https://www.andreabrownlit.com
https://www.andreabrownlit.com/Team/sally-m.-kim
https://querymanager.com/query/SallyABLA
https://aalitagents.org/author/sallymkim/

Literary Agency: Andrea Brown Literary Agency, Inc.
Professional Body: Association of American Literary Agents (AALA)

CHILDREN'S
Fiction
Chapter Books; Graphic Novels; Middle Grade; Picture Books
Nonfiction
Chapter Books; Graphic Nonfiction; Middle Grade; Picture Books

How to send: Query Tracker

Please send fiction and non-fiction submissions in the following categories: picture books, chapter books, middle grade, and graphic novels. Across all categories, she is especially eager to see authentic explorations of underrepresented cultures, relationships, and identities. No rhyming picture books, horror, sports, or time travel.

L336 Natalie Kimber
Literary Agent
Canada

Literary Agency: The Rights Factory

ADULT
Fiction
Graphic Novels: General
Novels: Adventure; Commercial; Cookery; Historical Fiction; Literary; Science Fiction
Nonfiction > *Nonfiction Books*
Creative Nonfiction; Memoir; Popular Culture; Science; Spirituality; Sustainable Living

YOUNG ADULT > **Fiction** > *Novels*: Boy Books

Send: Query; Author bio; Writing sample
How to send: Email

L337 Kimberley Cameron & Associates
Literary Agency
1550 Tiburon Blvd #704, Tiberon, CA 94920
United States

info@kimberleycameron.com

https://www.kimberleycameron.com
https://www.facebook.com/kimberleycameronandassociates
https://twitter.com/K_C_Associates
https://www.instagram.com/kcandaliterary/

Fiction > *Novels*

Nonfiction > *Nonfiction Books*

How to send: Query Tracker

See website for specific agent interests and submit to most suitable agent through their online submission system.

Literary Agents: Lisa Abellera; Kimberley Cameron (**L093**); Amy Cloughley; Camille Kantor (**L317**); Elizabeth Kracht (**L341**); Dorian Maffei

L338 Robert Kirby
Literary Agent; Company Director
United Kingdom

https://www.unitedagents.co.uk/rkirbyunitedagentscouk

Literary Agency: United Agents

Fiction > *Novels*
Adventure; Commercial; Speculative

Nonfiction > *Nonfiction Books*
Cultural History; Environment; Psychology; Science

Send: Synopsis; Writing sample
How to send: Email
How not to send: Post

I have an interest in science, psychology, cultural history and environmental issues. I enjoy gripping adventure fiction, speculative fiction and emotionally driven commercial fiction. Submissions should be sent to my assistant by via email, with a synopsis and first three chapters. Please do not send submissions via the post.

Assistant Agent: Olivia Davies (**L147**)

L339 Sheyla Knigge
Literary Agent
United States

https://www.highlineliterary.com/agent-sheyla
https://querymanager.com/query/sheylaknigge

Literary Agency: High Line Literary Collective (**L279**)

ADULT > **Fiction** > *Novels*
Erotic; Fantasy; Folklore, Myths, and Legends; LGBTQIA; Magic

CHILDREN'S > **Fiction** > *Middle Grade*: Fantasy

YOUNG ADULT > **Fiction** > *Novels*: Romance

Closed to approaches.

Very interested in books by marginalized creators who have yet to have the opportunity to have their voices heard particularly BIPOC, LGBTQIA, and other #OwnVoices as a fellow queer woman of color. She longs to see uplifting stories from these communities rather than ones that focus on the trauma that comes from being a part of them. She would love to see stories filled with myth, magic, and a healthy dose of smut when appropriate. Alternatively, she would love to see Percy Jackson-esque Middle Grade fiction; the type she can giggle along with as she reads them to her own children. Stories set in other lands, or other worlds tend to be her go to choice.

L340 Knight Features
Literary Agency
Trident Business Centre, 89 Bickersteth Road,
London, SW17 9SH
United Kingdom

https://www.knightfeatures.com

Nonfiction > *Nonfiction Books*
Business; Communication; Military

Send: Query; Synopsis; Writing sample; Market info
How to send: Online submission system

Send query with synopsis and three sample chapters. Include information on whether you envisage the book being illustrated, and details of the target market, the level at which it might be pitched, and the likely readership. Include information about any works in the same field which might be seen as competition for your book, or give some indication of how yours differs from these.

Company Directors: Samantha Ferris; Gaby Martin

Managing Director: Andrew Knight

L341 Elizabeth Kracht
Literary Agent
United States

https://elizabethkracht.com
https://kimberleycameron.com/team/

Literary Agency: Kimberley Cameron & Associates (**L337**)

Fiction > *Novels*
Commercial; Historical Fiction; Literary; Mystery; Thrillers; Women's Fiction

Nonfiction > *Nonfiction Books*
Animals; Crime; Environment; Health; High Concept; Investigative Journalism; Memoir; Pets; Prescriptive Nonfiction; Science; Sexuality; Spirituality

How to send: Conferences; Online pitch events; By referral

Represents both literary and commercial fiction as well as nonfiction. In fiction, she represents literary, commercial, women's, thrillers, mysteries, historical, and crossover YA. In nonfiction, she is interested in high concept, health, science, environment, prescriptive, investigative, true crime, voice- or adventure-driven memoir, sexuality, spirituality, and animal/pet stories.

L342 Stuart Krichevsky
Literary Agent
United States

https://www.skagency.com

Literary Agency: Stuart Krichevsky Literary Agency, Inc. (**L556**)

Fiction > *Novels:* Commercial

Nonfiction > *Nonfiction Books*
Literary; Narrative Journalism

Closed to approaches.

Has represented dozens of New York Times Best Sellers, with a focus on literary non-fiction, narrative journalism, and commercial fiction. His clients have been recipients of the National Book Award, the Pulitzer Prize and countless other literary awards.

L343 Mary Krienke
Literary Agent
United States

https://www.sll.com/our-team

Literary Agency: Sterling Lord Literistic, Inc.

Fiction > *Novels*
Culture; Disabilities; Literary; Mental Health; Sexuality; Upmarket

Nonfiction
Illustrated Books: General
Nonfiction Books: Culture; Disabilities; Health; Mental Health; Narrative Nonfiction; Prescriptive Nonfiction; Sexuality

Send: Query; Synopsis; Writing sample
How to send: Online submission system

Represents literary and upmarket fiction, narrative nonfiction, and select memoir, prescriptive, and illustrated projects. In both fiction and nonfiction, work that investigates culture, identity, sexuality, disability, and mental health is especially welcome.

L344 Kruger Cowne
Literary Agency
Unit 7C, Chelsea Wharf, 15 Lots Road,
London, SW10 0QJ
United Kingdom
Tel: +44 (0) 20 7352 2277

hello@krugercowne.com

https://www.krugercowne.com
https://twitter.com/krugercowne
https://www.instagram.com/krugercowne/
https://www.facebook.com/krugercowne
https://www.linkedin.com/company/kruger-cowne
https://www.youtube.com/user/KrugerCowneTalent

Professional Body: The Association of Authors' Agents (AAA)

Nonfiction > *Nonfiction Books*
General, and in particular: Celebrity; Entrepreneurship; Futurism; Journalism

How to send: Email

A talent management agency, with an extremely strong literary arm.

The majority of the works handled by the agency fall into the category of celebrity nonfiction. However, also regularly work with journalists, entrepreneurs and influencers on projects, with a speciality in polemics, and speculative works on the future.

Authors: Akala; Steven Bartlett; Kelly Holmes; Lia Leendertz; Jennifer Medhurst; Jack Monroe; Christine Morgan; Selene Nelson; John Simpson; Nicholas Boys Smith; Dave Stewart

L345 KT Literary
Literary Agency
United States

queries@ktliterary.com

https://ktliterary.com
https://twitter.com/ktliterary
https://www.instagram.com/ktliterary/

ADULT > **Fiction** > *Novels*

CHILDREN'S > **Fiction** > *Middle Grade*

YOUNG ADULT > **Fiction** > *Novels*

Send: Query
How to send: Query Tracker; Email
How not to send: Post; Social Media

Please see each individual agent's bio for instructions on how to best query them. If QueryManager provides an accessibility issue, send an email addressed to the specific agent in question. No snail mail queries or pitches via social media.

Authors: Samantha Chiusolo; Vikki Chu; Ebony Glenn; Jen Gubicza; Haejin Park; Lisa Wee

Foreign Rights Manager / Literary Agent: Maria Napolitano (**L431**)

Literary Agents: Savannah Brooks (**L080**); Kait Lee Feldmann (**L190**); Tara Gilbert (**L233**); Adria Goetz (**L241**); Renee Nyen (*L443*); Kelly Van Sant (**L518**); Arley Sorg (**L546**); Kari Sutherland (**L559**); Laurel Symonds (**L565**); Kate Testerman (*L571*)

L346 Hazel Kyle
Literary Agent

Literary Agency: Independent Talent Group Ltd

L347 Natalie Lakosil
Literary Agent
United States

https://www.adventuresinagentland.com
https://www.lookingglasslit.com/natalie-lakosil
https://querymanager.com/query/natlak
https://aalitagents.org/author/natalie_lakosil/
https://twitter.com/Natalie_Lakosil
http://www.manuscriptwishlist.com/mswl-post/natalie-lakosil/

Literary Agency: Looking Glass Literary & Media Management (**L370**)
Professional Body: Association of American Literary Agents (AALA)

ADULT
Fiction > *Novels*
Cozy Mysteries; Crime; Thrillers; Upmarket Women's Fiction; Upmarket

Nonfiction > *Nonfiction Books*

CHILDREN'S
Fiction
Chapter Books; *Middle Grade*; *Picture Books*
Nonfiction
Chapter Books; *Middle Grade*; *Picture Books*

YOUNG ADULT
Fiction > *Novels*
Nonfiction > *Nonfiction Books*

Closed to approaches.

Represents adult nonfiction, adult cozy mystery/crime, female-driven thrillers, upmarket women's/general fiction, illustrators, and all ages (picture book, chapter book, MG, YA) of children's literature, both fiction and nonfiction.

L348 Sophie Lambert
Literary Agent
United Kingdom
Tel: +44 (0) 20 7393 4200

sophie.lambert@cwagency.co.uk

https://cwagency.co.uk/agent/sophie-lambert

Literary Agency: C&W (Conville & Walsh)

Fiction > *Novels*
Commercial; Crime; Literary; Thrillers

Nonfiction > *Nonfiction Books*
Anthropology; Arts; Environment; Food; History; Memoir; Narrative Nonfiction; Nature; Travel

Closed to approaches.

I love fiction which is voice driven and introduces readers to different perspectives and singular narrators, as well as beautifully written literary fiction which has a strong sense of place, and commercial crime and thrillers which keep the reader on the edge of their seats and continually surprise and excite me. Where nonfiction is concerned I am drawn to narrative nonfiction which straddles genre and I'm especially interested in nature writing, travel, history, anthropology, art and the environment. I represent lots of memoir, as well as books by experts in their field and specialists. I would love to find a gorgeous, all-consuming love story, or a food writer who matches Bill Burford or Anthony Bourdain. Essentially, I'm looking for an exquisite writer to take me by the hand and show me a different way to see the world, whether that's through fiction or nonfiction.

Author / Literary Agent: Catherine Cho (**L114**)

Authors: Amy Abdelnoor; Gaar Adams; Gwen Adshead; Karen Angelico; Lisa Ballantyne; Leo Benedictus; Michael Bhaskar; Hannah Bourne-Taylor; Megan Bradbury; Iain Broome; Dea Brovig; Tom Burgis; Tim Clare; Jennifer Coolidge; Yvette Cooper; Caroline Crampton; Fiona Cummins; Howard Cunnell; Lara Dearman; Claire Dederer; Juano Diaz; Katherine Dunn; Nathan Filer; Cal Flyn; Julia Forster; Sam Fowles; James Fox; Karrie Fransman; Sara Freeman; Gabriel Gbadamosi; Karl Geary; Ruth Gilligan; Colin Grant; Guy Gunaratne; Karen Hamilton; Alexandra Heminsley; Adam Higginbotham; Matt Rowland Hill; Eileen Horne; Nicola Kelly; Amana Fontanella Khan; Rosie Kinchen; Martin Latham; Jemima Lewis; Rebecca Ley; Katy Mahood; Shiv Malik; Charlotte McDonald-Gibson; Emmett de Monterey; Priscilla Morris; Ramita Navai; Tom Newlands; Louise Newson; Hollie Newton; Charlotte Northedge; Marcus O'Dair; Nathan Oates; Elizabeth Oldfield; Emily Ostlere; Sara Pascoe; Jon Plackett; Charlene Prempeh; Laura Price; Elizabeth Prochaska; Jamie Quatro; Chitra Ramaswamy; Ben Rawlence; Ebony Reid; CE Riley; Catherine Riley; Sophy Roberts; Callum Robinson; Rhik Samadder; David Savill; Fíona Scarlett; Holly Seddon; Tali Sharot; Gail Simmons; Nikki Smith; Alex South; Tim Spector; Michelle Sterling; Michelle Min Sterling; Mustafa Suleyman; Michelle Thomas; Nafissa Thomson-Spires; Jane Turner; Tash Walker; Christie Watson; Jonathan Watts; Adam Weymouth; Zoe Williams; Antoine Wilson; Alice Winn; Tod Wodicka; Adam Zmith

L349 Helen Lane
Literary Agent
United Kingdom

helen@ki-agency.co.uk

https://www.ki-agency.co.uk
https://www.ki-agency.co.uk/about-us
https://www.manuscriptwishlist.com/mswl-post/helen-lane/

Literary Agency: Ki Agency Ltd (**L331**)

Fiction > *Novels*
Romantasy; Supernatural / Paranormal Romance; Urban Fantasy

How to send: Query Tracker

Represents Adult (and select YA) genre fiction. She is presently only open to Adult Paranormal Romance, Urban Fantasy, Romantasy, Fantasy Romance.

L350 Kirsten Lang
Literary Agent

Literary Agency: Zeno Agency (**L617**)

L351 Sara Langham
Literary Agent
United Kingdom

Literary Agency: David Higham Associates Ltd (**L146**)

L352 Lina Langlee
Literary Agent
United Kingdom

http://thenorthlitagency.com/our-friends-in-the-north/
https://twitter.com/LinaLanglee

Literary Agency: The North Literary Agency

ADULT > **Fiction** > *Novels*
General, and in particular: Commercial; Crime; Fantasy; High Concept; Horror; Literary; Romance; Science Fiction; Speculative; Thrillers

CHILDREN'S > **Fiction** > *Middle Grade*

YOUNG ADULT > **Fiction** > *Novels*

Closed to approaches.

Looking for books across genres: commercial/high concept fiction with a great hook (be that romance, crime, thriller or general fiction), accessible literary fiction, and intriguing speculative fiction, SFF & horror. Also looking for fun, fantastical, and moving Middle Grade, and "big emotion" Young Adult across genres. Actively welcomes authors from all backgrounds and would like to see more diverse stories and voices. She is less keen on political or gangland thrillers. As a general rule, she would not offer representation to US-based authors since they are better served by US-based agents, except in the very rare situation where their story ought to originate from the UK.

L353 Becca Langton
Literary Agent
United Kingdom

https://www.darleyanderson.com/our-team

Literary Agency: The Darley Anderson Agency (**L143**)

CHILDREN'S > **Fiction**
Graphic Novels: General
Middle Grade: General, and in particular: Adventure

TEEN > **Fiction** > *Novels*

YOUNG ADULT > **Fiction** > *Novels*
General, and in particular: Contemporary; Fantasy; LGBTQIA; Romantic Comedy

Closed to approaches.

Looking for new stories in all shapes and sizes, from middle grade and graphic novel to teen and YA fiction. Reads widely but loves books with compelling voices, twists and brave new ideas. In YA she would love to see some Queer fantasy, rom-coms with plenty of 'com' and contemporary stories told from a new perspective. For younger readers she love/hates the books that make her cry and is on the search for characters that stay with her long after the final page. High-stakes adventure stories are welcome as are graphic novels and books that make you want to read just one more chapter...

Author: Faith Williams Schesventer

L354 Langtons International
Literary Agency
United States

llangton@earthlink.net
langtonsinternational@gmail.com

https://langtonsinternational.com
https://www.facebook.com/
LangtonsInternationalAgency

Fiction > *Novels*
 Mystery; Thrillers; Women's Fiction

Nonfiction > *Nonfiction Books*
 Business; Crime; Memoir

Literary agency based in New York, specializing in business, self-help, memoir, and true crime, as well as mystery, thrillers, women's and literary fiction.

Literary Agent: Linda Langton

L355 Katherine Latshaw
Literary Agent; Vice President
United States

klatshaw@foliolit.com

https://www.foliolit.com/agents-1/katherine-latshaw

Literary Agency: Folio Literary Management, LLC (**L207**)

ADULT
 Fiction > *Novels*

 Nonfiction
  Essays: General
  Illustrated Books: General
  Nonfiction Books: Commercial; Cookery; Feminism; Health; Lifestyle; Memoir; Narrative Nonfiction; Popular Culture; Prescriptive Nonfiction; Wellbeing

CHILDREN'S > Fiction > *Middle Grade*

YOUNG ADULT > Fiction > *Novels*

How to send: Email

L356 Laxfield Literary Associates
Literary Agency
United Kingdom

submissions@laxfieldliterary.com

https://laxfieldliterary.com

Professional Body: The Association of Authors' Agents (AAA)

Fiction > *Novels*
 Commercial; Literary; Magical Realism; Speculative

Nonfiction > *Nonfiction Books*
 Creative Nonfiction; Memoir; Nature; Travel

Send: Query; Synopsis; Writing sample; Author bio; Outline; Table of contents
How to send: Email

We are looking for fiction and non-fiction of the highest quality. We are keen to receive literary and commercial fiction. We are also looking for non-fiction, particularly creative non-fiction, travel writing, memoir and nature writing. We do not represent plays, screenwriting, children's books, science fiction, horror or high fantasy; please do not send manuscripts within these genres as submissions will not be read. On the speculative fiction side, I lean towards books with a toehold in the 'real' world and literary fiction with elements of magical realism.

L357 Saskia Leach
Junior Agent
United Kingdom

https://katenashlit.co.uk
https://katenashlit.co.uk/people/
https://querymanager.com/query/Saskia
https://twitter.com/saskialeach_

Literary Agency: Kate Nash Literary Agency (**L321**)

Fiction > *Novels*

Closed to approaches.

Enjoys reading a wide range of genres and is fascinated by stories written from multiple perspectives. She also loves books which feature complex and dynamic characters.

L358 Jessica Leeke
Literary Agent
United Kingdom

info@madeleinemilburn.com

https://www.madeleinemilburn.co.uk
https://www.madeleinemilburn.co.uk/agents/jessica-leeke/
https://x.com/JessicaLeeke

Literary Agency: Madeleine Milburn Literary, TV & Film Agency (**L385**)

Fiction > *Novels*
 Book Club Fiction; Upmarket

How to send: Online submission system

Represents book club fiction with global appeal and upmarket general fiction.

L359 Leigh Feldman Literary
Literary Agency
United States

query@lfliterary.com
assistant@lfliterary.com

https://www.lfliterary.com

ADULT
 Fiction > *Novels*
  Historical Fiction; Literary

 Nonfiction > *Nonfiction Books*
  Memoir; Narrative Nonfiction

YOUNG ADULT > Fiction > *Novels*: Contemporary

Send: Query; Writing sample; Proposal
How to send: Email

Particularly interested in historical fiction, contemporary YA, literary fiction, memoir, and narrative nonfiction. No adult and YA paranormal, fantasy, science fiction, romance, thrillers, mysteries, or picture books. Send query by email with first ten pages or proposal. Only makes personal response if interested.

Literary Agent: Leigh Feldman (*L189*)

L360 Nina Leon
Associate Agent
United Kingdom

https://www.perezliterary.com/about-us/the-team/
https://querymanager.com/query/NinaLeon

Literary Agency: Perez Literary & Entertainment (**L463**)

ADULT > Fiction > *Novels*
 Adventure; Chick Lit; Commercial; Contemporary Romance; Contemporary; Crime; Fantasy; Gothic; Historical Fiction; Historical Romance; Horror; LGBTQIA; Literary; Magic; Magical Realism; Mystery; Romance; Romantasy; Romantic Suspense; Romantic Thrillers; Science Fiction; Supernatural / Paranormal Romance; Suspense; Thrillers; Upmarket; Urban Fantasy; Women's Fiction

CHILDREN'S > Fiction > *Middle Grade*
 Contemporary; Fantasy; Historical Fiction; Mystery

NEW ADULT > Fiction > *Novels*
 Fantasy; Romance

YOUNG ADULT > Fiction > *Novels*
 Contemporary; Fantasy; Historical Fiction; Literary; Mystery; Romance; Supernatural / Paranormal Romance; Supernatural / Paranormal; Thrillers

How to send: Query Tracker

Knew from a young age that the magic and power of stories was something she would always need in her life. She now proudly champions authors whose magic shines through every story they write. Works closely with her clients from day one. Editorially focused, she enjoys the collaborative back and forth of polishing a manuscript before guiding clients through the publishing process. Believes that all voices have value and deserve to be heard.

L361 Sarah Levitt
Literary Agent
New York
United States

https://aevitascreative.com/agents/
https://querymanager.com/query/2585

Literary Agency: Aevitas

Fiction > *Novels*: Literary

Nonfiction > *Nonfiction Books*
Comedy / Humour; History; Journalism; Memoir; Narrative Nonfiction; Popular Culture; Popular Science

Closed to approaches.

Most interested in narrative nonfiction in the areas of popular science, big ideas, history, humor, pop culture, memoir, and reportage, in addition to voice-driven literary fiction with a bold plot and fresh, imaginative characters. She's excited by strong female and underrepresented voices, the strange and speculative, and projects that ignite cultural conversation.

Authors: Ruha Benjamin; Laura Bliss; Marc Bojanowski; Elizabeth Brooks; Adam Chandler; Bloomberg CityLab; Daniel M. Davis; Sarah Ditum; Baz Dreisinger; Sarah Duenwald; Mieke Eerkens; Claire Evans; Ruth Feldman; Becky Ferreira; Marion Gibson; Annette Giesecke; Eliese Colette Goldbach; Elyse Graham; Wade Graham; Reina Hardy; Ayanna Howard; Tung-Hui Hu; Perrin Ireland; Saru Jayaraman; Nancy McSharry Jensen; Robin Wall Kimmerer; Doma Mahmood; Sara Majka; Antonia Malchik; Maggie Mertens; Ann Morgan; Laine Nooney; Jenni Nuttall; Amelia Possanza; Elizabeth Preston; Steve Ramirez; Ashanté Reese; Charlotte Rixon; Anjali Sachdeva; Suzanne Scanlon; Kathleen Sheppard; Lauren Shields; Josh Sokol; Ly Ky Tran; Phuc Tran; Sarah Turner; Sarah Vallance; Lizzie Wade; Peter von Ziegesar

L362 Yael Levy
Associate Agent
United States

yael@olswangerliterary.com

https://www.olswanger.com
https://www.manuscriptwishlist.com/mswl-post/yael-levy/
https://querytracker.net/query/3262
http://www.twitter.com/YaelLevy19
https://www.linkedin.com/in/yael-levy-9b55aab

Literary Agency: Olswanger Literary LLC (**L449**)

Fiction > *Novels*
Literary; Speculative

Nonfiction > *Nonfiction Books*
Arts; Biography; Business; Comedy / Humour; Cookery; Crafts; Cultural Criticism; Current Affairs; Family; Fashion; Feminism; Fitness; Health; History; Journalism; Memoir; Parenting; Popular Culture; Psychology; Relationships; Science; Self Help; Spirituality; Travel; Wellbeing; Women's Issues

Closed to approaches.

I'm a Literary Associate with years of experience in publishing as an author and developmental editor. I'm seeking to champion projects that illuminate identity, resilience, and connection.

L363 Lewinsohn Literary
Literary Agency
58 Old Compton Street, London, W1D 4UF
United Kingdom

queries@lewinsohnliterary.com

https://www.lewinsohnliterary.com
https://www.instagram.com/lewinsohnliterary

Professional Body: The Association of Authors' Agents (AAA)

Fiction
Graphic Novels: General
Novels: Family; Friends; Relationships; Romance; Romantic Comedy
Nonfiction
Gift Books: General
Illustrated Books: Cookery
Nonfiction Books: Memoir; Nature; Popular Culture

Closed to approaches.

We will be especially keen to read romcoms or anything with interesting relationship dynamics, be it about friendships, families, colleagues or romantic, tales set in cities or unusual places, even or especially if they seem outwardly mundane, memoir that elicits a strong emotional response and shines a light on the familiar in new ways, nature and pop culture writing that captures the zeitgeist but has timeless weight and resonance, and the occasional dabble with beautifully designed illustrated books, such as graphic novels, cookery, photo or gift books.

L364 Alison Lewis
Senior Agent
United States

atl@goldinlit.com

https://www.goldinlit.com/alison-lewis
https://twitter.com/atatelewis

Literary Agency: Frances Goldin Literary Agency, Inc.

Fiction > *Novels*: Literary

Nonfiction > *Nonfiction Books*
Cultural Criticism; History; Journalism; Literary Memoir; Science

Send: Query; Writing sample; Proposal
How to send: Email

Represents a wide range of nonfiction, spanning journalism, cultural criticism, history, science, literary memoir, and essays, as well as select literary fiction. She is particularly drawn to writers with a distinctive voice and perspective, a sense of social or political imagination and responsibility, scholars and researchers who can translate their expertise for a wide readership, and writers pushing the boundaries of form, preconceived ideas, and histories of representation in literature.

L365 Kayla Lightner
Literary Agent
United States

https://www.pandeliterary.com/our-team-pandeliterary
https://www.manuscriptwishlist.com/mswl-post/kayla-lightner/
https://twitter.com/LightnerKayla
https://www.linkedin.com/in/kayla-lightner-362406ab/

Literary Agency: Ayesha Pande Literary
Professional Body: Association of American Literary Agents (AALA)

Fiction
Graphic Novels: General
Novels: Book Club Fiction; Fantasy; Folklore, Myths, and Legends; Gothic; Historical Fiction; Literary; Magical Realism; Science Fiction; Speculative; Upmarket
Nonfiction > *Nonfiction Books*
Culture; Finance; Health; History; Internet Culture; Internet; Memoir; Mental Health; Narrative Nonfiction; Technology

Send: Pitch; Synopsis; Author bio; Writing sample
How to send: Online submission system

I love discovering diverse and fresh new perspectives across adult literary and upmarket fiction, non-fiction, and graphic novels. I'm particularly a fan of authors with singular voices that masterfully straddle the line between storytelling and teaching readers something new (about themselves, their communities, or the world we live in).

L366 Lindsay Literary Agency
Literary Agency
United Kingdom
Tel: +44 (0) 1420 831430

info@lindsayliteraryagency.co.uk

http://www.lindsayliteraryagency.co.uk
https://twitter.com/lindsaylit

Professional Body: The Association of Authors' Agents (AAA)

CHILDREN'S > **Fiction**
Middle Grade: General, and in particular: High / Epic Fantasy
Picture Books: General

YOUNG ADULT > Fiction > *Novels*
General, and in particular: Contemporary Romance; High Concept; Romantasy

Send: Query; Author bio; Pitch; Synopsis; Writing sample; Full text
How to send: Email

Send query by email only, including cover letter in the body of the email, single-page synopsis and first three chapters, or complete ms in the case of picture books. No submissions by post.

Authors: Helen Brandom; Pamela Butchart; Sital Gorasia Chapman; Christina Collins; Jim Daly; Donna David; James Davis; Keighley Douglas; Rachel Emily; Louise Finch; Sam Gayton; Ruth Hatfield; Larry Hayes; Sharon Hopwood; Peter Jones; Jay Joseph; Titania Krimpas; Mike Lancaster; Beth O'Brien; Kate Peridot; Josh Silver; Daniel Tawse; Sharon Tregenza; Rachel Valentine; Sue Wallman; Jacqueline Whitehart; Joe Wilson

Literary Agent: Becky Bagnell

L367 Isabel Lineberry
Junior Agent
United Kingdom

https://www.perezliterary.com
https://www.perezliterary.com/submit/submit-to-isabel/
https://querymanager.com/query/IsabelLineberry

Literary Agency: Perez Literary & Entertainment (**L463**)

NEW ADULT > Fiction > *Novels*
Contemporary Romance; Fantasy; Romantasy

YOUNG ADULT > Fiction > *Novels*
Contemporary Romance; Fantasy; Romantasy

How to send: Submittable

I represent YA and New Adult and am particularly interested in Contemporary Romance, Romantasy and Fantasy. I am always attracted to the character and voice first, so give me romantic tension that has me giggling, a villain who is as charming as they are evil or a group of characters who have me watching their conversations as if it's a tennis match.

L368 Laurie Liss
Literary Agent; Executive Vice President
United States

https://www.sll.com/our-team
http://aaronline.org/Sys/PublicProfile/2176754/417813

Literary Agency: Sterling Lord Literistic, Inc.
Professional Body: Association of American Literary Agents (AALA)

Fiction > *Novels*

Nonfiction > *Nonfiction Books*

Send: Query; Synopsis; Writing sample
How to send: Online submission system

L369 The Liverpool Literary Agency
Literary Agency
Liverpool
United Kingdom

submissions@liverpool-literary.agency

https://www.liverpool-literary.agency/
https://twitter.com/LiverpoolLit
https://www.instagram.com/liverpool_literary_agency/

Professional Body: The Association of Authors' Agents (AAA)

ADULT > Fiction > *Novels*

YOUNG ADULT > Fiction > *Novels*
Dystopian Fiction; Fantasy; Post-Apocalyptic; Science Fiction; Steampunk; Urban Fantasy

Closed to approaches.

Costs: Offers services that writers have to pay for. Also offers editorial services.

Literary agency based in Liverpool, focusing on helping writers from Northern England break into the publishing industry.

Associate Agent / Editor: Laura Bennett (**L050**)

Literary Agent: Clare Coombes (**L127**)

L370 Looking Glass Literary & Media Management
Literary Agency
United States

https://www.lookingglasslit.com
https://twitter.com/LookingGlassLit
https://www.instagram.com/lookingglasslit/

We are a boutique agency with a full-service team of fierce advocates who support all facets of our clients' careers. Our priority is championing authors and books that reflect the diverse world around us. The books we work with leave lasting impressions that inspire growth, thought, and joy in the world.

Associate Agents: Grace Milusich (**L412**); Antoinette Van Sluytman (**L541**)

Literary Agents: Natalie Lakosil (**L347**); Patricia Nelson (**L437**); Lee O'Brien (**L444**); Desiree Wilson (**L606**)

L371 Lotus Lane Literary
Literary Agency
United States

contact@lotuslit.com

https://lotuslit.com

Fiction > *Novels*

Nonfiction > *Nonfiction Books*

Send: Query; Author bio; Synopsis; Writing sample
How to send: Email

Independent literary agency based in New Jersey, representing a diverse list of debut and seasoned authors. Handles adult fiction and nonfiction, and sells rights to the US, UK, Europe, and India.

Literary Agent: Priya Doraswamy

L372 Jake Lovell
Literary Agent
United States

https://www.dijkstraagency.com
https://www.dijkstraagency.com/agent-page.php?agent_id=Lovell
https://querymanager.com/query/jakelovell

Literary Agency: Sandra Dijkstra Literary Agency

Fiction > *Novels*
Dark; Gothic; Horror; Speculative; Supernatural / Paranormal; Thrillers; UFOs; Upmarket; Westerns

Nonfiction > *Nonfiction Books*
General, and in particular: History; Military; Westerns

Actively looking for adult fiction and non-fiction. He is interested in upmarket fiction, with an emphasis on: Gothic, horror, thrillers, westerns, and speculative fiction (supernatural, paranormal, UFOs, etc…; think Jordan Peele or 10 Cloverfield Lane). When it comes to fiction, he loves dark stories that cause readers to question turning off the lights before bed. Dark stories permeate through all cultures, backgrounds, and histories, and he wants to hear them. His tastes lean more in the vein of The Hunger by Alma Katsu, The Only Good Indians by Stephen Graham Jones, Tender is the Flesh by Agustina Bazterrica, and works by Paul Tremblay, Mona Awad, and Colson Whitehead. In general, he's especially drawn to character driven stories written in distinct and diverse voices.

On the non-fiction front, he is looking for captivating stories and perspectives that stay with readers and keep them coming back. He is especially interested in working with historians, up-and-coming scholars looking to transition to trade readership, journalists, doctors, veterans, and people with unique takes on important issues. Think: Freakonomics, Outliers, A Molecule Away From Madness, Columbine, American Sniper, Empire's Workshop, and The Fact of a Body.

Open to queries the first week of every month.

L373 Amanda Luedeke
Literary Agent; President
United States

amanda@macgregorliterary.com

http://www.macgregorandluedeke.com
https://www.macgregorandluedeke.com/agents

Literary Agency: MacGregor & Luedeke (**L380**)

Nonfiction > *Nonfiction Books*

Open to seeing the right project but generally closed to submissions. Looking for: Nonfiction across most genres, nonreligious and religious. No memoir unless the author has a newsworthy story or a significant platform.

L374 Nicky Lund
Literary Agent
United Kingdom

Literary Agency: David Higham Associates Ltd (**L146**)

L375 Lutyens and Rubinstein
Literary Agency
17 Powis Mews, London, W11 1JN
United Kingdom
Tel: +44 (0) 20 7792 4855

submissions@lutyensrubinstein.co.uk

https://www.lutyensrubinstein.co.uk
https://twitter.com/LandRAgency
https://instagram.com/LandRAgency

Professional Body: The Association of Authors' Agents (AAA)

Fiction > *Novels*
  Commercial; Literary

Nonfiction > *Nonfiction Books*

Send: Query; Synopsis; Writing sample
How to send: Email
How not to send: Post

Send up to 5,000 words or first three chapters by email with covering letter and short synopsis. No film or TV scripts, or unsolicited submissions by hand or by post.

Literary Agent: Susannah Godman

L376 Rebecca Lyon
Literary Agent
United Kingdom

https://www.sheilland.com/about

Literary Agency: Sheil Land Associates Ltd

Scripts
  Film Scripts; *TV Scripts*; *Theatre Scripts*

L377 Donald Maass
Literary Agent
United States

Literary Agency: Donald Maass Literary Agency (**L160**)

L378 Emily MacDonald
Literary Agent
United Kingdom

emilymacdonald@42mp.com

https://www.42mp.com/agents
https://twitter.com/Ebh_mac

Literary Agency: 42 Management and Production

Fiction > *Novels*
  Book Club Fiction; Crime; High Concept; Literary; Romantic Comedy; Thrillers; Upmarket

Nonfiction > *Nonfiction Books*
  History; Memoir; Narrative Nonfiction; Nature; Regional; Scotland; Social Commentary

Closed to approaches.

Bring me a story with characters that never leave you and a narrative that pulls you in, keeping you in the world well after you've finished reading. I read across a wide-range and have a particular interest in; book club, high-concept crime/thriller, upmarket and literary fiction (with a real soft spot for witty romcoms with an unassailable hook!) In both fiction and non-fiction, I love stories woven into their natural landscape, where the setting is as central a character as those who drive the narrative. I'm actively looking for narrative non-fiction which immerses the reader into an untold true story (personal or historical), exploring a new point of view, and providing a compelling social commentary, with an investigative twist! I want to have my horizons expanded when I read. I'd also love to find a story which blends nature writing and memoir.

L379 Laura Macdougall
Literary Agent
United Kingdom

LMacdougall@unitedagents.co.uk

https://www.unitedagents.co.uk/lmacdougallunitedagentscouk
https://twitter.com/L_Macdougall
https://www.instagram.com/lmac_84/?hl=en
https://www.pinterest.co.uk/lmvmacdougall/

Literary Agency: United Agents

Fiction > *Novels*
  Book Club Fiction; Comedy / Humour; Commercial; Family Saga; Family; Friends; Historical Fiction; LGBTQIA; Literary; Menopause; Romance; Saga

Nonfiction
  Illustrated Books: General
  Nonfiction Books: Culture; Ethnic Groups; Gender; History; LGBTQIA; Midwifery; Narrative Nonfiction; Parenting; Philosophy; Politics; Popular Science; Psychology; Science; Scotland; Sexuality; Social Class; Sport

Send: Synopsis; Writing sample; Proposal
How to send: Email

I represent a diverse spectrum of commercial fiction – saga, romance, historical, book club and 'up-lit' – and literary fiction, ranging from the quirky to the daring and experimental. I've always been a big fan of historical fiction and also have a soft spot for novels that explore the complexities of relationships and family life.

My non-fiction list is equally varied, spanning illustrated books to parenting titles, history and popular philosophy. I also represent a fascinating wealth of narrative non-fiction, from Scottish nature writing to death, materials science, politics, manufacturing, midwifery and the recent history of gay bars. A writer who can successfully communicate their passion, whether that's about something niche or obscure or a global phenomenon, will always be of interest to me.

As a queer woman, I represent a large number of LGBTQ+ writers and I'm particularly keen to hear from those who also identify as LGBTQ+ and who are exploring the full spectrum of LGBTQ+ lives in their writing.

Authors: Ferdie Addis; Malcolm Alexander; Celia J Anderson; Leaf Arbuthnot; Hannah Bardell; Duncan Barrett; C F Barrington; Dan Beaumont; Pippa Beecheno; Roxy Bourdillon; Jim Broadbent; P Burton-Morgan; Nuala Calvi; Hayley Campbell; Laura Carlin; Georgina Clarke; Sandra Daniels; Dix; Margot Douaihy; Helen Erichsen; Anthony Price Estate; Katharine Briggs Estate; Alex Evans; Harper Ford; Eve Fraser; Laura Godfrey-Isaacs; Abbie Greaves; Mish Harris; Anneka Harry; Sabrin Hasbun; Julie Haworth; Jason Hazeley; Joe Heap; Beatrice Hitchman; Antonia Honeywell; Jane Housham; Jules Howard; Alice Hutton; E A Jackson; Craig Jordan-Baker; Michael Langan; CN Lester; Jeremy Atherton Lin; Phoebe Luckhurst; Annie Lyons; Kate MacDougall; Beezy Marsh; Rebecca Mascull; Alexandra Masters; Freddy McConnell; Kate McNaughton; Tim Minshall; Ada Moncrieff; Beth Mosley; Bernard O'Keeffe; Jess Phillips; Anna Ploszajski; Elizabeth Reeder; Genevieve Roberts; Gemma Rolls-Bentley; Lucy Jane Santos; Florence Schechter; Shelley Silas; Francesca Steele; Emily Steer; J I M Stewart; Wes Streeting; Joelle Taylor; Amanda Thomson; Katy Turner; Harriet Walker; Mollie Walton; Sophie Ward; Jenny Wells; Kaite Welsh; Bryony White; Dee Whitnell; Ellen Wiles; Susannah Wise; Keio Yoshida

L380 MacGregor & Luedeke
Literary Agency
United States

http://www.macgregorandluedeke.com
https://twitter.com/MacGregorLit

Fiction > *Novels*

Nonfiction > *Nonfiction Books*
Send: Query; Market info; Author bio; Writing sample
Don't send: Full text
How to send: Email

Costs: Author covers sundry admin costs.

We are a boutique literary agency, and since 2006, we have supported writers and their careers. We've agented over one thousand books and guided hundreds of authors. We've always been more interested in doing what's best for the client rather than chasing one-and-done book deals. In other words, we'll pick up the phone whether or not there's money to be made. It's a promise that has established us as a trustworthy, reliable literary agency that authors and publishers enjoy doing business with.

Authors: Don Brown; Davis Bunn; Rashawn Copeland; Sheila Gregoire; Rachel Hauck; James Byron Huggins; Steve Jackson; Jessica Kate; Rachel Linden; Holly Lorincz; Evelyn Lozada; Scott Parazynski; Jay Payleitner; Tom Satterly; Kimberly Stuart; David Thomas; Vincent Zandri

Literary Agent / President: Amanda Luedeke (**L373**)

Literary Agents: Alina Mitchell (*L413*); Colleen Oefelein (*L448*); Elisa Saphier (*L519*)

L381 Kate Mack
Literary Agent; Vice President; Company Director
United States

https://www.aevitascreative.com/agent/kate-mack

Literary Agency: Aevitas

Nonfiction
  Illustrated Books: General
  Nonfiction Books: Comedy / Humour; Culture; Fashion; History; Music

Closed to approaches.

She is most interested in cultural history, fashion, music, illustrated books for adults, strong female voices, and stories that give a voice to a person or community that's historically been silenced or ostracized.

Authors: Joana Avillez; Karen Azoulay; Tayler Carraway; Robyn Crawford; Liza Donnelly; America Ferrera; Patricia Field; Katy Fishell; Lucretia Tye Jasmine; Betsey Johnson; Sam Kashner; Rookie Magazine; Ian Purkayastha; Kate Schelter; Ramin Setoodeh; Amber Share; Kate Sidley; Kevin West; Alden Wicker

L382 Joanna MacKenzie
Literary Agent
United States

https://nelsonagency.com/joanna-mackenzie/
https://www.publishersmarketplace.com/members/JoannaMacKenzie/
https://twitter.com/joannamackenzie
https://www.facebook.com/joanna.topor.mackenzie

Literary Agency: Nelson Literary Agency, LLC (**L435**)

Fiction > *Novels*
  American Midwest; Commercial; Family; Friends; High Concept; Immigration; Magic; Mystery; Speculative; Thrillers; Women's Fiction

Closed to approaches.

Interested in high-concept, twisty stories with a strong voice in the areas of women's fiction, thriller, and speculative; timely commercial fiction in which the personal intersects with the world at large, offering a biting commentary on the times we're living in and making readers sit up and say, "Yes, that, exactly!"; stories that explore complex and challenging family dynamics and unlikely (and possibly toxic) friendships; stories about reinvention and second acts – especially with touches of magic, time slips, or other speculative elements; voicey, confident, atmospheric mysteries set in close-knit communities; creepy islands and Midwest-set stories are a plus; because I came to Chicago by way of Poland and Canada, I'm always looking for stories about the immigrant experience; and Elin Hilderbrand and/or Louise Penny for the Third Coast – I'd love to see a clever sleuth out of a resort town in Michigan.

Authors: Brooke Abrams; Kate Baer; Gina Banks; Ali Brady; Lina Chern; Laura Danger; Shana Galen; John Galligan; Jill Grunenwald; Alison Hammer; Sarah Zachrich Jeng; Sierra Kincade; Karen Koh; Gillian Libby; Jonathan Messinger; Meghan Scott Molin; Katrina Monroe; Lyndsay Rush; Erinn Salge; Kristen Simmons; Jennifer Springsteen; Stacy Stokes; Joy Sullivan; Ben Tanzer; Vikki VanSickle; Kathleen West

L383 Lauren MacLeod
Senior Agent
United States

https://www.aevitascreative.com/agent/lauren-macleod
https://www.strothmanagency.com/about
https://querymanager.com/query/LMacLeod
https://twitter.com/Lauren_MacLeod
http://aaronline.org/Sys/PublicProfile/12259463/417813

Literary Agencies: Aevitas; The Strothman Agency
Professional Body: Association of American Literary Agents (AALA)

ADULT > **Nonfiction** > *Nonfiction Books*
  Cookery; Crime; Food; History; Memoir; Narrative Nonfiction; Popular Culture

CHILDREN'S > **Fiction** > *Middle Grade*

YOUNG ADULT > **Fiction** > *Novels*
Send: Query
How to send: Email; Query Tracker; By referral

Only accepting nonfiction queries for food writing, cookbooks, true crime, and pop culture without a referral. If you have a memoir, narrative nonfiction, or YA or MG fiction project and have been referred by a friend or client, make contact directly.

Authors: Hélène Boudreau; Bridget Crocker; Helene Dunbar; Rogelio Garcia; Kenny Gilbert; Tyler Gillespie; Ron Goldberg; Steven Hale; Rachel Herz; Allison Horrocks; Sashi Kaufman; Claire and Alan Linic; Mary Mahoney; Nicole Maines; Jodi Meadows; Andrea Mosqueda; Frederick Douglass Opie; Erik Rebain; Beck Rourke-Mooney; Aminah Mae Safi; Alora Young; Marlene Zuk

L384 Mad Woman Literary Agency
Literary Agency
United States

https://www.madwomanliterary.com

A queer-woman-owned, full-service literary agency founded in 2021. The agency has a particular focus on DEAI and prides itself on its highly curated list of talented authors. Values transparency, a spirit of partnership, and author empowerment. We work to foster a sense of community among our clients through annual retreats and virtual educational presentations. We are by each client's side throughout the publishing process from the development of ideas all the way through publication and beyond to support sustainable, long-term writing careers.

Literary Agents: Danielle Burby (**L087**); Chelsea Hensley (**L274**)

L385 Madeleine Milburn Literary, TV & Film Agency
Literary Agency
The Factory, 1 Park Hill, London, SW4 9NS
United Kingdom
Tel: +44 (0) 20 7499 7550

submissions@madeleinemilburn.com
childrens@madeleinemilburn.com
info@madeleinemilburn.com

https://madeleinemilburn.co.uk
https://twitter.com/MMLitAgency
https://www.instagram.com/madeleinemilburn/?hl=en
https://www.facebook.com/MadeleineMilburnLiteraryAgency

Professional Body: The Association of Authors' Agents (AAA)

ADULT
  Fiction > *Novels*
  Nonfiction > *Nonfiction Books*

CHILDREN'S
Fiction > *Novels*
Nonfiction > *Nonfiction Books*

NEW ADULT
Fiction > *Novels*
Nonfiction > *Nonfiction Books*

TEEN
Fiction > *Novels*
Nonfiction > *Nonfiction Books*

YOUNG ADULT
Fiction > *Novels*
Nonfiction > *Nonfiction Books*

Send: Query; Synopsis; Pitch; Market info; Writing sample
How to send: Online submission system
How not to send: Post; Email

Represents award-winning and bestselling authors of adult and children's fiction and non-fiction. Submit via online submissions system. No submissions by post or by email.

Company Director / Literary Agent: Madeleine Milburn (**L411**)

Literary Agents: Emma Bal (**L032**); Maddy Belton (**L049**); Jessica Leeke (**L358**); Olivia Maidment (**L386**); Rachel Yeoh (**L612**)

Managing Director: Giles Milburn

Senior Agent: Chloe Seager (**L524**)

L386 Olivia Maidment
Literary Agent
United Kingdom

submissions@madeleinemilburn.com
https://www.madeleinemilburn.co.uk/agents/olivia-maidment/
https://twitter.com/liv_maidment

Literary Agency: Madeleine Milburn Literary, TV & Film Agency (**L385**)

Fiction > *Novels*
Book Club Fiction; Contemporary; Crime; Family; Historical Fiction; Horror; Literary; Mystery; Postcolonialism; Society; Speculative; Upmarket

Send: Synopsis; Writing sample
How to send: Email
How not to send: Post

I represent literary, upmarket, and book club fiction.

I am drawn to powerful novels layered with texture, character, and atmosphere that will stay with the reader long after they have finished reading. I'm excited by themes of family, history, society, self-discovery, and ambition, and I am eager to read global stories and postcolonial narratives.

I also represent literary or upmarket leaning fiction that blends with shades of genre – in particular with speculative, crime, mystery, or horror. For me, writing in this area needs to be grounded in the human stories at the heart of the novel.

L387 Alyssa Maltese
Literary Agent
United States

https://www.alyssamaltese.com
https://www.rootliterary.com/team
https://querymanager.com/query/alyssamaltese
https://www.publishersmarketplace.com/members/alyssamaltese/

Literary Agency: Root Literary (**L503**)

ADULT
Fiction > *Novels*
Contemporary Romance; Domestic Suspense; Historical Fiction; Horror; Psychological Thrillers; Speculative

Nonfiction > *Nonfiction Books*
Animals; Mental Health; Narrative Nonfiction; Nature; Popular Culture; Prescriptive Nonfiction; Psychology; Science; Sex

YOUNG ADULT > Fiction > *Novels*
Coming of Age; Contemporary; Fantasy; Historical Fiction; Horror; Romance; Speculative

Does not want:

ADULT > Fiction > *Novels*: Supernatural / Paranormal Romance
YOUNG ADULT > Fiction > *Novels*
High / Epic Fantasy; Supernatural / Paranormal Romance

Closed to approaches.

In the YA space, I'm seeking fiction that helps young readers discover their own voice and sense of self-worth. I love kids and have a background in early childhood education, and feel strongly that if a child is old enough to experience something, then they are old enough to read about it. I'm particularly drawn to contemporary coming-of-age stories with a healthy dose of angst. I'm open to genre elements (particularly speculative, fantasy, romance, historical), but in general I prefer fiction grounded in our world, so I'm not the best fit for straightforward fantasy. I'm also seeking YA horror. In this space, I love high stakes and work embedded with social commentary. I would be absolutely tickled to find a YA project exploring 2000s emo culture. (It's not a phase, mom!) If your book is set at Warped Tour or Bamboozle, I want to see it! In adult fiction, I'm casting a bit of a wider net. I'm looking for weird upmarket speculative novels. I'm also seeking commercial psychological thrillers, domestic suspense, and horror. Propulsive pacing is a must, and twists that really surprise me are a bonus! My very favorite kind of historical fiction is slice-of-life revealing untold stories of interesting women.

I'd also love some contemporary romance to round out my list. One of my favorite tropes is when love is reciprocated, but one or both love interests doesn't realize it... think enemies to lovers; best friends to lovers; sunshine and grumpy. My ideal romance is torturously slow burn with a healthy dose of angst and substantial emotional growth. In adult nonfiction, I'm seeking prescriptive and research-driven narrative nonfiction from authors with an established expertise and audience. Topics of interest in nonfiction include psychology, mental health, taboo topics such as death and sex, science pertaining to nature and animals, and pop culture. I am not accepting submissions for poetry, short story collections, screenplays, novellas, early reader books, chapter books, religious texts, picture books, graphic novels, or illustrations of any kind. I am not the best fit for high/epic fantasy, space operas, paranormal romance, crime fiction/detective novels, cozy mysteries, legal thrillers, romantic thrillers, pulp fiction, sick lit, stories set in mental hospitals, most things related to sports, grifter-themed stories, torture porn/gratuitous gore, or fairytale retellings (though I do have a soft spot for Arthurian legend).

L388 Victoria Marini
Literary Agent
United States

https://www.highlineliterary.com/agent-victoria
https://querymanager.com/query/2982
https://twitter.com/LitAgentMarini

Literary Agency: High Line Literary Collective (**L279**)

ADULT > Fiction > *Novels*
Adventure; Commercial; Fabulism; High / Epic Fantasy; Literary; Magical Realism; Romance; Romantasy; Romantic Comedy; Science Fiction; Speculative Thrillers; Speculative; Supernatural / Paranormal Horror; Suspense; Upmarket

YOUNG ADULT > Fiction > *Novels*
Commercial; Upmarket

Closed to approaches.

Has represented numerous award winning and bestselling authors across audiences and is interested in a broad range of sub-genres for both Upmarket & Commercial Adult and Young Adult readers. Her list is made up of everything from Literary page-turners to commercial suspense, supernatural horrors, whimsical speculative romantasy, big world fantasies, adventures, romance, edgy sci-fi, grounded magical fabulism, rom-coms, speculative thrillers, etc. What unites her eclectic list is a sense of unforgettable authentic characters, hooky concepts with strong plotting and an emotional core, and unique voices or visions!

She is a sucker for quirk, mystery, small town hysteria, atmosphere, secrets, things that go bump in the night, a bit of charm, a twist of magic, or a dash of humor.

L389 Jill Marr

Literary Agent
United States

https://www.dijkstraagency.com/agent-page.php?agent_id=Marr
https://querymanager.com/query/JillMarr

Literary Agency: Sandra Dijkstra Literary Agency

ADULT

Fiction > *Novels*
Commercial; Fantasy; Folklore, Myths, and Legends; Food; Gothic; Historical Fiction; Horror; Magical Realism; Mystery; Psychological Suspense; Romance; Romantasy; Romantic Comedy; Speculative; Thrillers; Upmarket

Nonfiction > *Nonfiction Books*
Comedy / Humour; Crime; Current Affairs; Health; History; Memoir; Music; Narrative Nonfiction; Nutrition; Politics; Popular Culture; Science; Social Commentary; Sport

CHILDREN'S > **Fiction** > *Picture Books*

Closed to approaches.

Looking for fiction and non-fiction by unrepresented voices, BIPOC and Latinx writers, disabled persons, and people identifying as LGBTQ+, among others. She is interested in commercial and upmarket fiction, with an emphasis on mysteries, thrillers, Gothic, horror, romantasy, romance, fantasy, speculative fiction, and historical fiction. She loves food-centric novels, no matter what the genre. She is looking to find more rom coms with a fresh voice, perspective and a strong hook. When it comes to suspense she likes it dark and psychological. Her tastes lean more in the vein of The Silent Patient, The Lost Apothecary or Mexican Gothic than Private Investigator and CIA stories. And she almost never takes on military or Western projects. However she is a sucker for novels with grounded magical realism, and is always looking for a new take on mythology or folklore. She is also looking for non-fiction by authors with a big, timely, smart message. She'd like to see work that does a deep dive into subcultures and social commentary as well as historical projects that look at big picture issues. She is looking for non-fiction projects in the areas of current events, true crime, science, history, narrative non-fiction, sports, politics, health and nutrition, pop culture, humor, music, and very select memoir.

L390 The Marsh Agency

Literary Agency
50 Albemarle Street, London, W1S 4BD United Kingdom
Tel: +44 (0) 20 7493 4361

http://www.marsh-agency.co.uk

Professional Body: The Association of Authors' Agents (AAA)
Types: Fiction; Nonfiction
Subjects: Literary
Markets: Adult; Young Adult

Closed to approaches.

Not currently accepting unsolicited mss as at March 2018. Most new clients come through recommendations.

Authors: Jill Bays; Ian Dear; Ed Halliwell; Tendai Huchu; Sam Kriss; Anita Nair; Alan Palmer; Allyson Pollock; Alfred Price; Gillian Riley; Richard Seymour; Christine Shaw

Literary Agent: Susie Nicklin

L391 Jen Marshall

Literary Agent
New York
United States

https://www.aevitascreative.com/agent/jen-marshall
https://querymanager.com/query/JenMarshall
https://twitter.com/jenmarshall3

Literary Agency: Aevitas

ADULT

Fiction
Graphic Novels: General
Novels: Adventure; Commercial; Crime; Drama; Horror; Literary; Popular Culture; Romance

Nonfiction > *Nonfiction Books*
Arts; Business; Crime; Design; Fashion; Health; History; Investigative Journalism; Mathematics; Narrative Nonfiction; Popular Culture; Science; Social Justice; Technology

CHILDREN'S > **Fiction** > *Novels*

Closed to approaches.

Represents acclaimed and bestselling narrative nonfiction projects. Also represents select literary and commercial fiction projects. Areas of interest in nonfiction are wide-ranging: investigative journalism, untold histories, fashion and design, social justice, true crime, tech, business, science, cities, and pop culture. In fiction, she primarily seeks literary and commercial works for adults.

Authors: Natasha S. Barrett; Elena Brower; Maggie Bullock; Windy Chien; Hopwood DePree; Danielle Dreilinger; Amanda FitzSimons; Neil Gross; Ericka Hart; Gabrielle Hartley; Katherine Sharp Landdeck; Nana Malone; Marisa Meltzer; Jenny Minton; Azadeh Moaveni; Vanessa O'Brien; Joe Pompeo; Gene Pressman; Paul Pringle; Kate Schapira; Chris Smalls; Keziah Weir; Eric Wilson; Sheryl Gonzalez Ziegler

L392 Caroline Marsiglia

Literary Agent
United States

https://www.aevitascreative.com
https://www.aevitascreative.com/agent/caroline-marsiglia

Nonfiction > *Nonfiction Books*
Investigative Journalism; Memoir; Narrative Nonfiction; Self Help

Closed to approaches.

Primarily interested in non-fiction, focusing on investigative journalism, memoir, evidence-based self-help, and narrative non-fiction. Across all genres, she is eager to work with authors who share her dedication to creating a more diverse and accessible literary landscape.

L393 Olivia Martin

Associate Agent
United Kingdom
Tel: +44 (0) 20 3214 0778

omartin@unitedagents.co.uk

https://www.unitedagents.co.uk/omartinunitedagentscouk

Literary Agency: United Agents
Literary Agent: Charles Walker

Authors: Anjana Appachana; Neil Ely; Lloyd Eyre-Morgan; Jack Hartley; Lucas Sogas López; Max Tobin; Ryan Walker-Edwards

L394 Massie McQuilkin & Altman

Literary Agency
27 West 20th Street, Suite 305, New York, NY 10011
United States
Tel: +1 (212) 352-2055

info@mmqlit.com

https://www.mmqalit.com
https://www.facebook.com/mmqalit
https://www.instagram.com/mmqalit

Fiction > *Novels*

Nonfiction > *Nonfiction Books*

Send: Query
Don't send: Full text
How to send: Email

Costs: Author covers sundry admin costs.

See website for specific agent interests and contact details. Query only one agent at a time.

Literary Agents: Stephanie Abou; Elias Altman; Ethan Bassoff; Aram Fox (**L212**); Maria Massie; Rob McQuilkin; Max Moorhead (**L416**); Neil Olson; Sandra Pareja; Rayhane Sanders (**L517**); Julie Stevenson; Lane Zachary; Renee Zuckerbrot (**L618**)

L395 Rebecca Matte
Literary Agent
United States

https://bradfordlit.com/about/rebecca-matte/
https://querymanager.com/query/RMatte
https://www.manuscriptwishlist.com/mswl-post/rebecca-matte/
https://twitter.com/rebeccalmatte

Literary Agency: Bradford Literary Agency (**L073**)

ADULT > **Fiction** > *Novels*
  Disabilities; Fantasy; Queer Romance; Romance; Romantasy; Science Fiction

YOUNG ADULT > **Fiction** > *Novels*
  Disabilities; Fantasy; Queer Romance; Romance; Romantasy; Science Fiction

How to send: Query Tracker

Loves adult and YA science fiction/fantasy and queer romance. But no matter the setting—be it a far off kingdom beset by magic or around the corner in Brooklyn—she seeks out books that feature diverse, complex characters in deeply rooted relationships, platonic and romantic. A well-crafted romance will make her heart sing, while a beautifully detailed friendship will elevate any book to an instant favorite. She also gravitates towards inherently hopeful stories of self-discovery and reinvention at all ages, particularly those that center questions of gender and sexuality. She tries to bring magic to every moment of life, and loves books that do the same.

L396 Jennifer Mattson
Senior Agent
United States

jmatt@andreabrownlit.com

https://www.andreabrownlit.com/Team/Jennifer-Mattson
http://twitter.com/jannmatt
http://instagram.com/jennmattson
https://www.publishersmarketplace.com/members/JenMatt/
https://www.manuscriptwishlist.com/mswl-post/jennifer-mattson/
https://querymanager.com/query/JenniferMattson

Literary Agency: Andrea Brown Literary Agency, Inc.

CHILDREN'S > **Fiction** > *Middle Grade*

YOUNG ADULT > **Fiction** > *Novels*

Closed to approaches.

Represents authors, illustrators, and author-illustrators who bring a distinct point of view to their work, and who tell stories with multiple layers. In middle grade and YA both, her heart beats faster for stories that cascade from a mind-expanding premise. She also loves survival stories and losing herself in Dickensian sagas (WOLVES OF WILLOUGHBY CHASE!), and enjoys watching characters puzzle their way through problems. She has a special soft spot for middle grade about resilient kids sorting out the messiness of life.

L397 Shari Maurer
Literary Agent
United States

https://www.stringerlit.com
https://querymanager.com/query/1434
https://aalitagents.org/author/sharimaurer/

Literary Agency: The Stringer Literary Agency LLC (**L553**)
Professional Body: Association of American Literary Agents (AALA)

ADULT > **Nonfiction** > *Nonfiction Books*
  Memoir; Narrative Nonfiction; Parenting; Popular Science

CHILDREN'S
  Fiction
    Middle Grade: Contemporary; Historical Fiction; Literary; Mystery
    Picture Books: General

  Nonfiction > *Middle Grade*

YOUNG ADULT
  Fiction > *Novels*
    Contemporary; Historical Fiction; Literary; Mystery

  Nonfiction > *Nonfiction Books*

Send: Query; Synopsis; Writing sample; Pitch
How to send: Query Tracker

L398 Jane Graham Maw
Literary Agent
United Kingdom
Tel: +44 (0) 7971 268342

jane@grahammawchristie.com

https://www.grahammawchristie.com
https://www.grahammawchristie.com/about

Literary Agency: Graham Maw Christie Literary Agency (**L246**)

Nonfiction > *Nonfiction Books*
  General, and in particular: Activism; Memoir; Narrative Nonfiction; Psychology

Send: Outline; Author bio; Market info; Writing sample; Proposal; Pitch
How to send: Email

For general non-fiction she seeks out activists, psychologists, creatives, change-makers and thought-leaders. On the narrative/memoir side she is looking for beautifully crafted books that take the reader somewhere new – a time, a place, or an experience, while managing to be universally appealing.

L399 Juliana McBride
Literary Agent
United States

https://rfliterary.com/about/
https://querymanager.com/query/JulianaMcBride
https://twitter.com/juliananotabot
https://www.instagram.com/julianalovesbooks/
https://www.manuscriptwishlist.com/mswl-post/juliana-mcbride/

Literary Agency: Rebecca Friedman Literary Agency

ADULT > **Fiction** > *Novels*
  Commercial; Literary

CHILDREN'S > **Fiction** > *Middle Grade*
  Contemporary; Relationships; Speculative

YOUNG ADULT > **Fiction** > *Novels*

Closed to approaches.

Loves commercial and literary fiction, young adult novels, and middle grade novels; mostly grounded contemporary stories with a speculative element, and honest stories that explore relationships and make her laugh.

L400 McCormick Literary
Literary Agency
United States
Tel: +1 (212) 691-9726

queries@mccormicklit.com

http://mccormicklit.com

ADULT
  Fiction > *Novels*
    Commercial; Literary

  Nonfiction > *Nonfiction Books*
    Arts; Biography; Cookery; Cultural History; Memoir; Narrative Nonfiction; Politics

YOUNG ADULT > **Fiction** > *Novels*

Send: Query; Author bio; Writing sample
How to send: Email
How not to send: Email attachment

Send queries by email with short bio and ten sample pages, indicating in the subject line which agent you are querying (see website for individual agent interests). No attachments. Response only if interested.

Literary Agents: Bridget McCarthy; David McCormick; Edward Orloff; Pilar Queen

L401 Christabel McKinley
Literary Agent
United Kingdom

Literary Agency: David Higham Associates Ltd (**L146**)

L402 Andy McNicol
Senior Agent
United States

https://www.aevitascreative.com
https://www.aevitascreative.com/agent/andy-mcnicol

Literary Agency: Aevitas

Nonfiction > *Nonfiction Books*

Closed to approaches.

Has represented New York Times bestselling books, including a #1 New York Times bestselling memoir and lifestyle brands.

L403 Isabel Mendia
Associate Agent
United States

https://www.cheneyagency.com/isabel-mendia

Literary Agency: The Cheney Agency

Nonfiction > *Nonfiction Books*
Climate Science; Cultural Criticism; History; Immigration; Narrative Journalism; Politics; Progressive Politics; Racism; Science

Send: Query; Self-addressed stamped envelope (SASE)
How to send: Post; Email

Interested in representing a range of nonfiction, including cultural criticism, narrative reportage, science, and history. A native Spanish speaker, she is particularly interested in Latinx stories, and in writing that makes sense of first- and second-generation immigrant experiences. She is also attracted to projects that have a progressive political mission, and that are responding in some way to colonialism, capitalism, racism, and the climate crisis. She also loves pop culture, and projects that provide entertainment, humor, and hope.

L404 Meridian Artists
Literary Agency
43 Britain Street, Suite A02, Toronto, Ontario
M5A 1R7
Canada
Tel: +1 (416) 961-2777

info@meridianartists.com

https://www.meridianartists.com

Fiction > *Novels*

Nonfiction > *Nonfiction Books*

Scripts
Film Scripts; *TV Scripts*

Send: Synopsis; Author bio; Writing sample
How to send: Online submission system

Offers premier full-service entertainment industry representation with principal offices in Toronto and Los Angeles. An established leader in the representation and management of Talent, Screenwriters, Directors, Authors, and Key Creatives.

L405 Annabel Merullo
Senior Agent
United Kingdom

amerullo@pfd.co.uk

https://petersfraserdunlop.com/agent/annabel-merullo/

Literary Agency: Peters Fraser + Dunlop

Fiction > *Novels*
Commercial; Literary

Nonfiction > *Nonfiction Books*
Commercial; Literary

Send: Query; Author bio; Synopsis; Writing sample; Proposal
How to send: Email

Represents literary and commercial writers of fiction and non-fiction. Only taking nonfiction submissions at this time.

Authors: Alba Arikha; Michael Banissy; Harry Benson; Patrick Bishop; James Blunt; Simon Booker; Jimmy Burns; Brian Cathcart; Monique Charlesworth; Richard Charlton; Paul Conroy; Adam Croft; Bob Cryer; Mark Dawson; Mike Dowling; Miriam Gonzalez Durantez; Patrick Flood; Adrian Fort; Jonathan Franklin

L406 Metamorphosis Literary Agency
Literary Agency
United States

info@metamorphosisliteraryagency.com

https://www.metamorphosisliteraryagency.com
https://www.facebook.com/metamorphosislitagent
https://twitter.com/MetamorphLitAg
https://www.linkedin.com/company/metamorphosis-literary-agency
https://www.instagram.com/metamorphosis_literary_agency/

ADULT
Fiction > *Novels*
Nonfiction > *Nonfiction Books*

YOUNG ADULT > **Fiction** > *Novels*

Send: Query; Author bio; Writing sample; Synopsis
How to send: Query Tracker

Costs: Author covers sundry admin costs.

Our mission is to help authors become traditionally published. We represent well-crafted commercial fiction and nonfiction. We work with authors to ensure that every book is in the best presentable form. Our publishing connections come from experience, numerous conferences, hard work, and genuine care.

Assistant Agent: Kaylyn Aldridge (**L010**)

Authors: Suleena Bibra; Kelly Cain; Natalie Cammaratta; Ashley M. Coleman; Stephanie Eding; Caroline Flynn; Charlee James; Karen Lynch; LaRonda Gardner Middlemiss; Janice Milusich; Anitra Rowe Schulte; Samara Shanker; Angela Shanté; Bruce Smith; Laura Snider; Heather Grace Stewart; Shannon Stults

Literary Agents: Des Salazar (**L515**); Shania N. Soler (**L543**)

Senior Agents: Amy Brewer; Erica Christensen (**L115**); Stephanie Hansen (**L264**)

L407 Mic Cheetham Literary Agency
Literary Agency
62 Grafton Way, London, W1T 5DW
United Kingdom
Tel: +44 (0) 20 3976 7713

submissions@miccheetham.co.uk

https://miccheetham.com

Fiction > *Novels*

Nonfiction > *Nonfiction Books*

Send: Query; Outline; Writing sample; Author bio
How to send: Email

Agency with a deliberately small list. Only takes on two or three new writers each year. New writers are advised to acquaint themselves with the work of the writers currently represented by the agency before submitting their own work.

Authors: Carol Birch; Nm Browne; Pat Cadigan; Alan Campbell; Gregory Doran; Barbara Ewing; Ian Green; M John Harrison; Alice James; Ken MacLeod; Paul Mcauley; China Miéville; Sharon Penman; Antony Sher; Adrian Tchaikovsky

Literary Agents: Mic Cheetham; Simon Kavanagh

L408 Caroline Michel
Literary Agent; Chief Executive Officer
United Kingdom
Tel: +44 (0) 20 7344 1000

cmichelsubmissions@pfd.co.uk

https://petersfraserdunlop.com/agent/caroline-michel/

Literary Agency: Peters Fraser + Dunlop

Fiction > *Novels*

Nonfiction > *Nonfiction Books*
Biography; History; Science

Send: Query; Synopsis; Writing sample; Proposal; Author bio
How to send: Email
How not to send: Post

Loves everything and anything. She is endlessly curious about people's ideas, what's going on in the world and how to understand it, whether it's through history, fiction, biography, science. She is an eternal optimist and loves working with people who believe that everything is possible.

Authors: Ellen Alpsten; Jamie Bartlett; Camila Batmanghelidjh; Elaine Bedell; Lesley Blanch; Peter Bowles; Rosie Boycott; Pattie Boyd;

Melvyn Bragg; Jonathan Bryan; Michael Caine; Emma Calder; Mark Carney; Augustus Casely-Hayford; Mavis Cheek; Helen Chislett; Rita Clifton; Sebastian Coe; Natalia Conroy; Chi-chi Nwanoku

L409 Leah Middleton
Literary Agent
United Kingdom

leah@marjacq.com

http://www.marjacq.com/leah-middleton.html

Literary Agency: Marjacq Scripts Ltd

Scripts
  Film Scripts; *TV Scripts*

Send: Full text; Synopsis; Author bio
How to send: Email

Open to submissions from screenwriters with at least one broadcast credit. Works with writers across genres and formats. Send one full screenplay written to format (feature or TV), a full synopsis (including spoilers!) and writing CV. No submissions from newer writers who haven't yet received their first credit.

L410 Natasha Mihell
Associate Agent
Canada

https://www.therightsfactory.com/Agents/Natasha-Mihell
https://querymanager.com/query/natashatrf

Literary Agency: The Rights Factory

ADULT
  Fiction > *Novels*
    Fantasy; Horror; Science Fiction

  Nonfiction > *Nonfiction Books*
    Biography; Memoir

CHILDREN'S > **Fiction** > *Middle Grade*
  Fantasy; Horror; Science Fiction

YOUNG ADULT > **Fiction** > *Novels*
  Fantasy; Horror; Science Fiction

Closed to approaches.

Loves stories that sing, move, and shimmer, and most especially, those that are fearless in speaking their truths. She is a great fan of conceptual depth and courage and will consider any story that has clear heart and vision. She is always keen to support voices from the 2SLGBTQQIA+, BIPOC, #ownvoices, disabled and neurodiverse communities.

Authors: Sylvie Cathrall; Kodie Van Dusen; Joe Frye; C.C. Graystone; Taryn Herlich; R.J. Joseph; Carolina Munhóz; Jasmine Ng; Nicholas Pullen; Ana Toumine; Vani Varshney; Fatemeh Zarei

L411 Madeleine Milburn
Literary Agent; Company Director
United Kingdom

https://madeleinemilburn.co.uk/team-member/madeleine-milburn/
https://twitter.com/agentmilburn

Literary Agency: Madeleine Milburn Literary, TV & Film Agency (**L385**)

Fiction > *Novels*
  General, and in particular: Book Club Fiction; Commercial; Crime; Family Saga; Historical Fiction; Literary; Romantic Mystery; Suspense; Thrillers; Upmarket

Send: Query; Pitch; Market info; Author bio; Synopsis; Writing sample
How to send: Email
How not to send: Post

Open to submissions from writers based in the UK and internationally, with strong ties in Canada and the US, and looking for upmarket and accessible literary fiction with a strong hook, compelling characters and propulsive storytelling. I'm looking to build on the crime and thriller side of my list with a big new suspense, and also looking for an epic multi-generational family drama, or a powerful love story with a mystery at its heart.

L412 Grace Milusich
Associate Agent
United States

https://www.lookingglasslit.com
https://www.lookingglasslit.com/grace-milusich
https://querymanager.com/query/2859
https://twitter.com/gracemilusich
https://gracemilusich.weebly.com/

Literary Agency: Looking Glass Literary & Media Management (**L370**)

ADULT > **Fiction** > *Novels*
  Contemporary; Horror; Romantasy; Thrillers

YOUNG ADULT > **Fiction** > *Novels*
  Contemporary; Horror; Romantasy; Thrillers

Closed to approaches.

Interested in pursuing both YA and adult pieces. She is passionate about horror, thrillers, and contemporary fiction featuring powerful/challenging themes. She is also a lover of the found family trope in all its forms. She is hoping to work on horror projects that feature BIPOC protagonists.

L413 Alina Mitchell
Literary Agent

Literary Agency: MacGregor & Luedeke (**L380**)

L414 Jess Molloy
Literary Agent
United Kingdom
Tel: +44 (0) 20 7393 4281

jess.molloy@curtisbrown.co.uk

https://curtisbrown.co.uk
https://curtisbrown.co.uk/agent/jess-molloy

Literary Agency: Curtis Brown (**L135**)

Fiction > *Novels*
  Crime; Fantasy; Ireland; Romance

Nonfiction > *Nonfiction Books*
  Crime; Narrative Nonfiction; Psychology

I read broadly across fiction and narrative non-fiction. I am usually first pulled in by a unique concept or setting, but what keeps me reading are beautifully drawn, complex characters, relationships, and family dynamics. I enjoy reading fantasy and romance and I am particularly on the lookout for a story which has a slow burn at its heart, full of angst and drama. I have a deep love for Irish fiction both in terms of Irish writers, and novels set in Ireland. I enjoy crime fiction and true crime writing that subverts the genre and focuses on the victim or the fallout for their family. In terms of non-fiction, I enjoy issues led narrative writing with a personal story at its heart and particularly love hearing from underrepresented voices. I am also interested in psychology and therapy. My non-fiction reading varies broadly from comedians to experts and journalists, but what I am always looking for is an authentic voice that will teach me something fascinating or share a very personal journey with me.

Authors: Casey Jay Andrews; Sui Annukka; Fern Brady; Georgina Charles; Ken Cheng; Laura Coffey; Babak Ganjei; Rebecca Gibson; Daniel Howell; Greg Keen; Danny James King; Tatty Macleod; Gráinne Maguire; Tara O'Sullivan; Lucy Webster; Claire Whatley

L415 Mary C. Moore
Literary Agent
United States

https://www.aevitascreative.com/agent/mary-c-moore
https://querymanager.com/query/Mary_C_Moore

Literary Agency: Aevitas

Fiction > *Novels*
  Book Club Fiction; Detective Fiction; Speculative; Upmarket

Closed to approaches.

Represents a wide range of fiction. She likes to work with clients long-term, and is comfortable representing multiple genres/age-ranges that an author is interested in, although prefers to begin a partnership in one genre before jumping to another. She is currently hoping to find layered and deeply satisfying upmarket fiction, bookclub fiction with light speculative elements, and smart female sleuth stories.

L416 Max Moorhead
Literary Agent
United States

max@mmqlit.com

http://www.mmqlit.com/about/

Literary Agency: Massie McQuilkin & Altman (**L394**)

Fiction > *Novels*: Literary

Nonfiction > *Nonfiction Books*
  Biography; Cultural History; Journalism; Memoir; Narrative Nonfiction; Politics

How to send: Email

Represents literary fiction and nonfiction in the areas of memoir, politics, journalism, cultural history, and biography. In fiction: he is drawn to beautiful writing, unforgettable characters, family stories, socially engaged writing, and compelling plots.

L417 Imogen Morrell
Literary Agent
United Kingdom

https://greeneheaton.co.uk/agents/imogen-morrell/
https://twitter.com/imogen_morrell

Literary Agency: Greene & Heaton Ltd (**L251**)

Fiction > *Novels*
  Dark; Detective Fiction; Ghost Stories; Historical Fiction; Horror; LGBTQIA; Literary; Politics; Science Fiction; Speculative; Suspense

Nonfiction > *Nonfiction Books*
  Biography; Crime; Cultural Criticism; Food; Investigative Journalism; Literary; Memoir; Nature; Politics; Social History

Send: Query; Synopsis; Writing sample
How to send: Word file email attachment

My fiction taste is broad, but I'm drawn to a distinctive style, a sense of strangeness or darkness, emotional stakes, and beauty! I love to read literary novels that inhabit genres or lean on plot -- be it a slanted take on a detective novel, science fiction, a ghost story -- to deal with wider moral or political complexity.

I'd like to find a clever, taut suspense; a campy queer horror; a sideways novel about desire; something bighearted and funny.

I like books that are speculative or ghostly; historical fiction of all stripes; novels that feel bendy and unusual.

I'm keen to work with academics and journalists, and I'm interested in social history, political writing, investigative journalism, cultural criticism, memoir, biography, nature,

and food. I'm looking for writers that can spark curiosity no matter the subject and marry vivid narrative with deep research. I enjoy working on proposals, too, and I'm happy to speak to non-fiction writers in the early stages of a project.

Authors: Juliana Adelman; Prudence Bussey-Chamberlain; Robin Craig; Avery Curran; Rachel Dawson; Sharanya Deepak; Vittoria Fallanca; Gareth Gavin; Mara Gold; Evie Hatch; Kat Hill; Sarah Housley; Daisy J. Hung; Sam Johnson-Schlee; Fiona Keating; Kerry McInerney; Anna Parker; Georgia Poplett; Eddie Scott; Margaux Vialleron; Joe Zadeh

L418 Michele Mortimer
Literary Agent
United States

submissions@dvagency.com

https://www.dvagency.com/aboutus

Literary Agency: Darhansoff & Verrill Literary Agents (**L142**)

ADULT
  Fiction > *Novels*
    Crime; Historical Fiction; Horror; Literary; Mystery; Romance; Thrillers; Upmarket Women's Fiction

  Nonfiction > *Nonfiction Books*
    Animals; Crime; Culture; Feminism; Memoir; Music; Narrative Nonfiction; Nature; Popular Culture; Sociology; Sport; Wellbeing

YOUNG ADULT > **Fiction** > *Novels*: Realistic

Send: Query; Writing sample
How to send: In the body of an email

Currently considers literary fiction; historical fiction; sophisticated genre (crime, mystery, thrillers, horror); upmarket character-rich women's fiction and smart romance; realism-based young adult fiction; memoirs, essays, and narrative nonfiction. Nonfiction interests include music, sports, wellness, the natural world, animal welfare, feminism, true crime, sociology, and culture both pop and serious.

L419 Tasneem Motala
Assistant Agent
Canada

https://www.therightsfactory.com/submissions
https://querymanager.com/query/2005

Literary Agency: The Rights Factory

ADULT > **Fiction**
  Graphic Novels; Novels; Short Fiction Collections
YOUNG ADULT > **Fiction**
  Graphic Novels; Novels; Short Fiction Collections

Closed to approaches.

I'm currently looking for character-driven young adult, adult, short story collections, and graphic novels written with a touch of magic. I'm also on the hunt for artists and illustrators who are interested in doing work for picture books, covers work, and graphic novels.

L420 Movable Type Management
Literary Agency
244 Madison Avenue, Suite 334, New York, NY 10016
United States
Tel: +1 (646) 431-6134

Submission@MovableTM.com

https://www.movabletm.com

Fiction > *Novels*: Commercial

Nonfiction > *Nonfiction Books*: Commercial

How to send: Email

Looking for authors of high quality commercial fiction and nonfiction with archetypal themes, stories, and characters, especially if they have strong film/TV potential. Response only if interested.

Literary Agent: Adam Chromy

L421 Lisa Moylett
Literary Agent
United Kingdom

https://cmm.agency/about-us.php
http://twitter.com/MoylettLisa

Literary Agency: Coombs Moylett & Maclean Literary Agency

Fiction > *Novels*: Commercial Women's Fiction

Send: Synopsis; Writing sample
How to send: Online submission system
How not to send: Email

represents an eclectic list of authors and writers and is currently looking for well-written, commercial women's fiction with a strong hook, twisty plots, lots of emotion and lots of drama.

L422 Jack Mozley
Literary Agent
United Kingdom

https://www.perezliterary.com/submit/submit-to-jack/

Literary Agency: Perez Literary & Entertainment (**L463**)

Fiction > *Novels*
  Alien Fiction; Alternative History; Dystopian Fiction; High Concept; Literary; Post-Apocalyptic; Science Fiction; Social Commentary; Speculative; Utopian Fiction

The son of a mining engineer and a poet, I naturally ended up with a doctorate in quantum physics and a love of Science Fiction, each using, as they do, a little of the extraordinary to understand the everyday.

SF's capacity to disrupt and subvert dominant perspectives is central to why I fell for it, and I encourage submissions from writers from underrepresented backgrounds.

What I look for above all else is the visceral impact of a story which leaves you changed. I first found this, in distilled form, in 2000AD Future Shocks, particularly those by Alan Moore, and I appreciate anything holding a Black Mirror up to our world, and to ourselves.

L423 Mulcahy Sweeney Literary Agency

Literary Agency
United Kingdom

https://mmbcreative.com
https://mmbcreative.com/literary-agency/books/

Talent Agency: MMB Creative

ADULT
  Fiction > *Novels*

  Nonfiction > *Nonfiction Books*
    Biography; Cultural History; Current Affairs; Food and Drink; History; Memoir; Popular Culture

CHILDREN'S > **Fiction** > *Picture Books*

YOUNG ADULT > **Fiction** > *Novels*

Send: Query; Market info; Synopsis; Author bio; Writing sample
How to send: Email

London-based literary agency specialising in representing Irish and Korean authors (not exclusively). Email submissions as per our website guidelines only. Non-fiction, literary fiction, and certain fiction genres which vary during the year. Please refer to the submissions page on our website for more details.

Literary Agents: Edwina de Charnace (**L110**); Ivan Mulcahy (*L424*); Sallyanne Sweeney (*L562*)

L424 Ivan Mulcahy

Literary Agent
United Kingdom

Literary Agency: Mulcahy Sweeney Literary Agency (**L423**)

L425 Helen Mumby

Literary Agent
United Kingdom

https://thesohoagency.co.uk

Literary Agency: The Soho Agency

Scripts
  Film Scripts; *TV Scripts*; *Theatre Scripts*

Represents a wide range of talented and award-winning writers and directors working across theatre, film, TV and media and creatives including designers (set, costume, lighting, video and sound), choreographers, movement directors, composers, musical directors and librettists. Interested in artists who are great storytellers and creative collaborators. She loves working with a great variety of talent and to help nurture the careers of all her clients working across theatre, film and TV.

L426 Toby Mundy

Senior Agent; Vice President
United Kingdom

https://aevitascreative.com/agents/#agent-7413

Literary Agency: Aevitas Creative Management (ACM) UK (**L006**)

Fiction > *Novels*
  Literary; Thrillers

Nonfiction > *Nonfiction Books*
  Biography; Current Affairs; History; Memoir; Narrative Nonfiction; Popular Culture; Popular Science; Sport

Send: Query; Writing sample
How to send: Online submission system

Looking for gripping narrative nonfiction, and well written, mind-expanding works in the areas of history, biography, memoir, current affairs, sport, popular culture and popular science. Also represents a small number of thriller writers and literary novelists.

Authors: Tim Adams; James Aldred; James Ashton; Odafe Atogun; Philip Augar; Hannah Barnes; Rahul Bhatia; Chris Bickerton; Innes Bowen; Ruth Brandon; Marcus Bridgewater; Tobias Buck; Stephen Bush; Joshua Chaffin; James Crabtree; Graham Daseler; Jonathan Derbyshire; Michael Dine; John Dunn; Armand D'Angour; Iyad El-Baghdadi; Graham Farmelo; Eliza Filby; Danny Finkelstein; John Gapper; Michael Gibson; Julian Glover; David Goodhart; Samuel Graydon; Rachel Halliburton; Liam Halligan; Charles Handy; Andrew Hankinson; Jonathan Hillman; Katja Hoyer; Nicholas Humphrey; Gavin Jacobson; Tiffany Jenkins; Joanna Jolly; Andrew Keen; Ivan Krastev; Graham Lawton; Charles Leadbeater; Frances Leech; Mark Leonard; Ian Leslie; Oliver Letwin; John Lloyd; Isabel Losada; Andrew Lycett; Polly Mackenzie; Gary Madden; Mark Makepeace; Kenan Malik; Owen Matthews; Tom McTague; Anand Menon; Daniel Metcalfe; Chris Miller; Munira Mirza; Paul Morland; Geoff Mulgan; Clive Myrie; David Omand; Arkady Ostrovsky; Tomiwa Owolade; Nicolas Pelham; Leigh Phillips; Mary Poffenroth; Alice Rawsthorn; Assaad Razzouk; Richard Reeves; Tim Revell; Peter Ricketts; Jonathan Rowson; Donald Sassoon; Mark Sedgwick; Nigel Shadbolt; Oliver Shah; Raymond Tallis; Sudhir Thomas Vadaketh; Georgios Varouxakis;
Jeevan Vasagar; James Vogl; James Waddell; Owen Walker; Dan Wang; Justin Webb; Frances Weetman; Geoffrey Wheatcroft; James Williams; Keely Winstone; Christian Wolmar; Jon Yates; Emma Young

L427 Karen Murgolo

Literary Agent
United States

https://www.aevitascreative.com/agent/karen-murgolo
https://querymanager.com/query/KarenMurgoloQueries

Literary Agency: Aevitas

Nonfiction > *Nonfiction Books*
  Cookery; Health; Memoir; Narrative Nonfiction; Psychology; Science; Spirituality; Wellbeing

Closed to approaches.

Interested in authoritative health, wellness, science and psychology, spirituality, inspirational (or just really fun) memoirs; original cookbooks, and narratives that illuminate a compelling subject or start a conversation.

Authors: Allison M. Alford; Cathy Barrow; Whitney Casares; Judith Choate; Shannah Game; Chelsey Goodan; Jaime Knopman; Illyanna Maisonet; Lauretta Malloy; Bernadette Murphy; LeeAnet Noble; Brittany Piper; Mike Sapiro; Eric Tipler; Kevin Tracey; Cassandra Vieten; Brigid Washington; Stephanie Venn Watson; Veronica Webb

L428 Judith Murray

Literary Agent
United Kingdom

https://greeneheaton.co.uk
https://greeneheaton.co.uk/agents/judith-murray/

Literary Agency: Greene & Heaton Ltd (**L251**)

Fiction > *Novels*
  Crime; Fantasy; Historical Fiction; Literary Horror; Literary; Romance; Science Fiction; Thrillers

Nonfiction > *Nonfiction Books*
  Biography; History; Literary; Memoir

Send: Query; Synopsis; Full text
How to send: Email

I am looking for well-written genre fiction, including thrillers, crime, historical novels, clever literary horror (not too gory), science-fiction, fantasy, romance, literary fiction that is well written with great characters and a propulsive narrative drive; and literary non-fiction including history, biography and memoir.

Authors: Poppy Adams; Mark Alder; Lucy Atkins; Raffaella Barker; Laura Barnett; Mark Barrowcliffe; Charlotte Bauer; Darcey Bell;

Caroline Bond; Lynne Bryan; Elizabeth Buchan; Wren Burke; Helen Callaghan; Clare Cavenagh; Lucy Clarke; Emma Cook; Kate Davies; Lydia Davis; Sabine Durrant; Samantha Ellis; Helen Fisher; Susanna Forrest; Andrea Gillies; Paula Gosling; Victoria Gosling; Stella Grey; Joanna Hall; Maeve Haran; Belinda Harley; Phil Harrison; Julia Hollander; Helen Jones; Jacqueline Jones; Anjali Joseph; Vedashree Khambete-Sharma; Esme King; Rebecca Dinerstein Knight; M.D. Lachlan; Reif Larsen; Jardine Libaire; Rebecca Mackenzie; Ruth Mancini; Ben Marcus; Ian McGuire; Laura McHugh; Ben McPherson; Kamin Mohammadi; Gemma Morr; Emily Morris; Kate Morrison; Pippa Nixon; Jenny Offill; Temi Oh; Sean O'Connor; Helen Paris; Miranda Popkey; Jonathan Ray; Maria Realf; Karen Russell; Indyana Schneider; Polly Stewart; Jacqueline Sutherland; Sonya Vatomsky; Patricia Wastvedt; Sarah Waters; Melissa Wellham; Benjamin Wood; Susie Yang; Anne Youngson

L429 Nate Muscato

Literary Agent
New York
United States

https://aevitascreative.com/agents/

Literary Agency: Aevitas

Fiction > *Novels*
Fantasy; Literary; Science Fiction

Nonfiction > *Nonfiction Books*
Arts; Education; Politics; Popular Culture; Sociology; Technology

Send: Author bio; Outline; Pitch; Market info; Writing sample
How to send: Online submission system

Drawn to nonfiction that illuminates the past and present—from arts and pop culture to education, politics, sociology, and technology—and envisions more just and equitable futures. He is also interested in select genre fiction with literary trappings, sci-fi/fantasy stories that leap into new worlds yet reveal something radical about our own.

Authors: Pamela Anderson; Carl Sferrazza Anthony; Samara Bay; Elizabeth Beller; Joshua Bennett; Charles Blow; Patricia Bosworth; Holly Brubach; Kevin Burke; Jim Carrey; Kimberlé Crenshaw; Hugh Eakin; Rhonda Garelick; Arline T. Geronimus; John Giorno; Karl Taro Greenfeld; Bob Greifeld; Michael Grynbaum; David Hallberg; Linda Hirshman; Sam Huber; Charlayne Hunter-Gault; Elise Jordan; Henry Louis Gates Jr.; Amy Larocca; Melissa Auf der Maur; Andrew McCarthy; Adam Moss; Mary Norris; Mark Oppenheimer; Holly Peterson; Gerald Posner; Peter Rader; James Reginato; Karin Roffman; James Romm; Mark Ronson; Thaddeus Russell; Alexandra Sacks; Elizabeth Samet; Michael Schulman; Erich Schwartzel;

Elizabeth Shackelford; Colin Spoelman; Greg Steinmetz; Lili Taylor; Craig Unger; Dana Vachon; Darren Walker; Jesse Wegman; Genevieve West; Casey Wilson

L430 Juliet Mushens

Literary Agent
United Kingdom

submissions@mushens-entertainment.com

https://www.mushens-entertainment.com/juliet-mushens
https://twitter.com/mushenska

Literary Agency: Mushens Entertainment

Fiction > *Novels*
Book Club Fiction; Commercial Women's Fiction; Crime; Fantasy; High / Epic Fantasy; High Concept; Historical Fiction; Romance; Romantasy; Science Fiction; Suspense; Thrillers; Upmarket

Send: Query; Synopsis; Writing sample
How to send: Email

Looking for: adult fiction across the genres – from reading group, to SFF, and most things in between. She has had major success selling crime/thriller, historical fiction, fantasy and reading group fiction and is actively focusing on these areas currently. She is naturally drawn to books with high concept hooks, and page-turning plots. She is looking for novels which make for good book-club reads; historical fiction which centres characters often side lined by history; twisty and thrilling novels with heaps of suspense; fantasy with immersive worldbuilding and a great sense of pace to the story be it romantasy or epic; and commercial women's fiction/romance.

Author / Literary Agent: Sarah Hornsley (**L287**)

Authors: Claire Alexander; Aliya Ali-Afzal; Luke Allnutt; Marie-Claire Amuah; Sussie Anie; Krystle Zara Appiah; Stephen Aryan; Joanna Barnard; Jessica Bull; Jessie Burton; Mary Chamberlain; Katy Colins; Polly Crosby; Sarah Day; Abigail Dean; LM Dillsworth; Claire Douglas; Saara El-Arifi; Fiona Erskine; Maria Farrer; Robert Gold; Kate Gray; Jack Guinness; Francesca Haig; Stacey Halls; Lou Morgan / Maggie Harcourt; Elodie Harper; Sophie Haydock; Debbie Howells; Theresa Howes; Ali Imdad; Liz De Jager; Hannah Kaner; Katie Khan; L.R. Lam; Ali Land; Lia Louis; Katie Lowe; Chris MacDonald; Taran Matharu; Amy McCulloch; Elvin James Mensah; Jo Monroe; Hester Musson; Peter Newman; Louise O'Neill; Richard Osman; James Oswald; Buki Papillon; Nell Pattison; Laura Purcell; Andrew Reid; Laure Van Rensburg; Jennifer Saint; Vanessa Savage; Boris Starling; Andrea Stewart; Susan Stokes-Chapman; Sonia Tagliareni; Rob Temple; Liz Tipping; Rajasree Variyar; Sonia Velton; Gray Williams; Hattie Williams; Jen Williams; Nick Clark Windo; Tom Winter

L431 Maria Napolitano

Literary Agent; Foreign Rights Manager
United States

maria@ktliterary.com

https://www.maria-regina.com
https://ktliterary.com/agents

Literary Agency: KT Literary (**L345**)

Fiction > *Novels*
Book Club Fiction; Commercial; High Concept; Romantic Comedy; Speculative; Thrillers; Upmarket

Closed to approaches.

Represents a broad range of fiction, from commercial rom-coms to radical speculative fiction, subversive thrillers, and upmarket book club fiction. She is drawn to character-driven stories, unusual perspectives, genre-bending works, and supremely pitchable high concepts.

L432 The Narrow Road Company

Literary Agency
First floor, The Dutch House, 307–308 High Holborn, London, WC1V 7LL
United Kingdom
Tel: +44 (0) 20 7831 4450

creatives@narrowroad.co.uk
agents@narrowroad.co.uk

https://narrowroad.co.uk
https://x.com/thenarrowroadco
https://www.instagram.com/narrowroadagency/

Scripts
Film Scripts: General
Radio Scripts: General
TV Scripts: General
Theatre Scripts: Theatre

Send: Query
How to send: Email

Based in West London, represents actors and creatives, including writers and screenwriters. Creatives seeking representation should send query by email. Response not guaranteed due to volume of applications.

Authors: Joe Graham; Richard Groves; Lincoln Hudson; Simon Macallum

Literary Agents: Amy Ireson; Dan Ireson; James Ireson; Richard Ireson; Rozzy Lloyd; Adam Mendlesohn; Sarah Veecock

L433 Abigail Nathan

Literary Agent
Sydney
Australia

https://alexadsett.com.au/literary-agency/
https://querymanager.com/query/AbigailNathanQueries

Literary Agency: Alex Adsett Literary

ADULT > **Fiction** > *Novels*
Commercial; Cozy Fantasy; Cozy Mysteries; Crime; Fantasy; Historical Romance; Mystery; Romance; Romantasy; Romantic Comedy; Romantic Mystery; Science Fiction; Thrillers

CHILDREN'S > **Fiction** > *Middle Grade*

YOUNG ADULT > **Fiction** > *Novels*

Closed to approaches.

Looking for engaging plots and convincing characters. Something that will keep her turning the pages and that will stay with her after she's finished reading. There are some rules and conventions it pays to follow, but something a bit weird or slightly (or very) unexpected will pique her interest, and characters that touch a nerve or worlds that make us question the status quo are always welcome. Above all, she's looking for great stories, told well – fiction in general and all things genre: sci-fi, fantasy, paranormal, horror, crime, thriller, romance (and any combination of those), for adult, YA or middle grade.

L434 Rachel Neely
Literary Agent
United Kingdom

submissions@mushens-entertainment.com

https://www.mushens-entertainment.com/rachel-neely

Literary Agency: Mushens Entertainment

Fiction > *Novels*
Book Club Fiction; Crime; Fantasy; Gothic; High Concept; Horror; Romance; Thrillers

Send: Query; Synopsis; Writing sample
How to send: Email

Rachel is looking for: Crime, thrillers, fantasy, dark academia, horror, tragic love stories and high-concept book club fiction. Would love to see: novels about cults, novels about cannibalism, horror, a commercial locked-room thriller, compelling dark academia, a tragic love story that will make me ugly cry, and anything that has an outsider trying to break into the world of the privileged and morally bankrupt.

Authors: Rhiannon Barnsley; Mimi Deb; Rachel Devine; Kate Dylan; Claire Frances; Faith Gladwin; Sue Hincenbergs; Carmella Lowkis; Emma Lowther; Elle Machray; Fiona McPhillips; Emily Slapper; Teresa Jacinta Tomás; Charlotte Wightwick

L435 Nelson Literary Agency, LLC
Literary Agency
1732 Wazee Street, Suite 207, Denver, CO 80202
United States
Tel: +1 (303) 292-2805

info@nelsonagency.com

https://nelsonagency.com

Professional Body: Association of American Literary Agents (AALA)

ADULT > **Fiction** > *Novels*

CHILDREN'S > **Fiction**
Middle Grade; *Picture Books*

YOUNG ADULT > **Fiction** > *Novels*

Send: Query; Author bio; Writing sample
How to send: Query Tracker
How not to send: Post; Phone

View individual agent interests and submit to one agent only.

Authors: Brooke Abrams; Kate Baer; Gina Banks; L. Biehler; Jillian Boehme; Ali Brady; Lina Chern; Kristen Ciccarelli; Jessi Cole; Laura Danger; Lisa Duffy; Doug Engstrom; Reese Eschmann; Shana Galen; John Galligan; Florence Gonsalves; Jill Grunenwald; Alison Hammer; Sarah Zachrich Jeng; Becca Jones; Chloe Jory; Ausma Zehanat Khan; Sierra Kincade; Karen Koh; Gillian Libby; Maryann Jacob Macias; Jonathan Messinger; Meghan Scott Molin; Katrina Monroe; Vanessa Montalban; Rosaria Munda; Jennifer Nissley; Lynette Noni; James Persichetti; Celesta Rimington; Laura Brooke Robson; Lyndsay Rush; Ehsaneh Sadr; Erinn Salge; Jeff Seymour; Kristen Simmons; Lisa Springer; Jennifer Springsteen; Stacy Stokes; Joy Sullivan; Ben Tanzer; Jordyn Taylor; Vikki VanSickle; Kathleen West

Literary Agents: Joanna MacKenzie (**L382**); Kristin Nelson (**L436**)

L436 Kristin Nelson
Literary Agent
United States

https://nelsonagency.com/kristin-nelson/
https://twitter.com/agentkristinNLA
https://querymanager.com/query/1350

Literary Agency: Nelson Literary Agency, LLC (**L435**)
Professional Body: Association of American Literary Agents (AALA)

ADULT > **Fiction** > *Novels*
Commercial; Fantasy; High Concept; Historical Fiction; Literary; Science Fiction; Speculative; Thrillers

YOUNG ADULT > **Fiction** > *Novels*

Closed to approaches.

My goal as an agent is simple: I want every client of mine to make a living solely from writing and 90% of my authors do without help from any other source of income.

L437 Patricia Nelson
Literary Agent
United States

https://www.lookingglasslit.com
https://www.lookingglasslit.com/patricia-nelson
https://querytracker.net/query/querypatricia

Literary Agency: Looking Glass Literary & Media Management (**L370**)

ADULT > **Fiction** > *Novels*
Book Club Fiction; Commercial Women's Fiction; Dark; Horror; Mystery; Romantic Comedy; Speculative; Suspense; Upmarket

CHILDREN'S > **Fiction** > *Middle Grade*

YOUNG ADULT > **Fiction** > *Novels*

How to send: Query Tracker

Represents young adult and middle grade fiction in all genres, adult book club/upmarket fiction (including upmarket fiction with speculative and horror elements), and the whole spectrum of commercial women's fiction – everything from lighter beach reads and romcoms to darker stories with a mystery or suspense thread. Across the board, she looks for stories that hook her with a unique plot, fantastic writing, and complex characters that jump off the page. She enjoys working closely with both debut and established authors to build successful long-term careers.

L438 Mariah Nichols
Literary Agent
United States

https://www.mariahlovesliterary.com
https://www.d4eoliteraryagency.com/p/mariah-nichols.html
https://twitter.com/litagentmariah

Literary Agency: D4EO Literary Agency

ADULT

Fiction > *Novels*
Contemporary Romance; Psychological Thrillers; Romantic Comedy; Women's Fiction

Nonfiction > *Nonfiction Books*
Cookery; Diversity; How To; Lifestyle; Mental Health; Romance; Self Help

YOUNG ADULT > **Fiction** > *Novels*
Contemporary Romance; Science Fiction; Supernatural / Paranormal Romance; Thrillers

Closed to approaches.

Interested in upmarket and commercial adult fiction focusing on women's fiction, psychological thrillers, and contemporary romance/rom-coms, along with representing young adult fiction with genres including science fiction, paranormal romance, thrillers, and contemporary romance. She is also wanting to represent nonfiction in categories such as cookbooks, memoirs, self-help, lifestyle, and how-to. Stories that showcase diversity and highlight mental health or special needs is something that she would especially like to see.

L439 Erin Niumata
Literary Agent; Senior Vice President
United States
Tel: +1 (212) 400-1494

erin@foliolit.com

https://www.foliolit.com/agents-1/erin-niumata
https://www.instagram.com/ecniumata/?hl=en
https://twitter.com/ecniumata?ref_src=twsrc%5Egoogle%7Ctwcamp%5Eserp%7Ctwgr%5Eauthor

Literary Agency: Folio Literary Management, LLC (**L207**)

Fiction > *Novels*
  Book Club Fiction; Commercial Women's Fiction; Commercial; Historical Fiction; Mystery; Romance; Romantic Comedy; Thrillers; Women's Fiction

Nonfiction > *Nonfiction Books*
  Commercial; Cookery; Memoir; Narrative Nonfiction; Prescriptive Nonfiction

Send: Query; Synopsis; Writing sample
How to send: In the body of an email

Looking for commercial nonfiction, from prescriptive and practical to narrative and memoir, as well as a select list of fiction including mysteries, rom-coms, and commercial women's fiction.

L440 Daniel Niv
Associate Agent
United States

Daniel@Olswangerliterary.com

https://www.danielniv.com
https://www.olswanger.com
https://querytracker.net/query/3561/
https://x.com/_DanielNiv

Literary Agency: Olswanger Literary LLC (**L449**)

ADULT
  Fiction > *Novels*
    Dark Academia; Family Saga; Fantasy; Gothic; Historical Fiction; Historical Romance; Magical Realism; Romance; Romantasy; Supernatural / Paranormal Romance

  Nonfiction > *Nonfiction Books*
    History; Spirituality

NEW ADULT > **Fiction** > *Novels*

Does not want:

  Nonfiction > *Nonfiction Books*: Religion

How to send: Query Tracker

Overall, I love stories with a compelling hook, an emphasis on character development, high stakes, and plot twists. I enjoy reading stories with diverse voices from all backgrounds. I am always intrigued by historical or unique settings! The most important thing for me when reading a manuscript is to connect to the protagonist. I often connect to vulnerable protagonists who discover their strengths. I am also very captivated by morally gray or flawed characters. In romance, my favorite tropes are slow-burn, banter, forced proximity, enemies to lovers, and forbidden love.

L441 Laura Nolan
Literary Agent; Senior Partner
United States

https://aevitascreative.com/agents/

Literary Agency: Aevitas
Professional Body: Association of American Literary Agents (AALA)

Nonfiction > *Nonfiction Books*
  Celebrity; Culture; Investigative Journalism; Medicine; Music; Performing Arts; Psychology; Sub-Culture

Send: Query; Writing sample
How to send: Online submission system

Represents investigative journalists, thought leaders, doctors, psychologists, musicians, and celebrities who inspire, entertain, educate and are striving to upend the culture. Seeks clients who are asking the "big" questions, exploring fascinating sub-cultures, and are paradigm-shifters in their fields, as well as performing artists who are successful in one medium but whose talents and passion translate into narrative.

Authors: Aaron Ayscough; Michael Azerrad; Sara Bareilles; Hunter Biden; Jill Blakeway; Kenneth Bock; Mariann Edgar Budde; Gesine Bullock-Prado; David Burtka; Scott Carney; Ratha Chaupoly; Charles R. Cross; Ben Daitz; Zayd Ayers Dohrn; Dagmara Dominczyk; Madeleine Dore; Charlotte Druckman; Aria Finger; John Fogerty; Ben Folds; Holly George-Warren; Rhiannon Giddens; Danny Goldberg; Andrea Gutiérrez-Glik; Neil Patrick Harris; Josiah Hesse; Bonnie J. Kaplan; Angela Jia Kim; Laura Krantz; Carson Kressley; Leah Lagos; Christine Lahti; Jennifer Lapidus; Alan Light; Anita Lo; Danica McKellar; Sara C. Mednick; Allison Moorer; Mandy Morris; Meagan B Murphy; Einat Nathan; Sabina Nawaz; Oliver Niño; David Peisner; Wendell Pierce; Matt Pinfield; Nicole Ponseca; Elizabeth Poynor; Eric Prum; National Public Radio; Julia J. Rucklidge; Anneli Rufus; Erika Schickel; Joseph Shuldiner; Rachel Signer; Julie Smolyansky; Charisma Sydnor; Gayla Trail; Miguel Trinidad; Nia Vardalos; Lynx Vilden; Martha Wainwright; Tionne Watkins; Elettra Wiedemann; Josh Williams; Vern Yip; Kristal Zook; Alan Zweibel

L442 Northbank Talent Management
Literary Agency
United Kingdom
Tel: +44 (0) 20 3973 0836

info@northbanktalent.com
fiction@northbanktalent.com
nonfiction@northbanktalent.com
childrens@northbanktalent.com

https://www.northbanktalent.com
https://twitter.com/NorthbankTalent
https://www.facebook.com/northbanktalent/
https://www.instagram.com/northbanktalent
https://www.linkedin.com/company/northbank-talent-management/
https://www.youtube.com/channel/UCKEAHOg6Y2G3NOy146k9y4A?view_as=subscriber

Professional Body: The Association of Authors' Agents (AAA)

ADULT
  Fiction > *Novels*
  Nonfiction > *Nonfiction Books*

YOUNG ADULT > **Fiction** > *Novels*

Send: Query; Synopsis; Writing sample
How to send: Email

Literary and talent agency based in central London. Actively seeking new clients. Send query by email with synopsis and first three chapters as Word or Open Document attachments to appropriate email address.

L443 Renee Nyen
Literary Agent
United States

Literary Agency: KT Literary (**L345**)

Closed to approaches.

L444 Lee O'Brien
Literary Agent
United States

leesubmissions@lookingglasslit.com

https://www.lookingglasslit.com/lee-obrien
https://twitter.com/leepaigeobrien
https://www.leepaigeobrien.com/

Literary Agency: Looking Glass Literary & Media Management (**L370**)

ADULT > **Fiction** > *Novels*
  Commercial; Fantasy; High Concept; LGBTQIA; Romantic Comedy; Thrillers

CHILDREN'S > **Fiction** > *Novels*
  Commercial; Fantasy; High Concept; LGBTQIA; Romantic Comedy; Thrillers

YOUNG ADULT > **Fiction** > *Novels*
  Commercial; Fantasy; High Concept; LGBTQIA; Romantic Comedy; Thrillers

Send: Query; Writing sample
How to send: Email

Focuses on MG, YA, and Adult, and he's interested in a range of genres, from fantasy to thrillers to romcoms. Within the genres he represents, he's especially looking for stories with a strong commercial hook or a compelling high-concept, and he loves anything full of twists and turns, an unforgettable cast of characters, or a mystery he can't put down. He's actively seeking diverse books and marginalized voices, and has a particular love for anything queer.

L445 Niamh O'Grady
Literary Agent
United Kingdom

https://www.thesohoagency.co.uk/agent/niamh-ogrady

Literary Agency: The Soho Agency

Fiction > *Novels*
   Book Club Fiction; Comedy / Humour; Family; Literary; Relationships

Nonfiction > *Nonfiction Books*
   Comedy / Humour; Narrative Nonfiction

Send: Query; Synopsis; Writing sample
How to send: Email attachment

Actively looking for accessible literary and reading-group fiction, and narrative non-fiction. She is drawn to books with heart and humour, thought-provoking writing and distinctive, compelling voices. She particularly loves novels that explore family and relationships and wants to read stories that leave an emotional impact, with characters that stay with her long after the final page. She is keen to find new Irish and Northern writing talent.

L446 Molly O'Neill
Literary Agent
United States

submissions@rootliterary.com

https://www.rootliterary.com/agents
https://querymanager.com/query/mollyoneillbooks
https://www.publishersmarketplace.com/members/mollyoneillagent/
https://twitter.com/molly_oneill

Literary Agency: Root Literary (**L503**)

ADULT > **Nonfiction** > *Nonfiction Books*
   Creativity; Culture; Family; Friends; Narrative Nonfiction

CHILDREN'S > **Fiction** > *Middle Grade*
   General, and in particular: Comedy / Humour; Fabulism; Magical Realism

YOUNG ADULT > **Fiction** > *Novels*

Closed to approaches.

If I can visualize exactly how to form a web of connections around a book and its creator while I'm reading an early draft, then it's a fantastic signal that I also know how to help that author or artist build their way into a meaningful, and potentially lucrative, career.

L447 Amy O'Shea
Junior Agent
United Kingdom

submissions@grahammawchristie.com

https://www.grahammawchristie.com
https://www.grahammawchristie.com/about

Literary Agency: Graham Maw Christie Literary Agency (**L246**)

Fiction > *Novels*
   Crime; Speculative

Nonfiction > *Nonfiction Books*
   Comedy / Humour; Crime; History; Lifestyle; Memoir; Prescriptive Nonfiction

Interested in a wide variety of non-fiction, from prescriptions for thinking and living better by experts in their field, to humour, history, and memoir whereby the author immerses the reader in a lived experience. In an ever-changing landscape, she is looking for books that bring fresh, practical and accessible solutions to their audience – anything that can teach us more about who we are and the world we share. She is particularly interested in receiving true crime submissions from experts, journalists and historians that are both meticulously researched and compellingly written. She is also building a select list of crime fiction and speculative fiction.

L448 Colleen Oefelein
Literary Agent
United States

Literary Agency: MacGregor & Luedeke (**L380**)

L449 Olswanger Literary LLC
Literary Agency
United States

https://www.olswanger.com

Associate Agents: Jared Johnson (**L303**); Yael Levy (**L362**); Daniel Niv (**L440**); Annie Romano (**L502**)

Literary Agents: Kimberly Fernando (**L198**); Anna Olswanger (**L450**); Madison Potter (**L481**)

L450 Anna Olswanger
Literary Agent
United States

anna@olswangerliterary.com

https://www.olswanger.com
https://aalitagents.org/author/olswanger/
https://twitter.com/annaolswanger
https://www.facebook.com/AnnaOlswanger
https://www.instagram.com/annaolswanger
https://www.pinterest.com/olswanger/anna-olswanger-literary-agent/
https://www.linkedin.com/in/olswanger

Literary Agency: Olswanger Literary LLC (**L449**)
Professional Body: Association of American Literary Agents (AALA)

CHILDREN'S > **Fiction**
   Graphic Novels; Picture Books

How to send: Email

Has been an agent since 2005. Represents a wide variety of genres but is currently focused on illustrated books (picture books and graphic novels).

L451 Originate Literary Agency
Literary Agency
United Kingdom

https://twitter.com/OriginateLit
https://linktr.ee/nataliejerome

Professional Body: The Association of Authors' Agents (AAA)

L452 Kristin Ostby
Literary Agent
United States

https://www.greenhouseliterary.com/the-team/kristin-ostby/
https://querymanager.com/query/kristinostby

Literary Agency: The Greenhouse Literary Agency

ADULT > **Fiction** > *Novels*
   Mystery; Upmarket

CHILDREN'S
   Fiction
      Chapter Books: Comedy / Humour
      Middle Grade: Adventure; Comedy / Humour; Contemporary; Cozy Mysteries; Friends; Historical Fiction; Light Fantasy; Mystery; Supernatural / Paranormal; Thrillers
   Poetry > *Novels in Verse*

YOUNG ADULT > **Fiction** > *Novels*
   Comedy / Humour; Contemporary; Cozy Mysteries; Friends; Historical Fiction; Historical Romance; Light Fantasy; Mystery; Romance; Speculative Romance; Supernatural / Paranormal; Thrillers

Closed to approaches.

Represents authors of middle grade and young adult fiction, as well as picture book author/illustrators. She is primarily seeking voice- and character-driven contemporary middle-grade and young adult fiction, with a focus on BIPOC creators. Not currently accepting picture book manuscripts, graphic novel scripts, issue books, or nonfiction. No manuscripts over 95,000 words.

L453 Saribel Pages

Literary Agent
United States

saribel@galltzacker.com

https://www.galltzacker.com
https://www.galltzacker.com/submissions.html
https://querymanager.com/query/2945
https://www.manuscriptwishlist.com/mswl-post/saribel-pages/

Literary Agency: Gallt & Zacker Literary Agency

CHILDREN'S > *Fiction*
  Graphic Novels: Adventure; Contemporary; Fantasy; Horror; Mystery; Speculative
  Picture Books: General

Closed to approaches.

Only seeking to represent picture books and graphic novels. Interested in contemporary, adventure, fantasy, speculative, horror, and mysteries. Accepts queries from the 1st to 7th of each month.

L454 Paradigm Talent and Literary Agency

Literary Agency
810 Seventh Avenue, Suite 205, New York, NY 10019
United States
Tel: +1 (212) 897-6400
Fax: +1 (310) 288-2000

books@paradigmagency.com

https://www.paradigmagency.com

Fiction > *Novels*

Nonfiction > *Nonfiction Books*

Scripts
  Film Scripts; *TV Scripts*; *Theatre Scripts*

Send: Query; Writing sample
How to send: In the body of an email

Talent and literary agency with offices in Los Angeles, New York, and London. Represents books in all areas and genres, as well as scriptwriters for film, TV, and theatre.

L455 Elana Roth Parker

Literary Agent
United States

http://www.ldlainc.com/submissions/
http://www.manuscriptwishlist.com/mswl-post/elana-roth-parker/
https://querymanager.com/query/queryelana
http://aaronline.org/Sys/PublicProfile/43775067/417813

Literary Agency: Laura Dail Literary Agency
Professional Body: Association of American Literary Agents (AALA)

ADULT > Fiction > *Novels*
  Commercial; Contemporary; Mystery; Romance; Romantic Comedy; Thrillers; Upmarket Women's Fiction

CHILDREN'S > Fiction > *Middle Grade*
  Adventure; Comedy / Humour; High / Epic Fantasy; High Concept

YOUNG ADULT > Fiction > *Novels*
  Adventure; Comedy / Humour; Commercial; High Concept; Romance

Closed to approaches.

Handles middle grade and young adult fiction. Closed to picture book submissions.

L456 Marina de Pass

Literary Agent
United Kingdom

https://www.thesohoagency.co.uk/agent/marina-de-pass
https://twitter.com/marinadepass

Literary Agency: The Soho Agency

ADULT
  Fiction > *Novels*
    General, and in particular: Animals; Book Club Fiction; Commercial; Contemporary; Crime; Dark Academia; Dogs; Family Saga; Folklore, Myths, and Legends; Historical Fiction; Literary; Police Procedural; Speculative; Spy Thrillers; Thrillers; Upmarket; Vikings Fiction

  Nonfiction > *Nonfiction Books*: Narrative Nonfiction

YOUNG ADULT > Fiction > *Novels*
  Mystery; Thrillers

Does not want:

ADULT > Fiction > *Novels*: Science Fiction

YOUNG ADULT > Fiction > *Novels*: Science Fiction

Send: Query; Synopsis; Writing sample
How to send: Email attachment

Looking for big stories, compelling writing and unforgettable characters. She reads across all genres in adult and YA fiction, except for straight sci-fi, and gravitates towards stories told through a female lens.

L457 David Patterson

Literary Agent
United States

dpquery@skagency.com

https://www.skagency.com
https://www.skagency.com/team

Literary Agency: Stuart Krichevsky Literary Agency, Inc. (**L556**)

Fiction > *Novels*: Literary

Nonfiction > *Nonfiction Books*

Send: Query; Writing sample; Proposal
How to send: In the body of an email

Represents a wide variety of narrative and idea-driven nonfiction and literary fiction, with an emphasis on journalists, public figures, scholars, and performers.

L458 Emma Patterson

Literary Agent
United States

epatterson@bromasite.com

Literary Agency: Brandt & Hochman Literary Agents, Inc.
Professional Body: Association of American Literary Agents (AALA)

Fiction > *Novels*
  Historical Fiction; Literary; Upmarket

Nonfiction > *Nonfiction Books*
  Investigative Journalism; Memoir; Narrative Nonfiction; Popular History

Send: Query
How to send: Email

Represents fiction ranging from dark, literary novels to historical and upmarket fiction; narrative non-fiction that includes memoir, investigative journalism, and popular history; and select children's projects. She is looking for fresh, lyrical, and voice-driven writing, suspenseful plots, emotional narratives, transporting settings, and unforgettable characters. Books that grapple with the dynamics of relationships (of all kinds, but especially from a female perspective), have a grounded speculative bent, or explore the current cultural landscape are all of perennial interest. Query by email only.

L459 Paul S. Levine Literary Agency

Literary Agency
1054 Superba Avenue, Venice, CA 90291-3940
United States
Tel: +1 (310) 450-6711
Fax: +1 (310) 450-0181

paul@paulslevinelit.com

https://paulslevinelit.com

ADULT
  Fiction
    Graphic Novels; *Novels*
  Nonfiction > *Nonfiction Books*

CHILDREN'S
  Fiction
    Graphic Novels; *Novels*
  Nonfiction > *Nonfiction Books*

YOUNG ADULT
  Fiction
    Graphic Novels; *Novels*
  Nonfiction > *Nonfiction Books*

Send: Query
How to send: Email; Post
How not to send: Phone

Send query by email preferably, or by post with SASE. No phone calls.

Literary Agents: Loren R. Grossman; Paul S. Levine

L460 Kay Peddle
Literary Agent
United Kingdom

submissions@colwillandpeddle.com

https://www.colwillandpeddle.com/about

Literary Agency: Colwill & Peddle

Nonfiction > *Nonfiction Books*
  Cookery; Current Affairs; Food; History; Journalism; Literary Memoir; Narrative Nonfiction; Nature; Politics; Popular Science; Social Justice; Travel

Send: Query; Proposal; Author bio; Market info; Writing sample; Outline; Pitch
How to send: Word file email attachment

Looking for books that spark discussion, that have the potential to change opinions and reveal hidden aspects of a familiar story. Interested in narrative nonfiction; literary memoir; cookery and food writing; travel writing; nature writing; journalism with a social justice angle; politics; current affairs; history and popular science.

L461 Imogen Pelham
Literary Agent
United Kingdom

imogen@marjacq.com

https://www.marjacq.com
https://www.marjacq.com/imogen-pelham.html

Literary Agency: Marjacq Scripts Ltd

Fiction > *Novels*
  Literary Thrillers; Literary; Upmarket; Women's Fiction

Nonfiction > *Nonfiction Books*
  General, and in particular: Arts; Cookery; Cultural Criticism; History; Investigative Journalism; Memoir; Psychology; Science; Social Issues

How to send: Email

Represents non-fiction which looks at serious subjects in innovative ways, and literary and upmarket fiction. In non-fiction, her list covers history, science, memoir, cookery, cultural criticism, social issues, and psychology. She is particularly interested in identity, the arts, and investigative journalism. She is drawn to books which have interesting takes on the everyday, which shine a light on an unexplored aspect of history or ourselves, and which encourage us to think more deeply about our place in the world. In fiction, she is looking for outstanding writing which shines a light on humanity, an unforgettable cast of characters, literary thrillers, and smart women's fiction.

Authors: Antonia Bolingbroke-Kent; Gabriella Braun; Kassia St Clair; Marie Le Conte; Hattie Crisell; Jimi Famurewa; Yara Rodrigues Fowler; Harry Gallon; Annie Garthwaite; Olivia Glazebrook; Sally Howard; Jo Jakeman; Brydie Lee-Kennedy; Emily Mayhew; Chris McQueer; Marianne Moore; Alya Mooro; Laura Mucha; Sam Parker; Emily Phillips; Angela Readman; Carl Shuker; Max Sydney Smith; Philippa Snow; David Whelan; Kylie Whitehead

L462 Kim Perel
Literary Agent
United States

https://www.highlineliterary.com/agent-kim

Literary Agency: High Line Literary Collective (**L279**)

Closed to approaches.

L463 Perez Literary & Entertainment
Literary Agency
49 Greek Street, London, W1D 4EG
United Kingdom
Tel: +44 (0) 20 7193 4792

assist@perezliterary.com

https://www.perezliterary.com
http://querymanager.com/KristinaPerez
https://www.instagram.com/perezliterary/
https://twitter.com/perez_literary
https://www.linkedin.com/company/perezliterary/
https://www.facebook.com/perezliterary

Professional Body: The Association of Authors' Agents (AAA)

ADULT
  Fiction > *Novels*
    Book Club Fiction; Commercial; Crime; Thrillers; Upmarket

  Nonfiction > *Nonfiction Books*
    Biography; Cultural History; Current Affairs; Feminism; Popular Science

YOUNG ADULT > **Fiction** > *Novels*
  Fantasy; Romance

Send: Query; Writing sample
How to send: Query Tracker
How not to send: Email

A full-service agency dedicated to storytelling in all of its forms. We believe in the power of words to open minds and change lives. In today's fast moving marketplace, we are on the constant lookout for opportunities in both traditional and non-traditional media. We are committed to empowering our clients and helping them to formulate the best strategies to achieve their storytelling goals.

Associate Agent: Nina Leon (**L360**)

Authors: Alexia Casale; Shauna Clinning; Sharon Emmerichs; Marina Evans; Jennifer Wolf Kam; Erin Rose Kim; S. K. Meekings; Kim Mykura; Troy Tassier; Vincent Tirado; Amy Trueblood; Khadijah VanBrakle; Johanna van Veen; Stephen Vines; Cristin Williams; Josh Winning; Kelly deVos

Junior Agent: Isabel Lineberry (**L367**)

Literary Agent: Jack Mozley (**L422**)

Literary Agent / Managing Director: Kristina Perez (**L464**)

L464 Kristina Perez
Literary Agent; Managing Director
United Kingdom

https://www.perezliterary.com/about-us/the-team/
http://querymanager.com/KristinaPerez
https://twitter.com/kperezagent

Literary Agency: Perez Literary & Entertainment (**L463**)

ADULT
  Fiction > *Novels*
    Book Club Fiction; Commercial; Crime; Thrillers; Upmarket

  Nonfiction > *Nonfiction Books*
    Biography; Cultural History; Current Affairs; Feminism; Popular Science

YOUNG ADULT > **Fiction** > *Novels*
  Fantasy; Romance

Send: Query; Writing sample
How to send: Query Tracker

Being both an agent and an author allows her to fully guide her clients through every step of the publishing process. She loves launching debut authors' careers as well as working with mid-career authors looking for new challenges. She sees each client relationship as a true partnership in which they develop the right strategy for a client's career together. Author care is paramount and she prides herself on using her multifaceted understanding of the industry to help her clients achieve their goals. She is eager to work with writers from around the globe.

Authors: Alexia Casale; Shauna Clinning; Sharon Emmerichs; Marina Evans; Jennifer Wolf Kam; Erin Rose Kim; S. K. Meekings; Kim Mykura; Martin Purbrick; Troy Tassier; Vincent Tirado; Amy Trueblood; Amy True / Amy Trueblood; Khadija L. VanBrakle; Khadijah VanBrakle; Johanna van Veen; Stephen Vines; Cristin Williams; Josh Winning; Kelly deVos

L465 Martha Perotto-Wills
Associate Agent
United Kingdom

http://www.thebentagency.com/martha-perotto-wills
https://twitter.com/martha_again

Literary Agency: The Bent Agency (UK) (**L051**)

ADULT
   Fiction > *Novels*
      Fantasy; Horror; Literary; Science Fiction

   Nonfiction > *Nonfiction Books*

YOUNG ADULT > **Fiction** > *Novels*

Closed to approaches.

Representing authors of adult literary fiction and sci-fi/fantasy/horror, as well as select adult non-fiction and young adult fiction. Particularly enjoys authorial confidence; unexpected, singular narrative voices; good, stylish sentences; humour/wit; knotty interpersonal relationships; and transportive writing that immerse the reader in a fully-formed world, whether fantastical, geographical, or emotional.

L466 Perry Literary
Literary Agency
United States

jperry@perryliterary.com
https://www.perryliterary.com

Nonfiction > *Nonfiction Books*
   Business; Cookery; Crime; Journalism; Memoir; Narrative Nonfiction; Parenting; Popular Culture; Psychology; Science; Self Help; Sociology; Sport; Technology

Send: Query; Writing sample
How to send: In the body of an email

Send query by email with first ten pages in the body of the email (or full manuscript for picture books). No attachments. See website for full guidelines.

Literary Agent: Joseph Perry

L467 Carrie Pestritto
Literary Agent
United States

http://www.ldlainc.com/about
http://aaronline.org/Sys/PublicProfile/53765008/417813
http://twitter.com/literarycarrie
https://literarycarrie.wixsite.com/blog
http://www.manuscriptwishlist.com/mswl-post/carrie-pestritto/

Literary Agency: Laura Dail Literary Agency
Professional Body: Association of American Literary Agents (AALA)

ADULT
   Fiction > *Novels*
      Chick Lit; Commercial; Cozy Mysteries; Historical Fiction; Literary; Mystery; Romance; Thrillers; Upmarket Women's Fiction

   Nonfiction > *Nonfiction Books*
      Biography; Memoir; Narrative Nonfiction

CHILDREN'S > **Fiction** > *Middle Grade*
   Commercial; High Concept

YOUNG ADULT > **Fiction** > *Novels*
   Contemporary; Fantasy; Historical Fiction; Horror; Mystery; Thrillers

Closed to approaches.

Loves the thrill of finding new authors with strong, unique voices and working closely with her clients. Always strives to help create books that will introduce readers to new worlds and is drawn in by relatable characters, meticulous world-building, and unusual, compelling premises.

L468 PEW Literary
Literary Agency
46 Lexington Street, London, W1F 0LP
United Kingdom
Tel: +44 (0) 20 7734 4464

submissions@pewliterary.com
https://www.pewliterary.com

Professional Body: The Association of Authors' Agents (AAA)

Fiction > *Novels*
   General, and in particular: Crime; Literary; Thrillers

Nonfiction > *Nonfiction Books*

Send: Query; Synopsis; Writing sample; Author bio; Proposal; Market info; Outline
How to send: Email; Post

Send query by post or by email, with synopsis and first three chapters (or fifty pages) (fiction); or proposal (nonfiction). If submitting by email, send material in Word or PDF attachment. If submitting by post, do not include SAE as material will be recycled once read. Include email address for response. Aims to respond within six weeks.

Literary Agent: Patrick Walsh

L469 Rubin Pfeffer
Literary Agent
United States

Literary Agencies: Rubin Pfeffer Content, LLC (**L509**); Aevitas

Authors: Micha Archer; Elana K. Arnold; Patricia MacLachlan; Kara Storti; Ellen Surrey; Ellen Tarlow; Jing Jing Tsong; Eric Velasquez; Jesse Joshua Watson; Richard Jesse Watson; Carole Boston Weatherford; Jeffery Boston Weatherford; Annie Won; Brian Won; Helen Yoon

L470 Beth Phelan
Literary Agent
United States

bethqueries@galltzacker.com
beth@galltzacker.com

https://www.galltzacker.com/submissions.html
https://querymanager.com/query/querybeth

Literary Agency: Gallt & Zacker Literary Agency

CHILDREN'S
   Fiction > *Middle Grade*
      Contemporary; Fantasy

   Nonfiction > *Middle Grade*

YOUNG ADULT
   Fiction > *Novels*
      Contemporary; Fantasy

   Nonfiction > *Nonfiction Books*

Closed to approaches.

Gravitates toward stories and characters that inspire, and anything with a touch of humor and the bittersweet. She is very interested in powerful and unique storytelling, offbeat contemporary fiction, immersive fantasy, and profoundly resonant voices. Open to queries from the 1st to the 7th of every month.

L471 Ariana Philips
Literary Agent
United States

https://www.jvnla.com/our-team.php
https://twitter.com/ArianaPhilips

Literary Agency: The Jean V. Naggar Literary Agency (**L299**)

ADULT
   Fiction > *Novels*
      Commercial; Family Saga; Historical Fiction; Literary; Romantic Comedy; Upmarket Women's Fiction

   Nonfiction
      Gift Books: General
      Illustrated Books: General
      Nonfiction Books: Comedy / Humour; Cookery; Crime; Food; Lifestyle; Literary Memoir; Narrative Nonfiction; Popular Culture; Popular History; Prescriptive Nonfiction; Science; Social Issues; Sport; Travel

CHILDREN'S > **Fiction** > *Middle Grade*
   Adventure; Magic; Mystery

YOUNG ADULT > **Fiction** > *Novels*
   Contemporary; Romantic Comedy

Closed to approaches.

Loves to find new talent and work with her clients to develop strong proposals and manuscripts. She enjoys being the author's advocate, often being their first editor, business manager, and trusted confidante. Her personal agenting philosophy is to take on an author for the duration of their career and help guide them through the ever-changing publishing landscape. She is actively building her client list while also handling audio, permissions, and electronic rights for the agency.

L472 Aemilia Phillips
Literary Agent
United States

apquery@skagency.com

http://skagency.com
http://skagency.com/agents/aemilia-phillips/

Literary Agency: Stuart Krichevsky Literary Agency, Inc. (**L556**)

Fiction > *Novels*
General, and in particular: Culture; Dark; Literary; Magic; Politics; Social Justice

Nonfiction > *Nonfiction Books*
Central America; Commercial; Cultural Criticism; Feminism; Journalism; Narrative Nonfiction; South America

How to send: Email

Works with a range of fiction and non-fiction writers. She is particularly interested in writers who push conventional boundaries in order to address cultural, political, and social justice issues. Interested in journalism, narrative non-fiction, literary fiction, and poetry, she looks for diverse, smart writing with an impactful story to tell. For non-fiction she's looking for driven, obsessed writers and topics that challenge the way we think about the world, with a particular interest in Latin American and feminist voices. She loves books that at first glance appear to be commercial, but that are also smart cultural critiques that force readers to examine new viewpoints. She's fascinated by darker, complex fictional characters who upend preconceptions, and stories with just a touch of magic.

Authors: Ahmed Badr; Sol Brager; Shavone Charles; Gabriel Dozal; Adriana Gallardo; Karen Ho; Lizz Huerta; Charlotte Kaufman; Cassidy Krug; Dan Lewis; Julie Lunde; Farah Nayeri; Okezie Nwoka; José Olivarez; José R. Ralat; Reyes Ramirez; Raquel Reichard; Ruben Reyes; Prisca Dorcas Mojica Rodriguez; David Schonfeld; Kim Thai; Sarah Weinman; Christina Wilcox

L473 Juliet Pickering
Literary Agent
United Kingdom

juliet@blakefriedmann.co.uk

http://blakefriedmann.co.uk/juliet-pickering
https://twitter.com/julietpickering

Literary Agency: Blake Friedmann Literary Agency Ltd (**L065**)

Fiction > *Novels*
Book Club Fiction; Commercial; Literary

Nonfiction
Illustrated Books: General
Nonfiction Books: Cookery; Food; Narrative Nonfiction; Popular Culture; Relationships; Social History

Closed to approaches.

Alongside literary, book club and commercial fiction, I represent non-fiction writers across the board, including memoir, pop culture, social history, writing on issues of race, gender and class, and cookery and food.

Authors: Diane Abbott; Saskia Alais; Kasim Ali; Graeme Armstrong; MiMi Aye; Trezza Azzopardi; Bolu Babalola; Tomas Bellamy; Jendella Benson; Meliz Berg; Ian Birch; Rachel Blackmore; Nora Anne Brown; Erin Bunting; Karen Campbell; Natasha Carthew; Fran Chang; Norie Clarke; Julia Cole; Sue Cook; Sara Crowe; Tuyen Do; Michael Donkor; Jo Facer; Alix Fox; Sarah Franklin; Roxy Freeman; Janice Galloway; Gabriella Griffith; Sarah Hartley; David Haslam; Emma Forsyth Haslett; Kate Hodges; Michael Hogan; Kerry Hudson; Leah Hyslop; Alexandra Jellicoe; Benjamin Johncock; Konditor; Kat Lister; Richard Littler; Clayton Littlewood; Anneliese Mackintosh; Ailbhe Malone; Lucy Mangan; Nina-Sophia Miralles; Emma Mitchell; Sue Moorcroft; Grace Mortimer; Nina Parker; Rosalind Powell; Julie Rea; Annie Robertson; Elliot Ryan; Lora Stimson; Jack Urwin; Helen Walmsley-Johnson; Jemma Wayne; Andrew Wong

L474 Rosie Pierce
Literary Agent
United Kingdom

piercesubmissions@curtisbrowngroup.co.uk
rosie.pierce@curtisbrown.co.uk

https://curtisbrown.co.uk
https://curtisbrown.co.uk/agent/rosie-pierce

Literary Agency: Curtis Brown (**L135**)

Fiction > *Novels*
Coming of Age; Commercial; Dark Academia; Family Saga; Friends; Ghost Stories; Horror; Literary; Mystery; Psychological Suspense; Romantic Comedy; Thrillers

Nonfiction > *Nonfiction Books*
Alternative History; Celebrity; Internet; Memoir; Narrative Nonfiction; Popular Culture; Psychology

Send: Query; Synopsis; Proposal; Writing sample
How to send: Email

I read widely and across genres, and I am looking for both literary and commercial fiction. I love family dramas, ghost and horror stories, psychological suspense, murder mysteries, gripping thrillers, and big-hearted romantic comedies. In storytelling I am most often drawn to distinctive, original voices; vivid characterisation and world building; confident, engaging prose; and astute social observation. I particularly love to read about the relationships that shape – or even define – a life. I am looking for expansive, character-driven novels that explore complicated family dynamics, enduring friendships, love affairs, coming of age, the best and worst things we do for love. I am also always keen to read novels that explore occultism, séances, the uncanny, dark academia, and thrillers with emotional punch and nail-biting plot. And if a novel can make me laugh, I am sold. In non-fiction, I'd love to hear from writers who bring their expertise and/or experiences to the page in an accessible, compelling and original way. I am looking for narrative non-fiction, memoir, and books exploring pop and celebrity culture, alternative histories, psychology, the internet.

Authors: Nicole Adams; Henry Agg; Alice Bell; Kaddy Benyon; Kate van der Borgh; Melanie Cantor; Toni Coppers; Matt Cunningham; Sarah Daniels; Rebecca Fallon; A.D. Garrett; Caroline Green; Susanna Kearsley; Euan Kitson; Sarah Lawton; Gytha Lodge; Laura Marshall; Laura McCluskey; Margaret Murphy; Madeleine Norton; Lauren O'Donoghue; Leah Pitt; Joanna Pritchard; Stephanie Sowden; Orla Thomas; Dan Whitlam

L475 Gideon Pine
Literary Agent
United States

submissions@inkwellmanagement.com

https://inkwellmanagement.com
https://inkwellmanagement.com/staff/gideon-pine

Literary Agency: InkWell Management

Fiction > *Novels*
Book Club Fiction; Commercial; Domestic; Literary; Mystery; Supernatural / Paranormal; Suspense; Thrillers

Nonfiction > *Nonfiction Books*
Crime; Health; Investigative Journalism; Narrative Nonfiction; Wellbeing

Send: Query; Writing sample
How to send: In the body of an email

A sucker for a good premise whether it is a thriller/mystery/suspense, domestic fiction and literary fiction. If you think your book is destined to be the next book club bestseller or a cult classic that will live on forever, he wants to read it. He's looking for thrillers in any form, whether they're commercial or have a healthy literary injection. Strong sense of place is a major plus. Literary novels are always welcome, as long as there's a plot. Also looking for suburban dysfunction (aka, domestic fiction) in any form, whether it's suspenseful or darkly comedic or even with a dose of supernatural, he wants to read it. He is also interested in narrative nonfiction with a compelling point of view, true crime, health and wellness, and long form investigative journalism.

L476 Zoe Plant
Literary Agent
United States

plantqueries@thebentagency.com

http://www.thebentagency.com/zoe-plant
https://www.twitter.com/zoeplant89

Literary Agency: The Bent Agency (**L052**)

ADULT > Fiction > *Novels*
Commercial; Fantasy; Gothic; High Concept; Horror; Mystery; Science Fiction; Speculative; Thrillers

CHILDREN'S > Fiction > *Middle Grade*
General, and in particular: Commercial

YOUNG ADULT > Fiction > *Novels*
General, and in particular: Commercial; Horror; Magic; Science Fiction; Speculative; Thrillers

Closed to approaches.

I am looking for middle-grade and young adult fiction across all genres, as well as adult science fiction, fantasy, horror and speculative fiction. Across the board, my tastes lean towards commercial, entertaining, accessible books that also have something to say about the world. I am particularly interested in seeing submissions from writers from traditionally underrepresented backgrounds.

L477 Carrie Plitt
Literary Agent; Company Director
United Kingdom

https://felicitybryan.com/fba-agent/carrie-plitt/

Literary Agency: Felicity Bryan Associates (**L192**)

Fiction
Novels: Book Club Fiction; Coming of Age; Family; Friends; Literary; Romance
Short Fiction Collections: General

Nonfiction > *Nonfiction Books*
History; Investigative Journalism; Memoir; Narrative Essays; Narrative Nonfiction; Nature; Popular Psychology; Popular Science; Social Issues; Travel

Closed to approaches.

I am actively building a list of non-fiction and fiction. In non-fiction, I love to represent expert authors who are passionate about their subject, who have something new to say, and who can convey their argument in a clear and invigorating manner. I have a particular interest in books about the issues our society faces today, narrative non-fiction, investigative journalism, popular science, popular psychology, big ideas, nature writing, history and travel. I also love book-length essays or cohesive essay collections, and memoirs that explore wider themes like freedom or education. In fiction, the books I represent range from the very literary to those you might read in a book club. Besides excellent writing, I am often drawn to emotionally complex novels; coming of age stories; sprawling narratives about love, friendship or families; and stories that capture the zeitgeist in some way – even when they are set in the past. I love a good short story collection, especially if the stories are linked together.

Authors: Sally Adee; Frances Ashcroft; Emily Baughan; Roderick Beaton; Catherine Belton; Tim Birkhead; Ursula Buchan; Julia Bueno; Emma Byrne; Fernando Cervantes; Simukai Chigudu; Marcus Chown; Serena Dyer; Will Eaves; Reni Eddo-Lodge; David Farrier; Peter Gatrell; Susan Golombok; James Hamilton; Tim Hecker; Lindsey Hilsum; Sarah Jasmon; Joseph Jebelli; Nick Jubber; Chelsea Kwakye; Grace Lavery; Suzannah Lipscomb; Tess Little; Rebecca Lowe; Natasha Lunn; Fiona Maddocks; Henry Mance; Ben Martynoga; Vanessa Nakate; Tom Nancollas; Camilla Nord; Jenny Odell; Ore Ogunbiyi; Elsa Panciroli; Alex Reeve; Dan Richards; Eloise Rickman; Alex Riley; Charlotte Lydia Riley; David Robson; Nicola Rollock; Farhan Samanani; Zakia Sewell; Tiffany Watt Smith; Miriam Stoppard; Cathy Thomas; Samantha Walton; Michael Wooldridge; Kieran Yates

L478 The Plot Agency
Literary Agency
United Kingdom

https://www.theplotagency.com

Professional Body: The Association of Authors' Agents (AAA)

Founded in 2024, with a commitment to centering and championing authors and great stories.

Literary Agent: Marilia Savvides (**L520**)

L479 Portobello Literary
Literary Agency
United Kingdom

info@portobelloliterary.co.uk
submissions@portobelloliterary.co.uk

https://www.portobelloliterary.co.uk
https://twitter.com/portyliterary
https://instagram.com/portyliterary

Professional Body: The Association of Authors' Agents (AAA)

Fiction > *Novels*

Nonfiction > *Nonfiction Books*

Send: Synopsis; Author bio; Writing sample
How to send: Email
How not to send: Post

Literary agency based in Edinburgh. Looking for clients and happy to chat to writers at any stage of their career. Response only if interested. No postal submissions, or submissions originated, written or edited by Artificial Intelligence (AI) technology.

Authors: Polly Atkin; Louis Bailey; Laura Basu; Victoria Bennett; Meg Bertera-Berwick; Fiona Black; Gill Booles; Jenny Chamarette; Rachel Charlton-Dailey; Mona Dash; Joe Donnelly; Samantha Dooey-Miles; Ashley Douglas; Laura Elliott; Harry Josephine Giles; CL Hellisen; Lindsay Johnstone; Louise Kenward; Wenying Li; Annie Lord; Aefa Mulholland; JC Niala; Eleanor Noyce; Andrés N. Ordorica; Alycia Pirmohamed; Wendy Pratt; Adam Ramsay; Christina Riley; Maud Rowell; Sarah Stewart; Elizabeth Lewis Williams; Elspeth Wilson

Literary Agent: Caro Clarke (**L118**)

L480 Marcy Posner
Literary Agent; Senior Vice President
United States

marcy@foliolit.com

https://www.foliolit.com/agents-1/marcy-posner
https://querymanager.com/query/marcyposner

Literary Agency: Folio Literary Management, LLC (**L207**)

ADULT

Fiction > *Novels*
Historical Fiction; Mystery; Psychological Suspense; Thrillers; Women's Fiction

Nonfiction > *Nonfiction Books*
Culture; Environment; Journalism; Narrative Nonfiction; Nature; Psychology; Social Issues; Women's Issues

CHILDREN'S > Fiction > *Middle Grade*
Contemporary; Fantasy; Historical Fiction; Mystery; Science Fiction

YOUNG ADULT > Fiction > *Novels*
Contemporary; Historical Fiction; Mystery; Romance

How to send: Query Tracker
How not to send: Email

Looking for Thrillers, Psychological suspense, Historical fiction, Women's fiction, Mystery, YA (contemporary, historical, romance, mystery), Middle grade (contemporary, SFF, historical, mystery, Narrative non-fiction, Cultural/social issues, Journalism, Nature and ecology, Psychology and Women's issues. No longer accepts queries through email. Submit through online submission system only.

Authors: Christi Clancy; Christina Clancy; Lexie Elliott; Jacqueline Kelly; Erika J. Kendrick; Michael McGarrity; Tanya Pell; Sheri Reynolds; Rebecca Stafford; Rachel J. Webster; Patricia Wood

L481 Madison Potter
Literary Agent
United States

madison@olswangerliterary.com

https://www.madisonpotterliteraryagent.com
https://www.olswanger.com
https://www.manuscriptwishlist.com/mswl-post/madison-scalera/
http://www.twitter.com/MadisonScalera

Literary Agency: Olswanger Literary LLC (**L449**)

Fiction > *Novels*
General, and in particular: Contemporary Fantasy; Contemporary Romance; Cozy Fantasy; Dark Academia; Dark Fantasy; Fantasy; Gothic; Grounded Fantasy; High / Epic Fantasy; LGBTQIA; Low Fantasy; Magical Realism; Romance; Romantasy

Send: Query; Synopsis; Writing sample; Author bio
How to send: Email

I'm looking for stories with romanticized worlds and literary merit. I'd love to indulge in magical realism, low fantasies, high fantasies, and romantasies with whimsical worlds and undeniable chemistry. As a hopeless romantic, I'm a sucker for byronic heroes and anti-heroes – any complex characters I can guiltily love and defend against friends and family. You can also query me with any love story that's contemporary but feels like it's from a different time.

L482 Anna Power
Literary Agent; Managing Director
Bloomsbury House, 74-77 Great Russell Street, London, WC1B 3DA
United Kingdom

anna@johnsonandalcock.co.uk

http://www.johnsonandalcock.co.uk/anna-power
https://twitter.com/APowerAgent

Literary Agency: Johnson & Alcock (**L302**)

Fiction
Graphic Novels: General
Novels: Book Club Fiction; Crime; Historical Fiction; Literary; Suspense
Nonfiction > *Nonfiction Books*
Cultural Criticism; Current Affairs; Food; History; Memoir; Popular Science; Psychology

Send: Query; Synopsis; Writing sample
How to send: Email attachment
How not to send: Post

In fiction, she is looking for literary, book club and historical fiction, as well as suspense and crime. Whatever the genre, she looks for a distinctive and compelling voice, and worldbuilding that immerses the reader. She is drawn especially to a moral dilemma, stories about families and relationships, and novels that combine darkness and humour. She is also interested to see graphic novels which appeal to a crossover readership.

In non-fiction, she invites submissions of history, memoir, current affairs, cultural criticism, popular science, psychology and food writing; anything that communicates an author's passion in an inventive and inspiring way. She welcomes approaches from experts with new and surprising takes on their subject, which alter the way we think about and engage with the world.

L483 Deirdre Power
Literary Agent
United Kingdom

Literary Agency: David Higham Associates Ltd (**L146**)

L484 Amanda Preston
Literary Agent
United Kingdom

amandasubmissions@lbabooks.com

http://www.lbabooks.com/agent/amanda-preston/

Literary Agency: LBA Books Ltd

ADULT
Fiction > *Novels*
Book Club Fiction; Commercial; Crime; High Concept Thrillers; Historical Fiction; Romance

Nonfiction > *Nonfiction Books*
Contemporary; Crime; Environment; History; Memoir; Narrative Nonfiction; Nature; Psychology; Science; Wellbeing

YOUNG ADULT > **Fiction** > *Novels*
Contemporary; Historical Fiction; Speculative

Represents a wide range of best-selling and award-winning authors across fiction and non-fiction. On the hunt for a high-concept thriller which is character and plot driven, but also has a discussable issue at its heart. Would also love a novel where the location is as integral to the plot as the crime. Would love a new crime series. On the hunt for a glorious book club love story that is doing something a bit different and special. For nonfiction, would love more true crime. It can be contemporary or historical, an unsolved case or a different perspective on a well known case. Not looking for any child-related crime stories. Looking for narrative non-fiction predominately in science, the environment, psychology, nature writing, well-being and memoir.

Authors: Emily Adlam; Jaimie Admans; Sarah Alderson; Dominique Antiglio; Kerry Barrett; A.L. Bird; Darcie Boleyn; Christina Bradley; Catherine Brookes; Jo Carnegie; Lucie Cave; Rebecca Chance; Emma Cooper; Susie Donkin; Hannah Doyle; Katherine Dyson; Kate Hackworthy; Sue Heath; Natalie Heaton; Holly Jade; Jane Jesmond; Lesley Kara; Simon Kernick; Emily Kerr; Ella King; Caedis Knight; Amy Lavelle; Georgina Lees; Freda Lightfoot; Jane Linfoot; Fiona Lucas; Rachael Lucas; Dee MacDonald; Ian Marber; Colin McDowell; Lisa Medved; L. C. North; Angelique Panagos; Catherine Piddington; Anna Pointer; Gillian Richmond; Natali Simmonds; Tom Simons; Johanna Spiers; Heidi Swain; Karen Swan; Sophie Tanner; Jonathan Trigell; Anna Turns; Claire Wade; Kate Wells; Kate Winter; Dalton Wong

L485 Rachel Mills Literary
Literary Agency
M27, South Wing, Somerset House, Strand, London, WC2R 1LA
United Kingdom

https://www.rachelmillsliterary.co.uk
https://twitter.com/bookishyogini
https://www.instagram.com/rachelmillsliterary/

Professional Body: The Association of Authors' Agents (AAA)

How to send: Email

As an agency we are particularly interested in female voices, and in showcasing talent which deserves to be heard, regardless of age or background. We seek to work with authors whose careers we can help build over the long term, across multiple projects.

Company Director / Literary Agent: Rachel Mills

Literary Agent: Nelle Andrew

L486 Susan Ramer
Literary Agent
United States

dca@doncongdon.com

https://doncongdon.com/agents

Literary Agency: Don Congdon Associates, Inc. (**L159**)

Fiction > *Novels*
Book Club Fiction; Contemporary; Literary; Upmarket

Nonfiction > *Nonfiction Books*
Arts; Cultural History; Fashion; Food; Literary Memoir; Music; Narrative Nonfiction; Popular Culture; Social History; Women's Issues

How to send: Email

Looks for literary fiction, upmarket 'book club' fiction (contemporary and historical, American in particular), and narrative non-fiction. Is drawn to an authentic voice, unforgettable characters with an edge, and an unfamiliar, well-crafted story that is emotional in unpredictable ways. For non-fiction, her interests include social history, cultural history, smart pop culture (fashion, food, art, music), women's issues, and literary memoir with a distinctive theme. She particularly likes a narrative that combines a personal thread with reporting and analysis of a broader social or cultural issue. In everything, she appreciates a sense of humor, especially when it's on the dark side. No queries in the following categories: romance, sci-fi, fantasy, espionage, mysteries, politics, health/diet/fitness, self-help sports or children's (young adult, middle grade or picture book); and she does not represent screenplays.

L487 Rebecca Carter Literary
Literary Agency
c/o PEW Literary, 46 Lexington Street, London, W1F 0LP
United Kingdom

info@rebeccacarterliterary.com

https://www.rebeccacarterliterary.com
https://twitter.com/rebeccasbooks
https://www.instagram.com/rebeccacarterliteraryagent/

Professional Body: The Association of Authors' Agents (AAA)

Literary Agent: Rebecca Carter (**L103**)

L488 Redhammer
Literary Agency
United Kingdom

https://redhammer.info
https://www.facebook.com/RealLitopia
https://twitter.com/Litopia
https://www.linkedin.com/in/petecox/
https://studio.youtube.com/channel/UCmbrM2ciaxb4hHQFfnSeOpg

Fiction > *Novels*

Nonfiction > *Nonfiction Books*

Send: Pitch; Writing sample
How to send: Online submission system

Suggests aspiring writers join their writers' colony. Interested in hearing from previously published authors, self-published authors, celebrities, whistleblowers, and people with a unique life story.

Literary Agent: Peter Cox

L489 Regina Ryan Books
Literary Agency
United States

queries@reginaryanbooks.com

https://www.reginaryanbooks.com

Professional Body: Association of American Literary Agents (AALA)

ADULT > Nonfiction
  Nonfiction Books: Architecture; Birds; Business; Cookery; Crime; Diet; Environment; Gardening; Health; History; Leisure; Lifestyle; Narrative Nonfiction; Nature; Parenting; Politics; Psychology; Science; Spirituality; Sport; Sustainable Living; Travel; Wellbeing; Women's Issues
  Reference: Popular

CHILDREN'S > Nonfiction > *Picture Books*

Does not want:

> **Nonfiction** > *Nonfiction Books*: Religion

Send: Query; Proposal; Writing sample; Full text; Author bio; Market info; Marketing plan
How to send: Word file email attachment

Costs: Offers services that writers have to pay for. Offers publishing consultation services and book packaging and production (print and electronic).

We are a Manhattan-based boutique literary agency primarily representing adult nonfiction. We also offer publishing consultation services and book packaging and production (print and electronic).

We are always looking for new and exciting books in our areas of interest, including well-written narrative nonfiction, architecture, history, politics, natural history (especially birds), true crime, science (especially the brain), the environment, women's issues, parenting, cooking, psychology, health, wellness, diet, business, non-religious contemporary spirituality, children's picture books, lifestyle, sustainability, popular reference, and leisure activities including sports, narrative travel, and gardening. We represent books that have something new to say, are well-written and that will, if possible, make the world a better place.

Authors: Ben Austro; Randi Minetor; Doug Whynott

Literary Agent: Regina Ryan

L490 Janet Reid
Literary Agent
United States

Janet@JetReidLiterary.com

http://www.jetreidliterary.com
http://jetreidliterary.blogspot.com/
https://queryshark.blogspot.com/
http://aaronline.org/Sys/PublicProfile/2176820/417813
https://www.publishersmarketplace.com/members/JanetReid/

Professional Bodies: Association of American Literary Agents (AALA); Mystery Writers of America (MWA)

Fiction > *Novels*
  Commercial; Crime; Domestic Suspense; Literary; Mystery; Thrillers

Nonfiction > *Nonfiction Books*
  Biography; History; Memoir; Narrative Nonfiction; Science

Send: Query; Writing sample; Author bio; Proposal
How to send: In the body of an email
How not to send: Email attachment

New York literary agent with a list consisting mainly of crime novels and thrillers, and narrative nonfiction in history and biography.

Authors: Robin Becker; Bill Cameron; Gary Corby; Phillip DePoy; Stephanie Evans; Kennedy Foster; Lee Goodman; Dana Haynes; Patrick Lee; Thomas Lippman; Jeff Marks; Warren Richey; Terry Shames; Jeff Somers; Robert Stubblefield; Deb Vlock

L491 Milly Reilly
Literary Agent
United Kingdom

submissions@colwillandpeddle.com

https://www.colwillandpeddle.com/about

Literary Agency: Colwill & Peddle

Fiction > *Novels*: Literary

Nonfiction > *Nonfiction Books*
  Arts; Comedy / Humour; Food; Health; Nature; Politics; Psychology; Society

Send: Query; Synopsis; Writing sample; Author bio; Market info; Outline
How to send: Email

I represent a broad range of non-fiction and a select amount of literary fiction. I'm on the look-out for informed, illuminating writing that challenges readers to think and live critically and imaginatively. Topics that interest me include food, art, comedy, the natural world, psychology, health and the social and political. I represent writers of memoir and creative non-fiction, where I'm particularly excited by bold, perceptive writing that interrogates the means of telling a story.

Authors: Alexina Anatole; Xanthi Barker; Aimee Cliff; Lucy Easthope; Benjamina Ebuehi; Melek Erdal; Josie Gill; Gabby Jahanshahi-Edlin; Shona Minson; Marie Mitchell; Jennifer Neal; Vic Parsons; Clare Rose; Jacqueline Roy; Ben Smoke; Annabel Sowemimo; Özlem Warren; Sophie Williams; Corina Zappia

L492 Francesca Riccardi
Literary Agent
United Kingdom

https://katenashlit.co.uk/people/
https://twitter.com/friccar_

Literary Agency: Kate Nash Literary Agency (**L321**)

Fiction > *Novels*
  Commercial; Crime; Detective Fiction; Family; Friends; Thrillers

Reads widely, especially across popular commercial genres, but is a particular fan of crime and thrillers, and loves a dogged detective or unusual sleuth. She also enjoys books about unusual family dynamics, toxic friendships and people keeping secrets.

L493 Rick Richter
Literary Agent; Senior Partner
United States

https://aevitascreative.com/agents/
https://querymanager.com/query/RickRichter

Literary Agency: Aevitas

ADULT
  Fiction > *Novels*
    Commercial; Horror; Psychological Thrillers

  Nonfiction > *Nonfiction Books*
    Celebrity Memoir; Crime; Food; History; Memoir; Music; Narrative Nonfiction; Politics; Popular Culture; Religion; Science; Self Help; Social Justice; Sports Celebrity

CHILDREN'S
  Fiction
    Chapter Books; *Early Readers*; *Middle Grade*; *Picture Books*
  Nonfiction
    Early Readers; *Middle Grade*; *Picture Books*

YOUNG ADULT
  Fiction > *Novels*
  Nonfiction > *Nonfiction Books*

Closed to approaches.

Areas of interest include self-help, pop culture, memoir, history, thriller, true crime, political and social issues, narrative food writing, and faith. He has deep experience and interest in children's books.

Authors: John Bainbridge; Rob Barnett; Mary Jane Begin; Sheryl Berk; Tom Booth; Marcus Brotherton; Kyle Buchanan; Libby Buck; Andrew Bustamante; Marc and Angel Chernoff; Pan Cooke; Amanda Craig; Matt Diffee; Geoff Edgers; Jeremy Egner; Michael Emberley; Nona Footz; JR and Vanessa Ford; Michael and Ava Gardner; Dan Goldman; Margaret Greanais; Andy Greene; Erik Gude; Peter Guralnick; Michael Hendrix; James Hibberd; Barry Jackson; Jeffrey H. Jackson; Alegra Kastens; Erin Kimmerle; Rebecca Kling; William J. Kole; Deb Miller Landau; Neil Lane; Nico Lang; Derek Lawrence; Kim Mager; Aaron Mahnke; Amanda Marrone; Scott Meslow; Darcy Michael; SSG Travis Mills; Kara Mitchell; Malcolm Mitchell; Real Sports Entertainment Network; Chris and Emily Norton; Cate Osborn; Panos Panay; Madeline Pendleton; Shawn Peters; Greg Presto; Jessica Radloff; Michael Relth; David Ricciardi; Geo Rutherford; Kate Schroeder; Hannah Selinger; Tim Sommer; Isaiah Stephens; Melanie Sumrow; Leah Tinari; Neil Tomba; Sheree Tomba; Allison Varnes; Sara Vladic; Molly Webster; Paige Wetzel; Sean Fay Wolfe

L494 Louise Ripley-Duggan
Literary Agent
United Kingdom

https://www.theseus.agency/team

Literary Agency: The Theseus Agency (**L573**)

L495 Soumeya Bendimerad Roberts
Literary Agent; Vice President
United States

soumeya@hgliterary.com

https://www.hgliterary.com/soumeya
https://querymanager.com/query/SBR
https://www.publishersmarketplace.com/members/SoumeyaRoberts/

Literary Agency: HG Literary
Professional Body: Association of American Literary Agents (AALA)

Fiction > *Novels*
  Animals; Family; Literary; Motherhood; Nature; Postcolonialism; Social Commentary; Sub-Culture; Upmarket

Nonfiction > *Nonfiction Books*
  Animals; Crafts; Design; Family; Lifestyle; Memoir; Motherhood; Narrative Nonfiction; Nature; Personal Essays; Social Commentary; Sub-Culture

Send: Query; Synopsis; Writing sample
How to send: Query Tracker

Represents award-winning and best-selling authors in literary and upmarket fiction, narrative non-fiction, and memoir. She also represents a curated list across creative fields including design, craft, and lifestyle. She is seeking new voices in fiction and narrative nonfiction, especially stories about dynamic relationships between complex but sympathetic characters; families, siblings, and motherhood; social commentary; unconventional settings and subcultures; our relationship with land, nature, and animals; and controlled experiments with form. She is particularly, but not exclusively, interested in work that investigates or reflects on the post-colonial world, marginalized and liminal spaces, and narratives by people of color. In non-fiction, she is primarily looking for idea-driven or voice-forward memoirs, personal essay collections, and narrative non-fiction of all stripes. She is not looking for fantasy, science fiction, religious books, commercial romance, middle grade, young adult, or picture books.

L496 Robertson Murray Literary Agency
Literary Agency
3rd Floor, 37 Great Portland Street, London, W1W 8QH
United Kingdom
Tel: +44 (0) 20 7580 0702

info@robertsonmurray.com

https://robertsonmurray.com

Nonfiction > *Nonfiction Books*

Represents a diverse range of writing talent, including established bestselling authors and exciting new voices.

Literary Agents: Jenny Heller; Hilary Murray; Charlotte Robertson

L497 Quressa Robinson
Literary Agent
United States

https://querymanager.com/query/1066
https://www.publishersmarketplace.com/members/QuressaRobinson/
https://twitter.com/qnrisawesome

Literary Agency: Folio Literary Management, LLC (**L207**)

ADULT
  Fiction > *Novels*
    Fantasy; Science Fiction

  Nonfiction > *Nonfiction Books*
    Commercial; Literary Memoir; Literary; Narrative Nonfiction; Popular Science; Westerns

CHILDREN'S > Fiction > *Middle Grade*
  Contemporary; Fantasy; Literary; Science Fiction

YOUNG ADULT > Fiction > *Novels*
  Contemporary; Fantasy; Romantic Comedy; Science Fiction

How to send: By referral

Looking for:

Modern-day blue stockings, BIPOC fangirls/fanboys, #blackgirlmagic, #carefreeblackgirls, #blackboyjoy, LGBTQ+, BIPOC falling in love, neuroatypical / neurodivergent, and disabled BIPOCs as leads.

Middle Grade (contemporary, literary, and SF/F). Cute, quirky, charming, and fun. Along the lines of Kiki's Delivery Service, Spirited Away, The Girl that Drank the Moon, the Pandava series, Hurricane Child.

Young adult (contemporary, Rom Coms, and SF/F) *I have TONS of SF/F on my current list so I am extremely selective with this genre*

Adult SF/F with strong genre-bending/crossover appeal. (Think the All Souls Trilogy by Deborah Harkness, The Night Circus by Erin Morgenstern, and The Age of Miracles by Karen Thompson Walker. I'm also a fan of Anne Bishop and Naomi Novik. More recent books that I've loved: Trail of Lightning, The Ten Thousand Doors of January, and Empire of Sand.)

Passion projects in narrative nonfiction with a strong literary voice and commercial appeal (Wild by Cheryl Strayed, Black Man in a White Coat by Damon Tweedy, When Breath Becomes Air by Paul Kalanithi). Would love to see non-whitewashed cowboy stories; pop science by women, specifically women of color; and literary, voice-driven memoir with commercial appeal.

#ownvoices and marginalized authors in all genres mentioned above. Inclusive narratives in all genres.

L498 Rochelle Stevens & Co.
Literary Agency
2 Terretts Place, Upper Street, London, N1 1QZ
United Kingdom
Tel: +44 (0) 20 7359 3900

info@rochellestevens.com

http://www.rochellestevens.com
http://twitter.com/TerrettsPlace
http://www.rochellestevens.com/submissions/#

Scripts
Film Scripts; *Radio Scripts*; *TV Scripts*; *Theatre Scripts*

Send: Query; Author bio
How to send: By referral

Handles script writers for film, television, theatre, and radio. No longer handles writers of fiction, nonfiction, or children's books. See website for full submission guidelines.

Literary Agents: Frances Arnold; Rochelle Stevens

L499 Rocking Chair Books
Literary Agency
United Kingdom
Tel: +44 (0) 7809 461342

representme@rockingchairbooks.com

http://www.rockingchairbooks.com
https://twitter.com/rockingbooks
https://www.instagram.com/rockingchairbooks/

Professional Body: The Association of Authors' Agents (AAA)

Fiction
Graphic Novels: General
Novels: Commercial; Literary
Nonfiction > *Nonfiction Books*

Send: Query; Full text; Writing sample
How to send: Email

Founded in 2011 after the founder worked for five years as a Director at an established London literary agency. Send complete ms or a few chapters by email only. No Children's, YA or Science Fiction / Fantasy.

Authors: Mike Medaglia; John Rensten; Lakimbini Sitoy; Brian Turner

Literary Agent: Samar Hammam

L500 Jennifer Rofe
Senior Agent
United States

jennifer@andreabrownlit.com

https://www.andreabrownlit.com/Team/Jennifer-Rof%C3%A9
http://twitter.com/jenrofe
http://instagram.com/jenrofe
https://www.publishersmarketplace.com/members/jenrofe/
https://www.manuscriptwishlist.com/mswl-post/jennifer-rofe/
http://queryme.online/jenrofe

Literary Agency: Andrea Brown Literary Agency, Inc.

CHILDREN'S > **Fiction**
Chapter Books: General
Middle Grade: General, and in particular: Commercial; Contemporary; Fantasy; Historical Fiction; Literary; Magic
Picture Books: General

Send: Query; Author bio; Writing sample
How to send: Query Tracker

Always seeking distinct voices and richly developed characters. Middle grade has long been her soft spot and she's open to all genres in this category—literary, commercial, contemporary, magical, fantastical, historical, and everything in between. She especially appreciates stories that make her both laugh and cry, and that offer an unexpected view into the pre-teen experience. In picture books, she likes funny, character-driven projects; beautifully imagined and written stories; and milestone moments with a twist.

Open to picture book texts only on the first day of each month. Not currently accepting queries for YA texts. However, if you write in multiple spaces, please query for one of the listed categories and mention your other areas of interest.

L501 Rogers, Coleridge & White Ltd
Literary Agency
20 Powis Mews, London, W11 1JN
United Kingdom
Tel: +44 (0) 20 7221 3717

info@rcwlitagency.com

https://www.rcwlitagency.com
https://www.instagram.com/rcwliteraryagency/
https://twitter.com/RCWLitAgency

Professional Body: The Association of Authors' Agents (AAA)

ADULT > **Fiction** > *Novels*
Commercial; Crime; Literary; Thrillers

CHILDREN'S > **Fiction** > *Novels*

YOUNG ADULT > **Fiction** > *Novels*

Send: Query; Writing sample; Synopsis; Proposal
How to send: Word file email attachment; PDF file email attachment

Submissions should include a covering letter telling us about yourself and the background to the book. In the case of fiction they should consist of the first three chapters or approximately the first fifty pages of the work to a natural break, and a brief synopsis. Non-fiction submissions should take the form of a proposal up to twenty pages in length explaining what the work is about and why you are best placed to write it. Submissions must be the original work of the author and not generated or co-written using artificial intelligence. Attachments in either Word or PDF formats are acceptable, otherwise sample chapters or proposals can be pasted into the body of the submission email.

Literary Agents: Gill Coleridge; Sam Copeland; Stephen Edwards; Natasha Fairweather; Georgia Garrett; Jenny Hewson; Cara Jones; Rebecca Jones; Tristan Kendrick; Laurence Laluyaux; Matthew Marland; Zoe Nelson; Peter Robinson; Caroline Sheldon (**L530**); Peter Straus; Matthew Turner; Zoe Waldie; Pat White; Claire Wilson

L502 Annie Romano
Associate Agent
United States

https://www.anniecroninromano.com
https://www.olswanger.com
https://querytracker.net/query/AnnieRomano

Literary Agency: Olswanger Literary LLC (**L449**)

Fiction > *Novels*
General, and in particular: Book Club Fiction; Comedy / Humour; Commercial; Contemporary; Horror; LGBTQIA; Literary; Magical Realism; Multicultural; Mystery; Romantic Comedy; Suspense; Thrillers; Upmarket; Women's Fiction

Nonfiction > *Nonfiction Books*
Crime; Narrative Nonfiction

Closed to approaches.

I accept submissions of adult fiction and select narrative nonfiction. For adult fiction, I am currently on the hunt for lighter fare with smart humor and a unique hook. I also am seeking upmarket and commercial fiction in the following areas: contemporary fiction, women's fiction, sharp romantic comedy (do not send me romance if there's no comedic element or original hook), psychological thrillers/suspense, mystery, and light/clever horror (not slasher; think more Grady Hendrix style for this). I welcome diverse narratives, including but not limited to LGBTQ+ and underrepresented ethnicities/cultures. I adore stories with humor, well-done ensemble casts, and plots that deliver the unexpected. Send me something unique that will make me laugh! I'd love to see book club fiction or something spooky and atmospheric. I will consider literary fiction so long as there is a discernible structure/plot; I am not the best fit for stories focused on an emotional or sensory journey—beautiful as the writing may be—if the storyline is vague or absent. I am not seeking historical fiction at this time. I'm not a match for science fiction/fantasy but will consider stories with light elements of fantasy or magical realism grounded in a familiar world (think The House in the Cerulean Sea). Note: I do not represent any children's/YA projects.

L503 Root Literary
Literary Agency
United States

info@rootliterary.com
submissions@rootliterary.com

https://www.rootliterary.com
https://www.instagram.com/rootliterary/
https://twitter.com/RootLiterary
https://www.pinterest.com/rootliterary/_created/

We're a boutique, future-focused literary agency, representing award-winning, bestselling, and up-and-coming authors, illustrators, and graphic novelists. We're committed to helping our clients confidently define and redefine their vision of success while they build a lasting body of work and a meaningful career, and we do so by advocating, empowering, educating, negotiating, problem-solving, and revenue-generating in innovative ways to support our clients' creative work.

Literary Agents: Kurestin Armada (**L024**); Samantha Fabien (**L186**); Melanie Figueroa (**L199**); Taylor Haggerty (**L258**); Alyssa Maltese (**L387**); Molly O'Neill (**L446**); Holly Root (**L504**)

L504 Holly Root
Literary Agent
United States

https://www.rootliterary.com/agents
https://www.publishersmarketplace.com/members/hroot/

Literary Agency: Root Literary (**L503**)

Fiction > *Novels*

How to send: By referral

Currently only considering new submissions by referral.

L505 The Rosenberg Group
Literary Agency
United States

http://www.rosenberggroup.com
https://querymanager.com/query/QueryManagerRosenbergGroup

Professional Body: Association of American Literary Agents (AALA)

ACADEMIC > *Nonfiction* > *Nonfiction Books*

ADULT
Fiction > *Novels*
Romance; Women's Fiction

Nonfiction > *Nonfiction Books*
General, and in particular: Apiculture (Beekeeping); History; Psychology; Wine

How to send: Query Tracker

Represents romance and women's fiction for an adult audience, nonfiction, and college textbooks.

Literary Agent: Barbara Collins Rosenberg (**L506**)

L506 Barbara Collins Rosenberg
Literary Agent
United States

Literary Agency: The Rosenberg Group (**L505**)

Closed to approaches.

L507 Whitney Ross
Literary Agent
United States

https://www.highlineliterary.com/agent-whitney
https://querymanager.com/query/WhitneyRoss

Literary Agency: High Line Literary Collective (**L279**)

ADULT
Fiction > *Novels*
General, and in particular: Contemporary; Fantasy; Romance; Science Fiction

Nonfiction > *Nonfiction Books*
Cookery; Design; Fashion

CHILDREN'S > **Fiction** > *Middle Grade*

YOUNG ADULT > **Fiction** > *Novels*

Closed to approaches.

Looking for middle grade, young adult, and adult fiction across all genres, with an emphasis on historical, SF and fantasy, romance, and contemporary fiction. She is also open to non-fiction submissions in the areas of design, cooking, and fashion.

L508 Stefanie Rossitto
Literary Agent
United States

https://www.thetobiasagency.com/stefanie-rossitto
https://querymanager.com/query/1927

Literary Agency: The Tobias Literary Agency

Fiction > *Novels*
Historical Fiction; Historical Romance; Medieval; Romance

Currently looking for historical fiction, and funny, witty, modern romances. She also enjoys anything and everything medieval as well as exciting historical romances and/or fiction based on real characters. Open to queries during the final week of each month.

L509 Rubin Pfeffer Content, LLC
Literary Agency
648 Hammond Street, Chestnut Hill, MA 02467
United States

info@rpcontent.com

http://www.rpcontent.com

Literary Agency: Aevitas

Types: Fiction; Nonfiction
Markets: Children's; Young Adult

Send: Query
Don't send: Full text
How to send: Email

Focuses on children's books and digital content for all ages and genres. Send query by email. See website for full guidelines.

Literary Agents: Melissa Nasson; Rubin Pfeffer (**L469**)

L510 The Rudy Agency
Literary Agency
United States
Tel: +1 (970) 577-8500

https://www.rudyagency.com

ADULT
Fiction > *Novels*

Nonfiction > *Nonfiction Books*
Business; Health; History; Investigative Journalism; Legal; Medicine; Politics; Science; Sport

CHILDREN'S
Fiction > *Picture Books*
Nonfiction > *Illustrated Books*

YOUNG ADULT > **Fiction** > *Novels*

Send: Query
Don't send: Proposal; Full text
How to send: Email

Agency representing both fiction and nonfiction. Send query before sending proposal or manuscript. Approach only one agent.

Literary Agents: Maryann Karinch; Geoffrey Stone

L511 Rupert Crew Ltd
Literary Agency
Southgate, 7 Linden Avenue, Dorchester, Dorset, DT1 1EJ
United Kingdom
Tel: +44 (0) 1305 260335

info@rupertcrew.co.uk

http://www.rupertcrew.co.uk

Professional Body: The Association of Authors' Agents (AAA)

Fiction > *Novels*

Nonfiction > *Nonfiction Books*

Closed to approaches.

Closed to submissions as at July 2023. Check website for current status.

Send query with SAE, synopsis, and first two or three consecutive chapters. International representation, handling volume and subsidiary rights in fiction and nonfiction properties. No Short Stories, Science Fiction, Fantasy, Horror, Poetry or original scripts for Theatre, Television and Film. Email address for correspondence only. No response by post and no return of material with insufficient return postage.

Literary Agent: Caroline Montgomery

L512 Kathleen Rushall

Senior Agent
United States

kathleen@andreabrownlit.com

https://www.kathleenrushall.com
https://www.andreabrownlit.com/Team/Kathleen-Rushall
https://www.facebook.com/kathleen.rushall.5/
https://www.publishersmarketplace.com/members/KatRushall/
https://www.manuscriptwishlist.com/mswl-post/kathleen-rushall/

Literary Agency: Andrea Brown Literary Agency, Inc.

CHILDREN'S > **Fiction**
  Middle Grade: Animals; Astrology; Contemporary; Environment; Family Saga; High Concept; Magic; Romance; Tarot; Witches
  Picture Books: Animals; Astrology; Environment; Tarot; Witches

YOUNG ADULT > **Fiction** > *Novels*

Closed to approaches.

Represents a wide range of children's literature. She represents NYT bestselling and award-winning authors. She's drawn to empowering stories, and environmental and whimsical themes, particularly for the youngest set. She loves animals and books about their welfare and science. She's always interested in picture books that inspire emotional intelligence, self-awareness, and empathy.

L513 Laetitia Rutherford

Literary Agent
United Kingdom

https://www.watsonlittle.com/agent/laetitia-rutherford/
https://x.com/laetitialit

Literary Agency: Watson, Little Ltd (**L590**)

Fiction > *Novels*
  Historical Fiction; Literary; Upmarket

Nonfiction > *Nonfiction Books*
  Cats; Comedy / Humour; Contemporary; Cookery; Food; How To; Nature

Send: Query; Synopsis; Writing sample
How to send: Email

My current focus is on literary and upmarket fiction and non-fiction (including lifestyle and wellbeing). I am currently not looking for Crime fiction.

In my fifteen years as a literary agent, I have worked with many extraordinary, award-winning writers. I firmly believe that what you have to say matters more than your grammar; but also look for brilliance, originality, and accomplishment in your writing. I have built a successful Crime Fiction list, and my forward focus is about curating a small list of Literary writers. Within this, I continue to look for creativity and diversity. I welcome stand-out stories driven by a strong leading idea and emotional depth, with fresh perspectives and transporting arcs. If historical, let your novel speak for today.

Tones of charm and humour also work well for me. I love cats, food and cooking, and nature, and I love how-to-live concepts from experts, activists, or new cultural voices. A deft and delightful eternity-in-a-grain-of-sand concept would be a delight to take to readers around the world.

Author Estate: The Estate of Akemi Tanaka

Authors: Rebecca Abrams; Wendy Allen; Jenny Blackhurst; Ajay Chowdhury; Vivianne Crowley; Rebecca Elliott; Timna Fibert; Samson Kambalu; Holan Liang; Alex Marwood; Diana McCaulay; Barbara Nadel; Tam Omond; Anna Reading; Matt Rendell; Richard Owain Roberts; Anika Scott; Hannah Silva; Shane Spall; Geeta Vara; Jeremy Williams

L514 Jim Rutman

Vice President; Literary Agent
United States

https://www.sll.com/our-team
http://aaronline.org/Sys/PublicProfile/4090054/417813

Literary Agency: Sterling Lord Literistic, Inc.
Professional Body: Association of American Literary Agents (AALA)

Fiction > *Novels*: Literary

Nonfiction
  Essays: General
  Nonfiction Books: Biography; Films; History; Journalism; Literary Criticism; Music; Narrative Nonfiction; Sport

Send: Query; Synopsis; Writing sample
How to send: Online submission system

Represents adult literary fiction and non-fiction. In fiction, he is interested in audacious novels that test the form and prioritize language. His non-fiction interests are wide ranging, from history, journalism, music, film, sports, and biography, to traditional narrative approaches, criticism, and essays. He is often drawn to interdisciplinary and hybrid treatments, authorities seeking to complicate long held assumptions.

L515 Des Salazar

Literary Agent
United States

https://www.metamorphosisliteraryagency.com
https://querymanager.com/query/3486

Literary Agency: Metamorphosis Literary Agency (**L406**)

ADULT > **Fiction** > *Novels*
  Fantasy; Horror; LGBTQIA; Literary; Mystery; Romance; Science Fiction; Thrillers

NEW ADULT > **Fiction** > *Novels*

YOUNG ADULT > **Fiction** > *Novels*

Open to queries in January and July.

L516 Kaitlyn Sanchez

Literary Agent
United States

https://bradfordlit.com/kaitlyn-sanchez/
https://querymanager.com/query/2049
https://twitter.com/KaitlynLeann17

Literary Agency: Bradford Literary Agency (**L073**)

CHILDREN'S
  Fiction
    Graphic Novels: General
    Middle Grade: Adventure; Comedy / Humour; Coming of Age; Friends; Magic
    Picture Books: General

Nonfiction > *Nonfiction Books*

Closed to approaches.

Looking for children's books (picture books through middle grade) in all categories, including graphic novels, nonfiction, and illustration. She is incredibly eclectic in her tastes, with a great affinity for emotional stories as well as funny stories. Always looking for diversity in all forms, including but not limited to BIPOC, neurodiversity, and LGBTQ+. Loves working with artists, so she's always on the lookout for great illustrators, author-illustrators, and graphic novelists. Generally leans PG and PG-13 for most submissions, though some intensity here and there is fine.

L517 Rayhane Sanders
Literary Agent
United States

https://www.mmqlit.com
https://www.mmqlit.com/about/

Literary Agency: Massie McQuilkin & Altman (**L394**)
Professional Body: Association of American Literary Agents (AALA)

Fiction > *Novels*
  Culture; Ethnic Groups; Immigration; Sexuality

Nonfiction > *Nonfiction Books*
  Culture; Ethnic Groups; Immigration; Sexuality

Send: Query; Writing sample
How to send: In the body of an email

She is particularly interested in representing a diversity of voices from around the world, and in fresh voices telling stories we haven't heard before. She is fond of immigrant tales and stories concerned with race, sexuality, cross-cultural themes, and notions of identity.

L518 Kelly Van Sant
Literary Agent
United States

https://www.penandparsley.com
https://querymanager.com/query/kellyvansant
https://www.manuscriptwishlist.com/mswl-post/kelly-van-sant/

Literary Agency: KT Literary (**L345**)

CHILDREN'S > **Fiction** > *Middle Grade*

YOUNG ADULT > **Fiction** > *Novels*

How to send: Query Tracker

Seeks young adult and middle grade fiction, with a particular interest in projects by marginalized creators. Accepts queries in the first week of every month only.

L519 Elisa Saphier
Literary Agent

Literary Agency: MacGregor & Luedeke (**L380**)

L520 Marilia Savvides
Literary Agent
United Kingdom

marilia@theplotagency.com

https://www.theplotagency.com
https://www.theplotagency.com/submissions
https://twitter.com/MariliaSavvides

Literary Agency: The Plot Agency (**L478**)

Fiction > *Novels*
  Book Club Fiction; Crime; Dystopian Fiction; Grounded Science Fiction; High Concept; Horror; Romance; Romantic Comedy; Speculative; Suspense; Thrillers

Nonfiction > *Nonfiction Books*
  Crime; Investigative Journalism; Narrative History; Popular Science; Psychology

Closed to approaches.

I am particularly interested in fiction that is beautifully written and cleverly constructed, but still accessible to a wide readership. I am often drawn to darker tales that weave together excellent characters and an impossible-to-put-down story, from immersive book club novels with a splash of suspense, crime and thrillers, accessible horror, and speculative, genre-bending or dystopian stories. I also love smart, witty, contemporary rom-com. I have a smaller non-fiction list, and I'm especially interested in pop science / psychology, narrative history, true crime and investigative journalism.

L521 The Sayle Literary Agency
Literary Agency
1 Petersfield, Cambridge, CB1 1BB
United Kingdom
Tel: +44 (0) 1223 303035

info@sayleliteraryagency.com

http://www.sayleliteraryagency.com

Professional Body: The Association of Authors' Agents (AAA)

Fiction > *Novels*

Nonfiction > *Nonfiction Books*

Closed to approaches.

Established in 1896, we are an independent, full-service literary agency dedicated to representing the finest writers and experts in their fields. We work with experienced editors and publishers and in collaboration with dedicated co-agents to give these writers the best chance of success in a highly competitive and international industry.

Literary Agent: Rachel Calder

L522 Hannah Schofield
Literary Agent
United Kingdom

hannahsubmissions@lbabooks.com

http://www.lbabooks.com/agent/hannah-schofield/

Literary Agency: LBA Books Ltd

ADULT
  Fiction > *Novels*
    Book Club Fiction; Commercial; Historical Fiction; Romantasy; Romantic Comedy; Suspense; Thrillers; Women's Fiction

  Nonfiction > *Nonfiction Books*
    Crime; History; Memoir; Narrative Nonfiction; Personal Development; Social History

YOUNG ADULT > **Fiction** > *Novels*

How to send: Email

Represents a broad list of commercial and reading-group fiction, and select non-fiction.

Authors: Emad Ahmed; Darby Bozeman; Chris Bridges; Amanda Brooke; Charlotte Butterfield; Sam Caporn; Erin Connor; Kim Donovan; Elizabeth Drummond; Chloe Duckworth; Moyette Gibbons; Lucy Goacher; Isabella Harcourt; Anam Iqbal; Hannah Karena Jones; Jenni Keer; Amy Lavelle; Nicole Louie; Marina McCarron; Heather Mottershead; Nicole Nagaki; Grace Noakes; Stephanie Parente; Katy Phoon; Eleanor Pilcher; Ande Pliego; Heidi Shertok; Celia Silvani; Crystal Sung; Tania Tay; David Turner; Catherine Walsh

L523 Fabienne Schwizer
Literary Agent
United Kingdom

fabienne@ki-agency.co.uk

https://www.ki-agency.co.uk
https://www.manuscriptwishlist.com/mswl-post/fabienne-schwizer/

Literary Agency: Ki Agency Ltd (**L331**)

ADULT
  Fiction > *Novels*
    Fantasy; Horror; Science Fiction

  Nonfiction > *Nonfiction Books*: History

YOUNG ADULT > **Fiction** > *Novels*
  Fantasy; Horror; Science Fiction

Closed to approaches.

Represents adult and YA science fiction, fantasy, horror and related genres, as well as serious non-fiction in the broad history space. She is not a great fit for memoir, women's fiction or very spicy stories.

L524 Chloe Seager
Senior Agent
United Kingdom

https://www.madeleinemilburn.co.uk/agents/chloe-seager/
https://x.com/ChloeSeager

Literary Agency: Madeleine Milburn Literary, TV & Film Agency (**L385**)

ADULT > **Fiction** > *Novels*
  Comedy / Humour; Dark Academia; Fantasy; Folklore, Myths, and Legends; Ghost Stories; Horror; Romantasy; Science Fiction

CHILDREN'S
  Fiction > *Middle Grade*
    Comedy / Humour; Coming of Age; Contemporary; Family; Fantasy; Friends

  Nonfiction > *Nonfiction Books*

YOUNG ADULT > **Fiction** > *Novels*
  Comedy / Humour; Dark Academia; Fairy Tales; Fantasy; Folklore, Myths, and Legends; Ghost Stories; Gothic; Horror;

Magic; Romantasy; Romantic Comedy; Science Fiction; Thrillers

Send: Query; Pitch; Market info; Author bio; Synopsis; Writing sample
How to send: Email
How not to send: Post

I'm on the hunt for SFF in the crossover space that could sit on an adult or a YA list, especially dark academia, horror and romantasy. (Bonus points if you can write me a horror romance!) I am drawn to dark humour, forbidden love, morally grey characters and terrible people doing terrible things. I'm a huge horror fan. From ghost stories to gore, I love it all. I especially want a YA horror that deals with real world issues. I'm always a fan of gripping YA thrillers, too, with a voice, hook or twist that stands out from other popular books in this area. In YA fantasy, I tend to veer toward the gothic and fairytale-esque and I'm always interested when magic is used as a vehicle to comment on the real world. I'm a fan of sci-fi, although it has to have an intriguing hook. I'll always enjoy contemporary YA romance with a strong hook. Broadly, I'm on the lookout for writers exploring mythology – particularly those from previously underrepresented cultures. In children's, I'm looking for books that capture the pain and joy of growing up. I love fantasy middle-grade packed with atmosphere, adventure and distinctive magic. I am also drawn to contemporary middle-grade centred around family or friendship, or books that tackle an issue in an accessible, child-friendly and uplifting way. I'm forever on the hunt for funny fiction across all ages. We represent all sorts of non-fiction for young people – from politics, to science, to history. I'd love to see anything inspirational or that takes a fresh angle on an interesting topic.

L525 Selectric Artists

Literary Agency
9 Union Square #123, Southbury, CT 06488
United States
Tel: +1 (347) 668-5426

query@selectricartists.com

https://www.selectricartists.com

ADULT
  Fiction
    Graphic Novels: General
    Novels: Commercial; Domestic Thriller; Science Fiction
  Nonfiction
    Graphic Nonfiction: General
    Nonfiction Books: Memoir; Narrative Nonfiction
YOUNG ADULT > **Fiction** > *Novels*
    Fantasy; Science Fiction

Closed to approaches.

Some categories have become tougher to sell – memoir, YA fantasy, science fiction (both adult and YA), domestic thrillers – so the bar is set even higher since I already have good writers in those areas. But I'm always looking for commercial fiction, literary fiction, narrative nonfiction, graphic novels and graphic nonfiction, and new work from previously under-represented voices. Send query by email with your manuscript attached as a .doc, .pdf, or .pages file. Put the word "query" in the subject line. No queries by phone. Response only if interested.

Literary Agent: Christopher Schelling

L526 Maria Cardona Serra

Literary Agent
Spain

https://www.aevitascreative.com/agent/maria-cardona-serra
https://querymanager.com/query/MariaCardona_Queries

Literary Agency: Aevitas Creative Management (ACM) UK (**L006**)

Fiction > *Novels*
    Literary; Romance; Upmarket Crime; Upmarket

Nonfiction > *Nonfiction Books*
    Narrative Nonfiction; Women's Issues

Closed to approaches.

Focuses in upmarket and literary fiction by authors who write in English and Spanish. Maria is an editorially minded agent that works closely with her authors with a long-term career plan. She is passionate about international voices and is used to working with authors that live in different corners of the world. She reads broadly yet is particularly drawn by character-driven, heart-wrenching fiction, modern love stories, and genre-bending upmarket crime. She is always looking for that perfect line that makes her thrill, paying special attention to the voice on the page and is always up for a surprise in a manuscript, looking for stories she hasn't read before. She is also interested in narrative non-fiction about women's experiences.

Authors: Safia El Aaddam; Ayesha Harruna Attah; Federico Axat; Lucía Baskaran; Meaghan Beatley; Lucía Benavides; Victor Lloret Blackburn; Maame Blue; Emily Cunningham; Rijula Das; Avni Doshi; Guillermo Erades; Eudald Espluga; Sujatha Fernandes; Karen Havelin; Sunnah Khan; Natalia Litvinova; Lucía Alba Martínez; Elena Medel; Elizabeth Morris; Irene Muchemi-Ndiritu; Maria Nicolau; Gemma Ruiz Palà; Mariane Pearl; Claudia Polo; Alana S. Portero; Zara Raheem; Devika Rege; Yaffa S. Santos; Marta Sanz; Shubhangi Swarup; María Sánchez; Cristina Sánchez-Andrade; Begoña Gómez Urzaiz

L527 Seventh Agency

Literary Agency
United Kingdom

info@seventhagency.co.uk

https://www.seventhagency.co.uk

ADULT > **Fiction** > *Novels*
    Commercial; Fantasy; Historical Fiction; Literary; Mystery; Romance; Science Fiction; Thrillers

CHILDREN'S > **Fiction** > *Middle Grade*

NEW ADULT > **Fiction** > *Novels*

YOUNG ADULT > **Fiction** > *Novels*

Accepts submissions in March, July, and November. To submit, sign up to mailing list on website. During open submission periods you will receive a link to the submissions form within 48 hours. If you sign up outside of a submission period, you will be notified a week before the next submission period opens. Currently prioritises UK writers but will accept English language submissions from writers based in other parts of the world.

L528 Charlotte Seymour

Literary Agent
United Kingdom

charlotte@johnsonandalcock.co.uk

http://www.johnsonandalcock.co.uk/charlotte-seymour

Literary Agency: Johnson & Alcock (**L302**)

Fiction > *Novels*
    Book Club Fiction; Crime; Literary; Suspense; Thrillers

Nonfiction > *Nonfiction Books*
    Arts; Cookery; Cultural History; Food; Journalism; Nature; Popular Science; Social History

Closed to approaches.

In fiction, looks for book club and literary fiction as well as outstanding character – and voice-driven crime, thriller and suspense. She loves writing that crosses boundaries, whether geographic or linguistic or in bringing a twist to a genre.

In non-fiction, she is interested in accessible, engaging writing on a range of subjects including popular science, social and cultural history, reportage, nature, the arts, food and cookery. She especially loves hybrid books, for example, when in a memoir, the personal is interwoven with a bigger story or subject.

L529 The Shaw Agency

Literary Agency
United Kingdom

https://www.theshawagency.co.uk

ADULT
Fiction > *Novels*
  Commercial; Literary
Nonfiction > *Nonfiction Books*
  Lifestyle; Narrative Nonfiction; Wellbeing
CHILDREN'S
Fiction > *Novels*
Nonfiction > *Nonfiction Books*
TEEN > Fiction > *Novels*

Closed to approaches.

Handles literary and commercial fiction, fact and fiction books for children (6+) and teenagers/young adults, and narrative nonfiction. Send query through online form with one-page synopsis, first 10 pages, and email address for response. See website for full guidelines.

Literary Agent: Kate Shaw

L530 Caroline Sheldon
Literary Agent
United Kingdom

Literary Agency: Rogers, Coleridge & White Ltd (**L501**)

L531 Hannah Sheppard
Literary Agent
United Kingdom

Literary Agency: Hannah Sheppard Literary Agency (**L262**)

L532 Sheree Bykofsky Associates, Inc.
Literary Agency
4326 Harbor Beach Boulevard, PO Box 706, Brigantine, NJ 08203
United States

shereebee@aol.com

http://www.shereebee.com

Nonfiction > *Nonfiction Books*
  Biography; Business; Comedy / Humour; Cookery; Current Affairs; Films; Games; Health; Multicultural; Music; Parenting; Personal Development; Psychology; Spirituality; Women's Interests

Send: Query
Don't send: Full text
How to send: Email
How not to send: Fax; Post

Send query by email only. Include one page query in the body of the email. No attachments.

Authors: Jeffrey Fox; Sue Hitzmann; Jason Kelly

Literary Agent: Sheree Bykofsky

L533 Shesto Literary
Literary Agency
United Kingdom

https://shesto-literary.com

Professional Body: The Association of Authors' Agents (AAA)

Fiction > *Novels*

Nonfiction > *Nonfiction Books*

Representing authors of fiction and nonfiction.

Literary Agent: Camilla Shestopal (**L534**)

L534 Camilla Shestopal
Literary Agent
United Kingdom

https://shesto-literary.com
https://shesto-literary.com/about/

Literary Agency: Shesto Literary (**L533**)

ADULT
Fiction > *Novels*
  Crime; Ghost Stories; Historical Fiction; Horror; Mystery; Psychological Thrillers; Romantic Suspense; Supernatural / Paranormal; Suspense; Thrillers; Women's Fiction
Nonfiction > *Nonfiction Books*
  General, and in particular: Memoir; Narrative Nonfiction; Self Help
CHILDREN'S > Fiction > *Middle Grade*
YOUNG ADULT > Fiction > *Novels*

Send: Query; Author bio; Synopsis; Writing sample; Proposal; Outline
How to send: Online contact form

Looking for: crime fiction (encompassing thriller, mystery, psychological thriller); supernatural suspense; Ghost stories; romantic suspense; historical fiction; women's fiction; children's (middle grade and YA only); horror; and non-fiction (including anything which is topical, appealing, accessible such as self-help, narrative and memoir).

Do not send science-fiction, fantasy, short stories, poetry collections, erotica, or picture books for children.

L535 Julia Silk
Literary Agent
United Kingdom

julia@greyhoundliterary.co.uk

https://greyhoundliterary.co.uk/agent/julia-silk/
https://twitter.com/juliasreading
https://www.instagram.com/juliasreading/
https://www.pinterest.co.uk/juliasreadingbo/my-favourite-books/

Literary Agency: Greyhound Literary

Fiction > *Novels*
  Commercial; Historical Fiction; Literary; Upmarket Crime; Upmarket Thrillers

Nonfiction > *Nonfiction Books*
  Crime; Health; Journalism; Lifestyle; Memoir; Narrative Nonfiction; Wellbeing

Send: Query; Writing sample
How to send: Email

In fiction she is looking for smart, compelling writing across the spectrum from commercial to literary, particularly when it opens a door into a previously inaccessible world or experience, exposes our flaws and hypocrisies in new ways, or upends expectations with wit and energy. She is also drawn to the combination of the acutely personal and the universal that makes great memoir, as well as the blurring of the lines of form and genre in books across categories such as true crime/memoir. She is a huge fan of upmarket crime and thrillers and is also on the lookout for immaculately voiced historical fiction. In narrative non-fiction she is keen to hear from journalists and experts illuminating new stories and previously unexplored subjects; on the practical side she represents a number of writers in health, wellbeing and lifestyle, and is interested in original evidence-based proposals in this area from experts with a strong platform. She loves to work with writers and on books that shape and change readers' view of the world.

Authors: Tobi Asare; Juliet Bell; Leona Nichole Black; Owen Booth; Luce Brett; Sarah Jane Butler; Kirsty Eyre; Marchelle Farrell; A P Firdaus; Clare Fisher; Liz Fraser; Claire Gleeson; Janet Gover; Sarah Graham; Elaine Gregersen; Hayley Gullen; Karen Gurney; Maisie Hill; Heidi James; Ginger Jones; Fiona Longmuir; Amanda Mason; Jen Moore; Charlotte Ord; Rebecca Rogers; Rebecca Schiller; Clare Seal; Carry Somers; Gemma Tizzard; Nikki Trott; Hayley Webster; Penny Wincer; Laura Wyatt-Smith

L536 Tanera Simons
Literary Agent; Company Director
United Kingdom

Tanera@greenstoneliterary.com

https://www.greenstoneliterary.com
https://www.greenstoneliterary.com/agents/eiusmod-sed-et-magna
https://x.com/tanera_simons
https://www.instagram.com/tanera.simons/

Literary Agency: Greenstone Literary (**L252**)

Fiction > *Novels*
  Book Club Fiction; Commercial; Domestic Suspense; Historical Fiction; Psychology; Romance; Romantasy; Romantic Comedy; Thrillers; Women's Fiction

Send: Query; Author bio; Pitch; Market info; Synopsis; Writing sample
How to send: Online submission system
How not to send: Email

I am looking to acquire commercial fiction across a wide range of genres, including rom-com, love stories, historical fiction, book club, romantic fantasy, and female-driven narratives with a darker edge. Across all genres I am always looking for very clear hooks; a pitch that can be easily summarised and leave readers wanting more. I want to see stand-out, memorable characters whose journeys readers can't help but invest in.

L537 Cara Lee Simpson
Literary Agent
United Kingdom

clsimpson@pfd.co.uk

https://petersfraserdunlop.com/agent/cara-lee-simpson/

Literary Agency: Peters Fraser + Dunlop

Fiction > *Novels*
General, and in particular: Book Club Fiction; Ethnic Groups; Family Saga; Gender; Literary; Relationships; Social Class; Speculative

Nonfiction > *Nonfiction Books*
Memoir; Narrative Nonfiction; Nature; Real Life Stories; Social Commentary

Send: Query; Synopsis; Writing sample; Proposal; Author bio
How to send: Email

I am on the lookout for general fiction, immersive book club novels and literary fiction. I generally lean towards fiction that is accessible to a wide readership while remaining beautifully written, and I'm always interested in stories that explore gender, race, class, sexuality, and those which offer a profound look at relationship dynamics. I would love to find a traditional intergenerational family or friendship story (contemporary or historical), something sweeping in scope with a richly imagined setting, exploring an unusual event or unexpected setup. I would also love to find something speculative. I work on a select number of narrative non-fiction titles and am interested in memoirs and real-life stories, nature writing, and social commentaries told through an interesting lens and with a strong sense of personal journey.

Authors: Tufayel Ahmed; Jacqueline Bublitz; Abi Canepa-Anson; Angela Chadwick; Roxy Dunn; Ben Halls; C.R. Howell; Kiprop Kimutai; Shilo Kino; Kira Mcpherson; Niamh Ní Mhaoileoin; Okechukwu Nzelu; Jonathan Page; Dan Spencer

L538 Amandeep Singh
Associate Agent
United Kingdom

https://www.grahammawchristie.com
https://www.grahammawchristie.com/about

Literary Agency: Graham Maw Christie Literary Agency (**L246**)

Fiction > *Novels*
Book Club Fiction; Fantasy; Grimdark; Historical Fiction; Romance; Speculative; Upmarket

Nonfiction > *Nonfiction Books*
Climate Science; Current Affairs; Economics; Memoir; Nature; Personal Development; Politics; Relationships; Science

Send: Query; Proposal; Outline; Pitch; Synopsis; Author bio; Writing sample; Market info; Marketing plan
How to send: Email

For non-fiction, she is looking for compelling memoir about universal experiences. She would also like to hear from academics and journalists writing for a trade audience in the areas of politics and current affairs, relationships, nature and climate crisis, science and economy. She is seeking science writing that illuminates and drives topical conversation. In personal development, she is looking for books that cut through the noise and offer research-based or expert insights. For fiction, she is building a select list of book club and upmarket fiction – character-led stories with lots of heart. She is also seeking select fantasy and speculative fiction, from grimdark historical to whimsical cosy romance.

L539 Aiden Siobhan
Associate Agent
United States

asiobhan@ldlainc.com

https://aidensiobhan.com
http://www.ldlainc.com/about
https://querymanager.com/query/asiobhan
https://twitter.com/aiden_png
http://instagram.com/aiden.png

Literary Agency: Laura Dail Literary Agency

ADULT
  Fiction
    Graphic Novels: General
    Novels: Contemporary; Historical Fiction; LGBTQIA; Psychological Horror; Romance; Speculative; Supernatural / Paranormal
  Nonfiction > *Graphic Nonfiction*

CHILDREN'S > **Fiction**
  Graphic Novels: General
  Middle Grade: General, and in particular: Fantasy

YOUNG ADULT > **Fiction**
  Graphic Novels: General
  Novels: General, and in particular: Fantasy

How to send: Query Tracker

Loves any story that is diverse, heartfelt, beautifully written, and makes them stay up reading until 3 A.M. Send them your trope-filled, high-stakes, addicting novels that will hook them so well they'll have to draw fan art (and they will)!

L540 Skylark Literary
Literary Agency
19 Parkway, Weybridge, Surrey, KT13 9HD
United Kingdom

submissions@skylark-literary.com
info@skylark-literary.com

https://www.skylark-literary.com
https://twitter.com/SkylarkLit
http://www.facebook.com/skylarkliteraryltd

Professional Body: The Association of Authors' Agents (AAA)

CHILDREN'S > **Fiction**
  Chapter Books; *Early Readers*; *Middle Grade*
YOUNG ADULT > **Fiction** > *Novels*

Send: Full text; Synopsis
How to send: Word file email attachment

Handles fiction for children, from chapter books for emerging readers up to young adult / crossover titles. No picture books. Send query by email with one-page synopsis and full ms. No postal submissions.

Literary Agents: Amber J. Caravéo; Joanna Moult

L541 Antoinette Van Sluytman
Associate Agent
United States

https://www.lookingglasslit.com/antoinette-van-sluytman
https://querymanager.com/query/2783
https://aalitagents.org/author/antoinette-van-sluytman/
https://twitter.com/antoinight
https://www.instagram.com/toni_vansluy
https://www.linkedin.com/in/antoinette-van-sluytman-83b5a423a/

Literary Agency: Looking Glass Literary & Media Management (**L370**)
Professional Body: Association of American Literary Agents (AALA)

ADULT > **Fiction**
  Graphic Novels: General
  Novels: Adventure; Dark Fantasy; High / Epic Fantasy; Historical Fiction; Horror; Science Fiction; Speculative
YOUNG ADULT > **Fiction**
  Graphic Novels; *Novels*

Closed to approaches.

Interested in all genres of speculative fiction, specifically cosmic horror, dark fantasy, epic fantasy, sci-fi, in addition to historical fiction. Antoinette maintains special interest in adult projects but is also open to select YA and graphic novels. In general she loves lyrical prose that challenges narrative conventions, ambitiously immersive worlds inspired by different cultures, morally gray and dysfunctional but lovable characters with fun dynamics, and new takes on old tropes. She is drawn to atmospheric and lyrical prose and complex philosophical/psychological themes across all genres. Some general themes she enjoys are adventures, antiheroines, quirky concepts you might find in an anime, dark fantasy, and anticolonialism. In historical fiction she's interested in finding stories inspired by non-western mythologies or about the untold stories of female heroines around the world.

L542 Georgie Smith
Literary Agent
United Kingdom

Literary Agency: David Higham Associates Ltd (**L146**)

L543 Shania N. Soler
Literary Agent
United States

https://www.metamorphosisliteraryagency.com
https://www.metamorphosisliteraryagency.com/submissions
https://querymanager.com/query/shaniansoler
https://x.com/beyond_literary

Literary Agency: Metamorphosis Literary Agency (**L406**)

ADULT > Fiction > *Novels*
  Book Club Fiction; Comedy / Humour; Dystopian Fiction; Folklore, Myths, and Legends; Gothic; High / Epic Fantasy; Historical Fiction; Horror; Low Fantasy; Magical Realism; Romance; Romantasy

CHILDREN'S > Fiction > *Middle Grade*

NEW ADULT > Fiction > *Novels*

YOUNG ADULT > Fiction > *Novels*

Closed to approaches.

Has been an avid book lover from the moment she picked up Richelle Mead's Vampire Academy. Ever since then, her TBR pile has steadily grown. Currently working on an MA at the University of Leeds, she has received her Bachelor of Arts in English from the University of Maine and plans to pursue a PhD in Japan, where she spent 7 months during her undergrad studying the language and culture.

L544 Jennifer March Soloway
Literary Agent
United States

soloway@andreabrownlit.com

https://querymanager.com/query/JenniferMarchSoloway
https://twitter.com/marchsoloway

Literary Agency: Andrea Brown Literary Agency, Inc.

ADULT > Fiction > *Novels*
  Commercial; Crime; Literary; Psychological Suspense

CHILDREN'S > Fiction
  Middle Grade: Adventure; Comedy / Humour; Contemporary; Fantasy; Ghost Stories; Mystery; Realistic
  Picture Books: General, and in particular: Comedy / Humour

YOUNG ADULT > Fiction > *Novels*
  Family; Literary; Mental Health; Psychological Horror; Relationships; Romance; Sexuality; Suspense; Thrillers

Send: Query
How to send: Email; By referral

Represents authors and illustrators of picture book, middle grade, and YA stories, and is actively building her list. Although she specializes in children's literature, she also represents adult fiction, both literary and commercial, particularly crime and psychological suspense projects.

Currently accepting queries by referral only.

L545 Sophie Hicks Agency
Literary Agency
Providence Yard, Ezra Street, London, E2 7RJ
United Kingdom
Tel: +44 (0) 20 3617 0997

info@sophiehicksagency.com

https://www.sophiehicksagency.com
https://twitter.com/SophieHicksAg
https://www.instagram.com/sophiehicksagency/

Professional Body: The Association of Authors' Agents (AAA)

ADULT
  Fiction > *Novels*
  Nonfiction > *Nonfiction Books*

CHILDREN'S > Fiction > *Novels*

Send: Query; Writing sample; Synopsis
How to send: Email

Welcomes submissions. Send query by email with sample pages attached as Word or PDF documents. See website for full guidelines and specific submissions email addresses. No poetry or scripts for theatre, film or television, and not currently accepting illustrated books for children.

Authors: Sarah Bannan; Lee Boyce; William Butler-Adams; Helen Chandler-Wilde; Carl Cox; Sarah Crosby; Michaela Dunbar; Ruth Fitzmaurice; Kate Ford; Lewis Hine; Shahroo Izadi; Signe Johansen; Sophie Monks Kaufman; Jesse McClure; Phil McNulty; Andrew Meehan; Katie Treggiden; Claire Walsh; Tom Whipple; Jim White

Literary Agents: Sophie Hicks; Sarah Williams

L546 Arley Sorg
Literary Agent
United States

https://arleysorg.com
https://ktliterary.com/submissions/
https://querymanager.com/query/QueryArley

Literary Agency: KT Literary (**L345**)

Fiction > *Novels*
  Environment; Fantasy; Horror; Literary; Science Fiction; Speculative

Closed to approaches.

Primarily interested in adult speculative titles, including science fiction, fantasy, and horror with speculative/fantastic elements, literary speculative fiction, and climate fiction.

L547 James Spackman
Literary Agent
United Kingdom

https://www.thebksagency.com/about
https://www.thebksagency.com/submissions

Literary Agency: The BKS Agency (**L063**)

Fiction > *Graphic Novels*

Nonfiction
  Graphic Nonfiction: General
  Nonfiction Books: Culture; Music; Sport

Closed to approaches.

Looking for sport, music, culture and smart thinking.

L548 Hayley Steed
Literary Agent
United Kingdom

https://www.janklowandnesbit.co.uk
https://janklowandnesbit.co.uk/agency/hayley-steed

Literary Agency: Janklow & Nesbit UK Ltd (**L297**)

Fiction > *Novels*
  Book Club Fiction; Commercial; Dark Academia; Dark; Dystopian Fiction; Family; High Concept; Historical Fiction; Horror; Light Fantasy; Mystery; Romance; Romantasy; Romantic Comedy; Speculative; Thrillers; Women's Fiction

Send: Query; Synopsis; Writing sample
How to send: Email
How not to send: Post

I'm looking for commercial and book club fiction across all genres. I'm particularly drawn to a strong hook – a setting, scenario or a 'what if' that captures my attention immediately and leads the way into a gripping story. I love to find compelling and distinctive voices that draw me in but are matched with well-paced plots and commercial appeal. I'm always open to books that cross genres, or which feel a little different.

L549 Jenny Stephens
Literary Agent
United States

https://www.sll.com/our-team

Literary Agency: Sterling Lord Literistic, Inc.

Nonfiction > *Nonfiction Books*
 Cookery; Cultural Criticism; Food; History; How To; Lifestyle; Mind, Body, Spirit; Narrative Nonfiction; Nature; Social Justice; Wellbeing

Send: Query; Synopsis; Writing sample
How to send: Online submission system

Represents award-winning nonfiction in a variety of categories including practical lifestyle and thoughtful how-to projects, particularly in the wellness and mindfulness spaces; cookbooks; and narrative nonfiction about history, cultural criticism, ecology and the natural world, food, and social justice. For both adults and kids, she loves highly designed books that inform and inspire through both text and image.

L550 Sternig & Byrne Literary Agency
Literary Agency
2370 S. 107th Street, Apt 4, Milwaukee, Wisconsin 53227-2036
United States
Tel: +1 (414) 328-8034

jackbyrne@hotmail.com

https://sternig-byrne-agency.com

Professional Bodies: Science Fiction and Fantasy Writers of America (SFWA); Mystery Writers of America (MWA)

Fiction > *Novels*
 Fantasy; Science Fiction

Closed to approaches.

Send brief query by post or email in first instance (if sending by email send in the body of the mail, do not send attachments). Will request further materials if interested. Currently only considering science fiction and fantasy. Preference given to writers with a publishing history.

Authors: Katherine Addison; John Haefele; Lael Littke; Kelly McCullough; Sarah Monette; Moira Moore; Jo Walton; David Michael Williams; John C. Wright

Literary Agent: Jack Byrne

L551 Rupert Stonehill
Literary Agent

Literary Agency: Independent Talent Group Ltd

L552 StoryWise
Literary Agency
41 Jubilee Road, Swanage, Dorset, BH19 2SE
United Kingdom

submissions@storywise.uk

https://storywise.uk
https://www.facebook.com/storywiseagency
https://twitter.com/StoryWiseAgency
https://www.instagram.com/storywiseagency/

Professional Body: The Association of Authors' Agents (AAA)

CHILDREN'S
 Fiction
  Middle Grade; Picture Books
 Nonfiction > *Nonfiction Books*

Closed to approaches.

Specialist children's literary agency representing bestselling and award-winning authors and illustrators of picture books, fiction and non-fiction.

L553 The Stringer Literary Agency LLC
Literary Agency
8429 Lorraine Road #408, Lakewood Ranch, FL 34202
United States

https://www.stringerlit.com
https://www.instagram.com/stringerlit/
https://www.pinterest.com/stringerlit/
https://www.facebook.com/StringerLit
https://twitter.com/MarleneStringer

Professional Bodies: Association of American Literary Agents (AALA); Mystery Writers of America (MWA); Society of Children's Book Writers and Illustrators (SCBWI); The Authors Guild; Women's Fiction Writers Association (WFWA)

ADULT > **Fiction** > *Novels*

CHILDREN'S > **Fiction**
 Middle Grade; Picture Books
YOUNG ADULT > **Fiction** > *Novels*

Send: Query; Synopsis; Pitch; Outline; Author bio
How to send: Query Tracker

A full-service literary agency specializing in commercial fiction since 2008.

Authors: Michelle Collins Anderson; Ciaran Bartlett; Emily Bleeker; Jen K Blom; Anna Bradley; Anabelle Bryant; Judy Campbell-Smith; Melinda Chiu Cook; Phyllis Dixon; Charlie Donlea; Trish Esden; Alyxandra Harvey; Erica Hayes; Lucy Hedrick; Isabella Kamal; Celina Kamler; Kristin Kisska; Caroline Lesniak; David Lewis; Guy Mace; Liane Merciel; Terri Parlato; Liz Perrine; Molly Pierce; Marianeli Rodriguez; Travis Simpson; Luanne G. Smith; Kate Pawson Studer; Bethany Wiggins; Sophie Williamson; Clare Zeschky

Literary Agents: Shari Maurer (**L397**); Marlene Stringer (**L554**)

L554 Marlene Stringer
Literary Agent
United States

https://aalitagents.org/author/marlenes/
https://querymanager.com/query/StringerLit

Literary Agency: The Stringer Literary Agency LLC (**L553**)
Professional Body: Association of American Literary Agents (AALA)

ADULT > **Fiction** > *Novels*
 Commercial; Historical Fiction; Literary; Psychological Horror; Women's Fiction

YOUNG ADULT > **Fiction** > *Novels*
 Contemporary; Crime; Fantasy; Magical Realism; Mystery; Romance; Suspense; Thrillers

Does not want:

Fiction > *Novels*: Erotic Romance

How to send: Query Tracker

Open to Book club fiction that straddles the commercial/literary line; Historical fiction; Women's Fiction, both contemporary and historical; Older YA, both fantasy and contemporary; Crime Fiction; Thrillers of all types; Suspense; Mysteries of all types; Romance (except erotic); Psychological Horror; Magical Realism.

L555 Wendy Strothman
Literary Agent; Partner
United States

https://www.aevitascreative.com/agent/wendy-strothman
https://www.strothmanagency.com/about
https://querymanager.com/query/WStrothman
http://aaronline.org/Sys/PublicProfile/2176866/417813

Literary Agencies: Aevitas; The Strothman Agency
Professional Body: Association of American Literary Agents (AALA)

Nonfiction > *Nonfiction Books*
 Current Affairs; History; Narrative Journalism; Narrative Nonfiction; Nature; Science

Closed to approaches.

Looking for books that matter, books that change the way we think about things we take for granted, that tell stories that readers can't forget, and advance scholarship and knowledge. History, narrative nonfiction, narrative journalism, science and nature, and current affairs.

Accepts referrals by email; otherwise approach through Query Manager.

L556 Stuart Krichevsky Literary Agency, Inc.

Literary Agency
118 East 28th Street, Suite 908, New York, NY 10016
United States

https://www.skagency.com

ADULT
  Fiction > *Novels*
  Nonfiction > *Nonfiction Books*

YOUNG ADULT
  Fiction > *Novels*
  Nonfiction > *Nonfiction Books*

Send: Query; Writing sample
How to send: In the body of an email

Send a query letter and the first ten pages of your manuscript or proposal in the body of an email (not an attachment) to one agent. Response only if interested.

Authors: Addison Armstrong; Roxanna Asgarian; Ahmed Badr; Emily Bloom; Katherine Blunt; Lyndsie Bourgon; Sol Brager; Hannah Brencher; Shavone Charles; Angela Chen; Carla Ciccone; Georgia Cloepfil; Chelsea Conaboy; Caren Cooper; Michelle Cyca; Ella Delany; Helen Donahue; Gabriel Dozal; Hope Ewing; Victoria Facelli; Chelsea Fairless; Anita Felicelli; Kathryn Finney; Kit Fox; John Fram; Katie Fricas; Adriana Gallardo; Lauren Garroni; Olivia Gatwood; Elyssa Goodman; Jessica Goudeau; Rose Hackman; Anita Hannig; Karen Ho; Lizz Huerta; Gabino Iglesias; Sarah Jaffe; Rachel McCarthy James; Amanda Jayatissa; R. Dean Johnson; Sophie Lucido Johnson; Charlotte Kaufman; Megan Kimble; Cassidy Krug; Dan Lewis; Audrea Lim; Catherine Lo; Michael Loynd; Julie Lunde; Jennifer Lunden; Bernice McFadden; Peter Mercurio; Sarafina Nance; Farah Nayeri; Okezie Nwoka; José Olivarez; Madeline Ostrander; Robin Page; Soraya Palmer; Amy Peterson; Karen Pinchin; Mira Ptacin; Shelley Puhak; José R. Ralat; Reyes Ramirez; Lydia Reeder; Raquel Reichard; Victoria Reihana; Ruben Reyes; Nadim Roberts; Prisca Dorcas Mojica Rodriguez; Zoë Schiffer; David Schonfeld; A. Brad Schwartz; Marina Scott; Margot Lee Shetterly; David Shih; Brie Spangler; Rachel Swaby; Kim Thai; Sofi Thanhauser; Kaitlyn Tiffany; Carson Vaughan; Sarah Vogel; Sarah Weinman; Kimberley Welman; Christina Wilcox; Nina Willner; Bernice Yeung; Charlyne Yi; Tom Zeller; Sara Zin

Literary Agents: Melissa Danaczko (**L139**); Barbara Jones (**L305**); Stuart Krichevsky (**L342**); David Patterson (**L457**); Aemilia Phillips (**L472**); Hannah Schwartz; Laura Usselman (**L581**); Mackenzie Brady Watson; Chandler Wickers (**L600**)

L557 Susan Schulman Literary Agency

Literary Agency
454 West 44th Street, New York, NY 10036
United States
Tel: +1 (212) 713-1633

Susan@Schulmanagency.com

https://twitter.com/SusanSchulman

Professional Body: Association of American Literary Agents (AALA)

ADULT
  Fiction > *Novels*
    General, and in particular: Commercial; Literary; Women's Fiction

  Nonfiction > *Nonfiction Books*
    Commercial; Creativity; Economics; Finance; Health; History; Legal; Literary; Memoir; Mind, Body, Spirit; Politics; Psychology; Social Issues; Writing

CHILDREN'S
  Fiction
    Board Books; Chapter Books; Middle Grade; Picture Books
  Nonfiction > *Nonfiction Books*
    History; Memoir; Popular Culture; Science

YOUNG ADULT > **Fiction** > *Novels*

Send: Query; Synopsis; Writing sample; Author bio
How to send: Email

Specializes in representing motion picture, television and allied rights, foreign rights, live stage including commercial theater, opera and dance adaptations, new media rights including e-book and digital applications, and other subsidiary rights on behalf of North American publishers and literary agents. The agency also represents its own clients domestically and internationally in all markets. The agency has a particular interest in fiction and non-fiction books for, by and about women and women's issues and interests, as well as all levels of children's books including picture books, middle-grade and young adult, history, science, pop culture, and memoir. Our primary interest however is in authors and their projects which explore big ideas about the world and being human. The agency's areas of focus include: commercial and literary fiction and non-fiction, specifically narrative memoir, politics, economics, social issues, history, urban planning, finance, law, health, psychology, body/mind/sprit, and creativity and writing.

Associate Agent: Emelie Burl

Literary Agent: Susan Schulman

L558 Susanna Lea Associates

Literary Agency
551 Fifth Avenue, Suite 616, New York, NY 10176
United States
Tel: +1 (646) 638-1435

ny@susannalea.com

http://www.susannaleaassociates.com

Fiction > *Novels*

Nonfiction > *Nonfiction Books*

Send: Query; Synopsis; Writing sample
How to send: Email
How not to send: Post; Fax

Agency based in France with US office in New York and UK office in London. No poetry, plays, screenplays, academic texts, or illustrated works., or queries by fax or post. Submit by email. See website for specific email addresses for US, UK, and French submissions. Include query letter, brief synopsis, first three chapters and/or proposal. Response not guaranteed.

L559 Kari Sutherland

Literary Agent
United States

kari@ktliterary.com

https://ktliterary.com/about/
https://querymanager.com/query/Kari_Sutherland_Query_Form
https://twitter.com/KariSutherland

Literary Agency: KT Literary (**L345**)

ADULT > **Fiction** > *Novels*: Upmarket

CHILDREN'S > **Fiction**
  Chapter Books; *Graphic Novels*; *Middle Grade*; *Picture Books*
YOUNG ADULT > **Fiction** > *Novels*

Closed to approaches.

Middle grade and YA are at the heart of her list, but she also represents picture books, chapter books, graphic novels, and upmarket fiction.

L560 Alice Sutherland-Hawes
Literary Agent
United Kingdom

https://www.ashliterary.com/#about

Literary Agency: ASH Literary

Closed to approaches.

Authors: Dina Al-Sabawi; Rebecca Ann; HF Brownfield; Ryan Crawford; Becki Jayne Crossley; Alex Falase-Koya; Abimbola Fashola; Kereen Getten; Tamika Gibson; Adina Glickman; Erica Gomez; Gina Gonzales; Sarah Guillory; Ravena Guron; Radiya Hafiza; Anika Hussain; Jennifer Iacopelli; Tess James-Mackey; Miranda Leiggi; Richard Mercado; Yasmine Naghdi; Samuel Pollen; Rebecca R; Cynthia So; Chitra Soundar; Claire Tomasi; Adelle Yeung

L561 Joanna Swainson
Literary Agent
United Kingdom

submissions@hardmanswainson.com
http://www.hardmanswainson.com/agents/joanna-swainson/
https://twitter.com/JoannaSwainson

Literary Agency: Hardman & Swainson (**L265**)

Fiction > *Novels*
Comedy / Humour; Commercial; Contemporary; Crime; Folk Horror; Ghost Stories; Historical Fiction; Horror; Literary; Speculative; Thrillers

Nonfiction > *Nonfiction Books*
Folklore, Myths, and Legends; Memoir; Narrative Nonfiction; Nature; Popular History; Science

Send: Synopsis; Full text
How to send: Email
How not to send: Post

In fiction, I'm looking for complex, larger-than-life characters. I love crime and thrillers at both ends of the commercial / literary spectrum. I also love a good ghost story and accessible speculative fiction, as well as a bit of horror, especially folk horror. Whatever the genre, whether literary or commercial, historical or contemporary, thriller or crime, I'm looking for originality and distinctive voices. I especially like fiction threaded with humour – not necessarily of the laugh out loud kind, it's often much subtler than that, but you can't have too many arresting observations and insights. On the non-fiction front, I enjoy narrative non-fiction, especially popular history (and prehistory) and science. I'm very partial to a memoir. I also enjoy nature writing and am interested in folklore.

Authors: Jon Bounds; Oggy Boytchev; Paul Braddon; Elizabeth Brooks; Mark Broomfield; Adrienne Chinn; Helen Cox; Jeremy Craddock; Sara Crowe; Emma Darwin; Stuart David; Caroline Davison; Carol Donaldson; Simon David Eden; Nicola Ford; Harry Freedman; James Gould-Bourn; Tom Higham; Michael Jecks; Oskar Cox Jensen; Stuart Johnstone; Lucy Lawrie; Peter Laws; David B. Lyons; Kevin Macneil; S R Masters; Lauren Price; Philip C Quaintrell; Patrick Roberts; Nick Russell-Pavier; Catherine Simpson; Danny Smith; Hollie Starling; Eliska Tanzer; Sarah Tierney; B P Walter; Samantha Wilson

L562 Sallyanne Sweeney
Literary Agent
United Kingdom

Literary Agency: Mulcahy Sweeney Literary Agency (**L423**)

L563 Emily Sweet
Literary Agent
United Kingdom

https://www.emilysweetassociates.com
https://www.aevitascreative.com/agent/emily-sweet

Literary Agencies: Emily Sweet Associates; Aevitas Creative Management (ACM) UK (**L006**)

Nonfiction > *Nonfiction Books*
Biography; Cookery; Current Affairs; Food and Drink; History; Lifestyle; Memoir

Send: Query; Synopsis
How to send: Online contact form

Particularly looks for exciting, original and useful cookery and lifestyle books, as well as innovative storytelling in the areas of history, memoir, biography, current affairs and topical non-fiction.

Authors: Fliss Chester; Amelia Christie-Miller; Nicky Corbishley; N.J. Crosskey; Anja Dunk; Becky Excell; Xanthe Gladstone; Alex Jackson; Tom Jackson; Irina Janakievska; Genevieve Jenner; Philip Khoury; Anna Koska; Nicola Lamb; Mitch Lane; Shu Han Lee; Ben Lippett; David Mountain; Tanya Mukendi; Amy Newsome; Emily Roz; Matthew Ryle; Su Scott; Tim Siadatan; Alex Stacey; Emma Tarlo; Katie Taylor; Joe Trivelli; Sumayya Usmani; Joe Woodhouse

L564 Becky Sweren
Senior Agent
United States

https://aevitascreative.com/agents/#agent-7413

Literary Agency: Aevitas

Nonfiction > *Nonfiction Books*
Culture; History; Investigative Journalism; Memoir

Closed to approaches.

Authors: Jesse Ball; Mark Braude; Adin Dobkin; Beck Dorey-Stein; Renee Dudley; Penina Eilberg-Schwartz; Valerie Fridland; Nicholas Griffin; Lawrence Jackson; Mohamad Jebara; Faith Jones; Jillian Keenan; Jake Keiser; Sulaiman Khatib; Ali Kriegsman; Daniel Levin; Maya Wei-Haas; Eric M. O'Neill; Matteson Perry; Pen Rhodeen; Mohammed Al Samawi; Laurie Segall; Shabtai Shavit; Gabourey Sidibe; Judith E. Stein; Noa Tishby; Steven Ujifusa; Jack Viertel; Payam Zamani; Lijia Zhang

L565 Laurel Symonds
Literary Agent
United States

https://ktliterary.com/about/
https://www.manuscriptwishlist.com/mswl-post/laurel-symonds/
https://twitter.com/laurelsymonds
https://www.facebook.com/laurelsymondsagent
https://www.linkedin.com/in/laurelsymonds/

Literary Agency: KT Literary (**L345**)

CHILDREN'S
Fiction
Graphic Novels: General
Middle Grade: General, and in particular: Contemporary; Fantasy; Historical Fiction; Literary
Picture Books: General

Nonfiction > *Nonfiction Books*
General, and in particular: Engineering; History; Mathematics; Science; Technology

YOUNG ADULT
Fiction
Graphic Novels: General
Novels: General, and in particular: Commercial; Contemporary; Fantasy; Historical Fiction
Nonfiction > *Nonfiction Books*
General, and in particular: Engineering; History; Mathematics; Science; Technology

Closed to approaches.

I represent young adult and middle grade fiction, and I have a special interest in contemporary, historical fiction, and genre-blending fantasy. I look for engaging voices, commercial hooks, and immersive worlds. My YA tastes are pretty commercial but my middle grade tastes can skew more literary, and I'm especially interested in middle grade that might lend itself to illustration.

I also represent picture books, graphic novels, and other illustrated work, and I am open to new clients who are both authors and illustrators. My tastes are diverse, ranging from sophisticated to quirky to gently humorous. I especially appreciate a smart use of color and perspective.

Additionally, I represent select nonfiction for children and young adults, especially projects about STEM or history with age-appropriate hooks and series potential.

L566 Marin Takikawa
Associate Agent
United States

mtakikawa@friedrichagency.com

http://www.friedrichagency.com/marin
https://twitter.com/marintakikawa
https://www.instagram.com/marintakikawa

Literary Agency: The Friedrich Agency LLC (**L220**)

ADULT
  Fiction > *Novels*
    Environment; Family Saga; Folklore, Myths, and Legends; Ghost Stories; Literary; Magical Realism; Social Issues; Speculative; Upmarket

  Nonfiction > *Nonfiction Books*
    Cultural History; Narrative Nonfiction; Postcolonialism; Social History

YOUNG ADULT > **Fiction** > *Novels*
  Adventure; Contemporary; Dark; Gothic; Literary; Mystery; Speculative

Send: Query; Writing sample
How to send: In the body of an email
How not to send: Email attachment

For adult fiction, I'm always seeking innovative—both in idea and structure—literary/upmarket fiction that's lush, evocative, and full of heart(break). I'm also looking for family sagas, novels that subvert forms of power, specifically relating to colonialism/imperialism, and engages with social and environmental issues. I'm also particularly enamored by genre-bending works: speculative concepts, ghost stories, magical realism, and anything that plays with myth and folklore will always catch my eye! For YA, I'm looking for voice-driven and literary-leaning novels with the emotional breadth and depth in the tradition of authors like Emily X. R. Pan and Kelly Loy Gilbert—although I won't say no to sweeter contemporary YA (my comfort reads are Anna & the French Kiss, Love & Gelato, and Better Than the Movies)! I'm also excited by speculative concepts and am not afraid of going dark. Give me all your gothic, atmospheric, haunting books (especially with a sense of mystery and adventure)! Some of my recent favorite YA books are If You Could See the Sun by Ann Liang, All My Rage by Sabaa Tahir, and Firekeeper's Daughter by Angeline Boulley. In adult nonfiction, I gravitate toward community-oriented narrative nonfiction with engaging and insightful research or reportage, as well as social/cultural histories and criticisms. I'm also looking for narrative nonfiction that is intersectional, resistant, and radical in nature, that questions why we have the institutions, ideas, and systems we have in place. I often think about the legacies of colonialism, how it haunts and perpetuates in various forms in the modern age (such as the environment and in capitalism), but also about collective action/liberation and its sense of possibilities and what an equitable future could look like. I'd love to hear from you if your work is in this space.

L567 Emily Talbot
Literary Agent
United Kingdom

etalbot@unitedagents.co.uk

https://www.unitedagents.co.uk/etalbotunitedagentscouk

Literary Agency: United Agents
Literary Agent: Jodie Hodges (**L282**)

ADULT > **Nonfiction** > *Nonfiction Books*

CHILDREN'S > **Fiction**
  Middle Grade; *Picture Books*

YOUNG ADULT > **Fiction** > *Novels*

Closed to approaches.

Represents hildren's illustrators and authors of picture books, middle grade, YA and non-fiction.

Authors: Aysha Awwad; Susanna Bailey; Abigail Balfe; Alex Barrow; Becky Baur; Gabby Dawnay; Sophie Deen; Chloe Douglass; Ed Eaves; Alison Guile; James Harris; Sam Hearn; Benjamin Hughes; James Lent; Rebecca Lewis-Oakes; Maggie Li; Roger McGough; Becka Moor; Polly Owen; Keith Robinson; Andy Sagar; Jion Sheibani; Qian Shi; Georgina Stevens; Barry Timms; Jacqueline Tucker; Kael Tudor; Lucy Unwin; Maddy Vian; Lucia Vinti

L568 Amy Tannenbaum
Literary Agent
United States

atannenbaum@janerotrosen.com

https://www.janerotrosen.com/agents
https://www.janerotrosen.com/contact-amy-tannenbaum

Literary Agency: Jane Rotrosen Agency

Fiction > *Novels*
  Commercial; Contemporary Romance; Historical Fiction; Literary; Psychological Suspense; Speculative; Thrillers; Women's Fiction

Send: Query
How to send: In the body of an email
How not to send: Email attachment

represents clients who write across a variety of genres including women's fiction, historical fiction, grounded speculative, contemporary romance, thriller and psychological suspense. She is particularly interested in those categories, as well as fiction that falls into the sweet spot between literary and commercial and works by marginalized voices.

L569 Alice Tasman
Literary Agent
United States

https://www.jvnla.com
https://www.jvnla.com/submitat

Literary Agency: The Jean V. Naggar Literary Agency (**L299**)

ADULT
  Fiction > *Novels*
    Commercial; Literary

  Nonfiction > *Nonfiction Books*
    Biography; Music; Narrative Nonfiction; Popular Culture

CHILDREN'S > **Fiction** > *Middle Grade*

YOUNG ADULT > **Fiction** > *Novels*

Send: Query; Outline; Author bio
How to send: Online submission system

Focuses on literary and commercial fiction and is always on the lookout for debut writers. She is especially interested in novels – whether adult, young adult, or middle grade – that combine excellent writing, voice, and characters with a great plot. She is also drawn to smart, off-beat non-fiction, particularly works of narrative non-fiction on biography, music, or pop-culture.

L570 Paige Terlip
Literary Agent
United States

paige@andreabrownlit.com

https://www.andreabrownlit.com/agents.html
https://twitter.com/pterlip
https://www.instagram.com/pterlip/

Literary Agency: Andrea Brown Literary Agency, Inc.

ADULT
  Fiction > *Novels*
    Cozy Mysteries; Fantasy; High Concept; Magic; Psychological Suspense; Science Fiction; Thrillers; Upmarket

  Nonfiction > *Nonfiction Books*
    Mind, Body, Spirit; Narrative Nonfiction; Self Help

CHILDREN'S > **Fiction**
  Chapter Books; *Middle Grade*; *Picture Books*

YOUNG ADULT > **Fiction** > *Novels*
  High Concept; Magic

Send: Author bio; Query; Writing sample; Pitch; Market info
How to send: Query Tracker

Represents all categories of children's books from picture books to young adult, as well as select adult fiction and nonfiction. She is also actively building her list of illustrators and is especially looking for author-illustrators and graphic novel illustrators.

L571 Kate Testerman
Literary Agent
United States

Literary Agency: KT Literary (**L345**)

Closed to approaches.

L572 Henry Thayer
Literary Agent
United States

hthayer@bromasite.com

Literary Agency: Brandt & Hochman Literary Agents, Inc.
Professional Body: Association of American Literary Agents (AALA)

Fiction > *Novels*
General, and in particular: Literary

Nonfiction > *Nonfiction Books*
General, and in particular: American History; Arts; Basketball; Biography; Current Affairs; Films; History; Politics; Popular Culture; Popular Music; Science; Sport

Send: Query
How to send: Email

Primarily represents nonfiction, including biography, history, current affairs, international relations, politics, the arts and sciences, sports, and popular culture. He is looking for engaging stories that make complex ideas accessible to the curious reader and bold arguments that challenge the conventional wisdom. He is also interested in finding new, compelling voices in literary and genre fiction, especially novels that bridge the gap between the two. His wide-ranging interests, within the world of books and beyond it, include American history, popular music, film, and basketball. Query by email only.

L573 The Theseus Agency
Literary Agency
29 Rosslyn Hill, London, NW3 5UJ
United Kingdom
Tel: +44 (0) 20 4559 9421

info@theseus.agency

https://www.theseus.agency

Fiction > *Novels*

Nonfiction > *Nonfiction Books*

We help brands, rights-holders, and creators pinpoint and harness what makes them matter to the wider world and shape their development.

Our work blends creative strategy with proactive rights and brand management to deliver practical outcomes: growing revenue, reach, and relevance.

Literary Agent: Louise Ripley-Duggan (**L494**)

L574 Euan Thorneycroft
Literary Agent
United Kingdom

https://amheath.com/agents/euan-thorneycroft/
http://twitter.com/EuanThorneycrof

Literary Agency: A.M. Heath & Company Limited, Author's Agents (**L002**)

Fiction > *Novels*
Adventure; Book Club Fiction; Commercial; Crime; Historical Fiction; Historical Mystery Fiction; Literary; Police Procedural; Psychological Suspense; Spy Thrilllers; Thrillers

Nonfiction > *Nonfiction Books*
History; Memoir; Nature; Politics; Science; Technology

How to send: Online submission system

I love novels with propulsive stories, fascinating characters, and great heart, whether it is commercial fiction or something more literary. I want first-in-class storytelling. And I want to be made to care. I love crossover literary/commercial fiction (Bookclub fiction). I read a lot of crime and thrillers from police procedurals to spy fiction, psychological suspense and full-throttle action adventure, and if they have a really unusual and imaginative hook, so much the better. Historical fiction is also a big passion of mine, and that might be a historical crime series. In non-fiction, I love memoirs in all shapes and sizes. I am also interested in working with experts in their field and helping them turn their ideas into something that will appeal to a broad readership. I am most interested in those ideas which can be told through stories and narratives, in the areas of history, science, technology, politics and nature.

Agency Assistant: Jessica Lee

L575 Steph Thwaites
Literary Agent
United Kingdom

thwaitesoffice@curtisbrown.co.uk

https://curtisbrown.co.uk
https://curtisbrown.co.uk/agent/steph-thwaites

Literary Agency: Curtis Brown (**L135**)

Fiction > *Novels*
Book Club Fiction; Commercial; Dark Humour; Family; Gothic; Horror; Judaism; Middle East; Politics; Romance; Thrillers; United States; Upmarket

Nonfiction > *Nonfiction Books*
High Concept; Memoir; Middle East; Politics; United States

Send: Query; Synopsis; Author bio; Writing sample
How to send: Email

Represents a broad range of writers from debut authors to bestselling brand authors and is drawn to a variety of genres including thrillers and espionage, book club fiction and romance with a twist, gothic stories, horror and dark humour. On the non-fiction side, she enjoys smart thinking and big ideas books appeal, as well as conversation starters, politics, memoir plus and "stealth" help.

She's on the hunt for commercial upmarket writing that is powerful and cinematic but feels different and fresh. She wants to read a story that feels unlike anything encountered before. A gripping plot is necessary, as well as a strong voice across all genres. Anything effortlessly quick-witted and funny, or with memorable characters.

She enjoys the unexpected and books which explore family relationships and dynamics. At the moment she's particularly interested in compelling stories with Jewish themes and politics of the US and the Middle East.

L576 Anne Tibbets
Literary Agent
United States

http://maassagency.com/anne-tibbets/
https://querymanager.com/query/AnneTibbets

Literary Agency: Donald Maass Literary Agency (**L160**)

Fiction > *Novels*
Cozy Mysteries; Domestic Mystery; Domestic; Fantasy; Horror; International; Literary Horror; Mystery; Police Procedural; Psychological Horror; Science Fiction; Suspense; Thrillers

Closed to approaches.

Represents adult commercial genre, primarily thrillers, mysteries, science fiction, fantasy, horror and select non-fiction.

L577 Antony Topping
Literary Agent
United Kingdom

http://greeneheaton.co.uk/agents/antony-topping/

Literary Agency: Greene & Heaton Ltd (**L251**)

Fiction > *Novels*
Book Club Fiction; Contemporary; Crime; Historical Literary; Historical Thrillers; Thrillers; Upmarket

Nonfiction > *Nonfiction Books*
Comedy / Humour; Food; History; Memoir; Music; Nature; Science

I represent historical thriller writers, contemporary and historical literary novelists, upmarket genre and bookclub fiction, science writers, food writers, historians, nature writers, music journalists, memoirists, and cultural critics.

Authors: Clayton Page Aldern; Amen Alonge; Peter Apps; Lucy Ashe; Helena Attlee; Mevan

Babakar; Lucy Brazier; James Bridle; Jason Byrne; Tom Campbell; Charles Cockell; Pam Corbin; Russell Davies; Anna Davis; Marie Derome; Patrick Drake; Suzannah Dunn; Jeremy Duns; Jonn Elledge; Olaf Falafel; Hugh Fearnley-Whittingstall; Jane Fearnley-Whittingstall; Christopher Fitz-Simon; Felix Flicker; Nick Foster; Christophe Galfard; Stuart Heritage; Julian Hitch; Andrew Holmes; Alex Hourston; Ferris Jabr; D.B. John; Keith Kahn-Harris; Max Kinnings; David Kirk; Rikke Schmidt Kjærgaard; Joseph Knox; Manon Lagrève; William Leith; Dan Lepard; Robert Lewis; Caroline Litman; Kieran Long; Dorian Lynskey; Rob Manuel; Jolyon Maugham; James McGee; Gill Meller; Thomasina Miers; Lottie Moggach; Cathy Newman; Mary-Ann Ochota; Christopher Osborn; Iain Overton; John O'Connell; Pete Paphides; Marie Phillips; Tom Phillips; Shivi Ramoutar; Richard Reed; Sam Rice; Tony Robinson; Stephen Sackur; C. J. Sansom; Marcus du Sautoy; Alev Scott; Rebecca Seal; Laura Shepherd-Robinson; Mimi Spencer; Count Arthur Strong; Andrew Taylor; Ian Vince; John Vincent; Adam Wagner; Jennie Walker; Rob Watts; Andrew Webb; Robyn Wilder; Will Wiles; John L Williams; Jason Wilson; Erin Young; Robyn Young; Andrew Ziminski

L578 Jennifer Chen Tran
Literary Agent
United States

https://glassliterary.com/team/jennifer-chen-tran/
https://twitter.com/jenchentran
https://querymanager.com/query/jct

Literary Agency: Glass Literary Management LLC (**L236**)

ADULT > **Fiction**
   Graphic Novels: General
   Novels: Chick Lit; Commercial; Contemporary; Family Saga; Literary; Multicultural; Romance; Upmarket; Women's Fiction
CHILDREN'S > **Fiction** > *Middle Grade*
   Contemporary; Literary; Mystery

NEW ADULT > **Fiction** > *Novels*

YOUNG ADULT > **Fiction** > *Novels*
   Contemporary; Historical Fiction; Literary

Closed to approaches.

Works with a wide range of award-winning talent, including entrepreneurs, journalists, physicians, thought leaders, James Beard nominated chefs, and graphic novelists, among others. Deeply committed to amplifying voices from persons with disabilities, BIPOC, LGBTQ, underrepresented, marginalized, and neurodiverse communities.

L579 Jes Trudel
Assistant Agent
Canada

https://www.therightsfactory.com
https://www.therightsfactory.com/Agents/jes-trudel
https://querymanager.com/query/jestrudel
https://writingcommunity.ca/agentjestrudel/

Literary Agency: The Rights Factory

CHILDREN'S > **Fiction**
   Board Books: General, and in particular: Commercial; High Concept
   Chapter Books: General, and in particular: Commercial; High Concept
   Middle Grade: General, and in particular: Adventure; Contemporary; Low Fantasy; Mystery; Romance; Speculative; Suspense; Thrillers
   Picture Books: General, and in particular: Commercial; High Concept
YOUNG ADULT
   Fiction > *Novels*
   General, and in particular: Adventure; Contemporary; Low Fantasy; Mystery; Romance; Speculative; Suspense; Thrillers

   Nonfiction > *Nonfiction Books*
   General, and in particular: Arts; Entrepreneurship; Environment; Mental Health; Social Justice

Closed to approaches.

In Board Book, Picture Book and Chapter Book categories, I'm especially interested in high concept, commercial stories (I already have several clients who excel at quiet, lyrical stories). I love both kid characters and animal characters. I prefer lyrical over rhyming texts, but if you do have a rhyming story, please make sure the meter is perfect and the rhymes are not cliche/forced.

In Middle Grade and Young Adult, I especially like action/adventure, contemporary, mystery, romance, low fantasy, present or near future speculative, and suspense/thriller. I prefer kid characters in these categories, though I will still look at stories with anthropomorphized characters in MG. I'm not a fan of vampires, werewolves, aliens, zombies, ghosts, fairies, fae, or other supernatural creatures in MG or YA.

I'm eager to take on nonfiction projects across all age groups, especially related to mental health, DEI, social justice, arts, community building, environmentalism, and entrepreneurship.

Authors: Dorothy Bentley; Katie Bono; Carrie Golus; Nancy Goulet; Christine Rose Henderson; Eileen Manes; Carol Nissenson; Howard Pearlstein; Rachel Rizzuto

L580 Jennifer Udden
Literary Agent
United States

https://www.ldlainc.com
https://querymanager.com/query/QueryJenniferUdden

Literary Agency: Laura Dail Literary Agency

Fiction > *Novels*
   Fantasy; Historical Romance; Horror; Mystery; Psychological Horror; Romance; Romantasy; Science Fiction; Thrillers

How to send: Query Tracker

Fantasy: from epic secondary world to historical or more contemporary fantasy, character-driven fantasy of all stripes with strong world building and a distinctive voice.

Science Fiction: science fiction of all stripes, particularly if there is a cross-genre element or an interesting hook.

Romance: innovative historical romance, sports romance, and romantasy.

Mystery/Thriller: Anything with a classic British feel, particularly if those tropes are subverted or there is a nontraditional narrator/setting.

Horror: Psychological and body horror, especially if there is a fresh take on an old trope.

L581 Laura Usselman
Literary Agent
United States

luquery@skagency.com

http://skagency.com/agents/laura-usselman/

Literary Agency: Stuart Krichevsky Literary Agency, Inc. (**L556**)

Fiction > *Novels*: Literary

Nonfiction > *Nonfiction Books*
   General, and in particular: Business; Cultural Criticism; Legal; Memoir; Parenting

How to send: Email

Represents adult nonfiction and select literary fiction. Her favorite novels are written in distinctive prose and have memorable characters at their heart. For nonfiction, she is interested in thoughtful narrative nonfiction, restlessly curious idea books, and reported memoir. Special areas of interest include legal and business narratives, cultural criticism, and contemporary parenthood.

Authors: Emily Bloom; Katherine Blunt; Angela Chen; Carla Ciccone; Georgia Cloepfil; Michelle Cyca; Victoria Facelli; Sarah Jaffe; Rachel McCarthy James; Peter Mercurio; Madeline Ostrander; Robin Page; Soraya Palmer; Nadim Roberts; Zoë Schiffer; A. Brad Schwartz; David Shih; Sofi Thanhauser; Kaitlyn Tiffany

L582 Valerie Hoskins Associates
Literary Agency
20 Charlotte Street, London, W1T 2NA
United Kingdom
Tel: +44 (0) 20 7637 4490

info@vhassociates.co.uk

https://vhassociates.co.uk

Scripts
  Film Scripts; *Radio Scripts*; *TV Scripts*

Send: Query
How to send: Email

Small agency extremely limited as to the number of new clients that can be taken on. Allow up to eight weeks for response to submissions.

Literary Agents: Valerie Hoskins; Rebecca Watson

L583 Lisa Erbach Vance
Literary Agent
United States

queryvance@aaronpriest.com

https://aaronpriest.com
https://aaronpriest.com/member/lisa-erbach-vance/

Literary Agency: Aaron M. Priest Literary Agency

Fiction > *Novels*
  Comedy / Humour; Commercial; Domestic Suspense; Family; Friends; Ghost Stories; Literary; Psychological Suspense; Relationships; Romantic Comedy; Speculative; Supernatural / Paranormal; Thrillers

Nonfiction > *Nonfiction Books*: Narrative Nonfiction

Send: Query; Writing sample
How to send: In the body of an email
How not to send: Email attachment

Currently most interested in and actively seeking out fiction, literary or commercial, especially works featuring female characters, as well as some narrative non-fiction. Types of work include: Propulsive, emotionally engaging thrillers—domestic or international. Moody psychological and domestic suspense. Speculative fiction set in a recognizable near future. Ghost or supernatural stories that go beyond chills and speak to current culture but are not graphically violent. Observant, thoughtful fiction about families and friends, with fresh perspectives on modern relationships. Narratives with a witty or lovingly humorous spin, including rom-coms. Diverse and unique narrative voices that speak to the human condition and the world today; underrepresented voices of all backgrounds and identities.

L584 Victoria Sanders & Associates LLC
Literary Agency
440 Buck Road, Stone Ridge, NY 12484
United States
Tel: +1 (212) 633-8811

queriesvsa@gmail.com

http://www.victoriasanders.com

Types: Fiction; Nonfiction; Translations
Formats: Film Scripts; Theatre Scripts
Subjects: Adventure; Arts; Autobiography; Comedy / Humour; Commercial; Contemporary; Crime; Culture; Current Affairs; Fantasy; History; Legal; Literary; Literature; Music; Mystery; Politics; Psychology; Satire; Society; Suspense; Thrillers; Women's Interests
Markets: Adult; Children's; Young Adult

Closed to approaches.

Send one-page query describing the work and the author by email only, with the first 25 pages pasted into the body of the email. No attachments or submissions by post. Response usually between 1 and 4 weeks.

Literary Agents: Bernadette Baker-Baughman; Victoria Sanders

L585 The Viney Agency
Literary Agency
64 New Cavendish Street, London, W1G 8TB
United Kingdom

https://www.thevineyagency.com

Professional Body: The Association of Authors' Agents (AAA)

ADULT
  Fiction > *Novels*

  Nonfiction > *Nonfiction Books*
    Biography; Narrative Nonfiction

CHILDREN'S > **Fiction** > *Novels*

Closed to approaches.

A London-based literary agency founded in 2008. The agency represents a diverse range of authors primarily handling their book deals with publishers worldwide, and providing a full range of services including selling film and TV options to broadcasters and production companies. Represents over 100 authors, writing across many genres, including adult and children's fiction and a wide variety of narrative nonfiction and biography.

Company Director / Senior Agent: Charlie Viney (**L586**)

L586 Charlie Viney
Company Director; Senior Agent
21 Dartmouth Park Avenue, London, NW5 1JL
United Kingdom

Charlie@thevineyagency.com

https://www.aevitascreative.com/agent/charlie-viney
https://www.thevineyagency.com/about

Literary Agencies: The Viney Agency (**L585**); Aevitas Creative Management (ACM) UK (**L006**)

Fiction > *Novels*

Nonfiction > *Nonfiction Books*

I have been a literary agent since 2002 and founded the agency in 2008. The agency represents a diverse range of clients writing across a wide range of subjects. I first started in the book trade as a bookseller and then enjoyed a twenty-five-year career in general trade publishing, mostly working in international sales and marketing, later becoming a board director at a major British publishing house. Being a literary agent combines my love of books and an enjoyment of business while enabling me to work very closely with our wonderful authors and manage their careers across all media.

Authors: Denise Allen; David Ambrose; David Andress; Paul Arnott; Stephen Bates; Chris Blackhurst; Jeremy Borum; Chris Bradford; Mike Bryan; David Charter; Charlie Charters; Paul Clammer; Lloyd Clark; Mark Cooper; Robin Cross; Richard Dannatt; David Downing; Paul Dowswell; Simon Elliott; Tim Fitzhigham; Lilia Giugni; Michael Harrison; David Hepworth; Justin Hill; Janet Hoggarth; Mark Hollingsworth; John Howkins; Graham Hoyland; Robin Ince; Andrew Jackson; Hannah Jewell; Michael Jones; Don Jordan; Miranda Kaufmann; Robert Kershaw; Philippa Langley; John Lazenby; Maurice Leitch; Grevel Lindop; David Loyn; Monty Lyman; Robert Lyman; S.I. Martin; Mark Mason; Roisin McAuley; Rosalind Miles; Kate Mossman; Michael Ohajura; Andrew Parker; Anna Perera; William Philpott; David Mark Price; Tom Pugh; David Richards; Cate Sevilla; Emma Southon; Siena Sterling; Mark Stevenson; Miranda Wilson; Alistair Wood; Duncan Wu

L587 Orli Vogt-Vincent
Literary Agent
United Kingdom

Literary Agency: David Higham Associates Ltd (**L146**)

L588 Wade & Co Literary Agency
Literary Agency
Poplar Hall, Brookland, Romney Marsh, Kent, TN29 9TD
United Kingdom

rw@rwla.com

https://www.rwla.com

ADULT
  Fiction > *Novels*

Nonfiction > *Nonfiction Books*

YOUNG ADULT
Fiction > *Novels*
Nonfiction > *Nonfiction Books*

Closed to approaches.

We handle fiction and non-fiction for adults and young adults. We do not handle poetry, plays, short stories, children's books, screenplays or film scripts.

Author Estate: The Estate of Louise Cooper

Authors: Darrell Alden; Steve Alton; Steuart Campbell; Ed Davey; Jack Dixon; Kimberly Greene; Nick Griffiths; Adam Guillain; Matthew Harffy; Brenda James; Jackie Kabler; Chris Kissling; Chris Luttichau; Andy McDermott; Mike McInnes; Richard Newman; Stephen Norman; Nigel Perrin; Lorna Read; Anthony Riches; Jos Sharrer; Andrea Shavick; Ewen Southby-Tailyour; Colin Sutton; Ayowa Taylor; John Tiffin; Russell Whitfield; Stuart Wyatt

Literary Agent: Robin Wade

L589 Caroline Walsh
Literary Agent
United Kingdom

childrenssubmissions@davidhigham.co.uk
carolinewalsh@davidhigham.co.uk

https://www.davidhigham.co.uk/agents-dh/caroline-walsh/

Literary Agency: David Higham Associates Ltd (**L146**)

ADULT
Fiction > *Novels*
Book Club Fiction; Commercial; Upmarket

Nonfiction > *Nonfiction Books*

CHILDREN'S
Fiction
Board Books; Chapter Books; Middle Grade; Novels; Picture Books
Nonfiction > *Nonfiction Books*
Poetry > *Poetry Collections*

TEEN > Fiction > *Novels*

YOUNG ADULT > Fiction > *Novels*

Send: Query; Synopsis; Writing sample
How to send: Email

Many of my clients have gone on to write award-wining and bestselling books and their output covers the whole range of children's books, from pre-school board books, through picture books, poetry, middle-grade fiction, non-fiction and Teen/YA novels. I also represent a handful of adult fiction writers where my tastes are for upmarket book club fiction and classy commercial page-turners.

Authors: R. J. Anderson; Kelly Andrew; Antonia Barber; Ella Beech; Joe Berger; Theresa Breslin; Martin Brown; Mike Brownlow; Kathryn Cave; Jason Chapman; Emma Chichester Clark; Trish Cooke; Susie Day; Kady MacDonald Denton; Lucy Dillamore; Eve Edwards; Jonathan Emmett; Ben Faulks; Corina Fletcher; P. M. Freestone; Jane Gardam; Sarah Garland; Susan Gates; Adèle Geras; Julia Golding; Kester Grant; Ryan Graudin; Candida Harper; Leigh Hodgkinson; Jesse Hodgson; Anna Hoghton; Meredith Hooper; Julia Jarman; Clive King; Bert Kitchen; Jay Kristoff; Fifi Kuo; Eleanor Lavender; Jo Lodge; Tim Lott; Jan Mark; Ellie Marney; Tom McLaughlin; Myfanwy Millward; Kate Milner; Tony Mitton; Laura Mucha; Jenny Nimmo; C. S. Pacat; Liz Pichon; Chris Powling; Kathryn Purdie; Madhvi Ramani; Catherine Rayner; Jacqui Rayner; Fiona Roberton; Rachel Rooney; Megan Shepherd; Alexander McCall Smith; Meagan Spooner; Joss Stirling; James L. Sutter; Sally Symes; Vanessa Tait; Frances Thomas; Pat Thomson; Theresa Tomlinson; Ann Turnbull; Martin Waddell; Melanie Walsh; Jacqueline Wilson; David Wojtowycz

L590 Watson, Little Ltd
Literary Agency
Suite 315, ScreenWorks, 22 Highbury Grove, London, N5 2ER
United Kingdom
Tel: +44 (0) 20 7388 7529

office@watsonlittle.com
submissions@watsonlittle.com

https://www.watsonlittle.com
https://twitter.com/watsonlittle

Professional Body: The Association of Authors' Agents (AAA)

ADULT
Fiction > *Novels*
Nonfiction > *Nonfiction Books*

CHILDREN'S
Fiction > *Novels*
Nonfiction > *Nonfiction Books*

Send: Query; Author bio; Writing sample; Market info; Outline
How to send: Word file email attachment; PDF file email attachment; In the body of an email
How not to send: Post

Send query by email only with outline in the body of the email, and synopsis and sample material as Word document attachments (or PDF attachments, if illustrated), addressed to a specific agent. See website for full guidelines and details of specific agents. No scripts, poetry, or unsolicited MSS.

Author Estate: The Estate of Akemi Tanaka

Authors: Rebecca Abrams; Luci Adams; Tom Adams; Jean Adamson; Rose Alexander; Wendy Allen; Rosie Archer; Faima Bakar; Louise Soraya Black; Kay Brellend; Laura Chamberlain; Sophie Claire; Sarah J. Coleman; Tara Costello; Bryony Cousins; Alex Day; Marianne Eloise; Timna Fibert; Lauren Ford; Tessa Gibbs; Natasha Holmes; Hayley Hoskins; Elias Jahshan; Hiba Noor Khan; Mary Mackie; Lindiwe Maqhubela; Diana McCaulay; Erin Murgatroyd; Barbara Nadel; Grace Newman; Briana J. Newstead; Sheila Norton; Fiona O'Brien; Ben Pechey; Anna Reading; Rhian Parry; Will Richard; Richard Owain Roberts; Alan Robinson; Kohinoor Sahota; Tara Sexton; Hannah Silva; Pam Weaver; Jeremy Williams; Alex Woolhouse

Foreign Rights Manager / Literary Agent: Gabrielle Demblon (**L150**)

Literary Agents: Megan Carroll (**L102**); Mandy Little; Laetitia Rutherford (**L513**); James Wills; Donald Winchester

L591 Jessica Watterson
Literary Agent
United States

https://www.dijkstraagency.com/agent-page.php?agent_id=Watterson
https://querymanager.com/query/jessicawatterson

Literary Agency: Sandra Dijkstra Literary Agency

ADULT
Fiction > *Novels*
Fantasy; Romance

Nonfiction > *Nonfiction Books*
Millennial; Popular Culture

CHILDREN'S > Fiction > *Novels*: Comedy / Humour

How to send: By referral

Most drawn to riveting and heart pounding romance. She loves fun, fresh voices and character driven stories that keep a reader turning the page because they need to know what happens next. Independent heroines are a must, in addition to well realized heroes who aren't alpha-holes. She also loves fantasy that will appeal to a broad readership, especially if it has some spice in it!

In the children's realm, she connects with anything that has heart and humor.

She does like the occasional pop-culture or millenial leaning non-fiction project.

She is only open to queries by referral at this time.

L592 Paula Weiman
Literary Agent
United States

submissions@ashliterary.com

https://ashliterary.com
https://ashliterary.com/#paulawishlist
https://querymanager.com/query/paulaashliterary

Literary Agency: ASH Literary

CHILDREN'S > Fiction > *Middle Grade*
Adventure; Contemporary

YOUNG ADULT > Fiction > *Novels*
Contemporary; Fantasy; High / Epic Fantasy; Magic; Romantic Comedy; Suspense; Thrillers

Closed to approaches.

I'm most actively seeking YA rom-coms at the moment. I want to see rom-coms with teeth, romances that are rooted in a larger social or cultural topic so the story has interest beyond the love story. My favorite tropes are fake dating and rivals-to-lovers where one character is way more into the rivalry than the other. In YA suspense, I want to see well-developed plots with beautiful prose, following teenagers who tackle systemic injustice and corrupt power systems. For YA thrillers I want heists, either contemporary or historical, where the team is trying to fight injustice or right a wrong from behind the scenes. In YA fantasy, I look for rich atmosphere and a propulsive plot, whether the stories are high fantasy or contemporary with a dash of magic. In middle grade, I want clever adventures with active narrators whose voice is so strong that they direct the plot. I'm also looking for contemporary middle grade that touches on grief and/or queer identity. I'm really eager for a middle grade story that tackles child labor rights or student activism.

L593 Alexandra Weiss
Associate Agent
United States

http://www.azantianlitagency.com/pages/team-awe.html
https://querymanager.com/query/AlexandraWeiss

Literary Agency: Azantian Literary Agency

ADULT
Fiction > *Novels*
Contemporary; Cozy Fantasy; High Concept; Literary; Mystery; Speculative; Thrillers

Nonfiction > *Nonfiction Books*
Animals; Climate Science; Environment; Gender; Internet; LGBTQIA; Media; Mental Health; Science; Space

CHILDREN'S > Fiction
Graphic Novels: General
Middle Grade: Contemporary; Fantasy; Horror; Suspense
Picture Books: General

YOUNG ADULT > Fiction
Graphic Novels: General
Novels: Coming of Age; Contemporary; Cozy Fantasy; Folklore, Myths, and Legends; Low Fantasy; Magical Realism; Romantic Comedy; Soft Science Fiction; Thrillers

How to send: Query Tracker

Represents fiction and nonfiction picture books, middle grade, young adult, graphic novels, and a handful of genres within adult fiction and nonfiction.

L594 Tess Weitzner
Literary Agent
United States

tw@goldinlit.com

https://www.goldinlit.com
https://www.goldinlit.com/tess-weitzner
https://twitter.com/TessWeitzner

Literary Agency: Frances Goldin Literary Agency, Inc.

ADULT
Fiction > *Novels*
Horror; Literary; Magical Realism; Upmarket

Nonfiction > *Nonfiction Books*: Narrative Nonfiction

CHILDREN'S > Fiction > *Middle Grade*: Contemporary

YOUNG ADULT > Fiction > *Novels*

Send: Query; Writing sample; Proposal
How to send: Email

Primarily looking for upmarket fiction, literary fiction, and narrative nonfiction narrow and deep in scope that might play with unreliable narrators, interrogations of power and violence, reclamations of identity, or dark-as-night humor. Fresh takes on horror, magical realism, camp, and kitsch will always be met with zeal. In the children's space, she is looking for contemporary middle-grade and YA stories that are fun, engaging, and seemingly "quiet" that crack open larger questions or underrepresented experiences. As part of their brilliant storytelling, they respect young readers and approach tough topics with warmth, humor, and edge. She is not accepting queries in science fiction, fantasy, or picture books at this time.

Authors: Sara Cody; David Dabel; Leora Fridman; Christina Frigo; Kathryn Kramer; Davey Lawson; Loretta Lopez; Suchi Rudra

L595 Karmen Wells
Literary Agent
Canada

karmen@therightsfactory.com

https://www.therightsfactory.com/Agents/Karmen-Wells
https://twitter.com/KarmenEdits

Literary Agency: The Rights Factory

Fiction > *Novels*
Comedy / Humour; Coming of Age; Commercial; Drama; Dystopian Fiction; High Concept; Horror; LGBTQIA; Literary; Popular Culture; Science Fiction

Nonfiction > *Nonfiction Books*: Narrative Nonfiction

Send: Query; Pitch; Author bio; Writing sample
How to send: Email

Looking for published or to-be-published books to represent to producers for film or TV adaptation.

Authors: Daniel Barnett; Kelly Florence; Rhonda J. Garcia; Jessica Guess; Meg Hafdahl

L596 Jennifer Weltz
Literary Agent; President
United States

https://www.jvnla.com
https://www.jvnla.com/submitjw
https://aalitagents.org/author/jweltzjvnla-com/

Literary Agency: The Jean V. Naggar Literary Agency (**L299**)
Professional Body: Association of American Literary Agents (AALA)

ADULT
Fiction > *Novels*
Nonfiction > *Nonfiction Books*

CHILDREN'S > Fiction > *Middle Grade*

YOUNG ADULT > Fiction > *Novels*

Send: Query; Outline; Author bio
How to send: Online submission system

Has sold books domestically, internationally, and for film for over two decades. Coming from a mediation background, she sees herself as a liaison between her author and the editor and publishing house that acquire her author's work.

L597 Erin Casey Westin
Literary Agent
United States

https://querymanager.com/query/erincaseywestin
https://twitter.com/erincaseywestin

Literary Agency: Gallt & Zacker Literary Agency

CHILDREN'S > Fiction
Middle Grade; *Picture Books*
YOUNG ADULT
Fiction
Graphic Novels; *Novels*
Nonfiction > *Nonfiction Books*

Closed to approaches.

Open to queries from the 1st to the 7th of every month.

L598 Michaela Whatnall
Literary Agent
United States

mwhatnall@dystel.com

https://www.dystel.com/michaela-whatnall
https://querymanager.com/query/michaelawhatnall
https://twitter.com/mwhatnall

Literary Agency: Dystel, Goderich & Bourret LLC

ADULT
  Fiction
    Graphic Novels: General
    Novels: Contemporary; Grounded Fantasy; Historical Fiction; Speculative; Upmarket
    Nonfiction > *Nonfiction Books*: Narrative Nonfiction

CHILDREN'S
  Fiction
    Graphic Novels; *Middle Grade*; *Picture Books*
    Nonfiction > *Nonfiction Books*: Narrative Nonfiction

YOUNG ADULT > **Fiction**
    Graphic Novels: General
    Novels: General, and in particular: Adventure; Contemporary; Fantasy; Historical Fiction; Horror; Romantic Comedy; Science Fiction

How to send: Query Tracker

Strong interest in children's literature, particularly middle grade and young adult fiction of all genres, including contemporary, fantasy, science fiction, historical, adventure, horror, and rom-com. In the adult fiction space, they are particularly seeking contemporary, speculative, and historical upmarket fiction, as well as character-driven, grounded fantasy. They are also open to select narrative nonfiction for both children and adults, graphic novels, and picture books.

L599 Whispering Buffalo Literary Agency

Literary Agency
97 Chesson Road, London, W14 9QS
United Kingdom
Tel: +44 (0) 20 7385 4655

info@whisperingbuffalo.com

https://www.whisperingbuffalo.com

ADULT
  Fiction > *Novels*
    Commercial; Literary
  Nonfiction > *Nonfiction Books*: Commercial

CHILDREN'S > **Fiction** > *Novels*

YOUNG ADULT > **Fiction** > *Novels*

Send: Query; Author bio; Synopsis; Writing sample; Proposal
How to send: Word file email attachment

Represents a growing stable of storytellers including individuals with a high media profile in a variety of fields. The agency is building its list and welcomes unsolicited submissions.

Literary Agent: Mariam Keen

L600 Chandler Wickers

Literary Agent
United States

cw@skagency.com

http://skagency.com/agents/chandler-wickers/

Literary Agency: Stuart Krichevsky Literary Agency, Inc. (**L556**)

Fiction > *Novels*
    Coming of Age; Family Saga; Literary; Upmarket

Nonfiction > *Nonfiction Books*
    Adventure; History; Journalism; Popular Culture; Technology; Warfare

Send: Query; Writing sample; Proposal
How to send: In the body of an email
How not to send: Email attachment

Interested in representing adult fiction and non-fiction.

She is drawn to voice-driven literary and upmarket fiction with a strong sense of place, novels featuring darkly funny narrators, flawed protagonists, coming of age stories, and family sagas. She's especially excited about writing that plays with form, stories that explore visceral experiences of body and mind, and characters grappling with philosophical questions about faith and desire.

In non-fiction, she looks for novelistic journalism, comprehensive histories, war reporting, wilderness adventures, and journeys to the edges of the Earth. As a San Francisco native and Brooklyn transplant she is keen on stories that intersect tech and pop culture, converge scholarly with personal narratives, and those that demystify a subculture or reveal an underbelly.

L601 Alice Williams

Literary Agent
United Kingdom

alice@alicewilliamsliterary.co.uk

https://www.instagram.com/agentalicewilliams/

Literary Agency: Alice Williams Literary (**L012**)

L602 Katie Williams

Literary Agent
United Kingdom

https://theagency.co.uk/the-agents/katie-williams/

Literary Agency: The Agency (London) Ltd (**L008**)

Scripts
    Film Scripts: Comedy / Humour; Drama
    TV Scripts: Comedy / Humour; Drama
    Theatre Scripts: Comedy / Humour; Drama

Represents drama and comedy writers in television, theatre and film.

L603 Laura Williams

Literary Agent
United Kingdom

lwilliams@greeneheaton.co.uk

https://greeneheaton.co.uk/agents/laura-williams/

https://twitter.com/laurabirdland

Literary Agency: Greene & Heaton Ltd (**L251**)

ADULT
  Fiction > *Novels*
    20th Century; Comedy / Humour; Commercial; Crime; Dark; Friends; Ghost Stories; Gothic; High Concept Romance; Historical Fiction; Historical Mystery Fiction; Horror; LGBTQIA; Literary; Magical Realism; Mystery; Police Procedural; Psychological Thrillers; Romance; Romantic Comedy; Speculative; Upmarket Commercial Fiction

  Nonfiction > *Nonfiction Books*
    Crime; History; Memoir; Mental Health; Narrative Nonfiction; Popular Culture; Popular Science

CHILDREN'S > **Fiction** > *Middle Grade*: Contemporary

YOUNG ADULT > **Fiction** > *Novels*: Contemporary

I love working on literary fiction and upmarket commercial fiction, of all different kinds, and I'm always on the lookout for meditative or moving novels about modern life. I prefer warmth and heart to coldness or ennui, although I love novels with a bit of bite and sharpness to them.

I'm also always on the lookout for a high concept love story that will sweep me away and make me cry happy or sad tears. At the more commercial end of fiction, I love funny novels with warmth and romantic comedies with a bit of depth. I think I've probably read every book by the masterful Marian Keyes. I love feeling feelings – give me your worn-worn beloved romantic tropes with a fresh angle and gorgeous writing.

I'm keen on darkness and a claustrophobic feel in novels, from gothic to horror to murder mysteries to ghost stories to psychological thrillers to speculative/magical realist fiction to novels that feel like true crime, or intense and emotional narratives about dark things, and I think being truly scared by a story is one of the most difficult things a writer can achieve. I love weird and wonderful stories with unexpected twists, I love being amazed by an author's imagination, but I also love brilliantly plotted conventional murder mysteries or procedurals, as long as there's something fresh and exciting about it.

Most of all I'm looking for novels I haven't read before – something unusual structurally or thematically, something that shines a light on a subject the author is passionate about, something that'll break my heart or raise my blood in an entirely new way. I don't want protagonists in novels to hold a mirror up to my own life, I want them to show me an open door into theirs. I'm always looking to promote diverse voices from across the globe, and I'm particularly keen on LGBTQI+ stories.

I also have a very small list of young adult and middle grade fiction, which I love working on. I'm looking for something that feels current and contemporary, with a real conversation at its core. I'm not currently looking for fantasy, or anything younger than middle grade.

On the non-fiction side, I love working on memoirs of extraordinary people, or narrative non-fiction about something the author feels passionately about. I've worked on many books about mental health, and I'm interested in untold stories across popular science, history and popular culture. I'd also really like to find a brilliant true crime book. Cookery, wellness and lifestyle would be a better fit for one of my brilliant colleagues.

Authors: Eve Ainsworth; David M Barnett; Catherine Barter; Laura Blake; SB Caves; Anne Corlett; Anna Day; Leona Deakin; Sue Divin; Helen Dring; Hayley Dunlop; Mari Ellis Dunning; Maggy Van Eijk; Lauren Farnsworth; Zoe Feeney; Gabrielle Fernie; Louise Finnigan; Hayley Gelfuso; Olesya Salnikova Gilmore; Sarah Goodwin; Oliver Grant; Molly Greeley; Cat Hepburn; Rebecca Hooper; Scott Alexander Howard; Maria Hummer; Gaynor Jones; Jem Lester; Matilda Leyser; Paddy Magrane; Claire McGlasson; Rebecca Taylor McKay; Gemma Milne; Bryan Moriarty; Hélène Mulholland; Barney Norris; Nina De Pass; Ben Reeves; Zuzana Ruzickova; James Smythe; Nancy Springer; John Sutherland; Lisa Timoney; Alyssa Warren; Anna Wickins; Gill Wyness; Bella Younger

L604 Jo Williamson

Literary Agent
United Kingdom

jo@antonyharwood.com
mail@antonyharwood.com

http://antonyharwood.com/jo-williamson/

Literary Agency: Antony Harwood Limited (**L022**)

ADULT > Fiction > *Novels*
Contemporary Romance; Dark; Psychological Thrillers; Romantic Comedy; Women's Fiction

CHILDREN'S > Fiction
Middle Grade: Adventure; Comedy / Humour; Contemporary; Folklore, Myths, and Legends
Picture Books: General

YOUNG ADULT > Fiction > *Novels*: Romance

Looking for compelling stories with strong voices. More specifically, Middle Grade adventures that feel fresh, as well as laugh-out-loud fiction with an engaging central character and series potential. She loves myths and legends so is keen to find something that blends contemporary with mythology for MG readers. She is also looking for YA romance with a strong hook. She is actively building her list of adult fiction and would like to find women's fiction, dark psychological thrillers, or a contemporary and funny romantic adventure. Follow agency submission guidelines (see website) and approach via general agency email address.

L605 Kathryn Willms

Literary Agent
Canada

kathryn@therightsfactory.com

https://www.therightsfactory.com/Agents/Kathryn-Willms
https://www.therightsfactory.com/submit-kathryn
https://querymanager.com/query/2039

Literary Agency: The Rights Factory

Fiction > *Novels*
Hard Science Fiction; Literary; Speculative

Nonfiction
Gift Books: General
Nonfiction Books: Biography; Business; Culture; Environment; Food and Drink; Health; History; Lifestyle; Narrative Nonfiction; Nature; Personal Development; Psychology; Science; Social Justice; Wellbeing; Women's Issues

Send: Query; Author bio; Writing sample
How to send: Query Tracker; Email attachment

Specializes in nonfiction. She is particularly interested in ambitious, unconventional, smart, and well-written book projects that contribute new perspectives, revel in the quirkiness of the world, and change the way we see it. She's passionate about work that translates specialist knowledge to the mainstream to push cultural conversations in new and surprising directions. She enthusiastically welcomes submissions from BIPOC and LGBTQ-2S creators. She is starting to acquire hard science fiction and speculative literary fiction. She's attracted to the same qualities in fiction and nonfiction: big ideas; ambitious and/or clever premises; a sense of humour; and engagement with the big questions of our times.

Authors: Lisa Brahin; Sam Chaiton; Meghan Chayka; Dustin Galer; Alyssa Huizing; Andrew Mayeda; Michelle McIvor; Riley E. Moynes; Nancy Pearson; Karen Pierce; Laura Pratt; Krista Towns; Jaime Weinman; Zed Zha

L606 Desiree Wilson

Literary Agent
United States

https://www.lookingglasslit.com/desiree-wilson
https://desir.ee/submissions/
https://twitter.com/swindlesoiree

Literary Agency: Looking Glass Literary & Media Management (**L370**)

ADULT
Fiction
Graphic Novels: Contemporary; Fantasy; Horror; Magical Realism; Science Fiction; Speculative
Novels: Contemporary; Fantasy; Horror; Magical Realism; Romantic Comedy; Science Fiction; Speculative; Thrillers; Upmarket
Short Fiction: General

Nonfiction > *Nonfiction Books*: Narrative Nonfiction

CHILDREN'S
Fiction
Graphic Novels: General
Middle Grade: Gender; Horror; Mental Health
Nonfiction > *Middle Grade*
Engineering; History; Mathematics; Science; Technology

YOUNG ADULT > Fiction
Graphic Novels: High Concept; Relationships
Novels: Fairy Tales; Fantasy; High Concept; Horror; LGBTQIA; Romance; Romantic Comedy; Science Fiction; Urban Fantasy

Does not want:

Fiction > *Novels*: Hard Science Fiction

Closed to approaches.

I represent upper middle grade, YA, and adult genre fiction, especially horror (and kid-horror), high-concept fantasy, speculative fiction, magical realism, and accessible or near-future science fiction. I am also looking for select middle grade nonfiction about history or STEM.

L607 Ed Wilson

Literary Agent; Company Director
United Kingdom
Tel: +44 (0) 20 7251 0125

ed@johnsonandalcock.co.uk

https://www.johnsonandalcock.co.uk/ed-wilson
https://twitter.com/literarywhore

Literary Agency: Johnson & Alcock (**L302**)

Fiction > *Novels*
Commercial; Crime; Experimental; Fantasy; High Concept; Literary; Science Fiction; Speculative; Thrillers

Nonfiction > *Nonfiction Books*
History; Memoir; Nature; Politics; Popular Culture; Sport

Send: Query; Synopsis; Writing sample
How to send: Email attachment

In fiction, he looks for anything with originality and style, and his list covers the full gamut from literary to commercial writing. He likes books with an imaginative setting, strong narrative voice, and compelling premise. He has an active SFF list, representing multiple award-winning authors, and is always on the lookout for new writers. Think of him for high concept writing, intelligent crime and thrillers, and books that transcend genre. Ed is not currently taking on any new YA or children's authors and does not represent plays or film scripts.

His non-fiction tastes cover a wide range: from serious politics and sweeping narrative history, to sport, natural history, quirky memoir and popular culture. He loves writers that find a new and inventive way into a well-known subject and works editorially with all his authors to make their books the best they can be.

L608 Caroline Wood
Literary Agent; Company Director
United Kingdom

https://felicitybryan.com/fba-agent/caroline-wood/

Literary Agency: Felicity Bryan Associates (**L192**)

Fiction > *Novels*
Book Club Fiction; Crime; Literary; Romance; Upmarket

I represent a range of fiction, from literary prize-winners to upmarket reading group fiction, and well-written crime novels. I'm looking for work that is ambitious and surprising, both satisfying to read and deep enough to warrant rereading. I love books with heart and prefer the complexity to be in the characters and their relationships than in the prose. I'm particularly drawn to messy family stories, books about human connection and misconnection, and books full of longing.

Authors: Carlos Acosta; Modern Baker; Kay Barron; Susan Beale; Louis De Bernières; Mary Berry; Nina Bhadreshwar; Francesca Brill; Rhidian Brook; Stephen Burke; Lucy Cavendish; Sarah Challis; Jonathan Coe; Will Cohu; T.A. Cotterell; Benjamin Daniels; Nick Edwards; James Fearnley; Rebecca Fleet; Damon Galgut; Kat Gordon; Catherine Hall; Anna Hope; Gill Hornby; Richard House; Allegra Huston; Stanley Kenani; Liza Klaussmann; Phyllida Law; Tim Leach; Simon Lelic; Sarah K Marr; Alistair Morgan; Alan Murrin; Jennifer Nadel; Svenja O'donnell; Colm O'gorman; Iain Pears; Nick Potter; Melody Razak; Adam Ruck; Penny Rudge; Edward Russell-Walling; Sue Stuart-Smith; Henry Sutton; Katherine Swift; Edmund De Waal; Martin Walker; Kirsty Wark; Greg Wise; James Wythe; Lucy Young

L609 Ed Wood
Literary Agent
United Kingdom

edsubmissions@theblairpartnership.com
https://www.theblairpartnership.com
https://www.theblairpartnership.com/literary-agents/ed-wood/

Literary Agency: The Blair Partnership (**L064**)

Fiction > *Novels*
Book Club Fiction; Crime; High Concept; Mystery; Psychological Thrillers; Thrillers

How to send: Email

After twelve years publishing some of the biggest and best commercial fiction authors, I'm thrilled to take on clients in crime, thriller, mystery and book club fiction – and to be their creative and commercial champion.

Authors: Sheena Cook; Charlotte Essex; Daisy Pearce

L610 Bryony Woods
Literary Agent
United Kingdom

submissions.bryony@dkwlitagency.co.uk
https://dkwlitagency.co.uk
https://dkwlitagency.co.uk/agents/bryony/
https://twitter.com/BryonyWoods

Literary Agency: Diamond Kahn and Woods (DKW) Literary Agency Ltd (**L153**)

ADULT
Fiction > *Novels*
General, and in particular: Commercial; Dark Magic; Fairy Tales; Friends; Literary; Romance; Science Fiction; Upmarket Contemporary Fiction

Nonfiction
Essays: General
Nonfiction Books: Memoir

CHILDREN'S > **Fiction** > *Middle Grade*
YOUNG ADULT > **Fiction** > *Novels*

Does not want:

> **Fiction** > *Novels*
> Crime; Psychological Thrillers

Send: Query; Writing sample; Synopsis; Author bio
How to send: Email attachment

I'm open to books in almost any genre, whether for adult readers, young adults or children from age 7+. My reading taste is fairly eclectic, and covers commercial to literary and everything in between.

At the moment I'd particularly love to find some beautifully written, upmarket contemporary novels; books about friendships and platonic love; thought-provoking sci-fi or richly imagined fantasy worlds; brilliant, sweeping love stories on an epic canvas; found families, or novels about finding love in unexpected places; something that truly makes me laugh; fairy tales, or anything darkly magical; books that surprise me; books that will break my heart; books that ask big questions of the world and our place within it; books that are full of hope.

I tend to avoid anything particularly gritty or depressing, so crime novels or harrowing psychological thrillers are likely to be a no. I also don't represent children's picture books, or poetry collections. The non-fiction side of my list is small, but I have been known to fall for a beautiful memoir or a moving collection of essays.

L611 Jessica Woollard
Literary Agent
United Kingdom

jessicawoollard@davidhigham.co.uk
https://davidhigham.co.uk
https://davidhigham.co.uk/agents-dh/jessica-woollard/

Literary Agency: David Higham Associates Ltd (**L146**)

Fiction > *Novels:* Literary

Nonfiction > *Nonfiction Books*
Memoir; Narrative Nonfiction

How to send: Email

I represent a diverse range of narrative non-fiction and have always been attracted to memoir. I also represent some literary fiction – the way we relate to land often plays a key role here – and international literary fiction with a particular focus on Southeast Asia, Japan and Africa.

Authors: Kerry Andrew; Lamorna Ash; Santanu Bhattacharya; Paco Calvo; Rob Cowen; Stanley Donwood; Caroline Eden; Tan Twan Eng; Charles Foster; Jay Griffiths; Nick Hayes; Liu Hong; Masud Husain; Lucy Jones; Helen Jukes; Jonathan Kennedy; Natalie Lawrence; Julia Lovell; Robert Macfarlane; Manchan Magan; Ben Masters; Jackie Morris; Benjamin Myers; Fred Pearce; Martin Shaw; Merlin Sheldrake; Lola Shoneyin; Hannah Stowe; Nigel Toon; Taichi Yamada

L612 Rachel Yeoh
Literary Agent
United Kingdom

submissions@madeleinemilburn.com

https://madeleinemilburn.co.uk/team-member/rachel-yeoh/
https://x.com/rachel_yeoh

Literary Agency: Madeleine Milburn Literary, TV & Film Agency (**L385**)

Fiction in Translation > *Novels*

Fiction > *Novels*
 Book Club Fiction; Contemporary; Family Saga; Literary; Postcolonialism; Psychological Thrillers; Retellings; Social Class; Society; Speculative; Suspense; Upmarket

Nonfiction > *Nonfiction Books*: Memoir

Send: Query; Pitch; Market info; Author bio
How to send: Email

Actively looking for: literary, upmarket, book club, global stories, human experience, social critique, class conflict, speculative fiction, family sagas, contemporary fiction, upmarket suspense, psychological thriller, postcolonial literature, translated fiction, classical retellings, narrative memoir.

L613 YMU Books
Literary Agency
United Kingdom

enquiries@ymugroup.com

https://www.ymugroup.com
https://books.ymugroup.com

Professional Body: The Association of Authors' Agents (AAA)

Nonfiction > *Nonfiction Books*
 Celebrity; Commercial

Closed to approaches.

A market-leading literary agency in premium brand and platform representation, working with writers and creators who excel in their genres.

Authors: Federica Amati; Rebecca Bainbridge; Whitney Bauman; Francis Bourgeois; Stephanie Bramwell-Lawes; Corey Brotherson; Deborah Chu; Emma Cowing; Rosie Day; Melvyn Downes; Jane Dunn; Sindri Eldon; Emily Fairbairn; Paloma Faith; Noel Fitzpatrick; Lizzie Frainier; Karissa Hamilton-Bannis; Cherry Healey; Sarah Hehir; Imran Khan; Sam Marsden; Alissa Jones Nelson; Poppy O'Neill; Kayleigh Rattle; Cat Sims; Jemma Solomon; Airy Something; KT Tunstall; Dakota Warren

L614 Claudia Young
Literary Agent
United Kingdom

http://greeneheaton.co.uk/agents/claudia-young/
https://twitter.com/ClaudiaL_Young

Literary Agency: Greene & Heaton Ltd (**L251**)

Fiction > *Novels*
 Contemporary; Crime; Historical Fiction; Literary; Thrillers

Nonfiction > *Nonfiction Books*
 Comedy / Humour; Cookery; Food Journalism; Travel

Closed to approaches.

Interested in all types of writing, in particular cooking and food journalism, comedy and travel writing. Loves literary fiction, contemporary as well as historical novels, crime fiction and thrillers.

Authors: Sam Akbar; Anthony Anaxagorou; Ros Atkinson; Lily Blacksell; Jordan Bourke; Áine Carlin; Matt Chapple; Martha Collison; Jack Cooke; Kevan Davis; Kim Duke; Gabriela Evangelou; Lucia Evangelou; Ella Frears; Francis Gimblett; Lewis Goodall; Peter Harper; Alice Hart; Wayne Holloway-Smith; Lizzie King; Vanessa King; Jenny Lee; Janina Matthewson; Ciara Ohartghaile; Val Payne; Alice Procter; Rejina Pyo; James Ramsden; Rosie Ramsden; Charlie Ryrie; Viviane Schwarz; Tim Sebastian; Dale Shaw; Rachel de Thample; Georgie Tilney; Regina Wong; David Wright

L615 The Zack Company, Inc
Literary Agency
United States

https://zackcompany.com
https://www.facebook.com/literaryagency
https://twitter.com/thezackcompany

Fiction
 Graphic Novels: General
 Novels: African American; Chick Lit; Comedy / Humour; Commercial Women's Fiction; Cozy Mysteries; Erotic; Fantasy; Hard Science Fiction; High / Epic Fantasy; Historical Fiction; Horror; International; Literary; Mystery; Native Americans; Post-Apocalyptic; Romance; Romantasy; Romantic Suspense; Science Fiction; Speculative Romance; Supernatural / Paranormal Romance; Suspense; Thrillers; Urban Fantasy; Women's Fiction

Nonfiction > *Nonfiction Books*
 Alternative Health; American History; Animals; Autobiography; Aviation; Biography; British History; Career Development; Childcare; Classics / Ancient World; Comedy / Humour; Cookery; Crime; Cultural History; Current Affairs; Diet; Economics; Entertainment; Entrepreneurship; Environment; European History; Films; Finance; Fitness; Food; Gardening; Health; Home Improvement; Inspirational; Investigative Journalism; Judaism; Leadership; Management; Medieval; Meditation; Memoir; Military History; Military; Mind, Body, Spirit; Music; National Security; Nature; Nutrition; Outdoor Activities; Painting; Parenting; Personal Development; Personal Finance; Pets; Politics; Popular Science; Relationships; Religion; Science; Secret Intelligence; Sex; Spirituality; Sports Celebrity; TV; Technology; Wellbeing; Women's Issues; Yoga

Send: Author bio; Synopsis; Full text; Proposal
How to send: Online submission system
How not to send: Post; Email

Requirements change frequently, so check the agency website before approaching. Approaches must be made via the form on the website.

Literary Agent: Andrew Zack

L616 Marietta B. Zacker
Literary Agent
United States

https://www.galltzacker.com/submissions.html
https://querymanager.com/query/querymarietta

Literary Agency: Gallt & Zacker Literary Agency

CHILDREN'S > **Fiction**
 Middle Grade; *Picture Books*
YOUNG ADULT
 Fiction
  Graphic Novels; *Novels*
 Nonfiction > *Nonfiction Books*

How to send: Query Tracker

Open to queries from the 1st to the 7th of every month.

L617 Zeno Agency
Literary Agency
Primrose Hill Business Centre, 110 Gloucester Avenue, London, NW1 8HX
United Kingdom
Tel: +44 (0) 20 7096 0927

info@zenoagency.com

http://zenoagency.com

Professional Body: The Association of Authors' Agents (AAA)

Fiction > *Novels*
 General, and in particular: Fantasy; Horror; Science Fiction

Nonfiction > *Nonfiction Books*

London-based literary agency that works with writers, illustrators and photographers. We cover fiction, non-fiction and children's books, with a specialism in adult fantasy, science fiction and horror. We represent a top-drawer range of authors, both as primary agent and in association with a number of well-known agencies abroad. Our list comprises major brand-names, high profile award winners, talented debut authors and prestigious literary estates.

Authors: Travis Baldree; Shannon Lee Barry; Alice Bell; Cierra Block; Marie Brennan; Rebecca Brownlie; Andrew Cartmel; Mário Coelho; Vida Cruz-Borja; J.R. Dawson; Clio Evans; Georgia Gailey; Craig Laurance Gidney; J.T. Greathouse; Elizabeth Helen; Grady Hendrix; Jesse J. Holland; Shannon Mayer; Anna McNuff; Katy Nyquist; Adam Oyebanji; Taylor Riley Parham; Martin Purbrick; Sian Radford; Emily Rath; Farrah Riaz; Cassidy Ellis Salter; Yah Yah Scholfield; Calah Singleton; Tracy Townsend; Amy True / Amy Trueblood; R.R. Virdi; M.A. Wardell; MJ Wassmer; Gary Wigglesworth; Jasmine Wigham; Yudhanjaya Wijeratne; Catelyn Wilson

Literary Agents: John Berlyne (**L055**); Stevie Finegan (**L203**); Bianca Gillam (**L234**); Kirsten Lang (*L350*)

L618 Renee Zuckerbrot
Literary Agent
United States

https://www.mmqalit.com
https://www.mmqalit.com/about/

Literary Agency: Massie McQuilkin & Altman (**L394**)
Professional Bodies: Association of American Literary Agents (AALA); The Authors Guild

Fiction
  Novels: Commercial; Literary
  Short Fiction Collections: General

Nonfiction > *Nonfiction Books*
  History; Popular Culture; Science

Represents commercial and literary fiction. She has a soft spot for short story collections and science, popular culture, and history in the nonfiction space.

L619 Ayla Zuraw-Friedland
Literary Agent
United States

azf@goldinlit.com
https://www.goldinlit.com/ayla-zuraw-friedland
https://twitter.com/aylazeef

Literary Agency: Frances Goldin Literary Agency, Inc.

Fiction
  Graphic Novels: General
  Novels: Literary

Nonfiction > *Nonfiction Books*
  Arts; LGBTQIA; Social Class; Technology

Send: Query; Writing sample
How to send: Email

Interested in literary fiction and nonfiction that inspect big questions about queer identity, class, community, and art & technology through a personal lens. Please note that she does not represent Young Adult, Middle Grade, or Picture Books.

Magazines

For the most up-to-date listings of these and hundreds of other magazines, visit https://www.firstwriter.com/magazines

To claim your free access to the site, please see the back of this book.

M001 30 North
Magazine
United States

30north@noctrl.edu

https://30northliterarymagazine.com

Fiction > *Short Fiction*: Literary

Nonfiction > *Short Nonfiction*: Creative Nonfiction

Poetry > *Any Poetic Form*

Send: Full text
How to send: Submittable

Welcomes submissions from students and alumni of the college and from student artists and writers across the nation and world. We welcome creative writing in all genres, as well as visual art and songwriting.

M002 32 Poems
Magazine
Washington & Jefferson College, Department of English, 60 S. Lincoln Street, Washington, PA 15301
United States

submissions@32poems.com

http://32poems.com

Nonfiction > *Reviews*: Poetry as a Subject

Poetry > *Any Poetic Form*

Send: Full text
How to send: Submittable; Duosuma; Post

Costs: A fee is charged for online submissions. $3 fee for online submissions.

Welcomes submissions from January 1st to April 30th and from July 1st to October 31st. We respond quickly, often within a few weeks, and poets who have not received a response within 90 days are encouraged to query regarding their manuscript's status. As a rule, we publish shorter poems that fit on a single page, but we regularly make exceptions to accommodate remarkable work that runs a little longer. Please send no more than five poems (in a single document) and no more than one active submission at a time. We do not accept translations or work that has been previously published in print or online.

Editor: George David Clark

Managing Editor: Elisabeth Clark

M003 aaduna
Online Magazine
144 Genesee Street Suite 102-259, Auburn, NY 13021
United States

submissionsmanager@aaduna.org

https://www.aaduna.net
https://www.facebook.com/AadunaInc
https://aadunanotes.blogspot.com/
https://twitter.com/aadunaspeaks

Fiction
 Novel Excerpts; *Short Fiction*

Nonfiction > *Essays*

Poetry > *Any Poetic Form*

Send: Query; Author bio; Full text
How to send: Word file email attachment
How not to send: PDF file email attachment

Publishes fiction, poetry, and nonfiction. Primarily interested in providing a viable publishing platform for people of color. Submissions must be sent by email and writers are also strongly encouraged to send a copy by post as well, however this is no longer required. See website for full guidelines.

M004 About Place Journal
Magazine
PO Box 24, Black Earth, WI 53515-0424
United States

blackearthinstitute@gmail.com

https://aboutplacejournal.org
https://aboutplacejournal.submittable.com/submit

Fiction > *Short Fiction*: Literary

Nonfiction
 Essays: General
 Short Nonfiction: Creative Nonfiction

Poetry > *Any Poetic Form*

Closed to approaches.

Publishes poetry, fiction, and essays / creative nonfiction. Accepts submissions during specific submission windows. See website for details and for themes.

M005 Abridged
Print Magazine
United Kingdom

abridged@ymail.com

https://www.abridged.zone
https://www.facebook.com/profile.php?id=100042275333261
https://twitter.com/Abridged030

Poetry > *Any Poetic Form*
 Contemporary; Experimental

Aims to publish and exhibit contemporary/experimental poetry plus contemporary art. Each issue is themed. Themes focus on contemporary concerns in a rapidly changing society. We are offering an alternative and complete integration of poetry, art and design. We experiment continually.

M006 The Account
Online Magazine
United States

poetryprosethought@gmail.com

https://theaccountmagazine.com
https://theaccountajournalofpoetryprosethought.submittable.com/submit
https://twitter.com/TheAccountMag
https://www.facebook.com/TheAccountAJournalOfPoetryProseAndThought

Fiction > *Short Fiction*

Nonfiction > *Short Nonfiction*: Creative Nonfiction

Poetry > *Any Poetic Form*

Send: Full text

Accepts poetry, fiction, and creative nonfiction. Send 3-5 poems, essays up to 6,000 words, or fiction between 1,000 and 6,000 words, through online submission system. Each piece of work must be accompanied by an account between 150 and 500 words, giving voice to the artist's approach.

Editors: Brianna Noll, Poetry Editor; Jennifer Hawe, Nonfiction Editor; M. Milks, Fiction Editor; Tyler Mills, Editor-in-Chief; Christina Stoddard, Managing Editor/ Publicist

M007 Acumen

Magazine
4 Thornhill Bridge Wharf, Caledonian Road,
London, N1 0RU
United Kingdom
Tel: +44 (0) 20 7278 6674

hello@acumen-poetry.co.uk

https://acumen-poetry.co.uk

Nonfiction
  Articles: Poetry as a Subject
  Essays: Poetry as a Subject
  Reviews: Books; Poetry as a Subject
Poetry in Translation > *Any Poetic Form*

Poetry > *Any Poetic Form*

Send: Full text
How to send: Online submission system;
Email; Post

We aim to publish the best in new poetry and poetry translations, alongside articles, debate, comment and reviews of recent poetry publications. We publish new and established writers and are proud to have discovered many new voices. All poems are considered on merit. We welcome unpublished and unsubmitted poems, translations of poems, articles and debate on poetry covering a wide variety of topics and with different writing styles.

Editor: Patricia Oxley

M008 African American Golfer's Digest

Magazine
99 Wall Street, Suite 720, New York, NY 10005
United States
Tel: +1 (212) 571-6559

editors@africanamericangolfersdigest.com

https://africanamericangolfersdigest.com
https://www.facebook.com/africanamericangolfersdigest
https://twitter.com/DebertCook
https://www.instagram.com/africanamericangolfersdigest/
https://www.pinterest.com/AfricanAmerGolf/

Nonfiction > *Articles*
  African American; Golf

Send: Pitch
How to send: Email; Online contact form

Designed to promote the exchange of information and ideas among golfers with a particular focus on the African American golfing community. Articles cover all areas of the golf lifestyle spectrum, including equipment, golf etiquette, travel, clothing, leisure, resorts, profiles, destination reviews, food and beverage, and more. Regular features include in-depth reviews of players, instructors, books, various consumer products and other items of interest.

M009 African American Review

Magazine
United States

aileen.keenan@slu.edu

https://afamreview.org
https://twitter.com/afamreview

Book Publisher: The Johns Hopkins University Press

Fiction > *Short Fiction*: African American

Nonfiction
  Essays: African American; Arts; Culture; Films; Literature; Theatre; Visual Culture
  Interviews: African American
  Reviews: African American; Books
Poetry > *Any Poetic Form*: African American

Closed to approaches.

Publishes insightful essays on African American literature, theatre, film, the visual arts, and culture; "Forgotten Manuscript" features; interviews; poetry; fiction; and book reviews.

Editor: Aileen Keenan

M010 African Voices

Magazine
325 Lafayette Avenue, C.F. Suite, Brooklyn, NY 11238
United States
Tel: +1 (212) 865-2982

https://africanvoices.com
https://africanvoices.submittable.com/submit/
https://www.facebook.com/africanvoicesmag
https://www.instagram.com/africanvoices/
https://x.com/africanvoices

Fiction
  Novel Excerpts; *Short Fiction*
Poetry > *Any Poetic Form*

Scripts > *Theatre Scripts*

How to send: Submittable

Costs: A fee is charged upon submission. $3.77 per submission.

An international, literary magazine devoted to the promotion of fiction, non-fiction, poetry and visual arts created by people of color. Published three times a year (2 print issues and 1 digital issue) and distributed throughout the United States and abroad. Encourages writers and artists to review sample copies before submitting work so they are familiar with the editorial style. Publishes short stories and poetry online on a monthly basis.

Open to submissions all year round. Prioritizes and publishes work from writers from the African Diaspora and people of color. Encourages people to submit work that is transgressive, creative and thought provoking. Accepts all genres and styles (i.e. speculative fiction, humor, mystery and drama). Short one to three act plays and novel excerpts are accepted as well. All styles of poetry are considered including avant-garde, free verse, haiku, light verse and traditional. All subject matter of poems are considered for publication.

No AI generated poems, short stories, essays or art. Submissions must be 100 percent created by human writers and artists.

M011 Agni

Magazine
Boston University, 236 Bay State Road,
Boston, MA 02215
United States

agni@bu.edu

https://agnionline.bu.edu
https://www.bu.edu/dbin/agni/
https://twitter.com/AGNIMagazine
https://facebook.com/agnimag

Fiction > *Short Fiction*

Nonfiction > *Essays*

Poetry > *Any Poetic Form*

Closed to approaches.

Costs: A fee is charged upon submission. $3 submission fee.

Submit one story, one essay, or up to five poems, and wait for reply before sending more. Accepts submissions by post with SASE or via online submission system. No submissions by email. Open to submissions between September 1 and December 15; and between January 15 and May 31.

Editor: Sven Birkerts

M012 Agricultural History

Magazine
Department of History, Georgia Southern University, Interdisciplinary Academic Building, #3009, PO Box 8054, Statesboro, GA 30460
United States

https://www.aghistorysociety.org/the-journal
https://read.dukeupress.edu/agricultural-history/pages/Submission_Guidelines
https://mc04.manuscriptcentral.com/aghistory

ACADEMIC > **Nonfiction** > *Articles*
  Agriculture; History

Send: Full text

Publishes articles on all aspects of the history of agriculture and rural life with no geographical or temporal limits. Submit via online submission system. See website for full guidelines.

Editor: Drew Swanson

M013 Alabama Heritage

Magazine
Box 870342, Tuscaloosa, AL 35487-0342

United States
Tel: +1 (205) 348-7467

alabama.heritage@ua.edu

https://www.alabamaheritage.com
https://www.facebook.com/alabamaheritage
https://www.instagram.com/alabamaheritage
https://www.linkedin.com/company/alabama-heritage-magazine/
https://www.youtube.com/channel/UC5nc1Um0_Kn4jr-HXC1b10A

Nonfiction > *Articles*
  Alabama; Culture; History; US Southern States

Publishes stories of the history and culture of Alabama and the South.

M014 Alaska Quarterly Review
Magazine
United States

https://aqreview.org
https://alaskaquarterlyreview.submittable.com/submit
https://www.facebook.com/AlaskaQuarterlyReview/
https://www.youtube.com/channel/UCvtOaG2FJ7tuEs8Vsd-rbFQ
https://twitter.com/AQReview

Fiction
  Novel Excerpts: Experimental; Traditional
  Novellas: Experimental; Traditional
  Short Fiction: Experimental; Traditional
Nonfiction > *Short Nonfiction*
  Experimental; Literary; Traditional
Poetry > *Any Poetic Form*
  Experimental; Traditional
Scripts > *Theatre Scripts*
  Drama; Experimental; Traditional

Closed to approaches.

Costs: A fee is charged upon submission. $3 submission fee.

The editors invite submissions of fiction, short plays, poetry, photo essays, and literary nonfiction in traditional and experimental styles.

M015 Albemarle
Magazine
United States

heather@albemarlemagazine.com

https://albemarlemagazine.com

Nonfiction > *Essays*
  Charlottesville; Culture; History; Virginia

Magazine highlighting the history, culture, and notable people of Central Virginia. It offers in-depth articles that explore the region's rich heritage, local traditions, and influential figures, providing readers with engaging stories that capture the essence of the area.

M016 Alfred Hitchcock Mystery Magazine
Magazine
6 Prowitt Street, Norwalk, CT 06855
United States

https://www.alfredhitchcockmysterymagazine.com

Fiction > *Short Fiction*
  Courtroom Dramas; Crime; Mystery; Police Procedural; Suspense

How to send: Online submission system

Interested in nearly every kind of mystery: stories of detection of the classic kind, police procedurals, private eye tales, suspense, courtroom dramas, stories of espionage, and so on. Only requirement is that the story be about a crime (or the threat or fear of one).

Editor: Linda Landrigan

M017 Allegro Poetry Magazine
Online Magazine
United Kingdom

https://www.allegropoetry.org

Poetry > *Any Poetic Form*: Contemporary

Send: Full text; Author bio
How to send: In the body of an email

Biannual online poetry magazine. Accepts poetry submissions up to 40 lines by email between June 1 and July 31, and between December 1 and January 31. Each year the March issue is a general issue, and the September issue is a themed one.

M018 American Short Fiction
Magazine
United States

editors@americanshortfiction.org

https://americanshortfiction.org
https://americanshortfiction.submittable.com/submit
https://www.facebook.com/americanshortfiction
https://x.com/asfmag
https://www.instagram.com/americanshortfiction/

Fiction in Translation > *Short Fiction*

Fiction > *Short Fiction*

Send: Full text
How to send: Submittable
How not to send: Post

Costs: A fee is charged upon submission. $3 submission fee.

Has published, and continues to seek, short fiction by some of the finest writers working in contemporary literature, whether they are established or new or lesser-known authors. In addition to its triannual print magazine, also publishes stories online. Unsolicited submissions are accepted from September to December. Short fiction submitted to the magazine must be original and previously unpublished. All manuscripts must be written in English. Translations are acceptable but must be accompanied by a copy of the original text. Considers simultaneous submissions on the condition that if the manuscript is accepted for publication elsewhere, the author immediately withdraws the submission through the Submittable site. No poetry, plays, nonfiction, reviews, etc.

M019 Amethyst Review
Online Magazine
United Kingdom

editor@amethystmagazine.org
Sarah.Poet@gmail.com

https://amethystmagazine.org
https://www.facebook.com/AmethystReview/

Fiction > *Short Fiction*: Spirituality
Nonfiction > *Short Nonfiction*: Spirituality
Poetry > *Any Poetic Form*: Spirituality

Closed to approaches.

Publishes work that engages in some way with spirituality or the sacred. Submit up to five poems (of any length) and / or prose pieces of up to 2,000 words. Simultaneous submissions if notification of acceptance elsewhere is provided. No previously published work. Send submissions by email with author bio of around 50 words. See website for full guidelines.

Editor: Sarah Law

M020 And Other Poems
Online Magazine
United Kingdom

editor.andotherpoems@gmail.com

https://andotherpoems.com
https://www.instagram.com/and_otherpoems/
https://x.com/And_OtherPoems
https://bsky.app/profile/andotherpoems.bsky.social

Nonfiction > *Essays*: Poetry as a Subject
Poetry > *Any Poetic Form*

How to send: Email

Costs: A fee is charged upon submission in some cases. £2 submission fee for up to four poems.

Online magazine publishing poems and essays on poetry. Accepts essay submissions year-round. Open to poetry submissions in January, May, and September.

M021 Angela Poetry Magazine
Online Magazine
Canada

info@waxpoetryart.com

https://waxpoetryart.com
https://waxpoetryart.com/angela/

Magazine Publisher: Wax Poetry and Art Network

Poetry > *Any Poetic Form*: Contemporary

How to send: Email

Accepts poems that are curious, humorous, joyful, playful, and generally on the lighter side of life. Accepts submissions from everyone all over the world.

M022 Ann Arbor Observer
Magazine
PO Box 1187, Ann Arbor, MI 48106
United States
Tel: +1 (734) 769-3175
Fax: +1 (734) 769-3775

editor@aaobserver.com

https://annarborobserver.com
https://x.com/aaobserver
https://www.facebook.com/AnnArborObserver/
https://www.instagram.com/aaobserver/

Nonfiction > *News*
  Ann Arbor; Education; Entertainment; Food and Drink; Politics

How to send: Email

Publishes news of Ann Arbor people, politics, education, shopping, dining, and entertainment. Welcomes freelance material.

Editor: John Hilton

M023 Arboreal
Online Magazine
United States

https://arborealmag.com
https://arboreal.submittable.com/submit
https://www.instagram.com/arborealmagazine/
https://twitter.com/arborealmag
https://www.facebook.com/ArborealMag
https://www.linkedin.com/company/arborealmag/

Fiction > *Short Fiction*

Nonfiction > *Essays*

Poetry > *Any Poetic Form*

Closed to approaches.

Online magazine that came about when two friends sought to create something of value, something for pure enjoyment, something to encourage creativity.

M024 Arc
Magazine
PO Box 269 Stn B, Ottawa, ON, K1P 6C4
Canada

arc@arcpoetry.ca
prose@arcpoetry.ca
coordinatingeditor@arcpoetry.ca

https://arcpoetry.ca
https://arcpoetry.submittable.com/submit
https://www.facebook.com/ArcPoetryMagazine/
https://x.com/arcpoetry
https://www.instagram.com/arcpoetrymag/
https://www.youtube.com/user/ArcPoetry

Nonfiction
  Articles: Poetry as a Subject
  Essays: Poetry as a Subject
  Interviews: Poetry as a Subject
  Reviews: Poetry as a Subject

Poetry > *Any Poetic Form*

Send: Full text; Pitch
How to send: Submittable; Email

Costs: A fee is charged upon submission in some cases. Poets based in the US must pay a submission fee of $2 per poem. If this fee is a barrier for anyone wishing to submit, poets may enquire about having the fee waived.

Accepts unsolicited submissions from poets at all stages of their writing careers during Spring and Fall submission periods, via Submittable. Send up to three poems, up to 360 lines in total. Also publishes essays, articles, interviews and reviews relating to poetry. Send pitches by email.

M025 The Architectural Review
Magazine
15 Bouverie Street, London, EC4Y 8DP
United Kingdom
Tel: +44 (0) 20 3953 2000

https://www.architectural-review.com

Magazine Publisher: EMAP Publishing

PROFESSIONAL > **Nonfiction** > *Articles*
  Architecture; Design

Magazine of architecture and design aimed at professionals.

Editor: Paul Finch

M026 Art Quarterly
Magazine
PO Box 4387, Chippenham, SN15 9NY
United Kingdom
Tel: +44 (0) 20 3757 9772

artquarterly@artfund.org

https://www.artfund.org/about-us/art-quarterly

Nonfiction > *Articles*: Arts

Arts magazine publishing features on artists, galleries and museums.

M027 Arts & Letters
Magazine
United States
Tel: +1 (478) 445-1289

https://artsandletters.gcsu.edu
https://artsandletters.submittable.com/submit
https://www.facebook.com/artslettersgc
https://twitter.com/ArtsLettersGC
https://artsandlettersjournal.tumblr.com/

Fiction > *Short Fiction*: Literary

Nonfiction > *Short Nonfiction*: Creative Nonfiction

Poetry > *Any Poetic Form*

Closed to approaches.

Costs: A fee is charged upon submission. $3 submission fee.

Send between four and six poems, or up to 25 pages (typed, double-spaced) of fiction or creative nonfiction. Accepts submissions between August 1 and September 30.

M028 Asian Social Science
Magazine
Canada

ass@ccsenet.org

https://www.ccsenet.org
https://www.ccsenet.org/journal/index.php/ass

ACADEMIC > **Nonfiction** > *Articles*
  Asia; Sociology

An international, double-blind peer-reviewed, open-access journal. The journal publishes high quality reviews and research articles that focus on social science, especially in Asian area. It provides an academic platform for professionals and researchers to contribute innovative work in the field. The journal carries original and full-length articles that reflect the latest research and developments in both theoretical and practical aspects of society and human behaviours.

M029 Asimov's Science Fiction
Magazine
United States

asimovs@dellmagazines.com

https://www.asimovs.com
http://asimovs.magazinesubmissions.com/

Magazine Publisher: Dell Magazines

Fiction > *Short Fiction*
  Fantasy; Science Fiction; Slipstream; Surreal

Poetry > *Any Poetic Form*
  Fantasy; Science Fiction; Slipstream; Surreal

Does not want:

> **Fiction** > *Short Fiction*: Sword and Sorcery

How to send: Online submission system; Post

Seeks serious, character-orientated science fiction and (borderline) fantasy, slipstream, and surreal. The characters should always be the main focus, rather than the science. Humour will be considered. No simultaneous submissions, sword-and-sorcery, horror, explicit sex, violence, or works written, developed, or assisted by AI.

M030 Atlanta Magazine
Magazine
5901-A Peachtree Dunwoody Rd NE, Suite 350, Atlanta, GA 30328
United States
Tel: +1 (404) 527-5500

https://www.atlantamagazine.com
https://www.facebook.com/atlantamag
http://instagram.com/atlantamagazine
https://www.linkedin.com/company/atlantamagazine
https://twitter.com/atlantamagazine

Nonfiction
   Articles: Arts; Atlanta; Culture; Design; Food and Drink; Gardening; Health; Lifestyle; Property / Real Estate; Travel; Wellbeing
   News: Atlanta

Send: Query
How to send: Email

We focus on Atlanta and the metro region. We're looking for stories that haven't been told before, that help us see the city, the state, the region, and ourselves in new ways.

M031 Atlanta Review
Magazine
Suite 333, 686 Cherry St. NW, Atlanta, GA 30332-0161
United States

atlantareview@gatech.edu

http://atlantareview.com
https://atlantareview.submittable.com/submit
https://twitter.com/ATLReview
https://www.facebook.com/atlantareview
https://www.instagram.com/atlantareviewpojo/

Poetry > *Any Poetic Form*

Closed to approaches.

Costs: A fee is charged for online submissions. $3. Also runs competitions for which a fee is charged.

Accepts submissions of poetry between January 1 and June 1, and between September 15 and December 1. Submit online ($3 submission fee) or by post with SASE. Also runs competitions.

M032 Atlantic Northeast
Magazine
United States

https://atlanticnortheastmag.com
https://www.instagram.com/atlanticnemag/
https://twitter.com/AtlanticNEMag

Fiction > *Short Fiction*
   Atlantic Northeast; Culture; History

Nonfiction > *Short Nonfiction*
   Atlantic Northeast; Creative Nonfiction; Culture; History

Closed to approaches.

A magazine dedicated to exploring the history, culture, and spirit of the Northeastern United States and Canada.

M033 Atrium
Online Magazine
Worcestershire
United Kingdom

https://atriumpoetry.com
https://www.facebook.com/AtriumPoetry
https://twitter.com/Atrium_Poetry

Poetry > *Any Poetic Form*

Closed to approaches.

A poetry webzine based in Worcestershire, UK. A new poem is published twice a week, on Tuesdays and Fridays. Aims to publish poems that allow readers to think, feel and see things in a new way.

M034 Aurealis
Magazine
Australia

editors@aurealis.com.au
submissions@aurealis.com.au
nonfiction@aurealis.com.au
reviews@aurealis.com.au

https://aurealis.com.au
https://www.facebook.com/AurealisFSF
https://x.com/AurealisMag

Fiction > *Short Fiction*
   Fantasy; Horror; Science Fiction

Nonfiction
   Articles: Fantasy; Horror; Science Fiction
   Interviews: Fantasy; Horror; Science Fiction
   Reviews: Books; Fantasy; Horror; Science Fiction

Looking for science fiction, fantasy or horror short stories between 2000 and 8000 words. All types of science fiction, fantasy and horror that are of a "speculative" nature will be considered, but we do not want stories that are derivative in nature. We do not publish horror without a supernatural element. Although we are an Australian-based publication, we are open to submissions in English from anywhere in the multiverse during specific reading periods. Accepts submissions from Australian and New Zealand writers February 1 to September 30. Accepts submissions from anyone anywhere during March.

M035 Auroras & Blossoms PoArtMo Anthology
Online Magazine
United Kingdom

info@abpositiveart.com

https://abpositiveart.com
https://www.facebook.com/abpositiveart
https://twitter.com/ab_positiveart
https://www.youtube.com/channel/UCkAh-EnwcJbd865SEXJQsEw

ADULT
   Fiction > *Short Fiction*
   Nonfiction > *Essays*

TEEN
   Fiction > *Short Fiction*
   Nonfiction > *Essays*

Send: Query; Author bio; Writing sample
How to send: Email

Annual anthology sold in ebook format.

Editors / Poets: David Ellis; Cendrine Marrouat

M036 AZ Foothills Magazine
Magazine
530 E McDowell Road #107, PMB 607, Phoenix, AZ 85004
United States

https://www.arizonafoothillsmagazine.com
https://www.facebook.com/azfoothillsmag
https://x.com/azfoothills
http://www.tiktok.com/@azfoothills
https://www.instagram.com/azfoothills

Nonfiction > *Articles*
   Arizona; Lifestyle; Upmarket

Upscale lifestyle magazine that reaches affluent, well-educated readers in the prestigious desert foothills communities of Arizona.

Editor: Elizabeth Smith, Executive Editor

M037 Babybug
Magazine
United States

https://cricketmedia.com
https://cricketmedia.com/babybug-submission-guidelines/
https://cricketmag.submittable.com/submit

Magazine Publisher: Cricket Media, Inc.

CHILDREN'S
   Fiction > *Short Fiction*
   Nonfiction > *Short Nonfiction*
   Poetry > *Any Poetic Form*

Closed to approaches.

Publishes poetry, stories, and nonfiction (including activities and parent–child interaction) for children aged 6 months to 3 years. Stories should be up to six short sentences; poems should be rhythmic and rhyming and up to eight lines long.

M038 Bacopa Literary Review
Magazine
United States

https://writersalliance.org/bacopa-literary-review/

Fiction > *Short Fiction*: Literary

Nonfiction > *Short Nonfiction*: Creative Nonfiction

Poetry > *Any Poetic Form*

How to send: Submittable

Annual print journal publishing short stories, creative nonfiction, poetry, and prose poetry. Accepts submissions only through free annual contest.

M039 The Baffler
Magazine
234 5th Avenue, New York, NY 10001
United States
Tel: +1 (844) 523-4680

https://thebaffler.com
https://www.facebook.com/TheBafflerMagazine/
https://twitter.com/thebafflermag

Fiction > *Short Fiction*
Comedy / Humour; Politics; Satire

Nonfiction > *Articles*
Culture; Left Wing Politics

Poetry > *Any Poetic Form*

Send: Pitch
How to send: Online submission system

Describes itself as "America's leading voice of interesting and unexpected left-wing political criticism, cultural analysis, short stories, poems and art". Submit pitch using online form on website.

M040 Bandit Fiction
Online Magazine
United Kingdom

https://banditfiction.com
https://www.facebook.com/banditfiction/
https://twitter.com/BanditFiction
https://www.instagram.com/banditfiction/
https://open.spotify.com/show/4roZtA65SdavXAwfflm1eE

Fiction > *Short Fiction*

Poetry > *Any Poetic Form*

We are digital publishers who believe in outstanding fiction. Our community is a place where readers and writers can grow and engage with the literary scene. Championing new, high quality and entertaining writing that is in touch with the craft of fiction, every piece of short fiction we publish is hand-picked by The Editor, edited alongside the author, and published direct to our website, always free to read. There are no limits on the genres, styles, perspectives or traditions we accept, and we aim to select pieces that represent something great about the current and future literary scene.

M041 Barren Magazine
Magazine
United States

info@barrenmagazine.com
poetry@barrenmagazine.com
fiction@barrenmagazine.com
flashcnf@barrenmagazine.com
creativenonfiction@barrenmagazine.com

https://barrenmagazine.com
http://twitter.com/BarrenMagazine
http://facebook.com/BarrenMagazine
http://instagram.com/barrenmagazine

Fiction > *Short Fiction*

Nonfiction > *Nonfiction Books*: Creative Nonfiction

Poetry > *Any Poetic Form*

Closed to approaches.

An Alt.Lit Introspective.

A literary publication that features fiction, poetry, creative nonfiction, and photography for hard truths, long stares, and gritty lenses. We revel in the shadow-spaces that make up the human condition, and aim to find antitheses to that which defines us: light in darkness; beauty in ugliness; peace in disarray. We invite you to explore it with us.

Editor: Jason D. Ramsey

M042 BBC History Magazine
Magazine
United Kingdom
Tel: +44 (0) 117 300 8699

historymagazine@historyextra.com

https://www.historyextra.com
https://www.facebook.com/HistoryExtra
https://twitter.com/HistoryExtra
https://www.instagram.com/historyextra
https://www.youtube.com/channel/historyextra

Magazine Publisher: Immediate Media Co.

Nonfiction > *Articles*: History

Magazine publishing articles about history.

M043 The Beano
Magazine
185 Fleet Street, London, EC4A 2HS
United Kingdom
Tel: +44 (0) 20 7400 1030

hello@beano.com

https://www.beano.com

Newspaper Publisher / Magazine Publisher: DC Thomson Media

CHILDREN'S > *Fiction* > *Cartoons*: Comedy / Humour

Publishes comic strips for children aged 6-12.

M044 The Bear Deluxe Magazine
Magazine
1881 NW Vaughn Street, Portland, OR 97209
United States
Tel: +1 (971) 235-2734

thebear@orlo.org
beardeluxe@orlo.org

https://orlo.org
https://www.facebook.com/pages/Bear-Deluxe-Magazine/115925931775159
https://twitter.com/orlobear

Fiction > *Short Fiction*

Nonfiction > *Articles*
Arts; Culture; Environment

Poetry > *Any Poetic Form*

Send: Full text
How to send: Email

Magazine of the arts, culture and environment. Send submissions by email.

Editor: Tom Webb

M045 The Bee
Online Magazine
New Writing North, 120 Squires Building, Northumbria University, Sandyford Road, Newcastle upon Tyne, NE1 8ST
United Kingdom

hello@thebeemagazine.com

https://thebeemagazine.com
https://www.facebook.com/beelitmag/
https://x.com/BeeLitMag
https://www.instagram.com/beelitmag/
https://bsky.app/profile/beelitmag.bsky.social

Fiction > *Short Fiction*

Nonfiction
  Articles; *Essays*; *Short Nonfiction*

We welcome work from writers who are working class or from working-class origins.

All submissions must be the original work of the writer.

We are interested in work of all lengths and in fiction, non-fiction, commentary, essays, and journalism. We are also interested in visual arts and photography submissions. Work will be published on the website and considered for a forthcoming print edition.

Any work submitted for consideration must not have been published online or in print previously.

M046 Bella

Magazine
The Lantern, 75 Hampstead Road, London, NW1 2PL
United Kingdom

Bella.Hotline@bauermedia.co.uk

https://www.bellamagazine.co.uk
https://twitter.com/#!/bellamagazineUK
http://facebook.com/bellamagazineUK
https://www.instagram.com/bellamagazineuk/

Magazine Publisher: Bauer Media Group

Nonfiction > *Articles*
  Celebrity; Diet; Fashion; Real Life Stories; Travel

Send: Query
How to send: Email

Human interest magazine for women, publishing articles on celebs, diet, style, travel, and real-life stories. Send query by email.

M047 Belmont Story Review

Magazine
United States

belmontstoryreview@gmail.com

https://belmontstoryreview.wixsite.com/website
https://belmontstoryreview.submittable.com/submit

Fiction > *Short Fiction*

Nonfiction > *Short Nonfiction*: Creative Nonfiction

Poetry > *Any Poetic Form*

Closed to approaches.

Established in 2016, the magazine aims to surprise and delight readers through an eclectic mix of storytelling which includes fiction, personal essay, poetry, songwriting, drama, graphic narrative, and photography; as well as creative reportage, including coverage of music, film, creativity and collaboration, and the intersection of faith and culture. "Faith" is not a specific religious perspective but a broad idea of faith is important for all selected publications.

We seek to publish new and established writers passionate about their craft, fearlessly encountering difficult ideas, seeking to explore human experience in all its broken blessedness.

M048 Beloit Fiction Journal

Magazine
Box 11, Beloit College, 700 College Street, Beloit, WI 53511
United States

https://www.beloit.edu/fiction-journal/
https://beloitfictionjournal.submittable.com/submit

Fiction > *Short Fiction*: Literary

Closed to approaches.

Costs: A fee is charged upon submission. $3 per submission.

Open to literary fiction on any subject or theme, up to 11,000 words. Also accepts flash fiction. Showcases new writers as well as established writers. Simultaneous submissions are accepted.

M049 Berks County Living

Magazine
GoggleWorks Center for the Arts, 201 Washington St., Suite 525, Reading, PA 19601
United States
Tel: +1 (610) 923-0385
Fax: +1 (610) 923-0389

info@berkscountyliving.com

https://berkscountyliving.com
https://www.facebook.com/BerksCountyLiving/
https://www.pinterest.com/bclmagazine/
https://www.instagram.com/bclmag/

Nonfiction > *Articles*
  Beauty; Berks County; Business; Food and Drink; Home Improvement; Lifestyle; Recipes; Restaurants; Weddings; Wellbeing

The only regional magazine dedicated to highlighting all that is unique and wonderful about the Greater Reading/Berks area. The monthly lifestyle magazine continues to inform readers about what makes Berks County an exceptional place to live.

M050 Best of British

Magazine
Morton Way, Horncastle, Lincolnshire, LN9 6JR
United Kingdom

https://www.bestofbritishmag.co.uk
https://www.facebook.com/bestbritishmag/
https://twitter.com/bestofbritishuk

Magazine Publisher: Mortons Media Group

Nonfiction > *Articles*
  History; Nostalgia; United Kingdom

Describes itself as "the UK's premier nostalgia magazine", covering every aspect of life from the 1930s to today.

M051 Better Homes and Gardens

Magazine
1716 Locust St, Des Moines, IA 50309
United States

bhgeditor@dotdashmdp.com

https://www.bhg.com
https://www.facebook.com/mybhg/
https://twitter.com/bhg/
https://www.pinterest.com/bhg/
https://www.instagram.com/betterhomesandgardens/

Magazine Publisher: Dotdash Meredith

Nonfiction > *Articles*
  Cookery; Gardening; Home Improvement; Recipes

The fourth best-selling magazine in the United States. Publishes articles on gardening, home improvement, cleaning and organizing, and cooking and recipes.

M052 Better Than Starbucks

Magazine
1524 Camino Real, Hobbs, NM 88240
United States
Tel: +1 (575) 441-5417

betterthanstarbucks2@gmail.com

https://www.betterthanstarbucks.org

ADULT
  Fiction > *Short Fiction*

  Nonfiction > *Short Nonfiction*: Creative Nonfiction

  Poetry in Translation > *Any Poetic Form*

  Poetry
    Any Poetic Form: Africa; Comedy / Humour; International
    Experimental Poetry: General
    Formal Poetry: General
    Free Verse: General
    Haiku: General
    Prose Poetry: General

CHILDREN'S > **Poetry** > *Any Poetic Form*

Closed to approaches.

Publishes African Poetry, International Poetry, Prose Poetry, Forms as well as Formal Poetry, Poetry Translations, Experimental Poetry and poetry for children. Encourages sentiment in poetry. Also publishes Fiction, Flash Fiction, Micro Fiction and Creative Nonfiction. Submitted opinion pieces will be considered.

Editor: Vera Ignatowitsch

M053 BFS Horizons

Magazine
United Kingdom

bfshorizons@britishfantasysociety.org
poetry@britishfantasysociety.org

https://britishfantasysociety.org
https://britishfantasysociety.org/get-in-touch/bfs-horizons/

Association: The British Fantasy Society

Fiction > *Short Fiction*
  Fantasy; Horror

Poetry > *Any Poetic Form*
  Fantasy; Horror

Send: Full text; Author bio
How to send: Word file email attachment; In the body of an email

We welcome short fiction submissions in any Fantasy or Horror genre or sub-genre, of 500 –

5000 words. In poetry, any form will be accepted. To be honest, rhyming poetry in iambic pentameters will be a hard sell. However, it would be good to see sonnets, Villanelles or the odd Rondeau, or any other form you care to tackle. Tip: Before submitting, read your poem out loud. Does it work? Check the metre. Does it scan? Look at your line lengths. Lengthy poems or sagas will be considered but should follow instead the submission guidelines for fiction.

M054 BFS Journal
Magazine
United Kingdom

kmanwaring@aub.ac.uk

https://www.britishfantasysociety.org/
https://britishfantasysociety.org/get-in-touch/bfs-journal/
https://twitter.com/BritFantasySoc

Association: The British Fantasy Society

ACADEMIC > **Nonfiction** > *Articles*: Fantasy

ADULT > **Nonfiction**
  Articles: Fantasy
  Interviews: Fantasy
  Reviews: Fantasy

How to send: Email

Fantasy journal devoted to non-fiction: interviews, academic articles, reviews and features.

M055 Big Fiction
Online Magazine
Seattle University, English Dept, c/o Juan Carlos Reyes, P.O. Box 222000, Seattle, WA 98122-1090
United States

editors@bigfiction.com

https://www.bigfictionmagazine.com

Fiction > *Novelettes*

Nonfiction
  Essays: General
  Reviews: Fiction as a Subject
  Short Nonfiction: Creative Nonfiction

Closed to approaches.

Costs: A fee is charged upon submission. $5 for novelettes; $3 for essays.

Literary magazine devoted to longer short fiction, between 7,500 and 20,000 words.

M056 Black Moon Magazine
Online Magazine
United States

blackmoonmageditors@gmail.com

http://www.blackmoonmag.com
https://www.facebook.com/BlackMoonMagazine

https://www.instagram.com/black.moon.mag/
https://twitter.com/Black_Moon_Mag

Fiction > *Short Fiction*

Nonfiction
  Interviews: Literature
  Reviews: Books

Poetry > *Any Poetic Form*

Send: Full text; Query; Author bio
How to send: Email attachment

Submit up to three short stories between 1,000 and 8,000 words, or up to five poems of up to five pages each. Also accepts book reviews and interviews with professionals in the writing community for online publication. No submissions in January or July.

M057 Black Static
Magazine
United Kingdom

blackstatic@ttapress.com

http://ttapress.com/blackstatic/

Magazine Publisher / Book Publisher: TTA Press

Fiction > *Short Fiction*
  Dark; Horror

Closed to approaches.

Always open to unsolicited submissions of new dark/horror stories up to a maximum of 10,000 words.

Editor: Andy Cox

M058 Black Warrior Review
Magazine
United States

blackwarriorreview@gmail.com
managingeditor.bwr@gmail.com

https://bwr.ua.edu
https://www.facebook.com/pages/Black-Warrior-Review/335215809212
https://twitter.com/BlackWarriorRev

Fiction
  Cartoons: General
  Short Fiction: General, and in particular: Experimental
Nonfiction
  Graphic Nonfiction; *Short Nonfiction*
Poetry
  Any Poetic Form; *Visual Poetry*

How to send: Submittable; Email

Costs: A fee is charged upon submission. $5. $10 for expedited response.

Accepts short stories and nonfiction up to 7,000 words, up to three pieces of flash fiction up to 1,000 words or submit up to five poems up to 10 pages total. Accepts work that takes risk or is experimental, in lieu of convention and/or grammatical cleanliness. Seeks nonfiction pieces outside western traditions; pieces that defy any such categorization. Welcomes submissions of striking visual narratives (think: graphic novel or memoir in short form).

Online Magazine: Boyfriend Village (**M064**)

M059 Blue Earth Review
Magazine
136 Nelson Hall, Minnesota State University, Mankato, Mankato, MN 56001
United States

blueearthreview@gmail.com

https://blueearthreview.mnsu.edu
https://www.facebook.com/theblueearthreview/
https://twitter.com/BlueEarthReview

Fiction > *Short Fiction*

Nonfiction
  Essays: Personal Essays
  Short Nonfiction: Creative Nonfiction; Memoir
Poetry > *Any Poetic Form*

Send: Full text
How to send: Submittable

Publishes fiction, creative nonfiction and poetry. Interested in creative nonfiction (memoir and personal essay) with contemporary themes. No literary criticism. Submit up to five poems at a time.

M060 Blue Mesa Review
Magazine
Department of English Language and Literature, Humanities Building, Second Floor, MSC03 2170, 1 University of New Mexico, Albuquerque, NM 87131-0001
United States

https://bmr.unm.edu/
https://bluemesareview.submittable.com/submit
https://www.instagram.com/bluemesareview/

Fiction > *Short Fiction*

Nonfiction > *Short Nonfiction*: Creative Nonfiction

Poetry > *Any Poetic Form*

How to send: Submittable

We accept previously unpublished work in Fiction (up to 6,000 words), Nonfiction (up to 6,000 words), Poetry (up to 3 poems), and Visual Art. We have a rotating editorial board, so each issue is fresh and unique. In general, we are seeking strong voices and lively, compelling narratives with a fine eye for craft. We look forward to reading your best work!

M061 Bluegrass Unlimited
Magazine
311 W 2nd St, Owensboro, KY 42301
United States
Tel: +1 (800) 258-4727

https://www.bluegrassunlimited.com
https://www.facebook.com/BluegrassUnlimited/
https://www.instagram.com/bluegrassunlimited/
https://twitter.com/bgunlimitedmag
https://www.youtube.com/channel/UCxNYVomNcDl-5mrOy3KgoHA

Nonfiction
Articles: Bluegrass
Interviews: Bluegrass
News: Bluegrass
Reviews: Bluegrass

A print magazine that has been dedicated to the furtherance of bluegrass music for over 50 years.

Managing Editor: Dan Miller

M062 Boston Review
Print Magazine; Online Magazine
PO Box 390568, Cambridge, MA 02139
United States
Tel: +1 (617) 356-8198

review@bostonreview.net

https://www.bostonreview.net
https://bostonreview.submittable.com/submit
https://www.facebook.com/bostonreview/
https://twitter.com/BostonReview/

Fiction > *Short Fiction*

Nonfiction
Essays: Culture; Politics
Reviews: Books

Poetry > *Any Poetic Form*

How to send: Submittable; Post

A web and print magazine of ideas, politics, and culture. Independent and nonprofit, animated by hope and committed to equality, we believe in the power of collective reasoning and imagination to create a more just world.

M063 Bowhunter
Magazine
United States

https://www.bowhunter.com
https://www.facebook.com/BowHunterMag/
https://twitter.com/BowHunterMag
https://www.instagram.com/bowhunter/
https://www.youtube.com/channel/UCyW-6pItixp7xZ4gD0GUrGw
https://www.pinterest.com/bowhunter0028/

Magazine Publisher: Outdoor Sportsman Group

Nonfiction > *Articles*
Archery; Hunting

Magazine publishing articles relating to hunting with a bow and arrow.

M064 Boyfriend Village
Online Magazine
United States

https://bwr.ua.edu/about-boyfriend-village/

Magazine: Black Warrior Review (**M058**)

Fiction > *Short Fiction*

Nonfiction > *Short Nonfiction*

Poetry > *Any Poetic Form*

How to send: Submittable

Costs: A fee is charged upon submission. $5.

There is one submission category for all genres. Accepts fiction, poetry, nonfiction, hybrid, visual and multimedia art, as well as sound collage, video, games, and more.

M065 Brick
Magazine
P.O. Box 609, STN P, Toronto, ON, M5S 2Y4
Canada

info@brickmag.com

https://brickmag.com/
https://brickmag.submittable.com/submit
https://twitter.com/brickMAG
https://facebook.com/brickmagazine
https://instagram.com/brickliterary

Nonfiction
Essays: Arts; City and Town Planning; Dance; Food; History; Literature; Music; Photography; Science; Sport; Travel; Writing
Interviews: Arts; Literature; Performing Arts
Short Nonfiction: Literary; Memoir

Closed to approaches.

Send entire submission in first instance. Please read magazine before submitting. Accepts unsolicited nonfiction submissions on a variety of subjects during April and October each year. No unsolicited fiction or poetry.

M066 Britain Magazine
Magazine
The Chelsea Magazine Company, 111 Buckingham Palace Road, London, SW1 0DT
United Kingdom
Tel: +44 (0) 20 7349 3700

editor@britain-magazine.co.uk

https://www.britain-magazine.com
https://www.facebook.com/BritainMagazine
https://www.instagram.com/britain_magazine/
https://twitter.com/BritainMagazine

Magazine Publisher: The Chelsea Magazine Company

Nonfiction > *Articles*
Culture; History; Nature; Royalty; Travel; United Kingdom

Magazine of UK travel, culture, heritage and style, and the go-to publication for visitors fascinated by British history. Each issue is packed with tales of kings and queens, heroes and villains and the stories behind British castles, cathedrals, stately homes and gardens, countryside, and coastline.

M067 The BSFA Review
Online Magazine
United Kingdom

https://bsfa.co.uk
https://bsfa.co.uk/bsfa-publications

Professional Body: BSFA (British Science Fiction Association)

Nonfiction > *Reviews*
Arts; Comic Books; Fantasy; Films; Horror; Science Fiction; Theatre; Warfare

A digital magazine filled with reviews of the latest genre fiction. We aim to cover as much of the SFF field as possible, whether it is traditional or contemporary science fiction and/or fantasy. We are also interested in fiction and non-fiction material that is not directly SFF but may be of related interest to the genre, including themes like horror and war. This means that as well as fiction and non-fiction we also try to feature reviews of comics, graphic novels, spoken word, films, plays, and exhibitions.

M068 Business & Accountancy Daily
Online Magazine
240 Blackfriars Road, London, SE1 8NW
United Kingdom

accountancynews@croneri.co.uk

https://www.accountancydaily.co
https://twitter.com/accountancylive
https://www.linkedin.com/company/accountancy-daily/

Book Publisher: Croner-i Limited

PROFESSIONAL > **Nonfiction** > *News*
Accounting; Business; Finance

Specialises in technical analysis, news and comment on business, tax, finance, accounting, audit and HR for finance professionals, accountants and business leaders.

M069 Business Traveller
Magazine
Blackburn House, Blackburn Road, London, NW6 1RZ
United Kingdom

bt@ink-global.com

https://www.businesstraveller.com
https://www.linkedin.com/groups/2136397
https://www.facebook.com/BusinessTraveller
https://www.twitter.com/BTUK
https://www.instagram.com/businesstravelleruk/

Nonfiction > *Articles*
Business; Travel

The leading magazine around the world for the frequent corporate traveller. A consumer publication, it is aimed at entertaining business travellers, saving them money and making their travelling life easier. Each edition is packed with editorial on the latest news about airlines, airports, hotels and car rental.

Editor: Tom Otley

M070 Butcher's Dog
Print Magazine
United Kingdom

https://www.butchersdogmagazine.co.uk
https://butchersdogpoetry.submittable.com/submit
https://www.facebook.com/ButchersDogPoetry
https://twitter.com/butchersdogmag
https://www.instagram.com/butchersdogmag/

Poetry > *Any Poetic Form*

Closed to approaches.

Proudly edited and published in the heart of North East England. We print two unthemed poetry magazines each year in Spring and Autumn. Every issue features original cover artwork and contains a selection of up to twenty-five exceptional poems. Poems are selected on their merit in an anonymous reading process, supporting a more inclusive body of contemporary writing than the publishing industry currently represents.

M071 The Cafe Irreal
Magazine
United States

editors@cafeirreal.com

http://cafeirreal.alicewhittenburg.com

Fiction > *Short Fiction*: Literary

Send: Full text
How to send: Email

Quarterly webzine publishing fantastic fiction resembling the work of writers such as Franz Kafka and Jorge Luis Borges. Send stories up to 2,000 in the body of an email. No simultaneous submissions.

M072 Canadian Dimension
Online Magazine
D-91 Albert Street, Winnipeg, Manitoba, R3B 1G5
Canada

info@canadiandimension.com

https://canadiandimension.com
https://twitter.com/CDN_Dimension
https://www.facebook.com/CDNDimension
https://www.instagram.com/cdn_dimension/

Nonfiction
  Articles: Current Affairs; Economics; Environment; Left Wing Politics
  Reviews: Books; Films

Send: Full text
How to send: Word file email attachment

The longest-standing voice of the left in Canada. For more than half-a-century, has provided a forum for lively and radical debate where red meets green, socialists take on social democrats, Indigenous voices are heard, activists report from every corner of the country, and the latest books and films are critically reviewed. Our dedicated and longstanding readership is comprised of activists, organisers, academics, economists, workers, trade unionists, feminists, environmentalists, Indigenous peoples, and members of the LGBTQ2 community.

Editor: Cy Gonick

M073 The Caribbean Writer
Magazine
University of the Virgin Islands, 10,000 Castle Burke, Kingshill, St. Croix USVI 00850-9960
United States
Tel: +1 (340) 692-4152
Fax: +1 (340) 692-4122

info@thecaribbeanwriter.org
submit@TheCaribbeanWriter.com
thecaribbeanwriter@uvi.edu

https://www.thecaribbeanwriter.org
https://www.facebook.com/profile.php?id=100069147405842#
https://www.instagram.com/thecaribbeanwriter/
https://x.com/TheCaribbeanWri
https://www.linkedin.com/company/thecaribbeanwriter
https://www.youtube.com/channel/UCCfIPff1O9j5oYTQom-JtNw

Fiction > *Short Fiction*
  Caribbean; Culture; Literary

Nonfiction
  Essays: Caribbean; Culture; Literary; Personal Essays
  Interviews: Caribbean; Culture
  Reviews: Books
  Short Nonfiction: Caribbean; Creative Nonfiction; Culture; Literary
Poetry > *Any Poetic Form*
  Caribbean; Culture; Literary
Scripts > *Theatre Scripts*
  Caribbean; Culture; Literary

Send: Full text
How to send: Online submission system

An international, refereed, literary journal with a Caribbean focus, founded in 1986. Our mission is to publish quality writing by established writers that reflects the culture of the Caribbean; promotes and foster a strong literary tradition; and serves as an institute for the development of emerging writers. Publishes exciting voices from the region, and beyond, that explore the diverse and multi-ethnic culture in poetry, short fiction, personal essays, creative non-fiction, and short plays. Social, cultural, economic and sometimes controversial issues are also explored, employing a wide array of literary devices. Also publishes translations, book reviews, interviews, and special sections offering insight into the dynamics of Caribbean society and showcases visual art by leading and emerging artists of the region.

Editor: Alscess Lewis-Brown

M074 Carolina Woman
Online Magazine
United States

articles@carolinawoman.com
info@carolinawoman.com

https://www.carolinawoman.com
https://www.facebook.com/profile.php?id=100063516732380
https://x.com/carolina_woman
https://www.linkedin.com/company/carolina-woman-inc.
http://www.pinterest.com/carolinawmag/
http://instagram.com/carolinawomanmagazine/

Nonfiction > *Articles*
  Lifestyle; Women's Interests

Send: Pitch
How to send: Email

Lifestyle magazine for women. Generally does not accept unsolicited articles or hire freelance writers, but is open to article ideas by email.

M075 Chapman
Magazine
4 Broughton Place, Edinburgh, EH1 3RX
United Kingdom
Tel: +44 (0) 131 557 2207

chapman-pub@blueyonder.co.uk

http://www.chapman-pub.co.uk

Book Publisher: Chapman Publishing

Fiction > *Short Fiction*: Literary

Nonfiction > *Articles*: Literary Criticism

Poetry > *Any Poetic Form*

Closed to approaches.

Describes itself as Scotland's leading literary magazine, publishing new creative writing: poetry, fiction, discussion of cultural affairs, theatre, reviews and the arts in general, plus critical essays. It publishes international as well as Scottish writers and is a dynamic force for artistic and cultural change and development. Always open to new writers and ideas.

Fiction may be of any length, but average is around 3,000 words. Send one piece at a time. Poetry submissions should contain between four and ten poems. Single poems are not usually published.

Articles and reviews are usually commissioned and ideas should be discussed with the editor in advance.

All submissions must include an SAE or IRCs or email address for response. No submissions by email.

M076 CharlottesvilleFamily
Magazine
United States

sales@ivylifeandstylemedia.com

https://www.charlottesvillefamily.com
https://www.facebook.com/CharlottesvilleFamily
https://twitter.com/ChvilleFamily
https://www.linkedin.com/company/ivylifeandstylemedia/

Magazine Publisher: Ivy Life & Style Media

Nonfiction > *Articles*
   Albemarle; Charlottesville; Education; Family; Food; Health; Houses and Homes; Leisure; Lifestyle; Parenting

Town and country living at its best! An award-winning quarterly magazine dedicated to serving families in Virginia's Charlottesville-Albemarle area with engaging feature stories on parenting, education, health and recreation as well as useful resources designed to help "Make Parenting Easier and Growing Up Fun".

M077 Chautauqua Literary Journal
Magazine
United States

chautauquajournal@gmail.com

https://chautauquajournal.wixsite.com/website
https://chautauqua.submittable.com/submit
https://www.instagram.com/chautauquajournal/
https://www.facebook.com/chautauqualiteraryjournal/
https://twitter.com/chautauqualit
http://chautauqualit.tumblr.com/

Fiction > *Short Fiction*

Nonfiction > *Short Nonfiction*: Creative Nonfiction

Poetry > *Any Poetic Form*

Closed to approaches.

Costs: A fee is charged upon submission. $2 submission fee.

Welcomes unsolicited submissions of poetry, flash, fiction, and creative nonfiction from February 15 to March 15 and from September 1 to September 30.

M078 Cheshire
Online Magazine
United States

infoccr00@gmail.com

https://uwm.edu/creamcityreview/i-o/
https://uwm.edu/creamcityreview/general/
https://creamcityreview.submittable.com/submit

Magazine: Cream City Review (**M094**)

Fiction > *Short Fiction*

Nonfiction > *Essays*

Poetry > *Any Poetic Form*

Closed to approaches.

Online magazine for writing that operates outside the printed page, including asemic writing, concrete poetry, interactive fiction and poetry, video, collage, hypertext essay, GIFpoetics, programmatic, gamic, and all hybrid and multimodal points along the way, things that capture process and procedure, lines and the signs between. Not interested in text-based work that engages very little with mixed and/or digital medium.

M079 Cobblestone
Magazine
United States

cobblestone@cricketmedia.com

https://cricketmedia.com
https://cricketmedia.com/cobblestone-submission-guidelines/

Magazine Publisher: Cricket Media, Inc.

CHILDREN'S
   Fiction > *Short Fiction*: American History
   Nonfiction
      Articles: Activities; American History
      Puzzles: General
   Poetry > *Any Poetic Form*: American History

Send: Query
Don't send: Full text
How to send: Email

American history magazine for kids ages 9 to 14 that knows that history doesn't have to be dull and dry. It can be vibrant and alive – and so much fun. That's why every page is a living, breathing guide to how Americans lived, worked, played, and died from the 1600s to today. Filled with fascinating true stories from all decades of our country's history, augmented with dramatic photographs and beautiful illustrations, this magazine is designed to take kids on a journey through history while it excites their imaginations and brings the past to life.

Editor: Meg Chorlian

M080 Cocoa Girl
Print Magazine
United Kingdom

admin@thecocoadream.com

https://www.cocoagirl.com
https://www.instagram.com/cocoagirlmag/

Magazine Publisher: Cocoa Publishing

CHILDREN'S
   Nonfiction
      Articles: Black People; Culture
      Interviews: Black People; Culture
   Poetry > *Any Poetic Form*
      Black People; Culture

How to send: Email

Magazine for Black girls. This magazine gives Black children a voice whilst educating the community about the Black culture. Filled with inspiring and empowering content for children aged 7-11 years old. Particularly looking for children aged 7-11 to contribute as writers, poets, artists, and young journalists.

M081 Cola
Print Magazine
United States

https://www.colaliteraryreview.com
https://colaliteraryreview.submittable.com/submit
https://twitter.com/ColaLitReview

Fiction > *Short Fiction*: Literary

Poetry > *Any Poetic Form*

Closed to approaches.

Costs: A fee is charged upon submission in some cases. $3 submission fee during spring submission period. Autumn submissions are free.

Annual print journal edited by graduate students. Publishes poetry and fiction. Submit 3-5 poems or pieces of flash fiction up to 1,000 words, or a longer short story up to 8,000 words (1,000 words to 5,000 words preferred), via online submission system. See website for full guidelines.

M082 Commonweal
Magazine
475 Riverside Drive, Room 244, New York, NY 10115
United States
Tel: +1 (212) 662-4200

editors@commonwealmagazine.org
poetryeditor@commonwealmagazine.org

https://www.commonwealmagazine.org
https://www.facebook.com/commonwealmagazine
https://twitter.com/commonwealmag

Nonfiction > *Articles*
   Culture; Politics; Religion

Poetry > *Any Poetic Form*

Send: Pitch; Full text; Author bio
How to send: Submittable; Email

Journal of opinion edited by Catholic lay people. Publishes articles on religion, literature, and the arts. More interested in articles which examine the links between "worldly" concerns and religious beliefs than churchy or devotional pieces. Submit pitches by email. Also publishes poetry. Submit through online submission system and include a short bio that could accompany your poem in print.

M083 Concho River Review
Magazine
United States

http://www.conchoriverreview.org
https://www.facebook.com/conchoriverreview

Fiction > *Short Fiction*

Nonfiction
  Essays: General
  Reviews: Books
  Short Nonfiction: Creative Nonfiction

Poetry > *Any Poetic Form*

Closed to approaches.

Costs: A fee is charged upon submission. $3 per submission.

Published biannually, welcomes submissions of high-quality fiction, nonfiction, poetry, and book reviews year-round.

Accepts only original work that has not been published previously.

Accepts submissions from writers residing outside the United States, however, international contributors should provide a domestic address to which a contributor's copy can be mailed.

M084 Conjunctions
Magazine
21 East 10th St., #3E, New York, NY 10003
United States

conjunctions@bard.edu

https://www.conjunctions.com
https://conjunctions.submittable.com/submit
http://www.facebook.com/pages/Conjunctions/133404885505
https://www.instagram.com/_conjunctions/
https://twitter.com/_conjunctions

Fiction > *Short Fiction*: Literary

Nonfiction > *Short Nonfiction*: Creative Nonfiction

Poetry > *Any Poetic Form*

Send: Full text; Self-addressed stamped envelope (SASE)
How to send: Post; Submittable

Publishes short and long form fiction, poetry, and creative nonfiction. No academic essays or book reviews. Do not query or send samples – submit complete ms by post with SASE (year-round) or using online submission system (during specific online submission windows in autumn and winter). See website for full guidelines.

Editor: Bradford Morrow

Online Magazine: Conjunctions Online (**M085**)

M085 Conjunctions Online
Online Magazine
21 E 10th Street, #3E, New York, NY 10003
United States

http://www.conjunctions.com/online/
https://conjunctions.submittable.com/submit
http://www.facebook.com/pages/Conjunctions/133404885505
https://www.instagram.com/_conjunctions/
https://twitter.com/_conjunctions

Magazine: Conjunctions (**M084**)

Fiction > *Short Fiction*

Nonfiction > *Short Nonfiction*: Creative Nonfiction

Poetry > *Any Poetic Form*

Closed to approaches.

Weekly online magazine. No thematic restrictions. Postal submissions are accepted year-round, but online submissions are open only during specific windows.

M086 Contemporary Verse 2
Magazine
502-100 Arthur Street, Winnipeg, Manitoba, R3B 1H3
Canada

submissions@contemporaryverse2.ca
editor@contemporaryverse2.ca

https://contemporaryverse2.ca
https://contemporaryverse2.submittable.com/submit
http://www.facebook.com/pages/CV2-magazine/116555781749958
https://www.instagram.com/cv2magazine/
http://twitter.com/CV2magazine

Nonfiction
  Articles: Poetry as a Subject
  Essays: Poetry as a Subject
  Interviews: Poetry as a Subject
  Reviews: Poetry as a Subject

Poetry > *Any Poetic Form*

How to send: Submittable

Costs: A fee is charged upon submission in some cases. $3 submission fee for submitters outside of Canada.

A quarterly literary journal that publishes poetry and critical writing about poetry, including interviews, articles, essays, and reviews. It is our policy to publish new writing by both emerging and established poets. The writing we encourage reflects a diversity representing a range of social and cultural experience along with literary excellence.

M087 The Conversation (UK)
Online Magazine
Shropshire House (4th Floor), 11-20 Capper Street, London, WC1E 6JA
United Kingdom

uk-support@theconversation.com

https://theconversation.com
https://www.facebook.com/ConversationUK
https://twitter.com/ConversationUK
https://www.instagram.com/theconversationdotcom
https://www.linkedin.com/company/the-conversation-uk
https://newsie.social/@TheConversationUK

Nonfiction
  Articles: Arts; Business; Culture; Economics; Education; Environment; Health; Politics; Science; Society; Technology
  News: Arts; Business; Culture; Economics; Education; Environment; Health; Politics; Science; Society; Technology

How to send: Online submission system

Online magazine describing itself as "the world's leading publisher of research-based news and analysis... a unique collaboration between academics and journalists." Publishes news and articles researchers and academics currently employed by a university or research institution. This includes PhD students under supervision, but nor Masters students.

M088 Cornwall Life
Magazine

Magazine Publisher: Great British Life

M089 Cosmos
Print Magazine
PO Box 10041, Adelaide, SA 5001
Australia
Tel: +61 (0) 1300 719623

info@cosmos.csiro.au

https://cosmosmagazine.com

Nonfiction
  Articles: Health; History; Nature; Popular Science; Space; Technology
  News: Health; History; Nature; Popular Science; Space; Technology

A quarterly science magazine. We aim to inspire curiosity in the science of everything and make the world of science accessible to everyone. We deliver the latest in science with beautiful pictures, clear explanations of the latest discoveries and breakthroughs and great writing.

M090 Cottage Life
Magazine
99 Atlantic Avenue, Suite 400, Toronto, ON, M6K 3J8
Canada
Tel: +1 (416) 599-2000

edit@cottagelife.com

https://cottagelife.com
https://www.facebook.com/cottagelife/
https://x.com/cottagelife/
http://instagram.com/cottagelife/
http://pinterest.com/cottagelife/
http://youtube.com/user/CottagelifeMagazine/

Nonfiction > *Articles*
   Architecture; Boats; Building / Construction; Design; Environment; Finance; How To; Lifestyle; Nature; Politics; Property / Real Estate

Send: Query
How to send: Email

The magazine has a strong service slant, combining useful "how-to" journalism with coverage of the people, trends, and issues in cottage country. We run columns and shorter features on subjects such as boating, real estate, building projects, cottage design and architecture, nature, personal cottage experience, and environmental, political, and financial issues of concern to cottagers. Depending on the subject, these can be anywhere from 1,000 to 1,800 words long. Our front-of-the-book department, Waterfront, features short news, humour, human interest, and service items, with a maximum length of 400 words. Our other front-of-book department, Workshop, is a place for "hammer and nails" DIY stories of the same length about maintaining a cottage. Major features range from 1,500 to 3,000 words and cover every aspect of cottage living—including profiles of cottagers, cottages, and cottage communities, investigations of relevant environmental and political issues, and in-depth service pieces that help readers solve common cottage problems. The fee varies with the length and complexity of the story, whether it's for digital or print, and the writer's experience. The editor and writer will agree on the fee when the story is assigned.

M091 Cowboys & Indians

Magazine
12801 North Central Expressway, Suite 565, Dallas, TX 75243
United States
Tel: +1 (386) 246-0179

editorial@cowboysindians.com

https://www.cowboysindians.com
https://www.facebook.com/cowboysindians/
http://pinterest.com/cowboysindians/
http://www.twitter.com/CI_Magazine
http://instagram.com/cowboysindiansmagazine#

Nonfiction > *Articles*
   American West; Arts; Culture; Entertainment; Fashion; Food and Drink; Houses and Homes; Ranch Lifestyle; Ranches; Travel

Magazine focusing on the past and present of the American West, including both historical and lifestyle material.

M092 Crannog Magazine

Magazine
47 Dominick, St Lower, Galway, H91 X0AP
Ireland

hello@crannogmagazine.com
submissions@crannogmagazine.com

https://crannogmagazine.com
https://twitter.com/crannogm
https://www.facebook.com/crannogmagazine/

Book Publisher / Magazine Publisher: Wordsonthestreet (**P434**)

Fiction > *Short Fiction*: Literary

Poetry > *Any Poetic Form*

Send: Full text; Author bio
How to send: Online submission system
How not to send: Post

Costs: A purchase is required. Authors who have not previously been published in the magazine must purchase the current issue before submitting.

A literary magazine publishing fiction and poetry only. No reviews or nonfiction. Published twice yearly in March and September. Accepts submissions in May and November. Authors who have been previously published in the magazine are required to purchase a copy of the current issue (or take out a subscription); for authors who have not been previously published in the magazine this is a requirement. Send up to one story or up to three poems via online submission system.

M093 Crazyhorse / Swamp Pink

Magazine
Department of English, College of Charleston, 66 George Street, Charleston, SC 29424
United States
Tel: +1 (843) 953-4470

crazyhorse@cofc.edu

https://crazyhorse.cofc.edu
https://www.facebook.com/CrazyhorseLiteraryJournal
https://twitter.com/crazyhorselitjo

Fiction > *Short Fiction*

Nonfiction > *Short Nonfiction*: Creative Nonfiction

Poetry > *Any Poetic Form*

Send: Full text
How to send: Submittable

Publishes fiction, poetry, and nonfiction on a semi-monthly basis. Aims to publish exceptional work from writers at all stages of their careers. Particularly interested in submissions from writers of color and writers from marginalized and underrepresented communities. Submissions of fiction and nonfiction can be up to 7,500 words in length. Has published exceptional work that falls outside this range, but it is an unusual occurrence. For poetry, submit a set of 3-6 poems.

Not accepting submissions from white people as of July 2025. Check website for current status.

M094 Cream City Review

Magazine
Department of English, University of Wisconsin-Milwaukee, P.O. Box 413, Milwaukee, WI 53201
United States

infoccr00@gmail.com
poetryccr@gmail.com
fictionccr@gmail.com
nonfictionccr@gmail.com

https://uwm.edu/creamcityreview/
https://www.facebook.com/creamcityreview/
https://twitter.com/creamcityreview
https://www.instagram.com/cream_city_review/

Fiction > *Short Fiction*

Nonfiction > *Short Nonfiction*: Creative Nonfiction

Poetry > *Any Poetic Form*

Closed to approaches.

Send prose up to 20 pages, or up to five poems of any length. Open to submissions January 2 to April 1 and August 1 to October 31.

Online Magazine: Cheshire (**M078**)

M095 Creative Nonfiction

Magazine
United States

information@creativenonfiction.org

https://creativenonfiction.org
https://creativenonfiction.submittable.com/submit/
https://www.facebook.com/creativenonfiction
https://twitter.com/cnfonline
https://instagram.com/creativenonfiction/

Nonfiction > *Essays*
   Creative Nonfiction; Memoir; Personal Essays

Closed to approaches.

Publishes all types of creative nonfiction, from immersion reportage to lyric essay to memoir and personal essays. See website for specific submission calls and their topics, or submit a pitch for a column year-round.

M096 Cricket

Magazine
United States

http://www.cricketmag.com

Magazine Publisher: Cricket Media, Inc.

CHILDREN'S > *Nonfiction* > *Articles*
   Arts; Culture; History; Science

Closed to approaches.

Magazine for children aged 9-14. Publishes only the highest quality fiction and classic literature and nonfiction stories on culture, history, science, and the arts. Each issue includes a signature cast of rambunctious bug characters who offer humorous commentary on the stories.

M097 Cruising World

Magazine
605 Chestnut Street, Suite 800, Chattanooga, TN 37450
United States
Tel: +1 (407) 628-4802

editor@cruisingworld.com

https://www.cruisingworld.com
https://www.facebook.com/cruisingworld/
https://twitter.com/cruisingworld/
https://www.instagram.com/cruisingworldmag/
https://www.youtube.com/c/cruisingworld

Media Company: Bonnier Corporation

Nonfiction > *Articles*
   Boats; Sailing

Send: Full text; Author bio
How to send: Word file email attachment

Magazine for owners of sailboats between 20 and 50 feet in length. Authors should familiarise themselves with the magazine before approaching.

M098 Crystal Magazine

Magazine
3 Bowness Avenue, Prenton, Birkenhead, CH43 0SD
United Kingdom
Tel: +44 (0) 7769 790676

christinecrystal@hotmail.com

http://www.christinecrystal.blogspot.com

Fiction > *Short Fiction*
   Adventure; Comedy / Humour; Fantasy; Horror; Mystery; Romance; Science Fiction; Suspense; Thrillers; Westerns

Nonfiction
   Articles: Literature; Nature; Travel
   News: General

Poetry > *Any Poetic Form*

Send: Full text
How to send: Email

An A4, 40-page, spiral-bound, print only bi-monthly with colour images. Subscribers receive six issues a year. £21 UK/£32.70 overseas. £2 for a sample to see if you want to subscribe.

Non-subscribers may send in work and purchase the issue it appears in for £3.50.

The magazine is very popular. There is a Feedback page on the website.

Contents: stories, poems and articles. Letters – kind comments or none at all. News – an opportunity to share writing achievements and anything of interest to writers.

Also accepting fillers and very long stories which could be turned into serials.

Wordsmithing. Titters Tips Titillations. Pay special attention to the second item in each section because there you will find useful information on writing (the "tips" part of the title).

Also Word Wise. In the July issue we learn about the hyphen.

There are yearly Surprise Competitions open to everybody. The competitions are called "Surprise" because you don't know what you could win. But every winner has been really pleased. There are pictures of previous prizes and winning entries on the website.

The current Surprise Competition is called "Dribble". Write a 50-word story.

Editor: Christine Carr

M099 CutBank

Magazine
University of Montana, English Dept, LA 133, Missoula, MT 59812
United States

editor.cutbank@gmail.com
cutbankonline@gmail.com
cutbankreview@gmail.com

http://www.cutbankonline.org
https://cutbank.submittable.com/submit
https://twitter.com/cutbankonline
http://instagram.com/cutbankmag
https://www.facebook.com/cutbanklitmag/

Fiction > *Short Fiction*

Nonfiction > *Short Nonfiction*: Creative Nonfiction

Poetry > *Any Poetic Form*

Closed to approaches.

Costs: A fee is charged upon submission. $5 reading fee.

Accepts poetry, fiction, creative nonfiction, and visual art submissions. Please only submit online; paper submissions will be recycled.

M100 The Dalhousie Review

Magazine
Dalhousie University, Halifax, Nova Scotia, B3H 4R2
Canada

dalhousie.review@dal.ca

https://ojs.library.dal.ca/dalhousiereview

Fiction > *Short Fiction*

Nonfiction
   Essays: Literary
   Reviews: Books

Poetry > *Any Poetic Form*

Send: Full text
How to send: Email

Publishes fiction, poetry, essays, and book reviews. Submit up to five poems at a time. Query before submitting reviews. See website for full submission guidelines.

M101 The Dark Horse

Magazine
PO Box 8351, Irvine, KA12 2DD
United Kingdom

https://www.thedarkhorsemagazine.com
https://www.facebook.com/The-Dark-Horse-Magazine-184043168311270/
https://twitter.com/thedarkhorsemag

Poetry > *Any Poetic Form*

Send: Full text; Self-addressed stamped envelope (SASE)
How to send: Post
How not to send: Email

International literary magazine committed to British, Irish and American poetry. Send submissions by post only, to UK or US editorial addresses. No simultaneous submissions. See website for full guidelines.

Editor: Gerry Cambridge

M102 The Dawntreader

Magazine
24 Forest Houses, Halwill, Beaworthy, Devon, EX21 5UU
United Kingdom

dawnidp@indigodreams.co.uk

https://www.indigodreams.co.uk/magazines

Book Publisher: Indigo Dreams Publishing

Fiction > *Short Fiction*
   Environment; Folklore, Myths, and Legends; Mysticism; Nature; Spirituality

Nonfiction > *Articles*
   Environment; Folklore, Myths, and Legends; Mysticism; Nature; Spirituality

Poetry > *Any Poetic Form*
   Environment; Folklore, Myths, and Legends; Mysticism; Nature; Spirituality

Send: Full text
How to send: Email attachment

A quarterly publication specialising in myth, legend; in the landscape, nature; spirituality and love; the mystic, the environment. Submit up to five poems (40 lines or fewer), and prose, articles, and local legends up to 1,000 words.

Editor: Ronnie Goodyer

M103 Deep Overstock Magazine
Magazine
United States

submissions@deepoverstock.com

https://deepoverstock.com/issues/
https://deepoverstock.com/submission-guidelines/

Book Publisher / Magazine Publisher: Deep Overstock Publishing

Fiction > *Short Fiction*

Closed to approaches.

Accepts fiction. Issues are themed. Check website for current theme. Prefers fiction to be under 6,000 words. Submissions over 3,000 words may not be considered. Submit one or two pieces of fiction per theme, or up to three if they are each under 1,000 words. Send up to seven poems per theme.

M104 Descent
Magazine
PO Box 297, Kendal, LA9 9GQ
United Kingdom
Tel: +44 (0) 7354 794240

info@descentmagazine.co.uk

https://www.descentmagazine.co.uk
https://twitter.com/CavingMagazine
https://www.facebook.com/profile.php?id=100083468112084
https://www.instagram.com/descentcavingmagazine/

Magazine Publisher: Stalactite Publishing

Nonfiction > *Articles*: Caving and Potholing

Send: Query
How to send: Email; Post

Magazine written by cavers, for cavers. Contact with ideas prior to submission.

Editor: Chris Howes

M105 Diver
Magazine
216 East Esplanade St., North Vancouver, BC, V7L 1A3
Canada
Tel: +1 (604) 988-0711

mail@divermag.com

https://divermag.com
https://www.facebook.com/divermagazine

Nonfiction > *Articles*: Scuba Diving

North America's longest established scuba diving magazine.

M106 Dream Catcher
Magazine
109 Wensley Drive, Leeds, LS7 2LU
United Kingdom

https://www.dreamcatchermagazine.co.uk

Fiction > *Short Fiction*

Nonfiction > *Interviews*

Poetry > *Any Poetic Form*

Send: Full text
How to send: Post

Send submissions by post, following guidelines on website. No electronic submissions.

M107 The Dublin Review
Magazine
Ireland

enquiry@thedublinreview.com

https://thedublinreview.com
https://twitter.com/thedublinreview
https://www.instagram.com/thedublinreview/
https://www.facebook.com/TheDublinReview/

Fiction > *Short Fiction*

Nonfiction
  Essays: General
  Short Nonfiction: Memoir

Send: Full text
How to send: Online submission system

Publishes essays, criticism, reportage, and fiction for a general, intelligent readership. No poetry. Accepts submissions via form on website.

M108 Dumfries and Galloway Life
Print Magazine
United Kingdom

Magazine Publisher: Great British Life

M109 The Ekphrastic Review
Online Magazine
Canada

theekphrasticreview@gmail.com

https://www.ekphrastic.net

Fiction > *Short Fiction*

Nonfiction
  Articles: Arts
  Interviews: Literature
  Reviews: Literature
  Short Nonfiction: General

Poetry in Translation > *Any Poetic Form*: Arts

Poetry > *Any Poetic Form*: Arts

Send: Full text
How to send: Email

Costs: A fee is charged upon submission. $5 CAD submission fee.

Publishes poetry that responds to, explores, or is inspired by a piece of art, and fiction and nonfiction of any kind, including book interviews or profiles, and articles about ekphrastic writing. Accepts submissions in January, April, July and October only. Submissions sent in other months will be deleted unread.

Editor: Lorette C. Luzajic

M110 El Portal
Magazine
United States

el.portal@enmu.edu

https://elportaljournal.com
https://elportal.submittable.com/submit
https://twitter.com/elportaljournal

Fiction > *Short Fiction*

Nonfiction > *Short Nonfiction*: Creative Nonfiction

Poetry > *Any Poetic Form*

Closed to approaches.

Accepts submissions of flash fiction up to 500 words, short stories and creative nonfiction up to 4,000 words, or up to five poems. Open reading periods run from July 1st to August 31st and from December 1st to January 31st.

M111 Emerge Literary Journal
Online Magazine
PO Box 815, Washingtonville, NY
United States

elj.editions@gmail.com

https://emergeliteraryjournal.com
https://eljpublications.submittable.com/submit
https://x.com/EmergeJournal/
https://www.facebook.com/eljeditions/
https://www.youtube.com/channel/UCh_gp_b2kOIa4XCJPuVq1Xg
https://www.instagram.com/elj_editions_ltd/

Fiction > *Short Fiction*: Literary

Nonfiction > *Short Nonfiction*
  Creative Nonfiction; Literary

Poetry > *Any Poetic Form*

A quarterly online journal of poetry and prose dedicated to emerging writers and their words. We love free verse, flash and creative non-fiction – words with passion, voice, and place. We look for succinct images and dialogue that linger, narrative that we can take with us to bed at night, ideas used in magnificent ways. Bring us your castles. We read during specified reading windows only and submissions will always be free. We publish exclusively online quarterly, although an annual "best-of" print issue may be a future possibility. Accepts submissions in January, February, July and August.

M112 Entrepreneur
Magazine
1651 East Fourth Street, Suite 125, Santa Ana,

Ca 92701
United States

https://www.entrepreneur.com/
https://www.facebook.com/EntMagazine
https://twitter.com/entrepreneur
https://www.linkedin.com/company/entrepreneur-media
https://www.pinterest.com/entrepreneurmedia
https://www.instagram.com/entrepreneur/
https://www.youtube.com/user/EntrepreneurOnline

Nonfiction > *Articles*
  Business; Entrepreneurship; Finance; How To

Magazine for people who have started and are running their own business, providing news o current trends, practical how-to articles, features on combining work and life, etc. Runs features and several regular columns, as well as an inner magazine on start-ups.

M113 Event
Magazine
PO Box 2503, New Westminster, BC, V3L 5B2
Canada
Tel: +1 (604) 527-5293

event@douglascollege.ca

https://www.eventmagazine.ca
https://eventmagazine.submittable.com/submit
https://twitter.com/EVENTmags
https://www.facebook.com/eventmagazine
http://www.youtube.com/channel/UCKuYlH5b3uRaitKO4lCk8zA?feature=watch

Fiction > *Short Fiction*

Nonfiction
  Reviews: Books
  Short Nonfiction: Creative Nonfiction

Poetry > *Any Poetic Form*

Closed to approaches.

One of Western Canada's longest-running literary magazines. Welcomes submissions in English from around the world during specific submission windows. Submissions must be entirely human created. No work written, developed, or assisted in any capacity by Artificial Intelligence.

M114 Every Day Fiction
Online Magazine
Canada

camille@everydayfiction.com

https://everydayfiction.com
https://everydayfiction.submittable.com/submit

Fiction > *Short Fiction*
  General, and in particular: Comedy / Humour; Fantasy; Historical Fiction; Horror; Inspirational; Literary; Mystery; Romance; Science Fiction; Surreal; Suspense

Send: Full text
How to send: Submittable

Online magazine publishing flash fiction up to 1,000 words. All fiction genres are acceptable. No previously published material, including material posted online to personal blogs, etc.

M115 Fabula Argentea
Magazine
United States

FAsubmits@gmail.com
fabargmagazine@gmail.com

https://fabulaargentea.com

Fiction > *Short Fiction*

Send: Full text
How to send: Email attachment
How not to send: PDF file email attachment

Online magazine publishing fiction up to 8,000 words. Submit fiction up to 8,000 words as an email attachment.

M116 Facts & Fiction
Magazine
United Kingdom
Tel: +44 (0) 1773 822829

steel.carpet@tiscali.co.uk

http://www.factsandfiction.co.uk
https://petecastle.co.uk/fandf

Nonfiction
  Articles: Storytelling
  Interviews: Storytelling
  News: Storytelling
  Reviews: Storytelling

How to send: Email

The magazine for everyone interested in (oral) storytelling. Not a short story or poetry mag. We deal with storytelling as an oral art form, in many ways as a traditional art form – so articles and other material should reflect that.

Editor: Pete Castle

M117 Fate
Magazine
PO Box 774, Hendersonville, NC 28793
United States
Tel: +1 (612) 965-5515

Phyllis@fatemag.com

https://www.fatemag.com
https://www.youtube.com/channel/UCAjXG-tsjV5VJM-i-afsvqA
https://twitter.com/Fate_Magazine
https://instagram.com/fatemagazine

Nonfiction > *Articles*
  Mystery; Science; Supernatural / Paranormal

How to send: Post; Email

Magazine of mysterious and unexplained phenomena.

Editor-in-Chief: Phyllis Galde

M118 Faultline
Magazine
UCI Department of English, 435 Humanities Instructional Building, Irvine, CA 92697-2650
United States
Tel: +1 (949) 824-1573

faultline@uci.edu
ucifaultline@gmail.com

https://faultline.sites.uci.edu/
https://www.facebook.com/uci.faultline
https://twitter.com/faultline_journ

Fiction in Translation > *Short Fiction*

Fiction > *Short Fiction*

Nonfiction in Translation > *Short Nonfiction*: Creative Nonfiction

Nonfiction > *Short Nonfiction*: Creative Nonfiction

Poetry in Translation > *Any Poetic Form*

Poetry > *Any Poetic Form*

Closed to approaches.

Send up to five poems or up to 20 pages of fiction or creative nonfiction, between October 15 and December 15 only.

Fiction Editor: Sara Joyce Robinson

Poetry Editor: Lisa P. Sutton

M119 Feminist Studies
Magazine
677 Rome Hall, 801 22nd Street, NW, George Washington University, Washington, DC 20052
United States

info@feministstudies.org
submit@feministstudies.org
creative@feministstudies.org
art@feministstudies.org
review@feministstudies.org

http://www.feministstudies.org

ACADEMIC > **Nonfiction** > *Essays*
  Cultural Criticism; Literary Criticism

ADULT
  Fiction > *Short Fiction*: Feminism

  Nonfiction > *Articles*
    Arts; Culture; Feminism

  Poetry > *Any Poetic Form*: Feminism

Send: Full text; Proposal; Writing sample; Author bio
How to send: Email

Feminist journal publishing research and criticism, creative writing, art, essays, and other forms of writing and visual expression. See website for submission guidelines and specific submission email addresses.

M120 Fiction
Magazine
c/o Department of English, City College of

New York, Convent Ave. at 138th Street, New York, NY 10031
United States

fictionmageditors@gmail.com

http://www.fictioninc.com
http://submissions.fictioninc.com/
http://instagram.com/fiction.magazine
https://twitter.com/fictionmag
https://www.facebook.com/fiction.mag/

Fiction in Translation > *Short Fiction*

Fiction > *Short Fiction*
Experimental; Literary

Closed to approaches.

We publish literary and experimental fiction and translations of works previously unpublished in English. We favor stories of under 7,500 words. We do not accept unsolicited artwork, graphic stories, novel excerpts, or interviews. Reading period runs from October 15 to April 15 annually.

M121 The Fiddlehead
Magazine
Campus House, 11 Garland Court, University of New Brunswick, PO Box 4400, Fredericton NB, E3B 5A3
Canada
Tel: +1 (506) 453-3501

fiddlehd@unb.ca

https://thefiddlehead.ca
https://twitter.com/TheFiddlehd
http://www.facebook.com/pages/The-Fiddlehead-Atlantic-Canadas-International-Literary-Journal/174825212565312

Fiction
Novel Excerpts; *Short Fiction*

Nonfiction > *Short Nonfiction*: Creative Nonfiction

Poetry > *Any Poetic Form*

Closed to approaches.

Publishes poetry, fiction, and creative nonfiction in a variety of styles, including experimental genres. Also publishes excerpts from longer works, and reviews. Submit up to six poems (up to 12 pages total), or a piece of fiction up to 6,000 words. All submissions must be original and unpublished. Prefers submissions through online submission system (January 1 to March 31 and September 15 to November 30 only), but will accept submissions by post all year round. See website for full details.

M122 First For Women
Magazine
270 Sylvan Avenue, Englewood Cliffs, NJ 07632
United States

contactus@firstforwomen.com

https://www.firstforwomen.com
https://www.facebook.com/firstforwomenmag
https://www.instagram.com/firstmag
https://www.pinterest.com/firstforwomen

Nonfiction > *Articles*
Beauty; Diet; Fashion; Food; Health; Menopause; Personal Finance; Wellbeing

Magazine where active women in all eras of life come for the tools and inspiration that they need to look good, feel great and enjoy every aspect of their experiences.

M123 The First Line
Magazine
PO Box 250382, Plano, Texas 75025-0382
United States

submission@thefirstline.com

http://www.thefirstline.com

Fiction > *Short Fiction*

Nonfiction > *Essays*: Literary Criticism

Poetry > *Any Poetic Form*

Send: Full text; Self-addressed stamped envelope (SASE)
How to send: Word file email attachment; Post
How not to send: PDF file email attachment; Google Docs shared document

Prefers submissions by email, but will also accept submissions by post with SASE. Prefers attachments as a Word or Word Perfect file. Stories must begin with the appropriate first line for that issue, as provided on the website. Occasionally accepts poems starting with the specified first line. Also accepts essays on your favourite first line from a book.

M124 Five Points
Magazine
Georgia State University, P.O. Box 3999, Atlanta, GA 30302-3999
United States

http://fivepoints.gsu.edu

Fiction in Translation > *Short Fiction*: Literary

Fiction > *Short Fiction*: Literary

Nonfiction in Translation > *Essays*

Nonfiction > *Short Nonfiction*
General, and in particular: Literary

Poetry in Translation > *Any Poetic Form*

Poetry > *Any Poetic Form*

Closed to approaches.

Costs: A fee is charged upon submission.

Welcomes unsolicited submissions of fiction, poetry, flash fiction, literary non-fiction, and translations in these genres. Submit through online submission system.

Editor: Megan Sexton

M125 Flash: The International Short-Short Story Magazine
Magazine
International Flash Fiction Association, Department of English, University of Chester, Parkgate Road, Chester, CH1 4BJ
United Kingdom

flash.magazine@chester.ac.uk

https://www.chester.ac.uk
https://www.chester.ac.uk/about/faculties/arts-humanities-and-social-sciences/school-for-the-creative-industries/flash-fiction/
https://www.facebook.com/groups/28291339826/

Fiction > *Short Fiction*

Flash fiction magazine based in Chester.

Editors: Dr Peter Blair; Dr Ashley Chantler

M126 Folio
Magazine
United States

folio.editors@gmail.com

https://www.american.edu/cas/literature/folio/
https://foliolitjournal.submittable.com/submit
https://www.facebook.com/FolioLitJournal/
https://twitter.com/FolioLitJournal
https://www.linkedin.com/in/folio-literary-journal-a235a8b4
http://folio-lit-journal.tumblr.com/

Fiction > *Short Fiction*: Literary

Nonfiction > *Essays*: Creative Nonfiction

Poetry > *Any Poetic Form*

Closed to approaches.

Accepts submissions of fiction, nonfiction, and poetry on specific themes during specific submission windows. See website for details.

M127 Fortean Times: The Journal of Strange Phenomena
Magazine
Diamond Publishing Ltd, Harmsworth House, 13-15 Bouverie Street, London, EC4Y 8DP
United Kingdom

hello@metropolis.co.uk

http://subscribe.forteantimes.com
https://www.instagram.com/forteantimes/
https://www.facebook.com/ForteanTimes
https://twitter.com/forteantimes

Magazine Publisher: Diamond Publishing

Nonfiction > *Articles*: Supernatural / Paranormal

Publishes accounts of strange phenomena, experiences, curiosities, mysteries, prodigies, and portents. No fiction or poetry.

Editor: David Sutton

M128 Forty20

Magazine
47 Street Lane, Leeds, West Yorkshire, LS8 1AP
United Kingdom
Tel: +44 (0) 113 225 9797
Fax: +44 (0) 113 225 2515

editorial@forty-20.com
admin@scratchingshedpublishing.com

https://www.scratchingshedpublishing.com/magazine/
https://www.facebook.com/forty20magazine
https://twitter.com/forty20magazine

Book Publisher / Magazine Publisher: Scratching Shed Publishing (**P331**)

Nonfiction
Articles: Rugby League
Interviews: Rugby League
News: Rugby League

How to send: Email

The alternative voice of rugby league. Intelligent, thought-provoking, informative and fun, it covers rugby league at every level. Features thought-provoking articles by the game's most respected writers and best-known personalities, and face-to-face interviews with rugby league's most engaging characters, be they in the European Super League, Australasian NRL or anywhere else in the world.

M129 Foundation: The International Review of Science Fiction

Magazine
28 St John's Road, Guildford, GU2 7UH
United Kingdom

sff@beccon.org

https://www.sf-foundation.org/about-the-sff-journal

Nonfiction
Articles: Science Fiction
Reviews: Books; Science Fiction

Describes itself as the essential critical review of science fiction, publishing articles 5,000 to 8,000 words and reviews of about 1,500 words.

M130 Fourteen Poems

Print Magazine
United Kingdom

hello@14poems.com

https://www.fourteenpoems.com
https://twitter.com/fourteenpoems
http://instagram.com/14poems

Poetry > *Any Poetic Form*: LGBTQIA

Send: Full text; Author bio
How to send: PDF file email attachment; Word file email attachment

Print magazine published three times a year. Each issue includes work by fourteen LGBTQ+ poets, printing their queer takes on sex, love, race, gender and life in the LGBTQ+ global community.

M131 The Fourth River

Magazine
United States

4thriver@gmail.com

https://www.thefourthriver.com
https://twitter.com/thefourthriver
https://www.instagram.com/thefourthriver/
https://www.facebook.com/TheFourthRiver

Fiction > *Short Fiction*: Literary

Nonfiction > *Short Nonfiction*: Creative Nonfiction

Poetry > *Any Poetic Form*

Closed to approaches.

Costs: A fee is charged upon submission. $2 submission fee.

Print and digital literary magazine publishing creative writing that explores the relationship between humans and their environments, whether natural or man-made. Submit 3-5 poems or prose up to 4,000 words between July 1 and September 1 for print, or December 1 and February 1 for online, via online submission system. No submissions by email.

Online Magazine: Tributaries (**M320**)

M132 The Frogmore Papers

Magazine
21 Mildmay Road, Lewes, East Sussex, BN7 1PJ
United Kingdom

frogmorepress@gmail.com

https://www.frogmorepress.co.uk

Fiction
Novel Excerpts; *Short Fiction*
Poetry > *Any Poetic Form*

Poetry and prose by new and established authors. There is no house style, but the extremes of tradition and experiment are equally unlikely to find favour. Send between four and six poems, or up to two prose pieces. Accepts submissions in April and October only.

Editor: Jeremy Page

M133 Fugue

Magazine
United States

fugue@uidaho.edu

https://fuguejournal.com
https://twitter.com/FugueJournal
https://www.instagram.com/fugue_journal/
https://www.facebook.com/fuguejournal/

Fiction > *Short Fiction*

Nonfiction
Essays: General
Reviews: Books

Poetry > *Any Poetic Form*

Closed to approaches.

Costs: A fee is charged upon submission. $3.

Submit 3 to 5 poems, up to two short shorts, one story, or one essay per submission. Accepts submissions online only, between August 15 and December 15. Submission service charges $3 per submission.

M134 Funeral Business Solutions

Magazine
1801 South Bay Street, Eustis, FL 32726-5666
United States
Tel: +1 (352) 242-8111

https://fbsmagazine.com
https://www.facebook.com/profile.php?id=100088592525602
https://www.linkedin.com/company/funeralbusinesssolutions/

Magazine Publisher: Radcliffe Media, Inc.

PROFESSIONAL > **Nonfiction**
Articles: Funeral Industry
Interviews: Funeral Industry
News: Funeral Industry
Reviews: Funeral Industry

Send: Full text
How to send: Email

Different from traditional association magazines or trade journals because it is specially-crafted to bring you the best industry specific business news and solutions that will help you to make effective business decisions for your staff, company, and client families.

Our magazine design and layout is purposefully easy to read and digest in short segments. We know that the average funeral professional has an unpredictable schedule and an effective business magazine gives the reader shorter editorials that get to the point without fluff.

Our writers provide actionable ideas and effective strategies that will help you, the industry professional, run a more profitable business. Issues are published every two months, giving you ample time to digest 8-12 articles, latest industry headlines, the included Funeral Home Success Stories, Vendor Company Spotlights, Industry Book Overviews and more.

Our goal is to never bore you or waste your precious time, so our editors consider each article, press release, and spotlight carefully to make sure it can in some way benefit a funeral director running a business.

At the end of each day, we are primarily a magazine of business solutions for an industry that our publisher, editors, and writers love.

Publisher: Timothy Totten

M135 The Future Fire
Online Magazine
United Kingdom

fiction@futurefire.net
nonfiction@futurefire.net

http://futurefire.net

Fiction in Translation > *Short Fiction*

Fiction > *Short Fiction*
  Crime; Environment; Feminism; LGBTQIA; Mystery; Noir; Postcolonialism; Speculative

Poetry in Translation > *Any Poetic Form*

Poetry > *Any Poetic Form*
  Environment; Feminism; LGBTQIA; Postcolonialism; Speculative

Send: Full text
How to send: Email attachment

Magazine of social political and speculative cyber fiction. Publishes short stories up to 17,500. Accepts email submissions for fiction. See website for full submission guidelines.

M136 Garden Answers
Magazine
Bauer Media, Media House, Lynch Wood, PE2 6EA
United Kingdom

https://www.gardenanswersmagazine.co.uk/
https://www.facebook.com/gardenanswers
https://twitter.com/GardenAnswers

Magazine Publisher: Bauer Media Group

Nonfiction > *Articles*: Gardening

A vibrant and inspiring gardening magazine filled with ingenious design ideas and exciting plant combinations guaranteed to make your garden beautiful.

M137 Gargoyle Online
Online Magazine
3819 13th Street North, Arlington, VA 22201
United States
Tel: +1 (703) 380-4893

https://gargoylemagazine.com
https://gargoylemagazinepaycockpress.submittable.com/submit
https://www.facebook.com/profile.php?id=100063527378646

Magazine Publisher / Ebook Publisher: Paycock Press

Fiction > *Short Fiction*

Poetry > *Any Poetic Form*

Closed to approaches.

Dedicated to publishing work by unknown poets and fiction writers, as well as seeking out the overlooked or neglected. The mag was on something of an extended hiatus from 1990-1997 and then resurfaced. After 46 years and 76 issues the magazine has ended the print run and shifted to an online presence from mid-2022 onward.

M138 The Geographical Journal
Online Magazine
United Kingdom

https://rgs-ibg.onlinelibrary.wiley.com/journal/14754959

ACADEMIC > **Nonfiction** > *Articles*: Geography

How to send: Online submission system

Academic journal founded in 1893. In order to minimise environmental impact, online only from 2024.

M139 The Georgia Review
Magazine
706A Main Library, 320 S. Jackson St., The University of Georgia, Athens, GA 30602-9009
United States
Tel: +1 (800) 542-3481

https://thegeorgiareview.com
https://thegeorgiareview.submittable.com/submit
https://www.instagram.com/georgiareview/
https://www.facebook.com/thegeorgiareview/
https://twitter.com/home

Fiction > *Short Fiction*: Literary

Nonfiction
  Essays: General
  Reviews: Books

Poetry > *Any Poetic Form*

Closed to approaches.

Costs: A fee is charged upon submission in some cases. $3 for non-subscribers. Subscribers submit for free.

Publishes literary fiction, poetry (submit 6-10 pages of poetry or one long poem), essays and book reviews. Submissions accepted between August 15 and May 15 only. Submissions received between May 15 and August 15 are returned unread.

M140 Ginosko Literary Journal
Magazine
United States

https://ginoskoliteraryjournal.com
https://ginosko.submittable.com/submit/

Fiction > *Short Fiction*

Nonfiction > *Short Nonfiction*: Creative Nonfiction

Poetry > *Any Poetic Form*

Send: Full text
How to send: Submittable

Costs: A fee is charged upon submission. $3 submission fee.

Semi-annual literary journal accepting short fiction, poetry, creative nonfiction, social justice issues, and literary and spiritual insights.

Editor: Robert Cesaretti

M141 The Glacier
Online Magazine
United States

https://theglacierjournal.com
https://42miles.submittable.com/submit

Book Publisher: 42 Miles Press

Fiction > *Short Fiction*
  General, and in particular: Experimental

Poetry > *Any Poetic Form*
  General, and in particular: Lyrical

How to send: Submittable

Costs: A fee is charged upon submission. $3 per submission.

Online magazine published once a year, in the autumn. Publishes poetry, fiction, and visual art. Accepts simultaneous submissions, but no previously published work. Prefers lyric/associative poetry over straight narrative, but does not have a house style. Send up to seven poems, all within a single file. In fiction, prefers more experimental work to straight narrative. Likes fiction that gets to the point and that keeps burning in a reader's mind after the last word is read . . . 1300 words max. Send up to three stories, single or double spaced is fine.

M142 Go World Travel Magazine
Online Magazine
United States

submissions@goworldtravel.com

https://www.goworldtravel.com
https://www.facebook.com/Go.World.Travel
https://www.instagram.com/goworldtravelmagazine/
https://pinterest.com/goworldtravel/
https://twitter.com/GoWorldMagazine
https://www.youtube.com/user/GoWorldPublishing

Nonfiction > *Articles*: Travel

How to send: Email

A digital publication for world travelers. We work with journalists around the world, and partner with destination marketing organizations and other tourism and travel businesses to promote travel.

Editor: Heike Schmidt, Senior Editor

M143 Grain Literary Magazine
Magazine
Saskatchewan Writers' Guild, PO Box 3986,
Regina, SK S4P 3R9
Canada
Tel: +1 (306) 791-7740

grainmag@skwriter.com

https://grainmagazine.ca
https://grainmagazine.submittable.com/submit
https://www.facebook.com/GrainLitMag
https://x.com/GrainLitMag
https://instagram.com/grainlitmag

Fiction > *Short Fiction*

Nonfiction > *Short Nonfiction*: Literary

Poetry > *Any Poetic Form*

How to send: Submittable

An internationally acclaimed literary journal that publishes engaging, surprising, eclectic, and challenging writing and art by Canadian and international writers and artists. Nine-month reading period, September 15 to June 15.

M144 Granta
Magazine
12 Addison Avenue, Holland Park, London, W11 4QR
United Kingdom
Tel: +44 (0) 20 7605 1360

editorial@granta.com

https://granta.com

Fiction > *Short Fiction*

Nonfiction > *Short Nonfiction*

Poetry > *Any Poetic Form*

Closed to approaches.

Costs: A fee is charged upon submission. £3.50 for prose; £2 for poems.

Submit one story or essay, or up to four poems, via online submission system. £3.50 charge for prose submissions; £2 for poems. No specific length limits for prose, but most pieces are between 3,000 and 6,000 words. Unlikely to read anything over 10,000 words.

Editor: Sigrid Rausing

M145 Graywolf Lab
Online Magazine
United States

https://graywolflab.org

Book Publisher: Graywolf Press (**P152**)

Fiction > *Short Fiction*

Nonfiction > *Articles*
  Arts; Literature; Music; Visual Arts

Poetry > *Any Poetic Form*

Closed to approaches.

An online platform for interdisciplinary conversations and new writing. Each issue starts by gathering a small group of artists for a roundtable discussing a theme. Over several months, we invite responses to that conversation from more artists, writers, and thinkers.

M146 The Great Outdoors (TGO)
Magazine
Kelsey Media Ltd, The Granary, Downs Court, Yalding Hil, Yalding, Kent, ME18 6AL
United Kingdom

https://www.thegreatoutdoorsmag.com

Magazine Publisher: Kelsey Media

Nonfiction > *Articles*: Walking

Magazine publishing articles on walking and back-packing.

M147 Gulf Coast: A Journal of Literature and Fine Arts
Magazine
University of Houston, Department of English, Roy G. Cullen Building, 3687 Cullen Boulevard, Room 203, Houston, Texas 77204-3013
United States
Tel: +1 (713) 743-3223

gulfcoastea@gmail.com
gcmagreviews@gmail.com

http://www.gulfcoastmag.org
https://www.facebook.com/GulfCoastJournal
https://twitter.com/Gulf_Coast
https://www.instagram.com/gulfcoastjournal/

Fiction in Translation > *Short Fiction*

Fiction > *Short Fiction*

Nonfiction
  Essays: Art Criticism
  Interviews: Literature
  Reviews: Books

Poetry in Translation > *Any Poetic Form*

Poetry > *Any Poetic Form*

How to send: Submittable

Costs: A fee is charged upon submission. $3 submission fee.

Submit up to five poems, or fiction or essays up to 7,000 words, by post or via online submission manager. For other material, send query by email to address on website. $3.00 submission fee. Accepts material September 1 to March 1, annually.

Editor: Luisa Muradyan Tannahill

M148 Gutter Magazine
Magazine
United Kingdom

contactguttermagazine@gmail.com

https://www.guttermag.co.uk/

Fiction > *Short Fiction*
  International; Literary; Scotland

Nonfiction > *Essays*
  Creative Nonfiction; International; Literary; Scotland

Poetry > *Any Poetic Form*
  International; Scotland

Closed to approaches.

Publishes poetry, short stories, and essays. Publishes work by writers born or living in Scotland alongside international writing. Send up to three poems up to 100 lines total or prose up to 2,500 words. Submit through online submission system. See website for full guidelines.

Editors: Colin Begg; Kate MacLeary; Laura Waddell

M149 Half Mystic Journal
Print Magazine
United States

hello@halfmystic.com

https://www.halfmystic.com

Book Publisher: Half Mystic Press (**P157**)

Fiction in Translation > *Short Fiction*
  Experimental; Music

Fiction > *Short Fiction*
  Experimental; Music

Nonfiction in Translation > *Short Nonfiction*
  Creative Nonfiction; Experimental; Music

Nonfiction > *Short Nonfiction*
  Creative Nonfiction; Experimental; Music

Poetry in Translation
  Any Poetic Form: Music
  Experimental Poetry: Music

Poetry
  Any Poetic Form: Music
  Experimental Poetry: Music

Closed to approaches.

Publishes all genres of poetry, prose, creative nonfiction, translations, and experimental work—as long as each piece pertains in some way to music. See website for the theme of the current issue.

M150 Hanging Loose
Magazine
PO Box 150608, Brooklyn, NY 11215
United States
Tel: +1 (857) 998-9473

highschool@hangingloosepress.com

https://www.hangingloosepress.com
https://www.facebook.com/hangingloosepress
https://twitter.com/HangingLooseNY

Fiction > *Short Fiction*

Poetry > *Any Poetic Form*

Send: Full text; Self-addressed stamped envelope (SASE)
How to send: Email

Send up to six poems, or flash fiction, or short fiction (up to 1000 words). Potential contributors should familiarise themselves with the magazine before submitting. Includes regular section of High School writers. Send submissions by email. Allow up to three months for a response.

M151 Harpur Palate
Magazine
Binghamton University, English Department, P.O. Box 6000, Binghamton, NY 13902-6000
United States

harpur.palate@gmail.com

https://harpurpalate.binghamton.edu
https://twitter.com/harpurpalate
https://www.instagram.com/harpurpalate
https://www.facebook.com/harpurpalate
https://harpurpalate.submittable.com/submit

Fiction > *Short Fiction*

Nonfiction > *Short Nonfiction*: Creative Nonfiction

Poetry > *Any Poetic Form*

Closed to approaches.

Submit up to three poems, up to five pages total; fiction up to 4,500 words; creative nonfiction up to 5,500 words; or three pieces of short prose up to 1,000 words each. Submit through online submission system.

M152 Healthy
Magazine
United Kingdom

healthy@therivergroup.co.uk

https://www.healthy-magazine.co.uk
https://www.facebook.com/HealthyMagazine
https://twitter.com/healthymag
http://instagram.com/healthymagdaily

Magazine Publisher: The River Group

Nonfiction > *Articles*
Beauty; Fitness; Food; Health; Lifestyle

Magazine of holistic health and lifestyle. Send query by email in first instance.

Editor: Heather Beresford

M153 Heavy Traffic
Print Magazine
United States

info@heavytrafficmagazine.com

https://heavytrafficmagazine.com
https://twitter.com/heavytrafficmag
https://www.instagram.com/heavy_traffic_mag/

Fiction > *Short Fiction*

Send: Full text
How to send: Email

Fiction magazine with open submissions and no criteria. Send submissions by email.

M154 The Helix
Magazine
United States

helixmagazine@gmail.com

https://helixmagazine.org

Fiction > *Short Fiction*

Nonfiction > *Short Nonfiction*

Poetry > *Any Poetic Form*

Send: Full text; Author bio
How to send: Submittable

Publishes fiction, creative nonfiction, poetry, plays, and art. Submit prose up to 3,000 words each, or up to four poems.

Editor: Victoria-Lynn Bell

M155 Hello!
Magazine
230 Blackfriars Rd, London, SE1 8NW
United Kingdom
Tel: +44 (0) 20 7667 8721

digitalteam@hellomagazine.com

https://www.hellomagazine.com
https://www.instagram.com/hellomag
https://www.facebook.com/hello
https://twitter.com/hellomag
https://www.tiktok.com/@hellomag
https://www.youtube.com/user/HelloTVuk
https://www.snapchat.com/discover/Hello/4038796137
https://www.pinterest.com/hellomag
https://app.weare8.com/@hellomag
https://chat.whatsapp.com/LoxKQrJ72CTKJtaUawtywi

Nonfiction > *Articles*
Beauty; Celebrity; Fashion; Lifestyle; Women's Interests

Magazine of celebrity and lifestyle.

M156 Hertfordshire Life
Print Magazine
United Kingdom

Magazine Publisher: Great British Life

M157 History Today
Magazine
2nd Floor (North), 55 Goswell Road, London, EC1V 7EN
United Kingdom
Tel: +44 (0) 20 3219 7810

contact@historytoday.com
enquiries@historytoday.com

https://www.historytoday.com

Nonfiction > *Articles*: History

Send: Query; Author bio
How to send: Email

Historical magazine publishing short articles (up to 1,000 words); mid-length articles (1,300-2,200 words) and feature articles (3,000 to 3,400 words). Send query by email with proposal and details of your career / academic background. See website for full guidelines.

M158 Homes & Antiques
Magazine
United Kingdom

https://www.homesandantiques.com
https://www.facebook.com/homesantiques
http://uk.pinterest.com/homesantiques
https://twitter.com/@homes_antiques
https://www.youtube.com/channel/UChlvNbVVoLcWle1xHnuAZlQ
https://www.instagram.com/homes_antiques

Magazine Publisher: Our Media

Nonfiction > *Articles*
Antiques; Decorating; Interior Design

Magazine of home interest, antiques, and collectibles.

Editor: Angela Linforth

M159 Horse & Rider
Magazine
7500 Alamo Road NW, Albuquerque, NM 87120
United States

https://my.horseandrider.com
https://www.facebook.com/HorseandRider
https://www.pinterest.com/hrsdrmag/
https://www.instagram.com/horseandridermag/
https://twitter.com/Horse_and_Rider

Magazine Publisher: Equine Network

Nonfiction > *Articles*
American West; Horses; Travel

Provides all you need for today's Western horse life. Learn from top professional trainers, clinicians, and horse-keeping experts. Experience Western life. Travel to Western destinations and scenic trails. Your resource to live today's Western horse life.

M160 Hotel Amerika
Magazine
C/O The Department of Creative Writing, Columbia College Chicago, 600 South Michigan Avenue, Chicago, IL 60605
United States
Tel: +1 (312) 369-8175

http://www.hotelamerika.net

Fiction > *Short Fiction*: Literary

Nonfiction > *Essays*

Poetry > *Any Poetic Form*

Closed to approaches.

Costs: A fee is charged upon submission. $3.00.

Submissions will be considered between September 1 and April 1. Materials received after April 1 and before September 1 will not be considered.

Editor: David Lazar

M161 Hunger Mountain
Magazine
36 College Street, Montpelier, VT 05602
United States

hungermtn@vcfa.edu

https://hungermtn.org

Fiction in Translation > *Short Fiction*: Literary

Fiction > *Short Fiction*: Literary

Nonfiction in Translation > *Short Nonfiction*: Creative Nonfiction

Nonfiction > *Short Nonfiction*: Creative Nonfiction

Poetry in Translation > *Any Poetic Form*

Poetry > *Any Poetic Form*

Closed to approaches.

Costs: A fee is charged upon submission.

Seeks to provide a platform for traditionally silenced voices, to expand representation in literature and to examine culture with a critical eye. Publishes fiction, nonfiction, poetry, hybrid work, and translations of all of these forms. Welcomes work that is genre-less and the traditional genres some magazines shun. Wants more speculative fiction. Doesn't believe in the divide between literary and genre fiction. Wants to read your science fiction, fantasy, magical realism, ecofabulism, irrealism and slipstream. Submit prose up to 5,000 words, or up to three flash pieces, or up to five poems, via online submission system.

Editor: Caroline Mercurio

M162 I-70 Review
Magazine
913 Joseph Drive, Lawrence, KS 66044
United States

i70review@gmail.com

http://i70review.fieldinfoserv.com

Fiction > *Short Fiction*

Poetry > *Any Poetic Form*

Send: Full text; Author bio
How to send: Word file email attachment

Accepts submissions of fiction and flash fiction or 3-5 poems, by email, during the reading period that runs from July 1 to December 31. Accepts simultaneous submissions. See website for full details.

M163 Idaho Review
Magazine
Boise State University, 1910 University Drive, Boise, Idaho 83725
United States

kiracompton@u.boisestate.edu

https://www.idahoreview.org
https://theidahoreview.submittable.com/submit
http://www.facebook.com/10213528569031037
http://twitter.com/idahoreview
http://www.instagram.com/theidahoreview

Fiction
  Novel Excerpts: Literary
  Short Fiction: Literary

Nonfiction
  Essays: General
  Short Nonfiction: Creative Nonfiction

Poetry > *Any Poetic Form*

Closed to approaches.

Costs: A fee is charged for online submissions. $3 to submit online.

Annual literary journal publishing poetry and fiction. No specific limit for fiction, but most of the stories accepted are under 25 double-spaced pages. For poetry, submit up to five poems. Accepts submissions by post with SASE, but prefers submissions through online submission system ($3 fee).

M164 Identity Theory
Online Magazine
United States

fiction@identitytheory.com
essays@identitytheory.com
poetry@identitytheory.com

http://www.identitytheory.com
https://identitytheory.submittable.com/submit

Fiction > *Short Fiction*

Nonfiction
  Essays: Lyric Essays; Personal Essays
  Interviews: General
  Short Nonfiction: Creative Nonfiction; Memoir

Poetry > *Any Poetic Form*

Send: Full text
How to send: Submittable; Email

Online literary magazine publishing short fiction, including flash fiction and microfiction. Send fiction or essays up to 4,000 words through Submittable or through specific email address, or 3-5 unpublished poems in the body of an email.

Editor: Matt Borondy

M165 The Idler
Print Magazine
Great Western Studios, 65 Alfred Road,
London, W2 5EU
United Kingdom

mail@idler.co.uk

https://www.idler.co.uk

Nonfiction > *Articles*: Lifestyle

Send: Pitch
How to send: Email

Please email pitches addressed to the editor. We rarely publish unsolicited material, but we do read everything that's sent to us. Please note that we cannot offer feedback on rejected articles and pitches.

M166 Image
Magazine
16915 SE 272nd St, Suite #100-213,
Covington, WA 98042
United States
Tel: +1 (206) 659-6008

image@imagejournal.org

https://imagejournal.org
http://facebook.com/imagejournal
http://twitter.com/image_journal
https://www.instagram.com/image_journal

Fiction > *Short Fiction*
  Culture; Literary; Religion; Spirituality

Nonfiction > *Essays*
  Arts; Culture; Literature; Religion; Spirituality

Poetry > *Any Poetic Form*
  Culture; Religion; Spirituality

Fosters contemporary art and writing that grapple with the mystery of being human by curating, cultivating, convening, and celebrating work that explores religious faith and faces spiritual questions. A vibrant thread in the fabric of culture, contributing to mainstream literary and artistic communities by demonstrating the vitality of contemporary art and literature invigorated by religious faith.

M167 Indiana Review
Magazine
United States

https://indianareview.iu.edu
https://indianareview.submittable.com/submit
https://twitter.com/indianareview
https://www.facebook.com/IndianaReview

Fiction in Translation > *Short Fiction*: Literary

Fiction > *Short Fiction*: Literary

Nonfiction in Translation > *Essays*

Nonfiction > *Essays*

Poetry in Translation > *Any Poetic Form*

Poetry > *Any Poetic Form*

Send: Full text
Don't send: Query
How to send: Submittable

Costs: A fee is charged upon submission. $3 per submission.

Send fiction or nonfiction up 6,000 words or 3-6 poems (up to 12 pages total) per submission, during specific submission windows only (see website for details). No submissions by post or by email – all submissions must be made through online submission manager ($3 fee). See website for full guidelines, and to submit.

M168 Ink Sweat and Tears
Online Magazine
United Kingdom

submissions@inksweatandtears.co.uk
interns@inksweatandtears.co.uk
enquries@inksweatandtears.co.uk
inksweatandtears@aol.com

https://inksweatandtears.co.uk
https://twitter.com/InkSweatTears
https://www.facebook.com/InkSweatandTears
https://www.instagram.com/insta.inksweatandtears/

Nonfiction > *Reviews*
 Literature; Poetry as a Subject

Poetry
 Any Poetic Form; *Haibun*; *Haiga*; *Haiku*; *Prose Poetry*

Send: Full text
How to send: Email

UK-based webzine publishing poetry, prose, prose-poetry, word and image pieces, and poetry reviews. Send 4-6 pieces of poetry (or 1-2 short prose/flash fiction works) by email only. Accepts unsolicited reviews of poetry and short story collections. See website for full guidelines.

Editor: Helen Ivory

M169 Insurance Post
Online Magazine
Infopro Digital, 133 Houndsditch, London, EC3A 7BX
United Kingdom
Tel: +44 (0) 20 7316 9000

postonline@infopro-digital.com

https://www.postonline.co.uk
https://twitter.com/Insurance_Post
https://www.linkedin.com/showcase/10580270
https://www.facebook.com/InsurancePost

PROFESSIONAL > **Nonfiction**
 Articles: Insurance
 News: Insurance

Publishes news and articles of interest to insurance professionals in the UK, Europe, and Asia.

M170 International Piano
Magazine
United Kingdom

https://www.markallengroup.com/brands/international-piano/
https://twitter.com/IP_mag
https://www.facebook.com/internationalpiano/
https://www.instagram.com/internationalpianomagazine
https://www.youtube.com/channel/UCOKPU5skkhcvQRjXVkou10Q

Media Company: Mark Allen Group

ACADEMIC > **Nonfiction** > *Articles*: Piano

ADULT > **Nonfiction** > *Articles*: Piano

PROFESSIONAL > **Nonfiction** > *Articles*: Piano

Describes itself as the leading magazine for pianists and piano fans around the world. Wide-ranging reviews and in-depth features meet inspiring practical advice from top performers and teachers in this indispensable guide to the piano in all its forms, published 10 times per year.

Editor: Tim Parry

M171 Interzone
Magazine
United Kingdom

submissions@interzone.press
editors@interzone.press

https://interzone.press
https://interzone.press/submissions/

Magazine Publisher: MYY Press

Fiction in Translation > *Short Fiction*
 Fantasy; Horror; Science Fiction

Fiction > *Short Fiction*
 Fantasy; Horror; Science Fiction

Send: Full text
How to send: Email

Publishes fantastika (including science fiction, fantasy, and horror) short stories up to 17,500 words. See website for full guidelines.

Editor / Publisher: Gareth Jelley

M172 Ireland's Own
Magazine
Channing House, Rowe Street, Wexford
Ireland
Tel: +353 1 7055 454

submissions@irelandsown.ie
info@irelandsown.ie

https://irelandsown.ie
https://www.facebook.com/irelandsown1902/
https://twitter.com/irelandsown1902

Fiction > *Short Fiction*: Ireland

Nonfiction > *Articles*
 Books; Cookery; Entertainment; Films; Health; History; Ireland; Literature; Science; Sport

How to send: Email

Magazine publishing stories and articles of Irish interest for the whole family, plus puzzles and games.

Editor: Sean Nolan

M173 Irish Pages
Magazine
129 Ormeau Road, Belfast, BT7 1SH
United Kingdom
Tel: +44 (0) 2890 434800

editor@irishpages.org
managingeditor@irishpages.org
sales@irishpages.org
gaeilge@irishpages.org

https://irishpages.org
https://twitter.com/irishpages
https://www.youtube.com/channel/UC08ArKYYmKVUpP5eHfEMz0w

Fiction in Translation > *Short Fiction*

Fiction > *Short Fiction*

Nonfiction in Translation
 Essays: General
 Short Nonfiction: Autobiography; Creative Nonfiction; History; Literary Journalism; Memoir; Nature; Religion; Science
Nonfiction
 Essays: General
 Short Nonfiction: Autobiography; Creative Nonfiction; History; Literary Journalism; Memoir; Nature; Religion; Science
Poetry in Translation > *Any Poetic Form*

Poetry > *Any Poetic Form*

Send: Full text
How to send: Post
How not to send: Email

Non-partisan and non-sectarian literary journal publishing writing from the island of Ireland and elsewhere in equal measure. Publishes work in English, and in the Irish Language or Ulster Scots with English translations or glosses. Accepts submissions throughout the year by post only with stamps, coupons or cash for return postage (no self-addressed envelope is needed). See website for more details.

M174 Island
Magazine
GPO Box 4703, Hobart TAS 7000
Australia
Tel: +61 (0) 3 6234 1462

admin@islandmag.com

https://islandmag.com
https://island.submittable.com/submit

Fiction > *Short Fiction*
 General, and in particular: Experimental; Literary

Nonfiction
 Articles; *Essays*

Poetry > Any Poetic Form
   General, and in particular: Experimental;
   Literary

Closed to approaches.

Welcomes submissions of nonfiction, fiction and poetry from Australia, New Zealand and the Pacific, as well as from Australians living abroad. Will consider more traditional forms but has a strong interest in experimental and literary approaches to form and content. See website for details and to submit using online submission system.

Online Magazine: Island Online (**M175**)

M175 Island Online
Online Magazine
Australia

admin@islandmag.com
ben@islandmag.com

https://islandmag.com/online
https://island.submittable.com/submit
http://www.facebook.com/islandmagtas
http://instagram.com/islandmagtas
https://twitter.com/IslandMagTas

Magazine: Island (**M174**)

Fiction > *Short Fiction*
   Arts; Culture; Environment; Experimental;
   Literary; Nature; Society

Nonfiction > *Essays*
   Arts; Culture; Environment; Nature; Society

Closed to approaches.

Digital publishing platform operated in conjunction with longstanding print magazine. Will consider more traditional forms but has a strong interest in experimental and literary approaches to form and content.

M176 The Journal
Magazine
38 Pwllcarn Terrace, Blaengarw, Bridgend, CF32 8AS
United Kingdom

asamsmith@hotmail.com

https://thesamsmith.com
https://thesamsmith.com/the-journal/

Nonfiction
   Interviews: Poetry as a Subject
   Reviews: Poetry as a Subject

Poetry in Translation > *Any Poetic Form*

Poetry > *Any Poetic Form*

Closed to approaches.

Accepts poems in English, or translations into English (about 6 at a time). Also welcome are interviews with poets, reviews, appreciations or appraisals of current poetry scenes. If a reply is desired within the UK, enclose SAE.

Editor: Sam Smith

M177 Kavya Kishor
Online Magazine
Bangladesh

editor.kavyakishor@gmail.com

https://en.kavyakishor.com

Fiction > *Short Fiction*

Nonfiction
   Articles; *Essays*; *Interviews*; *Reviews*

Poetry > *Any Poetic Form*

How to send: Email

An online literary magazine of English and Bengali language from Bangladesh.

M178 Kent Life
Magazine
United Kingdom

https://www.greatbritishlife.co.uk/magazines/kent/

Magazine Publisher: Great British Life

Nonfiction > *Articles*
   Arts; Celebrity; Countryside; Culture; Food
   and Drink; Gardening; Houses and Homes;
   Kent; Lifestyle; Local History; Nature;
   Recipes; Travel; Walking Guides

Every month you'll find within our pages a wealth of fresh ideas on how you can best explore our area's glorious countryside, beautiful coastline, thriving towns and villages and fascinating history. Whether you want to sample great local food and drink, dip into our exciting arts scene or revel in the glorious natural beauty that surrounds us, we've got suggestions galore. You'll hear Kent voices loud and clear, too, of course, with our top-notch writers highlighting the energy and sheer diversity of our community via their stories and interviews, and our columnists adding their unique take on county life. Add to the mix our inspiring monthly features on gorgeous homes and gardens, our town guides, walk suggestions and fascinating stories from local history, and you've got an unmissable monthly blend of ideas, lifestyle, nature and personalities.

M179 The Kenyon Review
Magazine
102 W. Wiggin St., Gambier, OH 43022
United States
Tel: +1 (740) 427-5208
Fax: +1 (740) 427-5417

kenyonreview@kenyon.edu

https://kenyonreview.org
https://thekenyonreview.submittable.com/submit

Fiction in Translation
   Novel Excerpts; *Short Fiction*
Fiction
   Novel Excerpts; *Short Fiction*
Nonfiction in Translation > *Essays*

Nonfiction > *Essays*

Poetry in Translation > *Any Poetic Form*

Poetry > *Any Poetic Form*

Scripts > *Theatre Scripts*

Closed to approaches.

Submit through online submission system. Send short fiction up to 7,500 words, poetry up to six poems, or plays or excerpts up to 30 pages. Translations are also accepted, but author is responsible for permissions. No unsolicited interviews, book reviews, or artwork, or submissions by email or post.

M180 Kids Alive!
Magazine
The Salvation Army Territorial Headquarters, 1 Champion Park, London, SE5 8FJ
United Kingdom
Tel: +44 (0) 20 7367 4910

kidsalive@salvationarmy.org.uk

https://www.salvationist.org.uk/media/kidsalive

CHILDREN'S
   Fiction > *Cartoons*: Christianity

   Nonfiction > *Articles*: Christianity

Christian children's magazine publishing puzzles, comic strips, etc.

M181 The Lake
Online Magazine
United Kingdom

poetry@thelakepoetry.co.uk

http://www.thelakepoetry.co.uk

Nonfiction > *Reviews*: Poetry as a Subject

Poetry > *Any Poetic Form*

Send: Full text; Author bio
How to send: In the body of an email; Word file email attachment

Submit up to five poems within the body of an email or attach one Word document with POETRY SUBMISSION in the Subject line. Please also include a short third person biography (50 words max.). If you have a publication or personal web site then you can also include a link to the site. I will respond to all submissions within two to three weeks. If after that time you haven't heard from me let me know via email.

M182 Landfall
Magazine
Otago University Press, PO Box 56, Dunedin 9054
New Zealand
Tel: +64 (0) 3 479 4155

landfall@otago.ac.nz

https://www.otago.ac.nz/press/landfall/index.html

https://www.facebook.com/landfall.journal
https://twitter.com/landfallnz

Book Publisher: Otago University Press (**P269**)

Fiction > *Short Fiction*: Literary

Nonfiction
  Articles: Arts; Culture; New Zealand
  Essays: General
  Reviews: Books; Local
Poetry > *Any Poetic Form*

Send: Full text; Author bio
How to send: Email

Publishes literary fiction and essays, poetry, extracts from work in progress, commentary on New Zealand arts and culture, work by visual artists including photographers, and reviews of local books.

M183 Leisure Group Travel
Magazine
United States

Jason@ptmgroups.com

https://leisuregrouptravel.com
https://www.facebook.com/LeisureGroupTravel
https://twitter.com/leisuregroup
https://www.linkedin.com/showcase/leisure-group-travel/

PROFESSIONAL > **Nonfiction** > *Articles*
  Business; Travel

How to send: Email; Online contact form

Magazine aimed at group travel buyers. Submit news and press releases that relate to the group travel industry by email or through contact form on website.

M184 Leisure Painter
Magazine
The Maltings, West Street, Bourne, Lincolnshire, PE10 9PH
United Kingdom
Tel: +44 (0) 1778 395174

https://www.painters-online.co.uk

Magazine Publisher: Warners Group Publications

Nonfiction > *Articles*: Painting

Magazine offering artistic inspiration, guidance, tuition and encouragement for beginners and amateur artists. Includes features and step-by-step painting and drawing demonstrations.

M185 Lighthouse
Magazine
United Kingdom

subs.lighthouse@gmail.com
lighthouseprosesubmissions@gmail.com

https://storymachines.co.uk/portfolio/lighthouse/

Fiction > *Short Fiction*
Poetry > *Any Poetic Form*

Send: Full text
How to send: Email

A literary journal dedicated to publishing new writing and championing new writers. Aims to publish the best short fiction, poetry, and art emerging from the UK scene. No submissions generated by AI (Artificial Intelligence) or other machine learning means.

M186 The Linguist
Magazine
Chartered Institute of Linguists (CIOL), Thanet House, 231-232 Strand, London, WC2R 1DA
United Kingdom
Tel: +44 (0) 20 7940 3100

info@ciol.org.uk

https://www.ciol.org.uk/the-linguist

PROFESSIONAL > **Nonfiction** > *Articles*: Language

Magazine for language professionals.

M187 Literary Mama
Online Magazine
United States

LMinfo@literarymama.com
LMreviews@literarymama.com
LMnonfiction@literarymama.com
lmfiction@literarymama.com
LMreflections@literarymama.com
lmpoetry@literarymama.com

https://literarymama.com
http://www.facebook.com/litmama
http://twitter.com/literarymama
https://www.instagram.com/literary_mama/

Fiction > *Short Fiction*: Motherhood

Nonfiction
  Essays: Creativity; Motherhood; Writing
  Reviews: Books; Motherhood
  Short Nonfiction: Creative Nonfiction; Motherhood
Poetry > *Any Poetic Form*: Motherhood

Send: Full text; Query
How to send: Online submission system

Online magazine publishing fiction, poetry, creative nonfiction, and book reviews focusing on mother writers, and the complexities and many faces of motherhood. Accepts submissions in the text of emails only – no snail mail submissions. See website for full submission guidelines. Contact again if no response after three months.

M188 London Grip
Online Magazine
United Kingdom

editor@londongrip.co.uk

https://londongrip.co.uk

Nonfiction
  Articles: General, and in particular: Arts; Culture
  Reviews: Books; Drama

How to send: Email

A wholly independent online cultural omnibus offering intelligent reviews of current shows, events and books and providing space for well-argued articles on a wide range of topics. Intended to act as an exhibition space for cross-media arts and includes an in-house poetry magazine with its own editor. The site's name reflects its place of origin rather than signalling any wish to focus on one city.

Online Magazine: London Grip New Poetry (**M189**)

M189 London Grip New Poetry
Online Magazine
United Kingdom

poetry@londongrip.co.uk

https://londongrip.co.uk

Online Magazine: London Grip (**M188**)

Nonfiction
  Articles: Poetry as a Subject
  Reviews: Poetry as a Subject
Poetry > *Any Poetic Form*

How to send: Email

Quarterly online poetry magazine. Poetry may be submitted in December/January, March/April, June/July, or September/October. Proposals for poetry reviews (or other articles on poetry) may be submitted at any time.

M190 The London Magazine
Magazine
11 Queen's Gate, London, SW7 5EL
United Kingdom
Tel: +44 (0) 20 7584 5977

editorial@thelondonmagazine.org
admin@thelondonmagazine.org

https://thelondonmagazine.org
https://thelondonmagazine.submittable.com/submit
https://www.facebook.com/thelondonmagazine1732/
https://twitter.com/thelondonmag
https://www.instagram.com/thelondonmagazine/?hl=en

Fiction > *Short Fiction*

Nonfiction
  Essays; *Interviews*; *Reviews*
Poetry > *Any Poetic Form*

Does not want:

> **Fiction** > *Short Fiction*
>   Erotic; Fantasy; Science Fiction

Send: Full text
How to send: Submittable
How not to send: Post

Costs: A fee is charged upon submission in some cases. £3 fee per submission every other month. Free submissions in September, November, January, March, May, and July.

Send submissions through online submission system. Does not normally publish science fiction or fantasy writing, or erotica. No submissions by post. See website for full guidelines.

M191 London Review of Books
Magazine
28 Little Russell Street, London, WC1A 2HN
United Kingdom
Tel: +44 (0) 20 7209 1101

edit@lrb.co.uk

https://www.lrb.co.uk
https://www.facebook.com/LondonReviewOfBooks
https://twitter.com/lrb
https://www.youtube.com/londonreviewofbooks
https://www.instagram.com/londonreviewofbooks/

Nonfiction
Articles: Anthropology; Arts; Biography; Classics / Ancient World; Culture; Economics; History; Legal; Literary Criticism; Literature; Memoir; Philosophy; Politics; Psychology; Science; Technology
Reviews: General

Poetry > *Any Poetic Form*

Send: Full text; Proposal; Self-addressed stamped envelope (SASE)
How to send: Email; Post

Publishes poems, reviews, reportage, memoir, articles, and blogposts. Send submissions by email or by post (with SAE).

M192 Long Poem Magazine
Magazine
20 Spencer Rise, London, NW5 1AP
United Kingdom

longpoemmagazine@gmail.com

http://longpoemmagazine.org.uk
https://www.facebook.com/groups/longpoemmagazine/
https://twitter.com/LongPoemMag

Nonfiction
Essays: Poetry as a Subject
Reviews: Books

Poetry > *Long Form Poetry*

Magazine dedicated to publishing long poems and sequences. Publishes unpublished poems of at least 75 lines (but no book length poems). Also publishes essays on aspects of the long poem and reviews of books featuring long poems or sequences. Send submissions by email as Word file attachments. Does not accept poems submitted in the body of emails. See website for full guidelines and submission months. Poems submitted outside submission months will be discarded.

M193 Lost Lake Folk Opera Magazine
Print Magazine
United States

https://shipwrecktbooks.press
https://shipwrecktbooks.submittable.com/submit

Book Publisher: Shipwreckt Books Publishing Company (**P336**)

Fiction > *Short Fiction*

Nonfiction > *Essays*

Poetry > *Any Poetic Form*

Scripts > *Theatre Scripts*

Send: Full text; Author bio
How to send: Submittable

Literary magazine published twice annually. Accepts short fiction (1000-6000 wds); one-act and other short plays or scenes (1000-6000 wds); essays and opinion (500-300 wds); poetry (no more than 10 poems or 10 pages).

M194 Louisiana Literature
Magazine
United States

lalit@selu.edu

http://www.louisianaliterature.org
https://twitter.com/LaLiterature
https://louisianaliterature.submittable.com/submit

Fiction > *Short Fiction*: Literary

Nonfiction > *Essays*: Creative Nonfiction

Poetry > *Any Poetic Form*

Send: Full text
How to send: Submittable

Literary journal publishing fiction, poetry, and creative nonfiction. Submit via online system available at the website.

Editor: Dr Jack Bedell

M195 The MacGuffin
Magazine
Schoolcraft College, 18600 Haggerty Road, Livonia, MI 48152
United States
Tel: +1 (734) 462-5327

macguffin@schoolcraft.edu

https://schoolcraft.edu/macguffin
https://themacguffin.submittable.com/submit

Fiction > *Short Fiction*

Nonfiction > *Short Nonfiction*: Creative Nonfiction

Poetry
Any Poetic Form; *Experimental Poetry*; *Free Verse*

Send: Full text
How to send: Submittable

Publishes fiction, creative nonfiction, and poetry. Submit up to five poems or up to two pieces of prose via online submission system.

M196 Magma
Magazine
23 Pine Walk, Carshalton, SM5 4ES
United Kingdom

info@magmapoetry.com
reviews@magmapoetry.com

https://magmapoetry.com
https://magmapoetry.submittable.com/submit
https://www.facebook.com/MagmaPoetry/

Nonfiction > *Reviews*: Poetry as a Subject

Poetry > *Any Poetic Form*

Closed to approaches.

Each issue has a different theme and different editors. The editorship circulates among the group that runs the magazine, with frequent guest editors. This allows for greater diversity of editorship, opportunities for mentoring new editors and publication of a very wide range of work.

Editor: Laurie Smith

M197 The Malahat Review
Magazine
Clearihue Bldg, Rm A405, University of Victoria, P.O. Box 1700, Stn CSC, Victoria, B.C., V8W 2Y2
Canada
Tel: +1 (250) 721-8524

malahat@uvic.ca

http://www.malahatreview.ca
https://twitter.com/malahatreview

Fiction > *Short Fiction*

Nonfiction
Essays: Personal Essays
Reviews: Books
Short Nonfiction: Biography; Creative Nonfiction; History; Memoir; Narrative Nonfiction; Social Commentary; Travel

Poetry > *Any Poetic Form*

How to send: Submittable

Publishes poetry, short fiction, and creative nonfiction by new and established writers mostly from Canada, reviews of Canadian books, and the best writing from abroad. Submissions from Canadian writers are accepted from January to June. Fiction and poetry submissions from international writers only accepted in January and May.

M198 The Manchester Review

Online Magazine
Centre for New Writing, S1.20, Samuel Alexander Building, The University of Manchester, Manchester, M13 9PL
United Kingdom

manreviewsubmissions@gmail.com

https://www.themanchesterreview.co.uk
https://x.com/mancreview
https://www.facebook.com/themanchesterreview/

Fiction > *Short Fiction*

Nonfiction
  Essays; *Reviews*
Poetry > *Any Poetic Form*

Closed to approaches.

Publishes two issues per year in Summer and Winter. During our submission period we welcome unpublished fiction, poetry and essays from both established and new writers. Please make no more than one submission per issue. Simultaneous submissions are permitted. In the subject line of your email, please include your name and the category of your submission (Fiction/Poetry/Non-Fiction). You should include a short bio in your cover email, and please make sure that identifying details are also on your submission. Please note: we only accept Word documents. We strongly encourage online submission. Alternatively, submissions can be sent by post.

M199 Manoa

Magazine
United States

manoaeds@hawaii.edu

https://manoajournal.org
https://www.instagram.com/manoa_journal/
https://www.facebook.com/manoajournal/
https://twitter.com/manoajournal

ACADEMIC > **Nonfiction** > *Essays*
  Asia; Culture; Literature; Pacific

ADULT
  Fiction in Translation > *Short Fiction*
    Asia; Pacific

  Fiction > *Short Fiction*
    Asia; Pacific

  Poetry in Translation > *Any Poetic Form*
    Asia; Pacific

  Poetry > *Any Poetic Form*
    Asia; Pacific

Closed to approaches.

A Pacific journal, however material does not need to be related to the Pacific, or by authors from the region.

M200 marie claire

Magazine
United States

pr@futurenet.com

https://www.marieclaire.com
https://www.facebook.com/MarieClaire
https://twitter.com/marieclaire
https://www.pinterest.com/MarieClaire
https://instagram.com/marieclairemag
https://www.youtube.com/c/MarieClaire

Magazine Publisher: Future

Nonfiction > *Articles*
  Beauty; Career Development; Celebrity; Culture; Fashion; Finance; Fitness; Food and Drink; Health; Horoscopes; Politics; Relationships; Sex; Travel; Women's Interests

Lifestyle magazine aimed at the younger working woman.

M201 Marlin

Magazine
PO Box 8500, Winter Park, FL 32790-8500
United States

https://www.marlinmag.com
https://www.facebook.com/marlinmag/
https://twitter.com/MarlinMagazine/
http://instagram.com/marlinmag/
http://www.youtube.com/MarlinMagazine/

Nonfiction > *Articles*
  Boats; How To; Offshore Gamefishing; Travel

Publishes articles, features, and news items relating to offshore fishing, destinations, personalities, fishery regulations, the boating industry and related topics, including how-to and technical information.

Editor: Jack Vitek

M202 The Massachusetts Review

Magazine
400 Venture Way, Hadley, MA 01035
United States
Tel: +1 (413) 545-2689
Fax: +1 (413) 577-0740

massrev@external.umass.edu

http://www.massreview.org
https://www.facebook.com/pages/The-Massachusetts-Review/40580092594
https://twitter.com/MassReview
http://instagram.com/themassachusettsreview?ref=badge
http://themassreview.tumblr.com/

Fiction in Translation > *Short Fiction*: Literary

Fiction > *Short Fiction*: Literary

Nonfiction in Translation > *Essays*
  Arts; Current Affairs; Drama; Literature; Music; Philosophy; Science

Nonfiction
  Articles: Arts; Current Affairs; Drama; Literature; Music; Philosophy; Science
  Essays: Arts; Current Affairs; Drama; Literature; Music; Philosophy; Science

Poetry in Translation > *Any Poetic Form*

Poetry > *Any Poetic Form*

Send: Full text; Self-addressed stamped envelope (SASE)
How to send: Post; Online submission system; Email

Costs: A fee is charged for online submissions. $3.

Send one story of up to 25–30 pages or up to six poems of any length (though rarely publishes poems of more than 100 lines). White people may not submit between May 1 and September 30. Others may submit year-round, and may use email if the online submission system is closed. White people are not permitted to submit by email. Articles and essays of breadth and depth are considered, as well as discussions of leading writers; of art, music, and drama; analyses of trends in literature, science, philosophy, and public affairs. No plays, reviews of single books, or submissions by fax or email.

M203 Meetinghouse

Magazine
United States

submissions@meetinghousemag.org

https://www.meetinghousemag.org
https://twitter.com/meethousemag

Fiction > *Short Fiction*

Poetry > *Any Poetic Form*

Closed to approaches.

A literary magazine that provides a space for diverse voices to speak with one another. Submit up to two pieces of prose and up to five poems per submission.

M204 Michigan Quarterly Review

Magazine
3277 Angell Hall, 435 S. State Street, Ann Arbor, MI 48109-1003
United States
Tel: +1 (734) 764-9265

mqr@umich.edu

https://sites.lsa.umich.edu/mqr/
https://mqr.submittable.com/submit

Fiction in Translation > *Short Fiction*

Fiction > *Short Fiction*

Nonfiction
  Articles; *Essays*
Poetry in Translation > *Any Poetic Form*

Poetry > *Any Poetic Form*

Closed to approaches.

Costs: A fee is charged upon submission. $3 submission fee.

An interdisciplinary and international literary journal, combining distinctive voices in poetry, fiction, and nonfiction, as well as works in translation.

Online Magazine: MQR Mixtape (**M214**)

M205 Micromance Magazine
Online Magazine
Cookeville, TN
United States

micromancemagazine@gmail.com

https://micromancemagazine.substack.com

Fiction > *Short Fiction*: Romance

How to send: Email

A flash fiction lit mag dedicated to romance, love stories and romantic poetry. Publishes one story or poem a day on both the site and directly to the inbox of its nearly 400 subscribers. Receives 10,500 views a month and was just voted by readers and writers the 4th favorite flash fiction lit mag in Chill Subs' Community Favorites. Submissions are open year-round with special anthology calls throughout the year. Considers submissions of all writers regardless of experience level and is all inclusive.

M206 Mid-American Review
Magazine
Department of English, Bowling Green State University, Bowling Green, OH 43403
United States
Tel: +1 (419) 372-2725

mar@bgsu.edu

https://casit.bgsu.edu/midamericanreview/

Fiction in Translation > *Short Fiction*: Literary

Fiction > *Short Fiction*: Literary

Nonfiction
  Essays: General
  Reviews: Books

Poetry in Translation > *Any Poetic Form*

Poetry > *Any Poetic Form*

How to send: Online submission system; Post

Accepts fiction, poetry, translations, and nonfiction (including personal essays, essays on writing, and short reviews). Submit by post with SASE or through online submission system.

M207 Midsummer Dream House
Magazine
4833 Santa Monica Ave #7341, San Diego, CA 92167
United States
Tel: +1 (619) 438 5129

editor@midsummerdream.house

https://midsummerdream.house
https://twitter.com/msdreamhouse
https://instagram.com/midsummerdream.house
https://midsummerdreamhouse.tumblr.com/
https://www.facebook.com/midsummerdream.house/

Fiction > *Short Fiction*
  Avant-Garde; Contemporary; Experimental; Literary; Traditional

Nonfiction > *Short Nonfiction*
  Avant-Garde; Contemporary; Experimental; Literary; Traditional

Poetry > *Any Poetic Form*
  Avant-Garde; Contemporary; Experimental; Literary; Traditional

Send: Full text
How to send: Email

An independent literary and arts magazine based in San Diego, California, that includes a wide variety of artistic and thought-provoking work, including the experimental and avant-garde.

M208 Midway Journal
Online Magazine; Editorial Service
United States

editors@midwayjournal.com

https://midwayjournal.com
https://www.facebook.com/midway.journal
https://twitter.com/MidwayJournal
https://www.instagram.com/the_midway_journal_/

Fiction > *Short Fiction*

Nonfiction
  Essays: General
  Interviews: General
  Short Nonfiction: Creative Nonfiction

Poetry > *Any Poetic Form*

Send: Full text
How to send: Submittable

Costs: A fee is charged; Offers services that writers have to pay for. $2.50 for expedited submissions, available year-round. Free submissions during specific windows only. Also offers editorial services.

Aims to act as a bridge between aesthetics (and coasts), and create an engaging sense of place. Publishes work that aims to complicate and question the boundaries of genre, binary, and perspective. It offers surprises and ways of re-seeing, re-thinking, and re-feeling.

Fiction Editor: Ralph Pennel

Nonfiction Editor: Allie Mariano

Poetry Editor: Samantha Sharp

M209 The Missouri Review
Magazine
453 McReynolds Hall, University of Missouri, Columbia, MO 65211
United States

question@moreview.com

https://www.missourireview.com
https://www.facebook.com/themissourireview
https://twitter.com/missouri_review
https://www.instagram.com/themissourireview/

Fiction > *Short Fiction*

Nonfiction
  Essays: General
  Reviews: Books

Poetry > *Any Poetic Form*

Does not want:

Nonfiction > *Essays*: Literary Criticism

Send: Query; Self-addressed stamped envelope (SASE); Full text
How to send: Post; Online submission system

Costs: A fee is charged for online submissions. $4 submission fee for online submissions.

Publishes poetry, fiction, and essays of general interest. No literary criticism. Submit by post with SASE, or via online system. There is a $4 charge for online submissions. Also considers omnibus reviews of 3-6 recently published books that share a common feature or address a similar topic. Especially interested in essays that respond to books from smaller presses and/or emerging authors

Editor: Speer Morgan

M210 Modern Applied Science
Magazine
1595 Sixteenth Ave, Suite 301, Richmond Hill, Ontario, L4B 3N9
Canada
Tel: +1 (416) 642-2606

mas@ccsenet.org

https://www.ccsenet.org
https://www.ccsenet.org/journal/index.php/mas

ACADEMIC > **Nonfiction** > *Articles*: Science

Send: Full text
How to send: Online submission system; Email

An international, double-blind peer-reviewed, open-access journal, publishing original research, applied, and educational articles in all areas of applied science. It provides an academic platform for professionals and researchers to contribute innovative work in the field. Authors are encouraged to submit complete, unpublished, original works that are not under review in any other journals.

M211 Modern Haiku

Magazine
PO Box 1570, Santa Rosa Beach, FL 32459
United States

modernhaiku@gmail.com

https://www.modernhaiku.org

Nonfiction
Essays: Poetry as a Subject
Reviews: Books; Poetry as a Subject
Poetry
Haibun; *Haiga*; *Haikai*; *Haiku*; *Renku*; *Senryu*; *Tanka*

Send: Full text
How to send: Email; Post

Publishes English poetry in a variety of Japanese forms, such as haiku. Also publishes essays and book reviews relevant to the same field.

M212 Modern Poetry in Translation

Magazine
United Kingdom

webeditor@mptmagazine.com

http://modernpoetryintranslation.com
https://modernpoetryintranslation.submittable.com/submit
https://twitter.com/MPTmagazine
https://www.instagram.com/modernpoetryintranslation/

Poetry in Translation > *Any Poetic Form*

Closed to approaches.

Respected poetry series originally founded by prominent poets in the sixties. New Series continues their editorial policy: translation of good poets by translators who are often themselves poets, fluent in the foreign language, and sometimes working with the original poet. Publishes translations into English only. No original English language poetry. Send submissions via online submission system.

M213 Moonday Mag

Print Magazine
United States

moondaymag@gmail.com

https://moondaymag.com
https://www.instagram.com/moondaymag/

Fiction > *Short Fiction*
Fantasy; Gothic; Horror; Literary; Science Fiction; Speculative; Surreal

Nonfiction > *Short Nonfiction*: Creative Nonfiction

Poetry > *Any Poetic Form*
Speculative; Surreal

How to send: In the body of an email

A quarterly speculative art and literary magazine founded in 2023, dedicated to celebrating all things fantastic and fantastically strange. Born in the place that rests between here and the uncanny valley, it wonders what else might be out there, beyond the veil. From sci-fi to fantasy, to the horrors only a quiet mind can imagine, to the witching hour caught on camera in 35mm, it wants it all and welcomes all.

M214 MQR Mixtape

Online Magazine
United States

https://sites.lsa.umich.edu/mqr/mqr-mixtape/
https://mqr.submittable.com/submit

Magazine: Michigan Quarterly Review (M204)

Fiction > *Short Fiction*

Poetry > *Any Poetic Form*

How to send: Submittable

Costs: A fee is charged upon submission. $3 submission fee.

An eclectic, online zine guest curated by university graduate students.

M215 My Weekly

Magazine
D C Thomson & Co Ltd, My Weekly, 2 Albert Square, Dundee, DD1 1DD
United Kingdom
Tel: +44 (0) 1382 223131

swatson@dcthomson.co.uk
kirstyn.smith@dcthomson.co.uk

https://www.myweekly.co.uk/
https://www.facebook.com/My-Weekly-199671216711852/
http://twitter.com/My_Weekly
https://www.instagram.com/my_weekly_magazine/

Newspaper Publisher / Magazine Publisher: DC Thomson Media

Fiction > *Short Fiction*

Nonfiction > *Articles*
Beauty; Cookery; Crafts; Fashion; Films; Food and Drink; Gardening; Health; Lifestyle; Personal Finance; Real Life Stories; TV; Travel; Women's Interests

Weekly women's magazine aged at the over-50s, publishing a mix of lifestyle features, true life stories, and fiction.

M216 Mystery Magazine

Magazine
United States

https://www.mysteryweekly.com
https://www.facebook.com/MysteryWeekly
https://twitter.com/MysteryWeekly
https://www.instagram.com/mystery_magazine/
https://www.linkedin.com/in/mystery-magazine-85598110a/

Fiction > *Short Fiction*: Mystery

Closed to approaches.

Submit mysteries between 2,500 and 7,500 words through online submission system available on website. No multiple submissions.

M217 Nashville Review

Magazine
United States

thenashvillereview@gmail.com

https://as.vanderbilt.edu/nashvillereview

Fiction in Translation > *Short Fiction*

Fiction
Comics; Short Fiction
Nonfiction in Translation
Essays: General
Short Nonfiction: Creative Nonfiction; Memoir
Nonfiction
Essays: General
Short Nonfiction: Creative Nonfiction; Memoir
Poetry in Translation > *Any Poetic Form*

Poetry > *Any Poetic Form*

Send: Query; Author bio; Full text
How to send: Submittable

Submit short stories and novel excerpts up to 8,000 words, or three flash fiction pieces (1,000 words each), 1-3 poems (up to ten pages total), or creative nonfiction including memoir excerpts, essays, imaginative meditations, up to 8,000 words, via online submission system during the two annual reading periods: August and January. Art and comic submissions are accepted year-round. Looking for anything from one-page comics to excerpts from graphic novels, but no single-frame cartoons.

M218 Neo-opsis Science Fiction Magazine

Magazine
4129 Carey Road, Victoria, BC, V8Z 4G5
Canada

neoopsis@shaw.ca

http://www.neo-opsis.ca
https://www.facebook.com/groups/48525080175/
https://x.com/OpsisNeo
https://www.youtube.com/user/KarlJohanson42

Fiction > *Short Fiction*
Fantasy; Science Fiction

Poetry > *Any Poetic Form*
Fantasy; Science Fiction

Closed to approaches.

Magazine publishing science fiction and fantasy stories and poems. Send complete MS by email as Word or .rtf attachment or in the body of the email, or by post. See website for full details. No simultaneous submissions.

M219 Neon
Magazine
United Kingdom

subs@neonmagazine.co.uk

https://www.neonmagazine.co.uk

Fiction > *Short Fiction*
  Dark; Literary; Speculative; Surreal

Poetry
  Any Poetic Form: Dark; Literary; Surreal
  Graphic Poems: Dark; Literary; Surreal

Closed to approaches.

Quarterly online magazine publishing stylised poetry and prose, particularly the new, experimental, and strange. Welcomes genre fiction. Dark material preferred over humour; free verse preferred over rhyme. Send work pasted into the body of an email with a biographical note and the word "Submission" in the subject line.

Editor: Krishan Coupland

M220 New England Review
Magazine
Middlebury College, Middlebury, VT 05753
United States
Tel: +1 (802) 443-5075

nereview@middlebury.edu

https://www.nereview.com
https://newenglandreview.submittable.com/submit
https://www.facebook.com/NewEnglandReviewMiddlebury/
https://twitter.com/nerweb

Fiction
  Novel Excerpts; *Novellas*; *Short Fiction*
Nonfiction in Translation > *Essays*

Nonfiction
  Essays: Personal Essays
  Short Nonfiction: Arts; Cultural Criticism; Environment; Films; Literary Criticism; Travel
Poetry > *Any Poetic Form*

Scripts > *Theatre Scripts*: Drama

How to send: Submittable; Post

Costs: A fee is charged for online submissions. $3 per submission.

Welcomes submissions in fiction, poetry, nonfiction, drama, and translation. Different submission windows for different categories of work. See website for details.

M221 New Internationalist
Magazine
United Kingdom

https://newint.org
https://twitter.com/newint
https://www.facebook.com/newint
https://www.instagram.com/newinternationalist

Nonfiction
  Articles: Civil Rights; Environment; Feminism; Politics; Social Issues; Social Justice
  News: Civil Rights; Environment; Feminism; Politics; Social Issues; Social Justice

How to send: Online submission system

Independent, non-profit magazine that has been producing in-depth journalism on human rights, politics, and social and environmental justice since 1973. Welcomes pitches for articles: stories range from features on under-covered topics around the world, important social movements and struggles in the fight for global justice, to radical opinion pieces with an international – or internationalist – perspective, making interesting and original arguments you wouldn't see elsewhere. Topics span social justice, global inequality, the environment, feminism and liberatory struggles, tech politics and more. Generally publishes articles of between 800-2000 words in length. Occasionally publishes investigative reports and in-depth features of up to 5000 words.

Editors: Vanessa Baird; Chris Brazier; Dinyar Godrej; David Ransom

M222 New Statesman
Magazine
Studio 5 Salters House, 156 High Street, Hull, HU1 1NQ
United Kingdom

comments@newstatesman.co.uk

https://www.newstatesman.com
https://www.facebook.com/NewStatesman/
https://twitter.com/newstatesman
https://www.linkedin.com/company/new-statesman/
https://www.instagram.com/newstatesman

Nonfiction > *Articles*
  Arts; Books; Business; Culture; Current Affairs; Politics

Describes itself as the leading progressive political and cultural magazine in the United Kingdom. Founded as a weekly review of politics and literature in 1913, it has notably recognised and published new writers and critics, as well as encouraged notable careers. Today, it is a vibrant print-digital hybrid.

Author / Editor-in-Chief: Jason Cowley

M223 New Welsh Reader
Print Magazine
The Old Surgery, Napier Street, Cardigan, SA43 1ED
United Kingdom
Tel: +44 (0) 7890 968246

newwelshreview.submissions@gmail.com

https://newwelshreview.com
https://newwelshreview.com/new-welsh-reader
https://newwelshreview.com/about-us/submissions

Fiction > *Short Fiction*: Literary

Nonfiction
  Essays: Literary Criticism
  Short Nonfiction: Creative Nonfiction

How to send: Email

Original Creative Nonfiction, Stories, Photography, Illustration: We continue to seek exclusive creative nonfiction, photography, stories and illustration. We also want incisive, engaging and innovative essays of critical interest in the study and discussion of Welsh writing in English (particularly the latest generations of writers) or contemporary European literature in translation into English. These pieces should be between 2,500 and 6,000 words and focus on 2 or 3 books of any vintage.

Editor: Gwen Davies

M224 Norfolk & Suffolk Bride
Print Magazine
United Kingdom

https://www.greatbritishlife.co.uk/magazines/bride/

Magazine Publisher: Great British Life

Nonfiction > *Articles*
  Fashion; Norfolk; Suffolk; Weddings

For engaged couples in the region. Filled with inspiration, information and advice, this annual publication is geared towards planning your wedding the local way. From fashion features and expert articles, to real weddings and venue listings, it makes easy work of your wedmin by providing everything you need to plan the perfect day. Glean ideas for your wedding in every aspect and connect with the local suppliers who can bring your vision to life.

M225 The North
Magazine
The Poetry Business, Campo House, 54 Campo Lane, Sheffield, S1 2EG
United Kingdom
Tel: +44 (0) 1144 384074

office@poetrybusiness.co.uk

https://poetrybusiness.co.uk

Poetry > *Any Poetic Form*: Contemporary

Closed to approaches.

Send up to 6 poems with SASE / return postage. We publish the best of contemporary poetry. No "genre" or derivative poetry. Submitters should be aware of, should preferably have read, the magazine before submitting. See our website for notes on submitting poems. No submissions by email. Overseas submissions may be made through online submission system.

Editors: Ann Sansom; Peter Sansom

M226 Northern Gravy
Magazine
United Kingdom

info@northerngravy.com
Submissions@NorthernGravy.com

https://northerngravy.com
https://www.facebook.com/NorthernGravy/
https://x.com/NorthGravy
https://www.instagram.com/northerngravy/

ADULT
  Fiction > *Short Fiction*
  Poetry > *Any Poetic Form*

CHILDREN'S > **Fiction** > *Short Fiction*

YOUNG ADULT > **Fiction** > *Short Fiction*

Closed to approaches.

Accepts submissions over three areas: Fiction, Poetry and Kid Lit (writing for Middle Grade and Young Adult audiences), from writers either born or currently residing in the UK or Ireland. Submit one story or up to four poems.

M227 Obsidian: Literature in the African Diaspora
Magazine
Illinois State University, Williams Hall Annex, Normal, IL 61790
United States

https://obsidianlit.org
https://obsidian.submittable.com/submit

Fiction > *Short Fiction*: African Diaspora

Poetry > *Any Poetic Form*: African Diaspora

Scripts > *Theatre Scripts*: African Diaspora

Send: Full text
How to send: Submittable

Publishes scripts, fiction, and poetry focused on Africa and her Diaspora. See website for submission guidelines and to submit via online submission system.

M228 OK! Magazine
Magazine
One Canada Square, Canary Wharf, London, E14 5AB
United Kingdom
Tel: +44 (0) 20 7293 3000

https://www.ok.co.uk

Magazine Publisher: Reach Magazines Publishing

Nonfiction
  Articles: Lifestyle; Women's Interests
  Interviews: Celebrity
  News: Celebrity

Celebrity magazine, welcoming ideas for features and interviews/pictures of celebrities.

Editor-in-Chief: Caroline Waterston

M229 Oxford Poetry
Magazine
c/o Partus Press, 266 Banbury Road, Oxford, OX2 7DL
United Kingdom

editors@oxfordpoetry.co.uk
reviews@oxfordpoetry.co.uk

https://www.oxfordpoetry.com
https://www.instagram.com/oxford_poetry
https://www.facebook.com/OxfordPoetryMag/
https://twitter.com/oxfordpoetry

Book Publisher / Magazine Publisher: Partus Press

Nonfiction
  Articles: Literature
  Essays: Literature
  Interviews: Literature
  Reviews: Literature

Poetry in Translation > *Any Poetic Form*

Poetry > *Any Poetic Form*

How to send: Submittable

Costs: A fee is charged upon submission. £3 submission fee.

Publishes poems, interviews, reviews, and essays. Accepts unpublished poems on any theme and of any length during specific biannual submission windows, which are announced on the website. Send up to four poems by email. See website for full details. To suggest a book for review, email the reviews editor.

M230 Oxford Review of Books
Print Magazine; Online Magazine
Radcliffe Humanities Building, Radcliffe Observatory Quarter, Woodstock Road, Oxford, OX2 6GG
United Kingdom

orbeditor@gmail.com
orbpoetry@gmail.com

https://www.the-orb.org
https://www.facebook.com/this.is.the.ORB/
https://twitter.com/oxreviewofbooks
https://www.instagram.com/oxfordreviewofbooks/

Fiction > *Short Fiction*

Nonfiction
  Essays: Current Affairs
  Interviews: Activism; Classics / Ancient World; History; Philosophy; Poetry as a Subject; Politics
  Reviews: Books; Culture; Films; TV

Poetry > *Any Poetic Form*

Send: Pitch; Full text
How to send: Email

Publishes reviews of films, books, TV shows (think culture in the broadest sense); interviews with politicians, actors, philosophers, historians, poets, classicists, and activists; essays that provide a new and fresh take on current affairs; and poetry and fiction. Submit 3-4 poems, or pitches for prose, by email. Pitches are accepted on a rolling basis for online, and during specific windows for print. See website for more details.

M231 Pacifica Literary Review
Online Magazine
Seattle, WA
United States

pacificalitreview@gmail.com

http://www.pacificareview.com
https://pacificaliteraryreview.submittable.com/submit
https://www.facebook.com/PacificaLiteraryReview
https://twitter.com/PacificaReview

Fiction
  Novel Excerpts; *Short Fiction*
Nonfiction > *Short Nonfiction*: Creative Nonfiction

Poetry > *Any Poetic Form*

Send: Full text
How to send: Submittable

Costs: A fee is charged upon submission. $3 per submission.

Accepts poetry, fiction, creative non-fiction, and folios. Prose submissions must be under 5,000 words. Flash fiction submissions must be no more than 1000 words individually. Novel excerpts are acceptable but must be able to stand alone. For poetry, please submit no more than three poems in a single document. For flash fiction, please submit no more than three pieces in a single document.

Editor: Matt Muth

M232 Panorama
Online Magazine
Panorama Enterprises, 3rd Floor, 86-90 Paul Street, London, EC2A 4NE
United Kingdom

https://panoramajournal.org
https://www.facebook.com/panoramathejournaloftravelplaceandnature/
https://panoramajournal.submittable.com/submit
https://twitter.com/Panorama_J
https://www.linkedin.com/company/panorama-

the-journal-of-travel-place-and-nature/
https://www.instagram.com/panorama_journal/

Fiction > *Short Fiction*
Literary; Nature; Travel

Nonfiction > *Short Nonfiction*
Literary; Nature; Travel

Poetry > *Any Poetic Form*
Literary; Nature; Travel

Send: Query; Author bio; Full text
How to send: Submittable

We publish contemporary, literary-themed travel works of nonfiction, fiction, poetry, illustration, as well as travel-themed photo essays and film stills. We are looking for exquisite, rich, surprising work capable of unbinding readers from their expectations and routines. Make us get lost on a journey in your hometown. Be the verbal cartographer of your own exile. Bring us the fictional realities of characters who take us places we can't go on our own. Offer us poetry that leaves us stranded in the natural world. Most of all, write evocative, experiential, descriptive prose that takes our readers with you, and confirms our belief in the power of place. We have a particular interest in travel memoir, real or imagined, but we invite memoir with an edge. This is not the place for traditional travel memoir: give us something different.

M233 The Paris Review

Magazine
544 West 27th Street, Floor 3, New York, NY 10001
United States
Tel: +1 (212) 343-1333

queries@theparisreview.org

https://www.theparisreview.org
https://theparisreview.submittable.com/submit
https://www.facebook.com/parisreview
https://twitter.com/parisreview
http://theparisreview.tumblr.com/

Fiction > *Short Fiction*: Literary

Nonfiction
Interviews; *Short Nonfiction*

Poetry > *Any Poetic Form*

Closed to approaches.

Send submissions through online submission system or by post. All submissions must be in English and previously unpublished, though translations are acceptable if accompanied by copy of the original text. Simultaneous submissions accepted as long as immediate notification is given of acceptance elsewhere.

M234 The Passionfruit Review

Online Magazine
United Kingdom

editor@passionfruitreview.com

https://passionfruitreview.com
https://duotrope.com/duosuma/submit/the-passionfruit-review-1o4uh

Fiction > *Short Fiction*: Love

Nonfiction > *Short Nonfiction*
Creative Nonfiction; Love

Poetry > *Any Poetic Form*: Love

How to send: Duosuma

Costs: A fee is charged upon submission in some cases.

The theme for general submissions is love: the romantic, the familial, the platonic, the intimate, the lost, the young, the wretched. Above all, Passionfruit seeks to be a home for that which illuminates something of the human spirit – pieces that explore what love is (or isn't, or might be), when we love, how we love, what we love, and why we love.

Our focus is on poetry, but there are no particular restrictions on genre, type, or style – we will consider poetry, prose, and visual art for each issue.

M235 PC Pro

Magazine
Quay House, The Ambury, Bath, BA1 1UA
United Kingdom
Tel: +44 (0) 330 333 9493

customercare@subscribe.pcpro.co.uk

https://subscribe.pcpro.co.uk
https://www.facebook.com/pcpro
https://twitter.com/pcpro

Magazine Publisher: Future

ADULT > **Nonfiction** > *Articles*: Computers

PROFESSIONAL > **Nonfiction** > *Articles*: Computers

IT magazine for professionals in the IT industry and enthusiasts.

M236 People's Friend Pocket Novels

Magazine
United Kingdom

pfeditor@dcthomson.co.uk

https://www.thepeoplesfriend.co.uk

Magazine: The People's Friend (**M237**)

Fiction > *Novellas*
Family Saga; Romance

Send: Query
How to send: Email

Publishes romance and family fiction between 37,000 and 39,000 words, aimed at adults aged over 30. Send query by email See website for more information.

M237 The People's Friend

Magazine
United Kingdom

pfeditor@dcthomson.co.uk

https://www.thepeoplesfriend.co.uk

Newspaper Publisher / Magazine Publisher: DC Thomson Media

Fiction > *Short Fiction*: Women's Fiction

Nonfiction > *Nonfiction Books*
Cookery; Crafts; Lifestyle; Women's Interests

Publishes complete short stories (1,200-3,000 words (4,000 for specials)) and serials, focusing on character development rather than complex plots, plus 10,000-word crime thrillers. Also considers nonfiction from nature to nostalgia and from holidays to hobbies, and poetry. Guidelines available on website.

Magazine: People's Friend Pocket Novels (**M236**)

M238 Pleiades

Magazine
Department of English, Martin 336, University of Central Missouri, 415 E. Clark St., Warrensburg, MO 64093
United States
Tel: +1 (660) 543-4268

pleiadespoetryeditor@gmail.com
pleiadesfictioninquiries@gmail.com
pleiadescnf@gmail.com
pleiadesreviews@gmail.com

https://pleiadesmag.com
https://twitter.com/pleiadesmag
https://www.facebook.com/UCMPleiades
http://websta.me/n/pleiades_magazine
https://www.pinterest.com/pleiadesUCM/

Fiction > *Short Fiction*

Nonfiction
Reviews: Books
Short Nonfiction: Creative Nonfiction

Poetry > *Any Poetic Form*

Closed to approaches.

Send submissions through online submission system during specific windows only.

M239 Ploughshares

Magazine
Emerson College, 120 Boylston St., Boston, MA 02116-4624
United States

https://www.pshares.org
http://facebook.com/ploughshares
http://www.pinterest.com/pshares
http://twitter.com/pshares
https://instagram.com/psharesjournal/

Fiction > *Short Fiction*

Nonfiction > *Short Nonfiction*

Poetry > *Any Poetic Form*

Closed to approaches.

Costs: A fee is charged for online submissions. $3 fee for online submissions, except for subscribers, who may submit for free.

Welcomes unsolicited submissions of fiction, poetry, and nonfiction during the regular reading period, which runs from June 1 to January 15. The literary journal is published four times a year: mixed issues of poetry and prose in the Spring and Winter, a prose issue in the summer, and a longform prose issue in the Fall, with two of the four issues per year guest-edited by a different writer of prominence.

Editor: Don Lee

M240 PN Review
Magazine
4th Floor, Alliance House, 30 Cross Street,
Manchester, M2 7AQ
United Kingdom
Tel: +44 (0) 161 834 8730

PNRsubmissions@carcanet.co.uk

https://www.pnreview.co.uk

Nonfiction
  Essays: Poetry as a Subject
  Reviews: Poetry as a Subject

Poetry > *Any Poetic Form*

Send: Query; Full text
How to send: Email; Post

Poetry may be submitted during the months of June and December. Subscribers may submit by email; otherwise submissions should be by post. Queries for nonfiction submissions may be sent to the editor at any time, by email.

Editor: Michael Schmidt

M241 Poetry
Magazine
61 West Superior Street, Chicago, IL 60654
United States
Tel: +1 (312) 787-7070

submissions@poetrymagazine.org
info@poetryfoundation.org

https://www.poetrymagazine.org
https://poetry.submittable.com/submit
https://twitter.com/poetrymagazine

Nonfiction
  Essays: Poetry as a Subject
  Reviews: Books; Poetry as a Subject
Poetry in Translation > *Any Poetic Form*
Poetry > *Any Poetic Form*

How to send: Submittable

Submit up to four poems, up to 10 pages in total. Also publishes essays on poetry of about 1,500 to 2,500 words (maximum 10 pages in total) and reviews of poetry books, typically 1,200 to 1,800 words.

M242 Poetry Birmingham Literary Journal
Print Magazine
PO Box 18757, Oldbury, B69 9HS
United Kingdom

poetrybirmingham@gmail.com
naush@poetrybirmingham.com

https://poetrybirmingham.com
https://www.instagram.com/poetrybrum
https://www.facebook.com/PoetryBrum/
https://x.com/poetrybrum/

Nonfiction
  Essays: Literary Criticism; Personal Essays; Poetry as a Subject
  Interviews: Poetry as a Subject
  Reviews: Poetry as a Subject

Poetry > *Any Poetic Form*

Closed to approaches.

We are looking for previously unpublished work that is original, well-crafted, intriguing, and demonstrates a sensitivity to lyric. We are also interested in engaging visual, experimental, constrained, collaborative, mixed media, or hybrid work. We will consider longer poems and sequences that fit within our five-page limit. Submit up to five poems using the online submission form if possible. Otherwise, send submissions by post with email address for response. For prose about poetry: send a proposal of up to 150 words by email with a Word document containing a 500-word extract of your prose writing and a writer's CV. We welcome essays—both creative-critical or personal—reviews, reportage, interviews, and are open to more experimental forms. We seek honest, informed, interesting writing.

M243 Poetry Ireland Review
Magazine
3 Great Denmark Street, Dublin 1, D01 NV63
Ireland
Tel: +353 (0)1 6789815

pir@poetryireland.ie
info@poetryireland.ie

https://www.poetryireland.ie
https://poetryireland.submittable.com/submit/

Nonfiction
  Articles: Poetry as a Subject
  Essays: Poetry as a Subject
  Interviews: Poetry as a Subject

Poetry > *Any Poetic Form*

Send: Full text; Proposal
How to send: Post; Submittable

Send up to four poems through online submission system, or by post. Poetry is accepted from around the world but must be previously unpublished. No sexism or racism. Prose is generally commissioned; however, proposals are welcome. No unsolicited prose.

M244 Poetry London
Magazine
Goldsmiths, University of London, New Cross,
London, SE14 6NW
United Kingdom

admin@poetrylondon.co.uk

https://poetrylondon.co.uk
https://poetrylondon.submittable.com/submit
https://twitter.com/Poetry_London
https://www.instagram.com/poetry_london/
https://www.facebook.com/poetrylondon
https://www.youtube.com/c/PoetryLondon

Poetry in Translation > *Any Poetic Form*

Poetry > *Any Poetic Form*

Send: Full text; Self-addressed stamped envelope (SASE)
How to send: Submittable; Post

Send up to six poems via online submission system, or by post with SASE or adequate return postage (if within the UK) or email address for response (if overseas). Considers poems by both new and established poets. Also publishes book reviews.

M245 Poetry Wales
Magazine
Suite 6, 4 Derwen Road, Bridgend, CF31 1LH
United Kingdom
Tel: +44 (0) 1656 663018

poetrywalessubmissions@gmail.com
info@poetrywales.co.uk
editor@poetrywales.co.uk

https://poetrywales.co.uk
https://poetrywales.submittable.com/submit
http://twitter.com/poetrywales
http://facebook.com/poetrywales
http://instagram.com/poetrywales

Nonfiction
  Articles: Poetry as a Subject
  Reviews: Books; Poetry as a Subject
Poetry > *Any Poetic Form*

Send: Full text
How to send: Submittable; Post; Email

Publishes poetry, features, and reviews from Wales and beyond. Submit via online submission system, or by post. If online form is not working, use email. Also runs competitions.

M246 The Political Quarterly
Magazine
Department of Politics, Birkbeck, University of London, Malet Street, London, WC1E 7HX
United Kingdom

submissions@politicalquarterly.net

https://politicalquarterly.org.uk
https://twitter.com/po_qu
https://www.facebook.com/PoliticalQuarterly

Nonfiction
  Articles: Politics
  Reviews: Books

How to send: Email

Magazine covering national and international politics. Accepts unsolicited articles.

M247 Power Cut Lite
Magazine
United Kingdom

submissions@powercutmag.co.uk

https://powercutmag.co.uk
https://www.facebook.com/powercutmag
https://twitter.com/powercutmag
https://www.pinterest.co.uk/powercutmag/
https://www.linkedin.com/in/kristina-stevens-28790b294/
https://www.instagram.com/powercutmag/

Fiction > *Short Fiction*
  20th Century; Historical Fiction

Nonfiction
  Essays: 20th Century; Arts; Culture; Films; History; Literature; Photography
  Reviews: 20th Century; Films; Literature

Poetry > *Any Poetic Form*: 20th Century

Send: Full text
How to send: Email

Magazine exploring 20th century pop culture and focusing on 1930-1999. All work should be set in or explore this period. See website for submission guidelines.

M248 Preservation Magazine
Magazine
600 14th Street NW, Suite 500, Washington, DC 20005
United States
Tel: +1 (202) 588-6013

preservation@savingplaces.org
editorial@savingplaces.org

https://savingplaces.org/preservation-magazine

Nonfiction > *Articles*
  History; Travel

Send: Query
How to send: Phone; Email

Magazine publishing material on the preservation of historic buildings and neighbourhoods in the United States.

M249 Pride
Magazine
1 Garrat Lane, London, SW18 4AQ
United Kingdom
Tel: +44 (0) 20 3442 3310

editor@pridemagazine.com

http://pridemagazine.com
http://www.facebook.com/PrideMagazine
http://www.instagram.com/pridemaguk

Nonfiction
  Articles: Beauty; Career Development; Entertainment; Fashion; Hairstyles; Health; Lifestyle
  News: Ethnic Groups; Social Issues

Magazine aimed at black women. Publishes news, and articles and features on entertainment, hair, beauty, and fashion.

M250 Prole
Magazine
United Kingdom

submissionspoetry@prolebooks.co.uk
submissionsprose@prolebooks.co.uk

https://prolebooks.co.uk
https://facebook.com/Prole-236155444300
https://twitter.com/Prolebooks

Fiction > *Short Fiction*: Literary

Nonfiction > *Short Nonfiction*: Creative Nonfiction

Poetry > *Any Poetic Form*

Send: Full text
How to send: In the body of an email

We promote accessible literature of high quality. Anything that we publish will be intelligent, engaging and impact the reader in a variety of ways. It's the reader who comes first. We want to appeal to a wide audience and reconnect a broad readership with excellent examples of poetry and short prose. We do not accept previously published material, either in paper journals or e-zines. We will consider pieces that have been shared on personal sites or membership writing sites but ask you to remove them prior to submission. We do not accept simultaneous submissions.

M251 Pulsar Poetry Magazine
Online Magazine
90 Beechwood Drive, Camelford, Cornwall, PL32 9NB
United Kingdom
Tel: +44 (0) 1840 213633

pulsar.ed@btinternet.com

https://www.pulsarpoetry.com

Poetry > *Any Poetic Form*

Send: Full text; Self-addressed stamped envelope (SASE)
How to send: In the body of an email; Domestic Post

The editor's preference is for hard hitting poems that have a message, meaning, and are well written. Not keen on deeply religious poems or de-dah de-dah poems where everything chimes annoyingly like a cheap clock. Please don't send poems about cute and cuddly kittens. Simultaneous submissions are not considered. Postal submissions from within the UK only.

Editor: David Pike

M252 Pushing Out the Boat
Magazine
United Kingdom

info@pushingouttheboat.co.uk

https://www.pushingouttheboat.co.uk

Fiction > *Short Fiction*: Literary

Poetry > *Any Poetic Form*

Scripts > *Theatre Scripts*

Closed to approaches.

Magazine of prose, poetry and visual arts, based in North-East Scotland. Welcomes work in English, Doric or Scots. Submit via online submission system during open reading periods. See website for details.

M253 Qu Literary Magazine
Magazine
United States

qulitmag@queens.edu

http://www.qulitmag.com

Fiction > *Short Fiction*: Literary

Nonfiction > *Essays*

Poetry > *Any Poetic Form*

Scripts
  Film Scripts; *TV Scripts*; *Theatre Scripts*

Send: Full text
How to send: Submittable
How not to send: Email

Costs: A fee is charged upon submission. $2.50 per submission.

Literary journal published by a university MFA program. Editorial staff is comprised of current students. Publishes fiction, poetry, essays and script excerpts.

M254 Quadrant Magazine
Magazine
PO Box 82, Balmain NSW 2041
Australia
Tel: +61 (0) 3 8317 8147

https://quadrant.org.au
https://www.facebook.com/QuadrantAus/
https://x.com/quadrantorgau
https://au.linkedin.com/company/quadrant-magazine-ltd

Fiction > *Short Fiction*

Nonfiction
  Articles: Culture; History; Literature; Music; Poetry as a Subject; Politics
  Essays: Literary Criticism

Poetry > *Any Poetic Form*

Send: Full text
How to send: Email

Accepts unsolicited, previously unpublished articles that fit within its general profile of a journal of ideas, essays, literature, poetry and historical and political debate. Although it retains its founding bias towards cultural freedom, anti-totalitarianism and classical liberalism, its pages are open to any well-written and thoughtful contribution. Also accepts poems, literary criticism, and short fiction between 1,000 and 4,000 words.

M255 Racecar Engineering
Magazine
The Chelsea Magazine Company, 111 Buckingham Palace Road, London, SW1 0DT
United Kingdom
Tel: +44 (0) 20 7349 3700

editorial@racecarengineering.com

https://www.racecar-engineering.com
https://www.facebook.com/RacecarEngineering/
https://twitter.com/RacecarEngineer

Magazine Publisher: The Chelsea Magazine Company

Nonfiction
Articles: Engineering; Racecars
News: Engineering; Racecars

Publishes news articles and in-depth features on racing cars and related products and technology. No material on road cars or racing drivers.

M256 Radar Poetry
Magazine
United States

radarpoetry@gmail.com

https://www.radarpoetry.com

Poetry > *Any Poetic Form*

Closed to approaches.

Costs: A fee is charged upon submission; Offers services that writers have to pay for. $3 submission fee, or optional $25 fee for submission with feedback.

Electronic journal of poetry and artwork, published quarterly. Interested in the interplay between poetry and visual media. Each issue features pairings of poetry and artwork, selected by the editors. Submit up to three original, previously unpublished poems through online submission system. Accepts submissions November 1 to January 1 (free), and March 1 to May 1 ($3) annually.

Editors: Rachel Marie Patterson; Dara-Lyn Shrager

M257 Rail Express
Magazine
United Kingdom
Tel: +44 (0) 1507 529529

RailExpressEditor@mortons.co.uk

https://www.railexpress.co.uk
https://www.facebook.com/RailExpressMag
https://www.instagram.com/railexpressmagazine/
https://twitter.com/railexpress

Magazine Publisher: Mortons Media Group

Nonfiction > *Articles:* Railways

Magazine publishing news and features on railways in the UK.

M258 Reactor
Online Magazine
United States

blogsubmissions@tor.com

https://reactormag.com
https://reactormag.com/submissions-guidelines/

Nonfiction
Articles: Fantasy; Science Fiction
Essays: Fantasy; Science Fiction
Reviews: Books; Fantasy; Science Fiction

Send: Pitch; Writing sample
How to send: Email

Most interested in pitches for essays, think pieces, list posts, reaction pieces, and reviews in the 1000-2500 word range (although also open to longer essays). If possible, please include 2-3 writing samples and/or links to your published work on other sites.

M259 Red Magazine
Magazine
30 Panton Street, London, SW1Y 4AJ
United Kingdom

https://www.redonline.co.uk
https://www.facebook.com/redmagazine/
https://twitter.com/RedMagDaily
https://www.pinterest.co.uk/redmagazine/
https://www.instagram.com/redmagazine/?hl=en
https://www.youtube.com/user/RedMagazineOnline

Magazine Publisher: Hearst Magazines UK

Nonfiction
Articles: Beauty; Decorating; Fashion; Fitness; Food; Hairstyles; Health; Interior Design; Parenting; Relationships; Sex; Travel; Wellbeing
Interviews: Women's Interests
Reviews: Books; Films; Music; TV

Magazine aimed at women in their thirties.

M260 Research Journal of Pharmacy and Technology
Magazine
India
Tel: +91-8871102662

editor.rjpt@gmail.com

https://www.rjptonline.org

ACADEMIC > **Nonfiction** > *Articles*
Medicine; Technology

Send: Full text
How to send: Online submission system

An international, peer-reviewed, multidisciplinary journal, devoted to pharmaceutical sciences. The aim is to increase the impact of pharmaceutical research both in academia and industry, with strong emphasis on quality and originality. The journal publishes Original Research Articles, Short Communications, Review Articles in all areas of pharmaceutical sciences from the discovery of a drug up to clinical evaluation. Topics covered are: Pharmaceutics and Pharmacokinetics; Pharmaceutical chemistry including medicinal and analytical chemistry; Pharmacognosy including herbal products standardization and Phytochemistry; Pharmacology: Allied sciences including drug regulatory affairs, Pharmaceutical Marketing, Pharmaceutical Microbiology, Pharmaceutical biochemistry, Pharmaceutical Education and Hospital Pharmacy.

Editor: Dr. R. B. Saudagar

M261 The Rialto
Magazine
74 Britannia Road, Norwich, NR1 4HS
United Kingdom

info@therialto.co.uk

https://www.therialto.co.uk
https://therialto.submittable.com/submit
https://www.facebook.com/rialtopoetry/
https://twitter.com/RialtoPoetry
https://www.instagram.com/rialtopoetry/

Poetry > *Any Poetic Form*

Closed to approaches.

Send up to six poems with SASE or adequate return postage or submit through online submission system. No submissions by email.

Editor: Michael Mackmin

M262 Riposte
Print Magazine
United Kingdom

studio@ripostemagazine.com

https://www.ripostemagazine.com
https://x.com/RiposteMagazine
https://www.instagram.com/ripostemagazine/

Nonfiction
Articles: Arts; Business; Design; Environment; Music; Politics; Social Justice; Women
Essays: Arts; Business; Design; Environment; Music; Politics; Social Justice; Women
Interviews: Women

We profile bold and fascinating women who challenge power structures and stereotypes. Our interviews are honest rather than being full of media-trained responses as the women we feature candidly discuss their successes and failures, their work, their passions and perspectives. Essays and features cover a broad range of issues including art, design, music, business, innovation, politics, social justice and environmental issues.

M263 River Hills Traveler
Magazine
212 E Main Street, Neosho, MO 64850
United States
Tel: +1 (417) 451-3798

https://www.riverhillstraveler.com

Nonfiction
Articles: Boats; Camping; Fishing; Hunting; Lifestyle; Missouri; Outdoor Activities; Ozarks
News: Animals; Missouri; Nature; Ozarks; Travel

Magazine covering outdoor sports and nature in the southeast quarter of Missouri, the east and central Ozarks.

Managing Editor: Madeleine Link
Publisher: Jimmy Sexton

M264 River Styx
Online Magazine
3301 Washington Ave, Suite 2C, St. Louis, MO 63103
United States

https://www.riverstyx.org
https://riverstyx.submittable.com/submit
https://twitter.com/riverstyxmag
https://www.facebook.com/RiverStyxLiteraryMagazine/
https://www.linkedin.com/company/river-styx/
https://www.instagram.com/riverstyxmag/

Fiction > *Short Fiction*

Nonfiction > *Short Nonfiction*: Creative Nonfiction

Poetry > *Any Poetic Form*

Scripts > *Theatre Scripts*

How to send: Submittable
How not to send: Email; Post

Costs: A fee is charged upon submission. $3 submission fee.

A multicultural magazine of poetry, short fiction, creative nonfiction, short plays, and art. Seeks to publish work that is striking in its originality, energy, and craft, from both new and established writers.

M265 Rugby World
Magazine
121-141 Westbourne Terrace, Paddington, London, W2 6QA
United Kingdom

rugbyworldletters@futurenet.com

https://www.rugbyworld.com
https://www.facebook.com/

rugbyworldmagazine
https://www.youtube.com/user/rugbyworld08
https://twitter.com/rugbyworldmag

Magazine Publisher: Future

Nonfiction
Articles: Rugby
News: Rugby

Send: Query; Author bio; Synopsis

Magazine publishing news and articles related to rugby. Send idea with coverline, headline, and 50-word synopsis, along with brief resume of your experience.

M266 Ruralite
Magazine
5625 NE Elam Young Parkway Suite 100, Hillsboro, OR 97124
United States
Tel: +1 (503) 357-2105

editor@pur.coop
info@pur.coop

https://www.ruralite.com
https://www.facebook.com/Ruralite
https://www.instagram.com/ruralitemag/
https://twitter.com/RuraliteMag
https://vimeo.com/showcase/5668282

Nonfiction > *Articles*
Energy; Lifestyle; Photography; Recipes; Travel

Send: Pitch
How to send: Email

Serves members of publicly owned electric utilities, delivering engaging human-interest features, energy-related content, travel and photography tips, scrumptious recipes, reader submissions and important information about electric service.

M267 Saddlebag Dispatches
Magazine
United States

submissions@saddlebagdispatches.com

https://saddlebagdispatches.com

Fiction > *Short Fiction*: American West

Nonfiction > *Articles*: American West

Poetry > *Any Poetic Form*: American West

Send: Full text
How to send: Email

Publishes fiction, nonfiction, and poetry about the American West. Looks for themes of open country, unforgiving nature, struggles to survive and settle the land, freedom from authority, cooperation with fellow adventurers, and other experiences that human beings encounter on the frontier. Send submissions by email. See website for full guidelines.

M268 Sailing Today
Magazine
The Chelsea Magazine Company, 111 Buckingham Palace Road, London, SW1 0DT
United Kingdom
Tel: +44 (0) 20 7349 3700

editor@sailingtoday.co.uk

https://www.sailingtoday.co.uk
https://www.facebook.com/sailingtoday/
https://twitter.com/SailingTodayMag
https://www.youtube.com/channel/UCah1Wlfp86HD0tpbhW1LP1Q

Nonfiction > *Articles*: Sailing

Practical magazine for cruising sailors. Offers a wealth of practical advice and a dynamic mix of in-depth boat, gear and equipment news.

M269 Savannah Magazine
Magazine
United States
Tel: +1 (912) 652-0293

https://www.savannahmagazine.com
https://www.facebook.com/SavannahMagazine
https://twitter.com/savmag
https://www.pinterest.com/savmagazine/
https://www.instagram.com/savannahmagazine/
https://www.youtube.com/user/SavannahMagazineLive

Nonfiction > *Articles*
Culture; Food; Health; Houses and Homes; Lifestyle; Savannah, GA; Weddings

Send: Query
How to send: Email
How not to send: Phone

Our mission is to celebrate the inimitable Savannah lifestyle and serve the city as thought leaders. We discover and uplift the talented individuals of the city's creative class. With smart, layered, inclusive content, we interpret Savannah's unique cultural identity – and become the change we want to see in the city.

M270 Scifaikuest
Print Magazine; Online Magazine
United States

gatrix65@yahoo.com

https://www.hiraethsffh.com/scifaikuest

Book Publisher / Ebook Publisher / Online Publisher: Hiraeth Books

Nonfiction > *Articles*
Biography; Creative Writing; Poetry as a Subject

Poetry
Haibun: Horror; Science Fiction
Haiku: Horror; Science Fiction
Senryu: Horror; Science Fiction
Tanka: Horror; Science Fiction

Send: Full text; Author bio
How to send: Email

Print and online magazine publishing science fiction and horror poetry in forms such as scifaiku, haibun, senryu, and tanka. Also publishes articles. No simultaneous submissions. See website for full submission guidelines.

M271 The Scots Magazine
Magazine
D.C. Thomson & Co. Ltd, 2 Albert Square, Dundee, DD1 1DD
United Kingdom
Tel: +44 (0) 1382 223131

mail@scotsmagazine.com

https://www.scotsmagazine.com
https://www.facebook.com/scotsmagazine/
https://twitter.com/ScotsMagazine
https://www.instagram.com/scots_magazine/
https://www.youtube.com/channel/UCQQRFhCCyaPvpY8uWpBmHtg?

Newspaper Publisher / Magazine Publisher: DC Thomson Media

Nonfiction > *Articles*
Folklore, Myths, and Legends; History; Outdoor Activities; Scotland; Wildlife

Send: Query
Don't send: Full text
How to send: Email

Scottish interest magazine publishing material covering history, folklore, wildlife, outdoor pursuits, Scottish personalities, etc.

Editor: John Methven

M272 Scottish Field
Magazine
Fettes Park, 496 Ferry Road, Edinburgh, EH5 2DL
United Kingdom
Tel: +44 (0) 1315 511000

editor@scottishfield.co.uk

https://www.scottishfield.co.uk
https://www.facebook.com/scottishfield
http://www.twitter.com/scottishfield

Nonfiction > *Articles*
Beauty; Culture; Fashion; Food and Drink; Gardening; Interior Design; Lifestyle; Outdoor Activities; Scotland; Travel

Lifestyle magazine publishing articles and features of general Scottish interest.

Editor: Richard Bath

M273 Scribble
Magazine
14 The Park, Stow on the Wold, Cheltenham, Glos., GL54 1DX
United Kingdom
Tel: +44 (0) 1451 831053

enquiries@parkpublications.co.uk
http://www.parkpublications.co.uk/scribble.html

Magazine Publisher: Park Publications

Fiction > *Short Fiction*

Send: Full text
How to send: Email; Post

Costs: A fee is charged upon submission. £5. Free for subscribers.

Accepts short stories on any subject from new and experienced writers. Each quarter prizes of £75, £25, and £15 will be awarded for the best three stories in the edition. These competitions are free to annual subscribers. See website for further details.

M274 Second Factory
Print Magazine
United States

https://uglyducklingpresse.org/about/submissions/
https://udp.submittable.com/submit

Book Publisher: Ugly Duckling Presse (**P399**)

Fiction > *Short Fiction*
General, and in particular: Experimental
Nonfiction > *Short Nonfiction*
General, and in particular: Experimental
Poetry > *Any Poetic Form*

Closed to approaches.

Publishes mainly poetry. Fiction and nonfiction will have a better chance if it is fairly short (more than 4 pages per contributor are not usually published) and if it has a fairly experimental and/or playful nature. 'Traditional' fiction and prose submissions are not as likely to be accepted, but open to surprises.

M275 Seventeen
Magazine
United States

mail@seventeen.com

https://www.seventeen.com
https://www.youtube.com/user/SeventeenMagazine
https://www.instagram.com/seventeen/
https://www.facebook.com/seventeen/

Magazine Publisher: Hearst Magazines International

YOUNG ADULT > **Nonfiction** > *Articles*
Beauty; Celebrity; Fashion; Health; Lifestyle; Politics; Wellbeing

Fashion beauty and lifestyle magazine for young women in their late teens and early twenties.

M276 Shearsman
Print Magazine
PO Box 4239, Swindon, SN3 9FN
United Kingdom

editor@shearsman.com

https://www.shearsman.com
https://www.facebook.com/profile.php?id=100063797880717
https://twitter.com/ShearsmanBooks
https://www.pinterest.com/shearsmanbooks/pins

Book Publisher: Shearsman Books

Poetry > *Any Poetic Form*

Now operates two reading windows for submissions: March and September. Send submissions with SAE for return. If outside UK please send disposable MS and email address for response. Do not send IRCs. Email submissions accepted if submission is sent in body of email, not as an attachment. PDFs accepted through online upload system. Please study magazine or at least website before deciding whether or not to submit your work. Publishes poetry in the modernist tradition, plus some prose, including reviews.

M277 Shenandoah
Magazine
United States

shenandoah@wlu.edu

https://shenandoahliterary.org
https://www.facebook.com/ShenandoahLiterary
https://www.instagram.com/shenandoah_literary
https://x.com/ShenandoahWLU

Fiction in Translation
Comics; Novel Excerpts, Short Fiction
Fiction
Comics; Novel Excerpts; Short Fiction
Nonfiction in Translation
Essays: General
Short Nonfiction: Creative Nonfiction; Memoir
Nonfiction
Essays: General
Short Nonfiction: Creative Nonfiction; Memoir
Poetry in Translation > *Any Poetic Form*
Poetry > *Any Poetic Form*

How to send: Submittable
How not to send: Post

Aims to showcase a wide variety of voices and perspectives in terms of gender identity, race, ethnicity, class, age, ability, nationality, regionality, sexuality, and educational background. Considers short stories, essays, excerpts of novels in progress, poems, comics, and translations of all the above.

M278 Ships Monthly Magazine
Magazine
Kelsey Media, The Granary, Downs Court,
Yalding Hil, Yalding, Kent, ME18 6AL
United Kingdom
Tel: +44 (0) 1959 543747

https://shipsmonthly.com

Magazine Publisher: Kelsey Media

ADULT > **Nonfiction** > *Articles*: Ships

PROFESSIONAL > **Nonfiction** > *Articles*
  Shipping; Ships

Magazine aimed at ship enthusiasts and maritime professionals. Publishes news and illustrated articles related to all kinds of ships, including reports on the ferry, cruise, new building and cargo ship scene as well as navies across the world.

Editor: Nicholas Leach

M279 Shooter Literary Magazine
Magazine
United Kingdom

submissions.shooterlitmag@gmail.com

https://shooterlitmag.com

Fiction > *Short Fiction*

Nonfiction
  Essays: General
  Short Nonfiction: Memoir

Poetry > *Any Poetic Form*

Send: Full text; Author bio
How to send: Email

Publishes literary fiction, poetry, creative nonfiction and memoir relating to specific themes for each issue. See website for current theme and full submission guidelines.

M280 Shoreline of Infinity
Magazine
United Kingdom

editor@shorelineofinfinity.com

https://www.shorelineofinfinity.com
https://duotrope.com/duosuma/submit/shoreline-of-infinity-6a37K
https://www.facebook.com/ShorelineOfInfinity/
https://twitter.com/shoreinf
https://www.youtube.com/channel/UCm2N3L9V2rvnkS5dCRzttCg
https://www.instagram.com/shoreinf/

Fiction > *Short Fiction*
  Fantasy; Science Fiction

Poetry > *Any Poetic Form*: Science Fiction

Closed to approaches.

Science Fiction magazine from Scotland. We want stories that explore our unknown future. We want to play around with the big ideas and the little ones. We want writers to tell us stories to inspire us, give us hope, provide some laughs. Or to scare the stuffing out of us. We want good stories: we want to be entertained. We want to read how people cope in our exotic new world, we want to be in their minds, in their bodies, in their souls.

M281 Sierra
Print Magazine; Online Magazine
United States

https://www.sierraclub.org
https://www.sierraclub.org/sierra
https://www.facebook.com/SierraMagazine/
https://www.instagram.com/sierramagazine/
https://twitter.com/sierra_magazine
https://www.pinterest.com/sierramagazine/

Nonfiction
  Articles: Adventure; Climate Science; Culture; Environment; Narrative Nonfiction; Nature; Social Justice; Sustainable Living; Travel; Wildlife
  Reviews: Books; Films

Send: Query; Pitch
How to send: Online submission system

A quarterly national print and digital magazine publishing award-winning journalism and cutting-edge photography, art, and video dedicated to protecting the natural world. Looking for reported stories on a wide range of environmental and social justice issues from writers who can bring to our audience a broad array of perspectives and writing styles.

M282 Sinister Wisdom
Magazine
2333 McIntosh Road, Dover, FL 33527
United States
Tel: +1 (301) 537-6570

julie@sinisterwisdom.org

https://www.sinisterwisdom.org
http://sinisterwisdom.submittable.com/submit
https://www.facebook.com/SinisterWisdom
https://www.instagram.com/sinister_wisdom/
https://twitter.com/Sinister_Wisdom
https://www.youtube.com/channel/UCtbGssCcCgE4WIwjGYL_qDA
https://www.linkedin.com/company/sinister-wisdom

Fiction > *Short Fiction*: LGBTQIA

Nonfiction
  Essays: LGBTQIA
  Reviews: Books

Poetry > *Any Poetic Form*: LGBTQIA

Send: Full text; Author bio
How to send: Submittable; Post

Multicultural lesbian literary and art journal. Material may be in any style or form, or combination of forms. Submit five poems, two short stories or essays, OR one longer piece of up to 5,000 words. Prefers submissions via online submission system, but will accept submissions by post if necessary.

Editor: Julie R. Enszer

M283 SmokeLong Quarterly
Online Magazine
United States

editor@smokelong.com

https://www.smokelong.com
https://smokelong.submittable.com/Submit
https://www.facebook.com/smokelong
https://twitter.com/SmokeLong

Fiction > *Short Fiction*

Nonfiction
  Articles: Creative Writing
  Essays: Creative Writing
  Reviews: Literature

How to send: Submittable

Publishes flash narratives up to 1,000 words. We do not consider poetry. We consider reviews of flash collections, essays on craft, and articles on teaching flash for the blog.

M284 Snowflake Magazine
Print Magazine
United Kingdom

info@snowflakeculture.com

https://www.snowflakeculture.com
https://twitter.com/SnowflakeMag
https://www.instagram.com/snowflake_magazine

Fiction > *Short Fiction*
  General, and in particular: LGBTQIA

Nonfiction
  Articles: General, and in particular: LGBTQIA
  Essays: General, and in particular: LGBTQIA
  Interviews: General, and in particular: LGBTQIA

Poetry > *Any Poetic Form*
  General, and in particular: LGBTQIA

Closed to approaches.

Publishes art, poetry, essays, flash fiction, photography, interviews and articles that are either queer themed or from an artist who identifies as LGBTQ+ (or both).

M285 SOMA
Magazine
888 O'Farrell Street, Suite 103, San Francisco, CA 94109
United States

http://www.somamagazine.com
http://www.twitter.com/SOMAmagazine
http://www.facebook.com/SOMA.Magazine
http://www.youtube.com/user/somamagazine
http://www.myspace.com/somamagazine

Nonfiction > *Articles*
 Arts; Design; Fashion; Films; Music

Magazine of music, film, the arts, fashion, design, architecture, and nightlife.

M286 Somerset Life

Magazine
United Kingdom

https://www.greatbritishlife.co.uk/magazines/somerset/

Magazine Publisher: Great British Life

Nonfiction
 Articles: Food; Gardening; History; Houses and Homes; Lifestyle; Somerset; Travel
 Reviews: Restaurants

Magazine that puts the gloss on life in Somerset. Every month it's packed with features about this picturesque part of England – from characters and personalities to heritage and traditions. We turn the focus on our towns and villages, and give comprehensive guides to enjoying life in Somerset – including what's on, restaurant reviews and topical features on major events.

M287 Sonder Magazine

Print Magazine
Dublin
Ireland

sonderlit@gmail.com

https://sonderlit.com
https://www.instagram.com/sonder_lit/
https://twitter.com/MagazineSonder
https://www.facebook.com/sonderlit
https://www.linkedin.com/company/sonder-magazine/
https://www.youtube.com/channel/UCm3GnFrr2QXkz14LeOe7IHA

Fiction > *Short Fiction*

Nonfiction > *Short Nonfiction*: Creative Nonfiction

Closed to approaches.

A Dublin-based print journal, focused on the idea of sonder, the self, and others: that existential feeling you get when you're walking down the street or sitting in the pub and are overcome by the realization that everyone you pass is just out there doing their own thing, thinking their own thoughts and living their own lives. Publishes short stories, flash fiction, and creative non-fiction, all based around the individual and how we interact with each other.

M288 South

Magazine
PO Box 9338, Wimborne, BH21 9JA
United Kingdom

south@southpoetry.org

http://www.southpoetry.org

Poetry > *Any Poetic Form*

Send: Full text
How to send: Post
How not to send: Email

Submit up to three poems up to 40 lines each by post (two copies of each), along with submission form available on website. No previously published poems (including poems that have appeared on the internet). Submissions are not returned. See website for full details. No translations or submissions by email.

Editors: Peter Keeble; Anne Peterson; Chrissie Williams

M289 South Carolina Review

Magazine
314 Strode Tower, Clemson, SC 29634
United States
Tel: +1 (864) 656-3151

km@clemson.edu

https://www.clemson.edu/caah/sites/south-carolina-review
https://thesouthcarolinareview.submittable.com/submit

Fiction > *Short Fiction*

Nonfiction
 Essays: General
 Reviews: Books
 Short Nonfiction: Creative Nonfiction

Poetry > *Any Poetic Form*

Closed to approaches.

Publishes fiction and poetry primarily, but will also consider creative nonfiction, scholarly essays, and book reviews.

Editor: Wayne Chapman

M290 Southern Humanities Review

Magazine
9088 Haley Center, Auburn University, Auburn, AL 36849
United States
Tel: +1 (334) 844-9088

shr@auburn.edu

https://www.southernhumanitiesreview.com
https://southernhumanitiesreview.submittable.com/submit
https://www.facebook.com/southernhumanitiesreview
https://twitter.com/SouthernHReview
https://www.instagram.com/southernhumanitiesreview/
https://www.youtube.com/channel/UCnywOlZbBtEX7OFYMUMSQsg

Fiction > *Short Fiction*

Nonfiction > *Essays*
 Creative Nonfiction; Literary Journalism; Literary; Lyric Essays; Memoir; Personal Essays; Travel

Poetry > *Any Poetic Form*

Send: Full text
How to send: Submittable
How not to send: Post; Email

Costs: A fee is charged upon submission. $3 submission fee.

Submissions for all fiction and nonfiction are open from August 1 until October 15 in the fall and from January 15 until March 14 in the spring. Poetry submissions are open from August 24 until September 7 in the fall and from January 15 until March 14 in the spring. Nonfiction submissions are open year-round.

M291 The Southern Review

Magazine
338 Johnston Hall, Louisiana State University, Baton Rouge, LA 70803
United States
Tel: +1 (225) 578-6467
Fax: +1 (225) 578-6461

southernreview@lsu.edu

https://thesouthernreview.org
https://www.facebook.com/lsusouthernreview
https://twitter.com/southern_review
https://soundcloud.com/lsupress_and_tsr

Fiction in Translation > *Short Fiction*

Fiction > *Short Fiction*

Nonfiction in Translation > *Essays*

Nonfiction > *Essays*

Poetry in Translation > *Any Poetic Form*

Poetry > *Any Poetic Form*

Closed to approaches.

Costs: A fee is charged upon submission. $3 per submission.

Strives to discover and promote a diverse array of engaging, relevant, and challenging literature—including fiction, nonfiction, poetry, and translation from literary luminaries as well as the best established and emerging writers.

M292 Southern Theatre

Magazine
5710 N Gate City Blvd, Ste K Box 186, Greensboro, NC 27407
United States
Tel: +1 (336) 265-6148

info@setc.org

https://setc.org/publications/
https://www.facebook.com/setc.org/
https://twitter.com/setctweet
https://www.instagram.com/setc/
https://www.linkedin.com/company/setcorg

Nonfiction > *Articles*: Theatre

Magazine covering theatre around the nation and beyond. Published quarterly and sent to all individual and organizational members.

M293 Southwest Review

Magazine
3225 Daniel Avenue, Room G09, Heroy Science Hall Basement, Dallas, TX 75205-1437
United States
Tel: +1 (214) 768-1037
Fax: +1 (214) 768-1408

contact@southwestreview.com

https://southwestreview.com
https://southwestreview.submittable.com/submit
https://www.facebook.com/SouthwestRev/
https://twitter.com/SouthwestReview
https://www.instagram.com/southwest_review/

Fiction > *Short Fiction*

Nonfiction > *Articles*
   Arts; Current Affairs; History; Literature; Music

Poetry > *Any Poetic Form*

Closed to approaches.

Costs: A fee is charged upon submission. $3 submission fee.

The third-longest-running literary quarterly in the United States.

M294 Southword Journal

Magazine
Frank O'Connor House, 84 Douglas Street, Cork
Ireland
Tel: +353 (0) 21 4322396

info@munsterlit.ie

http://www.munsterlit.ie/Southword%20Journal.html
https://www.facebook.com/Southword.Journal/
https://southword.submittable.com/submit

Fiction > *Short Fiction*

Poetry > *Any Poetic Form*

Closed to approaches.

Accepts submissions during specific submission windows only. See website for details.

M295 Spa Magazine

Print Magazine
P.O. Box 278, Pilot Hill, CA 95664
United States
Tel: +1 (916) 467-9118

editor@spamagazine.com

https://spamagazine.com

PROFESSIONAL > **Nonfiction**
   Articles: Business; Spas and Hot Tubs
   News: Business; Spas and Hot Tubs

Magazine covering spas and hot tubs. Digital version is available for free by email. Print version is free to anyone in the pool and spa industry.

M296 Speciality Food

Magazine
United Kingdom
Tel: +44 (0) 1206 505981

holly.shackleton@artichokehq.com

https://www.specialityfoodmagazine.com
https://twitter.com/specialityfood
https://www.linkedin.com/company/speciality-food/
https://www.instagram.com/specialityfoodmagazine/

Media Company: Artichoke Media

PROFESSIONAL > **Nonfiction**
   Articles: Business; Food and Drink
   News: Business; Food and Drink

Trade magazine for the food and drink industry.

Editor: Holly Shackleton

M297 Spitball

Magazine
536 Lassing Way, Walton, KY 41094
United States

spitball5@hotmail.com

https://www.spitballmag.com

Fiction > *Short Fiction*: Baseball

Nonfiction
   Reviews: Baseball; Books
   Short Nonfiction: Baseball

Poetry > *Any Poetic Form*: Baseball

Send: Full text
How not to send: Email

Costs: A purchase is required. Potential contributors must purchase a sample copy ($7.50) before submitting.

Literary baseball magazine, publishing poems, fiction, prose, art, and book reviews relating to baseball. See website for full guidelines.

M298 Square Mile Magazine

Magazine
United Kingdom

https://squaremile.com
https://twitter.com/squaremile_com
https://www.facebook.com/squaremileuk/
https://instagram.com/squaremile_com

Magazine Publisher: Threadneedle Media

Nonfiction > *Articles*
   Arts; Books; Boxing; Cars; Comedy / Humour; Culture; Films; Fitness; Food and Drink; Formula One; Golf; Investments; London; Motorbikes; Music; Photography; Property / Real Estate; Pubs; Sport; TV; Technology; Travel; Whisky; Wine; Yachts

Luxury lifestyle magazine targeting wealthy men working in London's financial districts.

Editor: Martin Deeson

M299 The Stinging Fly

Magazine
PO Box 6016, Dublin 1
Ireland

stingingfly@gmail.com
submissions.stingingfly@gmail.com

https://stingingfly.org
https://www.facebook.com/StingingFly
http://twitter.com/stingingfly

Fiction in Translation > *Short Fiction*

Fiction
   Graphic Short Fiction; *Novel Excerpts*; *Short Fiction*

Nonfiction
   Essays: General
   Interviews: Books; Creative Writing

Poetry in Translation > *Any Poetic Form*

Poetry > *Any Poetic Form*

Closed to approaches.

A literary magazine, a book publisher, an education provider, and an online platform. Independent and not for profit. Aims to seek out, nurture, publish and promote the very best new Irish and international writing.

Publisher: Declan Meade

M300 Story Unlikely

Online Magazine
United States

storyunlikely@mailbox.org

https://www.storyunlikely.com

Fiction > *Short Fiction*
   General, and in particular: Adventure; Alternative History; Comedy / Humour; Crime; Cyberpunk; Fantasy; Horror; Literary; Magical Realism; Mystery; Romance; Science Fiction; Speculative; Suspense; Thrillers; Westerns

Nonfiction > *Short Nonfiction*
   Creative Nonfiction; Memoir; Narrative Nonfiction

How to send: Email; Online submission system

A monthly literary magazine with subscribers all over the globe featuring a new short story every month in our online magazine. We are simply looking for good stories, not author backgrounds, pedigrees, number of followers or how high your social credit score is. If you resonate with the idea of just getting back to telling good stories simply for the love of the game and the art of the craft, paying authors fairly and treating them like they're actually human, then you've come to the right place.

Editors: Danny Hankner; Megan Hankner

M301 Strange Horizons
Online Magazine
United States

management@strangehorizons.com

http://strangehorizons.com
https://strangehorizons.moksha.io/publication/strange-horizons/guidelines
https://www.facebook.com/groups/strangehorizons/
https://twitter.com/strangehorizons
https://www.patreon.com/strangehorizons

Fiction > *Short Fiction*
  Fantasy; Science Fiction; Slipstream; Speculative

Nonfiction
  Articles: Fantasy; Science Fiction; Slipstream; Speculative
  Essays: Fantasy; Science Fiction; Slipstream; Speculative
  Interviews: Fantasy; Science Fiction; Slipstream; Speculative
  Reviews: Fantasy; Science Fiction; Slipstream; Speculative

Poetry > *Any Poetic Form*
  Fantasy; Science Fiction; Slipstream; Speculative

Send: Full text
How to send: Moksha
How not to send: Email

Weekly online magazine of speculative fiction, poetry, and nonfiction on related topics. Submit via online submission system only.

M302 Strategic Finance
Magazine
United States

productpublications@imanet.org

https://sfmagazine.com

PROFESSIONAL > **Nonfiction** > *Articles*: Finance

Send: Submission form

Publishes articles that help financial professionals perform their jobs more effectively, advance their careers, grow personally and professionally, and make their organisations more profitable.

M303 Structo Magazine
Print Magazine; Online Magazine
United Kingdom

https://structomagazine.co.uk

Magazine Publisher: Structo Press

Fiction in Translation > *Short Fiction*

Fiction > *Short Fiction*

Poetry in Translation > *Any Poetic Form*

Poetry > *Any Poetic Form*

Closed to approaches.

Short stories of up to approximately 4,000 words will be considered, both original stories and new translations of non-English language texts; or up to three previously unpublished poems in English or new translations from other languages. Hybrid forms are welcome.

M304 Studio One
Print Magazine; Online Magazine
United States

studio1@csbsju.edu

https://digitalcommons.csbsju.edu/studio_one/
https://www.csbsju.edu/forms/MNDYVGOZ4Z

Fiction > *Short Fiction*

Nonfiction > *Short Nonfiction*: Creative Nonfiction

Poetry > *Any Poetic Form*

Closed to approaches.

Literary and visual arts magazine published each spring. Founded in 1976 as a print publication with a print run of between 400 and 600 copies. Also, online since 2012.

M305 Sunspot Literary Journal
Print Magazine; Online Magazine
Durham, NC
United States
Tel: +1 (919) 928-2245

Sunspotlit@gmail.com

https://sunspotlit.com
https://sunspotlit.submittable.com/submit

Fiction in Translation > *Short Fiction*

Fiction
  Graphic Novels; Graphic Short Fiction; Novelettes; Novellas; Short Fiction

Nonfiction > *Essays*

Poetry in Translation > *Any Poetic Form*

Poetry > *Any Poetic Form*

Scripts
  Film Scripts; Theatre Scripts

How to send: Submittable

Costs: Offers services that writers have to pay for; A fee is charged upon submission in some cases. Offers a poetry feedback service and competitions for which there is an entry fee.

Since launching in January of 2019, this journal has amplified diverse multinational voices. New works have been published in their original language side-by-side with English translations. Boundaries that exclude meaningful and important works have been broken by accepting extremely long-form pieces, a rarity in publishing today.

M306 The Supplement
Magazine
Atlantean Publishing, 4 Pierrot Steps, 71 Kursaal Way, Southend-on-Sea, Essex, SS1 2UY
United Kingdom

atlanteanpublishing@hotmail.com

https://atlanteanpublishing.wordpress.com/
https://atlanteanpublishing.fandom.com/wiki/The_Supplement

Book Publisher / Magazine Publisher: Atlantean Publishing

Fiction > *Short Fiction*

Nonfiction
  Articles: General
  News: Small Press
  Reviews: Books; Films

Poetry > *Any Poetic Form*

Send: Full text; Self-addressed stamped envelope (SASE)
How to send: Email; Post

Publishes small-press news and advertisements, reviews covering new publications from small presses, independent and mainstream books, films and much more beside, and various articles on an equally wide variety of topics – as well as the occasional poem or very short piece of fiction, often related to the non-fiction content.

Editor: David-John Tyrer

M307 Swimming Pool News
Magazine
United Kingdom

jon@aqua-publishing.co.uk

https://www.swimmingpoolnews.co.uk

Magazine Publisher: Aqua Publishing

PROFESSIONAL > **Nonfiction** > *Articles*
  Spas and Hot Tubs; Swimming Pools

How to send: Email

Informing the pool and spa industry since 1959. Covering the UK's wet leisure market, this magazine is the UK's longest running and most respected trade title. Produced bi-monthly, the magazine covers swimming pools, covers, enclosures, spas, swim spas, hot tubs, saunas, chemicals, accessories and much, much more!

M308 Tahoma Literary Review
Magazine
United States

poetry@tahomaliteraryreview.com
fiction@tahomaliteraryreview.com
nonfiction@tahomaliteraryreview.com

https://tahomaliteraryreview.com

Fiction > *Short Fiction*
  Experimental; Literary

Magazines

Nonfiction
  Essays: General, and in particular: Experimental; Lyric Essays
  Short Nonfiction: Narrative Nonfiction

Poetry
  Formal Poetry; *Free Verse*; *Long Form Poetry*

Closed to approaches.

Costs: A fee is charged upon submission; Offers services that writers have to pay for. $4 for poetry and flash prose; $5 for longer prose. Critiques available for an additional fee.

Publishes poetry, fiction, and nonfiction. Charges $4 submission fee for short works; $5 submission fee for long works. Submit online through online submission system.

M309 Takahe
Magazine
New Zealand

https://www.takahe.org.nz
https://takahemagazine.submittable.com/submit
https://twitter.com/takahemagazine

Fiction > *Short Fiction*: Literary

Nonfiction
  Essays: Cultural Criticism; New Zealand; South Pacific
  Reviews: Books

Poetry > *Any Poetic Form*

How to send: Submittable

Exists to foster and promote art and literature that represents the diverse voices of Aotearoa New Zealand within the global context. It does this by publishing innovative prose, poetry, art, and critique by emerging and established writers and artists.

Art Editor: Andrew Paul Wood

Fiction Editor: Zoë Meager

Poetry Editor: Erik Kennedy

M310 Take a Break's Take a Puzzle
Magazine
Media House, Peterborough Business Park, Lynch Wood, Peterborough, PE2 6EA
United Kingdom

https://www.puzzleshq.com/puzzles-magazines/mixed/take-a-puzzle/

Magazine: Take a Break
Magazine Publisher: Bauer Media Group

Nonfiction > *Puzzles*

Magazine of puzzles.

M311 Tears in the Fence
Magazine
Flats, Durweston Mill, Mill Lane, Durweston, Blandford Forum, Dorset, DT11 0QD
United Kingdom

tearsinthefence@gmail.com

https://tearsinthefence.com

Fiction > *Short Fiction*

Nonfiction
  Essays: General
  Interviews: General
  Reviews: General
  Short Nonfiction: Creative Nonfiction

Poetry
  Any Poetic Form; *Prose Poetry*

Send: Full text
How to send: Email attachment; In the body of an email
How not to send: PDF file email attachment

International literary magazine publishing poetry, fiction, prose poems, essays, translations, interviews and reviews. Publishes fiction as short as 100 words or as long as 3,500. Maximum 6 poems per poet per issue. No simultaneous or PDF submissions, or previously published material. Send submissions by email as both an attachment and in the body of the email.

M312 The Temz Review
Online Magazine
London, ON
Canada

thetemzreview@gmail.com

https://www.thetemzreview.com

Fiction > *Short Fiction*: Literary

Nonfiction
  Interviews: Literature
  Reviews: Literature

Poetry > *Any Poetic Form*

Send: Full text; Query
How to send: Moksha; Email

Quarterly online magazine. Submit one piece of fiction or creative nonfiction (or more than one if under 1,000 words) or 1-8 poems via online submission system. For reviews and interviews, send query by email.

M313 That's Life!
Magazine
The Lantern, 75 Hampstead Road, London, NW1 2PL
United Kingdom

stories@thatslife.co.uk

http://www.thatslife.co.uk

Types: Nonfiction
Formats: Articles; News
Subjects: Lifestyle
Markets: Adult

Publishes nonfiction true life stories. See website for details.

M314 Thin Air Magazine
Print Magazine
United States

https://thinairmagazine.org
https://www.instagram.com/thinairmagazine/
https://twitter.com/thinairmagazine
https://www.facebook.com/thinairmagazine/

Fiction > *Short Fiction*: Literary

Nonfiction > *Short Nonfiction*

Poetry > *Any Poetic Form*

Send: Full text
How to send: Submittable

Costs: A fee is charged upon submission. $3 per submission.

A non-profit, graduate-student-run, literary magazine. Submit up to three poems, or prose up to 3,000 words.

M315 Third Coast
Magazine
United States

editors@thirdcoastmagazine.com

http://thirdcoastmagazine.com
https://thirdcoastmagazine.submittable.com/submit
http://facebook.com/thirdcoastmagazine
http://twitter.com/thirdcoastmag
http://instagram.com/thirdcoastmag

Fiction > *Short Fiction*

Nonfiction > *Short Nonfiction*: Creative Nonfiction

Poetry > *Any Poetic Form*

Scripts > *Theatre Scripts*

Closed to approaches.

Costs: A fee is charged upon submission. $3 submission fee.

All submissions should be sent via Submittable, through the portals of their respective genres. All attachments sent by email will be deleted, and any submissions sent via postal mail or social media will not be read. Accepts simultaneous submissions, but not multiple submissions; please submit no more than one manuscript at a time. No previously published works.

M316 This England
Magazine
185 Fleet Street, Holborn, London, EC4A 2HS
United Kingdom
Tel: +44 (0) 20 7400 1083

thisengland@dcthomson.co.uk
editor@thisengland.co.uk

https://www.thisengland.co.uk
https://www.dcthomson.co.uk/brands/this-england/
https://www.facebook.com/ThisEnglandMagazine/

Newspaper Publisher / Magazine Publisher:
DC Thomson Media

Nonfiction > *Articles*
Culture; England; History; Nature

Poetry > *Any Poetic Form*: England

The quarterly magazine for everyone who loves England's scenery, heritage, history and people. Launched in 1968 with the light-hearted slogan, "as refreshing as a pot of tea" and with a mission of "poetry not politics", it is packed with absorbing articles, beautiful photography and uplifting stories and poems celebrating all that is best about England.

M317 The Threepenny Review
Magazine
PO Box 9131, Berkeley, CA 94709
United States

wlesser@threepennyreview.com

https://www.threepennyreview.com

Fiction > *Short Fiction*: Literary

Nonfiction > *Articles*
Arts; Culture; Literature

Poetry > *Any Poetic Form*

Closed to approaches.

National literary magazine with coverage of the visual and performing arts. Send complete MS by post with SASE or via online submission system. No previously published material, simultaneous submissions, or submissions from May to December. Prospective contributors are advised to read the magazine before submitting.

Editor: Wendy Lesser

M318 The Times Literary Supplement (TLS)
Magazine
1 London Bridge Street, London, SE1 9GF
United Kingdom

queries@the-tls.co.uk
camille.ralphs@the-tls.co.uk
letters@the-tls.co.uk

https://www.the-tls.co.uk
https://www.facebook.com/Times-Literary-Supplement-221115152587/
https://x.com/TheTLS
https://www.instagram.com/the.tls

Nonfiction
Articles: Arts; Books; Culture; Literature; Poetry as a Subject; Theatre
Essays: Arts; Books; Culture; Literature; Poetry as a Subject; Theatre
Reviews: Arts; Books; Literature; Poetry as a Subject; Theatre
Poetry > *Any Poetic Form*

Send: Query; Full text
How to send: Email; Post

Publishes coverage of the latest and most important publications, as well as current theatre, opera, exhibitions and film. Also publishes letters to the editor and poetry. Send books for review by post. For poetry, submit up to six poems by email or by post. Letters to the Editor may be sent by post or by email.

M319 Tolka
Magazine
Ireland

https://www.tolkajournal.org
https://www.instagram.com/tolkajournal/
https://twitter.com/tolkajournal

Fiction > *Short Fiction*: Autofiction

Nonfiction
Essays: Personal Essays
Short Nonfiction: Memoir; Travel

Closed to approaches.

Biannual literary journal of non-fiction: publishing essays, reportage, travel writing, auto-fiction, individual stories and the writing that flows in between.

M320 Tributaries
Online Magazine
United States

https://www.thefourthriver.com
https://4thriver.submittable.com/submit

Magazine: The Fourth River (**M131**)

Fiction in Translation > *Short Fiction*

Fiction > *Short Fiction*

Nonfiction in Translation > *Short Nonfiction*

Nonfiction > *Short Nonfiction*

Poetry in Translation > *Any Poetic Form*

Poetry > *Any Poetic Form*

How to send: Submittable

Weekly online publication, showcasing the brief and the inspiring, that which sustains us and takes us through unexpected courses. Each week we will feature one short piece on our website. Submit one poem or up to 500 words of fiction or nonfiction prose, translations in any genre, and hybridity that addresses the mission. Multiple submissions are not accepted. Simultaneous submissions are fine as long as you notify us immediately. We do not accept previously published work.

M321 The Tusculum Review
Magazine
P.O. Box 5113, 60 Shiloh Rd, Greeneville, TN 37745-0595
United States
Tel: +1 (423) 636-7300 ext. 5420

review@tusculum.edu

https://ttr.tusculum.edu

Fiction > *Short Fiction*: Literary

Nonfiction
Essays: General
Reviews: Books

Poetry > *Any Poetic Form*

Scripts > *Theatre Scripts*: Drama

Send: Full text; Self-addressed stamped envelope (SASE)
How to send: Submittable; Email; Post

Costs: A fee is charged for online submissions. $2.

We seek well-crafted writing that takes risks. We publish work in and between all genres: poetry, fiction, essays, and plays--we appreciate work in experimental and traditional modes. We accept prose submissions of less than 7,000 words (24 double-spaced pages) and poetry submissions under five pages. We publish scripts in the 10-minute format (10 pages) and book reviews of under two pages. Generally, no submissions by mail or email, but if Submittable is a hardship make contact by email. If you do not have internet access send submissions by post with SASE.

M322 UCity Review
Online Magazine
United States

editors@ucityreview.com

http://www.ucityreview.com
https://twitter.com/UCityReview

Poetry > *Any Poetic Form*

Closed to approaches.

Online magazine accepting submissions of poetry in February / March and August / September. Submit 10-12 poems in .doc or .docx format, by email.

M323 Ulster Business
Magazine
Belfast Telegraph House, 33 Clarendon Road, Clarendon Dock, Belfast, BT1 3BG
United Kingdom
Tel: +44 (0) 28 9568 5246

https://www.ulsterbusiness.com
https://www.belfasttelegraph.co.uk/business/ulsterbusiness/

Newspaper: Belfast Telegraph

PROFESSIONAL > **Nonfiction**
Articles: Business
Interviews: Business
News: Business

Business magazine for Ulster, publishing news, articles, features, and interviews with local businessmen.

M324 Uncut
Magazine
United Kingdom

editors@uncut.co.uk

http://www.uncut.co.uk
https://www.facebook.com/UncutMagazine/
https://www.instagram.com/uncut_magazine/
https://twitter.com/uncutmagazine/

Nonfiction
   Articles: Films; Music
   Reviews: Films; Music

Magazine covering film and music.

M325 Under the Radar
Magazine
United Kingdom

mail@ninearchespress.com

https://ninearchespress.com/magazine
https://ninearchespress.submittable.com/submit

Book Publisher: Nine Arches Press (**P257**)

Fiction > *Short Fiction*

Poetry > *Any Poetic Form*

How to send: Submittable

A magazine of new contemporary poetry and fiction. Submit up to six poems, or short fiction up to 2,500 words. Submit only previously unpublished work.

M326 Unfit Magazine
Magazine
United States

https://unfitmag.com

Fiction > *Short Fiction*: Science Fiction

Nonfiction > *Articles*
   Culture; Futurism; Media; Science Fiction; Science; Writing

A boundary-pushing platform for bold science fiction – stories that challenge convention, question the future, and ignite imagination. We publish a blend of original sci-fi stories from emerging and established voices; writing craft advice tailored for speculative fiction creators; futurism and thought experiments grounded in real-world science and philosophical inquiry; and coverage of sci-fi media and culture, from books and films to games and fan communities.

M327 Vagabond City
Online Magazine
United States

vagabondcitypoetry@gmail.com
vagabondcityfiction@gmail.com
vagabondcitynonfic@gmail.com
vagabondcityliterary@gmail.com

https://vagabondcitylit.com

Fiction > *Short Fiction*

Nonfiction
   Essays: Creative Nonfiction
   Interviews: General
   Reviews: Books

Poetry > *Any Poetic Form*

Send: Full text
How to send: Email

Electronic magazine featuring poetry, fiction, art, creative nonfiction and essays by marginalised creators. Also publishes book reviews and interviews. Submit up to five pieces at a time in the body of an email or as a Word file attachment. See website for full guidelines.

M328 Vallum
Magazine
5038 Sherbrooke West, P.O. Box 23077 CP Vendome Station, Montreal, Quebec, H4A 1T0
Canada

info@vallummag.com

https://vallummag.com
https://www.facebook.com/VallumMagazine
https://twitter.com/vallummag
https://www.instagram.com/vallummag/
https://soundcloud.com/vallum-magazine
https://www.youtube.com/channel/UCARH_nOH0vXwmpXSxzpgQZg

Nonfiction
   Essays; *Interviews*; *Reviews*
Poetry > *Any Poetic Form*: Contemporary

Closed to approaches.

Send 4-7 poems, essays of 4-6 pages, interviews of 3-5 pages, reviews of 1-3 pages, through online submission system only. No fiction, plays, movie scripts, memoir, or creative nonfiction. Check website for submission windows and themes.

M329 Vestal Review
Online Magazine
United States

info@vestalreview.org

https://www.vestalreview.net
https://vestalreview.submittable.com/submit
https://www.facebook.com/VestalReview
https://www.instagram.com/vestalreview/
https://twitter.com/VestalReview

Fiction > *Short Fiction*

Nonfiction
   Interviews; *Reviews*

Send: Full text
How to send: Submittable

Publishes flash fiction up to 500 words. Accepts submissions between February 1 and May 31, and between August 1 and November 30. Also accepts proposals for interviews and reviews.

M330 The Virginia Quarterly Review
Magazine
5 Boar's Head Lane, PO Box 400223, Charlottesville, VA 22904
United States

Tel: +1 (434) 924-3675
Fax: +1 (434) 924-1397

editors@vqronline.org

https://www.vqronline.org
https://www.facebook.com/vqreview
https://twitter.com/vqr

Fiction > *Short Fiction*

Nonfiction > *Short Nonfiction*
   Arts; Creative Nonfiction; Cultural Criticism; History; Literary Criticism; Politics

Poetry > *Any Poetic Form*

Does not want:

> *Fiction* > *Short Fiction*
> Fantasy; Romance; Science Fiction

Closed to approaches.

Strives to publish the best writing they can find. Has a long history of publishing accomplished and award-winning authors, but they also seek and support emerging writers.

M331 Virginia Wine & Country Life
Magazine
United States

Concierge@ivypublications.com
editor@ivylifeandstylemedia.com

https://wineandcountrylife.com
https://www.facebook.com/WineAndCountryLife/
https://www.instagram.com/wineandcountrylife/
https://www.pinterest.com/wclifeva/

Magazine Publisher: Ivy Life & Style Media

Nonfiction > *Articles*
   Architecture; Arts; Beer Making; Country Lifestyle; Entertainment; Farm Equipment; Food and Drink; Gardening; Interior Design; Literature; Music; Virginia; Wine

Send: Query
How to send: Email

We tell the stories of the makers and celebrate the art of living well in the heart of Virginia Wine Country. Each luxury print magazine highlights Virginia wine, farm-to-table food, architecture, gardening, the arts and elegant entertaining, as well as Virginia craft drinks.

M332 Virginia Wine & Country Weddings
Magazine
4282 Ivy Road, Charlottesville, VA 22903
United States
Tel: +1 (434) 984-4713

Concierge@ivypublications.com

https://wineandcountryweddings.com

Magazine Publisher: Ivy Life & Style Media

Nonfiction > *Articles*
Lifestyle; Virginia; Weddings

Send: Query
How not to send: Email

A uniquely curated magazine for creating the elegant country wedding in Jefferson's Virginia, one that will inspire couples as well as top event planners across the nation from New York City to Beverly Hills.

M333 Viz
Magazine
4th Floor, Harmsworth House, 13-15 Bouverie Street, London, EC4Y 8DP
United Kingdom

hello@metropolis.co.uk

https://viz.co.uk
https://www.facebook.com/VizComic/
https://twitter.com/vizcomic

Magazine Publisher: Diamond Publishing

Fiction > *Cartoons:* Comedy / Humour

Nonfiction > *Articles*
Comedy / Humour; Satire

Magazine of adult humour, including cartoons, spoof articles, etc.

M334 Vogue
Magazine
United Kingdom

https://www.vogue.co.uk
https://www.facebook.com/BritishVogue
https://www.instagram.com/britishvogue
https://twitter.com/BritishVogue
https://www.youtube.com/user/vogue

Media Company: Condé Nast

Nonfiction > *Articles*
Arts; Beauty; Fashion; Lifestyle

Upmarket women's magazine. Generally commissions required pieces from known writers.

M335 Waccamaw
Online Magazine
United States

http://waccamawjournal.com
https://www.facebook.com/Waccamaw-A-Journal-of-Contemporary-Literature-164290950299653/
https://twitter.com/waccamawjournal
https://www.instagram.com/waccamawjournal/

Book Publisher: Athenaeum Press

Fiction > *Short Fiction:* Literary

Nonfiction > *Essays*

Poetry > *Any Poetic Form*

Closed to approaches.

Online literary journal publishing poems, stories, and essays. Submit prose up to 6,000 words or 3-5 poems between August 1 and September 8 annually. Submit via online submission system only.

M336 The Wallace Stevens Journal
Magazine
University of Antwerp, Prinsstraat 13, 2000 Antwerp
Belgium

https://www.press.jhu.edu/journals/wallace-stevens-journal

ACADEMIC > **Nonfiction**
Articles: Biography; Literary Criticism; Poetry as a Subject
Essays: Biography; Literary Criticism; Poetry as a Subject
News: Literature
Reviews: Books

ADULT > **Poetry** > *Any Poetic Form*

Send: Full text
How to send: Word file email attachment

Publishes articles and essays on all aspects of Wallace Stevens' poetry and life. Also accepts poetry inspired by the poet. See website for full submission guidelines.

Editor: Bart Eeckhout

M337 Wallpaper
Print Magazine; Online Magazine
United Kingdom

contact@wallpaper.com

https://www.wallpaper.com
https://www.instagram.com/wallpapermag
https://twitter.com/wallpapermag
https://www.facebook.com/wallpapermagazine
https://www.pinterest.co.uk/wallpapermag/
https://flipboard.com/@wallpapermag
https://foursquare.com/wallpapermag

Magazine Publisher: Future

Nonfiction > *Articles*
Architecture; Arts; Beauty; Design; Fashion; Technology; Transport

Magazine of architecture, design, art, entertaining, beauty & grooming, transport, technology, fashion, and watches and jewellery.

M338 Wasafiri
Magazine
c/o School of English and Drama, Queen Mary, University of London, Mile End Road, London, E1 4NS
United Kingdom
Tel: +44 (0) 20 7882 2686

wasafiri@qmul.ac.uk

https://www.wasafiri.org
https://www.facebook.com/wasafiri.magazine
https://twitter.com/Wasafirimag
https://www.youtube.com/channel/UC4J-lxAIL8iBiaRR2AOpGFg
https://www.linkedin.com/groups/8343914/profile

Fiction > *Short Fiction:* Literary

Nonfiction
Articles: Culture; Literature
Essays: Culture; Literature

Poetry > *Any Poetic Form*

Send: Full text
How to send: Online submission system

The indispensable journal of contemporary African, Asian Black British, Caribbean and transnational literatures.

In over fifteen years of publishing, this magazine has changed the face of contemporary writing in Britain. As a literary magazine primarily concerned with new and postcolonial writers, it continues to stress the diversity and range of black and diasporic writers world-wide. It remains committed to its original aims: to create a definitive forum for the voices of new writers and to open up lively spaces for serious critical discussion not available elsewhere. It is Britain's only international magazine for Black British, African, Asian and Caribbean literatures. Get the whole picture, get the magazine at the core of contemporary international literature today.

Submit via online submissions portal only (see website).

M339 West Branch
Magazine
Stadler Center, Bucknell University, 1 Dent Drive, Lewisburg, PA 17837
United States

westbranch@bucknell.edu

https://westbranch.blogs.bucknell.edu

Fiction > *Short Fiction*

Nonfiction
Essays; Reviews

Poetry > *Any Poetic Form*

Closed to approaches.

Send all submissions via online submission system, between August 1 and April 1 annually.

M340 WestWard Quarterly
Magazine
PO Box 375, Genoa, IL 60135
United States
Tel: +1 (800) 440-4043

editorwwq@mail.com

https://www.wwquarterly.com

Poetry > *Any Poetic Form*

How to send: Email; Post

We accept all styles of poetry and look for good imagery and grammar and a fresh outlook. If rhyming, we look for consistency and natural word order in the rhyme scheme. If metrical, we look for consistent scansion or "beat." If free verse, we look for some kind of rhythm, flow, and harmony that makes a poem differ from prose. We do not publish material with a negative or cynical outlook (possibly excepting in a humorous vein) or material with profanity or crudity. Additionally, poetry that is obscure (with references or meanings not readily accessible to most readers) is not likely to be acceptable for this magazine.

M341 Wet Grain
Print Magazine
United Kingdom

wetgrainpoetry@protonmail.com

https://wetgrainpoetry.co.uk

Nonfiction
 Essays: Poetry as a Subject
 Interviews: Poetry as a Subject
 Reviews: Poetry as a Subject

Poetry in Translation > *Any Poetic Form*

Poetry > *Any Poetic Form*

Closed to approaches.

Annual print magazine for new poetry in English. Since 2020, the magazine has included the work of emerging poets alongside recipients of awards including the Pulitzer, a MacArthur Fellowship, the Pushcart Prize, the German Book Prize, and the Eric Gregory. Each issue, selected poets are invited to contribute a short piece of commentary on a poem included in the issue. Also publishes interviews, reviews, and essays.

M342 Windsor Review
Magazine
Department of English, University of Windsor, 401 Sunset Ave, Windsor, Ontario, N9B 3P4
Canada

thewindsorreview@uwindsor.ca

https://ojs.uwindsor.ca
https://ojs.uwindsor.ca/index.php/windsor_review

Fiction > *Short Fiction*

Nonfiction
 Essays: Literature
 Short Nonfiction: Creative Nonfiction

Poetry > *Any Poetic Form*

Closed to approaches.

Features poetry, fiction, creative nonfiction, and review essays. We welcome material from all writers, with a focus on new and emerging voices.

M343 Wine Enthusiast
Magazine
United States

https://www.wineenthusiast.com
https://www.instagram.com/wineenthusiast/
https://www.facebook.com/WineEnthusiast
https://twitter.com/WineEnthusiast
https://www.pinterest.com/wineenthusiast/
https://www.tiktok.com/@wineenthusiast
https://www.youtube.com/@WineEnthusiastCatalog

Nonfiction > *Articles*: Wine

For more than 40 years we've been the premier source for all things wine, creating and delivering unique wine lifestyle products and content that inspires and empowers everyone to enjoy wine to its fullest. We started with a humble mission to make the wine experience accessible to everyone and have grown into a dynamic commerce and media company regarded around the world for our unmatched passion and expertise.

Editor: Tim Moriarty

M344 The Yale Review
Magazine
United States

theyalereview@yale.edu

https://yalereview.yale.edu
https://www.facebook.com/YaleReview/
https://www.instagram.com/yalereview/
https://twitter.com/YaleReview

Fiction > *Short Fiction*: Literary

Nonfiction > *Essays*
 Arts; Cultural Criticism; Films; History; Literary Criticism; Memoir; Music; Politics; TV

Poetry > *Any Poetic Form*

Closed to approaches.

Opens for submissions of poetry, nonfiction, and fiction in September of each year, via online submission system. Accepts pitches for essays and criticism on a rolling basis by email.

Editor: Meghan O'Rourke

M345 Yankee Magazine
Magazine
United States

https://newengland.com
https://www.facebook.com/YankeeMagazine/
https://www.instagram.com/yankeemagazine/
https://www.pinterest.com/yankeemagazine

Nonfiction > *Articles*
 Arts; Culture; Current Affairs; Food; History; Houses and Homes; Lifestyle; New England; Travel

Magazine covering the finest that New England has to offer, from home, food and travel coverage to arts and culture, current events, and history. Drawing readers from across generations and around the country, this magazine is New England's storyteller: exploring the future, present, and past of this fabled region, and sharing the lifestyle secrets that only the locals know. Through beautiful photos, artwork, and unforgettable stories, the magazine paints a portrait of New England that feels like home to all who live here and inspires people everywhere to discover the New England they dream of.

M346 Yellow Mama Webzine
Magazine
United States

crosmus@hotmail.com

http://blackpetalsks.tripod.com/yellowmama

Types: Fiction
Subjects: Horror; Literary
Markets: Adult

Send: Full text
How to send: Email

Webzine publishing fiction and poetry. Seeks cutting edge, hardboiled, horror, literary, noir, psychological / horror. No fanfiction, romance, swords & sorcery, fantasy, or erotica. Send submissions by email. See website for full guidelines.

M347 The Yorkshire Dalesman
Magazine
The Gatehouse, Skipton Castle, Skipton, North Yorkshire, BD23 1AL
United Kingdom
Tel: +44 (0) 1756 701033

https://www.dalesman.co.uk
https://www.facebook.com/yorkshire.dalesman
https://twitter.com/The_Dalesman
https://www.youtube.com/user/TheYorkshireDalesman
https://www.instagram.com/dalesmanmagazine/

Book Publisher / Magazine Publisher: Dalesman Publishing Co. Ltd

Nonfiction > *Articles*: Yorkshire

Magazine publishing material of Yorkshire interest.

Editor: Mick Smith

M348 Yorkshire Life
Magazine
United Kingdom

https://www.greatbritishlife.co.uk/magazines/yorkshire/

Magazine Publisher: Great British Life

Nonfiction
 Articles: Culture; Food and Drink; Houses and Homes; Lifestyle; Outdoor Activities; Travel; Walking; Yorkshire
 Interviews: Yorkshire

Magazine covering the people, places, history, arts, food and events of Yorkshire.

M349 Yorkshire Women's Life Magazine
Print Magazine
PO Box 113, Leeds, LS8 2WX
United Kingdom

ywleditorial@btinternet.com

https://www.yorkshirewomenslife.co.uk

Nonfiction > *Articles*
  Fashion; Lifestyle; Travel; Wellbeing; Women's Issues; Yorkshire

We believe every woman has a right to be who she wants to be; that's why our magazine is inclusive to everyone. Our title encourages and supports new women writers by providing a platform via the magazine to profile new women's writing. The title works with new writers while covering women focused issues both regionally and internationally.

M350 Yours
Magazine
The Lantern, 75 Hampstead Road, London, NW1 2PL
United Kingdom

yours@bauermedia.co.uk

https://www.yours.co.uk
https://www.facebook.com/Yoursmagazine
https://twitter.com/yoursmagazine
https://www.pinterest.com/yoursmagazine/

Magazine Publisher: Bauer Media Group

Nonfiction > *Articles*
  Activities; Beauty; Celebrity; Crafts; Fashion; Fitness; Food; Gardening; Health; Leisure; Lifestyle; Nostalgia; Pets; Relationships; TV; Travel; Wellbeing; Women's Interests

Magazine for women over 50. Publishes tips and expert advice on a range of topics from travel to financial guidance as well as discovering the latest fashion trends, beauty, and health tips. Also exclusive celebrity interviews and recipes for healthy meals or hearty treats.

M351 Yours Fiction – Women's Special Series
Print Magazine
The Lantern, 75 Hampstead Road, London, NW1 2PL
United Kingdom

yours@bauermedia.co.uk

https://www.yours.co.uk/yours-fiction/

Magazine Publisher: Bauer Media Group

Fiction > *Short Fiction*
  General, and in particular: Ghost Stories; Historical Fiction; Mystery; Romance; Saga

Closed to approaches.

Publishes 26 stories per issue. Stories can be of any genre, but we especially keen on romance, murder mystery, historical fiction, ghost stories, sagas and stories to make you smile. Any length between 450 and 2,700 words.

M352 Zoetrope: All-Story
Magazine
916 Kearny Street, San Francisco, CA 94133
United States

info@all-story.com

https://store.all-story.com

Fiction > *Short Fiction*

Closed to approaches.

Magazine of short fiction.

M353 Zone 3
Magazine
United States

https://www.zone3press.com
https://ceca.submittable.com/submit

Book Publisher / Magazine Publisher: Zone 3 Press

Fiction > *Short Fiction*
  Contemporary; Literary

Nonfiction > *Short Nonfiction*
  Contemporary; Creative Nonfiction; Literary

Poetry > *Any Poetic Form*

Closed to approaches.

Costs: A fee is charged upon submission. $3.

Publishes fiction, poetry, and creative nonfiction. Accepts submissions through online submission system between August 1 and April 1 annually. $3 submission fee.

Book Publishers

For the most up-to-date listings of these and hundreds of other book publishers, visit https://www.firstwriter.com/publishers

To claim your free access to the site, please see the back of this book.

P001 404 Ink
Book Publisher
United Kingdom

hello@404ink.com

https://www.404ink.com
https://www.facebook.com/404ink/
http://instagram.com/404ink
https://twitter.com/404Ink

Fiction
 Novels; *Short Fiction Collections*
Nonfiction > *Nonfiction Books*
 General, and in particular: Inspirational; Politics; Social Issues

Poetry > *Poetry Collections*

Closed to approaches.

Publishes fiction, non-fiction, short stories and poetry. No children's books. Particularly likes humour, gritty women-led fiction, anti-heroes, parodies, the weird and wonderful, hard-hitting social issue non-fiction, inspirational stories and accessible political engagement. Would quite like to publish a crime book that's an unusual take on the genre.

P002 ABC-CLIO
Book Publisher
1385 Broadway Fifth Floor, New York, NY 10018
United States
Tel: +1 (800) 368-6868
Fax: +1 (805) 968-1911

CustomerService@abc-clio.com

https://www.abc-clio.com/
https://www.facebook.com/ABCCLIO
https://twitter.com/ABC_CLIO
https://www.youtube.com/user/ABCCLIOLive
https://www.linkedin.com/company/abc-clio/

Book Publisher: Bloomsbury Academic (**P053**)

ACADEMIC > **Nonfiction** > *Reference*
 General, and in particular: History; Sociology

Publishes academic reference works and periodicals primarily on topics such as history and social sciences for educational and public library settings.

Publishing Imprints: ABC-CLIO / Greenwood; Libraries Unlimited; Praeger

P003 Able Muse Press
Book Publisher
United States

submission@ablemuse.com

https://www.ablemusepress.com
https://www.facebook.com/groups/eratosphere.ablemuse/
https://twitter.com/ablemuse
https://www.youtube.com/user/ablemuse
https://www.instagram.com/ablemusepress/
https://www.linkedin.com/in/alex-pepple-8657359/
https://www.pinterest.com/ablemuse/

Fiction > *Novels*

Nonfiction > *Nonfiction Books*

Poetry > *Poetry Collections*

Send: Full text
How to send: Online submission system; Email attachment
How not to send: In the body of an email

Publishes fiction and poetry. Prefers submissions via online form, but will also accept submissions by email with ms attached as a separate document. Do not paste material in the body of the email. See website for full details.

P004 Adventure Books by Vertebrate Publishing
Book Publisher
Omega Court, 352 Cemetery Road, Sheffield, S11 8FT
United Kingdom
Tel: +44 (0) 114 267 9277

info@adventurebooks.com

https://www.adventurebooks.com
https://twitter.com/VertebratePub
https://www.facebook.com/vertebratepublishing
https://www.instagram.com/vertebrate_publishing

Nonfiction > *Nonfiction Books*
 Climbing; Gravel Cycling; Outdoor / Wild Swimming; Running; Stand-Up Paddleboarding (SUP); Walking

Send: Query; Outline; Market info; Author bio; Table of contents; Writing sample
How to send: Email

Publishes books on climbing; walking; gravel cycling; running; outdoor swimming; and stand-up paddleboarding (SUP). Looking for books which inspire and equip people to plan their own adventures, with great photos and well-researched information; and practical guides to training, technique, nutrition; and injury in the above areas. Specifically, we'd currently love to hear from you if you have a proposal for: an outdoor swimming guide to Wales or London and the Southeast; gravel cycling guides; books aimed at climbing/running/cycling training.

Publishing Imprint: Sandstone Press (**P323**)

P005 Afsana Press
Book Publisher
United Kingdom

submission@afsanapress.uk

https://www.afsana-press.com
https://www.facebook.com/afsanapress/
https://x.com/afsana_press
https://www.linkedin.com/in/afsana-press-53592727b/
https://www.instagram.com/afsana_press/

Fiction > *Novels*
 General, and in particular: Climate Science; Culture; Gender; Immigration; Literary; Politics; Refugees; Social Issues; Social Justice

Closed to approaches.

We will consider fiction of any genre, but our preference inclines towards the literary. Our stories have a direct relation to social, political or cultural issues in countries and communities around the world, often exploring issues relating to migration and refugees, climate change, gender and social justice.

P006 Afterglow Books
Publishing Imprint
United States

https://bookpages.harlequin.com/afterglow-books/
https://harlequin.submittable.com/submit

Fiction > *Novels*: Romance

Does not want:

> Fiction > *Novels*
> Historical Romance; Romantic Suspense; Supernatural / Paranormal Romance

Send: Full text; Synopsis; Writing sample
How to send: Submittable

Depth, relatability and sizzling spice, too: these characters are determined to live their best lives – and find the romance that makes them feel seen, unapologetically. In the pages of these books, characters from all walks of life, all types of diverse identities, will pursue their dreams and discover love isn't far behind. Because everyone deserves a happily ever after that's true to who they are. Seeks books that are: proof that happy endings are meant for everyone; explicitly sexy with chemistry that pops; unique plots and strong emotional conflicts that embrace the world around us; and the journey of complex characters who aren't afraid to make mistakes or stand up for what they believe in. No paranormal, romantic suspense, dark or historical romances, or billionaires at this time.

P007 Albert Whitman & Company
Book Publisher
250 South Northwest Highway, Suite 320, Park Ridge, Illinois 60068
United States
Tel: +1 (800) 255-7675
Fax: +1 (847) 581-0039

submissions@albertwhitman.com

https://www.albertwhitman.com
https://www.facebook.com/AlbertWhitmanCompany
https://twitter.com/albertwhitman
https://instagram.com/albertwhitman
https://www.pinterest.com/albertwhitmanco/

CHILDREN'S > Fiction
  Middle Grade; *Picture Books*
YOUNG ADULT > Fiction > *Novels*

Send: Query; Full text
How to send: Email attachment

Publishes picture books, middle-grade fiction, and young adult novels. Will consider fiction and nonfiction manuscripts for picture books for children ages 1 to 8, up to 1,000 words; middle-grade novels up to 35,000 words for children up to the age of 12; and young adult novels up to 70,000 words for ages 12-18. See website for full submission guidelines.

Editor-in-Chief: Kathleen Tucker

P008 Algonquin Books
Publishing Imprint
1290 Avenue of the Americas, New York, NY 10104
United States

Marisol.Salaman@hbgusa.com

https://www.hachettebookgroup.com/imprint/workman-publishing-company/algonquin-books/
http://twitter.com/algonquinbooks
http://facebook.com/AlgonquinBooks
http://instagram.com/algonquinbooks

Fiction > *Novels*

Nonfiction > *Nonfiction Books*

Closed to approaches.

Publishes both fiction and nonfiction. Does not accept unsolicited submissions.

P009 Allen & Unwin
Book Publisher
SYDNEY:, 83 Alexander St, Crows Nest, NSW 2065, MELBOURNE:, 406 Albert Street, East Melbourne, Vic 3002
Australia
Tel: +61 (0) 2 8425 0100

fridaypitch@allenandunwin.com

https://www.allenandunwin.com
https://www.allenandunwin.com/about/submission-guidelines/the-friday-pitch
https://www.facebook.com/AllenandUnwinBooks
https://twitter.com/AllenAndUnwin
http://instagram.com/allenandunwin

ADULT
  Fiction > *Novels*
  Nonfiction > *Nonfiction Books*
CHILDREN'S > Fiction
  Board Books; *Chapter Books*; *Early Readers*; *Middle Grade*; *Picture Books*
YOUNG ADULT > Fiction > *Novels*

Send: Query; Synopsis; Writing sample
How to send: Email

Publisher with offices in Australia, New Zealand, and the UK. Accepts queries by email. See website for detailed instructions.

Book Publisher: Murdoch Books Australia (**P249**)

P010 Alternating Current Press
Book Publisher
2525 Arapahoe Ave, Ste E4 #162, Boulder, CO 80302
United States

info@altcurrentpress.com

https://altcurrentpress.com

ADULT
  Fiction > *Novels*
  Nonfiction > *Nonfiction Books*
CHILDREN'S > Fiction > *Chapter Books*

Indie press dedicated to publishing and promoting incredible literature that challenges readers and has an innate sense of self, timelessness, and atmosphere:

Online Magazine: The Coil

P011 Amber Books Ltd
Book Publisher
United House, North Road, London, N7 9DP
United Kingdom
Tel: +44 (0) 20 7520 7600

editorial@amberbooks.co.uk
enquiries@amberbooks.co.uk

https://www.amberbooks.co.uk
https://www.facebook.com/amberbooks
https://twitter.com/AmberBooks
https://www.pinterest.co.uk/amberbooksltd/
https://www.instagram.com/amberbooksltd/

Nonfiction > *Illustrated Books*
  General, and in particular: History; Military

Send: Synopsis; Table of contents; Writing sample; Author bio
Don't send: Full text
How to send: Post; Email

Publishes illustrated nonfiction books in a wide range of formats and subject areas for an international audience. Particularly interested in submissions on military topics, but not exclusively so, and welcomes good ideas on any nonfiction subject suitable for treatment as an illustrated book.

P012 American Mystery Classics
Publishing Imprint
United States

https://penzlerpublishers.com/product-category/american-mystery-classics/

Book Publisher: Penzler Publishers (**P282**)

Fiction > *Novels*: Mystery

Dedicated to reissuing classic American mystery fiction in new hardcover and paperback editions.

P013 And Other Stories
Book Publisher
Central Library, Surrey Street, Sheffield, S1 1XZ
United Kingdom

info@andotherstories.org

https://www.andotherstories.org
https://twitter.com/andothertweets
https://www.facebook.com/AndOtherStoriesBooks/
https://www.instagram.com/andotherpics/

Fiction in Translation > *Novels*: Literary

Fiction > *Novels*: Literary

Nonfiction in Translation > *Nonfiction Books*: Narrative Nonfiction

Nonfiction > *Nonfiction Books*: Narrative Nonfiction

Poetry > *Poetry Collections*

How to send: Through a literary agent

Our focus has always been on literary fiction, but increasingly on poetry and narrative/literary kinds of non-fiction too. We publish mainly contemporary writing, which for us means written in the last 50 years or so.

P014 Andersen Press Ltd
Book Publisher
6 Coptic Street, London, WC1A 1NH
United Kingdom

andersenpublicity@penguinrandomhouse.co.uk

https://www.andersenpress.co.uk
https://x.com/andersenpress
https://www.facebook.com/andersenpress

CHILDREN'S > Fiction > *Picture Books*

Closed to approaches.

Publishes rhyming stories, but no poetry, adult fiction, fiction for older children, nonfiction, or short story collections. Accepts submissions through literary agents only.

P015 Andrews McMeel Publishing
Book Publisher
ATTN: Submissions (Please specify Books or Calendars), 1130 Walnut St., Kansas City, MO 64106
United States

corpcommunications@amuniversal.com

https://publishing.andrewsmcmeel.com

ADULT
 Nonfiction
  Gift Books: General
  Nonfiction Books: Comedy / Humour; Food and Drink
  Puzzles: General

 Poetry > *Poetry Collections*

CHILDREN'S
 Fiction > *Middle Grade*
 Nonfiction > *Nonfiction Books*

How to send: Online submission system; Post

A leading publisher of poetry, inspiration, humor, and children's books and licensed, popular calendars. We publish as many as 150 books and 200 calendars annually. We are happy to consider submissions from creators and literary agents via email or regular mail, but materials submitted by any other means will not be considered. Please keep in mind that we receive a high volume of submissions and we do not answer calls or visits regarding submissions.

P016 Anhinga Press
Book Publisher
PO Box 3665, Tallahassee, FL 32315
United States

info@anhinga.org

http://www.anhinga.org
https://twitter.com/Anhinga_Press
https://www.facebook.com/anhingapress

Poetry
 Chapbooks; *Poetry Collections*

A non-profit, 501(c)3 operating in Tallahassee, Florida. Since 1974 our mission has been to bring quality poetry to a broad audience by publishing poetry, sponsoring poetry events and educational activities, participating in writers conferences, working with area colleges, making our books available as textbooks for students, and networking with other arts organizations as a good citizen of the arts community and the community at large.

P017 Anvil Press Publishers
Book Publisher
P.O. Box 3008, MPO, Vancouver, B.C., V6B 3X5
Canada
Tel: +1 (604) 876-8710

info@anvilpress.com

https://www.anvilpress.com
https://www.facebook.com/Anvil-Press-115437275199047/
https://www.twitter.com/anvilpress
https://www.instagram.com/anvilpress_publishers/

Fiction > *Novels*

Nonfiction > *Nonfiction Books*
 Arts; Photography

Poetry > *Poetry Collections*

Scripts > *Theatre Scripts*: Drama

Send: Query; Synopsis; Writing sample; Author bio
Don't send: Full text
How to send: Email

Publisher designed to discover and nurture Canadian literary talent. Considers work from Canadian authors only.

Editor: Brian Kaufman

P018 April Gloaming
Book Publisher
PO Box 2131, Nashville, TN 37011
United States

inquiries.aprilgloaming@gmail.com

https://aprilgloaming.com
https://aprilgloamingpublishing.submittable.com/submit
https://www.facebook.com/aprilgloaming
https://x.com/April_Gloaming
https://www.instagram.com/aprilgloamingpublishing/
https://www.youtube.com/channel/UCeV1j5608nTf2yD4nw-rA9A

Fiction
 Graphic Novels; *Novels*
Nonfiction > *Nonfiction Books*: Memoir

Poetry > *Poetry Collections*

Nashville-based independent press that aims to capture and better understand the Southern soul, Southern writing, and the Southern holler.

P019 Arachne Press
Book Publisher
100 Grierson Road, London, SE23 1NX
United Kingdom
Tel: +44 (0) 20 8699 0206

https://arachnepress.com
https://arachnepress.submittable.com/submit
https://www.facebook.com/ArachnePress

Fiction > *Short Fiction Collections*

Poetry > *Poetry Collections*

Closed to approaches.

A small, independent publisher of award-winning short fiction, award winning poetry and (very) select non-fiction, for adults and children. Only accepts responses to call outs (mainly for inclusion in anthologies). No AI generated or AI assisted work. See website for full details and current calls.

P020 Arcadia Publishing
Book Publisher
United States

https://www.arcadiapublishing.com
https://www.facebook.com/ArcadiaPublishing
https://twitter.com/arcadiapub
http://pinterest.com/imagesofamerica/
https://www.instagram.com/arcadia_publishing

ADULT
 Fiction > *Novels*

 Nonfiction
  Nonfiction Books: Activities; American History; Antiques; Architecture; Arts; Autobiography; Biography; Business; Collectibles; Comedy / Humour; Cookery; Crafts; Crime; Design; Economics; Education; Engineering; Family; Fitness; Games; Gardening; Health; History; Hobbies; Houses and Homes; Language; Legal; Leisure; Literary Criticism; Medicine; Mind, Body, Spirit; Music; Nature; Performing Arts; Pets; Philosophy; Photography; Politics; Psychology; Recreation; Relationships; Religion; Science; Self Help; Sociology; Sport; Technology; Transport; Travel
  Reference: General

 Poetry > *Poetry Collections*

CHILDREN'S
Fiction
Board Books; *Chapter Books*; *Early Readers*; *Middle Grade*; *Picture Books*
Nonfiction > *Nonfiction Books*

YOUNG ADULT > Fiction > *Novels*

How to send: Online submission system

Publishes books on over 70 different subjects of American history, including stories of true crime and passion in their crime series, past wars in military history books, and books on the history of sports. No fiction submissions.

Book Publisher: Pelican Publishing Company

P021 Arte Publico Press
Book Publisher
University of Houston, 4902 Gulf Fwy, Bldg. 19, Room 100, Houston, TX 77204-2004
United States

submapp@uh.edu

https://artepublicopress.com
https://www.facebook.com/artepublico/
https://twitter.com/artepublico
https://www.instagram.com/artepublico/
https://www.pinterest.com/artepublico/
http://artepublicopress.tumblr.com/

Fiction > *Novels*
Central America; Culture; History; Politics; South America

Nonfiction > *Nonfiction Books*
Central America; Culture; History; Politics; South America

Send: Writing sample
How to send: Online submission system
How not to send: Post

Publisher of contemporary and recovered literature by US Hispanic authors.

Publishing Imprint: Pinata Books

P022 Asabi Publishing
Book Publisher
United States

https://www.asabipublishing.com

ADULT
Fiction > *Novels*
Crime; Erotic; Historical Fiction; Horror; LGBTQIA; Mystery; Noir; Thrillers

Nonfiction > *Nonfiction Books*
Autobiography; Biography; Memoir; Narrative Nonfiction; Outdoor Survival Skills; Travel

CHILDREN'S
Fiction > *Novels*: Culture

Nonfiction > *Nonfiction Books*
Cultural History; Games

TEEN
Fiction > *Novels*: Culture

Nonfiction > *Nonfiction Books*
Cultural History; Games

YOUNG ADULT
Fiction > *Novels*: Culture

Nonfiction > *Nonfiction Books*
Cultural History; Games

Check website for submission windows. Submit query letter / proposal through form on website. No religious or spiritual books of any kind.

P023 Astra Publishing House
Book Publisher
United States

https://astrapublishinghouse.com/

Closed to approaches.

Dedicated to publishing books for children and adults that celebrate excellent storytelling, have a strong point of view, and introduce readers to new perspectives about their everyday lives as well as the lives of others.

Publishing Imprints: Astra House; Astra Young Readers; Calkins Creek; DAW Books; Hippo Park; Kane Press (**P202**); MineditionUS; Toon Books; WordSong

P024 Aurora Metro Press
Book Publisher
80 Hill Rise, Richmond, TW10 6UB
United Kingdom
Tel: +44 (0) 20 8948 1427

submissions@aurametro.com
editor@aurametro.com

https://aurametro.com
https://www.facebook.com/AuroraMetroBooks/
https://twitter.com/aurametro

ADULT
Fiction
Novels; *Short Fiction*
Nonfiction > *Nonfiction Books*
Arts; Biography; History; Popular Culture; Travel; Wellbeing

Scripts
Film Scripts; *Theatre Scripts*
YOUNG ADULT > Fiction > *Novels*

Send: Query; Synopsis; Author bio; Writing sample

Publishes adult fiction, YA fiction, drama, and non-fiction biography and books about the arts and popular culture.

P025 Autumn Publishing Ltd
Publishing Imprint
Cottage Farm, Mears Ashby Road, Sywell, Northants, NN6 0BJ
United Kingdom
Tel: +44 (0) 1604 741116

customerservice@igloobooks.com

https://autumnpublishing.co.uk

Book Publisher: Igloo Books Limited (**P184**)

CHILDREN'S > Nonfiction
Activity Books: General
Nonfiction Books: English; Health; Mathematics; Nature; Science

Deals in books for babies and toddlers, activity books, early learning books, and sticker books. Publisher's philosophy is that children should enjoy learning with books, and to this end combines activity and learning by turning simple workbooks into activity books, allowing children to learn whilst they play.

Publishing Imprint: Byeway Books

P026 AUWA Books
Publishing Imprint
United States

https://auwabooks.com

Book Publisher: Macmillan Publishers

P027 Backbeat Books
Book Publisher
United States

BackbeatSubmissions@rowman.com

http://www.backbeatbooks.com

Book Publisher: The Globe Pequot Press (**P145**)

Nonfiction > *Nonfiction Books*
Autobiography; Biography; Business; History; Music; Musical Instruments

Send: Query; Outline; Table of contents; Writing sample; Author bio; Market info; Marketing plan
How to send: Email; Post

Founded in 1991, we have grown to become the world's leading imprint dedicated solely to music. Passionate fans and musicians know to look to our brand to find the highest quality titles on their favorite topics. Specifically, our books are known for their depth, spirit, and authority, offering a diverse range of titles—from biographies and memoirs, critical examinations, and histories to authoritative volumes on musical instruments and instruction—covering all areas of popular music and beyond.

Editor: Mike Edison

P028 Bad Betty
Book Publisher
United Kingdom

info@badbettypress.com
littlebetty@badbettypress.com
submissions@badbettypress.com

https://badbettypress.com
https://www.facebook.com/badbettypress/
https://x.com/badbettypress
https://www.instagram.com/badbettypress/

Poetry > *Poetry Collections*
Publishes collections of new poems in book and pamphlet form. Send up to 10 pages by email during June for pamphlets or July for full collections.

P029 Baen Books
Book Publisher
PO Box 1188, Wake Forest, NC 27588
United States
Tel: +1 (919) 570-1640
Fax: +1 (919) 570-1644

https://www.baen.com
https://www.baen.com/slush/index/submit
https://twitter.com/BaenBooks

Fiction > *Novels*
  Fantasy; Science Fiction

Send: Full text
How to send: Online submission system
How not to send: Email

Publishes only science fiction and fantasy. Interested in science fiction with powerful plots and solid scientific and philosophical underpinnings. For fantasy, any magical system must be both rigorously coherent and integral to the plot. Work must at least strive for originality. Prefers manuscripts between 100,000 and 130,000 words. No submissions via email. Full manuscripts can be submitted online, in rtf format, via an electronic submission system. Postal submission accepted from those who are unable to submit electronically. Do not send material generated by AI, or material which derives from other creative people (e.g. fan fiction, media tie-in fiction, fiction related to properties created by others) without the express written permission of the copyright owners.

P030 Bald and Bonkers Network LLC
Book Publisher
United States
Tel: +1 (208) 421-2330

admin@baldandbonkers.net

https://baldandbonkers.net
https://www.facebook.com/BaldandBonkers
https://twitter.com/PRF_Dakota
https://www.instagram.com/baldandbonkersnetwork/
https://baldandbonkersnetwork.tumblr.com/
https://www.youtube.com/c/BaldandBonkers

Fiction > *Novels*

Nonfiction > *Nonfiction Books*

Poetry > *Any Poetic Form*

How to send: Email

Founded on the premise of helping unknown authors gain the exposure they would from big time publishing outlets. Every author accepted is guaranteed one-on-one attention and an interview at book launch to help gain immediate exposure.

P031 Ballantine Books
Publishing Imprint

Book Publisher: Random House

P032 Bantam (UK)
Publishing Imprint

Book Publisher: Transworld Publishers (**P393**)

Authors: Trisha Ashley; Dan Brown; Derren Brown; Lee Child; Jilly Cooper; Tess Daly; Sara Davies; Nell Frizzell; Ed Gamble; Tess Gerritsen; Paula Hawkins; David Hepworth; James Holland; Ruth Jones; Sophie Kinsella; Shari Lapena; Andrea Mara; Gina Martin; Guenther Steiner

P033 Banter Press
Book Publisher
561 Hudson Street, #57, New York, NY 10014
United States

banter@wordsupply.com

https://www.banterpress.com

Nonfiction > *Nonfiction Books*
  Business; Communication; Marketing; Writing

Send: Query; Outline; Author bio; Writing sample; Market info; Marketing plan
How to send: PDF file email attachment
How not to send: Post

We seek nonfiction authors who are active speakers and writers within their industry, especially those who do seminars or consulting. Currently, we're eager to see topics in business communication, writing, professional services marketing, personal branding, and marketing technology. We are open to works that have unfairly gone out of print.

Editor: David McClintock

P034 Basalt Books
Publishing Imprint
WSU Press, Cooper Publications Building, PO Box 645910, Pullman, WA 99164-5910, 509-335-7630
United States

https://wsupress.wsu.edu/basalt-books-submission-guidelines/

Book Publisher: Washington State University Press

ADULT > **Nonfiction** > *Nonfiction Books*
  Arts; Biography; Cookery; Culture; Environment; Food; History; Memoir; Nature; Pacific Northwest; Science

CHILDREN'S > **Nonfiction** > *Nonfiction Books*
  Arts; Biography; Cookery; Culture; Environment; Food; History; Memoir; Nature; Pacific Northwest; Science

Send: Query; Market info; Table of contents; Writing sample; Author bio
How to send: Email

Welcomes proposals for book projects anchored in the Pacific Northwest, particularly those focusing on the people, places, and cultures of the greater Northwest region. We encourage both established and first-time writers to contact us with your ideas. We are committed to publishing well-written and well-told stories.

P035 Basic Books
Publishing Imprint
United States

https://www.basicbooks.com
https://www.hachettebookgroup.com/imprint/basic-books-group/

Book Publisher: Basic Books Group (**P036**)

Nonfiction > *Nonfiction Books*
  Current Affairs; History; Politics; Psychology; Science; Sociology

Publishes award-winning books in history, science, sociology, psychology, politics, and current affairs.

P036 Basic Books Group
Book Publisher
United States

https://www.hachettebookgroup.com
https://www.hachettebookgroup.com/imprint/basic-books-group/

Book Publisher: Hachette Book Group (**P156**)

Publishing Imprints: Basic Books (**P035**); Basic Liberty (**P038**); Basic Venture (**P039**); Bold Type Books (**P058**); PublicAffairs (**P304**); Seal Press (**P332**)

P037 Basic Health Publications, Inc.
Publishing Imprint
United States

submissions@turnerpublishing.com

https://turnerbookstore.com/collections/basic-health

Book Publisher: Turner Publishing (**P394**)

Nonfiction > *Nonfiction Books*: Health

Send: Full text; Author bio; Market info
How to send: Word file email attachment; PDF file email attachment

Submit by email, including your manuscript as an attached Word Doc or PDF to your email (a completed manuscript is preferred, but partial manuscripts or detailed outlines/pitches are also accepted); author details including platform, following, qualifications, etc.; and pertinent marketing details, including intended audience and the sales angle of the book.

P038 Basic Liberty
Publishing Imprint
United States

Book Publisher: Basic Books Group (**P036**)

P039 Basic Venture
Publishing Imprint
United States

Book Publisher: Basic Books Group (**P036**)

P040 BatCat Press
Book Publisher
c/o Lincoln Park Performing Arts Charter School, One Lincoln Park, Midland, PA 15059
United States

batcatpress@gmail.com

https://batcatpress.com

Fiction > *Short Fiction*

Nonfiction > *Nonfiction Books*: Creative Nonfiction

Poetry > *Any Poetic Form*

Publishes literary fiction, poetry, and creative nonfiction. Submit via online submission system.

P041 Baylor University Press
Book Publisher
1920 S. 4th St., Waco, TX 76706
United States
Tel: +1 (254) 710-3164

BUP_Acquisitions@baylor.edu

https://www.baylorpress.com
https://www.facebook.com/BaylorPress/
https://x.com/Baylor_Press

ACADEMIC > **Nonfiction** > *Nonfiction Books*
  Anthropology; Christianity; Culture; History; Islam; Judaism; Literature; Philosophy; Politics; Religion; Science; Sociology

Send: Query
How to send: Email

The Press publishes technical scholarship for researchers, tools for teachers, and textbooks for students. All Press publications under our primary academic imprint enjoy rigorous peer review and project development. The list focuses on scriptural, historical, and theological studies of Christianity, Judaism, and Islam. Press publications also investigate the relationship between religion and politics, the sciences, sociology, anthropology, literature, philosophy, history, and culture.

P042 BCS (British Computer Society)
Book Publisher
United Kingdom
Tel: +44 (0) 1793 417417

publishing@bcs.uk

https://www.bcs.org/
https://shop.bcs.org/page/submissions-form/

PROFESSIONAL > **Nonfiction** > *Nonfiction Books*
  Business; Cyber Security; Data and Information Systems; Finance; Leadership; Legal; Management; Procurement; Project Management; Service Management; Software Development

How to send: Online submission system

Publishes books for business and technology professionals.

P043 Bearded Badger Publishing Co.
Book Publisher
United Kingdom

paulh@beardedbadgerpublishing.com

https://www.beardedbadgerpublishing.com
https://www.facebook.com/beardedbadgerpublishing/
https://www.instagram.com/bearded_badger_books/

Fiction > *Novels*
  Contemporary; East Midlands

Poetry > *Poetry Collections*: East Midlands

Independent book publisher with a focus on the East Midlands.

Publishing Imprints: East of Centre (**P119**); Tra[verse] (**P392**)

P044 Bentley Publishers
Book Publisher
United States

http://www.bentleypublishers.com
https://www.facebook.com/bentleypubs
https://www.youtube.com/bentleypublishers

Nonfiction
  Nonfiction Books: Cars
  Reference: Cars

Publishes books for motoring enthusiasts, including technical, motor sports, and service manuals.

P045 Berghahn Books Ltd
Book Publisher
3 Newtec Place, Magdalen Rd, Oxford, OX4 1RE
United Kingdom
Tel: +44 (0) 1865 250011

editorial@berghahnbooks.com

https://www.berghahnbooks.com
https://www.facebook.com/BerghahnBooks
https://twitter.com/berghahnbooks
https://www.youtube.com/channel/UCuh-JFDwm_HfzX1zJ92tzcw
https://www.instagram.com/berghahnbooks/

ACADEMIC > **Nonfiction** > *Nonfiction Books*
  Anthropology; Archaeology; Culture; Education; Environment; Films; Gender; History; Politics; Sociology; TV; Warfare

Send: Query; Submission form; Outline
How to send: Email attachment

Academic publisher of books and journals covering the social sciences. Download New Book Outline form from website, complete, and submit by email with an outline and/or chapter summary.

Editor: Marion Berghahn

P046 Berrett-Koehler Publishers
Book Publisher
1333 Broadway, Suite P-100, Oakland, CA 94612
United States
Tel: +1 (510) 817-2277
Fax: +1 (510) 817-2278

submissions@bkpub.com
bkpub@bkpub.com

https://www.bkconnection.com
https://www.facebook.com/BerrettKoehler
https://twitter.com/Bkpub
https://www.linkedin.com/company/berrett-koehler-publishers/
https://www.pinterest.com/berrettkoehler/
https://www.youtube.com/berrettkoehler

Nonfiction > *Nonfiction Books*
  Business; Career Development; Communication; Creativity; Economics; Equality; Leadership; Management

Send: Proposal; Outline; Writing sample; Market info
How to send: PDF file email attachment; Word file email attachment

Connecting people and ideas to create a world that works for all. Publishes titles that promote positive change at personal, organizational, and societal levels.

P047 Bess Press
Book Publisher
3565 Harding Avenue, Honolulu, HI 96816
United States
Tel: +1 (808) 734-7159
Fax: +1 (808) 732-3627

https://www.besspress.com

ACADEMIC > **Nonfiction** > *Nonfiction Books*
  Hawai'i; Pacific

ADULT
  Fiction > *Novels*
    Hawai'i; Pacific

  Nonfiction > *Nonfiction Books*
    Biography; Hawai'i; Memoir; Pacific

CHILDREN'S > Fiction
  Activity Books: Hawai'i; Pacific
  Board Books: Hawai'i; Pacific
  Picture Books: Hawai'i; Pacific

How to send: Online submission system

Publishes books about Hawai'i and the Pacific. All submissions should be sent via the online form. See website for full guidelines.

P048 Bird Eye Books
Publishing Imprint
United Kingdom

https://birdeyebooks.com
https://twitter.com/BirdEyeBooks/

Book Publisher: Graffeg (**P150**)

Nonfiction > *Illustrated Books*
  Architecture; Crafts; Photography; Visual Arts; Visual Culture

How to send: Online submission system

Imprint publishing high quality illustrated books about the visual arts. We plan to work with authors, artists, sculptors, ceramicists, photographers, illustrators, crafts people, architects and other creatives to publish beautiful books about our visual culture.

P049 Black & White Publishing Ltd
Book Publisher
Nautical House, 104 Commercial Street,
Edinburgh, EH6 6NF
United Kingdom
Tel: +44 (0) 1316 254500

submissions@blackandwhitepublishing.com
mail@blackandwhitepublishing.com

https://blackandwhitepublishing.com
https://twitter.com/bwpublishing
https://www.facebook.com/blackandwhitepublishing/
https://www.instagram.com/bwpublishing/
https://www.youtube.com/user/blackandwhitePub

Fiction > *Novels*

Nonfiction > *Nonfiction Books*
  Celebrity Memoir; Comedy / Humour; Food and Drink; Ireland; Lifestyle; Nature; Scotland; Sport

Send: Query; Proposal
How to send: Email; Through a literary agent

Publisher of general fiction and nonfiction. See website for an idea of the kind of books normally published. For nonfiction submissions, send one-page proposal. Accepts fiction submissions during specific submission windows only, or through a literary agent year-round. Check website for details and to submit via online submission system. No poetry, short stories, or work in languages other than English.

Editors: Campbell Brown; Alison McBride

Publishing Imprints: Ink Road; Itchy Coo

P050 Black Dog & Leventhal
Publishing Imprint
United States

Book Publisher: Workman Publishing (**P437**)

P051 Blackstaff Press
Book Publisher
Jubilee Business Park, 21 Jubilee Road,
Newtownards, BT23 4YH
United Kingdom
Tel: +44 (0) 28 9182 0505

sales@colourpoint.co.uk

https://blackstaffpress.com
https://facebook.com/Blackstaffpressni
https://twitter.com/BlackstaffNI

Book Publisher: Colourpoint Educational (**P095**)

Fiction > *Novels*

Nonfiction > *Nonfiction Books*
  General, and in particular: Biography; History; Ireland; Memoir; Northern Ireland; Politics; Sport

Does not want:

> **Fiction** > *Novels*
>   Erotic; Fantasy; Horror; Science Fiction

Closed to approaches.

Focuses on subjects of interest to the Irish market, both north and south. Not taking on any new projects.

P052 Bloodhound Books
Book Publisher
Nine Hills Road, Cambridge, CB2 1GE
United Kingdom

info@bloodhoundbooks.com
submissions@bloodhoundbooks.com

https://www.bloodhoundbooks.com
https://www.facebook.com/bloodhoundbooks/
https://twitter.com/Bloodhoundbook
https://www.instagram.com/bloodhound.books/

Professional Bodies: Independent Publishers Guild (IPG); The Crime Writers' Association

Fiction > *Novels*
  Contemporary Romance; Cozy Mysteries; Crime; Domestic Suspense; Historical Fiction; Literary; Police Procedural; Psychological Thrillers; Romantic Comedy; Saga; Thrillers; Women's Fiction

Nonfiction > *Nonfiction Books*: Crime

Closed to approaches.

Looking for entertaining, fresh and distinctive fiction that stands out from the crowd. We accept unsolicited submissions, manuscripts from agents, previously published authors, including self-published authors, and debut writers. We're looking for gripping, commercial stories with memorable characters. If your style of storytelling is unique, and readers are going to remember your novel, we want to hear from you.

P053 Bloomsbury Academic
Book Publisher
50 Bedford Square, London, WC1B 3DP
United Kingdom
Tel: +44 (0) 20 7631 5600

contact@bloomsbury.com

http://www.bloomsburyacademic.com

Book Publisher: Bloomsbury Publishing Plc

ACADEMIC > **Nonfiction** > *Nonfiction Books*
  Africa; Archaeology; Architecture; Artificial Intelligence (AI); Arts; Asia; Business; Classics / Ancient World; Communication; Computer Science; Creative Writing; Crime; Design; Drama; Economics; Education; Engineering; Environment; Ethnic Groups; Exercise; Fashion; Films; Food; Gender; Geography; Health; History; Information Science; Interior Design; Language; Legal; Literature; Management; Mathematics; Media; Medicine; Middle East; Music; Nursing; Philosophy; Politics; Psychology; Psychotherapy; Religion; Science; Sexuality; Society; Sociology; Sport; Technology; Visual Culture; Wellbeing

Publishes books for students, researchers, and independent thinkers.

Book Publishers: ABC-CLIO (**P002**); BFI Publishing

P054 Blue Diode Publishing
Book Publisher
Leith, Scotland
United Kingdom

bluedioderob@gmail.com

https://www.bluediode.co.uk
https://www.facebook.com/bluediodepress
https://x.com/DiodeBlue

Poetry > *Poetry Collections*

Closed to approaches.

We are a publisher of quality books, mainly poetry, based in Leith, Scotland.

P055 Blue Poppy Enterprises
Book Publisher
4804 SE 69th Avenue, Portland, OR 97206
United States
Tel: +1 (503) 650-6077
Fax: +1 (503) 650-6076

info@bluepoppy.com

https://www.bluepoppy.com
https://www.facebook.com/bluepoppy1
https://www.youtube.com/channel/UCSDGdeyprhpKC3imL9JCVcw
https://instagram.com/bluepoppyenterprises

ADULT > **Nonfiction** > *Nonfiction Books*
  Acupuncture; Chinese Medicine; Chinese Philosophy

PROFESSIONAL > **Nonfiction** > *Nonfiction Books*
  Acupuncture; Chinese Medicine; Chinese Philosophy

Publishes books on acupuncture, oriental medicine, and Chinese philosophy, for professional practitioners and lay readers.

Editor-in-Chief: Bob Flaws

P056 Blue Star Press
Book Publisher
Bend, OR
United States
Tel: +1 (458) 202-9530

submissions@bluestarpress.com
contact@bluestarpress.com

https://www.bluestarpress.com
https://www.instagram.com/bluestarpress/
https://www.facebook.com/bluestarpresslegacy/
https://www.tiktok.com/@bluestarpress
https://www.pinterest.com/bluestarpress/

Nonfiction > *Nonfiction Books*
  Arts; Comedy / Humour; Creativity; Wellbeing

Send: Submission form
How to send: Email

Focuses on the arts, creative processes, wellness, and witty non-fiction.

P057 BOA Editions, Ltd
Book Publisher
250 North Goodman Street, Suite 306, Rochester, NY 14607
United States
Tel: +1 (585) 546-3410

contact@boaeditions.org

https://www.boaeditions.org

Fiction > *Short Fiction Collections*: Literary

Nonfiction > *Nonfiction Books*
  Literature; Poetry as a Subject

Poetry in Translation > *Poetry Collections*

Poetry > *Poetry Collections*

Closed to approaches.

Publisher of literary fiction, poetry, and prose about poetry and poetics. Specific reading periods (see website). Also runs annual poetry and fiction competitions. See website for more details.

P058 Bold Type Books
Publishing Imprint

Book Publisher: Basic Books Group (**P036**)

P059 Bonnier Books (UK)
Book Publisher
5th Floor, HYLO, 105 Bunhill Row, London, EC1Y 8LZ
United Kingdom
Tel: +44 (0) 20 3770 8888

hello@bonnierbooks.co.uk

https://www.bonnierbooks.co.uk

ADULT
  Fiction > *Novels*
  Nonfiction > *Nonfiction Books*

CHILDREN'S
  Fiction
    Chapter Books; Early Readers; Picture Books
  Nonfiction > *Nonfiction Books*

How to send: Through a literary agent

Publishes adult fiction and nonfiction, and children's books. Accepts approaches through a literary agent only.

Publishing Imprints: Manilla Press (**P227**); Templar Books

P060 Books For All Times
Book Publisher
PO Box 202, Warrenton, VA 20188
United States
Tel: +1 (540) 428-3175

staff@bfat.com

https://bfat.com

Fiction > *Novels*

Nonfiction > *Nonfiction Books*

Independent press based in Warrenton, Virginia. Publishes fiction and nonfiction.

Editor: Joe David

P061 Bramble
Publishing Imprint
United States

Publishing Imprint: Tor Publishing Group (**P388**)

P062 Brewin Books Ltd
Book Publisher
19 Enfield Ind. Estate, Redditch, Worcestershire, B97 6BY
United Kingdom
Tel: +44 (0) 1527 854228
Fax: +44 (0) 1527 60451

admin@brewinbooks.com

https://www.brewinbooks.com
http://www.facebook.com/brewinbooks
http://www.twitter.com/brewinbooks

ADULT
  Fiction > *Novels*
    Contemporary; Ghost Stories

  Nonfiction > *Nonfiction Books*
    Arts; Biography; Comedy / Humour; Creativity; Family; Health; History; Memoir; Military History; Military; Music; Police; Social History; Sport; The Midlands; Transport; Travel; Wellbeing

CHILDREN'S
  Fiction
    Novels; Picture Books
  Nonfiction > *Nonfiction Books*

Send: Query; Synopsis; Author bio
How to send: Email; Post

Publishes regional books on Midland history in the areas of the police, hospitals, the military, family, social and biographies. Also publishes contemporary fiction and books for children. Welcomes submissions from aspiring authors.

Authors: Rob Blakeman; Carl Chinn; Alton Douglas; Brian Drew; Audrey Duggan; Jean Field; Jill Fraser; Gwen Freeman; Patrick Hayes; Nick Owen; Shirley Thompson

Publishing Imprints: Breedon Books; Brewin Books; History into Print; Hunt End Books; Richards Publishing

P063 The British Academy
Book Publisher
10–11 Carlton House Terrace, London, SW1Y 5AH
United Kingdom
Tel: +44 (0) 20 7969 5200

publishing@thebritishacademy.ac.uk

https://www.thebritishacademy.ac.uk
https://www.thebritishacademy.ac.uk/publishing/

ACADEMIC > **Nonfiction** > *Nonfiction Books*
  Archaeology; Culture; History; Philosophy; Society

Registered charity publishing not for profit. Publishes humanities and social sciences, particularly history, philosophy, and archaeology.

P064 The British Museum Press
Book Publisher
British Museum, Great Russell Street, London, WC1B 3DG
United Kingdom

publicity@britishmuseum.org

https://www.britishmuseum.org/commercial/british-museum-press

ACADEMIC > **Nonfiction** > *Nonfiction Books*
  Archaeology; Arts; Culture; History

ADULT > **Nonfiction** > *Nonfiction Books*
  Archaeology; Arts; Culture; History

Publishes books inspired by the collections of the British Museum, covering fine and decorative arts, history, archaeology and world cultures.

P065 Broadview Press
Book Publisher
PO Box 1243, Peterborough, ON, K9J 7H5
Canada
Tel: +1 (705) 482-5915
Fax: +1 (705) 743-8353

customerservice@broadviewpress.com

https://broadviewpress.com
https://www.facebook.com/thebroadviewpress/
https://twitter.com/broadviewpress
https://www.instagram.com/broadviewpress/

ACADEMIC > **Nonfiction** > *Nonfiction Books*
  History; Literature; Philosophy; Politics; Writing

Send: Query
Don't send: Proposal; Full text
How to send: Email

Publishes academic books on literature, philosophy, and history. Before sending a proposal send an email query to the appropriate editor (see website).

P066 Broken Sleep Books
Book Publisher
PO Box 102, Llandysul, SA44 9BG
United Kingdom

submissions@brokensleepbooks.com

https://www.brokensleepbooks.com
https://x.com/BrokenSleep
https://www.facebook.com/brokensleepbooks
http://instagram.com/brokensleepbooks

Nonfiction > *Pamphlets*

Poetry
  Pamphlets; Poetry Collections

A working-class, small, innovative press, who publish a range of poetry and prose, from a range of writers. Our primary focus is in increasing access to the arts, in ensuring more people are able to engage with creativity regardless of their socioeconomic status. We particularly wish to dismantle the gentrification of creative arts, and we encourage more working-class, LGBTQ+, and POC writers to submit. Politically we are left wing, and have no interest in misogynists, racist, sexists, or the alt-right. Submissions accepted during specific windows only (see website for details).

P067 Cadno
Publishing Imprint
United Kingdom

https://graffeg.com

Book Publisher: Graffeg (**P150**)

CHILDREN'S > **Fiction** > *Middle Grade*

How to send: Online submission system

Imprint handling middle grade fiction. Submissions welcome using online submission system (see website).

P068 Cambridge University Press
Book Publisher
University Printing House, Shaftesbury Road, Cambridge, CB2 8BS
United Kingdom
Tel: +44 (0) 1223 358331

information@cambridge.org
directcs@cambridge.org

https://www.cambridge.org
https://www.facebook.com/CambridgeUniversityPress
https://x.com/CambridgeUP
https://www.youtube.com/CambridgeUP
https://www.linkedin.com/company/cambridge-university-press
https://instagram.com/cambridgeuniversitypress

ACADEMIC > **Nonfiction** > *Nonfiction Books*
  Animals; Anthropology; Archaeology; Arts; Astronomy; Biology; Chemistry; Classics / Ancient World; Computer Science; Culture; Economics; Education; Engineering; Environment; Geography; History; Language; Legal; Literature; Management; Mathematics; Medicine; Music; Philosophy; Physics; Politics; Psychology; Religion; Science; Sociology; Statistics; Theatre

World's oldest publisher, with offices around the world. Publishes nonfiction, reference, academic textbooks, educational material, and academic journals. No fiction or poetry.

P069 Candlemark & Gleam
Book Publisher
United States

eloi@candlemarkandgleam.com
Morlocks@candlemarkandgleam.com

https://www.candlemarkandgleam.com

Fiction > *Novels*
  Alternative History; Fantasy; Magical Realism; Science Fiction; Speculative

How to send: By referral

We specialize in speculative fiction—we're eager to explore infinite possibilities. We believe wholeheartedly in the power of the imagination, and we want to shape speculative fiction (science fiction, fantasy, magical realism, alternative history) as it deserves to develop: not a genre, but a way of looking at things with fresh eyes.

P070 Candy Jar Books
Book Publisher
Mackintosh House, 136 Newport Road, Cardiff, CF24 1DJ
United Kingdom
Tel: +44 (0) 2921 157202

hello@candyjarbooks.co.uk
submissions@candyjarbooks.co.uk

https://www.candy-jar.co.uk

ADULT
  Fiction > *Novels*
  Nonfiction > *Nonfiction Books*

CHILDREN'S > **Fiction** > *Middle Grade*

YOUNG ADULT > **Fiction** > *Novels*

Send: Query; Synopsis; Writing sample
How to send: Email; Post

Costs: Offers services that writers have to pay for. Also offers self publishing services through a sister imprint.

We are always on the lookout for new ideas and talent, for stories that are fresh and engaging. We'd love to read what you have been working on. If you have an agent, great, but don't worry if not; we welcome unsolicited manuscripts. We do not accept children's picture books.

Publishing Director: Shaun Russell

P071 Canterbury Press
Publishing Imprint
Hymns Ancient and Modern Ltd, 3rd Floor, Invicta House, 110 Golden Lane, London, EC1Y 0TG
United Kingdom
Tel: +44 (0) 20 7776 7540
Fax: +44 (0) 20 7776 7556

https://canterburypress.hymnsam.co.uk
https://twitter.com/canterburypress
https://www.facebook.com/Canterbury-Press-176777199005586/

Book Publisher: Hymns Ancient & Modern Ltd

Nonfiction > *Nonfiction Books*
  Biography; Christianity; Comedy / Humour; Spirituality; Travel

Supplier of popular religious books. Publishes a wide range of titles, covering liturgy, worship, mission, ministry, spirituality, biography, travel and even humour.

P072 Captivate Press
Book Publisher
United States

captivatepress@gmail.com

https://captivatepress.site

Fiction > *Novels*

Nonfiction > *Nonfiction Books*

Does not want:

> **Fiction** > *Novels*
> Erotic Romance; Science Fiction; Thrillers

Send: Query; Market info; Writing sample
How to send: Email

We are accepting manuscripts from writers in the U.S. and Canada only and are particularly interested in writers who have an advance social media presence. Please do not send Sci-fi, Smutty Romance, or Thrillers. We accept un-agented submissions. We do not require exclusive submissions. Please be sure that your manuscript is properly formatted according to basic manuscript format guidelines.

P073 Carina Press
Publishing Imprint
United States

CustomerService@Harlequin.com

https://www.carinapress.com
https://www.writeforharlequin.com/carina-press-submission-guidelines/
https://www.facebook.com/CarinaPress
https://carinapress.submittable.com/submit

Book Publisher: Harlequin Enterprises

Fiction > *Novels*
Contemporary Romance; Erotic Romance; Historical Romance; Mystery; Romantasy; Romantic Suspense; Science Fiction; Supernatural / Paranormal Romance; Urban Fantasy

Send: Query; Full text; Synopsis
How to send: Submittable
How not to send: Email

Digital-first adult fiction imprint. See website for details submission guidelines and to submit via online submission system.

Editors: Kerri Buckley; Stephanie Doig

P074 Cassava Republic Press UK
Book Publisher
Studio C11, Mainyard Studios, 94 Wallis Rd, London, E9 5LN
United Kingdom

https://cassavarepublic.biz
https://cassavarepublicpress.submittable.com/submit
https://www.facebook.com/CassavaRepublic
https://www.instagram.com/cassavarepublicpress
https://www.tiktok.com/@cassavarepublic
https://twitter.com/cassavarepublic
https://ng.linkedin.com/company/cassava-republic-press
https://www.youtube.com/channel/UCXVcuTjK-xHk3dKygMVaVew

Fiction > *Novels*: Africa

Nonfiction > *Nonfiction Books*: Africa

Closed to approaches.

Founded in Abuja, Nigeria, 2006 with the aim of bringing high quality fiction and non-fiction for adults and children alike to a global audience. We have offices in Abuja and London.

Our mission is to change the way we all think about African writing. We think that contemporary African prose should be rooted in African experience in all its diversity, whether set in filthy-yet-sexy megacities such as Lagos or Kinshasa, in little-known communities outside of Bahia, in the recent past or indeed the near future.

We also think the time has come to build a new body of African writing that links writers and readers from Benin to Bahia. It's therefore the right time to ask challenging questions of African writing – where have we come from, where are we now, where are we going? Our role is to facilitate and participate in addressing these questions, as our list grows. We are still just beginning.

P075 CB Editions
Book Publisher
United Kingdom

info@cbeditions.com

https://www.cbeditions.com

Fiction in Translation > *Short Fiction Collections*

Fiction > *Short Fiction Collections*

Poetry in Translation > *Poetry Collections*

Poetry > *Poetry Collections*

Publishes short fiction, poetry, translations and other work which might otherwise fall through the cracks between big publishers. No submission guidelines. Writers wishing to send work may do so in whatever form they choose.

P076 Cedar Fort
Book Publisher
2373 W 700 S, Suite 100, Springville, UT 84663
United States
Tel: +1 (801) 489-4084

marketinginfo@cedarfort.com

https://www.cedarfort.com
https://cedarfort.submittable.com/submit
https://facebook.com/cedarfortbooks
https://www.instagram.com/cedarfort
https://www.youtube.com/@CedarFort

ADULT > **Nonfiction**
Gift Books: Church of Jesus Christ of Latter-Day Saints (LDS)
Nonfiction Books: Business; Church of Jesus Christ of Latter-Day Saints (LDS); Cookery; Crafts; Design; Entertainment; Family; Games; Gardening; Health; History; Hobbies; Outdoor Activities; Personal Experiences; Relationships; Religion; Science; Self Help; Wellbeing
Reference: General

CHILDREN'S
Fiction > *Picture Books*
Church of Jesus Christ of Latter-Day Saints (LDS); Religion

Nonfiction
Chapter Books: General, and in particular: Crafts; Health; History; Science
Picture Books: Church of Jesus Christ of Latter-Day Saints (LDS); Religion

How to send: Submittable

Publishes books with strong moral or religious values that inspire readers to be better people. No poetry, short stories, or erotica. See website for full submission guidelines, and to submit using online submission system.

Publishing Imprints: Bonneville Books; CFI; Council Press; Front Table Books; Hobble Creek Press; Horizon Publishers; King Dragon Press; Pioneer Plus; Plain Sight Publishing; Sweetwater Books

P077 Celadon Books
Publishing Imprint
United States

Book Publisher: Macmillan Publishers

P078 CGI (Chartered Governance Institute) Publishing
Book Publisher
Saffron House, 6–10 Kirby Street, London, EC1N 8TS
United Kingdom
Tel: +44 (0) 20 7580 4741

https://www.cgi.org.uk
https://www.cgi.org.uk/shop
https://www.linkedin.com/school/cgiuki
https://www.facebook.com/CGIUKI
https://twitter.com/CGIUKI
https://www.flickr.com/photos/icsaglobal

PROFESSIONAL > **Nonfiction** > *Nonfiction Books*: Business

Practical governance books and media on business skills; boards; risk and compliance; company secretarial practice; governance; and study texts.

P079 Charisma House
Publishing Imprint
600 Rinehart Rd, Lake Mary, FL 32746
United States
Tel: +1 (407) 333-0600

info@charismamedia.com

https://charismahouse.com
https://www.facebook.com/CharismaHouse/
https://twitter.com/charismahouse
https://www.instagram.com/charismahousebooks/

Media Company: Charisma Media

Fiction > *Novels*: Christianity

Nonfiction > *Nonfiction Books*
  Christian Living; Christianity; Politics

After fifty years, we're just as passionate about helping you discover the life-changing power of the Holy Spirit as we were half a century ago. We believe a life surrendered to the Holy Spirit brings transformation, joy, and purpose. We call this Spirit-led living, and it's why millions of readers trust us as their go-to resource for books that embrace the fullness of the Spirit-led life.

P080 Charles River Press
Book Publisher
United States

info@charlesriverpress.com

http://www.charlesriverpress.com
https://www.facebook.com/charles.r.press/
https://twitter.com/CharlesRiverLLC
https://www.youtube.com/user/CharlesRiverPress/

Fiction > *Novels*: Erotic

Nonfiction > *Nonfiction Books*: Sport

Send: Author bio; Market info; Synopsis; Full text

Costs: Offers services that writers have to pay for. Also offers editing and design services.

Currently accepting sports and erotica manuscripts.

Authors: Richard Herrick; John McMullen; Mike Ryan; Tony Schiavone; Jonathan Womack; Rowena Womack

P081 Charlesbridge Publishing
Book Publisher
9 Galen Street, Watertown, MA 02472
United States
Tel: +1 (617) 926-0329

tradeeditorial@charlesbridge.com

https://www.charlesbridge.com
https://twitter.com/charlesbridge
https://www.facebook.com/CharlesbridgePublishingInc
https://www.pinterest.com/charlesbridge/
https://www.instagram.com/charlesbridgepublishing/
https://charlesbridgebooks.tumblr.com/
https://www.youtube.com/user/Charlesbridge1

CHILDREN'S
  Fiction
    Board Books; Early Readers; Middle Grade; Picture Books
  Nonfiction
    Board Books: General
    Early Readers: General
    Middle Grade: Arts; Biography; History; Mathematics; Nature; Science; Social Issues
    Picture Books: General

Send: Full text
How to send: Word file email attachment; PDF file email attachment
How not to send: In the body of an email

Publishes books for children, with teen and adult imprints. No text or art generated by artificial intelligence.

Publishing Imprints: Charlesbridge Teen; Imagine Publishing (**P186**)

P082 Chelsea House Publishers
Publishing Imprint
8 The Green Suite 19225, Dover, DE 19901
United States
Tel: +1 (800) 322-8755
Fax: +1 (800) 678-3633

CustServ@Infobase.com

https://chelseahouse.infobasepublishing.com

Book Publisher: Infobase Publishing

ACADEMIC > **Nonfiction** > *Nonfiction Books*
  Biography; Contemporary; Geography; Health; History; Science; Sociology

Publishes curriculum-based nonfiction books for middle school and high school students, spanning historical and contemporary biographies, social studies, geography, science, health, high-interest titles, and more. Provides educators and librarians with colorful, engaging books and eBooks that can be used as supplemental reading for the school curriculum and as solid resources for research projects.

P083 Cherry Lake Publishing Group
Book Publisher
2395 South Huron Parkway, Suite 200, Ann Arbor, MI 48104
United States
Tel: +1 (866) 918-3956

submissions@sleepingbearpress.com

https://cherrylakepublishing.com
https://www.facebook.com/CherryLakePublishing
https://www.instagram.com/cherrylakepublishing

CHILDREN'S
  Fiction
    Board Books; Early Readers; Middle Grade; Picture Books
  Nonfiction
    Board Books; Early Readers; Middle Grade; Picture Books

Send: Query; Author bio; Outline
How to send: In the body of an email

We are a publisher of quality children's books. We publish a wide range of books, including board books, beginning readers, picture books, and select middle grade titles. We accept both fiction and nonfiction submissions. We are committed to the principles of diversity, equity and inclusion and welcome stories from diverse authors. Please browse our website or catalog for examples of the types of books we publish.

Publishing Imprint: Tilbury House Publishers (**P385**)

P084 Child's Play (International) Ltd
Book Publisher
Ashworth Road, Bridgemead, Swindon, Wiltshire, SN5 7YD
United Kingdom
Tel: +44 (0) 1793 616286

office@childs-play.com

http://www.childs-play.com
https://www.facebook.com/ChildsPlayBooks/
https://twitter.com/ChildsPlayBooks
http://pinterest.com/childsplaybooks/
http://www.instagram.com/childsplaybooks/
https://www.youtube.com/channel/UCik8Eew5rGc2LfpggFgX4Qg

CHILDREN'S
  Fiction
    Activity Books; Board Books; Picture Books
  Poetry > *Picture Books*

Closed to approaches.

Specialises in publishing books that allow children to learn through play. No novels. No AI-generated stories.

P085 Choc Lit
Book Publisher
United Kingdom

choc-lit@joffebooks.com

https://www.choc-lit.com
https://twitter.com/choclituk
https://www.facebook.com/Choc-Lit-30680012481/
https://www.instagram.com/choclituk/
https://www.youtube.com/channel/UCLZBZ2qeR5gtOyDoqEjMbQw

Book Publisher: Joffe Books (**P199**)

Fiction > *Novels*
Book Club Women's Fiction; Contemporary Romance; Domestic Noir; Family Saga; Historical Fiction; Historical Romance; Psychological Thrillers; Romance; Romantasy; Romantic Comedy; Romantic Suspense; Suspense; Time Travel; Timeslip Romance; World War II

Send: Query; Synopsis; Submission form; Author bio
How to send: Email attachment

Our favourite genres include contemporary uplit, spicy grump-sunshine, laugh-out-loud romantic comedy, cosy village romance, beachy escapes, time travel romantasy, sweeping historical sagas and WWII romances, spicy happily-ever-afters, and gripping women's book club fiction. We also love psychological thrillers, suspense and domestic noir. We want to read #OwnVoices submissions that bring characters who represent the same marginalised identities as their author, including but not limited to BIPOC, LGBT+ and differently abled people, people living in underrepresented cultures and socioeconomic backgrounds, and more. We encourage authors from diverse backgrounds to submit their work and make their voices heard. We especially look for great stories, fresh ideas, excellent writing and original voices; in short authors who say something interesting about the world as they see it. We publish writers we believe in, from debut novelists and agented authors, to self-represented writers and authors who are already well-established. Submissions are welcome from anywhere in the world, however, we only publish books in the English language. We accept submissions from agents, previously published authors (including self-published authors) with long backlists, first-time writers with only one book under their belt, and anyone in between. We do NOT publish non-fiction, poetry, YA fiction, children's fiction, sci-fi or erotica. If these are your genres, we are probably not the publisher for you.

Author: Juliet Archer

Publishing Imprint: Ruby Fiction (**P319**)

P086 Chosen Books
Book Publisher

Book Publisher: Baker Publishing Group

Closed to approaches.

P087 Cicada Books
Book Publisher
Studio 31A, Archway Studios, Bickerton House, 25-27 Bickerton Road, London, N19 5JT
United Kingdom

info@cicadabooks.co.uk
https://www.cicadabooks.co.uk
https://x.com/cicadabooks
https://www.instagram.com/cicadabooks/

ADULT > **Nonfiction** > *Nonfiction Books*
CHILDREN'S
Fiction
Graphic Novels; Picture Books
Nonfiction
Activity Books; Picture Books

Send: Query; Synopsis
How to send: Email

A New York Times Award winning children's book publisher based in London. We started out making adult art and design books, but now specialise in beautiful, high-end books for kids aged 4–11. We have an eclectic list that includes activity books, picture books and non-fiction.

P088 Cinnamon Press
Book Publisher
Lytchett House, 13 Freeland Park, Wareham Road, Poole, Dorset, BH16 6FA
United Kingdom

info@cinnamonpress.com
https://www.cinnamonpress.com

Fiction > *Novels*

Nonfiction > *Nonfiction Books*

Poetry > *Poetry Collections*

Small-press publisher of full length poetry collections, unique and imaginative novels, and practical and informative nonfiction with wide appeal. Willing to consider most genres as long as writing is thought-provoking, enjoyable, and accessible; but does not publish genre fiction (romantic, erotica, horror or crime), biography, autobiography, academic, technical or how-to. No unsolicited MSS. See website for submission details.

Editor: Jan Fortune

P089 Claret Press
Book Publisher
51 Iveley Road, London, SW4 0EN
United Kingdom
Tel: +44 (0) 7736 716927

contact@claretpress.com
https://www.claretpress.com
https://www.facebook.com/ClaretPublisher
https://twitter.com/ClaretPress

Fiction > *Novels*
Mystery; Thrillers

Nonfiction > *Nonfiction Books*
Memoir; Politics; Travel

Closed to approaches.

A Micro Publisher specialising in narratives that encourage conversations about contemporary politics, issues and places. We love a great read about our shared world, about politics, people and places. Our page turners percolate with ideas, entertain and enlighten. We're London-based and the majority of our books are about Britain. But our travelogues take you around the world. So do many of our thrillers. Hearts and minds are opened by our memoirs and novels.

P090 Classical Comics
Book Publisher
PO Box 177, Ludlow, SY8 9DL
United Kingdom

https://www.classicalcomics.com
https://www.facebook.com/ClassicalComics/
https://www.instagram.com/classcomeducation

CHILDREN'S > **Fiction** > *Graphic Novels*: Literature

Closed to approaches.

Publishes graphic novel adaptations of classical literature.

Creative Director: Jo Wheeler

Managing Director: Gary Bryant

P091 Cleis Press
Book Publisher
221 River St, 9th Fl, Hoboken, NJ 07030
United States
Tel: +1 (212) 431-5455

cleis@cleispress.com
acquisitions@cleispress.com

https://cleispress.com
https://instagram.com/cleis_press
https://twitter.com/cleispress
https://www.facebook.com/CleisPress.Page
https://www.pinterest.com/cleispress/
https://cleispress.tumblr.com/

Fiction > *Novels*
Erotic Romance; Erotic

Nonfiction > *Nonfiction Books*
Feminism; Health; LGBTQIA; Memoir; Relationships; Self Help; Sex; Sexuality; Women's Studies

How to send: Through a literary agent

The largest independent sexuality publishing company in the United States. With a focus on LGBTQ, BDSM, romance, and erotic writing for all sexual preferences. Agented approaches only.

P092 Coach House Books
Book Publisher
80 bpNichol Lane, Toronto, Ontario M5S 3J4
Canada
Tel: +1 (416) 979-2217
Fax: +1 (416) 977-1158

editor@chbooks.com
mail@chbooks.com

https://chbooks.com
https://www.facebook.com/coachhousebooks
https://x.com/coachhousebooks
https://www.goodreads.com/chbooks
https://instagram.com/coachhousebooks

Fiction > *Novels*: Literary

Nonfiction > *Nonfiction Books*

Poetry > *Poetry Collections*

Scripts > *Theatre Scripts*

Send: Full text; Author bio
How to send: Email

Publishes literary fiction, poetry, drama, and books about Toronto. Publishes primarily Canadian authors. Send complete MS with cover letter describing your work and comparing to at least two current authors published by this company. Include CV outlining any previous publishing experience.

P093 Coaches Choice
Book Publisher
311 – 21st Street, Camanche, IA 52730
United States
Tel: +1 (888) 229-5745

submissions@coacheschoice.com

https://coacheschoice.com

ADULT > Nonfiction > *Nonfiction Books*: Sports Coaching

PROFESSIONAL > Nonfiction > *Nonfiction Books*: Sports Coaching

Send: Query
How to send: Email

Always looking for people passionate about about sports instruction with the goal of improvement for coaches of all sports in all facets of their lives.

P094 College Press Publishing
Book Publisher
1307 W 20th Street, Joplin, MO 64804
United States

collpressjoplin@gmail.com

https://collegepress.com
https://www.facebook.com/collpresspublishing/

Nonfiction > *Nonfiction Books*
Bible Studies; Biography; Christianity; Evangelism; History

Send: Query; Proposal
How to send: Post; Email

Publishes Bible studies, topical studies (biblically based), apologetic studies, historical biographies of Christians, Sunday/Bible School curriculum (adult electives). No poetry, game or puzzle books, books on prophecy from a premillennial or dispensational viewpoint, or any books that do not contain a Christian message.

Publishing Imprint: HeartSpring Publishing

P095 Colourpoint Educational
Book Publisher
Colourpoint House, Jubilee Business Park, 21 Jubilee Road, Newtownards, Northern Ireland, BT23 4YH
United Kingdom
Tel: +44 (0) 28 9182 0505

sales@colourpoint.co.uk

https://colourpointeducational.com
https://twitter.com/ColourpointEdu

ACADEMIC > Nonfiction > *Nonfiction Books*
Biology; Chemistry; Design; Digital Technology; Education; French; Gaelic; Geography; Health; History; Home Economics / Domestic Science; Legal; Lifestyle; Mathematics; Physical Education; Physics; Politics; Religion; Technology

Send: Query
How to send: Email

Provides textbooks, ebooks and digital resources for Northern Ireland students at Key Stage 3 level, and the CCEA revised specification at GCSE and AS/A2/A-level.

Book Publisher: Blackstaff Press (**P051**)

Editor: Wesley Johnston

P096 Comma Press
Book Publisher
Studio 510a, 5th Floor, Hope Mill, 113 Pollard Street, Manchester, M4 7JA
United Kingdom

ra.page@commapress.co.uk

http://commapress.co.uk
https://faccbook.com/commapressmcr
https://twitter.com/commapress
https://instagram.com/commapress

Fiction > *Short Fiction*

A not-for-profit publisher and development agency specialising in short fiction from the UK and beyond.

P097 Compassiviste Publishing
Book Publisher
United Kingdom

submissions@compassivistepublishing.com

https://compassivistepublishing.com
https://x.com/compassiviste
https://www.tiktok.com/@compassiviste
https://www.instagram.com/compassiviste/
https://www.facebook.com/CompassivisteOfficial/
https://www.linkedin.com/company/compassiviste

Fiction
Novels: Adventure; Commercial; Contemporary; Drama; Experimental; Fantasy; Literary; Mainstream; Popular; Science Fiction; Thrillers; Traditional
Short Fiction Collections: General

Nonfiction > *Nonfiction Books*
Anthropology; Arts; Autobiography; Biography; Comedy / Humour; Culture; Current Affairs; Entertainment; Health; History; How To; Leisure; Lifestyle; Literature; Men's Interests; Music; Nature; New Age; Philosophy; Photography; Politics; Psychology; Science; Self Help; Sociology; Spirituality; Technology; Travel; Women's Interests

Send: Query; Synopsis; Outline; Author bio; Writing sample
How to send: Email; Online submission system

Welcomes unsolicited full-length manuscripts and submissions to our quarterly anthology. We welcome writers at any stage of their career, and support authors from disadvantaged and diverse backgrounds. Our work includes fiction and non-fiction books across a wide range of genres, covering important social, cultural and environmental topics aligned with our foundation's charitable causes. We invest 100% of our net profits back into the charity.

P098 Convergent
Publishing Imprint

Book Publisher: Random House

P099 Countryside Books
Book Publisher
3 Catherine Road, Newbury, Berkshire, RG14 7NA
United Kingdom
Tel: +44 (0) 1635 43816

info@countrysidebooks.co.uk

https://countrysidebooks.co.uk
https://twitter.com/countrysidebook
https://www.facebook.com/CountrysideBooks/
https://www.instagram.com/countrysidebooks/

Nonfiction > *Nonfiction Books*
Architecture; Aviation; Comedy / Humour; Crime; Cycling; Dialects; Ghosts; History; Local History; Mystery; Nostalgia; Railways; Supernatural / Paranormal; Walking; World War I; World War II

Publishes nonfiction only, mostly regional books relating to specific English counties. Covers topics such as local history, walks, photography, dialect, genealogy, military and aviation, and some transport; but not interested in natural history books or personal memories. No fiction or poetry.

P100 Crossway
Publishing Imprint
1300 Crescent Street, Wheaton, IL 60187

United States
Tel: +1 (630) 682-4300

info@crossway.org

http://www.crossway.org

ACADEMIC > *Nonfiction* > *Nonfiction Books*
  Bible Studies; Christianity; Church History

ADULT > *Nonfiction* > *Nonfiction Books*
  Christian Living; Christianity

PROFESSIONAL > *Nonfiction* > *Nonfiction Books*: Christianity

Send: Query
How to send: Email

Publishes nonfiction books that engage believers' minds, stir their affections, and motivate their wills. Focuses on key issues facing Christians; Christian life; the Christian worldview; and academic and professional volumes directed toward college and seminary students, pastors, and others in full-time Christian work.

P101 Crown
Publishing Imprint
United States

https://crownpublishing.com/archives/imprint/crown-publishers
https://www.instagram.com/crownpublishing
https://twitter.com/CrownPublishing
https://www.facebook.com/CrownPublishing

Book Publisher: The Crown Publishing Group (**P103**)

Nonfiction > *Nonfiction Books*
  Biography; Business; Cultural Criticism; Current Affairs; Economics; History; Politics; Psychology; Science; Social Justice

Publishes across a wide range of nonfiction genres with an emphasis on politics, current affairs, social justice, personal narrative, biography, history, economics, business, cultural criticism, science, social science, and psychology. As a team, we are committed to publishing a diverse array of leading and emerging voices who enlarge our understanding of the world; help us navigate and succeed in a rapidly evolving climate; challenge legacy narratives; and harness the power of storytelling to illuminate, entertain, inspire, and connect readers everywhere.

P102 Crown Currency
Publishing Imprint

Book Publisher: The Crown Publishing Group (**P103**)

P103 The Crown Publishing Group
Book Publisher
United States

customerservice@prh.com

https://crownpublishing.com
https://www.facebook.com/CrownPublishing
https://twitter.com/crownpublishing
http://instagram.com/crownpublishing
http://www.goodreads.com/user/show/2504245-crown-publishing-group
https://www.pinterest.com/crownpublishing/

Book Publisher: Penguin Random House

Fiction > *Novels*

Nonfiction
  Gift Books: General
  Nonfiction Books: Arts; Biography; Business; Comedy / Humour; Cookery; Crafts; Fitness; Gardening; Health; History; Hobbies; Memoir; Politics; Self Help

Division of large international publisher.

Publishing Imprints: 4 Color Books; Clarkson Potter; Crown (**P101**); Crown Currency (*P102*); Currency; Ten Speed Graphic (*P379*); Ten Speed Press (**P380**); Watson-Guptill Publications

P104 Dahlia Books
Book Publisher
United Kingdom

submissions@dahliapublishing.co.uk

http://www.dahliapublishing.co.uk
https://twitter.com/dahliabooks

Fiction > *Short Fiction Collections*
  Contemporary; Diversity; Regional

Send: Query; Outline; Writing sample
How to send: Word file email attachment

We only accept proposals for short fiction and short stories when presented as a collection from UK based writers. Please do not send us single short stories. We are particularly keen on publishing diverse voices and actively encourage submissions from first-time writers.

Print Magazine: Present Tense

P105 Dancing Girl Press
Book Publisher
United States

dancinggirlpress@yahoo.com

http://www.dancinggirlpress.com

Poetry > *Chapbooks*

Send: Full text

Publishes chapbooks by female poets between 12 and 32 pages. No payment, but free 10 copies and 40% discount on further copies.

P106 Daunt Books Publishing
Book Publisher
207-209 Kentish Town Rd, London, NW5 2JU
United Kingdom

publishing@dauntbooks.co.uk

https://dauntbookspublishing.co.uk
https://twitter.com/dauntbookspub

Fiction in Translation
  Novels: Literary
  Short Fiction Collections: Literary

Fiction
  Novels: Literary
  Short Fiction Collections: Literary

Nonfiction in Translation
  Essays: General
  Nonfiction Books: Memoir; Narrative Nonfiction

Nonfiction
  Essays: General
  Nonfiction Books: Memoir; Narrative Nonfiction

Closed to approaches.

We publish the finest and most exciting new writing in English and in translation, whether that's literary fiction – novels and short stories – or narrative non-fiction including essays and memoir. We also publish modern classics, reviving authors who have been overlooked and publishing them in bold editions with introductions from the best contemporary writers.

P107 Dedalus Ltd
Book Publisher
Langford Lodge, St Judith's Lane, Sawtry, PE28 5XE
United Kingdom
Tel: +44 (0) 1487 832382

info@dedalusbooks.com

https://www.dedalusbooks.com
https://www.facebook.com/profile.php?id=100063653493212
https://twitter.com/dedalusbooks
http://vimeo.com/dedalusbooks

Fiction in Translation > *Novels*
  Contemporary; Literary

Fiction > *Novels*
  Contemporary; Literary

Send: Query; Writing sample; Self-addressed stamped envelope (SASE)
How to send: Post

Publisher of literary fiction, including contemporary English language fiction and translated European fiction. Most books are translations.

Book Publisher: Dedalus European Classics

P108 Del Rey
Publishing Imprint
United States

Book Publisher: Random House

P109 Denis Kitchen Publishing Company Co., LLC
Book Publisher
P.O. Box 2250, Amherst, MA 01004
United States
Tel: +1 (413) 259-1627

help@deniskitchen.com

http://deniskitchenpublishing.com

Fiction
   Cartoons; *Comics*; *Graphic Novels*
Nonfiction > *Nonfiction Books*
   Arts; Comic Books

Publishes comics and graphic novels and books on the subject.

P110 The Dial Press
Publishing Imprint

Book Publisher: Random House

P111 Diversion Books
Book Publisher
United States
Tel: +1 (212) 961-6390

info@diversionbooks.com
submit@diversionbooks.com

http://www.diversionbooks.com

Fiction > *Novels*
   Fantasy; Horror; Mystery; Romantasy; Science Fiction; Thrillers

Nonfiction > *Nonfiction Books*
   Business; Crime; Current Affairs; History; Music; Science; Sport

How to send: Through a literary agent

An independent publisher with a focus on both non-fiction and fiction. The company specialises in general interest non-fiction across categories such as current events, music, history, business, sports, true crime, and science. Additionally, it has expanded its portfolio to include a growing range of fiction titles, with a particular focus on Science Fiction/Fantasy, Romantasy, Mystery/Thriller, and Horror.

Acquisitions Editors: Dan Ambrosio; Toni Kirkpatrick; Evan Phail; Keith Wallman

P112 DK Publishing
Book Publisher
1745 Broadway, 20th Floor, New York, NY 10019
United States

ecustomerservice@randomhouse.com

https://www.dk.com

Book Publisher: DK (Dorling Kindersley Ltd)

ADULT > **Nonfiction**
   Nonfiction Books: Arts; Beauty; Business; Career Development; Comic Books; Crafts; Culture; Education; Films; Fitness; Food and Drink; Gardening; Health; History; Hobbies; Language; Medicine; Nature; Parenting; Photography; Popular Culture; Pregnancy; Relationships; Religion; Science; Sport; TV; Travel
   Reference: General

CHILDREN'S > **Nonfiction**
   Board Books; *Early Readers*; *Middle Grade*; *Picture Books*

How to send: Through a literary agent

A global publisher of internationally bestselling authors and illustrators across non-fiction, adult and children's publishing. We have been pioneering ways to bring knowledge and adventure to people around the world for over 50 years.

P113 Dodo Ink
Book Publisher
United Kingdom

dodopublishingco@gmail.com

http://www.dodoink.com
https://twitter.com/DodoInk
https://www.facebook.com/profile.php?id=100064126986391

Fiction > *Novels*: Literary

Closed to approaches.

Independent UK publisher aiming to publish three novels per year, in paperback and digital formats. Publishes risk-taking, imaginative novels, that don't fall into easy marketing categories. Closed to submissions as at August 2023.

Editor: Sam Mills

P114 Doubleday (UK)
Publishing Imprint
United Kingdom

https://www.penguin.co.uk/company/publishers/transworld#Doubleday

Book Publisher: Transworld Publishers (**P393**)

Fiction > *Novels*

Nonfiction > *Nonfiction Books*: Narrative Nonfiction

A boutique literary imprint with a vibrant and dynamic list that publishes prize winners, international bestsellers and fresh new voices with passion and creative flair. We seek out ground-breaking books that engage the heart and mind; that speak to the zeitgeist but will also resonate for years to come.

Authors: Kate Atkinson; Sue Black; John Boyne; Bill Bryson; Nicola Dinan; Lottie Hazell; Rachel Joyce; Tracy King; John Lewis-Stempel; Catherine Newman; Elliot Page; Terry Pratchett; Hallie Rubenhold; Curtis Sittenfeld; Christopher Somerville; Clover Stroud

P115 Dreamspinner Press
Book Publisher
PO Box 1245, Woodville, FL 32362
United States
Tel: +1 (448) 488-4235

submissions@dreamspinnerpress.com
contact@dreamspinnerpress.com

https://www.dreamspinnerpress.com
https://www.facebook.com/dreamspinnerpress/
https://twitter.com/dreamspinners
https://www.instagram.com/dreamspinner_press/

Fiction > *Novels*
   Coming of Age; Erotic Romance; Erotic; Fantasy; Gay; Historical Fantasy; Mystery; Romance; Science Fiction; Supernatural / Paranormal Romance; Suspense; Westerns

Send: Synopsis; Full text
How to send: Email

Publishes gay male romance in all genres. While works do not need to be graphic, they must contain a primary or strong secondary romance plotline and focus on the interaction between two or more male characters. The main characters of the story must end in a gay or gay polyamorous relationship. Other relationships (heterosexual, lesbian, mixed gender polyamory) are acceptable in secondary pairings or as part of the development of a main character.

Authors: M. Jules Aedin; Rhianne Aile; Maria Albert; Eric Arvin; Mickie B. Ashling; Connie Bailey; Alix Bekins; Nicki Bennett; Sienna Bishop; Scarlett Blackwell; S. Blaise; Steven Blue-Williams; Anne Brooke; Bethany Brown; Janey Chapel; J. M. Colail; Jaymz Connelly; Lisa Marie Davis; Remmy Duchene; Giselle Ellis; Catt Ford; Lacey-Anne Frye; Reve Garrison; Andrew Grey; Felicitas Ivey; Ashlyn Kane; Sean Kennedy; V.B. Kildaire; Shay Kincaid; Marguerite Labbe; Clare London; Dar Mavison; Anais Morten; Chrissy Munder; Zahra Owens; D. G. Parker; Michael Powers; Angela Romano; Abigail Roux; Isabella Rowan; Steve Sampson; Ian Sentelik; Jane Seville; John Simpson; Jenna Hilary Sinclair; Dan Skinner; Sasha Skye; Sonja Spencer; Jaxx Steele; Jaelyn Storm; Rowena Sudbury; Fae Sutherland; Ariel Tachna; Madeleine Urban; G.S. Wiley

Publishing Imprints: DSP Publications (**P116**); Harmony Ink Press

P116 DSP Publications
Publishing Imprint
PO Box 1245, Woodville, FL 32362
United States
Tel: +1 (800) 970-3759
Fax: +1 (888) 308-3739

contact@dreamspinnerpress.com

https://www.dsppublications.com
https://twitter.com/DSPPublications
https://www.facebook.com/dsppublications/

Book Publisher: Dreamspinner Press (**P115**)

Fiction > *Novels*
  Fantasy; Historical Fiction; Horror; Mystery; Science Fiction; Spirituality; Supernatural / Paranormal

We are a boutique imprint producing quality fiction that pushes the envelope to present immersive, unique, and unforgettable reading experiences. We choose stories that beg to be told, tales that depart from mainstream concepts to create fantastic and compelling journeys of the mind.

P117 Duncan Petersen Publishing Limited

Book Publisher
United Kingdom

http://duncanpetersen.blogspot.com

Nonfiction > *Nonfiction Books*
  Cycling; Travel; Walking Guides

Travel publishing house. Publishes Hotel Guides, along with a variety of walking and cycling guides for Britain.

P118 Dundurn

Book Publisher
PO Box 75090 RPO Hudson Bay, Toronto, ON M4W 3T3
Canada
Tel: +1 (416) 214-5544

submissions@dundurn.com

https://www.dundurn.com
https://www.facebook.com/dundurnpress
https://x.com/dundurnpress
https://www.tiktok.com/@dundurnpress
http://instagram.com/dundurnpress
https://pinterest.com/dundurnpress
http://www.goodreads.com/user/show/8566676-dundurn-press

Fiction > *Novels*
  Contemporary; Literary

Nonfiction > *Nonfiction Books*
  Architecture; Biography; Business; Canada; Crime; Culture; Economics; History; Literary; Local; Memoir; Music; Politics; Popular Science; Self Help; Social History; Sociology; Sport; Supernatural / Paranormal; Travel; Wellbeing

Send: Query; Proposal; Full text; Synopsis; Author bio; Writing sample; Table of contents; Outline
How to send: Word file email attachment; PDF file email attachment

One of the largest independent publishing houses in Canada, with over 2,500 Canadian-authored titles in print. Best known for its robust publishing program spanning these five decades as well as its fiction titles that speak to diverse and international audiences. Publishes books that reflect the world, satisfy curiosity, enlighten, and entertain. Seeks to amplify and elevate exceptional Canadian voices, particularly those that have not yet been discovered or have been previously underrepresented in trade publishing. Publishes across numerous genres, from literary and genre fiction to true crime, memoir and biography, sport, history and public policy. Accepts international submissions but prioritises submissions from Canadian citizens. Response not guaranteed unless interested. If no response within six months, assume rejection.

P119 East of Centre

Publishing Imprint
United Kingdom

paulh@beardedbadgerpublishing.com

https://www.beardedbadgerpublishing.com

Book Publisher: Bearded Badger Publishing Co. (**P043**)

Fiction > *Novels*
  Contemporary; East Midlands

Publishes a range of contemporary and modern fiction by East Midlands writers.

P120 Eerdmans Books for Young Readers

Publishing Imprint
United States

ebyrsubmissions@eerdmans.com

https://www.eerdmans.com
https://www.eerdmans.com/youngreaders/

Book Publisher: William B. Eerdmans Publishing Co.

CHILDREN'S > **Fiction**
  Board Books; *Middle Grade*; *Picture Books*
YOUNG ADULT
  Fiction > *Novels*
  Nonfiction > *Nonfiction Books*

Send: Query; Synopsis; Writing sample; Full text
How to send: Email

Publishes board books, picture books, novels, and nonfiction. Seeks manuscripts that are honest, wise, and hopeful; but also publishes stories that simply delight with their storyline, characters, or good humor. Stories that celebrate diversity, stories of historical significance, and stories that relate to contemporary social issues are of special interest at this time. Currently publishes 18 to 20 books a year. Prefers agented submissions but accepts unsolicited submissions by email. Response only if interested.

P121 Elsevier Ltd

Book Publisher
125 London Wall, London, EC2Y 5AS
United Kingdom
Tel: +44 (0) 20 7424 4200
Fax: +44 (0) 20 7483 2293

https://www.elsevier.com

ACADEMIC > **Nonfiction** > *Nonfiction Books*
  Health; Medicine; Science; Technology
PROFESSIONAL > **Nonfiction** > *Nonfiction Books*
  Health; Medicine; Science; Technology

Send: Query
Don't send: Full text

Publisher of medical, scientific, and technical books for the professional and academic markets.

Book Publisher: Morgan Kaufmann Publishers

P122 Enitharmon Editions

Book Publisher
United Kingdom
Tel: +44 (0) 20 7430 0844

info@enitharmon.co.uk

https://www.enitharmon.co.uk
https://www.facebook.com/EnitharmonEditions/
https://twitter.com/enitharmonpress
https://instagram.com/enitharmon.editions
https://www.youtube.com/channel/UCIRq9ScqeBrQ4_HdqELUzaw
https://www.pinterest.co.uk/enitharmoneditions/

Fiction > *Short Fiction Collections*

Nonfiction
  Illustrated Books: Arts; Photography
  Nonfiction Books: Arts; Literary Criticism; Literary
Poetry > *Poetry Collections*

Closed to approaches.

An independent British publisher. We specialise in artists' books, artworks and literary editions. Our artists' books, which are in the tradition of the livre d'artiste, contain loose-leaf signed limited edition prints by such artists as Peter Blake, Jim Dine and Duane Michals. The artworks we publish include etchings, lithographs, photographs and paintings by artists including David Hockney, Paula Rego and Caroline Walker.

P123 Enslow Publishers, Inc.

Book Publisher
2544 Clinton Street, Buffalo, NY 14224
United States

CustomerService@enslow.com

https://www.enslow.com

ACADEMIC > Nonfiction > *Nonfiction Books*
Biography; Current Affairs; Drugs; Health; History; Holidays; Mathematics; Politics; Recreation; Science; Sport; Technology

Send: Query
How to send: Email

Publishes high-quality educational nonfiction books for children and young adults, who will access these materials in schools and public libraries. Our goals are that readers will be able to trust our products and that the books will satisfy their needs. The primary markets are school and public libraries. Books cover subjects including biography, contemporary issues, health & drug education, history and government, holidays and customs, math, science and technology, science projects and experiments, sports and recreation.

P124 Epicenter Press Inc.
Book Publisher
United States

info@epicenterpress.com

https://epicenterpress.com
https://www.facebook.com/EpicenterPressInc/
https://x.com/epicenterpress

Fiction > *Novels*: Alaska

Nonfiction > *Nonfiction Books*
Alaska; Biography; Comedy / Humour; Crime; Culture; History; Memoir; Native Americans

Send: Query; Pitch; Writing sample; Synopsis; Author bio
How to send: Email

Publishes nonfiction and fiction that relates to Alaska including biography, fiction, select memoirs, history, humor, life in the North, Native American culture, true crime.

Editor: Lael Morgan

P125 Evan-Moor Educational Publishers
Book Publisher
10 Harris Court, Ste C-3, Monterey, CA 93940
United States
Tel: +1 (800) 777-4362
Fax: +1 (800) 777-4332

customerservice@evan-moor.com

https://www.evan-moor.com
http://www.facebook.com/evanmoorcorp
https://twitter.com/evanmoor
https://www.youtube.com/channel/UCW1uyTjhrULw-vnU8PRwk0A
https://www.instagram.com/evanmoor_publisher/?hl=en

CHILDREN'S > **Nonfiction** > *Nonfiction Books*: Education

PROFESSIONAL > **Nonfiction** > *Nonfiction Books*: Education

Publishes practical, creative, and engaging PreK-8 educational materials.

P126 Everything With Words
Book Publisher
United Kingdom

info@everythingwithwords.com

http://www.everythingwithwords.com

ADULT > **Fiction** > *Novels*: Literary

CHILDREN'S > **Fiction** > *Novels*

Send: Query; Outline; Author bio; Writing sample
How to send: Email

We are open to submissions from both agents and authors.

At the moment, we don't publish picture books and we're not very interested in books with a strong moral or didactic aim – fine books do change people's view of the world but we find that books where the author's views are the main driving force tend to be heavy and predictable.

We don't publish adult horror fiction or crime.

Your book must be full length which means at least forty thousand words.

We try to respond to every query but we do receive a lot of submissions.

Please send a brief summary, something about yourself and three chapters or the first fifty pages.

P127 Facet Publishing
Book Publisher
Room 150, C/O British Library, 96 Euston Road, NW1 2DB
United Kingdom

info@facetpublishing.co.uk

https://www.facetpublishing.co.uk
https://www.facebook.com/facetpublishing
https://twitter.com/facetpublishing
https://www.youtube.com/user/facetpublishing
https://www.linkedin.com/company/facet-publishing

PROFESSIONAL > **Nonfiction** > *Nonfiction Books*
Data and Information Systems; Information Science

Describes itself as the leading publisher of books for library, information and heritage professionals worldwide.

P128 Fairlight Books
Book Publisher; Online Publisher
Summertown Pavilion, 18-24 Middle Way, Oxford, OX2 7LG
United Kingdom
Tel: +44 (0) 1865 957790

contact@fairlightbooks.com
Submissions@FairlightBooks.com

https://www.fairlightbooks.co.uk
https://www.facebook.com/FairlightBooks/
https://twitter.com/FairlightBooks
https://www.instagram.com/fairlightbooks/

Fiction
Novellas: Literary
Novels: Literary
Short Fiction: Literary

Closed to approaches.

Publishes literary fiction. Accepts novels and novellas for print publication and short stories up to 10,000 words (including flash fiction) for online publication. Send query by email with synopsis and writing sample up to 10,000 words for long fiction, or full text for short stories.

P129 Farrar, Straus & Giroux
Publishing Imprint
United States

Book Publisher: Macmillan Publishers

P130 The Feminist Press
Book Publisher
365 Fifth Avenue, Suite 5406, New York, NY 10016
United States

editor@feministpress.org

https://www.feministpress.org
https://www.facebook.com/FeministPress/
http://thefeministpress.tumblr.com/
https://www.youtube.com/channel/UCClCd_SsorK5JGKCE7rD7vw
https://twitter.com/FeministPress
https://www.instagram.com/feministpress/

ADULT
Fiction
Graphic Novels: Feminism
Novels: Contemporary; Fantasy; Feminism; Literary; Mystery; Speculative
Nonfiction > *Nonfiction Books*
Activism; Africa; African American; Arts; Asia; Asian American; Biography; Education; Feminism; Films; Health; History; Italian American; Italy; Journalism; Judaism; LGBTQIA; Legal; Media; Medicine; Memoir; Middle East; Popular Culture; Postcolonialism; Science; Sexuality; South America

Poetry > *Poetry Collections*: Feminism

CHILDREN'S > **Fiction** > *Novels*: Feminism

Closed to approaches.

Feminist publisher, publishing an array of genres including cutting-edge fiction, activist nonfiction, literature in translation, hybrid memoirs, children's books, and more.

P131 Fernwood Publishing
Book Publisher
2970 Oxford Street, Halifax, NS, B3L 2W4
Canada
Tel: +1 (902) 857-1388

editorial@fernpub.ca

https://fernwoodpublishing.ca
https://twitter.com/fernpub
https://www.facebook.com/fernwood.publishing
https://instagram.com/fernpub

ACADEMIC > **Nonfiction** > *Nonfiction Books*
  Activism; African Diaspora; Biography; Canada; Climate Science; Crime; Culture; Disabilities; Economics; Education; Family; Feminism; Gender; Health; History; Legal; Memoir; Politics; Postcolonialism; Racism; Sexuality; Social Class; Social Issues; Sociology; Urban

Send: Proposal
Don't send: Full text
How to send: Email

A non-fiction publisher specializing in books that provide a critical analysis of society. Publishes books that address issues of activism and social change, Indigenous resistance and decolonization, global justice, law, politics, social work, sociology, anti-racism, feminism, social theory, and more.

Acquisitions Editors: Tanya Andrusieczko; Wayne Antony; Jazz Cook; Fiona Jeffries; Fazeela Jiwa; Errol Sharpe

Managing Editor: Beverley Rach

Publishing Imprint: Roseway (**P317**)

P132 Fighting High
Book Publisher
23 Hitchin Road, Stotfold, Hitchin, Herts, SG5 4HP
United Kingdom
Tel: +44 (0) 7936 415843

fightinghigh@btinternet.com

https://fighting-high-books.myshopify.com
https://twitter.com/FightingHigh
https://www.facebook.com/groups/24337176057

Nonfiction > *Nonfiction Books*
  Adventure; Military History

Send: Query; Proposal; Synopsis; Writing sample
Don't send: Full text
How to send: Email

We specialise in non-fiction books that focus on human endeavour, particularly in a historical military setting. We also consider other stories of human enterprise and adventure.

P133 Firefly
Book Publisher
Britannia House, Caerphilly Business Park, Van Road, Caerphilly, CF83 3GG
United Kingdom

submissions@fireflypress.co.uk
hello@fireflypress.co.uk

https://fireflypress.co.uk
https://www.facebook.com/FireflyPress/
https://twitter.com/FireflyPress
https://www.instagram.com/fireflypress/
https://www.youtube.com/channel/UCqzaLmXCoGJEQuaooZcnb4Q

CHILDREN'S > **Fiction**
  Early Readers; *Middle Grade*
TEEN > **Fiction** > *Novels*
YOUNG ADULT > **Fiction** > *Novels*

Closed to approaches.

Publishes fiction and nonfiction for children and young adults aged 5-19. Not currently accepting nonfiction submissions. Fiction submissions through agents only. Not currently publishing any picture books or colour illustrated book for any age group.

P134 Forum Books
Publishing Imprint

Book Publisher: Random House

P135 Free Association Books Ltd
Book Publisher
1 Angel Cottages, Milespit Hill, London, NW7 1RD
United Kingdom

freeassociationbooks@gmail.com

https://freeassociationpublishing.com

Nonfiction > *Nonfiction Books*
  Health; History; Politics; Psychotherapy; Social Issues

Closed to approaches.

Send submissions by post or by email. Publishes books on a wide range of topics including psychotherapy, social work, health studies, history, public policy and more.

P136 Free Spirit Publishing
Book Publisher
Attn: Acquisitions, 9850 51st Ave. N, Suite 100, Minneapolis, MN 55442
United States
Tel: +1 (714) 891-2273
Fax: +1 (888) 877-7606

acquisitions@freespirit.com

https://www.freespirit.com
https://freespiritpublishing.submittable.com/submit
https://www.facebook.com/freespiritpublishing
https://twitter.com/FreeSpiritBooks
http://www.pinterest.com/freespiritbooks
https://www.instagram.com/freespiritpublishing
http://www.youtube.com/user/FreeSpiritPublishing

CHILDREN'S
  Fiction
    Board Books: Bullying; Disabilities; Personal Development; Wellbeing
    Novels: Bullying; Depression; Disabilities; Family; Health; Personal Development; Wellbeing
    Picture Books: Bullying; Disabilities; Personal Development; Wellbeing
  Nonfiction
    Board Books: Bullying; Disabilities; Education; Personal Development; Wellbeing
    Nonfiction Books: Bullying; Depression; Disabilities; Education; Family; Health; Personal Development; Social Justice; Wellbeing
    Picture Books: Biography; Bullying; Disabilities; Education; Personal Development; Wellbeing
TEEN
  Fiction > *Novels*
    Bullying; Depression; Disabilities; Family; Health; LGBTQIA; Personal Development; Wellbeing

  Nonfiction > *Nonfiction Books*
    Bullying; Depression; Disabilities; Education; Family; Health; LGBTQIA; Personal Development; Social Justice; Wellbeing

Send: Proposal
How to send: Post; Submittable

Publishes nonfiction books and learning materials for children and teens, parents, educators, counselors, and others who live and work with young people. Also publishes fiction relevant to the mission of providing children and teens with the tools they need to succeed in life, e.g.: self-esteem; conflict resolution, etc. No general fiction or storybooks; books with animal or mythical characters; books with religious or New Age content; or single biographies, autobiographies, or memoirs. Submit by proposals by post or through online submission system. See website for full submission guidelines.

P137 FrontLine
Publishing Imprint
United States

Media Company: Charisma Media

P138 Future Horizons
Book Publisher
2201 N Collins St, Ste 250, Arlington, TX 76011
United States
Tel: +1 (817) 277-0727
Fax: +1 (817) 277-2270

https://www.fhautism.com
https://www.facebook.com/futurehorizons
https://www.linkedin.com/company/future-horizons-inc-
https://www.instagram.com/futurehorizons/
https://www.youtube.com/@futurehorizonsautismchannne5331

ADULT > **Nonfiction** > *Nonfiction Books*: Autism

PROFESSIONAL > **Nonfiction** > *Nonfiction Books*: Autism

Publishes books on autism, Asperger's Syndrome, and other related disorders.

P139 Gale

Book Publisher
27555 Executive Dr. Ste 270, Farmington Hills, MI 48331
United States
Tel: +1 (800) 877-4253
Fax: +1 (877) 363-4253

gale.customerexperience@cengage.com

https://www.gale.com
https://www.facebook.com/GaleCengage/
https://www.linkedin.com/company/gale
https://twitter.com/galecengage
https://www.youtube.com/user/GaleCengage

Book Publisher: Cengage

ACADEMIC > **Nonfiction**
Nonfiction Books: Business; Chemistry; Computer Science; Earth Science; Economics; Education; Finance; Health; History; Legal; Literature; Mathematics; Medicine; Physics; Science; Sociology; Technology
Reference: General

ADULT > **Nonfiction**
Nonfiction Books: Agriculture; Antiques; Arts; Astronomy; Business; Chemistry; Crafts; Earth Science; Economics; Education; Finance; Gardening; Health; History; Hobbies; Legal; Literature; Medicine; Science; Sport; Technology
Reference: General

PROFESSIONAL > **Nonfiction**
Nonfiction Books: Business; Economics; Education; Finance; Health; Legal; Medicine; Science; Sociology; Technology
Reference: General

Supplies businesses, schools, and libraries with books and electronic reference materials.

Book Publisher: KidHaven Press

Publishing Imprints: The Taft Group; Blackbird Press; Charles Scribner & Sons; Five Star; G.K. Hall & Co.; Graham & Whiteside Ltd; Greenhaven Publishing; KG Saur Verlag GmbH & Co. KG; Lucent Books; Macmillan Reference USA; Primary Source Media; Schirmer Reference; St James Press; Thorndike Press; Twayne Publishers; UXL; Wheeler Publishing

P140 Gemini Books

Book Publisher
United Kingdom

customerservice@geminibooks.com

https://geminibooks.com

ADULT
Fiction > *Graphic Novels*

Nonfiction
Nonfiction Books: Arts; Biography; Comedy / Humour; Design; Fashion; Lifestyle; Memoir; Popular Culture
Puzzles: General

CHILDREN'S
Fiction
Board Books; *Chapter Books*; *Early Readers*; *Middle Grade*; *Picture Books*
Nonfiction
Activity Books; *Board Books*; *Colouring Books*; *Nonfiction Books*

Closed to approaches.

An independent publisher, established in 2023. We make beautiful, illustrated books for children and adults that spark readers' imagination. With the energy of a start-up, and a publishing pedigree spanning over twenty-five years, we champion exciting new authors and illustrators and publish brilliant books that entertain readers of all ages.

Book Publisher: Pimpernel Press (**P292**)

P141 Gill

Book Publisher
Ireland

https://www.gill.ie

Publishing Imprints: Gill Books (**P142**); Gill Education (**P143**)

P142 Gill Books

Publishing Imprint
Hume Avenue, Park West, Dublin, D12 YV96
Ireland
Tel: +353 (01) 500 9500

https://www.gillbooks.ie
http://www.facebook.com/GillBooks
http://www.twitter.com/Gill_Books
http://www.instagram.com/GillBooks

Book Publisher: Gill (**P141**)

ADULT > **Nonfiction**
Gift Books: Ireland
Nonfiction Books: Biography; Comedy / Humour; Crafts; Crime; Current Affairs; Food and Drink; History; Hobbies; Ireland; Lifestyle; Mind, Body, Spirit; Nature; Parenting; Politics; Sport
Reference: General, and in particular: Ireland
CHILDREN'S
Fiction > *Novels*
Nonfiction > *Nonfiction Books*

Send: Query; Outline; Synopsis; Table of contents; Writing sample; Author bio
How to send: Online submission system; Post

Publishes adult nonfiction and children's fiction and nonfiction. No adult fiction, poetry, short stories or plays. In general, focuses on books of Irish interest. Prefers proposals through online submission system, but will also accept proposals by post. See website for full submission guidelines.

P143 Gill Education

Publishing Imprint
Hume Avenue, Park West, D12 YV96
Ireland
Tel: +353 (1) 500 9500

primarysubmissions@gill.ie
secondarysubmissions@gill.ie

https://www.gilleducation.ie
https://www.facebook.com/GillEducation
https://twitter.com/GillEducation
https://www.instagram.com/GillEducation

Book Publisher: Gill (**P141**)

ACADEMIC > **Nonfiction** > *Nonfiction Books*
Accounting; Arts; Building / Construction; Business; Communication; Computer Programming; Design; Economics; Education; English; French; Geography; German; Graphic Design; Health; History; Home Economics / Domestic Science; Information Science; Irish (Gaeilge); Legal; Management; Marketing; Mathematics; Music; Nursing; Physical Education; Physics; Politics; Psychology; Religion; Science; Sociology

Send: Proposal
How to send: Email

Publishes books for the primary, secondary, and further education markets. Welcomes proposals from first time and experienced authors alike. All subject areas are of interest. See website for full guidelines.

P144 Glass Poetry Press

Book Publisher
United States

chaps@glass-poetry.com
editor@glass-poetry.com

https://www.glass-poetry.com
https://www.glass-poetry.com/submissions.html

Poetry > *Chapbooks*

Publishes poetry chapbooks between 15 and 25 pages. Open to submissions between October 1 and October 31 each year.

P145 The Globe Pequot Press

Book Publisher
64 South Main Street, Essex, CT 06426
United States

GPSubmissions@rowman.com

http://www.globepequot.com
https://rowman.com/Page/GlobePequot
https://www.facebook.com/globepequot/
https://twitter.com/globepequot

Book Publisher: Rowman & Littlefield Publishing Group

Nonfiction > *Nonfiction Books*
  Biography; Business; Cookery; Gardening; History; Mind, Body, Spirit; Nature; Travel

Send: Outline; Table of contents; Writing sample; Author bio; Market info
How to send: Email; Post

Publishes books about iconic brands and people, regional interest, history, lifestyle, cooking and food culture, and folklore – books that hit the intersection of a reader's interest in a specific place and their passion for a specific topic.

Book Publisher: Backbeat Books (**P027**)

Publishing Imprints: Applause; Astragal Press; Down East Books; FalconGuides; Lyons Press; Mcbooks Press; Muddy Boots; Pineapple Press (**P293**); Prometheus; Skip Jack Press; Stackpole Books; TwoDot; Union Park Press

P146 Gold SF
Publishing Imprint
United States

goldsmithspress@gold.ac.uk

https://www.gold.ac.uk/goldsmiths-press/submissions/

Book Publisher: Goldsmiths Press

Fiction > *Novels*
  Economics; Environment; Ethnic Groups; Experimental; Gender; Intersectional Feminism; LGBTQIA; Politics; Postcolonialism; Science Fiction; Sexuality; Social Class; Social Justice; Speculative

Send: Proposal; Writing sample
How to send: Email

Dedicated to discovering and publishing new intersectional feminist science fiction, promoting voices that answer to the unprecedented times in which we find ourselves, and orientated towards to social, economic, and environmental justice.

P147 Goodman Beck Publishing
Book Publisher
United States

info@goodmanbeck.com

https://www.goodmanbeck.com
https://www.facebook.com/goodmanbeck
https://twitter.com/goodmanbeck

Fiction > *Novels*

Nonfiction > *Nonfiction Books*
  Mental Health; Personal Development; Psychology; Self Help; Spirituality

Does not want:

> **Fiction** > *Novels*
>   Fantasy; Romance; Science Fiction
> **Nonfiction** > *Nonfiction Books*
>   How To; Politics; Religion

Send: Query
How to send: Email
How not to send: Post

Interested in helping people feel better about themselves and their lives. Focuses on mental health, personal growth, aging well, positive psychology, accessible spirituality, and overall self-help. Not interested in science fiction, fantasy, religious or political works, romance novels, textbooks, or how-to books.

Editor: Michael Pearson

P148 Goose Lane Editions
Book Publisher
Suite 330, 500 Beaverbrook Court,
Fredericton, NB, E3B 5X4
Canada
Tel: +1 (506) 450-4251
Fax: +1 (888) 926-8377

info@gooselane.com

https://gooselane.com
https://www.twitter.com/goose_lane
https://www.facebook.com/GooseLaneEditions/
https://www.instagram.com/goose_lane

Fiction
  Novels: General, and in particular: Historical Fiction
  Short Fiction Collections: General

Nonfiction > *Nonfiction Books*
  Architecture; Arts; Biography; Business; Crime; History; LGBTQIA; Memoir; Military History; Mind, Body, Spirit; Nature; New Brunswick; Philosophy; Politics; Sociology; Travel; Walking Guides

Poetry > *Poetry Collections*

Send: Query; Author bio; Synopsis; Writing sample
How to send: Online submission system

Publishes literary fiction and nonfiction (and poetry through its poetry imprint) by established and up-and-coming Canadian authors. Submissions will only be considered from outside Canada if the author is Canadian and the book is of extraordinary interest to Canadian readers. No unsolicited MSS, children's, or young adult. See website for full submission details.

Editor: Angela Williams

Publishing Imprint: Icehouse (**P179**)

P149 Goss & Crested China Club
Book Publisher
Forestside House, Broadwalk, Forestside,
Rowlands Castle, PO9 6EE
United Kingdom
Tel: +44 (0) 7738 842856

http://www.gosschinaclub.co.uk

ADULT > **Nonfiction** > *Reference*
  Antiques; Collectibles

PROFESSIONAL > **Nonfiction** > *Reference*
  Antiques; Collectibles

Publishes books on crested heraldic china and antique porcelain.

Managing Director: Andrew Pine

P150 Graffeg
Book Publisher
24 Stradey Park Business Centre, Mwrwg Road, Llangennech, Llanelli, SA14 8YP
United Kingdom
Tel: +44 (0) 1554 824000

croeso@graffeg.com

https://graffeg.com
https://www.facebook.com/graffegbooks
https://twitter.com/graffeg_books
https://www.pinterest.co.uk/GraffegBooks/
http://instagram.com/graffegbooks
https://www.youtube.com/channel/UCqnEBIarxraMZEYD8IlXh-A

Nonfiction > *Illustrated Books*
  Food; History; Nature

Send: Outline; Full text; Table of contents; Author bio
How to send: Online submission system

Always pleased to receive submissions from new and published authors. Publishes illustrated books on nature, heritage and food. Imprints welcome submissions for children's books up to young adult reads. Books with the potential of being serialised are also of special interest.

Publishing Imprints: Bird Eye Books (**P048**); Cadno (**P067**); Graffeg Childrens (**P151**)

P151 Graffeg Childrens
Publishing Imprint
United Kingdom

https://graffeg.com

Book Publisher: Graffeg (**P150**)

CHILDREN'S
  Fiction > *Picture Books*
  Nonfiction > *Illustrated Books*

Send: Outline; Full text; Table of contents; Author bio
How to send: Online submission system

Welcomes submissions for children's books.

P152 Graywolf Press
Book Publisher
212 Third Avenue North, Suite 485,
Minneapolis, MN 55401
United States
Tel: +1 (651) 641-0077
Fax: +1 (651) 641-0036

wolves@graywolfpress.org

https://www.graywolfpress.org
https://graywolfpress.submittable.com/submit
https://www.facebook.com/GraywolfPress/
https://twitter.com/GraywolfPress
https://www.instagram.com/graywolfpress/

Fiction
Novels: Literary
Short Fiction Collections: Literary

Nonfiction
Essays: Creative Writing; Cultural Criticism; Literary Criticism; Literary
Nonfiction Books: Creative Writing; Cultural Criticism; Literary Criticism; Memoir
Poetry > *Poetry Collections*

How to send: Through a contest; Through a literary agent; Submittable

Publishes about 30 books annually, mostly poetry, memoirs, essays, novels, and short stories. Accepts submissions through literary agents, or via competitions during specific windows.

Online Magazine: Graywolf Lab (**M145**)

P153 Guernica Editions
Book Publisher
1241 Marble Rock Road, Gananoque, ON,
K7G 2V4
Canada

michaelmirolla@guernicaeditions.com

https://guernicaeditions.com
https://x.com/guernica_ed
https://www.facebook.com/guernicaed
https://www.instagram.com/guernicaeditions/?hl=en
https://www.youtube.com/channel/UCjCv1d7ARSS9couCoMYwVkw

Fiction
Novels; *Short Fiction Collections*
Nonfiction > *Nonfiction Books*: Narrative Essays

Poetry > *Poetry Collections*

Publishes Essential Prose, Poetry, Essays, Writers Series, Anthologies and First Poets Series. No submissions by post. Send queries by email with manuscripts as attachments during open submission periods. See website for details.

P154 Guinness World Records
Book Publisher
Ground Floor, The Rookery, 2 Dyott Street,
London, WC1A 1DE
United Kingdom

https://www.guinnessworldrecords.com

Nonfiction > *Reference*

Publishes books of amazing facts, figures, and feats of outstanding human endeavour.

P155 Guppy Books
Book Publisher
United Kingdom

https://guppybooks.co.uk
https://twitter.com/guppybooks
https://www.instagram.com/guppypublishin/

CHILDREN'S > **Fiction**
Chapter Books; *Early Readers*; *Middle Grade*

How to send: Through a literary agent

A small and independent publisher of children's fiction. No nonfiction or picture books. No submissions from unagented or unpublished authors.

P156 Hachette Book Group
Book Publisher
United States

https://www.hachettebookgroup.com

Book Publisher: Hachette Livre

Fiction > *Novels*

Nonfiction > *Nonfiction Books*

How to send: Through a literary agent

Includes 24 imprints covering the entire array of contemporary fiction and nonfiction, from the most popular to the most literary.

Book Publishers: Basic Books Group (**P036**); Grand Central Publishing; Little, Brown and Company; Perseus Books; Workman Publishing (**P437**)

P157 Half Mystic Press
Book Publisher
United States

hello@halfmystic.com

https://www.halfmystic.com
https://halfmystic.submittable.com/submit

Fiction
Novellas; *Novels*; *Short Fiction Collections*
Nonfiction > *Nonfiction Books*
Memoir; Music

Poetry > *Poetry Collections*

How to send: Submittable

Publishes poetry, essay, and short story collections; drama; memoirs; novellas; full-length novels; experimental work. Publishes full-length manuscripts only—no chapbooks. See website for full submission guidelines.

Print Magazine: Half Mystic Journal (**M149**)

P158 Hammersmith Books
Book Publisher
4/4A Bloomsbury Square, London, WC1A 2RP
United Kingdom

https://www.hammersmithbooks.co.uk
https://www.facebook.com/HammersmithHealthBooks
http://twitter.com/HHealthBooks
https://www.instagram.com/hhealthbooks/?hl=en
https://www.pinterest.com/hhealthbooks/

ACADEMIC > **Nonfiction** > *Nonfiction Books*
Diet; Health; Medicine; Mental Health; Nutrition; Wellbeing

ADULT > **Nonfiction** > *Nonfiction Books*
Diet; Health; Medicine; Mental Health; Nutrition; Wellbeing

PROFESSIONAL > **Nonfiction** > *Nonfiction Books*
Diet; Health; Medicine; Mental Health; Nutrition; Wellbeing

Publisher of health, medicine, and nutrition books for the general public, health professionals, and academic markets.

Editor: Georgina Bentliff

P159 Hancock House Publishers
Book Publisher
Unit 104- 4550 Birch Bay-Lynden Rd, Blaine, WA 98230-9436
United States
Tel: +1 (800) 938-1114
Fax: +1 (800) 983-2262

submissions@hancockhouse.com
info@hancockhouse.com

https://www.hancockhouse.com
https://x.com/hancockhousepub
https://www.facebook.com/hancockhousepublishers/
https://www.pinterest.ca/hancockhousepub/
https://www.instagram.com/hancockhousepublishers/
https://www.youtube.com/user/HancockWildlifeFndn

ACADEMIC > **Nonfiction** > *Nonfiction Books*

ADULT
Nonfiction > *Nonfiction Books*
Alaska; Arctic; Bigfoot; Biography; Birds; British Columbia; Cookery; Culture; Falconry; Fishing; Folklore, Myths, and Legends; History; Nature; Regional; Wildlife

Poetry > *Poetry Collections*
Native Americans; Westerns

CHILDREN'S > Nonfiction
  Colouring Books: Animals; Bigfoot; Birds; Folklore, Myths, and Legends; Native Americans; Nature
  Nonfiction Books: Animals; Bigfoot; Birds; Folklore, Myths, and Legends; Native Americans; Nature

Send: Query; Table of contents; Writing sample; Synopsis; Author bio; Market info
How to send: Email

Focus has from the beginning been on nonfiction, regional titles, emphasizing western and northern history and biographies, indigenous art and culture, natural history, wildlife and folklore. Through the years, we have established an international reputation on specialized niche topics such as cryptozoology, falconry and Canadiana, among others. We continue to seek to define ourselves through exploring related and emerging genres.

Editor: David Hancock

P160 Handspring Publishing
Publishing Imprint
United Kingdom

Publishing Imprint: Jessica Kingsley Publishers (**P197**)

P161 Happy Yak
Publishing Imprint
1 Triptych Place, Second Floor, London, SE1 9SH
United Kingdom
Tel: +44 (0) 20 7700 9000

https://www.quartoknows.com/happy-yak

Book Publisher: The Quarto Group, Inc. (**P307**)

CHILDREN'S
  Fiction
    Board Books; Picture Books
  Nonfiction > Nonfiction Books

Send: Proposal
How to send: Email

A publisher of innovative preschool concepts, laugh-out-loud picture books, and illustrated nonfiction titles. If you have a book idea in one of our focus areas that you'd like to share with us, we'd love to hear it.

P162 Hardie Grant
Book Publisher
Level 11, 36 Wellington Street, Collingwood, VIC 3066
Australia
Tel: +61 3 8520 6444

hello@hardiegrant.com

https://www.hardiegrant.com

Nonfiction > *Nonfiction Books*

A global media and publishing business on a mission to help emerging ideas thrive. Since 1997, we've been creating culture, sharing stories, and re-imagining the way brands connect with audiences.

Book Publisher: Hardie Grant (North America) (**P163**)

P163 Hardie Grant (North America)
Book Publisher
2912 Telegraph Avenue, Berkeley, CA 94705
United States

https://www.hardiegrant.com

Book Publisher: Hardie Grant (**P162**)

Nonfiction > *Nonfiction Books*

P164 Harmony
Publishing Imprint

Book Publisher: Random House

P165 Harvard University Press
Book Publisher
79 Garden Street, Cambridge, MA 02138
United States
Tel: +1 (617) 495-2600

contact_hup@harvard.edu

https://www.hup.harvard.edu
https://www.facebook.com/HarvardPress
https://twitter.com/Harvard_Press
https://www.instagram.com/harvardpress/
https://www.linkedin.com/company/harvard-university-press-hup/
https://medium.com/@hup

ACADEMIC > Nonfiction
  Nonfiction Books: Architecture; Arts; Biography; Business; Classics / Ancient World; Economics; Education; Health; History; Legal; Literature; Media; Medicine; Music; Nature; Performing Arts; Philosophy; Politics; Popular Culture; Psychology; Religion; Science; Sociology
  Reference: General

Publishes humanities, sciences, social sciences, etc. Academic nonfiction only. See website for manuscript guidelines and appropriate editorial contacts.

Publishing Imprint: Belknap Press

P166 Hashtag Press
Book Publisher
United Kingdom

info@hashtagpress.co.uk
submissions@hashtagpress.co.uk

https://www.hashtagpress.co.uk
https://twitter.com/hashtag_press
https://www.instagram.com/hashtag_press/
https://www.tiktok.com/@hashtag_press
https://www.facebook.com/hashtagpressbooks

ADULT > Nonfiction > *Nonfiction Books*
  Memoir; Parenting; Self Help

CHILDREN'S > Fiction > *Middle Grade*
  Adventure; Comedy / Humour; Coming of Age; Friends; Mental Health
YOUNG ADULT > Fiction > *Novels*

Send: Query; Pitch; Synopsis; Writing sample; Author bio
How to send: Word file email attachment

We are looking for excellent writers with brilliant diverse stories to tell.

Please read the about us before submitting to us. We would prefer books that haven't been published already.

We love diverse and inclusive books! We are open to debut authors especially those from an underrepresented background. We publish commercial fiction books for young people that are plot driven with relatable, inspiring characters.

We are a tiny publishing house, so we are incredibly selective.

Any books that are not diverse or inclusive will be a no.

P167 Hawthorne Books
Book Publisher
2201 NE 23rd Avenue Third Floor, Portland, OR 97212
United States
Tel: +1 (503) 327-8849

rhughes@hawthornebooks.com

http://www.hawthornebooks.com
https://www.facebook.com/HawthorneBooks
http://twitter.com/hawthornebooks
http://pinterest.com/hawthornebooks/

Fiction > *Novels*: Literary

Nonfiction > *Nonfiction Books*
  Memoir; Narrative Essays

Closed to approaches.

An independent literary press based in Portland, Oregon, with a national scope and deep regional roots. Focuses on literary fiction and nonfiction with innovative and varied approaches to the relationships between essay, memoir, and narrative.

Authors: Kassten Alonso; Poe Ballantine; Peter Donahue; Monica Drake; D'Arcy Fallon; Peter Fogtdal; Jeff Meyers; Mark Mordue; Scott Nadelson; Toby Olson; Gin Phillips; Lynne Sharon Schwartz; Tom Spanbauer; Michael Strelow; Richard Wiley

P168 Hay House Publishers
Book Publisher
1st Floor, Crawford Corner, 91–93 Baker Street, London, W1U 6QQ
United Kingdom
Tel: +44 (0) 20 3927 7290
Fax: +44 (0) 20 3675 2451

https://www.hayhouse.co.uk
https://www.facebook.com/hayhouse
https://www.instagram.com/hayhouseuk
https://twitter.com/hayhouseuk

Nonfiction > *Nonfiction Books*
Alternative Health; Angels; Anxiety Disorders; Astrology; Business; Communication; Finance; Health; New Age; Parenting; Personal Development; Pets; Psychological Trauma; Relationships; Self Help; Spirituality; Tarot; Vegetarianism

Send: Query; Synopsis
How to send: Online submission system

Describes itself as the world's leading mind body and spirit publisher. Approach via form on website. See website for full submission guidelines.

P169 Hearing Eye
Book Publisher
Box 1, 99 Torriano Avenue, London, NW5 2RX
United Kingdom
Tel: +44 (0) 7519 917915

https://hearingeye.org
https://www.facebook.com/hearingeyepoetry

Poetry > *Poetry Collections*

Small independent poetry publisher. Rarely publishes unsolicited material.

P170 Hell's Hundred
Publishing Imprint
United States

Book Publisher: Soho Press (**P348**)

P171 Henley Hall Press
Book Publisher
United Kingdom

https://henleyhallpress.co.uk
https://twitter.com/HenleyHallPress

Nonfiction > *Nonfiction Books*
Farming; Gardening; History; Politics

Send: Pitch
How to send: Online contact form

An independent publisher of thought-provoking non-fiction books.

Our categories are: farming, politics, history, garden design and that all-encompassing category 'misc'.

No cancel culture here. We are happy to publish books that challenge received wisdom – or wokedom – and we support the work of the Free Speech Union.

We aim to publish just two to four books a year. This is to devote the time to help your book succeed in a crowded market.

P172 Henry Holt & Co.
Publishing Imprint
United States

Book Publisher: Macmillan Publishers

P173 High Stakes Publishing
Publishing Imprint
Harpenden, AL5 1EQ
United Kingdom

https://highstakespublishing.co.uk

Book Publisher: Oldcastle Books Group (**P264**)

Nonfiction > *Nonfiction Books*: Gambling

Imprint publishing books on gambling.

P174 The History Press
Book Publisher
United Kingdom

submissions@thehistorypress.co.uk

https://www.thehistorypress.co.uk
https://www.facebook.com/thehistorypressuk/
https://twitter.com/TheHistoryPress/
https://www.pinterest.com/thehistorypress/

Nonfiction > *Nonfiction Books*
General, and in particular: Archaeology; Aviation; Biography; Crime; Culture; Entertainment; Folklore, Myths, and Legends; History; Local History; Maritime History; Memoir; Military; Nature; Society; Sport; Transport

Send: Query; Synopsis; Author bio; Market info; Proposal
Don't send: Full text
How to send: Email

Publishes books on history, from local to international, and general nonfiction. Welcomes submissions from both new and established authors. Send query by email. No unsolicited mss. See website for full guidelines.

Publishing Imprint: Phillimore

P175 Hodder & Stoughton Ltd
Book Publisher
Carmelite House, 50 Victoria Embankment, London, EC4Y 0DZ
United Kingdom
Tel: +44 (0) 20 3122 6777

enquiries@hachette.co.uk

https://www.hodder.co.uk
https://www.facebook.com/hodderbooks/
https://twitter.com/HodderBooks
https://www.instagram.com/hodderbooks/

Fiction > *Novels*

Nonfiction > *Nonfiction Books*

How to send: Through a literary agent

Large London-based publisher of nonfiction and fiction.

Book Publisher: Hodder Faith

Publishing Imprint: Nicholas Brealey Publishing

P176 HopeRoad
Book Publisher
PO Box 55544, Exhibition Road, London, SW7 2DB
United Kingdom

info@hoperoadpublishing.com

https://www.hoperoadpublishing.com
https://www.facebook.com/HopeRoadPublishing
https://twitter.com/hoperoadpublish
https://www.instagram.com/hoperoadpublishing/
https://www.youtube.com/channel/UCd3aU4rc8zWAnB3dgnV-xhw?view_as=subscriber

ADULT > **Fiction** > *Novels*
Africa; Asia; Caribbean; Culture; Disabilities; Social Justice

YOUNG ADULT > **Fiction** > *Novels*
Africa; Asia; Caribbean; Culture; Disabilities; Social Justice

How to send: Through a literary agent

Promotes the best writing from and about Africa, Asia and the Caribbean, with themes of identity, cultural stereotyping, disability and injustices of particular interest.

P177 Host Publications
Book Publisher
PO BOX 302920, Austin, TX 78703
United States

editors@hostpublications.com

https://hostpublications.com
https://hostpublications.submittable.com/submit
http://instagram.com/HostPublications

Fiction in Translation > *Short Fiction Collections*

Fiction > *Short Fiction Collections*

Poetry in Translation > *Poetry Collections*

Poetry > *Poetry Collections*

How to send: Submittable

Publishes literature from across the United States and around the world, including Nobel Prize winners. In 2018, shifted its focus from international authors to authors based in the United States, and committed to creating a seat at the table for marginalized groups: primarily women, people of color, immigrants, and LGBTQ+ writers.

P178 Howgate Publishing
Book Publisher
United Kingdom

info@howgatepublishing.com

https://www.howgatepublishing.com
https://twitter.com/kirstin_howgate

Nonfiction > *Nonfiction Books*
  Military; Warfare

Send: Proposal; Table of contents; Synopsis; Author bio; Market info
How to send: Email

Our vision is simple: to positively impact the way we collectively think about war and warfare, to provide a specific resource and expertise for authors and readers, to be the 'go-to' place for military thought.

P179 Icehouse
Publishing Imprint
Canada

https://gooselane.com/pages/poetry-submission

Book Publisher: Goose Lane Editions (**P148**)

Poetry > *Poetry Collections*

Closed to approaches.

Publishes full-length poetry collections of roughly 48-100 pages, by new and established writers. Consider submissions by Canadian citizens or permanent residents only. Accepts submissions annually between April 1 and June 30.

P180 Icon Books Ltd
Book Publisher
Omnibus Business Centre, 39-41 North Road, London, N7 9DP
United Kingdom
Tel: +44 (0) 20 7697 9695
Fax: +44 (0) 20 7697 9501

info@iconbooks.com
submissions@iconbooks.net

https://iconbooks.com
https://twitter.com/iconbooks
https://www.facebook.com/iconbooks
https://www.instagram.com/iconbooks/
http://www.youtube.com/iconbooksuk

Nonfiction > *Nonfiction Books*
  Biography; Business; Crime; Cultural History; Current Affairs; Economics; Environment; Health; History; Language; Lifestyle; Literature; Mathematics; Memoir; Military History; Nature; Philosophy; Politics; Popular Science; Psychology; Religion; Self Help; Social History; Sport; Transport; Travel

Send: Submission form
How to send: Email
How not to send: Post

We are an adult non-fiction publisher and are happy to read manuscripts from potential new authors. We accept unsolicited adult non-fiction manuscripts only. We do not accept adult fiction, poetry, or children's fiction. If you would like to submit, please download and fill in our submissions form, and send it by email.

P181 Idyll Arbor
Book Publisher
2432 39th Street, Bedford, IN 47421
United States
Tel: +1 (812) 675-6623

editors@idyllarbor.com

https://www.idyllarbor.com

ADULT > **Nonfiction** > *Nonfiction Books*: Health

PROFESSIONAL > **Nonfiction** > *Nonfiction Books*
  Health; Medicine

How to send: Email

Provides information and tools you can use for Recreational Therapists, Activity Professionals, and Allied Therapists. We have texts for educators and students; books for specific areas of your practice; assessments for patients, clients, and residents; and therapeutic games.

We also have books that will improve your personal health and the health of people you work with. Other books from our imprint look at ways we can work to heal our culture.

As we move forward, we continue our commitment to provide material that tracks the trends in the fields we cover and helps you find the energy, ideas, and inspiration you need to succeed in your practice.

P182 Ig Publishing
Book Publisher
PO Box 2547, New York, NY 10163
United States
Tel: +1 (718) 797-0676

submissions@igpub.com

https://www.igpub.com
https://twitter.com/Igpublishing
https://www.facebook.com/pages/Ig-Publishing/176428769078839
https://www.pinterest.com/igpublishing/
https://www.instagram.com/igpublishing/

Fiction > *Novels*: Literary

Nonfiction > *Nonfiction Books*
  Culture; Politics

Send: Query
How to send: Email

A New York-based award-winning independent press dedicated to publishing original literary fiction and political and cultural nonfiction. Send query by email only.

Editor-in-Chief: Robert Lasner

Publishing Imprint: IgKids (**P183**)

P183 IgKids
Publishing Imprint
United States

https://www.igpub.com/
https://www.igpub.com/category/titles/igkids/

Book Publisher: Ig Publishing (**P182**)

CHILDREN'S > **Fiction** > *Middle Grade*
YOUNG ADULT > **Fiction** > *Novels*

Send: Query
How to send: Email

Publishes a curated list of middle grade and YA fiction.

P184 Igloo Books Limited
Book Publisher
Cottage Farm, Mears Ashby Road, Sywell, Northants, NN6 0BJ
United Kingdom
Tel: +44 (0) 1604 741116

customerservice@igloobooks.com

https://igloobooks.com
https://www.facebook.com/igloobooks/
https://instagram.com/igloobooks/
https://www.tiktok.com/@igloobooks

ADULT > **Nonfiction**
  Activity Books; *Colouring Books*; *Gift Books*; *Puzzles*
CHILDREN'S
  Fiction
    Board Books; *Picture Books*
  Nonfiction
    Activity Books; *Board Books*; *Reference*

Publishes nonfiction and gift and puzzle books for adults, and fiction, nonfiction, and novelty books for children.

Publishing Imprint: Autumn Publishing Ltd (**P025**)

P185 Image
Publishing Imprint

Book Publisher: Random House

P186 Imagine Publishing
Publishing Imprint
United States

https://www.imaginebooks.net
https://twitter.com/Imagine_CB
https://www.facebook.com/ImaginePress/
https://www.pinterest.com/charlesbridge/adult-books-from-imagine-publishing/
https://www.instagram.com/imagine_cb/

Book Publisher: Charlesbridge Publishing (**P081**)

Nonfiction
  Coffee Table Books: General
  Nonfiction Books: Arts; Comedy / Humour; Cookery; History; Nature; Politics; Women's Studies
  Puzzles: General

Closed to approaches.

Publishes 8-10 titles a year, primarily focused on history, politics, women's studies, and nature.

P187 Indiana University Press
Book Publisher
IU Office of Scholarly Publishing, Herman B Wells Library E350, 1320 E 10th Street E4, Bloomington, IN 47405-3907
United States
Tel: +1 (812) 855-8817

https://iupress.org
https://www.facebook.com/iupress
https://twitter.com/iupress
https://www.instagram.com/iu.press/
https://www.youtube.com/c/IndianaUniversityPress/videos

ACADEMIC > **Nonfiction** > *Nonfiction Books*
Africa; American Civil War; American Midwest; Eastern Europe; Films; Folklore, Myths, and Legends; Gender; International; Ireland; Jewish Holocaust; Judaism; Media; Middle East; Military History; Music; Paleontology; Performing Arts; Philosophy; Railways; Refugees; Regional; Religion; Russia; Sexuality; Transport

Send: Proposal; Outline; Table of contents; Writing sample; Author bio
How to send: Online submission system

Submit proposals via online proposal submission form.

P188 Information Today, Inc.
Book Publisher
143 Old Marlton Pike, Medford, NJ 08055-8750
United States
Tel: +1 (609) 654-6266
Fax: +1 (609) 654-4209

custserv@infotoday.com

https://www.infotoday.com

Nonfiction > *Nonfiction Books*
Computers; Data and Information Systems; Information Science; Technology

Publishes books and magazines on information technology.

P189 Ink & Willow
Publishing Imprint

Book Publisher: Random House

P190 Inkandescent
Book Publisher
United Kingdom

https://www.inkandescent.co.uk
https://www.facebook.com/InkandescentPublishing/
https://twitter.com/InkandescentUK
https://www.instagram.com/inkandescentuk/
https://www.youtube.com/channel/UC65iDI_gjHKDzJfQSeyDdPA

Fiction
Novellas; *Novels*
Nonfiction > *Nonfiction Books*
Poetry > *Poetry Collections*

Closed to approaches.

We are committed to outsider voices underrepresented in mainstream publishing. In the context of what we do, that primarily means writers who identify as LGBTQ+ or working class, or come from BAME backgrounds. We discover and celebrate original and diverse writing that challenges the status quo. We welcome submissions from new talent and not so new talent, particularly in the form of novellas and short novels.

P191 International Publishers
Book Publisher
235 W 23rd Street, New York, NY 10011-2302
United States
Tel: +1 (212) 366-9816

service@intpubnyc.com

https://www.intpubnyc.com

Nonfiction > *Nonfiction Books*
Culture; Gender Issues; History; Marxism; Philosophy; Politics; Social Issues

Marxist publishers of books on labour rights, race and gender issues, Marxist science, etc.

P192 International Society for Technology in Education (ISTE)
Book Publisher
2111 Wilson Boulevard, Suite 300, Arlington, VA 22201
United States
Tel: +1 (503) 342-2848
Fax: +1 (541) 302-3778

iste@iste.org

https://www.iste.org
https://www.iste.org/professional-development/books
https://twitter.com/iste
https://www.instagram.com/isteconnects/
https://www.facebook.com/ISTEconnects
https://www.iste.org/youtube

ACADEMIC > **Nonfiction** > *Nonfiction Books*
Computer Programming; Digital Technology
PROFESSIONAL > **Nonfiction** > *Nonfiction Books*
Computer Programming; Digital Technology; Education

Publishes books and resources focused on technology in education.

P193 InterVarsity Press (IVP)
Book Publisher
Studio 101, The Record Hall, 16-16A Baldwins Gardens, London, EC1N 7RJ
United Kingdom
Tel: +44 (0) 20 7592 3900

submissions@ivpbooks.com

https://ivpbooks.com
https://www.facebook.com/ivpbooks
https://www.instagram.com/ivpbooks/
https://twitter.com/IVPbookcentre

ACADEMIC > **Nonfiction** > *Nonfiction Books*: Religion
ADULT > **Nonfiction** > *Nonfiction Books*
Biography; Christian Living; Church History; Contemporary Culture; Religion

Closed to approaches.

Aims to produce quality, Evangelical books for the digital age. Send query through form on website.

P194 J. Gordon Shillingford Publishing
Book Publisher
PO Box 86, RPO Corydon Avenue, Winnipeg, MB R3M 3S3
Canada
Tel: +1 (204) 779-6967

jgshill2@mymts.net
jgshillingford@jgshillingford.com

https://www.jgshillingford.com
https://www.facebook.com/jgshillingford/
https://x.com/BooksJgs

Nonfiction > *Nonfiction Books*
Biography; Canada; Crime; Politics; Religion; Social History
Poetry > *Poetry Collections*
Scripts > *Theatre Scripts*

Send: Query; Author bio; Writing sample
How to send: Post; Email

We publish Canadian authored drama, poetry, and certain types of non-fiction. We do not publish fiction. Look through the titles on our website and you'll get a pretty good idea of the kinds of books we're interested in.

Publishing Imprints: The Muses Company; J. Gordon Shillingford; Scirozzo Drama; Watson & Dwyer

P195 Jain Publishing Company, Inc.
Book Publisher
Fremont, CA 94539
United States

mail@jainpub.com

https://www.jainpub.com

ACADEMIC > **Nonfiction** > *Reference*: Asia

ADULT > **Nonfiction** > *Nonfiction Books*: Asia

Send: Query; Proposal; Market info; Outline; Author bio
Don't send: Full text

Primarily publishes Asia related scholarly / academic references, and books for general readers. Complete manuscripts should only be sent on request. Send proposal in first instance. See website for full guidelines.

Editor: M. Jain

P196 Jamii Publishing
Book Publisher
United States

https://jamiipublishing.com
https://jamiipublishing.submittable.com/submit
https://twitter.com/jamiipub
https://www.facebook.com/jamiipublishing/

ADULT
  Fiction > *Short Fiction Collections*
  Nonfiction > *Essays*: Lyric Essays
  Poetry > *Poetry Collections*
    Literary; Slipstream
CHILDREN'S > **Poetry** > *Poetry Collections*

Closed to approaches.

Publishes literary poetry, including slipstream, hybrid, children's poetry, multiple authors, short story, lyric essay, visual/textual. Manuscripts must be a part of a larger community based project. No royalties.

Editor: Nikia Chaney

P197 Jessica Kingsley Publishers
Publishing Imprint
Carmelite House, 50 Victoria Embankment, London, EC4Y 0DZ
United Kingdom
Tel: +44 (0) 20 3122 6000

hello@jkp.com
proposals@jkp.com

https://www.jkp.com
https://jkp.submittable.com/submit
https://www.facebook.com/jessicakingsleypublishers
https://twitter.com/JKPBooks
http://www.pinterest.com/jkpbooks
http://instagram.com/JKPbooks

Book Publisher: John Murray Press (**P200**)

ACADEMIC > **Nonfiction** > *Nonfiction Books*
  Autism; Culture; Gender Issues; Health; Mental Health; Parenting; Religion; Social Issues
CHILDREN'S > **Nonfiction** > *Nonfiction Books*

PROFESSIONAL > **Nonfiction** > *Nonfiction Books*
  Autism; Culture; Gender Issues; Health; Mental Health; Parenting; Religion; Social Issues

Send: Proposal
How to send: Submittable

Publishes books on autism, social work and arts therapies.

Publishing Imprints: Handspring Publishing (*P160*); Singing Dragon (**P340**)

P198 JMD Media / DB Publishing
Book Publisher
United Kingdom
Tel: +44 (0) 7914 647382

https://www.jmdmedia.co.uk

Fiction > *Novels*

Nonfiction > *Nonfiction Books*
  Autobiography; Biography; Comedy / Humour; Crime; Football / Soccer; Ghosts; Local History; Local; Magic; Motorsports; Social History; Sport; Supernatural / Paranormal; Travel; Walking

Send: Query; Outline; Author bio
How to send: Email
How not to send: Post

Considers all types of books, but focuses on local interest, sport, biography, autobiography and social history. Approach by email or phone – no submissions by post. See website for full guidelines.

Editor: Steve Caron

P199 Joffe Books
Book Publisher
United Kingdom

submissions@joffebooks.com

https://www.joffebooks.com
https://www.facebook.com/joffebooks
https://twitter.com/joffebooks
https://www.instagram.com/joffebooks

Fiction > *Novels*
  Cozy Mysteries; Crime; Domestic Noir; Fantasy; Historical Fiction; Mystery; Police Procedural; Psychological Thrillers; Romance; Saga; Suspense; Women's Fiction; World War II

Send: Full text; Synopsis; Author bio
How to send: Email

Publishes crime fiction, mysteries, psychological thrillers, cosy crime, police procedurals, chillers, suspense and domestic noir. Will also consider women's fiction, fantasy, historical fiction and romance novels, including WWII romances and sagas. Manuscripts must be at least 60,000 words. Send query by email with complete manuscript as an attachment, a synopsis in the body of the email, and 100 words about yourself. Include the word "submission" in the subject line, along with your name and the book genre. Reply not guaranteed unless interested. See website for full guidelines.

Book Publisher: Choc Lit (**P085**)

Editor: Jasper Joffe

P200 John Murray Press
Book Publisher
Carmelite House, 50 Victoria Embankment, London, EC4Y 0DZ
United Kingdom
Tel: +44 (0) 20 3122 7222

enquiries@hachette.co.uk

https://www.johnmurraypress.co.uk

Book Publisher: Hachette UK

Fiction > *Novels*

Nonfiction > *Nonfiction Books*

Publisher of fiction and nonfiction, founded in the eighteenth century.

Publishing Imprints: Chambers; Jessica Kingsley Publishers (**P197**)

P201 Judson Press
Book Publisher
1075 First Avenue, King of Prussia, PA 19406
United States
Tel: +1 (800) 458-3766

acquisitions@judsonpress.com
info@judsonpress.com

https://www.judsonpress.com

Nonfiction > *Nonfiction Books*: Religion

Publishes adult nonfiction for Christians.

P202 Kane Press
Publishing Imprint
United States

https://astrapublishinghouse.com/imprints/kane-press/

Book Publisher: Astra Publishing House (**P023**)

CHILDREN'S
  Fiction
    Chapter Books; *Early Readers*; *Middle Grade*; *Picture Books*
  Nonfiction > *Nonfiction Books*
    Arts; Engineering; Mathematics; Science; Technology

An award-winning publisher of illustrated STEAM and literacy titles. Fiction and nonfiction books for ages 3–11 feature fun stories with curriculum connections and are the perfect springboard for learning in classrooms, libraries, and homes. Currently accepting proposals for series only, from published authors and literary agents.

P203 The Kates Hill Press
Book Publisher
8 Chapel Street, Wall Heath, Kingswinford,
West Midlands, DY6 0JU
United Kingdom
Tel: +44 (0) 1384 254719

kateshillpress1992@gmail.com

https://kateshillpress.com

Fiction
  Novels; *Short Fiction Collections*
Nonfiction > *Nonfiction Books*
  History; Local History; Memoir

Poetry > *Poetry Collections*

Small independent publisher producing short runs of fiction and social history books with a west midlands theme or by a west midlands writer. Also publishes booklets of poetry and dialect verse by Black Country/West Midlands poets.

P204 Kensington Publishing Corp.
Book Publisher
900 Third Avenue, 26th Floor, New York, NY 10022
United States
Tel: +1 (800) 221-2647

https://www.kensingtonbooks.com
https://www.facebook.com/kensingtonpublishing
https://twitter.com/KensingtonBooks
https://www.instagram.com/kensingtonbooks/
https://www.youtube.com/user/KensingtonPublishing
https://www.pinterest.co.uk/kensingtonbooks/
https://www.tiktok.com/@kensingtonbooks

ADULT
  Fiction
    Comics: General
    Graphic Novels: General
    Novels: Cozy Mysteries; Fantasy; Literary; Mystery; Romance; Thrillers; Westerns
  Nonfiction
    Nonfiction Books: Activities; Autobiography; Biography; Business; Comedy / Humour; Computers; Cookery; Crafts; Crime; Economics; Education; Engineering; Family; Fitness; Games; Gardening; Health; History; Hobbies; Houses and Homes; Language; Legal; Medicine; Mind, Body, Spirit; Music; Nature; Performing Arts; Pets; Philosophy; Photography; Politics; Psychology; Recreation; Relationships; Religion; Science; Self Help; Sociology; Sport; Technology; Transport; Travel
    Reference: General

CHILDREN'S > **Fiction** > *Novels*
YOUNG ADULT
  Fiction > *Novels*
  Nonfiction > *Nonfiction Books*

Send: Query
Don't send: Full text
How to send: In the body of an email

Send query only, in the body of the email. Submit to one editor only. See website for full guidelines and individual editor contact details.

Editor: John Scognamiglio

Publishing Imprints: Aphrodisia; Brava; Citadel Press; Dafina; Holloway House; John Scognamiglio Books; KTeen; KTeen Dafina; Kensington Hardcover; Kensington Mass-Market; Kensington Trade Paperback; Lyle Stuart Books; Lyrical Caress; Lyrical Liaison; Lyrical Press (**P225**); Lyrical Shine; Lyrical Underground; Pinnacle; Rebel Base Books; Zebra; Zebra Shout

P205 Kitchen Press
Book Publisher
1 Windsor Place, Dundee, DD2 1BG
United Kingdom
Tel: +44 (0) 1382 660890

https://kitchenpress.co.uk
https://www.facebook.com/kitchenpress

Nonfiction > *Nonfiction Books*
  Cookery; Food and Drink

Send: Outline; Author bio
Don't send: Full text
How to send: Online contact form

Cookbook publisher founded in 2011. We work with food writers, chefs and restaurants throughout the UK. We take our food and drink seriously. Our aim is to publish the freshest food writing, with recipes that work and images that make you hungry.

P206 Kogan Page Ltd
Book Publisher
45 Gee Street, 2nd Floor, London, EC1V 3RS
United Kingdom
Tel: +44 (0) 20 7278 0433

kpinfo@koganpage.com

https://www.koganpage.com
https://www.facebook.com/KoganPage
https://twitter.com/Koganpage
https://www.instagram.com/koganpage/
https://www.linkedin.com/company/kogan-page_2/
https://www.youtube.com/user/KoganPageBooks

Nonfiction > *Nonfiction Books*
  Business; Career Development; Finance

Publishes award-winning content from the world's leading business experts to help organizations and professionals develop the skills, competencies and knowledge to thrive.

P207 Kore Press
Book Publisher
PO Box 40682, Tucson, AZ 85717
United States

https://www.facebook.com/korepress

Fiction > *Novels*
Nonfiction > *Nonfiction Books*
Poetry > *Poetry Collections*

Closed to approaches.

Publishes fiction, poetry, nonfiction, hybrid, and cultural criticism. Accepts submissions both through open submission windows and competitions.

Managing Editor: Ann Dernier

P208 Korero Press
Book Publisher
London
United Kingdom
Fax: +44 (0) 7906 314098

info@koreropress.com
contact@koreropress.com

https://www.koreropress.com
https://www.facebook.com/koreropress
https://twitter.com/KoreroPress
http://www.pinterest.com/koreropress
https://instagram.com/koreropress/

Nonfiction > *Illustrated Books*
  Arts; Comic Books; Drawing; Graphic Design; Horror; How To; Music; Painting; Popular Culture; Sex

Send: Query; Outline; Author bio; Market info
How to send: Email

A London-based publisher of illustrated books only. No novels.

P209 Kube Publishing
Book Publisher
MCC, Ratby Lane, Markfield, Leicestershire, LE67 9SY
United Kingdom
Tel: +44 (0) 1530 249230

info@kubepublishing.com

https://www.kubepublishing.com
https://kubepublishing.submittable.com/submit
https://www.facebook.com/kubepublishing
https://twitter.com/Kube_Publishing
http://pinterest.com/kubepub/
https://www.instagram.com/kubepublishing/
http://www.youtube.com/user/KubeVideos/feed
https://www.tiktok.com/@kubepublishing?lang=en

ACADEMIC > **Nonfiction** > *Nonfiction Books*: Islam

ADULT > **Nonfiction** > *Nonfiction Books*
  Biography; Creativity; Culture; Current Affairs; History; Islam; Memoir; Politics; Spirituality

CHILDREN'S
  Fiction
    Board Books: Islam
    Chapter Books: Islam

Early Readers: Islam
Middle Grade: Islam
Picture Books: Islam

Nonfiction
Activity Books: Islam
Nonfiction Books: Islam
Picture Books: Islam

Poetry > *Any Poetic Form*: Islam

Send: Query
How to send: Submittable

Independent publisher of general interest, academic, and children's books on Islam and the Muslim experience. Publishes nonfiction for children, young people, and adults, but fiction and poetry for children. See website for full guidelines.

P210 Lantana Publishing
Book Publisher
Clavier House, 21 Fifth Road, Newbury, RG14 6DN
United Kingdom

submissions@lantanapublishing.com

https://www.lantanapublishing.com
https://www.instagram.com/lantana_publishing/
https://www.facebook.com/lantanapublishing
https://twitter.com/lantanapub
https://www.youtube.com/channel/UC_edBCMh3Y2wDID2X9qMSkA

CHILDREN'S
Fiction
Chapter Books; *Early Readers*; *Graphic Novels*; *Middle Grade*; *Picture Books*
Nonfiction > *Nonfiction Books*

Poetry > *Any Poetic Form*

Send: Full text; Synopsis
How to send: Email

We are looking for manuscripts and book dummies by authors and illustrators from under-represented groups. We particularly love stories that make us laugh, cry or move us in some way.

P211 Leamington Books
Book Publisher
32 Leamington Terrace, Edinburgh, EH10 4JL
United Kingdom

https://leamingtonbooks.com

Fiction > *Novels*
Commercial; Crime; Literary

Nonfiction > *Nonfiction Books*

Poetry > *Poetry Collections*

Closed to approaches.

Founded in 2020 to publish new fiction and poetry, and since 2021 has published debut novels each year, in the commercial, literary and crime styles. We have published two poetry collections each year, a mixture of new and established authors and performers, in Scottish Gaelic as well as English. We have published six anthologies, on diverse themes and non-fiction titles on Nordic runes, cryptocurrency, and the lyrics of Bob Dylan.

P212 Leapfrog Press
Book Publisher
PO Box 1293, Dunkirk, NY 14048
United States

leapfrog@leapfrogpress.com

https://leapfrogpress.com
https://www.facebook.com/Leapfrogpress
https://twitter.com/leapfrogpress1
https://instagram.com/leapfrogpress

ADULT
Fiction > *Novels*
Nonfiction > *Nonfiction Books*
Poetry > *Poetry Collections*

CHILDREN'S > **Fiction** > *Middle Grade*

YOUNG ADULT > **Fiction** > *Novels*

Publisher with an eclectic list of fiction, poetry, and nonfiction, including paperback originals of adult, young adult and middle-grade fiction, and nonfiction.

P213 Lerner Publishing Group
Book Publisher
241 First Avenue North, Minneapolis, MN 55401-1607
United States
Tel: +1 (800) 328-4929

custserve@lernerbooks.com

https://lernerbooks.com
https://www.facebook.com/lernerbooks
https://twitter.com/lernerbooks

CHILDREN'S
Fiction
Audiobooks; *Ebooks*; *Graphic Novels*; *Middle Grade*; *Novels*; *Picture Books*
Nonfiction
Audiobooks; *Ebooks*; *Nonfiction Books*
YOUNG ADULT
Fiction
Audiobooks; *Ebooks*; *Novels*
Nonfiction
Audiobooks; *Ebooks*; *Nonfiction Books*

How to send: Through a literary agent; By referral

Publishes fiction and nonfiction for children and young adults. No submissions or queries from unagented or unreferred authors.

Publishing Imprints: Carolrhoda Books; Carolrhoda Lab; Darby Creek; Ediciones Lerner; First Avenue Editions; Graphic Universe; Kar-Ben Publishing; Lerner Digital; Lerner Publications; LernerClassroom; Millbrook Press; Twenty-First Century Books; Zest Books

P214 LexisNexis
Book Publisher
Lexis House, 30 Farringdon Street, EC4A 4HH
United Kingdom
Tel: +44 (0) 330 161 1234

BIS@lexisnexis.co.uk

https://www.lexisnexis.com/en-gb

PROFESSIONAL > **Nonfiction** > *Reference*: Legal

Publishes books, looseleafs, journals etc. for legal professionals.

Book Publisher: Jordan Publishing

P215 Lightning Books
Publishing Imprint
United Kingdom

dan@eye-books.com

https://www.eye-books.com

Book Publisher: Eye Books

Fiction > *Novels*

Send: Query; Pitch; Synopsis; Writing sample
How to send: Word file email attachment

Query by email with the word SUBMISSION in capitals at the beginning of the subject field, followed by your name and book title. Attach a single Word file containing a pitch of up to 250 words, a synopsis of up to 500 words, and the first three chapters, up to 10,000 words.

P216 Liguori Publications
Book Publisher
One Liguori Drive, Liguori, MO 63057-9999
United States
Tel: +1 (800) 325-9521

manuscript_submission@liguori.org

https://www.liguori.org

Nonfiction > *Nonfiction Books*: Catholicism

Send: Query; Author bio; Outline; Table of contents; Writing sample; Market info
How to send: Email attachment

Publishes books founded in the Roman Catholic belief and tradition, including meditations on the seasons of the Church Year (Advent/Christmas, Lent/Easter) or on liturgical readings and texts; stories on, or reflections with, the life, words, and works of the saints; and studies, guides, and books for receiving, ministering and experiencing the sacraments.

Editor: Daniel Michaels

P217 The Lilliput Press
Book Publisher
62-63 Sitric Road, Arbour Hill, Dublin 7, D07 AE27
Ireland
Tel: +353 (01) 671 16 47

editorial@lilliputpress.ie

https://www.lilliputpress.ie
https://www.facebook.com/thelilliputpress/
https://twitter.com/LilliputPress
https://www.instagram.com/lilliputpress/

Fiction > *Novels*: Ireland

Nonfiction
Nonfiction Books: Architecture; Arts; Biography; Cultural Criticism; Environment; Food; Genealogy; History; Ireland; Literary Criticism; Literature; Local History; Memoir; Mind, Body, Spirit; Music; Nature; Philosophy; Photography; Travel
Reference: Ireland

Poetry > *Any Poetic Form*: Ireland

Closed to approaches.

Publishes books broadly focused on Irish themes. No genre literature, such as children's literature, crime fiction or science fiction. See website for full guidelines.

P218 Little Bigfoot
Publishing Imprint
United States

submissions@sasquatchbooks.com

Book Publisher: Sasquatch Books (**P325**)

CHILDREN'S
Fiction
Board Books: General, and in particular: American West; Nature; Pacific Northwest
Chapter Books: General, and in particular: American West; Nature; Pacific Northwest
Early Readers: General, and in particular: American West; Nature; Pacific Northwest
Picture Books: General, and in particular: American West; Nature; Pacific Northwest

Nonfiction > *Nonfiction Books*
General, and in particular: American West; Nature; Pacific Northwest

Send: Query; Author bio; Proposal; Full text
How to send: Email

Publishes fiction and nonfiction books for kids ages four to twelve and board books for kids ages zero to three.

P219 Llewellyn Worldwide Ltd
Book Publisher
Acquisitions Department, 2143 Wooddale Drive, Woodbury, MN 55125
United States
Tel: +1 (612) 291-1970
Fax: +1 (612) 291-1908

submissions@llewellyn.com

http://www.llewellyn.com

Nonfiction > *Nonfiction Books*
Alternative Health; Angels; Astral Projection; Astrology; Chakras; Cryptozoology; Ghost Hunting; Kabbalah; Meditation; Mind, Body, Spirit; Paganism; Psychic Abilities; Reiki; Reincarnation; Shamanism; Spirit Guides; Spirituality; Tarot; UFOs; Wicca; Witchcraft; Yoga

Send: Query; Proposal; Full text; Outline; Table of contents; Market info; Author bio; Writing sample
How to send: Word file email attachment; Post; PDF file email attachment

As the world's oldest and largest independent publisher of books for body, mind, and spirit, we are dedicated to bringing our readers the very best in metaphysical books and resources. Since 1901, we've been at the forefront of holistic and metaphysical publishing and thought. We've been a source of illumination, instruction, and new perspectives on a wealth of topics, including astrology, tarot, wellness, earth-based spirituality, magic, and the paranormal.

P220 Loft Press, Inc.
Book Publisher
9293 Fort Valley Road, Fort Valley, VA 22652
United States
Tel: +1 (540) 933-6210
Fax: +1 (540) 933-6523

books@loftpress.com

http://www.loftpress.com

ADULT
Fiction > *Novels*

Nonfiction > *Nonfiction Books*
History; Memoir; Philosophy

Poetry > *Poetry Collections*

PROFESSIONAL > **Nonfiction** > *Nonfiction Books*
Business; Logistics; Supply Chain Management; Transport; Warehousing

Does not want:

> **Fiction** > *Novels*
> Coming of Age; Fantasy; Feminism; Gender; Science Fiction; Women's Fiction

Send: Query; Writing sample; Outline; Market info; Self-addressed stamped envelope (SASE)
How to send: Post
How not to send: Email

Publishes books for both the business community and the general reading public. Business books specialize in transportation loss and damage, logistics, warehousing, and supply chain management. For the general reading public, publishes Poetry, history, philosophy, and memoirs. Publishes very little fiction. No "coming of age" works, science fiction, fantasy, feminist-, gender-, or women-oriented works, or any manuscript with inappropriate coarse language.

P221 Logaston Press
Book Publisher
The Holme, Church Road, Eardisley, Herefordshire, HR3 6NJ
United Kingdom
Tel: +44 (0) 1544 327182

info@logastonpress.co.uk

https://logastonpress.co.uk
https://twitter.com/LogastonPress

Nonfiction > *Nonfiction Books*
Archaeology; Architecture; Biography; Breconshire; Gloucestershire; Herefordshire; Local History; Montgomeryshire; Radnorshire; Shropshire; Walking Guides; Worcestershire

Send: Query; Submission form; Table of contents; Writing sample; Author bio
How to send: Email

Publishes local history, biography, archaeology, architecture, landscape and topography, and walk guides; and also books about the Southern Marches region: the English counties of Herefordshire, Shropshire, Worcestershire and Gloucestershire, and the Welsh counties of Radnorshire, Breconshire and Montgomeryshire.

Publishing Imprint: Fircone Books Ltd

P222 Loudhailer Books
Book Publisher
United Kingdom

info@loudhailerbooks.com

https://www.loudhailerbooks.com
https://www.facebook.com/loudhailerbooks
https://twitter.com/LoudhailerBooks

Fiction > *Novels*

Nonfiction > *Nonfiction Books*

Poetry > *Poetry Collections*

Send: Query; Synopsis; Writing sample; Author bio; Proposal
How to send: Email

A publisher of quality fiction, non-fiction and poetry.

We are currently accepting submissions from authors, either directly or via a literary agent.

For fiction, we ask to see a synopsis and the first three chapters.

For non-fiction, please send a brief proposal including a synopsis, author profile and sample material.

Please send all submissions and enquiries by email.

P223 LSU Press
Book Publisher
338 Johnston Hall, Louisiana State University,
Baton Rouge, LA 70803
United States
Tel: +1 (225) 578-6294

https://lsupress.org
https://www.facebook.com/LSUPress/
https://twitter.com/lsupress
https://www.instagram.com/lsupress/

ACADEMIC > **Nonfiction** > *Nonfiction Books*
    African American; American Civil War; American History; Architecture; Caribbean History; Culture; Environment; Food; History; Literature; Louisiana; Media; Roots Music; Social Justice; World War II

ADULT > **Poetry** > *Poetry Collections*

Send: Query; Proposal; Writing sample; Author bio; Table of contents; Self-addressed stamped envelope (SASE)
How to send: Email; Post

Publishes works of scholarly and creative excellence, amplifying diverse voices while promoting dialogue about the rich and varied cultures of Louisiana, the South, and the world beyond.

P224 Lund Humphries Limited
Publishing Imprint
Second Home Spitalfields, 68-80 Hanbury Street, London, E1 5JL
United Kingdom
Tel: +44 (0) 7955 290870

info@lundhumphries.com

https://www.lundhumphries.com
http://facebook.com/LHArtBooks
https://www.twitter.com/LHArtBooks
https://instagram.com/lhartbooks
https://www.youtube.com/channel/UCt-2V5NDuUGTzJOxNGSqR7w

Book Publisher: Ashgate Publishing Ltd

ACADEMIC > **Nonfiction** > *Nonfiction Books*
    Architecture; Arts; Design

ADULT > **Nonfiction** > *Nonfiction Books*
    Architecture; Arts; Design

PROFESSIONAL > **Nonfiction** > *Nonfiction Books*
    Architecture; Arts; Design

Send: Query; Proposal
How to send: Email

Publishes books on art, art history, and design. See website for guidelines on submitting a proposal.

Editor: Lucy Clark

P225 Lyrical Press
Publishing Imprint
United States

https://www.kensingtonbooks.com

Book Publisher: Kensington Publishing Corp. (**P204**)

Fiction > *Novels*
    Cozy Mysteries; Erotic; Historical Romance; Thrillers

A digital first imprint that offers readers a prolific catalogue of titles ranging from sweeping historical romances and edgy erotic titles to chilling thrillers and cozy mysteries.

Editor: John Scognamiglio

P226 Macmillan Children's Books
Publishing Imprint
United Kingdom

https://www.panmacmillan.com/mcb
https://twitter.com/MacmillanKidsUK
https://www.facebook.com/panmacmillanbooks/
https://www.instagram.com/panmacmillan
https://www.tiktok.com/@panmacmillan

Book Publisher: Pan Macmillan

CHILDREN'S > **Fiction**
    Board Books; *Chapter Books*; *Middle Grade*; *Picture Books*

YOUNG ADULT > **Fiction** > *Novels*

How to send: Through a literary agent

One of the UK's leading children's publishers, creating and publishing absorbing and exciting stories for children of all ages for over 150 years.

P227 Manilla Press
Publishing Imprint
United Kingdom

https://www.bonnierbooks.co.uk/imprints/manilla-press/

Book Publisher: Bonnier Books (UK) (**P059**)

Fiction > *Novels*

Nonfiction > *Nonfiction Books*

How to send: Through a literary agent

A boutique literary imprint dedicated to publishing unique author-led fiction and non-fiction. Boasting a carefully curated list and international reach, our books aspire to capture the mood of the times and the hearts and minds of our readers.

A home for novelists, journalists, memoirists, thinkers, dreamers, influencers, and experts. We are driven by our passion for bold and distinctive storytelling – seeking out a broad range of voices and underrepresented talents as we publish for readers from all walks of life.

P228 Margaret K. McElderry Books
Publishing Imprint
United States

https://www.simonandschuster.biz/m/mkm/margaret-mcelderry

Book Publisher: Simon & Schuster Children's Publishing

CHILDREN'S
    Fiction
        Middle Grade: Contemporary; Historical Fiction; Literary Fantasy
        Picture Books: General

    Poetry > *Any Poetic Form*

TEEN
    Fiction > *Novels*
        Contemporary; Historical Fiction; Literary Fantasy

    Poetry > *Any Poetic Form*

Publisher of literary author-driven fiction and nonfiction for the teen, middle grade, picture book, and poetry markets. Specializes in high quality literary fantasy, contemporary, and historical fiction, as well as character-driven picture books and poetry for all ages.

P229 Marion Boyars Publishers
Book Publisher
26 Parke Road, London, SW13 9NG
United Kingdom

jjoyce@equinoxpub.com

http://www.marionboyars.co.uk

Types: Fiction; Nonfiction
Formats: Film Scripts; Theatre Scripts
Subjects: Anthropology; Autobiography; Culture; Drama; Literary Criticism; Music; Philosophy; Psychology; Sociology; Women's Interests
Markets: Adult; Children's

Closed to approaches.

Not accepting new submissions as at April 2024. Check website for current status.

Editor: Catheryn Kilgarriff

P230 MB Media
Book Publisher
United States

mbmediafamily@gmail.com

https://mbmediacorp.com/

Provides publishing and related services to individuals and professionals within and outside the writing industry. Whether you're an individual seeking editing services before self-publishing your book, a company in need of a website, a writer looking for a publishing offer, or anything in between, we're here to help!

Publishing Imprint: Oh MG Press (**P260**)

P231 MCD Books
Publishing Imprint
United States

https://www.mcdbooks.com
https://twitter.com/mcdbooks
https://www.instagram.com/mcdbooks/
https://www.facebook.com/MCDBooks/

Book Publisher: Macmillan Publishers

P232 McNidder & Grace
Book Publisher; Ebook Publisher
United Kingdom
Tel: +44 (0) 7788 219370

andy@mcnidderandgrace.co.uk

https://mcnidderandgrace.com
https://www.instagram.com/mcniddergrace/
https://twitter.com/McNidderGrace
https://www.facebook.com/mcnidder.grace

Fiction > *Novels*
General, and in particular: Crime; Popular Culture; Thrillers

Nonfiction > *Nonfiction Books*
General, and in particular: Arts; Biography; Country Lifestyle; Health; History; Music; Photography; Popular Culture; Wellbeing

How to send: Email

We specialise in non-fiction and fiction titles for adults. With a particular emphasis on popular culture, our non-fiction list includes books on photography, art, music, biography, history, country pursuits and more recently health and well-being. Our fiction list concentrates primarily on Crime and Thrillers.

P233 Media Lab Books
Publishing Imprint

https://us.macmillan.com/publishers/media-lab-books

Book Publisher: Macmillan Publishers

A premier publishing imprint in New York City that partners with expert authors and high-profile brands like Smithsonian, John Wayne, Hasbro, Steve Spangler, Disney and more in order to publish a wide variety of titles designed to inform, educate and entertain readers around the world.

P234 Medical Physics Publishing
Book Publisher; Ebook Publisher
4555 Helgesen Drive, Madison, WI 53718
United States
Tel: +1 (608) 224-4508
Fax: +1 (608) 224-5016

bobbett@medicalphysics.org
mpp@medicalphysics.org

https://medicalphysics.org
https://www.facebook.com/medicalphysics

https://www.linkedin.com/company/medical-physics-publishing-inc

PROFESSIONAL > **Nonfiction** > *Nonfiction Books*
Medicine; Physics

Send: Query
How to send: Email

Aims to provide affordable books in medical physics and related fields. A nonprofit, tax-exempt 501(c)3 organization. Books are written by and for physicists, residents, radiologists, and technologists.

P235 Medina Publishing
Book Publisher
50 High Street, Cowes, Isle Of Wight, PO31 7RR
United Kingdom

info@medinapublishing.com
submissions@medinapublishing.com

https://medinapublishing.com

Nonfiction > *Nonfiction Books*
General, and in particular: Comedy / Humour; Memoir; Travel

Closed to approaches.

We specialise in non-fiction, particularly travel memoirs, and also publish humour under our imprint. Always interested in daring new literature. Whether you are an up-and-coming author or a well-established hand with something a little different up your sleeve, get in touch.

P236 Mentor Books
Book Publisher
43 Furze Road, Sandyford Industrial Estate, Dublin 18
Ireland
Tel: 01 2952112

admin@mentorbooks.ie

https://www.mentorbooks.ie

ACADEMIC > **Nonfiction** > *Nonfiction Books*
Biology; Business; Economics; English; French; Geography; German; History; Irish (Gaeilge); Physical Education; Religion; Science; Spanish

PROFESSIONAL > **Nonfiction** > *Nonfiction Books*: Education

Publishes educational books.

P237 Merlin Unwin Books
Book Publisher
6 Rural Enterprise Centre, Eco Park Road, Ludlow, Shropshire, SY8 1FF
United Kingdom
Tel: +44 (0) 1584 877456

books@merlinunwin.co.uk

https://merlinunwin.co.uk
https://x.com/merlinunwin
https://www.facebook.com/merlinunwinbooks
https://www.instagram.com/merlinunwinbooks/
https://www.pinterest.co.uk/business/hub/
https://www.youtube.com/channel/UCoLf4JXKK_QOBFwOE6bpLWQ

Fiction > *Novels*
Countryside; Nature

Nonfiction > *Nonfiction Books*
Cookery; Countryside; Dogs; Equestrian; Fishing; Herbal Remedies; How To; Hunting; Memoir; Nature; Self-Sufficiency; Shooting

Poetry > *Poetry Collections*
Countryside; Nature

Publishes books on the countryside and countryside pursuits, covering such topics as nature, fishing, shooting, etc.

P238 Methuen Publishing Ltd
Book Publisher
1 Wheelgate, Malton, YO17 7HT
United Kingdom

methuenenquiries@methuen.co.uk

http://www.methuen.co.uk
https://twitter.com/MethuenandCo

Fiction > *Novels*

Nonfiction
Essays: General
Nonfiction Books: Autobiography; Biography; Classics / Ancient World; Literature; Politics; Sport; Theatre; Travel; World War II

Send: Query
How to send: Email
How not to send: Phone

If you would like to check whether our publishing list is a fit for your manuscript, please send a brief enquiry only. Thank you. Please note that we do not publish works for children or young adults (including science fiction).

P239 Milkweed Editions
Book Publisher
1011 Washington Avenue South, Open Book, Suite 300, Minneapolis, MN 55415
United States

orders@milkweed.org

https://milkweed.org
http://www.facebook.com/milkweed.books
http://twitter.com/#!/Milkweed_Books
https://www.instagram.com/milkweed_books/
http://www.youtube.com/MilkweedEditions
https://www.pinterest.com/Milkfolk/

Fiction > *Novels*

Nonfiction > *Nonfiction Books*

Poetry > *Poetry Collections*
Closed to approaches.

An independent publisher of fiction, nonfiction, and poetry.

P240 Mills & Boon
Publishing Imprint
1 London Bridge Street, London, SE1 9GF
United Kingdom

info@millsandboon.co.uk
submissions@harlequin.com

https://www.millsandboon.co.uk
https://harlequin.submittable.com/submit
https://www.facebook.com/millsandboon/
https://twitter.com/MillsandBoon
https://www.instagram.com/millsandboonuk/
https://www.tiktok.com/@millsandboonuk

Book Publishers: Harlequin Enterprises; HarperCollins UK

Fiction > *Novels*
Adventure; Crime; Historical Romance; Medicine; Romance; Romantic Suspense; Romantic Thrillers

How to send: Submittable

Across every romance genre, from historical to contemporary, rom-com to erotica, our compelling, uplifting romances guarantee an instant escape to fantasy worlds, and the heart-warming reassurance of 'happily ever after'. We are proud to publish over 1,300 authors, 700 new titles a year, with manuscripts from 200 authors living in the UK and a further 1,300 worldwide.

P241 Minnesota Historical Society Press
Book Publisher
345 Kellogg Blvd. West, Saint Paul, MN 55102-1906
United States
Tel: +1 (651) 259-3205
Fax: +1 (651) 297-1345

https://www.mnhs.org/mnhspress
https://www.facebook.com/Mnhspress
https://twitter.com/MNHSPress
https://www.youtube.com/playlist?list=PLRrmlN6cO7LvpRkbuLYO6paOGLjrKCoXP

ADULT > **Nonfiction** > *Nonfiction Books*
American Midwest; Arts; Cookery; Culture; Environment; History; Literary; Memoir; Military History; Minnesota; Native Americans; Nature; Political History; Social History; Sport

CHILDREN'S > **Nonfiction** > *Picture Books*
American Midwest; Culture; Environment; History; Minnesota; Native Americans; Nature

Send: Query; Market info; Author bio; Table of contents; Outline; Writing sample
How to send: Email; Post

Publishes adult nonfiction titles, cookbooks, and children's picture books that reflect the history and culture of Minnesota and the Upper Midwest in several general areas: Native American history and culture; political and military history; natural history and the environment; cultural and social history; arts, culture, and sports; memoir and literary nonfiction.

Publishing Imprint: Borealis Books

P242 Minotaur Books
Publishing Imprint
United States

Book Publisher: Macmillan Publishers

P243 Missouri Historical Society Press
Book Publisher
PO Box 775460, St. Louis, MO 63177
United States

https://mohistory.org
https://mohistory.org/publications/submissions

Nonfiction > *Nonfiction Books*
History; St Louis

Send: Query; Full text; Outline
How to send: Word file email attachment

Welcomes book submissions that illuminate the history of the St Louis region and its people in an accessible way for the general public.

Publishing Director: Lauren Mitchell

P244 The MIT Press
Book Publisher
255 Main Street, 9th Floor, Cambridge, MA 02142
United States
Tel: +1 (617) 253-5646

https://mitpress.mit.edu
https://www.facebook.com/mitpress
https://twitter.com/mitpress
https://www.linkedin.com/company/11587565/
https://www.pinterest.com/mitpress/
https://www.instagram.com/mitpress/
https://www.youtube.com/c/TheMITPress

ACADEMIC > **Nonfiction** > *Nonfiction Books*
Arts; Design; Science; Sociology; Technology

University press publishing books and journals at the intersection of science, technology, art, social science, and design.

Acquisitions Editors: Matthew Browne; Susan Buckley; Beth Clevenger; Katie Helke; Victoria Hindley; Justin Kehoe; Philip Laughlin; Marc Lowenthal; Gita Manaktala; Jermey Matthews; Robert Prior; Elizabeth Swayze; Emily Taber; Thomas Weaver

P245 The Monacelli Press
Publishing Imprint
Attn: Acquisitions, 111 Broadway, Suite 301, New York, New York 10006
United States

submissions@monacellipress.com

https://www.phaidon.com/store/the-monacelli-press/

Book Publisher: Phaidon Press (**P287**)

Nonfiction > *Nonfiction Books*
Architecture; Arts; Gardening; Interior Design; Photography

How to send: Post; Email

Will review book proposals in the fields of architecture and landscape architecture, fine and decorative arts, design, and photography.

P246 Monoray
Publishing Imprint
United Kingdom

https://www.octopusbooks.co.uk
https://www.octopusbooks.co.uk/imprint/monoray/page/monoray/

Book Publisher: Octopus Publishing Group Limited

Nonfiction > *Nonfiction Books*
Arts; Business; Crime; History; Memoir; Narrative Nonfiction; Politics; Social Commentary; Spirituality; Sport

Publishes narrative non-fiction at its most immersive, inspiring and entertaining. Our authors have lived every moment of the stories they want to tell, and we are proud to bring these stories into the world. From the arts to politics and sport; from spiritual memoir to business; from socially conscious polemic to history or even crime – whatever the subject, our books always have a highly distinctive and authentic author voice and aim each time to be breakout bestsellers.

P247 Moody Publishers
Book Publisher
820 North LaSalle Boulevard, Chicago, IL 60610
United States
Tel: +1 (800) 678-8812

moody.publishers@moody.edu
Submissions@moody.edu

https://www.moodypublishers.com
https://www.instagram.com/moodypublishers/
https://www.facebook.com/moodypublishers/
https://twitter.com/MoodyPublishers
https://www.youtube.com/user/MoodyPro

ADULT > **Nonfiction** > *Nonfiction Books*
Bible Studies; Christian Living; Christianity

CHILDREN'S
    Fiction > *Middle Grade*: Christianity

    Nonfiction > *Nonfiction Books*
        Bible Stories; Bible Studies

    TEEN > Nonfiction > *Nonfiction Books*
        Christian Living; Christianity; Relationships

Send: Query; Author bio; Synopsis; Table of contents; Outline; Market info; Writing sample
How to send: Email; Through a literary agent; By referral; Conferences

Titles are designed to glorify God in content and style. Titles are selected for publication based upon fit with this goal, quality of writing, and potential for market success. Accepts unsolicited manuscripts, but priority given to submissions sent through a professional literary agent, an author already published by the company, an associate who works for a ministry, or personal contact at a writers' conference.

Publishing Imprints: Lift Every Voice; Northfield Publishing

P248 Multnomah
Publishing Imprint

Book Publisher: Random House

P249 Murdoch Books Australia
Book Publisher
Sydney
Australia

fridaypitch@allenandunwin.com

https://www.murdochbooks.com

Book Publisher: Allen & Unwin (**P009**)

Nonfiction > *Nonfiction Books*
    Family; Food; Health; Houses and Homes; Personal Development; Sustainable Living

Send: Submission form; Proposal; Synopsis
How to send: Email

We publish commercially appealing and visually outstanding books written by fresh, brave authors and creatives with unique points of view. Our bestselling and award-winning titles span our four pillars: Food, Home, Gift and Life. While we are Australian owned and operated, we are an international publisher, with offices in London, Auckland, as well as Sydney, and an extensive network of international publishing partners including in the US and across more than 20 languages.

Book Publisher: Murdoch Books UK Ltd

P250 Muswell Press
Book Publisher
United Kingdom

info@muswell-press.co.uk

https://muswell-press.co.uk
https://twitter.com/muswellpress
https://www.facebook.com/MuswellPress
https://www.instagram.com/muswellpress

Fiction > *Novels*
    Crime; LGBTQIA; Thrillers; Upmarket

Nonfiction > *Nonfiction Books*
    Biography; LGBTQIA; Memoir; Travel

Send: Query; Pitch; Author bio; Synopsis; Writing sample; Full text
How to send: Word file email attachment; PDF file email attachment

We are a small publisher and take on a maximum of 12 new books each year, both agented and non-agented, so both our time and space on the list is limited. That said, we love discovering new writers, so please bear with us, it may take up to three months to respond. We are interested in upmarket fiction, crime and thriller, memoir, biography and travel. Our queer list publishes both fiction and biography. Please consider whether your book would work on our list by browsing our recent titles on the website. We do not publish children's books, YA, military history, cookery, lifestyle, sci fi, fantasy or poetry.

P251 Myrmidon Books Ltd
Book Publisher
18 High Buston, Alnwick, Northumberland, NE66 3QH
United Kingdom
Tel: +44 (0) 1912 064005
Fax: +44 (0) 1912 064001

ed@myrmidonbooks.com

http://www.myrmidonbooks.com

Fiction > *Novels*
    Commercial; Literary

Send: Query; Writing sample; Author bio
How to send: Post
How not to send: Email; Fax

Submit your initial three chapters and a one-page covering letter providing information about yourself and your work. A synopsis or structure plan may be useful for a non-fiction proposal, but a synopsis is not required for fiction submissions and will not be read.

P252 The Mysterious Press
Publishing Imprint
United States

https://www.mysteriouspress.com
https://penzlerpublishers.com/product-category/mysterious-press/
https://twitter.com/eMysteries
https://www.facebook.com/MysteriousPressCom

Book Publisher: Penzler Publishers (**P282**)

Fiction > *Novels*
    Crime; Mystery

Publishes the very best in crime fiction from around the globe.

P253 NAHB BuilderBooks
Book Publisher
United States
Tel: +1 (800) 888-4741

https://www.builderbooks.com
https://www.facebook.com/NAHBhome

PROFESSIONAL > **Nonfiction** > *Nonfiction Books*: Building / Construction

Publishes education and training products aimed at professionals in the construction industry.

P254 NBM Publishing
Book Publisher
160 Broadway, Suite 700 East Wing, New York, NY 10038
United States

tnantier@nbmpub.com

https://nbmpub.com
https://twitter.com/NBMPUB
https://www.facebook.com/NBMGraphicNovels
https://www.instagram.com/nbmgraphicnovels/
https://www.tiktok.com/@nbmgraphicnovels
https://www.youtube.com/@NBMGraphicNovels

Fiction > *Graphic Novels*
    General, and in particular: Comedy / Humour; Erotic; Fantasy; Historical Fiction; Literary; Mystery; Science Fiction

Nonfiction > *Graphic Nonfiction*
    General, and in particular: Autobiography; Biography; Crime; How To; Journalism

Send: Query; Synopsis; Self-addressed stamped envelope (SASE)
How to send: Email; Post

We are interested in literary fiction, non-fiction and biographies. We are not interested in superheroes or any genre. We have no need for illustrations alone including covers. To submit please send a one-page synopsis of your story which will include any pertinent background and some character development. For the art, please send copies of a few finished pages or pencils for the project or at least of previous work in the same style you plan on using. Please do not at first send a complete finished story as that will only delay an answer greatly. To submit electronically: Send a low-resolution pdf of no more than 10 megs as attachment. You may submit a link to a website as an extra source but not by itself. If sending by mail and you want anything back, including an answer, please include a SASE.

Editor: Terry Nantier

P255 New Harbinger Publications
Book Publisher
5720 Shattuck Avenue, Oakland, CA 94609
United States

proposals@newharbinger.com

https://www.newharbinger.com
https://www.facebook.com/NewHarbinger
https://www.instagram.com/newharbinger/
https://twitter.com/NewHarbinger
https://www.linkedin.com/company/new-harbinger-publications/
https://www.youtube.com/newharbinger

ADULT > **Nonfiction** > *Nonfiction Books*
  Health; Mental Health; Psychology; Self Help

PROFESSIONAL > **Nonfiction** > *Nonfiction Books*
  Health; Mental Health; Psychology

Send: Query; Proposal; Market info; Author bio; Writing sample
How to send: Email

Publishes psychology and health self-help books that must be simple and easy to understand, but also complete and authoritative. Most authors for this publisher are therapists or other helping professionals. See website for extensive author guidelines.

P256 New Walk Editions
Book Publisher
c/o Nick Everett, School of English, Leicester University, University Road, Leicester, LE1 7RH
United Kingdom

newwalkmagazine@gmail.com

https://newwalkmagazine.com

Poetry > *Poetry Collections*

Send: Full text; Author bio
How to send: Word file email attachment; Post

A small press specialising in extremely high quality poetry pamphlets. Interested in poetic plurality: equally interested in established and new poets, and a broad church stylistically and thematically. Send 12-24 pages of poems by email or by post.

Editor: Nick Everett

P257 Nine Arches Press
Book Publisher
Unit 14, Frank Whittle Business Centre, Great Central Way, Rugby, Warwickshire, CV21 3XH
United Kingdom
Tel: +44 (0) 1788 226005

mail@ninearchespress.com

https://ninearchespress.com
https://ninearchespress.submittable.com/submit
https://twitter.com/NineArchesPress

Poetry > *Poetry Collections*
Closed to approaches.

Publishes poetry collections. Accepts submissions during specific submission windows. See website for details.

Magazine: Under the Radar (**M325**)

P258 No Starch Press, Inc.
Book Publisher
329 Primrose Road, #42, Burlingame, CA 94010-4093
United States
Tel: +1 (415) 863-9900
Fax: +1 (415) 863-9950

editors@nostarch.com
support@nostarch.com

https://nostarch.com

ADULT > **Nonfiction** > *Nonfiction Books*
  Arts; Computer Programming; Computer Science; Computers; Design

CHILDREN'S > **Nonfiction** > *Nonfiction Books*
  Arts; Computer Programming; Computer Science; Computers; Design

Send: Query; Outline; Synopsis; Market info; Author bio
How to send: Email

Publishes unique books on computer programming, security, hacking, alternative operating systems, STEM, and LEGO.

P259 Oak Tree Press
Book Publisher
Suite 309, NSC Campus Mahon, Cork, T12 XY2N
Ireland
Tel: +353 21 230 7021

https://oaktreepress.ie

PROFESSIONAL > **Nonfiction** > *Nonfiction Books*: Business

How to send: Online submission system

Publishes books on business, particularly for small business owners and managers.

P260 Oh MG Press
Publishing Imprint
United States

ohmgpress@gmail.com

https://ohmgpress.com
https://www.facebook.com/OhMGPress/
https://x.com/OhMGpress

Book Publisher: MB Media (**P230**)

CHILDREN'S > **Fiction** > *Middle Grade*

Does not want:

> **CHILDREN'S** > **Fiction** > *Middle Grade*
> Dark Magic; Gender; Science Fiction; Sex; Witchcraft

Send: Full text
How to send: Email

Costs: Offers services that writers have to pay for. Offers manuscript editing services.

Traditional middle grade publisher. No advance. High royalties. Welcomes submissions from authors based in the United States and Canada exclusively. Accepts early middle grade fiction between 16,000 and 30,000 words, and middle grade fiction between 30,000 and 65,000 words. Offers manuscript editing services for a fee.

P261 Ohio University Press
Book Publisher
Alden Library, Suite 101, 30 Park Place, Athens, OH 45701-2909
United States
Tel: +1 (740) 593-1154

https://www.ohioswallow.com

ACADEMIC > **Nonfiction** > *Nonfiction Books*
  Africa; American History; American Midwest; Anthropology; Appalachia; Art History; Arts; Asia; Central America; Crafts; Environment; Europe; Films; Food; Gender; Health; History; Hobbies; Japan; Journalism; Language; Legal; Literature; Media; Nature; North America; Ohio; Performing Arts; Philosophy; Poetry as a Subject; Politics; Religion; South America; Sport; TV; Theatre; Women; Writing

Send: Query; Table of contents; Writing sample; Author bio
Don't send: Full text
How to send: Email

Publishes primarily nonfiction. See website for full guidelines.

Editor: Ricky S. Huard

Publishing Imprint: Swallow Press

P262 Old Pond Publishing
Publishing Imprint
United Kingdom

contact@oldpond.com

https://www.foxchapelpublishing.co.uk
https://www.foxchapelpublishing.co.uk/old-pond

Book Publisher: Fox Chapel Publishing

Nonfiction > *Nonfiction Books*
  Agriculture; Comedy / Humour; Farm Equipment; Farming; Vehicles

Specialist UK publisher of agriculture, trucking and machinery books and DVDs, ranging from titles about tractor and haulage brands to practical farming and humorous books.

P263 Old Street Publishing Ltd
Book Publisher
Notaries House, Exeter, EX1 1AJ
United Kingdom

info@oldstreetpublishing.co.uk

http://www.oldstreetpublishing.co.uk
https://twitter.com/oldstpublishing

Fiction > *Novels*

Nonfiction > *Nonfiction Books*

Send: Query; Outline
Don't send: Full text
How to send: Email

Independent British publisher of fiction and nonfiction.

P264 Oldcastle Books Group
Book Publisher
18 Coleswood Road, Harpenden, Hertfordshire, AL5 1EQ
United Kingdom

publicity@oldcastlebooks.com

http://www.oldcastlebooks.co.uk

Fiction > *Novels*

Nonfiction > *Nonfiction Books*

How to send: Through a literary agent

Accepts submissions through literary agents only.

Publishing Imprints: Creative Essentials; Crime & Mystery Club; High Stakes Publishing (**P173**); Kamera Books; No Exit Press; Oldcastle Books; Pocketessentials; Pulp! The Classics

P265 Ooligan Press
Book Publisher
PO Box 751, Portland, OR 97207
United States
Tel: +1 (503) 725-9748
Fax: +1 (503) 725-3561

ooligan@ooliganpress.pdx.edu
publisher@ooliganpress.pdx.edu

https://www.ooliganpress.com
https://ooliganpress.submittable.com/submit
https://www.facebook.com/ooliganpress/
https://twitter.com/ooliganpress
https://www.instagram.com/ooliganpress
https://www.youtube.com/user/OoliganPress
https://sk.pinterest.com/ooliganpress/_saved/

ADULT
  Fiction > *Novels*: Literary

  Nonfiction > *Nonfiction Books*
    General, and in particular: Publishing; Sustainable Living; Writing

YOUNG ADULT > **Fiction** > *Novels*

Does not want:

> **Nonfiction** > *Nonfiction Books*
> Memoir; Religion; Self Help

Send: Query; Proposal; Writing sample
How to send: Submittable
How not to send: Through a literary agent

A student-run trade press rooted in the Pacific Northwest dedicated to cultivating the next generation of publishing professionals. Prioritizes literary equity and inclusion. Strives to publish culturally relevant titles from local, marginalized voices in order to make literature accessible and redefine who has a place within its pages.

P266 Orca Book Publishers
Book Publisher
Canada
Tel: +1 (800) 210-5277

orca@orcabook.com

https://www.orcabook.com
https://www.instagram.com/orcabook/
https://www.facebook.com/OrcaBook
https://www.pinterest.com/orcabook/
https://www.youtube.com/user/OrcaBookPublishers
https://www.tiktok.com/@orcabook

CHILDREN'S
  Fiction
    Board Books; *Graphic Novels*; *Middle Grade*; *Picture Books*
  Nonfiction
    Board Books; *Middle Grade*; *Picture Books*
YOUNG ADULT
  Fiction > *Novels*
  Nonfiction > *Nonfiction Books*

Send: Query; Author bio; Synopsis; Writing sample; Full text
How to send: CanSubmit

Publishes fiction and nonfiction for children. No adult fiction, nonfiction, or poetry. Accepts submissions in February and August from Canadian citizens or permanent residents of Canada only.

Editorial Director: Bob Tyrrell

Publisher: Andrew Wooldridge

P267 Orenda Books
Book Publisher
16 Carson Road, West Dulwich, London, SE21 8HU
United Kingdom

info@orendabooks.co.uk
submissions@orendabooks.co.uk

https://orendabooks.co.uk
https://twitter.com/orendabooks
https://www.facebook.com/orendabooks
https://www.instagram.com/orendabooks

Fiction in Translation > *Novels*

Fiction
  Novels: Adventure; Comedy / Humour; Crime; Ghost Stories; Historical Fiction; Horror; Legal Thrillers; Literary; Mystery; Political Thrillers; Psychological Thrillers; Romance; Suspense; Thrillers
  Short Fiction Collections: General

Closed to approaches.

Publishes literary fiction and upmarket genre fiction (in particular, crime fiction) only. No nonfiction, screenplays, children's books, or young adult. Send one-page synopsis and full ms (or three-chapter sample) by email.

P268 Orphans Publishing
Book Publisher
3 Arrow Close, Leominster Enterprise Park, Leominster, Herefordshire, HR6 0LD
United Kingdom
Tel: +44 (0) 1568 612460

books@orphanspublishing.co.uk

https://www.orphanspublishing.co.uk

Fiction > *Novels*

Nonfiction > *Nonfiction Books*
  Biography; Gardening; History; Lifestyle; Music

Send: Query; Synopsis
How to send: Email

Our ethos is producing beautiful books with a sense of place. Whether it's coffee table design-led non-fiction or a beautifully written memoir, we're interested in hearing from those who are passionate about their specialist subject. We're not worried about mass-market appeal; it's the niche interests explained through intricate narrative that we're interested in most. We strongly believe in the power of a beautifully produced book. Print and design is at the heart of everything we do. It's our heritage. From creative endpapers and beautiful jackets to gorgeous illustration and typesetting, we take pride in even the smallest details.

P269 Otago University Press
Book Publisher
PO Box 56, Dunedin 9054
New Zealand
Tel: +64 3 471 6344

oup.submissions@otago.ac.nz
university.press@otago.ac.nz

https://www.otago.ac.nz
https://www.otago.ac.nz/press/index.html

ACADEMIC > **Nonfiction** > *Nonfiction Books*
  Arts; Biography; Contemporary; Creative Nonfiction; History; Literature; Maori; Memoir; Narrative Essays; Nature; Pacific

ADULT > **Poetry** > *Poetry Collections*

Send: Table of contents; Synopsis; Writing sample; Full text; Proposal; Market info; Author bio
How to send: Email
How not to send: Post

Publishes books of scholarly and cultural significance that enrich society. Produces a range of non-fiction books on New Zealand and the Pacific, focusing on history, Māori/Pacific, natural history, contemporary issues, biography/memoir, essays and creative non-fiction, literature and the arts. Also publishes a small amount of poetry as well as New Zealand's longest-running and leading journal of new writing and art.

Magazine: Landfall **(M182)**

P270 Out-Spoken Press
Book Publisher
United Kingdom

press@outspokenldn.com

https://www.outspokenldn.com
https://out-spoken.submittable.com/submit
https://www.facebook.com/outspokenldn
https://twitter.com/OutSpokenLDN
https://instagram.com/outspokenldn

Poetry > *Poetry Collections*

Closed to approaches.

A London-based independent publisher of poetry and critical writing. Founded in 2015 with the aim of challenging a lack of diversity in publishing, the press was shortlisted for the British Book Awards' Small Publisher of the Year three years running in 2020, 2021 and 2022.

P271 Oxbow Books
Book Publisher
The Wheelhouse, Angel Court, 81 St Clement's Street, Oxford, OX4 1AW
United Kingdom
Tel: +44 (0) 1865 241249
Fax: +44 (0) 1865 794449

bookadmin@Oxbowbooks.com

https://www.oxbowbooks.com
https://www.facebook.com/oxbowbooks
https://www.twitter.com/oxbowbooks
https://www.linkedin.com/company/oxbow-books

ACADEMIC > **Nonfiction** > *Nonfiction Books*
  Archaeology; Classics / Ancient World; Medieval

Publisher of academic books on archaeology, ancient history and medieval studies.

Editor: Richard Purslow

Publishing Imprint: Aris & Phillips

P272 Oxford University Press
Book Publisher
Great Clarendon Street, Oxford, OX2 6DP
United Kingdom

groupcommunications@oup.com

https://corp.oup.com
https://www.linkedin.com/company/oup/
https://www.instagram.com/oxunipress
https://www.youtube.com/oxforduniversitypress
https://x.com/oxunipress

ACADEMIC > **Nonfiction** > *Nonfiction Books*
  Anthropology; Archaeology; Architecture; Arts; Biography; Business; Classics / Ancient World; Computer Science; Culture; Engineering; Environment; Health; History; Journalism; Language; Legal; Literature; Management; Mathematics; Media; Medicine; Music; Neuroscience; Performing Arts; Philosophy; Politics; Psychology; Publishing; Religion; Science; Society; Sociology; Technology

Describes itself as the world's leading university press with the widest global presence. Our academic publishing programme serves scholars, teachers and researchers, publishing important and rigorous research and scholarship across subject areas stretching from History to Life Sciences to Economics.

P273 Pacific Press Publishing Association
Book Publisher
1350 North Kings Road, Nampa, ID 83687
United States
Tel: +1 (208) 465-2500
Fax: +1 (208) 465-2531

booksubmissions@pacificpress.com

https://www.pacificpress.com

ADULT > **Nonfiction** > *Nonfiction Books*
  Bible Studies; Biography; Christian Living; Christianity; Church History; Cookery; Health; Parenting; Relationships

CHILDREN'S
  Fiction
    Chapter Books: Christianity
    Middle Grade: Christianity
    Picture Books: Christianity

  Nonfiction
    Chapter Books: Christianity
    Middle Grade: Christianity
    Picture Books: Christianity

Send: Query
How to send: Email
How not to send: Post

Seventh-day Adventist publisher publishing mainly nonfiction, but some fiction especially children's fiction. All titles are religious and Christian and confirm to Seventh-day Adventist beliefs. Send query by email only.

P274 Pan Macmillan Australia
Book Publisher
Australia
Tel: +61 2 92859100

pan.reception@macmillan.com.au

https://www.panmacmillan.com.au

Book Publisher: Pan Macmillan

ADULT
  Fiction > *Novels*
    Contemporary; Crime; Drama; Historical Fiction; Literary; Psychological Suspense; Saga; Thrillers

  Nonfiction > *Nonfiction Books*
    Contemporary; Crime; Health; History; Lifestyle; Memoir; Mind, Body, Spirit; Narrative Nonfiction

CHILDREN'S > **Fiction** > *Middle Grade*

YOUNG ADULT > **Fiction** > *Novels*

Send: Query; Author bio; Market info; Synopsis; Proposal; Writing sample
How to send: Online submission system

Accepts submissions via online submission system.

P275 Parthian Books
Book Publisher
The Old Surgery, Napier Street, Cardigan, SA43 1ED
United Kingdom
Tel: +44 (0) 7890 968246

parthiansubmissions@gmail.com

https://www.parthianbooks.com

Fiction
  Novels: Literary
  Short Fiction: Literary

Nonfiction > *Nonfiction Books*

Poetry > *Poetry Collections*

Closed to approaches.

Publisher of poetry, fiction, and creative nonfiction, of Welsh origin, in the English language. Also publishes English language translations of Welsh language work. Send query with SAE, and (for fiction) a one-page synopsis and first 30 pages, or (for poetry) a sample of 15-20 poems. No email submissions, genre fiction of any kind, or children's / teenage fiction. See website for full submission guidelines.

Author: Richard Owain Roberts

P276 Pavilion Poetry
Publishing Imprint
United Kingdom

reviewslup@liverpool.ac.uk

https://www.liverpooluniversitypress.co.uk/topic/imprints/pavilion-poetry/
https://twitter.com/PavilionPoetry

Book Publisher: Liverpool University Press

Poetry > *Poetry Collections*

Closed to approaches.

Seeks to publish the very best in contemporary poetry. Always international in its reach, it publishes poetry that takes a risk. Whether by new or established and award-winning writers, this is poetry sure to challenge and delight.

P277 PB and Yay! Books
Book Publisher
United States

pbandyaybooks@gmail.com

https://pbandyay.site

CHILDREN'S > *Fiction* > *Picture Books*

Does not want:

> **CHILDREN'S** > *Fiction* > *Picture Books*
> Bullying; Dark Magic; Gender; Science Fiction; Sex; Witchcraft

Send: Full text
How to send: Email

Traditional publisher. No advance. High royalties. Picture books only. Welcomes submissions from authors based in the United States and Canada exclusively.

P278 Peepal Tree Press
Book Publisher
17 King's Avenue, Leeds, LS6 1QS
United Kingdom
Tel: +44 (0) 113 245 1703

contact@peepaltreepress.com

https://www.peepaltreepress.com

Fiction > *Short Fiction Collections*
  Black People; Caribbean Diaspora; Caribbean

Nonfiction > *Nonfiction Books*
  Arts; Black People; Caribbean Diaspora; Caribbean; Cultural Criticism; Literary Criticism; Memoir

Poetry > *Poetry Collections*
  Black People; Caribbean Diaspora; Caribbean

Closed to approaches.

Publishes international Caribbean, Black British, and south Asian writing. Submit through online submission system.

P279 Pelagic
Book Publisher; Ebook Publisher
United Kingdom

editor@pelagicpublishing.com

https://pelagicpublishing.com
https://www.youtube.com/channel/UCIf1cxk0Q8rd0_XkhdAiQBQ

https://www.facebook.com/pelagicpublishing/
https://twitter.com/pelagicpublish

ACADEMIC > **Nonfiction** > *Nonfiction Books*
  Environment; Nature; Science; Wildlife

Send: Query; Proposal; Submission form
How to send: Email

A leading independent publisher of books on ecology, wildlife and environmental science. We publish for academics, libraries and natural history enthusiasts, and are actively commissioning in subjects including: ecology, wildlife, conservation, research methods, data collection, data analysis, fieldwork, identification, taxonomy and phylogenetics, environmental science and technology in nature.

P280 Pen & Ink Designs Publishing
Book Publisher; Self Publishing Service; Editorial Service
United Kingdom

https://www.penandinkdesigns.co.uk

ADULT
  Fiction
    Novels: Crime; Historical Fiction; Mystery
    Short Fiction Collections: General

  Nonfiction > *Nonfiction Books*: Self Help

  Poetry > *Poetry Collections*

CHILDREN'S > **Fiction**
  Chapter Books; *Colouring Books*; *Novels*; *Picture Books*; *Short Fiction Collections*
YOUNG ADULT > **Nonfiction** > *Nonfiction Books*: Self Help

Send: Query
How to send: Online contact form

Costs: Offers services that writers have to pay for.

The publisher has been operating since 2012 on a small basis originally by publishing a selection of children's picture books and other short story books. This was followed by the publication of an award winning historical novel and due to a physical move of the business to Wales the company began working with another small independent publisher. Due to the pandemic this publisher had to retire from the business leaving the business to continue under the ownership of the original proprietor. Since then the publisher has become a member of and been accepted as a small independent Welsh Publisher by the CCPW Group (backed by Literature Wales). They have published a small quantity of manuscripts both fiction and non-fiction and offer a variety of services aimed at assisting new and developing writers.

P281 Pen & Sword Books Ltd
Book Publisher
George House, Units 12 & 13, Beevor Street, Off Pontefract Road, Barnsley, South Yorkshire, S71 1HN
United Kingdom
Tel: +44 (0) 1226 734222

editorialoffice@pen-and-sword.co.uk

https://www.pen-and-sword.co.uk

Nonfiction > *Nonfiction Books*
  Local History; Maritime History; Military Aviation; Military History

Send: Query
Don't send: Full text

Publishes across a number of areas including military history, naval and maritime history, aviation, local history, family history, transport, discovery and exploration, collectables and antiques, nostalgia and true crime. In 2017, launched a new lifestyle imprint which publishes books on areas such as health and diet, hobbies and sport, gardening and wildlife and space. Submit proposal using form on website.

Editor: Lisa Hooson

Publishing Imprints: Frontline Books; Leo Cooper; Pen & Sword Aviation; Pen & Sword Maritime; Remember When; Wharncliffe Books; White Owl

P282 Penzler Publishers
Book Publisher
United States

https://penzlerpublishers.com
https://twitter.com/PenzlerPub
https://www.instagram.com/PenzlerPub/

Fiction > *Novels*
  Mystery; Suspense; Thrillers

An independent publisher of mysteries, thrillers, and suspense.

Publishing Imprints: American Mystery Classics (**P012**); The Mysterious Press (**P252**); Scarlet (**P327**)

P283 Perspectives Books
Book Publisher
United Kingdom

https://perspectivesbooks.com

Fiction
  Novels; *Short Fiction Collections*
Nonfiction > *Nonfiction Books*: Autobiography

Send: Query; Full text; Writing sample

Predominately seeking autobiographical works but will consider fiction also. Novels should be more than 70,000 words and less than 140,000. Also accepts short stories up to 8,000 words. Open minded with regard to the subject of short stories and will consider submissions across all genres.

P284 Perugia Press
Book Publisher
PO Box 60364, Florence, MA 01062
United States
Tel: +1 (413) 537-2588

https://www.perugiapress.com
https://www.facebook.com/perugiapress/
https://www.instagram.com/perugiapress/
https://www.youtube.com/channel/UCWzpqxJIXcK08VKNGzU0OxA

Poetry > *Poetry Collections*

Closed to approaches.

Publishes one book of poetry by a female US resident each year. Accepts submissions through annual competition running August 1 to November 15 annually ($30 entry fee).

P285 Peter Lang
Book Publisher
John Eccles House, Science Park, Robert Robinson Avenue, Littlemore, OX4 4GP
United Kingdom

Editorial@peterlang.com
info@peterlang.com

https://www.peterlang.com
https://www.facebook.com/pages/Peter-Lang-Oxford/260315267419469
https://twitter.com/peterlangoxford
http://peterlangoxford.wordpress.com/

Book Publisher: Peter Lang Group

ACADEMIC > **Nonfiction** > *Nonfiction Books*
Arts; Communication; Culture; Economics; Education; English; France; Germany; History; Italy; Language; Legal; Management; Media; Philosophy; Politics; Religion; Romania; Science; Slavs; Society; Spain

Send: Query
How to send: Email

Select appropriate editor from website and query by email.

Editor: Na Li

Publishing Director: Lucy Melville

Senior Editors: Tony Mason; Dr Laurel Plapp

P286 Peter Pauper Press
Book Publisher
3 International Drive, Suite 310, Rye Brook, NY 10573-7501
United States
Tel: +1 (914) 681-0144
Fax: +1 (914) 681-0389

customerservice@peterpauper.com
orders@peterpauper.com
https://www.peterpauper.com
https://www.facebook.com/pages/Peter-Pauper-Press-Inc/137389080124
https://twitter.com/PeterPauperPres
https://pinterest.com/peterpauperpres/

ADULT > **Nonfiction** > *Gift Books*

CHILDREN'S > **Nonfiction** > *Activity Books*

Closed to approaches.

Described as a preeminent gift and stationery publisher.

P287 Phaidon Press
Book Publisher
United Kingdom

submissions@phaidon.com
submissions.children@phaidon.com

https://www.phaidon.com
https://www.instagram.com/phaidonsnaps/
https://twitter.com/Phaidon
https://www.facebook.com/phaidoncom/
https://youtube.com/phaidonpress
https://linkedin.com/company/phaidon-press

ADULT > **Nonfiction** > *Nonfiction Books*
Architecture; Arts; Contemporary; Cookery; Cultural History; Culture; Design; Fashion; Films; Food; Interior Design; Music; Performing Arts; Photography; Travel

CHILDREN'S > **Nonfiction** > *Nonfiction Books*

Send: Outline; Author bio
How to send: Email

Publishes books in the areas of art, architecture, design, photography, film, fashion, contemporary culture, decorative arts, interior design, music, performing arts, cultural history, food, and cookery, travel, and books for children. No fiction or approaches by post. Send query by email only, with CV and short description of the project. Response only if interested.

Publishing Imprint: The Monacelli Press (**P245**)

P288 Phoenix Moirai
Book Publisher
United States

https://whimsillusion.com
https://twitter.com/whimsillusion

ADULT > **Fiction**
Novellas; *Novels*; *Short Fiction Collections*; *Short Fiction*

CHILDREN'S > **Fiction**
Chapter Books; *Middle Grade*

YOUNG ADULT > **Fiction**
Novellas; *Novels*; *Short Fiction Collections*; *Short Fiction*

How to send: Online submission system
How not to send: Email

Started in 2014 as a graphic design, writing, and video production company, with a goal of growing into a full publisher. They have reached that goal and are currently accepting manuscripts from all writers, including unagented and first-time authors. They also created a forum for writers and readers to come together to be and find beta readers for their works in progress. This is also the platform in which writers submit their manuscripts for publication. No membership to the site is needed or requested to submit. Submissions are open to all genre writers, regardless of social media following or manuscript length. Simply wants to read and publish fresh new voices who may not fit in a simple genre bubble, and writers struggling to find a way to have their voices heard.

P289 Piatkus Books
Publishing Imprint
50 Victoria Embankment, London, EC4Y 0DZ
United Kingdom
Tel: +44 (0) 20 3122 7000

info@littlebrown.co.uk

https://www.littlebrown.co.uk/imprint/piatkus/page/lbbg-imprint-piatkus/
https://business.facebook.com/piatkusfiction/?business_id=873802706096561
https://twitter.com/PiatkusBooks

Publishing Imprint: Little, Brown Book Group

Fiction > *Novels*
Fantasy; Historical Fiction; Popular; Romance; Supernatural / Paranormal; Suspense

Nonfiction > *Nonfiction Books*
Business; Health; Mind, Body, Spirit; Parenting; Personal Development; Popular Psychology; Self Help

How to send: Through a literary agent

No longer accepts unsolicited submissions. Accepts material through a literary agent only.

P290 Picador
Publishing Imprint
United States

Book Publisher: Macmillan Publishers

P291 Piccadilly Press
Publishing Imprint
United Kingdom
Tel: +44 (0) 20 3770 8888

hello@bonnierbooks.co.uk

https://www.bonnierbooks.co.uk/imprints/piccadilly-press/
https://www.instagram.com/piccadilly.press/
https://twitter.com/piccadillypress
https://www.facebook.com/piccadillypressbooks/

CHILDREN'S > Fiction
  Chapter Books; Early Readers; Graphic Novels; Middle Grade

Publishes books aimed at readers aged 5 to 12 years old – everything from highly illustrated first chapter books to groundbreaking new stories for confident readers. Whether it's a fast-paced and funny graphic novel or an immersive fantasy world, there are choices for every kind of young fiction fan.

P292 Pimpernel Press
Book Publisher
United Kingdom

https://geminibooks.com
https://geminibooks.com/pimpernel

Book Publisher: Gemini Books (**P140**)

Nonfiction > *Nonfiction Books*
  Arts; Design; Gardening; Houses and Homes

Publishes books on art, design, houses, and gardens.

P293 Pineapple Press
Publishing Imprint
United States

https://www.globepequot.com
https://www.globepequot.com/imprint/pineapple-press/
https://www.facebook.com/PineapplePress/

Book Publisher: The Globe Pequot Press (**P145**)

ADULT
  Fiction > *Novels*
    Florida; Folklore, Myths, and Legends
  Nonfiction
    Nonfiction Books: Animals; Arts; Florida; Gardening; History; Nature; Travel
    Reference: Florida

CHILDREN'S
  Fiction > *Novels*: Florida
  Nonfiction > *Nonfiction Books*: Florida

Publishes quality books that educate and entertain while making the real Florida accessible to readers nationwide. Topics include gardening, nature, art, folklore, history, travel, and children's books and fiction that feature the sunshine state.

P294 Plexus Publishing Limited
Book Publisher
United Kingdom

editorialassistant@plexusbooks.com

http://www.plexusbooks.com
https://www.instagram.com/plexusbooks/
https://twitter.com/plexusbooks

Nonfiction > *Illustrated Books*
  Biography; Films; Music; Popular Culture

Publishes illustrated nonfiction books specialising in biography, popular culture, movies and music.

P295 Pluto Press
Book Publisher
New Wing, Somerset House, Strand, London, WC2R 1LA
United Kingdom
Tel: +44 (0) 20 8348 2724

pluto@plutobooks.com
submissions@plutobooks.com

https://www.plutobooks.com

Nonfiction > *Nonfiction Books*
  Africa; Asia; Caribbean; Economics; Environment; Ethnic Groups; Feminism; Gender; History; Middle East; Police; Politics; Science; Sexuality; Socio-Political; Sociology; South America; Technology; United States; Warfare

Send: Query; Proposal; Synopsis; Table of contents; Market info; Author bio
How to send: Email

An independent, radical publisher of non-fiction books. No poetry collections or novels. Send proposal by email to relevant editor. See website for individual editor subject areas and email addresses.

Associate Editors: Ken Barlow; Anne Beech; Jakob Horstmann

Editorial Director: David Castle

Editors: David Shulman; Neda Tehrani

P296 Pocket Mountains
Book Publisher
The Old Church, Annanside, Moffat, DG10 9HB
United Kingdom
Tel: +44 (0) 1683 221641

https://pocketmountains.com
https://www.facebook.com/Pocket-Mountains-Ltd-107054847745288/
https://twitter.com/pocketmountains
https://www.instagram.com/pocketmountainsltd/

Nonfiction > *Nonfiction Books*
  Adventure; Cycling; Nature; Running; Walking Guides

Publishes accessible and inspiring pocket-sized guidebooks for anyone who likes a bit of an adventure, including cycling, easy walking, wildlife and running guides to various parts of Scotland, England and Wales.

Editors: Robbie Porteous; April Simmons

P297 Poisoned Pen Press
Publishing Imprint
United States

https://sourcebooks.com

Book Publisher: Sourcebooks (**P350**)

Fiction > *Novels*
  Amateur Investigator; Crime; Hardboiled Crime; Mystery

How to send: Through a literary agent

Adult mystery imprint, featuring exceptional crime writing from hardboiled detectives to amateur sleuths.

P298 Polygon
Publishing Imprint
West Newington House, 10 Newington Road, Edinburgh, EH9 1QS
United Kingdom
Tel: +44 (0) 1316 684371

info@birlinn.co.uk

https://birlinn.co.uk/polygon/

Book Publisher: Birlinn Ltd

Fiction > *Novels*
  Book Club Fiction; Commercial; Literary

Nonfiction > *Nonfiction Books*
  Crime; Films; Memoir; Music; Narrative Nonfiction; Nature; Popular Culture; Travel

Poetry > *Poetry Collections*

Send: Query; Synopsis; Writing sample; Author bio
How to send: Email; Online submission system

Publishes literary fiction and poetry, both classic and modern. Send query by email with synopsis and sample material.

P299 Popular Chess
Publishing Imprint
United Kingdom

info@everymanchess.com

https://popularchess.com
https://www.facebook.com/everymanchess
https://www.twitter.com/everymanchess
https://www.youtube.com/user/EverymanChessChannel
https://vimeo.com/everymanchess

Nonfiction > *Nonfiction Books*: Chess

Describes itself as the world's preeminent chess book publisher.

P300 Practical Pre-School Books
Book Publisher
Unit A Buildings 1-5, Dinton Business Park, Catherine Ford Road, Dinton, Salisbury, SP3 5HZ
United Kingdom
Tel: +44 (0) 1722 716997

bookscustomerservice@markallengroup.com

https://www.practicalpreschoolbooks.com

PROFESSIONAL > **Nonfiction** > *Nonfiction Books*: Education

Specialises in resources that support practitioners in delivering the EYFS with ease. Our titles range from planning and observation to child development, health and wellbeing and leadership and management, with key issues focusing on how children learn.

P301 Press 53
Book Publisher
560 N. Trade Street, Suite 103, Winston-Salem, NC 27101
United States
Tel: +1 (336) 770-5353

kevin@Press53.com

https://www.press53.com

Fiction > *Short Fiction Collections*

Poetry > *Poetry Collections*

Publishes collections of poetry and short stories by US-based authors. No novels or book length fiction. Finds authors through its competitions, and through writers being active in the literary community and literary magazines.

Editor: Kevin Morgan Watson

P302 Prestel Publishing Ltd
Book Publisher
First Floor, 15 Adeline Place, London, WC1B 3AJ
United Kingdom
Tel: +44 (0) 20 7323 5004

sales@prestel-uk.co.uk

https://prestelpublishing.penguinrandomhouse.de

Book Publisher: Penguin Random House Verlagsgruppe

Nonfiction > *Nonfiction Books*
   Architecture; Arts; Design; Photography

Send: Proposal
How to send: Email

One of the world's leading publishers in the fields of art, architecture, photography and design. The company has its headquarters in Munich, offices in New York and London, and an international sales network.

P303 Procrastinating Writers United
Writing Group; Book Publisher; Ebook Publisher
United States

info@pwritersu.com

https://pwritersu.com
https://instagram.com/pwritersu/
https://bsky.app/profile/pwritersu.com

Fiction > *Short Fiction Collections*

Poetry > *Poetry Collections*

How to send: File sharing service

A group of people that enjoy fiddling about with words. Their goals include sharing and improving their work and exchanging constructive critique and encouragement. Publish print and ebook anthologies of poetry and short fiction. See website for specific submission calls.

P304 PublicAffairs
Publishing Imprint
United States

Book Publisher: Basic Books Group (**P036**)

P305 Purdue University Press
Book Publisher
504 Mitch Daniels Blvd., West Lafayette, IN 47907-2058
United States
Tel: +1 (765) 494-2038

pupress@purdue.edu

https://thepress.purdue.edu
https://www.facebook.com/purduepress
https://twitter.com/purduepress

ACADEMIC > **Nonfiction** > *Nonfiction Books*
   Agriculture; Animals; Central Europe; Culture; Dementia; Engineering; Environment; Genocide; History; Indiana; Jewish Holocaust; Literature; Politics; Public Health; Science; Technology

ADULT > **Nonfiction** > *Nonfiction Books*
   Agriculture; Animals; Central Europe; Culture; Dementia; Engineering; Environment; Genocide; History; Indiana; Jewish Holocaust; Literature; Politics; Public Health; Science; Technology

Send: Query; Author bio; Table of contents; Proposal; Writing sample
How to send: Email

Dedicated to publishing works for academic and general readers. Welcomes proposals in its core subjects, which should be emailed to the Director.

Editorial Directors: Andrea Gapsch; Justin Race

Publishing Imprint: PuP

P306 Pureplay Press
Book Publisher
United States

info@pureplaypress.com

https://www.pureplaypress.com

Fiction > *Novels*

Nonfiction > *Nonfiction Books*
   Cuba; Culture; History; Politics

Poetry > *Poetry Collections*

Send: Query
Don't send: Full text
How to send: Email

Publishes books with Cuban themes, in English and Spanish, and is beginning to publish on other subjects. No unsolicited MSS. Send query of up to 250 words, similar to the book blurb you would expect on the back of a book.

P307 The Quarto Group, Inc.
Book Publisher
1 Triptych Place 2nd Floor, 185 Park Street, London, SE1 9BL
United Kingdom
Tel: +44 (0) 20 7700 9000

https://www.quarto.com
https://www.instagram.com/quartobooksus
https://www.youtube.com/channel/UCg6_9Q3TbEXRPspas_bqPHw
https://www.pinterest.com/quartoknows
https://www.tiktok.com/@quartobooks

ADULT > **Nonfiction** > *Nonfiction Books*

CHILDREN'S > **Nonfiction** > *Nonfiction Books*

Publisher of illustrated nonfiction books for adults and children.

Publishing Imprints: Book Sales; Bright Press; Burgess Lea Press; Cool Springs Press; Epic Ink; Fair Winds Press; Frances Lincoln Children's Books; Happy Yak (**P161**); Harvard Common Press; Iqon Editions; Ivy Kids; Ivy Press; Leaping Hare Press; Lincoln First Editions; Motorbooks; Quarry; Quarto Children's Books; Quarto Publishing; Race Point Publishing; Rock Point Gift & Stationery; Rockport Publishing; SmartLab Toys; Union Books; Voyageur Press; Walter Foster Jr.; Walter Foster Publishing; Wellfleet Press; White Lion Publishing; Wide-Eyed Editions (**P429**); Words & Pictures (**P433**); becker&mayer! books; becker&mayer! kids; small world creations

P308 Quirk Books
Book Publisher
215 Church Street, Philadelphia, PA 19106
United States
Tel: +1 (215) 627-3581
Fax: +1 (215) 627-5220

https://www.quirkbooks.com
https://www.facebook.com/QuirkBooks/
https://twitter.com/quirkbooks
https://www.tiktok.com/@quirkbooks
https://www.pinterest.com/quirkbooks
http://www.youtube.com/irreference
https://instagram.com/quirkbooks

ADULT

Fiction > *Novels*
   General, and in particular: Romance

Nonfiction > *Nonfiction Books*
   Comedy / Humour; Crafts; Food and Drink; Games; Gardening; History; Horror; LGBTQIA; Parenting; Pets; Popular Culture; Relationships; Sport

CHILDREN'S
Fiction > *Middle Grade*
Nonfiction > *Nonfiction Books*

How to send: Through a literary agent

Publishes unconventional books across a broad range of categories. Agents should approach individual editors directly. Unagented submissions should be directed to the unsolicited submissions inbox, which is only open at certain times (see website for current status).

P309 Radio Society of Great Britain
Book Publisher
3 Abbey Court, Fraser Road, Priory Business Park, MK44 3WH
United Kingdom
Tel: +44 (0) 1234 832700

https://rsgb.org
https://www.rsgbshop.org
https://www.facebook.com/theRSGB
https://x.com/theRSGB
https://www.youtube.com/user/TheRSGB

Nonfiction > *Nonfiction Books*
Amateur Radio; Radio Technology

Publishes books for amateur radio enthusiasts.

P310 Rand McNally
Book Publisher
United States
Tel: +1 (877) 446-4863

tndsupport@randmcnally.com

https://www.randmcnally.com
https://www.randmcnally.com/publishing

ADULT > **Nonfiction** > *Reference*
Road Atlases; Travel

CHILDREN'S > **Nonfiction** > *Activity Books*: Travel

Publishes road atlases and activity books for children, focusing on travel.

P311 Random House Worlds
Publishing Imprint

Book Publisher: Random House

P312 Ransom Publishing Ltd
Book Publisher
Unit 7, Brocklands Farm, West Meon, Hampshire, GU32 1JN
United Kingdom
Tel: +44 (0) 1730 829091

ransom@ransom.co.uk

https://www.ransom.co.uk

ADULT
Fiction > *Short Fiction*: High-Low Literacy
Nonfiction > *Nonfiction Books*: High-Low Literacy

CHILDREN'S
Fiction > *Middle Grade*: High-Low Literacy
Nonfiction > *Nonfiction Books*: High-Low Literacy

YOUNG ADULT
Fiction > *Short Fiction*: High-Low Literacy
Nonfiction > *Nonfiction Books*: High-Low Literacy

Send: Author bio
How to send: Email

An independent specialist publisher of high quality, inspirational books that encourage and help children, young adults, and adults to develop their reading skills. Books are intended to have content which is age appropriate and engaging, but reading levels that would normally be appropriate for younger readers. Writers with experience in writing phonics or guided readers, or hi lo readers, may send their CV by email.

Editor: Steve Rickard

P313 Renard Press Ltd
Book Publisher
124 City Road, London, EC1V 2NX
United Kingdom
Tel: +44 (0) 20 8050 2928

info@renardpress.com

https://renardpress.com
https://querymanager.com/query/renardpress
https://twitter.com/renardpress/
https://www.instagram.com/renardpress/
https://www.facebook.com/therenardpress/
https://www.pinterest.co.uk/renardpress/

Fiction > *Novels*: Literary
Nonfiction > *Nonfiction Books*: Literary
Poetry > *Poetry Collections*
Scripts > *Theatre Scripts*

Closed to approaches.

We're currently considering both non-fiction and fiction with a literary bent, as well as poetry (collections only) and playscripts. Generally speaking, we're not looking for science-fiction, romance or crime – but if you feel your work is literary and only partially defined by one of these categories, please feel free to send it our way.

P314 Roc Lit 101
Publishing Imprint

Book Publisher: Random House

P315 Rocky Mountain Books
Book Publisher
Canada

don@rmbooks.com

https://rmbooks.com
https://www.facebook.com/rmbooks/

ADULT > **Nonfiction** > *Nonfiction Books*
Adventure; Arts; Culture; Environment; History; Nature; Outdoor Activities; Photography; Travel; Walking Guides

CHILDREN'S > **Nonfiction** > *Nonfiction Books*
Adventure; Arts; Culture; Environment; History; Nature; Outdoor Activities; Photography; Travel; Walking Guides

Send: Query
How to send: Email

Established to specialize primarily in guidebooks for hikers, climbers and skiers, this publisher has repositioned itself for the 21st century and now publishes and promotes a dynamic, growing list of provocative, engaging and award-winning books on mountain history, adventure travel, outdoor lifestyle, environmental consciousness, Indigenous culture, and contemporary photography—as well as a growing selection of bestselling books for children.

Editor: Fraser Seely

P316 Rodale
Publishing Imprint

Book Publisher: Random House

P317 Roseway
Publishing Imprint
2970 Oxford Street, Halifax, NS, B3L 2W4
Canada
Tel: +1 (902) 857-1388

roseway@fernpub.ca

https://fernwoodpublishing.ca/publish/roseway

Book Publisher: Fernwood Publishing (**P131**)

Fiction > *Novels*
General, and in particular: Politics

Nonfiction > *Nonfiction Books*
Biography; Creative Nonfiction; Memoir; Politics

Poetry > *Poetry Collections*

Send: Proposal; Author bio; Pitch; Market info; Marketing plan; Writing sample; Full text
How to send: Email attachment

Publishes works of fiction, creative non-fiction, poetry, memoirs, biographies, and politically infused literary compositions. Publishes primarily for an adult audience but has occasionally published material for younger readers. Through diverse content, aims to spark critical thought and inclusively engage readers.

P318 Round Hall
Publishing Imprint; Magazine Publisher
Spaces, Office 313, 77 Sir John Rogerson's Quay, Block C, Dublin 2, D02YK60
Ireland

https://www.sweetandmaxwell.co.uk/roundhall/

Book Publisher: Thomson Reuters

PROFESSIONAL > **Nonfiction**
  Articles: Legal
  Nonfiction Books: Legal

Send: Query
How to send: Email

Publishes information on Irish law in the form of books, journals, periodicals, looseleaf services, CD-ROMs and online services. Contact by email.

Company Director: Martin McCann

Editor: Pamela Moran

P319 Ruby Fiction
Publishing Imprint
Finsgate, 5-7 Cranwood Street, London, EC1V 9EE
United Kingdom

info@rubyfiction.com
submissions@rubyfiction.com

https://www.rubyfiction.com
https://twitter.com/rubyfiction
https://www.facebook.com/pages/RubyFiction

Book Publisher: Choc Lit (**P085**)

Fiction > *Novels*
  Romance; Thrillers; Women's Fiction

Send: Author bio; Synopsis
How to send: Online submission system

Publishes thrillers, women's fiction and romances without the hero's point of view, between 60,000 and 100,000 words, suitable for a female adult audience.

P320 Running Press
Publishing Imprint
United States

Book Publisher: Workman Publishing (**P437**)

P321 Saga Press
Publishing Imprint

Book Publisher: Simon & Schuster Adult Publishing

P322 Salt Publishing
Book Publisher
12 Norwich Road, CROMER, Norfolk, NR27 0AX
United Kingdom

submissions@saltpublishing.com

https://www.saltpublishing.com
https://twitter.com/saltpublishing
https://www.facebook.com/SaltPublishing
https://instagram.com/saltpublishing/

Fiction > *Novels*
  General, and in particular: Comedy / Humour; Dark; Folk Horror; Gothic; Historical Fiction

Nonfiction > *Nonfiction Books*
  Climate Science; Creative Writing; Culture; Finance; Health; Narrative Nonfiction; Nature; Northern England; Social Issues

Send: Query; Synopsis; Author bio; Writing sample
How to send: Through a literary agent; Word file email attachment
How not to send: Post

We love historical fiction, folk horror, and are particularly interested in dark, uncanny and edgy fiction, comic fiction, eerie novels, and Gothic novels. We have a particular interest in narrative non-fiction writing about the natural world. We are also happy to consider life-writing projects, creative writing guides, and works that centre on the North of England. We are also happy to consider introductory or brief polemical works on key issues of the day – for example, ageing, climate change, cultural capital, energy security, health, housing, identity, social mobility, and wealth.

P323 Sandstone Press
Publishing Imprint
United Kingdom

https://www.adventurebooks.com
https://www.adventurebooks.com/collections/sandstone-press

Book Publisher: Adventure Books by Vertebrate Publishing (**P004**)

Fiction > *Novels*

Nonfiction > *Nonfiction Books*

P324 Saqi Books
Book Publisher
Gable House, 18-24 Turnham Green Terrace, London, W4 1QP
United Kingdom
Tel: +44 (0) 20 7221 9347

submissions@saqibooks.com

https://saqibooks.com
http://www.twitter.com/SaqiBooks
https://www.facebook.com/SaqiBooks/
https://www.youtube.com/channel/UCqvwvEp1N5rHauJEmmXq16g
http://instagram.com/saqibooks

ACADEMIC > **Nonfiction** > *Nonfiction Books*
  Middle East; North Africa

ADULT > **Nonfiction** > *Nonfiction Books*
  Middle East; North Africa

Send: Query; Synopsis; Table of contents; Writing sample; Author bio; Market info
How to send: Email

Publisher of books related to the Arab world and the Middle East. See website for full submission guidelines.

Publishing Imprint: Telegram Books

P325 Sasquatch Books
Book Publisher
1904 Third Avenue, Suite 710, Seattle, Washington 98101
United States

submissions@sasquatchbooks.com

https://sasquatchbooks.com
https://www.facebook.com/SasquatchBooksSeattle/
https://twitter.com/sasquatchbooks
https://www.instagram.com/sasquatchbooks/

Nonfiction > *Nonfiction Books*
  Arts; Business; Family; Food; Gardening; Literature; Nature; Politics; Wine

Send: Query; Proposal; Full text
How to send: Email

Publishes books by the most gifted writers, artists, chefs, naturalists, and thought leaders in the Pacific Northwest and on the West Coast, and brings their talents to a national audience. Welcomes agented and unagented submissions from both debut and experienced writers.

Publishing Imprints: Little Bigfoot (**P218**); Spruce Books

P326 Scala Arts & Heritage Publishers
Book Publisher
43 Great Ormond Street, London, SW2 5UA
United Kingdom

https://scalapublishers.com

Nonfiction > *Illustrated Books*
  Antiques; Architecture; Arts; History

Specialises in producing illustrated books for museums, galleries, libraries, cathedrals, heritage sites and educational institutions.

P327 Scarlet
Publishing Imprint
United States

https://penzlerpublishers.com/product-category/scarlet/

Book Publisher: Penzler Publishers (**P282**)

Fiction > *Novels*
  Domestic Thriller; Psychological Suspense

Aims to bring audiences fresh voices in psychological suspense and domestic thrillers.

P328 Schiffer Military History
Publishing Imprint
United States

proposals@schifferbooks.com

https://www.schiffermilitary.com
https://schifferbooks.com/pages/schiffer-imprints

Book Publisher: Schiffer Publishing

Nonfiction > *Nonfiction Books*
Aviation; History; Military

Send: Query; Outline; Pitch; Author bio; Table of contents; Writing sample; Market info
How to send: Email

Dedicated to publishing definitive books on military and aviation history by the world's leading historians.

P329 Scholastic
Book Publisher
557 Broadway, New York, NY 10012
United States

TeachingResources@Scholastic.com

https://www.scholastic.com
https://scholastic.force.com/scholasticfaqs/s/article/How-do-I-submit-a-manuscript-for-teaching-ideas

CHILDREN'S
Fiction
Chapter Books; *Early Readers*; *Middle Grade*; *Novels*; *Picture Books*
Nonfiction
Chapter Books; *Early Readers*; *Illustrated Books*; *Middle Grade*
PROFESSIONAL > **Nonfiction** > *Nonfiction Books*: Education

How to send: Through a literary agent

The world's largest publisher and distributor of children's books. Provides professional services, classroom magazines, and produces educational and popular children's media.

Book Publishers: Arthur A. Levine Books; Chicken House Publishing; Scholastic UK (**P330**)

Publishing Imprints: AFK; Cartwheel Books; Graphix; Klutz; Orchard Books; PUSH; Scholastic Audio; Scholastic Focus; Scholastic Inc.; Scholastic Press; Scholastic Reference

P330 Scholastic UK
Book Publisher
1 London Bridge, London, SE1 9BG, WITNEY:, Unit 18F, Thorney Leys Park, Witney, Oxfordshire, OX28 4GE
United Kingdom
Tel: +44 (0) 800 212281

enquiries@scholastic.co.uk

https://www.scholastic.co.uk
https://www.facebook.com/ScholasticUK
https://twitter.com/scholasticuk
https://instagram.com/scholastic_uk
https://www.pinterest.co.uk/scholasticuk
https://www.youtube.com/user/scholasticfilmsuk

Book Publisher: Scholastic (**P329**)

CHILDREN'S
Fiction
Board Books; *Chapter Books*; *Early Readers*; *Middle Grade*; *Novels*; *Picture Books*
Nonfiction
Board Books; *Chapter Books*; *Early Readers*; *Middle Grade*; *Nonfiction Books*; *Picture Books*

Publisher of fiction and nonfiction for children, as well as educational material for primary schools.

Book Publisher: Scholastic Children's Books

P331 Scratching Shed Publishing
Book Publisher; Magazine Publisher
47 Street Lane, Leeds, West Yorkshire, LS8 1AP
United Kingdom
Tel: +44 (0) 0113 225 9797
Fax: +44 (0) 0113 225 2515

admin@scratchingshedpublishing.com

https://www.scratchingshedpublishing.com
https://www.facebook.com/scratching.shed

ADULT
Fiction > *Novels*
Northern England; Sport

Nonfiction > *Nonfiction Books*
General, and in particular: Autobiography; Biography; Boxing; Children; Comedy / Humour; Cricket; Current Affairs; Football / Soccer; History; Horse Racing; Local History; Music; Northern England; Performing Arts; Politics; Rugby League; Sport; Travel

CHILDREN'S
Fiction > *Picture Books*: Sport

Poetry > *Poetry Collections*: Comedy / Humour

Send: Query; Author bio; Synopsis; Outline; Market info; Writing sample; Self-addressed stamped envelope (SASE)
How to send: Email; Post

Primary aim is to produce high-quality books inspired by aspects of northern English culture, though in recent years that brief has widened considerably to include several national and international titles and a monthly rugby league magazine.

Magazine: Forty20 (**M128**)

P332 Seal Press
Publishing Imprint
United States

https://www.sealpress.com
https://www.facebook.com/sealpress
https://x.com/sealpress
https://www.instagram.com/sealpress/

Book Publisher: Basic Books Group (**P036**)

Nonfiction > *Nonfiction Books*: Feminism

Founded in 1976 and stands as one of the most enduring feminist publishing houses to emerge from the women's press movement of the 1970s. Publishes radical and groundbreaking books that inspire and challenge readers, that humanize urgent issues, that build much-needed bridges in divisive times, and help us see the world in a new light.

P333 Seaworthy Publications
Book Publisher
6300 N Wickham Road, Unit #130-416, Melbourne, FL 32940
United States
Tel: +1 (321) 389-2506

queries@seaworthy.com

http://www.seaworthy.com

Nonfiction > *Articles*
Boats; Sailing

Send: Full text

Nautical book publisher specialising in recreational boating. Send query by email outlining your work and attaching sample table of contents and two or three sample chapters. See website for full submission guidelines.

P334 Sentient Publications
Book Publisher
PO Box 1851, Boulder, CO 80306
United States
Tel: +1 (303) 443-2188

submissions@sentientpublications.com

https://www.sentientpublications.com

Fiction > *Novels*: Literary

Nonfiction > *Nonfiction Books*
Education; Holistic Health; Spirituality

Send: Query; Author bio; Synopsis; Full text; Writing sample
How to send: Email

We have typically published titles with content related to the areas of holistic health, alternative education, and spirituality. While our primary focus is non-fiction in those genres, we're open to evaluating very well-written literary fiction and other work which may cross over into new territory for us.

P335 Seren Books
Book Publisher
Suite 6, 4 Derwen Road, Bridgend, CF31 1LH
United Kingdom
Tel: +44 (0) 1656 663018

seren@serenbooks.com
poetrysubmissions@serenbooks.com
mickfelton@serenbooks.com

https://www.serenbooks.com
https://www.facebook.com/SerenBooks

http://www.twitter.com/SerenBooks
http://www.pinterest.com/SerenBooks

Fiction
Novels: Literary
Short Fiction: Literary

Nonfiction > *Nonfiction Books*
Arts; Biography; Current Affairs; Drama; History; Literary Criticism; Memoir; Music; Photography; Sport; Travel

Poetry > *Poetry Collections*

Send: Query; Full text; Proposal; Author bio; Synopsis; Outline; Market info
How to send: Email; Post

Publishes fiction, nonfiction, and poetry. Specialises in English-language writing from Wales and aims to bring Welsh culture, art, literature, and politics to a wider audience. Accepts nonfiction submissions by post or by email. Prefers poetry submissions by email, but will accept hard copies. Accepts fiction only from authors with whom there is an existing publishing relationship.

Poetry Editor: Amy Wack

Publisher: Mick Felton

P336 Shipwreckt Books Publishing Company
Book Publisher
153 Franklin Street, Winona, MN 55987
United States

contact@shipwrecktbooks.com

https://shipwrecktbooks.press
https://shipwrecktbooks.submittable.com/submit
https://www.facebook.com/SWBPC/
https://twitter.com/shipwrecktbook/

Fiction
Novels; *Short Fiction Collections*

Nonfiction
Essays: General
Nonfiction Books: General, and in particular: Biography; Family; Memoir

Poetry > *Poetry Collections*

Closed to approaches.

Publishes books and literary magazine. Submit query letter, brief bio, synopsis, and/or writing sample via online submission system.

Print Magazine: Lost Lake Folk Opera Magazine (**M193**)

Publishing Imprints: Lost Lake Folk Art; Rocket Science Press; Up On Big Rock Poetry

P337 Sigma Press
Book Publisher
Stobart House, Pontyclerc, Penybanc Road, Ammanford, Carmarthenshire, SA18 3HP
United Kingdom
Tel: +44 (0) 1269 593100

info@sigmapress.co.uk

https://www.sigmapress.co.uk
https://www.facebook.com/sigmawalkingbooks/
https://twitter.com/Sigma_Press

Nonfiction > *Nonfiction Books*
Cycling Guides; Regional; Walking Guides

An independent publisher of regional walking and cycling guides and local interest books.

Editors: Jane Evans; Nigel Evans

P338 Siloam
Publishing Imprint
United States

Media Company: Charisma Media

P339 Simply Read Books
Book Publisher
501-5525 West Boulevard, Vancouver, BC, V6M 3W6
Canada

go@simplyreadbooks.com

https://simplyreadbooks.com
https://www.instagram.com/simply_read_books/
https://twitter.com/simplyreadbooks

CHILDREN'S > **Fiction**
Chapter Books; *Early Readers*; *Graphic Novels*; *Middle Grade*; *Picture Books*

Send: Query; Synopsis; Full text
Don't send: Self-addressed stamped envelope (SASE)
How to send: Post
How not to send: Email; Disk

Small publishing house specialising in high-quality, unique picture books and fiction.

P340 Singing Dragon
Publishing Imprint
Carmelite House, 50 Victoria Embankment, London, EC4Y 0DZ
United Kingdom
Tel: +44 (0) 20 3122 6000

hello@singingdragon.com
proposals@jkp.com

https://uk.singingdragon.com
https://jkp.submittable.com/submit
https://twitter.com/Singing_Dragon_
https://www.facebook.com/SingingDragon
http://instagram.com/singingdragonbooks

Publishing Imprint: Jessica Kingsley Publishers (**P197**)

ADULT > **Nonfiction**
Graphic Nonfiction: Alternative Health; Health; Wellbeing
Nonfiction Books: Alternative Health; Aromatherapy; Ayurveda; Childbirth; Chinese Medicine; Culture; Ethnic Groups; Fertility; Health; Herbal Remedies; Lifestyle; Martial Arts; Nutrition; Pregnancy; Qigong; Tai Chi; Taoism / Daoism; Wellbeing; Yoga

CHILDREN'S > **Nonfiction** > *Nonfiction Books*
Depression; Mental Health; Wellbeing

PROFESSIONAL > **Nonfiction** > *Nonfiction Books*
Career Development; Health; Medicine

Send: Proposal
How to send: Submittable
How not to send: Post

Publishes authoritative books on complementary and alternative health, Tai Chi, Qigong and ancient wisdom traditions for health, wellbeing, and professional and personal development. Our books are for professionals and general readers. We also publish graphic novels across our subject areas, and books for children on issues such as bereavement, depression and anger.

P341 Sinister Stoat Press
Publishing Imprint
United States

https://www.weaselpress.com/sinisterstoatpress
https://www.facebook.com/sinisterstoat
https://twitter.com/sinisterstoat

Fiction
Chapbooks: Dark Fantasy; Furries; Ghost Stories; Horror; LGBTQIA; Psychological Horror; Science Fiction; Sex; Supernatural / Paranormal Horror; Vampires; Werewolves
Novellas: Dark Fantasy; Furries; Ghost Stories; Horror; LGBTQIA; Psychological Horror; Science Fiction; Sex; Supernatural / Paranormal Horror; Vampires; Werewolves
Novels: Dark Fantasy; Furries; Ghost Stories; Horror; LGBTQIA; Psychological Horror; Science Fiction; Sex; Supernatural / Paranormal Horror; Vampires; Werewolves
Short Fiction Collections: Dark Fantasy; Furries; Ghost Stories; Horror; LGBTQIA; Psychological Horror; Science Fiction; Sex; Supernatural / Paranormal Horror; Vampires; Werewolves

Closed to approaches.

Horror publisher publishing Furry works, Queer Horror, Extreme Horror, Splatter Punk, Slashers, Paranormal Horror, Weird Horror, Vampires, Werewolves, Monsters, Cryptids (within reason), Sci-Fi horror, and Dark Fantasy. Only accepting work from Authors of Color, Authors who Identify as LGBTQ+, Authors with Disabilities, and Current and Former Sex Workers.

P342 SmashBear Publishing
Book Publisher
Office 6945, London, W1A 6US
United Kingdom

info@smashbearpublishing.co.uk

https://www.smashbearpublishing.com
https://www.linkedin.com/company/

smashbearpublishing
https://www.facebook.com/smashbearpublishing
https://x.com/SmashBearPH
https://www.instagram.com/smashbearpublishing/

Fiction > *Novels*
Fantasy; Horror; Science Fiction; Supernatural / Paranormal Romance; Urban Fantasy

We specialise in urban fantasy, fantasy, and paranormal romance but will also consider horror and Sci-Fi.

P343 Smokestack Books
Book Publisher
School Farm, Nether Silton, Thirsk, North Yorkshire, YO7 2JZ
United Kingdom
Tel: +44 (0) 1765 658917

info@smokestack-books.co.uk

https://smokestack-books.co.uk

Poetry > *Poetry Collections*

Closed to approaches.

Publishes poetry which is unconventional, unfashionable, radical or left-field. No fiction, short-stories, drama, nonfiction, or books for children.

Editor: Andy Croft

P344 Snowbooks
Book Publisher
United Kingdom

emma@snowbooks.com

https://www.snowbooks.com

Fiction > *Novels*
Fantasy; Horror; Science Fiction; Thrillers

Nonfiction > *Nonfiction Books*
Crafts; Crime; Leisure; Sport

Closed to approaches.

Publishes horror, science fiction, and fantasy novels over 70,000 words. Named joint Small Publisher of the Year at the 2006 British book Trade Awards. Friendly attitude towards authors and unsolicited approaches. See website for guidelines.

Managing Director: Emma Barnes

P345 Society for Promoting Christian Knowledge (SPCK)
Book Publisher
The Record Hall, 16-16A Baldwins Gardens, London
United Kingdom

contact@spck.org.uk

https://spckpublishing.co.uk
https://www.facebook.com/pages/SPCK-Publishing/205059496214486
https://www.instagram.com/spck_publishing/
https://twitter.com/SPCKPublishing

ADULT
  Fiction > *Novels*: Christianity

  Nonfiction > *Nonfiction Books*
  Arts; Bible Studies; Biography; Christian Living; Christianity; Culture; Family; Health; History; Meditation; Personal Development; Relationships; Society; Spirituality

CHILDREN'S > **Fiction** > *Picture Books*: Christianity

Send: Query; Table of contents; Outline; Market info
How to send: Online submission system

A recognised market-leader in the areas of Theology and Christian Spirituality. Nearly all books are commissioned so rarely accepts unsolicited projects for publication.

P346 Society of Genealogists
Book Publisher
40 Wharf Road, London, N1 7GS
United Kingdom
Tel: +44 (0) 20 7251 8799

hello@sog.org.uk

https://www.sog.org.uk
https://www.facebook.com/societyofgenealogists
https://twitter.com/soggenealogist
https://www.pinterest.co.uk/societyofgeneal/

Nonfiction > *Nonfiction Books*
Genealogy; History

Publishes a wide variety of family history and genealogy publications.

P347 Soho Crime
Publishing Imprint
United States

Book Publisher: Soho Press (**P348**)

P348 Soho Press
Book Publisher
United States

https://sohopress.com
https://twitter.com/soho_press
https://www.facebook.com/SohoPress

ADULT > **Fiction** > *Novels*
Crime; Literary

YOUNG ADULT > **Fiction** > *Novels*

An independent book publisher based in Manhattan. Founded in 1986, Soho publishes 80-100 books a year across its imprints, and is known for introducing bold literary voices, award-winning crime fiction, and ground-breaking young adult fiction.

Publishing Imprints: Hell's Hundred (*P170*); Soho Crime (*P347*); Soho Teen (*P349*)

P349 Soho Teen
Publishing Imprint
United States

Book Publisher: Soho Press (**P348**)

P350 Sourcebooks
Book Publisher
PO Box 4410, Naperville, IL 60567-4410
United States
Tel: +1 (800) 432-7444
Fax: +1 (630) 961-2168

info@sourcebooks.com

https://www.sourcebooks.com
https://linkedin.com/company/50434/
https://twitter.com/sourcebooks
https://facebook.com/sourcebooks
https://www.pinterest.com/sbjabberwockykids/
https://www.instagram.com/sourcebooks/
https://www.sourcebooks.com/contact-us.html

Nonfiction > *Nonfiction Books*

How to send: Through a literary agent

Publishes adult nonfiction. No submissions from unagented authors.

Publishing Imprints: Poisoned Pen Press (**P297**); Sourcebooks Casablanca (**P351**); Sourcebooks Fire (**P353**); Sourcebooks Horror (**P354**); Sourcebooks Jabberwocky (**P355**); Sourcebooks Landmark (**P356**); Sourcebooks Wonderland (**P357**); Sourcebooks Young Readers (**P358**); Sourcebooks eXplore (**P352**)

P351 Sourcebooks Casablanca
Publishing Imprint
United States

romance@sourcebooks.com

https://sourcebooks.com

Book Publisher: Sourcebooks (**P350**)

Fiction > *Novels*
Contemporary Romance; Historical Romance; Romance; Romantic Suspense; Supernatural / Paranormal Romance

Send: Query; Author bio; Synopsis; Full text
How to send: Word file email attachment

We publish all genres of romance, including paranormal, historical, contemporary, and romantic suspense.

P352 Sourcebooks eXplore
Publishing Imprint
United States

https://sourcebooks.com

Book Publisher: Sourcebooks (**P350**)

CHILDREN'S > **Nonfiction** > *Nonfiction Books*

How to send: Online submission system

Children's nonfiction imprint dedicated to educating and entertaining young readers on a variety of subjects. Accepts submissions only from expert professionals in their fields.

P353 Sourcebooks Fire
Publishing Imprint
United States

https://sourcebooks.com

Book Publisher: Sourcebooks (**P350**)

YOUNG ADULT
  Fiction > *Novels*
  Nonfiction > *Nonfiction Books*

How to send: Through a literary agent

Dedicated to publishing quality, break-out fiction and nonfiction for young adults. We are passionate about producing books with authentic teen voices that create – and validate – the teen experience in all of its diversity, whether it's heart-wrenching romance, laugh-out-loud humor, intense and issue-driven drama, haunting mystery, thrilling suspense, or heart-pounding action. Bridging the commercial and the literary, our books have dynamic, engaging, and innovative storytelling that teens want to read, then share with their friends. We build and grow authors in the market, creating brands that teens will trust and return to for a fantastic reading experience.

P354 Sourcebooks Horror
Publishing Imprint
United States

horror@sourcebooks.com

https://sourcebooks.com

Book Publisher: Sourcebooks (**P350**)

Fiction > *Novels*: Horror

Send: Query; Synopsis; Full text; Author bio
How to send: Word file email attachment

We are actively acquiring agented and unagented Horror fiction including Own Voices, marginalized voices, inclusive and diverse stories. We're looking for strong writers of all ethnicities, races, sexualities, gender identities, abilities and ages, whose stories have something fresh to offer in the Horror genre.

P355 Sourcebooks Jabberwocky
Publishing Imprint
United Kingdom

https://sourcebooks.com

Book Publisher: Sourcebooks (**P350**)

CHILDREN'S > **Fiction**
  Board Books; *Picture Books*

How to send: Through a literary agent

Believes in engaging children in the pure fun of books and the wonder of learning new things. Focused on all things children's fiction, delivers unique voices, education and entertainment to the next generation of picture and board book readers.

P356 Sourcebooks Landmark
Publishing Imprint
United States

https://sourcebooks.com

Book Publisher: Sourcebooks (**P350**)

Fiction > *Novels*
  General, and in particular: Book Club Fiction; Contemporary Women's Fiction; Historical Fiction; Suspense

How to send: Through a literary agent

Adult fiction imprint featuring many styles and authors with particular sweet spots in historical fiction, contemporary women's fiction, suspense, and book club fiction. Submissions are closed to unagented projects.

P357 Sourcebooks Wonderland
Publishing Imprint
United States

https://sourcebooks.com

Book Publisher: Sourcebooks (**P350**)

CHILDREN'S > **Fiction** > *Picture Books*

How to send: Through a literary agent

Publishes proprietary, customized, and regional children's books.

P358 Sourcebooks Young Readers
Publishing Imprint
United States

https://sourcebooks.com

Book Publisher: Sourcebooks (**P350**)

CHILDREN'S > **Fiction** > *Middle Grade*

How to send: Through a literary agent

Believes in promoting accessible, fun, and new voices in fiction for ages 8–12.

P359 Sparsile Books
Book Publisher
United Kingdom
Tel: +44 (0) 7938 864485

enquiries@sparsilebooks.com
Submissions@sparsilebooks.com

https://www.sparsilebooks.com
https://www.facebook.com/sparsilebooks/
https://twitter.com/SparsileBooks
https://www.instagram.com/sparsile_books_ltd/

Fiction > *Novels*
  Contemporary; Crime; Historical Fiction; Literary; Scotland; Thrillers
Nonfiction > *Nonfiction Books*
  General, and in particular: Scotland

Send: Query; Synopsis; Writing sample; Market info; Author bio
How to send: Email

A small boutique publisher, specializing in literary fiction and high quality non-fiction. We have an old-fashioned approach, which sees publishing in terms of an art. We have undertaken only to publish original and beautifully-crafted works with attention to historical detail and the poetry of language.

P360 Spout Press
Book Publisher
PO Box 581067, Minneapolis, MN 55458-1067
United States

spoutpress@gmail.com

https://www.spoutpress.org

Fiction
  Novels: Contemporary; Experimental; Literary
  Short Fiction Collections: Contemporary; Experimental; Literary
Poetry > *Poetry Collections*
  Contemporary; Experimental; Literary

Closed to approaches.

A small, all-volunteer, non-profit literary publisher. Publishes and promotes the finest in contemporary experimental writing – mentoring young writers and bringing new and/or under-appreciated voices to the attention of a larger audience. This is accomplished through the publishing of books and the production of live events within the community. Both strive to combine artistic genres to facilitate dialogue between the film, music, visual art, and literary communities creating synergy that expands possibilities for both artists and audiences.

P361 SRL Publishing
Book Publisher
Office 47396, PO Box 6945, London, W1A 6US
United Kingdom

admin@srlpublishing.co.uk
submissions@srlpublishing.co.uk

https://srlpublishing.co.uk
https://www.facebook.com/srlpublishing
https://www.instagram.com/srlpublishing
https://twitter.com/@srlpublishing
https://www.tiktok.com/@srlpublishing
https://www.threads.net/@srlpublishing
https://www.linkedin.com/company/srlpublishing

Fiction > *Novels*

Nonfiction > *Nonfiction Books*

Does not want:

> **Fiction** > *Novels*
> Erotic; Religion
> **Nonfiction** > *Nonfiction Books*
> Religion; Self Help

Send: Query; Author bio; Synopsis; Full text; Pitch
How to send: Word file email attachment

We don't care about your colour; we care about your words.

Writers will never be asked their sexuality, race, or religion – only if the author wishes to disclose, and we will never use this information to generate sales. We advise anyone who is thinking of submitting their work to us, to not put their race in the subject heading. We view all submissions as equal and will not prioritise any submissions from certain minority groups.

We love stories – fiction or non-fiction. We will consider most genres, topics, or formats.

No graphic or eroticised incest/rape; necrophilia; paedophilia; bestiality; erotica, fetishes or porn; or anything that encourages violence, hate, or racism. No poetry, self-help titles, short story collections, anthologies, or faith-based books. No AI-generated submissions in any form. These include works that are written or co-written by AI technology.

P362 St Martin's Press
Publishing Imprint
United States

Book Publisher: Macmillan Publishers

P363 St. Martin's Essentials
Publishing Imprint
United States

Book Publisher: Macmillan Publishers

P364 St. Martin's Griffin
Publishing Imprint
United States

Book Publisher: Macmillan Publishers

P365 St. Martin's Publishing Group
Publishing Imprint
United States

Book Publisher: Macmillan Publishers

P366 Stainer & Bell Ltd
Book Publisher
Victoria House, 23 Gruneisen Road, London, England, N3 1DZ
United Kingdom
Tel: +44 (0) 20 8343 3303

post@stainer.co.uk
https://stainer.co.uk

Nonfiction > *Nonfiction Books*: Music

An independent music publisher with a catalogue of choral, orchestral, vocal and instrumental music representing the highest achievements of British composers from the sixteenth century to the present, an extensive list of contemporary hymnody and religious song, and a range of collected editions.

P367 Stanford University Press
Book Publisher
485 Broadway, First Floor, Redwood City CA 94063-8460
United States
Tel: +1 (650) 723-9434

https://www.sup.org
http://www.facebook.com/stanforduniversitypress
http://www.twitter.com/stanfordpress
https://www.youtube.com/channel/UCmd8xj7yu0WGeLRqL39UjLA
http://instagram.com/stanfordupress

ACADEMIC > **Nonfiction** > *Nonfiction Books*
Anthropology; Asia; Business; History; Judaism; Legal; Literature; Media; Middle East; Philosophy; Politics; Religion; Sociology; South America

Send: Query; Proposal; Author bio; Table of contents
How to send: Email; Post

Submit proposals by post, or see website for list of editors and submit proposal to the appropriate editor by email.

P368 Stanley Gibbons
Book Publisher; Magazine Publisher
399 Strand, London, WC2R 0LP
United Kingdom

support@stanleygibbons.com

https://www.stanleygibbons.com
https://www.stanleygibbons.com/publishing/publishing-house
https://www.facebook.com/stanleygibbonsgroup
https://twitter.com/StanleyGibbons
https://www.instagram.com/stanleygibbons/

Nonfiction > *Reference*: Stamp Collecting

Publishes handbooks and reference guides on stamps and stamp collecting.

P369 Steward House Publishers
Book Publisher
2307 Steamboat Lp E #202, Port Orchard, WA 98366
United States

query@stewardhouse.com
submissions@stewardhouse.com

https://www.stewardhouse.com

Fiction > *Novels*

Nonfiction > *Nonfiction Books*

Send: Full text; Query; Synopsis; Writing sample
How to send: Email attachment

Generally publishes works between 15,000 and 150,000 words in length, and is open to a variety of genres, both fiction and non-fiction, if the writing shows skill and care with words. Not accepting book proposals: only finished manuscripts will be considered for publication. All submissions must contain either a full manuscript (preferred) or a partial manuscript that includes at least three sample chapters, a cover letter, and a synopsis of the whole manuscript.

P370 Stewed Rhubarb Press
Book Publisher
United Kingdom

https://stewedrhubarb.org

Poetry > *Poetry Collections*

Closed to approaches.

A small independent Scottish press with its roots in Edinburgh. We are an inclusive, friendly press that champions new and diverse poetry written across a wide range of styles, always with a strong (but not exclusive!) interest in spoken word performance. Poetry pamphlets are our mainstay.

P371 Stipes Publishing
Book Publisher
204 W. University Avenue, Champaign, IL 61820
United States
Tel: +1 (217) 356-8391
Fax: +1 (217) 356-5753

stipes01@sbcglobal.net

https://stipes.com

ACADEMIC > **Nonfiction** > *Nonfiction Books*
Agriculture; American Literature; Anatomy; Architecture; Arts; Audio Visual Technology; Building / Construction; Business Law; Chemistry; Classics / Ancient World; Computer Science; Creativity; Economics; Engineering; Environment; French; Health; Journalism; Mathematics; Music; Physics; Physiology; Police; Science; Sociology; Spanish

A trusted source for quality educational materials at the university, college, community college, and high school levels. Founded in the 1920s, it is a second and third generation family business and one of the few remaining family-owned and operated educational publishers in the United States.

P372 Summit Books
Publishing Imprint

Book Publisher: Simon & Schuster Adult Publishing

P373 Sunbelt Publications, Inc.
Book Publisher
664 Marsat Court, Suite A, Chula Vista, CA 91911
United States
Tel: +1 (619) 258-4911
Fax: +1 (619) 258-4916

info@sunbeltpub.com

https://sunbeltpublications.com
https://www.facebook.com/SunbeltPub/
https://twitter.com/sunbeltpub

ADULT
  Fiction > *Novels*
    California; Southwestern United States; United States

  Nonfiction > *Nonfiction Books*
    California; Central America; Cookery; Finance; Folklore, Myths, and Legends; Gardening; Health; History; Houses and Homes; Legal; Native Americans; Nature; Science; Self Help; United States

CHILDREN'S > **Nonfiction**
  Colouring Books: California; Nature
  Nonfiction Books: California; Native Americans; Nature
  Picture Books: California; Native Americans; Nature

Publishes and distributes award-winning books, specializing in regional interest for the Pacific Southwest including Baja California.

Editor: Jennifer Redmond

P374 Sweet & Maxwell
Publishing Imprint
United Kingdom

https://www.sweetandmaxwell.co.uk

Book Publisher: Thomson Reuters

PROFESSIONAL > **Nonfiction** > *Nonfiction Books*: Legal

Send: Proposal
How to send: Email

Our branded legal business in the UK has over 200 years of heritage in legal publishing and is well-recognised for its commitment to quality in the legal industry, both in the UK and globally. Send proposal by email.

Editorial Manager: Judith Hudson

P375 Sweetgum Press
Book Publisher
United States

https://sweetgumpress.com

Fiction > *Short Fiction Collections*
  American Midwest; Historical Fiction; Missouri

Poetry > *Poetry Collections*
  American Midwest; History; Missouri

Closed to approaches.

Publishes book-length works (70-250 pages) by writers from the Midwest, particularly Missouri. The editors look for manuscripts that are unlikely to attract mainstream publishers but are worthy of publication because of one or more qualities, among them originality, authenticity, beauty, regional or historical appeal.

P376 Tailwinds Press
Book Publisher
PO Box 2283, Radio City Station, New York, NY 10101-2283
United States

submissions@tailwindspress.com

http://www.tailwindspress.com

Fiction > *Novels*: Literary

Closed to approaches.

New York City-based independent press specialising in high-quality literary fiction and nonfiction. Send submissions by post or email. See website for full guidelines.

P377 Tall-Lighthouse
Book Publisher
United Kingdom

tall.lighthouse@yahoo.com

https://tall-lighthouse.co.uk
https://www.facebook.com/talllighthousekeeper/

Poetry > *Poetry Collections*

Closed to approaches.

An independent poetry press renowned for publishing exciting new poets.

P378 Taylor & Francis Group
Book Publisher
4 Park Square, Milton Park, Abingdon, OX14 4RN
United Kingdom
Tel: +44 (0) 20 8052 0500

https://taylorandfrancis.com
https://www.facebook.com/TaylorandFrancisGroup
https://twitter.com/wearetandf
https://www.linkedin.com/company/taylor-&-francis-group/

Book Publisher: Informa PLC

ACADEMIC > **Nonfiction** > *Nonfiction Books*
  Agriculture; Arts; Biomedical Science; Business; Chemistry; Computer Science; Earth Science; Economics; Education; Engineering; Environment; Finance; Geography; Health; History; Information Science; Language; Legal; Literature; Management; Mathematics; Medicine; Nursing; Philosophy; Physics; Politics; Psychiatry; Psychology; Religion; Science; Sociology; Statistics; Sustainable Living; Technology

PROFESSIONAL > **Nonfiction** > *Nonfiction Books*
  Agriculture; Biomedical Science; Business; Chemistry; Computer Science; Earth Science; Economics; Education; Engineering; Environment; Finance; Geography; Health; History; Information Science; Language; Legal; Literature; Management; Mathematics; Medicine; Nursing; Philosophy; Physics; Politics; Psychiatry; Psychology; Religion; Science; Sociology; Statistics; Sustainable Living; Technology

One of the leading research publishers in the world, serving academia and professionals in industry and government.

Book Publishers: Ashgate Publishing Limited; Focal Press; Routledge

Publishing Imprint: Psychology Press

P379 Ten Speed Graphic
Publishing Imprint

Book Publisher: The Crown Publishing Group (P103)

P380 Ten Speed Press
Publishing Imprint
United States

https://crownpublishing.com/archives/imprint/ten-speed-press

Book Publisher: The Crown Publishing Group (P103)

Nonfiction > *Illustrated Books*
  Design; Food and Drink; Gardening; Health; Popular Culture

Known for creating beautiful illustrated books with innovative design and award-winning content. Actively seeks out new and established authors who are authorities and tastemakers in the world of food, drink, pop culture, graphic novels, illustration, design, reference, gardening, and health.

Publishing Imprint: Crossing Press

P381 Texas A&M University Press
Book Publisher; Ebook Publisher
John H. Lindsey Building, Lewis Street,

College Station, Texas 77843-4354
United States
Tel: +1 (800) 826-8911

tamupressproposals@gmail.com

https://www.tamupress.com
https://twitter.com/TAMUPress
https://www.instagram.com/tamupress
https://www.goodreads.com/user/show/
82064706-texas-a-m-university-press

ACADEMIC > **Nonfiction** > *Nonfiction Books*
African American; Agriculture; American History; Anthropology; Archaeology; Arts; Biography; Cookery; Culture; Environment; Ethnic; Food; Gardening; History; Immigration; Military History; Music; Nature; Political History; Politics; Science; Sport; Texas; Veterinary; Women's Studies

ADULT
Fiction > *Novels*

Nonfiction > *Nonfiction Books*
African American; Agriculture; American History; Anthropology; Archaeology; Arts; Biography; Cookery; Culture; Environment; Food; Gardening; Health; Military History; Music; Nature; Political History; Politics; Science; Sport; Texas; Veterinary

Poetry > *Poetry Collections*

Send: Query
How to send: Email

Publishes fifty to sixty new titles a year, including both works of science and scholarship and books that educate and entertain the general reader. All books are published simultaneously in print and ebook editions and sold all over the world.

P382 Thames & Hudson Inc.
Book Publisher
500 Fifth Avenue, New York, NY 10110
United States
Tel: +1 (212) 354-3763
Fax: +1 (212) 398-1252

bookinfo@thames.wwnorton.com

https://www.thamesandhudsonusa.com
https://www.instagram.com/thamesandhudsonusa
https://twitter.com/ThamesHudsonUSA
https://www.facebook.com/ThamesandHudsonUSA

Book Publisher: Thames and Hudson Ltd (**P383**)

ADULT > **Nonfiction**
Nonfiction Books: Anthropology; Antiques; Archaeology; Architecture; Arts; Biography; Business; Classics / Ancient World; Comedy / Humour; Comic Books; Computer and Video Games; Crafts; Design; Drawing; Evolution; Fashion; Food; History; Interior Design; Lifestyle; Literary Criticism; Medicine; Military History; Music; Performing Arts; Philosophy; Photography; Popular Culture; Religion; Science; Spirituality; Sport; TV; Travel
Reference: General

CHILDREN'S
Fiction
Chapter Books; *Early Readers*; *Picture Books*
Nonfiction
Activity Books; *Nonfiction Books*; *Picture Books*

YOUNG ADULT > **Nonfiction** > *Nonfiction Books*

Send: Query
Don't send: Full text
How to send: In the body of an email
How not to send: Email attachment

Send proposals up to six pages by email. No attachments or unsolicited mss.

P383 Thames and Hudson Ltd
Book Publisher
6–24 Britannia St, London, WC1X 9JD
United Kingdom
Tel: +44 (0) 20 7845 5000

submissions@thameshudson.co.uk

https://thamesandhudson.com

ADULT > **Nonfiction** > *Nonfiction Books*
Advertising; Archaeology; Architecture; Arts; Biography; Business; Classics / Ancient World; Crafts; Design; Fashion; Folklore, Myths, and Legends; History; Hobbies; Jewellery; Language; Lifestyle; Literature; Nature; Philosophy; Photography; Popular Culture; Practical Art; Religion; Science

CHILDREN'S
Fiction
Picture Books; *Pop-Up Books*
Nonfiction
Activity Books; *Picture Books*; *Pop-Up Books*

Send: Proposal; Outline; Market info; Author bio; Writing sample

We are always open to suggestions and submissions from authors, photographers, designers and illustrators with new proposals for books. Art, Architecture, Photography, Design, Fashion, Popular Culture, History and Archaeology are the best-known areas of our adult list, and we also have a highly successful children's list. We do not publish adult fiction or poetry and tend not to publish outside our existing subject areas.

Book Publisher: Thames & Hudson Inc. (**P382**)

P384 Thinkwell Books, UK
Book Publisher
United Kingdom

https://thinkwellbooks.org

Fiction > *Novels*
Commercial; Literary; Science Fiction; Warfare

Nonfiction > *Nonfiction Books*
Politics; Social Issues; Sport

Send: Query; Synopsis; Full text
How to send: Email

We welcome fiction, sport and political/social works that make us sit up and thirst for the next line, the next profound, humorous, emotional, devastating or stupefying glimpse of originality.

Publishing Imprint: Scruff Whan

P385 Tilbury House Publishers
Publishing Imprint
United States

submissions@sleepingbearpress.com

https://www.tilburyhouse.com

Book Publisher: Cherry Lake Publishing Group (**P083**)

CHILDREN'S
Fiction
Board Books; *Early Readers*; *Middle Grade*; *Picture Books*
Nonfiction
Board Books; *Early Readers*; *Middle Grade*; *Picture Books*

How to send: Email
How not to send: Post

Publishes a wide range of children's books, including board books, beginning readers, picture books, and middle grade titles. Publishes both fiction and nonfiction. Committed to the principles of diversity, equity, and inclusion, and welcomes stories from diverse authors.

P386 Tippermuir Books
Book Publisher
Perth, Scotland
United Kingdom

https://tippermuirbooks.co.uk
https://www.facebook.com/profile.php?id=100076236727041
https://www.instagram.com/tippermuirbooks/
https://x.com/tippermuirbooks

ADULT
Fiction > *Novels*
General, and in particular: Scotland

Nonfiction > *Nonfiction Books*
General, and in particular: Scotland

CHILDREN'S > **Fiction**
Early Readers: General, and in particular: Scotland
Picture Books: General, and in particular: Scotland

Our mission is to add to the cultural life of Scotland by publishing interesting and worthy books in English and Scots. The company's strength is our smallness (actually, we are not that small anymore) and love of the written word. We publish books that appeal to us and/or we feel are important culturally, socially, and most importantly, because they are great reads.

P387 Toad Hall Editions
Book Publisher; Self Publishing Service; Magazine Publisher
United States

hello@toadhalleditions.ink

https://www.toadhalleditions.ink
https://www.instagram.com/toadhalleditions/

Fiction
  Novels; Short Fiction Collections
Nonfiction > *Nonfiction Books*
  Creative Nonfiction; Memoir; Personal Essays
Poetry > *Poetry Collections*

Does not want:

> **Fiction** > *Novels*
>   Fantasy; Historical Fiction; Horror; Mystery; Romance; Science Fiction; Thrillers
> **Nonfiction** > *Nonfiction Books*
>   Finance; Motivational Self-Help

Costs: Offers services that writers have to pay for.

Small press publisher that also provides self-publishing services. Publishes 1-3 per year, written by women or gender-diverse people.

P388 Tor Publishing Group
Publishing Imprint
120 Broadway, New York, NY 10271
United States

https://us.macmillan.com/torpublishinggroup/
https://www.facebook.com/torbooks
https://twitter.com/torbooks
https://www.youtube.com/user/torforge

Book Publisher: Macmillan Publishers

ADULT > **Fiction** > *Novels*
  Fantasy; Horror; Mystery; Science Fiction; Thrillers
TEEN > **Fiction** > *Novels*
  Fantasy; Science Fiction; Speculative

Publisher of Science Fiction, Fantasy, Horror, Mystery, Thriller and Suspense, and Other Speculative Fiction.

Publishing Imprints: Bramble (*P061*); Forge; Nightfire; Tor; Tor Teen (**P389**); Tor.com Publishing

P389 Tor Teen
Publishing Imprint
United States

https://torteen.com
https://www.instagram.com/torteen/
https://twitter.com/torteen
https://www.facebook.com/torteen
http://torteen.tumblr.com/

Publishing Imprint: Tor Publishing Group (**P388**)

TEEN > **Fiction** > *Novels*
  General, and in particular: Fantasy; Science Fiction
YOUNG ADULT > **Fiction** > *Novels*
  General, and in particular: Fantasy; Science Fiction

Launched as an imprint dedicated to publishing quality science fiction, fantasy, and general fiction for young adults.

P390 Torrey House Press, LLC
Book Publisher
370 S 300 E, Suite 103, Salt Lake City, UT 84111
United States

Gray@TorreyHouse.org

https://www.torreyhouse.org
https://torreyhousepress.submittable.com/submit/
https://www.facebook.com/TorreyHousePress/
https://twitter.com/torreyhouse
https://www.instagram.com/torreyhousepress

ADULT
Fiction
  Graphic Novels: General
  Novels: Contemporary; Fantasy; Futurism; Historical Fiction; Horror; LGBTQIA; Literary; Magical Realism; Mystery; Romance; Science Fiction; Thrillers; Urban
  Short Fiction Collections: General
Nonfiction
  Essays: General
  Nonfiction Books: Creative Nonfiction; Investigative Journalism; Literary Journalism; Memoir
Poetry > *Poetry Collections*
YOUNG ADULT > **Fiction** > *Novels*

How to send: Submittable

Interested in great writing that engages, in a wide variety of ways, with place, the natural world, and/or issues that link the Western United States to the past, present, and future of the ever-changing Earth. Originally founded with a specific focus on the Intermountain West but, over the past thirteen years, has expanded its scope to include literature from the plains to the Pacific. (And yes, that includes Alaska and Hawaii!)

Editors: Kirsten Johanna Allen; Mark Bailey

P391 Torva
Publishing Imprint
United Kingdom

https://www.penguin.co.uk/company/publishers/transworld#Torva

Book Publisher: Transworld Publishers (**P393**)

Nonfiction > *Nonfiction Books*

Imprint for bold ideas that ignite debate. Publishes expert voices who challenge how we live and work, and books that tackle some of the biggest questions about our world, from the birth of the universe to how we have a good life.

Authors: Dawn Butler; Helen Czerski; Hannah Fry; Emma Gannon; Viv Groskop; Jonathan Kennedy; Monty Lyman; Thomas Hertog

P392 Tra[verse]
Publishing Imprint
United Kingdom

https://www.beardedbadgerpublishing.com

Book Publisher: Bearded Badger Publishing Co. (**P043**)

Poetry > *Poetry Collections*: East Midlands

Publishes chapbook-sized poetry publications, showcasing the best poetry the East Midlands has to offer.

P393 Transworld Publishers
Book Publisher
United Kingdom

https://www.penguin.co.uk/company/publishers/transworld.html

Book Publisher: Penguin Random House UK

Types: Fiction; Nonfiction
Subjects: Biography; Comedy / Humour; Cookery; Crime; Fantasy; Health; History; Literary; Literature; Music; Romance; Science; Science Fiction; Spirituality; Sport; Thrillers; Travel
Markets: Adult; Children's

How to send: Through a literary agent

Large publisher publishing a wide range of fiction and nonfiction for children and adults. No unsolicited MSS. Approach via a literary agent only.

Publishing Imprints: Bantam (UK) (**P032**); Doubleday (UK) (**P114**); Torva (**P391**)

P394 Turner Publishing
Book Publisher
Nashville, TN
United States

submissions@turnerpublishing.com

https://turnerbookstore.com
https://www.facebook.com/turner.publishing/
https://twitter.com/TurnerPub
https://www.pinterest.com/turnerpub

https://www.instagram.com/turnerpub/
https://www.youtube.com/@turnerpublishing3277

ADULT
  Fiction > *Novels*
    Contemporary Romance; Dystopian Fiction; Fantasy; Historical Fiction; Horror; Literary; Mystery; Romance; Romantasy; Science Fiction; Suspense; Thrillers

  Nonfiction > *Nonfiction Books*
    Animals; Autobiography; Biography; Business; Cookery; Crafts; Crime; Current Affairs; Drinks; Economics; Entertainment; Family; Genealogy; Health; History; Hobbies; Medicine; Mind, Body, Spirit; Nature; Pets; Politics; Psychology; Relationships; Religion; Science; Travel; Wellbeing

CHILDREN'S
  Fiction
    Chapter Books; *Comics*; *Graphic Novels*; *Middle Grade*; *Novels*; *Picture Books*
  Nonfiction > *Nonfiction Books*

TEEN > **Fiction** > *Novels*

YOUNG ADULT > **Fiction** > *Novels*

Send: Proposal; Full text; Author bio; Outline; Pitch; Market info
How to send: Word file email attachment; PDF file email attachment

An award-winning, independent publisher of books. The company is in the top 101 independent publishing companies in the U.S. as compiled by Bookmarket.com and has been named five times to Publishers Weekly's Fastest Growing Publishers List. Currently accepting submissions of fiction and non-fiction manuscripts. Submissions can be made by agents or authors directly.

Publishing Imprints: Basic Health Publications, Inc. (**P037**); Jewish Lights Publishing

P395 Turtle Press
Book Publisher
United States

https://www.turtlepress.com
https://www.youtube.com/channel/UCQg1AWsmVgRPFTB-CQOVoyQ

Nonfiction > *Nonfiction Books*
  Martial Arts; Mind, Body, Spirit; Philosophy

Publisher of books on martial arts.

P396 Two Fine Crows Books
Publishing Imprint
United States

https://twofinecrowsbooks.com
https://saddleroadpress.submittable.com/submit

Book Publisher / Ebook Publisher: Saddle Road Press

Nonfiction > *Nonfiction Books*
  Nature; Spirituality

Publishes books of nature and spirit.

P397 Tyndale House Publishers, Inc.
Book Publisher
351 Executive Drive, Carol Stream, IL 60188
United States
Tel: +1 (855) 277-9400
Fax: +1 (866) 622-9474

https://www.tyndale.com
https://facebook.com/TyndaleHouse
https://twitter.com/TyndaleHouse
https://pinterest.com/TyndaleHouse/
https://instagram.com/tyndalehouse/
https://youtube.com/user/TyndaleHP/

ADULT
  Fiction > *Novels*
    Allegory; Christianity; Contemporary Romance; Contemporary; Historical Fiction; Mystery; Romantic Suspense; Suspense; Thrillers

  Nonfiction
    Nonfiction Books: Arts; Biography; Business; Career Development; Christianity; Comedy / Humour; Culture; Current Affairs; Education; Evangelism; Family; Finance; Fitness; Friends; Health; History; Inspirational; Leadership; Love; Memoir; Mental Health; Motivational Self-Help; Parenting; Personal Development; Politics; Psychology; Recreation; Relationships; Romance; Self Help; Social Justice; Spirituality; Sport; Women
    Reference: Bible Studies; Christianity

CHILDREN'S
  Fiction
    Chapbooks: Christianity
    Picture Books: Christianity

  Nonfiction > *Nonfiction Books*
    Christian Living; Christianity

TEEN
  Fiction > *Novels*: Christianity

  Nonfiction > *Nonfiction Books*
    Christian Living; Christianity; Relationships; Sex

How to send: Through a literary agent

Christian publisher, publishing bibles, nonfiction, fiction, and books for kids and teens.

P398 UCL Press
Book Publisher
United Kingdom

https://uclpress.co.uk

ACADEMIC > **Nonfiction** > *Nonfiction Books*
  Archaeology; Education; History; Language; Legal; Politics; Sociology; Sustainable Living

Send: Query; Proposal
How to send: Email

Publishes monographs, short monographs, edited collections and textbooks. Welcomes proposals.

Acquisitions Editors: Pat Gordon-Smith; Chris Penfold; Dhara Snowden

P399 Ugly Duckling Presse
Book Publisher
The Old American Can Factory, 232 Third Street, #E303 (corner Third Avenue), Brooklyn, NY 11215
United States
Tel: +1 (347) 948-5170

office@uglyducklingpresse.org

https://uglyducklingpresse.org

Nonfiction > *Nonfiction Books*: Experimental

Poetry in Translation > *Poetry Collections*

Poetry > *Poetry Collections*

Closed to approaches.

Nonprofit publisher of poetry, translation, experimental nonfiction, performance texts, and books by artists. Check website for specific calls for submissions.

Print Magazine: Second Factory (**M274**)

P400 Unbound Press
Book Publisher
United Kingdom

customerservices@boundlesspublishinggroup.com

https://unbound.com
https://facebook.com/unbound
https://x.com/unboundsocials
https://www.instagram.com/unboundsocials/
https://tiktok.com/@unboundsocials
https://bsky.app/profile/unboundsocials.bsky.social

Fiction > *Novels*

Nonfiction > *Nonfiction Books*

The home of unexpected stories – a place where bold ideas and brave voices thrive.

P401 Unbridled Books
Book Publisher
United States

contact@unbridledbooks.com

https://www.unbridledbooks.com

Fiction > *Novels*

Nonfiction > *Nonfiction Books*: Memoir

Closed to approaches.

Publishes fiction and memoir. Not accepting unsolicited submissions as at February 2025. Check website for current status.

Editors: Greg Michalson; Fred Ramey

P402 Unicorn
Publishing Imprint
United Kingdom

https://www.unicornpublishing.org/page/about/

Book Publisher: Unicorn Publishing Group

Nonfiction > *Nonfiction Books*
  Cultural History; Visual Arts

Send: Query
How to send: Email

We are always looking for new and exciting projects relating to the visual arts and cultural history. Email the chairman in the first instance.

Chair: Ian Macpherson

P403 The University of Akron Press
Book Publisher
185 E. Mill St., University of Akron, Akron, OH 44325-1703
United States

uapress@uakron.edu

https://www.uakron.edu/uapress/
https://theuniversityofakronpress.submittable.com/submit

ACADEMIC > **Nonfiction** > *Nonfiction Books*
  Culture; History; Ohio; Poetry as a Subject; Politics; Psychology

ADULT
  Nonfiction > *Nonfiction Books*
    Cookery; Culture; Food; History; Ohio; Sport

  Poetry > *Poetry Collections*

Closed to approaches.

For nonfiction, download and complete form on website, or submit through online submission system. Also publishes books of poetry, mainly through its annual competition.

P404 University of Alberta Press
Book Publisher
1-16 Rutherford Library South, 11204 89 Avenue NW, Edmonton, AB, T6G 2J4
Canada
Tel: +1 (780) 492-3662

https://ualbertapress.ca
https://ualbertapress.submittable.com/submit
https://www.facebook.com/UAlbertaPress
https://x.com/UAlbertaPress
https://www.instagram.com/ualbertapress/

ACADEMIC > **Nonfiction** > *Nonfiction Books*
  Activism; Africa; Alberta; Animals; Anthropology; Arts; Asia; Australasia / Oceania; Canada; City and Town Planning; Climate Science; Crime; Culture; Design; Disabilities; Education; Environment; Ethnic Groups; Europe; Films; Food; Gender; Geography; Health; History; Immigration; LGBTQIA; Language; Legal; Literary Criticism; Literature; Medicine; Middle East; Native Americans; Nature; Performing Arts; Philosophy; Politics; Psychology; Racism; Refugees; Religion; Science; Sexuality; Society; Sociology; Sport; TV; Technology; Urban

ADULT
  Fiction > *Short Fiction Collections*

  Nonfiction > *Nonfiction Books*
    Autobiography; Literary; Memoir; Travel

  Poetry > *Poetry Collections*

Send: Query; Proposal; Full text
How to send: Submittable

A contemporary, award-winning publisher of scholarly and creative books distinguished by their editorial care, exceptional design, and global reach. We publish scholarly work by established and emerging authors in the Humanities and Social Sciences, as well as works of poetry and literary nonfiction. We actively work to diversify our publishing program, and welcome submissions by authors from diverse and marginalized backgrounds.

P405 University of Calgary Press
Book Publisher
2500 University Drive N.W., Calgary, Alberta, T2N 1N4
Canada
Tel: +1 (403) 220-7578

ucpbooks@ucalgary.ca
editorial@ucalgary.ca

https://press.ucalgary.ca
https://www.facebook.com/UCalgaryPress/
https://twitter.com/UCalgaryPress
https://www.instagram.com/ucalgarypress/

ACADEMIC > **Nonfiction** > *Nonfiction Books*

How to send: Email

We publish peer-reviewed scholarly books that connect local experience to the global community, helping to create a deeper understanding of human dynamics in a changing world. Through open access publishing, we make our authors' research accessible to the widest possible audience.

Editor: John King

P406 University of California Press
Book Publisher
United States

krobinson@ucpress.edu

https://www.ucpress.edu
https://twitter.com/ucpress
https://www.facebook.com/ucpress
https://www.instagram.com/uc_press/
https://www.youtube.com/channel/UCX5V8BHO32jgshduh7nbR8Q
https://www.linkedin.com/company/university-of-california-press

ACADEMIC > **Nonfiction** > *Nonfiction Books*
  Africa; Anthropology; Arts; Asia; Classics / Ancient World; Crime; Economics; Environment; Films; Food; Gender; Geography; Health; History; Language; Legal; Literature; Media; Middle East; Music; Philosophy; Politics; Psychology; Religion; Science; Sexuality; Sociology; South America; Technology; United States; Wine

Scholarly publisher based in California.

Acquisitions Editors: Naja Pulliam Collins; Niels Hooper; LeKeisha Hughes; Chloe Layman; Michelle Lipinski; Kate Marshall; Enrique Ochoa-Kaup; Raina Polivka; Maura Roessner; Naomi Schneider

Editorial Director: Kim Robinson

P407 University of Georgia Press
Book Publisher
Main Library, Third Floor, 320 South Jackson Street, Athens, GA 30602
United States

books@uga.edu

https://ugapress.org
https://www.facebook.com/UGAPress
https://twitter.com/UGAPress
https://www.instagram.com/ugapress/
https://www.goodreads.com/user/show/23695305-university-of-georgia-press
https://ugapress.wordpress.com/

ACADEMIC > **Nonfiction** > *Nonfiction Books*
  African American; American History; American Literature; Current Affairs; Environment; Food; Geography; Georgia (US State); National Security; Nature; US Southern States; United States; Urban

ADULT > **Nonfiction** > *Nonfiction Books*
  African American; American History; American Literature; Current Affairs; Environment; Food; Geography; Georgia (US State); National Security; Nature; US Southern States; United States; Urban

Send: Query; Proposal; Author bio; Market info
How to send: Email

Publishes scholarly and general-interest books in the areas indicated. See website for full submission guidelines.

P408 University of Iowa Press
Book Publisher
119 West Park Road, 100 Kuhl House, Iowa City IA 52242-1000
United States
Tel: +1 (319) 335-2000

uipress@uiowa.edu

https://www.uipress.uiowa.edu

ACADEMIC > Nonfiction > *Nonfiction Books*
American Midwest; Archaeology; Books; Culture; Food; History; Literature; Nature; Poetry as a Subject; Theatre; Writing

ADULT
Fiction
Novels; Short Fiction
Poetry > *Any Poetic Form*

Send: Outline; Market info; Table of contents; Writing sample; Author bio
How to send: Email; Through a contest

Send proposals for nonfiction by email. Accepts short fiction and poetry through annual competitions only. Also publishes novels.

P409 University of Maine Press
Book Publisher
5729 Fogler Library, Orono, ME 04469-5729
United States
Tel: +1 (207) 581-1652

um.press@maine.edu

https://umaine.edu/umpress/

ACADEMIC > Nonfiction > *Nonfiction Books*
Arts; Maine; Science

ADULT > Fiction > *Novels*: Maine

Closed to approaches.

Publishes scholarly books and original writing in science, the arts and the humanities, focusing on the intellectual concerns of the Maine region. Occasionally publishes regional fiction. Send query by email or by post with SASE between September 1 and October 31.

P410 The University of Michigan Press
Book Publisher
4190 Shapiro Library, 919 S. University Avenue, Ann Arbor, MI 48109-1185
United States
Tel: +1 (734) 764-4388
Fax: +1 (734) 615-1540

http://www.press.umich.edu

ACADEMIC > Nonfiction
Nonfiction Books: Africa; African American; Anthropology; Archaeology; Arts; Asia; Biography; Business; Caribbean; Classics / Ancient World; Cookery; Culture; Dance; Disabilities; Economics; Education; Engineering; Environment; Ethnic Groups; Gender; German; Health; History; Ireland; Islam; Judaism; Language; Legal; Literature; Mathematics; Media; Medicine; Medieval; Memoir; Michigan; Middle East; Music; Native Americans; Nature; Philosophy; Politics; Psychology; Religion; Renaissance; Sexuality; Social Class; Sociology; South America; Sport; Theatre; Travel; United States; Urban; Women's Studies; Writing
Reference: General

ADULT > Fiction > *Novels*

Send query with table of contents, outline of chapters, overview, and CV. Queries should include statements on the rationale of your book, similar and competing books in the field, your target audience, why you think it is right for this list, the length of MS, number of illustrations, and what your anticipated date of completion is. Send queries and proposals by email to specific editor (guidelines on website). See website for particular guidelines relating to fiction and certain series published by the press.

P411 University of Missouri Press
Book Publisher
113 Heinkel Building, 201 S 7th Street, Columbia, MO 65211
United States
Tel: +1 (573) 882-7641
Fax: +1 (573) 884-4498

upress@missouri.edu

https://upress.missouri.edu
https://www.facebook.com/umissouripress#
https://x.com/umissouripress

ACADEMIC > Nonfiction > *Nonfiction Books*
African American; American History; American Midwest; Journalism; Literary Criticism; Military; Missouri; Native Americans; Nature; Politics; Sport

Send: Proposal
How to send: Email

Publishes books on American history, with a special emphasis on topics including the U.S. Military since the turn of the twentieth century, the Early American Republic, African and Indigenous Americans, and Sports. In addition, publishes works in Journalism, Political Science, and scholarly studies related to Missouri and the Midwest, including Natural History. Also acquires works in Literary Criticism, focusing on Twain studies and regional literary figures.

Editor-in-Chief: Andrew J. Davidson

P412 University of North Texas Press
Book Publisher
1155 Union Circle #311336, Denton, TX 76203-5017
United States
Tel: +1 (940) 565-2142

https://untpress.unt.edu
https://www.facebook.com/UniversityOfNorthTexasPress/
https://twitter.com/untpress
https://www.pinterest.com/untpress0263/

ACADEMIC > Nonfiction > *Nonfiction Books*
Crime; Culture; Environment; Folklore, Myths, and Legends; Food History; History; Legal; Military History; Multicultural; Music; Nature; Texas; Women's Studies

ADULT
Fiction > *Short Fiction*
Poetry > *Any Poetic Form*

Send: Query
How to send: Post; Email
How not to send: Phone

Publishes in the humanities and social sciences, with an emphasis on Texas. Also publishes fiction and poetry through its annual competitions. See website for more details.

P413 University of Tennessee Press
Book Publisher
Hodges Library 323, 1015 Volunteer Blvd, Knoxville, TN 37996-4108
United States
Tel: +1 (865) 974-3321

utpress@utk.edu

https://utpress.org
https://www.facebook.com/utennpress/
https://twitter.com/utennpress

ACADEMIC > Nonfiction > *Nonfiction Books*
American Civil War; American History; Anthropology; Folklore, Myths, and Legends; Literature; Music; Popular Culture; Religion; Sport

Send: Query; Table of contents; Writing sample; Author bio

The press is committed to preserving knowledge about Tennessee and the region and, by expanding its unique publishing program, it promotes a broad base of cultural understanding and, ultimately, improves life in the state.

Acquisitions Editor: Scot Danforth

P414 University of Texas Press
Book Publisher
3001 Lake Austin Blvd, 2.200, Stop E4800,
Austin, TX 78703-4206
United States

https://utpress.utexas.edu

ACADEMIC > Nonfiction > *Nonfiction Books*
  Anthropology; Archaeology; Architecture; Arts; Biography; Caribbean; Classics / Ancient World; Comic Books; Cookery; Environment; Films; Food; Gender; History; Judaism; Literary Criticism; Literature; Media; Middle East; Music; Nature; Photography; Sexuality; South America; Southwestern United States; Texas; United States

ADULT > Nonfiction > *Nonfiction Books*
  Art History; Arts; Culture; Current Affairs; Food; History; Music; Nature; Texas

Send: Query; Proposal; Table of contents; Writing sample; Author bio; Submission form
How to send: Email

Send query with proposal, table of contents, sample chapter, and CV. Publishes scholarly books and some general readership nonfiction. See website for full details.

P415 University of Virginia Press
Book Publisher
P.O. Box 400318, Charlottesville, VA 22904-4318
United States
Tel: +1 (434) 924-3468
Fax: +1 (434) 982-2655

vapress@virginia.edu

https://www.upress.virginia.edu/

ACADEMIC > Nonfiction > *Nonfiction Books*
  18th Century; Africa; African American; American Civil War; American History; Anthropology; Archaeology; Architecture; Arts; Autobiography; Biography; Business; Caribbean; Cookery; Culture; Current Affairs; Education; Environment; European History; Food; Geography; History; Legal; Literary Criticism; Literature; Memoir; Music; Nature; Philosophy; Photography; Politics; Publishing; Religion; Science; Sociology; Technology; Virginia; Women's Studies

ADULT
Nonfiction > *Nonfiction Books*: Virginia
Poetry > *Any Poetic Form*

Send: Submission form

Has a reputation for publishing quality scholarship in American history and government, eighteenth-century and Victorian literature, Afro-Caribbean studies, cultural religion, architectural and environmental history, and trade books of regional interest.

P416 University Press of Colorado
Book Publisher
1580 N Logan St, Ste 660, PMB 39883,
Denver, CO, 80203-1942
United States
Tel: +1 (720) 406-8849

https://upcolorado.com
https://twitter.com/UPColorado
https://www.facebook.com/profile.php?id=100069378078836

ACADEMIC > Nonfiction > *Nonfiction Books*
  American West; Anthropology; Archaeology; Colorado; Environment; Ethnic; History; Native Americans; Science

Send: Proposal; Table of contents; Market info; Author bio
How to send: Online submission system

Currently accepting manuscript proposals in anthropology, archaeology, ethnohistory, environmental justice, history of the American West, indigenous studies, and the natural sciences as well as projects about the state of Colorado and the Rocky Mountain region.

Publishing Imprint: Utah State University Press

P417 Unseen Press
Book Publisher
United States

https://www.unseenpress.com
https://www.facebook.com/ghosttoursIN/
https://twitter.com/ghosts_IN
https://www.youtube.com/channel/UCinXzwCZ2_qj-xRO62SULaw
https://instagram.com/ghosts_in/

Nonfiction
  Colouring Books: Crime; Folklore, Myths, and Legends; Ghosts; History; Indiana; Supernatural / Paranormal
  Nonfiction Books: Crime; Folklore, Myths, and Legends; Ghosts; History; Indiana; Supernatural / Paranormal

Dedicated to bringing the information about ghosts to the public. Promotes ghost research as a source of folklore and also as viable scientific area of study.

P418 Valley Press
Book Publisher; Publishing Service
Woodend, The Crescent, Scarborough, YO11 2PW
United Kingdom

hello@valleypressuk.com

https://www.valleypressuk.com
https://www.facebook.com/valleypress
https://twitter.com/valleypress
https://www.pinterest.com/valleypress

Fiction
  Novels; Short Fiction Collections
Nonfiction > *Nonfiction Books*
  Memoir; Travel
Poetry > *Poetry Collections*

Closed to approaches.

Costs: Offers services that writers have to pay for.

Publishes poetry, fiction, and nonfiction.

P419 Vane Women Press
Book Publisher
United Kingdom

submissions@vanewomen.co.uk

https://www.vanewomen.co.uk
https://www.facebook.com/profile.php?id=100064798383906

Fiction > *Short Fiction Collections*
Poetry > *Poetry Collections*

Closed to approaches.

Publishes poetry by women of the North East. Send query by email in first instance. You will then be provided with a postal address to which you will need to send a hard copy submission. See website for full details.

P420 Velocity Press
Book Publisher
United Kingdom

info@velocitypress.uk

https://velocitypress.uk
https://twitter.com/PressVelocity
https://www.instagram.com/velocitypress/
https://www.facebook.com/velocitypressbooks
https://www.youtube.com/channel/UC2BdIfx5ljzDKwp49tDO_Vw
https://soundcloud.com/velocitypress

Fiction > *Novels*: Electronic Music
Nonfiction > *Nonfiction Books*: Electronic Music

Send: Query; Outline; Table of contents
How to send: Email

Publishes fiction and nonfiction about the history and innovation of electronic music and club culture.

P421 Verve Poetry Press
Book Publisher
United Kingdom
Tel: +44 (0) 7713 236205

mail@vervepoetrypress.com

https://vervepoetrypress.com
https://www.facebook.com/VervePoetry
https://twitter.com/VervePoetryPres

https://www.instagram.com/verve.publisherofpoetry/

Poetry
Chapbooks; *Poetry Collections*

Closed to approaches.

A prize-winning Birmingham based publisher dedicated to promoting and showcasing unnoticed and overlooked poetic talent in colourful and exciting ways. We publish debut collections from poets with both page and performance backgrounds, and we have a broad sense of what poetry is and can be. We are keen that the poets we publish reflect the variety of our city and our festival – in terms of culture, age and class. We are keen that voices and works that aren't fully represented in the national poetry discussion get heard. We also publish debut and between-collection pamphlets by poets we love and also books to accompany poetry shows which capture the life and vibe of performance focussed poetry experiences. We are looking for colour, energy and open heartedness in all the works we publish. We are looking for poetry that works in performance and performances that work on the page. We think poetry should be read and heard, spoken and thought. And of course, celebrated.

P422 W.W. Norton & Company Ltd
Book Publisher
15 Carlisle Street, London, W1D 3BS
United Kingdom
Tel: +44 (0) 20 7323 1579

ukcustomerservice@wwnorton.com

https://wwnorton.co.uk
https://twitter.com/wwnortonUK
https://www.instagram.com/wwnortonuk/
https://medium.com/@W.W.NortonUK
https://www.pinterest.com/wwnortonuk/

ACADEMIC > **Nonfiction** > *Nonfiction Books*
African American; Anthropology; Astronomy; Biology; Chemistry; Classics / Ancient World; Computer Science; Films; Geology; History; Literature; Music; Philosophy; Physics; Politics; Psychology; Religion; Sociology; Statistics

ADULT
Fiction
Graphic Novels; *Novels*
Nonfiction
Essays: General
Nonfiction Books: Adventure; African American; Archaeology; Architecture; Arts; Astronomy; Biography; Business; Classics / Ancient World; Comedy / Humour; Crafts; Crime; Culture; Current Affairs; Design; Drama; Economics; Education; Environment; Films; Folklore, Myths, and Legends; Food and Drink; Games; Gardening; Health; History; Hobbies; Houses and Homes; LGBTQIA; Legal; Literature; Medicine; Memoir; Music; Nature; Neuropsychology; Neuroscience; Oceanography; Parenting; Pets; Philosophy; Photography; Politics; Psychology; Psychotherapy; Religion; Self Help; Sociology; Sport; Statistics; Technology; Transport; Travel; Women's Studies; Writing
Poetry > *Poetry Collections*

CHILDREN'S
Fiction
Chapter Books; *Early Readers*; *Picture Books*
Nonfiction > *Nonfiction Books*

PROFESSIONAL > **Nonfiction** > *Nonfiction Books*
Addiction; Anxiety Disorders; Architecture; Autism; Child Psychotherapy; Couple Therapy; Depression; Design; Diversity; Eating Disorders; Education; Family Therapy; Genetics; Geriatrics; Health; Hypnosis; Juvenile Psychotherapy; Medicine; Multicultural; Neurobiology; Neuropsychology; Neuroscience; Personal Coaching; Post Traumatic Stress Disorder; Psychiatry; Psychoanalysis; Psychological Trauma; Psychotherapy; Self Help; Sexuality; Writing

UK branch of a US publisher. No editorial office in the UK – contact the main office in New York (see separate listing).

P423 W.W. Norton & Company, Inc.
Book Publisher
500 Fifth Avenue, New York, NY 10110
United States
Tel: +1 (212) 354-5500
Fax: +1 (212) 869-0856

https://wwnorton.com
https://www.facebook.com/wwnorton/
https://twitter.com/wwnorton
https://www.instagram.com/w.w.norton/

ACADEMIC > **Nonfiction** > *Nonfiction Books*
Anthropology; Architecture; Arts; Astronomy; Biology; Chemistry; Communication; Computer Science; Design; Economics; Education; English; Films; Geology; History; Literature; Mathematics; Music; Science; Sociology

ADULT
Fiction
Graphic Novels: General
Novels: Adventure; African American; Alternative History; Animals; Asian American; Coming of Age; Crime; Culture; Disabilities; Dystopian Fiction; Epistolary; Erotic; Family; Fantasy; Folklore, Myths, and Legends; Mystery; Thrillers
Short Fiction Collections: General

Nonfiction
Nonfiction Books: Architecture; Biography; Business; Comedy / Humour; Cookery; Design; Economics; Education; History; Hobbies; Houses and Homes; Legal; Literary Criticism; Mathematics; Memoir; Mental Health; Mind, Body, Spirit; Performing Arts; Philosophy; Politics; Psychology; Religion; Visual Arts
Reference: General

Poetry > *Poetry Collections*

PROFESSIONAL > **Nonfiction** > *Nonfiction Books*: Education

How to send: Through a literary agent

No longer accepts submissions directly – submissions through a literary agent only.

P424 Walker Books
Book Publisher
87 Vauxhall Walk, London, SE11 5HJ
United Kingdom
Tel: +44 (0) 20 7793 0909

illustratorsubmissions@walker.co.uk

https://www.walker.co.uk
https://x.com/WalkerBooksUK
https://www.instagram.com/walkerbooksuk/
https://www.facebook.com/walkerbooks
https://www.tiktok.com/@walkerbooksuk
https://bsky.app/profile/walkerbooksuk.bsky.social

CHILDREN'S
Fiction
Board Books; *Chapter Books*; *Early Readers*; *Middle Grade*; *Picture Books*
Nonfiction > *Nonfiction Books*

How to send: Email

Publishes fiction and nonfiction for children, including illustrated books. Accepts illustrated picture-book stories and/or artwork samples via email only.

P425 Washington Writers' Publishing House
Book Publisher
United States

wwphpress@gmail.com

https://www.washingtonwriters.org
https://wwph.submittable.com/submit
https://www.instagram.com/writingfromwwph/
https://www.facebook.com/WashingtonWritersPublishingHouse/
https://x.com/WWPHPress
https://bsky.app/profile/wwph.bsky.social

Fiction
Novels; *Short Fiction Collections*
Nonfiction > *Nonfiction Books*

Poetry > *Poetry Collections*

A non-profit, cooperative literary organization that has published over 100 volumes of poetry since 1975 as well as fiction and nonfiction. The press sponsors three annual competitions for writers living in DC, Maryland, and Virginia, and the winners of each category (one each in poetry, fiction, and creative nonfiction) comprise our annual slate.

P426 Waterbrook
Publishing Imprint

Book Publisher: Random House

P427 The Wee Book Company
Book Publisher
United Kingdom

sales@theweebookcompany.com

https://www.theweebookcompany.com
https://www.facebook.com/theweebookcompany
https://x.com/theweebookco_
https://www.youtube.com/channel/UC5uerOQRCVXv9v_0UXheSmw

ADULT > **Nonfiction** > *Nonfiction Books*
  Comedy / Humour; Scotland

CHILDREN'S > **Fiction** > *Picture Books*

Closed to approaches.

Aims to produce quality, modern nonfiction Scottish humour and children's fiction.

P428 Whitford Press
Publishing Imprint
United States

https://schifferbooks.com/pages/schiffer-imprints

Book Publisher: Schiffer Publishing

Nonfiction > *Nonfiction Books*
  Mind, Body, Spirit; Supernatural / Paranormal

Publishes books on paranormal activities and mind and spirit lifestyles.

P429 Wide-Eyed Editions
Publishing Imprint
1 Triptych Place, Second Floor, London, SE1 9SH
United Kingdom
Tel: +44 (0) 20 7700 9000

QuartoExploresSubmissions@Quartous.com

https://www.quartoknows.com/Wide-Eyed-Editions

Book Publisher: The Quarto Group, Inc. (**P307**)

CHILDREN'S > **Nonfiction** > *Nonfiction Books*
  Arts; Nature; Travel

Send: Query
Don't send: Full text

Publishes books on the arts, natural history and armchair travel. Send query with proposal by email. See website for full guidelines.

P430 Windhorse Publications Ltd
Book Publisher
38 Newmarket Road, Cambridge, CB5 8DT
United Kingdom

info@windhorsepublications.com
dhammamegha@windhorsepublications.com

https://www.windhorsepublications.com
https://www.facebook.com/windhorse.publications/
https://twitter.com/WindhorsePubs
https://www.instagram.com/windhorsepubs/
https://issuu.com/windhorsepublications
https://vimeo.com/windhorsepublications
https://soundcloud.com/windhorsepublications
https://thebuddhistcentre.com/windhorsepublications?display=latest

Nonfiction > *Nonfiction Books*: Buddhism

Send: Query; Proposal
Don't send: Full text
How to send: Email

An independent publisher of English-language non-fiction books on Buddhism, meditation and mindfulness. Based in the UK, we publish and distribute internationally. We publish books for practitioners at all stages in the path as well as for a wider non-Buddhist readership. We are also interested in books exploring new directions in Buddhist scholarship.

P431 Wisdom Publications
Book Publisher
199 Elm Street, Somerville, MA 02144
United States

submissions@wisdompubs.org

https://wisdomexperience.org
https://twitter.com/wisdompubs
https://www.facebook.com/wisdompubs
https://instagram.com/wisdompubs
https://www.youtube.com/channel/UCKrdx4usaugOhLzjvYmzpIg

Nonfiction > *Nonfiction Books*: Buddhism

Send: Submission form
How to send: Email

Will only consider books directly related to Buddhism, written by people with relevant credentials. Download submission questionnaire from website, then complete and return by email.

P432 Wolfpack Publishing
Book Publisher
1707 E. Diana Street, Tampa, FL 33610
United States

submissions@wolfpackpublishing.com

https://wolfpackpublishing.com
https://www.goodreads.com/group/show/138635-wolfpack-publishing
https://www.facebook.com/WolfpackPub/
https://twitter.com/wolfpackpub

Fiction > *Novels*
  Adventure; Crime; Historical Fiction; Thrillers; Westerns

Closed to approaches.

An award winning indie publisher that began life as a small Western Fiction publishing company, but which now publishes across a variety of genres.

P433 Words & Pictures
Publishing Imprint
1 Triptych Place, Second Floor, London, SE1 9SH
United Kingdom
Tel: +44 (0) 20 770 9000

QuartoHomesSubmissions@Quarto.com

https://www.quartoknows.com/words-pictures

Book Publisher: The Quarto Group, Inc. (**P307**)

CHILDREN'S > **Fiction** > *Picture Books*

How to send: Email

Always on the lookout for authors and artists with creative ideas to enhance and broaden their list of children's books. See website for submission guidelines.

Publisher: Holly Willsher

P434 Wordsonthestreet
Book Publisher; Magazine Publisher
Six San Antonio Park, Salthill, Galway
Ireland

publisher@wordsonthestreet.com

http://www.wordsonthestreet.com

Fiction
  Novellas; Novels; Short Fiction Collections
Poetry > *Poetry Collections*

How to send: Post
How not to send: Email

Independent publisher based in Galway, Ireland, publishing novels, novellas, short story and poetry collections, and Ireland's premier fiction and poetry magazine.

Editor: Tony O'Dwyer

Magazine: Crannog Magazine (**M092**)

Publishing Imprint: 6th House

P435 Wordsworth Editions
Book Publisher
PO Box 13147, Stansted, CM21 1BT
United Kingdom
Tel: +44 (0) 1920 465167

enquiries@wordsworth-editions.com

http://www.wordsworth-editions.com
https://twitter.com/WordsworthEd
https://en-gb.facebook.com/wordsworth.editions/

ADULT
Fiction > *Novels*
Poetry > *Poetry Collections*

CHILDREN'S > **Fiction** > *Novels*

Closed to approaches.

Publishes out-of-copyright titles.

Managing Director: Helen Trayler

P436 Workman
Publishing Imprint

Book Publisher: Workman Publishing (**P437**)

P437 Workman Publishing
Book Publisher
1290 Avenue of the Americas, New York, NY 10104
United States
Tel: +1 (800) 759-0190
Fax: +1 (212) 364-0950

Workman-Inquiry@hbgusa.com

https://www.workman.com
https://www.instagram.com/workmanpub
https://www.tiktok.com/@workmanpub
https://twitter.com/workmanpub
https://www.facebook.com/WorkmanPublishing/
https://www.linkedin.com/company/workman-publishing/
https://www.pinterest.com/workmanpub/

Book Publisher: Hachette Book Group (**P156**)

ADULT
Fiction > *Novels*

Nonfiction
Gift Books: General
Nonfiction Books: Comedy / Humour; Cookery; Country Lifestyle; Gardening; Parenting; Pregnancy

CHILDREN'S > **Nonfiction** > *Nonfiction Books*

We are publishers of award-winning cookbooks, parenting/pregnancy guides, books on gardening, country living, and humor, as well as children's books, gift books, fiction, and the bestselling calendar line in the business.

Publishing Imprints: Artisan Books; Black Dog & Leventhal (*P050*); Running Press (*P320*); Storey Publishing; Timber Press; Workman (*P436*)

P438 Yale University Press (London)
Book Publisher
47 Bedford Square, London, WC1B 3DP
United Kingdom
Tel: +44 (0) 20 7079 4900

sales@yaleup.co.uk

https://www.yalebooks.co.uk

ADULT > **Nonfiction**
Nonfiction Books: Architecture; Arts; Biography; Business; Computers; Current Affairs; Economics; Fashion; Health; History; Language; Legal; Literature; Mathematics; Medicine; Memoir; Music; Philosophy; Politics; Religion; Science; Society; Sociology; Technology; Wellbeing
Reference: General

CHILDREN'S > **Nonfiction** > *Nonfiction Books*: Education

Send: Query; Author bio; Market info; Table of contents; Writing sample
How to send: Post; Email

Publishes world class scholarship for a broad readership.

Editors: Mark Eastment; Joanna Godfrey; Julian Loose; Heather McCallum; Sophie Neve

P439 YesYes Books
Book Publisher
1631 Broadway St #121, Portland, OR 97232-1425
United States
Tel: +1 (503) 446-3851

info@yesyesbooks.com

https://www.yesyesbooks.com
https://yesyesbooks.submittable.com/submit
https://www.facebook.com/yesyesbooks/
https://twitter.com/YesYesBooks
https://www.instagram.com/yesyesbooks

Fiction
Novellas; *Novels*; *Short Fiction Collections*
Poetry > *Poetry Collections*

Closed to approaches.

A dynamic independent press that publishes poetry and prose collections from bold fresh voices.

P440 Zibby Books
Book Publisher
United States

info@zibbybooks.com
submissions@zibbybooks.com

https://www.zibbybooks.com
https://www.instagram.com/zibbybooks
https://www.facebook.com/zibbybooks
https://twitter.com/zibbybooks

Fiction > *Novels*

Nonfiction > *Nonfiction Books*: Memoir

How to send: Email

A publishing home for fiction and memoir.

Index

17th Century
See more broadly: History
18th Century
See more broadly: History
University of Virginia Press............... P415
19th Century
See more broadly: History
20th Century
See more broadly: History
Power Cut Lite M247
Williams, Laura L603
ADHD
See more broadly: Neurodiversity
Academic
ABC-CLIO P002
Agricultural History M012
Asian Social Science M028
Baylor University Press P041
Berghahn Books Ltd P045
Bess Press P047
BFS Journal M054
Bloomsbury Academic P053
British Academy, The P063
British Museum Press, The P064
Broadview Press P065
Cambridge University Press......................P068
Chelsea House Publishers P082
Colourpoint Educational P095
Crossway P100
Curious Minds L133
Elsevier Ltd P121
Enslow Publishers, Inc. P123
Feminist Studies.......................................M119
Fernwood Publishing P131
Gale P139
Geographical Journal, The M138
Gill Education P143
Hammersmith Books P158
Hancock House Publishers........................P159
Harvard University Press P165
Indiana University Press P187
International Piano M170
International Society for Technology in
 Education (ISTE)...................................P192
InterVarsity Press (IVP) P193
Jain Publishing Company, Inc. P195
Jessica Kingsley Publishers.......................P197
Kube Publishing.......................................P209
LSU Press P223
Lund Humphries Limited P224
Manoa M199
Mentor Books P236
MIT Press, The P244
Modern Applied Science M210
Ohio University Press P261
Otago University Press..............................P269
Oxbow Books P271
Oxford University Press P272
Pelagic P279
Peter Lang P285
Purdue University Press P305
Research Journal of Pharmacy and
 Technology...M260
Rosenberg Group, The L505
Saqi Books P324
Stanford University Press..........................P367
Stipes Publishing P371

Taylor & Francis Group P378
Texas A&M University Press P381
UCL Press P398
University of Akron Press, The P403
University of Alberta Press........................P404
University of Calgary Press P405
University of California Press....................P406
University of Georgia Press.......................P407
University of Iowa Press............................P408
University of Maine Press P409
University of Michigan Press, The P410
University of Missouri Press P411
University of North Texas Press P412
University of Tennessee Press P413
University of Texas Press P414
University of Virginia Press P415
University Press of Colorado P416
W.W. Norton & Company Ltd P422
W.W. Norton & Company, Inc. P423
Wallace Stevens Journal, The...................M336
Accounting
See more broadly: Finance
Business & Accountancy Daily M068
Gill Education P143
Activism
See more broadly: Politics; Society
Borstel, Stefanie Sanchez Von...................L070
Feminist Press, The P130
Fernwood Publishing P131
Maw, Jane Graham L398
Oxford Review of Books M230
University of Alberta Press........................P404
Activities
See more specifically: Outdoor Activities
Arcadia Publishing P020
Cobblestone M079
Kensington Publishing Corp.....................P204
Yours...M350
Activity Books
Autumn Publishing Ltd P025
Bess Press P047
Child's Play (International) Ltd P084
Cicada Books P087
Gemini Books P140
Igloo Books Limited..................................P184
Kube Publishing.......................................P209
Peter Pauper Press P286
Rand McNally P310
Thames & Hudson Inc. P382
Thames and Hudson Ltd...........................P383
Acupuncture
See more broadly: Alternative Health
Blue Poppy Enterprises P055
Addiction
See more broadly: Social Issues
W.W. Norton & Company Ltd P422
Adventure
Armada, Kurestin L024
Blair Partnership, The................................L064
Burby, Danielle L087
Carroll, Megan L102
Compassiviste Publishing.........................L097
Cooper, Gemma L128
Crystal Magazine.....................................M098
Diana Finch Literary Agency L154
Doug Grad Literary Agency L161
Ferguson, T.S. L195

Fighting High..P132
Gisondi, Katie L235
Gordon, Andrew L245
Gunic, Masha L256
Haley, Jolene L260
Hashtag Press..P166
Hensley, Chelsea......................................L274
Hodges, Jodie..L282
Irvine, Lucy L292
Kimber, Natalie..L336
Kirby, Robert L338
Langton, Becca L353
Leon, Nina L360
Marini, Victoria L388
Marshall, Jen L391
Mills & Boon P240
Orenda Books P267
Ostby, Kristin...L452
Pages, Saribel L453
Parker, Elana Roth L455
Philips, Ariana L471
Pocket Mountains P296
Rocky Mountain Books P315
Sanchez, Kaitlyn L516
Sierra M281
Sluytman, Antoinette Van.........................L541
Soloway, Jennifer March L544
Story Unlikely..M300
Takikawa, Marin L566
Thorneycroft, Euan L574
Trudel, Jes...L579
Victoria Sanders & Associates LLC...........L584
W.W. Norton & Company Ltd P422
W.W. Norton & Company, Inc. P423
Weiman, Paula...L592
Whatnall, Michaela L598
Wickers, Chandler L600
Williamson, Jo L604
Wolfpack Publishing P432
Advertising
See more broadly: Marketing
Thames and Hudson Ltd P383
Africa
See more broadly: Regional
See more specifically: African Diaspora; North Africa
Better Than Starbucks..............................M052
Bloomsbury Academic P053
Cassava Republic Press UK P074
Feminist Press, The..................................P130
HopeRoad P176
Indiana University Press P187
Ohio University Press P261
Pluto Press P295
University of Alberta Press P404
University of California Press P406
University of Michigan Press, The............P410
University of Virginia Press......................P415
African American
See more broadly: Ethnic Groups
See more specifically: African American Issues
African American Golfer's Digest M008
African American Review.........................M009
Feminist Press, The..................................P130
LSU Press P223
Texas A&M University Press P381
University of Georgia Press P407

University of Michigan Press, The.............P410
University of Missouri Press.....................P411
University of Virginia Press......................P415
W.W. Norton & Company Ltd P422
W.W. Norton & Company, Inc...................P423
Zack Company, Inc, The L615
African American Issues
See more broadly: African American
African Diaspora
See more broadly: Africa
Fernwood Publishing................................P131
Julien, Ria..L312
Obsidian: Literature in the African
    Diaspora..M227
Agriculture
See more specifically: Farming; Self-Sufficiency; Smallholdings
Agricultural History..................................M012
Gale..P139
Old Pond Publishing.................................P262
Purdue University Press............................P305
Stipes Publishing......................................P371
Taylor & Francis Group.............................P378
Texas A&M University Press....................P381
Air Travel
See more broadly: Travel
Alabama
See more broadly: United States
Alabama Heritage.....................................M013
Alaska
See more broadly: United States
Epicenter Press Inc...................................P124
Hancock House Publishers.......................P159
Albemarle
See more broadly: Virginia
See more specifically: Charlottesville
CharlottesvilleFamily................................M076
Alberta
See more broadly: Canada
University of Alberta Press........................P404
Alien Fiction
See more broadly: Science Fiction
See more specifically: Alien Invasion
Mozley, Jack...L422
Alien Invasion
See more broadly: Alien Fiction
Allegory
Tyndale House Publishers, Inc. P397
Alternative Health
See more broadly: Health
See more specifically: Acupuncture; Aromatherapy; Ayurveda; Chinese Medicine; Herbal Remedies; Reiki
Hay House Publishers..............................P168
Llewellyn Worldwide Ltd...........................P219
Singing Dragon..P340
Zack Company, Inc, The L615
Alternative History
See more broadly: Speculative
Candlemark & Gleam...............................P069
Harris, Erin...L268
Mozley, Jack...L422
Pierce, Rosie..L474
Story Unlikely..M300
W.W. Norton & Company, Inc...................P423
Alternative Lifestyles
See more broadly: Lifestyle
Alzheimer's
See more broadly: Dementia
Amateur Investigator
See more broadly: Mystery
Poisoned Pen Press..................................P297
Amateur Radio
See more broadly: Radio Technology
Radio Society of Great Britain..................P309

Amateur Winemaking
See more broadly: Winemaking
American Civil War
See more broadly: Warfare
Indiana University Press P187
LSU Press P223
University of Tennessee Press..................P413
University of Virginia Press.......................P415
American History
See more broadly: History
Arcadia Publishing P020
Brattle Agency LLC, The..........................L077
Cobblestone M079
LSU Press P223
Ohio University Press P261
Texas A&M University Press....................P381
Thayer, Henry..L572
University of Georgia Press P407
University of Missouri Press.....................P411
University of Tennessee Press..................P413
University of Virginia Press.......................P415
Zack Company, Inc, The..........................L615
American Literature
See more broadly: Literature
Stipes Publishing P371
University of Georgia Press P407
American Midwest
See more broadly: United States
Indiana University Press P187
MacKenzie, Joanna.................................L382
Minnesota Historical Society Press P241
Ohio University Press P261
Sweetgum Press......................................P375
University of Iowa Press P408
University of Missouri Press.....................P411
American Revolution
See more broadly: Warfare
American West
See more broadly: United States
Cowboys & Indians..................................M091
Horse & Rider..M159
Little Bigfoot P218
Saddlebag Dispatches.............................M267
University Press of Colorado P416
Americana
See more broadly: United States
Amish
See more broadly: Christianity
Amish Romance
See more broadly: Christian Romance
Anatomy
See more broadly: Medicine
Stipes Publishing P371
Angels
See more broadly: Religion
Hay House Publishers..............................P168
Llewellyn Worldwide Ltd..........................P219
Animal Husbandry
See more broadly: Farming
See more specifically: Apiculture (Beekeeping)
Animal Rights
See more broadly: Animals
Animals
See more broadly: Nature
See more specifically: Animal Rights; Birds; Deer; Furries; Horses; Pets; Prehistoric Animals; Veterinary; Wildlife
Barrett, Emily...L040
Cambridge University Press.....................P068
Hancock House Publishers.......................P159
Hensley, Chelsea.....................................L274
Kracht, Elizabeth L341
Maltese, Alyssa.......................................L387
Mortimer, Michele L418
Pass, Marina de.......................................L456
Pineapple Press P293

Purdue University Press............................P305
River Hills Traveler M263
Roberts, Soumeya Bendimerad................L495
Rushall, Kathleen L512
Turner Publishing.....................................P394
University of Alberta Press........................P404
W.W. Norton & Company, Inc...................P423
Weiss, Alexandra.....................................L593
Zack Company, Inc, The L615
Ann Arbor
See more broadly: Michigan
Ann Arbor Observer M022
Antarctica
See more broadly: Regional
Anthropology
Baylor University Press.............................P041
Berghahn Books Ltd.................................P045
Cambridge University Press P068
Compassiviste Publishing.........................P097
Lambert, Sophie......................................L348
London Review of Books M191
Marion Boyars Publishers.........................P229
Ohio University Press...............................P261
Oxford University Press P272
Stanford University Press.........................P367
Texas A&M University Press....................P381
Thames & Hudson Inc..............................P382
University of Alberta Press........................P404
University of California Press....................P406
University of Michigan Press, The.............P410
University of Tennessee Press..................P413
University of Texas Press P414
University of Virginia Press.......................P415
University Press of Colorado P416
W.W. Norton & Company Ltd P422
W.W. Norton & Company, Inc...................P423
Antiques
Arcadia Publishing P020
Gale..P139
Goss & Crested China Club.....................P149
Graham, Stacey.......................................L247
Homes & Antiques M158
Scala Arts & Heritage Publishers..............P326
Thames & Hudson Inc..............................P382
Anxiety Disorders
See more broadly: Psychology
Hay House Publishers..............................P168
W.W. Norton & Company Ltd P422
Any Poetic Form
30 North M001
32 Poems M002
aaduna M003
About Place Journal.................................M004
Abridged..M005
Account, The M006
Acumen...M007
African American Review M009
African Voices..M010
Agni M011
Alaska Quarterly Review.........................M014
Allegro Poetry Magazine..........................M017
Amethyst Review M019
And Other Poems M020
Angela Poetry Magazine..........................M021
Arboreal M023
Arc M024
Arts & Letters..M027
Asimov's Science Fiction M029
Atlanta Review..M031
Atrium M033
Babybug..M037
Bacopa Literary Review M038
Baffler, The M039
Bald and Bonkers Network LLC P030
Bandit Fiction M040
Barren Magazine M041

BatCat Press ... P040
Bear Deluxe Magazine, The ... M044
Belmont Story Review ... M047
Better Than Starbucks ... M052
BFS Horizons ... M053
Black Moon Magazine ... M056
Black Warrior Review ... M058
Blue Earth Review ... M059
Blue Mesa Review ... M060
Bookseeker Agency ... L069
Boston Review ... M062
Boyfriend Village ... M064
Butcher's Dog ... M070
Caribbean Writer, The ... M073
Chang, Nicola ... L109
Chapman ... M075
Chautauqua Literary Journal ... M077
Cheshire ... M078
Cobblestone ... M079
Cocoa Girl ... M080
Cola ... M081
Commonweal ... M082
Concho River Review ... M083
Conjunctions ... M084
Conjunctions Online ... M085
Contemporary Verse 2 ... M086
Crannog Magazine ... M092
Crazyhorse / Swamp Pink ... M093
Cream City Review ... M094
Crystal Magazine ... M098
CutBank ... M099
Dalhousie Review, The ... M100
Dark Horse, The ... M101
Dawntreader, The ... M102
Dream Catcher ... M106
Eddison Pearson Ltd ... L170
Ekphrastic Review, The ... M109
El Portal ... M110
Emerge Literary Journal ... M111
Event ... M113
Faultline ... M118
Feminist Studies ... M119
Fiddlehead, The ... M121
First Line, The ... M123
Five Points ... M124
Folio ... M126
Fourteen Poems ... M130
Fourth River, The ... M131
Frogmore Papers, The ... M132
Fugue ... M133
Future Fire, The ... M135
Gargoyle Online ... M137
Georgia Review, The ... M139
Ginosko Literary Journal ... M140
Glacier, The ... M141
Grain Literary Magazine ... M143
Granta ... M144
Graywolf Lab ... M145
Gulf Coast: A Journal of Literature and
  Fine Arts ... M147
Gutter Magazine ... M148
Half Mystic Journal ... M149
Hanging Loose ... M150
Harpur Palate ... M151
Helix, The ... M154
Hotel Amerika ... M160
Hunger Mountain ... M161
I-70 Review ... M162
Idaho Review ... M163
Identity Theory ... M164
Image ... M166
Indiana Review ... M167
Ink Sweat and Tears ... M168
Irish Pages ... M173
Island ... M174
Journal, The ... M176

Kavya Kishor ... M177
Kenyon Review, The ... M179
Kube Publishing ... P209
Lake, The ... M181
Landfall ... M182
Lantana Publishing ... P210
Lighthouse ... M185
Lilliput Press, The ... P217
Literary Mama ... M187
London Grip New Poetry ... M189
London Magazine, The ... M190
London Review of Books ... M191
Lost Lake Folk Opera Magazine ... M193
Louisiana Literature ... M194
MacGuffin, The ... M195
Magma ... M196
Malahat Review, The ... M197
Manchester Review, The ... M198
Manoa ... M199
Margaret K. McElderry Books ... P228
Massachusetts Review, The ... M202
Meetinghouse ... M203
Michigan Quarterly Review ... M204
Mid-American Review ... M206
Midsummer Dream House ... M207
Midway Journal ... M208
Missouri Review, The ... M209
Modern Poetry in Translation ... M212
Moonday Mag ... M213
MQR Mixtape ... M214
Nashville Review ... M217
Neo-opsis Science Fiction Magazine ... M218
Neon ... M219
New England Review ... M220
North, The ... M225
Northern Gravy ... M226
Obsidian: Literature in the African
  Diaspora ... M227
Oxford Poetry ... M229
Oxford Review of Books ... M230
Pacifica Literary Review ... M231
Panorama ... M232
Paris Review, The ... M233
Passionfruit Review, The ... M234
Pleiades ... M238
Ploughshares ... M239
PN Review ... M240
Poetry ... M241
Poetry Birmingham Literary Journal ... M242
Poetry Ireland Review ... M243
Poetry London ... M244
Poetry Wales ... M245
Power Cut Lite ... M247
Prole ... M250
Pulsar Poetry Magazine ... M251
Pushing Out the Boat ... M252
Qu Literary Magazine ... M253
Quadrant Magazine ... M254
Radar Poetry ... M256
Rialto, The ... M261
River Styx ... M264
Saddlebag Dispatches ... M267
Second Factory ... M274
Shearsman ... M276
Shenandoah ... M277
Shooter Literary Magazine ... M279
Shoreline of Infinity ... M280
Sinister Wisdom ... M282
Snowflake Magazine ... M284
South ... M288
South Carolina Review ... M289
Southern Humanities Review ... M290
Southern Review, The ... M291
Southwest Review ... M293
Southword Journal ... M294
Spitball ... M297

Stinging Fly, The ... M299
Strange Horizons ... M301
Structo Magazine ... M303
Studio One ... M304
Sunspot Literary Journal ... M305
Supplement, The ... M306
Takahe ... M309
Tears in the Fence ... M311
Temz Review, The ... M312
Thin Air Magazine ... M314
Third Coast ... M315
This England ... M316
Threepenny Review, The ... M317
Times Literary Supplement (TLS), The ... M318
Tributaries ... M320
Tusculum Review, The ... M321
UCity Review ... M322
Under the Radar ... M325
University of Iowa Press ... P408
University of North Texas Press ... P412
University of Virginia Press ... P415
Vagabond City ... M327
Vallum ... M328
Virginia Quarterly Review, The ... M330
Waccamaw ... M335
Wallace Stevens Journal, The ... M336
Wasafiri ... M338
West Branch ... M339
WestWard Quarterly ... M340
Wet Grain ... M341
Windsor Review ... M342
Yale Review, The ... M344
Zone 3 ... M353

Apiculture (Beekeeping)
See more broadly: Animal Husbandry
Rosenberg Group, The ... L505

Appalachia
See more broadly: United States
Ohio University Press ... P261

Archaeology
Berghahn Books Ltd ... P045
Bloomsbury Academic ... P053
British Academy, The ... P063
British Museum Press, The ... P064
Cambridge University Press ... P068
Fazzari, Hillary ... L188
History Press, The ... P174
Kahn, Ella Diamond ... L314
Logaston Press ... P221
Oxbow Books ... P271
Oxford University Press ... P272
Texas A&M University Press ... P381
Thames & Hudson Inc. ... P382
Thames and Hudson Ltd ... P383
UCL Press ... P398
University of Iowa Press ... P408
University of Michigan Press, The ... P410
University of Texas Press ... P414
University of Virginia Press ... P415
University Press of Colorado ... P416
W.W. Norton & Company Ltd ... P422

Archery
See more broadly: Sport
Bowhunter ... M063

Architecture
See more specifically: Church Architecture; City and Town Planning
Arcadia Publishing ... P020
Architectural Review, The ... M025
Bird Eye Books ... P048
Bloomsbury Academic ... P053
Cottage Life ... M090
Countryside Books ... P099
Dundurn ... P118
Goose Lane Editions ... P148
Harvard University Press ... P165

296 Index | Arctic

Lilliput Press, The P217
Logaston Press....P221
LSU Press P223
Lund Humphries Limited P224
Monacelli Press, The P245
Oxford University Press P272
Phaidon Press P287
Prestel Publishing Ltd....P302
Regina Ryan Books L489
Scala Arts & Heritage Publishers....P326
Stipes Publishing P371
Thames & Hudson Inc. P382
Thames and Hudson Ltd....P383
University of Texas Press P414
University of Virginia Press P415
Virginia Wine & Country Life.... M331
W.W. Norton & Company Ltd P422
W.W. Norton & Company, Inc. P423
Wallpaper M337
Yale University Press (London)....P438

Arctic

See more broadly: Regional

Hancock House Publishers P159

Arizona

See more broadly: United States

AZ Foothills Magazine M036

Aromatherapy

See more broadly: Alternative Health

Singing Dragon P340

Art Criticism

See more broadly: Arts

Gulf Coast: A Journal of Literature and Fine Arts M147

Art History

See more broadly: Arts; History

Brattle Agency LLC, The L077
Charnace, Edwina de L110
Curran, Sabhbh....L134
Derviskadic, Dado L151
Ohio University Press....P261
University of Texas Press P414

Articles

Acumen M007
African American Golfer's Digest M008
Agricultural History.... M012
Alabama Heritage.... M013
Arc M024
Architectural Review, The.... M025
Art Quarterly M026
Asian Social Science M028
Atlanta Magazine M030
Aurealis M034
AZ Foothills Magazine.... M036
Baffler, The M039
BBC History Magazine M042
Bear Deluxe Magazine, The M044
Bee, The M045
Bella M046
Berks County Living M049
Best of British.... M050
Better Homes and Gardens M051
BFS Journal M054
Bluegrass Unlimited M061
Bowhunter M063
Britain Magazine M066
Business Traveller M069
Canadian Dimension M072
Carolina Woman.... M074
Chapman M075
CharlottesvilleFamily M076
Cobblestone.... M079
Cocoa Girl M080
Commonweal M082
Contemporary Verse 2.... M086
Conversation (UK), The M087
Cosmos.... M089
Cottage Life M090
Cowboys & Indians....M091
Cricket....M096
Cruising World M097
Crystal Magazine M098
Dawntreader, The....M102
Descent M104
Diver....M105
Ekphrastic Review, The M109
Entrepreneur M112
Facts & Fiction M116
Fate....M117
Feminist Studies....M119
First For Women....M122
Fortean Times: The Journal of Strange Phenomena M127
Forty20 ....M128
Foundation: The International Review of Science Fiction M129
Funeral Business Solutions M134
Garden Answers....M136
Geographical Journal, The M138
Go World Travel Magazine....M142
Graywolf Lab....M145
Great Outdoors (TGO), The M146
Healthy M152
Hello!....M155
History Today M157
Homes & Antiques....M158
Horse & Rider....M159
Idler, The M165
Insurance Post....M169
International Piano....M170
Ireland's Own M172
Island M174
Kavya Kishor....M177
Kent Life....M178
Kids Alive! M180
Landfall M182
Leisure Group Travel M183
Leisure Painter M184
Linguist, The....M186
London Grip M188
London Grip New Poetry M189
London Review of Books....M191
marie claire M200
Marlin....M201
Massachusetts Review, The M202
Michigan Quarterly Review M204
Modern Applied Science....M210
My Weekly M215
New Internationalist....M221
New Statesman M222
Norfolk & Suffolk Bride M224
OK! Magazine M228
Oxford Poetry M229
PC Pro....M235
Poetry Ireland Review....M243
Poetry Wales....M245
Political Quarterly, The....M246
Preservation Magazine....M248
Pride M249
Quadrant Magazine....M254
Racecar Engineering M255
Rail Express....M257
Reactor....M258
Red Magazine....M259
Research Journal of Pharmacy and Technology....M260
Riposte....M262
River Hills Traveler M263
Round Hall.... P318
Rugby World M265
Ruralite....M266
Saddlebag Dispatches M267
Sailing Today....M268
Savannah Magazine.... M269
Scifaikuest.... M270
Scots Magazine, The M271
Scottish Field.... M272
Seaworthy Publications P333
Seventeen M275
Ships Monthly Magazine.... M278
Sierra M281
SmokeLong Quarterly M283
Snowflake Magazine M284
SOMA.... M285
Somerset Life M286
Southern Theatre M292
Southwest Review M293
Spa Magazine M295
Speciality Food.... M296
Square Mile Magazine.... M298
Strange Horizons M301
Strategic Finance M302
Supplement, The.... M306
Swimming Pool News M307
That's Life!.... M313
This England M316
Threepenny Review, The.... M317
Times Literary Supplement (TLS), The... M318
Ulster Business.... M323
Uncut.... M324
Unfit Magazine.... M326
Virginia Wine & Country Life.... M331
Virginia Wine & Country Weddings M332
Viz.... M333
Vogue.... M334
Wallace Stevens Journal, The.... M336
Wallpaper M337
Wasafiri.... M338
Wine Enthusiast.... M343
Yankee Magazine.... M345
Yorkshire Dalesman, The M347
Yorkshire Life M348
Yorkshire Women's Life Magazine.... M349
Yours.... M350

Artificial Intelligence (AI)

See more broadly: Computer Science

Bloomsbury Academic P053

Arts

See more specifically: Art Criticism; Art History; Church Art; Drawing; Painting; Performing Arts; Photography; Practical Art; Visual Arts

African American Review M009
Alcock, Michael L009
Anvil Press Publishers....P017
Arcadia Publishing P020
Art Quarterly M026
Atlanta Magazine M030
Aurora Metro Press....P024
Bal, Emma....L032
Barr, Anjanette L038
Basalt Books....P034
Bear Deluxe Magazine, The M044
Bernardi, Amanda L056
Bloomsbury Academic P053
Blue Star Press P056
Brailsford, Karen L075
Brewin Books Ltd P062
Brick.... M065
British Museum Press, The....P064
BSFA Review, The.... M067
Cambridge University Press P068
Cavanagh, Claire L107
Charlesbridge Publishing....P081
Compassiviste Publishing....P097
Conversation (UK), The M087
Cowboys & Indians M091
Cricket.... M096
Crown Publishing Group, The P103

Index | *Beauty* **297**

Curran, Sabhbh L134
Davies, Olivia L147
Denis Kitchen Publishing Company Co., LLC P109
DK Publishing P112
Draper, Claire L162
Ekphrastic Review, The M109
Enitharmon Editions P122
Feminist Press, The P130
Feminist Studies M119
Gale P139
Gemini Books P140
Gill Education P143
Global Lion Intellectual Property Management, Inc. L239
Goldblatt, Rachel L243
Goose Lane Editions P148
Graywolf Lab M145
Harvard University Press P165
Hildebrand, Cole L280
Image M166
Imagine Publishing P186
Island Online M175
Kane Press P202
Kent Life M178
Kim, Julia L334
Korero Press P208
Lambert, Sophie L348
Landfall M182
Levy, Yael L362
Lilliput Press, The P217
London Grip M188
London Review of Books M191
Lund Humphries Limited P224
Marshall, Jen L391
Massachusetts Review, The M202
McCormick Literary L400
McNidder & Grace P232
Minnesota Historical Society Press P241
MIT Press, The P244
Monacelli Press, The P245
Monoray P246
Muscato, Nate L429
New England Review M220
New Statesman M222
No Starch Press, Inc. P258
Ohio University Press P261
Otago University Press P269
Oxford University Press P272
Peepal Tree Press P278
Pelham, Imogen L461
Peter Lang P285
Phaidon Press P287
Pimpernel Press P292
Pineapple Press P293
Power Cut Lite M247
Prestel Publishing Ltd P302
Ramer, Susan L486
Reilly, Milly L491
Riposte M262
Rocky Mountain Books P315
Sasquatch Books P325
Scala Arts & Heritage Publishers P326
Seren Books P335
Seymour, Charlotte L528
Society for Promoting Christian Knowledge (SPCK) P345
SOMA M285
Southwest Review M293
Square Mile Magazine M298
Stipes Publishing P371
Taylor & Francis Group P378
Texas A&M University Press P381
Thames & Hudson Inc. P382
Thames and Hudson Ltd P383
Thayer, Henry L572
Threepenny Review, The M317
Times Literary Supplement (TLS), The M318
Trudel, Jes L579
Tyndale House Publishers, Inc. P397
University of Alberta Press P404
University of California Press P406
University of Maine Press P409
University of Michigan Press, The P410
University of Texas Press P414
University of Virginia Press P415
Victoria Sanders & Associates LLC L584
Virginia Quarterly Review, The M330
Virginia Wine & Country Life M331
Vogue M334
W.W. Norton & Company Ltd P422
W.W. Norton & Company, Inc. P423
Wallpaper M337
Wide-Eyed Editions P429
Yale Review, The M344
Yale University Press (London) P438
Yankee Magazine M345
Zuraw-Friedland, Ayla L619

Asia
See more broadly: Regional
See more specifically: East Asia; Japan; South-East Asia
Asian Social Science M028
Bloomsbury Academic P053
Feminist Press, The P130
HopeRoad P176
Jain Publishing Company, Inc. P195
Manoa M199
Ohio University Press P261
Pluto Press P295
Stanford University Press P367
University of Alberta Press P404
University of California Press P406
University of Michigan Press, The P410

Asian American
See more broadly: Ethnic Groups
Feminist Press, The P130
W.W. Norton & Company, Inc. P423

Astral Projection
See more broadly: Psychic Abilities
Llewellyn Worldwide Ltd P219

Astrology
See more broadly: Fortune Telling and Divination
Hay House Publishers P168
Hensley, Chelsea L274
Llewellyn Worldwide Ltd P219
Rushall, Kathleen L512

Astronomy
See more broadly: Science
Cambridge University Press P068
Gale P139
W.W. Norton & Company Ltd P422
W.W. Norton & Company, Inc. P423

Atlanta
See more broadly: Georgia (US State)
Atlanta Magazine M030

Atlantic
See more broadly: Regional

Atlantic Northeast
See more broadly: North America
Atlantic Northeast M032

Audio Technology
See more broadly: Audio Visual Technology
See more specifically: Radio Technology

Audio Visual Technology
See more broadly: Technology
See more specifically: Audio Technology
Stipes Publishing P371

Audiobooks
Lerner Publishing Group P213

Augmented Reality
See more broadly: Technology

Australasia / Oceania
See more broadly: Regional
See more specifically: New Zealand
University of Alberta Press P404

Austria
See more broadly: Europe

Autism
See more broadly: Neuropsychology
Future Horizons P138
Jessica Kingsley Publishers P197
W.W. Norton & Company Ltd P422

AutoHotKey
See more broadly: Computer Programming

Autobiography
See more broadly: Biography
See more specifically: Autofiction; Memoir; Personal Essays; Personal Experiences
Arcadia Publishing P020
Asabi Publishing P022
Backbeat Books P027
Canterbury Literary Agency L096
Compassiviste Publishing P097
Dillsworth, Elise L156
Glenister, Emily L238
Irish Pages M173
JMD Media / DB Publishing P198
Joy Harris Literary Agency, Inc. L308
Kensington Publishing Corp. P204
Marion Boyars Publishers P229
Methuen Publishing Ltd P238
NBM Publishing P254
Perspectives Books P283
Scratching Shed Publishing P331
Turner Publishing P394
University of Alberta Press P404
University of Virginia Press P415
Victoria Sanders & Associates LLC L584
Zack Company, Inc, The L615

Autofiction
See more broadly: Autobiography
Goldstein, Veronica L244
Tolka M319

Avant-Garde
Midsummer Dream House M207

Aviation
See more broadly: Transport
See more specifically: Military Aviation
Countryside Books P099
History Press, The P174
Schiffer Military History P328
Zack Company, Inc, The L615

Ayurveda
See more broadly: Alternative Health
Singing Dragon P340

Baha'i
See more broadly: Religion

Baseball
See more broadly: Sport
Spitball M297

Basketball
See more broadly: Sport
Thayer, Henry L572

Beat Generation
See more broadly: Literature

Beauty
See more specifically: Hairstyles; Make-Up
Berks County Living M049
DK Publishing P112
Finan, Ciara L200
First For Women M122
Healthy M152
Hello! M155
marie claire M200
My Weekly M215
Pride M249
Red Magazine M259

Scottish Field................................. M272
Seventeen M275
Vogue M334
Wallpaper M337
Yours... M350

Beer
See more broadly: Drinks
See more specifically: Beer Making

Beer Making
See more broadly: Beer
Virginia Wine & Country Life................ M331

Berks County
See more broadly: Pennsylvania
Berks County Living M049

Bible Stories
See more broadly: Christianity
Moody Publishers................................ P247

Bible Studies
See more broadly: Christianity
Brown, Megan L084
College Press Publishing P094
Crossway P100
Moody Publishers................................ P247
Pacific Press Publishing Association P273
Society for Promoting Christian
  Knowledge (SPCK)........................... P345
Tyndale House Publishers, Inc. P397

Bibles
See more broadly: Christianity

Bigfoot
See more broadly: Folklore, Myths, and Legends
Hancock House Publishers P159

Biker Lifestyle
See more broadly: Lifestyle

Biochemistry
See more broadly: Biology; Chemistry

Bioethics
See more broadly: Biology

Biography
See more specifically: Autobiography
Alcock, Michael L009
Annette Green Authors' Agency............ L021
Arcadia Publishing P020
Asabi Publishing................................ P022
Aurora Metro Press............................ P024
Backbeat Books P027
Barr, Anjanette L038
Bartholomew, Jason L041
Basalt Books..................................... L034
Bess Press....................................... P047
Betsy Amster Literary Enterprises L059
Blackstaff Press................................ P051
Bradford Literary Agency L073
Brailsford, Karen L075
Brewin Books Ltd P062
Canterbury Literary Agency L096
Canterbury Press............................... P071
Carter, Rebecca L103
Cavanagh, Claire L107
Charlesbridge Publishing..................... P081
Chelsea House Publishers P082
Clarke, Catherine.............................. L119
College Press Publishing P094
Compassiviste Publishing P097
Crown.. P101
Crown Publishing Group, The P103
Dana Newman Literary, LLC................ L138
Darga, Jon Michael........................... L141
Derviskadic, Dado............................. L151
Doug Grad Literary Agency L161
Dundurn P118
Dystel, Jane..................................... L167
Einstein, Susanna............................. L173
Eisenmann, Caroline.......................... L175
Enslow Publishers, Inc. P123
Epicenter Press Inc........................... P124

Feminist Press, The............................ P130
Fernwood Publishing........................... P131
Free Spirit Publishing.......................... P136
Furniss, Eugenie................................. L224
Geiger, Ellen...................................... L227
Gemini Books P140
Gill Books P142
Glenister, Emily.................................. L238
Globe Pequot Press, The P145
Goderich, Miriam................................. L240
Goldblatt, Rachel................................ L243
Goose Lane Editions P148
Gordon, Andrew.................................. L245
Hancock House Publishers P159
Harvard University Press P165
Hensley, Chelsea................................ L274
History Press, The.............................. P174
Holloway, Sally.................................. L284
Icon Books Ltd P180
InterVarsity Press (IVP)....................... P193
J. Gordon Shillingford Publishing........... P194
JMD Media / DB Publishing................... P198
Joelle Delbourgo Associates, Inc........... L301
Kahn, Ella Diamond............................. L314
Kensington Publishing Corp. P204
Kim, Julia L334
Kube Publishing.................................. P209
Levy, Yael L362
Lilliput Press, The............................... P217
Logaston Press P221
London Review of Books...................... M191
Malahat Review, The M197
McCormick Literary L400
McNidder & Grace.............................. P232
Methuen Publishing Ltd....................... P238
Michel, Caroline................................. L408
Mihell, Natasha L410
Moorhead, Max.................................. L416
Morrell, Imogen L417
Mulcahy Sweeney Literary Agency L423
Mundy, Toby..................................... L426
Murray, Judith................................... L428
Muswell Press P250
NBM Publishing P254
Orphans Publishing............................. P268
Otago University Press P269
Oxford University Press....................... P272
Pacific Press Publishing Association...... P273
Perez Literary & Entertainment............. L463
Perez, Kristina................................... L464
Pestritto, Carrie L467
Plexus Publishing Limited P294
Reid, Janet L490
Roseway P317
Rutman, Jim...................................... L514
Scifaikuest M270
Scratching Shed Publishing.................. P331
Seren Books..................................... P335
Sheree Bykofsky Associates, Inc. L532
Shipwreckt Books Publishing
  Company P336
Society for Promoting Christian
  Knowledge (SPCK)........................... P345
Sweet, Emily..................................... L563
Tasman, Alice L569
Texas A&M University Press................. P381
Thames & Hudson Inc......................... P382
Thames and Hudson Ltd P383
Thayer, Henry L572
Transworld Publishers......................... P393
Turner Publishing P394
Tyndale House Publishers, Inc. P397
University of Michigan Press, The P410
University of Texas Press P414
University of Virginia Press.................. P415
Viney Agency, The.............................. L585

W.W. Norton & Company Ltd P422
W.W. Norton & Company, Inc............... P423
Wallace Stevens Journal, The M336
Willms, Kathryn.................................. L605
Yale University Press (London)............. P438
Zack Company, Inc, The L615

Biology
See more broadly: Science
See more specifically: Biochemistry; Bioethics; Biomedical Science; Evolution; Human Biology; Neurobiology; Paleontology
Cambridge University Press P068
Colourpoint Educational P095
Conrad, Claire Paterson...................... L125
Mentor Books.................................... P236
W.W. Norton & Company Ltd P422
W.W. Norton & Company, Inc.............. P423

Biomedical Science
See more broadly: Biology; Medicine
Taylor & Francis Group....................... P378

Birds
See more broadly: Animals
Hancock House Publishers P159
Regina Ryan Books L489

Black People
See more broadly: Ethnic Groups
Cocoa Girl M080
Peepal Tree Press.............................. P278

Bluegrass
See more broadly: Music
Bluegrass Unlimited M061

Board Books
Allen & Unwin P009
Arcadia Publishing P020
Bess Press....................................... P047
Charlesbridge Publishing P081
Cherry Lake Publishing Group P083
Child's Play (International) Ltd............. P084
DK Publishing................................... P112
Eerdmans Books for Young Readers P120
Free Spirit Publishing......................... P136
Gemini Books P140
Happy Yak P161
Hare, Jessica L266
Holroyde, Penny................................ L285
Igloo Books Limited........................... P184
Kube Publishing................................ P209
Little Bigfoot.................................... P218
Macmillan Children's Books P226
Orca Book Publishers P266
Scholastic UK................................... P330
Sourcebooks Jabberwocky P355
Susan Schulman Literary Agency L557
Tilbury House Publishers P385
Trudel, Jes L579
Walker Books P424
Walsh, Caroline L589

Boats
See more broadly: Vehicles
See more specifically: Motor Boats; Shipping; Yachts
Cottage Life M090
Cruising World M097
Marlin.. M201
River Hills Traveler M263
Seaworthy Publications P333

Book Club Fiction
See more specifically: Book Club Women's Fiction
Armstrong, Susan L026
Baxter, Veronique.............................. L045
Beaumont, Diana L046
Berdinsky, Kendall............................. L054
Blair Partnership, The L064
Bolton, Camilla L067
Brace, Samantha L072

Index | *Business* 299

Brannan, Maria L076
Buckley, Louise L085
Carroll, Megan L102
Caskie, Robert L105
Chanchani, Sonali L108
Cho, Catherine L114
Crowley, Sheila L132
Curran, Sabhbh L134
Danaczko, Melissa L139
Dawson, Liza L148
Dunn, Ben L164
Fabien, Samantha L186
Fazzari, Hillary L188
Ferguson, Hannah L194
Fergusson, Julie L196
Finan, Ciara L200
Forrester, Jemima L210
Foxx, Kat L213
Friedman, Claire L217
Glenister, Emily L238
Grunewald, Hattie L254
Haggerty, Taylor L258
Harper, Logan L267
Harris, Erin L268
Hayden, Viola L271
Heathfield, Laura L273
Hordern, Kate L286
Hornsley, Sarah L287
Kaliszewska, Joanna L315
Kate Barker Literary, TV, & Film Agency L320
Kavanagh, Jade L323
Keane Kataria Literary Agency L325
Keeffe, Sara O' L326
Leeke, Jessica L358
Lightner, Kayla L365
MacDonald, Emily L378
Macdougall, Laura L379
Maidment, Olivia L386
Milburn, Madeleine L411
Moore, Mary C. L415
Mushens, Juliet L430
Napolitano, Maria L431
Neely, Rachel L434
Nelson, Patricia L437
Niumata, Erin L439
O'Grady, Niamh L445
Pass, Marina de L456
Perez Literary & Entertainment L463
Perez, Kristina L464
Pickering, Juliet L473
Pine, Gideon L475
Plitt, Carrie L477
Polygon P298
Power, Anna L482
Preston, Amanda L484
Ramer, Susan L486
Romano, Annie L502
Savvides, Marilia L520
Schofield, Hannah L522
Seymour, Charlotte L528
Simons, Tanera L536
Simpson, Cara Lee L537
Singh, Amandeep L538
Soler, Shania N. L543
Sourcebooks Landmark P356
Steed, Hayley L548
Thorneycroft, Euan L574
Thwaites, Steph L575
Topping, Antony L577
Walsh, Caroline L589
Wood, Caroline L608
Wood, Ed L609
Yeoh, Rachel L612

Book Club Women's Fiction
See more broadly: Book Club Fiction; Women's Fiction
Burke, Kate L088
Choc Lit P085

Book Publishing
See more broadly: Publishing

Books
See more broadly: Media
Acumen M007
African American Review M009
Aurealis M034
Black Moon Magazine M056
Boston Review M062
Canadian Dimension M072
Caribbean Writer, The M073
Concho River Review M083
Dalhousie Review, The M100
Event M113
Foundation: The International Review of Science Fiction M129
Fugue M133
Georgia Review, The M139
Gulf Coast: A Journal of Literature and Fine Arts M147
Ireland's Own M172
Landfall M182
Literary Mama M187
London Grip M188
Long Poem Magazine M192
Malahat Review, The M197
Mid-American Review M206
Missouri Review, The M209
Modern Haiku M211
New Statesman M222
Oxford Review of Books M230
Pleiades M238
Poetry M241
Poetry Wales M245
Political Quarterly, The M246
Reactor M258
Red Magazine M259
Sierra M281
Sinister Wisdom M282
South Carolina Review M289
Spitball M297
Square Mile Magazine M298
Stinging Fly, The M299
Supplement, The M306
Takahe M309
Times Literary Supplement (TLS), The M318
Tusculum Review, The M321
University of Iowa Press P408
Vagabond City M327
Wallace Stevens Journal, The M336

Boxing
See more broadly: Sport
Scratching Shed Publishing P331
Square Mile Magazine M298

Boy Books
Kimber, Natalie L336

Brazil
See more broadly: South America

Breconshire
See more broadly: Wales
Logaston Press P221

British Columbia
See more broadly: Canada
See more specifically: Vancouver Island
Hancock House Publishers P159

British History
See more broadly: History
Zack Company, Inc, The L615

Buddhism
See more broadly: Religion
See more specifically: Mahayana Buddhism; Theravada Buddhism
Ericka T. Phillips L181
Windhorse Publications Ltd P430
Wisdom Publications P431

Building / Construction
See more broadly: Business
See more specifically: Electrical Contracting
Cottage Life M090
Gill Education P143
NAHB BuilderBooks P253
Stipes Publishing P371

Buildings
See more specifically: Houses and Homes

Bullying
See more broadly: Social Issues
Free Spirit Publishing P136

Burton upon Trent
See more broadly: Staffordshire

Business
See more specifically: Building / Construction; Business Law; Entrepreneurship; Film Industry; Funeral Industry; Insurance; Investments; Logistics; Management; Marketing; Procurement; Publishing; Trade; Warehousing; Women in Business
Arcadia Publishing P020
Backbeat Books P027
Banter Press P033
Baumer, Jan L044
BCS (British Computer Society) P042
Berks County Living M049
Berrett-Koehler Publishers P046
Bloomsbury Academic P053
Bradford Literary Agency L073
Business & Accountancy Daily M068
Business Traveller M069
Campos, Vanessa L095
Cedar Fort P076
CGI (Chartered Governance Institute) Publishing P078
Christie, Jennifer L116
Conversation (UK), The M087
Crown P101
Crown Publishing Group, The P103
Dana Newman Literary, LLC L138
Diana Finch Literary Agency L154
Dickerson, Donya L155
Diversion Books P111
DK Publishing P112
Doug Grad Literary Agency L161
Dundurn P118
Einstein, Susanna L173
Entrepreneur M112
Fogg, Jack L206
Frankel, Valerie L215
Gale P139
Getzler, Josh L229
Gill Education P143
Global Lion Intellectual Property Management, Inc. L239
Globe Pequot Press, The P145
Goose Lane Editions P148
Gordon, Andrew L245
Harvard University Press P165
Hay House Publishers P168
Hiyate, Sam L281
Holloway, Sally L284
Icon Books Ltd P180
Irene Goodman Literary Agency (IGLA) L291
Kensington Publishing Corp. P204
Killingley, Jessica L332
Knight Features L340
Kogan Page Ltd P206
Langtons International L354

300 Index | Business Law

Leisure Group Travel M183
Levy, Yael L362
Loft Press, Inc. P220
Marshall, Jen L391
Mentor Books P236
Monoray P246
New Statesman M222
Oak Tree Press P259
Oxford University Press P272
Perry Literary L466
Piatkus Books P289
Regina Ryan Books L489
Riposte M262
Rudy Agency, The L510
Sasquatch Books P325
Sheree Bykofsky Associates, Inc. L532
Spa Magazine M295
Speciality Food M296
Stanford University Press P367
Taylor & Francis Group P378
Thames & Hudson Inc. P382
Thames and Hudson Ltd P383
Turner Publishing P394
Tyndale House Publishers, Inc. P397
Ulster Business M323
University of Michigan Press, The P410
University of Virginia Press P415
Usselman, Laura L581
W.W. Norton & Company Ltd P422
W.W. Norton & Company, Inc. P423
Willms, Kathryn L605
Yale University Press (London) P438

Business Law
See more broadly: Business; Legal
Stipes Publishing P371

CIA
See more broadly: Secret Intelligence

California
See more broadly: United States
Sunbelt Publications, Inc. P373

Cambridgeshire
See more broadly: England

Camping
See more broadly: Outdoor Activities
River Hills Traveler M263

Campus Novels
See more specifically: Dark Academia

Canada
See more broadly: North America
See more specifically: Alberta; British Columbia; New Brunswick; Yukon
Dundurn P118
Fernwood Publishing P131
J. Gordon Shillingford Publishing P194
University of Alberta Press P404

Cannabis
See more broadly: Drugs

Canoeing
See more broadly: Sport

Caravans
See more broadly: Vehicles

Career Development
See more broadly: Personal Development
Barrett, Emily L040
Berrett-Koehler Publishers P046
Betsy Amster Literary Enterprises L059
Demblon, Gabrielle L150
DK Publishing P112
Kogan Page Ltd P206
marie claire M200
Pride M249
Singing Dragon P340
Tyndale House Publishers, Inc. P397
Zack Company, Inc, The L615

Caribbean
See more broadly: Regional
See more specifically: Cuba
Caribbean Writer, The M073
HopeRoad P176
Peepal Tree Press P278
Pluto Press P295
University of Michigan Press, The P410
University of Texas Press P414
University of Virginia Press P415

Caribbean Diaspora
See more broadly: Ethnic Groups
Peepal Tree Press P278

Caribbean History
See more broadly: History
LSU Press P223

Cars
See more broadly: Vehicles
See more specifically: Classic Cars; Mini Cars; Racecars; Sports Cars
Bentley Publishers P044
Doug Grad Literary Agency L161
Square Mile Magazine M298

Cartoons
Beano, The M043
Black Warrior Review M058
Denis Kitchen Publishing Company
   Co., LLC P109
Kids Alive! M180
Viz M333

Catholicism
See more broadly: Christianity
See more specifically: Ignation Spirituality
Liguori Publications P216

Cats
See more broadly: Pets
Rutherford, Laetitia L513

Caving and Potholing
See more broadly: Outdoor Activities
Descent M104

Celebrity
See more broadly: Entertainment
See more specifically: Sports Celebrity
Bella M046
Cavanagh, Claire L107
Granger, David L250
Hello! M155
Heymont, Lane L277
Kent Life M178
Kruger Cowne L344
marie claire M200
Nolan, Laura L441
OK! Magazine M228
Pierce, Rosie L474
Seventeen M275
YMU Books L613
Yours M350

Celebrity Memoir
See more broadly: Memoir
Black & White Publishing Ltd P049
Richter, Rick L493

Central America
See more broadly: Regional
Arte Publico Press P021
Ohio University Press P261
Phillips, Aemilia L472
Sunbelt Publications, Inc. P373

Central Europe
See more broadly: Europe
Purdue University Press P305

Ceramics
See more broadly: Collectibles; Crafts

Chakras
See more broadly: Psychic Abilities
Llewellyn Worldwide Ltd P219

Chapbooks
Anhinga Press P016
Dancing Girl Press P105
Glass Poetry Press P144
Sinister Stoat Press P341
Tyndale House Publishers, Inc. P397
Verve Poetry Press P421

Chapter Books
Allen & Unwin P009
Alternating Current Press P010
Andlyn L014
Arcadia Publishing P020
Armada, Kurestin L024
Bent Agency (UK), The L051
Bent Agency, The L052
Bonnier Books (UK) P059
Bright Agency (UK), The L078
Bright Agency (US), The L079
Brooks, Savannah L080
Cedar Fort P076
Children's Books North Agency L112
Cooper, Gemma L128
Darley Anderson Children's L144
Dunow, Carlson & Lerner Agency L166
Flynn, Amy Thrall L205
Gemini Books P140
Guppy Books P155
Hare, Jessica L266
Hawk, Susan L269
Holroyde, Penny L285
Irvine, Lucy L292
Kane Press P202
Kim, Sally M. L335
Kube Publishing P209
Lakosil, Natalie L347
Lantana Publishing P210
Little Bigfoot P218
Macmillan Children's Books P226
Ostby, Kristin L452
Pacific Press Publishing Association P273
Pen & Ink Designs Publishing P280
Phoenix Moirai P288
Piccadilly Press P291
Richter, Rick L493
Rofe, Jennifer L500
Scholastic P329
Scholastic UK P330
Simply Read Books P339
Skylark Literary L540
Susan Schulman Literary Agency L557
Sutherland, Kari L559
Terlip, Paige L570
Thames & Hudson Inc. P382
Trudel, Jes L579
Turner Publishing P394
W.W. Norton & Company Ltd P422
Walker Books P424
Walsh, Caroline L589

Charlottesville
See more broadly: Albemarle
Albemarle M015
CharlottesvilleFamily M076

Chemistry
See more broadly: Science
See more specifically: Biochemistry
Cambridge University Press P068
Colourpoint Educational P095
Gale P139
Stipes Publishing P371
Taylor & Francis Group P378
W.W. Norton & Company Ltd P422
W.W. Norton & Company, Inc. P423

Chesapeake Bay
See more broadly: United States

Cheshire
See more broadly: England
See more specifically: Chester

Chess
See more broadly: Games

Popular Chess P299
Chester
See more broadly: Cheshire
Chicago
See more broadly: Illinois
Chick Lit
See more broadly: Women's Fiction
Leon, Nina L360
Pestritto, Carrie L467
Tran, Jennifer Chen L578
Zack Company, Inc, The L615
Child Psychotherapy
See more broadly: Juvenile Psychotherapy
W.W. Norton & Company Ltd P422
Childbirth
See more broadly: Pregnancy
Foxx, Kat L213
Singing Dragon P340
Childcare
See more broadly: Children
Zack Company, Inc, The L615
Children
See more broadly: Family
See more specifically: Childcare
Scratching Shed Publishing P331
Children's
3 Seas Literary Agency L001
Agency (London) Ltd, The L008
Albert Whitman & Company P007
Alice Williams Literary L012
Allen & Unwin P009
Alternating Current Press P010
Andersen Press Ltd P014
Andlyn L014
Andrade, Hannah L015
Andrew Nurnberg Associates, Ltd L016
Andrews McMeel Publishing P015
Ange, Anna L019
Anne Clark Literary Agency L020
Annette Green Authors' Agency L021
Arcadia Publishing P020
Armada, Kurestin L024
Arms, Victoria Wells L025
Asabi Publishing P022
Atyeo, Charlotte L028
Autumn Publishing Ltd P025
Babybug M037
Baror International, Inc. L037
Barr, Anjanette L038
Basalt Books P034
Bath Literary Agency L042
Bauman, Erica L043
Baxter, Veronique L045
Beano, The M043
Belton, Maddy L049
Bent Agency (UK), The L051
Bent Agency, The L052
Bess Press P047
Better Than Starbucks M052
Bewley, Elizabeth L061
Blair Partnership, The L064
Bonnier Books (UK) P059
Borstel, Stefanie Sanchez Von L070
Bradford Literary Agency L073
Bradford, Laura L074
Brewin Books Ltd P062
Bright Agency (UK), The L078
Bright Agency (US), The L079
Brooks, Savannah L080
Burby, Danielle L087
Burns, Camille L089
CAA (London) L091
Cabello, Analia L092
Cadno P067
Candy Jar Books P070
Carroll, Megan L102

Carter, Rebecca L103
Cartey, Claire L104
Cedar Fort P076
Charlesbridge Publishing P081
Cherry Lake Publishing Group P083
Chevais, Jennifer L111
Child's Play (International) Ltd P084
Children's Books North Agency L112
Chiotti, Danielle L113
Cicada Books P087
Cichello, Kayla L117
Clarke, Catherine L119
Classical Comics P090
Cobblestone M079
Cocoa Girl M080
Colwill, Charlotte L121
Comparato, Andrea L123
Cooper, Gemma L128
Crandall, Becca L130
Creative Roots Studio L131
Cricket M096
Curtis Brown L135
Cusick, John L136
Darley Anderson Children's L144
DHH Literary Agency Ltd L152
DK Publishing P112
Dominguez, Adriana L158
Draper, Claire L162
Dunham Literary, Inc. L163
Dunow, Carlson & Lerner Agency L166
Eddison Pearson Ltd L170
Eerdmans Books for Young Readers ... P120
Einstein, Susanna L173
Eisenbraun, Nicole L174
Eunice McMullen Children's Literary
  Agent Ltd L182
Evan-Moor Educational Publishers P125
Everything With Words P126
Fabien, Samantha L186
Fazzari, Hillary L188
Feldmann, Kait Lee L190
Fellows, Abi L193
Feminist Press, The P130
Ferguson, T.S. L195
Fernandez, Rochelle L197
Figueroa, Melanie L199
Finegan, Stevie L203
Firefly P133
Flannery Literary L204
Flynn, Amy Thrall L205
Fraser Ross Associates L216
Free Spirit Publishing P136
Friedman, Claire L217
Fuller, Lisa L223
Gahan, Isobel L225
Gemini Books P140
Getzler, Josh L229
Ghahremani, Lilly L230
Gilbert, Tara L233
Gill Books P142
Gisondi, Katie L235
Glass Literary Management LLC L236
Goetz, Adria L241
Goff, Ellen L242
Graffeg Childrens P151
Graham, Susan L248
Grajkowski, Kara L249
Gruber, Pam L253
Gunic, Masha L256
Guppy Books P155
Hakim, Serene L259
Haley, Jolene L260
Hancock House Publishers P159
Hannah Sheppard Literary Agency L262
Hannigan, Carrie L263
Happy Yak P161

Hare, Jessica L266
Hashtag Press P166
Hawk, Susan L269
Hawn, Molly Ker L270
Hensley, Chelsea L274
Hernandez, Saritza L275
Hernando, Paloma L276
Hodges, Jodie L282
Holroyde, Penny L285
Hordern, Kate L286
IgKids P183
Igloo Books Limited P184
Inscriptions Literary Agency L289
Irvine, Lucy L292
Jamieson, Molly L296
Jamii Publishing P196
Janklow & Nesbit UK Ltd L297
Jean V. Naggar Literary Agency, The ... L299
Jessica Kingsley Publishers P197
Joelle Delbourgo Associates, Inc. L301
K2 Literary L313
Kahn, Ella Diamond L314
Kane Press P202
Kate Nash Literary Agency L321
Kathryn Green Literary Agency, LLC ... L322
Kean, Taylor Martindale L324
Kensington Publishing Corp. P204
Kids Alive! M180
Kim, Sally M. L335
Knigge, Sheyla L339
KT Literary L345
Kube Publishing P209
Lakosil, Natalie L347
Langlee, Lina L352
Langton, Becca L353
Lantana Publishing P210
Latshaw, Katherine L355
Leapfrog Press P212
Leon, Nina L360
Lerner Publishing Group P213
Lindsay Literary Agency L366
Little Bigfoot P218
MacLeod, Lauren L383
Macmillan Children's Books P226
Madeleine Milburn Literary, TV &
  Film Agency L385
Margaret K. McElderry Books P228
Marion Boyars Publishers P229
Marr, Jill L389
Marshall, Jen L391
Mattson, Jennifer L396
Maurer, Shari L397
McBride, Juliana L399
Mihell, Natasha L410
Minnesota Historical Society Press ... P241
Moody Publishers P247
Mulcahy Sweeney Literary Agency ... L423
Nathan, Abigail L433
Nelson Literary Agency, LLC L435
Nelson, Patricia L437
No Starch Press, Inc. P258
Northern Gravy M226
O'Brien, Lee L444
O'Neill, Molly L446
Oh MG Press P260
Olswanger, Anna L450
Orca Book Publishers P266
Ostby, Kristin L452
Pacific Press Publishing Association ... P273
Pages, Saribel L453
Pan Macmillan Australia P274
Parker, Elana Roth L455
Paul S. Levine Literary Agency L459
PB and Yay! Books P277
Pen & Ink Designs Publishing P280
Pestritto, Carrie L467

Claim your free access to www.firstwriter.com: See p.367

Peter Pauper Press P286
Phaidon Press P287
Phelan, Beth L470
Philips, Ariana L471
Phoenix Moirai P288
Piccadilly Press P291
Pineapple Press P293
Plant, Zoe L476
Posner, Marcy L480
Quarto Group, Inc., The P307
Quirk Books P308
Rand McNally P310
Ransom Publishing Ltd P312
Regina Ryan Books L489
Richter, Rick L493
Robinson, Quressa L497
Rocky Mountain Books P315
Rofe, Jennifer L500
Rogers, Coleridge & White Ltd L501
Ross, Whitney L507
Rubin Pfeffer Content, LLC L509
Rudy Agency, The L510
Rushall, Kathleen L512
Sanchez, Kaitlyn L516
Sant, Kelly Van L518
Scholastic P329
Scholastic UK P330
Scratching Shed Publishing P331
Seager, Chloe L524
Seventh Agency L527
Shaw Agency, The L529
Shestopal, Camilla L534
Simply Read Books P339
Singing Dragon P340
Siobhan, Aiden L539
Skylark Literary L540
Society for Promoting Christian
   Knowledge (SPCK) P345
Soler, Shania N. L543
Soloway, Jennifer March L544
Sophie Hicks Agency L545
Sourcebooks eXplore P352
Sourcebooks Jabberwocky P355
Sourcebooks Wonderland P357
Sourcebooks Young Readers P358
StoryWise L552
Stringer Literary Agency LLC, The L553
Sunbelt Publications, Inc. P373
Susan Schulman Literary Agency L557
Sutherland, Kari L559
Symonds, Laurel L565
Talbot, Emily L567
Tasman, Alice L569
Terlip, Paige L570
Thames & Hudson Inc. P382
Thames and Hudson Ltd P383
Tilbury House Publishers P385
Tippermuir Books P386
Tran, Jennifer Chen L578
Transworld Publishers P393
Trudel, Jes L579
Turner Publishing P394
Tyndale House Publishers, Inc. P397
Victoria Sanders & Associates LLC L584
Viney Agency, The L585
W.W. Norton & Company Ltd P422
Walker Books P424
Walsh, Caroline L589
Watson, Little Ltd L590
Watterson, Jessica L591
Wee Book Company, The P427
Weiman, Paula L592
Weiss, Alexandra L593
Weitzner, Tess L594
Weltz, Jennifer L596
Westin, Erin Casey L597

Whatnall, Michaela L598
Whispering Buffalo Literary Agency L599
Wide-Eyed Editions P429
Williams, Laura L603
Williamson, Jo L604
Wilson, Desiree L606
Woods, Bryony L610
Words & Pictures P433
Wordsworth Editions P435
Workman Publishing P437
Yale University Press (London) P438
Zacker, Marietta B. L616

China
See more broadly: South-East Asia

Chinese Medicine
See more broadly: Alternative Health
Blue Poppy Enterprises P055
Singing Dragon P340

Chinese Philosophy
See more broadly: Philosophy
Blue Poppy Enterprises P055

Choral Music
See more broadly: Music

Christian Living
See more broadly: Christianity
Brown, Megan L084
Charisma House P079
Crossway P100
InterVarsity Press (IVP) P193
Moody Publishers P247
Pacific Press Publishing Association P273
Society for Promoting Christian
   Knowledge (SPCK) P345
Tyndale House Publishers, Inc. P397

Christian Romance
See more broadly: Romance
See more specifically: Amish Romance
Inscriptions Literary Agency L289

Christianity
See more broadly: Religion
See more specifically: Amish; Bible Stories; Bible Studies; Bibles; Catholicism; Christian Living; Church of Jesus Christ of Latter-Day Saints (LDS); Evangelism; Methodism; Mormonism; Quakerism
Ambassador Speakers Bureau &
   Literary Agency L013
Balow, Dan L033
Baylor University Press P041
Brown, Megan L084
Canterbury Press P071
Charisma House P079
College Press Publishing P094
Crossway P100
Eason, Lynette L169
Inscriptions Literary Agency L289
Kids Alive! M180
Moody Publishers P247
Pacific Press Publishing Association P273
Society for Promoting Christian
   Knowledge (SPCK) P345
Tyndale House Publishers, Inc. P397

Church Architecture
See more broadly: Architecture

Church Art
See more broadly: Arts

Church History
See more broadly: History
Crossway P100
InterVarsity Press (IVP) P193
Pacific Press Publishing Association P273

Church Music
See more broadly: Music
See more specifically: Hymnals

Church of Jesus Christ of Latter-Day Saints (LDS)
See more broadly: Christianity

Cedar Fort P076

Cider
See more broadly: Drinks

Cinemas / Movie Theaters
See more broadly: Film Industry

City and Town Planning
See more broadly: Architecture
Brick M065
University of Alberta Press P404

Civil Rights
See more broadly: Politics
New Internationalist M221

Classic Cars
See more broadly: Cars

Classical Music
See more broadly: Music
Edenborough, Sam L172

Classics / Ancient World
Bloomsbury Academic P053
Cambridge University Press P068
Foxx, Kat L213
Harvard University Press P165
London Review of Books M191
Methuen Publishing Ltd P238
Oxbow Books P271
Oxford Review of Books M230
Oxford University Press P272
Stipes Publishing P371
Thames & Hudson Inc. P382
Thames and Hudson Ltd P383
University of California Press P406
University of Michigan Press, The P410
University of Texas Press P414
W.W. Norton & Company Ltd P422
Zack Company, Inc, The L615

Climate Science
See more broadly: Earth Science; Environment
Afsana Press P005
Barrett, Emily L040
Cooper, Maggie L129
Fernwood Publishing P131
Mendia, Isabel L403
Salt Publishing P322
Sierra M281
Singh, Amandeep L538
University of Alberta Press P404
Weiss, Alexandra L593

Climbing
See more broadly: Sport
Adventure Books by Vertebrate
   Publishing P004

Coffee Table Books
Imagine Publishing P186

Cognitive Science
See more broadly: Science

Collectibles
See more specifically: Ceramics
Arcadia Publishing P020
Goss & Crested China Club P149

College / University
See more broadly: School
See more specifically: Harvard

Colorado
See more broadly: United States
University Press of Colorado P416

Colouring Books
Gemini Books P140
Hancock House Publishers P159
Igloo Books Limited P184
Pen & Ink Designs Publishing P280
Sunbelt Publications, Inc. P373
Unseen Press P417

Comedy / Humour
See more specifically: Dark Humour; Romantic Comedy; Satire
Andrews McMeel Publishing P015

Annette Green Authors' Agency	L021	
Arcadia Publishing	P020	
Armada, Kurestin	L024	
Baffler, The	M039	
Barr, Nicola	L039	
Barrett, Emily	L040	
Baumer, Jan	L044	
Baxter, Veronique	L045	
Beano, The	M043	
Beaumont, Diana	L046	
Belton, Maddy	L049	
Better Than Starbucks	M052	
Black & White Publishing Ltd	P049	
Blue Star Press	P056	
Bowlin, Sarah	L071	
Bradford Literary Agency	L073	
Brewin Books Ltd	P062	
Canterbury Press	P071	
Carr, Jamie	L101	
Carroll, Megan	L102	
Chiotti, Danielle	L113	
Christie, Jennifer	L116	
Cichello, Kayla	L117	
Colwill, Charlotte	L121	
Compassiviste Publishing	P097	
Conville, Clare	L126	
Cooper, Gemma	L128	
Countryside Books	P099	
Crown Publishing Group, The	P103	
Crystal Magazine	M098	
Cusick, John	L136	
Danko, Margaret	L140	
Dawson, Liza	L148	
Doug Grad Literary Agency	L161	
Epicenter Press Inc.	P124	
Every Day Fiction	M114	
Forrester, Jemima	L210	
Fuentes, Sarah	L222	
Furniss, Eugenie	L224	
Gemini Books	P140	
Getzler, Josh	L229	
Ghahremani, Lilly	L230	
Gilbert, Tara	L233	
Gill Books	P142	
Graham, Stacey	L247	
Gunic, Masha	L256	
Haley, Jolene	L260	
Hannah Sheppard Literary Agency	L262	
Hannigan, Carrie	L263	
Hashtag Press	P166	
Hensley, Chelsea	L274	
Hernando, Paloma	L276	
Hodges, Jodie	L282	
Imagine Publishing	P186	
Irvine, Lucy	L292	
JMD Media / DB Publishing	P198	
Johnson, Jared	L303	
Joy Harris Literary Agency, Inc.	L308	
Kathryn Green Literary Agency, LLC	L322	
Kensington Publishing Corp.	P204	
Levitt, Sarah	L361	
Levy, Yael	L362	
Macdougall, Laura	L379	
Mack, Kate	L381	
Marr, Jill	L389	
Medina Publishing	L235	
NBM Publishing	P254	
O'Grady, Niamh	L445	
O'Neill, Molly	L446	
O'Shea, Amy	L447	
Old Pond Publishing	P262	
Orenda Books	P267	
Ostby, Kristin	L452	
Parker, Elana Roth	L455	
Philips, Ariana	L471	
Quirk Books	P308	
Reilly, Milly	L491	
Romano, Annie	L502	
Rutherford, Laetitia	L513	
Salt Publishing	P322	
Sanchez, Kaitlyn	L516	
Scratching Shed Publishing	P331	
Seager, Chloe	L524	
Sheree Bykofsky Associates, Inc.	L532	
Soler, Shania N.	L543	
Soloway, Jennifer March	L544	
Square Mile Magazine	M298	
Story Unlikely	M300	
Swainson, Joanna	L561	
Thames & Hudson Inc.	P382	
Topping, Antony	L577	
Transworld Publishers	P393	
Tyndale House Publishers, Inc.	P397	
Vance, Lisa Erbach	L583	
Victoria Sanders & Associates LLC	L584	
Viz	M333	
W.W. Norton & Company Ltd	P422	
W.W. Norton & Company, Inc.	P423	
Watterson, Jessica	L591	
Wee Book Company, The	L427	
Wells, Karmen	L595	
Williams, Katie	L602	
Williams, Laura	L603	
Williamson, Jo	L604	
Workman Publishing	P437	
Young, Claudia	L614	
Zack Company, Inc, The	L615	

Comic Books
- BSFA Review, The ... M067
- Denis Kitchen Publishing Company Co., LLC ... P109
- DK Publishing ... P112
- Korero Press ... P208
- Thames & Hudson Inc. ... P382
- University of Texas Press ... P414

Comics
- Denis Kitchen Publishing Company Co., LLC ... P109
- Hodges, Jodie ... L282
- Kensington Publishing Corp. ... P204
- Nashville Review ... M217
- Shenandoah ... M277
- Turner Publishing ... P394

Coming of Age
- Aldridge, Kaylyn ... L010
- Brace, Samantha ... L072
- Carroll, Megan ... L102
- Chanchani, Sonali ... L108
- Dreamspinner Press ... P115
- Ellis-Martin, Sian ... L180
- Gahan, Isobel ... L225
- Gruber, Pam ... L253
- Haley, Jolene ... L260
- Hashtag Press ... P166
- Maltese, Alyssa ... L387
- Pierce, Rosie ... L474
- Plitt, Carrie ... L477
- Sanchez, Kaitlyn ... L516
- Seager, Chloe ... L524
- W.W. Norton & Company, Inc. ... P423
- Weiss, Alexandra ... L593
- Wells, Karmen ... L595
- Wickers, Chandler ... L600

Commentary
See more specifically: Cultural Commentary; Social Commentary

Commercial
See more specifically: Commercial Fantasy; Commercial Women's Fiction; Upmarket Commercial Fiction
- Adsett, Alex ... L005
- Afonso, Thais ... L007
- Andrade, Hannah ... L015
- Baror International, Inc. ... L037
- Barr, Nicola ... L039
- Bauman, Erica ... L043
- Beaumont, Diana ... L046
- Bent, Jenny ... L053
- Beverley Slopen Literary Agency ... L060
- Blair Partnership, The ... L064
- Brannan, Maria ... L076
- Brotherstone Creative Management ... L081
- Brotherstone, Charlie ... L082
- Buckley, Louise ... L085
- Campbell, Charlie ... L094
- Carroll, Megan ... L102
- Caskie, Robert ... L105
- Cichello, Kayla ... L117
- Compassiviste Publishing ... P097
- Conrad, Claire Paterson ... L125
- Crowley, Sheila ... L132
- Danaczko, Melissa ... L139
- Danko, Margaret ... L140
- Darga, Jon Michael ... L141
- Darley Anderson Agency, The ... L143
- Dolin, Lily ... L157
- Dunow, Carlson & Lerner Agency ... L166
- Dystel, Jane ... L167
- Ellis-Martin, Sian ... L180
- Fabien, Samantha ... L186
- Faulks, Holly ... L187
- Fazzari, Hillary ... L188
- Fellows, Abi ... L193
- Ferguson, Hannah ... L194
- Ferguson, T.S. ... L195
- Fernandez, Rochelle ... L197
- Figueroa, Melanie ... L199
- Finan, Ciara ... L200
- Finch, Rebeka ... L202
- Folio Literary Management, LLC ... L207
- for Authors, A ... L209
- Forrester, Jemima ... L210
- Fox, Aram ... L212
- Foxx, Kat ... L213
- Friedman, Claire ... L217
- Friedman, Rebecca ... L219
- Glenister, Emily ... L238
- Global Lion Intellectual Property Management, Inc. ... L239
- Goderich, Miriam ... L240
- Gordon, Andrew ... L245
- Graham, Stacey ... L247
- Greenstone Literary ... L252
- Gruber, Pam ... L253
- Grunewald, Hattie ... L254
- Gunic, Masha ... L256
- Haggerty, Taylor ... L258
- Hayden, Viola ... L271
- Heathfield, Laura ... L273
- Heymont, Lane ... L277
- Hordern, Kate ... L286
- Hornsley, Sarah ... L287
- Irvine, Lucy ... L292
- Jamieson, Molly ... L296
- Janklow & Nesbit UK Ltd. ... L297
- Joelle Delbourgo Associates, Inc. ... L301
- Joy Harris Literary Agency, Inc. ... L308
- Judith Murdoch Literary Agency ... L309
- Kahn, Ella Diamond ... L314
- Kate Barker Literary, TV, & Film Agency ... L320
- Kate Nash Literary Agency ... L321
- Keren, Eli ... L330
- Kimber, Natalie ... L336
- Kirby, Robert ... L338
- Kracht, Elizabeth ... L341
- Krichevsky, Stuart ... L342
- Lambert, Sophie ... L348

304 Index | Commercial Fantasy

Langlee, Lina L352
Latshaw, Katherine L355
Laxfield Literary Associates L356
Leamington Books P211
Leon, Nina L360
Lutyens and Rubinstein L375
Macdougall, Laura L379
MacKenzie, Joanna L382
Marini, Victoria L388
Marr, Jill L389
Marshall, Jen L391
McBride, Juliana L399
McCormick Literary L400
Merullo, Annabel L405
Milburn, Madeleine L411
Movable Type Management L420
Myrmidon Books Ltd P251
Napolitano, Maria L431
Nathan, Abigail L433
Nelson, Kristin L436
Niumata, Erin L439
O'Brien, Lee L444
Parker, Elana Roth L455
Pass, Marina de L456
Perez Literary & Entertainment L463
Perez, Kristina L464
Pestritto, Carrie L467
Philips, Ariana L471
Phillips, Aemilia L472
Pickering, Juliet L473
Pierce, Rosie L474
Pine, Gideon L475
Plant, Zoe L476
Polygon P298
Preston, Amanda L484
Reid, Janet L490
Riccardi, Francesca L492
Richter, Rick L493
Robinson, Quressa L497
Rocking Chair Books L499
Rofe, Jennifer L500
Rogers, Coleridge & White Ltd L501
Romano, Annie L502
Schofield, Hannah L522
Selectric Artists L525
Seventh Agency L527
Shaw Agency, The L529
Silk, Julia L535
Simons, Tanera L536
Soloway, Jennifer March L544
Steed, Hayley L548
Stringer, Marlene L554
Susan Schulman Literary Agency L557
Swainson, Joanna L561
Symonds, Laurel L565
Tannenbaum, Amy L568
Tasman, Alice L569
Thinkwell Books, UK P384
Thorneycroft, Euan L574
Thwaites, Steph L575
Tran, Jennifer Chen L578
Trudel, Jes L579
Vance, Lisa Erbach L583
Victoria Sanders & Associates LLC L584
Walsh, Caroline L589
Wells, Karmen L595
Whispering Buffalo Literary Agency L599
Williams, Laura L603
Wilson, Ed L607
Woods, Bryony L610
YMU Books L613
Zuckerbrot, Renee L618

Commercial Fantasy
See more broadly: Commercial; Fantasy
Fazzari, Hillary L188

Commercial Women's Fiction
See more broadly: Commercial; Women's Fiction
Barr, Nicola L039
Curtis Brown L135
Dystel, Jane L167
Grunewald, Hattie L254
Keane Kataria Literary Agency L325
Moylett, Lisa L421
Mushens, Juliet L430
Nelson, Patricia L437
Niumata, Erin L439
Zack Company, Inc, The L615

Communication
Banter Press P033
Berrett-Koehler Publishers P046
Bloomsbury Academic P053
Gill Education P143
Hay House Publishers P168
Knight Features L340
Peter Lang P285
W.W. Norton & Company, Inc. P423

Computer Programming
See more broadly: Computers
See more specifically: AutoHotKey
Gill Education P143
International Society for Technology in Education (ISTE) P192
No Starch Press, Inc. P258

Computer Science
See more broadly: Computers
See more specifically: Artificial Intelligence (AI)
Bloomsbury Academic P053
Cambridge University Press P068
Gale P139
No Starch Press, Inc. P258
Oxford University Press P272
Stipes Publishing P371
Taylor & Francis Group P378
W.W. Norton & Company Ltd P422
W.W. Norton & Company, Inc. P423

Computer and Video Games
See more broadly: Computers; Games
Thames & Hudson Inc. P382

Computers
See more broadly: Technology
See more specifically: Computer Programming; Computer Science; Computer and Video Games; Cyber Security; Data and Information Systems; Internet; Software
Information Today, Inc. P188
Kensington Publishing Corp. P204
No Starch Press, Inc. P258
PC Pro M235
Yale University Press (London) P438

Conservative
See more broadly: Politics

Contemporary
See more specifically: Contemporary Crime; Contemporary Culture; Contemporary Fantasy; Contemporary Politics; Contemporary Women's Fiction; Upmarket Contemporary Fiction
Abridged M005
Alekseii, Keir L011
Allegro Poetry Magazine M017
Angela Poetry Magazine M021
Armada, Kurestin L024
Armstrong, Susan L026
Barr, Nicola L039
Bearded Badger Publishing Co. P043
Beaumont, Diana L046
Bent, Jenny L053
Borstel, Stefanie Sanchez Von L070
Brewin Books Ltd P062
Brooks, Savannah L080
Buckley, Louise L085
Burke, Kate L088
Cabello, Analia L092
Carroll, Megan L102
Chelsea House Publishers P082
Christensen, Erica L115
Colwill, Charlotte L121
Compassiviste Publishing P097
Cooper, Gemma L128
Cusick, John L136
Dahlia Books P104
Danaczko, Melissa L139
Danko, Margaret L140
Dawson, Liza L148
Dedalus Ltd P107
Dundurn P118
East of Centre P119
Eddison Pearson Ltd L170
Ellis-Martin, Sian L180
Feminist Press, The P130
Figueroa, Melanie L199
Finch, Rebeka L202
Getzler, Josh L229
Gilbert, Tara L233
Glenister, Emily L238
Goldstein, Veronica L244
Grajkowski, Kara L249
Gunic, Masha L256
Hakim, Serene L259
Haley, Jolene L260
Hannigan, Carrie L263
Hansen, Stephanie L264
Harris, Erin L268
Hensley, Chelsea L274
Hildebrand, Cole L280
Holloway, Sally L284
Irvine, Lucy L292
Kahn, Ella Diamond L314
Kate Barker Literary, TV, & Film Agency L320
Kean, Taylor Martindale L324
Keane Kataria Literary Agency L325
Langton, Becca L353
Leigh Feldman Literary L359
Leon, Nina L360
Maidment, Olivia L386
Maltese, Alyssa L387
Margaret K. McElderry Books P228
Maurer, Shari L397
McBride, Juliana L399
Midsummer Dream House M207
Milusich, Grace L412
North, The M225
Ostby, Kristin L452
Otago University Press P269
Pages, Saribel L453
Pan Macmillan Australia P274
Parker, Elana Roth L455
Pass, Marina de L456
Pestritto, Carrie L467
Phaidon Press P287
Phelan, Beth L470
Philips, Ariana L471
Posner, Marcy L480
Preston, Amanda L484
Ramer, Susan L486
Robinson, Quressa L497
Rofe, Jennifer L500
Romano, Annie L502
Ross, Whitney L507
Rushall, Kathleen L512
Rutherford, Laetitia L513
Seager, Chloe L524
Siobhan, Aiden L539
Soloway, Jennifer March L544
Sparsile Books P359
Spout Press P360

Stringer, Marlene	L554	
Swainson, Joanna	L561	
Symonds, Laurel	L565	
Takikawa, Marin	L566	
Topping, Antony	L577	
Torrey House Press, LLC	P390	
Tran, Jennifer Chen	L578	
Trudel, Jes	L579	
Tyndale House Publishers, Inc.	P397	
Vallum	M328	
Victoria Sanders & Associates LLC	L584	
Weiman, Paula	L592	
Weiss, Alexandra	L593	
Weitzner, Tess	L594	
Whatnall, Michaela	L598	
Williams, Laura	L603	
Williamson, Jo	L604	
Wilson, Desiree	L606	
Yeoh, Rachel	L612	
Young, Claudia	L614	
Zone 3	M353	

Contemporary Crime
See more broadly: Contemporary; Crime

Contemporary Culture
See more broadly: Contemporary; Culture
- InterVarsity Press (IVP) ... P193
- Kahn, Ella Diamond ... L314

Contemporary Fantasy
See more broadly: Contemporary; Fantasy
- Belton, Maddy ... L049
- Potter, Madison ... L481

Contemporary Politics
See more broadly: Contemporary; Politics

Contemporary Romance
See more broadly: Romance
- Afonso, Thais ... L007
- Aldridge, Kaylyn ... L010
- Bloodhound Books ... P052
- Bradford Literary Agency ... L073
- Bradford, Laura ... L074
- Carina Press ... P073
- Choc Lit ... P085
- Cichello, Kayla ... L117
- Fabien, Samantha ... L186
- Friedman, Rebecca ... L219
- Harper, Logan ... L267
- Inscriptions Literary Agency ... L289
- Leon, Nina ... L360
- Lindsay Literary Agency ... L366
- Lineberry, Isabel ... L367
- Maltese, Alyssa ... L387
- Nichols, Mariah ... L438
- Potter, Madison ... L481
- Sourcebooks Casablanca ... P351
- Tannenbaum, Amy ... L568
- Turner Publishing ... P394
- Tyndale House Publishers, Inc. ... P397
- Williamson, Jo ... L604

Contemporary Women's Fiction
See more broadly: Contemporary; Women's Fiction
- Danko, Margaret ... L140
- Eason, Lynette ... L169
- Sourcebooks Landmark ... P356

Cookery
See more broadly: Food and Drink
See more specifically: Recipes; Regional Cooking; Vegetarian Cooking
- Arcadia Publishing ... P020
- Bal, Emma ... L032
- Barrett, Emily ... L040
- Basalt Books ... P034
- Baumer, Jan ... L044
- Beaumont, Diana ... L046
- Bernardi, Amanda ... L056
- Betsy Amster Literary Enterprises ... L059

Better Homes and Gardens	M051	
Bradford Literary Agency	L073	
Cedar Fort	P076	
Chang, Nicola	L109	
Chiotti, Danielle	L113	
Clarke, Caro	L118	
Crown Publishing Group, The	P103	
Danko, Margaret	L140	
Darga, Jon Michael	L141	
DeBlock, Liza	L149	
Derviskadic, Dado	L151	
Doug Grad Literary Agency	L161	
Draper, Claire	L162	
Einstein, Susanna	L173	
Ekus Group, The	L176	
Ekus, Sally	L177	
Ellis-Martin, Sian	L180	
Evans, Kate	L185	
Fernando, Kimberly	L198	
Galvin, Lori	L226	
Globe Pequot Press, The	P145	
Graham, Stacey	L247	
Hancock House Publishers	P159	
Imagine Publishing	P186	
Ireland's Own	M172	
Irene Goodman Literary Agency (IGLA)	L291	
Joelle Delbourgo Associates, Inc.	L301	
Karen Gantz Literary Management	L319	
Kensington Publishing Corp.	P204	
Kimber, Natalie	L336	
Kitchen Press	P205	
Latshaw, Katherine	L355	
Levy, Yael	L362	
Lewinsohn Literary	L363	
MacLeod, Lauren	L383	
McCormick Literary	L400	
Merlin Unwin Books	P237	
Minnesota Historical Society Press	P241	
Murgolo, Karen	L427	
My Weekly	M215	
Nichols, Mariah	L438	
Niumata, Erin	L439	
Pacific Press Publishing Association	P273	
Peddle, Kay	L460	
Pelham, Imogen	L461	
People's Friend, The	M237	
Perry Literary	L466	
Phaidon Press	P287	
Philips, Ariana	L471	
Pickering, Juliet	L473	
Regina Ryan Books	L489	
Ross, Whitney	L507	
Rutherford, Laetitia	L513	
Seymour, Charlotte	L528	
Sheree Bykofsky Associates, Inc.	L532	
Stephens, Jenny	L549	
Sunbelt Publications, Inc.	P373	
Sweet, Emily	L563	
Texas A&M University Press	P381	
Transworld Publishers	P393	
Turner Publishing	P394	
University of Akron Press, The	P403	
University of Michigan Press, The	P410	
University of Texas Press	P414	
University of Virginia Press	P415	
W.W. Norton & Company, Inc.	P423	
Workman Publishing	P437	
Young, Claudia	L614	
Zack Company, Inc, The	L615	

Cotswolds
See more broadly: England

Country Lifestyle
See more broadly: Countryside; Lifestyle
- McNidder & Grace ... P232
- Virginia Wine & Country Life ... M331

Workman Publishing	P437	

Countryside
See more specifically: Country Lifestyle; Rural Living
- Kent Life ... M178
- Merlin Unwin Books ... P237

County Durham
See more broadly: England
See more specifically: Hartlepool

Couple Therapy
See more broadly: Relationships
- W.W. Norton & Company Ltd ... P422

Courtroom Dramas
See more broadly: Crime
- Alfred Hitchcock Mystery Magazine ... M016

Cozy Crime
See more broadly: Crime
- Cooper, Gemma ... L128

Cozy Fantasy
See more broadly: Fantasy
- Belton, Maddy ... L049
- Buckley, Louise ... L085
- Cooper, Maggie ... L129
- Faulks, Holly ... L187
- Finan, Ciara ... L200
- Goetz, Adria ... L241
- Irvine, Lucy ... L292
- Nathan, Abigail ... L433
- Potter, Madison ... L481
- Weiss, Alexandra ... L593

Cozy Mysteries
See more broadly: Mystery
- Bloodhound Books ... P052
- Buckley, Louise ... L085
- Gisondi, Katie ... L235
- Grunewald, Hattie ... L254
- Haley, Jolene ... L260
- Joffe Books ... P199
- Kathryn Green Literary Agency, LLC ... L322
- Keane Kataria Literary Agency ... L325
- Kensington Publishing Corp. ... P204
- Lakosil, Natalie ... L347
- Lyrical Press ... P225
- Nathan, Abigail ... L433
- Ostby, Kristin ... L452
- Pestritto, Carrie ... L467
- Terlip, Paige ... L570
- Tibbets, Anne ... L576
- Zack Company, Inc, The ... L615

Crafts
See more specifically: Ceramics; Crocheting; Embroidery; Knitting; Lacemaking; Model Making; Quilting; Sewing
- Arcadia Publishing ... P020
- Bajek, Lauren ... L031
- Bird Eye Books ... P048
- Cedar Fort ... P076
- Crown Publishing Group, The ... P103
- DK Publishing ... P112
- Draper, Claire ... L162
- Fogg, Jack ... L206
- Gale ... P139
- Gill Books ... P142
- Graham, Stacey ... L247
- Kensington Publishing Corp. ... P204
- Levy, Yael ... L362
- My Weekly ... M215
- Ohio University Press ... P261
- People's Friend, The ... M237
- Quirk Books ... P308
- Roberts, Soumeya Bendimerad ... L495
- Snowbooks ... P344
- Thames & Hudson Inc. ... P382
- Thames and Hudson Ltd ... P383
- Turner Publishing ... P394
- W.W. Norton & Company Ltd ... P422

306 Index | Creative Nonfiction

Yours ... M350
Creative Nonfiction
30 North ... M001
About Place Journal ... M004
Account, The ... M006
Arts & Letters ... M027
Atlantic Northeast ... M032
Bacopa Literary Review ... M038
Barren Magazine ... M041
BatCat Press ... P040
Belmont Story Review ... M047
Better Than Starbucks ... M052
Big Fiction ... M055
Blue Earth Review ... M059
Blue Mesa Review ... M060
Caribbean Writer, The ... M073
Carter, Rebecca ... L103
Chautauqua Literary Journal ... M077
Concho River Review ... M083
Conjunctions ... M084
Conjunctions Online ... M085
Conrad, Claire Paterson ... L125
Cooper, Maggie ... L129
Crazyhorse / Swamp Pink ... M093
Cream City Review ... M094
Creative Nonfiction ... M095
CutBank ... M099
El Portal ... M110
Emerge Literary Journal ... M111
Event ... M113
Faultline ... M118
Fiddlehead, The ... M121
Folio ... M126
Fourth River, The ... M131
Ginosko Literary Journal ... M140
Gutter Magazine ... M148
Half Mystic Journal ... M149
Harpur Palate ... M151
Hunger Mountain ... M161
Idaho Review ... M163
Identity Theory ... M164
Inspired Ink Literary ... L290
Irish Pages ... M173
Kimber, Natalie ... L336
Laxfield Literary Associates ... L356
Literary Mama ... M187
Louisiana Literature ... M194
MacGuffin, The ... M195
Malahat Review, The ... M197
Midway Journal ... M208
Moonday Mag ... M213
Nashville Review ... M217
New Welsh Reader ... M223
Otago University Press ... P269
Pacifica Literary Review ... M231
Passionfruit Review, The ... M234
Pleiades ... M238
Prole ... M250
River Styx ... M264
Roseway ... P317
Shenandoah ... M277
Sonder Magazine ... M287
South Carolina Review ... M289
Southern Humanities Review ... M290
Story Unlikely ... M300
Studio One ... M304
Tears in the Fence ... M311
Third Coast ... M315
Toad Hall Editions ... P387
Torrey House Press, LLC ... P390
Vagabond City ... M327
Virginia Quarterly Review, The ... M330
Windsor Review ... M342
Zone 3 ... M353
Creative Writing
See more broadly: Writing
Bloomsbury Academic ... P053
Graywolf Press ... P152
Salt Publishing ... P322
Scifaikuest ... M270
SmokeLong Quarterly ... M283
Stinging Fly, The ... M299
Creativity
Berrett-Koehler Publishers ... P046
Blue Star Press ... P056
Brewin Books Ltd ... P062
Kube Publishing ... P209
Literary Mama ... M187
O'Neill, Molly ... L446
Stipes Publishing ... P371
Susan Schulman Literary Agency ... L557
Cricket
See more broadly: Sport
Scratching Shed Publishing ... P331
Crime
See more specifically: Contemporary Crime; Courtroom Dramas; Cozy Crime; Crime Thrilllers; Detective Fiction; Domestic Noir; Hardboiled Crime; High Concept Crime; Historical Crime; Noir; Organised Crime; Police; Police Procedural; Upmarket Crime
Adams, Seren ... L004
Adsett, Alex ... L005
Alfred Hitchcock Mystery Magazine ... M016
Andrade, Hannah ... L015
Arcadia Publishing ... P020
Armstrong, Susan ... L026
Arthurson, Wayne ... L027
Asabi Publishing ... P022
Barr, Nicola ... L039
Barrett, Emily ... L040
Bartholomew, Jason ... L041
Baxter, Veronique ... L045
Berlyne, John ... L055
Blair Partnership, The ... L064
Bloodhound Books ... P052
Bloomsbury Academic ... P053
Bolton, Camilla ... L067
Brace, Samantha ... L072
Buckley, Louise ... L085
Burke, Kate ... L088
Campbell, Charlie ... L094
Carter, Rebecca ... L103
Clarke, Caro ... L118
Cochran, Alexander ... L120
Colwill, Charlotte ... L121
Coombes, Clare ... L127
Countryside Books ... P099
Curtis Brown ... L135
Danko, Margaret ... L140
Darley Anderson Agency, The ... L143
Demblon, Gabrielle ... L150
Diversion Books ... P111
Dolin, Lily ... L157
Doug Grad Literary Agency ... L161
Dundurn ... P118
Einstein, Susanna ... L173
Ellis-Martin, Sian ... L180
Epicenter Press Inc. ... P124
Faulks, Holly ... L187
Ferguson, Hannah ... L194
Fernandez, Rochelle ... L197
Fernando, Kimberly ... L198
Fernwood Publishing ... P131
Finan, Ciara ... L200
for Authors, A ... L209
Forrester, Jemima ... L210
Foxx, Kat ... L213
Furniss, Eugenie ... L224
Future Fire, The ... M135
Getzler, Josh ... L229
Gill Books ... P142
Glenister, Emily ... L238
Goose Lane Editions ... P148
Grunewald, Hattie ... L254
Haley, Jolene ... L260
Harper, Logan ... L267
Hayden, Viola ... L271
Heathfield, Laura ... L273
History Press, The ... P174
Hiyate, Sam ... L281
Hordern, Kate ... L286
Icon Books Ltd ... P180
Inscriptions Literary Agency ... L289
J. Gordon Shillingford Publishing ... P194
JMD Media / DB Publishing ... P198
Joffe Books ... P199
Judith Murdoch Literary Agency ... L309
Kahn, Ella Diamond ... L314
Kaliszewska, Joanna ... L315
Kane Literary Agency ... L316
Kensington Publishing Corp. ... P204
Keren, Eli ... L330
Kim, Julia ... L334
Kracht, Elizabeth ... L341
Lakosil, Natalie ... L347
Lambert, Sophie ... L348
Langlee, Lina ... L352
Langtons International ... L354
Leamington Books ... P211
Leon, Nina ... L360
MacDonald, Emily ... L378
MacLeod, Lauren ... L383
Maidment, Olivia ... L386
Marr, Jill ... L389
Marshall, Jen ... L391
McNidder & Grace ... P232
Milburn, Madeleine ... L411
Mills & Boon ... P240
Molloy, Jess ... L414
Monoray ... P246
Morrell, Imogen ... L417
Mortimer, Michele ... L418
Murray, Judith ... L428
Mushens, Juliet ... L430
Muswell Press ... P250
Mysterious Press, The ... P252
Nathan, Abigail ... L433
NBM Publishing ... P254
Neely, Rachel ... L434
O'Shea, Amy ... L447
Orenda Books ... P267
Pan Macmillan Australia ... P274
Pass, Marina de ... L456
Pen & Ink Designs Publishing ... P280
Perez Literary & Entertainment ... L463
Perez, Kristina ... L464
Perry Literary ... L466
PEW Literary ... L468
Philips, Ariana ... L471
Pine, Gideon ... L475
Poisoned Pen Press ... P297
Polygon ... P298
Power, Anna ... L482
Preston, Amanda ... L484
Regina Ryan Books ... L489
Reid, Janet ... L490
Riccardi, Francesca ... L492
Richter, Rick ... L493
Rogers, Coleridge & White Ltd ... L501
Romano, Annie ... L502
Savvides, Marilia ... L520
Schofield, Hannah ... L522
Seymour, Charlotte ... L528
Shestopal, Camilla ... L534
Silk, Julia ... L535
Snowbooks ... P344
Soho Press ... P348

Access more listings online at www.firstwriter.com

Index | Current Affairs 307

Soloway, Jennifer March L544
Sparsile Books P359
Story Unlikely M300
Stringer, Marlene L554
Swainson, Joanna L561
Thorneycroft, Euan L574
Topping, Antony L577
Transworld Publishers P393
Turner Publishing P394
University of Alberta Press P404
University of California Press P406
University of North Texas Press P412
Unseen Press P417
Victoria Sanders & Associates LLC L584
W.W. Norton & Company Ltd P422
W.W. Norton & Company, Inc. P423
Williams, Laura L603
Wilson, Ed L607
Wolfpack Publishing P432
Wood, Caroline L608
Wood, Ed L609
Young, Claudia L614
Zack Company, Inc, The L615

Crime Thrilllers
See more broadly: Crime; Thrillers
Hannah Sheppard Literary Agency L262

Crocheting
See more broadly: Crafts

Cryptozoology
See more broadly: Supernatural / Paranormal
Llewellyn Worldwide Ltd P219

Cuba
See more broadly: Caribbean
Pureplay Press P306

Cultural Commentary
See more broadly: Commentary; Culture
Carter, Rebecca L103

Cultural Criticism
See more broadly: Culture
Cavanagh, Claire L107
Combemale, Chris L122
Crown P101
Eisenmann, Caroline L175
Feminist Studies M119
Fuentes, Sarah L222
Graywolf Press P152
Levy, Yael L362
Lewis, Alison L364
Lilliput Press, The P217
Mendia, Isabel L403
Morrell, Imogen L417
New England Review M220
Peepal Tree Press P278
Pelham, Imogen L461
Phillips, Aemilia L472
Power, Anna L482
Stephens, Jenny L549
Takahe M309
Usselman, Laura L581
Virginia Quarterly Review, The M330
Yale Review, The M344

Cultural History
See more broadly: Culture; History
Asabi Publishing P022
Derviskadic, Dado L151
Icon Books Ltd P180
Kahn, Ella Diamond L314
Keren, Eli L330
Kirby, Robert L338
McCormick Literary L400
Moorhead, Max L416
Mulcahy Sweeney Literary Agency L423
Perez Literary & Entertainment L463
Perez, Kristina L464
Phaidon Press P287
Ramer, Susan L486
Seymour, Charlotte L528
Takikawa, Marin L566
Unicorn P402
Zack Company, Inc, The L615

Culture
See more specifically: Contemporary Culture; Cultural Commentary; Cultural Criticism; Cultural History; Ethnic; Folklore, Myths, and Legends; Jewish Culture; Multicultural; Popular Culture; Postcolonialism; Sub-Culture; Visual Culture; Youth Culture
African American Review M009
Afsana Press P005
Alabama Heritage M013
Albemarle M015
Arte Publico Press P021
Asabi Publishing P022
Atlanta Magazine M030
Atlantic Northeast M032
Baffler, The M039
Barr, Anjanette L038
Basalt Books P034
Baylor University Press P041
Bear Deluxe Magazine, The M044
Berghahn Books Ltd P045
Boston Review M062
Brattle Agency LLC, The L077
Britain Magazine M066
British Academy, The P063
British Museum Press, The P064
Cambridge University Press P068
Caribbean Writer, The M073
Carr, Jamie L101
Cavanagh, Claire L107
Chanchani, Sonali L108
Clarke, Caro L118
Cocoa Girl M080
Commonweal M082
Compassiviste Publishing P097
Conversation (UK), The M087
Cooper, Maggie L129
Cowboys & Indians M091
Cricket M096
Danko, Margaret L140
Dawson, Liza L148
DK Publishing P112
Dundurn P118
Edelstein, Anne L171
Edenborough, Sam L172
Epicenter Press Inc. P124
Fazzari, Hillary L188
Fellows, Abi L193
Feminist Studies M119
Fernwood Publishing P131
Foster, Clara L211
Fox, Aram L212
Geiger, Ellen L227
Ghahremani, Lilly L230
Goldstein, Veronica L244
Granger, David L250
Hakim, Serene L259
Hancock House Publishers P159
Heymont, Lane L277
Hildebrand, Cole L280
History Press, The P174
HopeRoad P176
Ig Publishing P182
Image M166
International Publishers P191
Island Online M175
Jessica Kingsley Publishers P197
Johnson, Jared L303
Joy Harris Literary Agency, Inc. L308
Julien, Ria L312
Kahn, Ella Diamond L314
Kent Life M178
Kim, Jennifer L333
Kim, Julia L334
Krienke, Mary L343
Kube Publishing P209
Landfall M182
Lightner, Kayla L365
London Grip M188
London Review of Books M191
LSU Press P223
Macdougall, Laura L379
Mack, Kate L381
Manoa M199
marie claire M200
Marion Boyars Publishers P229
Minnesota Historical Society Press P241
Mortimer, Michele L418
New Statesman M222
Nolan, Laura L441
O'Neill, Molly L446
Oxford Review of Books M230
Oxford University Press P272
Peter Lang P285
Phaidon Press P287
Phillips, Aemilia L472
Posner, Marcy L480
Power Cut Lite M247
Purdue University Press P305
Pureplay Press P306
Quadrant Magazine M254
Rocky Mountain Books P315
Salt Publishing P322
Sanders, Rayhane L517
Savannah Magazine M269
Scottish Field M272
Sierra M281
Singing Dragon P340
Society for Promoting Christian Knowledge (SPCK) P345
Spackman, James L547
Square Mile Magazine M298
Sweren, Becky L564
Texas A&M University Press P381
This England M316
Threepenny Review, The M317
Times Literary Supplement (TLS), The M318
Tyndale House Publishers, Inc. P397
Unfit Magazine M326
University of Akron Press, The P403
University of Alberta Press P404
University of Iowa Press P408
University of Michigan Press, The P410
University of North Texas Press P412
University of Texas Press P414
University of Virginia Press P415
Victoria Sanders & Associates LLC L584
W.W. Norton & Company Ltd P422
W.W. Norton & Company, Inc. P423
Wasafiri M338
Willms, Kathryn L605
Yankee Magazine M345
Yorkshire Life M348

Current Affairs
Alcock, Michael L009
Annette Green Authors' Agency L021
Bartholomew, Jason L041
Basic Books P035
Baxter, Veronique L045
Brouckaert, Justin L083
Canadian Dimension M072
Chiotti, Danielle L113
Compassiviste Publishing P097
Crown P101
Curran, Sabhbh L134
Dana Newman Literary, LLC L138
Diversion Books P111
Dystel, Jane L167

Enslow Publishers, Inc. P123
Gill Books P142
Gordon, Andrew L245
Hanbury Agency, The L261
Icon Books Ltd P180
Joelle Delbourgo Associates, Inc. L301
Karen Gantz Literary Management L319
Kim, Julia L334
Kube Publishing P209
Levy, Yael L362
Marr, Jill L389
Massachusetts Review, The M202
Mulcahy Sweeney Literary Agency L423
Mundy, Toby L426
New Statesman M222
Oxford Review of Books M230
Peddle, Kay L460
Perez Literary & Entertainment L463
Perez, Kristina L464
Power, Anna L482
Scratching Shed Publishing P331
Seren Books P335
Sheree Bykofsky Associates, Inc. L532
Singh, Amandeep L538
Southwest Review M293
Strothman, Wendy L555
Sweet, Emily L563
Thayer, Henry L572
Turner Publishing P394
Tyndale House Publishers, Inc. P397
University of Georgia Press P407
University of Texas Press P414
University of Virginia Press P415
Victoria Sanders & Associates LLC L584
W.W. Norton & Company Ltd P422
Yale University Press (London) P438
Yankee Magazine M345
Zack Company, Inc, The L615
Cyber Security
See more broadly: Computers
BCS (British Computer Society) P042
Cyberpunk
See more broadly: Science Fiction
Afonso, Thais L007
Edenborough, Sam L172
Story Unlikely M300
Cycling
See more broadly: Sport
See more specifically: Cycling Guides; Gravel Cycling
Countryside Books P099
Duncan Petersen Publishing Limited P117
Pocket Mountains P296
Cycling Guides
See more broadly: Cycling
Sigma Press P337
Dance
See more broadly: Performing Arts
Bowlin, Sarah L071
Brick M065
University of Michigan Press, The P410
Dark
See more specifically: Dark Academia; Dark Fantasy; Dark Humour; Dark Romance; Dark Thrillers
Belton, Maddy L049
Black Static M057
Burke, Kate L088
Curran, Sabhbh L134
Fellows, Abi L193
Ferguson, T.S. L195
Fuentes, Sarah L222
Goldblatt, Rachel L243
Kavanagh, Jade L323
Kenny, Julia L329
Lovell, Jake L372

Morrell, Imogen L417
Nelson, Patricia L437
Neon M219
Phillips, Aemilia L472
Salt Publishing P322
Steed, Hayley L548
Takikawa, Marin L566
Williams, Laura L603
Williamson, Jo L604
Dark Academia
See more broadly: Campus Novels; Dark
Buckley, Louise L085
Faulks, Holly L187
Niv, Daniel L440
Pass, Marina de L456
Pierce, Rosie L474
Potter, Madison L481
Seager, Chloe L524
Steed, Hayley L548
Dark Fantasy
See more broadly: Dark; Fantasy
Andrade, Hannah L015
Potter, Madison L481
Sinister Stoat Press P341
Sluytman, Antoinette Van L541
Dark Humour
See more broadly: Comedy / Humour; Dark
Andrade, Hannah L015
Carroll, Megan L102
Charnace, Edwina de L110
Cichello, Kayla L117
Dolin, Lily L157
Killingley, Jessica L332
Thwaites, Steph L575
Dark Magic
See more broadly: Magic
Woods, Bryony L610
Dark Romance
See more broadly: Dark; Romance
Fazzari, Hillary L188
Dark Thrillers
See more broadly: Dark; Thrillers
Cochran, Alexander L120
Darts
See more broadly: Sport
Data and Information Systems
See more broadly: Computers
BCS (British Computer Society) P042
Facet Publishing P127
Information Today, Inc. P188
Decorating
See more broadly: Interior Design
Homes & Antiques M158
Red Magazine M259
Deep Sea Fishing
See more broadly: Fishing
Deer
See more broadly: Animals
Dementia
See more broadly: Mental Health
See more specifically: Alzheimer's
Purdue University Press P305
Depression
See more broadly: Psychology
Free Spirit Publishing P136
Singing Dragon P340
W.W. Norton & Company Ltd P422
Derbyshire
See more broadly: England
Design
See more specifically: Graphic Design; Interior Design
Arcadia Publishing P020
Architectural Review, The M025
Atlanta Magazine M030
Bernardi, Amanda L056

Bloomsbury Academic P053
Carter, Rebecca L103
Cedar Fort P076
Colourpoint Educational P095
Cottage Life M090
Fogg, Jack L206
Gemini Books P140
Gill Education P143
Lund Humphries Limited P224
Marshall, Jen L391
MIT Press, The P244
No Starch Press, Inc. P258
Phaidon Press P287
Pimpernel Press P292
Prestel Publishing Ltd P302
Riposte M262
Roberts, Soumeya Bendimerad L495
Ross, Whitney L507
SOMA M285
Ten Speed Press P380
Thames & Hudson Inc. P382
Thames and Hudson Ltd P383
University of Alberta Press P404
W.W. Norton & Company Ltd P422
W.W. Norton & Company, Inc. P423
Wallpaper M337
Detective Fiction
See more broadly: Crime; Mystery
Blair Partnership, The L064
Grunewald, Hattie L254
Moore, Mary C. L415
Morrell, Imogen L417
Riccardi, Francesca L492
Detroit
See more broadly: Michigan
Devon
See more broadly: England
Diabetes
See more broadly: Health
Dialects
See more broadly: Language
Countryside Books P099
Diet
See more broadly: Food and Drink; Health
Bella M046
First For Women M122
Hammersmith Books P158
Regina Ryan Books L489
Zack Company, Inc, The L615
Digital Technology
See more broadly: Technology
Colourpoint Educational P095
International Society for Technology in Education (ISTE) P192
Dinosaurs
See more broadly: Prehistoric Animals
Disabilities
See more broadly: Health
Buckley, Louise L085
Fernwood Publishing P131
Free Spirit Publishing P136
HopeRoad P176
Krienke, Mary L343
Matte, Rebecca L395
University of Alberta Press P404
University of Michigan Press, The P410
W.W. Norton & Company, Inc. P423
Discrimination
See more broadly: Social Issues
See more specifically: Racism
Diverse Romance
See more broadly: Romance
Diversity
See more broadly: Social Issues
Dahlia Books P104
Nichols, Mariah L438

W.W. Norton & Company Ltd P422
Diving
See more broadly: Outdoor Activities
See more specifically: Scuba Diving
Dogs
See more broadly: Pets
Doug Grad Literary Agency L161
Merlin Unwin Books P237
Pass, Marina de L456
Domestic
See more specifically: Domestic Mystery;
Domestic Noir; Domestic Suspense;
Domestic Thriller
Baxter, Veronique L045
Goldblatt, Rachel L243
Hodges, Jodie L282
Pine, Gideon L475
Tibbets, Anne L576
Domestic Mystery
See more broadly: Domestic; Mystery
Tibbets, Anne L576
Domestic Noir
See more broadly: Crime; Domestic
Choc Lit P085
Joffe Books P199
Domestic Suspense
See more broadly: Domestic; Suspense
Bent, Jenny L053
Bloodhound Books P052
Fergusson, Julie L196
Galvin, Lori L226
Harper, Logan L267
Keren, Eli L330
Maltese, Alyssa L387
Reid, Janet L490
Simons, Tanera L536
Vance, Lisa Erbach L583
Domestic Thriller
See more broadly: Domestic; Thrillers
Kane Literary Agency L316
Scarlet P327
Selectric Artists L525
Dorset
See more broadly: England
Drama
Alaska Quarterly Review M014
Anvil Press Publishers P017
Bloomsbury Academic P053
Compassiviste Publishing P097
London Grip M188
Marion Boyars Publishers P229
Marshall, Jen L391
Massachusetts Review, The M202
New England Review M220
Pan Macmillan Australia P274
Seren Books P335
Tusculum Review, The M321
W.W. Norton & Company Ltd P422
Wells, Karmen L595
Williams, Katie L602
Drawing
See more broadly: Arts
Korero Press P208
Thames & Hudson Inc. P382
Drinks
See more broadly: Food and Drink
See more specifically: Beer; Cider; Whisky; Wine
Turner Publishing P394
Drugs
See more specifically: Cannabis
Enslow Publishers, Inc. P123
Dystopian Fiction
See more broadly: Speculative
Bennett, Laura L050
Blair Partnership, The L064
Liverpool Literary Agency, The L369

Mozley, Jack L422
Savvides, Marilia L520
Soler, Shania N. L543
Steed, Hayley L548
Turner Publishing P394
W.W. Norton & Company, Inc. P423
Wells, Karmen L595
Early Readers
Allen & Unwin P009
Andlyn L014
Arcadia Publishing P020
Bonnier Books (UK) P059
Charlesbridge Publishing P081
Cherry Lake Publishing Group P083
Curtis Brown L135
DK Publishing P112
Dunow, Carlson & Lerner Agency L166
Finegan, Stevie L203
Firefly P133
Flynn, Amy Thrall L205
Gemini Books P140
Guppy Books P155
Hare, Jessica L266
Holroyde, Penny L285
Irvine, Lucy L292
Kane Press P202
Kube Publishing P209
Lantana Publishing P210
Little Bigfoot P218
Piccadilly Press P291
Richter, Rick L493
Scholastic P329
Scholastic UK P330
Simply Read Books P339
Skylark Literary L540
Thames & Hudson Inc. P382
Tilbury House Publishers P385
Tippermuir Books P386
W.W. Norton & Company Ltd P422
Walker Books P424
Earth Science
See more broadly: Science
See more specifically: Climate Science; Geology;
Oceanography
Gale P139
Taylor & Francis Group P378
East Asia
See more broadly: Asia
Charnace, Edwina de L110
East Midlands
See more broadly: The Midlands
Bearded Badger Publishing Co. P043
East of Centre P119
Tra[verse] P392
Eastern Europe
See more broadly: Europe
Indiana University Press P187
Eating Disorders
See more broadly: Psychology
W.W. Norton & Company Ltd P422
Ebooks
Lerner Publishing Group P213
Economics
Arcadia Publishing P020
Berrett-Koehler Publishers P046
Bloomsbury Academic P053
Cambridge University Press P068
Campbell, Charlie L094
Canadian Dimension M072
Christie, Jennifer L116
Conversation (UK), The M087
Crown P101
Dundurn P118
Evans, Kate L185
Fernwood Publishing P131
Finan, Ciara L200

Gale P139
Gill Education P143
Gold SF P146
Gordon, Andrew L245
Harvard University Press P165
Holloway, Sally L284
Icon Books Ltd P180
Julien, Ria L312
Kensington Publishing Corp. P204
London Review of Books M191
Mentor Books P236
Peter Lang P285
Pluto Press P295
Singh, Amandeep L538
Stipes Publishing P371
Susan Schulman Literary Agency L557
Taylor & Francis Group P378
Turner Publishing P394
University of California Press P406
University of Michigan Press, The P410
W.W. Norton & Company Ltd P422
W.W. Norton & Company, Inc. P423
Yale University Press (London) P438
Zack Company, Inc, The L615
Education
See more specifically: Physical Education;
Reading
Ann Arbor Observer M022
Arcadia Publishing P020
Berghahn Books Ltd P045
Bloomsbury Academic P053
Cambridge University Press P068
CharlottesvilleFamily M076
Colourpoint Educational P095
Conversation (UK), The M087
DK Publishing P112
Evan-Moor Educational Publishers P125
Feminist Press, The P130
Fernwood Publishing P131
Free Spirit Publishing P136
Gale P139
Gill Education P143
Global Lion Intellectual Property
  Management, Inc. L239
Harvard University Press P165
International Society for Technology in
  Education (ISTE) P192
Kensington Publishing Corp. P204
Mentor Books P236
Muscato, Nate L429
Peter Lang P285
Practical Pre-School Books P300
Scholastic P329
Sentient Publications P334
Taylor & Francis Group P378
Tyndale House Publishers, Inc. P397
UCL Press P398
University of Alberta Press P404
University of Michigan Press, The P410
University of Virginia Press P415
W.W. Norton & Company Ltd P422
W.W. Norton & Company, Inc. P423
Yale University Press (London) P438
Electrical Contracting
See more broadly: Building / Construction
Electronic Music
See more broadly: Music
Velocity Press P420
Embroidery
See more broadly: Crafts; Hobbies
Emergency Services
See more specifically: Search and Rescue
Energy
See more broadly: Technology
Ruralite M266

Engineering
- Arcadia Publishing P020
- Bloomsbury Academic P053
- Cambridge University Press P068
- Kane Press............................... P202
- Kensington Publishing Corp. P204
- Oxford University Press P272
- Purdue University Press............ P305
- Racecar Engineering M255
- Stipes Publishing P371
- Symonds, Laurel L565
- Taylor & Francis Group P378
- University of Michigan Press, The............P410
- Wilson, Desiree L606

England
See more broadly: United Kingdom
See more specifically: Cambridgeshire; Cheshire; Cotswolds; County Durham; Derbyshire; Devon; Dorset; Essex; Gloucestershire; Herefordshire; Kent; Lancashire; Lincolnshire; London; Norfolk; Northern England; Shropshire; Somerset; Staffordshire; Suffolk; The Midlands; West Country; Worcestershire; Yorkshire
- This England M316

English
See more broadly: Language
- Autumn Publishing Ltd P025
- Gill Education P143
- Mentor Books P236
- Peter Lang P285
- W.W. Norton & Company, Inc. P423

Entertainment
See more specifically: Celebrity
- Ann Arbor Observer M022
- Brailsford, Karen L075
- Cedar Fort P076
- Compassiviste Publishing P097
- Cowboys & Indians M091
- FRA (Futerman, Rose, & Associates)....L214
- History Press, The P174
- Ireland's Own M172
- Pride M249
- Turner Publishing P394
- Virginia Wine & Country Life .. M331
- Zack Company, Inc, The L615

Entrepreneurship
See more broadly: Business
- Campos, Vanessa...................... L095
- Entrepreneur M112
- Kruger Cowne L344
- Trudel, Jes L579
- Zack Company, Inc, The L615

Environment
See more broadly: Nature
See more specifically: Climate Science; Sustainable Living
- Basalt Books............................ P034
- Bear Deluxe Magazine, The M044
- Berghahn Books Ltd P045
- Bernardi, Amanda L056
- Bloomsbury Academic P053
- Cambridge University Press P068
- Canadian Dimension M072
- Carter, Rebecca L103
- Conrad, Claire Paterson L125
- Conversation (UK), The M087
- Cottage Life M090
- Danko, Margaret L140
- Dawntreader, The M102
- Dawson, Liza.......................... L148
- Diana Finch Literary Agency... L154
- Future Fire, The M135
- Gold SF P146
- Hildebrand, Cole L280
- Icon Books Ltd P180
- Island Online........................... M175
- Julien, Ria L312
- Kirby, Robert L338
- Kracht, Elizabeth L341
- Lambert, Sophie L348
- Lilliput Press, The P217
- LSU Press P223
- Minnesota Historical Society Press P241
- New England Review............... M220
- New Internationalist................. M221
- Ohio University Press P261
- Oxford University Press P272
- Pelagic P279
- Pluto Press P295
- Posner, Marcy L480
- Preston, Amanda L484
- Purdue University Press........... P305
- Regina Ryan Books L489
- Riposte M262
- Rocky Mountain Books P315
- Rushall, Kathleen L512
- Sierra M281
- Sorg, Arley.............................. L546
- Stipes Publishing P371
- Takikawa, Marin L566
- Taylor & Francis Group P378
- Texas A&M University Press... P381
- Trudel, Jes L579
- University of Alberta Press P404
- University of California Press .. P406
- University of Georgia Press P407
- University of Michigan Press, The P410
- University of North Texas Press............. P412
- University of Texas Press......... P414
- University of Virginia Press P415
- University Press of Colorado ... P416
- W.W. Norton & Company Ltd .. P422
- Weiss, Alexandra L593
- Willms, Kathryn L605
- Zack Company, Inc, The L615

Epistolary
- W.W. Norton & Company, Inc. P423

Equality
See more broadly: Social Issues
- Atyeo, Charlotte L028
- Berrett-Koehler Publishers P046

Equestrian
See more broadly: Sport
- Merlin Unwin Books P237

Erotic
See more specifically: Erotic Romance
- Asabi Publishing P022
- Charles River Press P080
- Cleis Press P091
- Curtis Brown........................... L135
- Dreamspinner Press P115
- Knigge, Sheyla........................ L339
- Lyrical Press P225
- NBM Publishing P254
- W.W. Norton & Company, Inc. P423
- Zack Company, Inc, The L615

Erotic Romance
See more broadly: Erotic; Romance
- Barone Literary Agency L036
- Bradford Literary Agency L073
- Bradford, Laura....................... L074
- Carina Press P073
- Cleis Press P091
- Dreamspinner Press P115

Essays
- aaduna M003
- About Place Journal M004
- Acumen M007
- African American Review........ M009
- Agni M011
- Albemarle M015
- And Other Poems M020
- Arboreal M023
- Arc M024
- Auroras & Blossoms PoArtMo Anthology M035
- Bee, The.................................. M045
- Big Fiction M055
- Blue Earth Review.................. M059
- Boston Review M062
- Brick....................................... M065
- Caribbean Writer, The M073
- Cheshire M078
- Clarke, Caro L118
- Concho River Review.............. M083
- Contemporary Verse 2 .... M086
- Creative Nonfiction M095
- Dalhousie Review, The............ M100
- Daunt Books Publishing P106
- Dublin Review, The................. M107
- Eisenmann, Caroline................ L175
- Feminist Studies M119
- First Line, The M123
- Five Points M124
- Folio M126
- Fugue M133
- Georgia Review, The............... M139
- Graywolf Press........................ P152
- Gulf Coast: A Journal of Literature and Fine Arts M147
- Gutter Magazine M148
- Hotel Amerika M160
- Idaho Review M163
- Identity Theory M164
- Image M166
- Indiana Review........................ M167
- Irish Pages M173
- Island...................................... M174
- Island Online........................... M175
- Jamii Publishing P196
- Kavya Kishor M177
- Kenyon Review, The............... M179
- Landfall M182
- Latshaw, Katherine.................. L355
- Literary Mama......................... M187
- London Magazine, The............ M190
- Long Poem Magazine M192
- Lost Lake Folk Opera Magazine.............. M193
- Louisiana Literature................. M194
- Malahat Review, The............... M197
- Manchester Review, The M198
- Manoa M199
- Massachusetts Review, The..... M202
- Methuen Publishing Ltd P238
- Michigan Quarterly Review..... M204
- Mid-American Review M206
- Midway Journal M208
- Missouri Review, The.............. M209
- Modern Haiku M211
- Nashville Review..................... M217
- New England Review............... M220
- New Welsh Reader M223
- Oxford Poetry M229
- Oxford Review of Books M230
- PN Review M240
- Poetry M241
- Poetry Birmingham Literary Journal M242
- Poetry Ireland Review M243
- Power Cut Lite M247
- Qu Literary Magazine.............. M253
- Quadrant Magazine M254
- Reactor M258
- Riposte M262
- Rutman, Jim............................ L514
- Shenandoah M277
- Shipwreckt Books Publishing Company P336

Shooter Literary Magazine M279
Sinister Wisdom M282
SmokeLong Quarterly M283
Snowflake Magazine M284
South Carolina Review M289
Southern Humanities Review M290
Southern Review, The M291
Stinging Fly, The M299
Strange Horizons M301
Sunspot Literary Journal M305
Tahoma Literary Review M308
Takahe M309
Tears in the Fence M311
Times Literary Supplement (TLS), The ... M318
Tolka M319
Torrey House Press, LLC P390
Tusculum Review, The M321
Vagabond City M327
Vallum M328
W.W. Norton & Company Ltd P422
Waccamaw M335
Wallace Stevens Journal, The M336
Wasafiri M338
West Branch M339
Wet Grain M341
Windsor Review M342
Woods, Bryony L610
Yale Review, The M344

Essex
See more broadly: England

Ethnic
See more broadly: Culture
Texas A&M University Press P381
University Press of Colorado P416

Ethnic Groups
See more broadly: Society
See more specifically: African American; Asian American; Black People; Caribbean Diaspora; Italian American; Maori; Native Americans; Slavs
Bloomsbury Academic P053
Chanchani, Sonali L108
Dawson, Liza L148
Ellis-Martin, Sian L180
Gold SF P146
Macdougall, Laura L379
Pluto Press P295
Pride M249
Sanders, Rayhane L517
Simpson, Cara Lee L537
Singing Dragon P340
University of Alberta Press P404
University of Michigan Press, The ... P410

Ethnography
See more broadly: Sociology

Europe
See more broadly: Regional
See more specifically: Austria; Central Europe; Eastern Europe; France; Germany; Ireland; Italy; Romania; Russia; Scandinavia; Spain; Switzerland; United Kingdom
Barr, Nicola L039
Ohio University Press P261
University of Alberta Press P404

European History
See more broadly: History
Brattle Agency LLC, The L077
University of Virginia Press P415
Zack Company, Inc, The L615

Evangelism
See more broadly: Christianity
Brown, Megan L084
College Press Publishing P094
Tyndale House Publishers, Inc. P397

Events
See more specifically: Weddings

Evolution
See more broadly: Biology
Thames & Hudson Inc. P382

Exercise
See more broadly: Fitness
Bloomsbury Academic P053

Experimental
Abridged M005
Alaska Quarterly Review M014
Black Warrior Review M058
Carter, Rebecca L103
Compassiviste Publishing P097
Conrad, Claire Paterson L125
Fiction M120
Glacier, The M141
Gold SF P146
Goldstein, Veronica L244
Half Mystic Journal M149
Hildebrand, Cole L280
Island M174
Island Online M175
Joy Harris Literary Agency, Inc. L308
Midsummer Dream House M207
Second Factory M274
Spout Press P360
Tahoma Literary Review M308
Ugly Duckling Presse P399
Wilson, Ed. L607

Experimental Poetry
Better Than Starbucks M052
Half Mystic Journal M149
MacGuffin, The M195

FBI
See more broadly: Police

Fabulism
See more broadly: Magical Realism
Cooper, Maggie L129
Harris, Erin L268
Marini, Victoria L388
O'Neill, Molly L446

Fairy Tales
Belton, Maddy L049
Burby, Danielle L087
Eisenbraun, Nicole L174
Ferguson, T.S. L195
Harris, Erin L268
Seager, Chloe L524
Wilson, Desiree L606
Woods, Bryony L610

Falconry
See more broadly: Sport
Hancock House Publishers P159

Family
See more broadly: Relationships
See more specifically: Children; Family Therapy; Parenting
Arcadia Publishing P020
Brace, Samantha L072
Brewin Books Ltd P062
Brown, Megan L084
Burke, Kate L088
Cabello, Analia L092
Carroll, Megan L102
Cedar Fort P076
Chanchani, Sonali L108
CharlottesvilleFamily M076
Cho, Catherine L114
Conville, Clare L126
Cooper, Gemma L128
Crowley, Sheila L132
Danaczko, Melissa L139
Danko, Margaret L140
Ellis-Martin, Sian L180
Fazzari, Hillary L188
Fernwood Publishing P131
Free Spirit Publishing P136

Goldblatt, Rachel L243
Grunewald, Hattie L254
Haley, Jolene L260
Hannah Sheppard Literary Agency .. L262
Johnson, Jared L303
Kensington Publishing Corp. P204
Levy, Yael L362
Lewinsohn Literary L363
Macdougall, Laura L379
MacKenzie, Joanna L382
Maidment, Olivia L386
Murdoch Books Australia P249
O'Grady, Niamh L445
O'Neill, Molly L446
Plitt, Carrie L477
Riccardi, Francesca L492
Roberts, Soumeya Bendimerad L495
Sasquatch Books P325
Seager, Chloe L524
Shipwreckt Books Publishing
    Company P336
Society for Promoting Christian
    Knowledge (SPCK) P345
Soloway, Jennifer March L544
Steed, Hayley L548
Thwaites, Steph L575
Turner Publishing P394
Tyndale House Publishers, Inc. P397
Vance, Lisa Erbach L583
W.W. Norton & Company, Inc. P423

Family Saga
Armstrong, Susan L026
Baxter, Veronique L045
Beaumont, Diana L046
Charnace, Edwina de L110
Choc Lit P085
Dolin, Lily L157
Ellis-Martin, Sian L180
Evans, Kate L185
Figueroa, Melanie L199
Harris, Erin L268
Kim, Jennifer L333
Macdougall, Laura L379
Milburn, Madeleine L411
Niv, Daniel L440
Pass, Marina de L456
People's Friend Pocket Novels M236
Philips, Ariana L471
Pierce, Rosie L474
Rushall, Kathleen L512
Simpson, Cara Lee L537
Takikawa, Marin L566
Tran, Jennifer Chen L578
Wickers, Chandler L600
Yeoh, Rachel L612

Family Therapy
See more broadly: Family
W.W. Norton & Company Ltd P422

Fantasy
See more specifically: Commercial Fantasy; Contemporary Fantasy; Cozy Fantasy; Dark Fantasy; Gaslamp Fantasy; Grounded Fantasy; High / Epic Fantasy; Historical Fantasy; Light Fantasy; Literary Fantasy; Low Fantasy; Magic; Magical Realism; Romantasy; Science Fantasy; Slipstream; Superhero Fantasy; Sword and Sorcery; Upmarket Fantasy; Urban Fantasy
3 Seas Literary Agency L001
Adsett, Alex L005
Afonso, Thais L007
Alekseii, Keir L011
Ange, Anna L019
Armada, Kurestin L024
Armstrong, Susan L026
Arthurson, Wayne L027

Claim your free access to www.firstwriter.com: See p.367

Asimov's Science Fiction M029
Aurealis M034
Baen Books P029
Bajek, Lauren L031
Baror International, Inc. L037
Belton, Maddy L049
Bennett, Laura L050
Bent, Jenny L053
Berlyne, John L055
BFS Horizons M053
BFS Journal M054
Bhasin, Tamanna L062
Bradford Literary Agency L073
Brannan, Maria L076
BSFA Review, The M067
Burby, Danielle L087
Candlemark & Gleam P069
Carroll, Megan L102
Chevais, Jennifer L111
Cho, Catherine L114
Clarke, Caro L118
Cochran, Alexander L120
Colwill, Charlotte L121
Compassiviste Publishing P097
Cooper, Gemma L128
Crystal Magazine M098
Curtis Brown L135
Cusick, John L136
Danko, Margaret L140
Diversion Books P111
Dreamspinner Press P115
DSP Publications P116
Edenborough, Sam L172
Every Day Fiction M114
Fabien, Samantha L186
Feminist Press, The P130
Ferguson, T.S. L195
Fernandez, Rochelle L197
Figueroa, Melanie L199
Finan, Ciara L200
Forrester, Jemima L210
Foster, Clara L211
Gahan, Isobel L225
Gilbert, Tara L233
Gisondi, Katie L235
Global Lion Intellectual Property
   Management, Inc. L239
Goff, Ellen L242
Gunic, Masha L256
Hakim, Serene L259
Hannigan, Carrie L263
Hawn, Molly Ker L270
Hensley, Chelsea L274
Hodges, Jodie L282
Hogrebe, Christina L283
Interzone M171
Irvine, Lucy L292
Jamieson, Molly L296
Joelle Delbourgo Associates, Inc. L301
Joffe Books P199
Johnson, Jared L303
Julie Crisp Literary Agency L311
Kean, Taylor Martindale L324
Kensington Publishing Corp. P204
Killingley, Jessica L332
Kim, Jennifer L333
Knigge, Sheyla L339
Langlee, Lina L352
Langton, Becca L353
Leon, Nina L360
Lightner, Kayla L365
Lineberry, Isabel L367
Liverpool Literary Agency, The L369
Maltese, Alyssa L387
Marr, Jill L389
Matte, Rebecca L395
Mihell, Natasha L410
Molloy, Jess L414
Moonday Mag M213
Murray, Judith L428
Muscato, Nate L429
Mushens, Juliet L430
Nathan, Abigail L433
NBM Publishing P254
Neely, Rachel L434
Nelson, Kristin L436
Neo-opsis Science Fiction Magazine M218
Niv, Daniel L440
O'Brien, Lee L444
Pages, Saribel L453
Perez Literary & Entertainment L463
Perez, Kristina L464
Perotto-Wills, Martha L465
Pestritto, Carrie L467
Phelan, Beth L470
Piatkus Books P289
Plant, Zoe L476
Posner, Marcy L480
Potter, Madison L481
Reactor M258
Robinson, Quressa L497
Rofe, Jennifer L500
Ross, Whitney L507
Salazar, Des L515
Schwizer, Fabienne L523
Seager, Chloe L524
Selectric Artists L525
Seventh Agency L527
Shoreline of Infinity M280
Singh, Amandeep L538
Siobhan, Aiden L539
SmashBear Publishing P342
Snowbooks P344
Soloway, Jennifer March L544
Sorg, Arley L546
Sternig & Byrne Literary Agency L550
Story Unlikely M300
Strange Horizons M301
Stringer, Marlene L554
Symonds, Laurel L565
Terlip, Paige L570
Tibbets, Anne L576
Tor Publishing Group P388
Tor Teen P389
Torrey House Press, LLC P390
Transworld Publishers P393
Turner Publishing P394
Udden, Jennifer L580
Victoria Sanders & Associates LLC L584
W.W. Norton & Company, Inc. P423
Watterson, Jessica L591
Weiman, Paula L592
Weiss, Alexandra L593
Whatnall, Michaela L598
Wilson, Desiree L606
Wilson, Ed L607
Zack Company, Inc, The L615
Zeno Agency L617

Farm Equipment
See more broadly: Farming
Old Pond Publishing P262
Virginia Wine & Country Life M331

Farming
See more broadly: Agriculture
See more specifically: Animal Husbandry; Farm Equipment; Urban Farming
Henley Hall Press P171
Old Pond Publishing P262

Fashion
See more specifically: Hairstyles
Bella M046
Bloomsbury Academic P053
Cavanagh, Claire L107
Cowboys & Indians M091
Curran, Sabhbh L134
Derviskadic, Dado L151
First For Women M122
Gemini Books P140
Hello! M155
Levy, Yael L362
Mack, Kate L381
marie claire M200
Marshall, Jen L391
My Weekly M215
Norfolk & Suffolk Bride M224
Phaidon Press P287
Pride M249
Ramer, Susan L486
Red Magazine M259
Ross, Whitney L507
Scottish Field M272
Seventeen M275
SOMA M285
Thames & Hudson Inc. P382
Thames and Hudson Ltd P383
Vogue M334
Wallpaper M337
Yale University Press (London) P438
Yorkshire Women's Life Magazine M349
Yours M350

Feminism
See more broadly: Gender
See more specifically: Intersectional Feminism
Atyeo, Charlotte L028
Barr, Nicola L039
Baxter, Veronique L045
Burby, Danielle L087
Cleis Press P091
Conrad, Claire Paterson L125
Dolin, Lily L157
Draper, Claire L162
Feminist Press, The P130
Feminist Studies M119
Fernwood Publishing P131
Finan, Ciara L200
Finegan, Stevie L203
Forrester, Jemima L210
Future Fire, The M135
Hannah Sheppard Literary Agency L262
Latshaw, Katherine L355
Levy, Yael L362
Mortimer, Michele L418
New Internationalist M221
Perez Literary & Entertainment L463
Perez, Kristina L464
Phillips, Aemilia L472
Pluto Press P295
Seal Press P332

Feminist Romance
See more broadly: Romance
Cooper, Maggie L129

Fertility
See more broadly: Health
Singing Dragon P340

Fiction
3 Seas Literary Agency L001
30 North M001
404 Ink P001
A.M. Heath & Company Limited,
   Author's Agents L002
aaduna M003
Able Muse Press P003
About Place Journal M004
Account, The M006
Acheampong, Kwaku L003
Adams, Seren L004
Adsett, Alex L005
Afonso, Thais L007

Index | Fiction

African American Review … M009
African Voices … M010
Afsana Press … P005
Afterglow Books … P006
Agency (London) Ltd, The … L008
Agni … M011
Alaska Quarterly Review … M014
Albert Whitman & Company … P007
Aldridge, Kaylyn … L010
Alekseii, Keir … L011
Alfred Hitchcock Mystery Magazine … M016
Algonquin Books … P008
Alice Williams Literary … L012
Allen & Unwin … P009
Alternating Current Press … P010
Ambassador Speakers Bureau & Literary Agency … L013
American Mystery Classics … P012
American Short Fiction … M018
Amethyst Review … M019
And Other Stories … P013
Andersen Press Ltd … P014
Andlyn … L014
Andrade, Hannah … L015
Andrew Nurnberg Associates, Ltd … L016
Andrews McMeel Publishing … P015
Ange, Anna … L019
Anne Clark Literary Agency … L020
Annette Green Authors' Agency … L021
Antony Harwood Limited … L022
Anvil Press Publishers … P017
Apple Tree Literary Ltd … L023
April Gloaming … P018
Arachne Press … P019
Arboreal … M023
Arcadia Publishing … P020
Armada, Kurestin … L024
Arms, Victoria Wells … L025
Armstrong, Susan … L026
Arte Publico Press … P021
Arthurson, Wayne … L027
Arts & Letters … M027
Asabi Publishing … P022
Asimov's Science Fiction … M029
Atlantic Northeast … M032
Atyeo, Charlotte … L028
Aurealis … M034
Aurora Metro Press … P024
Auroras & Blossoms PoArtMo Anthology … M035
Babybug … M037
Bacopa Literary Review … M038
Baen Books … P029
Baffler, The … M039
Bajek, Lauren … L031
Bald and Bonkers Network LLC … P030
Bandit Fiction … M040
Barbara, Stephen … L034
Barone Literary Agency … L036
Baror International, Inc. … L037
Barr, Anjanette … L038
Barr, Nicola … L039
Barren Magazine … M041
Bartholomew, Jason … L041
BatCat Press … P040
Bath Literary Agency … L042
Bauman, Erica … L043
Baxter, Veronique … L045
Beano, The … M043
Bear Deluxe Magazine, The … M044
Bearded Badger Publishing Co. … P043
Beaumont, Diana … L046
Bee, The … M045
Begum, Salma … L047
Belmont Story Review … M047
Beloit Fiction Journal … M048

Belton, Maddy … L049
Bennett, Laura … L050
Bent Agency (UK), The … L051
Bent Agency, The … L052
Bent, Jenny … L053
Berdinsky, Kendall … L054
Berlyne, John … L055
Bess Press … P047
Betancourt Literary … L057
Betsy Amster Literary Enterprises … L059
Better Than Starbucks … M052
Beverley Slopen Literary Agency … L060
Bewley, Elizabeth … L061
BFS Horizons … M053
Bhasin, Tamanna … L062
Big Fiction … M055
Black & White Publishing Ltd … P049
Black Moon Magazine … M056
Black Static … M057
Black Warrior Review … M058
Blackstaff Press … P051
Blair Partnership, The … L064
Blake Friedmann Literary Agency Ltd … L065
Bloodhound Books … P052
Blue Earth Review … M059
Blue Mesa Review … M060
BOA Editions, Ltd. … P057
Bolton, Camilla … L067
Bonnier Books (UK) … P059
Book Group, The … L068
Books For All Times … P060
Bookseeker Agency … L069
Borstel, Stefanie Sanchez Von … L070
Boston Review … M062
Bowlin, Sarah … L071
Boyfriend Village … M064
Brace, Samantha … L072
Bradford Literary Agency … L073
Bradford, Laura … L074
Brannan, Maria … L076
Brattle Agency LLC, The … L077
Brewin Books Ltd … P062
Bright Agency (UK), The … L078
Bright Agency (US), The … L079
Brooks, Savannah … L080
Brotherstone Creative Management … L081
Brotherstone, Charlie … L082
Buckley, Louise … L085
Bukowski, Danielle … L086
Burby, Danielle … L087
Burke, Kate … L088
Burns, Camille … L089
CAA (London) … L091
Cabello, Analia … L092
Cadno … P067
Cafe Irreal, The … M071
Cameron, Kimberley … L093
Campbell, Charlie … L094
Candlemark & Gleam … P069
Candy Jar Books … P070
Canterbury Literary Agency … L096
Captivate Press … P072
Caribbean Writer, The … M073
Carina Press … P073
Caroline Davidson Literary Agency … L099
Carr, Jamie … L101
Carroll, Megan … L102
Carter, Rebecca … L103
Cartey, Claire … L104
Caskie, Robert … L105
Cassava Republic Press UK … P074
Cavanagh, Claire … L107
CB Editions … P075
Cedar Fort … P076
Chanchani, Sonali … L108
Chang, Nicola … L109

Chapman … M075
Charisma House … P079
Charles River Press … P080
Charlesbridge Publishing … P081
Charnace, Edwina de … L110
Chautauqua Literary Journal … M077
Cherry Lake Publishing Group … P083
Cheshire … M078
Chevais, Jennifer … L111
Child's Play (International) Ltd … P084
Children's Books North Agency … L112
Chiotti, Danielle … L113
Cho, Catherine … L114
Choc Lit … P085
Christensen, Erica … L115
Cicada Books … P087
Cichello, Kayla … L117
Cinnamon Press … P088
Claret Press … P089
Clarke, Caro … L118
Clarke, Catherine … L119
Classical Comics … P090
Cleis Press … P091
Coach House Books … P092
Cobblestone … M079
Cochran, Alexander … L120
Cola … M081
Colwill, Charlotte … L121
Combemale, Chris … L122
Comma Press … P096
Comparato, Andrea … L123
Compass Talent … L124
Compassiviste Publishing … P097
Concho River Review … M083
Conjunctions … M084
Conjunctions Online … M085
Conrad, Claire Paterson … L125
Conville, Clare … L126
Coombes, Clare … L127
Cooper, Gemma … L128
Cooper, Maggie … L129
Crandall, Becca … L130
Crannog Magazine … M092
Crazyhorse / Swamp Pink … M093
Cream City Review … M094
Creative Roots Studio … L131
Crowley, Sheila … L132
Crown Publishing Group, The … P103
Crystal Magazine … M098
Curran, Sabhbh … L134
Curtis Brown … L135
Cusick, John … L136
CutBank … M099
Dahlia Books … P104
Dalhousie Review, The … M100
Dana Newman Literary, LLC … L138
Danaczko, Melissa … L139
Danko, Margaret … L140
Darga, Jon Michael … L141
Darhansoff & Verrill Literary Agents … L142
Darley Anderson Agency, The … L143
Darley Anderson Children's … L144
Daunt Books Publishing … P106
David Godwin Associates … L145
Davies, Olivia … L147
Dawntreader, The … M102
Dawson, Liza … L148
DeBlock, Liza … L149
Dedalus Ltd … P107
Deep Overstock Magazine … M103
Demblon, Gabrielle … L150
Denis Kitchen Publishing Company Co., LLC … P109
DHH Literary Agency Ltd … L152
Diamond Kahn and Woods (DKW) Literary Agency Ltd … L153

Claim your free access to www.firstwriter.com: See p.367

Dillsworth, Elise	L156
Diversion Books	P111
Dodo Ink	P113
Dolin, Lily	L157
Dominguez, Adriana	L158
Don Congdon Associates, Inc.	L159
Donald Maass Literary Agency	L160
Doubleday (UK)	P114
Doug Grad Literary Agency	L161
Draper, Claire	L162
Dream Catcher	M106
Dreamspinner Press	P115
DSP Publications	P116
Dublin Review, The	M107
Dundurn	P118
Dunham Literary, Inc.	L163
Dunn, Ben	L164
DunnFogg	L165
Dunow, Carlson & Lerner Agency	L166
Dystel, Jane	L167
Eason, Lynette	L169
East of Centre	P119
Eddison Pearson Ltd	L170
Edelstein, Anne	L171
Edenborough, Sam	L172
Eerdmans Books for Young Readers	P120
Einstein, Susanna	L173
Eisenbraun, Nicole	L174
Eisenmann, Caroline	L175
Ekphrastic Review, The	M109
El Portal	M110
Elaine Markson Literary Agency	L178
Elaine Steel	L179
Ellis-Martin, Sian	L180
Emerge Literary Journal	M111
Enitharmon Editions	P122
Epicenter Press Inc.	P124
Eunice McMullen Children's Literary Agent Ltd	L182
Evan Marshall Agency, The	L183
Evans, Kate	L185
Event	M113
Every Day Fiction	M114
Everything With Words	P126
Fabien, Samantha	L186
Fabula Argentea	M115
Fairlight Books	P128
Faulks, Holly	L187
Faultline	M118
Fazzari, Hillary	L188
Feldmann, Kait Lee	L190
Feldstein Agency, The	L191
Felicity Bryan Associates	L192
Fellows, Abi	L193
Feminist Press, The	P130
Feminist Studies	M119
Ferguson, Hannah	L194
Ferguson, T.S.	L195
Fergusson, Julie	L196
Fernandez, Rochelle	L197
Fiction	M120
Fiddlehead, The	M121
Figueroa, Melanie	L199
Finan, Ciara	L200
Finch, Rebeka	L202
Finegan, Stevie	L203
Firefly	P133
First Line, The	M123
Five Points	M124
Flannery Literary	L204
Flash: The International Short-Short Story Magazine	M125
Flynn, Amy Thrall	L205
Fogg, Jack	L206
Folio	M126
Folio Literary Management, LLC	L207
for Authors, A	L209
Forrester, Jemima	L210
Foster, Clara	L211
Fourth River, The	M131
Fox, Aram	L212
Foxx, Kat	L213
Frankel, Valerie	L215
Fraser Ross Associates	L216
Free Spirit Publishing	P136
Friedman, Claire	L217
Friedman, Jessica	L218
Friedman, Rebecca	L219
Friedrich Agency LLC, The	L220
Frogmore Papers, The	M132
Fuentes, Sarah	L222
Fugue	M133
Fuller, Lisa	L223
Furniss, Eugenie	L224
Future Fire, The	M135
Gahan, Isobel	L225
Galvin, Lori	L226
Gargoyle Online	M137
Geiger, Ellen	L227
Gemini Books	P140
Georgia Review, The	M139
Getzler, Josh	L229
Ghahremani, Lilly	L230
Ghosh Literary	L231
Ghosh, Anna	L232
Gilbert, Tara	L233
Gill Books	P142
Gillam, Bianca	L234
Ginosko Literary Journal	M140
Gisondi, Katie	L235
Glacier, The	M141
Glass Literary Management LLC	L236
Glenister, Emily	L238
Global Lion Intellectual Property Management, Inc.	L239
Goderich, Miriam	L240
Goetz, Adria	L241
Goff, Ellen	L242
Gold SF	P146
Goldblatt, Rachel	L243
Goldstein, Veronica	L244
Goodman Beck Publishing	P147
Goose Lane Editions	P148
Gordon, Andrew	L245
Graffeg Childrens	P151
Graham Maw Christie Literary Agency	L246
Graham, Stacey	L247
Graham, Susan	L248
Grain Literary Magazine	M143
Grajkowski, Kara	L249
Granta	M144
Graywolf Lab	M145
Graywolf Press	P152
Greene & Heaton Ltd	L251
Greenstone Literary	L252
Gruber, Pam	L253
Grunewald, Hattie	L254
Guernica Editions	P153
Gulf Coast: A Journal of Literature and Fine Arts	M147
Gunic, Masha	L256
Guppy Books	P155
Gutter Magazine	M148
Hachette Book Group	P156
Haggerty, Taylor	L258
Hakim, Serene	L259
Haley, Jolene	L260
Half Mystic Journal	M149
Half Mystic Press	P157
Hanbury Agency, The	L261
Hanging Loose	M150
Hannah Sheppard Literary Agency	L262
Hannigan, Carrie	L263
Hansen, Stephanie	L264
Happy Yak	P161
Hare, Jessica	L266
Harper, Logan	L267
Harpur Palate	M151
Harris, Erin	L268
Hashtag Press	P166
Hawk, Susan	L269
Hawn, Molly Ker	L270
Hawthorne Books	P167
Hayden, Viola	L271
Headley, David H.	L272
Heathfield, Laura	L273
Heavy Traffic	M153
Helix, The	M154
Hensley, Chelsea	L274
Hernandez, Saritza	L275
Hernando, Paloma	L276
Heymont, Lane	L277
Hildebrand, Cole	L280
Hiyate, Sam	L281
Hodder & Stoughton Ltd	P175
Hodges, Jodie	L282
Hogrebe, Christina	L283
Holroyde, Penny	L285
HopeRoad	P176
Hordern, Kate	L286
Hornsley, Sarah	L287
Host Publications	P177
Hotel Amerika	M160
Hunger Mountain	M161
Hwang, Annie	L288
I-70 Review	M162
Idaho Review	M163
Identity Theory	M164
Ig Publishing	P182
IgKids	P183
Igloo Books Limited	P184
Image	M166
Indiana Review	M167
Inkandescent	P190
Inscriptions Literary Agency	L289
Inspired Ink Literary	L290
Interzone	M171
Ireland's Own	M172
Irene Goodman Literary Agency (IGLA)	L291
Irish Pages	M173
Irvine, Lucy	L292
Island	M174
Island Online	M175
Jamieson, Molly	L296
Jamii Publishing	P196
Janklow & Nesbit UK Ltd	L297
Jean V. Naggar Literary Agency, The	L299
JMD Media / DB Publishing	P198
Joelle Delbourgo Associates, Inc.	L301
Joffe Books	P199
John Murray Press	P200
Johnson, Jared	L303
Jonathan Clowes Ltd	L304
Jones, Philip Gwyn	L307
Joy Harris Literary Agency, Inc.	L308
Judith Murdoch Literary Agency	L309
Julie Crisp Literary Agency	L311
Julien, Ria	L312
K2 Literary	L313
Kahn, Ella Diamond	L314
Kaliszewska, Joanna	L315
Kane Literary Agency	L316
Kane Press	P202
Kantor, Camille	L317
Kardon, Julia	L318
Karen Gantz Literary Management	L319

Access more listings online at www.firstwriter.com

Index | *Fiction* **315**

Kate Barker Literary, TV, & Film Agency L320
Kate Nash Literary Agency L321
Kates Hill Press, The P203
Kathryn Green Literary Agency, LLC L322
Kavanagh, Jade L323
Kavya Kishor M177
Kean, Taylor Martindale L324
Keane Kataria Literary Agency L325
Keeffe, Sara O' L326
Kenny, Julia L329
Kensington Publishing Corp. P204
Kenyon Review, The M179
Keren, Eli L330
Ki Agency Ltd L331
Kids Alive! M180
Killingley, Jessica L332
Kim, Jennifer L333
Kim, Julia L334
Kim, Sally M. L335
Kimber, Natalie L336
Kimberley Cameron & Associates L337
Kirby, Robert L338
Knigge, Sheyla L339
Kore Press P207
Kracht, Elizabeth L341
Krichevsky, Stuart L342
Krienke, Mary L343
KT Literary L345
Kube Publishing P209
Lakosil, Natalie L347
Lambert, Sophie L348
Landfall M182
Lane, Helen L349
Langlee, Lina L352
Langton, Becca L353
Langtons International L354
Lantana Publishing P210
Latshaw, Katherine L355
Laxfield Literary Associates L356
Leach, Saskia L357
Leamington Books P211
Leapfrog Press P212
Leeke, Jessica L358
Leigh Feldman Literary L359
Leon, Nina L360
Lerner Publishing Group P213
Levitt, Sarah L361
Levy, Yael L362
Lewinsohn Literary L363
Lewis, Alison L364
Lighthouse M185
Lightner, Kayla L365
Lightning Books P215
Lilliput Press, The P217
Lindsay Literary Agency L366
Lineberry, Isabel L367
Liss, Laurie L368
Literary Mama M187
Little Bigfoot P218
Liverpool Literary Agency, The L369
Loft Press, Inc. P220
London Magazine, The M190
Lost Lake Folk Opera Magazine M193
Lotus Lane Literary L371
Loudhailer Books P222
Louisiana Literature M194
Lovell, Jake L372
Lutyens and Rubinstein L375
Lyrical Press P225
MacDonald, Emily L378
Macdougall, Laura L379
MacGregor & Luedeke L380
MacGuffin, The M195
MacKenzie, Joanna L382
MacLeod, Lauren L383
Macmillan Children's Books P226
Madeleine Milburn Literary, TV & Film Agency L385
Maidment, Olivia L386
Malahat Review, The M197
Maltese, Alyssa L387
Manchester Review, The M198
Manilla Press P227
Manoa M199
Margaret K. McElderry Books P228
Marini, Victoria L388
Marion Boyars Publishers P229
Marr, Jill L389
Marsh Agency, The L390
Marshall, Jen L391
Massachusetts Review, The M202
Massie McQuilkin & Altman L394
Matte, Rebecca L395
Mattson, Jennifer L396
Maurer, Shari L397
McBride, Juliana L399
McCormick Literary L400
McNidder & Grace P232
Meetinghouse M203
Meridian Artists L404
Merlin Unwin Books P237
Merullo, Annabel L405
Metamorphosis Literary Agency L406
Methuen Publishing Ltd P238
Mic Cheetham Literary Agency L407
Michel, Caroline L408
Michigan Quarterly Review M204
Micromance Magazine M205
Mid-American Review M206
Midsummer Dream House M207
Midway Journal M208
Mihell, Natasha L410
Milburn, Madeleine L411
Milkweed Editions P239
Mills & Boon P240
Milusich, Grace L412
Missouri Review, The M209
Molloy, Jess L414
Moody Publishers P247
Moonday Mag M213
Moore, Mary C. L415
Moorhead, Max L416
Morrell, Imogen L417
Mortimer, Michele L418
Motala, Tasneem L419
Movable Type Management L420
Moylett, Lisa L421
Mozley, Jack L422
MQR Mixtape M214
Mulcahy Sweeney Literary Agency L423
Mundy, Toby L426
Murray, Judith L428
Muscato, Nate L429
Mushens, Juliet L430
Muswell Press P250
My Weekly M215
Myrmidon Books Ltd P251
Mysterious Press, The P252
Mystery Magazine M216
Napolitano, Maria L431
Nashville Review M217
Nathan, Abigail L433
NBM Publishing P254
Neely, Rachel L434
Nelson Literary Agency, LLC L435
Nelson, Kristin L436
Nelson, Patricia L437
Neo-opsis Science Fiction Magazine M218
Neon M219
New England Review M220
New Welsh Reader M223
Nichols, Mariah L438
Niumata, Erin L439
Niv, Daniel L440
Northbank Talent Management L442
Northern Gravy M226
O'Brien, Lee L444
O'Grady, Niamh L445
O'Neill, Molly L446
O'Shea, Amy L447
Obsidian: Literature in the African Diaspora M227
Oh MG Press P260
Old Street Publishing Ltd P263
Oldcastle Books Group P264
Olswanger, Anna L450
Ooligan Press P265
Orca Book Publishers P266
Orenda Books P267
Orphans Publishing P268
Ostby, Kristin L452
Oxford Review of Books M230
Pacific Press Publishing Association P273
Pacifica Literary Review M231
Pages, Saribel L453
Pan Macmillan Australia P274
Panorama M232
Paradigm Talent and Literary Agency L454
Paris Review, The M233
Parker, Elana Roth L455
Parthian Books P275
Pass, Marina de L456
Passionfruit Review, The M234
Patterson, David L457
Patterson, Emma L458
Paul S. Levine Literary Agency L459
PB and Yay! Books P277
Peepal Tree Press P278
Pelham, Imogen L461
Pen & Ink Designs Publishing P280
Penzler Publishers P282
People's Friend Pocket Novels M236
People's Friend, The M237
Perez Literary & Entertainment L463
Perez, Kristina L464
Perotto-Wills, Martha L465
Perspectives Books P283
Pestritto, Carrie L467
PEW Literary L468
Phelan, Beth L470
Philips, Ariana L471
Phillips, Aemilia L472
Phoenix Moirai P288
Piatkus Books P289
Piccadilly Press P291
Pickering, Juliet L473
Pierce, Rosie L474
Pine, Gideon L475
Pineapple Press P293
Plant, Zoe L476
Pleiades M238
Plitt, Carrie L477
Ploughshares M239
Poisoned Pen Press P297
Polygon P298
Portobello Literary L479
Posner, Marcy L480
Potter, Madison L481
Power Cut Lite M247
Power, Anna L482
Press 53 ..... P301
Preston, Amanda L484
Procrastinating Writers United P303
Prole M250
Pureplay Press P306
Pushing Out the Boat M252
Qu Literary Magazine M253

Quadrant Magazine	M254	
Quirk Books	P308	
Ramer, Susan	L486	
Ransom Publishing Ltd	P312	
Redhammer	L488	
Reid, Janet	L490	
Reilly, Milly	L491	
Renard Press Ltd	P313	
Riccardi, Francesca	L492	
Richter, Rick	L493	
River Styx	M264	
Roberts, Soumeya Bendimerad	L495	
Robinson, Quressa	L497	
Rocking Chair Books	L499	
Rofe, Jennifer	L500	
Rogers, Coleridge & White Ltd	L501	
Romano, Annie	L502	
Root, Holly	L504	
Rosenberg Group, The	L505	
Roseway	P317	
Ross, Whitney	L507	
Rossito, Stefanie	L508	
Rubin Pfeffer Content, LLC	L509	
Ruby Fiction	P319	
Rudy Agency, The	L510	
Rupert Crew Ltd	L511	
Rushall, Kathleen	L512	
Rutherford, Laetitia	L513	
Rutman, Jim	L514	
Saddlebag Dispatches	M267	
Salazar, Des	L515	
Salt Publishing	P322	
Sanchez, Kaitlyn	L516	
Sanders, Rayhane	L517	
Sandstone Press	P323	
Sant, Kelly Van	L518	
Savvides, Marilia	L520	
Sayle Literary Agency, The	L521	
Scarlet	P327	
Schofield, Hannah	L522	
Scholastic	P329	
Scholastic UK	P330	
Schwizer, Fabienne	L523	
Scratching Shed Publishing	P331	
Scribble	M273	
Seager, Chloe	L524	
Second Factory	M274	
Selectric Artists	L525	
Sentient Publications	P334	
Seren Books	P335	
Serra, Maria Cardona	L526	
Seventh Agency	L527	
Seymour, Charlotte	L528	
Shaw Agency, The	L529	
Shenandoah	M277	
Shesto Literary	L533	
Shestopal, Camilla	L534	
Shipwreckt Books Publishing Company	P336	
Shooter Literary Magazine	M279	
Shoreline of Infinity	M280	
Silk, Julia	L535	
Simons, Tanera	L536	
Simply Read Books	P339	
Simpson, Cara Lee	L537	
Singh, Amandeep	L538	
Sinister Stoat Press	P341	
Sinister Wisdom	M282	
Siobhan, Aiden	L539	
Skylark Literary	L540	
Sluytman, Antoinette Van	L541	
SmashBear Publishing	P342	
SmokeLong Quarterly	M283	
Snowbooks	P344	
Snowflake Magazine	M284	
Society for Promoting Christian Knowledge (SPCK)	P345	
Soho Press	P348	
Soler, Shania N.	L543	
Soloway, Jennifer March	L544	
Sonder Magazine	M287	
Sophie Hicks Agency	L545	
Sorg, Arley	L546	
Sourcebooks Casablanca	P351	
Sourcebooks Fire	P353	
Sourcebooks Horror	P354	
Sourcebooks Jabberwocky	P355	
Sourcebooks Landmark	P356	
Sourcebooks Wonderland	P357	
Sourcebooks Young Readers	P358	
South Carolina Review	M289	
Southern Humanities Review	M290	
Southern Review, The	M291	
Southwest Review	M293	
Southword Journal	M294	
Spackman, James	L547	
Sparsile Books	P359	
Spitball	M297	
Spout Press	P360	
SRL Publishing	P361	
Steed, Hayley	L548	
Sternig & Byrne Literary Agency	L550	
Steward House Publishers	P369	
Stinging Fly, The	M299	
Story Unlikely	M300	
StoryWise	L552	
Strange Horizons	M301	
Stringer Literary Agency LLC, The	L553	
Stringer, Marlene	L554	
Structo Magazine	M303	
Stuart Krichevsky Literary Agency, Inc.	L556	
Studio One	M304	
Sunbelt Publications, Inc.	P373	
Sunspot Literary Journal	M305	
Supplement, The	M306	
Susan Schulman Literary Agency	L557	
Susanna Lea Associates	L558	
Sutherland, Kari	L559	
Swainson, Joanna	L561	
Sweetgum Press	P375	
Symonds, Laurel	L565	
Tahoma Literary Review	M308	
Tailwinds Press	P376	
Takahe	M309	
Takikawa, Marin	L566	
Talbot, Emily	L567	
Tannenbaum, Amy	L568	
Tasman, Alice	L569	
Tears in the Fence	M311	
Temz Review, The	M312	
Terlip, Paige	L570	
Texas A&M University Press	P381	
Thames & Hudson Inc.	P382	
Thames and Hudson Ltd	P383	
Thayer, Henry	L572	
Theseus Agency, The	L573	
Thin Air Magazine	M314	
Thinkwell Books, UK	P384	
Third Coast	M315	
Thorneycroft, Euan	L574	
Threepenny Review, The	M317	
Thwaites, Steph	L575	
Tibbets, Anne	L576	
Tilbury House Publishers	P385	
Tippermuir Books	P386	
Toad Hall Editions	P387	
Tolka	M319	
Topping, Antony	L577	
Tor Publishing Group	P388	
Tor Teen	P389	
Torrey House Press, LLC	P390	
Tran, Jennifer Chen	L578	
Transworld Publishers	P393	
Tributaries	M320	
Trudel, Jes	L579	
Turner Publishing	P394	
Tusculum Review, The	M321	
Tyndale House Publishers, Inc.	P397	
Udden, Jennifer	L580	
Unbound Press	P400	
Unbridled Books	P401	
Under the Radar	M325	
Unfit Magazine	M326	
University of Alberta Press	P404	
University of Iowa Press	P408	
University of Maine Press	P409	
University of Michigan Press, The	P410	
University of North Texas Press	P412	
Usselman, Laura	L581	
Vagabond City	M327	
Valley Press	P418	
Vance, Lisa Erbach	L583	
Vane Women Press	P419	
Velocity Press	P420	
Vestal Review	M329	
Victoria Sanders & Associates LLC	L584	
Viney Agency, The	L585	
Viney, Charlie	L586	
Virginia Quarterly Review, The	M330	
Viz	M333	
W.W. Norton & Company Ltd	P422	
W.W. Norton & Company, Inc.	P423	
Waccamaw	M335	
Wade & Co Literary Agency	L588	
Walker Books	P424	
Walsh, Caroline	L589	
Wasafiri	M338	
Washington Writers' Publishing House	P425	
Watson, Little Ltd	L590	
Watterson, Jessica	L591	
Wee Book Company, The	P427	
Weiman, Paula	L592	
Weiss, Alexandra	L593	
Weitzner, Tess	L594	
Wells, Karmen	L595	
Weltz, Jennifer	L596	
West Branch	M339	
Westin, Erin Casey	L597	
Whatnall, Michaela	L598	
Whispering Buffalo Literary Agency	L599	
Wickers, Chandler	L600	
Williams, Laura	L603	
Williamson, Jo	L604	
Willms, Kathryn	L605	
Wilson, Desiree	L606	
Wilson, Ed	L607	
Windsor Review	M342	
Wolfpack Publishing	P432	
Wood, Caroline	L608	
Wood, Ed	L609	
Woods, Bryony	L610	
Woollard, Jessica	L611	
Words & Pictures	P433	
Wordsonthestreet	P434	
Wordsworth Editions	P435	
Workman Publishing	P437	
Yale Review, The	M344	
Yellow Mama Webzine	M346	
Yeoh, Rachel	L612	
YesYes Books	P439	
Young, Claudia	L614	
Yours Fiction – Women's Special Series	M351	
Zack Company, Inc, The	L615	
Zacker, Marietta B.	L616	
Zeno Agency	L617	

Index | Food 317

Zibby Books P440
Zoetrope: All-Story M352
Zone 3 M353
Zuckerbrot, Renee L618
Zuraw-Friedland, Ayla L619

Fiction as a Subject
See more broadly: Literature
Big Fiction M055

Fiction in Translation
American Short Fiction M018
And Other Stories P013
CB Editions P075
Charnace, Edwina de L110
Daunt Books Publishing P106
Dedalus Ltd P107
Faultline M118
Fiction M120
Five Points M124
Friedman, Jessica L218
Future Fire, The M135
Gulf Coast: A Journal of Literature and Fine Arts M147
Half Mystic Journal M149
Host Publications P177
Hunger Mountain M161
Indiana Review M167
Interzone M171
Irish Pages M173
Julien, Ria L312
Kenyon Review, The M179
Kim, Jennifer L333
Manoa M199
Massachusetts Review, The M202
Michigan Quarterly Review M204
Mid-American Review M206
Nashville Review M217
Orenda Books P267
Shenandoah M277
Southern Review, The M291
Stinging Fly, The M299
Structo Magazine M303
Sunspot Literary Journal M305
Tributaries M320
Yeoh, Rachel L612

Film Industry
See more broadly: Business
See more specifically: Cinemas / Movie Theaters
Global Lion Intellectual Property Management, Inc. L239

Film Scripts
Agency (London) Ltd, The L008
Andrews, Gina L018
Aurora Metro Press P024
AVAnti Productions & Management L029
Barnard, Arthur L035
Bell, Eva L048
Bolger, Maeve L066
Comparato, Andrea L123
Curtis Brown L135
Elaine Steel L179
Hickman, Emily L278
Inscriptions Literary Agency L289
JFL Agency L300
Judy Daish Associates Ltd L310
Kelleher, Sophie L327
Ki Agency Ltd L331
Lyon, Rebecca L376
Marion Boyars Publishers P229
Meridian Artists L404
Middleton, Leah L409
Mumby, Helen L425
Narrow Road Company, The L432
Paradigm Talent and Literary Agency L454
Qu Literary Magazine M253
Rochelle Stevens & Co. L498
Sunspot Literary Journal M305
Valerie Hoskins Associates L582
Victoria Sanders & Associates LLC L584
Williams, Katie L602

Films
See more broadly: Media
African American Review M009
Annette Green Authors' Agency L021
Berghahn Books Ltd P045
Bloomsbury Academic P053
BSFA Review, The M067
Canadian Dimension M072
Derviskadic, Dado L151
DK Publishing P112
Doug Grad Literary Agency L161
Feminist Press, The P130
Gordon, Andrew L245
Indiana University Press P187
Ireland's Own M172
Kim, Julia L334
My Weekly M215
New England Review M220
Ohio University Press P261
Oxford Review of Books M230
Phaidon Press P287
Plexus Publishing Limited P294
Polygon P298
Power Cut Lite M247
Red Magazine M259
Rutman, Jim L514
Sheree Bykofsky Associates, Inc. L532
Sierra M281
SOMA M285
Square Mile Magazine M298
Supplement, The M306
Thayer, Henry L572
Uncut M324
University of Alberta Press P404
University of California Press P406
University of Texas Press P414
W.W. Norton & Company Ltd P422
W.W. Norton & Company, Inc. P423
Yale Review, The M344
Zack Company, Inc, The L615

Finance
See more specifically: Accounting; Investments; Personal Finance; Taxation
BCS (British Computer Society) P042
Business & Accountancy Daily M068
Carr, Jamie L101
Cottage Life M090
Dawson, Liza L148
Entrepreneur M112
Furniss, Eugenie L224
Gale P139
Hay House Publishers P168
Kogan Page Ltd P206
Lightner, Kayla L365
marie claire M200
Salt Publishing P322
Strategic Finance M302
Sunbelt Publications, Inc. P373
Susan Schulman Literary Agency L557
Taylor & Francis Group P378
Tyndale House Publishers, Inc. P397
Zack Company, Inc, The L615

Firearms
See more broadly: Weapons

Fishing
See more broadly: Hunting
See more specifically: Deep Sea Fishing; Fly Fishing; Offshore Gamefishing
Hancock House Publishers P159
Merlin Unwin Books P237
River Hills Traveler M263

Fitness
See more broadly: Health
See more specifically: Exercise; Running
Arcadia Publishing P020
Crown Publishing Group, The P103
Dana Newman Literary, LLC L138
DK Publishing P112
Fernando, Kimberly L198
Healthy M152
Kensington Publishing Corp. P204
Levy, Yael L362
marie claire M200
Red Magazine M259
Square Mile Magazine M298
Tyndale House Publishers, Inc. P397
Yours M350
Zack Company, Inc, The L615

Florida
See more broadly: United States
See more specifically: Pensacola
Pineapple Press P293

Fly Fishing
See more broadly: Fishing

Folk Horror
See more broadly: Horror
Jamieson, Molly L296
Salt Publishing P322
Swainson, Joanna L561

Folklore, Myths, and Legends
See more broadly: Culture
See more specifically: Bigfoot
Afonso, Thais L007
Andrade, Hannah L015
Barr, Anjanette L038
Bauman, Erica L043
Belton, Maddy L049
Burby, Danielle L087
Cho, Catherine L114
Dawntreader, The M102
Edenborough, Sam L172
Ferguson, T.S. L195
Finch, Rebeka L202
Foster, Clara L211
Gruber, Pam L253
Haley, Jolene L260
Hancock House Publishers P159
Harris, Erin L268
History Press, The P174
Indiana University Press P187
Irvine, Lucy L292
Knigge, Sheyla L339
Lightner, Kayla L365
Marr, Jill L389
Pass, Marina de L456
Pineapple Press P293
Scots Magazine, The M271
Seager, Chloe L524
Soler, Shania N. L543
Sunbelt Publications, Inc. P373
Swainson, Joanna L561
Takikawa, Marin L566
Thames and Hudson Ltd P383
University of North Texas Press P412
University of Tennessee Press P413
Unseen Press P417
W.W. Norton & Company Ltd P422
W.W. Norton & Company, Inc. P423
Weiss, Alexandra L593
Williamson, Jo L604

Food
See more broadly: Food and Drink
See more specifically: Food History; Vegetarian Food
Alcock, Michael L009
Arms, Victoria Wells L025
Bal, Emma L032
Basalt Books P034
Baxter, Veronique L045

Bloomsbury Academic P053
Bradford Literary Agency L073
Brick M065
Cabello, Analia L092
Carr, Jamie L101
Chang, Nicola L109
CharlottesvilleFamily M076
Chiotti, Danielle L113
Clarke, Caro L118
Compass Talent L124
Cooper, Maggie L129
Curran, Sabhbh L134
Davies, Olivia L147
Derviskadic, Dado L151
Dolin, Lily L157
Ellis-Martin, Sian L180
Evans, Kate L185
Fernando, Kimberly L198
First For Women M122
Fogg, Jack L206
Foxx, Kat L213
Galvin, Lori L226
Goff, Ellen L242
Graffeg P150
Granger, David L250
Healthy M152
Hiyate, Sam L281
Joelle Delbourgo Associates, Inc. L301
Kim, Julia L334
Lambert, Sophie L348
Lilliput Press, The P217
LSU Press P223
MacLeod, Lauren L383
Marr, Jill L389
Morrell, Imogen L417
Murdoch Books Australia P249
Ohio University Press P261
Peddle, Kay L460
Phaidon Press P287
Philips, Ariana L471
Pickering, Juliet L473
Power, Anna L482
Ramer, Susan L486
Red Magazine M259
Reilly, Milly L491
Richter, Rick L493
Rutherford, Laetitia L513
Sasquatch Books P325
Savannah Magazine M269
Seymour, Charlotte L528
Somerset Life M286
Stephens, Jenny L549
Texas A&M University Press P381
Thames & Hudson Inc. P382
Topping, Antony L577
University of Akron Press, The P403
University of Alberta Press P404
University of California Press P406
University of Georgia Press P407
University of Iowa Press P408
University of Texas Press P414
University of Virginia Press P415
Yankee Magazine M345
Yours M350
Zack Company, Inc, The L615

Food History
See more broadly: Food
Bowlin, Sarah L071
University of North Texas Press P412

Food Journalism
See more broadly: Food and Drink; Journalism
Young, Claudia L614

Food and Drink
See more specifically: Cookery; Diet; Drinks; Food; Food Journalism; Nutrition; Restaurants

Andrews McMeel Publishing P015
Ann Arbor Observer M022
Atlanta Magazine M030
Berks County Living M049
Black & White Publishing Ltd P049
Cowboys & Indians M091
DK Publishing P112
Gill Books P142
Hernandez, Saritza L275
Kent Life M178
Kitchen Press P205
marie claire M200
Mulcahy Sweeney Literary Agency L423
My Weekly M215
Quirk Books P308
Scottish Field M272
Speciality Food M296
Square Mile Magazine M298
Sweet, Emily L563
Ten Speed Press P380
Virginia Wine & Country Life M331
W.W. Norton & Company Ltd P422
Willms, Kathryn L605
Yorkshire Life M348

Football / Soccer
See more broadly: Sport
See more specifically: Women's Football / Soccer
JMD Media / DB Publishing P198
Scratching Shed Publishing P331

Formal Poetry
Better Than Starbucks M052
Tahoma Literary Review M308

Formula One
See more broadly: Motorsports
Square Mile Magazine M298

Fortune Telling and Divination
See more broadly: Mysticism
See more specifically: Astrology; Horoscopes; Numerology; Palmistry; Tarot

Fossils
See more broadly: Geology

France
See more broadly: Europe
Irene Goodman Literary Agency (IGLA) L291
Peter Lang P285

Free Verse
Better Than Starbucks M052
MacGuffin, The M195
Tahoma Literary Review M308

French
See more broadly: Language
Colourpoint Educational P095
Gill Education P143
Mentor Books P236
Stipes Publishing P371

Friends
See more broadly: Social Groups
Carr, Jamie L101
Chanchani, Sonali L108
Chang, Nicola L109
Cooper, Gemma L128
Danaczko, Melissa L139
Ellis-Martin, Sian L180
Hannah Sheppard Literary Agency L262
Hashtag Press P166
Lewinsohn Literary L363
Macdougall, Laura L379
MacKenzie, Joanna L382
O'Neill, Molly L446
Ostby, Kristin L452
Pierce, Rosie L474
Plitt, Carrie L477
Riccardi, Francesca L492
Sanchez, Kaitlyn L516
Seager, Chloe L524

Tyndale House Publishers, Inc. P397
Vance, Lisa Erbach L583
Williams, Laura L603
Woods, Bryony L610

Funeral Industry
See more broadly: Business
Funeral Business Solutions M134

Furries
See more broadly: Animals
Sinister Stoat Press P341

Futurism
Kruger Cowne L344
Torrey House Press, LLC P390
Unfit Magazine M326

Gaelic
See more broadly: Language
Colourpoint Educational P095

Gambling
High Stakes Publishing P173

Games
See more broadly: Leisure
See more specifically: Chess; Computer and Video Games
Arcadia Publishing P020
Asabi Publishing P022
Cedar Fort P076
Kensington Publishing Corp. P204
Quirk Books P308
Sheree Bykofsky Associates, Inc. L532
W.W. Norton & Company Ltd P422

Gardening
See more broadly: Hobbies
Arcadia Publishing P020
Atlanta Magazine M030
Betsy Amster Literary Enterprises L059
Better Homes and Gardens M051
Cabello, Analia L092
Cedar Fort P076
Crown Publishing Group, The P103
DK Publishing P112
Doug Grad Literary Agency L161
Fernando, Kimberly L198
Gale P139
Garden Answers M136
Globe Pequot Press, The P145
Henley Hall Press P171
Kensington Publishing Corp. P204
Kent Life M178
Monacelli Press, The P245
My Weekly M215
Orphans Publishing P268
Pimpernel Press P292
Pineapple Press P293
Quirk Books P308
Regina Ryan Books L489
Sasquatch Books P325
Scottish Field M272
Somerset Life M286
Sunbelt Publications, Inc. P373
Ten Speed Press P380
Texas A&M University Press P381
Virginia Wine & Country Life M331
W.W. Norton & Company Ltd P422
Workman Publishing P437
Yours M350
Zack Company, Inc, The L615

Gaslamp Fantasy
See more broadly: Fantasy; Historical Fiction

Gay
See more broadly: LGBTQIA
Dreamspinner Press P115

Gems
See more broadly: Geology

Gender
See more broadly: Social Groups

Index | Graphic Novels 319

See more specifically: Feminism; Gender Politics; Women; Women's Studies
Afsana Press P005
Berghahn Books Ltd P045
Bloomsbury Academic P053
Chanchani, Sonali L108
Cooper, Maggie L129
Fernwood Publishing P131
Goff, Ellen L242
Gold SF P146
Indiana University Press P187
Julien, Ria L312
Macdougall, Laura L379
Ohio University Press P261
Pluto Press P295
Simpson, Cara Lee L537
University of Alberta Press P404
University of California Press P406
University of Michigan Press, The P410
University of Texas Press P414
Weiss, Alexandra L593
Wilson, Desiree L606

Gender Issues
See more broadly: Social Issues
Atyeo, Charlotte L028
International Publishers P191
Jessica Kingsley Publishers P197

Gender Politics
See more broadly: Gender

Genealogy
See more broadly: History
Lilliput Press, The P217
Society of Genealogists P346
Turner Publishing P394

Genetics
See more broadly: Science
W.W. Norton & Company Ltd P422

Genocide
See more broadly: History
Purdue University Press P305

Geography
See more specifically: Rivers
Bloomsbury Academic P053
Cambridge University Press P068
Chelsea House Publishers P082
Colourpoint Educational P095
Geographical Journal, The M138
Gill Education P143
Mentor Books P236
Taylor & Francis Group P378
University of Alberta Press P404
University of California Press P406
University of Georgia Press P407
University of Virginia Press P415

Geology
See more broadly: Earth Science
See more specifically: Fossils; Gems; Lapidary; Minerals; Rocks
W.W. Norton & Company Ltd P422
W.W. Norton & Company, Inc. P423

Georgia (US State)
See more broadly: United States
See more specifically: Atlanta; Savannah, GA
University of Georgia Press P407

Geriatrics
See more broadly: Medicine
W.W. Norton & Company Ltd P422

German
See more broadly: Language
Gill Education P143
Mentor Books P236
University of Michigan Press, The P410

Germany
See more broadly: Europe
Peter Lang P285

Ghost Hunting
See more broadly: Ghosts
Llewellyn Worldwide Ltd P219

Ghost Stories
See more broadly: Supernatural / Paranormal
Andrade, Hannah L015
Brewin Books Ltd P062
Glenister, Emily L238
Goff, Ellen L242
Haley, Jolene L260
Hannah Sheppard Literary Agency L262
Kim, Jennifer L333
Morrell, Imogen L417
Orenda Books P267
Pierce, Rosie L474
Seager, Chloe L524
Shestopal, Camilla L534
Sinister Stoat Press P341
Soloway, Jennifer March L544
Swainson, Joanna L561
Takikawa, Marin L566
Vance, Lisa Erbach L583
Williams, Laura L603
Yours Fiction – Women's Special Series M351

Ghosts
See more broadly: Supernatural / Paranormal
See more specifically: Ghost Hunting
Countryside Books P099
JMD Media / DB Publishing P198
Unseen Press P417

Gift Books
Andrews McMeel Publishing P015
Betsy Amster Literary Enterprises L059
Cedar Fort P076
Crown Publishing Group, The P103
Davies, Olivia L147
Ghahremani, Lilly L230
Gill Books P142
Igloo Books Limited P184
Lewinsohn Literary L363
Peter Pauper Press P286
Philips, Ariana L471
Willms, Kathryn L605
Workman Publishing P437

Glasgow
See more broadly: Scotland

Gloucester
See more broadly: Gloucestershire

Gloucestershire
See more broadly: England
See more specifically: Gloucester
Logaston Press P221

Golf
See more broadly: Sport
African American Golfer's Digest M008
Square Mile Magazine M298

Gothic
See more broadly: Horror
Afonso, Thais L007
Ange, Anna L019
Armstrong, Susan L026
Barr, Anjanette L038
Beaumont, Diana L046
Brannan, Maria L076
Buckley, Louise L085
Burke, Kate L088
Fazzari, Hillary L188
Foxx, Kat L213
Glenister, Emily L238
Goff, Ellen L242
Jamieson, Molly L296
Kim, Jennifer L333
Leon, Nina L360
Lightner, Kayla L365
Lovell, Jake L372
Marr, Jill L389
Moonday Mag M213
Neely, Rachel L434
Niv, Daniel L440
Plant, Zoe L476
Potter, Madison L481
Salt Publishing P322
Seager, Chloe L524
Soler, Shania N. L543
Takikawa, Marin L566
Thwaites, Steph L575
Williams, Laura L603

Graphic Design
See more broadly: Design
Gill Education P143
Korero Press P208

Graphic Nonfiction
Ange, Anna L019
Black Warrior Review M058
Kim, Sally M. L335
NBM Publishing P254
Selectric Artists L525
Singing Dragon P340
Siobhan, Aiden L539
Spackman, James L547

Graphic Novels
Andrade, Hannah L015
Ange, Anna L019
April Gloaming P018
Armada, Kurestin L024
Bauman, Erica L043
Bent Agency (UK), The L051
Bent Agency, The L052
Bradford Literary Agency L073
Bradford, Laura L074
Brattle Agency LLC, The L077
Bright Agency (UK), The L078
Bright Agency (US), The L079
Burby, Danielle L087
Children's Books North Agency L112
Cicada Books P087
Classical Comics P090
Cooper, Gemma L128
Crandall, Becca L130
Denis Kitchen Publishing Company Co., LLC P109
Doug Grad Literary Agency L161
Draper, Claire L162
Feldmann, Kait Lee L190
Feminist Press, The P130
Ferguson, T.S. L195
Finegan, Stevie L203
Friedman, Jessica L218
Gahan, Isobel L225
Gemini Books P140
Gilbert, Tara L233
Gisondi, Katie L235
Goetz, Adria L241
Goff, Ellen L242
Graham, Stacey L247
Gruber, Pam L253
Hannah Sheppard Literary Agency L262
Hannigan, Carrie L263
Hawn, Molly Ker L270
Hernando, Paloma L276
Hodges, Jodie L282
Kensington Publishing Corp. P204
Kim, Sally M. L335
Kimber, Natalie L336
Langton, Becca L353
Lantana Publishing P210
Lerner Publishing Group P213
Lewinsohn Literary L363
Lightner, Kayla L365
Marshall, Jen L391
Motala, Tasneem L419

NBM Publishing P254
Olswanger, Anna L450
Orca Book Publishers P266
Pages, Saribel L453
Paul S. Levine Literary Agency L459
Piccadilly Press P291
Power, Anna L482
Rocking Chair Books L499
Sanchez, Kaitlyn L516
Selectric Artists L525
Simply Read Books P339
Siobhan, Aiden L539
Sluytman, Antoinette Van L541
Spackman, James L547
Sunspot Literary Journal M305
Sutherland, Kari L559
Symonds, Laurel L565
Torrey House Press, LLC P390
Tran, Jennifer Chen L578
Turner Publishing L594
W.W. Norton & Company Ltd P422
W.W. Norton & Company, Inc. P423
Weiss, Alexandra L593
Westin, Erin Casey L597
Whatnall, Michaela L598
Wilson, Desiree L606
Zack Company, Inc, The L615
Zacker, Marietta B. L616
Zuraw-Friedland, Ayla L619

Graphic Poems
Neon M219

Graphic Short Fiction
Stinging Fly, The M299
Sunspot Literary Journal M305

Gravel Cycling
See more broadly: Cycling
Adventure Books by Vertebrate
   Publishing P004

Greenock
See more broadly: Inverclyde

Grimdark
See more broadly: Speculative
Singh, Amandeep L538

Grimsby
See more broadly: Lincolnshire

Grounded Fantasy
See more broadly: Fantasy
Bent, Jenny L053
DeBlock, Liza L149
Gruber, Pam L253
Potter, Madison L481
Whatnall, Michaela L598

Grounded Science Fiction
See more broadly: Science Fiction
Savvides, Marilia L520

Haibun
Ink Sweat and Tears M168
Modern Haiku M211
Scifaikuest M270

Haiga
Ink Sweat and Tears M168
Modern Haiku M211

Haikai
Modern Haiku M211

Haiku
Better Than Starbucks M052
Ink Sweat and Tears M168
Modern Haiku M211
Scifaikuest M270

Hairstyles
See more broadly: Beauty; Fashion
Pride M249
Red Magazine M259

Hard Science Fiction
See more broadly: Science Fiction
Edenborough, Sam L172

Willms, Kathryn L605
Zack Company, Inc, The L615

Hardboiled Crime
See more broadly: Crime
Inscriptions Literary Agency L289
Poisoned Pen Press P297

Hartlepool
See more broadly: County Durham

Harvard
See more broadly: College / University

Hauliers
See more broadly: Transport

Hawai'i
See more broadly: United States
Bess Press P047

Health
See more specifically: Alternative Health; Diabetes; Diet; Disabilities; Fertility; Fitness; Holistic Health; Medicine; Mental Health; Mind, Body, Spirit; Nursing; Nutrition; Public Health; Wellbeing; Women's Health
Alcock, Michael L009
Arcadia Publishing P020
Atlanta Magazine M030
Autumn Publishing Ltd P025
Barrett, Emily L040
Basic Health Publications, Inc. P037
Baumer, Jan L044
Bernardi, Amanda L056
Betsy Amster Literary Enterprises L059
Bloomsbury Academic P053
Brailsford, Karen L075
Brewin Books Ltd P062
Cedar Fort P076
CharlottesvilleFamily M076
Chelsea House Publishers P082
Cleis Press P091
Colourpoint Educational P095
Compassiviste Publishing P097
Conversation (UK), The M087
Cosmos M089
Crown Publishing Group, The P103
Curious Minds L133
Dana Newman Literary, LLC L138
Derviskadic, Dado L151
DK Publishing P112
Doug Grad Literary Agency L161
Ekus, Sally L177
Elsevier Ltd P121
Enslow Publishers, Inc. P123
Ericka T. Phillips L181
Faulks, Holly L187
Feminist Press, The P130
Fernando, Kimberly L198
Fernwood Publishing P131
Finan, Ciara L200
First For Women M122
Frankel, Valerie L215
Free Association Books Ltd P135
Free Spirit Publishing P136
Gale P139
Gill Education P143
Hammersmith Books P158
Harvard University Press P165
Hay House Publishers P168
Healthy M152
Hiyate, Sam L281
Icon Books Ltd P180
Idyll Arbor P181
Ireland's Own M172
Irene Goodman Literary Agency
   (IGLA) L291
Jessica Kingsley Publishers P197
Joelle Delbourgo Associates, Inc. L301
Kaliszewska, Joanna L315

Kensington Publishing Corp. P204
Kracht, Elizabeth L341
Krienke, Mary L343
Latshaw, Katherine L355
Levy, Yael L362
Lightner, Kayla L365
marie claire M200
Marr, Jill L389
Marshall, Jen L391
McNidder & Grace P232
Murdoch Books Australia P249
Murgolo, Karen L427
My Weekly M215
New Harbinger Publications P255
Ohio University Press P261
Oxford University Press P272
Pacific Press Publishing Association ... P273
Pan Macmillan Australia P274
Piatkus Books P289
Pine, Gideon P422
Pride M249
Red Magazine M259
Regina Ryan Books L489
Reilly, Milly L491
Rudy Agency, The L510
Salt Publishing P322
Savannah Magazine M269
Seventeen M275
Sheree Bykofsky Associates, Inc. L532
Silk, Julia L535
Singing Dragon P340
Society for Promoting Christian
   Knowledge (SPCK) P345
Stipes Publishing P371
Sunbelt Publications, Inc. P373
Susan Schulman Literary Agency L557
Taylor & Francis Group P378
Ten Speed Press P380
Texas A&M University Press P381
Transworld Publishers P393
Turner Publishing P394
Tyndale House Publishers, Inc. P397
University of Alberta Press P404
University of California Press P406
University of Michigan Press, The P410
W.W. Norton & Company Ltd P422
Willms, Kathryn L605
Yale University Press (London) P438
Yours M350
Zack Company, Inc, The L615

Heavy Metal
See more broadly: Music

Hemp
See more broadly: Plants

Herbal Remedies
See more broadly: Alternative Health
Merlin Unwin Books P237
Singing Dragon P340

Herefordshire
See more broadly: England
Logaston Press P221

High / Epic Fantasy
See more broadly: Fantasy
Armada, Kurestin L024
Belton, Maddy L049
Carroll, Megan L102
Ferguson, T.S. L195
Finegan, Stevie L203
Hernando, Paloma L276
Irvine, Lucy L292
Lindsay Literary Agency L366
Marini, Victoria L388
Mushens, Juliet L430
Parker, Elana Roth L455
Potter, Madison L481
Sluytman, Antoinette Van L541

Index | Historical Fiction

Soler, Shania N. L543
Weiman, Paula L592
Zack Company, Inc, The L615

High Concept
See more specifically: High Concept Crime; High Concept Romance; High Concept Thrillers
Adams, Seren L004
Baxter, Veronique L045
Begum, Salma L047
Bent, Jenny L053
Blair Partnership, The L064
Brannan, Maria L076
Carroll, Megan L102
Cavanagh, Claire L107
Cho, Catherine L114
Colwill, Charlotte L121
Cooper, Gemma L128
DeBlock, Liza L149
Demblon, Gabrielle L150
Dunn, Ben L164
Fabien, Samantha L186
Faulks, Holly L187
Fazzari, Hillary L188
Ferguson, T.S. L195
Forrester, Jemima L210
Foster, Clara L211
Ghahremani, Lilly L230
Gisondi, Katie L235
Gunic, Masha L256
Hannah Sheppard Literary Agency L262
Harris, Erin L268
Headley, David H. L272
Holloway, Sally L284
Kantor, Camille L317
Kate Barker Literary, TV, & Film
  Agency L320
Killingley, Jessica L332
Kracht, Elizabeth L341
Langlee, Lina L352
Lindsay Literary Agency L366
MacDonald, Emily L378
MacKenzie, Joanna L382
Mozley, Jack L422
Mushens, Juliet L430
Napolitano, Maria L431
Neely, Rachel L434
Nelson, Kristin L436
O'Brien, Lee L444
Parker, Elana Roth L455
Pestritto, Carrie L467
Plant, Zoe L476
Rushall, Kathleen L512
Savvides, Marilia L520
Steed, Hayley L548
Terlip, Paige L570
Thwaites, Steph L575
Trudel, Jes L579
Weiss, Alexandra L593
Wells, Karmen L595
Wilson, Desiree L606
Wilson, Ed L607
Wood, Ed L609

High Concept Crime
See more broadly: Crime; High Concept
Beaumont, Diana L046
Gordon, Andrew L245

High Concept Romance
See more broadly: High Concept; Romance
Grunewald, Hattie L254
Williams, Laura L603

High Concept Thrillers
See more broadly: High Concept; Thrillers
Beaumont, Diana L046
Burke, Kate L088
Preston, Amanda L484

High School
See more broadly: School
High Society
See more broadly: Society
High-Low Literacy
See more broadly: Reading
Ransom Publishing Ltd P312
Hinduism
See more broadly: Religion
Historical Crime
See more broadly: Crime; Historical Fiction
Historical Fantasy
See more broadly: Fantasy; Historical Fiction
Ange, Anna L019
Dreamspinner Press P115
Foxx, Kat L213
Gahan, Isobel L225
Gilbert, Tara L233
Historical Fiction
See more specifically: Gaslamp Fantasy; Historical Crime; Historical Fantasy; Historical Literary; Historical Mystery Fiction; Historical Romance; Historical Thrillers; Saga; Speculative Historical Fiction; Vikings Fiction
Andrade, Hannah L015
Ange, Anna L019
Armada, Kurestin L024
Armstrong, Susan L026
Asabi Publishing P022
Barone Literary Agency L036
Baror International, Inc. L037
Baxter, Veronique L045
Beaumont, Diana L046
Belton, Maddy L049
Berlyne, John L055
Bewley, Elizabeth L061
Bhasin, Tamanna L062
Blair Partnership, The L064
Bloodhound Books P052
Borstel, Stefanie Sanchez Von L070
Brace, Samantha L072
Bradford, Laura L074
Buckley, Louise L085
Burke, Kate L088
Chang, Nicola L109
Cho, Catherine L114
Choc Lit P085
Coombes, Clare L127
Cooper, Gemma L128
Cooper, Maggie L129
Curran, Sabhbh L134
Curtis Brown L135
Danaczko, Melissa L139
Darley Anderson Agency, The L143
Dawson, Liza L148
DeBlock, Liza L149
Doug Grad Literary Agency L161
DSP Publications P116
Eason, Lynette L169
Eddison Pearson Ltd L170
Ellis-Martin, Sian L180
Every Day Fiction M114
Fazzari, Hillary L188
Fellows, Abi L193
Figueroa, Melanie L199
Finan, Ciara L200
for Authors, A L209
Forrester, Jemima L210
Foster, Clara L211
Foxx, Kat L213
Furniss, Eugenie L224
Geiger, Ellen L227
Getzler, Josh L229
Glenister, Emily L238
Goldblatt, Rachel L243

Goose Lane Editions P148
Grunewald, Hattie L254
Gunic, Masha L256
Harris, Erin L268
Hayden, Viola L271
Heathfield, Laura L273
Hodges, Jodie L282
Hordern, Kate L286
Hornsley, Sarah L287
Inspired Ink Literary L290
Irene Goodman Literary Agency
  (IGLA) L291
Joffe Books P199
Kahn, Ella Diamond L314
Kate Barker Literary, TV, & Film
  Agency L320
Kathryn Green Literary Agency, LLC ... L322
Kean, Taylor Martindale L324
Keane Kataria Literary Agency L325
Keren, Eli L330
Kim, Julia L334
Kimber, Natalie L336
Kracht, Elizabeth L341
Leigh Feldman Literary L359
Leon, Nina L360
Lightner, Kayla L365
Macdougall, Laura L379
Maidment, Olivia L386
Maltese, Alyssa L387
Margaret K. McElderry Books P228
Marr, Jill L389
Maurer, Shari L397
Milburn, Madeleine L411
Morrell, Imogen L417
Mortimer, Michele L418
Murray, Judith L428
Mushens, Juliet L430
NBM Publishing P254
Nelson, Kristin L436
Niumata, Erin L439
Niv, Daniel L440
Orenda Books P267
Ostby, Kristin L452
Pan Macmillan Australia P274
Pass, Marina de L456
Patterson, Emma L458
Pen & Ink Designs Publishing P280
Pestritto, Carrie L467
Philips, Ariana L471
Piatkus Books P289
Posner, Marcy L480
Power Cut Lite M247
Power, Anna L482
Preston, Amanda L484
Rofe, Jennifer L500
Rossitto, Stefanie L508
Rutherford, Laetitia L513
Salt Publishing P322
Schofield, Hannah L522
Seventh Agency L527
Shestopal, Camilla L534
Silk, Julia L535
Simons, Tanera L536
Singh, Amandeep L538
Siobhan, Aiden L539
Sluytman, Antoinette Van L541
Soler, Shania N. L543
Sourcebooks Landmark P356
Sparsile Books P359
Steed, Hayley L548
Stringer, Marlene L554
Swainson, Joanna L561
Sweetgum Press P375
Symonds, Laurel L565
Tannenbaum, Amy L568
Thorneycroft, Euan L574

322 Index | Historical Literary

Torrey House Press, LLC P390
Tran, Jennifer Chen L578
Turner Publishing P394
Tyndale House Publishers, Inc. P397
Whatnall, Michaela L598
Williams, Laura L603
Wolfpack Publishing P432
Young, Claudia L614
Yours Fiction – Women's Special Series M351
Zack Company, Inc, The L615

Historical Literary
See more broadly: Historical Fiction; Literary
Topping, Antony L577

Historical Mystery Fiction
See more broadly: Historical Fiction; Mystery
Thorneycroft, Euan L574
Williams, Laura L603

Historical Romance
See more broadly: Historical Fiction; Romance
Adsett, Alex L005
Armada, Kurestin L024
Bradford Literary Agency L073
Bradford, Laura L074
Carina Press P073
Choc Lit P085
Irvine, Lucy L292
Leon, Nina L360
Lyrical Press P225
Mills & Boon P240
Nathan, Abigail L433
Niv, Daniel L440
Ostby, Kristin L452
Rossitto, Stefanie L508
Sourcebooks Casablanca P351
Udden, Jennifer L580

Historical Thrillers
See more broadly: Historical Fiction; Thrillers
Topping, Antony L577

History
See more specifically: 17th Century; 18th Century; 19th Century; 20th Century; American History; Art History; British History; Caribbean History; Church History; Cultural History; European History; Genealogy; Genocide; Intellectual History; Jewish Holocaust; Local History; Maritime History; Medieval; Military History; Modern History; Narrative History; Nostalgia; Political History; Popular History; Regional History; Renaissance; Revisionist History; Social History
ABC-CLIO P002
Agricultural History M012
Alabama Heritage M013
Albemarle M015
Alcock, Michael L009
Amber Books Ltd P011
Ange, Anna L019
Annette Green Authors' Agency L021
Arcadia Publishing P020
Arte Publico Press P021
Atlantic Northeast M032
Aurora Metro Press P024
Backbeat Books P027
Barr, Anjanette L038
Barrett, Emily L040
Bartholomew, Jason L041
Basalt Books P034
Basic Books P035
Baxter, Veronique L045
Baylor University Press P041
BBC History Magazine M042
Berghahn Books Ltd P045
Best of British M050
Betsy Amster Literary Enterprises L059
Blackstaff Press P051
Bloomsbury Academic P053
Borstel, Stefanie Sanchez Von L070
Bowlin, Sarah L071
Bradford Literary Agency L073
Brannan, Maria L076
Brewin Books Ltd P062
Brick M065
Britain Magazine M066
British Academy, The P063
British Museum Press, The P064
Broadview Press P065
Brouckaert, Justin L083
Cambridge University Press P068
Carter, Rebecca L103
Cavanagh, Claire L107
Cedar Fort P076
Charlesbridge Publishing P081
Chelsea House Publishers P082
Christie, Jennifer L116
Clarke, Catherine L119
College Press Publishing P094
Colourpoint Educational P095
Compassiviste Publishing P097
Cosmos M089
Countryside Books P099
Cricket M096
Crown P101
Crown Publishing Group, The P103
Curious Minds L133
Curran, Sabhbh L134
Dana Newman Literary, LLC L138
Danaczko, Melissa L139
Danko, Margaret L140
Darga, Jon Michael L141
Davies, Olivia L147
Diana Finch Literary Agency L154
Dickerson, Donya L155
Diversion Books P111
DK Publishing P112
Dolin, Lily L157
Doug Grad Literary Agency L161
Dundurn P118
Dystel, Jane L167
Edenborough, Sam L172
Einstein, Susanna L173
Eisenmann, Caroline L175
Ellis-Martin, Sian L180
Enslow Publishers, Inc. P123
Epicenter Press Inc P124
Evans, Kate L185
Fazzari, Hillary L188
Fellows, Abi L193
Feminist Press, The P130
Fernwood Publishing P131
Finan, Ciara L200
Fox, Aram L212
Free Association Books Ltd P135
Fuentes, Sarah L222
Gale P139
Geiger, Ellen L227
Getzler, Josh L229
Gill Books P142
Gill Education P143
Glenister, Emily L238
Globe Pequot Press, The P145
Goldblatt, Rachel L243
Goose Lane Editions P148
Gordon, Andrew L245
Graffeg P150
Hanbury Agency, The L261
Hancock House Publishers P159
Harvard University Press P165
Henley Hall Press P171
Hernando, Paloma L276
Heymont, Lane L277
Hildebrand, Cole L280
History Press, The P174
History Today M157
Holloway, Sally L284
Hordern, Kate L286
Icon Books Ltd P180
Imagine Publishing P186
International Publishers P191
Ireland's Own M172
Irene Goodman Literary Agency (IGLA) L291
Irish Pages M173
Javelin L298
Joelle Delbourgo Associates, Inc. L301
Johnson, Jared L303
Joy Harris Literary Agency, Inc. L308
Julien, Ria L312
Kardon, Julia L318
Karen Gantz Literary Management L319
Kate Barker Literary, TV, & Film Agency L320
Kates Hill Press, The P203
Kathryn Green Literary Agency, LLC L322
Kensington Publishing Corp. P204
Kim, Jennifer L333
Kim, Julia L334
Kube Publishing P209
Lambert, Sophie L348
Levitt, Sarah L361
Levy, Yael L362
Lewis, Alison L364
Lightner, Kayla L365
Lilliput Press, The P217
Loft Press, Inc. P220
London Review of Books M191
Lovell, Jake L372
LSU Press P223
MacDonald, Emily L378
Macdougall, Laura L379
Mack, Kate L381
MacLeod, Lauren L383
Malahat Review, The M197
Marr, Jill L389
Marshall, Jen L391
McNidder & Grace P232
Mendia, Isabel L403
Mentor Books P236
Michel, Caroline L408
Minnesota Historical Society Press P241
Missouri Historical Society Press P243
Monoray P246
Mulcahy Sweeney Literary Agency L423
Mundy, Toby L426
Murray, Judith L428
Niv, Daniel L440
O'Shea, Amy L447
Ohio University Press P261
Orphans Publishing P268
Otago University Press P269
Oxford Review of Books M230
Oxford University Press P272
Pan Macmillan Australia P274
Peddle, Kay L460
Pelham, Imogen L461
Peter Lang P285
Pineapple Press P293
Plitt, Carrie L477
Pluto Press P295
Power Cut Lite M247
Power, Anna L482
Preservation Magazine M248
Preston, Amanda L484
Purdue University Press P305
Pureplay Press P306
Quadrant Magazine M254
Quirk Books P308

Index | Houses and Homes

Regina Ryan Books L489
Reid, Janet L490
Richter, Rick L493
Rocky Mountain Books P315
Rosenberg Group, The L505
Rudy Agency, The L510
Rutman, Jim L514
Scala Arts & Heritage Publishers P326
Schiffer Military History P328
Schofield, Hannah L522
Schwizer, Fabienne L523
Scots Magazine, The M271
Scratching Shed Publishing P331
Seren Books P335
Society for Promoting Christian
   Knowledge (SPCK) P345
Society of Genealogists P346
Somerset Life M286
Southwest Review M293
Stanford University Press P367
Stephens, Jenny L549
Strothman, Wendy L555
Sunbelt Publications, Inc. P373
Susan Schulman Literary Agency L557
Sweet, Emily L563
Sweetgum Press P375
Sweren, Becky L564
Symonds, Laurel L565
Taylor & Francis Group P378
Texas A&M University Press P381
Thames & Hudson Inc. P382
Thames and Hudson Ltd P383
Thayer, Henry L572
This England M316
Thorneycroft, Euan L574
Topping, Antony L577
Transworld Publishers P393
Turner Publishing P394
Tyndale House Publishers, Inc. P397
UCL Press P398
University of Akron Press, The P403
University of Alberta Press P404
University of California Press P406
University of Iowa Press P408
University of Michigan Press, The P410
University of North Texas Press P412
University of Texas Press P414
University of Virginia Press P415
University Press of Colorado P416
Unseen Press P417
Victoria Sanders & Associates LLC L584
Virginia Quarterly Review, The M330
W.W. Norton & Company Ltd P422
W.W. Norton & Company, Inc. P423
Wickers, Chandler L600
Williams, Laura L603
Willms, Kathryn L605
Wilson, Desiree L606
Wilson, Ed L607
Yale Review, The M344
Yale University Press (London) P438
Yankee Magazine M345
Zuckerbrot, Renee L618

Hobbies
*See more specifically: Embroidery; Gardening;
Knitting; Motorcycling; Numismatics (Coin /
Currency Collecting); Quilting; Rock
Collecting / Rockhounding; Sewing; Stamp
Collecting*
Arcadia Publishing P020
Cedar Fort P076
Crown Publishing Group, The P103
DK Publishing P112
Gale P139
Gill Books P142
Kensington Publishing Corp. P204

Ohio University Press P261
Thames and Hudson Ltd P383
Turner Publishing P394
W.W. Norton & Company Ltd P422
W.W. Norton & Company, Inc. P423

Hockey
See more broadly: Sport

Holiday Homes
See more broadly: Holidays

Holidays
See more specifically: Holiday Homes
Enslow Publishers, Inc. P123

Holistic Health
See more broadly: Health
Sentient Publications P334

Home Economics / Domestic Science
Colourpoint Educational P095
Gill Education P143

Home Improvement
See more broadly: Houses and Homes
Berks County Living M049
Better Homes and Gardens M051
Draper, Claire L162
Zack Company, Inc, The L615

Homelessness
See more broadly: Social Issues

Horoscopes
See more broadly: Fortune Telling and Divination
marie claire M200

Horror
*See more specifically: Folk Horror; Gothic;
Horrormance; Literary Horror;
Psychological Horror; Speculative Horror;
Supernatural / Paranormal Horror;
Werewolves; Zombies*
Afonso, Thais L007
Alekseii, Keir L011
Ange, Anna L019
Annette Green Authors' Agency L021
Armada, Kurestin L024
Armstrong, Susan L026
Asabi Publishing P022
Aurealis M034
Bajek, Lauren L031
Barone Literary Agency L036
Baxter, Veronique L045
Begum, Salma L047
Bent, Jenny L053
Berlyne, John L055
BFS Horizons M053
Black Static M057
Brannan, Maria L076
Brooks, Savannah L080
BSFA Review, The M067
Buckley, Louise L085
Carroll, Megan L102
Charnace, Edwina de L110
Chevais, Jennifer L111
Colwill, Charlotte L121
Crystal Magazine M098
Curtis Brown L135
Cusick, John L136
Demblon, Gabrielle L150
Diversion Books P111
DSP Publications P116
Edenborough, Sam L172
Every Day Fiction M114
Fabien, Samantha L186
Ferguson, T.S. L195
Figueroa, Melanie L199
Gilbert, Tara L233
Glenister, Emily L238
Gunic, Masha L256
Haley, Jolene L260
Hannah Sheppard Literary Agency L262
Harper, Logan L267

Harris, Erin L268
Hensley, Chelsea L274
Heymont, Lane L277
Interzone M171
Irvine, Lucy L292
Jamieson, Molly L296
Johnson, Jared L303
Kavanagh, Jade L323
Kim, Jennifer L333
Kim, Julia L334
Korero Press P208
Langlee, Lina L352
Leon, Nina L360
Lovell, Jake L372
Maidment, Olivia L386
Maltese, Alyssa L387
Marr, Jill L389
Marshall, Jen L391
Mihell, Natasha L410
Milusich, Grace L412
Moonday Mag M213
Morrell, Imogen L417
Mortimer, Michele L418
Neely, Rachel L434
Nelson, Patricia L437
Orenda Books P267
Pages, Saribel L453
Perotto-Wills, Martha L465
Pestritto, Carrie L467
Pierce, Rosie L474
Plant, Zoe L476
Quirk Books P308
Richter, Rick L493
Romano, Annie L502
Salazar, Des L515
Savvides, Marilia L520
Schwizer, Fabienne L523
Scifaikuest M270
Seager, Chloe L524
Shestopal, Camilla L534
Sinister Stoat Press P341
Sluytman, Antoinette Van L541
SmashBear Publishing P342
Snowbooks P344
Soler, Shania N. L543
Sorg, Arley L546
Sourcebooks Horror P354
Steed, Hayley L548
Story Unlikely M300
Swainson, Joanna L561
Thwaites, Steph L575
Tibbets, Anne L576
Tor Publishing Group P388
Torrey House Press, LLC P390
Turner Publishing P394
Udden, Jennifer L580
Weiss, Alexandra L593
Weitzner, Tess L594
Wells, Karmen L595
Whatnall, Michaela L598
Williams, Laura L603
Wilson, Desiree L606
Yellow Mama Webzine M346
Zack Company, Inc, The L615
Zeno Agency L617

Horrormance
See more broadly: Horror; Romance
Fazzari, Hillary L188

Horse Racing
See more broadly: Sport
Scratching Shed Publishing P331

Horses
See more broadly: Animals
Horse & Rider M159

Houses and Homes
See more broadly: Buildings

See more specifically: Home Improvement; Ranches; Spas and Hot Tubs
Arcadia Publishing ... P020
Barr, Nicola ... L039
Bernardi, Amanda ... L056
CharlottesvilleFamily ... M076
Cowboys & Indians ... M091
Kensington Publishing Corp. ... P204
Kent Life ... M178
Murdoch Books Australia ... P249
Pimpernel Press ... P292
Savannah Magazine ... M269
Somerset Life ... M286
Sunbelt Publications, Inc. ... P373
W.W. Norton & Company Ltd ... P422
W.W. Norton & Company, Inc. ... P423
Yankee Magazine ... M345
Yorkshire Life ... M348

How To
Compassiviste Publishing ... P097
Cottage Life ... M090
Doug Grad Literary Agency ... L161
Entrepreneur ... M112
Graham, Stacey ... L247
Korero Press ... P208
Marlin ... M201
Merlin Unwin Books ... P237
NBM Publishing ... P254
Nichols, Mariah ... L438
Rutherford, Laetitia ... L513
Stephens, Jenny ... L549

Huddersfield
See more broadly: Yorkshire

Human Biology
See more broadly: Biology

Hunting
See more broadly: Sport
See more specifically: Fishing
Bowhunter ... M063
Merlin Unwin Books ... P237
River Hills Traveler ... M263

Hymnals
See more broadly: Church Music

Hypnosis
See more broadly: Psychology
W.W. Norton & Company Ltd ... P422

Ignation Spirituality
See more broadly: Catholicism

Illinois
See more broadly: United States
See more specifically: Chicago

Illustrated Books
Amber Books Ltd ... P011
Bird Eye Books ... P048
Children's Books North Agency ... L112
Davies, Olivia ... L147
Doug Grad Literary Agency ... L161
Enitharmon Editions ... P122
Ghahremani, Lilly ... L230
Graffeg ... P150
Graffeg Childrens ... P151
Korero Press ... P208
Krienke, Mary ... L343
Latshaw, Katherine ... L355
Lewinsohn Literary ... L363
Macdougall, Laura ... L379
Mack, Kate ... L381
Philips, Ariana ... L471
Pickering, Juliet ... L473
Plexus Publishing Limited ... P294
Rudy Agency, The ... L510
Scala Arts & Heritage Publishers ... P326
Scholastic ... P329
Ten Speed Press ... P380

Immigration
See more broadly: Social Issues
Afsana Press ... P005
MacKenzie, Joanna ... L382
Mendia, Isabel ... L403
Sanders, Rayhane ... L517
Texas A&M University Press ... P381
University of Alberta Press ... P404

Immunology
See more broadly: Medicine

Indiana
See more broadly: United States
Purdue University Press ... P305
Unseen Press ... P417

Information Science
See more broadly: Science
Bloomsbury Academic ... P053
Facet Publishing ... P127
Gill Education ... P143
Information Today, Inc. ... P188
Taylor & Francis Group ... P378

Inspirational
See more broadly: Religion
See more specifically: Inspirational Memoir
404 Ink ... P001
Borstel, Stefanie Sanchez Von ... L070
Every Day Fiction ... M114
Tyndale House Publishers, Inc. ... P397
Zack Company, Inc, The ... L615

Inspirational Memoir
See more broadly: Inspirational; Memoir
Goderich, Miriam ... L240

Insurance
See more broadly: Business
Insurance Post ... M169

Intellectual History
See more broadly: History

Interior Design
See more broadly: Design
See more specifically: Decorating
Bloomsbury Academic ... P053
Homes & Antiques ... M158
Monacelli Press, The ... P245
Phaidon Press ... P287
Red Magazine ... M259
Scottish Field ... M272
Thames & Hudson Inc. ... P382
Virginia Wine & Country Life ... M331

International
Better Than Starbucks ... M052
Danaczko, Melissa ... L139
Dillsworth, Elise ... L156
Gutter Magazine ... M148
Hakim, Serene ... L259
Indiana University Press ... P187
Tibbets, Anne ... L576
Zack Company, Inc, The ... L615

Internet
See more broadly: Computers
See more specifically: Internet Culture
Lightner, Kayla ... L365
Pierce, Rosie ... L474
Weiss, Alexandra ... L593

Internet Culture
See more broadly: Internet
Brouckaert, Justin ... L083
Lightner, Kayla ... L365

Intersectional Feminism
See more broadly: Feminism
Clarke, Caro ... L118
Goff, Ellen ... L242
Gold SF ... P146

Interviews
African American Review ... M009
Arc ... M024
Aurealis ... M034
BFS Journal ... M054
Black Moon Magazine ... M056
Bluegrass Unlimited ... M061
Brick ... M065
Caribbean Writer, The ... M073
Cocoa Girl ... M080
Contemporary Verse 2 ... M086
Dream Catcher ... M106
Ekphrastic Review, The ... M109
Facts & Fiction ... M116
Forty20 ... M128
Funeral Business Solutions ... M134
Gulf Coast: A Journal of Literature and Fine Arts ... M147
Identity Theory ... M164
Journal, The ... M176
Kavya Kishor ... M177
London Magazine, The ... M190
Midway Journal ... M208
OK! Magazine ... M228
Oxford Poetry ... M229
Oxford Review of Books ... M230
Paris Review, The ... M233
Poetry Birmingham Literary Journal ... M242
Poetry Ireland Review ... M243
Red Magazine ... M259
Riposte ... M262
Snowflake Magazine ... M284
Stinging Fly, The ... M299
Strange Horizons ... M301
Tears in the Fence ... M311
Temz Review, The ... M312
Ulster Business ... M323
Vagabond City ... M327
Vallum ... M328
Vestal Review ... M329
Wet Grain ... M341
Yorkshire Life ... M348

Inverclyde
See more broadly: Scotland
See more specifically: Greenock

Investigative Journalism
See more broadly: Journalism
Andrade, Hannah ... L015
Bal, Emma ... L032
Bernardi, Amanda ... L056
Chanchani, Sonali ... L108
Charnace, Edwina de ... L110
Fogg, Jack ... L206
Fuentes, Sarah ... L222
Geiger, Ellen ... L227
Goldstein, Veronica ... L244
Hildebrand, Cole ... L280
Holloway, Sally ... L284
Kracht, Elizabeth ... L341
Marshall, Jen ... L391
Marsiglia, Caroline ... L392
Morrell, Imogen ... L417
Nolan, Laura ... L441
Patterson, Emma ... L458
Pelham, Imogen ... L461
Pine, Gideon ... L475
Plitt, Carrie ... L477
Rudy Agency, The ... L510
Savvides, Marilia ... L520
Sweren, Becky ... L564
Torrey House Press, LLC ... P390
Zack Company, Inc, The ... L615

Investments
See more broadly: Business; Finance
Square Mile Magazine ... M298

Ireland
See more broadly: Europe
Black & White Publishing Ltd ... P049
Blackstaff Press ... P051
Gill Books ... P142
Indiana University Press ... P187
Ireland's Own ... M172

Lilliput Press, The................................P217
Molloy, Jess...L414
University of Michigan Press, The............P410
Irish (Gaeilge)
See more broadly: Language
Gill Education......................................P143
Mentor Books.....................................P236
Islam
See more broadly: Religion
See more specifically: Sufism
Baylor University Press.......................P041
Kube Publishing..................................P209
University of Michigan Press, The............P410
Islamic Philosophy
See more broadly: Philosophy
Italian American
See more broadly: Ethnic Groups
Feminist Press, The..............................P130
Italy
See more broadly: Europe
Feminist Press, The..............................P130
Peter Lang..P285
Japan
See more broadly: Asia
Ohio University Press.........................P261
Jazz
See more broadly: Music
Edenborough, Sam.............................L172
Jewellery
Thames and Hudson Ltd....................P383
Jewish Culture
See more broadly: Culture
Jewish Holocaust
See more broadly: History
Indiana University Press.....................P187
Purdue University Press......................P305
Journalism
See more specifically: Food Journalism; Investigative Journalism; Literary Journalism; Narrative Journalism; Science Journalism
Begum, Salma....................................L047
Carr, Jamie...L101
Compass Talent..................................L124
Doug Grad Literary Agency................L161
Feminist Press, The..............................P130
Friedman, Rebecca..............................L219
Granger, David....................................L250
Javelin..L298
Kardon, Julia.......................................L318
Kim, Jennifer......................................L333
Kruger Cowne....................................L344
Levitt, Sarah.......................................L361
Levy, Yael...L362
Lewis, Alison......................................L364
Moorhead, Max..................................L416
NBM Publishing.................................P254
Ohio University Press.........................P261
Oxford University Press......................P272
Peddle, Kay..L460
Perry Literary.....................................L466
Phillips, Aemilia..................................L472
Posner, Marcy....................................L480
Rutman, Jim.......................................L514
Seymour, Charlotte............................L528
Silk, Julia..L535
Stipes Publishing................................P371
University of Missouri Press.................P411
Wickers, Chandler..............................L600
Judaism
See more broadly: Religion
See more specifically: Kabbalah
Baylor University Press.......................P041
Carr, Jamie...L101
Feminist Press, The..............................P130
Indiana University Press.....................P187

Irene Goodman Literary Agency (IGLA)...L291
Stanford University Press...................P367
Thwaites, Steph..................................L575
University of Michigan Press, The............P410
University of Texas Press....................P414
Zack Company, Inc, The.....................L615
Juvenile Psychotherapy
See more broadly: Psychotherapy
See more specifically: Child Psychotherapy
W.W. Norton & Company Ltd...........P422
Kabbalah
See more broadly: Judaism
Llewellyn Worldwide Ltd....................P219
Kent
See more broadly: England
Kent Life..M178
Knitting
See more broadly: Crafts; Hobbies
LGBTQIA
See more broadly: Sexuality
See more specifically: Gay
Afonso, Thais.....................................L007
Aldridge, Kaylyn.................................L010
Ange, Anna..L019
Asabi Publishing.................................P022
Belton, Maddy...................................L049
Burby, Danielle...................................L087
Clarke, Caro.......................................L118
Cleis Press..P091
Cooper, Maggie..................................L129
Demblon, Gabrielle.............................L150
Draper, Claire.....................................L162
Ellis-Martin, Sian.................................L180
Feminist Press, The..............................P130
Ferguson, T.S......................................L195
Finegan, Stevie...................................L203
Fourteen Poems.................................M130
Free Spirit Publishing..........................P136
Future Fire, The..................................M135
Gold SF..P146
Goose Lane Editions...........................P148
Hernando, Paloma.............................L276
Hildebrand, Cole................................L280
Keren, Eli..L330
Knigge, Sheyla....................................L339
Langton, Becca..................................L353
Leon, Nina...L360
Macdougall, Laura.............................L379
Morrell, Imogen.................................L417
Muswell Press.....................................P250
O'Brien, Lee..L444
Potter, Madison..................................L481
Quirk Books.......................................P308
Romano, Annie..................................L502
Salazar, Des..L515
Sinister Stoat Press..............................P341
Sinister Wisdom.................................M282
Siobhan, Aiden...................................L539
Snowflake Magazine..........................M284
Torrey House Press, LLC.....................P390
University of Alberta Press..................P404
W.W. Norton & Company Ltd...........P422
Weiss, Alexandra................................L593
Wells, Karmen....................................L595
Williams, Laura..................................L603
Wilson, Desiree...................................L606
Zuraw-Friedland, Ayla.........................L619
Lacemaking
See more broadly: Crafts
Lancashire
See more broadly: England
Language
See more specifically: Dialects; English; French; Gaelic; German; Irish (Gaeilge); Slang; Spanish; Writing

Arcadia Publishing..............................P020
Bloomsbury Academic........................P053
Cambridge University Press................P068
DK Publishing.....................................P112
Doug Grad Literary Agency................L161
Faulks, Holly.......................................L187
Icon Books Ltd...................................P180
Johnson, Jared....................................L303
Kensington Publishing Corp................P204
Linguist, The......................................M186
Ohio University Press.........................P261
Oxford University Press......................P272
Peter Lang..P285
Taylor & Francis Group.......................P378
Thames and Hudson Ltd....................P383
UCL Press...P398
University of Alberta Press..................P404
University of California Press..............P406
University of Michigan Press, The............P410
Yale University Press (London)............P438
Lapidary
See more broadly: Geology
Leadership
See more broadly: Personal Development
BCS (British Computer Society)...........P042
Berrett-Koehler Publishers...................P046
Ki Agency Ltd....................................L331
Tyndale House Publishers, Inc.............P397
Zack Company, Inc, The.....................L615
Left Wing Politics
See more broadly: Politics
Baffler, The...M039
Canadian Dimension..........................M072
Legal
See more specifically: Business Law; Legal Thrillers; Taxation
Arcadia Publishing..............................P020
BCS (British Computer Society)...........P042
Bloomsbury Academic........................P053
Cambridge University Press................P068
Colourpoint Educational.....................P095
Dystel, Jane..L167
Feminist Press, The..............................P130
Fernwood Publishing..........................P131
Gale..P139
Gill Education......................................P143
Harvard University Press....................P165
Julien, Ria...L312
Kensington Publishing Corp................P204
LexisNexis..P214
London Review of Books....................M191
Ohio University Press.........................P261
Oxford University Press......................P272
Peter Lang..P285
Round Hall...P318
Rudy Agency, The..............................L510
Stanford University Press...................P367
Sunbelt Publications, Inc....................P373
Susan Schulman Literary Agency........L557
Sweet & Maxwell...............................P374
Taylor & Francis Group.......................P378
UCL Press...P398
University of Alberta Press..................P404
University of California Press..............P406
University of Michigan Press, The............P410
University of North Texas Press..........P412
University of Virginia Press.................P415
Usselman, Laura.................................L581
Victoria Sanders & Associates LLC......L584
W.W. Norton & Company Ltd...........P422
W.W. Norton & Company, Inc...........P423
Yale University Press (London)............P438
Legal Thrillers
See more broadly: Legal; Thrillers
Orenda Books....................................P267

Leisure

See more specifically: Games; Pubs; Recreation; Sailing; Skiing; Snowboarding

Arcadia Publishing	P020
CharlottesvilleFamily	M076
Compassiviste Publishing	P097
Regina Ryan Books	L489
Snowbooks	P344
Yours	M350

Lifestyle

See more specifically: Alternative Lifestyles; Biker Lifestyle; Country Lifestyle; Luxury Lifestyle; Mountain Lifestyle; Ranch Lifestyle; Retirement; Rural Living; Self-Sufficiency; Vegetarianism

Atlanta Magazine	M030
AZ Foothills Magazine	M036
Beaumont, Diana	L046
Bent, Jenny	L053
Berks County Living	M049
Betsy Amster Literary Enterprises	L059
Black & White Publishing Ltd	P049
Blair Partnership, The	L064
Carolina Woman	M074
CharlottesvilleFamily	M076
Chiotti, Danielle	L113
Colourpoint Educational	P095
Compassiviste Publishing	P097
Cottage Life	M090
Danko, Margaret	L140
Diana Finch Literary Agency	L154
Ekus, Sally	L177
Faulks, Holly	L187
Fernando, Kimberly	L198
Forrester, Jemima	L210
Frankel, Valerie	L215
Gemini Books	P140
Gill Books	P142
Graham, Stacey	L247
Grunewald, Hattie	L254
Healthy	M152
Hello!	M155
Hiyate, Sam	L281
Icon Books Ltd	P180
Idler, The	M165
Irene Goodman Literary Agency (IGLA)	L291
Karen Gantz Literary Management	L319
Kate Barker Literary, TV, & Film Agency	L320
Kent Life	M178
Kim, Julia	L334
Latshaw, Katherine	L355
My Weekly	M215
Nichols, Mariah	L438
O'Shea, Amy	L447
OK! Magazine	M228
Orphans Publishing	P268
Pan Macmillan Australia	P274
People's Friend, The	M237
Philips, Ariana	L471
Pride	M249
Regina Ryan Books	L489
River Hills Traveler	M263
Roberts, Soumeya Bendimerad	L495
Ruralite	M266
Savannah Magazine	M269
Scottish Field	M272
Seventeen	M275
Shaw Agency, The	L529
Silk, Julia	L535
Singing Dragon	P340
Somerset Life	M286
Stephens, Jenny	L549
Sweet, Emily	L563
Thames & Hudson Inc.	P382
Thames and Hudson Ltd	P383
That's Life!	M313
Virginia Wine & Country Weddings	M332
Vogue	M334
Willms, Kathryn	L605
Yankee Magazine	M345
Yorkshire Life	M348
Yorkshire Women's Life Magazine	M349
Yours	M350

Light Fantasy

See more broadly: Fantasy

Ostby, Kristin	L452
Steed, Hayley	L548

Lincolnshire

See more broadly: England
See more specifically: Grimsby

Literary

See more specifically: Historical Literary; Literary Fantasy; Literary Horror; Literary Journalism; Literary Mystery; Literary Suspense; Literary Thrillers

30 North	M001
About Place Journal	M004
Adams, Seren	L004
Adsett, Alex	L005
Afsana Press	P005
Alaska Quarterly Review	M014
And Other Stories	P013
Ange, Anna	L019
Annette Green Authors' Agency	L021
Apple Tree Literary Ltd	L023
Armada, Kurestin	L024
Armstrong, Susan	L026
Arthurson, Wayne	L027
Arts & Letters	M027
Atyeo, Charlotte	L028
Bacopa Literary Review	M038
Bajek, Lauren	L031
Baror International, Inc.	L037
Barr, Nicola	L039
Baxter, Veronique	L045
Begum, Salma	L047
Beloit Fiction Journal	M048
Bent, Jenny	L053
Betancourt Literary	L057
Betsy Amster Literary Enterprises	L059
Beverley Slopen Literary Agency	L060
Blair Partnership, The	L064
Bloodhound Books	P052
BOA Editions, Ltd	P057
Bowlin, Sarah	L071
Brace, Samantha	L072
Bradford Literary Agency	L073
Brattle Agency LLC, The	L077
Brick	M065
Brotherstone Creative Management	L081
Brotherstone, Charlie	L082
Buckley, Louise	L085
Cafe Irreal, The	M071
Campbell, Charlie	L094
Caribbean Writer, The	M073
Caskie, Robert	L105
Chanchani, Sonali	L108
Chang, Nicola	L109
Chapman	M075
Chiotti, Danielle	L113
Cho, Catherine	L114
Cichello, Kayla	L117
Clarke, Caro	L118
Coach House Books	P092
Cochran, Alexander	L120
Cola	M081
Colwill, Charlotte	L121
Combemale, Chris	L122
Compassiviste Publishing	P097
Conjunctions	M084
Conrad, Claire Paterson	L125
Conville, Clare	L126
Cooper, Maggie	L129
Crannog Magazine	M092
Curran, Sabhbh	L134
Curtis Brown	L135
Dalhousie Review, The	M100
Dana Newman Literary, LLC	L138
Danaczko, Melissa	L139
Daunt Books Publishing	P106
Dawson, Liza	L148
DeBlock, Liza	L149
Dedalus Ltd	P107
Demblon, Gabrielle	L150
Dillsworth, Elise	L156
Dodo Ink	P113
Dolin, Lily	L157
Dundurn	P118
Dunow, Carlson & Lerner Agency	L166
Dystel, Jane	L167
Eisenmann, Caroline	L175
Ellis-Martin, Sian	L180
Emerge Literary Journal	M111
Enitharmon Editions	P122
Evans, Kate	L185
Every Day Fiction	M114
Everything With Words	P126
Fairlight Books	P128
Faulks, Holly	L187
Fazzari, Hillary	L188
Fellows, Abi	L193
Feminist Press, The	P130
Ferguson, Hannah	L194
Fergusson, Julie	L196
Fiction	M120
Figueroa, Melanie	L199
Five Points	M124
Fogg, Jack	L206
Folio	M126
Folio Literary Management, LLC	L207
for Authors, A	L209
Forrester, Jemima	L210
Foster, Clara	L211
Fourth River, The	M131
Fox, Aram	L212
Friedman, Jessica	L218
Friedman, Rebecca	L219
Fuentes, Sarah	L222
Georgia Review, The	M139
Goldstein, Veronica	L244
Gordon, Andrew	L245
Grain Literary Magazine	M143
Graywolf Press	P152
Gruber, Pam	L253
Gunic, Masha	L256
Gutter Magazine	M148
Hakim, Serene	L259
Harper, Logan	L267
Harris, Erin	L268
Hawthorne Books	P167
Hildebrand, Cole	L280
Hiyate, Sam	L281
Hotel Amerika	M160
Hunger Mountain	M161
Hwang, Annie	L288
Idaho Review	M163
Ig Publishing	P182
Image	M166
Indiana Review	M167
Island	M174
Island Online	M175
Jamii Publishing	P196
Janklow & Nesbit UK Ltd	L297
Joelle Delbourgo Associates, Inc.	L301
Joy Harris Literary Agency, Inc.	L308
Judith Murdoch Literary Agency	L309

Kantor, Camille	L317	
Kardon, Julia	L318	
Kate Barker Literary, TV, & Film Agency	L320	
Kean, Taylor Martindale	L324	
Keeffe, Sara O'	L326	
Kenny, Julia	L329	
Kensington Publishing Corp.	P204	
Keren, Eli	L330	
Killingley, Jessica	L332	
Kim, Jennifer	L333	
Kim, Julia	L334	
Kimber, Natalie	L336	
Kracht, Elizabeth	L341	
Krichevsky, Stuart	L342	
Krienke, Mary	L343	
Lambert, Sophie	L348	
Landfall	M182	
Langlee, Lina	L352	
Laxfield Literary Associates	L356	
Leamington Books	P211	
Leigh Feldman Literary	L359	
Leon, Nina	L360	
Levitt, Sarah	L361	
Levy, Yael	L362	
Lewis, Alison	L364	
Lightner, Kayla	L365	
Louisiana Literature	M194	
Lutyens and Rubinstein	L375	
MacDonald, Emily	L378	
Macdougall, Laura	L379	
Maidment, Olivia	L386	
Marini, Victoria	L388	
Marsh Agency, The	L390	
Marshall, Jen	L391	
Massachusetts Review, The	M202	
Maurer, Shari	L397	
McBride, Juliana	L399	
McCormick Literary	L400	
Merullo, Annabel	L405	
Mid-American Review	M206	
Midsummer Dream House	M207	
Milburn, Madeleine	L411	
Minnesota Historical Society Press	P241	
Moonday Mag	M213	
Moorhead, Max	L416	
Morrell, Imogen	L417	
Mortimer, Michele	L418	
Mozley, Jack	L422	
Mundy, Toby	L426	
Murray, Judith	L428	
Muscato, Nate	L429	
Myrmidon Books Ltd	P251	
NBM Publishing	P254	
Nelson, Kristin	L436	
Neon	M219	
New Welsh Reader	M223	
O'Grady, Niamh	L445	
Ooligan Press	P265	
Orenda Books	P267	
Pan Macmillan Australia	P274	
Panorama	M232	
Paris Review, The	M233	
Parthian Books	P275	
Pass, Marina de	L456	
Patterson, David	L457	
Patterson, Emma	L458	
Pelham, Imogen	L461	
Perotto-Wills, Martha	L465	
Pestritto, Carrie	L467	
PEW Literary	L468	
Philips, Ariana	L471	
Phillips, Aemilia	L472	
Pickering, Juliet	L473	
Pierce, Rosie	L474	
Pine, Gideon	L475	
Plitt, Carrie	L477	
Polygon	P298	
Power, Anna	L482	
Prole	M250	
Pushing Out the Boat	M252	
Qu Literary Magazine	M253	
Ramer, Susan	L486	
Reid, Janet	L490	
Reilly, Milly	L491	
Renard Press Ltd	P313	
Roberts, Soumeya Bendimerad	L495	
Robinson, Quressa	L497	
Rocking Chair Books	L499	
Rofe, Jennifer	L500	
Rogers, Coleridge & White Ltd	L501	
Romano, Annie	L502	
Rutherford, Laetitia	L513	
Rutman, Jim	L514	
Salazar, Des	L515	
Sentient Publications	P334	
Seren Books	P335	
Serra, Maria Cardona	L526	
Seventh Agency	L527	
Seymour, Charlotte	L528	
Shaw Agency, The	L529	
Silk, Julia	L535	
Simpson, Cara Lee	L537	
Soho Press	P348	
Soloway, Jennifer March	L544	
Sorg, Arley	L546	
Southern Humanities Review	M290	
Sparsile Books	P359	
Spout Press	P360	
Story Unlikely	M300	
Stringer, Marlene	L554	
Susan Schulman Literary Agency	L557	
Swainson, Joanna	L561	
Symonds, Laurel	L565	
Tahoma Literary Review	M308	
Tailwinds Press	P376	
Takahe	M309	
Takikawa, Marin	L566	
Tannenbaum, Amy	L568	
Tasman, Alice	L569	
Temz Review, The	M312	
Thayer, Henry	L572	
Thin Air Magazine	M314	
Thinkwell Books, UK	P384	
Thorneycroft, Euan	L574	
Threepenny Review, The	M317	
Torrey House Press, LLC	P390	
Tran, Jennifer Chen	L578	
Transworld Publishers	P393	
Turner Publishing	P394	
Tusculum Review, The	M321	
University of Alberta Press	P404	
Usselman, Laura	L581	
Vance, Lisa Erbach	L583	
Victoria Sanders & Associates LLC	L584	
Waccamaw	M335	
Wasafiri	M338	
Weiss, Alexandra	L593	
Weitzner, Tess	L594	
Wells, Karmen	L595	
Whispering Buffalo Literary Agency	L599	
Wickers, Chandler	L600	
Williams, Laura	L603	
Willms, Kathryn	L605	
Wilson, Ed	L607	
Wood, Caroline	L608	
Woods, Bryony	L610	
Woollard, Jessica	L611	
Yale Review, The	M344	
Yellow Mama Webzine	M346	
Yeoh, Rachel	L612	
Young, Claudia	L614	
Zack Company, Inc, The	L615	
Zone 3	M353	
Zuckerbrot, Renee	L618	
Zuraw-Friedland, Ayla	L619	

Literary Criticism
See more broadly: Literature

Arcadia Publishing	P020
Chapman	M075
Davies, Olivia	L147
Enitharmon Editions	P122
Feminist Studies	M119
First Line, The	M123
Goldblatt, Rachel	L243
Graywolf Press	P152
Lilliput Press, The	P217
London Review of Books	M191
Marion Boyars Publishers	P229
New England Review	M220
New Welsh Reader	M223
Peepal Tree Press	P278
Poetry Birmingham Literary Journal	M242
Quadrant Magazine	M254
Rutman, Jim	L514
Seren Books	P335
Thames & Hudson Inc.	P382
University of Alberta Press	P404
University of Missouri Press	P411
University of Texas Press	P414
University of Virginia Press	P415
Virginia Quarterly Review, The	M330
W.W. Norton & Company, Inc.	P423
Wallace Stevens Journal, The	M336
Yale Review, The	M344

Literary Fantasy
See more broadly: Fantasy; Literary

Margaret K. McElderry Books	P228

Literary Horror
See more broadly: Horror; Literary

Colwill, Charlotte	L121
Murray, Judith	L428
Tibbets, Anne	L576

Literary Journalism
See more broadly: Journalism; Literary

Irish Pages	M173
Southern Humanities Review	M290
Torrey House Press, LLC	P390

Literary Memoir
See more broadly: Memoir

Eisenmann, Caroline	L175
Fellows, Abi	L193
Fuentes, Sarah	L222
Lewis, Alison	L364
Peddle, Kay	L460
Philips, Ariana	L471
Ramer, Susan	L486
Robinson, Quressa	L497

Literary Mystery
See more broadly: Literary; Mystery

Chanchani, Sonali	L108
Harris, Erin	L268

Literary Suspense
See more broadly: Literary; Suspense

Evans, Kate	L185

Literary Thrillers
See more broadly: Literary; Thrillers

Chang, Nicola	L109
Geiger, Ellen	L227
Pelham, Imogen	L461

Literature
See more specifically: American Literature; Beat Generation; Fiction as a Subject; Literary Criticism; Medieval Literature; Metaphysical; Poetry as a Subject

African American Review	M009
Baylor University Press	P041
Black Moon Magazine	M056

Bloomsbury Academic P053
BOA Editions, Ltd. P057
Brick M065
Broadview Press P065
Cambridge University Press P068
Charnace, Edwina de L110
Classical Comics P090
Compassiviste Publishing P097
Crystal Magazine M098
Ekphrastic Review, The M109
Fazzari, Hillary L188
Gale P139
Graywolf Lab M145
Gulf Coast: A Journal of Literature and
    Fine Arts M147
Harvard University Press P165
Holloway, Sally L284
Icon Books Ltd P180
Image M166
Ink Sweat and Tears M168
Ireland's Own M172
Lilliput Press, The P217
London Review of Books M191
LSU Press P223
Manoa M199
Massachusetts Review, The M202
Methuen Publishing Ltd P238
Ohio University Press P261
Otago University Press P269
Oxford Poetry M229
Oxford University Press P272
Power Cut Lite M247
Purdue University Press P305
Quadrant Magazine M254
Sasquatch Books P325
SmokeLong Quarterly M283
Southwest Review M293
Stanford University Press P367
Taylor & Francis Group P378
Temz Review, The M312
Thames and Hudson Ltd P383
Threepenny Review, The M317
Times Literary Supplement (TLS), The ... M318
Transworld Publishers P393
University of Alberta Press P404
University of California Press P406
University of Iowa Press P408
University of Michigan Press, The P410
University of Tennessee Press P413
University of Texas Press P414
University of Virginia Press P415
Victoria Sanders & Associates LLC L584
Virginia Wine & Country Life M331
W.W. Norton & Company Ltd P422
W.W. Norton & Company, Inc. P423
Wallace Stevens Journal, The M336
Wasafiri M338
Windsor Review M342
Yale University Press (London) P438

Live Music
See more broadly: Music
Local
See more broadly: Regional
Dundurn P118
JMD Media / DB Publishing P198
Landfall M182
Local History
See more broadly: History
Countryside Books P099
History Press, The P174
JMD Media / DB Publishing P198
Kates Hill Press, The P203
Kent Life M178
Lilliput Press, The P217
Logaston Press P221
Pen & Sword Books Ltd P281

Scratching Shed Publishing P331
Logistics
See more broadly: Business
Loft Press, Inc. P220
London
See more broadly: England
Square Mile Magazine M298
Long Form Poetry
Long Poem Magazine M192
Tahoma Literary Review M308
Louisiana
See more broadly: United States
LSU Press P223
Love
See more broadly: Relationships
Ellis-Martin, Sian L180
Passionfruit Review, The M234
Tyndale House Publishers, Inc. P397
Low Fantasy
See more broadly: Fantasy
Gilbert, Tara L233
Potter, Madison L481
Soler, Shania N. L543
Trudel, Jes. L579
Weiss, Alexandra L593
Luxury Lifestyle
See more broadly: Lifestyle
Lyric Essays
Identity Theory M164
Jamii Publishing P196
Southern Humanities Review M290
Tahoma Literary Review M308
Lyrical
Glacier, The M141
Hensley, Chelsea L274
Mafia
See more broadly: Organised Crime
Magazines
See more broadly: Media
Magic
See more broadly: Fantasy
See more specifically: Dark Magic
Bauman, Erica L043
Belton, Maddy L049
Bent, Jenny L053
Buckley, Louise L085
Cabello, Analia L092
Danaczko, Melissa L139
Forrester, Jemima L210
Haley, Jolene L260
Harris, Erin L268
Hernando, Paloma L276
JMD Media / DB Publishing P198
Johnson, Jared L303
Knigge, Sheyla L339
Leon, Nina L360
MacKenzie, Joanna L382
Philips, Ariana L471
Phillips, Aemilia L472
Plant, Zoe L476
Rofe, Jennifer L500
Rushall, Kathleen L512
Sanchez, Kaitlyn L516
Seager, Chloe L524
Terlip, Paige L570
Weiman, Paula L592
Magical Realism
See more broadly: Fantasy
See more specifically: Fabulism
Armstrong, Susan L026
Barr, Anjanette L038
Cabello, Analia L092
Candlemark & Gleam P069
Cho, Catherine L114
Cichello, Kayla L117
Cooper, Maggie L129

Figueroa, Melanie L199
Foxx, Kat L213
Glenister, Emily L238
Gunic, Masha L256
Haley, Jolene L260
Julie Crisp Literary Agency L311
Kean, Taylor Martindale L324
Keren, Eli L330
Laxfield Literary Associates L356
Leon, Nina L360
Lightner, Kayla L365
Marini, Victoria L388
Marr, Jill L389
Niv, Daniel L440
O'Neill, Molly L446
Potter, Madison L481
Romano, Annie L502
Soler, Shania N. L543
Story Unlikely M300
Stringer, Marlene L554
Takikawa, Marin L566
Torrey House Press, LLC P390
Weiss, Alexandra L593
Weitzner, Tess. L594
Williams, Laura L603
Wilson, Desiree L606
Mahayana Buddhism
See more broadly: Buddhism
See more specifically: Zen
Maine
See more broadly: United States
University of Maine Press P409
Mainstream
Compassiviste Publishing P097
Make-Up
See more broadly: Beauty
Management
See more broadly: Business
See more specifically: Project Management;
    Service Management; Supply Chain
    Management
BCS (British Computer Society) P042
Berrett-Koehler Publishers P046
Bloomsbury Academic P053
Cambridge University Press P068
Gill Education P143
Oxford University Press P272
Peter Lang P285
Taylor & Francis Group P378
Zack Company, Inc, The L615
Maori
See more broadly: Ethnic Groups
Otago University Press P269
Maritime History
See more broadly: History
History Press, The P174
Pen & Sword Books Ltd P281
Marketing
See more broadly: Business
See more specifically: Advertising
Banter Press P033
Gill Education P143
Martial Arts
See more broadly: Sport
See more specifically: Qigong; Tai Chi
Singing Dragon P340
Turtle Press P395
Marxism
See more broadly: Philosophy; Politics
International Publishers P191
Maryland
See more broadly: United States
Mathematics
See more specifically: Statistics
Autumn Publishing Ltd P025
Bloomsbury Academic P053

Index | *Memoir* **329**

Cambridge University Press P068
Charlesbridge Publishing P081
Colourpoint Educational P095
Curious Minds L133
Diana Finch Literary Agency L154
Enslow Publishers, Inc. P123
Gale P139
Gill Education P143
Icon Books Ltd P180
Kane Press P202
Marshall, Jen L391
Oxford University Press P272
Stipes Publishing P371
Symonds, Laurel L565
Taylor & Francis Group P378
University of Michigan Press, The P410
W.W. Norton & Company, Inc. P423
Wilson, Desiree L606
Yale University Press (London) P438

Media

See more specifically: Books; Films; Magazines; Social Media; TV; Theatre

Bloomsbury Academic P053
Draper, Claire L162
Feminist Press, The P130
FRA (Futerman, Rose, & Associates) L214
Harvard University Press P165
Hensley, Chelsea L274
Hernando, Paloma L276
Indiana University Press P187
Joy Harris Literary Agency, Inc. L308
LSU Press P223
Ohio University Press P261
Oxford University Press P272
Peter Lang P285
Stanford University Press P367
Unfit Magazine M326
University of California Press P406
University of Michigan Press, The P410
University of Texas Press P414
Weiss, Alexandra L593

Medicine

See more broadly: Health

See more specifically: Anatomy; Biomedical Science; Geriatrics; Immunology; Physiology; Psychiatry

Arcadia Publishing P020
Betsy Amster Literary Enterprises L059
Bloomsbury Academic P053
Cambridge University Press P068
Curious Minds L133
DK Publishing P112
Dystel, Jane L167
Elsevier Ltd P121
Feminist Press, The P130
Gale P139
Glenister, Emily L238
Hammersmith Books P158
Harvard University Press P165
Idyll Arbor P181
Kensington Publishing Corp. P204
Medical Physics Publishing P234
Mills & Boon P240
Nolan, Laura L441
Oxford University Press P272
Research Journal of Pharmacy and Technology M260
Rudy Agency, The L510
Singing Dragon P340
Taylor & Francis Group P378
Thames & Hudson Inc. P382
Turner Publishing P394
University of Alberta Press P404
University of Michigan Press, The P410
W.W. Norton & Company Ltd P422
Yale University Press (London) P438

Medieval

See more broadly: History

Oxbow Books P271
Rossitto, Stefanie L508
University of Michigan Press, The P410
Zack Company, Inc, The L615

Medieval Literature

See more broadly: Literature

Meditation

See more broadly: Mind, Body, Spirit

Llewellyn Worldwide Ltd P219
Society for Promoting Christian Knowledge (SPCK) P345
Zack Company, Inc, The L615

Memoir

See more broadly: Autobiography

See more specifically: Celebrity Memoir; Inspirational Memoir; Literary Memoir

Ange, Anna L019
Annette Green Authors' Agency L021
April Gloaming P018
Arthurson, Wayne L027
Asabi Publishing P022
Bal, Emma L032
Barr, Anjanette L038
Bartholomew, Jason L041
Basalt Books P034
Baumer, Jan L044
Baxter, Veronique L045
Beaumont, Diana L046
Begum, Salma L047
Bess Press P047
Blackstaff Press P051
Blue Earth Review M059
Bradford Literary Agency L073
Brailsford, Karen L075
Brannan, Maria L076
Brewin Books Ltd P062
Brick M065
Carter, Rebecca L103
Caskie, Robert L105
Cavanagh, Claire L107
Chiotti, Danielle L113
Christie, Jennifer L116
Claret Press P089
Clarke, Caro L118
Clarke, Catherine L119
Cleis Press P091
Comparato, Andrea L123
Compass Talent L124
Conville, Clare L126
Creative Nonfiction M095
Crown Publishing Group, The P103
Curtis Brown L135
Dana Newman Literary, LLC L138
Danaczko, Melissa L139
Daunt Books Publishing P106
Dawson, Liza L148
Diana Finch Literary Agency L154
Dillsworth, Elise L156
Dolin, Lily L157
Doug Grad Literary Agency L161
Draper, Claire L162
Dublin Review, The M107
Dundurn P118
Dunn, Ben L164
Dystel, Jane L167
Edelstein, Anne L171
Einstein, Susanna L173
Epicenter Press Inc. P124
Evans, Kate L185
Feminist Press, The P130
Fernandez, Rochelle L197
Fernando, Kimberly L198
Fernwood Publishing P131
Fogg, Jack L206
Folio Literary Management, LLC L207
Fox, Aram L212
Foxx, Kat L213
Frankel, Valerie L215
Friedman, Rebecca L219
Furniss, Eugenie L224
Galvin, Lori L226
Gemini Books P140
Glenister, Emily L238
Goldblatt, Rachel L243
Goldstein, Veronica L244
Goose Lane Editions P148
Gordon, Andrew L245
Graywolf Press P152
Half Mystic Press P157
Harris, Erin L268
Hashtag Press P166
Hawthorne Books P167
Hayden, Viola L271
Hildebrand, Cole L280
History Press, The P174
Hiyate, Sam L281
Hordern, Kate L286
Icon Books Ltd P180
Identity Theory M164
Inscriptions Literary Agency L289
Irish Pages M173
Joelle Delbourgo Associates, Inc. L301
Kahn, Ella Diamond L314
Kardon, Julia L318
Karen Gantz Literary Management L319
Kate Barker Literary, TV, & Film Agency L320
Kates Hill Press, The P203
Kathryn Green Literary Agency, LLC L322
Kim, Julia L334
Kimber, Natalie L336
Kracht, Elizabeth L341
Kube Publishing P209
Lambert, Sophie L348
Langtons International L354
Latshaw, Katherine L355
Laxfield Literary Associates L356
Leigh Feldman Literary L359
Levitt, Sarah L361
Levy, Yael L362
Lewinsohn Literary L363
Lightner, Kayla L365
Lilliput Press, The P217
Loft Press, Inc. P220
London Review of Books M191
MacDonald, Emily L378
MacLeod, Lauren L383
Malahat Review, The M197
Marr, Jill L389
Marsiglia, Caroline L392
Maurer, Shari L397
Maw, Jane Graham L398
McCormick Literary L400
Medina Publishing P235
Merlin Unwin Books P237
Mihell, Natasha L410
Minnesota Historical Society Press P241
Monoray P246
Moorhead, Max L416
Morrell, Imogen L417
Mortimer, Michele L418
Mulcahy Sweeney Literary Agency L423
Mundy, Toby L426
Murgolo, Karen L427
Murray, Judith L428
Muswell Press P250
Nashville Review M217
Niumata, Erin L439
O'Shea, Amy L447
Otago University Press P269

330 Index | *Men's Interests*

Pan Macmillan Australia P274
Patterson, Emma L458
Peepal Tree Press P278
Pelham, Imogen L461
Perry Literary L466
Pestritto, Carrie L467
Pierce, Rosie L474
Plitt, Carrie L477
Polygon P298
Power, Anna L482
Preston, Amanda L484
Reid, Janet L490
Richter, Rick L493
Roberts, Soumeya Bendimerad L495
Roseway P317
Schofield, Hannah L522
Selectric Artists L525
Seren Books P335
Shenandoah M277
Shestopal, Camilla L534
Shipwreckt Books Publishing Company P336
Shooter Literary Magazine M279
Silk, Julia L535
Simpson, Cara Lee L537
Singh, Amandeep L538
Southern Humanities Review M290
Story Unlikely M300
Susan Schulman Literary Agency L557
Swainson, Joanna L561
Sweet, Emily L563
Sweren, Becky L564
Thorneycroft, Euan L574
Thwaites, Steph L575
Toad Hall Editions P387
Tolka M319
Topping, Antony L577
Torrey House Press, LLC P390
Tyndale House Publishers, Inc. P397
Unbridled Books P401
University of Alberta Press P404
University of Michigan Press, The P410
University of Virginia Press P415
Usselman, Laura L581
Valley Press P418
W.W. Norton & Company Ltd P422
W.W. Norton & Company, Inc. P423
Williams, Laura L603
Wilson, Ed L607
Woods, Bryony L610
Woollard, Jessica L611
Yale Review, The M344
Yale University Press (London) P438
Yeoh, Rachel L612
Zack Company, Inc, The L615
Zibby Books P440

Men's Interests
Compassiviste Publishing P097

Men's Issues
See more broadly: Social Issues

Menopause
See more broadly: Women's Health
First For Women M122
Macdougall, Laura L379

Mental Disorders
See more broadly: Psychiatry

Mental Health
See more broadly: Health
See more specifically: Dementia
Danko, Margaret L140
Finegan, Stevie L203
Goodman Beck Publishing P147
Grunewald, Hattie L254
Hammersmith Books P158
Hashtag Press P166
Hildebrand, Cole L280
Jessica Kingsley Publishers P197
Krienke, Mary L343
Lightner, Kayla L365
Maltese, Alyssa L387
New Harbinger Publications P255
Nichols, Mariah L438
Singing Dragon P340
Soloway, Jennifer March L544
Trudel, Jes L579
Tyndale House Publishers, Inc. P397
W.W. Norton & Company, Inc. P423
Weiss, Alexandra L593
Williams, Laura L603
Wilson, Desiree L606

Metaphysical
See more broadly: Literature

Methodism
See more broadly: Christianity

Michigan
See more broadly: United States
See more specifically: Ann Arbor; Detroit
University of Michigan Press, The P410

Middle East
See more broadly: Regional
Bloomsbury Academic P053
Feminist Press, The P130
Ghahremani, Lilly L230
Indiana University Press P187
Pluto Press P295
Saqi Books P324
Stanford University Press P367
Thwaites, Steph L575
University of Alberta Press P404
University of California Press P406
University of Michigan Press, The P410
University of Texas Press P414

Middle Grade
3 Seas Literary Agency L001
Agency (London) Ltd, The L008
Albert Whitman & Company P007
Alice Williams Literary L012
Allen & Unwin P009
Andlyn L014
Andrade, Hannah L015
Andrews McMeel Publishing P015
Ange, Anna L019
Anne Clark Literary Agency L020
Annette Green Authors' Agency L021
Arcadia Publishing P020
Armada, Kurestin L024
Arms, Victoria Wells L025
Atyeo, Charlotte L028
Baror International, Inc. L037
Bath Literary Agency L042
Baxter, Veronique L045
Belton, Maddy L049
Bent Agency (UK), The L051
Bent Agency, The L052
Bewley, Elizabeth L061
Blair Partnership, The L064
Borstel, Stefanie Sanchez Von L070
Bradford, Laura L074
Bright Agency (UK), The L078
Bright Agency (US), The L079
Brooks, Savannah L080
Burby, Danielle L087
Burns, Camille L089
Cabello, Analia L092
Cadno P067
Candy Jar Books P070
Carroll, Megan L102
Charlesbridge Publishing P081
Cherry Lake Publishing Group P083
Children's Books North Agency L112
Chiotti, Danielle L113
Cichello, Kayla L117
Colwill, Charlotte L121
Comparato, Andrea L123
Cooper, Gemma L128
Crandall, Becca L130
Curtis Brown L135
Cusick, John L136
Darley Anderson Children's L144
DK Publishing P112
Dominguez, Adriana L158
Draper, Claire L162
Dunow, Carlson & Lerner Agency L166
Eerdmans Books for Young Readers P120
Einstein, Susanna L173
Eisenbraun, Nicole L174
Eunice McMullen Children's Literary Agent Ltd L182
Fabien, Samantha L186
Fazzari, Hillary L188
Fellows, Abi L193
Ferguson, T.S. L195
Fernandez, Rochelle L197
Figueroa, Melanie L199
Finegan, Stevie L203
Firefly P133
Flannery Literary L204
Flynn, Amy Thrall L205
Gahan, Isobel L225
Gemini Books P140
Getzler, Josh L229
Ghahremani, Lilly L230
Gisondi, Katie L235
Goetz, Adria L241
Goff, Ellen L242
Gruber, Pam L253
Gunic, Masha L256
Guppy Books P155
Hakim, Serene L259
Haley, Jolene L260
Hannah Sheppard Literary Agency L262
Hare, Jessica L266
Hashtag Press P166
Hawk, Susan L269
Hawn, Molly Ker L270
Hensley, Chelsea L274
Hernandez, Saritza L275
Hernando, Paloma L276
Hodges, Jodie L282
Holroyde, Penny L285
Hordern, Kate L286
IgKids P183
Inscriptions Literary Agency L289
Irvine, Lucy L292
Jean V. Naggar Literary Agency, The L299
Joelle Delbourgo Associates, Inc. L301
Kahn, Ella Diamond L314
Kane Press P202
Kate Nash Literary Agency L321
Kathryn Green Literary Agency, LLC L322
Kean, Taylor Martindale L324
Kim, Sally M. L335
Knigge, Sheyla L339
KT Literary L345
Kube Publishing P209
Lakosil, Natalie L347
Langlee, Lina L352
Langton, Becca L353
Lantana Publishing P210
Latshaw, Katherine L355
Leapfrog Press P212
Leon, Nina L360
Lerner Publishing Group P213
Lindsay Literary Agency L366
MacLeod, Lauren L383
Macmillan Children's Books P226
Margaret K. McElderry Books P228
Mattson, Jennifer L396

Maurer, Shari	L397
McBride, Juliana	L399
Mihell, Natasha	L410
Moody Publishers	P247
Nathan, Abigail	L433
Nelson Literary Agency, LLC	L435
Nelson, Patricia	L437
O'Neill, Molly	L446
Oh MG Press	P260
Orca Book Publishers	P266
Ostby, Kristin	L452
Pacific Press Publishing Association	P273
Pan Macmillan Australia	P274
Parker, Elana Roth	L455
Pestritto, Carrie	L467
Phelan, Beth	L470
Philips, Ariana	L471
Phoenix Moirai	P288
Piccadilly Press	P291
Plant, Zoe	L476
Posner, Marcy	L480
Quirk Books	P308
Ransom Publishing Ltd	P312
Richter, Rick	L493
Robinson, Quressa	L497
Rofe, Jennifer	L500
Ross, Whitney	L507
Rushall, Kathleen	L512
Sanchez, Kaitlyn	L516
Sant, Kelly Van	L518
Scholastic	P329
Scholastic UK	P330
Seager, Chloe	L524
Seventh Agency	L527
Shestopal, Camilla	L534
Simply Read Books	P339
Siobhan, Aiden	L539
Skylark Literary	L540
Soler, Shania N.	L543
Soloway, Jennifer March	L544
Sourcebooks Young Readers	P358
StoryWise	L552
Stringer Literary Agency LLC, The	L553
Susan Schulman Literary Agency	L557
Sutherland, Kari	L559
Symonds, Laurel	L565
Talbot, Emily	L567
Tasman, Alice	L569
Terlip, Paige	L570
Tilbury House Publishers	P385
Tran, Jennifer Chen	L578
Trudel, Jes	L579
Turner Publishing	P394
Walker Books	P424
Walsh, Caroline	L589
Weiman, Paula	L592
Weiss, Alexandra	L593
Weitzner, Tess	L594
Weltz, Jennifer	L596
Westin, Erin Casey	L597
Whatnall, Michaela	L598
Williams, Laura	L603
Williamson, Jo	L604
Wilson, Desiree	L606
Woods, Bryony	L610
Zacker, Marietta B.	L616

Midwifery
See more broadly: Nursing
Macdougall, Laura	L379

Military
See more broadly: Warfare
See more specifically: Military Aviation; Military Vehicles; Special Forces
Amber Books Ltd	P011
Brewin Books Ltd	P062
Brown, Megan	L084
Doug Grad Literary Agency	L161
History Press, The	P174
Howgate Publishing	P178
Knight Features	L340
Lovell, Jake	L372
Schiffer Military History	P328
University of Missouri Press	P411
Zack Company, Inc, The	L615

Military Aviation
See more broadly: Aviation; Military
Pen & Sword Books Ltd	P281

Military History
See more broadly: History; Warfare
Brewin Books Ltd	P062
Fighting High	P132
Goose Lane Editions	P148
Icon Books Ltd	P180
Indiana University Press	P187
Minnesota Historical Society Press	P241
Pen & Sword Books Ltd	P281
Texas A&M University Press	P381
Thames & Hudson Inc.	P382
University of North Texas Press	P412
Zack Company, Inc, The	L615

Military Vehicles
See more broadly: Military; Vehicles

Millennial
Carr, Jamie	L101
Watterson, Jessica	L591

Mind, Body, Spirit
See more broadly: Health
See more specifically: Meditation; Yoga
Arcadia Publishing	P020
Curran, Sabhbh	L134
Dana Newman Literary, LLC	L138
Ericka T. Phillips	L181
Gill Books	P142
Globe Pequot Press, The	P145
Goose Lane Editions	P148
Haley, Jolene	L260
Joelle Delbourgo Associates, Inc.	L301
Kensington Publishing Corp.	P204
Lilliput Press, The	P217
Llewellyn Worldwide Ltd	P219
Pan Macmillan Australia	P274
Piatkus Books	P289
Stephens, Jenny	L549
Susan Schulman Literary Agency	L557
Terlip, Paige	L570
Turner Publishing	P394
Turtle Press	P395
W.W. Norton & Company, Inc.	P423
Whitford Press	P428
Zack Company, Inc, The	L615

Minerals
See more broadly: Geology

Mini Cars
See more broadly: Cars

Minnesota
See more broadly: United States
Minnesota Historical Society Press	P241

Missouri
See more broadly: United States
See more specifically: St Louis
River Hills Traveler	M263
Sweetgum Press	P375
University of Missouri Press	P411

Model Aircraft
See more broadly: Model Making

Model Making
See more broadly: Crafts
See more specifically: Model Aircraft; Model Ships and Boats

Model Ships and Boats
See more broadly: Model Making

Modern History
See more broadly: History

Montgomeryshire
See more broadly: Wales
Logaston Press	P221

Mormonism
See more broadly: Christianity

Motherhood
See more broadly: Parenting
Buckley, Louise	L085
Carr, Jamie	L101
Foxx, Kat	L213
Literary Mama	M187
Roberts, Soumeya Bendimerad	L495

Motivational Self-Help
See more broadly: Self Help
Derviskadic, Dado	L151
Tyndale House Publishers, Inc.	P397

Motor Boats
See more broadly: Boats

Motorbikes
See more broadly: Vehicles
Square Mile Magazine	M298

Motorcycling
See more broadly: Hobbies

Motorhomes
See more broadly: Vehicles

Motorsports
See more broadly: Sport
See more specifically: Formula One; NASCAR
JMD Media / DB Publishing	P198

Mountain Lifestyle
See more broadly: Lifestyle

Multicultural
See more broadly: Culture
Cho, Catherine	L114
Geiger, Ellen	L227
Romano, Annie	L502
Sheree Bykofsky Associates, Inc.	L532
Tran, Jennifer Chen	L578
University of North Texas Press	P412
W.W. Norton & Company Ltd	P422

Music
See more specifically: Bluegrass; Choral Music; Church Music; Classical Music; Electronic Music; Heavy Metal; Jazz; Live Music; Musical Instruments; Popular Music; Punk; Rock Music; Roots Music; Traditional Music
Annette Green Authors' Agency	L021
Arcadia Publishing	P020
Atyeo, Charlotte	L028
Backbeat Books	P027
Begum, Salma	L047
Bloomsbury Academic	P053
Brattle Agency LLC, The	L077
Brewin Books Ltd	P062
Brick	M065
Cambridge University Press	P068
Compassiviste Publishing	P097
Diversion Books	P111
Doug Grad Literary Agency	L161
Dundurn	P118
Edenborough, Sam	L172
FRA (Futerman, Rose, & Associates)	L214
Gill Education	P143
Gordon, Andrew	L245
Graywolf Lab	M145
Half Mystic Journal	M149
Half Mystic Press	P157
Harvard University Press	P165
Indiana University Press	P187
Kensington Publishing Corp.	P204
Kim, Jennifer	L333
Korero Press	P208
Lilliput Press, The	P217
Mack, Kate	L381

Marion Boyars Publishers	P229	
Marr, Jill	L389	
Massachusetts Review, The	M202	
McNidder & Grace	P232	
Mortimer, Michele	L418	
Nolan, Laura	L441	
Orphans Publishing	P268	
Oxford University Press	P272	
Phaidon Press	P287	
Plexus Publishing Limited	P294	
Polygon	P298	
Quadrant Magazine	M254	
Ramer, Susan	L486	
Red Magazine	M259	
Richter, Rick	L493	
Riposte	M262	
Rutman, Jim	L514	
Scratching Shed Publishing	P331	
Seren Books	P335	
Sheree Bykofsky Associates, Inc.	L532	
SOMA	M285	
Southwest Review	M293	
Spackman, James	L547	
Square Mile Magazine	M298	
Stainer & Bell Ltd	P366	
Stipes Publishing	P371	
Tasman, Alice	L569	
Texas A&M University Press	P381	
Thames & Hudson Inc.	P382	
Topping, Antony	L577	
Transworld Publishers	P393	
Uncut	M324	
University of California Press	P406	
University of Michigan Press, The	P410	
University of North Texas Press	P412	
University of Tennessee Press	P413	
University of Texas Press	P414	
University of Virginia Press	P415	
Victoria Sanders & Associates LLC	L584	
Virginia Wine & Country Life	M331	
W.W. Norton & Company Ltd	P422	
W.W. Norton & Company, Inc.	P423	
Yale Review, The	M344	
Yale University Press (London)	P438	
Zack Company, Inc, The	L615	

Musical Instruments
See more broadly: Music
See more specifically: Piano
Backbeat Books P027

Musicals
See more broadly: Theatre

Mystery
See more specifically: Amateur Investigator; Cozy Mysteries; Detective Fiction; Domestic Mystery; Historical Mystery Fiction; Literary Mystery; Romantic Mystery

Adsett, Alex	L005
Afonso, Thais	L007
Alfred Hitchcock Mystery Magazine	M016
American Mystery Classics	P012
Andrade, Hannah	L015
Armada, Kurestin	L024
Asabi Publishing	P022
Baxter, Veronique	L045
Betancourt Literary	L057
Betsy Amster Literary Enterprises	L059
Bolton, Camilla	L067
Brace, Samantha	L072
Bradford Literary Agency	L073
Bradford, Laura	L074
Brooks, Savannah	L080
Burke, Kate	L088
Carina Press	P073
Cichello, Kayla	L117
Claret Press	P089
Comparato, Andrea	L123
Cooper, Gemma	L128
Countryside Books	P099
Crowley, Sheila	L132
Crystal Magazine	M098
Dawson, Liza	L148
Diversion Books	P111
Doug Grad Literary Agency	L161
Dreamspinner Press	P115
DSP Publications	P116
Eason, Lynette	L169
Every Day Fiction	M114
Fabien, Samantha	L186
Fate	M117
Feminist Press, The	P130
Fernandez, Rochelle	L197
Figueroa, Melanie	L199
Foxx, Kat	L213
Frankel, Valerie	L215
Future Fire, The	M135
Galvin, Lori	L226
Getzler, Josh	L229
Gilbert, Tara	L233
Gisondi, Katie	L235
Graham, Stacey	L247
Grunewald, Hattie	L254
Gunic, Masha	L256
Haley, Jolene	L260
Harper, Logan	L267
Hensley, Chelsea	L274
Hiyate, Sam	L281
Inscriptions Literary Agency	L289
Irene Goodman Literary Agency (IGLA)	L291
Irvine, Lucy	L292
Joelle Delbourgo Associates, Inc.	L301
Joffe Books	P199
Joy Harris Literary Agency, Inc.	L308
Kensington Publishing Corp.	P204
Keren, Eli	L330
Kim, Julia	L334
Kracht, Elizabeth	L341
Langtons International	L354
Leon, Nina	L360
MacKenzie, Joanna	L382
Maidment, Olivia	L386
Marr, Jill	L389
Maurer, Shari	L397
Mortimer, Michele	L418
Mysterious Press, The	P252
Mystery Magazine	M216
Nathan, Abigail	L433
NBM Publishing	P254
Nelson, Patricia	L437
Niumata, Erin	L439
Orenda Books	P267
Ostby, Kristin	L452
Pages, Saribel	L453
Parker, Elana Roth	L455
Pass, Marina de	L456
Pen & Ink Designs Publishing	P280
Penzler Publishers	P282
Pestritto, Carrie	L467
Philips, Ariana	L471
Pierce, Rosie	L474
Pine, Gideon	L475
Plant, Zoe	L476
Poisoned Pen Press	P297
Posner, Marcy	L480
Reid, Janet	L490
Romano, Annie	L502
Salazar, Des	L515
Seventh Agency	L527
Shestopal, Camilla	L534
Soloway, Jennifer March	L544
Steed, Hayley	L548
Story Unlikely	M300
Stringer, Marlene	L554
Takikawa, Marin	L566
Tibbets, Anne	L576
Tor Publishing Group	P388
Torrey House Press, LLC	P390
Tran, Jennifer Chen	L578
Trudel, Jes	L579
Turner Publishing	P394
Tyndale House Publishers, Inc.	P397
Udden, Jennifer	L580
Victoria Sanders & Associates LLC	L584
W.W. Norton & Company, Inc.	P423
Weiss, Alexandra	L593
Williams, Laura	L603
Wood, Ed	L609
Yours Fiction – Women's Special Series	M351
Zack Company, Inc, The	L615

Mysticism
See more broadly: Supernatural / Paranormal
See more specifically: Fortune Telling and Divination
Dawntreader, The M102

NASCAR
See more broadly: Motorsports

Narrative Essays
See more broadly: Narrative Nonfiction
See more specifically: Personal Essays

Ange, Anna	L019
Danko, Margaret	L140
Dolin, Lily	L157
Guernica Editions	P153
Hawthorne Books	L167
Otago University Press	P269
Plitt, Carrie	L477

Narrative History
See more broadly: History; Narrative Nonfiction

Dawson, Liza	L148
Edelstein, Anne	L171
Savvides, Marilia	L520

Narrative Journalism
See more broadly: Journalism; Narrative Nonfiction

Krichevsky, Stuart	L342
Mendia, Isabel	L403
Strothman, Wendy	L555

Narrative Nonfiction
See more specifically: Narrative Essays; Narrative History; Narrative Journalism

Adams, Seren	L004
Adsett, Alex	L005
And Other Stories	P013
Andrade, Hannah	L015
Ange, Anna	L019
Arthurson, Wayne	L027
Asabi Publishing	P022
Bal, Emma	L032
Bartholomew, Jason	L041
Baumer, Jan	L044
Berdinsky, Kendall	L054
Betancourt Literary	L057
Betsy Amster Literary Enterprises	L059
Bowlin, Sarah	L071
Brouckaert, Justin	L083
Carr, Jamie	L101
Caskie, Robert	L105
Chanchani, Sonali	L108
Chiotti, Danielle	L113
Cho, Catherine	L114
Clarke, Caro	L118
Combemale, Chris	L122
Curran, Sabhbh	L134
Dana Newman Literary, LLC	L138
Daunt Books Publishing	P106
Diana Finch Literary Agency	L154
Dolin, Lily	L157

Index | Neurobiology

Dominguez, Adriana	L158
Doubleday (UK)	P114
Dunham Literary, Inc.	L163
Dunn, Ben	L164
Ellis-Martin, Sian	L180
Evans, Kate	L185
Ferguson, Hannah	L194
Fogg, Jack	L206
Folio Literary Management, LLC	L207
Fox, Aram	L212
Friedman, Claire	L217
Friedman, Jessica	L218
Gillam, Bianca	L234
Goderich, Miriam	L240
Goldblatt, Rachel	L243
Gordon, Andrew	L245
Gruber, Pam	L253
Hannah Sheppard Literary Agency	L262
Harris, Erin	L268
Hayden, Viola	L271
Hernandez, Saritza	L275
Hildebrand, Cole	L280
Holloway, Sally	L284
Hwang, Annie	L288
Irving, Dotti	L293
Joelle Delbourgo Associates, Inc.	L301
Kahn, Ella Diamond	L314
Kardon, Julia	L318
Karen Gantz Literary Management	L319
Krienke, Mary	L343
Lambert, Sophie	L348
Latshaw, Katherine	L355
Leigh Feldman Literary	L359
Levitt, Sarah	L361
Lightner, Kayla	L365
MacDonald, Emily	L378
Macdougall, Laura	L379
MacLeod, Lauren	L383
Malahat Review, The	M197
Maltese, Alyssa	L387
Marr, Jill	L389
Marshall, Jen	L391
Marsiglia, Caroline	L392
Maurer, Shari	L397
Maw, Jane Graham	L398
McCormick Literary	L400
Molloy, Jess	L414
Monoray	P246
Moorhead, Max	L416
Mortimer, Michele	L418
Mundy, Toby	L426
Murgolo, Karen	L427
Niumata, Erin	L439
O'Grady, Niamh	L445
O'Neill, Molly	L446
Pan Macmillan Australia	P274
Pass, Marina de	L456
Patterson, Emma	L458
Peddle, Kay	L460
Perry Literary	L466
Pestritto, Carrie	L467
Philips, Ariana	L471
Phillips, Aemilia	L472
Pickering, Juliet	L473
Pierce, Rosie	L474
Pine, Gideon	L475
Plitt, Carrie	L477
Polygon	P298
Posner, Marcy	L480
Preston, Amanda	L484
Ramer, Susan	L486
Regina Ryan Books	L489
Reid, Janet	L490
Richter, Rick	L493
Roberts, Soumeya Bendimerad	L495
Robinson, Quressa	L497
Romano, Annie	L502
Rutman, Jim	L514
Salt Publishing	P322
Schofield, Hannah	L522
Selectric Artists	L525
Serra, Maria Cardona	L526
Shaw Agency, The	L529
Shestopal, Camilla	L534
Sierra	M281
Silk, Julia	L535
Simpson, Cara Lee	L537
Stephens, Jenny	L549
Story Unlikely	M300
Strothman, Wendy	L555
Swainson, Joanna	L561
Tahoma Literary Review	M308
Takikawa, Marin	L566
Tasman, Alice	L569
Terlip, Paige	L570
Vance, Lisa Erbach	L583
Viney Agency, The	L585
Weitzner, Tess	L594
Wells, Karmen	L595
Whatnall, Michaela	L598
Williams, Laura	L603
Willms, Kathryn	L605
Wilson, Desiree	L606
Woollard, Jessica	L611

National Security
See more broadly: Warfare

University of Georgia Press	P407
Zack Company, Inc, The	L615

Native Americans
See more broadly: Ethnic Groups

Epicenter Press Inc.	P124
Hancock House Publishers	P159
Minnesota Historical Society Press	P241
Sunbelt Publications, Inc.	P373
University of Alberta Press	P404
University of Michigan Press, The	P410
University of Missouri Press	P411
University Press of Colorado	P416
Zack Company, Inc, The	L615

Nature
See more specifically: Animals; Environment

Adams, Seren	L004
Arcadia Publishing	P020
Atyeo, Charlotte	L028
Autumn Publishing Ltd	P025
Bajek, Lauren	L031
Bal, Emma	L032
Barr, Anjanette	L038
Barrett, Emily	L040
Basalt Books	P034
Bernardi, Amanda	L056
Black & White Publishing Ltd	P049
Brannan, Maria	L076
Britain Magazine	M066
Caskie, Robert	L105
Charlesbridge Publishing	P081
Clarke, Caro	L118
Clarke, Catherine	L119
Compassiviste Publishing	P097
Conrad, Claire Paterson	L125
Cosmos	M089
Cottage Life	M090
Crystal Magazine	M098
Curious Minds	L133
Dawntreader, The	M102
DK Publishing	P112
Dunn, Ben	L164
Evans, Kate	L185
Fogg, Jack	L206
Fox, Aram	L212
Gill Books	P142
Globe Pequot Press, The	P145
Goldblatt, Rachel	L243
Goldstein, Veronica	L244
Goose Lane Editions	P148
Graffeg	P150
Hancock House Publishers	P159
Harvard University Press	P165
History Press, The	P174
Icon Books Ltd	P180
Imagine Publishing	P186
Irish Pages	M173
Island Online	M175
Kantor, Camille	L317
Kate Barker Literary, TV, & Film Agency	L320
Kensington Publishing Corp.	P204
Kent Life	M178
Lambert, Sophie	L348
Laxfield Literary Associates	L356
Lewinsohn Literary	L363
Lilliput Press, The	P217
Little Bigfoot	P218
MacDonald, Emily	L378
Maltese, Alyssa	L387
Merlin Unwin Books	P237
Minnesota Historical Society Press	P241
Morrell, Imogen	L417
Mortimer, Michele	L418
Ohio University Press	P261
Otago University Press	P269
Panorama	M232
Peddle, Kay	L460
Pelagic	P279
Pineapple Press	P293
Plitt, Carrie	L477
Pocket Mountains	P296
Polygon	P298
Posner, Marcy	L480
Preston, Amanda	L484
Regina Ryan Books	L489
Reilly, Milly	L491
River Hills Traveler	M263
Roberts, Soumeya Bendimerad	L495
Rocky Mountain Books	P315
Rutherford, Laetitia	L513
Salt Publishing	P322
Sasquatch Books	P325
Seymour, Charlotte	L528
Sierra	M281
Simpson, Cara Lee	L537
Singh, Amandeep	L538
Stephens, Jenny	L549
Strothman, Wendy	L555
Sunbelt Publications, Inc.	P373
Swainson, Joanna	L561
Texas A&M University Press	P381
Thames and Hudson Ltd	P383
This England	M316
Thorneycroft, Euan	L574
Topping, Antony	L577
Turner Publishing	P394
Two Fine Crows Books	P396
University of Alberta Press	P404
University of Georgia Press	P407
University of Iowa Press	P408
University of Michigan Press, The	P410
University of Missouri Press	P411
University of North Texas Press	P412
University of Texas Press	P414
University of Virginia Press	P415
W.W. Norton & Company Ltd	P422
Wide-Eyed Editions	P429
Willms, Kathryn	L605
Wilson, Ed	L607
Zack Company, Inc, The	L615

Neurobiology
See more broadly: Biology

W.W. Norton & Company Ltd P422

Neurodiversity
See more broadly: Psychology
See more specifically: ADHD

Neuropsychology
See more broadly: Psychology
See more specifically: Autism
W.W. Norton & Company Ltd P422

Neuroscience
See more broadly: Science
Buckley, Louise L085
Oxford University Press P272
W.W. Norton & Company Ltd P422

Nevada
See more broadly: United States

New Adult
Acheampong, Kwaku L003
Barone Literary Agency L036
Brannan, Maria L076
Fazzari, Hillary L188
Finch, Rebeka L202
Leon, Nina L360
Lineberry, Isabel L367
Madeleine Milburn Literary, TV &
    Film Agency L385
Niv, Daniel L440
Salazar, Des L515
Seventh Agency L527
Soler, Shania N. L543
Tran, Jennifer Chen L578

New Age
See more broadly: Spirituality
Compassiviste Publishing P097
Danko, Margaret L140
Hay House Publishers P168

New Brunswick
See more broadly: Canada
Goose Lane Editions P148

New England
See more broadly: United States
Yankee Magazine M345

New Jersey
See more broadly: United States

New York City
See more broadly: New York State

New York State
See more broadly: United States
See more specifically: New York City; Westchester
    County

New Zealand
See more broadly: Australasia / Oceania
Landfall M182
Takahe M309

News
Ann Arbor Observer M022
Atlanta Magazine M030
Bluegrass Unlimited M061
Business & Accountancy Daily M068
Conversation (UK), The M087
Cosmos M089
Crystal Magazine M098
Facts & Fiction M116
Forty20 .... M128
Funeral Business Solutions M134
Insurance Post M169
New Internationalist M221
OK! Magazine M228
Pride M249
Racecar Engineering M255
River Hills Traveler M263
Rugby World M265
Spa Magazine M295
Speciality Food M296
Supplement, The M306
That's Life! M313
Ulster Business M323

Wallace Stevens Journal, The M336

Noir
See more broadly: Crime
Ange, Anna L019
Asabi Publishing P022
Future Fire, The M135
Kane Literary Agency L316

Nonfiction
30 North M001
32 Poems M002
404 Ink P001
A.M. Heath & Company Limited,
    Author's Agents L002
aaduna M003
ABC-CLIO P002
Able Muse Press P003
About Place Journal M004
Account, The M006
Acheampong, Kwaku L003
Acumen M007
Adams, Seren L004
Adsett, Alex L005
Adventure Books by Vertebrate
    Publishing P004
African American Golfer's Digest M008
African American Review M009
Agni M011
Agricultural History M012
Alabama Heritage M013
Alaska Quarterly Review M014
Albemarle M015
Alcock, Michael L009
Algonquin Books P008
Alice Williams Literary L012
Allen & Unwin P009
Alternating Current Press P010
Ambassador Speakers Bureau &
    Literary Agency L013
Amber Books Ltd P011
Amethyst Review M019
And Other Poems M020
And Other Stories P013
Andrade, Hannah L015
Andrew Nurnberg Associates, Ltd L016
Andrews McMeel Publishing P015
Ange, Anna L019
Ann Arbor Observer M022
Anne Clark Literary Agency L020
Annette Green Authors' Agency L021
Antony Harwood Limited L022
Anvil Press Publishers P017
Apple Tree Literary Ltd L023
April Gloaming P018
Arboreal M023
Arc M024
Arcadia Publishing P020
Architectural Review, The M025
Arms, Victoria Wells L025
Art Quarterly M026
Arte Publico Press P021
Arthurson, Wayne L027
Arts & Letters M027
Asabi Publishing P022
Asian Social Science M028
Atlanta Magazine M030
Atlantic Northeast M032
Atyeo, Charlotte L028
Aurealis M034
Aurora Metro Press P024
Auroras & Blossoms PoArtMo
    Anthology M035
Autumn Publishing Ltd P025
AZ Foothills Magazine M036
Babybug M037
Backbeat Books P027
Bacopa Literary Review M038

Baffler, The M039
Bajek, Lauren L031
Bal, Emma L032
Bald and Bonkers Network LLC P030
Balow, Dan L033
Banter Press P033
Barbara, Stephen L034
Baror International, Inc. L037
Barr, Anjanette L038
Barr, Nicola L039
Barren Magazine M041
Barrett, Emily L040
Bartholomew, Jason L041
Basalt Books P034
Basic Books P035
Basic Health Publications, Inc. P037
BatCat Press P040
Bath Literary Agency L042
Baumer, Jan L044
Baxter, Veronique L045
Baylor University Press P041
BBC History Magazine M042
BCS (British Computer Society) P042
Bear Deluxe Magazine, The M044
Beaumont, Diana L046
Bee, The M045
Begum, Salma L047
Bella M046
Belmont Story Review M047
Belton, Maddy L049
Bent Agency (UK), The L051
Bent Agency, The L052
Bent, Jenny L053
Bentley Publishers P044
Berdinsky, Kendall L054
Berghahn Books Ltd P045
Berks County Living M049
Bernardi, Amanda L056
Berrett-Koehler Publishers P046
Bess Press P047
Best of British M050
Betancourt Literary L057
Betsy Amster Literary Enterprises L059
Better Homes and Gardens M051
Better Than Starbucks M052
Beverley Slopen Literary Agency L060
BFS Journal M054
Big Fiction M055
Bird Eye Books P048
Black & White Publishing Ltd P049
Black Moon Magazine M056
Black Warrior Review M058
Blackstaff Press P051
Blair Partnership, The L064
Blake Friedmann Literary Agency Ltd .. L065
Bloodhound Books P052
Bloomsbury Academic P053
Blue Earth Review M059
Blue Mesa Review M060
Blue Poppy Enterprises P055
Blue Star Press P056
Bluegrass Unlimited M061
BOA Editions, Ltd. P057
Bonnier Books (UK) P059
Book Group, The L068
Books For All Times P060
Borstel, Stefanie Sanchez Von L070
Boston Review M062
Bowhunter M063
Bowlin, Sarah L071
Boyfriend Village M064
Bradford Literary Agency L073
Bradford, Laura L074
Brailsford, Karen L075
Brannan, Maria L076
Brattle Agency LLC, The L077

Brewin Books Ltd	P062
Brick	M065
Bright Agency (UK), The	L078
Bright Agency (US), The	L079
Britain Magazine	M066
British Academy, The	P063
British Museum Press, The	P064
Broadview Press	P065
Broken Sleep Books	P066
Brooks, Savannah	L080
Brotherstone Creative Management	L081
Brotherstone, Charlie	L082
Brouckaert, Justin	L083
Brown, Megan	L084
BSFA Review, The	M067
Buckley, Louise	L085
Bukowski, Danielle	L086
Burns, Camille	L089
Business & Accountancy Daily	M068
Business Traveller	M069
CAA (London)	L091
Cambridge University Press	P068
Cameron, Kimberley	L093
Campbell, Charlie	L094
Campos, Vanessa	L095
Canadian Dimension	M072
Candy Jar Books	P070
Canterbury Literary Agency	L096
Canterbury Press	P071
Captivate Press	P072
Caribbean Writer, The	M073
Carolina Woman	M074
Caroline Davidson Literary Agency	L099
Carr, Jamie	L101
Carroll, Megan	L102
Carter, Rebecca	L103
Cartey, Claire	L104
Caskie, Robert	L105
Cassava Republic Press UK	P074
Cavanagh, Claire	L107
Cedar Fort	P076
CGI (Chartered Governance Institute) Publishing	P078
Chanchani, Sonali	L108
Chang, Nicola	L109
Chapman	M075
Charisma House	P079
Charles River Press	P080
Charlesbridge Publishing	P081
CharlottesvilleFamily	M076
Charnace, Edwina de	L110
Chautauqua Literary Journal	M077
Chelsea House Publishers	P082
Cherry Lake Publishing Group	P083
Cheshire	M078
Chevais, Jennifer	L111
Children's Books North Agency	L112
Chiotti, Danielle	L113
Cho, Catherine	L114
Christie, Jennifer	L116
Cicada Books	P087
Cinnamon Press	P088
Claret Press	P089
Clarke, Caro	L118
Clarke, Catherine	L119
Cleis Press	P091
Coach House Books	P092
Coaches Choice	P093
Cobblestone	M079
Cochran, Alexander	L120
Cocoa Girl	M080
College Press Publishing	P094
Colourpoint Educational	P095
Colwill, Charlotte	L121
Combemale, Chris	L122
Commonweal	M082
Comparato, Andrea	L123
Compass Talent	L124
Compassiviste Publishing	P097
Concho River Review	M083
Conjunctions	M084
Conjunctions Online	M085
Conrad, Claire Paterson	L125
Contemporary Verse 2	M086
Conversation (UK), The	M087
Conville, Clare	L126
Cooper, Maggie	L129
Cosmos	M089
Cottage Life	M090
Countryside Books	P099
Cowboys & Indians	M091
Crandall, Becca	L130
Crazyhorse / Swamp Pink	M093
Cream City Review	M094
Creative Nonfiction	M095
Cricket	M096
Crossway	P100
Crowley, Sheila	L132
Crown	P101
Crown Publishing Group, The	P103
Cruising World	M097
Crystal Magazine	M098
Curious Minds	L133
Curran, Sabhbh	L134
Curtis Brown	L135
CutBank	M099
Dalhousie Review, The	M100
Dana Newman Literary, LLC	L138
Danaczko, Melissa	L139
Danko, Margaret	L140
Darga, Jon Michael	L141
Darhansoff & Verrill Literary Agents	L142
Darley Anderson Children's	L144
Daunt Books Publishing	P106
David Godwin Associates	L145
Davies, Olivia	L147
Dawntreader, The	M102
Dawson, Liza	L148
DeBlock, Liza	L149
Demblon, Gabrielle	L150
Denis Kitchen Publishing Company Co., LLC	P109
Derviskadic, Dado	L151
Descent	M104
DHH Literary Agency Ltd	L152
Diamond Kahn and Woods (DKW) Literary Agency Ltd	L153
Diana Finch Literary Agency	L154
Dickerson, Donya	L155
Dillsworth, Elise	L156
Diver	M105
Diversion Books	P111
DK Publishing	P112
Dolin, Lily	L157
Dominguez, Adriana	L158
Don Congdon Associates, Inc.	L159
Donald Maass Literary Agency	L160
Doubleday (UK)	P114
Doug Grad Literary Agency	L161
Draper, Claire	L162
Dream Catcher	M106
Dublin Review, The	M107
Duncan Petersen Publishing Limited	P117
Dundurn	P118
Dunham Literary, Inc.	L163
Dunn, Ben	L164
DunnFogg	L165
Dunow, Carlson & Lerner Agency	L166
Dystel, Jane	L167
Eason, Lynette	L169
Edelstein, Anne	L171
Edenborough, Sam	L172
Eerdmans Books for Young Readers	P120
Einstein, Susanna	L173
Eisenharth, Caroline	L175
Ekphrastic Review, The	M109
Ekus Group, The	L176
Ekus, Sally	L177
El Portal	M110
Elaine Markson Literary Agency	L178
Elaine Steel	L179
Ellis-Martin, Sian	L180
Elsevier Ltd	P121
Emerge Literary Journal	M111
Enitharmon Editions	P122
Enslow Publishers, Inc.	P123
Entrepreneur	M112
Epicenter Press Inc.	P124
Ericka T. Phillips	L181
Evan Marshall Agency, The	L183
Evan-Moor Educational Publishers	P125
Evans, Kate	L185
Event	M113
Facet Publishing	P127
Facts & Fiction	M116
Fate	M117
Faulks, Holly	L187
Faultline	M118
Fazzari, Hillary	L188
Feldstein Agency, The	L191
Felicity Bryan Associates	L192
Fellows, Abi	L193
Feminist Press, The	P130
Feminist Studies	M119
Ferguson, Hannah	L194
Fernandez, Rochelle	L197
Fernando, Kimberly	L198
Fernwood Publishing	P131
Fiddlehead, The	M121
Fighting High	P132
Finan, Ciara	L200
Finegan, Stevie	L203
First For Women	M122
First Line, The	M123
Five Points	M124
Flannery Literary	L204
Fogg, Jack	L206
Folio	P126
Folio Literary Management, LLC	L207
Forrester, Jemima	L210
Fortean Times: The Journal of Strange Phenomena	M127
Forty20	M128
Foster, Clara	L211
Foundation: The International Review of Science Fiction	M129
Fourth River, The	M131
Fox, Aram	L212
Foxx, Kat	L213
FRA (Futerman, Rose, & Associates)	L214
Frankel, Valerie	L215
Fraser Ross Associates	L216
Free Association Books Ltd	P135
Free Spirit Publishing	P136
Friedman, Claire	L217
Friedman, Jessica	L218
Friedman, Rebecca	L219
Friedrich Agency LLC, The	L220
Frog Literary Agency	L221
Fuentes, Sarah	L222
Fugue	M133
Funeral Business Solutions	M134
Furniss, Eugenie	L224
Future Horizons	P138
Gahan, Isobel	L225
Gale	P139
Galvin, Lori	L226
Garden Answers	M136

Geiger, Ellen	L227
Gemini Books	P140
Geographical Journal, The	M138
Georgia Review, The	M139
Getzler, Josh	L229
Ghahremani, Lilly	L230
Ghosh Literary	L231
Ghosh, Anna	L232
Gill Books	P142
Gill Education	P143
Gillam, Bianca	L234
Ginosko Literary Journal	M140
Glass Literary Management LLC	L236
Glenister, Emily	L238
Global Lion Intellectual Property Management, Inc.	L239
Globe Pequot Press, The	P145
Go World Travel Magazine	M142
Goderich, Miriam	L240
Goff, Ellen	L242
Goldblatt, Rachel	L243
Goldstein, Veronica	L244
Goodman Beck Publishing	P147
Goose Lane Editions	P148
Gordon, Andrew	L245
Goss & Crested China Club	P149
Graffeg	P150
Graffeg Childrens	P151
Graham Maw Christie Literary Agency	L246
Graham, Stacey	L247
Graham, Susan	L248
Grain Literary Magazine	M143
Granger, David	L250
Granta	M144
Graywolf Lab	M145
Graywolf Press	P152
Great Outdoors (TGO), The	M146
Greene & Heaton Ltd	L251
Gruber, Pam	L253
Grunewald, Hattie	L254
Guernica Editions	P153
Guinness World Records	P154
Guinsler, Robert	L255
Gulf Coast: A Journal of Literature and Fine Arts	M147
Gutter Magazine	M148
Hachette Book Group	P156
Haley, Jolene	L260
Half Mystic Journal	M149
Half Mystic Press	P157
Hammersmith Books	P158
Hanbury Agency, The	L261
Hancock House Publishers	P159
Hannah Sheppard Literary Agency	L262
Hannigan, Carrie	L263
Hansen, Stephanie	L264
Happy Yak	P161
Hardie Grant	P162
Hardie Grant (North America)	P163
Hare, Jessica	L266
Harpur Palate	M151
Harris, Erin	L268
Harvard University Press	P165
Hashtag Press	P166
Hawk, Susan	L269
Hawn, Molly Ker	L270
Hawthorne Books	P167
Hay House Publishers	P168
Hayden, Viola	L271
Healthy	M152
Heathfield, Laura	L273
Helix, The	M154
Hello!	M155
Henley Hall Press	P171
Hensley, Chelsea	L274
Hernandez, Saritza	L275
Hernando, Paloma	L276
Heymont, Lane	L277
High Stakes Publishing	P173
Hildebrand, Cole	L280
History Press, The	P174
History Today	M157
Hiyate, Sam	L281
Hodder & Stoughton Ltd	P175
Holloway, Sally	L284
Holroyde, Penny	L285
Homes & Antiques	M158
Hordern, Kate	L286
Hornsley, Sarah	L287
Horse & Rider	M159
Hotel Amerika	M160
Howgate Publishing	P178
Hunger Mountain	M161
Hwang, Annie	L288
Icon Books Ltd	P180
Idaho Review	M163
Identity Theory	M164
Idler, The	M165
Idyll Arbor	P181
Ig Publishing	P182
Igloo Books Limited	P184
Image	M166
Imagine Publishing	P186
Indiana Review	M167
Indiana University Press	P187
Information Today, Inc.	P188
Ink Sweat and Tears	M168
Inkandescent	P190
Inscriptions Literary Agency	L289
Inspired Ink Literary	L290
Insurance Post	M169
International Piano	M170
International Publishers	P191
International Society for Technology in Education (ISTE)	P192
InterVarsity Press (IVP)	P193
Ireland's Own	M172
Irene Goodman Literary Agency (IGLA)	L291
Irish Pages	M173
Irving, Dotti	L293
Island	M174
Island Online	M175
J. Gordon Shillingford Publishing	P194
Jain Publishing Company, Inc.	P195
Jamii Publishing	P196
Janklow & Nesbit UK Ltd	L297
Javelin	L298
Jean V. Naggar Literary Agency, The	L299
Jessica Kingsley Publishers	P197
JMD Media / DB Publishing	P198
Joelle Delbourgo Associates, Inc.	L301
John Murray Press	P200
Johnson, Jared	L303
Jonathan Clowes Ltd	L304
Journal, The	M176
Joy Harris Literary Agency, Inc.	L308
Judson Press	P201
Julien, Ria	L312
Kahn, Ella Diamond	L314
Kaliszewska, Joanna	L315
Kane Press	P202
Kantor, Camille	L317
Kardon, Julia	L318
Karen Gantz Literary Management	L319
Kate Barker Literary, TV, & Film Agency	L320
Kate Nash Literary Agency	L321
Kates Hill Press, The	P203
Kathryn Green Literary Agency, LLC	L322
Kavya Kishor	M177
Kellerman, Carly	L328
Kensington Publishing Corp.	P204
Kent Life	M178
Kenyon Review, The	M179
Keren, Eli	L330
Ki Agency Ltd	L331
Kids Alive!	M180
Killingley, Jessica	L332
Kim, Jennifer	L333
Kim, Julia	L334
Kim, Sally M.	L335
Kimber, Natalie	L336
Kimberley Cameron & Associates	L337
Kirby, Robert	L338
Kitchen Press	P205
Knight Features	L340
Kogan Page Ltd	P206
Kore Press	P207
Korero Press	P208
Kracht, Elizabeth	L341
Krichevsky, Stuart	L342
Krienke, Mary	L343
Kruger Cowne	L344
Kube Publishing	P209
Lake, The	M181
Lakosil, Natalie	L347
Lambert, Sophie	L348
Landfall	M182
Langtons International	L354
Lantana Publishing	P210
Latshaw, Katherine	L355
Laxfield Literary Associates	L356
Leamington Books	P211
Leapfrog Press	P212
Leigh Feldman Literary	L359
Leisure Group Travel	M183
Leisure Painter	M184
Lerner Publishing Group	P213
Levitt, Sarah	L361
Levy, Yael	L362
Lewinsohn Literary	L363
Lewis, Alison	L364
LexisNexis	P214
Lightner, Kayla	L365
Liguori Publications	P216
Lilliput Press, The	P217
Linguist, The	M186
Liss, Laurie	L368
Literary Mama	M187
Little Bigfoot	P218
Llewellyn Worldwide Ltd	P219
Loft Press, Inc.	P220
Logaston Press	P221
London Grip	M188
London Grip New Poetry	M189
London Magazine, The	M190
London Review of Books	M191
Long Poem Magazine	M192
Lost Lake Folk Opera Magazine	M193
Lotus Lane Literary	L371
Loudhailer Books	P222
Louisiana Literature	M194
Lovell, Jake	L372
LSU Press	P223
Luedeke, Amanda	L373
Lund Humphries Limited	P224
Lutyens and Rubinstein	L375
MacDonald, Emily	L378
Macdougall, Laura	L379
MacGregor & Luedeke	L380
MacGuffin, The	M195
Mack, Kate	L381
MacLeod, Lauren	L383
Madeleine Milburn Literary, TV & Film Agency	L385
Magma	M196
Malahat Review, The	M197

Maltese, Alyssa	L387
Manchester Review, The	M198
Manilla Press	P227
Manoa	M199
marie claire	M200
Marion Boyars Publishers	P229
Marlin	M201
Marr, Jill	L389
Marsh Agency, The	L390
Marshall, Jen	L391
Marsiglia, Caroline	L392
Massachusetts Review, The	M202
Massie McQuilkin & Altman	L394
Maurer, Shari	L397
Maw, Jane Graham	L398
McCormick Literary	L400
McNicol, Andy	L402
McNidder & Grace	P232
Medical Physics Publishing	P234
Medina Publishing	P235
Mendia, Isabel	L403
Mentor Books	P236
Meridian Artists	L404
Merlin Unwin Books	P237
Merullo, Annabel	L405
Metamorphosis Literary Agency	L406
Methuen Publishing Ltd	P238
Mic Cheetham Literary Agency	L407
Michel, Caroline	L408
Michigan Quarterly Review	M204
Mid-American Review	M206
Midsummer Dream House	M207
Midway Journal	M208
Mihell, Natasha	L410
Milkweed Editions	P239
Minnesota Historical Society Press	P241
Missouri Historical Society Press	P243
Missouri Review, The	M209
MIT Press, The	P244
Modern Applied Science	M210
Modern Haiku	M211
Molloy, Jess	L414
Monacelli Press, The	P245
Monoray	P246
Moody Publishers	P247
Moonday Mag	M213
Moorhead, Max	L416
Morrell, Imogen	L417
Mortimer, Michele	L418
Movable Type Management	L420
Mulcahy Sweeney Literary Agency	L423
Mundy, Toby	L426
Murdoch Books Australia	P249
Murgolo, Karen	L427
Murray, Judith	L428
Muscato, Nate	L429
Muswell Press	P250
My Weekly	M215
NAHB BuilderBooks	P253
Nashville Review	M217
NBM Publishing	P254
New England Review	M220
New Harbinger Publications	P255
New Internationalist	M221
New Statesman	M222
New Welsh Reader	M223
Nichols, Mariah	L438
Niumata, Erin	L439
Niv, Daniel	L440
No Starch Press, Inc.	P258
Nolan, Laura	L441
Norfolk & Suffolk Bride	M224
Northbank Talent Management	L442
O'Grady, Niamh	L445
O'Neill, Molly	L446
O'Shea, Amy	L447
Oak Tree Press	P259
Ohio University Press	P261
OK! Magazine	M228
Old Pond Publishing	P262
Old Street Publishing Ltd	P263
Oldcastle Books Group	P264
Ooligan Press	P265
Orca Book Publishers	P266
Orphans Publishing	P268
Otago University Press	P269
Oxbow Books	P271
Oxford Poetry	M229
Oxford Review of Books	M230
Oxford University Press	P272
Pacific Press Publishing Association	P273
Pacifica Literary Review	M231
Pan Macmillan Australia	P274
Panorama	M232
Paradigm Talent and Literary Agency	L454
Paris Review, The	M233
Parthian Books	P275
Pass, Marina de	L456
Passionfruit Review, The	M234
Patterson, David	L457
Patterson, Emma	L458
Paul S. Levine Literary Agency	L459
PC Pro	M235
Peddle, Kay	L460
Peepal Tree Press	P278
Pelagic	P279
Pelham, Imogen	L461
Pen & Ink Designs Publishing	P280
Pen & Sword Books Ltd	P281
People's Friend, The	M237
Perez Literary & Entertainment	L463
Perez, Kristina	L464
Perotto-Wills, Martha	L465
Perry Literary	L466
Perspectives Books	P283
Pestritto, Carrie	L467
Peter Lang	L285
Peter Pauper Press	P286
PEW Literary	L468
Phaidon Press	P287
Phelan, Beth	L470
Philips, Ariana	L471
Phillips, Aemilia	L472
Piatkus Books	P289
Pickering, Juliet	L473
Pierce, Rosie	L474
Pimpernel Press	P292
Pine, Gideon	L475
Pineapple Press	P293
Pleiades	M238
Plexus Publishing Limited	P294
Plitt, Carrie	L477
Ploughshares	M239
Pluto Press	P295
PN Review	M240
Pocket Mountains	P296
Poetry	M241
Poetry Birmingham Literary Journal	M242
Poetry Ireland Review	M243
Poetry Wales	M245
Political Quarterly, The	M246
Polygon	P298
Popular Chess	P299
Portobello Literary	L479
Posner, Marcy	L480
Power Cut Lite	M247
Power, Anna	L482
Practical Pre-School Books	P300
Preservation Magazine	P248
Prestel Publishing Ltd	P302
Preston, Amanda	L484
Pride	M249
Prole	M250
Purdue University Press	P305
Pureplay Press	P306
Qu Literary Magazine	M253
Quadrant Magazine	M254
Quarto Group, Inc., The	P307
Quirk Books	P308
Racecar Engineering	M255
Radio Society of Great Britain	P309
Rail Express	M257
Ramer, Susan	L486
Rand McNally	P310
Ransom Publishing Ltd	P312
Reactor	M258
Red Magazine	M259
Redhammer	L488
Regina Ryan Books	L489
Reid, Janet	L490
Reilly, Milly	L491
Renard Press Ltd	P313
Research Journal of Pharmacy and Technology	M260
Richter, Rick	L493
Riposte	M262
River Hills Traveler	M263
River Styx	M264
Roberts, Soumeya Bendimerad	L495
Robertson Murray Literary Agency	L496
Robinson, Quressa	L497
Rocking Chair Books	L499
Rocky Mountain Books	P315
Romano, Annie	L502
Rosenberg Group, The	L505
Roseway	P317
Ross, Whitney	L507
Round Hall	P318
Rubin Pfeffer Content, LLC	L509
Rudy Agency, The	L510
Rugby World	M265
Rupert Crew Ltd	L511
Ruralite	M266
Rutherford, Laetitia	L513
Rutman, Jim	L514
Saddlebag Dispatches	M267
Sailing Today	M268
Salt Publishing	P322
Sanchez, Kaitlyn	L516
Sanders, Rayhane	L517
Sandstone Press	P323
Saqi Books	P324
Sasquatch Books	P325
Savannah Magazine	M269
Savvides, Marilia	L520
Sayle Literary Agency, The	L521
Scala Arts & Heritage Publishers	P326
Schiffer Military History	P328
Schofield, Hannah	L522
Scholastic	P329
Scholastic UK	P330
Schwizer, Fabienne	L523
Scifaikuest	M270
Scots Magazine, The	M271
Scottish Field	M272
Scratching Shed Publishing	P331
Seager, Chloe	L524
Seal Press	P332
Seaworthy Publications	P333
Second Factory	M274
Selectric Artists	L525
Sentient Publications	P334
Seren Books	P335
Serra, Maria Cardona	L526
Seventeen	M275
Seymour, Charlotte	L528
Shaw Agency, The	L529
Shenandoah	M277

Index | Nonfiction Books

Sheree Bykofsky Associates, Inc. ...L532
Shesto Literary ...L533
Shestopal, Camilla ...L534
Ships Monthly Magazine ...M278
Shipwreckt Books Publishing Company ...P336
Shooter Literary Magazine ...M279
Sierra ...M281
Sigma Press ...P337
Silk, Julia ...L535
Simpson, Cara Lee ...L537
Singh, Amandeep ...L538
Singing Dragon ...P340
Sinister Wisdom ...M282
Siobhan, Aiden ...L539
SmokeLong Quarterly ...M283
Snowbooks ...P344
Snowflake Magazine ...M284
Society for Promoting Christian Knowledge (SPCK) ...P345
Society of Genealogists ...P346
SOMA ...M285
Somerset Life ...M286
Sonder Magazine ...M287
Sophie Hicks Agency ...L545
Sourcebooks ...P350
Sourcebooks eXplore ...P352
Sourcebooks Fire ...P353
South Carolina Review ...M289
Southern Humanities Review ...M290
Southern Review, The ...M291
Southern Theatre ...M292
Southwest Review ...M293
Spa Magazine ...M295
Spackman, James ...L547
Sparsile Books ...P359
Speciality Food ...M296
Spitball ...M297
Square Mile Magazine ...M298
SRL Publishing ...P361
Stainer & Bell Ltd ...P366
Stanford University Press ...P367
Stanley Gibbons ...P368
Stephens, Jenny ...L549
Steward House Publishers ...P369
Stinging Fly, The ...M299
Stipes Publishing ...P371
Story Unlikely ...M300
StoryWise ...L552
Strange Horizons ...M301
Strategic Finance ...M302
Strothman, Wendy ...L555
Stuart Krichevsky Literary Agency, Inc. ...L556
Studio One ...M304
Sunbelt Publications, Inc. ...P373
Sunspot Literary Journal ...M305
Supplement, The ...M306
Susan Schulman Literary Agency ...L557
Susanna Lea Associates ...L558
Swainson, Joanna ...L561
Sweet & Maxwell ...P374
Sweet, Emily ...L563
Sweren, Becky ...L564
Swimming Pool News ...M307
Symonds, Laurel ...L565
Tahoma Literary Review ...M308
Takahe ...M309
Take a Break's Take a Puzzle ...M310
Takikawa, Marin ...L566
Talbot, Emily ...L567
Tasman, Alice ...L569
Taylor & Francis Group ...P378
Tears in the Fence ...M311
Temz Review, The ...M312
Ten Speed Press ...P380
Terlip, Paige ...L570
Texas A&M University Press ...P381
Thames & Hudson Inc. ...P382
Thames and Hudson Ltd ...P383
That's Life! ...M313
Thayer, Henry ...L572
Theseus Agency, The ...L573
Thin Air Magazine ...M314
Thinkwell Books, UK ...P384
Third Coast ...M315
This England ...M316
Thorneycroft, Euan ...L574
Threepenny Review, The ...M317
Thwaites, Steph ...L575
Tilbury House Publishers ...P385
Times Literary Supplement (TLS), The ...M318
Tippermuir Books ...P386
Toad Hall Editions ...P387
Tolka ...M319
Topping, Antony ...L577
Torrey House Press, LLC ...P390
Torva ...P391
Transworld Publishers ...P393
Tributaries ...M320
Trudel, Jes ...L579
Turner Publishing ...P394
Turtle Press ...P395
Tusculum Review, The ...M321
Two Fine Crows Books ...P396
Tyndale House Publishers, Inc. ...P397
UCL Press ...P398
Ugly Duckling Presse ...P399
Ulster Business ...M323
Unbound Press ...P400
Unbridled Books ...P401
Uncut ...M324
Unfit Magazine ...M326
Unicorn ...P402
University of Akron Press, The ...P403
University of Alberta Press ...P404
University of Calgary Press ...P405
University of California Press ...P406
University of Georgia Press ...P407
University of Iowa Press ...P408
University of Maine Press ...P409
University of Michigan Press, The ...P410
University of Missouri Press ...P411
University of North Texas Press ...P412
University of Tennessee Press ...P413
University of Texas Press ...P414
University of Virginia Press ...P415
University Press of Colorado ...P416
Unseen Press ...P417
Usselman, Laura ...L581
Vagabond City ...M327
Valley Press ...P418
Vallum ...M328
Vance, Lisa Erbach ...L583
Velocity Press ...P420
Vestal Review ...M329
Victoria Sanders & Associates LLC ...L584
Viney Agency, The ...L585
Viney, Charlie ...L586
Virginia Quarterly Review, The ...M330
Virginia Wine & Country Life ...M331
Virginia Wine & Country Weddings ...M332
Viz ...M333
Vogue ...M334
W.W. Norton & Company Ltd ...P422
W.W. Norton & Company, Inc. ...P423
Waccamaw ...M335
Wade & Co Literary Agency ...L588
Walker Books ...P424
Wallace Stevens Journal, The ...M336
Wallpaper ...M337
Walsh, Caroline ...L589
Wasafiri ...M338
Washington Writers' Publishing House ...P425
Watson, Little Ltd ...L590
Watterson, Jessica ...L591
Wee Book Company, The ...P427
Weiss, Alexandra ...L593
Weitzner, Tess ...L594
Wells, Karmen ...L595
Weltz, Jennifer ...L596
West Branch ...M339
Westin, Erin Casey ...L597
Wet Grain ...M341
Whatnall, Michaela ...L598
Whispering Buffalo Literary Agency ...L599
Whitford Press ...P428
Wickers, Chandler ...L600
Wide-Eyed Editions ...P429
Williams, Laura ...L603
Willms, Kathryn ...L605
Wilson, Desiree ...L606
Wilson, Ed ...L607
Windhorse Publications Ltd ...P430
Windsor Review ...M342
Wine Enthusiast ...M343
Wisdom Publications ...P431
Woods, Bryony ...L610
Woollard, Jessica ...L611
Workman Publishing ...P437
Yale Review, The ...M344
Yale University Press (London) ...P438
Yankee Magazine ...M345
Yeoh, Rachel ...L612
YMU Books ...L613
Yorkshire Dalesman, The ...M347
Yorkshire Life ...M348
Yorkshire Women's Life Magazine ...M349
Young, Claudia ...L614
Yours ...M350
Zack Company, Inc, The ...L615
Zacker, Marietta B. ...L616
Zeno Agency ...L617
Zibby Books ...P440
Zone 3 ...M353
Zuckerbrot, Renee ...L618
Zuraw-Friedland, Ayla ...L619

Nonfiction Books
404 Ink ...P001
A.M. Heath & Company Limited, Author's Agents ...L002
Able Muse Press ...P003
Acheampong, Kwaku ...L003
Adams, Seren ...L004
Adsett, Alex ...L005
Adventure Books by Vertebrate Publishing ...P004
Alcock, Michael ...L009
Algonquin Books ...P008
Alice Williams Literary ...L012
Allen & Unwin ...P009
Alternating Current Press ...P010
Ambassador Speakers Bureau & Literary Agency ...L013
And Other Stories ...P013
Andrade, Hannah ...L015
Andrew Nurnberg Associates, Ltd ...L016
Andrews McMeel Publishing ...P015
Ange, Anna ...L019
Anne Clark Literary Agency ...L020
Annette Green Authors' Agency ...L021
Antony Harwood Limited ...L022
Anvil Press Publishers ...P017
Apple Tree Literary Ltd ...L023
April Gloaming ...P018
Arcadia Publishing ...P020
Arms, Victoria Wells ...L025
Arte Publico Press ...P021

Access more listings online at www.firstwriter.com

Index | Nonfiction Books

Arthurson, Wayne ... L027
Asabi Publishing ... P022
Atyeo, Charlotte ... L028
Aurora Metro Press ... P024
Autumn Publishing Ltd ... P025
Backbeat Books ... P027
Bajek, Lauren ... L031
Bal, Emma ... L032
Bald and Bonkers Network LLC ... P030
Balow, Dan ... L033
Banter Press ... P033
Barbara, Stephen ... L034
Baror International, Inc. ... L037
Barr, Anjanette ... L038
Barr, Nicola ... L039
Barren Magazine ... M041
Barrett, Emily ... L040
Bartholomew, Jason ... L041
Basalt Books ... P034
Basic Books ... P035
Basic Health Publications, Inc. ... P037
BatCat Press ... P040
Bath Literary Agency ... L042
Baumer, Jan ... L044
Baxter, Veronique ... L045
Baylor University Press ... P041
BCS (British Computer Society) ... P042
Beaumont, Diana ... L046
Begum, Salma ... L047
Belton, Maddy ... L049
Bent Agency (UK), The ... L051
Bent Agency, The ... L052
Bent, Jenny ... L053
Bentley Publishers ... P044
Berdinsky, Kendall ... L054
Berghahn Books Ltd ... P045
Bernardi, Amanda ... L056
Berrett-Koehler Publishers ... P046
Bess Press ... P047
Betancourt Literary ... L057
Betsy Amster Literary Enterprises ... L059
Beverley Slopen Literary Agency ... L060
Black & White Publishing Ltd ... P049
Blackstaff Press ... P051
Blair Partnership, The ... L064
Blake Friedmann Literary Agency Ltd ... L065
Bloodhound Books ... P052
Bloomsbury Academic ... P053
Blue Poppy Enterprises ... P055
Blue Star Press ... P056
BOA Editions, Ltd ... P057
Bonnier Books (UK) ... P059
Book Group, The ... L068
Books For All Times ... P060
Borstel, Stefanie Sanchez Von ... L070
Bowlin, Sarah ... L071
Bradford Literary Agency ... L073
Bradford, Laura ... L074
Brailsford, Karen ... L075
Brannan, Maria ... L076
Brattle Agency LLC, The ... L077
Brewin Books Ltd ... P062
Bright Agency (UK), The ... L078
Bright Agency (US), The ... L079
British Academy, The ... P063
British Museum Press, The ... P064
Broadview Press ... P065
Brooks, Savannah ... L080
Brotherstone Creative Management ... L081
Brotherstone, Charlie ... L082
Brouckaert, Justin ... L083
Brown, Megan ... L084
Buckley, Louise ... L085
Bukowski, Danielle ... L086
Burns, Camille ... L089
CAA (London) ... L091

Cambridge University Press ... P068
Cameron, Kimberley ... L093
Campbell, Charlie ... L094
Campos, Vanessa ... L095
Candy Jar Books ... P070
Canterbury Literary Agency ... L096
Canterbury Press ... P071
Captivate Press ... P072
Caroline Davidson Literary Agency ... L099
Carr, Jamie ... L101
Carroll, Megan ... L102
Carter, Rebecca ... L103
Cartey, Claire ... L104
Caskie, Robert ... L105
Cassava Republic Press UK ... P074
Cavanagh, Claire ... L107
Cedar Fort ... P076
CGI (Chartered Governance Institute) Publishing ... P078
Chanchani, Sonali ... L108
Chang, Nicola ... L109
Charisma House ... P079
Charles River Press ... P080
Charnace, Edwina de ... L110
Chelsea House Publishers ... P082
Chevais, Jennifer ... L111
Chiotti, Danielle ... L113
Cho, Catherine ... L114
Christie, Jennifer ... L116
Cicada Books ... P087
Cinnamon Press ... P088
Claret Press ... P089
Clarke, Caro ... L118
Clarke, Catherine ... L119
Cleis Press ... P091
Coach House Books ... P092
Coaches Choice ... P093
Cochran, Alexander ... L120
College Press Publishing ... P094
Colourpoint Educational ... P095
Colwill, Charlotte ... L121
Combemale, Chris ... L122
Comparato, Andrea ... L123
Compass Talent ... L124
Compassiviste Publishing ... P097
Conrad, Claire Paterson ... L125
Conville, Clare ... L126
Cooper, Maggie ... L129
Countryside Books ... P099
Crandall, Becca ... L130
Crossway ... P100
Crowley, Sheila ... L132
Crown ... P101
Crown Publishing Group, The ... P103
Curious Minds ... L133
Curran, Sabhbh ... L134
Curtis Brown ... L135
Dana Newman Literary, LLC ... L138
Danaczko, Melissa ... L139
Danko, Margaret ... L140
Darga, Jon Michael ... L141
Darhansoff & Verrill Literary Agents ... L142
Darley Anderson Children's ... L144
Daunt Books Publishing ... P106
David Godwin Associates ... L145
Davies, Olivia ... L147
Dawson, Liza ... L148
DeBlock, Liza ... L149
Demblon, Gabrielle ... L150
Denis Kitchen Publishing Company Co., LLC ... P109
Derviskadic, Dado ... L151
DHH Literary Agency Ltd ... L152
Diamond Kahn and Woods (DKW) Literary Agency Ltd ... L153
Diana Finch Literary Agency ... L154

Dickerson, Donya ... L155
Dillsworth, Elise ... L156
Diversion Books ... P111
DK Publishing ... P112
Dolin, Lily ... L157
Dominguez, Adriana ... L158
Don Congdon Associates, Inc. ... L159
Donald Maass Literary Agency ... L160
Doubleday (UK) ... P114
Doug Grad Literary Agency ... L161
Draper, Claire ... L162
Duncan Petersen Publishing Limited ... P117
Dundurn ... P118
Dunham Literary, Inc. ... L163
Dunn, Ben ... L164
DunnFogg ... L165
Dunow, Carlson & Lerner Agency ... L166
Dystel, Jane ... L167
Eason, Lynette ... L169
Edelstein, Anne ... L171
Edenborough, Sam ... L172
Eerdmans Books for Young Readers ... P120
Einstein, Susanna ... L173
Eisenmann, Caroline ... L175
Ekus Group, The ... L176
Ekus, Sally ... L177
Elaine Markson Literary Agency ... L178
Elaine Steel ... L179
Ellis-Martin, Sian ... L180
Elsevier Ltd ... P121
Enitharmon Editions ... P122
Enslow Publishers, Inc. ... P123
Epicenter Press Inc. ... P124
Ericka T. Phillips ... L181
Evan-Moor Educational Publishers ... P125
Evans, Kate ... L185
Facet Publishing ... P127
Faulks, Holly ... L187
Fazzari, Hillary ... L188
Feldstein Agency, The ... L191
Felicity Bryan Associates ... L192
Fellows, Abi ... L193
Feminist Press, The ... P130
Ferguson, Hannah ... L194
Fernandez, Rochelle ... L197
Fernando, Kimberly ... L198
Fernwood Publishing ... P131
Fighting High ... P132
Finan, Ciara ... L200
Finegan, Stevie ... L203
Flannery Literary ... L204
Fogg, Jack ... L206
Folio Literary Management, LLC ... L207
Forrester, Jemima ... L210
Foster, Clara ... L211
Fox, Aram ... L212
Foxx, Kat ... L213
FRA (Futerman, Rose, & Associates) ... L214
Frankel, Valerie ... L215
Fraser Ross Associates ... L216
Free Association Books Ltd ... P135
Free Spirit Publishing ... P136
Friedman, Claire ... L217
Friedman, Jessica ... L218
Friedman, Rebecca ... L219
Friedrich Agency LLC, The ... L220
Frog Literary Agency ... L221
Fuentes, Sarah ... L222
Furniss, Eugenie ... L224
Future Horizons ... P138
Gahan, Isobel ... L225
Gale ... P139
Galvin, Lori ... L226
Geiger, Ellen ... L227
Gemini Books ... P140
Getzler, Josh ... L229

Ghahremani, Lilly L230
Ghosh Literary L231
Ghosh, Anna L232
Gill Books P142
Gill Education P143
Gillam, Bianca L234
Glass Literary Management LLC L236
Glenister, Emily L238
Global Lion Intellectual Property Management, Inc. L239
Globe Pequot Press, The P145
Goderich, Miriam L240
Goff, Ellen L242
Goldblatt, Rachel L243
Goldstein, Veronica L244
Goodman Beck Publishing P147
Goose Lane Editions P148
Gordon, Andrew L245
Graham Maw Christie Literary Agency L246
Graham, Stacey L247
Graham, Susan L248
Granger, David L250
Graywolf Press P152
Greene & Heaton Ltd L251
Gruber, Pam L253
Grunewald, Hattie L254
Guernica Editions P153
Guinsler, Robert L255
Hachette Book Group P156
Haley, Jolene L260
Half Mystic Press P157
Hammersmith Books P158
Hanbury Agency, The L261
Hancock House Publishers P159
Hannah Sheppard Literary Agency L262
Hannigan, Carrie L263
Hansen, Stephanie L264
Happy Yak P161
Hardie Grant P162
Hardie Grant (North America) P163
Hare, Jessica L266
Harris, Erin L268
Harvard University Press P165
Hashtag Press P166
Hawk, Susan L269
Hawn, Molly Ker L270
Hawthorne Books P167
Hay House Publishers P168
Hayden, Viola L271
Heathfield, Laura L273
Henley Hall Press P171
Hensley, Chelsea L274
Hernandez, Saritza L275
Hernando, Paloma L276
Heymont, Lane L277
High Stakes Publishing P173
Hildebrand, Cole L280
History Press, The P174
Hiyate, Sam L281
Hodder & Stoughton Ltd P175
Holloway, Sally L284
Holroyde, Penny L285
Hordern, Kate L286
Hornsley, Sarah L287
Howgate Publishing P178
Hwang, Annie L288
Icon Books Ltd P180
Idyll Arbor P181
Ig Publishing P182
Imagine Publishing P186
Indiana University Press P187
Information Today, Inc. P188
Inkandescent P190
Inscriptions Literary Agency L289
Inspired Ink Literary L290
International Publishers P191
International Society for Technology in Education (ISTE) P192
InterVarsity Press (IVP) P193
Irene Goodman Literary Agency (IGLA) L291
Irving, Dotti L293
J. Gordon Shillingford Publishing P194
Jain Publishing Company, Inc. P195
Janklow & Nesbit UK Ltd L297
Javelin L298
Jean V. Naggar Literary Agency, The L299
Jessica Kingsley Publishers P197
JMD Media / DB Publishing P198
Joelle Delbourgo Associates, Inc. L301
John Murray Press P200
Johnson, Jared L303
Jonathan Clowes Ltd L304
Judson Press P201
Julien, Ria L312
Kahn, Ella Diamond L314
Kaliszewska, Joanna L315
Kane Press P202
Kantor, Camille L317
Kardon, Julia L318
Karen Gantz Literary Management L319
Kate Barker Literary, TV, & Film Agency L320
Kate Nash Literary Agency L321
Kates Hill Press, The P203
Kathryn Green Literary Agency, LLC L322
Kellerman, Carly L328
Kensington Publishing Corp. P204
Keren, Eli L330
Ki Agency Ltd L331
Killingley, Jessica L332
Kim, Jennifer L333
Kim, Julia L334
Kimber, Natalie L336
Kimberley Cameron & Associates L337
Kirby, Robert L338
Kitchen Press P205
Knight Features L340
Kogan Page Ltd P206
Kore Press P207
Kracht, Elizabeth L341
Krichevsky, Stuart L342
Krienke, Mary L343
Kruger Cowne L344
Kube Publishing P209
Lakosil, Natalie L347
Lambert, Sophie L348
Langtons International L354
Lantana Publishing P210
Latshaw, Katherine L355
Laxfield Literary Associates L356
Leamington Books P211
Leapfrog Press P212
Leigh Feldman Literary L359
Lerner Publishing Group P213
Levitt, Sarah L361
Levy, Yael L362
Lewinsohn Literary L363
Lewis, Alison L364
Lightner, Kayla L365
Liguori Publications P216
Lilliput Press, The P217
Liss, Laurie L368
Little Bigfoot P218
Llewellyn Worldwide Ltd P219
Loft Press, Inc. P220
Logaston Press P221
Lotus Lane Literary L371
Loudhailer Books P222
Lovell, Jake L372
LSU Press P223
Luedeke, Amanda L373
Lund Humphries Limited P224
Lutyens and Rubinstein L375
MacDonald, Emily L378
Macdougall, Laura L379
MacGregor & Luedeke L380
Mack, Kate L381
MacLeod, Lauren L383
Madeleine Milburn Literary, TV & Film Agency L385
Maltese, Alyssa L387
Manilla Press P227
Marr, Jill L389
Marshall, Jen L391
Marsiglia, Caroline L392
Massie McQuilkin & Altman L394
Maurer, Shari L397
Maw, Jane Graham L398
McCormick Literary L400
McNicol, Andy L402
McNidder & Grace P232
Medical Physics Publishing P234
Medina Publishing P235
Mendia, Isabel L403
Mentor Books P236
Meridian Artists L404
Merlin Unwin Books P237
Merullo, Annabel L405
Metamorphosis Literary Agency L406
Methuen Publishing Ltd P238
Mic Cheetham Literary Agency L407
Michel, Caroline L408
Mihell, Natasha L410
Milkweed Editions P239
Minnesota Historical Society Press P241
Missouri Historical Society Press P243
MIT Press, The P244
Molloy, Jess L414
Monacelli Press, The P245
Monoray P246
Moody Publishers P247
Moorhead, Max L416
Morrell, Imogen L417
Mortimer, Michele L418
Movable Type Management L420
Mulcahy Sweeney Literary Agency L423
Mundy, Toby L426
Murdoch Books Australia P249
Murgolo, Karen L427
Murray, Judith L428
Muscato, Nate L429
Muswell Press P250
NAHB BuilderBooks P253
New Harbinger Publications P255
Nichols, Mariah L438
Niumata, Erin L439
Niv, Daniel L440
No Starch Press, Inc. P258
Nolan, Laura L441
Northbank Talent Management L442
O'Grady, Niamh L445
O'Neill, Molly L446
O'Shea, Amy L447
Oak Tree Press P259
Ohio University Press P261
Old Pond Publishing P262
Old Street Publishing Ltd P263
Oldcastle Books Group P264
Ooligan Press P265
Orca Book Publishers P266
Orphans Publishing P268
Otago University Press P269
Oxbow Books P271
Oxford University Press P272
Pacific Press Publishing Association P273
Pan Macmillan Australia P274
Paradigm Talent and Literary Agency L454

Parthian Books	P275
Pass, Marina de	L456
Patterson, David	L457
Patterson, Emma	L458
Paul S. Levine Literary Agency	L459
Peddle, Kay	L460
Peepal Tree Press	P278
Pelagic	P279
Pelham, Imogen	L461
Pen & Ink Designs Publishing	P280
Pen & Sword Books Ltd	P281
People's Friend, The	M237
Perez Literary & Entertainment	L463
Perez, Kristina	L464
Perotto-Wills, Martha	L465
Perry Literary	L466
Perspectives Books	P283
Pestritto, Carrie	L467
Peter Lang	P285
PEW Literary	L468
Phaidon Press	P287
Phelan, Beth	L470
Philips, Ariana	L471
Phillips, Aemilia	L472
Piatkus Books	P289
Pickering, Juliet	L473
Pierce, Rosie	L474
Pimpernel Press	P292
Pine, Gideon	L475
Pineapple Press	P293
Plitt, Carrie	L477
Pluto Press	P295
Pocket Mountains	P296
Polygon	P298
Popular Chess	P299
Portobello Literary	L479
Posner, Marcy	L480
Power, Anna	L482
Practical Pre-School Books	P300
Prestel Publishing Ltd	P302
Preston, Amanda	L484
Purdue University Press	P305
Pureplay Press	P306
Quarto Group, Inc., The	P307
Quirk Books	P308
Radio Society of Great Britain	P309
Ramer, Susan	L486
Ransom Publishing Ltd	P312
Redhammer	L488
Regina Ryan Books	P489
Reid, Janet	L490
Reilly, Milly	L491
Renard Press Ltd	P313
Richter, Rick	L493
Roberts, Soumeya Bendimerad	L495
Robertson Murray Literary Agency	L496
Robinson, Quressa	L497
Rocking Chair Books	L499
Rocky Mountain Books	P315
Romano, Annie	L502
Rosenberg Group, The	L505
Roseway	P317
Ross, Whitney	L507
Round Hall	P318
Rudy Agency, The	L510
Rupert Crew Ltd	L511
Rutherford, Laetitia	L513
Rutman, Jim	L514
Salt Publishing	P322
Sanchez, Kaitlyn	L516
Sanders, Rayhane	L517
Sandstone Press	P323
Saqi Books	P324
Sasquatch Books	P325
Savvides, Marilia	L520
Sayle Literary Agency, The	L521
Schiffer Military History	P328
Schofield, Hannah	L522
Scholastic	P329
Scholastic UK	P330
Schwizer, Fabienne	L523
Scratching Shed Publishing	P331
Seager, Chloe	L524
Seal Press	P332
Selectric Artists	L525
Sentient Publications	P334
Seren Books	P335
Serra, Maria Cardona	L526
Seymour, Charlotte	L528
Shaw Agency, The	L529
Sheree Bykofsky Associates, Inc.	L532
Shesto Literary	L533
Shestopal, Camilla	L534
Shipwreckt Books Publishing Company	P336
Sigma Press	P337
Silk, Julia	L535
Simpson, Cara Lee	L537
Singh, Amandeep	L538
Singing Dragon	P340
Snowbooks	P344
Society for Promoting Christian Knowledge (SPCK)	P345
Society of Genealogists	P346
Sophie Hicks Agency	L545
Sourcebooks	P350
Sourcebooks eXplore	P352
Sourcebooks Fire	P353
Spackman, James	L547
Sparsile Books	P359
SRL Publishing	P361
Stainer & Bell Ltd	P366
Stanford University Press	P367
Stephens, Jenny	L549
Steward House Publishers	P369
Stipes Publishing	P371
StoryWise	L552
Strothman, Wendy	L555
Stuart Krichevsky Literary Agency, Inc.	L556
Sunbelt Publications, Inc.	P373
Susan Schulman Literary Agency	L557
Susanna Lea Associates	L558
Swainson, Joanna	L561
Sweet & Maxwell	P374
Sweet, Emily	L563
Sweren, Becky	L564
Symonds, Laurel	L565
Takikawa, Marin	L566
Talbot, Emily	L567
Tasman, Alice	L569
Taylor & Francis Group	P378
Terlip, Paige	L570
Texas A&M University Press	P381
Thames & Hudson Inc	P382
Thames and Hudson Ltd	P383
Thayer, Henry	L572
Theseus Agency, The	L573
Thinkwell Books, UK	P384
Thorneycroft, Euan	L574
Thwaites, Steph	L575
Tippermuir Books	P386
Toad Hall Editions	P387
Topping, Antony	L577
Torrey House Press, LLC	P390
Torva	P391
Trudel, Jes	L579
Turner Publishing	P394
Turtle Press	P395
Two Fine Crows Books	P396
Tyndale House Publishers, Inc.	P397
UCL Press	P398
Ugly Duckling Presse	P399
Unbound Press	P400
Unbridled Books	P401
Unicorn	P402
University of Akron Press, The	P403
University of Alberta Press	P404
University of Calgary Press	P405
University of California Press	P406
University of Georgia Press	P407
University of Iowa Press	P408
University of Maine Press	P409
University of Michigan Press, The	P410
University of Missouri Press	P411
University of North Texas Press	P412
University of Tennessee Press	P413
University of Texas Press	P414
University of Virginia Press	P415
University Press of Colorado	P416
Unseen Press	P417
Usselman, Laura	L581
Valley Press	P418
Vance, Lisa Erbach	L583
Velocity Press	P420
Viney Agency, The	L585
Viney, Charlie	L586
W.W. Norton & Company Ltd	P422
W.W. Norton & Company, Inc.	P423
Wade & Co Literary Agency	L588
Walker Books	P424
Walsh, Caroline	L589
Washington Writers' Publishing House	P425
Watson, Little Ltd	L590
Watterson, Jessica	L591
Wee Book Company, The	P427
Weiss, Alexandra	L593
Weitzner, Tess	L594
Wells, Karmen	L595
Weltz, Jennifer	L596
Westin, Erin Casey	L597
Whatnall, Michaela	L598
Whispering Buffalo Literary Agency	L599
Whitford Press	P428
Wickers, Chandler	L600
Wide-Eyed Editions	P429
Williams, Laura	L603
Willms, Kathryn	L605
Wilson, Desiree	L606
Wilson, Ed	L607
Windhorse Publications Ltd	P430
Wisdom Publications	P431
Woods, Bryony	L610
Woollard, Jessica	L611
Workman Publishing	P437
Yale University Press (London)	P438
Yeoh, Rachel	L612
YMU Books	L613
Young, Claudia	L614
Zack Company, Inc, The	L615
Zacker, Marietta B.	L616
Zeno Agency	L617
Zibby Books	P440
Zuckerbrot, Renee	L618
Zuraw-Friedland, Ayla	L619

Nonfiction in Translation

And Other Stories	P013
Charnace, Edwina de	L110
Daunt Books Publishing	P106
Faultline	M118
Five Points	M124
Half Mystic Journal	M149
Hunger Mountain	M161
Indiana Review	M167
Irish Pages	M173
Kenyon Review, The	M179
Massachusetts Review, The	M202
Nashville Review	M217

Index | Norfolk

New England Review M220
Shenandoah M277
Southern Review, The M291
Tributaries M320

Norfolk
See more broadly: England
Norfolk & Suffolk Bride M224

North Africa
See more broadly: Africa
Saqi Books P324

North America
See more broadly: Regional
See more specifically: Atlantic Northeast; Canada; United States
Ohio University Press P261

North Pacific Rim
See more broadly: Pacific

Northern England
See more broadly: England
Salt Publishing P322
Scratching Shed Publishing P331

Northern Ireland
See more broadly: United Kingdom
Blackstaff Press P051

Nostalgia
See more broadly: History
Best of British M050
Countryside Books P099
Foxx, Kat L213
Yours M350

Novel Excerpts
aaduna M003
African Voices M010
Alaska Quarterly Review M014
Fiddlehead, The M121
Frogmore Papers, The M132
Idaho Review M163
Kenyon Review, The M179
New England Review M220
Pacifica Literary Review M231
Shenandoah M277
Stinging Fly, The M299

Novelettes
Big Fiction M055
Sunspot Literary Journal M305

Novellas
Alaska Quarterly Review M014
Fairlight Books P128
Half Mystic Press P157
Inkandescent P190
New England Review M220
People's Friend Pocket Novels M236
Phoenix Moirai P288
Sinister Stoat Press P341
Sunspot Literary Journal M305
Wordsonthestreet P434
YesYes Books P439

Novels
3 Seas Literary Agency L001
404 Ink P001
A.M. Heath & Company Limited, Author's Agents L002
Able Muse Press P003
Acheampong, Kwaku L003
Adams, Seren L004
Adsett, Alex L005
Afonso, Thais L007
Afsana Press P005
Afterglow Books P006
Agency (London) Ltd, The L008
Albert Whitman & Company P007
Aldridge, Kaylyn L010
Alekseii, Keir L011
Algonquin Books P008
Alice Williams Literary L012
Allen & Unwin P009

Alternating Current Press P010
Ambassador Speakers Bureau & Literary Agency L013
American Mystery Classics P012
And Other Stories P013
Andlyn L014
Andrade, Hannah L015
Andrew Nurnberg Associates, Ltd L016
Ange, Anna L019
Anne Clark Literary Agency L020
Annette Green Authors' Agency L021
Antony Harwood Limited L022
Anvil Press Publishers P017
Apple Tree Literary Ltd L023
April Gloaming P018
Arcadia Publishing P020
Armada, Kurestin L024
Arms, Victoria Wells L025
Armstrong, Susan L026
Arte Publico Press P021
Arthurson, Wayne L027
Asabi Publishing P022
Atyeo, Charlotte L028
Aurora Metro Press L029
Baen Books P029
Bajek, Lauren L031
Bald and Bonkers Network LLC P030
Barbara, Stephen L034
Barone Literary Agency L036
Baror International, Inc. L037
Barr, Anjanette L038
Barr, Nicola L039
Bartholomew, Jason L041
Bath Literary Agency L042
Bauman, Erica L043
Baxter, Veronique L045
Bearded Badger Publishing Co. P043
Beaumont, Diana L046
Begum, Salma L047
Belton, Maddy L049
Bennett, Laura L050
Bent Agency (UK), The L051
Bent Agency, The L052
Bent, Jenny L053
Berdinsky, Kendall L054
Berlyne, John L055
Bess Press P047
Betancourt Literary L057
Betsy Amster Literary Enterprises L059
Beverley Slopen Literary Agency L060
Bewley, Elizabeth L061
Bhasin, Tamanna L062
Black & White Publishing Ltd P049
Blackstaff Press P051
Blair Partnership, The L064
Blake Friedmann Literary Agency Ltd ... L065
Bloodhound Books P052
Bolton, Camilla L067
Bonnier Books (UK) P059
Book Group, The L068
Books For All Times P060
Bookseeker Agency L069
Bowlin, Sarah L071
Brace, Samantha L072
Bradford Literary Agency L073
Bradford, Laura L074
Brannan, Maria L076
Brattle Agency LLC, The L077
Brewin Books Ltd P062
Brooks, Savannah L080
Brotherstone Creative Management .. L081
Brotherstone, Charlie L082
Buckley, Louise L085
Bukowski, Danielle L086
Burby, Danielle L087
Burke, Kate L088

Burns, Camille L089
CAA (London) L091
Cabello, Analia L092
Cameron, Kimberley L093
Campbell, Charlie L094
Candlemark & Gleam P069
Candy Jar Books P070
Canterbury Literary Agency L096
Captivate Press P072
Carina Press P073
Caroline Davidson Literary Agency . L099
Carr, Jamie L101
Carroll, Megan L102
Carter, Rebecca L103
Cartey, Claire L104
Caskie, Robert L105
Cassava Republic Press UK P074
Cavanagh, Claire L107
Chanchani, Sonali L108
Chang, Nicola L109
Charisma House P079
Charles River Press P080
Charnace, Edwina de L110
Chevais, Jennifer L111
Chiotti, Danielle L113
Cho, Catherine L114
Choc Lit P085
Christensen, Erica L115
Cichello, Kayla L117
Cinnamon Press P088
Claret Press P089
Clarke, Caro L118
Clarke, Catherine L119
Cleis Press P091
Coach House Books P092
Cochran, Alexander L120
Colwill, Charlotte L121
Combemale, Chris L122
Comparato, Andrea L123
Compass Talent L124
Compassiviste Publishing P097
Conrad, Claire Paterson L125
Conville, Clare L126
Coombes, Clare L127
Cooper, Gemma L128
Cooper, Maggie L129
Crandall, Becca L130
Crowley, Sheila L132
Crown Publishing Group, The P103
Curran, Sabhbh L134
Curtis Brown L135
Cusick, John L136
Dana Newman Literary, LLC L138
Danaczko, Melissa L139
Danko, Margaret L140
Darga, Jon Michael L141
Darhansoff & Verrill Literary Agents .. L142
Darley Anderson Agency, The L143
Darley Anderson Children's L144
Daunt Books Publishing P106
David Godwin Associates L145
Davies, Olivia L147
Dawson, Liza L148
DeBlock, Liza L149
Dedalus Ltd P107
Demblon, Gabrielle L150
DHH Literary Agency Ltd L152
Diamond Kahn and Woods (DKW) Literary Agency Ltd L153
Dillsworth, Elise L156
Diversion Books P111
Dodo Ink P113
Dolin, Lily L157
Don Congdon Associates, Inc. L159
Donald Maass Literary Agency L160
Doubleday (UK) P114

Access more listings online at www.firstwriter.com

Index | Novels

Doug Grad Literary Agency L161
Draper, Claire L162
Dreamspinner Press P115
DSP Publications P116
Dundurn P118
Dunham Literary, Inc. L163
Dunn, Ben L164
DunnFogg L165
Dunow, Carlson & Lerner Agency L166
Dystel, Jane L167
Eason, Lynette L169
East of Centre P119
Eddison Pearson Ltd L170
Edelstein, Anne L171
Edenborough, Sam L172
Eerdmans Books for Young Readers P120
Einstein, Susanna L173
Eisenbraun, Nicole L174
Eisenmann, Caroline L175
Elaine Markson Literary Agency L178
Elaine Steel L179
Ellis-Martin, Sian L180
Epicenter Press Inc P124
Eunice McMullen Children's Literary Agent Ltd L182
Evans, Kate L185
Everything With Words P126
Fabien, Samantha L186
Fairlight Books P128
Faulks, Holly L187
Fazzari, Hillary L188
Feldstein Agency, The L191
Felicity Bryan Associates L192
Fellows, Abi L193
Feminist Press, The P130
Ferguson, Hannah L194
Ferguson, T.S. L195
Fergusson, Julie L196
Fernandez, Rochelle L197
Figueroa, Melanie L199
Finan, Ciara L200
Finch, Rebeka L202
Finegan, Stevie L203
Firefly P133
Flannery Literary L204
Flynn, Amy Thrall L205
Fogg, Jack L206
Folio Literary Management, LLC L207
for Authors, A L209
Forrester, Jemima L210
Foster, Clara L211
Fox, Aram L212
Foxx, Kat L213
Frankel, Valerie L215
Fraser Ross Associates L216
Free Spirit Publishing P136
Friedman, Claire L217
Friedman, Jessica L218
Friedman, Rebecca L219
Friedrich Agency LLC, The L220
Fuentes, Sarah L222
Fuller, Lisa L223
Furniss, Eugenie L224
Gahan, Isobel L225
Galvin, Lori L226
Geiger, Ellen L227
Getzler, Josh L229
Ghahremani, Lilly L230
Ghosh Literary L231
Ghosh, Anna L232
Gilbert, Tara L233
Gill Books P142
Gillam, Bianca L234
Gisondi, Katie L235
Glass Literary Management LLC L236
Glenister, Emily L238
Global Lion Intellectual Property Management, Inc. L239
Goderich, Miriam L240
Goetz, Adria L241
Goff, Ellen L242
Gold SF P146
Goldblatt, Rachel L243
Goldstein, Veronica L244
Goodman Beck Publishing P147
Goose Lane Editions P148
Gordon, Andrew L245
Graham Maw Christie Literary Agency L246
Graham, Stacey L247
Graham, Susan L248
Grajkowski, Kara L249
Graywolf Press P152
Greene & Heaton Ltd L251
Greenstone Literary L252
Gruber, Pam L253
Grunewald, Hattie L254
Guernica Editions P153
Gunic, Masha L256
Hachette Book Group P156
Haggerty, Taylor L258
Hakim, Serene L259
Haley, Jolene L260
Half Mystic Press P157
Hanbury Agency, The L261
Hannah Sheppard Literary Agency L262
Hannigan, Carrie L263
Hansen, Stephanie L264
Harper, Logan L267
Harris, Erin L268
Hashtag Press P166
Hawk, Susan L269
Hawn, Molly Ker L270
Hawthorne Books P167
Hayden, Viola L271
Headley, David H. L272
Heathfield, Laura L273
Hensley, Chelsea L274
Hernandez, Saritza L275
Hernando, Paloma L276
Heymont, Lane L277
Hildebrand, Cole L280
Hiyate, Sam L281
Hodder & Stoughton Ltd P175
Hogrebe, Christina L283
HopeRoad P176
Hordern, Kate L286
Hornsley, Sarah L287
Hwang, Annie L288
Ig Publishing P182
IgKids P183
Inkandescent P190
Inscriptions Literary Agency L289
Inspired Ink Literary L290
Irene Goodman Literary Agency (IGLA) L291
Irvine, Lucy L292
Jamieson, Molly L296
Janklow & Nesbit UK Ltd L297
Jean V. Naggar Literary Agency, The L299
JMD Media / DB Publishing P198
Joelle Delbourgo Associates, Inc. .. L301
Joffe Books P199
John Murray Press P200
Johnson, Jared L303
Jonathan Clowes Ltd L304
Jones, Philip Gwyn L307
Judith Murdoch Literary Agency ... L309
Julie Crisp Literary Agency L311
Julien, Ria L312
K2 Literary L313
Kahn, Ella Diamond L314
Kaliszewska, Joanna L315
Kane Literary Agency L316
Kantor, Camille L317
Kardon, Julia L318
Karen Gantz Literary Management L319
Kate Barker Literary, TV, & Film Agency L320
Kate Nash Literary Agency L321
Kates Hill Press, The P203
Kathryn Green Literary Agency, LLC L322
Kavanagh, Jade L323
Kean, Taylor Martindale L324
Keane Kataria Literary Agency L325
Keeffe, Sara O' L326
Kenny, Julia L329
Kensington Publishing Corp. P204
Keren, Eli L330
Ki Agency Ltd L331
Killingley, Jessica L332
Kim, Jennifer L333
Kim, Julia L334
Kimber, Natalie L336
Kimberley Cameron & Associates .. L337
Kirby, Robert L338
Knigge, Sheyla L339
Kore Press P207
Kracht, Elizabeth L341
Krichevsky, Stuart L342
Krienke, Mary L343
KT Literary L345
Lakosil, Natalie L347
Lambert, Sophie L348
Lane, Helen L349
Langlee, Lina L352
Langton, Becca L353
Langtons International L354
Latshaw, Katherine L355
Laxfield Literary Associates L356
Leach, Saskia L357
Leamington Books P211
Leapfrog Press P212
Leeke, Jessica L358
Leigh Feldman Literary L359
Leon, Nina L360
Lerner Publishing Group P213
Levitt, Sarah L361
Levy, Yael L362
Lewinsohn Literary L363
Lewis, Alison L364
Lightner, Kayla L365
Lightning Books P215
Lilliput Press, The P217
Lindsay Literary Agency L366
Lineberry, Isabel L367
Liss, Laurie L368
Liverpool Literary Agency, The L369
Loft Press, Inc. P220
Lotus Lane Literary L371
Loudhailer Books P222
Lovell, Jake L372
Lutyens and Rubinstein L375
Lyrical Press P225
MacDonald, Emily L378
Macdougall, Laura L379
MacGregor & Luedeke L380
MacKenzie, Joanna L382
MacLeod, Lauren L383
Macmillan Children's Books P226
Madeleine Milburn Literary, TV & Film Agency L385
Maidment, Olivia L386
Maltese, Alyssa L387
Manilla Press P227
Margaret K. McElderry Books P228
Marini, Victoria L388
Marr, Jill L389
Marshall, Jen L391

Massie McQuilkin & Altman	L394
Matte, Rebecca	L395
Mattson, Jennifer	L396
Maurer, Shari	L397
McBride, Juliana	L399
McCormick Literary	L400
McNidder & Grace	P232
Meridian Artists	L404
Merlin Unwin Books	P237
Merullo, Annabel	L405
Metamorphosis Literary Agency	L406
Methuen Publishing Ltd	P238
Mic Cheetham Literary Agency	L407
Michel, Caroline	L408
Mihell, Natasha	L410
Milburn, Madeleine	L411
Milkweed Editions	P239
Mills & Boon	P240
Milusich, Grace	L412
Molloy, Jess	L414
Moore, Mary C.	L415
Moorhead, Max	L416
Morrell, Imogen	L417
Mortimer, Michele	L418
Motala, Tasneem	L419
Movable Type Management	L420
Moylett, Lisa	L421
Mozley, Jack	L422
Mulcahy Sweeney Literary Agency	L423
Mundy, Toby	L426
Murray, Judith	L428
Muscato, Nate	L429
Mushens, Juliet	L430
Muswell Press	P250
Myrmidon Books Ltd	P251
Mysterious Press, The	P252
Napolitano, Maria	L431
Nathan, Abigail	L433
Neely, Rachel	L434
Nelson Literary Agency, LLC	L435
Nelson, Kristin	L436
Nelson, Patricia	L437
Nichols, Mariah	L438
Niumata, Erin	L439
Niv, Daniel	L440
Northbank Talent Management	L442
O'Brien, Lee	L444
O'Grady, Niamh	L445
O'Neill, Molly	L446
O'Shea, Amy	L447
Old Street Publishing Ltd	P263
Oldcastle Books Group	P264
Ooligan Press	P265
Orca Book Publishers	P266
Orenda Books	P267
Orphans Publishing	P268
Ostby, Kristin	L452
Pan Macmillan Australia	P274
Paradigm Talent and Literary Agency	L454
Parker, Elana Roth	L455
Parthian Books	P275
Pass, Marina de	L456
Patterson, David	L457
Patterson, Emma	L458
Paul S. Levine Literary Agency	L459
Pelham, Imogen	L461
Pen & Ink Designs Publishing	P280
Penzler Publishers	P282
Perez Literary & Entertainment	L463
Perez, Kristina	L464
Perotto-Wills, Martha	L465
Perspectives Books	P283
Pestritto, Carrie	L467
PEW Literary	L468
Phelan, Beth	L470
Philips, Ariana	L471
Phillips, Aemilia	L472
Phoenix Moirai	P288
Piatkus Books	P289
Pickering, Juliet	L473
Pierce, Rosie	L474
Pine, Gideon	L475
Pineapple Press	P293
Plant, Zoe	L476
Plitt, Carrie	L477
Poisoned Pen Press	P297
Polygon	P298
Portobello Literary	L479
Posner, Marcy	L480
Potter, Madison	L481
Power, Anna	L482
Preston, Amanda	L484
Pureplay Press	P306
Quirk Books	P308
Ramer, Susan	L486
Redhammer	L488
Reid, Janet	L490
Reilly, Milly	L491
Renard Press Ltd	P313
Riccardi, Francesca	L492
Richter, Rick	L493
Roberts, Soumeya Bendimerad	L495
Robinson, Quressa	L497
Rocking Chair Books	L499
Rogers, Coleridge & White Ltd	L501
Romano, Annie	L502
Root, Holly	L504
Rosenberg Group, The	L505
Roseway	P317
Ross, Whitney	L507
Rossitto, Stefanie	L508
Ruby Fiction	P319
Rudy Agency, The	L510
Rupert Crew Ltd	L511
Rushall, Kathleen	L512
Rutherford, Laetitia	L513
Rutman, Jim	L514
Salazar, Des	L515
Salt Publishing	P322
Sanders, Rayhane	L517
Sandstone Press	P323
Sant, Kelly Van	L518
Savvides, Marilia	L520
Sayle Literary Agency, The	L521
Scarlet	P327
Schofield, Hannah	L522
Scholastic	P329
Scholastic UK	P330
Schwizer, Fabienne	L523
Scratching Shed Publishing	P331
Seager, Chloe	L524
Selectric Artists	L525
Sentient Publications	P334
Seren Books	P335
Serra, Maria Cardona	L526
Seventh Agency	L527
Seymour, Charlotte	L528
Shaw Agency, The	L529
Shesto Literary	L533
Shestopal, Camilla	L534
Shipwreckt Books Publishing Company	P336
Silk, Julia	L535
Simons, Tanera	L536
Simpson, Cara Lee	L537
Singh, Amandeep	L538
Sinister Stoat Press	P341
Siobhan, Aiden	L539
Skylark Literary	L540
Sluytman, Antoinette Van	L541
SmashBear Publishing	P342
Snowbooks	P344
Society for Promoting Christian Knowledge (SPCK)	P345
Soho Press	P348
Soler, Shania N.	L543
Soloway, Jennifer March	L544
Sophie Hicks Agency	L545
Sorg, Arley	L546
Sourcebooks Casablanca	P351
Sourcebooks Fire	P353
Sourcebooks Horror	P354
Sourcebooks Landmark	P356
Sparsile Books	P359
Spout Press	P360
SRL Publishing	P361
Steed, Hayley	L548
Sternig & Byrne Literary Agency	L550
Steward House Publishers	P369
Stringer Literary Agency LLC, The	L553
Stringer, Marlene	L554
Stuart Krichevsky Literary Agency, Inc.	L556
Sunbelt Publications, Inc.	P373
Susan Schulman Literary Agency	L557
Susanna Lea Associates	L558
Sutherland, Kari	L559
Swainson, Joanna	L561
Symonds, Laurel	L565
Tailwinds Press	P376
Takikawa, Marin	L566
Talbot, Emily	L567
Tannenbaum, Amy	L568
Tasman, Alice	L569
Terlip, Paige	L570
Texas A&M University Press	P381
Thayer, Henry	L572
Theseus Agency, The	L573
Thinkwell Books, UK	P384
Thorneycroft, Euan	L574
Thwaites, Steph	L575
Tibbets, Anne	L576
Tippermuir Books	P386
Toad Hall Editions	P387
Topping, Antony	L577
Tor Publishing Group	P388
Tor Teen	P389
Torrey House Press, LLC	P390
Tran, Jennifer Chen	L578
Trudel, Jes	L579
Turner Publishing	P394
Tyndale House Publishers, Inc.	P397
Udden, Jennifer	L580
Unbound Press	P400
Unbridled Books	P401
University of Iowa Press	P408
University of Maine Press	P409
University of Michigan Press, The	P410
Usselman, Laura	L581
Valley Press	P418
Vance, Lisa Erbach	L583
Velocity Press	P420
Viney Agency, The	L585
Viney, Charlie	L586
W.W. Norton & Company Ltd	P422
W.W. Norton & Company, Inc.	P423
Wade & Co Literary Agency	L588
Walsh, Caroline	L589
Washington Writers' Publishing House	P425
Watson, Little Ltd	L590
Watterson, Jessica	L591
Weiman, Paula	L592
Weiss, Alexandra	L593
Weitzner, Tess	L594
Wells, Karmen	L595
Weltz, Jennifer	L596
Westin, Erin Casey	L597
Whatnall, Michaela	L598

Whispering Buffalo Literary Agency L599
Wickers, Chandler L600
Williams, Laura L603
Williamson, Jo L604
Willms, Kathryn L605
Wilson, Desiree L606
Wilson, Ed L607
Wolfpack Publishing P432
Wood, Caroline L608
Wood, Ed L609
Woods, Bryony L610
Woollard, Jessica L611
Wordsonthestreet P434
Wordsworth Editions P435
Workman Publishing P437
Yeoh, Rachel L612
YesYes Books P439
Young, Claudia L614
Zack Company, Inc, The L615
Zacker, Marietta B. L616
Zeno Agency L617
Zibby Books P440
Zuckerbrot, Renee L618
Zuraw-Friedland, Ayla L619

Novels in Verse
    Borstel, Stefanie Sanchez Von L070
    Ostby, Kristin L452

Numerology
    See more broadly: Fortune Telling and Divination

Numismatics (Coin / Currency Collecting)
    See more broadly: Hobbies

Nursing
    See more broadly: Health
    See more specifically: Midwifery
    Bloomsbury Academic P053
    Gill Education P143
    Taylor & Francis Group P378

Nutrition
    See more broadly: Food and Drink; Health
    Betsy Amster Literary Enterprises L059
    Demblon, Gabrielle L150
    Derviskadic, Dado L151
    Hammersmith Books P158
    Marr, Jill L389
    Singing Dragon P340
    Zack Company, Inc, The L615

Oceanography
    See more broadly: Earth Science
    W.W. Norton & Company Ltd P422

Offshore Gamefishing
    See more broadly: Fishing
    Marlin M201

Ohio
    See more broadly: United States
    Ohio University Press P261
    University of Akron Press, The P403

Organised Crime
    See more broadly: Crime
    See more specifically: Mafia

Outdoor / Wild Swimming
    See more broadly: Swimming
    Adventure Books by Vertebrate Publishing P004

Outdoor Activities
    See more broadly: Activities
    See more specifically: Camping; Caving and Potholing; Diving; Outdoor Survival Skills; Walking
    Cedar Fort P076
    River Hills Traveler M263
    Rocky Mountain Books P315
    Scots Magazine, The M271
    Scottish Field M272
    Yorkshire Life M348
    Zack Company, Inc, The L615

Outdoor Survival Skills
    See more broadly: Outdoor Activities
    Asabi Publishing P022

Ozarks
    See more broadly: United States
    River Hills Traveler M263

Pacific
    See more broadly: Regional
    See more specifically: North Pacific Rim; South Pacific
    Bess Press P047
    Manoa M199
    Otago University Press P269

Pacific Northwest
    See more broadly: United States
    Basalt Books P034
    Little Bigfoot P218

Paganism
    See more broadly: Religion
    See more specifically: Wicca
    Llewellyn Worldwide Ltd P219

Painting
    See more broadly: Arts
    Korero Press P208
    Leisure Painter M184
    Zack Company, Inc, The L615

Paleontology
    See more broadly: Biology
    Indiana University Press P187

Palmistry
    See more broadly: Fortune Telling and Divination

Pamphlets
    Broken Sleep Books P066

Parenting
    See more broadly: Family
    See more specifically: Motherhood; Pregnancy
    Barrett, Emily L040
    Baumer, Jan L044
    Bernardi, Amanda L056
    Betsy Amster Literary Enterprises L059
    Bradford Literary Agency L073
    CharlottesvilleFamily M076
    Dana Newman Literary, LLC L138
    Demblon, Gabrielle L150
    Dickerson, Donya L155
    DK Publishing P112
    Draper, Claire L162
    Foxx, Kat L213
    Gill Books P142
    Hashtag Press P166
    Hay House Publishers P168
    Jessica Kingsley Publishers P197
    Joelle Delbourgo Associates, Inc. L301
    Kathryn Green Literary Agency, LLC L322
    Levy, Yael L362
    Macdougall, Laura L379
    Maurer, Shari L397
    Pacific Press Publishing Association P273
    Perry Literary L466
    Piatkus Books P289
    Quirk Books P308
    Red Magazine M259
    Regina Ryan Books L489
    Sheree Bykofsky Associates, Inc. L532
    Tyndale House Publishers, Inc. P397
    Usselman, Laura L581
    W.W. Norton & Company Ltd P422
    Workman Publishing P437
    Zack Company, Inc, The L615

Pennsylvania
    See more broadly: United States
    See more specifically: Berks County; Pittsburgh

Pensacola
    See more broadly: Florida

Performing Arts
    See more broadly: Arts
    See more specifically: Dance; Storytelling
    Arcadia Publishing P020
    Brick M065
    Harvard University Press P165
    Indiana University Press P187
    Kensington Publishing Corp. P204
    Nolan, Laura L441
    Ohio University Press P261
    Oxford University Press P272
    Phaidon Press P287
    Scratching Shed Publishing P331
    Thames & Hudson Ltd P382
    University of Alberta Press P404
    W.W. Norton & Company, Inc. P423

Personal Coaching
    See more broadly: Personal Development
    Ki Agency Ltd L331
    W.W. Norton & Company Ltd P422

Personal Development
    See more specifically: Career Development; Leadership; Personal Coaching; Self Help
    Barrett, Emily L040
    Blair Partnership, The L064
    Charnace, Edwina de L110
    Christie, Jennifer L116
    Dickerson, Donya L155
    Evans, Kate L185
    Free Spirit Publishing P136
    Goodman Beck Publishing P147
    Grunewald, Hattie L254
    Hay House Publishers P168
    Hiyate, Sam L281
    Ki Agency Ltd L331
    Killingley, Jessica L332
    Murdoch Books Australia P249
    Piatkus Books P289
    Schofield, Hannah L522
    Sheree Bykofsky Associates, Inc. L532
    Singh, Amandeep L538
    Society for Promoting Christian Knowledge (SPCK) P345
    Tyndale House Publishers, Inc. P397
    Willms, Kathryn L605
    Zack Company, Inc, The L615

Personal Essays
    See more broadly: Autobiography; Narrative Essays
    Blue Earth Review M059
    Caribbean Writer, The M073
    Creative Nonfiction M095
    Identity Theory M164
    Malahat Review, The M197
    New England Review M220
    Poetry Birmingham Literary Journal M242
    Roberts, Soumeya Bendimerad L495
    Southern Humanities Review M290
    Toad Hall Editions P387
    Tolka M319

Personal Experiences
    See more broadly: Autobiography
    Cedar Fort P076
    Christie, Jennifer L116

Personal Finance
    See more broadly: Finance
    Danko, Margaret L140
    Demblon, Gabrielle L150
    Faulks, Holly L187
    First For Women M122
    My Weekly M215
    Zack Company, Inc, The L615

Pet Fish
    See more broadly: Pets

Pets
    See more broadly: Animals
    See more specifically: Cats; Dogs; Pet Fish
    Arcadia Publishing P020

Graham, Stacey	L247	
Hay House Publishers	P168	
Kensington Publishing Corp.	P204	
Kracht, Elizabeth	L341	
Quirk Books	P308	
Turner Publishing	P394	
W.W. Norton & Company Ltd	P422	
Yours	M350	
Zack Company, Inc, The	L615	

Philosophy
See more specifically: Chinese Philosophy; Islamic Philosophy; Marxism; Taoism / Daoism

Arcadia Publishing	P020
Baylor University Press	P041
Bloomsbury Academic	P053
British Academy, The	P063
Broadview Press	P065
Cambridge University Press	P068
Christie, Jennifer	L116
Clarke, Catherine	L119
Compassiviste Publishing	P097
Curious Minds	L133
Derviskadic, Dado	L151
Edelstein, Anne	L171
Evans, Kate	L185
Goose Lane Editions	P148
Harvard University Press	P165
Icon Books Ltd	P180
Indiana University Press	P187
International Publishers	P191
Kensington Publishing Corp.	P204
Lilliput Press, The	P217
Loft Press, Inc.	P220
London Review of Books	M191
Macdougall, Laura	L379
Marion Boyars Publishers	P229
Massachusetts Review, The	M202
Ohio University Press	P261
Oxford Review of Books	M230
Oxford University Press	P272
Peter Lang	P285
Stanford University Press	P367
Taylor & Francis Group	P378
Thames & Hudson Inc.	P382
Thames and Hudson Ltd	P383
Turtle Press	P395
University of Alberta Press	P404
University of California Press	P406
University of Michigan Press, The	P410
University of Virginia Press	P415
W.W. Norton & Company Ltd	P422
W.W. Norton & Company, Inc.	P423
Yale University Press (London)	P438

Photography
See more broadly: Arts

Anvil Press Publishers	P017
Arcadia Publishing	P020
Bird Eye Books	P048
Brick	M065
Compassiviste Publishing	P097
Darga, Jon Michael	L141
DK Publishing	P112
Doug Grad Literary Agency	L161
Enitharmon Editions	P122
Ghahremani, Lilly	L230
Kensington Publishing Corp.	P204
Lilliput Press, The	P217
McNidder & Grace	P232
Monacelli Press, The	P245
Phaidon Press	P287
Power Cut Lite	M247
Prestel Publishing Ltd	P302
Rocky Mountain Books	P315
Ruralite	M266
Seren Books	P335

Square Mile Magazine	M298
Thames & Hudson Inc.	P382
Thames and Hudson Ltd	P383
University of Texas Press	P414
University of Virginia Press	P415
W.W. Norton & Company Ltd	P422

Physical Education
See more broadly: Education

Colourpoint Educational	P095
Gill Education	P143
Mentor Books	P236

Physics
See more broadly: Science

Cambridge University Press	P068
Colourpoint Educational	P095
Gale	P139
Gill Education	P143
Medical Physics Publishing	P234
Stipes Publishing	P371
Taylor & Francis Group	P378
W.W. Norton & Company Ltd	P422

Physiology
See more broadly: Medicine

Stipes Publishing	P371

Piano
See more broadly: Musical Instruments

International Piano	M170

Picture Books

Agency (London) Ltd, The	L008
Albert Whitman & Company	P007
Alice Williams Literary	L012
Allen & Unwin	P009
Andersen Press Ltd	P014
Andlyn	L014
Arcadia Publishing	P020
Armada, Kurestin	L024
Arms, Victoria Wells	L025
Atyeo, Charlotte	L028
Barr, Anjanette	L038
Bath Literary Agency	L042
Bess Press	P047
Bonnier Books (UK)	P059
Bradford Literary Agency	L073
Brewin Books Ltd	P062
Bright Agency (UK), The	L078
Bright Agency (US), The	L079
Brooks, Savannah	L080
Burby, Danielle	L087
CAA (London)	L091
Cabello, Analia	L092
Cartey, Claire	L104
Cedar Fort	P076
Charlesbridge Publishing	P081
Cherry Lake Publishing Group	P083
Child's Play (International) Ltd	P084
Children's Books North Agency	L112
Cicada Books	P087
Cichello, Kayla	L117
Comparato, Andrea	L123
Crandall, Becca	L130
Creative Roots Studio	L131
Curtis Brown	L135
Darley Anderson Children's	L144
DK Publishing	P112
Dominguez, Adriana	L158
Dunham Literary, Inc.	L163
Eddison Pearson Ltd	L170
Eerdmans Books for Young Readers	P120
Eunice McMullen Children's Literary Agent Ltd	L182
Feldman, Kait Lee	L190
Fernandez, Rochelle	L197
Finegan, Stevie	L203
Flynn, Amy Thrall	L205
Fraser Ross Associates	L216
Free Spirit Publishing	P136

Gemini Books	P140
Ghahremani, Lilly	L230
Goetz, Adria	L241
Goff, Ellen	L242
Graffeg Childrens	P151
Happy Yak	P161
Hare, Jessica	L266
Hawk, Susan	L269
Hensley, Chelsea	L274
Hodges, Jodie	L282
Holroyde, Penny	L285
Igloo Books Limited	P184
Inscriptions Literary Agency	L289
Irvine, Lucy	L292
Joelle Delbourgo Associates, Inc.	L301
Kane Press	P202
Kim, Sally M.	L335
Kube Publishing	P209
Lakosil, Natalie	L347
Lantana Publishing	P210
Lerner Publishing Group	P213
Lindsay Literary Agency	L366
Little Bigfoot	P218
Macmillan Children's Books	P226
Margaret K. McElderry Books	P228
Marr, Jill	L389
Maurer, Shari	L397
Minnesota Historical Society Press	P241
Mulcahy Sweeney Literary Agency	L423
Nelson Literary Agency, LLC	L435
Olswanger, Anna	L450
Orca Book Publishers	P266
Pacific Press Publishing Association	P273
Pages, Saribel	L453
PB and Yay! Books	P277
Pen & Ink Designs Publishing	P280
Regina Ryan Books	L489
Richter, Rick	L493
Rofe, Jennifer	L500
Rudy Agency, The	L510
Rushall, Kathleen	L512
Sanchez, Kaitlyn	L516
Scholastic	P329
Scholastic UK	P330
Scratching Shed Publishing	P331
Simply Read Books	P339
Society for Promoting Christian Knowledge (SPCK)	P345
Soloway, Jennifer March	L544
Sourcebooks Jabberwocky	P355
Sourcebooks Wonderland	P357
StoryWise	L552
Stringer Literary Agency LLC, The	L553
Sunbelt Publications, Inc.	P373
Susan Schulman Literary Agency	L557
Sutherland, Kari	L559
Symonds, Laurel	L565
Talbot, Emily	L567
Terlip, Paige	L570
Thames & Hudson Inc.	P382
Thames and Hudson Ltd	P383
Tilbury House Publishers	P385
Tippermuir Books	P386
Trudel, Jes	L579
Turner Publishing	P394
Tyndale House Publishers, Inc.	P397
W.W. Norton & Company Ltd	P422
Walker Books	P424
Walsh, Caroline	L589
Wee Book Company, The	P427
Weiss, Alexandra	L593
Westin, Erin Casey	L597
Whatnall, Michaela	L598
Williamson, Jo	L604
Words & Pictures	P433
Zacker, Marietta B.	L616

Access more listings online at www.firstwriter.com

Index | *Poetry* **347**

Piloting
See more broadly: Planes
Pittsburgh
See more broadly: Pennsylvania
Planes
See more broadly: Vehicles
See more specifically: Piloting
Plants
See more specifically: Hemp
Draper, Claire L162
Poetry
30 North M001
32 Poems M002
404 Ink P001
aaduna M003
Able Muse Press P003
About Place Journal M004
Abridged M005
Account, The M006
Acumen M007
African American Review M009
African Voices M010
Agni M011
Alaska Quarterly Review M014
Allegro Poetry Magazine M017
Amethyst Review M019
And Other Poems M020
And Other Stories P013
Andrews McMeel Publishing P015
Angela Poetry Magazine M021
Anhinga Press P016
Anvil Press Publishers P017
April Gloaming P018
Arachne Press P019
Arboreal M023
Arc M024
Arcadia Publishing P020
Arts & Letters M027
Asimov's Science Fiction M029
Atlanta Review M031
Atrium M033
Babybug M037
Bacopa Literary Review M038
Bad Betty P028
Baffler, The M039
Bald and Bonkers Network LLC P030
Bandit Fiction M040
Barren Magazine M041
BatCat Press P040
Bath Literary Agency L042
Bear Deluxe Magazine, The M044
Bearded Badger Publishing Co. P043
Begum, Salma L047
Belmont Story Review M047
Better Than Starbucks M052
BFS Horizons M053
Black Moon Magazine M056
Black Warrior Review M058
Blue Diode Publishing P054
Blue Earth Review M059
Blue Mesa Review M060
BOA Editions, Ltd P057
Bookseeker Agency L069
Borstel, Stefanie Sanchez Von L070
Boston Review M062
Boyfriend Village M064
Broken Sleep Books P066
Butcher's Dog M070
Caribbean Writer, The M073
CB Editions P075
Chang, Nicola L109
Chapman M075
Chautauqua Literary Journal M077
Cheshire M078
Child's Play (International) Ltd P084
Cinnamon Press P088
Coach House Books P092
Cobblestone M079
Cocoa Girl M080
Cola M081
Commonweal M082
Concho River Review M083
Conjunctions M084
Conjunctions Online M085
Contemporary Verse 2 .... M086
Crannog Magazine M092
Crazyhorse / Swamp Pink M093
Cream City Review M094
Crystal Magazine M098
CutBank M099
Dalhousie Review, The M100
Dancing Girl Press P105
Dark Horse, The M101
Dawntreader, The M102
Dream Catcher M106
Eddison Pearson Ltd L170
Ekphrastic Review, The M109
El Portal M110
Emerge Literary Journal M111
Enitharmon Editions P122
Event M113
Faultline M118
Feminist Press, The P130
Feminist Studies M119
Fiddlehead, The M121
First Line, The M123
Five Points M124
Folio M126
Fourteen Poems M130
Fourth River, The M131
Frogmore Papers, The M132
Fugue M133
Future Fire, The M135
Gargoyle Online M137
Georgia Review, The M139
Ginosko Literary Journal M140
Glacier, The M141
Glass Poetry Press P144
Goose Lane Editions P148
Grain Literary Magazine M143
Granta M144
Graywolf Lab M145
Graywolf Press P152
Guernica Editions P153
Gulf Coast: A Journal of Literature and Fine Arts M147
Gutter Magazine M148
Half Mystic Journal M149
Half Mystic Press P157
Hancock House Publishers P159
Hanging Loose M150
Harpur Palate M151
Harris, Erin L268
Hearing Eye P169
Helix, The M154
Host Publications P177
Hotel Amerika M160
Hunger Mountain M161
Hwang, Annie L288
I-70 Review M162
Icehouse P179
Idaho Review M163
Identity Theory M164
Image M166
Indiana Review M167
Ink Sweat and Tears M168
Inkandescent P190
Irish Pages M173
Island M174
J. Gordon Shillingford Publishing P194
Jamii Publishing P196
Journal, The M176
Kates Hill Press, The P203
Kavya Kishor M177
Kenyon Review, The M179
Kore Press P207
Kube Publishing P209
Lake, The M181
Landfall M182
Lantana Publishing P210
Leamington Books P211
Leapfrog Press P212
Lighthouse M185
Lilliput Press, The P217
Literary Mama M187
Loft Press, Inc. P220
London Grip New Poetry M189
London Magazine, The M190
London Review of Books M191
Long Poem Magazine M192
Lost Lake Folk Opera Magazine M193
Loudhailer Books P222
Louisiana Literature M194
LSU Press P223
MacGuffin, The M195
Magma M196
Malahat Review, The M197
Manchester Review, The M198
Manoa M199
Margaret K. McElderry Books P228
Massachusetts Review, The M202
Meetinghouse M203
Merlin Unwin Books P237
Michigan Quarterly Review M204
Mid-American Review M206
Midsummer Dream House M207
Midway Journal M208
Milkweed Editions P239
Missouri Review, The M209
Modern Haiku M211
Moonday Mag M213
MQR Mixtape M214
Nashville Review M217
Neo-opsis Science Fiction Magazine M218
Neon M219
New England Review M220
New Walk Editions P256
Nine Arches Press P257
North, The M225
Northern Gravy M226
Obsidian: Literature in the African Diaspora M227
Ostby, Kristin L452
Otago University Press P269
Out-Spoken Press P270
Oxford Poetry M229
Oxford Review of Books M230
Pacifica Literary Review M231
Panorama M232
Paris Review, The M233
Parthian Books P275
Passionfruit Review, The M234
Pavilion Poetry P276
Peepal Tree Press P278
Pen & Ink Designs Publishing P280
Perugia Press P284
Pleiades M238
Ploughshares M239
PN Review M240
Poetry M241
Poetry Birmingham Literary Journal M242
Poetry Ireland Review M243
Poetry London M244
Poetry Wales M245
Polygon P298
Power Cut Lite M247
Press 53 .... P301
Procrastinating Writers United P303

348 Index | Poetry Collections

Prole	M250
Pulsar Poetry Magazine	M251
Pureplay Press	P306
Pushing Out the Boat	M252
Qu Literary Magazine	M253
Quadrant Magazine	M254
Radar Poetry	M256
Renard Press Ltd	P313
Rialto, The	M261
River Styx	M264
Roseway	P317
Saddlebag Dispatches	M267
Scifaikuest	M270
Scratching Shed Publishing	P331
Second Factory	M274
Seren Books	P335
Shearsman	M276
Shenandoah	M277
Shipwreckt Books Publishing Company	P336
Shooter Literary Magazine	M279
Shoreline of Infinity	M280
Sinister Wisdom	M282
Smokestack Books	P343
Snowflake Magazine	M284
South	M288
South Carolina Review	M289
Southern Humanities Review	M290
Southern Review, The	M291
Southwest Review	M293
Southword Journal	M294
Spitball	M297
Spout Press	P360
Stewed Rhubarb Press	P370
Stinging Fly, The	M299
Strange Horizons	M301
Structo Magazine	M303
Studio One	M304
Sunspot Literary Journal	M305
Supplement, The	M306
Sweetgum Press	P375
Tahoma Literary Review	M308
Takahe	M309
Tall-Lighthouse	P377
Tears in the Fence	M311
Temz Review, The	M312
Texas A&M University Press	P381
Thin Air Magazine	M314
Third Coast	M315
This England	M316
Threepenny Review, The	M317
Times Literary Supplement (TLS), The	M318
Toad Hall Editions	P387
Torrey House Press, LLC	P390
Tra[verse]	P392
Tributaries	M320
Tusculum Review, The	M321
UCity Review	M322
Ugly Duckling Presse	P399
Under the Radar	M325
University of Akron Press, The	P403
University of Alberta Press	P404
University of Iowa Press	P408
University of North Texas Press	P412
University of Virginia Press	P415
Vagabond City	M327
Valley Press	P418
Vallum	M328
Vane Women Press	P419
Verve Poetry Press	P421
Virginia Quarterly Review, The	M330
W.W. Norton & Company Ltd	P422
W.W. Norton & Company, Inc.	P423
Waccamaw	M335
Wallace Stevens Journal, The	M336
Walsh, Caroline	L589
Wasafiri	M338
Washington Writers' Publishing House	P425
West Branch	M339
WestWard Quarterly	M340
Wet Grain	M341
Windsor Review	M342
Wordsonthestreet	P434
Wordsworth Editions	P435
Yale Review, The	M344
YesYes Books	P439
Zone 3	M353

Poetry Collections

404 Ink	P001
Able Muse Press	P003
And Other Stories	P013
Andrews McMeel Publishing	P015
Anhinga Press	P016
Anvil Press Publishers	P017
April Gloaming	P018
Arachne Press	P019
Arcadia Publishing	P020
Bad Betty	P028
Bearded Badger Publishing Co.	P043
Begum, Salma	L047
Blue Diode Publishing	P054
BOA Editions, Ltd	P057
Broken Sleep Books	P066
CB Editions	P075
Cinnamon Press	P088
Coach House Books	P092
Enitharmon Editions	P122
Feminist Press, The	P130
Goose Lane Editions	P148
Graywolf Press	P152
Guernica Editions	P153
Half Mystic Press	P157
Hancock House Publishers	P159
Harris, Erin	L268
Hearing Eye	P169
Host Publications	P177
Hwang, Annie	L288
Icehouse	P179
Inkandescent	P190
J. Gordon Shillingford Publishing	P194
Jamii Publishing	P196
Kates Hill Press, The	P203
Kore Press	P207
Leamington Books	P211
Leapfrog Press	P212
Loft Press, Inc.	P220
Loudhailer Books	P222
LSU Press	P223
Merlin Unwin Books	P237
Milkweed Editions	P239
New Walk Editions	P256
Nine Arches Press	P257
Otago University Press	P269
Out-Spoken Press	P270
Parthian Books	P275
Pavilion Poetry	P276
Peepal Tree Press	P278
Pen & Ink Designs Publishing	P280
Perugia Press	P284
Polygon	P298
Press 53	P301
Procrastinating Writers United	P303
Pureplay Press	P306
Renard Press Ltd	P313
Roseway	P317
Scratching Shed Publishing	P331
Seren Books	P335
Shipwreckt Books Publishing Company	P336
Smokestack Books	P343
Spout Press	P360
Stewed Rhubarb Press	P370
Sweetgum Press	P375
Tall-Lighthouse	P377
Texas A&M University Press	P381
Toad Hall Editions	P387
Torrey House Press, LLC	P390
Tra[verse]	P392
Ugly Duckling Presse	P399
University of Akron Press, The	P403
University of Alberta Press	P404
Valley Press	P418
Vane Women Press	P419
Verve Poetry Press	P421
W.W. Norton & Company Ltd	P422
W.W. Norton & Company, Inc.	P423
Walsh, Caroline	L589
Washington Writers' Publishing House	P425
Wordsonthestreet	P434
Wordsworth Editions	P435
YesYes Books	P439

Poetry as a Subject

See more broadly: Literature

32 Poems	M002
Acumen	M007
And Other Poems	M020
Arc	M024
BOA Editions, Ltd	P057
Contemporary Verse 2	M086
Ink Sweat and Tears	M168
Journal, The	M176
Lake, The	M181
London Grip New Poetry	M189
Long Poem Magazine	M192
Magma	M196
Modern Haiku	M211
Ohio University Press	P261
Oxford Review of Books	M230
PN Review	M240
Poetry	M241
Poetry Birmingham Literary Journal	M242
Poetry Ireland Review	M243
Poetry Wales	M245
Quadrant Magazine	M254
Scifaikuest	M270
Times Literary Supplement (TLS), The	M318
University of Akron Press, The	P403
University of Iowa Press	P408
Wallace Stevens Journal, The	M336
Wet Grain	M341

Poetry in Translation

Acumen	M007
Better Than Starbucks	M052
BOA Editions, Ltd	P057
CB Editions	P075
Ekphrastic Review, The	M109
Faultline	M118
Five Points	M124
Future Fire, The	M135
Gulf Coast: A Journal of Literature and Fine Arts	M147
Half Mystic Journal	M149
Host Publications	P177
Hunger Mountain	M161
Indiana Review	M167
Irish Pages	M173
Journal, The	M176
Kenyon Review, The	M179
Manoa	M199
Massachusetts Review, The	M202
Michigan Quarterly Review	M204
Mid-American Review	M206
Modern Poetry in Translation	M212
Nashville Review	M217
Oxford Poetry	M229
Poetry	M241
Poetry London	M244
Shenandoah	M277

Access more listings online at www.firstwriter.com

Index | *Popular Culture* 349

Southern Review, The M291
Stinging Fly, The M299
Structo Magazine M303
Sunspot Literary Journal M305
Tributaries M320
Ugly Duckling Presse P399
Wet Grain M341

Police

See more broadly: Crime
See more specifically: FBI; Police History
Brewin Books Ltd P062
Pluto Press P295
Stipes Publishing P371

Police History

See more broadly: Police

Police Procedural

See more broadly: Crime
Alfred Hitchcock Mystery Magazine M016
Bloodhound Books P052
Joffe Books P199
Kane Literary Agency L316
Pass, Marina de L456
Thorneycroft, Euan L574
Tibbets, Anne L576
Williams, Laura L603

Political History

See more broadly: History; Politics
Minnesota Historical Society Press P241
Texas A&M University Press P381

Political Thrillers

See more broadly: Politics; Thrillers
Orenda Books P267

Politics

See more specifically: Activism; Civil Rights; Conservative; Contemporary Politics; Left Wing Politics; Marxism; Political History; Political Thrillers; Progressive Politics; Socio-Political
404 Ink P001
Afsana Press P005
Ann Arbor Observer M022
Annette Green Authors' Agency L021
Arcadia Publishing P020
Arte Publico Press P021
Baffler, The M039
Barrett, Emily L040
Bartholomew, Jason L041
Basic Books P035
Baylor University Press P041
Berghahn Books Ltd P045
Blackstaff Press P051
Bloomsbury Academic P053
Boston Review M062
Brattle Agency LLC, The L077
Broadview Press P065
Brouckaert, Justin L083
Cambridge University Press P068
Carter, Rebecca L103
Caskie, Robert L105
Chanchani, Sonali L108
Charisma House P079
Claret Press P089
Colourpoint Educational P095
Commonweal M082
Compassiviste Publishing P097
Conversation (UK), The M087
Cottage Life M090
Crown P101
Crown Publishing Group, The P103
Danko, Margaret L140
Dawson, Liza L148
Demblon, Gabrielle L150
Diana Finch Literary Agency L154
Doug Grad Literary Agency L161
Dundurn P118
Dystel, Jane L167
Ellis-Martin, Sian L180
Enslow Publishers, Inc. P123
Evans, Kate L185
Faulks, Holly L187
Fernwood Publishing P131
Finan, Ciara L200
Finegan, Stevie L203
Foster, Clara L211
Fox, Aram L212
FRA (Futerman, Rose, & Associates) L214
Free Association Books Ltd P135
Furniss, Eugenie L224
Geiger, Ellen L227
Getzler, Josh L229
Gill Books P142
Gill Education P143
Gold SF P146
Goldstein, Veronica L244
Goose Lane Editions P148
Gordon, Andrew L245
Granger, David L250
Harvard University Press P165
Henley Hall Press P171
Hildebrand, Cole L280
Icon Books Ltd P180
Ig Publishing P182
Imagine Publishing P186
International Publishers P191
Irene Goodman Literary Agency (IGLA) L291
J. Gordon Shillingford Publishing P194
Javelin L298
Karen Gantz Literary Management L319
Kensington Publishing Corp. P204
Kim, Jennifer L333
Kim, Julia L334
Kube Publishing P209
London Review of Books M191
Macdougall, Laura L379
marie claire M200
Marr, Jill L389
McCormick Literary L400
Mendia, Isabel L403
Methuen Publishing Ltd P238
Monoray P246
Moorhead, Max L416
Morrell, Imogen L417
Muscato, Nate L429
New Internationalist M221
New Statesman M222
Ohio University Press P261
Oxford Review of Books M230
Oxford University Press P272
Peddle, Kay L460
Peter Lang P285
Phillips, Aemilia L472
Pluto Press P295
Political Quarterly, The M246
Purdue University Press P305
Pureplay Press P306
Quadrant Magazine M254
Regina Ryan Books L489
Reilly, Milly L491
Richter, Rick L493
Riposte M262
Roseway P317
Rudy Agency, The L510
Sasquatch Books P325
Scratching Shed Publishing P331
Seventeen M275
Singh, Amandeep L538
Stanford University Press P367
Susan Schulman Literary Agency L557
Taylor & Francis Group P378
Texas A&M University Press P381
Thayer, Henry L572
Thinkwell Books, UK P384
Thorneycroft, Euan L574
Thwaites, Steph L575
Turner Publishing P394
Tyndale House Publishers, Inc. P397
UCL Press P398
University of Akron Press, The P403
University of Alberta Press P404
University of California Press P406
University of Michigan Press, The P410
University of Missouri Press P411
University of Virginia Press P415
Victoria Sanders & Associates LLC L584
Virginia Quarterly Review, The M330
W.W. Norton & Company Ltd P422
W.W. Norton & Company, Inc. P423
Wilson, Ed L607
Yale Review, The M344
Yale University Press (London) P438
Zack Company, Inc, The L615

Pop-Up Books

Thames and Hudson Ltd P383

Popular

See more specifically: Popular Culture; Popular History; Popular Music; Popular Psychology; Popular Science
Compassiviste Publishing P097
Joelle Delbourgo Associates, Inc. L301
Piatkus Books P289
Regina Ryan Books L489

Popular Culture

See more broadly: Culture; Popular
Annette Green Authors' Agency L021
Aurora Metro Press P024
Bernardi, Amanda L056
Betsy Amster Literary Enterprises L059
Bowlin, Sarah L071
Bradford Literary Agency L073
Cavanagh, Claire L107
Curran, Sabhbh L134
Dana Newman Literary, LLC L138
Darga, Jon Michael L141
Davies, Olivia L147
Derviskadic, Dado L151
Dickerson, Donya L155
DK Publishing P112
Dolin, Lily L157
Ellis-Martin, Sian L180
Evans, Kate L185
Fazzari, Hillary L188
Feminist Press, The P130
Forrester, Jemima L210
Gemini Books P140
Glenister, Emily L238
Goldstein, Veronica L244
Gordon, Andrew L245
Graham, Stacey L247
Hanbury Agency, The L261
Harvard University Press P165
Hensley, Chelsea L274
Hernandez, Saritza L275
Heymont, Lane L277
Hildebrand, Cole L280
Holloway, Sally L284
Irene Goodman Literary Agency (IGLA) L291
Joelle Delbourgo Associates, Inc. L301
Kathryn Green Literary Agency, LLC L322
Kim, Jennifer L333
Kim, Julia L334
Kimber, Natalie L336
Korero Press P208
Latshaw, Katherine L355
Levitt, Sarah L361
Levy, Yael L362
Lewinsohn Literary L363

MacLeod, Lauren L383
Maltese, Alyssa L387
Marr, Jill L389
Marshall, Jen L391
McNidder & Grace P232
Mortimer, Michele L418
Mulcahy Sweeney Literary Agency L423
Mundy, Toby L426
Muscato, Nate L429
Perry Literary L466
Philips, Ariana L471
Pickering, Juliet L473
Pierce, Rosie L474
Plexus Publishing Limited P294
Polygon P298
Quirk Books P308
Ramer, Susan L486
Richter, Rick L493
Susan Schulman Literary Agency L557
Tasman, Alice L569
Ten Speed Press P380
Thames & Hudson Inc P382
Thames and Hudson Ltd P383
Thayer, Henry L572
University of Tennessee Press .. P413
Watterson, Jessica L591
Wells, Karmen L595
Wickers, Chandler L600
Williams, Laura L603
Wilson, Ed L607
Zuckerbrot, Renee L618

Popular History
See more broadly: History; Popular
Bernardi, Amanda L056
Furniss, Eugenie L224
Patterson, Emma L458
Philips, Ariana L471
Swainson, Joanna L561

Popular Music
See more broadly: Music; Popular
Thayer, Henry L572

Popular Psychology
See more broadly: Popular; Psychology
Holloway, Sally L284
Kate Barker Literary, TV, & Film Agency L320
Piatkus Books P289
Plitt, Carrie L477

Popular Science
See more broadly: Popular; Science
Alcock, Michael L009
Barr, Anjanette L038
Barrett, Emily L040
Bernardi, Amanda L056
Christie, Jennifer L116
Clarke, Caro L118
Conrad, Claire Paterson L125
Cosmos M089
Curran, Sabhbh L134
Danko, Margaret L140
DeBlock, Liza L149
Demblon, Gabrielle L150
Derviskadic, Dado L151
Dundurn P118
Dunn, Ben L164
Evans, Kate L185
Fuentes, Sarah L222
Gordon, Andrew L245
Holloway, Sally L284
Icon Books Ltd P180
Kantor, Camille L317
Keren, Eli L330
Levitt, Sarah L361
Macdougall, Laura L379
Maurer, Shari L397
Mundy, Toby L426

Peddle, Kay L460
Perez Literary & Entertainment L463
Perez, Kristina L464
Plitt, Carrie L477
Power, Anna L482
Robinson, Quressa L497
Savvides, Marilia L520
Seymour, Charlotte L528
Williams, Laura L603
Zack Company, Inc, The L615

Post Traumatic Stress Disorder
See more broadly: Psychological Trauma
W.W. Norton & Company Ltd P422

Post-Apocalyptic
See more broadly: Science Fiction
Bennett, Laura L050
Liverpool Literary Agency, The . L369
Mozley, Jack L422
Zack Company, Inc, The L615

Postcolonialism
See more broadly: Culture; Society
Feminist Press, The P130
Fernwood Publishing P131
Future Fire, The M135
Gold SF P146
Maidment, Olivia L386
Roberts, Soumeya Bendimerad L495
Takikawa, Marin L566
Yeoh, Rachel L612

Poverty
See more broadly: Social Issues
Barr, Anjanette L038

Practical Art
See more broadly: Arts
Thames and Hudson Ltd P383

Pregnancy
See more broadly: Parenting
See more specifically: Childbirth
DK Publishing P112
Foxx, Kat L213
Singing Dragon P340
Workman Publishing P437

Prehistoric Animals
See more broadly: Animals
See more specifically: Dinosaurs

Preschool
See more broadly: School

Prescriptive Nonfiction
Baumer, Jan L044
Kracht, Elizabeth L341
Krienke, Mary L343
Latshaw, Katherine L355
Maltese, Alyssa L387
Niumata, Erin L439
O'Shea, Amy L447
Philips, Ariana L471

Procurement
See more broadly: Business
BCS (British Computer Society) P042

Professional
Architectural Review, The M025
BCS (British Computer Society) P042
Blue Poppy Enterprises P055
Business & Accountancy Daily M068
CGI (Chartered Governance Institute) Publishing P078
Coaches Choice P093
Crossway P100
Elsevier Ltd P121
Evan-Moor Educational Publishers P125
Facet Publishing P127
Funeral Business Solutions M134
Future Horizons P138
Gale P139
Goss & Crested China Club P149
Hammersmith Books P158

Idyll Arbor P181
Insurance Post M169
International Piano M170
International Society for Technology in Education (ISTE) P192
Jessica Kingsley Publishers P197
Leisure Group Travel M183
LexisNexis P214
Linguist, The M186
Loft Press, Inc P220
Lund Humphries Limited P224
Medical Physics Publishing P234
Mentor Books P236
NAHB BuilderBooks P253
New Harbinger Publications P255
Oak Tree Press P259
PC Pro M235
Practical Pre-School Books P300
Round Hall P318
Scholastic P329
Ships Monthly Magazine M278
Singing Dragon P340
Spa Magazine M295
Speciality Food M296
Strategic Finance M302
Sweet & Maxwell P374
Swimming Pool News M307
Taylor & Francis Group P378
Ulster Business M323
W.W. Norton & Company Ltd ... P422
W.W. Norton & Company, Inc. . P423

Progressive Politics
See more broadly: Politics
Mendia, Isabel L403

Project Management
See more broadly: Management
BCS (British Computer Society) P042

Property / Real Estate
Atlanta Magazine M030
Cottage Life M090
Square Mile Magazine M298

Prose Poetry
Better Than Starbucks M052
Ink Sweat and Tears M168
Tears in the Fence M311

Prostitution
See more broadly: Sex

Psychiatry
See more broadly: Medicine
See more specifically: Mental Disorders
Taylor & Francis Group P378
W.W. Norton & Company Ltd ... P422

Psychic Abilities
See more broadly: Supernatural / Paranormal
See more specifically: Astral Projection; Chakras
Llewellyn Worldwide Ltd P219

Psychoanalysis
See more broadly: Psychology
W.W. Norton & Company Ltd ... P422

Psychological Horror
See more broadly: Horror
Sinister Stoat Press P341
Siobhan, Aiden L539
Soloway, Jennifer March L544
Stringer, Marlene L554
Tibbets, Anne L576
Udden, Jennifer L580

Psychological Suspense
See more broadly: Suspense
See more specifically: Psychological Suspense Thrillers
Brace, Samantha L072
Curran, Sabhbh L134
Danko, Margaret L140
Forrester, Jemima L210
Hordern, Kate L286

Kavanagh, Jade L323
Marr, Jill L389
Pan Macmillan Australia P274
Pierce, Rosie L474
Posner, Marcy L480
Scarlet P327
Soloway, Jennifer March L544
Tannenbaum, Amy L568
Terlip, Paige L570
Thorneycroft, Euan L574
Vance, Lisa Erbach L583

Psychological Suspense Thrillers
See more broadly: Psychological Suspense; Psychological Thrillers
Demblon, Gabrielle L150

Psychological Thrillers
See more broadly: Thrillers
See more specifically: Psychological Suspense Thrillers
Berdinsky, Kendall L054
Betancourt Literary L057
Bloodhound Books P052
Charnace, Edwina de L110
Choc Lit P085
Coombes, Clare L127
Danaczko, Melissa L139
Fergusson, Julie L196
Finan, Ciara L200
Galvin, Lori L226
Glenister, Emily L238
Harper, Logan L267
Joffe Books P199
Kane Literary Agency L316
Maltese, Alyssa L387
Nichols, Mariah L438
Orenda Books P267
Richter, Rick L493
Shestopal, Camilla L534
Williams, Laura L603
Williamson, Jo L604
Wood, Ed L609
Yeoh, Rachel L612

Psychological Trauma
See more broadly: Psychology
See more specifically: Post Traumatic Stress Disorder
Hay House Publishers P168
W.W. Norton & Company Ltd P422

Psychology
See more specifically: Anxiety Disorders; Depression; Eating Disorders; Hypnosis; Neurodiversity; Neuropsychology; Popular Psychology; Psychoanalysis; Psychological Trauma; Psychotherapy; Stress Management
Arcadia Publishing P020
Basic Books P035
Baxter, Veronique L045
Betsy Amster Literary Enterprises L059
Bloomsbury Academic P053
Cambridge University Press P068
Christie, Jennifer L116
Compassiviste Publishing P097
Crown P101
Curran, Sabhbh L134
Dana Newman Literary, LLC L138
Demblon, Gabrielle L150
Derviskadic, Dado L151
Fogg, Jack L206
Geiger, Ellen L227
Gill Education P143
Goodman Beck Publishing P147
Gordon, Andrew L245
Harvard University Press P165
Icon Books Ltd P180
Joelle Delbourgo Associates, Inc. L301
Karen Gantz Literary Management L319

Kensington Publishing Corp. P204
Kirby, Robert L338
Levy, Yael L362
London Review of Books M191
Macdougall, Laura L379
Maltese, Alyssa L387
Marion Boyars Publishers P229
Maw, Jane Graham L398
Molloy, Jess L414
Murgolo, Karen L427
New Harbinger Publications P255
Nolan, Laura L441
Oxford University Press P272
Pelham, Imogen L461
Perry Literary L466
Pierce, Rosie L474
Posner, Marcy L480
Power, Anna L482
Preston, Amanda L484
Regina Ryan Books L489
Reilly, Milly L491
Rosenberg Group, The L505
Savvides, Marilia L520
Sheree Bykofsky Associates, Inc. L532
Simons, Tanera L536
Susan Schulman Literary Agency L557
Taylor & Francis Group P378
Turner Publishing P394
Tyndale House Publishers, Inc. P397
University of Akron Press, The P403
University of Alberta Press P404
University of California Press P406
University of Michigan Press, The P410
Victoria Sanders & Associates LLC L584
W.W. Norton & Company Ltd P422
W.W. Norton & Company, Inc. P423
Willms, Kathryn L605

Psychotherapy
See more broadly: Psychology
See more specifically: Juvenile Psychotherapy
Bloomsbury Academic P053
Free Association Books Ltd P135
W.W. Norton & Company Ltd P422

Public Health
See more broadly: Health
Purdue University Press P305

Publishing
See more broadly: Business
See more specifically: Book Publishing; Small Press
Ooligan Press P265
Oxford University Press P272
University of Virginia Press P415

Pubs
See more broadly: Leisure
Square Mile Magazine M298

Punk
See more broadly: Music

Puzzles
Andrews McMeel Publishing P015
Barrett, Emily L040
Cobblestone M079
Gemini Books P140
Igloo Books Limited P184
Imagine Publishing P186
Take a Break's Take a Puzzle M310

Qigong
See more broadly: Martial Arts
Singing Dragon P340

Quakerism
See more broadly: Christianity

Queer Romance
See more broadly: Romance
Matte, Rebecca L395

Quilting
See more broadly: Crafts; Hobbies

Racecars
See more broadly: Cars
Racecar Engineering M255

Racism
See more broadly: Discrimination
Fernwood Publishing P131
Mendia, Isabel L403
University of Alberta Press P404

Radio Control
See more broadly: Technology

Radio Scripts
Bolger, Maeve L066
Elaine Steel L179
JFL Agency L300
Judy Daish Associates Ltd L310
Narrow Road Company, The L432
Rochelle Stevens & Co. L498
Valerie Hoskins Associates L582

Radio Technology
See more broadly: Audio Technology
See more specifically: Amateur Radio
Radio Society of Great Britain P309

Radnorshire
See more broadly: Wales
Logaston Press P221

Railways
See more broadly: Transport
Countryside Books P099
Indiana University Press P187
Rail Express M257

Ranch Lifestyle
See more broadly: Lifestyle
Cowboys & Indians M091

Ranches
See more broadly: Houses and Homes
Cowboys & Indians M091

Reading
See more broadly: Education
See more specifically: High-Low Literacy

Real Life Stories
Bella M046
Colwill, Charlotte L121
My Weekly M215
Simpson, Cara Lee L537

Realistic
Mortimer, Michele L418
Soloway, Jennifer March L544

Recipes
See more broadly: Cookery
Berks County Living M049
Better Homes and Gardens M051
Kent Life M178
Ruralite M266

Recreation
See more broadly: Leisure
See more specifically: Recreational Vehicles
Arcadia Publishing P020
Enslow Publishers, Inc. P123
Kensington Publishing Corp. P204
Tyndale House Publishers, Inc. P397

Recreational Vehicles
See more broadly: Recreation; Vehicles

Reference
ABC-CLIO P002
Arcadia Publishing P020
Bentley Publishers P044
Brown, Megan L084
Cedar Fort P076
DK Publishing P112
Gale P139
Gill Books P142
Goss & Crested China Club P149
Guinness World Records P154
Harvard University Press P165
Igloo Books Limited P184
Jain Publishing Company, Inc. P195

Claim your free access to www.firstwriter.com: See p.367

352 Index | Refugees

Joelle Delbourgo Associates, Inc. L301
Kensington Publishing Corp. P204
LexisNexis P214
Lilliput Press, The P217
Pineapple Press P293
Rand McNally P310
Regina Ryan Books L489
Stanley Gibbons P368
Thames & Hudson Inc. P382
Tyndale House Publishers, Inc. P397
University of Michigan Press, The P410
W.W. Norton & Company, Inc. P423
Yale University Press (London) P438

Refugees

See more broadly: Social Issues

Afsana Press P005
Indiana University Press P187
University of Alberta Press P404

Regency Romance

See more broadly: Romance

Regional

See more specifically: Africa; Antarctica; Arctic; Asia; Atlantic; Australasia / Oceania; Caribbean; Central America; Europe; Local; Middle East; North America; Pacific; Regional History; South America

Dahlia Books P104
Hancock House Publishers P159
Indiana University Press P187
MacDonald, Emily L378
Sigma Press P337

Regional Cooking

See more broadly: Cookery

Regional History

See more broadly: History; Regional

Reiki

See more broadly: Alternative Health

Llewellyn Worldwide Ltd. P219

Reincarnation

See more broadly: Supernatural / Paranormal

Llewellyn Worldwide Ltd. P219

Relationships

See more specifically: Couple Therapy; Family; Love; Sex; Sexuality

Arcadia Publishing P020
Bradford Literary Agency L073
Carr, Jamie L101
Cedar Fort P076
Chiotti, Danielle L113
Cho, Catherine L114
Cleis Press P091
Demblon, Gabrielle L150
DK Publishing P112
Ellis-Martin, Sian L180
Fernando, Kimberly L198
Finan, Ciara L200
Goldblatt, Rachel L243
Hay House Publishers P168
Kensington Publishing Corp. P204
Levy, Yael L362
Lewinsohn Literary L363
marie claire M200
McBride, Juliana L399
Moody Publishers P247
O'Grady, Niamh L445
Pacific Press Publishing Association P273
Pickering, Juliet L473
Quirk Books P308
Red Magazine M259
Simpson, Cara Lee L537
Singh, Amandeep L538
Society for Promoting Christian Knowledge (SPCK) P345
Soloway, Jennifer March L544
Turner Publishing P394
Tyndale House Publishers, Inc. P397
Vance, Lisa Erbach L583
Wilson, Desiree L606
Yours M350
Zack Company, Inc, The L615

Religion

See more broadly: Spirituality

See more specifically: Angels; Baha'i; Buddhism; Christianity; Hinduism; Inspirational; Islam; Judaism; Paganism; Shamanism; Voodoo

Arcadia Publishing P020
Barr, Anjanette L038
Baumer, Jan L044
Baylor University Press P041
Bloomsbury Academic P053
Cambridge University Press P068
Cedar Fort P076
Colourpoint Educational P095
Commonweal M082
Davies, Olivia L147
Derviskadic, Dado L151
DK Publishing P112
Doug Grad Literary Agency L161
Edelstein, Anne L171
Geiger, Ellen L227
Gill Education P143
Harvard University Press P165
Icon Books Ltd P180
Image M166
Indiana University Press P187
InterVarsity Press (IVP) P193
Irish Pages M173
J. Gordon Shillingford Publishing P194
Jessica Kingsley Publishers P197
Judson Press P201
Karen Gantz Literary Management L319
Kensington Publishing Corp. P204
Mentor Books P236
Ohio University Press P261
Oxford University Press P272
Peter Lang P285
Richter, Rick L493
Stanford University Press P367
Taylor & Francis Group P378
Thames & Hudson Inc. P382
Thames and Hudson Ltd P383
Turner Publishing P394
University of Alberta Press P404
University of California Press P406
University of Michigan Press, The P410
University of Tennessee Press P413
University of Virginia Press P415
W.W. Norton & Company Ltd P422
W.W. Norton & Company, Inc. P423
Yale University Press (London) P438
Zack Company, Inc, The L615

Renaissance

See more broadly: History

University of Michigan Press, The P410

Renku

Modern Haiku M211

Restaurants

See more broadly: Food and Drink

Berks County Living M049
Somerset Life M286

Retellings

Yeoh, Rachel L612

Retirement

See more broadly: Lifestyle

Retropunk

See more broadly: Science Fiction

Reviews

32 Poems M002
Acumen M007
African American Review M009
Arc M024
Aurealis M034
BFS Journal M054
Big Fiction M055
Black Moon Magazine M056
Bluegrass Unlimited M061
Boston Review M062
BSFA Review, The M067
Canadian Dimension M072
Caribbean Writer, The M073
Concho River Review M083
Contemporary Verse 2 ....M086
Dalhousie Review, The M100
Ekphrastic Review, The M109
Event M113
Facts & Fiction M116
Foundation: The International Review of Science Fiction M129
Fugue M133
Funeral Business Solutions M134
Georgia Review, The M139
Gulf Coast: A Journal of Literature and Fine Arts M147
Ink Sweat and Tears M168
Journal, The M176
Kavya Kishor M177
Lake, The M181
Landfall M182
Literary Mama M187
London Grip M188
London Grip New Poetry M189
London Magazine, The M190
London Review of Books M191
Long Poem Magazine M192
Magma M196
Malahat Review, The M197
Manchester Review, The M198
Mid-American Review M206
Missouri Review, The M209
Modern Haiku M211
Oxford Poetry M229
Oxford Review of Books M230
Pleiades M238
PN Review M240
Poetry M241
Poetry Birmingham Literary Journal M242
Poetry Wales M245
Political Quarterly, The M246
Power Cut Lite M247
Reactor M258
Red Magazine M259
Sierra M281
Sinister Wisdom M282
SmokeLong Quarterly M283
Somerset Life M286
South Carolina Review M289
Spitball M297
Strange Horizons M301
Supplement, The M306
Takahe M309
Tears in the Fence M311
Temz Review, The M312
Times Literary Supplement (TLS), The ...M318
Tusculum Review, The M321
Uncut M324
Vagabond City M327
Vallum M328
Vestal Review M329
Wallace Stevens Journal, The M336
West Branch M339
Wet Grain M341

Revisionist History

See more broadly: History

Rivers

See more broadly: Geography

Road Atlases

See more broadly: Travel

Index | *Romantic Comedy* 353

Rand McNally P310

Road Trips

See more broadly: Travel

Robots

See more broadly: Technology

Rock Collecting / Rockhounding

See more broadly: Hobbies

Rock Music

See more broadly: Music

Rocks

See more broadly: Geology

Romance

See more specifically: Christian Romance; Contemporary Romance; Dark Romance; Diverse Romance; Erotic Romance; Feminist Romance; High Concept Romance; Historical Romance; Horrormance; Queer Romance; Regency Romance; Romantasy; Romantic Comedy; Romantic Mystery; Romantic Suspense; Romantic Thrillers; Science Fiction Romance; Speculative Romance; Supernatural / Paranormal Romance; Timeslip Romance; Upmarket Romance

3 Seas Literary Agency L001
Afterglow Books P006
Aldridge, Kaylyn L010
Ange, Anna L019
Armada, Kurestin L024
Barone Literary Agency L036
Beaumont, Diana L046
Begum, Salma L047
Belton, Maddy L049
Bent, Jenny L053
Betancourt Literary L057
Bewley, Elizabeth L061
Bhasin, Tamanna L062
Bradford Literary Agency L073
Bradford, Laura L074
Brannan, Maria L076
Carroll, Megan L102
Chang, Nicola L109
Choc Lit P085
Christensen, Erica L115
Cichello, Kayla L117
Colwill, Charlotte L121
Crowley, Sheila L132
Crystal Magazine M098
Curtis Brown L135
Cusick, John L136
Danko, Margaret L140
Darley Anderson Agency, The L143
Doug Grad Literary Agency L161
Draper, Claire L162
Dreamspinner Press P115
Ellis-Martin, Sian L180
Evans, Kate L185
Every Day Fiction M114
Faulks, Holly L187
Fazzari, Hillary L188
Figueroa, Melanie L199
Finan, Ciara L200
Finch, Rebeka L202
Foster, Clara L211
Foxx, Kat L213
Frankel, Valerie L215
Friedman, Claire L217
Gilbert, Tara L233
Gisondi, Katie L235
Glenister, Emily L238
Goff, Ellen L242
Grunewald, Hattie L254
Haggerty, Taylor L258
Haley, Jolene L260
Hannah Sheppard Literary Agency L262
Heathfield, Laura L273
Hensley, Chelsea L274
Hernandez, Saritza L275
Hernando, Paloma L276
Hogrebe, Christina L283
Hornsley, Sarah L287
Irene Goodman Literary Agency (IGLA) L291
Irvine, Lucy L292
Jamieson, Molly L296
Joffe Books P199
Keane Kataria Literary Agency L325
Kensington Publishing Corp. P204
Knigge, Sheyla L339
Langlee, Lina L352
Leon, Nina L360
Lewinsohn Literary L363
Macdougall, Laura L379
Maltese, Alyssa L387
Marini, Victoria L388
Marr, Jill L389
Marshall, Jen L391
Matte, Rebecca L395
Micromance Magazine M205
Mills & Boon P240
Molloy, Jess L414
Mortimer, Michele L418
Murray, Judith L428
Mushens, Juliet L430
Nathan, Abigail L433
Neely, Rachel L434
Nichols, Mariah L438
Niumata, Erin L439
Niv, Daniel L440
Orenda Books P267
Ostby, Kristin L452
Parker, Elana Roth L455
People's Friend Pocket Novels M236
Perez Literary & Entertainment L463
Perez, Kristina L464
Pestritto, Carrie L467
Piatkus Books P289
Plitt, Carrie L477
Posner, Marcy L480
Potter, Madison L481
Preston, Amanda L484
Quirk Books P308
Rosenberg Group, The L505
Ross, Whitney L507
Rossitto, Stefanie L508
Ruby Fiction P319
Rushall, Kathleen L512
Salazar, Des L515
Savvides, Marilia L520
Serra, Maria Cardona L526
Seventh Agency L527
Simons, Tanera L536
Singh, Amandeep L538
Siobhan, Aiden L539
Soler, Shania N. L543
Soloway, Jennifer March L544
Sourcebooks Casablanca P351
Steed, Hayley L548
Story Unlikely M300
Stringer, Marlene L554
Thwaites, Steph L575
Torrey House Press, LLC P390
Tran, Jennifer Chen L578
Transworld Publishers P393
Trudel, Jes L579
Turner Publishing P394
Tyndale House Publishers, Inc. P397
Udden, Jennifer L580
Watterson, Jessica L591
Williams, Laura L603
Williamson, Jo L604
Wilson, Desiree L606
Wood, Caroline L608
Woods, Bryony L610
Yours Fiction – Women's Special Series M351
Zack Company, Inc, The L615

Romania

See more broadly: Europe

Peter Lang P285

Romantasy

See more broadly: Fantasy; Romance

Adsett, Alex L005
Afonso, Thais L007
Armada, Kurestin L024
Bradford Literary Agency L073
Carina Press P073
Carroll, Megan L102
Charnace, Edwina de L110
Choc Lit P085
Darley Anderson Agency, The L143
DeBlock, Liza L149
Diversion Books P111
Faulks, Holly L187
Fazzari, Hillary L188
Finan, Ciara L200
Finch, Rebeka L202
Gillam, Bianca L234
Gisondi, Katie L235
Goff, Ellen L242
Hannah Sheppard Literary Agency L262
Irvine, Lucy L292
Lane, Helen L349
Leon, Nina L360
Lindsay Literary Agency L366
Lineberry, Isabel L367
Marini, Victoria L388
Marr, Jill L389
Matte, Rebecca L395
Milusich, Grace L412
Mushens, Juliet L430
Nathan, Abigail L433
Niv, Daniel L440
Potter, Madison L481
Schofield, Hannah L522
Seager, Chloe L524
Simons, Tanera L536
Soler, Shania N. L543
Steed, Hayley L548
Turner Publishing P394
Udden, Jennifer L580
Zack Company, Inc, The L615

Romantic Comedy

See more broadly: Comedy / Humour; Romance

Adsett, Alex L005
Afonso, Thais L007
Aldridge, Kaylyn L010
Bauman, Erica L043
Beaumont, Diana L046
Bent, Jenny L053
Bloodhound Books P052
Bradford Literary Agency L073
Brannan, Maria L076
Brooks, Savannah L080
Cavanagh, Claire L107
Choc Lit P085
Cichello, Kayla L117
Cooper, Gemma L128
Cusick, John L136
Darley Anderson Agency, The L143
Ellis-Martin, Sian L180
Fabien, Samantha L186
Fazzari, Hillary L188
Fellows, Abi L193
Fergusson, Julie L196
Fernandez, Rochelle L197
Finan, Ciara L200
Finch, Rebeka L202

354 Index | *Romantic Mystery*

Foxx, Kat L213
Gilbert, Tara L233
Gillam, Bianca L234
Gisondi, Katie L235
Glenister, Emily L238
Goetz, Adria L241
Graham, Stacey L247
Grunewald, Hattie L254
Haley, Jolene L260
Harper, Logan L267
Langton, Becca L353
Lewinsohn Literary L363
MacDonald, Emily L378
Marini, Victoria L388
Marr, Jill L389
Napolitano, Maria L431
Nathan, Abigail L433
Nelson, Patricia L437
Nichols, Mariah L438
Niumata, Erin L439
O'Brien, Lee L444
Parker, Elana Roth L455
Philips, Ariana L471
Pierce, Rosie L474
Robinson, Quressa L497
Romano, Annie L502
Savvides, Marilia L520
Schofield, Hannah L522
Seager, Chloe L524
Simons, Tanera L536
Steed, Hayley L548
Vance, Lisa Erbach L583
Weiman, Paula L592
Weiss, Alexandra L593
Whatnall, Michaela L598
Williams, Laura L603
Williamson, Jo L604
Wilson, Desiree L606

Romantic Mystery
See more broadly: Mystery; Romance
Adsett, Alex L005
Milburn, Madeleine L411
Nathan, Abigail L433

Romantic Suspense
See more broadly: Romance; Suspense
Bradford Literary Agency L073
Bradford, Laura L074
Carina Press P073
Choc Lit P085
Eason, Lynette L169
Haley, Jolene L260
Leon, Nina L360
Mills & Boon P240
Shestopal, Camilla L534
Sourcebooks Casablanca P351
Tyndale House Publishers, Inc. P397
Zack Company, Inc, The L615

Romantic Thrillers
See more broadly: Romance; Thrillers
Leon, Nina L360
Mills & Boon P240

Roots Music
See more broadly: Music
LSU Press P223

Royalty
Britain Magazine M066
Glenister, Emily L238

Rugby
See more broadly: Sport
See more specifically: Rugby League
Rugby World M265

Rugby League
See more broadly: Rugby
Forty20 .... M128
Scratching Shed Publishing P331

Running
See more broadly: Fitness
Adventure Books by Vertebrate Publishing P004
Pocket Mountains P296

Rural Living
See more broadly: Countryside; Lifestyle

Russia
See more broadly: Europe
Indiana University Press P187

Saga
See more broadly: Historical Fiction
Bloodhound Books P052
Chang, Nicola L109
Crowley, Sheila L132
Joffe Books P199
Keane Kataria Literary Agency L325
Macdougall, Laura L379
Pan Macmillan Australia P274
Yours Fiction – Women's Special Series M351

Sailing
See more broadly: Leisure; Travel
Cruising World M097
Sailing Today M268
Seaworthy Publications P333

Satire
See more broadly: Comedy / Humour
Ange, Anna L019
Baffler, The M039
Joy Harris Literary Agency, Inc. L308
Victoria Sanders & Associates LLC L584
Viz M333

Savannah, GA
See more broadly: Georgia (US State)
Savannah Magazine M269

Scandinavia
See more broadly: Europe

School
See more specifically: College / University; High School; Preschool

Science
See more specifically: Astronomy; Biology; Chemistry; Cognitive Science; Earth Science; Genetics; Information Science; Neuroscience; Physics; Popular Science; Science Journalism; Space
Annette Green Authors' Agency L021
Arcadia Publishing P020
Autumn Publishing Ltd P025
Bajek, Lauren L031
Bal, Emma L032
Basalt Books P034
Basic Books P035
Baylor University Press P041
Bloomsbury Academic P053
Brannan, Maria L076
Brick M065
Brouckaert, Justin L083
Buckley, Louise L085
Cambridge University Press P068
Cedar Fort P076
Charlesbridge Publishing P081
Chelsea House Publishers P082
Christie, Jennifer L116
Compass Talent L124
Compassiviste Publishing P097
Conversation (UK), The M087
Cricket M096
Crown P101
Curious Minds L133
Danaczko, Melissa L139
Diana Finch Literary Agency L154
Dickerson, Donya L155
Diversion Books P111
DK Publishing P112
Dystel, Jane L167
Edelstein, Anne L171
Edenborough, Sam L172
Elsevier Ltd P121
Enslow Publishers, Inc. P123
Evans, Kate L185
Fate M117
Feminist Press, The P130
Foster, Clara L211
Fox, Aram L212
Gale P139
Gill Education P143
Goldstein, Veronica L244
Harvard University Press P165
Hernandez, Saritza L275
Heymont, Lane L277
Ireland's Own M172
Irish Pages M173
Javelin L298
Joelle Delbourgo Associates, Inc. L301
Kane Press P202
Kate Barker Literary, TV, & Film Agency L320
Kensington Publishing Corp. P204
Kimber, Natalie L336
Kirby, Robert L338
Kracht, Elizabeth L341
Levy, Yael L362
Lewis, Alison L364
London Review of Books M191
Macdougall, Laura L379
Maltese, Alyssa L387
Marr, Jill L389
Marshall, Jen L391
Massachusetts Review, The M202
Mendia, Isabel L403
Mentor Books P236
Michel, Caroline L408
MIT Press, The P244
Modern Applied Science M210
Murgolo, Karen L427
Oxford University Press P272
Pelagic P279
Pelham, Imogen L461
Perry Literary L466
Peter Lang P285
Philips, Ariana L471
Pluto Press P295
Preston, Amanda L484
Purdue University Press P305
Regina Ryan Books L489
Reid, Janet L490
Richter, Rick L493
Rudy Agency, The L510
Singh, Amandeep L538
Stipes Publishing P371
Strothman, Wendy L555
Sunbelt Publications, Inc. P373
Susan Schulman Literary Agency L557
Swainson, Joanna L561
Symonds, Laurel L565
Taylor & Francis Group P378
Texas A&M University Press P381
Thames & Hudson Inc. P382
Thames and Hudson Ltd P383
Thayer, Henry L572
Thorneycroft, Euan L574
Topping, Antony L577
Transworld Publishers P393
Turner Publishing P394
Unfit Magazine M326
University of Alberta Press P404
University of California Press P406
University of Maine Press P409
University of Virginia Press P415
University Press of Colorado P416

Index | Self Help 355

W.W. Norton & Company, Inc. P423
Weiss, Alexandra L593
Willms, Kathryn L605
Wilson, Desiree... L606
Yale University Press (London) P438
Zack Company, Inc, The L615
Zuckerbrot, Renee L618

Science Fantasy

See more broadly: Fantasy; Science Fiction

Science Fiction

See more specifically: Alien Fiction; Cyberpunk; Grounded Science Fiction; Hard Science Fiction; Post-Apocalyptic; Retropunk; Science Fantasy; Science Fiction Romance; Slipstream; Soft Science Fiction; Space Opera; Steampunk; Time Travel

3 Seas Literary Agency L001
Adsett, Alex L005
Afonso, Thais.. L007
Alekseii, Keir L011
Armada, Kurestin L024
Armstrong, Susan L026
Arthurson, Wayne L027
Asimov's Science Fiction M029
Aurealis M034
Baen Books P029
Bajek, Lauren L031
Baror International, Inc. L037
Belton, Maddy L049
Bennett, Laura L050
Berlyne, John L055
Bradford Literary Agency L073
BSFA Review, The M067
Candlemark & Gleam P069
Carina Press P073
Chevais, Jennifer L111
Cochran, Alexander L120
Compassiviste Publishing P097
Crystal Magazine M098
Curtis Brown L135
Cusick, John L136
Diversion Books P111
Doug Grad Literary Agency L161
Dreamspinner Press P115
DSP Publications P116
Every Day Fiction M114
Fernandez, Rochelle L197
Figueroa, Melanie L199
Foundation: The International Review of Science Fiction M129
Gahan, Isobel L225
Global Lion Intellectual Property Management, Inc. L239
Gold SF P146
Gunic, Masha L256
Harris, Erin L268
Hawn, Molly Ker L270
Hensley, Chelsea L274
Hernandez, Saritza L275
Hernando, Paloma L276
Inscriptions Literary Agency L289
Interzone M171
Irvine, Lucy L292
Jamieson, Molly L296
Joelle Delbourgo Associates, Inc. L301
Johnson, Jared L303
Julie Crisp Literary Agency L311
Killingley, Jessica L332
Kim, Jennifer L333
Kimber, Natalie L336
Langlee, Lina L352
Leon, Nina L360
Lightner, Kayla L365
Liverpool Literary Agency, The L369
Marini, Victoria L388
Matte, Rebecca L395
Mihell, Natasha L410
Moonday Mag M213
Morrell, Imogen L417
Mozley, Jack L422
Murray, Judith L428
Muscato, Nate L429
Mushens, Juliet L430
Nathan, Abigail L433
NBM Publishing P254
Nelson, Kristin L436
Neo-opsis Science Fiction Magazine M218
Nichols, Mariah L438
Perotto-Wills, Martha L465
Plant, Zoe L476
Posner, Marcy L480
Reactor M258
Robinson, Quressa L497
Ross, Whitney L507
Salazar, Des L515
Schwizer, Fabienne L523
Scifaikuest M270
Seager, Chloe L524
Selectric Artists L525
Seventh Agency L527
Shoreline of Infinity M280
Sinister Stoat Press P341
Sluytman, Antoinette Van L541
SmashBear Publishing P342
Snowbooks P344
Sorg, Arley L546
Sternig & Byrne Literary Agency L550
Story Unlikely M300
Strange Horizons M301
Terlip, Paige L570
Thinkwell Books, UK P384
Tibbets, Anne L576
Tor Publishing Group P388
Tor Teen P389
Torrey House Press, LLC P390
Transworld Publishers P393
Turner Publishing P394
Udden, Jennifer L580
Unfit Magazine M326
Wells, Karmen L595
Whatnall, Michaela L598
Wilson, Desiree L606
Wilson, Ed L607
Woods, Bryony L610
Zack Company, Inc, The L615
Zeno Agency L617

Science Fiction Romance

See more broadly: Romance; Science Fiction

Fazzari, Hillary L188

Science Journalism

See more broadly: Journalism; Science

Scotland

See more broadly: United Kingdom

See more specifically: Glasgow; Inverclyde; Shetland

Black & White Publishing Ltd P049
Gutter Magazine M148
MacDonald, Emily L378
Macdougall, Laura L379
Scots Magazine, The M271
Scottish Field M272
Sparsile Books P359
Tippermuir Books P386
Wee Book Company, The P427

Scripts

African Voices M010
Agency (London) Ltd, The L008
Alaska Quarterly Review M014
Andrews, Gina L018
Anvil Press Publishers P017
Aurora Metro Press P024
AVAnti Productions & Management L029
Barnard, Arthur L035
Bell, Eva L048
Bolger, Maeve L066
Caribbean Writer, The M073
Coach House Books P092
Comparato, Andrea L123
Curtis Brown L135
Elaine Steel L179
Fontaine, Melissa L208
Gurman Agency, LLC L257
Hickman, Emily L278
Inscriptions Literary Agency L289
J. Gordon Shillingford Publishing P194
JFL Agency L300
Judy Daish Associates Ltd L310
Kelleher, Sophie L327
Kenyon Review, The M179
Ki Agency Ltd L331
Lost Lake Folk Opera Magazine M193
Lyon, Rebecca L376
Meridian Artists L404
Middleton, Leah L409
Mumby, Helen L425
Narrow Road Company, The L432
New England Review M220
Obsidian: Literature in the African Diaspora M227
Paradigm Talent and Literary Agency L454
Pushing Out the Boat M252
Qu Literary Magazine M253
Renard Press Ltd P313
River Styx M264
Rochelle Stevens & Co. L498
Sunspot Literary Journal M305
Third Coast M315
Tusculum Review, The M321
Valerie Hoskins Associates L582
Williams, Katie L602

Scuba Diving

See more broadly: Diving

Diver M105

Search and Rescue

See more broadly: Emergency Services

Secret Intelligence

See more broadly: Warfare

See more specifically: CIA

Zack Company, Inc, The L615

Self Help

See more broadly: Personal Development

See more specifically: Motivational Self-Help

Arcadia Publishing P020
Baumer, Jan L044
Bent, Jenny L053
Betsy Amster Literary Enterprises L059
Bradford Literary Agency L073
Campos, Vanessa L095
Cedar Fort P076
Charnace, Edwina de L110
Cleis Press P091
Compassiviste Publishing P097
Crown Publishing Group, The P103
Danko, Margaret L140
Dickerson, Donya L155
Doug Grad Literary Agency L161
Dundurn P118
Fellows, Abi L193
Fernando, Kimberly L198
Global Lion Intellectual Property Management, Inc. L239
Goderich, Miriam L240
Goodman Beck Publishing P147
Hashtag Press P166
Hay House Publishers P168
Icon Books Ltd P180
Kensington Publishing Corp. P204
Levy, Yael L362

Claim your free access to www.firstwriter.com: See p.367

356 Index | Self-Sufficiency

Marsiglia, Caroline ... L392
New Harbinger Publications ... P255
Nichols, Mariah ... L438
Pen & Ink Designs Publishing ... P280
Perry Literary ... L466
Piatkus Books ... P289
Richter, Rick ... L493
Shestopal, Camilla ... L534
Sunbelt Publications, Inc. ... P373
Terlip, Paige ... L570
Tyndale House Publishers, Inc. ... P397
W.W. Norton & Company Ltd ... P422

Self-Sufficiency
See more broadly: Agriculture; Lifestyle
Merlin Unwin Books ... P237

Senryu
Modern Haiku ... M211
Scifaikuest ... M270

Service Management
See more broadly: Management
BCS (British Computer Society) ... P042

Sewing
See more broadly: Crafts; Hobbies

Sex
See more broadly: Relationships
See more specifically: Prostitution
Cleis Press ... P091
Ellis-Martin, Sian ... L180
Korero Press ... P208
Maltese, Alyssa ... L387
marie claire ... M200
Red Magazine ... M259
Sinister Stoat Press ... P341
Tyndale House Publishers, Inc. ... P397
Zack Company, Inc, The ... L615

Sexuality
See more broadly: Relationships
See more specifically: LGBTQIA
Bloomsbury Academic ... P053
Cleis Press ... P091
Ellis-Martin, Sian ... L180
Feminist Press, The ... P130
Fernwood Publishing ... P131
Gold SF ... P146
Indiana University Press ... P187
Kracht, Elizabeth ... L341
Krienke, Mary ... L343
Macdougall, Laura ... L379
Pluto Press ... P295
Sanders, Rayhane ... L517
Soloway, Jennifer March ... L544
University of Alberta Press ... P404
University of California Press ... P406
University of Michigan Press, The ... P410
University of Texas Press ... P414
W.W. Norton & Company Ltd ... P422

Shamanism
See more broadly: Religion
Llewellyn Worldwide Ltd ... P219

Shetland
See more broadly: Scotland

Shipping
See more broadly: Boats
Ships Monthly Magazine ... M278

Ships
See more broadly: Vehicles
Ships Monthly Magazine ... M278

Shooting
See more broadly: Sport
Merlin Unwin Books ... P237

Short Fiction
30 North ... M001
aaduna ... M003
About Place Journal ... M004
Account, The ... M006
African American Review ... M009
African Voices ... M010
Agni ... M011
Alaska Quarterly Review ... M014
Alfred Hitchcock Mystery Magazine ... M016
American Short Fiction ... M018
Amethyst Review ... M019
Arboreal ... M023
Arts & Letters ... M027
Asimov's Science Fiction ... M029
Atlantic Northeast ... M032
Aurealis ... M034
Aurora Metro Press ... P024
Auroras & Blossoms PoArtMo Anthology ... M035
Babybug ... M037
Bacopa Literary Review ... M038
Baffler, The ... M039
Bandit Fiction ... M040
Barren Magazine ... M041
BatCat Press ... P040
Bear Deluxe Magazine, The ... M044
Bee, The ... M045
Belmont Story Review ... M047
Beloit Fiction Journal ... M048
Better Than Starbucks ... M052
BFS Horizons ... M053
Black Moon Magazine ... M056
Black Static ... M057
Black Warrior Review ... M058
Blue Earth Review ... M059
Blue Mesa Review ... M060
Boston Review ... M062
Boyfriend Village ... M064
Cafe Irreal, The ... M071
Caribbean Writer, The ... M073
Chapman ... M075
Chautauqua Literary Journal ... M077
Cheshire ... M078
Cobblestone ... M079
Cola ... M081
Comma Press ... P096
Concho River Review ... M083
Conjunctions ... M084
Conjunctions Online ... M085
Crannog Magazine ... M092
Crazyhorse / Swamp Pink ... M093
Cream City Review ... M094
Crystal Magazine ... M098
CutBank ... M099
Dalhousie Review, The ... M100
Dawntreader, The ... M102
Deep Overstock Magazine ... M103
Dream Catcher ... M106
Dublin Review, The ... M107
Ekphrastic Review, The ... M109
El Portal ... M110
Emerge Literary Journal ... M111
Event ... M113
Every Day Fiction ... M114
Fabula Argentea ... M115
Fairlight Books ... P128
Faultline ... M118
Feminist Studies ... M119
Fiction ... M120
Fiddlehead, The ... M121
First Line, The ... M123
Five Points ... M124
Flash: The International Short-Short Story Magazine ... M125
Folio ... M126
Fourth River, The ... M131
Frogmore Papers, The ... M132
Fugue ... M133
Future Fire, The ... M135
Gargoyle Online ... M137
Georgia Review, The ... M139
Ginosko Literary Journal ... M140
Glacier, The ... M141
Grain Literary Magazine ... M143
Granta ... M144
Graywolf Lab ... M145
Gulf Coast: A Journal of Literature and Fine Arts ... M147
Gutter Magazine ... M148
Half Mystic Journal ... M149
Hanging Loose ... M150
Harpur Palate ... M151
Heavy Traffic ... M153
Helix, The ... M154
Hotel Amerika ... M160
Hunger Mountain ... M161
I-70 Review ... M162
Idaho Review ... M163
Identity Theory ... M164
Image ... M166
Indiana Review ... M167
Interzone ... M171
Ireland's Own ... M172
Irish Pages ... M173
Island ... M174
Island Online ... M175
Joy Harris Literary Agency, Inc. ... L308
Kavya Kishor ... M177
Kenyon Review, The ... M179
Landfall ... M182
Lighthouse ... M185
Literary Mama ... M187
London Magazine, The ... M190
Lost Lake Folk Opera Magazine ... M193
Louisiana Literature ... M194
MacGuffin, The ... M195
Malahat Review, The ... M197
Manchester Review, The ... M198
Manoa ... M199
Massachusetts Review, The ... M202
Meetinghouse ... M203
Michigan Quarterly Review ... M204
Micromance Magazine ... M205
Mid-American Review ... M206
Midsummer Dream House ... M207
Midway Journal ... M208
Missouri Review, The ... M209
Moonday Mag ... M213
MQR Mixtape ... M214
My Weekly ... M215
Mystery Magazine ... M216
Nashville Review ... M217
Neo-opsis Science Fiction Magazine ... M218
Neon ... M219
New England Review ... M220
New Welsh Reader ... M223
Northern Gravy ... M226
Obsidian: Literature in the African Diaspora ... M227
Oxford Review of Books ... M230
Pacifica Literary Review ... M231
Panorama ... M232
Paris Review, The ... M233
Parthian Books ... P275
Passionfruit Review, The ... M234
People's Friend, The ... M237
Phoenix Moirai ... P288
Pleiades ... M238
Ploughshares ... M239
Power Cut Lite ... M247
Prole ... M250
Pushing Out the Boat ... M252
Qu Literary Magazine ... M253
Quadrant Magazine ... M254
Ransom Publishing Ltd ... P312
River Styx ... M264
Saddlebag Dispatches ... M267

Access more listings online at www.firstwriter.com

Index | Social History 357

Scribble ... M273
Second Factory ... M274
Seren Books ... P335
Shenandoah ... M277
Shooter Literary Magazine ... M279
Shoreline of Infinity ... M280
Sinister Wisdom ... M282
SmokeLong Quarterly ... M283
Snowflake Magazine ... M284
Sonder Magazine ... M287
South Carolina Review ... M289
Southern Humanities Review ... M290
Southern Review, The ... M291
Southwest Review ... M293
Southword Journal ... M294
Spitball ... M297
Stinging Fly, The ... M299
Story Unlikely ... M300
Strange Horizons ... M301
Structo Magazine ... M303
Studio One ... M304
Sunspot Literary Journal ... M305
Supplement, The ... M306
Tahoma Literary Review ... M308
Takahe ... M309
Tears in the Fence ... M311
Temz Review, The ... M312
Thin Air Magazine ... M314
Third Coast ... M315
Threepenny Review, The ... M317
Tolka ... M319
Tributaries ... M320
Tusculum Review, The ... M321
Under the Radar ... M325
Unfit Magazine ... M326
University of Iowa Press ... P408
University of North Texas Press ... P412
Vagabond City ... M327
Vestal Review ... M329
Virginia Quarterly Review, The ... M330
Waccamaw ... M335
Wasafiri ... M338
West Branch ... M339
Wilson, Desiree ... L606
Windsor Review ... M342
Yale Review, The ... M344
Yours Fiction – Women's Special Series ... M351
Zoetrope: All-Story ... M352
Zone 3 ... M353

Short Fiction Collections
404 Ink ... P001
Arachne Press ... P019
BOA Editions, Ltd ... P057
Brooks, Savannah ... L080
CB Editions ... P075
Chang, Nicola ... L109
Compassiviste Publishing ... P097
Dahlia Books ... P104
Daunt Books Publishing ... P106
Enitharmon Editions ... P122
Glenister, Emily ... L238
Goose Lane Editions ... P148
Graywolf Press ... P152
Guernica Editions ... P153
Half Mystic Press ... P157
Host Publications ... P177
Jamii Publishing ... P196
Kates Hill Press, The ... P203
Motala, Tasneem ... L419
Orenda Books ... P267
Peepal Tree Press ... P278
Pen & Ink Designs Publishing ... P280
Perspectives Books ... P283
Phoenix Moirai ... P288
Plitt, Carrie ... L477
Press 53 ... P301
Procrastinating Writers United ... P303
Shipwreckt Books Publishing Company ... P336
Sinister Stoat Press ... P341
Spout Press ... P360
Sweetgum Press ... P375
Toad Hall Editions ... P387
Torrey House Press, LLC ... P390
University of Alberta Press ... P404
Valley Press ... P418
Vane Women Press ... P419
W.W. Norton & Company, Inc. ... P423
Washington Writers' Publishing House ... P425
Wordsonthestreet ... P434
YesYes Books ... P439
Zuckerbrot, Renee ... L618

Short Nonfiction
30 North ... M001
About Place Journal ... M004
Account, The ... M006
Alaska Quarterly Review ... M014
Amethyst Review ... M019
Arts & Letters ... M027
Atlantic Northeast ... M032
Babybug ... M037
Bacopa Literary Review ... M038
Bee, The ... M045
Belmont Story Review ... M047
Better Than Starbucks ... M052
Big Fiction ... M055
Black Warrior Review ... M058
Blue Earth Review ... M059
Blue Mesa Review ... M060
Boyfriend Village ... M064
Brick ... M065
Caribbean Writer, The ... M073
Chautauqua Literary Journal ... M077
Concho River Review ... M083
Conjunctions ... M084
Conjunctions Online ... M085
Crazyhorse / Swamp Pink ... M093
Cream City Review ... M094
CutBank ... M099
Dublin Review, The ... M107
Ekphrastic Review, The ... M109
El Portal ... M110
Emerge Literary Journal ... M111
Event ... M113
Faultline ... M118
Fiddlehead, The ... M121
Five Points ... M124
Fourth River, The ... M131
Ginosko Literary Journal ... M140
Grain Literary Magazine ... M143
Granta ... M144
Half Mystic Journal ... M149
Harpur Palate ... M151
Helix, The ... M154
Hunger Mountain ... M161
Idaho Review ... M163
Identity Theory ... M164
Irish Pages ... M173
Literary Mama ... M187
MacGuffin, The ... M195
Malahat Review, The ... M197
Midsummer Dream House ... M207
Midway Journal ... M208
Moonday Mag ... M213
Nashville Review ... M217
New England Review ... M220
New Welsh Reader ... M223
Pacifica Literary Review ... M231
Panorama ... M232
Paris Review, The ... M233
Passionfruit Review, The ... M234
Pleiades ... M238
Ploughshares ... M239
Prole ... M250
River Styx ... M264
Second Factory ... M274
Shenandoah ... M277
Shooter Literary Magazine ... M279
Sonder Magazine ... M287
South Carolina Review ... M289
Spitball ... M297
Story Unlikely ... M300
Studio One ... M304
Tahoma Literary Review ... M308
Tears in the Fence ... M311
Thin Air Magazine ... M314
Third Coast ... M315
Tolka ... M319
Tributaries ... M320
Virginia Quarterly Review, The ... M330
Windsor Review ... M342
Zone 3 ... M353

Shropshire
See more broadly: England
Logaston Press ... P221

Skiing
See more broadly: Leisure; Sport

Slang
See more broadly: Language

Slavs
See more broadly: Ethnic Groups
Peter Lang ... P285

Slipstream
See more broadly: Fantasy; Science Fiction
Asimov's Science Fiction ... M029
Jamii Publishing ... P196
Strange Horizons ... M301

Small Press
See more broadly: Publishing
Supplement, The ... M306

Smallholdings
See more broadly: Agriculture

Snowboarding
See more broadly: Leisure; Sport

Social Class
See more broadly: Social Groups
Chanchani, Sonali ... L108
Dawson, Liza ... L148
Ellis-Martin, Sian ... L180
Fernwood Publishing ... P131
Gold SF ... P146
Macdougall, Laura ... L379
Simpson, Cara Lee ... L537
University of Michigan Press, The ... P410
Yeoh, Rachel ... L612
Zuraw-Friedland, Ayla ... L619

Social Commentary
See more broadly: Commentary; Society
Carter, Rebecca ... L103
Danko, Margaret ... L140
Faulks, Holly ... L187
MacDonald, Emily ... L378
Malahat Review, The ... M197
Marr, Jill ... L389
Monoray ... P246
Mozley, Jack ... L422
Roberts, Soumeya Bendimerad ... L495
Simpson, Cara Lee ... L537

Social Groups
See more broadly: Society
See more specifically: Friends; Gender; Social Class; Working Class

Social History
See more broadly: History
Brewin Books Ltd ... P062
DeBlock, Liza ... L149
Dundurn ... P118

358 Index | *Social Issues*

Fuentes, Sarah ... L222
Icon Books Ltd ... P180
J. Gordon Shillingford Publishing ... P194
JMD Media / DB Publishing ... P198
Kahn, Ella Diamond ... L314
Minnesota Historical Society Press ... P241
Morrell, Imogen ... L417
Pickering, Juliet ... L473
Ramer, Susan ... L486
Schofield, Hannah ... L522
Seymour, Charlotte ... L528
Takikawa, Marin ... L566

Social Issues
See more broadly: Society
See more specifically: Addiction; Bullying; Discrimination; Diversity; Equality; Gender Issues; Homelessness; Immigration; Men's Issues; Poverty; Refugees; Women's Issues
404 Ink ... P001
Afsana Press ... P005
Barr, Nicola ... L039
Betsy Amster Literary Enterprises ... L059
Bradford Literary Agency ... L073
Caskie, Robert ... L105
Charlesbridge Publishing ... P081
Christie, Jennifer ... L116
Dana Newman Literary, LLC ... L138
Eisenmann, Caroline ... L175
Evans, Kate ... L185
Fernwood Publishing ... P131
Finegan, Stevie ... L203
Free Association Books Ltd ... P135
Geiger, Ellen ... L227
International Publishers ... P191
Jessica Kingsley Publishers ... P197
New Internationalist ... M221
Pelham, Imogen ... L461
Philips, Ariana ... L471
Plitt, Carrie ... L477
Posner, Marcy ... L480
Pride ... M249
Salt Publishing ... P322
Susan Schulman Literary Agency ... L557
Takikawa, Marin ... L566
Thinkwell Books, UK ... P384

Social Justice
See more broadly: Society
Afsana Press ... P005
Beaumont, Diana ... L046
Bernardi, Amanda ... L056
Burby, Danielle ... L087
Chanchani, Sonali ... L108
Cooper, Maggie ... L129
Crown ... P101
Free Spirit Publishing ... P136
Gold SF ... P146
HopeRoad ... P176
Julien, Ria ... L312
LSU Press ... P223
Marshall, Jen ... L391
New Internationalist ... M221
Peddle, Kay ... L460
Phillips, Aemilia ... L472
Richter, Rick ... L493
Riposte ... M262
Sierra ... M281
Stephens, Jenny ... L549
Trudel, Jes ... L579
Tyndale House Publishers, Inc. ... P397
Willms, Kathryn ... L605

Social Media
See more broadly: Media
Begum, Salma ... L047
Faulks, Holly ... L187

Society
See more specifically: Activism; Ethnic Groups; High Society; Postcolonialism; Social Commentary; Social Groups; Social Issues; Social Justice; Socio-Political; Sociology
Bloomsbury Academic ... P053
British Academy, The ... P063
Cavanagh, Claire ... L107
Chanchani, Sonali ... L108
Conversation (UK), The ... M087
Faulks, Holly ... L187
Goldstein, Veronica ... L244
History Press, The ... P174
Island Online ... M175
Johnson, Jared ... L303
Kahn, Ella Diamond ... L314
Maidment, Olivia ... L386
Oxford University Press ... P272
Peter Lang ... P285
Reilly, Milly ... L491
Society for Promoting Christian Knowledge (SPCK) ... P345
University of Alberta Press ... P404
Victoria Sanders & Associates LLC ... L584
Yale University Press (London) ... P438
Yeoh, Rachel ... L612

Socio-Political
See more broadly: Politics; Society
Pluto Press ... P295

Sociology
See more broadly: Society
See more specifically: Ethnography
ABC-CLIO ... P002
Arcadia Publishing ... P020
Asian Social Science ... M028
Basic Books ... P035
Baylor University Press ... P041
Berghahn Books Ltd ... P045
Bernardi, Amanda ... L056
Bloomsbury Academic ... P053
Cambridge University Press ... P068
Chelsea House Publishers ... P082
Compassiviste Publishing ... P097
Dundurn ... P118
Fernwood Publishing ... P131
Fogg, Jack ... L206
Gale ... P139
Gill Education ... P143
Goldblatt, Rachel ... L243
Goldstein, Veronica ... L244
Goose Lane Editions ... P148
Harvard University Press ... P165
Kensington Publishing Corp. ... P204
Marion Boyars Publishers ... P229
MIT Press, The ... P244
Mortimer, Michele ... L418
Muscato, Nate ... L429
Oxford University Press ... P272
Perry Literary ... L466
Pluto Press ... P295
Stanford University Press ... P367
Stipes Publishing ... P371
Taylor & Francis Group ... P378
UCL Press ... P398
University of Alberta Press ... P404
University of California Press ... P406
University of Michigan Press, The ... P410
University of Virginia Press ... P415
W.W. Norton & Company Ltd ... P422
W.W. Norton & Company, Inc. ... P423
Yale University Press (London) ... P438

Soft Science Fiction
See more broadly: Science Fiction
Brannan, Maria ... L076
Finegan, Stevie ... L203
Weiss, Alexandra ... L593

Software
See more broadly: Computers
See more specifically: Software Development

Software Development
See more broadly: Software
BCS (British Computer Society) ... P042

Somerset
See more broadly: England
Somerset Life ... M286

South America
See more broadly: Regional
See more specifically: Brazil
Arte Publico Press ... P021
Feminist Press, The ... P130
Ohio University Press ... P261
Phillips, Aemilia ... L472
Pluto Press ... P295
Stanford University Press ... P367
University of California Press ... P406
University of Michigan Press, The ... P410
University of Texas Press ... P414

South Pacific
See more broadly: Pacific
Takahe ... M309

South-East Asia
See more broadly: Asia
See more specifically: China

Southeastern United States
See more broadly: United States

Southwestern United States
See more broadly: United States
Sunbelt Publications, Inc. ... P373
University of Texas Press ... P414

Space
See more broadly: Science
Cosmos ... M089
Weiss, Alexandra ... L593

Space Opera
See more broadly: Science Fiction
Armada, Kurestin ... L024
Berlyne, John ... L055
Gahan, Isobel ... L225
Gunic, Masha ... L256
Irvine, Lucy ... L292

Spain
See more broadly: Europe
Peter Lang ... P285

Spanish
See more broadly: Language
Mentor Books ... P236
Stipes Publishing ... P371

Spas and Hot Tubs
See more broadly: Houses and Homes
Spa Magazine ... M295
Swimming Pool News ... M307

Special Forces
See more broadly: Military

Speculative
See more specifically: Alternative History; Dystopian Fiction; Grimdark; Speculative Historical Fiction; Speculative Horror; Speculative Romance; Speculative Thrillers; Utopian Fiction
Afonso, Thais ... L007
Ange, Anna ... L019
Apple Tree Literary Ltd ... L023
Armada, Kurestin ... L024
Armstrong, Susan ... L026
Bajek, Lauren ... L031
Bauman, Erica ... L043
Baxter, Veronique ... L045
Bent, Jenny ... L053
Blair Partnership, The ... L064
Bradford, Laura ... L074
Brannan, Maria ... L076
Brooks, Savannah ... L080

Index | *Sports Coaching* **359**

Candlemark & Gleam P069
Chanchani, Sonali L108
Cho, Catherine L114
Clarke, Caro L118
Cochran, Alexander L120
Cooper, Gemma L128
Cusick, John L136
DeBlock, Liza L149
Demblon, Gabrielle L150
Dolin, Lily L157
Dunn, Ben L164
Eason, Lynette L169
Edenborough, Sam L172
Fabien, Samantha L186
Feminist Press, The P130
Fergusson, Julie L196
Figueroa, Melanie L199
Fogg, Jack L206
Forrester, Jemima L210
Foster, Clara L211
Friedman, Claire L217
Fuentes, Sarah L222
Fuller, Lisa L223
Future Fire, The M135
Gilbert, Tara L233
Gold SF P146
Goldblatt, Rachel L243
Goldstein, Veronica L244
Graham, Susan L248
Gruber, Pam L253
Hannah Sheppard Literary Agency L262
Harris, Erin L268
Hawn, Molly Ker L270
Hordern, Kate L286
Hornsley, Sarah L287
Johnson, Jared L303
Kahn, Ella Diamond L314
Kavanagh, Jade L323
Keren, Eli L330
Killingley, Jessica L332
Kim, Jennifer L333
Kirby, Robert L338
Langlee, Lina L352
Laxfield Literary Associates L356
Levy, Yael L362
Lightner, Kayla L365
Lovell, Jake L372
MacKenzie, Joanna L382
Maidment, Olivia L386
Maltese, Alyssa L387
Marini, Victoria L388
Marr, Jill L389
McBride, Juliana L399
Moonday Mag M213
Moore, Mary C. L415
Morrell, Imogen L417
Mozley, Jack L422
Napolitano, Maria L431
Nelson, Kristin L436
Nelson, Patricia L437
Neon M219
O'Shea, Amy L447
Pages, Saribel L453
Pass, Marina de L456
Plant, Zoe L476
Preston, Amanda L484
Savvides, Marilia L520
Simpson, Cara Lee L537
Singh, Amandeep L538
Siobhan, Aiden L539
Sluytman, Antoinette Van L541
Sorg, Arley L546
Steed, Hayley L548
Story Unlikely M300
Strange Horizons M301
Swainson, Joanna L561
Takikawa, Marin L566
Tannenbaum, Amy L568
Tor Publishing Group P388
Trudel, Jes L579
Vance, Lisa Erbach L583
Weiss, Alexandra L593
Whatnall, Michaela L598
Williams, Laura L603
Willms, Kathryn L605
Wilson, Desiree L606
Wilson, Ed L607
Yeoh, Rachel L612

Speculative Historical Fiction
See more broadly: Historical Fiction; Speculative
Fazzari, Hillary L188

Speculative Horror
See more broadly: Horror; Speculative
Irvine, Lucy L292
Julie Crisp Literary Agency L311

Speculative Romance
See more broadly: Romance; Speculative
Danko, Margaret L140
Hannah Sheppard Literary Agency L262
Ostby, Kristin L452
Zack Company, Inc, The L615

Speculative Thrillers
See more broadly: Speculative; Thrillers
Marini, Victoria L388

Spirit Guides
See more broadly: Spirituality
Llewellyn Worldwide Ltd P219

Spirituality
See more specifically: New Age; Religion; Spirit Guides
Amethyst Review M019
Baumer, Jan L044
Brailsford, Karen L075
Brown, Megan L084
Canterbury Press P071
Compassiviste Publishing P097
Danko, Margaret L140
Dawntreader, The M102
Derviskadic, Dado L151
DSP Publications P116
Edelstein, Anne L171
Ericka T. Phillips L181
Fernando, Kimberly L198
Goodman Beck Publishing P147
Haley, Jolene L260
Hay House Publishers P168
Image M166
Joy Harris Literary Agency, Inc L308
Kimber, Natalie L336
Kracht, Elizabeth L341
Kube Publishing P209
Levy, Yael L362
Llewellyn Worldwide Ltd P219
Monoray P246
Murgolo, Karen L427
Niv, Daniel L440
Regina Ryan Books L489
Sentient Publications P334
Sheree Bykofsky Associates, Inc. L532
Society for Promoting Christian Knowledge (SPCK) P345
Thames & Hudson Inc. P382
Transworld Publishers P393
Two Fine Crows Books P396
Tyndale House Publishers, Inc. P397
Zack Company, Inc, The L615

Sport
See more specifically: Archery; Baseball; Basketball; Boxing; Canoeing; Climbing; Cricket; Cycling; Darts; Equestrian; Falconry; Football / Soccer; Golf; Hockey; Horse Racing; Hunting; Martial Arts; Motorsports; Rugby; Shooting; Skiing; Snowboarding; Sports Coaching; Swimming; Water Sports; Wilderness Sports; Women's Sports
Annette Green Authors' Agency L021
Arcadia Publishing P020
Atyeo, Charlotte L028
Barr, Nicola L039
Bernardi, Amanda L056
Black & White Publishing Ltd P049
Blackstaff Press P051
Bloomsbury Academic P053
Brattle Agency LLC, The L077
Brewin Books Ltd P062
Brick M065
Brouckaert, Justin L083
Campbell, Charlie L094
Charles River Press P080
Dana Newman Literary, LLC L138
Diversion Books P111
DK Publishing P112
Doug Grad Literary Agency L161
Dundurn P118
Enslow Publishers, Inc. P123
Fogg, Jack L206
Gale P139
Gill Books P142
Gordon, Andrew L245
History Press, The P174
Icon Books Ltd P180
Ireland's Own M172
JMD Media / DB Publishing P198
Kensington Publishing Corp. P204
Macdougall, Laura L379
Marr, Jill L389
Methuen Publishing Ltd P238
Minnesota Historical Society Press P241
Monoray P246
Mortimer, Michele L418
Mundy, Toby L426
Ohio University Press P261
Perry Literary L466
Philips, Ariana L471
Quirk Books P308
Regina Ryan Books L489
Rudy Agency, The L510
Rutman, Jim L514
Scratching Shed Publishing P331
Seren Books P335
Snowbooks P344
Spackman, James L547
Square Mile Magazine M298
Texas A&M University Press P381
Thames & Hudson Inc. P382
Thayer, Henry L572
Thinkwell Books, UK P384
Transworld Publishers P393
Tyndale House Publishers, Inc. P397
University of Akron Press, The P403
University of Alberta Press P404
University of Michigan Press, The P410
University of Missouri Press P411
University of Tennessee Press P413
W.W. Norton & Company Ltd P422
Wilson, Ed L607

Sports Cars
See more broadly: Cars

Sports Celebrity
See more broadly: Celebrity
FRA (Futerman, Rose, & Associates) L214
Richter, Rick L493
Zack Company, Inc, The L615

Sports Coaching
See more broadly: Sport
Coaches Choice P093

Spy Thrillers
See more broadly: Thrillers
Armada, Kurestin L024
Dawson, Liza..............................L148
Pass, Marina de L456
Thorneycroft, Euan.....................L574

St Louis
See more broadly: Missouri
Missouri Historical Society Press P243

Staffordshire
See more broadly: England
See more specifically: Burton upon Trent

Stamp Collecting
See more broadly: Hobbies
Stanley Gibbons........................P368

Stand-Up Paddleboarding (SUP)
See more broadly: Water Sports
Adventure Books by Vertebrate Publishing..............................P004

Statistics
See more broadly: Mathematics
Cambridge University Press.......P068
Taylor & Francis Group...............P378
W.W. Norton & Company Ltd P422

Steam Engines
See more broadly: Steam Power; Vehicles

Steam Power
See more broadly: Technology
See more specifically: Steam Engines

Steampunk
See more broadly: Science Fiction
Bennett, Laura L050
Irvine, Lucy L292
Liverpool Literary Agency, The ...L369

Storytelling
See more broadly: Performing Arts
Facts & Fiction M116

Stress Management
See more broadly: Psychology

Sub-Culture
See more broadly: Culture
Danaczko, Melissa.....................L139
Derviskadic, Dado L151
Eisenmann, Caroline.................L175
Nolan, Laura..............................L441
Roberts, Soumeya Bendimerad...............L495

Suffolk
See more broadly: England
Norfolk & Suffolk Bride..............M224

Sufism
See more broadly: Islam

Superhero Fantasy
See more broadly: Fantasy

Supernatural / Paranormal
See more specifically: Cryptozoology; Ghost Stories; Ghosts; Mysticism; Psychic Abilities; Reincarnation; Supernatural / Paranormal Horror; Supernatural / Paranormal Romance; Supernatural / Paranormal Thrillers; UFOs; Vampires; Witchcraft; Witches
Buckley, Louise.........................L085
Cabello, Analia..........................L092
Countryside Books P099
DSP Publications......................P116
Dundurn....................................P118
Fate...M117
Fortean Times: The Journal of Strange Phenomena...............M127
JMD Media / DB Publishing P198
Leon, Nina.................................L360
Lovell, Jake L372
Ostby, Kristin L452
Piatkus Books...........................P289
Pine, Gideon.............................L475
Shestopal, Camilla....................L534

Siobhan, Aiden L539
Unseen Press............................P417
Vance, Lisa Erbach L583
Whitford Press P428

Supernatural / Paranormal Horror
See more broadly: Horror; Supernatural / Paranormal
Foxx, Kat L213
Marini, Victoria..........................L388
Sinister Stoat Press..................P341

Supernatural / Paranormal Romance
See more broadly: Romance; Supernatural / Paranormal
Aldridge, Kaylyn L010
Bradford Literary Agency L073
Carina Press.............................P073
Dreamspinner Press P115
Lane, Helen L349
Leon, Nina.................................L360
Nichols, Mariah.........................L438
Niv, Daniel.................................L440
SmashBear Publishing P342
Sourcebooks Casablanca.........P351
Zack Company, Inc, The L615

Supernatural / Paranormal Thrillers
See more broadly: Supernatural / Paranormal; Thrillers
Afonso, Thais............................L007

Supply Chain Management
See more broadly: Management
Loft Press, Inc...........................P220

Surfing
See more broadly: Water Sports

Surreal
Asimov's Science Fiction M029
Every Day Fiction......................M114
Moonday Mag............................M213
Neon..M219

Suspense
See more specifically: Domestic Suspense; Literary Suspense; Psychological Suspense; Romantic Suspense
Afonso, Thais............................L007
Alfred Hitchcock Mystery Magazine.......M016
Armstrong, Susan......................L026
Baror International, Inc..............L037
Bent, Jenny...............................L053
Bolton, Camilla..........................L067
Brooks, Savannah.....................L080
Carr, Jamie................................L101
Cho, Catherine..........................L114
Choc Lit.....................................P085
Cichello, Kayla..........................L117
Comparato, Andrea L123
Crowley, Sheila.........................L132
Crystal Magazine......................M098
Cusick, John..............................L136
Dana Newman Literary, LLC.....L138
Dreamspinner Press P115
Every Day Fiction......................M114
Fabien, Samantha.....................L186
Figueroa, Melanie L199
Fogg, Jack.................................L206
Foxx, Kat L213
Friedman, Claire L217
Friedman, Rebecca...................L219
Gilbert, Tara L233
Harris, Erin................................L268
Hayden, Viola............................L271
Heathfield, Laura.......................L273
Hensley, Chelsea......................L274
Hornsley, Sarah.........................L287
Inscriptions Literary Agency......L289
Joffe Books...............................P199
Joy Harris Literary Agency, Inc..L308
Kavanagh, Jade L323

Kenny, Julia...............................L329
Leon, Nina.................................L360
Marini, Victoria..........................L388
Milburn, Madeleine....................L411
Morrell, Imogen.........................L417
Mushens, Juliet.........................L430
Nelson, Patricia.........................L437
Orenda Books...........................P267
Penzler Publishers....................P282
Piatkus Books...........................P289
Pine, Gideon.............................L475
Power, Anna..............................L482
Romano, Annie.........................L502
Savvides, Marilia.......................L520
Schofield, Hannah.....................L522
Seymour, Charlotte L528
Shestopal, Camilla....................L534
Soloway, Jennifer March...........L544
Sourcebooks Landmark............P356
Story Unlikely............................M300
Stringer, Marlene.......................L554
Tibbets, Anne............................L576
Trudel, Jes................................L579
Turner Publishing......................P394
Tyndale House Publishers, Inc..P397
Victoria Sanders & Associates LLC.............L584
Weiman, Paula..........................L592
Weiss, Alexandra......................L593
Yeoh, Rachel.............................L612
Zack Company, Inc, The L615

Sustainable Living
See more broadly: Environment
Cooper, Maggie.........................L129
Kimber, Natalie.........................L336
Murdoch Books Australia..........P249
Ooligan Press............................P265
Regina Ryan Books...................L489
Sierra..M281
Taylor & Francis Group..............P378
UCL Press.................................P398

Swimming
See more broadly: Sport
See more specifically: Outdoor / Wild Swimming; Swimming Pools

Swimming Pools
See more broadly: Swimming
Swimming Pool News M307

Switzerland
See more broadly: Europe

Sword and Sorcery
See more broadly: Fantasy

TV
See more broadly: Media
Annette Green Authors' Agency...........L021
Berghahn Books Ltd..................P045
DK Publishing...........................P112
Global Lion Intellectual Property Management, Inc....................L239
Kim, Julia..................................L334
My Weekly.................................M215
Ohio University Press................P261
Oxford Review of Books M230
Red Magazine...........................M259
Square Mile Magazine...............M298
Thames & Hudson Inc...............P382
University of Alberta Press........P404
Yale Review, The M344
Yours...M350
Zack Company, Inc, The L615

TV Scripts
Agency (London) Ltd, The L008
Andrews, Gina...........................L018
Barnard, Arthur L035
Bell, Eva....................................L048
Bolger, Maeve...........................L066
Curtis Brown.............................L135

Index | Thrillers 361

Elaine Steel L179
Fontaine, Melissa L208
Hickman, Emily L278
JFL Agency L300
Judy Daish Associates Ltd L310
Kelleher, Sophie L327
Ki Agency Ltd L331
Lyon, Rebecca L376
Meridian Artists L404
Middleton, Leah L409
Mumby, Helen L425
Narrow Road Company, The L432
Paradigm Talent and Literary Agency L454
Qu Literary Magazine M253
Rochelle Stevens & Co. L498
Valerie Hoskins Associates L582
Williams, Katie L602

Tai Chi

See more broadly: Martial Arts

Singing Dragon P340

Tanka

Modern Haiku M211
Scifaikuest M270

Taoism / Daoism

See more broadly: Philosophy

Singing Dragon P340

Tarot

See more broadly: Fortune Telling and Divination

Haley, Jolene L260
Hay House Publishers P168
Hensley, Chelsea L274
Llewellyn Worldwide Ltd P219
Rushall, Kathleen L512

Taxation

See more broadly: Finance; Legal

Technology

See more specifically: Audio Visual Technology; Augmented Reality; Computers; Digital Technology; Energy; Radio Control; Robots; Steam Power

Arcadia Publishing P020
Bloomsbury Academic P053
Carter, Rebecca L103
Colourpoint Educational P095
Compass Talent L124
Compassiviste Publishing P097
Conversation (UK), The M087
Cosmos M089
Curious Minds L133
Dana Newman Literary, LLC L138
Dickerson, Donya L155
Elsevier Ltd P121
Enslow Publishers, Inc. P123
Gale P139
Global Lion Intellectual Property Management, Inc. L239
Goldstein, Veronica L244
Information Today, Inc. P188
Kane Press P202
Kensington Publishing Corp. P204
Lightner, Kayla L365
London Review of Books M191
Marshall, Jen L391
MIT Press, The P244
Muscato, Nate L429
Oxford University Press P272
Perry Literary L466
Pluto Press P295
Purdue University Press P305
Research Journal of Pharmacy and Technology M260
Square Mile Magazine M298
Symonds, Laurel L565
Taylor & Francis Group P378
Thorneycroft, Euan L574
University of Alberta Press P404
University of California Press P406
University of Virginia Press P415
W.W. Norton & Company Ltd P422
Wallpaper M337
Wickers, Chandler L600
Wilson, Desiree L606
Yale University Press (London) P438
Zack Company, Inc, The L615
Zuraw-Friedland, Ayla L619

Teen

Agency (London) Ltd, The L008
Andlyn L014
Annette Green Authors' Agency L021
Asabi Publishing P022
Auroras & Blossoms PoArtMo Anthology M035
Blair Partnership, The L064
Eunice McMullen Children's Literary Agent Ltd L182
Firefly P133
Free Spirit Publishing P136
Haggerty, Taylor L258
Hawk, Susan L269
Langton, Becca L353
Madeleine Milburn Literary, TV & Film Agency L385
Margaret K. McElderry Books P228
Moody Publishers P247
Shaw Agency, The L529
Tor Publishing Group P388
Tor Teen P389
Turner Publishing P394
Tyndale House Publishers, Inc. P397
Walsh, Caroline L589

Tennessee

See more broadly: United States

Texas

See more broadly: United States

Texas A&M University Press P381
University of North Texas Press P412
University of Texas Press P414

The Midlands

See more broadly: England

See more specifically: East Midlands

Brewin Books Ltd P062

Theatre

See more broadly: Media

See more specifically: Musicals

African American Review M009
BSFA Review, The M067
Cambridge University Press P068
Doug Grad Literary Agency L161
Methuen Publishing Ltd P238
Narrow Road Company, The L432
Ohio University Press P261
Southern Theatre M292
Times Literary Supplement (TLS), The M318
University of Iowa Press P408
University of Michigan Press, The P410

Theatre Scripts

African Voices M010
Agency (London) Ltd, The L008
Alaska Quarterly Review M014
Anvil Press Publishers P017
Aurora Metro Press P024
Barnard, Arthur L035
Bell, Eva L048
Bolger, Maeve L066
Caribbean Writer, The M073
Coach House Books P092
Curtis Brown L135
Elaine Steel L179
Gurman Agency, LLC L257
Hickman, Emily L278
J. Gordon Shillingford Publishing P194
JFL Agency L300
Judy Daish Associates Ltd L310
Kelleher, Sophie L327
Kenyon Review, The M179
Ki Agency Ltd L331
Lost Lake Folk Opera Magazine M193
Lyon, Rebecca L376
Marion Boyars Publishers P229
Mumby, Helen L425
Narrow Road Company, The L432
New England Review M220
Obsidian: Literature in the African Diaspora M227
Paradigm Talent and Literary Agency L454
Pushing Out the Boat M252
Qu Literary Magazine M253
Renard Press Ltd P313
River Styx M264
Rochelle Stevens & Co. L498
Sunspot Literary Journal M305
Third Coast M315
Tusculum Review, The M321
Victoria Sanders & Associates LLC L584
Williams, Katie L602

Theravada Buddhism

See more broadly: Buddhism

Thrillers

See more specifically: Crime Thrilllers; Dark Thrillers; Domestic Thriller; High Concept Thrillers; Historical Thrillers; Legal Thrillers; Literary Thrillers; Political Thrillers; Psychological Thrillers; Romantic Thrillers; Speculative Thrillers; Spy Thrilllers; Supernatural / Paranormal Thrillers; Upmarket Thrillers

3 Seas Literary Agency L001
Afonso, Thais L007
Annette Green Authors' Agency L021
Armstrong, Susan L026
Asabi Publishing P022
Baror International, Inc. L037
Bartholomew, Jason L041
Baxter, Veronique L045
Belton, Maddy L049
Berlyne, John L055
Betsy Amster Literary Enterprises L059
Blair Partnership, The L064
Bloodhound Books P052
Bolton, Camilla L067
Brace, Samantha L072
Bradford Literary Agency L073
Bradford, Laura L074
Brannan, Maria L076
Brooks, Savannah L080
Buckley, Louise L085
Burke, Kate L088
Campbell, Charlie L094
Carroll, Megan L102
Chanchani, Sonali L108
Chevais, Jennifer L111
Christensen, Erica L115
Claret Press P089
Cochran, Alexander L120
Compassiviste Publishing P097
Cooper, Gemma L128
Crowley, Sheila L132
Crystal Magazine M098
Curtis Brown L135
Cusick, John L136
Dana Newman Literary, LLC L138
Darley Anderson Agency, The L143
Dawson, Liza L148
DeBlock, Liza L149
Demblon, Gabrielle L150
Diversion Books P111
Doug Grad Literary Agency L161
Dunn, Ben L164

Eason, Lynette	L169	Posner, Marcy	L480	Wallpaper	M337
Ellis-Martin, Sian	L180	Reid, Janet	L490	**Travel**	
Fabien, Samantha	L186	Riccardi, Francesca	L492	*See more specifically: Air Travel; Road Atlases; Road Trips; Sailing*	
Faulks, Holly	L187	Rogers, Coleridge & White Ltd	L501	Arcadia Publishing	P020
Ferguson, Hannah	L194	Romano, Annie	L502	Asabi Publishing	P022
Figueroa, Melanie	L199	Ruby Fiction	P319	Atlanta Magazine	M030
Finan, Ciara	L200	Salazar, Des	L515	Aurora Metro Press	P024
for Authors, A	L209	Savvides, Marilia	L520	Bal, Emma	L032
Forrester, Jemima	L210	Schofield, Hannah	L522	Baxter, Veronique	L045
Foxx, Kat	L213	Seager, Chloe	L524	Bella	M046
Frankel, Valerie	L215	Seventh Agency	L527	Betsy Amster Literary Enterprises	L059
Friedman, Claire	L217	Seymour, Charlotte	L528	Brewin Books Ltd	P062
Getzler, Josh	L229	Shestopal, Camilla	L534	Brick	M065
Gilbert, Tara	L233	Simons, Tanera	L536	Britain Magazine	M066
Gillam, Bianca	L234	Snowbooks	P344	Business Traveller	M069
Goetz, Adria	L241	Soloway, Jennifer March	L544	Campbell, Charlie	L094
Gordon, Andrew	L245	Sparsile Books	P359	Canterbury Press	P071
Grunewald, Hattie	L254	Steed, Hayley	L548	Carter, Rebecca	L103
Gunic, Masha	L256	Story Unlikely	M300	Claret Press	P089
Haley, Jolene	L260	Stringer, Marlene	L554	Clarke, Caro	L118
Hannah Sheppard Literary Agency	L262	Swainson, Joanna	L561	Compassiviste Publishing	P097
Hansen, Stephanie	L264	Tannenbaum, Amy	L568	Cowboys & Indians	M091
Heathfield, Laura	L273	Terlip, Paige	L570	Crystal Magazine	M098
Hensley, Chelsea	L274	Thorneycroft, Euan	L574	Curran, Sabhbh	L134
Hiyate, Sam	L281	Thwaites, Steph	L575	Davies, Olivia	L147
Hogrebe, Christina	L283	Tibbets, Anne	L576	DK Publishing	P112
Hornsley, Sarah	L287	Topping, Antony	L577	Doug Grad Literary Agency	L161
Irene Goodman Literary Agency (IGLA)	L291	Tor Publishing Group	P388	Duncan Petersen Publishing Limited	P117
Joelle Delbourgo Associates, Inc.	L301	Torrey House Press, LLC	P390	Dundurn	P118
Kahn, Ella Diamond	L314	Transworld Publishers	P393	Foxx, Kat	L213
Kaliszewska, Joanna	L315	Trudel, Jes	L579	Globe Pequot Press, The	P145
Kane Literary Agency	L316	Turner Publishing	P394	Go World Travel Magazine	M142
Kavanagh, Jade	L323	Tyndale House Publishers, Inc.	P397	Goose Lane Editions	P148
Keeffe, Sara O'	L326	Udden, Jennifer	L580	Horse & Rider	M159
Kensington Publishing Corp.	P204	Vance, Lisa Erbach	L583	Icon Books Ltd	P180
Keren, Eli	L330	Victoria Sanders & Associates LLC	L584	JMD Media / DB Publishing	P198
Kracht, Elizabeth	L341	W.W. Norton & Company, Inc.	P423	Kensington Publishing Corp.	P204
Lakosil, Natalie	L347	Weiman, Paula	L592	Kent Life	M178
Lambert, Sophie	L348	Weiss, Alexandra	L593	Lambert, Sophie	L348
Langlee, Lina	L352	Wilson, Desiree	L606	Laxfield Literary Associates	L356
Langtons International	L354	Wilson, Ed	L607	Leisure Group Travel	M183
Leon, Nina	L360	Wolfpack Publishing	P432	Levy, Yael	L362
Lovell, Jake	L372	Wood, Ed	L609	Lilliput Press, The	P217
Lyrical Press	P225	Young, Claudia	L614	Malahat Review, The	M197
MacDonald, Emily	L378	Zack Company, Inc, The	L615	marie claire	M200
MacKenzie, Joanna	L382	**Time Travel**		Marlin	M201
Marr, Jill	L389	*See more broadly: Science Fiction*		Medina Publishing	P235
McNidder & Grace	P232	Begum, Salma	L047	Methuen Publishing Ltd	P238
Milburn, Madeleine	L411	Choc Lit	P085	Muswell Press	P250
Milusich, Grace	L412	**Timeslip Romance**		My Weekly	M215
Mortimer, Michele	L418	*See more broadly: Romance*		New England Review	M220
Mundy, Toby	L426	Choc Lit	P085	Panorama	M232
Murray, Judith	L428	**Trade**		Peddle, Kay	L460
Mushens, Juliet	L430	*See more broadly: Business*		Phaidon Press	P287
Muswell Press	P250	**Traditional**		Philips, Ariana	L471
Napolitano, Maria	L431	Alaska Quarterly Review	M014	Pineapple Press	P293
Nathan, Abigail	L433	Compassiviste Publishing	P097	Plitt, Carrie	L477
Neely, Rachel	L434	Midsummer Dream House	M207	Polygon	P298
Nelson, Kristin	L436	**Traditional Music**		Preservation Magazine	M248
Nichols, Mariah	L438	*See more broadly: Music*		Rand McNally	P310
Niumata, Erin	L439	**Trains**		Red Magazine	M259
O'Brien, Lee	L444	*See more broadly: Vehicles*		Regina Ryan Books	L489
Orenda Books	P267	**Translations**		River Hills Traveler	M263
Ostby, Kristin	L452	Joy Harris Literary Agency, Inc.	L308	Rocky Mountain Books	P315
Pan Macmillan Australia	P274	Victoria Sanders & Associates LLC	L584	Ruralite	M266
Parker, Elana Roth	L455	**Transport**		Scottish Field	M272
Pass, Marina de	L456	*See more specifically: Aviation; Hauliers; Railways; Vehicles*		Scratching Shed Publishing	P331
Penzler Publishers	P282	Arcadia Publishing	P020	Seren Books	P335
Perez Literary & Entertainment	L463	Brewin Books Ltd	P062	Sierra	M281
Perez, Kristina	L464	History Press, The	P174	Somerset Life	M286
Pestritto, Carrie	L467	Icon Books Ltd	P180	Southern Humanities Review	M290
PEW Literary	L468	Indiana University Press	P187	Square Mile Magazine	M298
Pierce, Rosie	L474	Kensington Publishing Corp.	P204	Thames & Hudson Inc.	P382
Pine, Gideon	L475	Loft Press, Inc.	P220	Tolka	M319
Plant, Zoe	L476	W.W. Norton & Company Ltd	P422	Transworld Publishers	P393

Access more listings online at www.firstwriter.com

Turner Publishing P394
University of Alberta Press P404
University of Michigan Press, The P410
Valley Press P418
W.W. Norton & Company Ltd P422
Wide-Eyed Editions P429
Yankee Magazine M345
Yorkshire Life M348
Yorkshire Women's Life Magazine M349
Young, Claudia L614
Yours M350

UFOs
See more broadly: Supernatural / Paranormal
Llewellyn Worldwide Ltd P219
Lovell, Jake L372

US Southern States
See more broadly: United States
Alabama Heritage M013
Dawson, Liza L148
University of Georgia Press P407

United Kingdom
See more broadly: Europe
See more specifically: England; Northern Ireland; Scotland; Wales
Best of British M050
Britain Magazine M066

United States
See more broadly: North America
See more specifically: Alabama; Alaska; American Midwest; American West; Americana; Appalachia; Arizona; California; Chesapeake Bay; Colorado; Florida; Georgia (US State); Hawai'i; Illinois; Indiana; Louisiana; Maine; Maryland; Michigan; Minnesota; Missouri; Nevada; New England; New Jersey; New York State; Ohio; Ozarks; Pacific Northwest; Pennsylvania; Southeastern United States; Southwestern United States; Tennessee; Texas; US Southern States; Utah; Virginia; Wisconsin
Pluto Press P295
Sunbelt Publications, Inc. P373
Thwaites, Steph. L575
University of California Press P406
University of Georgia Press P407
University of Michigan Press, The P410
University of Texas Press P414

Upmarket
See more specifically: Upmarket Commercial Fiction; Upmarket Contemporary Fiction; Upmarket Crime; Upmarket Fantasy; Upmarket Romance; Upmarket Thrillers; Upmarket Women's Fiction
Armada, Kurestin L024
AZ Foothills Magazine M036
Bajek, Lauren L031
Blair Partnership, The L064
Brannan, Maria L076
Buckley, Louise L085
Carroll, Megan L102
Cichello, Kayla L117
Combemale, Chris L122
Dana Newman Literary, LLC L138
DeBlock, Liza L149
Demblon, Gabrielle L150
Edenborough, Sam L172
Eisenmann, Caroline L175
Fabien, Samantha L186
Fazzari, Hillary L188
Figueroa, Melanie L199
Folio Literary Management, LLC L207
Forrester, Jemima L210
Foster, Clara L211
Friedman, Claire L217
Friedman, Jessica L218

Fuentes, Sarah L222
Getzler, Josh L229
Gilbert, Tara L233
Goetz, Adria L241
Grunewald, Hattie L254
Harper, Logan L267
Hildebrand, Cole L280
Kahn, Ella Diamond L314
Kardon, Julia L318
Keren, Eli L330
Krienke, Mary L343
Lakosil, Natalie L347
Leeke, Jessica L358
Leon, Nina L360
Lightner, Kayla L365
Lovell, Jake L372
MacDonald, Emily L378
Maidment, Olivia L386
Marini, Victoria L388
Marr, Jill L389
Milburn, Madeleine L411
Moore, Mary C. L415
Mushens, Juliet L430
Muswell Press P250
Napolitano, Maria L431
Nelson, Patricia L437
Ostby, Kristin L452
Pass, Marina de L456
Patterson, Emma L458
Pelham, Imogen L461
Perez Literary & Entertainment L463
Perez, Kristina L464
Ramer, Susan L486
Roberts, Soumeya Bendimerad L495
Romano, Annie L502
Rutherford, Laetitia L513
Serra, Maria Cardona L526
Singh, Amandeep L538
Sutherland, Kari L559
Takikawa, Marin L566
Terlip, Paige L570
Thwaites, Steph. L575
Topping, Antony L577
Tran, Jennifer Chen L578
Walsh, Caroline L589
Weitzner, Tess L594
Whatnall, Michaela L598
Wickers, Chandler L600
Wilson, Desiree L606
Wood, Caroline L608
Yeoh, Rachel L612

Upmarket Commercial Fiction
See more broadly: Commercial; Upmarket
Armstrong, Susan L026
Barr, Nicola L039
Beaumont, Diana L046
Betsy Amster Literary Enterprises L059
Bradford Literary Agency L073
Chiotti, Danielle L113
Einstein, Susanna L173
Glenister, Emily L238
Hiyate, Sam L281
Kaliszewska, Joanna L315
Williams, Laura L603

Upmarket Contemporary Fiction
See more broadly: Contemporary; Upmarket
Woods, Bryony L610

Upmarket Crime
See more broadly: Crime; Upmarket
Serra, Maria Cardona L526
Silk, Julia L535

Upmarket Fantasy
See more broadly: Fantasy; Upmarket
Fazzari, Hillary L188

Upmarket Romance
See more broadly: Romance; Upmarket

Berdinsky, Kendall L054
Carroll, Megan L102

Upmarket Thrillers
See more broadly: Thrillers; Upmarket
Silk, Julia L535

Upmarket Women's Fiction
See more broadly: Upmarket; Women's Fiction
Bent, Jenny L053
Betsy Amster Literary Enterprises L059
Bewley, Elizabeth L061
Hordern, Kate L286
Lakosil, Natalie L347
Mortimer, Michele L418
Parker, Elana Roth L455
Pestritto, Carrie L467
Philips, Ariana L471

Urban
Begum, Salma L047
Fernwood Publishing P131
Torrey House Press, LLC P390
University of Alberta Press P404
University of Georgia Press P407
University of Michigan Press, The P410

Urban Fantasy
See more broadly: Fantasy
Bennett, Laura L050
Berlyne, John L055
Carina Press P073
DeBlock, Liza L149
Glenister, Emily L238
Irvine, Lucy L292
Lane, Helen L349
Leon, Nina L360
Liverpool Literary Agency, The L369
SmashBear Publishing P342
Wilson, Desiree L606
Zack Company, Inc, The L615

Urban Farming
See more broadly: Farming

Utah
See more broadly: United States

Utopian Fiction
See more broadly: Speculative
Mozley, Jack L422

Vampires
See more broadly: Supernatural / Paranormal
DeBlock, Liza L149
Sinister Stoat Press P341

Vancouver Island
See more broadly: British Columbia

Veganism
See more broadly: Vegetarianism

Vegetarian Cooking
See more broadly: Cookery; Vegetarianism

Vegetarian Food
See more broadly: Food; Vegetarianism

Vegetarianism
See more broadly: Lifestyle
See more specifically: Veganism; Vegetarian Cooking; Vegetarian Food
Hay House Publishers P168

Vehicles
See more broadly: Transport
See more specifically: Boats; Caravans; Cars; Military Vehicles; Motorbikes; Motorhomes; Planes; Recreational Vehicles; Ships; Steam Engines; Trains
Old Pond Publishing P262

Veterinary
See more broadly: Animals
Texas A&M University Press P381

Vikings Fiction
See more broadly: Historical Fiction
Pass, Marina de L456

Virginia
See more broadly: United States

See more specifically: Albemarle
Albemarle M015
University of Virginia Press P415
Virginia Wine & Country Life M331
Virginia Wine & Country Weddings M332
Visual Arts
See more broadly: Arts
Bird Eye Books P048
Graywolf Lab M145
Unicorn P402
W.W. Norton & Company, Inc. P423
Visual Culture
See more broadly: Culture
African American Review M009
Bird Eye Books P048
Bloomsbury Academic P053
Visual Poetry
Black Warrior Review M058
Voodoo
See more broadly: Religion
Wales
See more broadly: United Kingdom
See more specifically: Breconshire; Montgomeryshire; Radnorshire
Walking
See more broadly: Outdoor Activities
See more specifically: Walking Guides
Adventure Books by Vertebrate Publishing P004
Countryside Books P099
Great Outdoors (TGO), The M146
JMD Media / DB Publishing P198
Yorkshire Life M348
Walking Guides
See more broadly: Walking
Duncan Petersen Publishing Limited P117
Goose Lane Editions P148
Kent Life M178
Logaston Press P221
Pocket Mountains P296
Rocky Mountain Books P315
Sigma Press P337
Warehousing
See more broadly: Business
Loft Press, Inc. P220
Warfare
See more specifically: American Civil War; American Revolution; Military; Military History; National Security; Secret Intelligence; World War I; World War II
Berghahn Books Ltd P045
BSFA Review, The M067
Davies, Olivia L147
Howgate Publishing P178
Pluto Press P295
Thinkwell Books, UK P384
Wickers, Chandler L600
Water Sports
See more broadly: Sport
See more specifically: Stand-Up Paddleboarding (SUP); Surfing
Weapons
See more specifically: Firearms
Weddings
See more broadly: Events
Berks County Living M049
Norfolk & Suffolk Bride M224
Savannah Magazine M269
Virginia Wine & Country Weddings M332
Wellbeing
See more broadly: Health
Atlanta Magazine M030
Aurora Metro Press P024
Barrett, Emily L040
Baumer, Jan L044
Berks County Living M049

Bernardi, Amanda L056
Bloomsbury Academic P053
Blue Star Press P056
Brailsford, Karen L075
Brewin Books Ltd P062
Cedar Fort P076
Dana Newman Literary, LLC L138
Danko, Margaret L140
Dundurn P118
Ekus, Sally L177
Faulks, Holly L187
First For Women M122
Frankel, Valerie L215
Free Spirit Publishing P136
Hammersmith Books P158
Kaliszewska, Joanna L315
Kate Barker Literary, TV, & Film Agency L320
Latshaw, Katherine L355
Levy, Yael L362
McNidder & Grace P232
Mortimer, Michele L418
Murgolo, Karen L427
Pine, Gideon L475
Preston, Amanda L484
Red Magazine M259
Regina Ryan Books L489
Seventeen M275
Shaw Agency, The L529
Silk, Julia L535
Singing Dragon P340
Stephens, Jenny L549
Turner Publishing P394
Willms, Kathryn L605
Yale University Press (London) P438
Yorkshire Women's Life Magazine M349
Yours M350
Zack Company, Inc, The L615
Werewolves
See more broadly: Horror
DeBlock, Liza L149
Irvine, Lucy L292
Sinister Stoat Press P341
West Country
See more broadly: England
Westchester County
See more broadly: New York State
Westerns
Armada, Kurestin L024
Crystal Magazine M098
Doug Grad Literary Agency L161
Dreamspinner Press P115
Hancock House Publishers P159
Kensington Publishing Corp. P204
Lovell, Jake L372
Robinson, Quressa L497
Story Unlikely M300
Wolfpack Publishing P432
Whisky
See more broadly: Drinks
Square Mile Magazine M298
Wicca
See more broadly: Paganism
Llewellyn Worldwide Ltd P219
Wilderness Sports
See more broadly: Sport
Wildlife
See more broadly: Animals
Hancock House Publishers P159
Pelagic P279
Scots Magazine, The M271
Sierra M281
Wine
See more broadly: Drinks
See more specifically: Winemaking
Bowlin, Sarah L071

Chiotti, Danielle L113
Foxx, Kat L213
Rosenberg Group, The L505
Sasquatch Books P325
Square Mile Magazine M298
University of California Press P406
Virginia Wine & Country Life M331
Wine Enthusiast M343
Winemaking
See more broadly: Wine
See more specifically: Amateur Winemaking
Wisconsin
See more broadly: United States
Witchcraft
See more broadly: Supernatural / Paranormal
Danko, Margaret L140
Foxx, Kat L213
Haley, Jolene L260
Llewellyn Worldwide Ltd P219
Witches
See more broadly: Supernatural / Paranormal
Buckley, Louise L085
DeBlock, Liza L149
Foxx, Kat L213
Haley, Jolene L260
Rushall, Kathleen L512
Women
See more broadly: Gender
Danko, Margaret L140
Foster, Clara L211
Glenister, Emily L238
Goldblatt, Rachel L243
Julien, Ria L312
Ohio University Press P261
Riposte M262
Tyndale House Publishers, Inc. P397
Women in Business
See more broadly: Business
Women's Fiction
See more specifically: Book Club Women's Fiction; Chick Lit; Commercial Women's Fiction; Contemporary Women's Fiction; Upmarket Women's Fiction
3 Seas Literary Agency L001
Afonso, Thais L007
Armstrong, Susan L026
Barone Literary Agency L036
Betancourt Literary L057
Blair Partnership, The L064
Bloodhound Books P052
Bolton, Camilla L067
Bradford Literary Agency L073
Bradford, Laura L074
Burby, Danielle L087
Burke, Kate L088
Chanchani, Sonali L108
Coombes, Clare L127
Doug Grad Literary Agency L161
Dunn, Ben L164
Fabien, Samantha L186
Fazzari, Hillary L188
Ferguson, Hannah L194
Figueroa, Melanie L199
Finch, Rebeka L202
Forrester, Jemima L210
Friedman, Rebecca L219
Getzler, Josh L229
Gillam, Bianca L234
Hornsley, Sarah L287
Joelle Delbourgo Associates, Inc. L301
Joffe Books P199
Kahn, Ella Diamond L314
Kracht, Elizabeth L341
Langtons International L354
Leon, Nina L360
MacKenzie, Joanna L382

Index | Young Adult 365

Nichols, Mariah L438
Niumata, Erin L439
Pelham, Imogen L461
People's Friend, The M237
Posner, Marcy L480
Romano, Annie L502
Rosenberg Group, The L505
Ruby Fiction P319
Schofield, Hannah L522
Shestopal, Camilla L534
Simons, Tanera L536
Steed, Hayley L548
Stringer, Marlene L554
Susan Schulman Literary Agency L557
Tannenbaum, Amy L568
Tran, Jennifer Chen L578
Williamson, Jo L604
Zack Company, Inc, The L615

Women's Football / Soccer
See more broadly: Football / Soccer
Hensley, Chelsea L274

Women's Health
See more broadly: Health
See more specifically: Menopause

Women's Interests
Canterbury Literary Agency L096
Carolina Woman M074
Compassiviste Publishing P097
Dana Newman Literary, LLC L138
Hello! M155
Joy Harris Literary Agency, Inc. L308
marie claire M200
Marion Boyars Publishers P229
My Weekly M215
OK! Magazine M228
People's Friend, The M237
Red Magazine M259
Sheree Bykofsky Associates, Inc. L532
Victoria Sanders & Associates LLC L584
Yours M350

Women's Issues
See more broadly: Social Issues
Betsy Amster Literary Enterprises L059
Danko, Margaret L140
Dawson, Liza L148
Geiger, Ellen L227
Kim, Julia L334
Levy, Yael L362
Posner, Marcy L480
Ramer, Susan L486
Regina Ryan Books L489
Serra, Maria Cardona L526
Willms, Kathryn L605
Yorkshire Women's Life Magazine M349
Zack Company, Inc, The L615

Women's Sports
See more broadly: Sport
Hensley, Chelsea L274

Women's Studies
See more broadly: Gender
Cleis Press P091
Imagine Publishing P186
Texas A&M University Press P381
University of Michigan Press, The P410
University of North Texas Press P412
University of Virginia Press P415
W.W. Norton & Company Ltd P422

Worcestershire
See more broadly: England
Logaston Press P221

Working Class
See more broadly: Social Groups

World War I
See more broadly: Warfare
Countryside Books P099

World War II
See more broadly: Warfare
Choc Lit P085
Countryside Books P099
Joffe Books P199
LSU Press P223
Methuen Publishing Ltd P238

Writing
See more broadly: Language
See more specifically: Creative Writing
Banter Press P033
Brick M065
Broadview Press P065
Literary Mama M187
Ohio University Press P261
Ooligan Press P265
Susan Schulman Literary Agency L557
Unfit Magazine M326
University of Iowa Press P408
University of Michigan Press, The P410
W.W. Norton & Company Ltd P422

Yachts
See more broadly: Boats
Square Mile Magazine M298

Yoga
See more broadly: Mind, Body, Spirit
Llewellyn Worldwide Ltd P219
Singing Dragon P340
Zack Company, Inc, The L615

Yorkshire
See more broadly: England
See more specifically: Huddersfield
Yorkshire Dalesman, The M347
Yorkshire Life M348
Yorkshire Women's Life Magazine M349

Young Adult
3 Seas Literary Agency L001
Adsett, Alex L005
Afonso, Thais L007
Agency (London) Ltd, The L008
Albert Whitman & Company P007
Aldridge, Kaylyn L010
Alekseii, Keir L011
Alice Williams Literary L012
Allen & Unwin P009
Andlyn L014
Andrade, Hannah L015
Anne Clark Literary Agency L020
Apple Tree Literary Ltd L023
Arcadia Publishing P020
Arms, Victoria Wells L025
Arthurson, Wayne L027
Asabi Publishing P022
Atyeo, Charlotte L028
Aurora Metro Press P024
Barbara, Stephen L034
Barone Literary Agency L036
Baror International, Inc. L037
Barr, Nicola L039
Bath Literary Agency L042
Bauman, Erica L043
Belton, Maddy L049
Bennett, Laura L050
Bent Agency (UK), The L051
Bent Agency, The L052
Bent, Jenny L053
Berlyne, John L055
Bewley, Elizabeth L061
Bhasin, Tamanna L062
Blair Partnership, The L064
Bradford Literary Agency L073
Bradford, Laura L074
Brannan, Maria L076
Brooks, Savannah L080
Burby, Danielle L087
Burns, Camille L089
Cabello, Analia L092
Candy Jar Books P070
Carroll, Megan L102
Chiotti, Danielle L113
Cho, Catherine L114
Christensen, Erica L115
Cichello, Kayla L117
Colwill, Charlotte L121
Compass Talent L124
Cooper, Gemma L128
Crandall, Becca L130
Curtis Brown L135
Cusick, John L136
Danko, Margaret L140
Darhansoff & Verrill Literary Agents L142
Darley Anderson Children's L144
DHH Literary Agency Ltd L152
Dolin, Lily L157
Donald Maass Literary Agency L160
Draper, Claire L162
Eason, Lynette L169
Eddison Pearson Ltd L170
Eerdmans Books for Young Readers P120
Einstein, Susanna L173
Eisenbraun, Nicole L174
Evan Marshall Agency, The L183
Fabien, Samantha L186
Fazzari, Hillary L188
Fellows, Abi L193
Ferguson, T.S. L195
Figueroa, Melanie L199
Firefly P133
Flannery Literary L204
Flynn, Amy Thrall L205
Foster, Clara L211
Foxx, Kat L213
Frankel, Valerie L215
Friedman, Claire L217
Friedman, Rebecca L219
Fuller, Lisa L223
Gahan, Isobel L225
Ghahremani, Lilly L230
Gilbert, Tara L233
Gisondi, Katie L235
Goff, Ellen L242
Graham, Stacey L247
Graham, Susan L248
Grajkowski, Kara L249
Gruber, Pam L253
Gunic, Masha L256
Hakim, Serene L259
Haley, Jolene L260
Hannah Sheppard Literary Agency L262
Hansen, Stephanie L264
Harris, Erin L268
Hashtag Press P166
Hawk, Susan L269
Hawn, Molly Ker L270
Hensley, Chelsea L274
Hernandez, Saritza L275
Hernando, Paloma L276
Heymont, Lane L277
HopeRoad P176
IgKids P183
Irene Goodman Literary Agency (IGLA) L291
Irvine, Lucy L292
Janklow & Nesbit UK Ltd L297
Jean V. Naggar Literary Agency, The L299
Joelle Delbourgo Associates, Inc. L301
Joy Harris Literary Agency, Inc. L308
Kahn, Ella Diamond L314
Kate Nash Literary Agency L321
Kathryn Green Literary Agency, LLC L322
Kean, Taylor Martindale L324
Kensington Publishing Corp. P204

Kimber, Natalie	L336	
Knigge, Sheyla	L339	
KT Literary	L345	
Lakosil, Natalie	L347	
Langlee, Lina	L352	
Langton, Becca	L353	
Latshaw, Katherine	L355	
Leapfrog Press	P212	
Leigh Feldman Literary	L359	
Leon, Nina	L360	
Lerner Publishing Group	P213	
Lindsay Literary Agency	L366	
Lineberry, Isabel	L367	
Liverpool Literary Agency, The	L369	
MacLeod, Lauren	L383	
Macmillan Children's Books	P226	
Madeleine Milburn Literary, TV & Film Agency	L385	
Maltese, Alyssa	L387	
Marini, Victoria	L388	
Marsh Agency, The	L390	
Matte, Rebecca	L395	
Mattson, Jennifer	L396	
Maurer, Shari	L397	
McBride, Juliana	L399	
McCormick Literary	L400	
Metamorphosis Literary Agency	L406	
Mihell, Natasha	L410	
Milusich, Grace	L412	
Mortimer, Michele	L418	
Motala, Tasneem	L419	
Mulcahy Sweeney Literary Agency	L423	
Nathan, Abigail	L433	
Nelson Literary Agency, LLC	L435	
Nelson, Kristin	L436	
Nelson, Patricia	L437	
Nichols, Mariah	L438	
Northbank Talent Management	L442	
Northern Gravy	M226	
O'Brien, Lee	L444	
O'Neill, Molly	L446	
Ooligan Press	P265	
Orca Book Publishers	P266	
Ostby, Kristin	L452	
Pan Macmillan Australia	P274	
Parker, Elana Roth	L455	
Pass, Marina de	L456	
Paul S. Levine Literary Agency	L459	
Pen & Ink Designs Publishing	P280	
Perez Literary & Entertainment	L463	
Perez, Kristina	L464	
Perotto-Wills, Martha	L465	
Pestritto, Carrie	L467	
Phelan, Beth	L470	
Philips, Ariana	L471	
Phoenix Moirai	P288	
Plant, Zoe	L476	
Posner, Marcy	L480	
Preston, Amanda	L484	
Ransom Publishing Ltd	P312	
Richter, Rick	L493	
Robinson, Quressa	L497	
Rogers, Coleridge & White Ltd	L501	
Ross, Whitney	L507	
Rubin Pfeffer Content, LLC	L509	
Rudy Agency, The	L510	
Rushall, Kathleen	L512	
Salazar, Des	L515	
Sant, Kelly Van	L518	
Schofield, Hannah	L522	
Schwizer, Fabienne	L523	
Seager, Chloe	L524	
Selectric Artists	L525	
Seventeen	M275	
Seventh Agency	L527	
Shestopal, Camilla	L534	
Siobhan, Aiden	L539	
Skylark Literary	L540	
Sluytman, Antoinette Van	L541	
Soho Press	P348	
Soler, Shania N.	L543	
Soloway, Jennifer March	L544	
Sourcebooks Fire	P353	
Stringer Literary Agency LLC, The	L553	
Stringer, Marlene	L554	
Stuart Krichevsky Literary Agency, Inc.	L556	
Susan Schulman Literary Agency	L557	
Sutherland, Kari	L559	
Symonds, Laurel	L565	
Takikawa, Marin	L566	
Talbot, Emily	L567	
Tasman, Alice	L569	
Terlip, Paige	L570	
Thames & Hudson Inc.	P382	
Tor Teen	L389	
Torrey House Press, LLC	P390	
Tran, Jennifer Chen	L578	
Trudel, Jes	L579	
Turner Publishing	P394	
Victoria Sanders & Associates LLC	L584	
Wade & Co Literary Agency	L588	
Walsh, Caroline	L589	
Weiman, Paula	L592	
Weiss, Alexandra	L593	
Weitzner, Tess	L594	
Weltz, Jennifer	L596	
Westin, Erin Casey	L597	
Whatnall, Michaela	L598	
Whispering Buffalo Literary Agency	L599	
Williams, Laura	L603	
Williamson, Jo	L604	
Wilson, Desiree	L606	
Woods, Bryony	L610	
Zacker, Marietta B.	L616	

Youth Culture
See more broadly: Culture

Yukon
See more broadly: Canada

Zen
See more broadly: Mahayana Buddhism

Zombies
See more broadly: Horror

Get Free Access to the firstwriter.com Website

To claim your free access to the firstwriter.com website simply go to the website at https://www.firstwriter.com/subscribe and begin the subscription process as normal. On the second page, enter the required details (such as your name and address, etc.) then for "Voucher / coupon number" enter the following promotional code:

- **9APZ-83DU**

This will reduce the cost of creating a subscription by up to $18 / £15 / €18, making it free to create a monthly, quarterly, or combination subscription. Alternatively, you can use the discount to take out an annual or life subscription at a reduced rate.

Continue the process until your account is created. Please note that you will need to provide your payment details, even if there is no up-front payment. This is in case you choose to leave your subscription running after the free initial period, but there is no obligation for you to do so.

When you use this code to take out a free subscription you are under no obligation to make any payments whatsoever and you are free to cancel your account before you make any payments if you wish.

If you need any assistance, please email support@firstwriter.com.

If you have found this book useful, please consider leaving a review on the website where you bought it.

What you get

Once you have set up access to the site you will be able to benefit from all the following features:

Databases

All our databases are updated almost every day, and include powerful search facilities to help you find exactly what you need. Searches that used to take you hours or even days in print books or on search engines can now be done in seconds, and produce more accurate and up-to-date information. Our agents database also includes independent reports from at least three separate sources, showing you which are the top agencies and helping you avoid the scams that are all over the internet. You can try out any of our databases before you subscribe:

- Search dozens of **current competitions**.
- Search **over 2,400 literary agents and agencies**.
- Search **over 2,100 magazines**.
- Search **over 2,700 book publishers** that **don't** charge fees.

Plus advanced features to help you with your search:

- Save searches and save time – set multiple search parameters specific to your work, save them, and then access the search results with a single click whenever you log in. You can even save multiple different searches if you have different types of work you are looking to place.
- Add personal notes to listings, visible only to you and fully searchable – helping you to organise your actions.
- Set reminders on listings to notify you when to submit your work, when to follow up, when to expect a reply, or any other custom action.
- Track which listings you've viewed and when, to help you organise your search – any listings which have changed since you last viewed them will be highlighted for your attention!

Daily email updates

As a subscriber you will be able to take advantage of our email alert service, meaning you can specify your particular interests and we'll send you automatic email updates when we change or add a listing that matches them. So if you're interested in agents dealing in romantic fiction in the United States you can have us send you emails with the latest updates about them – keeping you up to date without even having to log in.

User feedback

Our agent, publisher, and magazine databases all include a user feedback feature that allows our subscribers to leave feedback on each listing – giving you not only the chance to have your say about the markets you contact, but giving a unique authors' perspective on the listings.

Save on copyright protection fees

If you're sending your work away to publishers, competitions, or literary agents, it's vital that you first protect your copyright. As a subscriber to firstwriter.com you can do this through our site and save 10% on the copyright registration fees normally payable for protecting your work internationally through the Intellectual Property Rights Office.

Monthly newsletter

When you subscribe to firstwriter.com you also receive our monthly email newsletter – described by one publishing company as "the best in the business" – including articles, news, and interviews for writers. And the best part is that you can continue to receive the newsletter even after you stop your paid subscription – at no cost!

Terms and conditions

The promotional code contained in this publication may be used by the owner of the book only to create one subscription to firstwriter.com at a reduced cost, or for free. It may not be used by or disseminated to third parties. Should the code be misused then the owner of the book will be liable for any costs incurred, including but not limited to payment in full at the standard rate for the subscription in question. The code may be used at any time until the end of the calendar year named in the title of the publication, after which time it will become invalid. The code may be redeemed against the creation of a new account only – it cannot be redeemed against the ongoing costs of keeping a subscription open. In order to create a subscription a method of payment must be provided, but there is no obligation to make any payment. Subscriptions may be cancelled at any time, and if an account is cancelled before any payment becomes due then no payment will be made. Once a subscription has been created, the normal schedule of payments will begin on a monthly, quarterly, or annual basis, unless a life Subscription is selected, or the subscription is cancelled prior to the first payment becoming due. Subscriptions may be cancelled at any time, but if they are left open beyond the date at which the first payment becomes due and is processed then payments will not be refundable.

www.ingramcontent.com/pod-product-compliance
Lightning Source LLC
Chambersburg PA
CBHW081153020426
42333CB00020B/2492